AMERICAN
DECADES
1980-1989

AMERICAN DECADES

1980 - 1989

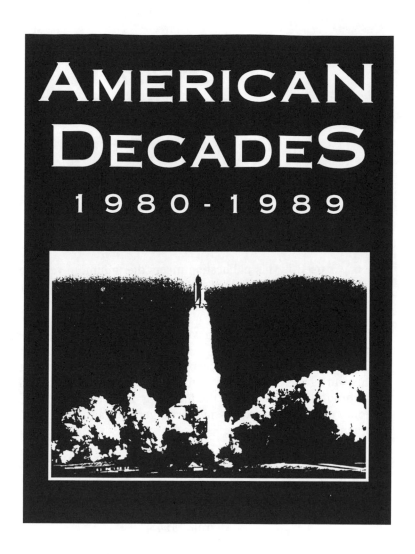

EDITED BY

VICTOR BONDI

A MANLY, INC. BOOK

 Gale Research Inc. • DETROIT • WASHINGTON, D.C. • LONDON

AMERICAN
DECADES
1980-1989

Matthew J. Bruccoli and Richard Layman, *Editorial Directors*

Printed in the United States of America

The paper used in this publication meets the minimum requirements of American National Standard for Information Sciences-Permanence Paper for Printed Library Materials, ANSI Z39.48-1984. ∞™

Library of Congress Catalog Card Number 95-081586
ISBN 0-8103-8881-2

I⒯P™ Gale Research, an ITP Information/Reference Group Company.
ITP logo is a trademark under license.

10 9

CONTENTS

INTRODUCTION

A Decade of Decades. In one sense nothing distinguished the 1980s as a decade; instead, its cultural preoccupations and political symbols were borrowed from other decades. Little during the time was original or new: almost universally the art and literature of the period required some sense of precedent in order to be understood; politics and culture seemed locked into agendas set prior to the decade. The dominant political figure of the era, President Ronald Reagan, expressed an economic philosophy derived from the 1920s (or, perhaps, from the 1890s), a populist rhetoric borrowed from the 1930s, the can-do optimism of the 1940s, and an anticommunism straight out of the 1950s. His political opponents attacked him via the liberalism of the 1930s and 1940s or through the social radicalism of the 1960s and 1970s. The arts and fashion in the 1980s were dominated by stylistic borrowings: Art Deco from the 1930s, Abstract Expressionism and film noir from the 1940s, commercial kitsch from the 1950s, rock music and countercultural experimentalism from the 1960s. American lifestyle during the decade witnessed a continuing clash between the Reagan generation, who derived their sense of the "normal" or "natural" from the 1940s and 1950s, and the baby boomers, who challenged these norms in the 1960s and 1970s. The 1980s, in other words, contained the volatile historical forces and cultural conflicts of much of twentieth-century America.

Pastiche. In another sense the retrospective character of the 1980s was the distinguishing feature of the decade. Even the mostly new or unprecedented part included reworkings or refashionings of older styles and ideas. Rap music, the most original musical style of the period, exemplified the reworking of the past implicit in most 1980s culture. Built on samples of sound and bits of rhythm borrowed from 1960s soul music and 1970s funk, rap was the most obvious type of expression that the literary critic Fredric Jameson termed *pastiche* — one based on arranging the fragments of the past in a new form rather than creating a wholly original art. Film, television, and literature were similarly marked by pastiche, gestures toward the conventions of the past rather than breaks with those conventions. The *Star Wars* and *Indiana Jones* films reworked the 1930s movie serial; *The Cosby Show* re-created the family sitcom of 1950s televi-

sion; *Less Than Zero* (1985), the best-selling novel of Bret Easton Ellis, was an extended homage to J. D. Salinger's 1951 novel *The Catcher in the Rye*. Jazz and country-and-western music were dominated by "traditional" stylings and gestures toward the past. Postmodern architecture combined the conventions of modernism, Art Deco, neoclassicism, and Renaissance architecture; the postmodern art of Julian Schnabel or the Starn twins literally fragmented and recombined earlier artistic styles. Even economics and politics in the 1980s were distinguished by pastiche, by their retro character. The "revolutionary" foundation of supply-side economics turned out to be a hodgepodge of traditional Republican economic theories. And even the new political phenomenon of the "sound bite" — a pithy, televisable quip to take the place of substantive rhetoric — was analogous to the samples of funk music in rap: quick blasts of the familiar in a seemingly new arrangement.

The Superficial. Rap samples and political sound bites both distinguish another dominant feature of the decade: the superficial. The 1980s were an insubstantial period, one given to surface and design rather than substance and content. The decade reveled in the glitzy and the glamorous, in the slightly trashy aesthetic of the newly wealthy. As hippies left their Vermont communes for Wall Street and traded in their Volkswagen vans for Audis, the symbols of "thirtysomething" success became the yuppies (young urban professionals or, more accurately, young upwardly mobile professionals — a play on the countercultural politcal party the Yippies). Television programs such as *Dallas, Dynasty,* and *Lifestyles of the Rich and Famous* parlayed the public's thirst for diamonds and dirt into success. Nancy Reagan's $45,000 inaugural gown set the tone for expensive style during a decade preoccupied with such wealthy figures as Donald Trump, Malcolm Forbes, and Tammy Faye Bakker. Pop singers such as Madonna and Michael Jackson became famous by striking poses, shedding and adopting multiple public personae, and always expressing an all-important attitude. Fashion models, famed for a depth that ran skin-deep, became international celebrities. Even the gritty television detectives of *Miami Vice* wore Armani suits. When ABC producer Roone Arledge moved from sports programming to the news division in the early 1980s, he brought with him slow-motion replays, quick editing, and flash — a style of attention-grabbing news presentation that, by the 1990s, set the industry standard. While critics deplored the emphasis on the sensational in culture, many intellectuals adopted bits and pieces of French poststructural philosophy to reassure the public that there was, in fact, no such thing as substance. To many, such as literary critic Paul de Man, life was the play of image and myth; the search for authenticity, for substance, betrayed a hopeless — if not reactionary — effort to secure meaning in a world that was ultimately meaningless. To poststructuralists the style and glitz of the 1980s represented nothing if not cultural and philosophical progress.

The Fundamentals. As poststructuralists often presented their arguments in an unreadable style, few outside of academia agreed with their propositions. Moreover, the success of classics scholar Allan Bloom's bestseller, *The Closing of the American Mind* (1987), was as telling of the philosophical sympathies of the decade as anything written by the poststructuralists. Against the embrace of the superficial offered by the poststructuralists, Bloom argued for a return to the fundamentals of philosophy, to the tried truths of Plato and Saint Augustine. His basic argument was reflected elsewhere in the culture. It was a decade in search of fundamentals, not only in philosophy but also in education, religion, lifestyle, and politics. After experiments with open classrooms and new curricula in the 1970s, conservative educators led by Secretary of Education William Bennett called for a return to "excellence" and to the fundamentals of education: English and mathematics. In religion fundamentalism was a small movement that began at the turn of the century, specifically in response to the challenge evolutionary theory presented to orthodox Protestantism. By the 1980s it superseded mainline Protestantism, becoming a formidable cultural presence capable of forcing high-school science classes to adopt the biblical story of creation as an alternative to Darwinism. The 1960s countercultural experiments with alternative lifestyles had all but fizzled out by the 1980s, leaving many in search of "fundamental" family structures and "traditional" lifestyles. And the political conservatism of the decade was dominated by a rhetorical call to the fundamentals of old-fashioned Republicanism: patriotism, anticommunism, and balanced budgets.

Contradictions of Conservatism. Conservatives and fundamentalists during the decade liked to think of themselves as restoring substance and values during an insubstantial and valueless decade. But as the overriding social movements of the decade, conservatism and fundamentalism were fraught with contradictions, not the least of which was the charge by critics such as essayist Barbara Ehrenreich that both were in fact superficial and shallow. Bloom's scale of philosophical virtue and truth were keyed toward a preindustrial age, and few actually read his best-selling book. Educational conservatives often touted twenty- or thirty-year-old curricula, as if they

were appropriate for a decade marked by the increasing use of computers in the classroom. Fundamentalists proved remarkably selective at reading the Bible, ignoring a host of injunctions regarding charity and pride, and were often more adept at political protest and self-enrichment than at pious practice. The reinvention of the family and "traditional" lifestyles had more in common with the fictional families of 1950s television sitcoms such as *Ozzie and Harriet* than it did with the actual history of families or the realities of making a living in the 1980s. And old-fashioned Republicanism was hardly in keeping with tradition, as 1980s conservatives expanded their definition of *patriot* to include men such as Oliver North, who violated the spirit, if not the letter, of the Constitution; hectored endlessly about anticommunism while pursuing business deals with the authoritarian leaders of Red China; and — under two successive Republican presidents — racked up the largest federal debt in American history.

Reagan. Conservatism was fraught with contradictions during the decade because — like liberalism during the 1960s — it was expressed by a variety of groups often working at cross-purposes. Religious fundamentalists pushed a Puritan evangelism at odds with anti-authoritarian libertarians; neoconservative intellectuals embraced a scale of values alien to free-market entrepreneurs. A common commitment to anticommunism, a disdain for the radicalism of the 1960s, and an antipathy for government regulation bound these groups together at the beginning of the decade. Even these bonds, however, were less important to conservatism than was the figure of President Ronald Reagan. Reagan took office in 1981 by appealing to the varied conservative groups, as well as to traditional Democratic voters disaffected by a poor economy. Reagan had the ability to represent almost all things to almost all his supporters. They saw in him what they wanted and glossed over the rest: fundamentalists loved him for his rhetorical invocation of piety despite the fact that his opponent in 1980, Jimmy Carter, was a more diligent, practicing Christian; millions saw Reagan as the champion of family values, although he was the first divorced president in American history; many were enamored of his populist image, while his closest associates were millionaires; Reagan was lauded for his tough approach to foreign affairs, despite the debacle of the 1983 marine deployment and withdrawal in Lebanon and even though Carter pursued more aggressive policies toward the Soviets; Reagan was cherished as a strong leader, even as the Iran-Contra scandal raised serious questions about his competence as president. None of it mattered. As a figure, as a symbol of the office of the presidency, Reagan was the perfect projection of the multitude of the nation's hopes and aspirations, suffering dearly after the defeat in Vietnam, the disgrace of Watergate, and the disintegration of the economy in the 1970s. The man acted like a president, and in the 1980s acting was enough.

From Acting to Being. The large electoral majorities by which Reagan won in 1980 and 1984 not only confirmed his skills as a actor, but in an indirect fashion reaffirmed a waning American confidence: that acting was the first step to doing, that one could project an image and in the process become it. The self-appointed global destiny of America was called to question by Vietnam; Reagan insisted that America project an image of world leadership and that the leadership would follow. If Nixon's illegalities undermined the luster of the presidency, Reagan's careful attention to the pomp and circumstance of the office could restore it. And proper confidence in economic possibility bootstrapped the return of prosperity. Confidence required conformity. If believing was precedent to doing, no one could afford to be skeptical. A Reagan opponent who suggested that it took more than an image of strength to make a strong nation was by his skepticism guilty of undermining the nation's power. Given a choice between such skeptics — or even the occasional realist — the public would turn every time to Reagan's genial and hale confidence that one could make things better by acting as though they were better. Hence the majority of the public's embrace of a glitzy 1980s style of patriotism that was found in movies such as *Rambo: First Blood Part II* (1985) and *Top Gun* (1986), patriotic country-and-western ballads, televised Fourth of July spectaculars — even commercials that equated buying trucks to national loyalty. But the fervor and insistence of patriotism during the 1980s always carried the hint of overstatement, a fear that things were no better in the 1980s than they were in the 1970s, so when skeptical voices arose in the culture during the decade they were often denounced.

Culture Wars. Partisans of the Reagan agenda saw divergences from their confidence as disloyalty and often attacked those who refused to conform to the program. Opponents of the Reagan program in turn enlisted the most incendiary tactics of the 1960s counterculture to antagonize and oppose conservatives. Disputes over 1960s legacies such as affirmative action, feminism, and gay rights were particularly heated. Artists versed in the street polemics of the 1960s, such as Cindy Sherman, Jenny Holzer, Barbara Kruger, and Keith Haring, attacked the conformities of the decade in word and image. Conservatives fired back with assaults on rock music, including those led by the Parents' Music Resource Center (PMRC), or with studies such as that published by Attorney General Edwin Meese's Commission on Pornography, or by denouncing public funding of the arts. Conservatives banned school textbooks that taught evolution and sex education; radicals responded with works such as "Dread" Scott Tyler's 1989 Art Institute of Chicago installation, *What Is The Proper Way to Display a U.S. Flag?*, whose dissent from mainstream values was profoundly alienating. From the speeches of Jesse Helms to the photographs of Robert Mapplethorpe, different groups in society appropriated culture and used it to argue against other groups — or perhaps more appropriately, to argue past them.

The Economy. Nothing undermined American confidence as much as the deplorable state of the economy. As the decade began, wracked by simultaneous double-digit inflation and unemployment and a growing trade and budget deficit, the American economy seemed antiquated, inefficient, and overburdened. The solution proposed by Reagan and his supply-side advisers combined tax cuts and assertive leadership to spark capital investment and modernization. But supply-side economics did not work exactly as planned. Profits on overseas investments paid a greater return than modernizing American industry. Tax cuts paid for transfers of capital and labor abroad. By middecade economists discussed "deindustrialization" — the dismantling of large-scale American manufacturing, especially in the steel industry — and Wall Street made new hay with "leveraged buyouts" (LBOs) — hostile stock takeovers that were the first step to the sell-off of industrial assets. The effect on American labor would have been devastating were it not for the astronomical amounts of borrowed money that the government spent on military goods. By 1989 the government was spending $303 billion per year on defense — more than $500,000 per minute — and that money propped up an important sector of the economy. Yet paying the money back would obviously be a major problem in the future. There were, moreover, industries doing well in the 1980s: the computer industry, making enormous profits and promising to facilitate a further revolution in communications; a healthy aviation industry; and retail discount merchants, notably the Wal-Mart retail chain. Working wives, often in the service industries, increasingly acted as primary contributors to individual households and kept paychecks flowing during the decade. But positive economic forces did not stop the overall decline in wages when adjusted for inflation, a disintegration ongoing since the early 1970s. Moreover, hidden tax increases in the form of rising Social Security withholding and the growing federal debt promised that despite Reagan's promises to get the government off the back of the individual taxpayer, in the future Washington would press the citizenry ever harder to repay federal debts to wealthy creditors. As economist Benjamin Friedman put it in his 1987 book *The Consequences of American Economic Policy Under Reagan and After*, "America has thrown itself a party and billed the tab to the future."

Boom. Supply-side economics not only facilitated the deindustrialization of the economy, it also advanced a growing divide between the economic classes in the 1980s, a transfer of wealth from the middle class to the wealthy unprecedented in American history. For the rich the 1980s were boom times. Because of Reagan's 1981 restructuring of the tax code, the rich had more disposable wealth. Wall Street soared in the greatest bull market in history. Corporate mergers and the creation of huge multinational concerns were news in the entertainment and communications industry, facilitated by government deregulation and lax antitrust enforcement. Entrepreneurs and buccaneer capitalists such as Donald Trump, Michael Milken, and Ivan Boesky were national celebrities, acclaimed for their "art of the deal." In every major American city, the status symbols of the new elite — foreign automobiles, hand-tailored suits, cellular phones — made an appearance. Prices for art works rocketed to new heights. Sotheby's and Christie's auction houses each surpassed $1 billion in sales in 1987, with individual paintings such as Vincent van Gogh's *Irises* selling for $53.9 million. Tickets for concerts and other cultural events also fetched dear prices. (On Broadway *Les Miserables* took in advanced sales of $12 million in 1987.) Bestselling novels such as *Bonfire of the Vanities* (1987) and *Slaves of New York* (1986) examined the lives of the new elite and the decadence their wealth purchased. Cinema also focused on money in movies such as *Wall Street* (1987), *Working Girl* (1987), and *Fatal Attraction* (1988). Even the defendents in the most sensational trials of the 1980s were rich and prominent people, including Jean Harris and Claus von Bulow. Judging from the books and movies of the 1980s one would think all America wealthy. But statistically less than 1 percent of wage earners were doing fantastically well. For much of the rest of America the 1980s revealed new depths of poverty and despair with levels of misery approaching that of the developing countries.

Hype. One reason many viewed the 1980s as a boom period was because of the "hype" that surrounded the decade. *Hype* was a slang term for a massive advertising campaign, usually implying that the goods to be sold were not all the advertisers promised. Hype was manifest in most every level of life during the decade. Advertising and marketing assumed new levels of sophistication, with children's television coordinating their activities with toy manufacturers, soft-drink manufacturers placing their products ostentatiously in mainstream films, and the creation of the world's first nonstop commercial cable channel — MTV, whose twenty-four hours of music videos acted as sensational advertisements for records and compact discs. Hype made rock superstars of more than a few mediocre artists, who used vocal overdubs and new music technology to gloss over their lack of talent. Sports became a multibillion-dollar business, and baseball and football players wrangled endlessly over contracts, while sporting-goods endorsements by athletes such as basketball star Michael Jordan filled the airwaves. Artists such as Julian Schnabel had savvy agents such as Mary Boone to advance their fortunes. Even opera star Luciano Pavarotti marketed himself like a rock star, with Pavarotti's *Greatest Hits!* becoming a best-seller. Hype promoted dubious medical and scientific technologies, such as the artificial heart and cold fusion. But hype was manifest most tellingly in politics, where along with "sound bite" and "spin" (to interpret a political act, usu-

ally from a partisan perspective), hype insisted that things were working even if they were not; or — as in the notorious "Willie Horton" ad campaign during the 1988 presidential election — hype insisted that some things were so, even if they were not. By the end of the decade politicians of every political persuasion, just like rock stars, businessmen, and baseball players, had a coterie of hired image makers and press managers to churn out photo opportunities and policy papers for the public. Hype had become a political and cultural science.

A Two-Tiered Society. As the 1980s closed, the hype ground on, but reality kept intervening: the stock market crashed; the federal debt soared; the paychecks kept getting smaller; test scores dropped; the space shuttle *Challenger* exploded; AIDS deaths multiplied; and taxpayers bailed out millionaires who gambled everything in dubious savings-and-loan transactions. The United States seemed to resemble a Third World nation, divided between rich and poor, powerful and weak, privileged and desperate. While the wealthy benefited from advances in medical technology such as laser surgery, gene therapy, artificial insemination, and fertility drugs, soaring medical costs stripped many middle-class Americans of their basic health benefits and their old-age security. (Overall prices rose 142 percent during the decade.) In the early part of the decade yuppies made fortunes speculating on extravagant real estate and condominiums, while the ranks of people living in the street — the homeless — grew by an estimated 25 percent per year, a consequence in part of a loss of $22 million in government funding for low-income housing from 1980 to 1987. Infant mortality rates in the inner city, and the mortality rate among minorities, approached and even exceeded those found in the Third World. As private schooling boomed around the nation, federal cuts in education spending, combined with state tax cuts such as Proposition 13 in California or Proposition 2½ in Massachusetts, had disastrous effects on public schools. In two of the nation's most prosperous school districts — California's Silicon Valley and Boston's Route 128 area — marked declines in educational scores were evident as schools tightened budgets and wealthy citizens put their children into private schools. Lacking educational opportunities or the prospects of high-wage manufacturing jobs, low-income students fell easily into despair, and the country's inner-city neighborhoods were rocked by violence and drug addiction throughout the decade.

Violence. Handgun sales boomed. New prisons were built and filled at such a rate that by the 1990s the United States had the highest rate of incarceration in the world. Child abuse became a national scandal with an astonishing 2.4 million cases reported by 1989. Gang violence became endemic to urban areas, with sensational, nihilistic crimes that shocked the public. By 1989 metal detectors were common in many urban schools, and 66 percent of teachers surveyed by the American Federation of Teachers said they feared violence from their students. A highly addictive new form of cocaine, crack, destroyed hundreds of thousands of lives, despite highly publicized administration efforts to interdict and wage war on drugs. By the end of the decade, as those in the highest quintile of income in America were predominately white while those in the lowest quintile of income were predominately black, the divide in economic classes widened the racial chasm of the nation. Police brutality became a common complaint of black neighborhoods, the impetus behind the Miami race riots of 1980; while race became the subtext to the stories of the 1984 presidential bid of Jesse Jackson, the MOVE bombing of 1985, the 1987 Tawana Brawley accusations, and the "Willie Horton" ad campaign during the presidential election of 1988. Many urban whites came to fear black crime, despite statistics showing that black-on-black crime was more common than interracial attacks, and a white New York vigilante, Bernhard Goetz, became a hero to some after he shot four black youths he claimed were trying to rob him on a train in 1984. Wealthy white neighborhoods, like those of Latin American land barons, erected walls around themselves and posted guards to keep out intruders. Rich urbanites, like Sherman McCoy, the fictional protagonist in Tom Wolfe's *The Bonfire of the Vanities*, sought desperately to insulate themselves from the misery of their poorer neighbors. The nation polarized, becoming economically, racially, and politically balkanized.

New Problems. Part of the problem was generational. The 1980s were locked into an ongoing dispute over values between baby boomers and their parents, using vocabularies and definitions rooted in the past. There were new problems during the decade: AIDS, growing environmental devastation, and gang violence; but the culture remained fragmented, addressing these issues in antithetical terms. Conservatives spoke the language of fundamentals, of nature; baby boomers rearticulated the language of expressive freedom. On hot-button political issues such as abortion virtually no consensus could be generated because groups were speaking at cross purposes. Some younger observers might note that both sides of the abortion debate were expressing a core desire that some element of the human experience be held sacred in a dehumanizing age or that at a time like the 1980s, when mice were patented and computers got viruses, older definitions of the natural needed to be rethought. Such views were rarely aired during the decade. Between the confrontations of World War II veteran and Vietnam War protester, black teenager and white policeman, religious fundamentalist and feminist, difference became more important than commonality; embracing divisiveness more important than building consensus. The irony, of course, was the 1980s were not supposed to be that way; to the partisan of the Reagan restoration, confidence in the future was a consequence of coming together. But it could never be that simple. Precisely because the 1980s embodied the tensions and forces of so many preceding periods, a World War II–style rallying around the flag was scarcely possible. Instead the 1980s were contested, acrimonious, diverse, and contradictory — like America and American history generally. Perhaps that diversity and acrimony can be a source of enduring strength to the next generation that studies the past carefully but not slavishly, confident enough to frame solutions appropriate to the problems of their time.

ACKNOWLEDGMENTS

This book was produced by Manly, Inc.

Production coordinator is James W. Hipp. Photography editor is Margaret Meriwether. Photographic copy work was performed by Joseph M. Bruccoli. Layout and graphics supervisor is Penney L. Haughton. Copyediting supervisor is Laurel M. Gladden. Typesetting supervisor is Kathleen M. Flanagan. Systems manager is George F. Dodge. Julie E. Frick is editorial associate. The production staff includes Phyllis A. Avant, Ann M. Cheschi, Patricia Coate, Joyce Fowler, Stephanie C. Hatchell, Kathy Lawler Merlette, Jeff Miller, Pamela D. Norton, Laura S. Pleicones, Emily R. Sharpe, William L. Thomas Jr., and Allison Trussell.

Walter W. Ross and Robert S. McConnell did library research. They were assisted by the following librarians at the Thomas Cooper Library of the University of South Carolina: Linda Holderfield and the interlibrary-loan staff; reference-department head Virginia Weathers; reference librarians Marilee Birchfield, Stefanie Buck, Cathy Eckman, Rebecca Feind, Jill Holman, Karen Joseph, Jean Rhyne, Kwamine Washington, and Connie Widney; circulation-department head Caroline Taylor; and acquisitions-searching supervisor David Haggard.

AMERICAN DECADES
1980-1989

WORLD EVENTS: SELECTED OCCURRENCES OUTSIDE THE UNITED STATES

1980

- Italian semiotics professor Umberto Eco publishes his medieval detective novel, *The Name of the Rose.*

- Anthony Burgess publishes *Earthly Powers.*

- *Nuns and Soldiers,* by Iris Murdoch, is published.

- German motion-picture director Rainer Werner Fassbinder completes his fifteen-and-a-half-hour *Berlin Alexanderplatz.*

- Japanese filmmaker Akira Kurosawa releases *Kagemusha.*

- *Man of Iron,* by Polish director Andrzej Wajda, is released.

- Alain Resnais's *Mon oncle d'Amérique* (My American Uncle), starring Gérard Depardieu, is released.

- The British rock group Joy Division disbands following the May suicide of their lead singer, Ian Curtis.

- British unemployment reaches 2.5 million by year's end, the highest number since 1935. Inflation climbs above 20 percent, double its rate when Prime Minister Margaret Thatcher took office in 1979.

- The Organization of Petroleum Exporting Countries (OPEC) raises the price of a barrel of crude oil to $32. Gasoline prices rise accordingly.

- The Church of England replaces the Book of Common Prayer, used in services since 1569, with the Alternative Service Book.

6 Jan. Former Indian prime minister Indira Gandhi is reelected to the office.

27 Feb. French officials announce the sale of weapons-grade uranium and a nuclear reactor to Iraq.

24 Mar. Human rights activist Archbishop Oscar A. Romero is murdered in El Salvador.

12 Apr. In Liberia a military coup led by Samuel K. Doe deposes President William R. Tolbert.

18 Apr. Zimbabwe, formerly known as Rhodesia, gains independence after years of civil war. The first autonomous government is headed by Prime Minister Robert Mugabe, 56, a Marxist.

21 Apr.	Cubans begin an exodus from the port of Mariel to the United States, resulting in a migration of 125,262 citizens before the Castro government halts the emigration on 26 September.
24 Apr.	An attempt by U.S. forces to rescue the fifty-two diplomatic hostages held by Islamic revolutionaries in Iran fails.
30 Apr.	Dutch queen Juliana abdicates and is succeeded by her daughter, Beatrix.
4 May	Yugoslav leader Josip Broz Tito dies after thirty-five years in power. The power vacuum precipitated by his death raises fears that Yugoslavia will be racked by long-standing but suppressed ethnic violence.
20 May	Quebec voters defeat an independence initiative.
12 June	Japanese prime minister Masayoshi Ohira dies. He is succeeded by Zenko Suzuki, 66.
23 June	The son of Indian prime minister Indira Gandhi, Sanjay Gandhi, dies in a plane crash.
26 June	France announces the successful test of a prototype neutron bomb.
27 June	Canada's House of Commons officially adopts "O, Canada" as the national anthem.
14 July	The American Defense Intelligence Agency (ADIA) announces that its members believe that South Africa exploded an atomic bomb in September 1979.
18 July	India launches its first successful staged rocket.
27 July	Shah Mohammad Reza Pahlavi of Iran, in exile following the 1979 Islamic Revolution, dies of cancer.
14 Aug.	Polish shipyard workers in Gdansk strike in protest of a new rise in meat prices. By 1 September, Communist Party leader Edward Gierek agrees to the demands set by a dissident labor union, Solidarity. Led by electrician Lech Walesa, Solidarity becomes the first independent labor union in the Soviet bloc.
19 Aug.	Willy Russell's play *Educating Rita* debuts at London's Piccadilly Theatre, following an opening at the Warehouse Theatre.
20 Aug.	In response to continuing unrest in the East Bloc, the Soviet Union jams western radio broadcasts, thus violating the 1975 Helsinki accords.
4–22 Sept.	Iraqi planes and a ten-thousand-man strike force attack Iranian airfields in the Shatt al Arab estuary, escalating border conflicts and beginning an eight-year war between Iran and Iraq.
17 Sept.	In Asunción, Paraguay, former Nicaraguan dictator Anastasio Somoza Debayle is assassinated by gunmen who destroy his Mercedes with a bazooka and machine guns.
1 Oct.	The European Economic Community (EEC) bans the use of growth hormones in cattle feed.
4 Oct.	A bomb explosion outside a Paris synagogue kills four, injures ten, and raises fear of neo-Nazi activities in France.

1981

- German author Heinrich Böll's *Fürsorgliche Belagerung: Roman* (1979) is translated into English by Leila Vennowitz and published as *The Safety Net.*

- University of Geneva literature professor George Steiner publishes *The Portage to San Cristobal of A. H.*

- British novelist Salman Rushdie completes *Midnight's Children.*

- West German writer Peter O. Chotjewitz publishes *The Thirty Years Peace.*

- Wolfgang Peterson's antiwar study, *Das Boot* (The Boat), starring Jurgen Prochnow, is released.

- Australian filmmaker Peter Weir completes *Gallipoli,* starring Mark Lee and Mel Gibson.

- The world population reaches 4.5 billion, up from 2.5 billion in 1950.

- Divorce is legalized in Spain.

- French psychoanalyst Jacques Lacan, 80, dies.

- Britain completes the building of the 4,626-foot Humber Bridge at Hull, the longest suspension bridge in the world.

- The new U.S. presidential administration of Ronald Reagan resumes grain exports to the Soviet Union and agrees that the United States will not suspend any future grain shipments. The grain embargo had been imposed by previous U.S. president, Jimmy Carter, in response to the 1979 Soviet invasion of Afghanistan.

17 Jan. Philippine president Ferdinand Marcos ends eight years of martial law and calls for free elections. He wins a second six-year term on 16 June.

20 Jan. On the day of U.S. president Ronald Reagan's inauguration, the United States releases almost $8 billion in Iranian assets, and Iran releases the fifty-two American diplomats held hostage for 444 days.

23 Jan. The Reagan administration suspends U.S. financial aid to the revolutionary Sandinista government of Nicaragua, charging that Nicaragua, with the aid of Cuba and the Soviet Union, is supplying arms to rebels in El Salvador. Later in the year the U.S. government begins to support the Contras, a counterrevolutionary guerrilla force opposing the Sandinistas.

5 May Following a sixty-five-day hunger strike, Irish nationalist Bobby Sands dies.

6 May Accusing Libya of supporting international terrorism, the Reagan administration closes the Libyan embassy in Washington.

10 May Socialist leader François Mitterrand is elected president of France.

13 May In Rome, Pope John Paul II survives an assassination attempt by a Bulgarian-trained Turk.

7 June In an effort to prevent Iraqi production of plutonium, Israeli jets destroy Iraq's Osirak nuclear reactor.

22 June Iranian president Abolhassan Bani-Sadr is removed from office and flees to France.

28 June   Islamic Republican Party chief Ayatollah Mohammed Beheshti, along with four aides, is killed in Teheran.

1 July   Nell Dunn's *Steaming* opens at London's Theatre Royal, Stratford East.

24 July   U.S. envoy Philip C. Habib negotiates a cease-fire following continuing clashes between Israeli and Palestinian forces in Lebanon.

28 July   Simon Gray's *Quartermaine's Terms,* starring Edward Fox, debuts at the Queen's Theatre in London.

29 July   Prince Charles of Great Britain, 32, marries Lady Diana Spencer, 20, at St. Paul's Cathedral in London, beginning a relationship that would keep tabloid writers occupied throughout the decade.

31 July   Brig. Gen. Omar Torrijos Herrera, dictator of Panama, is killed in a plane crash. By 1983 Col. Manuel Antonio Noriega, a U.S. Central Intelligence Agency (CIA) informant, will be the strong-arm de facto leader of Panama.

19 Aug.   After they are attacked in air space above the Gulf of Sidra, two U.S. Navy planes shoot down two Soviet-made Libyan air-force planes.

30 Aug.   Several top Iranian officials, including President Muhammad Ali Rajai and Prime Minister Mohammad Javar Bahonar, are killed by a bomb in the prime minister's office.

11 Sept.   A grenade attack kills Ayatollah Assadolah Madani, an aide to Iranian cleric and Islamic revolutionary leader Ayatollah Ruholla Khomeini.

21 Sept.   British Honduras, renamed Belize, becomes an independent state and member of the British Commonwealth of Nations.

22 Sept.   The 236 MPH high-speed train, the TGV, begins service from Paris to Lyon, France.

6 Oct.   In Cairo, Egyptian president Anwar Sadat is assassinated by Islamic extremists angered by his 1979 peace accord with Israel and recent crackdowns on political dissidents. Sadat will be succeeded by Hosni Mubarak, 53.

1 Nov.   The Caribbean islands of Antigua and Barbuda gain independence and together are recognized as one state in the British Commonwealth of Nations.

13 Dec.   Polish general Wojciech Jaruzelski, having assumed the office of prime minister in February, declares martial law, outlaws the independent labor union Solidarity, and imprisons opposition leaders.

14 Dec.   Israel annexes the Golan Heights, a Syrian territory taken in the 1967 Six-Day War.

1982

- Soviet poet Yevgeny A. Yevtushenko publishes his first novel, *Berry Patches.*

- Colombian novelist Gabriel García Márquez publishes *Crónica de una muerte anunciada* (translated as *Chronicle of a Death Foretold*) and wins the 1982 Nobel Prize for literature.

- *La tía Julia y el escribidor* (1977), by Peruvian novelist Mario Vargas Llosa, is translated into English by Helen R. Lane and published as *Aunt Julia and the Scriptwriter.*

- Andrzej Wajda's film about the French Revolution, *Danton*, starring Gérard Depardieu, is released.
- Klaus Kinski stars in Werner Herzog's *Fitzcarraldo*.
- Ben Kingsley plays the lead in Richard Attenborough's *Gandhi*.
- Beatrice Romand stars in Eric Rohmer's *Le Beau Mariage*.
- Placido Domingo stars in Franco Zeffirelli's movie version of *La Traviata*.
- Italy defeats West Germany, 3–1, to win the World Cup in international soccer competition.
- A national census reveals that the Chinese population is more than one billion.
- Many U.S. oil companies and thousands of U.S. citizens leave Libya.

23 Mar. In Guatemala a military coup overthrows the dictatorship of Gen. Romeo Lucas Garcia, who has been charged by Amnesty International with responsibility for thousands of political murders. Gen. José Efraín Ríos Montt becomes the new dictator in June.

1 Apr. Under the terms of the 1977 treaty with the United States, Panama formally takes over the policing of the Panama Canal Area.

2 Apr. A long-standing territorial dispute between Argentina and Great Britain over the disposition of the British-held Falkland Islands in the southern Atlantic leads to an Argentinean military invasion of the islands.

3 Apr. In Paris, terrorists assassinate an Israeli diplomat.

12 Apr. Great Britain imposes a blockade of the Falkland Islands.

17 Apr. In Ottawa, Queen Elizabeth II of Britain signs the Constitution Act, replacing the North American Act of 1867 with a new, fully autonomous Canadian constitution.

21 Apr. Israeli forces destroy Palestinian strongholds in southern Lebanon from which members of the Palestinian Liberation Organization (PLO) have been staging guerrilla attacks.

25 Apr. Under the terms of the 1978 Camp David Accords and 1979 Egyptian-Israeli peace treaty, Israel completes withdrawal of its troops from the Sinai.

4 May South African playwright Athol Fugard debuts *Master Harold . . . and the Boys* at New York's Lyceum Theater.

14 May British forces storm the Falkland Islands.

24 May Iranian forces retake the port city of Khurramshahr, seizing thirty thousand Iraqi prisoners.

3 June In London, terrorists critically wound the Israeli ambassador to Great Britain.

6 June Seeking to quell PLO guerrilla attacks, Israel invades Lebanon. Israeli forces reach the outskirts of Beirut on 10 June.

14 June Argentinean troops in the Falkland Islands surrender to the British. The Falkland Islands war has cost the British 243 lives and the Argentineans more than 1,000.

27 July Israeli jets bomb West Beirut, killing 120 and injuring 232.

20 Aug. Mexico defaults on a $60 billion foreign debt, the first of several Third World nations to do so. In response, First World bankers begin to grant delays in interest payments.

29 Aug. Two British explorers complete a three-year expedition to circumnavigate the globe by way of both the North and South poles.

14 Sept. Christian Phalangist leader Bashir Gemayel, the president-elect of Lebanon, is killed in a bomb explosion.

16 Sept. In West Beirut, Christian Phalangist militiamen massacre Palestinian civilians in refugee camps. Suspicions of Israeli complicity lead to demands for the resignation of Israeli prime minister Menachem Begin.

1 Oct. In West German elections the Christian Democrats defeat the Socialists. Christian Democratic leader Helmut Kohl replaces Helmut Schmidt as prime minister.

29 Oct. Spanish voters elect Socialist leader Felipe González as prime minister.

5 Nov. Brazil and Paraguay complete construction of the sluice gates on the Itaipu Dam, the world's largest hydroelectric project.

10 Nov. Soviet party secretary Leonid I. Brezhnev dies after seventeen years in power in the Soviet Union. He is succeeded by former KGB head Yuri V. Andropov.

16 Nov. Tom Stoppard's *The Real Thing* debuts at London's Strand Theatre.

1983

- The German magazine *Stern* reveals the existence of what are purported to be Adolf Hitler's diaries. The diaries are later exposed as a hoax.

- South African novelist J. M. Coetzee publishes *The Life and Times of Michael K.*

- *Stanley and the Women,* by British novelist Kingsley Amis, is published.

- Swedish director Ingmar Bergman releases *Fanny and Alexander.*

- Robert Bresson's *L'Argent* is released.

- The "New Romantic" style of British pop music, exemplified by artists such as A Flock of Seagulls, Duran Duran, and Culture Club, enjoys popularity.

- In a stunning upset, Australia strips the United States of the America's Cup for the first time since 1851 when the *Australia II* defeats *Liberty* four races to three in international sailboat racing.

- In a portent of a coming ecological disaster, Soviet haulers quit fishing the Aral Sea, once the source of 10 to 15 percent of the nation's freshwater catch. By the 1990s the sea will have shrunk massively, becoming primarily a desert.

- Gen. Oscar Mejía Victores organizes a coup and overthrows Guatemalan dictator José Efraín Ríos Montt.

9 Mar. Caryl Churchill's *Fen* opens at London's Almeida Theatre.

30 Mar. *Run for Your Wives,* by Ray Cooney, opens at London's Shaftesbury Theatre.

18 Apr.   In Beirut terrorists bomb the U.S. Embassy, killing sixty-three people.

6 Aug.   Off the coast of Cape Town, South Africa, the oil tanker *Castillo de Bellver* catches fire, spilling 250,000 tons of crude oil.

21 Aug.   After two years in exile, Philippine senator Benigno S. Aquino returns to Manila to organize political opposition to President Ferdinand Marcos. Aquino is murdered upon arrival by an assassin who is himself killed.

29 Aug.   Mortar shells landing in the U.S. Marine compound at the Beirut airport kill two and wound thirteen.

1 Sept.   Near Sakhalin Island in the north Pacific, a Korean Air Lines Boeing 747 strays into Soviet airspace and is shot down, killing all 269 passengers. The government of the Soviet Union issues no apology, insisting the airliner was part of a reconnaissance mission. The U.S. government condemns the attack but acknowledges that it has been conducting surveillance activities in the area. Despite the strain the incident causes to U.S.–Soviet relations, arms control negotiations resume soon after.

15 Sept.   Israeli prime minister Menachem Begin resigns. He is succeeded by Foreign Minister Yitzhak Shamir.

21 Sept.   David Mamet's study of greed, *Glengarry Glen Ross,* opens at London's Cottlesloe Theatre.

8 Oct.   In Tokyo the Metropolitan Teien Art Museum opens.

9 Oct.   In an attempt to assassinate South Korean president Chun Doo Hwan, North Korean terrorists destroy a ceremonial mausoleum in Rangoon, Burma, killing nineteen and wounding forty-nine. President Hwan, visiting Burma, had changed his scheduled visit to the mausoleum at the last minute and thus avoided the attack.

12 Oct.   In Tokyo former Japanese prime minister Kakuei Tanaka is convicted of accepting a $2.2 million bribe from Lockheed Corporation. Tanaka is fined the amount of the bribe and sentenced to four years in prison.

In the tiny Caribbean-island nation of Grenada, Prime Minister Maurice Bishop is overthrown in a coup engineered by Deputy Prime Minister Bernard Coard, a Marxist. One week later, Bishop is killed as his supporters engineer a prison break.

23 Oct.   Terrorists on suicide missions detonate trucks filled with explosives in the U.S. and French barracks in Lebanon, killing 241 U.S. Marines and 58 French paratroopers.

25 Oct.   Three thousand U.S. Marines invade Grenada. U.S. officials justify the intervention on the grounds that the new Marxist government is endangering the lives of American citizens on the island and that the Grenadan government is constructing an airstrip for use by Central American communists.

26 Oct.   London's Lyric Theatre debuts Hugh Williams's *Pack of Lies.*

4 Nov.   A suicide bomber attacks an Israeli military installation in Lebanon, killing sixty people.

26 Nov.   Masked gunmen steal $39 million in gold from Heathrow Airport in London.

31 Dec.   Nigeria's five-year-old democracy is overthrown in a military coup led by Maj. Gen. Mohammed Buhari.

1984

- Exiled Czech novelist Milan Kundera publishes *The Unbearable Lightness of Being*.

- *L'Amant*, by French novelist Marguerite Duras, is published.

- Mario Vargas Llosa publishes *Historia de Mayta* (translated as *The Real Life of Alejandro Mayta*).

- French sculptor Jean Dubuffet unveils his *Monument with Standing Beast* before the new State of Illinois building in Chicago.

- Louis Ducreux stars in Bertrand Tavernier's *A Sunday in the Country*.

- Famine and drought in sub-Saharan Africa kill three hundred thousand.

- British pop star Bob Geldof organizes Band Aid, a high-profile pop-music charity for African famine victims.

- Japan endures a scare as extortionists claim to have poisoned candy.

- Western experts estimate that casualties from the ongoing Iran-Iraq War have killed one hundred thousand Iranians and fifty thousand Iraqis.

- U.S., French, and Italian peacekeeping forces leave Lebanon.

- The World Court denounces the mining of Nicaraguan export harbors by the United States as a violation of international law.

- In the fall Great Britain is wracked by a debilitating national coal strike.

- Great Britain's Thatcher government privatizes its telephone service.

1 Jan.   With construction of the European-Soviet pipeline complete, France receives its first delivery of Soviet natural gas.

18 Jan.   In Beirut terrorists kill American University president Malcolm H. Kerr.

9 Feb.   Soviet general secretary Yuri V. Andropov dies. He is succeeded by Politburo member Konstantin U. Chernenko.

10 Feb.   The Soviet Union and China sign a $1.2 billion trade agreement.

16 Mar.   South Africa and Mozambique sign a peace accord, the first between South Africa's white government and a black nation.

27 Mar.   *Starlight Express*, a musical featuring roller skating, debuts at London's Apollo Theatre.

4 Apr.   Michael Frayn's *Benefactors* debuts at London's Vaudeville Theatre.

May   Junta leader and political moderate José Napoleón Duarte is elected president in El Salvador, defeating the ultra-right-wing candidate Roberto D'Aubuisson, a graduate of the United States School of the Americas and a leading figure linked to El Salvador's death squads.

5–6 June   Indian government efforts to expel Sikh separatists from the Golden Temple at Amritsar result in the deaths of six hundred to twelve hundred people.

30 June   Canadian prime minister Pierre Elliott Trudeau resigns from office and calls for national elections.

3 Aug.   The African nation of Upper Volta changes its name to Burkina Faso.

4 Sept.   In Canadian national elections, the Progressive Conservative Party enjoys a sweep of the House of Commons, winning 211 of 282 seats. Corporate lawyer Brian Mulroney becomes prime minister.

14 Sept.   Because no political party has earned a majority of votes in recent elections, the Israeli Knesset agrees to a coalition government headed first by Labor leader Shimon Peres, followed by a government headed by Likud head Yitzhak Shamir.

1 Oct.   Sikh extremists among her own bodyguards assassinate Indian prime minister Indira Gandhi, 66. She is succeeded by her son Rajiv, who wins the ministry in his own right by year's end.

19 Oct.   Members of the Polish security police murder pro-Solidarity priest Jerzy Popieluszko. Public outcry results in the arrest and trial of the murderers, who are convicted in February 1985.

20 Oct.   Beijing announces economic reforms leading to increased capitalism in Red China.

15 Nov.   Following demonstrations against dictator Augusto Pinochet, Chilean police arrest thirty-two thousand suspects in the Santiago slum district of La Victoria and hold them in a soccer stadium for questioning.

19 Nov.   A natural gas explosion in Mexico City kills five hundred people.

3 Dec.   The Union Carbide pesticide plant in Bhopal, India, leaks poison gas, killing two thousand and injuring two hundred thousand.

19 Dec.   In Beijing British prime minister Margaret Thatcher and Chinese premier Zhao Ziyang sign an agreement providing for the transfer of Hong Kong to China in 1997.

21 Dec.   In Montreal gunmen seize two Merrill Lynch couriers and escape with $51.3 million in securities.

1985

- Gabriel García Márquez publishes *El amor en los tiempos del cólera* (translated as *Love in the Time of Cholera*).

- New Zealand novelist Keri Hume publishes *The Bone People*.

- British author D. H. Lawrence is enshrined in Poet's Corner at London's Westminster Abbey.

- Masahiro Shinoda films *MacArthur's Children*.

- Stephen Frears's *My Beautiful Laundrette* is released.

- Europe experiences an unprecedented rash of terrorist attacks and bombings by Arab, French, Islamic, and Palestinian groups, the worst of which occurs in simultaneous attacks on the Rome and Vienna airports on 27 December. The attacks kill 18 people and injure 111.

- Guatemalan leader Gen. Oscar Mejía Victores turns over his power to the elected civilian president, Marco Vinicio Cerezo Arévalo.

4 Feb. New Zealand refuses to allow a U.S. warship entry into its waters on the grounds that the ship carries nuclear arms.

11 Mar. Soviet Communist Party general secretary Konstantin Chernenko, 73, dies. He is succeeded by agricultural minister Mikhail Sergeyevich Gorbachev, 54.

13 Mar. Following two widely publicized incidents of soccer rioting, British prime minister Margaret Thatcher commissions a group to study the problem of soccer hooliganism.

16 Mar. Terry Anderson, U.S. foreign correspondent for the Associated Press, is kidnapped by Lebanese terrorists in Beirut. He is held hostage until 4 December 1991.

11 Apr. Albanian dictator and Communist Party chief Enver Hoxha, 78, dies after forty-one years in power. He is succeeded by Ramiz Alia.

1 May U.S. president Ronald Reagan orders a trade embargo on Nicaragua, denouncing the Sandinista regime as a threat to U.S. national security.

29 May Thirty-eight people die during a riot by soccer fans and structural collapse at the European Cup Finals in Brussels.

10 July The French secret service bombs the antinuclear protest ship, *Rainbow Warrior*, in Auckland harbor, New Zealand, killing photographer Fernando Pereira. The bombing and subsequent cover-up will lead to the resignations of French defense minister Charles Hernu and French secret service chief, Adm. Pierre Lacoste.

13 July British pop star Bob Geldof stages Live Aid, simultaneous concerts in London and Philadelphia, as a benefit for African famine relief.

20 July In response to continuing racial violence, South Africa declares an indefinite state of emergency, the first declaration of its kind in twenty-five years.

17 Aug. In the continuing Iran-Iraq War, Iraqi forces armed with French Exocet missiles attack the Iranian oil terminal of Kharg Island.

13 Sept. Saudi Arabian oil minister Ahmad Zaki Yamani announces a new oil pricing discount system, spurring plummeting oil prices for the next six months.

7 Oct. Terrorists hijack the Italian cruise ship *Achille Lauro* in the Mediterranean and kill an American passenger the next day.

8 Oct. *Les Miserables* debuts at London's Palace Theatre.

15 Oct. Military ruler Gen. Samuel K. Doe is elected president of Liberia despite accusations of election fraud.

3 Nov. Tanzanian president Julius K. Nyerere, who led his nation to independence, resigns after twenty-one years in power. He is succeeded by Vice President Ali Hassan Mwinyi.

9 Nov. In Moscow, world chess master Anatoly Karpov is defeated by Soviet chess master Gary Kasparov.

11 Nov. Nicaraguan Sandinista president Daniel Ortega Saavedra rejects the latest peace plan drafted by the Contradora (neutral Latin American) nations, citing the absence of provisions forbidding U.S. military maneuvers in the region.

21 Nov. Soviet leader Mikhail Gorbachev and U.S. president Ronald Reagan meet for a summit on foreign affairs.

25 Nov. The musical *Black and Blue,* featuring vaudeville songs from the 1920s and 1930s, debuts at Paris's Chatelet theater.

30 Dec. Pakistani president Gen. Mohammad Zia ul-Haq declares an end to eight and one-half years of martial law.

1986

- British novelist Kingsley Amis publishes *The Old Devils.*

- Argentinean director Luis Puenzo's *La historia oficial* (The Official Story), a dramatization set during Argentina's Guerra Sucia (Dirty War) of 1976–1983 in which thousands of designated subversives "disappeared," is released. It wins an Oscar for best foreign film of 1986.

- French filmmaker Claude Berri releases *Jean de Florette,* starring Yves Montand and Gérard Depardieu.

- Barbara Sukowa stars in Margarethe von Trotta's *Rosa Luxemburg.*

- Juzo Itami's comedy *Tampopo,* with Ken Watanabe and Tsutomu Yamakazi, is released.

- Europe continues to be plagued by terrorist attacks and bombings.

- The Annacis Bridge in Vancouver, British Columbia, is completed, making it the world's longest cable-stayed bridge.

- Testing of the abortion drug, RU 486, begins in France.

- U.S. officials express alarm at the Soviet "peace offensive" led by General Secretary Mikhail Gorbachev, who is winning diplomatic gains throughout Western Europe.

1 Jan. In a sign of lessening Cold War tensions, U.S. president Ronald Reagan and Soviet general secretary Mikhail Gorbachev exchange New Year's greetings televised in the United States and Soviet Union.

6 Jan. Gen. Samuel K. Doe is inaugurated as president of Liberia. His government becomes famous for corruption and human-rights abuses.

6 Feb. Following a week-long state of siege, Haitian President-for-Life Jean-Claude "Baby Doc" Duvalier, 34, is forced to flee the island nation for exile in France.

11 Feb. Russian dissident Anatoly Shcharansky is freed by the Soviet Union in an East-West prisoner exchange.

26 Feb. Following ten days of national protests over a presidential election marked by widespread vote fraud, twenty-year Philippine ruler Ferdinand Marcos is forced into exile in Hawaii. He is succeeded by his opponent in the election, Corazon Aquino, widow of the opposition leader Benigno S. Aquino, who was assassinated in 1983.

28 Feb.   Swedish prime minister and peace activist Olof Palme, 59, is assassinated in Stockholm.

4 Mar.   During Austrian elections, evidence surfaces that presidential candidate Kurt Waldheim, former U.N. secretary general, had been a member of Nazi organizations during World War II. He is elected president nonetheless.

7 Mar.   South African president Pieter W. Botha lifts the martial law in place in black South African districts since 1985.

15 Mar.   Paris mayor Jacques Chirac is elected to head a Conservative Parliament and share power with Socialist president François Mitterrand, who has been in power since 1981.

5 Apr.   A terrorist bombing at a West Berlin discotheque kills two people, including a U.S. serviceman, and leaves 230 injured.

10 Apr.   After approximately twenty people die in Italy in within a few weeks as a result of drinking wine contaminated with methanol, the U.S. government warns consumers not to drink Italian wine.

13 Apr.   In what is believed to be the first papal visit to a Jewish house of worship, Pope John Paul II visits Rome's main synagogue.

14 Apr.   Civil rights leader Desmond Tutu is elected Anglican Archbishop of South Africa.

15 Apr.   After the U.S. government accuses Libya of sponsoring the bombing of a West Berlin discotheque, U.S. warplanes strike the Tripoli and Benghazi headquarters of Libyan strongman Mu'ammar Gadhafi. In reprisals for the attacks, three hostages in Beirut are killed.

18 Apr.   South African "pass laws," restricting the movement of blacks, are repealed.

26 Apr.   At the Chernobyl nuclear power plant near Kiev, Ukraine, a serious accident occurs, resulting in the release of an enormous radioactive cloud into the atmosphere. More than thirty firefighters and plant workers die in the weeks following the accident; predictions of future deaths from radiation exposure range from sixty-five hundred to forty-five thousand.

1 May   Nearly 1.5 million South Africans protest apartheid in the nation's largest strike.

24 May   Margaret Thatcher begins a three-day visit to Israel. She is the first British prime minister to visit the country.

27 May   The United States agrees to comply with the terms of the 1979 Strategic Arms Limitation Treaty, suspended since the Soviet invasion of Afghanistan.

12 June   Anticipating protests marking the tenth anniversary of the Soweto uprising, South Africa once again declares a state of emergency.

26 June   Irish voters reject a measure to end the nation's ban on divorce.

27 June   The International Court of Justice in The Hague rules that the United States has broken international law by mining the harbors of Nicaragua and by aiding antigovernment rebels. The United States ignores the ruling.

29 June   Argentina wins the World Cup by defeating West Germany, 3–2, in international soccer competition.

6 July	In parliamentary elections in Japan, the Liberal Democratic Party and Prime Minister Yasuhiro Nakasone win landslide reelection.
15 July	U.S. officials announce that army troops have been sent to Bolivia to aid in the war on drug trafficking.
26 July	Following a Reagan administration secret arms trade to Iran, Shiite Muslim terrorists release American priest Lawrence Jenco from captivity in Lebanon.
18 Aug.	The Soviet Union announces it will continue its yearlong moratorium on nuclear testing, which expired on 6 August.
21–26 Aug.	In Cameroon, volcanic explosions release toxic gas, killing fifteen hundred to seventeen hundred people.
11 Sept.	Egyptian president Hosni Mubarak and Israeli prime minister Shimon Peres meet in the first summit between the nations in five years.
16 Sept.	The EEC agrees to a series of economic sanctions directed against apartheid in South Africa.
5 Oct.	Nicaraguan military forces shoot down a U.S. cargo plane carrying arms and capture the pilot, Eugene Hasenfus of Wisconsin.
7 Oct.	In London a politically neutral daily, *The Independent*, begins publication.
9 Oct.	Andrew Lloyd Weber's musical *The Phantom of the Opera*, starring Michael Crawford, debuts at London's Majesty Theatre.
12 Oct.	During a summit in Reykjavík, Iceland, U.S. president Ronald Reagan offers Soviet general secretary Mikhail Gorbachev complete nuclear disarmament. The offer falls through when the Soviets insist that the American Strategic Defense Initiative, or "Star Wars," be included in the disarmament package.
14 Oct.	Holocaust survivor and human-rights activist Elie Wiesel wins the Nobel Peace Prize.
21 Oct.	English playwright Hugh Whitemore debuts *Breaking the Code*, a play about World War II codebreaker Alan Turing, at London's Haymarket Theater.
1 Nov.	A fire at the Sandoz pharmaceutical warehouse in Switzerland discharges one thousand tons of toxic chemicals into the Rhine, killing millions of fish and contaminating water supplies.
2 Nov.	As part of continuing Reagan administration arms trades with terrorists, American University administrator David Jacobsen is released by Shiite extremists in Lebanon.
25 Nov.	Soviet general secretary Mikhail Gorbachev visits India, the first Soviet leader to do so since 1980.
28 Nov.	The United States officially violates the 1979 Strategic Arms Limitation Treaty with the Soviet Union by deploying a B-52 bomber capable of carrying cruise missiles.
30 Nov.	Punjabi extremists commandeer a public bus and kill twenty-two Hindu prisoners.
8 Dec.	French prime minister Jacques Chirac withdraws a bill to reform the French university system following more than two weeks of violent student protests.

17 Dec.	Nicaragua releases American pilot Eugene Hasenfus.
20 Dec.	In Shanghai, China, some fifty thousand students march for democratic rights.

1987

- British novelist Penelope Lively publishes *Moon Tiger*.

- *Au revoir les enfants* (*Goodbye Children*), by Louis Malle, is released.

- Italian director Bernardo Bertolucci releases *The Last Emperor*.

- Mbongeni Ngema's *Sarafina!* debuts at Johannesburg's Market theater.

- The United States regains the America's Cup when *Stars and Stripes* sweeps Australia's *Kookaburra III* in international sailboat racing.

- Nearly eighty thousand square miles of Amazonian rain forest are burned in eighty days by Brazilian landowners, sparking environmental fears that razing the forest will contribute to a global "greenhouse effect."

- Canadian officials sign the Meech Lake Accord, granting Quebec special status as a "distinct society," beginning a ratification process that is to be completed by 1990.

- South African politics are rent by a bloody civil war between Zulus led by Mangosuthu Buthelezi's Inkatha Party and Nelson Mandela's African National Congress.

4 Jan.	The Communist Party of China expels dissidents.
22 Feb.	Syrian troops seize West Beirut in an attempt to stabilize the anarchical political situation in the city.
6 Mar.	The ferry *Herald of Free Enterprise* sinks in the English Channel, killing 192 people.
11 Apr.	Protests aimed at winning release for detainees are banned in South Africa.
17 May	Iraqi missiles hit the U.S. frigate *Stark* in the Persian Gulf, killing thirty-seven men. Iraqi president Saddam Hussein apologizes, explaining the attack as a mistake in the Iraq-Iran War.
11 June	British prime minister Margaret Thatcher is elected to a third term.
25 June	Soviet Party general secretary Mikhail Gorbachev announces perestroika, sweeping economic reforms designed to improve Russian industrial production.
4 July	A French court sentences former Gestapo chief Klaus Barbie, 73, to life in prison for war crimes during World War II.
1 Aug.	In Mecca clashes between Shiites and other Muslims on hajj (pilgrimage) leave nearly four hundred people dead.
7 Aug.	Five Central American nations agree to a peace process drafted by Costa Rican president Oscar Arias Sanchez.
1 Oct.	Nicaragua's anti-Sandinista newspaper, *La Prensa,* resumes publication.
2 Oct.	Great Britain begins tests of the French abortion pill, RU 486.

3 Oct. Canada and the United States sign a free-trade agreement opposed by Canadian liberals and socialists.

27 Oct. Peter Shaffer's *Lettice and Lovage*, starring Maggie Smith, opens at London's Globe Theater.

9 Nov. A bomb explosion in Colombo, Sri Lanka, leaves thirty-two dead and more than seventy injured. The bombing is the latest in continuing ethnic violence between Indians and Tamils.

7 Dec. Soviet leader Gorbachev arrives in Washington for a three-day summit with U.S. president Reagan. The summit results in the completion of a treaty to dismantle all Soviet and U.S. medium-range nuclear missiles.

16 Dec. Roh Tae Woo, the handpicked successor to South Korean military leader and president Chun Doo-Hwan, is elected by a direct popular vote.

A sensational Sicilian Mafia trial ends in the sentencing to prison of 338 of 452 defendants charged primarily with heroin trafficking.

17 Dec. Czech Communist Party leader Gustav Husak, who has ruled for eighteen years, is replaced by Milos Jakes, a Gorbachev-style reformer.

31 Dec. In a move that angers U.S. officials, Medellín drug lord Jorge Luis Ochoa is released from a Colombian prison.

1988

- British novelist Salman Rushdie's satire, *The Satanic Verses*, incenses Muslim readers with alleged "blasphemies," leading Islamic leader Ayatollah Khomeini of Iran to pronounce a death sentence against Rushdie and offer $1 million reward to any person who kills him.

- Indian novelist Bharati Mukherjee publishes *The Middleman and Other Stories*.

- *Foucault's Pendulum*, a mystery by Umberto Eco, is published.

- German filmmaker Wim Wenders releases *Wings of Desire*.

- Marcel Ophuls's documentary about Nazi war criminal Klaus Barbie, *Hotel Terminus*, is released.

- Spanish director Pedro Almodovar's comedy *Women on the Verge of a Nervous Breakdown* is released.

- In international sailboat racing, *Stars and Stripes* of the United States successfully defends the America's Cup against *New Zealand* by using a catamaran, which tends to be faster than monohulled ships. New Zealand protests, and the outcome of the race is contested in court for the next year and a half. Ultimately, *Stars and Stripes* is granted the cup.

- Floods in Bangladesh — the worst in seventy years — kill thousands and leave millions homeless.

- Palestinians in the Gaza Strip continue to stage protests in an *intifada* (uprising) against Israeli occupation. The protests will cost nearly three hundred Arabs their lives before the year is out.

- Political unrest racks Burma as the military dictatorship authorizes police to shoot and kill thousands of student protesters led by human-rights activist Aung San Suu Kyi.

- Seeking a return of the outlawed union Solidarity, Polish workers strike in August.

28 Jan. The Canadian Supreme Court rules that a law restricting abortion is unconstitutional.

5 Feb. A U.S. grand jury indicts Panamanian dictator and onetime CIA functionary Gen. Manuel Noriega on charges of accepting bribes from drug traffickers.

16 Mar. Iraqi troops drop poison gas on Kurdish civilians in the town of Halabja, killing four thousand to twelve thousand people.

14 Apr. The Soviet Union announces that its military forces will begin to withdraw from Afghanistan on 17 May. Experts estimate that the casualties total fifteen thousand Soviets and one million Afghans since the Soviet invasion was initiated in 1979.

1 July Delegates to a Communist conference in Moscow endorse Mikhail Gorbachev's reform proposals, including transfer of party power to a democratically elected legislature.

3 July The U.S. warship *Vincennes* mistakes an Iran Air A300 Airbus for an attacking plane and shoots it down, killing all aboard. Washington apologizes for the attack and offers reparations to the survivors of the 290 victims.

8 July French voters reelect President François Mitterrand.

13 July Peace talks brokered by U.S. assistant secretary of state Chester A. Crocker among Angolan, South African, and Cuban officials bring long hostilities in Angola and Namibia to an end.

20 July After nearly eight years of war, Iran and Iraq agree to a cease-fire. Direct talks to resolve the conflict follow. The war has cost an estimated 105,000 Iraqi and one million Iranian lives.

18 Aug. Pakistani president Gen. Mohammad Zia ul-Haq and U.S. ambassador Arnold I. Raphel are killed in a midair explosion of a Pakistani Air Force plane.

24 Sept. France and China authorize use of the abortion pill, RU 486.

1 Dec. Benazir Bhutto, daughter of former prime minister Zulfikar Ali Bhutto, is elected prime minister of Pakistan. She becomes the first woman to head a modern Islamic state and brings eleven years of military rule to an end.

5 Dec. The West German environmental ministry confirms that a serious accident occurred at a nuclear power plant near Frankfurt in December 1987, as reported by an American journal.

21 Dec. A Pan Am 747 explodes in midair over Lockerbie, Scotland, killing all 259 passengers and 11 persons on the ground. The explosion inaugurates a massive international search for Middle Eastern terrorists suspected of planting a bomb aboard the plane in Frankfurt, Germany.

22 Dec. Brazilian rubber tapper and environmentalist Francisco "Chico" Mendes is killed at his home in Xapuri. Mendes had been the foremost opponent of Brazilian landowners clearing the Amazonian rain forest.

1989

- Japanese-English novelist Kazuo Ishiguro writes *The Remains of the Day.*

- Spanish surrealist painter Salvador Dali dies.

- Italian filmmaker Giuseppe Tornatore's *Cinema Paradiso* is released.

- Kenneth Branagh directs and stars in a film version of William Shakespeare's *Henry V.*

- The World Health Organization estimates that the number of AIDS cases worldwide will increase from 450,000 in 1989 to five million in the year 2000.

7 Jan. Emperor Hirohito of Japan dies at age eighty-seven after sixty-two years of rule. He is succeeded by his fifty-five-year-old son, Akihito.

2–3 Feb. Alfredo Stroessner, for thirty-five years the dictator of Paraguay, is overthrown in a military coup.

26 Mar. Multicandidate parliamentary elections in the Soviet Union result in an embarrassing defeat for the Communist Party and the ascension of former Communist and Moscow city head Boris N. Yeltsin, who is now leader of the non-Communist opposition.

30 Mar. Following renovations the Louvre Museum in Paris reopens, featuring a striking glass pyramid entrance designed by architect I. M. Pei.

15 Apr. Chinese students meet in Beijing's Tiananmen Square to mourn the death of Politburo member Hu Yaobang, 73. The students remain in the square and turn the occasion into a prodemocracy demonstration that lasts for weeks, sparking similar demonstrations throughout China.

7 May Panamanians vote to oust strongman Gen. Manuel Noriega, but he ignores the election results.

11 May Fearing the extinction of African elephants, Kenya calls for a worldwide ban on the trade of ivory.

14 May In the first peaceful transfer of power since 1927, Argentinean voters elect Peronist leader Carlos Saúl Menem president.

24 May The Exxon *Valdez* hits a reef in Prince William Sound, Alaska, and spills approximately ten million gallons of oil.

4 June Iranian president Ayatollah Khomeini dies. He is succeeded in office by Ali Akbar Hashemi Rafsanjani.

8 June The prodemocracy demonstrations in China are crushed when government troops fire on protesters in Tiananmen Square and the leaders of the movement are executed. Despite worldwide condemnation Western powers, led by the United States, quickly normalize relations with the Chinese government.

23 July Plagued by scandal, Japan's ruling Liberal Democratic Party suffers electoral defeat for the first time since 1955.

15 Aug. South African president Pieter W. Botha resigns. He is replaced by F. W. de Klerk, who permits antiapartheid marches and releases some political prisoners in the fall.

18 Aug.	Following non-Communist victories in June parliamentary elections, the Polish government forms a cabinet with non-Communist figures — the first Polish multiparty government in forty years. Solidarity leader Lech Walesa is named president.
	Colombian presidential candidate Luis Carlos Galán is assassinated, reputedly by drug lords. President Virgilio Barco Vargas of Colombia declares war on the Medellín and Cali cocaine cartels. By year's end more than 187 civilians and officials have been killed; 265 bombings have occurred; and officials have made nearly five hundred arrests and seized $250 million worth of property.
23 Aug.	Hundreds of thousands of Lithuanians, Latvians, and Estonians form a human chain across their three states to demand autonomy from the Soviet Union.
26 Sept.	Following eleven years of occupation, the last Vietnamese military forces leave Cambodia.
5–7 Oct.	Soviet leader Mikhail Gorbachev visits East Germany to help celebrate the country's fortieth anniversary. Meanwhile, nearly 170,000 East Germans are migrating to the West via newly opened borders in Hungary, Poland, and Czechoslovakia.
7 Oct.	The Hungarian Communist Party renames itself the Hungarian Socialist Party and renounces communism in favor of democratic socialism.
9 Oct.	For the first time since 1917, the Supreme Soviet grants workers the legal right to strike, albeit under limited conditions.
18 Oct.	East German political leader Erich Honecker resigns and is replaced by Egon Krenz.
	The Hungarian National Assembly drafts a new constitution and sets new multiparty elections for 1990.
19 Oct.	The British Court of Appeals voids the conviction of the "Guildford Four," Irish prisoners convicted of 1974 bombings of pubs in Guildford and Woolwich.
23 Oct.	On the thirty-third anniversary of the 1956 uprising, Hungary declares itself a free republic.
28 Oct.	A ten-thousand-strong prodemocracy demonstration in Prague is broken up by Czechoslovakian police. Leading dissidents, including playwright Vaclav Havel, are arrested.
3 Nov.	An estimated nine thousand people demonstrate in Sofia, Bulgaria, for democratic reforms.
9 Nov.	East Germany allows citizens to visit the West without visas.
10 Nov.	President Todor Zhivkov of Bulgaria resigns after eighteen years in power. He also resigns as general secretary of the Communist Party, which he has directed since 1954.
11 Nov.	In El Salvador the rebel Farabundo Marti National Liberation Front (FMLN) launches a "final offensive" in its ten-year-old civil war against the government after the rightist leader Alberto Cristiani is elected to the presidency. The offensive fails, but the murder of six Jesuit priests on 16 November brings calls in the U.S. Congress for the cessation of U.S. financial and military support for El Salvador.

23 Nov.	Former Czechoslovakian leader Alexander Dubcek, who ushered in the reform "Prague Spring" of 1968, addresses seventy thousand prodemocracy demonstrators in Braislava.
24 Nov.	The Czechoslovakian Communist Party Presidium, including General Secretary Milos Jakes, resigns en masse.
29 Nov.	In Yugoslavia the southern republic of Serbia severs economic relations with the northern republic of Slovenia.
1 Dec.	Soviet president Mikhail Gorbachev meets Pope John Paul II at the Vatican, the first-ever meeting between the head of the Soviet Union and the head of the Catholic Church.
3 Dec.	The entire leadership of East Germany's ruling Socialist Unity party resigns, including all 163 members of the Central Committee.
7 Dec.	Czechoslovakian premier Ladislav Adamec resigns, creating a political crisis. President Gustav Husak resigns three days later. Dissident leaders Vaclav Havel and Alexander Dubcek announce their candidacies for the presidency. On 29 December Havel is elected president and Dubcek is elected chairman of parliament.
	The Lithuanian Supreme Soviet votes to remove the Communist Party's monopoly on power.
10 Dec.	Nearly fifty thousand people demonstrate in Sofia for an end to Communist rule in Bulgaria.
11 Dec.	Two hundred thousand people demonstrate in Leipzig for the reunification of Germany.
15 Dec.	Demonstrators in Timisoara, Romania, surround a church and prevent the secret police from arresting a popular cleric, Rev. Laszlo Tokes.
	Gen. Manuel Noriega's Panamanian regime declares war on insurgents. A U.S. Marine is killed by Panamanian soldiers.
16 Dec.	The United States launches an invasion of Panama City, "Operation Just Cause," to protect American citizens. The invasion, which results in the death of 22 Americans and 202–4,000 Panamanians, succeeds in seizing Gen. Manuel Noriega on 3 January 1990 and sending him to Florida to stand trial on drug trafficking charges. The United Nations denounces the invasion as a "flagrant violation of international law."
	Romanian security forces shoot antigovernment demonstrators in Timisoara.
20 Dec.	The Lithuanian Communist Party declares itself independent of the Soviet Communist Party.
21 Dec.	In Romania a speech by Communist dictator Nicolae Ceausescu is drowned out by prodemocracy demonstrators. In what has become a civil war, his security forces battle units of the army. On 22 December, Ceausescu and his wife are captured by the army, and three days later they are executed by a military firing squad.
22 Dec.	Germans celebrate the opening of the Brandenburg Gate between East and West Berlin, symbolically reuniting East and West Germany and symbolically ending the Cold War.

THE ARTS

by JAMES ZRIMSEK

CONTENTS

Sidebars and tables are listed in italics.

1980

Movies

Airplane!, starring Robert Hays and Julie Hagerty; *Altered States,* starring William Hurt and Blair Brown; *American Gigolo,* starring Richard Gere and Lauren Hutton; *The Blue Lagoon,* starring Brooke Shields and Christopher Atkins; *The Blues Brothers,* starring John Belushi and Dan Aykroyd; *Caddyshack,* starring Chevy Chase, Bill Murray, and Rodney Dangerfield; *Coal Miner's Daughter,* starring Sissy Spacek and Tommy Lee Jones; *Dressed to Kill,* directed by Brian De Palma and starring Michael Caine, Nancy Allen, and Angie Dickinson; *The Elephant Man,* directed by David Lynch and starring John Hurt, Anthony Hopkins, and Anne Bancroft; *The Empire Strikes Back,* starring Harrison Ford, Mark Hamill, and Carrie Fisher; *Fame,* starring Irene Cara; *The Great Santini,* starring Robert Duvall; *Melvin and Howard,* directed by Jonathan Demme and starring Paul LeMat, Mary Steenburgen, and Jason Robards; *Nine to Five,* starring Jane Fonda, Lily Tomlin, and Dolly Parton; *Ordinary People,* starring Donald Sutherland, Mary Tyler Moore, and Timothy Hutton; *Private Benjamin,* starring Goldie Hawn; *Raging Bull,* directed by Martin Scorsese and starring Robert De Niro; *The Shining,* starring Jack Nicholson and Shelley Duvall; *The Stunt Man,* starring Peter O'Toole; *Tess,* starring Nastassia Kinski; *Urban Cowboy,* starring John Travolta and Debra Winger; *Xanadu,* starring Michael Beck, Olivia Newton-John, and Gene Kelly.

Fiction

Jean M. Auel, *The Clan of the Cave Bear;* Ann Beattie, *Falling in Place;* Thomas Berger, *Neighbors;* E. L. Doctorow, *Loon Lake;* Ken Follett, *The Key to Rebecca;* Cynthia Freeman, *Come Pour the Wine;* Shirley Hazzard, *The Transit of Venus;* Erica Jong, *Fanny;* Stephen King, *Firestarter;* Maxine Hong Kingston, *China Men;* Judith Krantz, *Princess Daisy;* Robert Ludlum, *The Bourne Identity;* James Michener, *The Covenant;* Wright Morris, *Plains Song for Female Voices;* Joyce Carol Oates, *Bellefleur;* Walker Percy, *The Second Coming;* Belva Plain, *Random Winds;* Tom Robbins, *Still Life With Woodpecker;* Sidney Sheldon, *Rage of Angels;* John Kennedy Toole, *A Confederacy of Dunces;* Anne Tyler, *Morgan's Passing;* Eudora Welty, *The Collected Stories;* Gene Wolfe, *The Shadow of the Torturer.*

Popular Songs

Air Supply, "Lost in Love"; Pat Benatar, "Heartbreaker"; Blondie, "Call Me"; David Bowie, "Ashes to Ashes"; Captain and Tennille, "Do That to Me One More Time"; Irene Cara, "Fame"; The Clash, "Train in Vain"; The Commodores, "Still"; Christopher Cross, "Sailing" and "Ride Like the Wind"; Grandmaster Flash and the Furious Five, "Freedom"; Funkadelic, "Knee Deep"; Crystal Gayle, "Heart Mender"; Rupert Holmes, "Escape"; Jermaine Jackson, "Let's Get Serious"; Michael Jackson, "Don't Stop Til You Get Enough," "Off the Wall," and "Rock with You"; Billy Joel, "It's Still Rock & Roll to Me"; Kool & The Gang, "Ladies Night" and "Too Hot"; Lipps Inc., "Funkytown"; M, "Pop Muzik"; Paul McCartney, "Coming Up"; Bette Midler, "The Rose"; Ronnie Milsap, "In No Time at All"; Anne Murray, "Broken Hearted Me" and "Daydream Believer"; Willie Nelson, "On the Road Again"; Olivia Newton-John, "Magic" and "Xanadu"; Gary Numan, "Cars"; Tom Petty and the Heartbreakers, "Don't Do Me Like That" and "Refugee"; Pink Floyd, "Another Brick in the Wall"; The Pretenders, "Brass in Pocket"; Prince, "I Wanna Be Your Lover"; Queen, "Crazy Little Thing Called Love"; Smokey Robinson, "Cruisin' "; Kenny Rogers, "Coward of the County"; Rolling Stones, "Emotional Rescue"; Diana Ross, "Upside Down"; The S.O.S. Band, "Take Your Time"; Shalamar, "The Second Time Around"; Spinners, "Cupid/I've Loved You for a Long Time" and "Working My Way Back to You/Forgive Me Girl"; Sugar Hill Gang, "Rapper's Delight"; The Whispers, "And the Beat Goes On."

- Broadway box offices take in almost $200 million.

- The Metropolitan Museum of Art in New York City opens an American wing.

- Michael Cimino's movie *Heaven's Gate* loses $40 million, making Hollywood producers unwilling to finance other big-budget motion pictures by "auteur" directors.

- More than 1.5 million people tour a retrospective exhibit of one thousand works by Pablo Picasso at the Museum of Modern Art in New York City.

- President Jimmy Carter cancels a Washington exhibit of works from the Hermitage Museum in Leningrad to protest the Soviet invasion of Afghanistan.

- Mikhail Baryshnikov becomes director of the American Ballet Theater.

- The Metropolitan Opera receives a $5 million grant from Texaco.

29 Mar. The New York Metropolitan Opera production of *Manon Lescaut*, with Placido Domingo and Renata Scotto, is broadcast via satellite to twenty countries.

13 Apr. *Grease*, the longest-running show on Broadway to date, closes after 3,388 performances.

6 Sept. The Whitney Museum buys Jasper Johns's *Three Flags* for $1 million, the highest price yet paid for a work by a living artist.

1981

Movies *Arthur*, starring Dudley Moore, Liza Minnelli, and John Gielgud; *Atlantic City*, starring Burt Lancaster and Susan Sarandon; *Blow Out*, directed by Brian De Palma and starring John Travolta and Nancy Allen; *Body Heat*, starring William Hurt and Kathleen Turner; *Endless Love*, starring Brooke Shields; *Escape from New York*, starring Kurt Russell; *The French Lieutenant's Woman*, starring Meryl Streep and Jeremy Irons; *Heaven's Gate*, starring Christopher Walken and Kris Kristofferson; *Mommie Dearest*, starring Faye Dunaway; *My Dinner with Andre*, starring Wallace Shawn and Andre Gregory; *On Golden Pond*, starring Henry Fonda, Katharine Hepburn, and Jane Fonda; *Ragtime*, starring James Olson, Mary Steenburgen, Howard E. Rollins Jr., and James Cagney; *Raiders of the Lost Ark*, directed by Steven Spielberg and starring Harrison Ford; *Reds*, directed by Warren Beatty and starring Beatty, Diane Keaton, Jack Nicholson, and Maureen Stapleton; *S.O.B.*, starring William Holden and Julie Andrews; *Stripes*, starring Bill Murray; *Superman II*, starring Christopher Reeve, Gene Hackman, and Margot Kidder.

Fiction Thomas Berger, *Reinhart's Women*; Raymond Carver, *What We Talk About When We Talk About Love*; Howard Fast, *The Legacy*; Cynthia Freeman, *No Time for Tears*; Andrew M. Greeley, *The Cardinal Sins*; Frank Herbert, *God Emperor of Dune*; John Irving, *The Hotel New Hampshire*; Stephen King, *Cujo*; John D. Mac-Donald, *Free Fall in Crimson*; Leonard Michaels, *The Men's Club*; Toni Morrison, *Tar Baby*; Joyce Carol Oates, *Angel of Light*; Harold Robbins, *Goodbye, Janet*; Philip Roth, *Zuckerman Unbound*; Lawrence Sanders, *The Third Deadly Sin*; Martin Cruz Smith, *Gorky Park*; John Updike, *Rabbit Is Rich*; Joseph Wambaugh, *The Glitter Dome*.

Popular Songs

Air Supply, "The One That You Love"; Pat Benatar, "Hit Me with Your Best Shot"; Blondie, "Rapture" and "The Tide Is High"; Kim Carnes, "Bette Davis Eyes"; Rosanne Cash, "Seven Year Ache"; Eric Clapton and His Band, "I Can't Stand It"; The Commodores, "Lady (You Bring Me Up)"; Earl Thomas Conley, "Fire and Smoke"; Christopher Cross, "Arthur's Theme"; Devo, "Whip It"; Neil Diamond, "America," "Hello Again," and "Love on the Rocks"; Duran Duran, "Girls on Film" and "Planet Earth"; E.L.O., "Hold On Tight"; Sheena Easton, "For Your Eyes Only" and "Morning Train"; English Beat, "Mirror in the Bathroom"; Daryl Hall and John Oates, "Kiss on My List"; George Harrison, "All Those Years Ago"; Rick James, "Give It to Me Baby" and "Superfreak"; Kool & The Gang, "Celebration"; John Lennon, "Starting Over" and "Woman"; Manhattan Transfer, "Boy from New York City"; Ronnie Milsap, "No Gettin' Over Me"; Juice Newton, "Angel of the Morning" and "Queen of Hearts"; Oak Ridge Boys, "Elvira"; Dolly Parton, "9 to 5"; Pointer Sisters, "Slow Hand"; The Police, "De Do Do Do, De Da Da Da" and "Don't Stand So Close to Me"; Queen, "Another One Bites the Dust"; Eddie Rabbitt, "I Love a Rainy Night"; REO Speedwagon, "Keep on Loving You"; Kenny Rogers, "Lady" and "I Don't Need You"; Rolling Stones, "Start Me Up"; Diana Ross and Lionel Richie, "Endless Love"; Joey Scarbury, "The Theme from The Greatest American Hero"; Frankie Smith, "Double Dutch Bus"; Rick Springfield, "Jessie's Girl"; Bruce Springsteen, "Hungry Heart"; Billy Squier, "The Stroke"; Rod Stewart, "Passion"; Barbra Streisand, "Woman in Love"; Barbra Streisand and Barry Gibb, "Guilty" and "What Kind of Fool"; Styx, "The Best of Times" and "Too Much Time On My Hands"; Grover Washington Jr., "Just the Two of Us"; Stevie Wonder, "Master Blaster."

- The portable Sony Walkman becomes a huge seller, popularizing "mobile" music.

- The Whitney Museum opens its first branch, in Stamford, Connecticut.

- The $7.2 million San Antonio Museum opens.

- The University of Pennsylvania Press publishes the complete, unexpurgated version of Theodore Dreiser's novel *Sister Carrie,* including thirty-six thousand words that the original publisher, Frank Doubleday, considered too sexually explicit.

- The Rolling Stones earn a record $25 million during their forty-city U.S. tour.

21 May American collector Wendell Cherry buys Picasso's self-portrait *Yo Picasso* at Sotheby's auction house in New York City for $5.83 million, the highest price yet paid for a twentieth-century work of art.

1 Aug. MTV (Music Television) begins broadcasting. Its first video is the Buggles' "Video Killed the Radio Star."

4 Oct. *The Life and Adventures of Nicholas Nickleby* sets a record for Broadway ticket prices — $100 per seat.

1982

Movies

Blade Runner, starring Harrison Ford; *Cat People,* starring Nastassia Kinski and Malcolm McDowell; *Deathtrap,* starring Michael Caine and Christopher Reeve; *Diner,* starring Steve Guttenberg, Kevin Bacon, Mickey Rourke, Daniel Stern, Timothy Daly, Paul Reiser, and Ellen Barkin; *Eating Raoul,* starring Paul Bartel and Mary Woronov; *E.T.: The Extra-Terrestrial,* directed by Steven Spielberg and starring Henry Thomas and Drew Barrymore; *Fast Times at Ridgemont High,* starring Sean Penn, Phoebe Cates, and Jennifer Jason Leigh; *First Blood,* starring Sylvester Stallone; *48 Hrs.,* starring Nick Nolte and Eddie Murphy; *Frances,* starring Jessica Lange; *Making Love,* starring Michael Ontkean, Kate Jackson, Harry Hamlin, and Wendy Hiller; *Missing,* starring Sissy Spacek and Jack Lemmon; *My Favorite Year,* starring Peter O'Toole; *An Officer and a Gentleman,* starring Richard Gere and Debra Winger; *Personal Best,* starring Mariel Hemingway and Patrice Donnelly; *Poltergeist,* starring JoBeth Williams; *The Road Warrior,* starring Mel Gibson; *Sophie's Choice,* starring Meryl Streep and Kevin Kline; *Star Trek II: The Wrath of Khan,* starring William Shatner, Leonard Nimoy, and Ricardo Montalban; *Tootsie,* starring Dustin Hoffman, Jessica Lange, and Teri Garr; *The Verdict,* starring Paul Newman; *Victor/Victoria,* starring Julie Andrews, James Garner, and Robert Preston; *Wild Style,* directed by Charlie Ahearn and starring "Lee" Quinones, Sandra "Pink" Fabara, Fred Braithwaite, and Patti Astor; *The World According to Garp,* starring Robin Williams, Glenn Close, and John Lithgow.

Fiction

Isaac Asimov, *Foundation's Edge;* Jean M. Auel, *The Valley of Horses;* Ann Beattie, *The Burning House;* Saul Bellow, *The Dean's December;* Arthur C. Clarke, *2010: Odyssey Two;* Richard Condon, *Prizzi's Honor;* John M. Del Vecchio, *The 13th Valley;* Stephen R. Donaldson, *The One Tree;* Ken Follett, *The Man from St. Petersburg;* John Gardner, *Mickelsson's Ghosts;* John Jakes, *North and South;* Stephen King, *Different Seasons;* Judith Krantz, *Mistral's Daughter;* Robert Ludlum, *The Parsifal Mosaic;* Bobbie Ann Mason, *Shiloh and Other Stories;* James Michener, *Space;* Joyce Carol Oates, *A Bloodsmoor Romance;* Cynthia Ozick, *Levitation, Five Fictions;* Harold Robbins, *Spellbinder;* Mary Lee Settle, *The Killing Ground;* Sidney Sheldon, *Master of the Game;* Isaac Bashevis Singer, *The Collected Stories;* Danielle Steel, *Crossings;* Paul Theroux, *The Mosquito Coast;* Anne Tyler, *Dinner at the Homesick Restaurant;* Alice Walker, *The Color Purple;* William Wharton, *A Midnight Clear.*

Popular Songs

Alabama, "Love in the First Degree" and "Mountain Music"; Afrika Bambaataa, "Planet Rock"; Toni Basil, "Mickey"; Big Country, "In a Big Country"; Laura Branigan, "Gloria"; Buckner and Garcia, "Pac-Man Fever"; The Cars, "Shake It Up"; Chicago, "Hard to Say I'm Sorry"; Joe Cocker and Jennifer Warnes, "Up Where We Belong"; John Cougar, "Hurts So Good" and "Jack and Diane"; Crosby, Stills & Nash, "Southern Cross" and "Wasted On the Way"; Paul Davis, " '65 Love Affair"; Dazz Band, "Let It Whip"; Earth, Wind & Fire, "Let's Groove"; Fleetwood Mac, "Hold Me" and "Gypsy"; A Flock of Seagulls, "I Ran"; Foreigner, "Waiting For a Girl Like You"; Aretha Franklin, "Jump To It"; J. Geils Band, "Centerfold" and "Freeze-Frame"; The Go-Go's, "Our Lips Are Sealed," "Vacation," and "We Got the Beat"; Daryl Hall and John Oates, "I Can't Go for That (No Can Do)" and "Private Eyes"; Human League, "Don't You Want Me"; Billy Idol, "Hot in the City"; Joan Jett and the Blackhearts, "I Love Rock 'n' Roll"; Journey, "Open Arms"; Loverboy, "Working for the Weekend"; Paul McCartney and Stevie Wonder, "Ebony and Ivory"; Men at Work, "Who Can It Be Now"; Steve Miller Band, "Abracadabra"; Ronnie Milsap, "Any Day Now"; The Motels, "Suddenly Last Summer" and "Only the Lonely"; Willie Nelson, "Always On My Mind"; Juice Newton, "Love's Been a Little Bit Hard on Me"; Olivia Newton-John, "Physical"; The Alan Parsons Project, "Eye in the Sky"; The Police, "Every Little Thing She Does Is Magic"; Prince,

"Controversy"; Quarterflash, "Harden My Heart"; Ricky Skaggs, "Crying My Heart Out Over You"; Soft Cell, "Tainted Love/Where Did Our Love Go"; Rick Springfield, "Don't Talk to Strangers"; Rod Stewart, "Young Turks"; Survivor, "Eye of the Tiger"; Toto, "Rosanna"; Tommy Tutone, "867–5309 (Jenny)"; Twisted Sister, "We're Not Gonna Take It"; Vangelis, "Chariots of Fire"; Hank Williams Jr., "A Country Boy Can Survive"; Stevie Wonder, "That Girl."

- Michael Jackson releases *Thriller*, which becomes the top-selling album in history.

- The Library of America begins publishing collected editions of works by major American authors.

- Compact discs are introduced by the Sony Corporation of Japan and Philips of the Netherlands.

- The Salvador Dali Museum opens in Saint Petersburg, Florida.

- Carnegie Hall in New York City undergoes a $20 million renovation.

- The J. Paul Getty Museum in Malibu, California, receives a $1.1 billion bequest from oil magnate J. Paul Getty, making it the best-endowed museum in America.

- Steven Spielberg's movie *E.T.: The Extra-Terrestrial* earns a record $235 million at the box office in only three months.

7 June   Graceland, the Memphis, Tennessee, home of the late Elvis Presley, is opened to the public as a tourist attraction.

7 Oct.   *Cats*, which becomes the most popular musical of the 1980s, opens on Broadway.

1983

Movies   *The Big Chill*, starring William Hurt, Glenn Close, Kevin Kline, Jeff Goldblum, Tom Berenger, JoBeth Williams, Mary Kay Place, and Meg Tilly; *Breathless*, starring Richard Gere; *Flashdance*, starring Jennifer Beals; *The King of Comedy*, directed by Martin Scorsese and starring Robert De Niro, Jerry Lewis, and Sandra Bernhard; *Lianna*, directed by John Sayles; *Local Hero*, starring Burt Lancaster; *Mr. Mom*, starring Michael Keaton and Teri Garr; *The Outsiders*, starring Matt Dillon, Patrick Swayze, Rob Lowe, Tom Cruise, Emilio Estevez, and Ralph Macchio; *Return of the Jedi*, starring Harrison Ford, Mark Hamill, and Carrie Fisher; *The Right Stuff*, starring Sam Shepard, Scott Glenn, Ed Harris, Dennis Quaid, and Fred Ward; *Risky Business*, starring Tom Cruise and Rebecca DeMornay; *Rumble Fish*, starring Matt Dillon and Mickey Rourke; *Scarface*, directed by Brian De Palma and starring Al Pacino and Michelle Pfeiffer; *Silkwood*, starring Meryl Streep, Kurt Russell, and Cher; *Streamers*, directed by Robert Altman and starring Matthew Modine; *Sudden Impact*, starring Clint Eastwood; *Superman III*, starring Christopher Reeve and Richard Pryor; *Tender Mercies*, starring Robert Duvall; *Terms of Endearment*, starring Shirley MacLaine, Debra Winger, and Jack Nicholson; *Trading Places*, starring Eddie Murphy and Dan Aykroyd; *Twilight Zone — The Movie*, starring Vic Morrow and John Lithgow; *Valley Girl*, starring Nicolas Cage and Deborah Foreman; *War Games*, starring Matthew Broderick, Ally Sheedy, and Dabney Coleman; *The Year of Living Dangerously*, starring Mel Gibson, Sigourney Weaver, and Linda Hunt; *Yentl*, directed and produced by Barbra Streisand, starring Streisand and Mandy Patinkin; *Zelig*, starring Woody Allen and Mia Farrow.

Fiction   Isaac Asimov, *The Robots of Dawn;* Raymond Carver, *Cathedral;* Jackie Collins, *Hollywood Wives;* Stephen R. Donaldson, *White Gold Wielder;* George Garrett, *The Succession;* Mark Helprin, *Winter's Tale;* William Kennedy, *Ironweed;* Stephen King, *Pet Sematary* and *Christine;* Louis L'Amour, *The Lonesome Gods;* Norman Mailer, *Ancient Evenings;* Bernard Malamud, *The Stories;* Anne McCaffrey, *Moreta;* James Michener, *Poland;* Judith Rossner, *August;* Philip Roth, *The Anatomy Lesson;* Lee Smith, *Oral History;* Danielle Steel, *Changes;* Walter Tevis, *The Queen's Gambit;* John Edgar Wideman, *Sent for You Yesterday;* Roger Zelazny, *Unicorn Variations.*

Popular Songs   ABC, "The Look of Love"; Bryan Adams, "Straight from the Heart"; After the Fire, "Der Kommisar"; Air Supply, "Making Love Out of Nothing at All"; John Anderson, "Swingin' "; Adam Ant, "Goody Two Shoes"; Patti Austin with James Ingram, "Baby Come to Me"; David Bowie, "China Girl," "Let's Dance," and "Modern Love"; Irene Cara, "Flashdance . . . What a Feeling"; The Clash, "Rock the Casbah"; George Clinton, "Atomic Dog"; Culture Club, "Do You Really Want to Hurt Me," "I'll Tumble 4 Ya," and "Time"; Def Leppard, "Photograph"; Dexys Midnight Runners, "Come on Eileen"; Thomas Dolby, "She Blinded Me with Science"; Duran Duran, "Hungry Like the Wolf," "Is There Something I Should Know?," and "Rio"; Eurythmics, "Sweet Dreams (Are Made of This)"; Marvin Gaye, "Sexual Healing"; Golden Earring, "Twilight Zone"; Eddy Grant, "Electric Avenue"; Daryl Hall and John Oates, "Maneater"; Herbie Hancock, "Rockit"; Don Henley, "Dirty Laundry"; Michael Jackson, "Beat It," "Billie Jean," "Human Nature," and "Wanna Be Startin' Something"; Michael Jackson and Paul McCartney, "The Girl Is Mine"; Rick James, "Cold Blooded"; Billy Joel, "Allentown" and "Tell Her About It"; Journey, "Separate Ways"; Kajagoogoo, "Too Shy"; The Greg Kihn Band, "Jeopardy"; The Kinks, "Come Dancing"; Huey Lewis and the News, "Heart and Soul"; Men at Work, "Down Under"; Men Without Hats, "The Safety Dance"; Midnight Star, "Freak-a-zoid"; Mtume, "Juicy Fruit"; Musical Youth, "Pass the Dutchie"; The Police, "Every Breath You Take"; The Pretenders, "Back on the Chain Gang"; Charley Pride, "Night Games"; Prince, "1999," "Little Red Corvette," and "Delirious"; Eddie Rabbitt with Crystal Gayle, "You and I"; Lionel Richie, "My Love," "Truly," and "You Are"; Kenny Rogers and Sheena Easton, "We've Got Tonight"; Run-D.M.C., "It's Like That/Sucker M.C."; Bob Seger and the Silver Bullet Band, "Shame on the Moon"; Michael Sembello, "Maniac"; Stray Cats, "Sexy + 17" and "Stray Cat Strut"; Styx, "Mr. Roboto"; Donna Summer, "She Works Hard for the Money"; Talking Heads, "Speaking in Tongues"; Thompson Twins, "Lies"; Toto, "Africa"; Bonnie Tyler, "Total Eclipse of the Heart"; Shelly West, "Jose Cuervo."

- Conceptual artist Javacheff Christo wraps eleven islands in Biscayne Bay, Florida, with pink polypropylene at a cost of $3 million.

22 Apr.   The Dance Black America Festival in Brooklyn, New York, celebrates three hundred years of black dance.

25 May   The movie *Return of the Jedi* sets an opening-day box-office record, $6.2 million.

29 Sept.   After 3,389 performances, *A Chorus Line* becomes the longest-running show in the history of Broadway.

22 Oct.   The Metropolitan Opera in New York City celebrates its one hundredth anniversary with a gala featuring one hundred performers.

1984

Movies

All of Me, starring Steve Martin and Lily Tomlin; *Amadeus,* starring F. Murray Abraham and Tom Hulce; *Beat Street,* starring Robert Taylor, Rae Dawn Chong, and Guy Davis; *Beverly Hills Cop,* starring Eddie Murphy; *Body Double,* directed by Brian De Palma and starring Melanie Griffith; *Body Rock,* starring Lorenzo Lamas; *Breakin',* starring Lucinda Dickey, Adolfo (Shabba-Doo) Quinones, and Michael (Boogaloo Shrimp) Chambers; *Broadway Danny Rose,* starring Woody Allen and Mia Farrow; *Choose Me,* directed by Alan Rudolph and starring Genevieve Bujold; *Country,* starring Jessica Lange and Sam Shepard; *Footloose,* starring Kevin Bacon and Lori Singer; *Ghostbusters,* starring Bill Murray, Dan Aykroyd, Rick Moranis, and Sigourney Weaver; *Gremlins,* starring Zach Galligan and Phoebe Cates; *Indiana Jones and the Temple of Doom,* starring Harrison Ford; *The Karate Kid,* starring Ralph Macchio and Pat Morita; *The Killing Fields,* starring Sam Waterston and Haing S. Ngor; *Missing in Action,* starring Chuck Norris; *Mrs. Soffel,* starring Diane Keaton; *The Natural,* starring Robert Redford, Robert Duvall, and Glenn Close; *Once Upon a Time in America,* starring Robert De Niro and James Woods; *Paris, Texas,* starring Harry Dean Stanton and Nastassia Kinski; *Places in the Heart,* starring Sally Field; *Police Academy,* starring Steve Guttenberg; *Purple Rain,* starring Prince; *Reckless,* starring Aidan Quinn and Daryl Hannah; *Red Dawn,* starring Patrick Swayze; *Repo Man,* directed by Alex Cox and starring Emilio Estevez and Harry Dean Stanton; *The River,* starring Sissy Spacek and Mel Gibson; *Romancing the Stone,* starring Kathleen Turner and Michael Douglas; *Sixteen Candles,* starring Molly Ringwald and Anthony Michael Hall; *Splash,* starring Tom Hanks and Daryl Hannah; *Star Trek III: The Search for Spock,* starring William Shatner and Leonard Nimoy; *Stop Making Sense,* directed by Jonathan Demme and starring Talking Heads; *Stranger Than Paradise,* directed by Jim Jarmusch; *Streets of Fire,* starring Michael Paré, Diane Lane, Rick Moranis, and Amy Madigan; *The Terminator,* starring Arnold Schwarzenegger; *This Is Spinal Tap,* starring Christopher Guest and Michael McKean; *The Woman in Red,* starring Gene Wilder, Kelly LeBrock, and Gilda Radner.

Fiction

Rosellen Brown, *Civil Wars;* Mary Higgins Clark, *Stillwatch;* E. L. Doctorow, *Lives of the Poets: Six Stories and a Novella;* Louise Erdrich, *Love Medicine;* Ellen Gilchrist, *Victory Over Japan;* Robert A. Heinlein, *Job: A Comedy of Justice;* Joseph Heller, *God Knows;* Frank Herbert, *Heretics of Dune;* John Jakes, *Love and War;* Susan Kenney, *In Another Country;* Stephen King and Peter Straub, *The Talisman;* David Leavitt, *Family Dancing;* Robert Ludlum, *The Acquitaine Progression;* Alison Lurie, *Foreign Affairs;* Norman Mailer, *Tough Guys Don't Dance;* Jay McInerney, *Bright Lights, Big City;* Jayne Anne Phillips, *Machine Dreams;* Belva Plain, *Crescent City;* Mario Puzo, *The Sicilian;* Tom Robbins, *Jitterbug Perfume;* Helen Hooven Santmyer, *". . . And Ladies of the Club";* Danielle Steel, *Full Circle;* John Updike, *The Witches of Eastwick;* Leon Uris, *The Haj;* Gore Vidal, *Lincoln;* John Edgar Wideman, *Brothers and Keepers;* Richard Yates, *Young Hearts Crying.*

Popular Songs

Art of Noise, "Beat Box"; Bananarama, "Cruel Summer"; Pat Benatar, "Love Is a Battlefield"; Berlin, "No More Words"; Laura Branigan, "Self Control"; Cameo, "She's Strange"; The Cars, "You Might Think" and "Drive"; Chicago, "Hard Habit to Break"; Phil Collins, "Against All Odds (Take a Look at Me Now)"; Culture Club, "Church of the Poison Mind," "Karma Chameleon," "Miss Me Blind," and "It's a Miracle"; Duran Duran, "Union of the Snake," "New Moon on Monday," and "The Reflex"; Sheila E., "The Glamorous Life"; Eurythmics, "Here Comes the Rain Again"; Frankie Goes to Hollywood, "Two Tribes" and "War"; The Go-Go's, "Head Over Heels"; Daryl Hall and John Oates, "Out of Touch" and "Say It Isn't So"; Corey Hart, "Sunglasses at Night";

Dan Hartman, "I Can Dream About You"; Julio Iglesias and Willie Nelson, "To All the Girls I've Loved Before"; Michael Jackson, "Thriller"; Michael Jackson and Paul McCartney, "Say Say Say"; The Jacksons, "State of Shock"; Rick James, "17"; Billy Joel, "Uptown Girl"; Elton John, "I Guess That's Why They Call It the Blues" and "Sad Songs (Say So Much)"; Howard Jones, "New Song"; The Judds, "Mama He's Crazy"; Chaka Khan, "I Feel for You"; Laid Back, "White Horse"; Cyndi Lauper, "Girls Just Want to Have Fun," "She Bop," and "Time After Time"; John Lennon, "Nobody Told Me"; Huey Lewis and the News, "I Want a New Drug," "If This Is It," and "The Heart of Rock 'n' Roll"; Kenny Loggins, "Footloose"; Madonna, "Holiday," "Borderline," and "Lucky Star"; Barbara Mandrell, "Only a Lonely Heart Knows"; John Cougar Mellencamp, "Pink Houses"; Nena, "99 Luftballoons"; Billy Ocean, "Caribbean Queen"; Ollie and Jerry, "Breakin' . . . There's No Stopping Us"; Ray Parker Jr., "Ghostbusters"; The Alan Parsons Project, "Don't Answer Me"; The Pointer Sisters, "Automatic," "Jump (for My Love)," and "I'm So Excited"; Prince, "When Doves Cry" and "Purple Rain"; Prince & The Revolution, "Let's Go Crazy"; Psychedelic Furs, "Heartbeat"; Queen, "Radio Ga-Ga"; Quiet Riot, "Cum On Feel the Noize"; Ratt, "Round and Round"; Lionel Richie, "All Night Long," "Hello," "Running With the Night," and "Stuck on You"; Rockwell, "Somebody's Watching Me"; Kenny Rogers with Dolly Parton, "Islands in the Stream"; The Romantics, "Talking in Your Sleep"; Scandal featuring Patty Smyth, "The Warrior"; Peter Schilling, "Major Tom (Coming Home)"; Scorpions, "Rock You Like a Hurricane"; Shannon, "Let the Music Play"; Bruce Springsteen, "Born in the U.S.A.," "Cover Me" and "Dancing in the Dark"; George Strait, "Let's Fall to Pieces Together"; Talk Talk, "It's My Life"; Thompson Twins, "Hold Me Now"; Tina Turner, "What's Love Got to Do With It"; Twisted Sister, "We're Not Gonna Take It"; Conway Twitty, "I Don't Know a Thing About Love"; Van Halen, "Jump," "I'll Wait," and "Panama"; John Waite, "Missing You"; Wang Chung, "Dance Hall Days"; Wham!, "Wake Me Up Before You Go-Go"; Deniece Williams, "Let's Hear It for the Boy"; Stevie Wonder, "I Just Called to Say I Love You"; Yes, "Owner of a Lonely Heart"; Paul Young, "Come Back and Stay"; ZZ Top, "Legs."

- The New York Philharmonic Orchestra presents *Horizons 84: The New Romanticism,* a program mixing computer, synthesizer, and performance art.

- After four years of renovation costing $55 million, the Museum of Modern Art in New York City reopens with a new wing that doubles its gallery space.

- The Equitable Life Assurance Society buys ten Thomas Hart Benton murals.

- Forty-five Renaissance masterworks at the Metropolitan Museum are discovered to be forgeries.

- The Getty Museum acquires the Ludwig collection of medieval manuscripts and several major photograph collections, becoming one of the world's finest photograph museums.

- Run-D.M.C.'s self-titled debut album becomes the first rap album to be certified gold.

28 Feb. Michael Jackson wins eight Grammy awards for his album *Thriller,* which tops 37 million in sales and also earns him seven American Music Awards.

19 June The Motion Picture Association of America institutes the PG-13 rating.

1985

Movies

After Hours, directed by Martin Scorsese and starring Griffin Dunne; *Back to the Future,* starring Michael J. Fox; *Blood Simple,* directed by Joel and Ethan Coen; *Brazil,* directed by Terry Gilliam and starring Jonathan Pryce, Kim Greist, and Robert De Niro; *The Breakfast Club,* starring Molly Ringwald, Emilio Estevez, Judd Nelson, Anthony Michael Hall, and Ally Sheedy; *Cocoon,* starring Jessica Tandy, Steve Guttenberg, Don Ameche, Wilford Brimley, and Hume Cronyn; *The Color Purple,* directed by Steven Spielberg and starring Whoopi Goldberg, Danny Glover, Oprah Winfrey, and Margaret Avery; *Desert Hearts,* starring Helen Shaver and Patricia Charbonneau; *Desperately Seeking Susan,* starring Rosanna Arquette, Aidan Quinn, and Madonna; *The Goonies,* starring Sean Astin, Josh Brolin, and Corey Feldman; *Kiss of the Spider Woman,* starring William Hurt and Raul Julia; *Lost in America,* starring Albert Brooks and Julie Hagerty; *Mad Max Beyond Thunderdome,* starring Mel Gibson and Tina Turner; *Mask,* starring Cher, Sam Elliott, and Eric Stolz; *National Lampoon's European Vacation,* starring Chevy Chase; *Out of Africa,* starring Meryl Streep and Robert Redford; *Pee-Wee's Big Adventure,* directed by Tim Burton and starring Pee-Wee Herman; *Prizzi's Honor,* directed by John Huston and starring Jack Nicholson, Kathleen Turner, and Anjelica Huston; *The Purple Rose of Cairo,* directed by Woody Allen and starring Mia Farrow; *Rambo: First Blood, Part 2,* starring Sylvester Stallone; *Rocky IV,* starring Sylvester Stallone; *St. Elmo's Fire,* starring Rob Lowe, Demi Moore, Andrew McCarthy, Ally Sheedy, Emilio Estevez, and Martin Balsam; *The Sure Thing,* starring John Cusack and Daphne Zuniga; *Sweet Dreams,* starring Jessica Lange and Ed Harris; *The Trip to Bountiful,* starring Geraldine Page; *White Nights,* starring Mikhail Baryshnikov, Gregory Hines, and Isabella Rossellini; *Witness,* directed by Peter Weir and starring Harrison Ford and Kelly McGillis; *Young Sherlock Holmes,* starring Nicholas Rowe.

Fiction

Jean M. Auel, *The Mammoth Hunters;* Russell Banks, *Continental Drift;* Ann Beattie, *Love Always;* Barbara Taylor Bradford, *Hold the Dream;* Carolyn Chute, *The Beans of Egypt, Maine;* Tom Clancy, *The Hunt for Red October;* Jackie Collins, *Lucky;* Robin Cook, *Mindbend;* Don DeLillo, *White Noise;* E. L. Doctorow, *World's Fair;* Dominick Dunne, *The Two Mrs. Grenvilles;* Bret Easton Ellis, *Less Than Zero;* Cynthia Freeman, *Illusions of Love;* William Gaddis, *Carpenter's Gothic;* Mary Gordon, *Men and Angels;* Andrew M. Greeley, *Virgin and Martyr;* Robert A. Heinlein, *The Cat Who Walks Through Walls;* Frank Herbert, *Chapterhouse: Dune;* Rolando Hinojosa-Smith, *Partners in Crime;* John Irving, *Cider House Rules;* Garrison Keillor, *Lake Woebegon Days;* Stephen King, *Skeleton Crew;* Louis L'Amour, *Jubal Sackett;* Elmore Leonard, *Glitz;* John D. MacDonald, *The Lonely Silver Rain;* Bobbie Ann Mason, *In Country;* Larry McMurtry, *Lonesome Dove;* James Michener, *Texas;* Anne Rice, *The Vampire Lestat;* Philip Roth, *Zuckerman Bound;* Carl Sagan, *Contact;* Lawrence Sanders, *The Fourth Deadly Sin;* Erich Segal, *The Class;* Sidney Sheldon, *If Tomorrow Comes;* Danielle Steel, *Secrets* and *Family Album;* Irving Stone, *Depths of Glory;* Peter Taylor, *The Old Forest and Other Stories;* Anne Tyler, *The Accidental Tourist;* Kurt Vonnegut, *Galápagos;* Joseph Wambaugh, *Secrets of Harry Bright;* Herman Wouk, *Inside, Outside.*

Popular Songs

ABC, "Be Near Me"; Bryan Adams, "Heaven," "Run to You," "Somebody," and "Summer of '69"; Animotion, "Obsession"; Artists United Against Apartheid, "Sun City"; Philip Bailey with Phil Collins, "Easy Lover"; Pat Benatar, "We Belong"; Jellybean Benitez, "Sidewalk Talk"; Bronski Beat, "Smalltown Boy"; Phil Collins, "Sussudio" and "One More Night"; The Commodores, "Nightshift"; Dead or Alive, "You Spin Me Round (Like a Record)"; DeBarge, "Rhythm of the Night"; Dire Straits, "Money for Nothing"; Duran Duran, "A View to a Kill" and "The Wild Boys"; Sheena Easton, "Strut" and

"Sugar Walls"; Harold Faltermeyer, "Axel F"; Foreigner, "I Want to Know What Love Is"; Aretha Franklin, "Freeway of Love" and "Who's Zoomin' Who"; Glenn Frey, "The Heat Is On" and "You Belong to the City"; General Public, "Never You Done That"; Lee Greenwood, "Dixie Road"; Jan Hammer, "Miami Vice Theme"; Murray Head, "One Night in Bankok"; Don Henley, "The Boys of Summer"; The Hooters, "And We Danced"; Whitney Houston, "You Give Good Love" and "Saving All My Love for You"; Waylon Jennings, Willie Nelson, Johnny Cash, and Kris Kristofferson, "Highwayman"; Howard Jones, "Things Can Only Get Better"; Katrina and the Waves, "Walking on Sunshine"; Kool & The Gang, "Cherish," "Fresh," and "Misled"; Patti LaBelle, "New Attitude"; Julian Lennon, "Valotte"; Huey Lewis and the News, "The Power of Love"; Lisa Lisa and Cult Jam with Full Force, "I Wonder If I Take You Home"; Madonna, "Angel," "Crazy for You," "Dress You Up," "Into the Groove," "Like a Virgin," and "Material Girl"; John Cougar Mellencamp, "Lonely Ol' Night"; Miami Sound Machine, "Conga"; Ronnie Milsap, "Lost in the Fifties Tonight"; New Edition, "Cool It Now"; New Order, "The Perfect Kiss"; John Parr, "St. Elmo's Fire"; Prince & The Revolution, "Raspberry Beret" and "Pop Life"; Ready for the World, "Oh Sheila"; REO Speedwagon, "Can't Fight This Feeling"; David Lee Roth, "California Girls" and "Just a Gigolo"; Run-D.M.C., "King of Rock"; Sade, "Smooth Operator"; Simple Minds, "Don't You (Forget About Me)"; Simply Red, "Money's Too Tight to Mention"; Bruce Springsteen, "I'm on Fire," "Glory Days," and "My Hometown"; Starship, "We Built This City"; Sting, "If You Love Somebody Set Them Free" and "Fortress Around Your Heart"; Tears for Fears, "Everybody Wants to Rule the World," "Shout," and "Head Over Heels"; 'Til Tuesday, "Voices Carry"; The Time, "Jungle Love"; Tina Turner, "Better Be Good to Me," "Private Dancer," and "We Don't Need Another Hero (Thunderdome)"; USA for Africa, "We Are the World"; Wham!, "Careless Whisper" and "Everything She Wants"; Stevie Wonder, "Part-time Lover"; Paul Young, "Everytime You Go Away."

- Income from rental of movies on videocassette equals movie theater box office income.

- The Getty Museum buys Andrea Mantegna's *Adoration of the Magi* for a record $10.4 million.

- Sales of Bruce Springsteen's *Born in the U.S.A.* reach 15 million.

- Madonna's *Like a Virgin* becomes the first album by a female artist to sell more than 5 million copies.

- The all-star recording "We Are the World," released under the name USA for Africa, becomes the hottest-selling single of the decade and raises $50 million for African famine relief.

- Michael Jackson buys ATV Music for $40 million, acquiring the rights to some 250 songs written by John Lennon and Paul McCartney.

- The art magazine *ARTnews* pressures the Austrian government to return thirty-nine hundred artworks seized by the Nazis to their owners, with unclaimed works to be auctioned for Jewish charities.

- Frank Zappa, Dee Snider of Twisted Sister, and John Denver are among the musicians who testify at Senate hearings on explicit lyrics in rock music.

13 July   The "Live Aid" concert held in London and Philadelphia is broadcast to more than 1.6 billion people and raises $70 million for African famine relief.

22 Sept.   "Farm Aid," a concert organized by Willie Nelson, Neil Young, and John Cougar Mellencamp to raise funds for American farmers, is held in Champaign, Illinois.

2 Oct.   Movie actor Rock Hudson dies from an AIDS-related illness, raising public awareness of the disease.

Nov.   The Whitney Museum opens a branch in the new $200 million Equitable Building in New York; Roy Lichtenstein contributes a sixty-eight-foot mural to its entrance.

10–14 Nov.   The first American Music Week at Alice Tully Hall in New York City features three hundred performances of music by new and established American composers, including John Cage, Aaron Copland, and Robert Erickson.

1986

Movies   *Aliens,* starring Sigourney Weaver; *Blue Velvet,* directed by David Lynch and starring Kyle MacLachlan, Laura Dern, Dennis Hopper, Isabella Rossellini, and Dean Stockwell; *Children of a Lesser God,* starring William Hurt and Marlee Matlin; *The Color of Money,* directed by Martin Scorsese and starring Paul Newman and Tom Cruise; *Crimes of the Heart,* starring Diane Keaton, Sissy Spacek, and Jessica Lange; *Down and Out in Beverly Hills,* starring Nick Nolte, Bette Midler, and Richard Dreyfuss; *The Fly,* starring Jeff Goldblum and Geena Davis; *Hannah and Her Sisters,* starring Woody Allen, Mia Farrow, Dianne Wiest, and Michael Caine; *The Hitcher,* starring Rutger Hauer, C. Thomas Howell, and Jennifer Jason Leigh; *The Mission,* starring Robert De Niro and Jeremy Irons; *Mona Lisa,* starring Bob Hoskins; *Peggy Sue Got Married,* starring Kathleen Turner and Nicolas Cage; *Platoon,* directed by Oliver Stone and starring Charlie Sheen, Tom Berenger, and Willem Dafoe; *Round Midnight,* starring Dexter Gordon; *Ruthless People,* starring Danny DeVito and Bette Midler; *Salvador,* directed by Oliver Stone and starring James Woods and James Belushi; *Shanghai Surprise,* starring Madonna and Sean Penn; *She's Gotta Have It,* directed by Spike Lee; *Sid and Nancy,* directed by Alex Cox and starring Gary Oldman and Chloe Webb; *Something Wild,* directed by Jonathan Demme and starring Melanie Griffith and Jeff Daniels; *Stand by Me,* starring River Phoenix; *Star Trek IV: The Voyage Home,* starring William Shatner and Leonard Nimoy; *Top Gun,* starring Tom Cruise and Kelly McGillis; *Under the Cherry Moon,* starring Prince.

Fiction   Isaac Asimov, *Foundation and Earth;* Barbara Taylor Bradford, *Act of Will;* Tom Clancy, *Red Storm Rising;* Arthur C. Clarke, *The Songs of Distant Earth;* Jackie Collins, *Hollywood Husbands;* Pat Conroy, *The Prince of Tides;* Stephen Coonts, *Flight of the Intruder;* Patti Davis, *Homefront;* Stephen R. Donaldson, *Mordant's Need;* Louise Erdrich, *The Beet Queen;* Ken Follett, *Lie Down With Lions;* Richard Ford, *The Sportswriter;* Cynthia Freeman, *Seasons of the Heart;* Larry Heinemann, *Paco's Story;* Ernest Hemingway, *Garden of Eden;* Tama Janowitz, *Slaves of New York;* Stephen King, *It;* David Leavitt, *The Lost Language of Cranes;* Robert Ludlum, *The Bourne Supremacy;* Sue Miller, *The Good Mother;* Andre Norton, *Flight in Yiktor;* Belva Plain, *The Golden Cup;* Reynolds Price, *Kate Vaiden;* Sally Quinn, *Regrets Only;* Lawrence Sanders, *The Eighth Commandment;* Mary Lee Settle, *Celebration;* Clifford D. Simak, *Highway of Eternity;* Danielle Steel, *Wanderlust;* Robert Stone, *Children of Light;* Peter Taylor, *A Summons to Memphis;* John Updike, *Roger's Version.*

Popular Songs

Carl Anderson and Gloria Loring, "Friends and Lovers"; Art of Noise featuring Duane Eddy, "Peter Gunn"; Atlantic Starr, "Secret Lovers"; B-52's, "Summer of Love"; Bananarama, "Venus"; Bangles, "Manic Monday" and "If She Knew What She Wants"; Berlin, "Take My Breath Away"; Bon Jovi, "You Give Love a Bad Name"; Boston, "Amanda"; James Brown, "Living in America"; Cameo, "Word Up"; Belinda Carlisle, "Mad About You"; Rosanne Cash, "Never Be You"; Phil Collins, "Take Me Home"; Culture Club, "Move Away"; The Dream Academy, "Life in a Northern Town"; Sheila E., "A Love Bizarre"; Erasure, "Oh L'Amour"; Falco, "Rock Me Amadeus"; Peter Gabriel, "Sledgehammer"; Genesis, "Invisible Touch"; Gwen Guthrie, "Ain't Nothin' Goin' On But the Rent"; Heart, "Never" and "These Dreams"; Whitney Houston, "How Will I Know" and "Greatest Love of All"; Human League, "Human"; INXS, "What You Need"; Janet Jackson, "What Have You Done for Me Lately," "Nasty," and "When I Think of You"; The Jets, "Crush On You"; Grace Jones, "Slave to the Rhythm"; The Judds, "Have Mercy"; Patti LaBelle and Michael McDonald, "On My Own"; Cyndi Lauper, "True Colors"; Level 42, "Something About You"; Huey Lewis and the News, "Stuck with You"; Madonna, "Live to Tell," "Papa Don't Preach," and "True Blue"; Reba McEntire, "Whoever's in New England"; John Cougar Mellencamp, "R.O.C.K. in the U.S.A." and "Small Town"; Mr. Mister, "Broken Wings" and "Kyrie"; Eddie Murphy, "Party All the Time"; Nu Shooz, "I Can't Wait"; Orchestral Manoeuvres in the Dark, "If You Leave"; Robert Palmer, "Addicted to Love"; Pet Shop Boys, "West End Girls"; Prince & The Revolution, "Kiss" and "Mountains"; Regina, "Baby Love"; Lionel Richie, "Dancing on the Ceiling" and "Say You, Say Me"; Run-D.M.C., "Walk This Way"; Simply Red, "Holding Back the Years"; Stacey Q, "Two of Hearts"; Starship, "Sara"; The Statler Brothers, "Too Much On My Heart"; Jermaine Stewart, "We Don't Have to Take Our Clothes Off"; Timbuk 3, "The Future's So Bright, I Gotta Wear Shades"; Randy Travis, "On the Other Hand" and "1982"; Tina Turner, "Typical Male"; Dionne Warwick and Friends, "That's What Friends Are For"; Steve Winwood, "Higher Love"; Dwight Yoakam, "Honky Tonk Man" and "Guitars, Cadillacs"; ZZ Top, "Sleeping Bag."

- Dollywood, Dolly Parton's theme park in Pigeon Forge, Tennessee, opens to the public.

- Choreographer Martha Graham's dance company celebrates its sixtieth anniversary.

- The Joffrey Ballet celebrates its thirtieth anniversary.

26 Feb. Robert Penn Warren is named the first poet laureate of the United States.

5 May Cleveland is chosen as the site for the Rock and Roll Hall of Fame.

1987

Movies

Baby Boom, starring Diane Keaton; *Beverly Hills Cop II*, starring Eddie Murphy; *The Big Easy*, starring Dennis Quaid and Ellen Barkin; *Broadcast News*, starring Holly Hunter, William Hurt, and Albert Brooks; *Cry Freedom*, starring Kevin Kline and Denzel Washington; *Dirty Dancing*, starring Patrick Swayze and Jennifer Grey; *Empire of the Sun*, directed by Steven Spielberg and starring Christopher Bale, John Malkovich, and Miranda Richardson; *Fatal Attraction*, starring Michael Douglas and Glenn Close; *Full Metal Jacket*, directed by Stanley Kubrick and starring Matthew Modine; *Gardens of Stone*, directed by Francis

Ford Coppola and starring James Caan, Anjelica Huston, and James Earl Jones; *Good Morning, Vietnam,* starring Robin Williams; *Hamburger Hill,* starring Anthony Barrile and Michael Patrick Boatman; *House of Games,* directed by David Mamet and starring Lindsay Crouse and Joe Mantegna; *Ishtar,* starring Warren Beatty and Dustin Hoffman; *Lethal Weapon,* starring Mel Gibson and Danny Glover; *The Lost Boys,* starring Jason Patric, Kiefer Sutherland, and Corey Haim; *Matewan,* directed by John Sayles; *Moonstruck,* starring Cher, Nicolas Cage, Olympia Dukakis, and Danny Aiello; *Near Dark,* starring Adrian Pasdar and Jenny Wright; *Prick Up Your Ears,* starring Gary Oldman; *Radio Days,* directed by Woody Allen; *Raising Arizona,* directed by Joel and Ethan Coen and starring Nicolas Cage and Holly Hunter; *River's Edge,* starring Dennis Hopper and Keanu Reeves; *Robocop,* starring Peter Weller and Nancy Allen; *Roxanne,* starring Steve Martin and Daryl Hannah; *Sign o' the Times,* starring Prince, Sheila E., and Sheena Easton; *The Stepfather,* starring Terry O'Quinn and Shelley Hack; *Superman IV: The Quest for Peace,* starring Christopher Reeve; *Suspect,* starring Cher; *Three Men and a Baby,* starring Tom Selleck, Steve Guttenberg, and Ted Danson; *Tin Men,* starring Richard Dreyfuss and Danny DeVito; *The Untouchables,* directed by Brian De Palma and starring Kevin Costner, Sean Connery, and Robert De Niro; *Wall Street,* directed by Oliver Stone and starring Charlie Sheen, Michael Douglas, Martin Sheen, and Daryl Hannah; *Who's That Girl?,* starring Madonna and Griffin Dunne; *The Witches of Eastwick,* starring Jack Nicholson, Cher, Susan Sarandon, and Michelle Pfeiffer.

Fiction   Isaac Asimov, *Fantastic Voyage II;* Saul Bellow, *More Die of Heartbreak;* Truman Capote, *Answered Prayers;* Tom Clancy, *Patriot Games;* Mary Higgins Clark, *Weep No More My Lady;* Arthur C. Clarke, *2061: Odyssey Three;* Robin Cook, *Outbreak;* Janet Dailey, *Heiress;* Carrie Fisher, *Postcards from the Edge;* Thomas Flanagan, *The Tenants of Time;* John Jakes, *Heaven and Hell;* Garrison Keillor, *Leaving Home;* Stephen King, *Misery, The Tommyknockers,* and *The Eyes of the Dragon;* Louis L'Amour, *The Haunted Mesa;* Larry McMurtry, *Texasville;* James Michener, *The Legacy;* Toni Morrison, *Beloved;* Cynthia Ozick, *The Messiah of Stockholm;* Robert B. Parker, *Pale Kings and Princes;* Jayne Anne Phillips, *Fast Lanes;* Frederik Pohl, *The Annals of the Heechee;* Philip Roth, *The Counterlife;* Lawrence Sanders, *The Timothy Files;* Sidney Sheldon, *Windmills of the Gods;* Danielle Steel, *Kaleidoscope* and *Fine Things;* Scott Turow, *Presumed Innocent;* Kurt Vonnegut, *Bluebeard;* Tom Wolfe, *The Bonfire of the Vanities.*

Popular Songs   Herb Alpert, "Diamonds"; Bangles, "Walk Like an Egyptian"; Beastie Boys, "(You Gotta) Fight for Your Right (to Party)"; Bon Jovi, "Livin' on a Prayer" and "Wanted Dead or Alive"; Bobby Brown, "Girlfriend"; Peter Cetera with Amy Grant, "The Next Time I Fall"; Club Nouveau, "Lean on Me"; The Robert Cray Band, "Smoking Gun"; Crowded House, "Don't Dream It's Over"; Cutting Crew, "(I Just) Died in Your Arms"; Chris de Burgh, "The Lady in Red"; Duran Duran, "Notorious"; Gloria Estefan and Miami Sound Machine, "Rhythm Is Gonna Get You"; Exposé, "Come Go With Me"; Samantha Fox, "Touch Me (I Want Your Body)"; Aretha Franklin and George Michael, "I Knew You Were Waiting for Me"; Kenny G, "Songbird"; Peter Gabriel, "Big Time"; Georgia Satellites, "Keep Your Hands to Yourself"; Genesis, "Land of Confusion"; Debbie Gibson, "Only in My Dreams"; Lou Gramm, "Midnight Blue"; Grateful Dead, "Touch of Grey"; Heart, "Alone"; Bruce Hornsby and the Range, "Mandolin Rain" and "The Way It Is"; Whitney Houston, "Didn't We Almost Have It All" and "I Wanna Dance With Somebody (Who Loves Me)"; Billy Idol, "Mony Mony"; Janet Jackson, "Control" and "Let's Wait Awhile"; Michael Jackson "Bad"; Michael Jackson with Siedah Garrett, "I Just Can't Stop Loving You"; Michael Johnson, "Give Me Wings"; The Judds, "Cry Myself to Sleep"; L. L. Cool J, "I Need Love"; Cyndi Lauper, "Change of Heart"; LeVert,

"Casanova"; Huey Lewis and the News, "Hip to Be Square" and "Jacob's Ladder"; Lisa Lisa and Cult Jam, "Head to Toe" and "Lost in Emotion"; Los Lobos, "La Bamba"; Madonna, "Open Your Heart," "La Isla Bonita," "Who's That Girl," and "Causing a Commotion"; Reba McEntire, "What Am I Gonna Do About You"; Bill Medley and Jennifer Warnes, "(I've Had) The Time of My Life"; John Cougar Mellencamp, "Paper in Fire"; George Michael, "I Want Your Sex"; Robbie Nevil, "C'est la Vie"; K. T. Oslin, "80s Ladies"; Tom Petty and the Heartbreakers, "Jammin' Me"; Pink Floyd, "Learning to Fly"; Prince, "Sign O' the Times" and "U Got the Look"; R.E.M., "The One I Love"; Smokey Robinson, "Just to See Her"; Linda Ronstadt and James Ingram, "Somewhere Out There"; Bob Seger, "Shakedown"; Bruce Springsteen, "Brilliant Disguise"; Starship, "Nothing's Gonna Stop Us Now"; Tiffany, "I Think We're Alone Now"; Randy Travis, "Forever and Ever, Amen"; U2, "With or Without You," "I Still Haven't Found What I'm Looking For," and "Where the Streets Have No Name"; Luther Vandross, "Stop to Love"; Suzanne Vega, "Luka"; Billy Vera and the Beaters, "At This Moment"; Wang Chung, "Everybody Have Fun Tonight"; Jody Watley, "Looking for a New Love"; Whitesnake, "Here I Go Again"; Kim Wilde, "You Keep Me Hangin' On"; Bruce Willis, "Respect Yourself"; World Party, "Ship of Fools."

- Jasper Johns's *Out the Window* sells for $3.6 million; Rembrandt Peale's *Rubens Peale with a Geranium* fetches $4 million at auction.

- The Terra Museum of American Art opens in Chicago.

- The Metropolitan Museum opens a $26 million wing dedicated to twentieth-century art.

- Luciano Pavarotti and Yo-Yo Ma are among the performers at the AIDS benefit concert *Music for Life* held at Carnegie Hall in New York City.

- The Smithsonian Institution opens the Arthur M. Sackler Gallery of Asian and Near Eastern Art and the Museum of African Art in Washington, D.C.

- The Vienna Philharmonic performs the complete Beethoven symphonies and concerti at Carnegie Hall in New York.

- Christie's of New York sells Vincent van Gogh's *Sunflowers* for $39.9 million at auction; Sotheby's of New York sells his *Irises* for $53.9 million.

- George Michael's song "I Want Your Sex" is banned from many radio-station playlists because its lyrics are considered too suggestive to be heard by young listeners.

13 July   Madonna, Leontyne Price, and rapper Queen Latifah are among the performers at an AIDS benefit concert held at Madison Square Garden in New York City.

Aug.   More than fifty thousand fans gather in Memphis to commemorate the tenth anniversary of Elvis Presley's death.

5 Oct.   Thirteen New York dance companies perform a *Dancing for Life* benefit for AIDS research.

1988

Movies

The Accidental Tourist, starring William Hurt, Geena Davis, and Kathleen Turner; *The Accused,* starring Jodie Foster and Kelly McGillis; *Beetlejuice,* directed by Tim Burton and starring Michael Keaton, Alec Baldwin, Geena Davis, and Winona Ryder; *Big,* starring Tom Hanks; *Big Business,* starring Bette Midler and Lily Tomlin; *Bright Lights, Big City,* starring Michael J. Fox; *Bull Durham,* starring Kevin Costner, Susan Sarandon, and Tim Robbins; *Cocktail,* starring Tom Cruise; *Colors,* directed by Dennis Hopper and starring Sean Penn and Robert Duvall; *Coming to America,* starring Eddie Murphy; *A Cry in the Dark,* starring Meryl Streep and Sam Neill; *Dangerous Liaisons,* starring Glenn Close, John Malkovich, and Michelle Pfeiffer; *Die Hard,* starring Bruce Willis; *A Fish Called Wanda,* starring John Cleese, Jamie Lee Curtis, Kevin Kline, and Michael Palin; *The Good Mother,* starring Diane Keaton and Liam Neeson; *The Last Temptation of Christ,* directed by Martin Scorsese and starring Willem Dafoe; *Married to the Mob,* directed by Jonathan Demme and starring Michelle Pfeiffer; *Mississippi Burning,* starring Gene Hackman and Willem Dafoe; *The Naked Gun,* starring Leslie Nielsen, Priscilla Presley, and O. J. Simpson; *Rain Man,* starring Dustin Hoffman and Tom Cruise; *Running on Empty,* starring Christine Lahti, River Phoenix, Judd Hirsch, and Martha Plimpton; *Tucker,* starring Jeff Bridges; *Twins,* starring Arnold Schwarzenegger and Danny DeVito; *The Unbearable Lightness of Being,* starring Daniel Day-Lewis, Lena Olin, and Juliette Binoche; *Who Framed Roger Rabbit?,* starring Bob Hoskins; *Willow,* starring Val Kilmer; *Working Girl,* starring Melanie Griffith, Harrison Ford, and Sigourney Weaver.

Fiction

Poul Anderson, *The Year of the Ransom;* Richard Bach, *One;* Barbara Taylor Bradford, *To Be the Best;* Nash Candelaria, *The Day the Cisco Kid Shot John Wayne;* Raymond Carver, *Where I'm Coming From;* John Casey, *Spartina;* Tom Clancy, *The Cardinal of the Kremlin;* Jackie Collins, *Rock Star;* Joan Collins, *Prime Time;* Stephen Coonts, *Final Flight;* Don DeLillo, *Libra;* Pete Dexter, *Paris Trout;* Dominick Dunne, *People Like Us;* Louise Erdrich, *Tracks;* Alex Haley, *A Different Kind of Christmas;* Susan Isaacs, *Shining Through;* Dean R. Koontz, *Lightning;* Judith Krantz, *Till We Meet Again;* Robert Ludlum, *The Icarus Agenda;* Anne McCaffrey, *Dragonsdawn;* Larry McMurtry, *Anything for Billy;* James Michener, *Alaska;* Gloria Naylor, *Mama Day;* Belva Plain, *Tapestry;* Anne Rice, *The Queen of the Damned;* Lawrence Sanders, *Timothy's Game;* Erich Segal, *Doctors;* Sidney Sheldon, *The Sands of Time;* Lee Smith, *Fair and Tender Ladies;* Danielle Steel, *Zoya;* Peter Straub, *Koko;* Anne Tyler, *Breathing Lessons;* Leon Uris, *Mitla Pass.*

Popular Songs

Aerosmith, "Angel" and "Rag Doll"; Rick Astley, "Never Gonna Give You Up" and "Together Forever"; Anita Baker, "Giving You the Best That I Got"; The Beach Boys, "Kokomo"; Bon Jovi, "Bad Medicine"; Breathe, "Hands to Heaven"; Edie Brickell and the New Bohemians, "What I Am"; Bobby Brown, "Don't Be Cruel" and "My Prerogative"; James Brown, "I'm Real"; Belinda Carlisle, "Circle in the Sand," "Heaven Is a Place on Earth," and "I Get Weak"; Eric Carmen, "Hungry Eyes"; Rosanne Cash, "If You Could Change Your Mind"; Tracy Chapman, "Fast Car"; Cheap Trick, "The Flame"; Cher, "I Found Someone"; The Church, "Under the Milky Way"; Phil Collins, "Groovy Kind of Love"; D. J. Jazzy Jeff and the Fresh Prince, "Parents Just Don't Understand"; Terence Trent D'Arby, "Sign Your Name" and "Wishing Well"; Taylor Dayne, "Tell It to My Heart," "Prove Your Love," and "I'll Always Love You"; Def Leppard, "Love Bites" and "Pour Some Sugar on Me"; Depeche Mode, "Route 66"; E.U., "Da'Butt"; Erasure, "Chains of Love"; The Escape Club, "Wild Wild West"; Gloria Estefan and Miami Sound Machine, "1-2-3" and "Anything for You"; Exposé, "Seasons Change"; Samantha Fox, "Naughty Girls (Need Love Too)"; Debbie Gibson, "Foolish Beat," "Out of the Blue," and

"Shake Your Love"; Guns N' Roses, "Sweet Child O' Mine"; George Harrison, "Got My Mind Set on You"; Whitney Houston, "Where Do Broken Hearts Go," "One Moment in Time," and "So Emotional"; Ice-T, "Colors"; INXS, "Need You Tonight," "Devil Inside," "Never Tear Us Apart," and "New Sensation"; Michael Jackson, "Dirty Diana," "Man in the Mirror," and "The Way You Make Me Feel"; Jellybean, "Jingo (Remix)"; The Jets, "Make It Real" and "Rocket 2 U"; Elton John, "Candle in the Wind" and "I Don't Want to Go On with You Like That"; Johnny Kemp, "Just Got Paid"; Gladys Knight and the Pips, "Love Overboard"; L. L. Cool J, "I'm Goin Back to Cali"; M/A/R/R/S, "Pump Up the Volume"; Richard Marx, "Hold Onto the Nights"; Bobby McFerrin, "Don't Worry, Be Happy"; John Cougar Mellencamp, "Check It Out" and "Cherry Bomb"; George Michael, "Faith," "Father Figure," "Monkey," and "One More Try"; Midnight Oil, "Beds Are Burning"; New Edition, "If It Isn't Love"; New Kids On the Block, "Please Don't Go Girl"; Billy Ocean, "Get Outta My Dreams, Get Into My Car"; Robert Palmer, "Simply Irresistible"; Pebbles, "Girlfriend" and "Mercedes Boy"; Pet Shop Boys and Dusty Springfield, "What Have I Done to Deserve This?"; Robert Plant, "Tall Cool One"; Prince, "Alphabet St." and "I Could Never Take the Place of Your Man"; Psychedelic Furs, "All That Money Wants"; Brenda Russell featuring Joe Esposito, "Piano in the Dark"; Salt-N-Pepa, "Push It"; Salt-N-Pepa featuring E.U., "Shake Your Thang"; Siouxsie and the Banshees, "The Killing Jar" and "Peek-A-Boo"; The Smithereens, "Only a Memory"; Al B. Sure!, "Nite and Day"; Patrick Swayze featuring Wendy Frazer, "She's Like the Wind"; Keith Sweat, "I Want Her"; Tiffany, "Could've Been"; U2, "Desire"; Van Halen, "Finish What Ya Started"; Whitesnake, "Is This Love"; Keith Whitley, "Don't Close Your Eyes"; Vanessa Williams, "The Right Stuff"; Steve Winwood, "Roll With It"; Stevie Wonder, "Skeletons"; Dwight Yoakam and Buck Owens, "Streets of Bakersfield."

* Whitney Houston becomes the first recording artist in *Billboard* history to have four number one songs from a single album; only one month later Michael Jackson breaks this record with five number one singles from his *Bad* album.

* Religious fundamentalists picket Martin Scorsese's controversial movie *The Last Temptation of Christ*.

* Motown Records is sold to MCA and a Boston investment firm for $61 million.

* Total spending for cultural events ($3.4 billion) exceeds spending on spectator sports for the first time in American history.

* Picasso's *Acrobat and Young Harlequin* sells for $38.4 million, a record sum for a twentieth-century artist; Jasper Johns's *False Starts* sets an auction record for a living artist, $17 million.

2 Sept. Bruce Springsteen, Sting, Peter Gabriel, and Tracy Chapman launch a benefit concert tour for Amnesty International.

1989

Movies *Batman*, directed by Tim Burton and starring Jack Nicholson, Michael Keaton, and Kim Basinger; *Bill and Ted's Excellent Adventure*, starring Keanu Reeves and Alex Winter; *Born on the Fourth of July*, directed by Oliver Stone and starring Tom Cruise; *Casualties of War*, starring Sean Penn and Michael J. Fox; *Crimes and Misdemeanors*, directed by Woody Allen; *Dead Poets Society*, starring Robin Williams; *Do the Right Thing*, directed by Spike Lee and starring Danny Aiello,

Ossie Davis, Ruby Dee, John Turturro, and Lee; *Driving Miss Daisy*, starring Jessica Tandy and Morgan Freeman; *Drugstore Cowboy*, directed by Gus Van Sant and starring Matt Dillon and Kelly Lynch; *Enemies: A Love Story*, starring Ron Silver, Lena Olin, and Anjelica Huston; *The Fabulous Baker Boys*, starring Jeff Bridges, Beau Bridges, and Michelle Pfeiffer; *Field of Dreams*, starring Kevin Costner; *Ghostbusters II*, starring Bill Murray and Dan Aykroyd; *Glory*, starring Matthew Broderick, Denzel Washington, and Morgan Freeman; *Heathers*, starring Winona Ryder and Christian Slater; *Honey, I Shrunk the Kids*, starring Rick Moranis; *In Country*, starring Bruce Willis; *Indiana Jones and the Last Crusade*, starring Harrison Ford, Sean Connery, and River Phoenix; *Look Who's Talking*, starring John Travolta and Kirstie Alley; *National Lampoon's Christmas Vacation*, starring Chevy Chase; *Parenthood*, starring Steve Martin and Dianne Wiest; *Say Anything*, starring John Cusack; *Scandal*, starring Joanna Whalley-Kilmer and John Hurt; *sex, lies and videotape*, starring James Spader and Andie MacDowell; *Star Trek V: The Final Frontier*, starring William Shatner and Leonard Nimoy; *The War of the Roses*, starring Michael Douglas and Kathleen Turner; *When Harry Met Sally*, starring Billy Crystal and Meg Ryan.

Fiction

Jimmy Buffett, *Tales from Margaritaville*; Tom Clancy, *Clear and Present Danger*; Mary Higgins Clark, *While My Pretty One Sleeps*; Stephen Coonts, *Minotaur*; Len Deighton, *Spy Line*; E. L. Doctorow, *Billy Bathgate*; Ken Follett, *The Pillar of the Earth*; John Grisham, *A Time to Kill*; Allan Gurganus, *The Oldest Living Confederate Widow Tells All*; John Irving, *A Prayer for Owen Meany*; John Jakes, *California Gold*; Stephen King, *The Dark Half*; Dean R. Koontz, *Midnight*; Larry McMurtry, *Some Can Whistle*; James Michener, *Caribbean*; Belva Plain, *Blessings*; Lawrence Sanders, *Capital Crimes*; Martin Cruz Smith, *Polar Star*; Danielle Steel, *Star*; Amy Tan, *The Joy Luck Club*; Alice Walker, *The Temple of My Familiar*.

Popular Songs

Paula Abdul, "Straight Up," "Forever Your Girl," and "Cold Hearted"; Aerosmith, "Love in an Elevator"; Art of Noise featuring Tom Jones, "Kiss"; Rick Astley, "She Wants to Dance With Me"; B-52's, "Love Shack"; Bee Gees, "One"; Clint Black, "Better Man" and "Killin' Time"; Bon Jovi, "I'll Be There For You"; Boy Meets Girl, "Waiting for a Star to Fall"; Bobby Brown, "Every Little Step," "On Our Own," and "Roni"; Belinda Carlisle, "Leave a Light On"; Cher, "If I Could Turn Back Time"; Cher and Peter Cetera, "After All"; Neneh Cherry, "Buffalo Stance" and "Kisses on the Wind"; Chicago, "Look Away"; Phil Collins, "Another Day in Paradise" and "Two Hearts"; Alice Cooper, "Poison"; Elvis Costello, "Veronica"; Cowboy Junkies, "Sweet Jane"; The Cult, "Fire Woman"; The Cure, "Love Song" and "Fascination Street"; Taylor Dayne, "Don't Rush Me"; De La Soul, "Me, Myself and I"; Fine Young Cannibals, "She Drives Me Crazy" and "Good Thing"; Lita Ford (duet with Ozzy Osbourne), "Close My Eyes Forever"; Debbie Gibson, "Lost in Your Eyes" and "Electric Youth"; Great White, "Once Bitten, Twice Shy"; Guns N' Roses, "Paradise City," "Patience," and "Welcome to the Jungle"; Heavy D & The Boyz, "We Got Our Own Thang"; Highway 101, "Setting Me Up"; Hoodoo Gurus, "Come Anytime"; Janet Jackson, "Miss You Much" and "Rhythm Nation"; Michael Jackson, "Smooth Criminal"; Billy Joel, "We Didn't Start the Fire"; Kon Kan, "I Beg Your Pardon"; Kool Moe Dee, "They Want Money"; L. L. Cool J, "I'm That Type of Guy"; K. D. Lang, "Pulling Back the Reins"; Living Colour, "Cult of Personality"; Love & Rockets, "So Alive"; Madonna, "Cherish," "Express Yourself," "Like a Prayer," and "Oh Father"; Ziggy Marley and the Melody Makers, "Tumblin' Down"; Maurice, "This Is Acid"; Bette Midler, "Wind Beneath My Wings"; Mike + The Mechanics, "The Living Years"; Milli Vanilli, "Baby Don't Forget My Number," "Blame It on the Rain," "Girl I'm Gonna Miss You," and "Girl You Know It's True"; Bob Mould, "See a Little Light"; New Kids on the Block, "You Got It (The Right Stuff)," "I'll Be Loving You (Forever)," and "Hangin' Tough"; New Order, "Fine Time"; Roy Orbison, "You

Got It"; Donny Osmond, "Soldier of Love"; Tom Petty, "Free Fallin'," "I Won't Back Down," and "Runnin' Down a Dream"; Pixies, "Here Comes Your Man"; Poison, "Every Rose Has Its Thorn"; Prince, "Batdance"; Public Enemy, "Fight the Power"; Public Image Ltd., "Disappointed"; R.E.M., "Orange Crush" and "Stand"; The Replacements, "I'll Be You"; Linda Ronstadt and Aaron Neville, "Don't Know Much"; Roxette, "The Look"; Skid Row, "18 and Life"; Soul II Soul featuring Caron Wheeler, "Back to Life" and "Keep on Movin'"; Rod Stewart, "My Heart Can't Tell You No"; The Stop the Violence Movement, "Self-Destruction"; Donna Summer, "This Time I Know It's for Real"; Tears for Fears, "Sowing the Seeds of Love"; Technotronic, "Pump Up the Jam"; Tone Loc, "Funky Cold Medina" and "Wild Thing"; Traveling Wilburys, "End of the Line"; Conway Twitty, "She's Got a Single Thing in Mind"; Stevie Ray Vaughan and Double Trouble, "Crossfire"; Warrant, "Heaven"; Karyn White, "Superwoman"; White Lion, "When the Children Cry"; Will to Power, "Baby I Love Your Way/Freebird Medley"; XTC, "The Mayor of Simpleton"; Young M.C., "Bust a Move."

- A Picasso self-portrait sells for $47.85 million, a record sum for a twentieth-century work; later this year the record is broken by Picasso's *Pierrette's Wedding,* which fetches $51.3 million.

- Willem de Kooning's *Interchange* sells for $20.7 million, a record for a living artist.

- Movies gross a record $5 billion.

- Sony Corporation buys Columbia Pictures for $3.4 billion.

5 Mar.   Amid controversy, artist Richard Serra's mammoth sculpture *Tilted Arc* is removed from Federal Plaza in New York.

30 Mar.   The Louvre in Paris adds a new entrance, a glass and metal pyramid designed by American architect I. M. Pei.

21 June   The original script for the movie classic *Citizen Kane* (1941) is sold at auction for $210,000.

OVERVIEW

The Culture of Success. Much of American art in the 1980s was shaped by and responded to the consumerism and feel-good conservatism of the Reagan era. In a decade preoccupied with success and image, art got bigger: bigger in scope and ambition (elaborate sets, large casts, and complex narratives for commercial musicals), bigger in theme (epic visions in the works of Neo-Expressionist painters), bigger in budget (record advances for new novels), and bigger in promotion (hyping of pop albums and art auctions). Art also became far bigger as a cultural presence. From twenty-four-hour-a-day media coverage to in-your-face images of pop art, video, and graffiti, art was more immediate, available, and accessible than ever before. The new scale and influence of art suited Americans in the 1980s. With more disposable income than in the 1970s and weary of the pervasive pessimism of that decade, they wanted to enjoy themselves again. They began to spend more money on arts and entertainment, aided by the healthiest national economy since the 1960s. Prices in the art market reached new heights as the wealthy discovered that acquiring fine art was a way to parade their success. With increasing corporate, foreign, and private investment in Hollywood and the rapid growth of computer technology, American cinema became increasingly the province of big-budget adventure spectacles designed like thrill rides and packaged as pure escapist fun. Broadway was right behind, hawking high-end productions crammed with star names and special effects. There were other toys too: MTV served up one fantasy after another, while small, portable audiocassette players, videocassette recorders, and compact discs gave young urban professionals — "yuppies" — the freedom to enjoy books and music on the go and movies in their homes. As a result art packaged as entertainment became one of the most profitable (and exportable) American industries. The primary sources of art and entertainment — from galleries to movie studios to publishing houses to record labels — came more than ever to look on art as a business and to view the financial bottom line as the ultimate purpose of an art form.

Wealth and Status. Inevitably Americans' obsession with material success was reflected in the art of the 1980s. Appropriation artist Jeff Koons used status symbols such as bar accessories and sports equipment to celebrate and lampoon materialism. In 1985 Madonna's "Material Girl" video showed the budding starlet swathed in mink and fluttering greenbacks, trilling that "the boy with the cold hard cash is always Mr. Right." Rap singers such as L. L. Cool J boasted not only about sexual conquests but also about their fine clothing and sports cars. Popular movies — including *Risky Business* (1983), *Trading Places* (1983), *Baby Boom* (1987), and *Working Girl* (1988) — glorified "having it all": career, wealth, and family. *Wall Street* (1987), despite a finger-wagging preachiness, made a cultural hero of corporate raider Gordon Gekko, who declares that "greed . . . is good." Tom Wolfe's best-selling novel *The Bonfire of the Vanities* (1987) centered on a yuppie financier who imagines himself "Master of the Universe." Even John Updike's working-class protagonist Harry Angstrom reappeared to taste the good life in *Rabbit Is Rich* (1981). Bret Easton Ellis studied the decadent swimming-pool culture of rich California teens in *Less Than Zero* (1985), while "glitz" novelists such as Sidney Sheldon (*Master of the Game,* 1982), Shirley Conran (*Lace,* 1982), Jackie Collins (*Hollywood Wives,* 1983), and Judith Krantz (*I'll Take Manhattan,* 1986) set their potboilers in the international playgrounds of the nouveau riche. Far more cynical than these writers was playwright David Mamet, who skewered the American success ethic in *Glengarry Glen Ross* (1983) and *Speed-the-Plow* (1988), his explorations of greed and opportunism in the world of con artists, hustlers, and deal makers. Artist Jenny Holzer displayed a similar disaffection in her controversial "Inflammatory Essays," billboards, and posters: "Money creates taste" and "Private property created crime" were two of her best-known aphorisms.

The Art of Publicity. The media flourished in the 1980s, fed by a celebrity-starved public. It seemed as though virtually everyone, as Andy Warhol once predicted, was famous for fifteen minutes. Trend-spotting magazines such as *US* and *People* and "behind the scenes" television programs, including *Entertainment Tonight* and *Lifestyles of the Rich and Famous,* bombarded Americans with more information than ever before about actors, artists, writers, singers, and video performers. Some, such as novelist Salman Rushdie and painter Jean-Michel Basquiat, found themselves thrust into the spotlight overnight. Other celebrities were discovered in unlikely spots: Vanna White turned letters on a game show; Courteney Cox danced onstage in a rock video; La Toya Jackson bared all for centerfolds. A national taste for scandal boosted several careers; Vanessa Williams lost her Miss America crown after nude photographs of her were published in *Penthouse*, but she rebounded with a strong recording career. Meanwhile, the infidelities of Bruce Springsteen, Sylvester Stallone, and other celebrities were photographed by enquiring photographers from the supermarket tabloids. Riding trends with the savvy of advertising executives, many of the most successful artists and performers of the decade learned to use the media to package and market their public images and to create a demand for their projects and products. The expert in self-marketing and image mongering was Madonna, but she had plenty of competition from many others — including novelist Tom Wolfe, film actors Tom Cruise and Arnold Schwarzenegger, Broadway hit maker Andrew Lloyd Webber, artists Julian Schnabel and Robert Longo, movie moguls Michael Eisner and Jeffrey Katzenberg, and horror writer Stephen King.

Brats. Disillusioned in designer wear, underappreciated in urban lofts, misunderstood at the mall, and affecting boredom through a haze of designer drugs and alcohol — the" brats" were the 1980s version of the Lost Generation. The term began with a group of young actors known as the "Brat Pack," made notorious in movies such as *Sixteen Candles* (1984), *The Breakfast Club* (1985), and *St. Elmo's Fire* (1985). Demi Moore, Molly Ringwald, Rob Lowe, Charlie Sheen, Sean Penn, and a host of other petulant young actors flooded the multiplexes of America with hipness and "brattitude." Many of them starred in film versions of novels by another group of "brats," overnight literary sensations Tama Janowitz, Jay McInerney, and twenty-one-year-old Bret Easton Ellis. After hailing these three novelists as modern chroniclers of youthful alienation, the media later dismissed them as mere barometers of pop culture. Tom Cruise, one of the hottest movie stars of the 1980s, went deftly from one "brat" role to another. Music video produced several "brats" in the late 1980s, including Tiffany, Debbie Gibson, and New Kids on the Block, all of whom were still teenagers when they began selling millions of CDs in suburbia. Many of the most popular performers on the rap scenes were brats: D. J. Jazzy Jeff and the Fresh Prince, Kid 'N Play, L. L. Cool J, and Tone Loc. Eddie Murphy of the popular television show *Saturday Night Live* became a movie star at twenty-one. Meanwhile, in the world of jazz, audiences were amazed at the talents of boy wonders Wynton Marsalis and Harry Connick Jr., both of whom had recording contracts by the time they were twenty. "Brat" painters Julian Schnabel and Robert Longo competed for the attentions of the media and art community by bad-mouthing one another, boasting about their artistic prowess, and dressing in

black. By the time they were thirty their incomes were in six figures.

Bigshots. The most treasured American art form in the 1980s may have been the art of the deal. Increasingly, creative people learned to think like businesspeople, and those artists and performers who stayed on top learned to see their work as a commodity and an investment. It was not surprising, then, that some actors and movie directors shifted gears and became producers. In the 1980s, as in the studio era of the 1930s and 1940s, only Hollywood producers and a few superstars had the clout to get their projects on the screen. The A-list of movers and shakers included Barry Diller, Michael Eisner, Jeffrey Katzenberg, Sherry Lansing, Joel Silver, David Geffen, and Jon Peters. At the top were Steven Spielberg and George Lucas; between them they were responsible for producing and/or directing six of the top ten moneymakers of the decade. On Broadway it was much the same story; with audiences demanding ever-bigger shows, important producers (such as Cameron Mackintosh), directors (such as Trevor Nunn), and investors assembled new plays and musicals with the military strategy of generals. Andrew Lloyd Webber became the Midas of Broadway after composing the megahits *Evita* (1978), *Cats* (1982), and *The Phantom of the Opera* (1986). After the success of his first full-length novel, *The Bonfire of the Vanities*, Wolfe took potshots at established novelists in a manifesto on how to write fiction. Any work by Stephen King, the wealthiest and most-published novelist of the decade, was virtually guaranteed to make the best-seller lists (and be sold to Hollywood). Manhattan art dealers Tony Shafrazi and Mary Boone made their reputations, and vast amounts of money, by shrewdly investing in brash young artists with superstar potential, working the media machine to create demand, and jacking up prices accordingly. Film actors such as Eddie Murphy and Bruce Willis raised their fees exponentially after a single hit. Madonna was perhaps the most skillful entrepreneur of the decade, becoming a one-woman conglomerate as she marketed her movies, videos, recordings, and image and made millions.

Marketing. In the 1980s economic success required aggressive advertising and clever packaging. Spielberg and Lucas presold their blockbuster movies, often a year or more in advance, with teasers, trailers, and merchandising tie-ins that ranged from action figures to soft drink cups. Pop artist Keith Haring took marketing a step further, creating a line of products bearing his most popular graphic images and then opening a store to sell them. His contemporaries took note; Jenny Holzer and Mark Kostabi were among other artists of the 1980s with their own product lines. The marketers of *Batman* (1989) went still further, planning their media blitz around a single, simple graphic — a bat logo — and selling the movie as a shared public "event." By then, the makers of motion pictures such as *The Big Chill* (1983), *Flashdance* (1983), *Footloose* (1984), *Top Gun* (1986), and *Dirty Dancing* (1987) had revolutionized the film, video, and recording industries by using soundtrack albums and accompanying hit singles and videos as advertisements for movies. In 1984 Michael Jackson altered video production, packaging, and store sales with his $1 million high-tech "Thriller" clip and an accompanying cassette, *The Making of Michael Jackson's Thriller*. Within a few years, rock and pop performers were typically releasing "video albums" to be sold alongside new recordings. Madonna, Tama Janowitz, and Kenny Scharf were so skillful at marketing their work that the product itself became secondary; they became advertisements for themselves. Advance promotion, including advertisements on MTV, helped horror writers Stephen King and Peter Straub set a record for pre-publication sales of their collaborative novel *The Talisman* (1984). After the huge success of *Cats*, preselling also became the new standard on Broadway. Before the show opened in October 1982 the producer, Cameron Mackintosh, mounted massive advertising campaigns and used the media to attract large audiences long in advance. Similar techniques did the same for the big-budget, expensive-ticket musicals *Les Miserables, The Phantom of the Opera*, and *Miss Saigon*.

Style over Substance. "Where's the beef?" asked a much-quoted television commercial in the mid 1980s. The question might well be applied to the art of the decade, much of which was characterized by bloated budgets, endless hype, an obsession with technology, and the recycling of old ideas and images, usually from the media. In recording studios better and cheaper technology — from synthesizers to samplers — created an artificial, heavily "produced" sound on many pop, rock, jazz, country, and even classical releases. With the spectacular success of music videos, the "look" of a band or a singer became as important as the quality or content of a song. Record companies began to sign a barrage of new recording artists who were highly photogenic but had more to offer visually than musically. The pop duo Milli Vanilli were forced to return their 1989 Grammy Award for Best New Artist when it was discovered that someone else had done the singing on their hit records. Media-inspired artists such as Kenny Scharf and Keith Haring were often clever and fresh in their appropriation of popular culture, but their trendiness and insistence on fun as a theme undermined the possibility of enduring artistic reputations. Neo-Expressionist painters Julian Schnabel and Robert Longo and photographer Robert Mapplethorpe were also criticized as slick and superficial. The bottom-line, blockbuster mentality of Hollywood was a boon to the special-effects industry, but often the movies themselves seemed only excuses to show off computerized technology or, in the cases of *Return of the Jedi* (1983) and *Batman*, to merchandise toys. Action movies and big-star comedies — including *Stripes* (1981), *Beverly Hills Cop* (1984), *Lethal Weapon* (1987), and *Die Hard* (1988) — became exercises in crowd-pleasing irreverence and glib one-liners. Even "arty" cult movies such as *Blue Velvet* (1986), *Brazil* (1985), and *Blade Runner* (1982) attracted

more attention for their style and hip attitude than for content or character. Broadway hits suffered from the same high gloss; reviewers complained that most shows offered nothing special but effects. Andrew Lloyd Webber struck many critics as formulaic in his approach to musicals, while similar charges were leveled against Stephen King. The new wave of "brat" novelists were accused of peppering their fiction with hip cynicism, ironic wit, and pop-culture references while forgetting to supply the "beef" of plot and characters.

Pop Culture Crossover. Starting with hip-hop — an urban subculture that thrived in the Hispanic and African American communities during the early 1980s — American pop culture forms began to merge and overlap to a degree never seen before. Hip-hop unified the audiences for three different but interdependent arts: break dancing, graffiti art, and rap music. The hip-hop sensibility spread to the artistic community of New York City, which embraced its energy and forms. Suddenly multimedia was everywhere. New York "art clubs" such as Area and The Palladium drew huge and varied crowds by merging art, video, dance, music, and fashion. Pop artists became successful by appropriating images and ideas from other arts and from the mass culture. Music video was ignited from the sparks of dance, film, and pop music. The success of the movie *Flashdance* was the key to a new crossover marketing phenomenon that used soundtracks and videos to boost box office and used blockbuster movies to sell soundtracks and videos. This new merging of film, video, music, and other mass media also helped to create an ever-growing preoccupation with fashion, image, hipness, trendiness, and "attitude," especially among the young. Thanks to video and hip-hop, dance and choreography reached mainstream America as never before. Video stars such as Sting, Madonna, and Tina Turner and directors such as Adrian Lyne launched movie careers; respected motion picture directors, including Martin Scorsese and Brian De Palma, tried their hands at video. Painters Eric Fischl and Robert Longo; novelists Tama Janowitz and Jay McInerney; and playwrights Sam Shepard, David Mamet, and Beth Henley dabbled in film, video, and music projects.

Revisiting the 1960s. During the 1980s the media seemed obsessed with the baby-boom generation, the "thirtysomethings" who came of age in the 1960s and 1970s. A rash of Vietnam War movies — *Platoon* (1986), *Full Metal Jacket* (1987), *In Country* (1989), and *Casualties of War* (1989) — indicated that the 1960s generation was anxious to reexamine, or even make peace with, their troubling experiences in that decade. Other movies of the 1980s dealt with the changes the baby boom generation underwent between the 1960s and the 1980s. *The Big Chill* depicts a group of seven college friends who come together for the funeral of a compatriot. Once idealists and rebels, they have been calmed into complacency by material success in their thirties. Baby boomer nostalgia, thanks to the Motown soundtrack, was a key to the success of the movie. Such nostalgia was also expressed in pop songs by aging baby boomers such as Bruce Springsteen ("My Hometown," 1985; "Glory Days," 1985), John Cougar Mellencamp ("Check It Out," 1988; "Cherry Bomb," 1988), and Bryan Adams ("Summer of '69," 1985), each of whom looked back from adult responsibility to the simpler, more vital days of their youth in the 1960s. In 1986 Mellencamp also contributed "R.O.C.K. in the U.S.A.," a tribute to rock and soul music of the early 1960s. Other wistful backward glances were provided by Starship ("We Built This City," 1985), George Harrison ("All Those Years Ago," 1981), and the Grateful Dead ("Touch of Grey," 1987). Even the post–baby-boom generation could not resist nostalgia; in their work pop artists Ronnie Cutrone and Kenny Scharf resurrected the television cartoons they had watched during their childhoods in the 1960s. *Valley Girl* (1983) was the first movie to portray a new, inverted generation gap: conservative, materialistic teenagers of the 1980s attempting to tolerate the druggy excesses of their liberal former-hippie parents. In *Running on Empty* (1988) a teenager is forced to live on the run from the FBI because of his parents' radical political activism in the past. The message of such movies, like that of Tom Cruise movies and David Mamet plays, seemed to be that milking the system was far more enjoyable and profitable than rebelling against it.

Selling the Counterculture. One of the ironies of the conservative Reagan era was the way in which mainstream America embraced and canonized previously underground, countercultural, even subversive artists and images. An appetite for glamour and decadence brought the drug subculture, once the province of fringe dwellers and bohemians, into the living rooms of the wealthy, as chronicled by novelists Bret Easton Ellis, Tom Wolfe, and Jay McInerney. Largely for the same reason, Robert Mapplethorpe's glossy homoerotic photographs turned a tidy profit. Wolfe, the best-known chronicler of the hippie counterculture during the 1960s, became a dandyish literary star in the 1980s. Jack Nicholson repackaged his 1970s counterculture image for the 1980s in a series of crowd-pleasing "everyman" roles that allowed him to personify and celebrate lechery and madness. Jane Fonda reversed her legendary 1970s radicalism and became an exercise queen, selling millions of aerobics videos. Former burnout Glenn Frey of The Eagles reemerged in the mid 1980s with new hits and a new pumped-up body, which he showed off in a series of health club advertisements. Others who cleaned up their acts, mended their youthful ways, and polished their images for the 1980s marketplace included John Lennon, Steve Miller, and Brian Wilson of the Beach Boys. Even the Grateful Dead went mainstream, scoring their first Top 40 hit. Meanwhile, Eddie Murphy, Bill Murray, John Belushi, Dan Aykroyd, and other stars of the countercultural 1970s comedy program *Saturday Night Live* were showered with lucrative movie deals. The public cheered as

their cutting-edge irreverence and political satire were transformed by Hollywood into harmless and lovable fraternity-boy antics. The Manhattan underground of the late 1970s was repackaged and swallowed up as 1980s commerce. Bands once considered punk, including Talking Heads and Blondie, received full-scale promotion and posted Top 40 hits, while previously "alternative" and "fringe" artists Robert Longo, Laurie Anderson, Keith Haring, Jenny Holzer, Cindy Sherman, and Kenny Scharf began selling their work for small fortunes. Weird, arty personas and images, only recently considered hopelessly uncommercial by the recording industry, were used to peddle new pop stars such as Cyndi Lauper, Boy George, Annie Lennox, and Prince to the video generation. Some of the most "alternative" musical acts — including R.E.M., Metallica, and Run-D.M.C. — were catapulted into stardom and filled stadiums for their concerts.

Comebacks. In the 1980s "retro" was in, and faded pop-culture heroes returned to the limelight in droves as aging baby boomers became nostalgic. Andy Warhol returned to the limelight amid a new frenzy for pop art. Painter David Hockney, who had raised eyebrows in the late 1960s with his homoerotic poolside images, became one of the wealthiest and most collected artists of the 1980s. Dennis Hopper, best known as the hippie director of *Easy Rider* (1969), became a mainstream Hollywood hero after appearing in the cult hits *Blue Velvet* and *River's Edge* (1987). Cher was reborn as a movie actress, winning an Oscar for *Moonstruck* (1987). She also resurrected her recording career. Tina Turner emerged triumphantly from Ike Turner's shadow, strutting her stuff on stage, in videos, and in movies. Aretha Franklin returned to the top of the charts, and 1960s heartthrob Tom Jones broke into video with his version of Prince's "Kiss" (1989). The aging and ever-changing singing group Jefferson Airplane reemerged as Starship. The Beach Boys, John Lennon, and George Harrison all returned to the top of the charts. Pop music of the late 1980s began to resemble that of the 1970s, with Heart, Queen, Cheap Trick, the Bee Gees, Boston, and Aerosmith all scoring major hits. Meanwhile, Reagan-inspired nostalgia and a renewed taste for style and elegance made old-time crooners such as Frank Sinatra, Dean Martin, and Tony Bennett popular again. Golden Age movie actors — including Henry Fonda, Don Ameche, Katharine Hepburn, and Jessica Tandy — came out of retirement to capture press attention and Oscars. After a slump in the 1970s Disney became the most profitable Hollywood studio, resurrecting the careers of stars such as Bette Midler, Richard Dreyfuss, and Robin Williams.

Causes and Issues. The 1980s were not a decade of greed, style, and self-promotion for everyone. Some artists and entertainers involved themselves in 1960s-style social causes. Others used their work to make political statements. Bob Geldof organized the Band Aid project in 1984 and the Live Aid twin concerts in London and Philadelphia in 1985 to aid victims of famine in Africa, inspiring the USA for Africa collaboration that produced the all-star pop anthem "We Are the World" (1985). The Farm Aid concert held in 1985 sought to raise money to pay off the debts of American farmers, but its chief accomplishment was publicizing the farmers' plight in the 1980s. John Cougar Mellencamp's album *Scarecrow* and a trio of "save the farm" movies in 1984 — *Places in the Heart, Country,* and *The River* — had a similar effect, focusing media attention on foreclosures and the disappearance of private ownership. Jessica Lange of *Country* and Sissy Spacek of *The River* joined Jane Fonda on Capitol Hill to testify on behalf of American farmers. The AIDS epidemic, disregarded by the government during much of the decade, also prompted arts benefits, including auctions and performances, as well as fundraising efforts by celebrities such as Elizabeth Taylor. Larry Kramer used his play *The Normal Heart* (1985) to protest government apathy and raise public awareness of the AIDS crisis. Filmmaker Oliver Stone was openly critical of U.S. foreign policy in his movies; in *Salvador* (1986) he criticized the Reagan administration's military support of the anticommunist regime in Nicaragua. Hardcore punk bands such as the Dead Kennedys and Minor Threat also attacked the administration's policies, staging a Rock Against Reagan tour in 1983. Projects such as the movie *Cry Freedom* (1987) and Paul Simon's *Graceland* (1987) album helped to open American eyes to South African apartheid. The rock recording "Sun City" (1985) promoted a boycott of South African entertainment venues.

The Macho Decade. Despite the strong presence of women in the job market and in the culture at large, the arts in the 1980s remained largely a boys' club. In the art world the media focused much attention on the brash, all-male fraternity of Neo-Expressionists and on male pop artists. In Hollywood and on Broadway the decade was characterized by powerful producers and deal makers (almost exclusively men); macho action stars such as Sylvester Stallone and Arnold Schwarzenegger dominated movie screens. At the top of the pop-music scene were all-American-boy rockers such as Bruce Springsteen and all-male heavy metal acts. The burgeoning hip-hop culture was built on male assertiveness and competition, as was the underground punk-rock scene. The model for stage and screen dialogue was created by playwright/screenwriter David Mamet, a master of realistic and hypermasculine speech patterns. Men — especially white men — dominated mass culture so effortlessly that it was often easy to forget minority artists, who had struggled publicly, vocally, and often successfully to win respect and attention in the 1960s and 1970s. Racial and feminist issues, vital to the arts throughout the previous decade, seemed almost invisible for much of the 1980s.

Minorities. Yet American women did continue to make their mark in the arts. Meryl Streep, nominated for six Academy Awards during the 1980s, emerged as a model of strong, independent movie women. Other successful actresses of the 1980s included Glenn Close, Jessica Lange, Debra Winger, Sissy Spacek, and Kathleen Turner. Women began to get a foothold in Hollywood as directors and producers as well. Playwrights Beth Henley, Marsha Norman, and Wendy Wasserstein were all Pulitzer Prize winners, and novelists Anne Tyler and Anne Rice both won critical acclaim. Video stars such as Madonna, Cyndi Lauper, Tina Turner, and Pat Benatar proved that women could be strong, powerful, sexual, and fun. Artists Jenny Holzer and Laurie Anderson influenced the national culture with their provocative wordplay. Even country music, long the home of old-fashioned, docile women, boasted independent new stars such as Reba McIntire and Emmylou Harris. African American artists also achieved mainstream success. Eddie Murphy was a huge crossover star, as were Michael Jackson, Prince, Whitney Houston, Lionel Richie, and dozens of others. Wynton Marsalis became a jazz superstar, while playwright August Wilson was the new toast of Broadway. Bill T. Jones emerged as an influential dancer and choreographer; painter Jean-Michel Basquiat became a media sensation. Novelists Toni Morrison and Alice Walker both won Pulitzer Prizes. Hip-hop culture spread from urban ghettos to suburbia thanks to exposure in movies, videos, and galleries. Rap artists such as Run-D.M.C. attracted large interracial audiences.

Gay Visibility. Gay sensibilities and themes, long present in American art, moved closer to mainstream acceptance in the 1980s. Throughout the decade movies as varied as *Making Love* (1982), *Victor/Victoria* (1982), *Personal Best* (1982), *Deathtrap* (1982), *Lianna* (1983), *Streamers* (1983), *My Beautiful Laundrette* (1985), *Kiss of the Spider Woman* (1985), *Desert Hearts* (1985), *Maurice* (1987), and *Prick Up Your Ears* (1987) featured gay characters, story lines, and romances, usually in a sensitive and straightforward way. Novelist David Leavitt and playwrights Larry Kramer and Terence McNally received serious critical attention, while other popular novels and plays — including Ellis's *Less Than Zero*, Alice Walker's *The Color Purple* (1982), and Wendy Wasserstein's *The Heidi Chronicles* (1988) — treated homosexuality and bisexuality as commonplace. Keith Haring, Kenny Scharf, and David Hockney were among the best-selling artists of the decade. Popular music and video brought gay performers — especially those in British bands such as Culture Club, Erasure, Dead or Alive, Pet Shop Boys, and Bronski Beat — into American living rooms, while Madonna tweaked listeners and viewers with a defiant sexual ambiguity. Composer and lyricist Stephen Sondheim flourished on Broadway with his innovative musicals, while Harvey Fierstein won awards for his plays. Mark Morris and collaborators Bill T. Jones and Arnie Zane won acclaim for their dance performances and choreography. Film actor Rock Hudson's death from AIDS in 1985, followed by the AIDS-related deaths of Liberace, photographer Robert Mapplethorpe, and director-choreographer Michael Bennett increased awareness of gay issues throughout America. By the end of the decade emerging gay artists — including singer K. D. Lang, pianist Michael Feinstein, and Gus Van Sant, director of the movie *Drugstore Cowboy* (1989) — were finding new popularity with mainstream audiences.

Backlash. Despite the apparent assimilation of minorities into mainstream American culture, the arts in the 1980s mirrored continued societal friction over minority issues. The divisiveness of race became more pronounced as Ronald Reagan's economic policies swelled the ranks of the (largely white) rich and the (largely black) poor. The rap group Public Enemy vented their anger with the album *It Takes a Nation of Millions to Hold Us Back*. The movie *Colors* (1988) dealt with interracial violence among warring street gangs. Tom Wolfe's novel *The Bonfire of the Vanities* portrayed the uproar over a rich white New Yorker's hit-and-run killing of a poor black youth, while Spike Lee's movie *Do the Right Thing* (1989) depicted the mutual hostilities of a mixed-race ghetto. August Wilson's play *Fences* confronted the effect of racism on an aging ballplayer, while Alice Walker's postfeminist novel *The Color Purple* raised storms of protest over its scathing portrayal of African American men. Many Americans also sensed an antifeminist backlash during the decade, largely the result of Reagan-era conservatism that seemed to prefer women in their traditional cultural roles. This trend was most strongly reflected in Hollywood movies such as *Fatal Attraction* (1987), *Baby Boom*, and *The Good Mother* (1988), which "punished" career women and "rewarded" stay-at-home mothers. Jack Nicholson's crowd-pleasing lament over women in *The Witches of Eastwick* (1987) — "Do they exist just to torture us?" — was a typical sentiment in movies of the late 1980s. The decade-long wave of slasher and stalker movies also elicited protests that they victimized women, as did music videos (especially heavy metal), which frequently depicted women as passive sex toys. Works by feminist artists such as Cindy Sherman and Barbara Kruger protested society's continued sexism. Meanwhile, homosexuals found themselves targets of a conservative backlash during the decade, first as a result of AIDS hysteria and *Rambo*-era machismo and later as a result of a controversy over government funding of the arts.

The Culture War. The insurrectionary works of some minority artists shocked and angered conservative segments of the public in the 1980s, fueling a debate about the place of art in society and the relationship of art, law, and government. While on the whole, consumer spending on art increased during the decade (encouraged by the tax-cutting policies of Ronald Reagan), the president's agenda led to cuts in government funding for the arts. During the 1980s the Christian right spent much of its energy on fighting to censor "subversive" books, movies, recordings, and showings of fine art. In 1989 Sen. Jesse Helms (R–N.C.) spearheaded an attempt to make drastic cuts in government funding for the National Endowment for the Arts (NEA) after he became outraged over an NEA-funded exhibit that included "obscene" photographs by Robert Mapplethorpe. A compromise was reached — funding was curtailed, not eliminated — but Helms's battle was typical of the increasing politicization of the arts during the 1980s. Washington wife Tipper Gore and the Parents' Music Resource Center (PMRC) fought for warning labels on album covers to protect children from raunchy rock lyrics and cover art. Their efforts led to a series of highly publicized congressional hearings on "porn rock." Punk rocker Jello Biafra was acquitted of obscenity charges after a long trial in Los Angeles. Across the United States school boards made headlines by attempting to remove controversial books from school libraries, many of them classic novels by respected authors such as John Steinbeck, F. Scott Fitzgerald, and J. D. Salinger. Some of these cases escalated into court battles over students' First Amendment rights; one case reached the Supreme Court. Other popular targets of the Christian Right included "biased" history texts, rap music, "blasphemous" movies and videos, and the "desecration" by artists of the American flag.

Patriotism. If any single impression was left by the Reagan presidency, it was an almost fevered Cold War patriotism that echoed the strong anticommunist rhetoric of the 1950s. Reagan embraced entertainment legends such as liberal Democrat-turned-Republican Frank Sinatra, especially when they fit an image of national pride and religious faith. In 1982 he presented singer Kate Smith with the Medal of Freedom for "inspiring the nation" with her renditions of "God Bless America." He used country singer Lee Greenwood's song "God Bless the U.S.A." as his campaign theme in 1984; Greenwood sang it at the Republican National Convention. When Bruce Springsteen reached new heights of popularity with the release "Born in the U.S.A." (1984), Reagan praised the musician's "patriotic" message in his campaign speeches. He, and many of Springsteen's fans, cheerfully ignored the antigovernment rage of the song, and Springsteen rejected Reagan's attempt to appropriate him and his song for the conservative cause. In Hollywood a host of mid-1980s movies — from *Rambo: First Blood, Part 2* (1985) to *Missing in Action* (1984) to *Rocky IV* (1985) to *Red Dawn* (1984) — fought the Cold War on-screen, while flag-wavers such as *Top Gun* (1986) boosted Reagan's efforts to build a strong national defense. The overall result was a sometimes mindless patriotism not seen in Hollywood since World War II. This movie propaganda was hardly surprising, given Reagan's history as a film actor. In fact, he cultivated an image akin to that of a Western hero riding into town to restore peace, order, and prosperity. At the end of his second term he appeared, waving goodbye, on the cover of *Vanity Fair* over a title that read "Happy Trails." The Reagan persona was well suited to a decade in which many Americans valued style and image over substance and worshiped wealth and success.

TOPICS IN THE NEWS

THE ART BOOM

Money, Money. The wealth and prosperity enjoyed by upper- and middle-class Americans during much of the 1980s brought about tremendous growth in the art market, particularly in New York City, as Americans rushed to invest in art. Between 1983 and 1985 more than one hundred galleries opened in New York, seventy-eight of them in the East Village. Gallery sales in 1984 alone exceeded $1 billion. That year 50 percent of all auction transactions were under $1,000; only four years later the average price paid for a work of art had risen to between $7,000 and $11,000. Top auction prices for single works, paid mostly by dealers, hovered at about $3 million early in the decade. By the end of the 1980s individual works were selling to private bidders for ten to twenty times that amount. Sales at each of the two biggest New York auction houses, Sotheby's and Christie's, surpassed $1 billion in 1987 and accounted for a third of the world's art transactions. During the decade a few private collectors saw the works they owned appreciate in value by as much as 700 percent. By 1989 the worldwide cash turnover in the art industry was estimated at $50 billion per year.

Collectors. This huge increase in art collecting and investing was caused by several factors, including changes in taxes on capital gains, which favored accumulating all sorts of assets; the weakness of the dollar on the world market, which made traditional financial investments less attractive to Americans; and what seemed to be a resurgence of upper-class greed. Upper-income Americans, from young urban professionals to CEOs, began to see art, like real estate, as a commodity that could be bought and resold at a higher value. A new generation of "star" artists added to the cachet of investing in art. Unlike their Conceptualist and Minimalist predecessors in the 1970s, the artists who emerged in the 1980s aggressively marketed their work and were lavished with media attention. Often characterized by highly accessible imagery derived from media and "pop" sources, their art was embraced by the baby-boom generation, who found its cheek and cynicism appealing. Its market value was enhanced by the buying public's tireless thirst for newness, hipness, and trendiness. Many new buyers — including doctors, lawyers, advertising executives, and entrepreneurs — had lit-

tle or no art background or knowledge. While their interest was investment, not aesthetics or patronage for worthy artists, these collectors helped to make the visual arts one of the most vital American cultural forces of the 1980s.

Sponsorship. Corporations and museums also contributed to art awareness in the 1980s. They were especially supportive of contemporary artists. A Manhattan real-estate boom stimulated growth in corporate art sponsorship. IBM, Equitable Life Insurance, and Philip Morris opened free galleries in their New York headquarters. Both Philip Morris and IBM featured large-scale art installations in their new office towers, and in 1985 Equitable devoted the entire ground floor of its new fifty-four-story headquarters to galleries and public art shows, the largest corporate-sponsored art complex in the country. Two of the galleries at Equitable were run by the Whitney Museum, which also had three other corporate-sponsored branches. Major museums have traditionally been reluctant to include art from the previous twenty years in their permanent collections, but in 1987 the Metropolitan Museum added a wing for contemporary art. No longer able to ignore the popularity and innovations of the East Village art scene, the Museum of Modern Art hired a curator who had worked in alternative art spaces to assess the inclusion of works by younger artists in the museum collection. In 1985 the Brooklyn Museum began a series of large-scale multimedia installation projects in its lobby, including a massive work by Robert Longo.

Auctions. As the numbers of private bidders and dollars spent increased dramatically, art auctions became major public and media events during the 1980s. In previous decades the majority of bidders had been art dealers, who kept prices relatively stable. By the mid 1980s, however, more and more private collectors were bypassing dealers to bid on artworks directly. Many of these investors were Wall Street tycoons and overnight millionaires looking for new ways to display their wealth. Gilbert Edelson of the Art Dealers Association of America observed, "They buy art to celebrate their arrival." The often astonishing sums such collectors spent at auctions caused a stampede of media coverage, lending auctions an aura of gala social events. Sotheby's and Christie's became fierce competitors, each attracting business through slick marketing campaigns and trying to outdo the other with "star" auctions (such as the much-publicized Sotheby's sale of Andy Warhol's collection in 1988). While Christie's sales grew faster (by 49 percent in 1987 alone), Sotheby's commanded a greater share of the total art market (59 percent by 1988). Both houses used glossy catalogues, direct-mail services, and traveling exhibitions to create advance publicity for major auctions. Christie's even advertised its sale of artworks, antiques, and memorabilia from Liberace's estate in the supermarket tabloid *National Enquirer*. As Christie's chairman John Floyd commented, "There is practically nothing that we wouldn't have a market for. There is nothing which is faintly artistic which we wouldn't sell."

Inflated Prices. *Search,* a painting by Jackson Pollock, sold for $200,000 in 1971. It was auctioned again in 1988, for $4.8 million — an increase of 2,400 percent. Such price inflation was typical during the 1980s. Wendell Cherry, president of Humana, Inc., bought a work titled *Yo Picasso* for $5.83 million in 1981 and sold it eight years later for $47.85 million. In 1987 a Leonardo da Vinci drawing sold for $3.6 million. That same year an Edward Steichen photograph went for $82,500, breaking the previous auction record for a photographic work, set in 1983. Also in 1987 Christie's auctioned Vincent van Gogh's *Sunflowers* for an unheard-of $39.9 million, the highest auction price ever paid for a single work of art. Only months later Sotheby's sold van Gogh's *Irises* for a record-setting $53.9 million. The October 1987 stock-market crash had no negative effect on art prices. In May 1988 investors paid record-breaking prices for works of sculpture, for a work by a living American artist (Jasper Johns's *False Starts*), and for individual works by artists from Barbara Kruger to Man Ray.

Financing. Sotheby's and several large banks helped collectors afford such astronomical prices by offering loans and financing. Many observers felt that this practice was artificially inflating the market, since bidders commonly paid half the final price up front and the remainder in installments at regular interest rates. In 1989 Sotheby's loaned $27 million to Alan Bond, the buyer of van Gogh's *Irises*. Sotheby's began offering financing in 1984, with advances to consignors, generally limiting loans to works with estimated values of $50,000 or higher. Citibank started an art advisory service, first enlisting experts from Sotheby's to advise clients on their purchases and later adding an in-house staff to bid for clients at auctions. Citibank also offered a financing program for serious collectors. To encourage more owners to offer their works at auction, Sotheby's began giving them price guarantees. Another popular trend of the 1980s was the art fund, a kind of investment cooperative, which solicited cash for art purchases from investors. In 1989 the Chase Art Investors fund collected $300 million from various pension funds. Fred Kline of Santa Fe started the Aurora Art Fund to purchase unknown masterworks at low prices and resell them for far larger amounts. All these practices emphasized the investor's bottom line. One advertisement for Citicorp's art advisory service proclaimed, "The acquisition of art is itself an art."

Criticism. In the face of escalating art prices, museums increasingly found themselves shut out of the art market. In addition a 1986 revision of tax laws eliminated exemptions for art donations, effectively curbing the tradition of rich collectors giving their works to museums. As auction prices skyrocketed and many works became overvalued, museums were no longer able to insure works in exhibitions of those artists. Complaints about the auction houses prompted New York City Commissioner of Consumer Affairs Angelo Aponte to launch an investigation in 1985, but despite the finding of "gross irregularities," the industry remained self-regulating. The same year David Bathurst, a former president of Christie's, admitted to falsifying two major sales in 1981, claiming that his motive was to protect the market. Artists complained about "block buying" by collectors such as advertising mogul Charles Saatchi, who would resell whole catalogues of work at inflated prices. This practice, dubbed "raider dealing," caused unstable prices and cut artists and their dealers out of potential resale profits. The chief executive officer of Sotheby's CEO retorted that auction houses were being "arraigned for the crime of success."

Competition. In November 1989 a Picasso that had been expected to sell for as much as $60 million fetched a mere $40.7 million, indicating that perhaps the auction mania was at last beginning to subside. By the end of the decade American collectors and megadealers also faced new competition from the Japanese. In 1989 Japanese art buyers paid more than $26.4 million for a Picasso and $20.7 million for a de Kooning, a new record for a living artist and a contemporary artwork. By 1988 the Aichi Corporation of Japan had become one of the five largest shareholders of Christie's stock. Of $204 million worth of contemporary art sold in one week during November 1989, Americans bought only one quarter; Europeans purchased 35 percent, and the Japanese paid for an impressive 40 percent. These events seemed to signal the end of the 1980s art boom. As buyers of fine art, Americans no longer controlled the market or led the world.

Sources:

"After the Crash: So Far, So Good," *ARTnews,* 87 (February 1988): 23;

"Art Goes to Wall Street," *Esquire,* 112 (July 1989): 53–54;

"The Billion Dollar Picture?," *Art in America,* 76 (July 1988): 21–23;

"The New Grand Acquisitors," *ARTnews,* 84 (September 1985): 93;

"Plenty of Money for Big Spenders Only," *ARTnews,* 86 (Summer 1987): 29–30;

"Sold!," *Time,* 134 (27 November 1989): 60–65;

"Sold! The Art Auction Boom," *Newsweek,* 111 (18 April 1988): 65–72.

ART STARS

Self-Promotion. As the art market exploded in the 1980s, young artists were ready to take advantage of the public's desire to invest in art. By middecade many had become as well-known as pop-music stars — and as image conscious. Like their 1960s predecessors Andy Warhol, Roy Lichtenstein, Jasper Johns, and Robert Rauschenberg, artists of the 1980s learned to market not only their work but their own public personae. Neo-Expressionists Julian Schnabel and David Salle sought to make their lives as legendary as their work. Keith Haring and Kenny Scharf caught the zeitgeist of hip-hop culture and sold their street sensibility as fashion to the malls of suburbia. Others, such as Jeff Koons, "sampled" and recycled words and images from other media (and earlier eras) or, like Jenny Holzer, caught the public's appetite for slogans and sound bites. Much of 1980s art, from graffiti to sloganeering, functioned as advertising for the artist. The brash image mongering and self-promotion of many artists — like that of their much-hyped counterparts in music, literature, movies, and video — helped to inject a desire for urban hipness, for style over substance, into the culture at large. With the media at their feet and their works selling for often astonishing sums, fine artists were among the savviest of 1980s "players."

The Neo-Expressionists. The first art "stars" of the 1980s, the Neo-Expressionists were a loosely associated enclave of New York painters who worked with large canvases and even larger themes. While their individual styles were often strikingly different — Robert Longo's cinematic images, Eric Fischl's erotic scenes, David Salle's intellectual/pop juxtapositions — the Neo-Expressionists strove for grand statements and psychological impact in their work. They also shared great ambition, and ego. Noting a sense of entitlement among these artists, critic Donald Kuspit commented, "The megalomania that is rampant among artists is unbelievable, and so is the self-importance. Bankers must be the same, but the cry for attention from artists — the ruthlessness of their sense of what is due them — is extraordinary." By 1979, when Julian Schnabel began gaining media attention, the appetite of dealers and buyers for these hot new painters was already whetted. After a decade of largely unsalable, uncollectable conceptual and performance art and nameless, faceless artists, the art community was eager for stars. Helene Winer, who ran the successful Metro Pictures Gallery, noted that the Neo-Expressionists "already had an idea of what kind of public personalities they wanted to be and clearly expected to be. They could hardly wait to buy property and Armani suits." Soon they could afford to: by 1987 they were commonly selling individual works for as much as $60,000. There were also lucrative fringe benefits to being an artist-celebrity: Schnabel published an autobiography in 1987 (at age thirty-five); Longo wrote a movie script and directed a video for The Golden Palominos;

Two views of Robert Longo's *Men in the Cities* installation at Metro Pictures in New York City, 1981

and Fischl produced an album for musician Paul McMahon.

Schnabel. Julian Schnabel's imposing style was dubbed "Neo-Expressionism" by Hilton Kramer of *The New York Times*. With his oversize themes (history, myth, death), giant scale, earthy colors, and bold brushwork, Schnabel's works evoked the Abstract Expressionists of the 1950s. He also seemed taken with the romantic images of their lives, but in his appropriation and chaotic mixture of materials — copper, crockery, velvet, wood — Schnabel sought to move beyond his predecessors' art and provoke emotional, even religious, responses in the viewer. "I think people still have religious experiences in front of paintings," he once commented. With his sizable ego and need for attention he found a perfect counterpart in dealer Mary Boone, who gave Schnabel his first show in 1979 and later that year showed his infamous plate paintings — shards of pottery jutting out of huge painted canvases. In publicizing the plate-paintings exhibition she aggressively developed a public image for Schnabel through advertising, getting stories and interviews in art magazines and throwing impressive parties at hip nightclubs. Boone pitched Schnabel's works to potential collectors as investment opportunities, creating an advance demand for his work by publicizing its scarcity and then raising prices. The strategy worked. Collectors bought every available plate painting, for $6,000 each. By 1981 Schnabel was selling paintings for $40,000 or more, and by 1984 they were selling for $60,000. That year Schnabel left Boone for the conservative Pace Gallery in uptown Manhattan, which takes on only one artist per generation. Whatever his motivation, Schnabel was undoubtedly passionate about his work: "Painting makes me feel that I don't have to kill myself. If I didn't do what I'm doing I might as well lie down and die — or become a stockbroker."

Dealer-Celebrities. In using a corporate strategy to market her client to the level of superstardom, Mary Boone became a celebrity in her own right, and by 1984 she was representing other important artists, including Eric Fischl and David Salle. Her success with new artists benefited other dealers who began promoting untried talent to collectors afraid of missing out on the next big thing. Tony Shafrazi — notorious for having once spray-painted the message "Kill Lies, All Lies" on Picasso's *Guernica* at the Museum of Modern Art — became the wheeler-dealer of young hotshots such as Keith Haring and Jean-Michel Basquiat in the mid 1980s. In 1984 alone, Shafrazi spent $43,000 on advertising his stable of superstars. Mounting important shows often cost dealers upwards of $50,000, including money for photographers, opening-night galas, catalogues, and promotional dinners. Other notable Manhattan dealers and gallery owners of the decade included Gracie Mansion, who achieved fame after opening a gallery called the Loo Connection in her bathroom, and Bill Stelling and Patti Astor, whose Fun Gallery featured shows by Basquiat and Kenny Scharf.

Longo. A longtime Schnabel rival, Robert Longo admitted that "Schnabel brought back the American collectors. We all wanted to get in on that." In 1981 he did. *Men in the Cities,* his show at Metro Pictures Gallery, included his best-known and most-successful works — images that were much borrowed and parodied by other artists and the media. These provocative paintings depicted men and women, wearing business or semiformal attire, in contorted poses that suggested both dancing and death. Longo had achieved the poses by photographing friends on his roof as he threw rocks or tennis balls at them. His aim was a highly emotional, cinematic form of art: "In cinema, the big-impact moments are sex and the way people die," he explained. *Men in the Cities* was a sellout and made Longo an instant star. He started promoting himself in the media. "I want to make art that is going to kill you," he said. "I want my pictures to be like screams. I want the whole spectrum of emotions." By 1984 Longo was selling works for $40,000 apiece, making $300,000 a year, and employing as many as six assistants to help him. By 1986 his images were appearing in fashion advertisements. "Your artwork is your ego," Longo said. "I had to be successful, because there's nothing else I can do."

Kenny Scharf in the room he painted at The Palladium nightclub in New York City

The Bottom Line. Speaking of his success, Longo said, "I'm a good salesman, and I transfer my enthusiasm about my work to other people." By middecade he was not the only young artist with a six-figure income, with big names such as Salle and Schnabel pulling in yearly sales of more than $1 million. Clearly artists of the 1980s had an eye for the bottom line as well as for color and shape. Janelle Reiring, a founder of the Metro Pictures Gallery in Soho, put it bluntly: "This is a business we're in — not the pursuit of a 19th century gentleman.... Artists want galleries that are more progressive — that will promote their careers." Artists chose dealers carefully and worked closely with them on advertising, public appearances, the timing of shows, and, of course, prices. Several art schools began offering business courses; students at the School of the Art Institute in Chicago learned the fine arts of bookkeeping and contract negotiation. Gallery owners had to hire — or become — public-relations consultants, investment advisers, and legal and tax experts. Many in the art world complained, with some justification, that careerism and marketing had replaced aesthetics as the passion of young artists.

Basquiat. The career of Jean-Michel Basquiat might be said to exemplify the extremes of art stardom in the 1980s. His meteoric rise from obscurity to the heights of hype, and his quick burnout, illustrated the mania of 1980s art collectors for young, untried talent and instant reputations. Basquiat first attracted attention in 1980 as part of a two-man street-artist team called SAMO, leaving cryptic but thought-provoking graffiti tags on subway walls and the sides of New York City buildings. His first paintings appeared later that year at the influential Times

Keith Haring painting the Berlin Wall, October 1986

Square Show, and in 1981 they were shown at the Brooklyn alternative art space P.S. 1. With the help of several art dealers, including Mary Boone and Tony Shafrazi, Basquiat rode a wave of media enthusiasm and hype for graffiti art. At Christie's spring 1984 sale one of his works sold for an impressive $19,000. The following year Basquiat appeared on the cover of *The New York Times Magazine,* and he was befriended by future mentor and collaborator Andy Warhol. By this time jazz and African imagery were influencing his canvases, which were increasingly Neo-Expressionist in style. The pieces he created with Warhol received mixed responses in 1986, by which time Basquiat's drug use (which earned him the nickname "the Charlie Parker of SoHo") was already out of control. He died of a heroin overdose in 1988.

Neo-Geo. "Get ready for the artists of the next fifteen minutes," warned critic Kay Larson. Indeed, by 1986 the rage for Neo-Expressionism had been replaced by an even newer craze — Neo-Geo. Neo-Geo painters were neo-minimalists, fusing traditional minimalism with the brashness and arrogant attitudes of the Neo-Expressionist crowd. Like their predecessors they understood marketing: by publicizing themselves

as a new movement, Neo-Geo artists caused a stampede of collectors and the media. In early 1987, for example, the opening of a Neo-Geo show in SoHo far outdrew the latest Longo exhibition. The style of the Neo-Geo artists — led by Peter Halley, Jeff Koons, and Ashley Bickerton — was best exemplified by Halley's work: fluorescent colors, wirelike lines, and evocations of computers and modern electronics. Koons's work, which appropriated cultural objects, was more akin to pop art. The reaction of the "old guard" Neo-Expressionists to this new and much-hyped generation was predictable. Robert Longo — whose own work had once provoked the disgusted comment "Like soap opera! Like *Dynasty*!" from Eric Fischl — snarled at one Neo-Geo opening, "It's ridiculous. This show is like . . . *Bloomingdale's.*"

Media Appropriation. Having grown up watching television, the new artists of the 1980s included, or evoked, imagery from the mass media in their works. Artists such as Rhonda Zwillinger and Rodney Alan Greenblat were part of a 1980s trend known as *appropriation* — borrowing ideas, images, and materials from other sources. Like other art trends during the decade, appropriation owed much of its inspiration to 1960s pop artists such as Warhol and Lichtenstein, whose art also appropriated, and commented on, media and consumerism. Robert Longo's paintings and Cindy Sherman's photographs evoked movie images. Barbara Kruger used photographs from old magazines to provide visual impact for her disquieting slogans; Laurie Anderson recycled clips from old movies. While Kenny Scharf took his inspiration from 1960s television cartoons, David Salle's pieces incorporated comic strips and images from other artworks. Jeff Koons took appropriation to its limits by simply "enhancing" or re-creating familiar manufactured goods and consumer products and presenting them as art.

Koons. In his irreverent mid 1980s shows, stockbroker-turned-artist Jeff Koons sought to satirize and celebrate the decade's worship of luxury, material possessions, and status symbols. In one series he placed vacuum cleaners in huge, light-filled display containers and floated basketballs in water-filled aquariums; another group of his works featured sports equipment coated in bronze, and bar accessories — and even an inflatable rabbit — cast in stainless steel. In 1989 he caused a stir with a show at the Sonnabend Gallery, where he exhibited painted, carved figures he had commissioned from wood sculptors in Italy. Though many viewers were appalled by Koons's deliberate attempt to create kitsch, many more were irritated by the millions he earned selling work essentially created by others. One figurine had a blond beauty hugging the Pink Panther; another was a cream-and-gold-painted rendering of Michael Jackson and his pet chimpanzee, Bubbles. In 1990 he outraged the art community still further when he and his wife, former pornographic film star Ilona Staller, posed for a series of computer-enhanced, soft-core pornographic photo-paintings. For a garish series of silk-screen photographs exhibited the following year, Staller and Koons engaged in actual sex acts. Koons even took out prominent display advertisements to hype the show. He said, "I believe in advertisement and media completely. My art and my personal life are based on it." In 1992 he was found guilty of copyright infringement, after he used a greeting-card photograph to create a sculpture. The decision placed the future of art appropriation into question.

Marketing. Artists such as Koons were as hard-nosed as Madonna about reinventing their art and public selves periodically to keep the media and the buying public interested. Longo did an about-face in the mid 1980s, moving away from his famous contorted figures and experimenting with mixed-media pieces. "The whole idea is not to get stuck with a tired-out product like Atari," he commented. Painter Jedd Garet concurred, but he worried that collectors would resist such changes: "I have to make a conscious effort to fight typecasting and hope that they will want the next thing." Instead of making radical changes in style, many artists simply expanded their market to stay on top. By 1985 Keith Haring, Dan Friedman, Jenny Holzer, and Barbara Kruger had designed T-shirts that were distributed nationally by fashion designer Willi

Sign by Jenny Holzer on the Spectacolor billboard in Times Square, New York City, 1982

Smith. Holzer also marketed posters, caps, and T-shirts featuring her much-quoted "Truisms," and Kenny Scharf created a line of fabrics. Mark Kostabi designed shopping bags for Bloomingdale's department store, as well as jewelry, baseball caps, jackets, books, and postcards. Haring was perhaps the boldest self-retailer, opening his own store, The Pop Shop, which specialized in buttons, wristwatches, sheets, puzzles, radios, tote bags, and toys — all featuring his trademark figures. Such merchandising ventures often made art itself seem like just a sideline; or, as Kostabi put it, "marketing is a rest from painting, and painting is a rest from marketing."

Design. Americans were as design crazy as they were art happy in the 1980s, and many designers and artists were able to tap each other's markets. Products such as clocks, pens, and lamps became stylized, high-tech pieces akin to pop-art objects. Designers such as Stephen Sprouse, with his Day-Glo clothing, and Alex Locadia, with his signature wristwatches, marketed their fashion as art, blurring the distinction between the two. At the height of the art/design boom, lamp designer James Evanson sold more lamps in twelve months than he had in the previous ten years. Michael Graves sold a hundred thousand high-tech teakettles at $99.95 apiece. One of the most profitable design markets was furniture, which ranged from stark and minimal (Scott Burton's granite chaise lounges) to quirky and fun (Michael McDonough's Cadillac-shaped chair). McDonough and Greenblat specialized in "funature" — furniture designed more for aesthetic than for utilitarian value. As Greenblat explained, "You have to have furniture anyway, so why not have fun stuff?" His brightly colored, folk-art–influenced designs were among the most popular of the decade.

Fun Art. Greenblat was among the biggest promoters of Fun Art, which was part appropriation, part embellishment, part collage, and part camp. During the 1980s several New York galleries became successful by marketing the style, especially the media-influenced pop art of Haring, Scharf, Basquiat, and Ronnie Cutrone. Best friends Haring and Scharf were the leaders of the Fun Art movement, with Haring showing his work at Tony Shafrazi's SoHo gallery and Scharf showing his at the Fun Gallery (which he named) in the East Village. Although Cutrone's work featured familiar cartoon characters such as Casper and Mickey Mouse in political contexts, most Fun Art included no social commentary. Fun artists used bright colors, television-derived images, and childlike humor to convince large-scale audiences that art could be "fun." Several of them specialized in "customization," turning everyday functional objects — such as radios, toasters, telephones, pianos, and cars — into artworks by painting them and covering them with masses of smaller objects, including toys and hardware. Museum stores and catalogues sold one-of-a-kind objects that Scharf, Zwillinger, Haring, and Greenblat had "customized." Scharf in particular had a compulsion for customizing and once completely customized an apartment he was subletting for only one month.

Scharf. Fun was Kenny Scharf's only artistic guideline: "The whole thing about fun — I like to have fun. I think everyone wants to have fun. I think that having fun is being happy. I know it's not all fun, but maybe fun helps with the bad. I mean, you definitely cannot have too much fun. Okay, it's like I want to have fun when I'm painting. And I want people to have fun looking at the paintings. When I think, 'What should I do next?,' I think: more, newer, better, nower, funner." Scharf's art, best exemplified by his campy fur-lined and Day-Glo decoration of the Palladium in 1985, mixed colorful lines and shapes, richly textured ornamentation, and 1960s cartoon images such as the Flintstones and the Jetsons. Warehouses, dimestores, fabric outlets, surplus bins, and dumpsters were his sources and his inspiration. Scharf attracted considerable attention with his contribution to the 1984 *Art* show at Area. *Closet #7,* his installation at the Whitney Museum in 1985, featured black-lit rooms filled with salvage. *When Worlds Collide* (1984) celebrated the once-futuristic 1950s imagery of molecules, orbs, spi-

rals, and gases. Such showings made Scharf a celebrity. By 1985 he was appearing in *People* magazine and selling paintings for as much as $20,000 apiece.

The East Village Scene. By the time Haring and Scharf met in 1979, the East Village had long been a center for underground art, performance, and music. The punk rock and new-wave scene was still peaking at Village venues such as the Mudd Club and Hurrah's. New wavers began collaborating with painters and graffiti artists. Club 57 hosted theme parties that featured visual art, performance art, and stage skits. These "art parties" took off, and other night spots, including Danceteria, the Pyramid Club, and the Limbo Lounge, were soon holding similar events. In 1982 Area opened a nightclub that was given a completely revamped interior every six weeks. With art "theme" nights such as "Night," "Obelisks," and "The Color Red," Area became a huge success as the first art nightclub in New York City. In 1984 Area invited dozens of New York artists to participate in an installation called *Art.* During these same years hordes of young artists were gravitating to the East Village, driven out of SoHo by spiraling rents. Impatient with the snobbery and exclusiveness of SoHo galleries, many of these artists opened their own storefront spaces. In 1983 there were perhaps a dozen galleries in the East Village; by 1985 there were at least seventy. Art collectors, many of them wealthy uptown yuppies, rushed to the East Village to buy art at the trendy new galleries and hang out at the hot new clubs.

Club Art. The energy of the East Village art scene, the much-hyped Fun Art of the mid 1980s, and the pervasive lust for glamor that characterized much of the 1980s lifestyle all collided in 1985 at the opening of the Palladium by the former owners of the popular New York nightclub Studio 54. Sensing the East Village rage for art, they had decided to revamp the ancient Academy of Music as an art club. They had commissioned architect Arata Isozaki to convert the interior and hired Henry Geldzahler, the former New York commissioner for cultural affairs, as curator. Francesco Clemente, Kenny Scharf, Keith Haring, and Jean-Michel Basquiat were invited to design installations for the huge rooms. Basquiat painted two massive murals for the upstairs bar and lounge. Scharf covered the basement lounge between the restrooms with Day-Glo paint, fake fur, cartoon characters, and customized objects. Clemente painted a huge fresco on the walls and ceiling at the top of the main staircase. Haring contributed a forty-foot-high painting for a wall by the dance floor. In spring 1985 the Palladium opening was a giant media event, and its success led to other art experiments at clubs such as the Limelight. Andy Warhol commented, "When you call the kids up now, they're doing club art. They're fighting to be in it."

Haring. Keith Haring's stark, linear figures are perhaps the best-known art images of the 1980s. His stylized forms, which resemble a cross between cartoons, cave drawings, and hieroglyphs, have been supremely market-

By the mid 1980s the number of AIDS victims in the United States had climbed into the tens of thousands. Unfortunately, the public's fear and ignorance and the media's frequent misinformation and lack of coverage hindered efforts to educate Americans about the virus and to raise money for AIDS funding and research. The 1985 death of movie actor Rock Hudson called attention to the crisis, as did the deaths later in the decade of notable artists such as Michael Bennett and Robert Mapplethorpe. Yet these tragedies also fanned the fires of AIDS hysteria, and critically acclaimed AIDS-related plays such as Larry Kramer's *The Normal Heart* (1985) and William Hoffman's *As Is* (1985), and later in the decade Paul Monette's highly regarded AIDS memoir *Borrowed Time* (1988), reached primarily a homosexual audience — preaching mainly to the converted.

In the mid 1980s the New York art world attempted to close the funding gap with a series of benefit auctions. In May 1984 an auction for the Gay Men's Health Crisis, a national AIDS organization, raised $149,000. In 1985 and 1986 benefit auctions held for the organization at Sotheby's raised more than $1.5 million. In November 1986 another auction at Barney's, for which artists and fashion designers donated items, raised more than $100,000 for the AIDS hospice program at St. Vincent's Hospital in New York City.

In 1987, seeking to increase awareness and raise money to help AIDS sufferers, the New York art world mounted a campaign known as Art Against AIDS, conceived and organized by public-relations experts Anne Livet and Steven Reichard. With half of all proceeds going to AmFAR (The American Foundation for AIDS Research), major works by four hundred dead and living artists were exhibited for sale in almost sixty galleries. Instead of being auctioned publicly at a single event, works were offered to collectors over a period of several months in specially curated shows. "I'm not taking a cent," artist Robert Rauschenberg announced. "I could have taken 50 percent of the profits, but from what, the world? We're hoping to set an example for other contributors." The print he donated sold for $105,000.

Nathan Kolodner, director of a New York gallery, commented, "The art world has been one of the most responsive communities for the AIDS crisis, I think in part because it has been one of the most affected. We've had a very high toll here." William Olander, curator of an exhibit of videotapes by gay artists at the New Museum of Contemporary Art, concurred: "So many of the artists who are sick or who have already died are younger, and their careers have been cut relatively short. When someone dies at this young age, what's going to happen to their work, their reputation?"

Artist Ross Bleckner contributed the haunting *16,301 as of January 1987,* a painting that evokes images of medieval plagues. "It's about the brevity of what these lives were and are — the tragedy of that briefness," Bleckner said. "I'm trying to address the horror of it." Artist Peter Kunz Opfersei, an AIDS sufferer, said of his condition, "It didn't really change my art, but for me it is important to face death and explore it, too — not to run away from it — and at the same time to express life. That is what my art is about. I don't want to be classified as an AIDS artist. I'm just an artist who happens to have AIDS."

Source: "Art Against Aids," *ARTnews,* 86 (Summer 1987): 54–57.

able and much imitated. Haring started as a graffiti artist, leaving his quirky icons on empty advertising spaces in subways. In 1981 he began working as a gofer for Tony Shafrazi and was soon showing his highly accessible work in gallery shows. His graffiti tags led to frequent arrests for "criminal mischief," but Haring continued the practice even after achieving mainstream success. "The stuff I do in subways is every bit as important to me as the work I show in galleries," he said. "I give it just as much thought as a painting that I sell for 10 or 20 thousand dollars." By middecade the public was familiar with his alligator-headed dogs and crawling babies, and he was selling his work on large vinyl and fiberglass sheets for as much as $350,000 apiece. His success opened the gates to widespread acceptance of graffiti as an art form, and by making his work so available, particularly on mass-produced products, he took art marketing to a new level. "You don't communicate the same way you did 20 years ago, or 50," he said in defense of his merchandising efforts. "You can't just stay in your studio and paint; that's not the most effective way to communicate."

Messages. Because of his commitment to social causes such as AIDS prevention and research and his contributions to charities, Haring was never considered as mercenary as many of his contemporaries. "I want my art to make people think," he said. Though naive and playful in form, much of his work has a pointed social and political message. His radiant children and winged television sets evoke the perils of nuclear and technological advancement, while other works point out societal violence and prejudice. Several of his best paintings deal with the AIDS crisis; one depicts a pile of dying, writhing forms under a giant dollar sign that clearly represents the indifference and inaction of the U.S. government. In 1986 he painted a giant mural on the Berlin Wall as "a political and subversive act — an attempt to psychologically destroy the wall by painting it." Though in one way Haring personified the 1980s marriage of art and commerce, he also illustrated the growing polarization of the art world and society at large. While many artists continued to jump on the commercial bandwagon, others found themselves alienated by the consumerist mentality and male-dominated power structure of both the art world and the nation at large. Working increasingly outside the mainstream, these visual and performance artists created pieces whose intent ranged from the marginally political to the outright insurrectionary.

Sources:

"Bright Lights, Big City," *ARTnews,* 84 (September 1985): 82–91;

"Disco," *New Yorker,* 61 (22 July 1985): 64–66;

Jonathan Fineburg, *Art Since 1940: Strategies of Being* (New York: Abrams, 1995);

"The Four Brushmen of the Apocalypse," *Esquire,* 107 (March 1987): 76–84;

Peter Frank and Michael McKenzie, *New, Used & Improved: Art for the '80s* (New York: Abbeville Press, 1987);

"Golden Paintbrushes," *Newsweek,* 104 (15 October 1984): 82–83;

"Kenny Scharf's Fun–House Big Bang," *ARTnews,* 84 (September 1985): 73–81;

"Longo: Making Art for Brave Eyes," *ARTnews,* 84 (May 1985): 56–65;

"Neo–Geo: Art's Computer Hum," *Newsweek,* 110 (16 November 1987): 119;

Andreas Papadakis, Clare Farrow, and Nicola Hodges, eds., *New Art: An International Survey* (New York: Rizzoli, 1991);

"Requiem for a Featherweight," *New Republic,* 199 (21 November 1988): 34–36;

"Rituals of Consumption," *Art in America,* 76 (May 1988): 164–171;

Kirk Varnedoe and Adam Gopnik, *High and Low: Modern Art and Popular Culture* (New York: Abrams, 1990).

ART TRENDS: POLITICS AND PERFORMANCE

Holzer. In the late 1970s Jenny Holzer's wry, eye-catching, and vaguely subversive "Truisms" began showing up on posters all over Manhattan. Holzer's aphorisms gained effectiveness through their stark presentation: bland typography against passionless white backgrounds. By juxtaposing Truisms that were deliberately contradictory — such as "Everyone's work is equally important" followed by "Exceptional people deserve special concessions" — Holzer disquieted viewers who might otherwise have read her clichés as either truth or personal propaganda. Some of her best-known texts include: "Abuse of power should come as no surprise"; "Murder has its sexual side"; and "Romantic love was invented to manipulate women." By 1982 these and other Truisms were appear-ing in major gallery shows, and by middecade they were adorning T-shirts and other products. Holzer moved on from handbills to wall plaques, then finally to electronic display boards. A 1982 display on the Spectacolor board in Times Square caused a stir by including messages such as "Money creates taste" and "Private property created crime." In 1984 Holzer collaborated with twenty-two other artists to create *Sign on a Truck,* a public forum on the presidential campaign issues of that year. She called this experiment with political propaganda "art applied to rabble rousing." As her work, which included *Inflammatory Essays* (1980–1982) and the *Survival* series (1983–1985), became more personal, it also became more ominous, incorporating themes of violence, power, death, sex, religion, and authority. At the same time, however, it remained ambivalent. Sidestepping the question of intent, Holzer said simply, "I like information blitzes."

Kruger. Barbara Kruger's work, like Holzer's, evokes advertising and uses vaguely ominous declarations. Kruger mixed her statements with appropriated photographs whose images jar the viewer, especially because of their contrast with seemingly unrelated texts. Part black humor and part political message, Kruger's most popular works include *You are an experiment in terror,* in which this statement, in bold-face type, is superimposed on a photograph of a hand holding an exploding firecracker. Once a layout artist for *Mademoiselle,* Kruger drew on her experiences there to assemble and blend the right words with the most effective images, enclosing her stark black-and-white works in vivid red frames. Her breakthrough came with a solo show at P.S. 1 in 1981. Within five years her giant accusatory billboards were appearing regularly in major cities. "Your money or your life," screamed one. Her best works include pointed feminist messages. On a pro-choice poster Kruger placed the stark text "Your body is a battleground" over the divided image of a woman's face. Another work shows a woman subdued by giant needles embedded in her spine and legs; the text reads "We have received orders not to move." A photograph of a girl admiring a boy's bicep, accompanied by the statement that reads "We don't need another hero," is a wry commentary on male ego and hero worship. "We, as women, are spoken of but never addressed," Kruger once said. She saw her pieces as "a series of attempts to ruin certain representations and to welcome the female spectator into the audience of men." In 1987 she became the first female artist to be represented by the Mary Boone Gallery.

Anderson. Like Kruger, performance artist Laurie Anderson fused text with images from popular culture in her multimedia pieces, and, like Holzer, she sidestepped direct political statements, preferring to juxtapose ambiguous, contradictory, and even absurd texts to create a disquieting response in her audiences. Her androgynous appearance, coupled with the frequent use of a synthesizer that distorted her voice, allowed Anderson to blur the boundaries of sexual identity and gender roles.

United States I-IV, developed between 1979 and 1983, was funded partly by a grant from the National Endowment for the Arts. In this six-hour performance epic Anderson explored the political, cultural, social, and technological state of America by blending photographs, videos, cartoons, films, a variety of musical instruments, and her own voice. The project also produced a popular song, "O Superman," and the album *Big Science* (1981). "I try not to be didactic," Anderson said of this work. "I also try not to be alarmist. My purpose is not to tell people what the world is like or to tell them what to do about it. I can only, well, look at the landscape and paint it."

Sherman. Cindy Sherman first attracted serious critical attention with her *Untitled Film Stills* series (1977–1980), which she created with the help of a $3,000 NEA grant. In seventy-five black-and-white still photographs shot mostly in her own apartment building, Sherman satirized media-generated stereotypes of women by mimicking traditional female movie images. "My stills were about the fakeness of role-playing as well as contempt for the domineering 'male' audience who would mistakenly read the images as sexy," she said. In 1980 Sherman began to use color film and went on to create a series of horizontal prints that resemble centerfolds in men's magazines. The unsmiling poses and exaggerated femininity in these photographs address the sexualization and victimization of women by the mass culture. Sherman commented, "The male half of society has structured the whole language of how women see and think about themselves." To point up this tendency as well as to invert it, Sherman also posed as a man in some of her photographs. Her later work, which includes horrific landscapes and nightmarish fantasies, is more personal and less political.

Performance Artists. Actress, musician, and performance artist Ann Magnuson also parodied female sexual roles during the 1980s. In the late 1970s she opened Club 57 in the basement of the former Polish National Church in the East Village. A combination gallery, cabaret, and theater space, the club became a second home to Keith Haring and Kenny Scharf and became known for its wacky "art parties," comic revues, and showings of old B-movies. It also gave Magnuson a venue to try out new stage characters, many of whom she endowed with exaggerated femininity or sexuality. Magnuson's personae included Fallopia, a sex slave to a rock star; Babe Wrangler, a radical lesbian feminist; Anoushka, a Soviet pop singer; and Raven, the singer for a heavy metal band called Vulcan Death Grip. Magnuson and artist Joey Arias created a series of famous wax-museum figures come to life. Another Club 57 favorite was Magnuson's friend John Sex, who performed rock-star parodies in low-budget events that later won him gigs at the Palladium. Eric Bogosian was launched in the media with a series of street characters created at the Kitchen, a music and theater performance club he ran with Robert Longo. In

Dancer-choreographer Bill T. Jones performing in London, 1983; body paint by Keith Haring

1988 Bogosian appeared in the movie version of his stage piece *Talk Radio,* directed by Oliver Stone.

Finley. Performance artist Karen Finley screamed, howled, and ranted her way through the 1980s in series of confrontational, often witty pieces that mixed sex, feminism, and politics. Her topics included the abuse and oppression of women, racial minorities, gays, AIDS victims, and the homeless. Often appearing nude onstage as a commentary on society's obsession with female beauty and desirability, Finley used humor and anger to attack Americans' worship of male aggressiveness and power, explaining:

> Americans are not intuitive enough. We have to be feminized. The national ideology is to go for it, no matter what. We rape women and other countries. The way we treat the earth is the way we treat women. . . . As a female I am an outcast in every system. I can never dream of being president or pope. Men like to give us tokens: Margaret Thatcher or Sandra Day O'Connor. The way to have power as a woman is to act like a man.

In one controversial piece Finley compared American treatment of the disenfranchised with the concentration camps of Nazi Germany: "In principle we are not very different," she said. "It's just that our ovens are at a slower speed. We keep our victims ready." In 1990 Finley, long a recipient of state and federal grants, found herself at the center of a national debate over arts funding by the National Endowment for the Arts.

Guerrilla Girls. In 1984 the Museum of Modern Art in New York City held an International Survey of Painting and Sculpture; among 165 artists represented, only 14 were women. In response an unknown number of anonymous female artists formed the Guerrilla Girls, who became known for their eye-catching posters, nationwide lecture tours, and especially the gorilla masks and fishnet stockings they wore in public. Describing themselves as "an anonymous group of women seeking to transform anger into fun," the Guerrilla Girls also stated their goal as "exposing patterns of sexism, racism, and censorship in the art world." In the mid 1980s the group began displaying their first posters in New York. Far to one side of a mostly blank surface appeared the words: "You're seeing less than half the picture without the vision of women artists and artists of color." In 1989 they distributed another that showed a reclining female nude in a gorilla mask and read: "Do women have to be naked to get into the Met. Museum?" This poster referred to the fact that women represented less than 5 percent of all artists in the modern-art collection at the Metropolitan Museum of Art; yet 85 percent of the nudes in this collection were women. The Guerrilla Girls also made public appearances, taking on the white-male–dominated art establishment with statistics that showed the small numbers of women and minorities represented in museum shows and collections, in commercial galleries, and in critical reviews. They also attacked politicians who were working to restrict national arts funding and policies.

Jones. The explosive works of dancer-choreographer Bill T. Jones were highly autobiographical. As a black homosexual, Jones used his work to confront — and transcend — the racism, homophobia, and other forms of prejudice he witnessed in society. In 1982 he and Arnie Zane, his dance partner and companion, founded the Bill T. Jones/Arnie Zane Dance Company. Working in an experimental postmodernist style, they collaborated on a series of dances that were at once political, personal, and universal. Among these was the intimate duet *Intuitive Momentum* (1983), in which the physically mismatched Zane and Jones sprang at one another, hurled one another into the air, and traded passive-aggressive roles. One reviewer, impressed with the frankness and vitality of the work, called it an "instinctive locking of impulses." Also in 1983 Jones created *Fever Swamp* as guest choreographer for Alvin Ailey's American Dance Theater. This piece featured six male dancers in stylized motion and partnerings that many viewers found daring and insurgent. By the mid 1980s Jones and Zane enjoyed a reputation as two of the world's best postmodern choreographers. In 1986 they won the prestigious Bessie Award, one of the dance world's highest honors. That year Zane was diagnosed with AIDS; he died in 1988. Jones went on to receive three choreographic fellowships from the National Endowment for the Arts.

Morris. Like Jones, dancer-choreographer Mark Morris also gained attention with provocative works that included nontraditional partnerings. By the mid 1980s Morris, who formed his own dance company in 1980, was being compared to dance legends Martha Graham, Merce Cunningham, and Paul Taylor. Some critics considered him the most promising modern dance choreographer since Twyla Tharp. In many of his dances Morris abandoned any pretense of traditional gender roles, making solos random or interchangeable and creating frequent same-sex pairings. In others, such as *10 Suggestions* (1984), Morris himself danced female roles in a completely direct and unapologetic fashion, without the intent of camp or mockery, explaining: "I intend to dance sometimes as a woman. Then, my role *is* that of a woman, not a man playing a woman." Many reviewers noted a refreshing sense of utopianism, humanism, and universality in such "subversive" experiments. While some of Morris's works were humorous and playful, he could also be confrontational. In the ambitious *Mythologies* (1987) he created three satiric dances based on a series of essays that explored the frequent absurdity and exploitativeness of popular culture.

Mapplethorpe. To an often disturbing degree Robert Mapplethorpe's photographs mix commercial conceits with radical content, satisfying what one critic called the 1980s "appetite for both glamour and decadence, high fashion and subterranean sex." Like the works of Keith Haring, Mapplethorpe's slick, stylish photographs encompass both the mainstream and the underground factions of the 1980s art world, but his images are far more insurrectionary. Mapplethorpe achieved his most dramatic effects by wedding classical composition and surface perfection with subculture subject matter, from male homosexual acts to sadomasochism. By using perfect positioning and lighting, Mapplethorpe tried to instill what one critic called "dignity and beauty to a subject that was outside the accepted norms of behavior." His most commercial photographs, of flowers, are as highly sexual as his male nudes; the two types of photographs were often juxtaposed in the artist's exhibits. In many of these pictures Mapplethorpe's images look so abstract and unreal that they take on the appearance of sculpture, an effect which earned him both praise and criticism. His celebrity portraits, which earned him as much as $20,000 apiece, were equally glossy. "My work is about seeing things like they haven't been seen before," he noted. What was to Mapplethorpe an exploration of order, symmetry, and beauty was to many observers mere pornography, however well lit or well composed.

Sources:

Jonathan Fineburg, *Art Since 1940: Strategies of Being* (New York: Abrams, 1995);

Peter Frank and Michael McKenzie, *New, Used & Improved: Art for the '80s* (New York: Abbeville Press, 1987);

"Guerrilla Girls: From Broadsides to Broadsheets," *Ms.,* 22 (March/April 1993): 69;

"Jenny Holzer: The Message Is the Medium," *ARTnews,* 87 (Summer 1988): 122–127;

"A One-Woman Tour of Hell," *Newsweek,* 116 (6 August 1990): 60–61;

Andreas Papadakis, Clare Farrow, and Nicola Hodges, eds., *New Art: An International Survey* (New York: Rizzoli, 1991).

CULTURE WARS

Controversy. The conservative climate of the United States during the administrations of Presidents Ronald Reagan and George Bush set the stage for a series of controversies over the place of art in American culture. Many of these battles pitted members of the religious right against artists whose work they considered indecent, subversive, or blasphemous. Others were fought over issues of racism and patriotism, and some involved works of art long viewed as classics by the public at large. Inevitably most of these "culture wars" became political struggles, with proponents of "decency" and "moral values" butting heads with defenders of artistic expression and the right to free speech guaranteed by the First Amendment to the U.S. Constitution.

Helms versus the NEA. When the National Endowment for the Arts (NEA) came up for a five-year budget review in 1989, it came under fire from Sen. Jesse Helms, a conservative Republican from North Carolina. Helms was outraged that taxpayers were (indirectly) helping to fund art that he and many other religious conservatives considered indecent. One example he cited was an exhibit of photographs by Robert Mapplethorpe (who had recently died of an AIDS-related illness) that featured homoerotic and sadomasochistic imagery. The second, a traveling show organized by the Southeastern Center for Contemporary Art, featured *Piss Christ,* a photograph by Andres Serrano that showed a crucifix submerged in a glass of the artist's urine. Helms introduced an appropriation bill that would ban the NEA or any other federal agency from funding "obscene" art. On 18 May another conservative Republican, Sen. Alfonse D'Amato of New York, tore up a Serrano catalogue on the Senate floor and argued that although the artist may have the constitutional right to create "filth," taxpayers' money should not be used to promote it. On the same day 36 senators signed letters proposing changes in NEA procedures to prevent grants for "shocking, abhorrent and completely undeserving" art. On 8 June 107 representatives signed a similar letter. These congressmen found support among many who saw Mapplethorpe's work as pornography, but to many others Helms's bill amounted to government censorship that would allow politicians to judge the worthiness of art.

Outcry. The Corcoran Gallery of Art in Washington, D.C., had scheduled the Mapplethorpe exhibit for fall 1989, but in June director Christina Orr-Cahall, nervous about further assaults on the NEA by Helms, canceled the Mapplethorpe exhibit, causing instant outrage in the artistic community. Conceptual artist Annie Lemieux led a boycott of the Corcoran by canceling a scheduled Corcoran showing of her work, as did six sculptors who were part of an exhibit planned for the following winter. A traveling show of U.S. and Soviet artists also pulled out, reasoning that given the subject of their show — the emergence of free and uncensored speech in the Soviet Union — displaying their works at the Corcoran would be hypocritical. Artist Lowell Nesbitt withdrew a $1.5 million bequest to the gallery. Veteran curator Jane Livingston, who had arranged for the Mapplethorpe exhibit, resigned in September, as did the head of public relations. The night before the original opening date of the exhibit, outraged artists picketed the Corcoran and projected slides of Mapplethorpe's works on the outside of the building. After three months of controversy and a 10 percent drop in museum membership, the Corcoran board of trustees and Orr-Cahall issued an apology, voicing their regret for offending members of the art community. Many found this apology inadequate because it did not acknowledge what they saw as the real issue: the artist's First Amendment right to free speech.

Compromise. The Senate found Helms's definition of indecency too vague and too broad to implement and voted down his bill 62–35. In its place they suggested a compromise: the NEA would adopt the obscenity guidelines set by the Supreme Court in 1973, when it ruled that individual communities should set standards by which to judge the artistic merit of a work. This way certain obscene art could be denied funding, but at the discretion of the NEA, not Congress. Helms did not lose his battle altogether, however. Congress cut NEA funding by $45,000, the exact amount of the original grants for the Mapplethorpe exhibit and the Serrano show. In addition, they imposed a five-year ban on federal funding to the Institute for Contemporary Art and the Southeastern Center for Contemporary Art. Few were satisfied by this uneasy truce, and clearly the NEA controversy was far from over.

Responsibility. The following year performance artist Karen Finley, who had received state and federal funding since 1984, was deluged with unexpected publicity for her controversial performance piece "We Keep Our Victims Ready," in which a seminude Finley smeared her torso with chocolate frosting. Attempting to raise the specter of Mapplethorpe, syndicated columnists Rowland Evans and Robert Novak made her piece the NEA test case of 1990. In response the National Endowment for the Arts denied funding to Finley and three others who included political and sexual commentary in their performance pieces. After the incident Finley commented:

Because of the NEA decision, I'm not treated the way I was two years ago. People now look over my shoulder as I do my work. I know I am privileged in comparison with others, but the joy I used to have in my work is gone; now I feel anxiety. Because of [the NEA], places like the Kennedy Center refuse my work; they want to avoid controversy.... It's very difficult for me to create live work now, knowing I could affect some institution's funding. It's a horrible responsibility.

"Blasphemy." The NEA was not the only target of an outraged religious right in the 1980s. Director Martin Scorsese inadvertently caused a controversy with his 1988 movie *The Last Temptation of Christ.* In a protest led by Rev. Donald Wildmon of the National Federation for Decency, Christian groups picketed showings of the film, which depicted Jesus hallucinating that he was bypassing crucifixion in favor of a pleasurable life with Mary Magdalene. Many video stores reacted to the protest by refusing to carry the movie. Wildmon's charges that this fictional and speculative movie was "blasphemous" begged the question of whether blasphemy was relevant when the issue was constitutionally protected freedom of expression. Madonna enraged the religious right when her video for the song "Like a Prayer" aired on MTV in March 1989. The video depicts a black Christ crying tears of blood and kissing Madonna, who discovers stigmata on her hands and dances on a hill covered with burning crosses. The singer had just signed a $5 million contract with Pepsi, which had already aired a commercial with Madonna performing part of the song in a far less controversial setting. Fearing a boycott by fundamentalist groups, Pepsi asked her to pull or at least change the offending video. When she refused, Pepsi canceled her commercials, but Madonna kept the $5 million.

Art and Patriotism. Chicago artist "Dread" Scott Tyler found himself at the center of controversy early in 1989 when he showed at the School of the Art Institute a work titled *What Is the Proper Way to Display a U.S. Flag?* — which he called "an installation for audience participation." On a shelf below a collage that featured photographs of flag-draped coffins and South Koreans burning an American flag, Tyler placed a ledger in which viewers could write their answers to his question. To reach the ledger, however, they had to step on an American flag that Tyler had draped on the floor. Outraged veterans' groups picketed the Art Institute and continually picked up the flag, folding it and placing it on the shelf. Tyler and his mother received death threats, and a dozen students demonstrating in support of Tyler's First Amendment rights were attacked when more than twenty-five hundred veterans and their supporters marched on the school, demanding that officials remove the flag.

Flag Ruling. The reaction in Washington was equally strong: President Bush called the work "disgraceful," and Republican senator Robert Dole of Kansas sought to pass legislation making it a crime to display the American flag on the floor or the ground. The Senate agreed with Dole, passing his bill 97–0, and the Chicago City Council and the Illinois legislature passed similar flag-desecration laws. Yet a Cook County Circuit Court judge ruled against a coalition of veterans' groups who sued to close the exhibit, defending Tyler's First Amendment right as an artist to "communicate ideas and feelings." Soon after, the U.S. Supreme Court ruled, on an unrelated flag-burning case from 1984, that laws prohibiting use or desecration of the flag were unconstitutional. Justice William J. Brennan Jr. commented that "the government may not prohibit the expression of an idea simply because society finds the idea itself offensive or disagreeable." For the time being, Tyler and his fellow artists had been vindicated.

Art and Racism. Tyler was not the first School of the Art Institute student to become the center of controversy. In 1988 artist David Nelson invited charges of racism when he exhibited his *Mirth and Girth,* a satiric portrait of the late Harold Washington, the first African American mayor of Chicago. Nelson, who had depicted Washington clothed in women's underwear, apparently intended the irreverent piece as a satire on icons and myth-making, a response to a popular poster that showed Washington looking down on the city from the right hand of Jesus. An outraged group of black aldermen demanded the removal of Nelson's work and then stormed the exhibit, illegally seizing the painting. Alderman Allan Streeter called it "an insult to a great man and an affront to blacks," but Alton Miller, who had been Washington's press secretary, retorted that Washington would have supported Nelson's First Amendment right to display the picture. After police impounded the work on the grounds that angry citizens might riot or march on the Art Institute, students there demonstrated to show their support for Nelson's right of free speech. The school received bomb threats, and there were rumors of cuts in public funding. After a public apology to the community by the president of the Art Institute board of trustees, the painting was returned to Nelson, and the controversy subsided.

Book Banning. As conservatism spread during the early 1980s, efforts to ban books from community libraries were on the upswing. A 1980 survey of almost two thousand public-school administrators and librarians found increases in school censorship, with 22 percent reporting challenges to specific works. Of these challenges 95 percent were seen as attempts to limit information and points of view. Most complaints originated with parents concerned about sexual material and "dirty language," one-third of whom admitted they had never seen the books or materials they were challenging. A 1981 survey by the American Library Association revealed that in 1980 there were three to five episodes of book banning per day nationwide, up from three to five per week just a few years previously. In a poll of seventy-five hundred school administrators 25 percent reported an increase in attempts to ban books in their districts.

School Censorship. In 1980 Concerned Citizens of Montello, a group of parents in a small Wisconsin town, attempted to ban *The American Heritage Dictionary* because it included words they found objectionable. The following year they sought to remove Sol Stein's novel *The Magician* (1972) from the district high-school curriculum and libraries. One parent charged that the book "stimulates youngsters sexually." The school board rejected the petitions 6–1 after it learned that the teacher using the novel had first collected signed permission forms from the majority of the students' parents. Undaunted, and claiming the school system was teaching "filth" and impeding efforts of parents to instill "moral values" in their children, the group checked out of the library thirty-three other "objectionable" books for evaluation of their literary merit, including J. D. Salinger's *The Catcher in the Rye* (1951), F. Scott Fitzgerald's *The Great Gatsby* (1925), *The Diary of Anne Frank* (1952), several Judy Blume novels, and Gertrude Samuels's *Adam's Daughter* (1977). A school board in South Dakota banned another Samuels book, *Run, Shelley, Run* (1974), because, the board proclaimed, "Swear words aren't words children should be reading in the library." In this case the school board prevailed. In an Alabama community in 1982, Baptist ministers and two hundred congregation members forced their school board to remove seven books from two high-school libraries because they included vulgar language. These books included John Steinbeck's *The Grapes of Wrath* (1939) and *East of Eden* (1952), Anthony Burgess's *A Clockwork Orange* (1962), and *Doris Day: Her Own Story* (1976). After its legal counsel cited court decisions that made such removal illegal, the board decided to require parental permission before a student could have access to these books.

Publishers' Views. Author Ronald Glasser also heard charges of "offensive and abusive language" when the school committee of Baileyville, Maine, voted to remove his Vietnam novel *365 Days* (1971) from the high-school library in 1981. The managing editor at Braziller, which had published the novel, responded: "We shall not be protecting our youth if we swathe them in ignorance, nor shall we earn or deserve their respect if we cannot place enough trust or faith in them to reason and respond on their own behalves." Thomas Nelson, a publishing house specializing in Bibles and other religious books, took the conservative side when it acquired Dodd, Mead in 1982. The new management became nervous over complaints about existing Dodd, Mead titles containing the word *goddamn*. The publisher asked two authors whose books were currently in galley proofs to excise the offending word from their works. They refused. A third book, an anthology titled *The Devil's Book of Verse*, was already in print, but distribution was halted when editor Richard Conniff refused to remove an Ezra Pound poem that used "goddamn" several times. Conniff sued Dodd, Mead and Thomas Nelson for breach of contract and won. Calling the publishers hypocritical for acting not on religious or moral grounds but because they feared a drop in Bible sales, Conniff commented, "they object either because they are incapable of thought or they think other people are incapable of thought." Samuel Moore, president of Thomas Nelson, defended the actions of his company, publicly stating that he did not want to be involved in the publication of "trash."

The Island Trees Case. The most publicized instance of literary censorship of the 1980s originated in 1975, when the Board of Education in Island Trees, New York, banned nine books it considered "anti-American, anti-Semitic, and just plain filthy." These books included *Soul on Ice* (1968) by Eldridge Cleaver, *Slaughterhouse Five* (1969) by Kurt Vonnegut, and *The Fixer* (1966) by Bernard Malamud. A group of angry students sued the board for violating their First Amendment rights. When the case reached the Supreme Court in 1982, the court ordered a local court to decide the matter. Four justices stated that local school boards should not remove books "simply because they dislike the ideas contained in those books," nor should they "prescribe what shall be orthodox in politics, nationalism, religion, or other matters of opinion." The justices concluded, "Our Constitution does not permit the suppression of ideas." To avoid a trial that would give the courts control over schools, the board then voted to restore the books to the school library but to require parental notification. In 1983 this procedure was found in violation of a New York State law that protected the privacy of all library records. The students of Island Trees had prevailed. Their lawyer, Alan Levine, summed up their position: "Unpopular ideas are not for banning."

Rock-Music Crackdown. During the 1980s parents and public officials were as concerned with the content and message of rock and roll music as they were with library books. Soon after the Southland Corporation removed *Playboy* and *Penthouse* from its 7–11 chain of convenience stores, televangelist Jimmy Swaggart delivered an impassioned on-air speech against "the devil's music," which inspired the Wal-Mart chain to pull thirty-two rock-oriented magazines from eight hundred of its stores. During the same period the U.S. Department of Immigration began making it more difficult for foreign rock bands to obtain the visas they needed to perform in the United States. Many foreign underground bands were unable to provide the notarized and translated articles required to prove that they had "economic viability" in the United States and "distinguished merit or ability." In 1985, after Susan Baker, wife of former senator Howard Baker, heard the Prince song "Darling Nikki" (which mentions masturbation), seventeen wives of politicians, including Sen. Albert Gore's wife, Tipper Gore, founded the Parents' Music Resource Center (PMRC) "to educate and inform parents of this alarming new trend . . . toward lyrics that are sexually explicit, excessively violent, and glorify use of drugs and alcohol." Echoing the parental concern over rock 'n' roll in the 1950s, the PMRC claimed that modern rock music was "subversive to the values that constitute the fabric of American society." Rock came under more fire in 1985, when two teenagers shot themselves after hearing alleged "hidden commands" that said "Let's be dead" and "do it" in a Judas Priest song. The boys' parents unsuccessfully sued the band and their recording company.

"Porn Rock." Aided by well-known Reagan supporters such as Mike Love of the Beach Boys and beer mogul Joseph Coors, the PMRC made several controversial suggestions. Foremost, they wanted song lyrics printed on album covers so that parents could screen them; they requested that store owners be required to keep from public view albums with explicit pictures on their covers; and they proposed a ratings system for albums and concerts. They also asked that the contracts of "violent" or "sexual" performers be reassessed, and that broadcasters be pressured not to air songs by musicians with "questionable" talent. Charged with supporting government censorship of music, the PMRC insisted that they favored voluntary cooperation of artists and record companies — industry *self*-censorship. While they denied connections to any religious group, Rev. Jeff Ling wrote most PMRC literature, and Tipper Gore's book was advertised on televangelist Pat Robertson's program, *The 700 Club*. Under siege by a PMRC letter-writing campaign, the Recording Industry Association of America agreed in 1985 to record-display labels reading "Parental Advisory — Explicit Lyrics." Also in 1985, as thirteen states considered legislation to restrict young people's access to rock music, the Senate Commerce Committee began hearings on "porn rock." The hearings quickly turned into a media circus, as rock performers from Frank Zappa to Dee Snider of the metal band Twisted Sister turned up to testify on behalf of the First Amendment.

A Bad Rap for Rap. In 1986 Tipper Gore took on rap group Run-D.M.C. after a series of incidents on their summer tour. In June twenty-five people had been arrested for vandalism and assault after a Run-D.M.C. show in Pittsburgh; in July several muggings had been reported after the group had performed at Madison Square Garden in New York City; and in August gang fights had broken out at a Run-D.M.C. concert in Long Beach, California, injuring more than forty fans. "Disillusioned kids unite behind heavy metal or rap music, and the music says it's OK to beat people up," warned Gore. The group's management countered that the social problems of poverty and drugs caused the violence, not the music. The rap group 2 Live Crew incited controversy in 1988 when record-store owner Tommy Hammond was arrested in Alexander City, Alabama, for selling their recording "Move Somethin'," which featured explicitly sexual and misogynistic lyrics that — according to City Attorney Daniel Brown — violated "community standards of decency" and had "no redeeming social value." A

local judge fined Hammond $500 for selling an obscene work, and the town paper blasted the band. The group defended its work, claiming the lyrics were all in fun. "It's damn funny," said 2 Live Crew rapper and producer Luke Skyywalker. Hammond's attorney, calling the case frivolous, pointed out that raunchy sexual language was a long-standing tradition in pop music and that everyone's standards of decency are different: "You may be offended by it, but that doesn't make it obscene."

PMRC versus *Frankenchrist*. In late 1985 a fourteen-year-old California girl bought her younger brother the Dead Kennedys' album *Frankenchrist*, which included a foldout poster of *Landscape #20*, an artwork by Swiss surrealist painter H. R. Giger that depicts a bleak vista filled with stylized and disembodied genitalia engaged in copulation. When the girl's mother saw the poster, she complained to the state district attorney's office, which decided to prosecute the punk group's front man, Jello Biafra, and four others on charges of "obscenity based on potential harm to minors." Biafra countered that this action violated his First Amendment rights, especially since the album had carried a warning label about the artwork. Everyone saw something different in the poster. Prosecutor Michael Guarino saw dead body parts. Susan Baker of the PMRC saw "diseased genitalia engaged in anal intercourse." Biafra insisted that he intended the artwork, which he'd originally seen in an issue of *Penthouse*, as a "metaphor for consumer culture on parade." The Dead Kennedys, he asserted, played "antifascist" rock, intended to shake listeners out of their political apathy and "complacent consumerist cocoons." He and his codefendants faced fines of $2,000 and prison terms of up to a year. Since it was the first such charge ever filed against a recorded album, the outcome would set a precedent affecting thousands of artists, musicians, writers, and performers.

Defense. Biafra's supporters raised $75,000 in a NO MORE CENSORSHIP defense fund that received contributions from performers as varied as Frank Zappa, Steve Van Zandt, and Paul Kantner. The case finally came to trial in August 1987. Defense attorney Philip Schnayerson and Carol Sorbel, representing the American Civil Liberties Union (ACLU), argued for Biafra, who pleaded not guilty. Guarino's charge that the poster appealed to "prurient interest," that it "would be deemed offensive to minors by the average California adult," that it was "utterly without redeeming value," and that it "interfered with the quality of life" raised several unanswerable questions: Whose prurient interest did the poster appeal to? What was the "average" California adult? Who would or could objectively determine the aesthetic value of any artwork? Whose quality of life was at risk? The defense, meanwhile, insisted that the poster be judged only in the context of the entire album, leaving Guarino to prove that the entire album was harmful. The defense also called in expert witnesses, including an art professor to discuss Giger's artistic reputation and rock critic Greil

Marcus, who explained the Dead Kennedys' political and satirical stance. The courtroom atmosphere ranged from silly to surreal, with the prosecution refusing to read aloud the names of bands such as The Butthole Surfers, The Fartz, The Dicks, and The Crucifucks or the title of the song "Too Drunk to F—." By keeping the focus on the issue of free speech, the defense was able to secure a deadlocked jury, leading to a mistrial and Biafra's acquittal. The Dead Kennedys had already disbanded under the weight of Biafra's legal battles. After the trial the PMRC faded from the national scene.

Sources:

"Art Grants Under Fire," *Newsweek*, 114 (7 August 1989): 23;

"Author Frees Her Alabama Censors," *Publishers Weekly*, 223 (19 March 1983);

"Blaming Death on Hidden Messages," *Newsweek*, 116 (30 July 1990): 60;

"Conniff Sues Dodd, Mead, Thomas Nelson," *Publishers Weekly*, 225 (6 January 1984): 16;

"The First Amendment," *Publishers Weekly*, 219 (3 April 1981): 14;

"The First Amendment," *Publishers Weekly*, 219 (22 May 1981): 18;

"The First Amendment," *Publishers Weekly*, 220 (17 July 1981): 16;

"Flag Furor," *ARTnews*, 88 (Summer 1989): 43–44;

David Kennedy, "*Frankenchrist* vs. the State: The New Right, Rock Music and the Case of Jello Biafra," *Journal of Popular Culture*, 24 (Summer 1990): 131–148;

"The Growing Battle of the Books," *Time*, 219 (19 January 1981): 85–86;

"Interpreting G——n: Nelson Cancels 3 Dodd, Mead Books," *Publishers Weekly*, 224 (9 September 1983);

"Island Trees Board Restores Banned Books to Libraries," *Publishers Weekly*, 222 (27 August 1982): 260;

"Island Trees Decision, Though Split, Is Hailed," *Publishers Weekly*, 222 (9 July 1982): 10, 14–15;

"Island Trees School Ends Its Fight to Ban Books," *Publishers Weekly*, 223 (11 February 1983): 14;

John Mutter, "Study on School Censorship Finds Cases on Rise," *Publishers Weekly*, 220 (7 August 1981): 12;

"School for Scandal," *ARTnews*, 87 (November 1988): 37–38;

"Tipper De Doo Dah," *New Republic*, 197 (7 December 1987): 22–23;

"The War on Culture," *Art in America*, 77 (September 1989): 39–41;

"When Taxes Pay for Art," *Newsweek*, 114 (3 July 1989): 68;

"Whose Art Is It, Anyway?," *Time*, 134 (3 July 1989): 21.

HIP-HOP CULTURE

Background. During the late 1970s an underground urban movement known as "hip-hop" began to develop in the South Bronx area of New York City. Encompassing graffiti art, break dancing, rap music, and fashion, hip-hop became the dominant cultural movement of the African American and Hispanic communities in the 1980s. Tagging, rapping, and break dancing were all artistic variations on the male competition and one-upmanship of street gangs. Sensing that gang members' often violent urges could be turned into creative ones, Afrika Bambaataa founded the Zulu Nation, a loose confederation of street-dance crews, graffiti artists, and rap musicians. The popularity of hip-hop spread quickly to mainstream white consumers through movies, music vid-

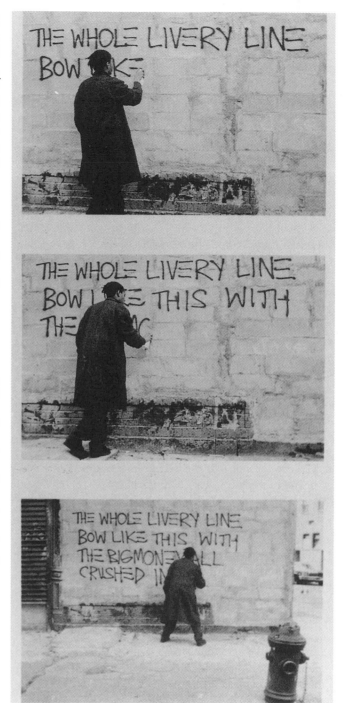

A member of SAMO spray painting a message in the SoHo section of New York City

eos, radio play, and media coverage. The resulting flood of attention from wealthy investors, art dealers, movie and video producers, and trend-conscious consumers made hip-hop a viable avenue to success for black and Hispanic ghetto youth. Rap music in particular found a huge interracial audience. After 1985, when the mania for graffiti art and break dancing began to wane, rap music continued to gain popularity, emerging as one of the most original music forms of the decade.

Graffiti Art. Gang graffiti, long a staple of urban life, was elevated to the status of a respected art form in the 1980s. The South Bronx storefront gallery Fashion/Moda, founded in 1978, was the early home of experimental graffiti art, and it soon attracted the attention of downtown artists such as Keith Haring, who began to gravitate uptown to meet other graffitists. Asked to curate an exhibition of graffiti art at the Mudd Club in the East Village, Haring was fired after he invited hundreds of black, white, and Hispanic graffiti artists, who literally covered the club and the surrounding area with their "tags." During these same years, a two-man graffiti team known as SAMO began leaving cryptic, poetic tags and spray-painted social critiques in SoHo and other bohemian neighborhoods. One member of SAMO was artist-musician Jean-Michel Basquiat, who in 1980 was asked to contribute graffiti art to the Times Square Show, an event that brought East Village and Bronx artists together. By this time graffiti-art styles had developed from simple words and symbols into "wild style" — colorful, character-filled art that was at times as beautiful and surreal as it was unintelligible. Some critics hailed graffiti as the first true democratic art form, a style anyone could try. Others decried it as simple vandalism. Alfred Oliveri, head of the New York City Transit Authority vandal squad, sneered, "If this is art, then to hell with art." Gallery owner Tony Shafrazi countered, "It's time to wake up to the fact that we are in a new era. The new artists are the heirs to the continuing tradition of rebellion, play and adventure which is art."

Commercialism. By 1981 graffiti was being featured in public art exhibitions at venues such as P.S. 1, an alternative-art space in a converted school building in Long Island City. Such shows attracted established art dealers and gallery owners. Also in 1981, independent-film actress Patti Astor acted in Charlie Ahearn's underground, semidocumentary movie *Wild Style* (1982), which features several young graffiti artists, and later that year she and Bill Stelling opened a storefront gallery in the East Village to show the work of her costars, who included Lee Quinones and Lady Pink. Tony Shafrazi, quick to spot any trend, began featuring works by Haring and Basquiat in his SoHo gallery. By 1983 collectors, including Europeans, were buying graffiti art at an astonishing rate. Though Basquiat emerged as the one African American superstar of the form, other black artists such as Futura 2000 and Fab Five Freddy, as well as artists' groups including United Artists, found success in the booming graffiti market. The Fun Gallery continued to attract ghetto kids such as ERO, whose exhibit there led to a subsequent show in Berlin in 1983. By 1984 graffiti art was being prominently featured in Hollywood hip-hop movies such as *Beat Street* and in music videos such as Madonna's "Borderline."

Break Dancing. A mixture of dancing, tumbling, and gymnastics, break dancing became one of the predominant dance forms of the 1980s, equaled only by the syn-

Run-D.M.C.

chronized choreography of music videos. Break-dancers used acrobatic moves — such as splits, headstands, flips, and handsprings — spinning on their shoulders, backs, and heads in an often dazzling display of athletics and choreography. Especially in California, some breakers spun partners overhead or interlocked with other dancers; many danced in pairs. Others incorporated related street moves, such as the robotic electric boogie made popular by Michael Jackson. Most dancing was competitive and, like graffiti art and rap music, performed by young inner-city males. This dance style began in the late 1970s as a type of mock urban warfare in which members of opposing street gangs, usually Hispanic, tried to one-up each other with hot moves. These teenagers started congregating to perform and compete in graffiti-art venues such as Fashion/MODA in the South Bronx and underground clubs such as the Fun House in New York. DJs such as John "Jellybean" Benitez tried out new records at the youth clubs. Dancers would meet on street corners, spinning on pieces of linoleum or cardboard boxes to the thunderous beats of ghetto blasters. In some inner-city schools, breaking started to replace fighting between rival gangs. "It's a way to be No. 1 without blowing somebody away," said the director of a Denver juvenile-delinquency program, who pushed for a city-sponsored break-dance contest. Said one San Francisco gang member, "If you told me a few years ago that I'd be dancing, I'd laugh. It's like a thing: gangs getting ready to fight, but instead we dance."

Mainstream. Breakers had been featured in *Wild Style*, released in 1982, but the mainstream breakthrough came in 1983, when Rock Steady Crew of New York performed break-dance moves in the hit movie *Flashdance*. Soon break-dancing was prominently featured in music videos and television commercials, performed by professional dance groups such as the New York City Breakers. It was also being taken seriously as a new art form: the San Francisco Ballet opened its 1984 season with a gala featuring forty-six break-dancers, and the Los Angeles Olympic Games used one hundred break-dancers in the closing ceremony. One ballet promoter who began working with breakers commented, "Changing the field of gravity of the dancer is as revolutionary as the addition of sound to moving pictures." In summer 1984 a book called *Breakdancing* topped *The New York Times* list of best-selling how-to books. By the time the motion pictures *Breakin'* and *Beat Street* opened in 1984, Hollywood had six more major break-dance movies in production. *Breakin*, shot on a shoestring budget and featuring dancers Shabba-Doo and Boogaloo Shrimp, grossed more than $30 million in two months; the soundtrack sold a million copies in six weeks. *Beat Street,* produced by Harry Belafonte and featuring sixteen-year-old dancer Robert Taylor, showed a slick Hollywood version of the South Bronx far removed from urban grit, gangs, and drugs of *Wild Style.* By the time *Beat Street* was released, much of the original style and charm of break dancing had been diluted by excessive commercialization. With how-to videos and break-dance lessons available in towns nationwide and white stars such as Lorenzo Lamas (*Body Rock,* 1984) and the elderly Don Ameche (*Cocoon,* 1985) break dancing in movies, the form began to seem both silly and surreal.

Mixing and Sampling. *Beat Street* featured several prominent urban-music trends of the 1980s, including mixing, sampling, and scratching. Mixing, popularized by club DJs such as Jellybean, required the skillful blending of different records that had similar beats into a single, seamless dance number. When DJs started recording and replaying their best mixes, the major record labels took notice, releasing extended-play dance mixes of big chart hits. By 1984 a third of the standard Top 20 pop singles were available as twelve-inch remixes. Jellybean did a remix for Michael Jackson, while Arthur Baker, the music coordinator for *Beat Street,* was hired to remix dance versions of songs for Cyndi Lauper and Bruce Springsteen. Mixing was taken a step further by DJs who employed scratching, which involved placing the needle in a record groove and manually turning the disc back and forth in rapid succession to achieve a staccato effect and thereby segue into another song. Sampling was akin to the appropriation used by many visual artists of the decade: samplers took snatches of existing records and wove them into new numbers, usually by scratching the records to cover the transition from one sample to another. In the song "Strictly Business" (1988) EPMD borrowed a familiar riff from Eric Clapton's version of "I Shot the Sheriff." Using two or more turntables to scratch and sample, DJs kept dance floors crowded with sound changes that appealed to MTV attention spans. Mixing, scratching, and sampling were all popular techniques with DJs.

Rap Music. Rap originated in the early 1970s in the South Bronx, where DJs played riffs from their favorite dance records at "house parties," creating new sounds by scratching over them or adding drum synthesizers. A partner, the MC, would add a rhyming, spoken vocal (a rap) over the mix, often using clever plays on words. Most rap songs were braggadocio, the aural equivalent of street gangs' strut and swagger. Boasting about their physical prowess and coolness, rappers used competitiveness with rival males as the motivation for creativity. Some early rap songs promoted global and interracial harmony, including The Sugar Hill Gang's "Rapper's Delight" (1980) and Afrika Bambaataa's "Planet Rock" (1982), which became a crossover hit on the dance charts and sold more than six hundred thousand copies. Other rappers expressed serious political and social messages, often addressing the effects of racism, poverty, and crime on the African American community. One such group was Grandmaster Flash and the Furious Five, formed in the Bronx in 1978 by Joseph Saddler. Flash first attracted attention with the song "Freedom," released on the rap label Sugar Hill in 1980. Their 1981 album was among the first to feature sampling, and in 1982 their seven-minute recording "The Message" — about black ghetto life — became an underground hit. When Flash went solo, another Furious Five member stepped forward to lead the group as Grandmaster Melle Mel. The new group released the antidrug anthem "White Lines (Don't Do It)" in 1983.

Crossover. Rap remained primarily an underground urban style until the mid 1980s, when it exploded into the mainstream with the unexpected popularity of Run-D.M.C. Formed in 1982 the trio released their first record the following year and watched it become the first rap-music gold album. Their 1985 LP *King of Rock* was an even bigger hit, reaching number fifty-three on the *Billboard* album chart and featuring two videos that achieved significant airplay on MTV. Run-D.M.C.'s heavy metal sampling increased its popularity with young white males, especially after the 1986 recording of "Walk This Way," a remake of an Aerosmith song with a video featuring Joe Perry and Steven Tyler of Aerosmith. The song was the crossover breakthrough for rap music, while the album that featured it, *Raising Hell,* sold more than 3 million copies and became the first platinum rap album. Inspired by the success of Run-D.M.C., MTV launched a daily *Yo! MTV Raps* program. Female rap artists such as Salt-N-Pepa, MC Lyte, and Queen Latifah began to make inroads in the late 1980s, and even white acts jumped on the bandwagon; in 1987 the Beastie Boys had a major hit with "(You've Gotta) Fight for Your Right (to Party)." By the end of the decade rappers such as L. L. Cool J ("I'm Goin Back to Cali," 1988) and Tone Loc ("Wild Thing," 1989) were regularly appearing in the Top 40, and in the 1990s the rap stars Ice-T, Fresh Prince, and Kid 'N Play were elevated to movie and television stars.

Controversy. While some rap songs were lighthearted and fun — for example, Run-D.M.C.'s "My Adidas" celebrated hip footwear — rap music became increasingly political as the decade progressed. Sensing nothing but indifference from the Reagan administration and white America to the escalating problems of crime, poverty, drugs, and unemployment in their communities, many rappers openly raged against the police, the government, big corporations, and other bastions of white male power. In response some critics attacked rap music in the late 1980s for the often overt violence, racism, sexual explicitness, and misogyny of its lyrics. In 1986 Tipper Gore of the Parents' Music Resource Center blamed the music of Run-D.M.C. for the eruption of violence at several stops on their summer tour. Others took issue with the militant, seemingly antiwhite stance of rap group Public Enemy, especially on their million-selling 1988 album *It Takes a Nation of Millions to Hold Us Back* and in the song "Fight the Power," featured in Spike Lee's controversial 1989 movie *Do the Right Thing.* Though candid about the evils of bigotry, group members Flavor Flav and Chuck D responded to such criticism by insisting that they advocated improving black life through empowerment. During a concert at Riker's Island Prison in New York, Chuck D announced, "Our goal is to get ourselves out of this mess and be responsible to our sons and daughters so they can lead a better life. My job is to build 5,000 potential black leaders through my means of communication." Also in 1988 the recording "Move Somethin' " by 2 Live Crew ignited controversy when an Alabama store owner was arrested and charged with selling an obscene work. In 1990, 2 Live Crew was again in court, successfully defending their music against obscenity charges.

Messages. Run-D.M.C. sought to be role models for black youth through their involvement in social causes. In addition to decrying the gang fighting at their live shows, they took part in the Live Aid and Artists United Against Apartheid projects, appeared in a promo video for the Martin Luther King national holiday campaign and at an anticrack awareness day, and came out with a strong antidrug message in the song "It's Tricky." Rappers Queen Latifah and N.W.A also spoke out against drugs. Ice-T used his chilling gangland rap "Colors," in the 1988 movie of the same name, as a commentary on the harsh realities of black life in the inner cities. In 1989 leading rappers joined together in the Stop the Violence (STV) movement. Denouncing gang warfare, Chuck D and Flavor Flav of Public Enemy joined KRS-One, Heavy D, MC Lyte, and others to record the single "Self-Destruction," which sold half a million copies. STV donated $500,000 in royalties to the National Urban League to combat illiteracy. "We wanted to reach the kids most affected by black-on-black crime," said Ann Carli, the Jive Records executive who helped organize STV. "Rap records can be a tool that can be used in education today." Black pride was also the message of rappers Sir Mix-a-Lot ("National Anthem"), Big Daddy Kane ("Young, Gifted and Black"), and Queen Latifah, who dressed in African-inspired garb. "Style is Afrocentric," she said, "and my style and music are one."

Fashion. The underground urban fashion and street language of hip-hop had also reached mainstream America by middecade. Inspired by rap performers such as the Furious Five, who sported head-to-toe leather, metal studs, and fur-trimmed coats, ghetto kids modified their street-gang uniforms to include gold rings and chains, personalized belt buckles, and high, knitted ski caps. Furious Five member Kurtis Blow noted, "Not only did our fans want to talk like we did, but they dressed like we did." Spotless jeans, baseball caps, and impeccable Adidas sneakers were standard for hip-hoppers as well. While "b-boys" tended to sport the flashiest clothes, "fly girls" adopted their own version of the look with leather pants and layered sweatshirts. Because of the pervasiveness of hip-hop culture in the mass media, bits of black street vocabulary — including *fresh, def, chill,* and *posse* — became common even in white suburbia. By the late 1980s white teenagers were as conscious of hip-hop fashion and status symbols as the black and Hispanic kids who had inspired them: the "right" Air Jordan sneakers with the most complex lacing, the hippest bandannas, the perfect layering of shorts over sweatpants. Hip-hop had struck the trendiest nerve in mainstream America — the need to be on the "cutting edge" of fashion.

Sources:

"Break Dancing the Night Away," *Newsweek,* 102 (21 March 1983): 72–73;

"Breaking Out: America Goes Dancing," *Newsweek,* 104 (2 July 1984): 46–52;

"Chilling Out on Rap Flash," *Time,* 121 (21 March 1983): 72–73;

Peter Frank and Michael McKenzie, *New, Used & Improved: Art for the '80s* (New York: Abbeville Press, 1987);

"Graffiti on Canvas," *Newsweek,* 102 (18 April 1983): 94;

"Some Bad Raps for Good Rap," *Newsweek,* 108 (1 September 1986): 85;

David P. Szatmary, *Rockin' in Time: A Social History of Rock and Roll* (Englewood Cliffs, N.J.: Prentice-Hall, 1987).

HOLLYWOOD: THE BOTTOM LINE

Blockbusters. While the summer adventure movies *Jaws* (1975) and *Star Wars* (1977) had seemed state-of-the-art in the 1970s, the screen spectaculars of the 1980s made them look like student films. The record-shattering profits of those two movies had created an insatiable demand by producers for even bigger successes. As box-office profits went through the roof, budgets went out the window. At the same time the demographic profile of the American movie audience was shifting increasingly to male teenage viewers. As a result American audiences were bombarded every summer with more and more slick special effects, juvenile comedies, futuristic fantasies, macho action adventures, rock-star soundtracks, and high-tech horror. Despite protests from the critics every big hit seemed to be followed by a parade of increasingly less original sequels. From the trend-setting science fiction of *The Empire Strikes Back* in 1980 through the spectacular comic-book spin-off *Batman* in 1989, the 1980s were the years of the blockbuster. Most of these

Henry Thomas with the lovable special-effects alien in *E.T.: The Extra-Terrestrial*

movies were created, or at least inspired, by Steven Spielberg or George Lucas. By the end of the decade Spielberg and/or Lucas were responsible for six of the top ten moneymakers of the 1980s and for eight of the ten top-grossing movies of all time. Their movies had rousing, crowd-pleasing scores by John Williams, the most successful soundtrack composer of the decade. Williams was nominated for nine Oscars during the 1980s — most notably for the *Star Wars* sequels and the *Indiana Jones* series — and won an Oscar for the music for *E.T: The Extra-Terrestrial* (1982).

Special Effects. Computerized visual effects dominated the biggest movies of the decade. *Star Wars* (1977) and its sequels *The Empire Strikes Back* (1980) and *Return of the Jedi* (1983) set the industry standard for technical wizardry. All three were produced by George Lucas, who was also responsible for the trio *Raiders of the Lost Ark* (1981), *Indiana Jones and the Temple of Doom* (1984), and *Indiana Jones and the Last Crusade* (1989) — which were also filled with spectacular special effects. The *Indiana Jones* movies were directed by Spielberg, whose 1982 space-alien fantasy *E.T.: The Extra-Terrestrial* set an American box-office record that even his 1993 monster

hit *Jurassic Park* could not beat. Following the example of Lucas, Spielberg also became a producer; his boyish love of toys, gadgetry, and alien creatures gave America the effects-laden hits *Poltergeist* (1982), *Twilight Zone — The Movie* (1983), *Gremlins* (1984), *The Goonies* (1985), *Back to the Future* (1985), *Young Sherlock Holmes* (1985), and *Who Framed Roger Rabbit?* (1988). Lucas also contributed the ill-fated, gnome-laden *Willow* (1988). Special effects were the motor that drove comic-book dramas such as *Batman* and the *Superman* sequels (1981, 1983, 1987); cyborg thrillers such as *Blade Runner* (1982), *The Terminator* (1984), and *Robocop* (1987); outer-space adventures such as *Aliens* (1986) and four *Star Trek* sequels (1982, 1984, 1986, 1989); and even comedies such as two *Ghostbusters* movies (1984, 1989), *Time Bandits* (1981), and *Brazil* (1985).

Producers. Not since the days of David O. Selznick, Irving Thalberg, Louis B. Mayer, and Darryl F. Zanuck had producers and studio moguls been so powerful and influential. "The producer is king again," trumpeted *Newsweek* in 1985, making official a trend that had been growing since the late 1970s, when the arty films of "auteur" directors such as Robert Altman, Francis Ford

When it was released in fall 1987, the movie *Fatal Attraction* looked like a slick, harmless thriller about a bunch of yuppies. *MacLean* reviewer Lawrence O'Toole called it a movie about "a crazy woman giving a nice guy and his family a hard time." Yet within weeks, as it was racking up huge profits at box offices nationwide, *Fatal Attraction* became the subject of heated controversy, as some viewers, particularly women, charged that its implied message was sexist and offensive. The debate became so intense that *Time* magazine sent its reviewers, who had originally shrugged off the movie, back for a second look. Shortly thereafter *Time* declared *Fatal Attraction* "the zeitgeist movie of the 1980s."

On the surface *Fatal Attraction* appeared to be nothing new. For almost a decade Americans had been inundated with stalker and slasher movies that outraged viewers had criticized for portraying women as victims and encouraging audience identification with their attackers. *Fatal Attraction* seemed to turn the tables because its stalker was a woman. In the movie Dan, a successful, married lawyer (Michael Douglas), has a weekend affair with Alex, a successful, single, book editor (Glenn Close). To avoid jeopardizing his apparently idyllic home life with his wife and young daughter he tries to break up with Alex, who attempts suicide and then begins to harass Dan and his family. In the harrowing climactic scene of the movie she attacks Dan's wife, Beth, with a knife in the family's bathroom; Dan tries unsuccessfully to drown the homicidal Alex in the bathtub, and Beth shoots and kills Alex as she is about to stab Dan.

The meaning of *Fatal Attraction* is open to interpretation. Is it a cautionary tale about the consequences of extramarital sex in the age of conservative "family values"? Does it attempt to compare the innocent family with the victims of worldwide terrorism? One reviewer likened the film to Velcro, since anyone's theory about it seemed to stick. Many concerned women saw the movie as a paranoid reaction to the "threat" of feminism as perceived by the Reagan Right: an implication that successful, independent career women are by nature vindictive, devouring monsters who threaten the sanctity of the traditional nuclear family. Director Adrian Lyne seemed to bear out this interpretation by openly stating his preference for "traditional," 1950s-style women like his own stay-at-home wife: "Maybe that thrusting career woman looks rather attractive for a brief fling, but you don't want to spend your life with a woman like that. It's kind of unattractive, no matter how liberated and emancipated it is. It sort of fights the whole wife role, the whole childbearing role. Sure you get your career and your success, but you are not fulfilled as a woman." According to him career women were "overcompensating for not being men."

To varying degrees other motion pictures of the mid to late 1980s portrayed independent women as unfulfilled romantic losers, power-driven manipulators, or bad mothers. Movies such as *Legal Eagles* (1986), *Baby Boom* (1987), *Broadcast News* (1987), *The Big Easy* (1987), *Suspect* (1987), *The Witches of Eastwick* (1987), *The Good Mother* (1988), and *Dangerous Liaisons* (1988) appeared to be symptomatic of an antifeminist backlash. In such movies strong, smart career women who did not "know their place" could not seek personal fulfillment without being punished for it.

Sources: Liahna Babener, "Patriarchal Politics in *Fatal Attraction*," *Journal of Popular Culture*, 26 (Winter 1992): 25–34;

Susan Bromley and Pamela Hewitt, "*Fatal Attraction*: The Sinister Side of Women's Conflict About Career and Family," *Journal of Popular Culture*, 26 (Winter 1992): 17–24;

John Rohrkemper, "*Fatal Attraction*: The Politics of Terror," *Journal of Popular Culture*, 26 (Winter 1992): 83–93.

Coppola, and Michael Cimino had begun to bomb. By then Spielberg and Lucas had shown Hollywood a new level of success — and a new bottom line. Because of them Hollywood movies increasingly became expensive high-tech packages that had to have a guaranteed audience and an easy-to-advertise formula to gain studio approval. By the mid 1980s, with a few creative exceptions, the identity of a movie's director was no longer remembered, or even discernible. If a movie became a hit, it was the producer who was in demand, not the director. British producer David Puttnam emerged from his Oscar-winning triumph with *Chariots of Fire* (1981) to produce *Local Hero* (1983) and *The Killing Fields* (1984). Craig Zadan landed a job with Tri-Star Pictures after the success of *Footloose* (1984). After producing the glossy megahits *American Gigolo* (1980), *Cat People* (1982), *Flashdance* (1983), and *Beverly Hills Cop* (1984), Jerry Bruckheimer renegotiated his contract with Paramount and went on to make *Top Gun* (1986). On the strength of *Trading Places* (1983), Aaron Russo cut a deal worth $72 million, while Brian Grazer was able to write his own ticket after *Splash*

(1984). America's fascination with "the art of the deal" turned studio heads Barry Diller, Michael Eisner, Dawn Steel, and Sherry Lansing and producers Jeffrey Katzenberg, Joel Silver, David Geffen, and Jon Peters into "stars" in their own right.

Spielberg. Steven Spielberg was a one-man hit factory throughout the 1980s. His signature movie, *E.T.: The Extra-Terrestrial* broke all box-office records, earning $367 million in the United States and almost twice that amount worldwide. Video sales brought in another $400 million. The success of *E.T.* was so staggering that it was difficult to remember that the movie was intended to be just a sweet, winsome tale of a lonely boy and his alien friend. It was equally hard to believe that just a year earlier Spielberg had directed the action-adventure movie *Raiders of the Lost Ark* for Lucas and brought in $242 million in revenue. Spielberg received Oscar nominations for both movies but failed to win for either, indicating that the Hollywood establishment respected his hit-making ability but not his aesthetics. Spielberg went for broad effects, big emotional responses, and awe-inspiring visuals in a filmmaking style that many fans and critics likened to the imagination of an overgrown child. Some applauded his evocation of an earlier, grander, and more innocent movie era, but his tendency to amplify his themes and messages — to imagine everything for his audience — led to a chorus of criticism. With his screen adaptation of Alice Walker's novel *The Color Purple* in 1985, most critics complained that Spielberg had turned an original and uncompromising work of African American fiction into a big, dumb Disney movie; movie critic Dave Kehr called it "Alice Walker and the Temple of Doom." The movie had eleven Oscar nominations, and Spielberg received an award for it from the Director's Guild, but he was passed over for an Academy Award for Best Director.

Big Bucks. Spielberg rebounded with the acclaimed *Empire of the Sun* (1987) and a host of producing projects, including the short-lived television series *Amazing Stories* and the innovative *Who Framed Roger Rabbit?* (1988), which combined cartoon animation and live action. Much of his attention was devoted to Amblin Entertainment, his production studio on the Universal Pictures lot. Universal built the headquarters as a gift to Spielberg — at a rumored cost of $4 million to $6 million. Through Amblin, Spielberg put his executive producer stamp on a huge variety of projects, including the gimmicky box-office duds *Innerspace* (1987) and *batteries not included* (1987). He could afford the risk, however, because the second and third *Indiana Jones* movies each grossed more than $150 million. By 1989 worldwide ticket sales for Spielberg films totaled $2 billion, and he had become the highest-paid producer and director in the movie industry. With flat fees of at least $1 million, Spielberg also had percentage guarantees of at least 10 percent. Budgets for his movies tended to set the same sort of records as his box-office takes; *Gremlins* (1984) was planned as a low-budget horror movie, but the producer's blockbuster touches upped the cost to $25 million. The original $27.5 million budget for *Who Framed Roger Rabbit?* swelled to $45 million after Spielberg advised the Disney studio to add more special effects. "I want people to love my movies," he said, "and I'll be a whore to get them into the theaters."

Lucas. Just as the cuddly E.T. will forever be associated with Spielberg, the endearing *Star Wars* characters R2D2, Chewbacca, and C3PO will always be connected with George Lucas. His 1977 movie *Star Wars* forever changed the way filmmakers and audiences looked at movies. The two follow-ups were the most successful sequels in movie history, with *Return of the Jedi* ranking only one place below *Star Wars* on the list of all-time moneymakers by the end of the decade. Lucas's movies established an entire new approach to marketing; *Raiders of the Lost Ark* touched off a safari fashion craze, while *The Empire Strikes Back* products — including notebooks, lunch boxes, and action figures — were quickly bought up by enthusiastic fans. When the endearing characters in *Return of the Jedi* became big sellers, Lucas was suspected of creating the movie specifically to peddle tie-in products. To those who complained that, like video games, Lucas's megabuck fantasies robbed children of the power of imagination, others replied that Lucas was just a high-tech version of Walt Disney, creating the classic myths and legends for tomorrow. The creation of the *Star Wars* movies took a major toll on Lucas; after finishing *Return of the Jedi*, he commented, "The sacrifice I've made for *Star Wars* may have been greater than I wanted. *Star Wars* has grabbed my life and taken it over against my will." After overseeing the production of *Indiana Jones and the Temple of Doom*, Lucas began a four-year hiatus from his production company, Lucasfilm. Its special-effects division, Industrial Light and Magic, had become the industry leader, providing effects for dozens of films, including *E.T.* and *Star Trek II*. Lucas returned to film production in 1988 with the fantasy-adventure movie *Willow*. Despite aggressive marketing of related toys, accessories, and clothing (or perhaps because of it), *Willow* wilted at the box office, but Lucas ended the decade on an upswing by producing *Indiana Jones and the Last Crusade*, which took in almost as much money during the first six weeks after it was released ($165 million) as *Indiana Jones and the Temple of Doom* had in its entire theatrical life.

Disney. The fairy-tale comeback of the decade was the rejuvenation of the Disney studio by its new chairman Michael Eisner and its new studio-operations head Jeffrey Katzenberg. In 1984, after more than a decade of lackluster box-office receipts and dwindling creative energy, Disney faced a takeover by corporate raider Saul Steinberg, who aimed to sell everything but the highly profitable theme parks. Walt Disney's nephew Roy Disney fended off Steinberg and persuaded the Disney board to regroup and restaff, starting at the top. Financial ad-

At 2:30 A.M. on 23 July 1982, tempers were beginning to fray on the set of *Twilight Zone — The Movie*. Reportedly behind schedule on his part of the anthology movie, which had four sequences shot by four different directors, John Landis was directing the shooting of a tricky stunt sequence involving actor Vic Morrow and two small children. As Morrow crossed a simulated bomb-torn river in Vietnam with the children in his arms, a special-effects explosion caused a camera helicopter hovering overhead to veer out of control and crash into the water, instantly decapitating Morrow and the children.

Speculation was rampant about Landis's responsibility for the tragedy. Witnesses on the set claimed Landis had ordered the helicopter to descend to just thirty feet above a hut that was to be blown up, and they said he had screamed obscenities at the pilot. Landis denied these allegations. At the very least Landis had violated child-labor laws; the accident occurred eight hours after the time that the children's work should legally have ended. There were also rumors that Landis had hired a helicopter pilot with little experience in filming motion pictures because he had agreed to work for lower wages. A veteran movie air coordinator who examined the scene of the crash noticed poor radio links among the pilot, the effects expert, and Landis.

Shortly after the accident, three wrongful death lawsuits seeking millions of dollars in damages were filed against Landis, and in June 1983 he and four associates were indicted on charges of involuntary manslaughter. Landis became the first director ever charged with causing a death on a movie set. (In 1928 Michael Curtiz was not charged after several extras were killed during dangerous stunts he had ordered them to perform on the set of *Noah's Ark*.) Facing a possible six-year prison term if convicted, Landis, who called the tragic crash "the most terrible experience of my life," pleaded not guilty. "I know in my head and I know in my heart that we did not cause the accident," he said in court.

In late 1983 Landis was acquitted. Those who had already worked with him on such hits as *National Lampoon's Animal House* (1978), *The Blues Brothers* (1980), and *Trading Places* (1983) were confident that Landis would rebound. "It won't affect his career," one insider predicted. "He's too good and Hollywood is too greedy." When *Twilight Zone — The Movie* movie was released that same year, reviews were mixed. The critic for *Time* observed that Landis's segment, which was released with the Morrow footage pared down, hardly seemed worth filming in the first place, much less worth the cost of three lives.

Source: *"Twilight Zone* Director John Landis Faces a Manslaughter Rap Over a Stunt That Went Tragically Wrong," *People*, 20 (18 July 1983): 59–60.

---

viser Frank Wells suggested replacing chairman Ron Miller with Eisner, already well known as the hit-making president at Paramount. With Miller gone and Eisner, Disney, and Wells installed as chairman, vice chairman, and president, further support was enlisted from Texas billionaire and Disney shareholder Sid Bass. Eisner then recruited Katzenberg, the dynamo head of production at Paramount, to complete the new team. Disney had just released one successful movie, *Splash* (1984), its first big hit in ten years. The next three years were even more promising; Touchstone Pictures, created as the adult movie division of the studio, released several substantial moneymakers, including *Down and Out in Beverly Hills* (1986) and *Ruthless People* (1986), both starring Bette Midler. These projects were developed under a tough new operating philosophy: to keep budgets at a minimum, low-demand performers were signed to multipicture deals, and movies were developed within the studio rather than bought from outside as expensive packages. In short Disney became an updated version of the old Hollywood studio system.

Payoff. Disney soon earned a reputation in Hollywood for its penny-pinching productions, paltry salaries, and aggressive deal making. Yet the results could not be ignored: Disney, which ranked dead last among the major studios in 1984 with just 3 percent of all domestic movie revenues, had rebounded to second place by 1987 and had 15 percent of the market, with surprise hits such as *Stakeout*, *Outrageous Fortune*, and *Tin Men*. The studio's 1987 profits of $444 million represented an 80 percent increase over its totals for 1986. Revenues more than doubled, and stock values shot from $2 billion in 1983 to $10 billion four years later. By early 1988 Disney was the top-ranking studio in Hollywood, with a whopping 30 percent share of all movie revenues and three of the top five motion pictures in the country. *Three Men and a Baby* (1987) was the biggest of these, earning more than $160 million. It was followed by *Good Morning, Vietnam* (1987) at $110 million and *Shoot to Kill* (1988) at $30 million. Later that year Disney increased its lead with *Who Framed Roger Rabbit?* — the blockbuster hit of 1988, and the Tom Cruise moneymaker *Cocktail*. There

Bob Hoskins handcuffed to the title character in *Who Framed Roger Rabbit?* — in which live actors interacted with cartoon characters

was more good news in 1989, with *Honey, I Shrunk the Kids* topping $100 million and *Dead Poets Society* not far behind. By this time 90 percent of the movies released under the new Disney management had become profitable, compared to the industry average of 30 percent. Production costs on Disney films also remained well below the norm. Yet Disney executives did not revise their bargain-hunting approach to deals or production. "We have the money," said one, "but we won't pay retail." Meanwhile, other Disney divisions were also making money: the Disney television channel took off, video sales of classic Disney movies soared, and attendance swelled at Disney World, Disneyland, and Tokyo Disneyland. With seemingly unlimited merchandising opportunities, Disney appeared to have found the formula for a whole new dynasty.

Japan. Even as world events signaled the impending end of the Cold War in 1989, America seemed poised to start a trade war with Japan. Aware of the "takeover" of many U.S. businesses by Japanese investors, especially during the last years of the decade, many Americans

openly cheered Japan-bashing entertainments such as the 1989 movie *Black Rain.* Japanese corporations looked to invest some of their excess capital in the one American industry that thrived during the 1980s: entertainment. Sony Corporation led the way, purchasing CBS Records for $2 billion in 1987 and then buying Columbia Pictures from Coca-Cola for $3.4 billion in fall 1989. It was the largest Japanese takeover of a U.S. company to date, and it involved more than just cash: the Columbia holdings included a 2,700-film library and 260 television properties. Also in 1989 Richard Englund closed the biggest Japanese-backed movie deal in history, receiving a $50 million budget to direct a space fantasy. Zeron, a Japanese venture-capital group, invested $20 million in a four-picture deal. Shochiku-Fuji, a film distributor, gave producer Jeremy Thomas $50 million to make six movies. Producer David Puttnam started a London-based production company with $50 million in Japanese financing. In August 1989 JVC/Victor of Japan sank $100 million into a production deal with Hollywood producer Lawrence Gordon. Though executives at Sony claimed they would not interfere with creative decisions at Columbia

Pictures, there was increasing talk of Japanese companies moving into movie development and production.

Retreads. When *The Empire Strikes Back* proved in 1980 that a sequel could rival its predecessor not only in ticket sales but also in originality, a sequel "mania" began with a vengeance. George Lucas's and Steven Spielberg's creativity with sequels turned out to be rare, however, as theatergoers were treated to second and third helpings of everything from *Porky's* (1983, 1985) to *Meatballs* (1984, 1987). Michael J. Fox of *Back to the Future* (1985) went back again (1989) and again (1990). Chevy Chase had three *National Lampoon* vacations (1983, 1985, 1989). The producer of *Alien* (1979) kept things simple by just adding *s*, but the producer of the second sequel to *First Blood* (1982) got confused and called the movie *Rambo III* (1988). *Mad Max* (1979) was followed by *The Road Warrior* (1982) and *Mad Max Beyond Thunderdome* (1985). *Rocky* (1976) and *Rocky* (1979) were followed by numbers III–V (1982, 1985, 1990). By 1987 *Superman* had reached number IV, and by 1991 *Star Trek* was at number VI. By 1989 *Friday the 13th* (1980) had seven sequels, and it began to seem as though movie producers had given up discovering new stars and gambling on untested material, preferring recycled versions of "sure-fire" product and cheap knockoffs of previous hits. Sequels seemed the ultimate expression of the 1980s Hollywood obsession with the bottom line.

Movies and Video. Even as television producers were adapting the style of music videos to series such as *Miami Vice*, Hollywood producers were discovering the power of videos in marketing movies. The runaway success of the MTV-influenced *Flashdance* in 1983 demonstrated the potential of video, especially when the soundtrack for the movie produced two number-one hit songs. Later in 1983 nostalgic, aging baby boomers spent millions of dollars on the Motown soundtrack for *The Big Chill*. The following year ten movie soundtracks went platinum, and all but one were rock-oriented; the *Beverly Hills Cop* soundtrack featured three Top 10 songs, and *Footloose* produced five Top 40 hits. By 1985 dozens of major studio releases featured rock-oriented soundtracks and big pop singles, among them "The Power of Love" (Huey Lewis & the News) from *Back to the Future*, "Into the Groove" (Madonna) from *Desperately Seeking Susan*, "Crazy for You" (Madonna) from *Vision Quest*, "We Don't Need Another Hero (Thunderdome)" (Tina Turner) from *Mad Max Beyond Thunderdome*, and "Don't You (Forget About Me)"(The Simple Minds) from *The Breakfast Club*. The soundtrack for *Dirty Dancing* (1987) became one of the top-selling albums of the year. By the time of the fighter-jock fantasy *Top Gun* in 1986, savvy movie marketers knew their potential audience and how to reach them with a big hit song ("Take My Breath Away," Berlin) on MTV. Independent film-music coordinator Becky Shargo noted that "movie producers today are trying to get a soundtrack attached to anything." *Top*

THE 20 TOP-GROSSING MOVIES OF THE 1980S	
1. *E.T.: The Extra-Terrestrial* (1982)	$228,618,939
2. *Return of the Jedi* (1983)	168,002,414
3. *Batman* (1989)	150,500,000
4. *The Empire Strikes Back* (1980)	141,600,000
5. *Ghostbusters* (1984)	130,211,324
6. *Raiders of the Lost Ark* (1981)	115,598,000
7. *Indiana Jones and the Last Crusade* (1989)	115,500,000
8. *Indiana Jones and the Temple of Doom* (1984)	109,000,000
9. *Beverly Hills Cop* (1984)	108,000,000
10. *Back to the Future* (1985)	104,408,738
11. *Tootsie* (1982)	96,292,736
12. *Rain Man* (1988)	86,000,000
13. *Three Men and a Baby* (1987)	81,313,000
14. *Who Framed Roger Rabbit?* (1988)	81,244,000
15. *Beverly Hills Cop II* (1987)	80,857,776
16. *Gremlins* (1984)	79,500,000
17. *Top Gun* (1986)	79,400,000
18. *Rambo: First Blood Part 2* (1985)	78,919,250
19. *Rocky IV* (1985)	76,023,246
20. *Honey, I Shrunk the Kids* (1989)	71,097,000

Source: *The World Almanac and Book of Facts* (New York: Newspaper Enterprise Association, 1991).

Gun producer Jerry Bruckheimer agreed, admitting, "We always saw the pilots as rock 'n' roll stars of the sky."

Hotshots. During the 1980s many new directors benefited from the Hollywood blockbuster mania by getting their own studio production deals. One was Ivan Reitman, who had gone unnoticed as a producer in the 1970s; he had produced the successful *National Lampoon's Animal House* in 1978, but director John Landis got all the credit. Reitman switched to directing and got noticed with the blockbuster comedies *Meatballs* (1979), *Stripes* (1981), and *Ghostbusters* and won the chance to pick his projects in the future. The huge success of *The Empire Strikes Back* got screenwriter Lawrence Kasdan his first job as a director. He followed *Body Heat* (1981) with a big

Michael Keaton and Jack Nicholson in *Batman*

hit, *The Big Chill* (1983), and by the end of the decade he was well established as the developer of prestigious projects such as *The Accidental Tourist* (1988). Adrian Lyne moved from music videos to features with the slick and trendy *Flashdance*. After the steamy *9 1/2 Weeks* (1986), he secured his position with the glossy yuppie thriller *Fatal Attraction* (1987). John Hughes got lucky with his first movie, the cute teen comedy *Sixteen Candles* (1984). Subsequent hits, including the "brat pack" drama *The Breakfast Club* (1985), gave him the clout to become a producer by 1989. Robert Zemeckis was able to cash in on the big box office for *Romancing the Stone* (1984) with the help of his mentor, Steven Spielberg, who produced Zemeckis's *Back to the Future* and *Who Framed Roger Rabbit?* Though they were directed by Zemeckis, they were in fact indistinguishable from movies directed by Spielberg. Perhaps luckiest of all the new big-money directors was the quirky visionary Tim Burton. He had caught the eye of Hollywood with his darkly subversive comedies *Pee-Wee's Big Adventure* (1985) and *Beetlejuice* (1988) and ended up with the plum directing job of the decade — *Batman*.

Batman. Hollywood's record-shattering success reached a peak in 1989. Summer box-office receipts approached $2 billion, taking just eight weeks to break the previous season record, set only one year earlier. Leading the field of blockbusters was *Batman*, which earned $167 million in the first twenty-five days after its release to become the fastest-grossing movie of all time. Its runaway success surprised almost no one; so great was the hype for *Batman* that after those first twenty-five days a majority of Americans had seen the movie. Batmania ruled America during the summer of 1989; the shiny, ominous, and wordless bat logo, which loomed on billboards and hovered on caps and T-shirts for months before the movie opened, was perhaps the simplest, most effective, and most influential marketing tool in Hollywood history. Warner Bros. carefully created anticipation and demand for the movie by releasing a well-edited trailer during the previous Christmas season and then slowly infusing merchandise into stores during subsequent months. The strategy worked: when the movie finally opened in June, the market exploded. More than one hundred designers and manufacturers created three hundred Batproducts, including pens, apparel, utility belts, capes, Batarangs, Batwings, and even miniature electric-powered Batmobiles for kids. Producer Jon Peters admitted, "We've made everything." A promotional tie-in with Taco Bell helped merchandising sales climb above $200 million. As for the movie, it received mixed responses from audiences and critics. Most loved Jack Nicholson's Joker, Tim Burton's brooding direction, and the set designer's nightmarish vision of Gotham City, but they did not care much for the story line, Michael Keaton's Bruce Wayne, or Kim Basinger's Vicki Vale. Such disapproval hardly mattered in the face of the staggering box office, which eventually totaled almost $250 million. It was sharing in the "event" of *Batman* that mattered, not the film itself. *Batman* was 1980s Hollywood in a nutshell, a triumph of marketing over content.

Sources:
"Batmania," *Newsweek*, 113 (26 June 1989): 70–74;

"Boffo Box Office Big Boost to Biz," *Newsweek*, 114 (31 July 1989): 60–62;

"Do You Believe in Magic?," *Time*, 132 (25 April 1988): 66–73;

"Fear Not, Hollywood: Golden Boy Is Still Golden," *Business Week*, no. 3107 (29 May 1989): 64–65;

"I Dream for a Living," *Time*, 126 (15 July 1985): 54–61;

"I've Got to Get My Life Back Again," *Time*, 121 (23 May 1983): 66–68;

"Japan Goes Hollywood," *Newsweek*, 114 (9 October 1989): 62–67;

"Michael Eisner's Hit Parade," *Business Week*, no. 3036 (1 February 1988): 27;

"Next Stop, Tinseltown," *Newsweek*, 113 (20 March 1989): 48–49;

"The Producer Is King Again," *Newsweek*, 106 (20 May 1985).

HOLLYWOOD UNDER REAGAN

The Movie President. During the era of Hollywood's megabuck resurgence, a former movie actor was in the White House. President Ronald Reagan retained his fondness for his old profession, making frequent allusions to movies during his campaigns. One of his best-known lines was "Win one for the Gipper," which he spoke while playing Notre Dame football star George Gipp in *Knute Rockne, All American* (1940). Reagan's political persona often resembled that of an old-fashioned Western

Sylvester Stallone in *Rambo: First Blood, Part 2*

hero. In fact, John Wayne's 1956 movie *The Searchers* was one of the president's favorites. So was *The Bridges at Toko-Ri* (1954), which he mentioned when praising acts of Korean War heroism. Reagan's Teflon-like media sheen was the envy of publicists, marketers, and advertising executives, all of whom benefited from his trademark use of sound bites and quotable quips. Perhaps his most quoted line was "Go ahead, make my day," which he lifted from the Clint Eastwood hit *Sudden Impact* (1983) and used to great and humorous effect during a 1984 debate with Democratic challenger Walter Mondale. The line reinforced the heroic, tough-guy image he used to promote his brand of conservatism and patriotism in the Cold War against the "evil empire" of the Soviet Union. The media, in turn, picked up on Reagan's movie mindset when they nicknamed his planned expensive, high-tech Strategic Defense Initiative "Star Wars."

Patriotism. Hollywood responded to Reagan's emphasis on patriotism with jingoistic Cold War movies celebrating American heroism. In *Red Dawn* (1984) and *Invasion U.S.A.* (1985) resourceful action stars violently thwart Russian invaders. In *Missing in Action* (1984) an American POW returns to Vietnam to take on the Communist regime and free other prisoners. Featuring a "war room" in which military experts frantically work to avoid Armageddon, *War Games* (1983) was the most paranoid nuclear-arms fable since *On the Beach* (1959) and *Dr. Strangelove* (1964). *An Officer and a Gentleman* (1982), starring Richard Gere, exudes simple military pride, but *Taps* (1981) goes beyond patriotism as Tom Cruise, playing a gung-ho cadet, screams "Beautiful!" as he opens fire

with a machine gun. Cruise later starred in *Top Gun* (1986), an old-fashioned propaganda piece in which he plays a hotshot pilot who becomes a big hero and even gets the girl — all to the beat of an MTV-style soundtrack. The success of *Top Gun*, the highest-grossing movie of 1986, prompted the U.S. Air Force to use it in recruiting. By contrast, *The Right Stuff* (1983) was ironic, mocking more than applauding the frenzy surrounding U.S. pilots and astronauts during the Soviet-American space race of the 1950s and 1960s. The media took the movie seriously, however, particularly its heroic portrayal of former astronaut John Glenn. In October 1983, after Glenn announced his intention to seek the Democratic presidential nomination, *Newsweek* ran a cover showing actor Ed Harris as Glenn and asking, "Can a Movie Elect a President?" Apparently it could not; Glenn's campaign folded well before the 1984 Democratic National Convention, and Reagan was reelected in 1984.

Rocky and *Rambo*. Sylvester Stallone hit the box-office jackpot in 1985 with *Rambo: First Blood, Part 2* and *Rocky IV*, the first two sequels in movie history to do substantially better at the box office than the originals. *Rocky IV* tapped into a popular fantasy, allowing audiences to go into the ring against the Soviet Union and win. The movie ends on Christmas Day in Moscow with Rocky defeating his evil, doped-up Soviet opponent (in red trunks) and getting draped in the American flag. The sweet but sorrowful loser of the first *Rocky* movie was transformed into a symbol of American might and freedom. In *Rambo* the angry Vietnam veteran John Rambo from *First Blood* travels back to the war-scarred jungles to take revenge on old enemies. "To survive war, you have to become war," Rambo announces, and he proceeds to prove his point by becoming a one-man battalion. To an America weary of bleak realism and antiheroes, the old-fashioned heroism in *Rambo* represented an opportunity for audiences to refight the war in Vietnam and win. The success inspired plenty of posturing, flag waving, and muscle flexing across America from Rambo water guns to look-alike contests and Rambo theme bars to a "Ronbo" poster of Ronald Reagan, portraying the president armed and ready for revenge. The zeitgeist Stallone so cleverly tapped in 1985 had shifted by 1988; in the wake of the 1987 stock-market crash and the Iran-Contra scandal, Reagan-inspired patriotism soured, and *Rambo III* was a box-office bust.

Vietnam. *Rambo* was the most commercial of a rash of Vietnam War movies released between 1984 and 1989, and none of the others share its jingoistic theme. The majority of them deal with the harsh realities of war and its high psychological and moral price. *The Killing Fields* (1984) paints a nightmarish portrait of Cambodian genocide. *Gardens of Stone* (1987) and *In Country* (1989) deal with the troubling aftereffects of the war on American veterans; *1969* (1988) depicts a group of young draftees. *Hamburger Hill* and *Full Metal Jacket* (both 1987) highlight the often horrific brutality of the war. *Good Morn-*

ing, Vietnam (1987), though publicized as a comedy, does not avoid the reality of its Saigon setting. *Casualties of War* (1989) is blunt about American atrocities committed overseas. The best-known chronicler of the Vietnam experience in the 1980s was Oliver Stone, who directed *Platoon* (1986) and *Born on the Fourth of July* (1989). Having served in the war, Stone was hailed by many other veterans, and the critics, for creating the most realistic movie depiction of the war in *Platoon*, a grim and uncompromising story of infighting among a company of soldiers. *Born on the Fourth of July*, based on a memoir by disabled veteran Ron Kovic, refights the war on the home front, as an embittered Kovic, played by Tom Cruise, rages against the "system." Stone himself generated a great deal of controversy for his open criticism, on- and offscreen, of the American government.

Real Men. With Ronald Reagan in Washington, American audiences in the 1980s once again embraced traditional masculine heroes and "regular guys." Some of these heroes — including Harrison Ford in the *Indiana Jones* movies and *Witness* (1985) or Kevin Costner in *Bull Durham* (1988) and *Field of Dreams* (1989) — were of the tough but tender variety. These actors projected integrity (like Gary Cooper) and an inner strength (like Gregory Peck) even when their characters displayed human weakness. Richard Gere excelled in playing charming but cocky hustlers in *American Gigolo* (1980), *An Officer and a Gentleman* (1982), and *Breathless* (1983). With his toothpaste-white grin and slick, well-groomed demeanor, Tom Cruise became the ultimate movie star in a decade of packaged film products. He was also the first young superstar whose onscreen image was more opportunist than rebellious; his characters enjoy playing the system's games, and they play to win. Cruise's teenage entrepreneur in *Risky Business* (1983) set the stage for the hustlers he played in *The Color of Money* (1986), *Cocktail* (1988), and *Rain Man* (1988). Other 1980s heroes tended to be larger than life and just as unbelievable. Paul Hogan emerged as an unlikely macho hero in the Australian movie *Crocodile Dundee* (1986), proving that aging Australian outbackers could be strong and sexy and sell a lot of tickets. Jack Nicholson packaged his trademark smart-guy lunacy to the point of self-parody. Audiences cheered at his leering, red-blooded, eyebrow-wiggling antics in *The Shining* (1980), *Terms of Endearment* (1983), *The Witches of Eastwick* (1987), and *Batman* (1989). By the end of the decade Nicholson had become the cinematic voice of a new "minority," the angry white American male.

Action Heroes. In *Sudden Impact* (1983) Clint Eastwood reprised his Dirty Harry character, perfecting the ice-cool action hero, complete with tag lines and sound bites ("Go ahead, make my day"). Suddenly action heroes, who had languished for a decade, were everywhere, tougher and more resourceful — and more quotable — than ever. Chuck Norris exploded onto screens with martial-arts fantasies such as *Forced Vengeance* (1982),

Silent Rage (1982), *Code of Silence* (1985), and *Delta Force* (1986). *Rocky IV* made Dolph Lundgren a star, and he followed up with movies such as *The Punisher* (1989) and *Red Scorpion* (1989). Kick-boxer Jean-Claude Van Damme, "The Muscles from Brussels," lunged his way through *Bloodsport* (1987), *Black Eagle* (1988), *Cyborg* (1989) and *Kickboxer* (1989). Steven Seagal made macho thrillers such as *Above the Law* (1988) and *Hard to Kill* (1990). Mel Gibson, best known as the angry, postapocalyptic loner in the Australian *Mad Max* movies, became an action hero with a screw loose in *Lethal Weapon* (1987). Bruce Willis graduated from television to movie superstardom with the action romp *Die Hard* (1988), in which his irreverent character single-handedly defeats a group of terrorists. Perhaps the biggest action star to emerge during the 1980s was Arnold Schwarzenegger, who turned the potential liability of his Austrian accent into box-office platinum by playing a monosyllabic killer robot in *The Terminator* (1984). Other roles as strong but silent cyborgs and foreigners followed in *Commando* (1985), *Predator* (1987), and *The Running Man* (1987). By 1988 Schwarzenegger was a big enough star to attempt a comedy, *Twins*.

Comedies. Comedies were serious business in the 1980s, rivaling fantasy and science fiction at the box office. Bette Midler and Robin Williams, faltering comedy stars in the early 1980s, had their careers resuscitated by Disney. After Disney's *Down and Out in Beverly Hills* (1986), Midler went on to appear with Danny DeVito in *Ruthless People* (1986), with Shelley Long in *Outrageous Fortune* (1987), and with Lily Tomlin in *Big Business* (1988). Williams received acclaim for *Good Morning, Vietnam* and *Dead Poets Society* (1989). Steve Martin twice won the New York Film Critics Circle awards for best actor during the 1980s — for *All of Me* (1984) and *Roxanne* (1987). Among the actors who received Oscar nominations for their comedy roles were Goldie Hawn for *Private Benjamin* (1980), Dudley Moore for *Arthur* (1981), and Tom Hanks for *Big* (1988). Hawn and Moore both capitalized on their success by playing variations on the same characters. DeVito carved out a string of comedic supporting roles in *Romancing the Stone* (1984), *Tin Men* (1987), and *The War of the Roses* (1989). In the late 1970s Chevy Chase and John Belushi had opened the cinema doors to other performers from the late-night television comedy programs *Saturday Night Live* and *SCTV*, including Joe Piscopo, Rick Moranis, Dave Thomas, and Harold Ramis. Chase went on to star in several 1980s comedies, most notably *National Lampoon's Vacation* (1983) and its sequels. Belushi and Dan Aykroyd expanded one of their best-known sketches into the full-length romp, *The Blues Brothers* (1980). After Belushi's drug-related death in 1982, Aykroyd continued to make comedies, including *Trading Places* (1983) and *Ghostbusters* (1984).

Murray and Murphy. The nutty irreverence Bill Murray displayed in *Meatballs* (1979) translated into comedy

Barbra Streisand on the set of *Yentl*

superstardom in the early 1980s. Chevy Chase and Rodney Dangerfield were ostensibly the stars of *Caddyshack* (1980), but it was Bill Murray's over-the-top cameo that turned the low-budget vehicle into a cult hit. His follow-up, *Stripes* (1982), a goofy military comedy perfectly tailored to his wise-guy persona, became an even bigger hit. In 1984 Murray topped his previous efforts yet again in *Ghostbusters,* a big-budget special effects comedy that made $220 million to become the eighth highest-grossing film in history. He played a dramatic role in *The Razor's Edge* (1984), but audiences were not interested. After a four-year layoff, Murray returned to movies with *Scrooged* (1988) and *Ghostbusters II* (1989). After the original *Saturday Night Live* cast departed in 1980, Eddie Murphy emerged as the only star of the replacement cast, winning an audience with a range of sly characters. In 1982 he was paired with Nick Nolte for his big-screen debut, *48 Hrs.* That film established his street-smart, take-no-prisoners comic persona, which was crystallized in *Trading Places* the following year. The peak of his popularity came in 1984, when he played hip detective Axel Foley in *Beverly Hills Cop,* the biggest comedy hit of the decade and the sixth largest moneymaker of all time. The movie is mainly a series of set pieces that enabled Murphy to do his lovable bad-boy schtick. Follow-ups — including *The Golden Child* (1986), *Coming to America* (1988), the concert movie *Eddie Murphy Raw* (1987), and

the inevitable *Beverly Hills Cop II* (1987) — more or less continued the winning Murphy formula.

Dumb Comedies. The unexpected success of the supremely silly *Airplane!* and *Caddyshack* in 1980 opened the door for a slew of "dumb" comedies during the decade. Bill Murray's goofy but lovable movies stood out from the crowd, largely because of his star talent. Many others, such as *Porky's* (1982) and its two sequels, were leering sex comedies (complete with holes in shower-room walls) about teenage boys' obsession with losing their virginity. *Bachelor Party* (1984) with Tom Hanks was more of the same, as were *Spring Break* (1983) and *Losin' It* (1983). *Police Academy* (1984), starring Steve Guttenberg, perfected the dumb-comedy formula of bathroom humor and good-natured anarchy. It also had five sequels by 1989. The heroes of *Bill & Ted's Excellent Adventure* (1989) are perfect examples of late-1980s "dudes," one-upping Sean Penn's dumb prototype in *Fast Times at Ridgemont High* (1982) with their dazzling displays of "air guitar." In 1988 *The Naked Gun* resurrected the bad puns, endless sight gags, and pratfalls of *Airplane!* and *Airplane II: The Sequel* (1982) and launched the previously staid Leslie Nielsen on a new career as an aging goofball.

Stalkers and Slashers. As tasteless as the dumb comedies of the 1980s were the "slasher" movies. Jason, the hockey-masked "star" of the seven sequels to *Friday the 13th,* proved that low-budget "quickies" could still make piles of money at the box office. The popularity of Jason and Freddie Kruger, the knife-fingered slasher of *A Nightmare on Elm Street* (1984) and its sequels, angered as many as it delighted. Most outraged were feminists, who were weary of seeing women portrayed as the victims of predatory violence in these "stalker" or "slasher" films. Many critics felt that the glut of stalker movies in the 1980s films represented an antifeminist backlash in Hollywood. *Halloween,* which had launched the slasher cycle in 1978, had four sequels in the 1980s, each with its sinister "hero" stalking a terrified woman. The three long-awaited *Psycho* sequels (1983, 1986, 1990) offered the same queasy dynamic as the original 1960 movie, minus the original genius of Alfred Hitchcock. Other suspense movies of the decade — including *The Terminator* (1984), *The Stepfather* (1987), and *Body Double* (1984) — not only offered such brutal and misogynistic violence as entertainment but encouraged viewers to identify with the killers. The effect of slasher movies on children was hotly debated, especially with the release of *Child's Play* (1988), featuring a murderous doll, and *Silent Night, Deadly Night* (1984), which depicted a homicidal Santa Claus. Rutger Hauer was one of the most chilling of the seemingly unkillable 1980s stalkers, most notably as an android in *Blade Runner* (1982) and as *The Hitcher* (1986). Director David Cronenberg offered a sinister variation of stalking in *Dead Ringers* (1988), with twin gynecologists pursuing an understandably frightened woman. Cronenberg also specialized in another popular horror genre, the "splatter" movie, so named for the tendency of blood and guts to splatter during acts of violence. *Scanners* (1981) featured heads blowing apart.

Independents. Cronenberg was one of the few directors with a discernible personal style to emerge during the 1980s. Brian De Palma also made a career of onscreen violence, while adding a touch of arty prestige to projects such as *Dressed to Kill* (1980), *Scarface* (1983), *Body Double* (1984), and *The Untouchables* (1987). Martin Scorsese, who had earned acclaim as an "auteur" in the 1970s, contributed one of the best movies of the 1980s, the gritty, atmospheric *Raging Bull* (1980). He continued to experiment with style and subject in *The King of Comedy* (1983), *After Hours* (1985), and *The Last Temptation of Christ* (1988). *The Year of Living Dangerously* (1983) and *Witness* (1985) earned Peter Weir a reputation for moody and dreamlike vision, while Terry Gilliam became known for fusing fantasy and comedy in *Time Bandits* (1981) and *Brazil* (1985). After the cult independent-film hit *Eraserhead* (1978) David Lynch found mainstream success with *The Elephant Man* (1980) and then went on to make the misguided epic *Dune* (1984). The decadent and disturbing *Blue Velvet* (1986), one of the most talked-about movies of the decade, restored Lynch's cult appeal. The directing team of Joel and Ethan Coen also outgrew the underground status they earned with *Blood Simple* (1984) when they made the big comedy hit *Raising Arizona* (1987). Alex Cox contributed two of the biggest cult successes of the 1980s, *Repo Man* (1984) and *Sid and Nancy* (1986). Jonathan Demme became known for his versatility after *Melvin and Howard* (1980), *Stop Making Sense* (1984), *Something Wild* (1986), and *Married to the Mob* (1988). John Sayles developed a following with uncommercial movies such as the comedy *The Brother from Another Planet* (1984) and the drama *Matewan* (1987). British director Bill Forsyth won critical acclaim for his refreshing comedies *Gregory's Girl* (1981) and *Local Hero* (1983). Alan Rudolph excelled at creating unusual moods and characters in *Choose Me* (1984) and *Trouble in Mind* (1985). Jim Jarmusch elevated minimalism to humorous heights in *Stranger Than Paradise* (1984), *Down by Law* (1986), and *Mystery Train* (1989). Spike Lee became the best-known black filmmaker of the decade with the independent comedy hit *She's Gotta Have It* (1986) and the controversial interracial drama *Do the Right Thing* (1989). Lee was often compared to Woody Allen in his use of ensembles and urban humor. Allen himself continued to make appealing and original comedies during the decade, including *Zelig* (1983), *Broadway Danny Rose* (1984), *The Purple Rose of Cairo* (1985), *Hannah and Her Sisters* (1986), and *Crimes & Misdemeanors* (1989). Several veteran actors had their careers revived with appearances in independent films and underground cult hits, most notably Dennis Hopper in *Blue Velvet* and *River's Edge* (1987), Harry Dean Stanton in *Paris, Texas* (1984), and *Repo Man*, and Dean Stockwell in *Blue Velvet* and *Married to the Mob*.

Jane Fonda, Katharine Hepburn, and Henry Fonda in *On Golden Pond*

Women. Except for top executives Sherry Lansing and Dawn Steel, producer Gale Anne Hurd, and actresses such as Sally Field and Goldie Hawn (who set up their own production companies), Hollywood remained largely a boys' club during the 1980s. Yet women directors did emerge during the decade, many to major acclaim. Barbra Streisand made a splash by producing, writing, and acting in her first directorial effort, *Yentl* (1983), and she made headlines when she was overlooked at Oscar time. Randa Haines was also denied a nomination for best director when her *Children of a Lesser God* (1986) was nominated for best picture. Veteran director Elaine May struck out with *Ishtar* (1987), one of the most expensive bombs, but Penny Marshall had a major comedy hit with *Big* (1988). Amy Heckerling won praise for adding a feminine perspective to the teen movie *Fast Times at Ridgemont High* (1982); then she made the $50 million hit *National Lampoon's European Vacation* (1985) and *Look Who's Talking* (1989). Martha Coolidge also raised the level of the teen movie, with *Valley Girl* (1983) and *Real Genius* (1985). Susan Seidelman earned raves for the hip urban sensibilities of *Smithereens* (1982) and *Desperately Seeking Susan* (1985). Penelope Spheeris contributed the two-part rock documentary *The Decline of Western Civilization* (1981, 1988), a hilarious but chilling dissection of the punk-rock and heavy-metal scenes. Australian Gillian Armstrong directed *Mrs. Soffel* (1984) and *High Tide* (1987), and Jane Campion of New Zealand attracted critical attention with *Sweetie* (1989). Other new directors included Kathryn Bigelow (*Near Dark*, 1987), Amy Jones (*Love Letters*, 1983), Joyce

Chopra (*Smooth Talk*, 1985), and Donna Deitch (*Desert Hearts*, 1985).

Blandness. Distinctive filmmaking styles like Spike Lee's were the cinematic exceptions in the 1980s. With Hollywood's emphasis on bigness most releases came to seem interchangeable. Stately, tasteful "prestige" movies such as *Gandhi* (1982), *Out of Africa* (1985), and *Driving Miss Daisy* (1989) seemed to exist only to win Oscars. Many others — such as *Ordinary People* (1980), *The Big Chill* (1983), *Silkwood* (1983), *Terms of Endearment* (1983), and *Mask* (1985) — seemed more like made-for-television movies than big-screen efforts. The queen of both types of movies was Meryl Streep, who was nominated six times in the 1980s for best-actress Oscars for her roles in movies that were tasteful but often lifeless. Oscar-winning "prestige" actors Robert De Niro and Dustin Hoffman gave excellent performances in well-received movies for "prestige" directors such as Martin Scorsese and Barry Levinson, but most of their other efforts were soggy. A few promising film actors emerged in the 1980s (including Anjelica Huston, Daniel Day-Lewis, Debra Winger, Jeremy Irons, Susan Sarandon, and Holly Hunter), but many of the most-acclaimed stars — Jessica Lange, Robert Duvall, Sally Field, Sissy Spacek — seemed committed to bland, "noble" film efforts. Directors became chameleons, reliably churning out hits without any noticeable personal stamp. After his hilarious heavy-metal parody *This Is Spinal Tap* (1984), Rob Reiner settled in into a yeomanlike pace with conventional comedies like *The Sure Thing* (1985) and *When Harry Met Sally* (1989). Ron Howard's efforts were similarly bland. He contributed *Splash* (1984), *Cocoon* (1985), and *Parenthood* (1989) like clockwork. Unlike the gritty and realistic experiments of the 1970s, more and more 1980s movies relied on happy endings, tidied-up plots, and crowd-pleasing climaxes. The Hollywood products of the Reagan years were bland, empty packages with feel-good labels.

Nostalgia. Reagan's vision of an America filled with white picket fences may have been more in line with the 1950s than the 1980s, but it worked well as a movie. Norman Rockwell–style nostalgia bloomed. *A Christmas Story* (1983) harkened back to home and hearth in the 1940s, as did Woody Allen's *Radio Days* (1987). *Stand by Me* (1986) was a sepia-tinged flashback to boyhood innocence in the 1950s, also evoked in *Dead Poets Society* (1989). *Diner* (1982) depicted the days of President John F. Kennedy's Camelot as experienced by six male friends, while *Dirty Dancing* (1987) set a story of first love during the same period. *Back to the Future* (1985) sent a typical 1980s kid back to the 1950s to change his family's destiny, while the heroine of *Peggy Sue Got Married* (1986) found herself back in 1962, with a second chance at life. Though set in the present, *Field of Dreams* (1989) created nostalgia for a simpler time with its midwestern landscapes and baseball, mom, and apple-pie sensibility. *Life* magazine Americana also popped up in

period pieces such as *The Right Stuff* (1983), *Driving Miss Daisy* (1989), and the romantic baseball saga *The Natural* (1984).

Veterans. The Hollywood nostalgia in the 1980s extended to its veteran actors, who popped up increasingly in important roles and major movies. During the 1980s nearly one quarter of the actors who won Oscars were past sixty, and six were over seventy. In 1981 fifty-six-year-old Maureen Stapleton was the youngest winner; the other winners that year were John Gielgud (seventy-seven), Katharine Hepburn (seventy-four), and Henry Fonda (seventy-six). Hepburn and Fonda were the oldest actors ever to win in the best-actor and best-actress categories until Jessica Tandy surpassed them in 1989, at eighty. The Hepburn-Fonda vehicle, *On Golden Pond*, was such a surprise hit that it triggered a demand for warm, fuzzy movies about folks in their sunset years. Veteran Don Ameche began a whole new career. He had major roles in *Trading Places* (1983) and *Things Change* (1989) and won an Oscar for his break-dancing and cannonball-diving performance in the retirement-home hit *Cocoon*, which also featured Tandy, Hume Cronyn, Wilford Brimley, Stapleton, and other older stars. Tandy suddenly became a major movie star with her Oscar-winning turn as a feisty widow in *Driving Miss Daisy* (1989). Geraldine Page won for her role as a determined retiree in *The Trip to Bountiful* (1985), and Paul Newman proved there was life after sixty when he won an Oscar for playing the aging pool hustler Eddie Felson in *The Color of Money* (1986). Sean Connery, Olympia Dukakis, Shirley MacLaine, and other veterans unexpectedly found themselves in demand, while top male stars such as Clint Eastwood, Dustin Hoffman, Warren Beatty, Robert Redford, and Jack Nicholson all passed fifty without losing their leading-man appeal.

Family Values. From cuddly oldsters to newborn babies, families hit the big time in Reagan-era movies. *Fatal Attraction* (1987) used a strong, traditional nuclear family, including a stay-at-home mom, to nail home its conservative moral about the evils of adultery and independent, "deviant" women. Career-minded women were staples of 1980s movies, but they sacrificed romantic and family fulfillment, as in *Legal Eagles* (1986), *Broadcast News* (1987), *The Big Easy* (1987), *House of Games* (1987), and *Suspect* (1987). The heroine of *The Good Mother* (1988) is punished for her sexuality by losing custody of her child. In *Baby Boom* (1987) a high-powered executive has motherhood literally thrust upon her, only to find herself loving it. After the success of *Kramer vs. Kramer* in 1979, fatherhood, never a big subject in Hollywood movies, was celebrated as both strong and nurturing in hits such as *Mr. Mom* (1983), *Three Men and a Baby* (1987), and *Look Who's Talking* (1989). *Parenthood* was almost an advertisement for the traditional nuclear family, while prospective parents in *The Big Chill* and *Immediate Family* (1989) resort to outside help to start families.

Amid the commotion surrounding the record-breaking auction of Andy Warhol's estate in 1988, a London newspaper observed dryly, "There is hype after death." The following year there was still more hoopla over the publication of his name-dropping diaries. Warhol once made the frequently quoted observation that everyone in the future would be famous for fifteen minutes. By that measure his posthumous fame in the late 1980s lasted for hours.

Warhol, who died of a heart attack following gall bladder surgery in February 1987, had been a compulsive shopper and collector. His tastes ran the gamut from classical sculpture and art deco furniture to cheap jewelry and kitsch. "Andy had no pretensions to connoisseurship," said executor Frederick Hughes, who hired Sotheby's auction house to sell Warhol's collection of some ten thousand items. Inventory took several weeks, as objects were grouped in three thousand lots according to their market value. Three floors of the auction house were devoted to the presale display.

In a statement that accurately reflected the capitalist spirit of the 1980s, Warhol had once remarked, "Making money is art and good business is the best art." Sotheby's was true to that spirit in their aggressive marketing of his possessions. A glossy six-volume catalogue was sold in bookstores for ninety-five dollars. To encourage advance bidding the auction house also sent a traveling exhibit of seventy objects to Chicago, Los Angeles, Europe, and Japan, and they hosted elegant parties, including several in Warhol's home, for important clients and the press.

By the time the auction was held on 23 April–3 May, Warhol was awash in the kind of media hype he would have loved, including a cover story in *Newsweek*, a feature on the television program *20/20*, and articles in *Forbes* and *Business Week*. For the ten days of the auction a record sixty thousand people, from serious bidders to gawkers and celebrity watchers, crowded Sotheby's, which opened telephone lines to prospective clients from all over the world and distributed a how-to book for novice bidders. Bidding paddles and ID tags from auctioned pieces became collector's items, as sought after as the actual merchandise.

Final sales totaled $25.3 million, $10 million above expectations. A pair of cookie jars estimated at $100 to $150 were sold for $23,100. One private collector spent $27,500 on an art piece that consisted of garbage sealed in Plexiglass. "Everyone wants a bit of Andy Warhol," commented a security guard. Prices for Warhol's collection of contemporary art, works by artists from Jean-Michel Basquiat to Roy Lichtenstein, far exceeded presale estimates. Warhol's own work *210 Coca-Cola Bottles* sold for $1.43 million, double the previous auction record for a work by Warhol.

The auction seemed like Warhol's last hurrah — until 1989 and the much-hyped publication of *The Warhol Diaries*. In 1976 Warhol had started tracking his expenditures by phoning his assistant Pat Hackett each morning with a rundown of the previous night's activities and a report of how much he had spent. Since those activities invariably included Warhol's galaxy of celebrity friends — from Liza Minnelli and Liz Taylor to Halston and Bianca Jagger — the "ledger" soon became a name-dropping time capsule of the Studio 54 disco era.

After Warhol's death Hackett edited the ten-thousand-page book down to eight hundred pages highlighting the period 1976–1987. Amid the media furor over the auction in 1988, the estate received a $1.2 million publisher's advance, and the appearance of *The Warhol Diaries* in 1989 caused another media stir. The best-seller status of the book at decade's end was a fitting close to a second Warhol era. The artist himself could not have planned a splashier exit.

Sources: "Andy Warhol Gets Another 15 Minutes," *ARTnews*, 87 (Summer 1988): 27–28;

"The Selling of Andy Warhol," *Newsweek*, 111 (18 April 1988): 60–64.

Field of Dreams, Honey, I Shrunk the Kids, and *Back to the Future* have family messages, and the comedy hit *Moonstruck* (1987) even ends with a toast to "la familia!"

Yuppies. The audience for family fare grew steadily during the decade with the aging of the baby boomers. Whether they were parenting, coupling, or simply reveling in singles-bar success, boomers and yuppies were everywhere, both in the culture and on movie screens. Michael Douglas, Glenn Close, and William Hurt became onscreen embodiments of yuppiedom. *The Big Chill* was the first movie to capture the zeitgeist; its seven aging boomers spend a weekend trying to reconcile their rebellion and idealism in the 1960s with their newfound success in the 1980s. In *Lost in America* (1985) a yuppie couple confront the same issue by junking their big-salary careers in order to drive cross-country and "touch Indians," in a 1980s version of *Easy Rider* (1969). Later, they crawl back to their urban meal tickets. Others were not as worried about integrity: the heroine of *Working Girl* (1988) trounces her evil yuppie boss by stealing her high-power job. *Arthur* (1981), *Trading Places* (1983), and *Big Business* (1988) also had it both ways, with evil entrepreneurs being ousted in favor of the good guys, who still get to keep all their money. The heroine of *Baby Boom* is rewarded with the jackpot of a new romance, a new business, and new motherhood. Such movies suggested to many boomers that they could have it all: wealth, career success, and family. Gordon Gekko, the corporate-raider "hero" of *Wall Street,* proclaims that "greed . . . is good," and he has the wife, beach house, clothes, and art collection to prove it.

The Brat Pack. A decade or more younger but just as successful onscreen as Douglas and Close were the Brat Pack, all with a similar well-clothed, well-groomed, well-paid, and well-housed angst. Tom Cruise kicked off the Pack attack with *Risky Business* (1983), in which he plays an upper-class, North Shore brat who throws a party, hires a hooker, drives his father's expensive car into Lake Michigan, and becomes an entrepreneur. Other movies about privileged but whiny 1980s suburbanites and mall rats included *Valley Girl* (1983) with Nicolas Cage; *Fast Times at Ridgemont High* (1982) with Sean Penn, Phoebe Cates, Judge Reinhold, and Jennifer Jason Leigh; and *Sixteen Candles* (1984) with Molly Ringwald and Anthony Michael Hall. *Valley Girl,* echoing the character Michael J. Fox played in the television hit *Family Ties,* became the first movie to depict acquisitive consumerist brats rolling their eyes at the 1960s ideals of their former hippie parents. Fox translated his Reagan-supporting television persona into the yuppie roles he played in *The Secret of My Success* (1987) and *Bright Lights, Big City* (1988). Charlie Sheen played a similar role in *Wall Street,* while his brother Emilio Estevez starred in the two biggest Brat Pack movies: *St. Elmo's Fire* (1985) with Rob Lowe, Demi Moore, Andrew McCarthy, Ally Sheedy, and Judd Nelson; and *The Breakfast Club* (1985) with Sheedy, Nelson, Ringwald, and Hall. Lowe and Moore reunited in *About Last Night . . .* (1986), while McCarthy moved on to *Less Than Zero* (1987), with up-and-coming brats Robert Downey Jr. and Jamie Gertz, and *Pretty in Pink* (1986), with Ringwald. Downey portrayed another brat in *The Pick-Up Artist* (1987). John Hughes was the top Brat Pack director, working with Ringwald on *Sixteen Candles, The Breakfast Club,* and *Pretty in Pink.* Several brat stars benefited from movie versions of best-selling novels by a new group of brat novelists who were taking the literary world by storm.

Sources:

Leonard Maltin, ed., *Leonard Maltin's Movie and Video Guide,* 1995 edition (New York: Signet, 1995);

"Rocky and Rambo," *Newsweek,* 107 (23 December 1985): 58–62;

David Thomson, *A Biographical Dictionary of Film* (New York: Knopf, 1994);

Tom Wolfe, whose novel *The Bonfire of the Vanities* satirized life in New York City during the 1980s

John Walker, ed., *Halliwell's Film Guide* (New York: HarperCollins, 1994);

Mason Wiley and Damien Bona, *Inside Oscar: The Unofficial History of the Academy Awards* (New York: Ballantine, 1991).

LITERARY STARS

Brats. In the mid 1980s a group of hotshot young writers attained celebrity with novels that explored the decade-long obsession with drugs, money, cheap sex, instant gratification — and celebrity. This literary "brat pack," which included Jay McInerney, Bret Easton Ellis, and Tama Janowitz, shrewdly tapped the passive MTV mindset of young Americans. Their chief subject — young, privileged urban hipsters disillusioned by the seeming decadence of their empty social scenes — made them the darlings of the yuppie-hungry media and millions of wanna-be-hip readers. These stories were light on plot and character but rich in dropped names, pop-culture references, and slick surface descriptions of galleries, lofts, offices, studios, and shopping malls. *The Village Voice* dubbed the style "socialite realism." McInerney's *Bright Lights, Big City* (1984), narrated in the second person, traces the aimless days and cocaine-laden nights of a young New York magazine fact checker whose fashion-model wife has left him. Ellis's *Less Than Zero* (1985) follows the cocaine-filled days and bleak nights of a rich, burned-out Los Angeles student and his rich, shopped-out friends. Janowitz's *Slaves of New York* (1986)

Stephen King, whose horror fiction made him the most popular American novelist of the 1980s

is a collection of stories loosely organized around the superficial days and cocaine-packed nights of a New York jewelry designer and her graffiti-artist boyfriend.

Media Spotlight. *Bright Lights, Big City* received mixed reviews, but it was an overnight success with the reading public. McInerney was soon living the nightlife his novel had satirized, appearing on magazine covers and at trendy New York parties with well-known artists, models, and film stars. Ellis was only twenty-one years old and still a student at Bennington College when *Less Than Zero* landed him an MTV interview. After *Slaves of New York* became a hit, the previously unknown Janowitz lent her face and name to a series of liquor ads. Janowitz's success was not harmed by a blurb from McInerney on the cover of the paperback edition of *Slaves of New York;* he pronounced her "a singular talent." By 1987 all three of these authors had six-figure movie deals, with McInerney and Janowitz contributing the screenplays for the movie versions of their books. All three shrewdly marketed their follow-up products. While McInerney attempted to prove he was no flash in the pan by exploring other themes in *Ransom* (1986) and *The Story of My Life* (1989), Ellis realized that spiritual and moral bankruptcy of the young and rich was a best-selling commodity and

simply repackaged it in a new setting for *The Rules of Attraction* (1987). Meanwhile, Janowitz peddled her modern fable *A Cannibal in Manhattan* (1987) to hipsters by packing the text with photos of celebrities such as Andy Warhol and Stephen Sprouse. By then several other brat novelists had joined the pack, among them Mark Lindquist with *Sad Movies* (1987), Jill Eisenstadt with *From Rockaway* (1987), and Peter Farrelly with *Outside Providence* (1988).

The Bonfire of the Vanities. When it came to tapping the American zeitgeist, the brats could not compete with Tom Wolfe. Nor did the media uproar surrounding them touch that generated by Wolfe's first novel, *The Bonfire of the Vanities* (1987). Wolfe, who had virtually invented New Journalism in the 1960s and coined the phrase "The Me Decade" in the 1970s, provided in *The Bonfire of the Vanities* both a comic novel of manners and an entertaining time capsule of New York life in the 1980s. Readers throughout America responded, often with outrage, to Wolfe's depiction of the racial clash between white yuppie Manhattan financier Sherman McCoy (self-proclaimed "Master of the Universe") and Reverend Bacon of the Bronx, who manipulates public opinion to win justice for a poor black youth McCoy has inadvertently killed. With his trademark breathless, often purple prose, Wolfe effectively skewered the pretensions and attitudes of both races; he also managed to satirize Wall Street, the media, and the entire legal and judicial system. The gigantic success of the novel with critics and the public led Wolfe to appoint himself almost a laureate of new fiction writing. In 1989 he published an article in *Harper's,* with the subtitle "a literary manifesto for the new social novel," in which he took pains to criticize "absurdist" writers, including Philip Roth and John Barth, for leading the American novel away from realism and reportage. Wolfe's self-serving piece proved as controversial as his novel; it also kept his name in the press after sales of the novel began to slack off.

Other Novelists. In 1983, after thirteen publishers rejected William Kennedy's fourth novel, *Ironweed,* Kennedy's novelist friend Saul Bellow persuaded Viking to publish it. The critics greeted it with high praise, and it won a Pulitzer Prize and a National Book Critics Circle Award. At fifty-six Kennedy found himself an overnight celebrity. His three earlier novels, *The Ink Truck* (1969), *Legs* (1975), and *Billy Phelan's Greatest Game* (1978) — all set, like *Ironweed,* in Albany, New York — were republished, winning him more acclaim, as did the appearance of a fifth Albany novel, *Quinn's Book,* in 1988. The success of *Ironweed* also led to his writing the script for Francis Ford Coppola's movie *The Cotton Club* (1984). Alice Walker also gained newfound fame when her novel *The Color Purple* (1982) won a Pulitzer Prize and a National Book Award. Though *The Color Purple* drew fire from some African American readers and critics for its harsh portrayal of black men, most praised its originality and the strength and spirit of its female characters. The story, told in a series of letters, traces the gradual liberation of Celie from virtual slave and victim to a woman who is master of her own destiny. Anne Tyler also won recognition in the 1980s. *Morgan's Passing* (1980) was nominated for a National Book Critics Circle Award. *Dinner at the Homesick Restaurant* (1982) and *The Accidental Tourist* (1985) won praise for their irony, humor, and characters, and *Breathing Lessons* (1988) won a Pulitzer Prize. Other Pulitzer Prize winners during the 1980s included John Updike for *Rabbit Is Rich* (1981), Toni Morrison for *Beloved* (1987), the late John Kennedy Toole for *A Confederacy of Dunces* (1980), and Larry McMurtry for *Lonesome Dove* (1985). Other notable literary voices of the decade included Reynolds Price (*Kate Vaiden*, 1986), Richard Ford (*The Sportswriter*, 1986), and David Leavitt (*Family Dancing*, 1984).

Page Turners. Many of the best-selling authors of the 1980s were "specialists" in genre fiction. Jean M. Auel won fans with novels that feature animals: *The Clan of the Cave Bear* (1980), *The Valley of the Horses* (1982), and *The Mammoth Hunters* (1985). Anne Rice capitalized on the popularity of her 1976 novel, *Interview with the Vampire*, with two successful sequels: *The Vampire Lestat* (1985) and *The Queen of the Damned* (1988). Robert Ludlum and British author John Le Carre virtually cornered the market in espionage fiction, while James Michener continued to crank out epics that seemed ready-made for adaptation as television miniseries. Tom Clancy traced the adventures of marine lieutenant Jack Ryan in *The Hunt for Red October* (1984), *Patriot Games* (1987), and *Clear and Present Danger* (1989) — all subsequently adapted for the big screen. Scott Turow found his legal thriller *Presumed Innocent* (1987) at the top of the best-seller list. Thousands of Americans read English translations of Italian novelist Umberto Eco's *The Name of the Rose* (1983) and *Foucault's Pendulum* (1989), mysteries/intellectual puzzles in religious/occult settings. Garrison Keillor built on the success of his *Prairie Home Companion* radio show with two best-sellers, *Lake Woebegone Days* (1985) and *Leaving Home* (1987). Andrew Greeley used the Catholic Church as a setting for his sensational best-sellers *The Cardinal Sins* (1981) and *Virgin and Martyr* (1985). Page-turners by specialists in glitz novels — including Jackie Collins, Danielle Steel, Sidney Sheldon, Judith Krantz, and Shirley Conran — dominated the best-seller lists and were frequently adapted into television miniseries.

The Horror Factory. Possibly the most prolific and most famous novelist of the 1980s was horror-fiction writer Stephen King, a one-man best-seller factory throughout the decade, turning out as many as four novels in a single fifteen-month period. By 1985 there were 50 million copies of King's books in print, earning him more than $20 million. He earned $3 million alone as an advance for *It* (1986), which already ranked number one on *The New York Times* best-seller list before it was officially published. Hollywood snatched up King's best-sellers, quickly adapting them into money-making mov-

ies, including *The Shining* (1980), *Creepshow* (1982), *The Dead Zone* (1983), *Christine* (1983), *Cujo* (1983), *Firestarter* (1984), *Stand by Me* (1986), and *Pet Sematary* (1989). In 1984 he and Peter Straub made publishing history with their co-authored novel *The Talisman*. An unheard-of $550,000 advertising budget and a television commercial rotated regularly on MTV helped the publisher earn back the authors' hefty advances in only twenty-four hours, and the novel sold faster than any other book ever printed. An unprecedented 1 million hardcover copies of the novel sold in only ten weeks. King also wrote movies such as *Silver Bullet* (1985) and *Maximum Overdrive* (1986), which he also directed.

Books on Tape. King was one of the best-selling authors whose books became readily available on audiocassette when that new industry took off in the mid and late 1980s. Recorded readings of books, once available only at libraries or through direct mail for the blind, suddenly became popular with busy professionals who found they had less and less time to read. For the cost of a compact disc, and for less than a hardcover book, they could listen in the car or at the gym to their favorite authors reading their own work or to a well-known actor's dramatic rendition. Usually abridged versions of well-known works, books on tape proved to be a money-making idea. Only a handful of publishers were testing the market with a few titles in 1985; by 1987 the market was flooded with audio books. Warner Audio Publishing led the way with sixty new titles a year. The most popular audio books tended to be best-sellers. Among the authors who read their own works were Garrison Keillor, John Updike, Richard Ford, Erica Jong, James Michener, John Updike, Toni Morrison, Gore Vidal, John Le Carre, Eudora Welty, and Stephen King. Actors who read books on tape included Mel Gibson, Claudette Colbert, Peter Ustinov, Sam Waterston, and Kathleen Turner. Though many of these celebrities' voices were used to maximum effect (such as Jason Robards reading William Kennedy's Albany trilogy), some seemed incongruous choices: F. Murray Abraham reading *The Two Mrs. Grenvilles*, Frank Langella reading *The Cardinal Sins*, Roger Moore reading *If Tomorrow Comes*, Darren McGavin reading *Space*, Lee Remick reading *Windmills of the Gods*, Juliet Mills reading *Valley of the Dolls*, and Genie Francis of the soap opera *General Hospital* reading Jacqueline Susann's *Once Is Not Enough*.

Sources:
"Advertisements for Themselves," *New Yorker,* 63 (26 October 1987): 142–146;

"Books That Speak for Themselves," *U.S. News & World Report,* 101 (14 July 1986): 49;

"Having the Time of His Life," *Newsweek,* 103 (6 February 1984): 78–79;

"Heard a Good Book Lately?," *Newsweek,* 106 (29 July 1985): 55;

"King of Horror," *Time,* 128 (6 October 1986): 74–83;

"A Long Road to Liberation," *Newsweek,* 99 (21 June 1982): 67–68;

"The MTV Novel Arrives," *Film Comment,* 21 (November/December 1985): 44–46;

Michael Jackson holding six of the eight Grammy Awards he won for his album *Thriller,* February 1984

"The Titans of Terror," *Newsweek,* 104 (24 December 1984): 61–62;

"Two Divine Decadents," *Newsweek,* 110 (7 September 1987): 72;

"An Unleashed Wolfe," *Newsweek,* 110 (26 October 1987): 84–85;

"An Unstoppable Thriller King," *Newsweek,* 105 (10 June 1985): 62–63;

"Wolfe Among the Pigeons," *Time,* 134 (27 November 1989): 78.

MUSIC VIDEO

Impact. The music video, in which short performances accompany and illustrate songs, appeared out of nowhere in the early 1980s to become the most influential — and the only new — art form of the decade. As advertisements for new recordings and as self-promotion for the artist, music videos captured the capitalist spirit of 1980s art. Artistically these videos were a mixed lot, ranging from electrifying to turgid. Most fell somewhere between these extremes — a typical video was a quirky, dreamlike montage of images (a "minimovie") designed to illustrate fantasies or approximate the live performances of the artist or band. In their cultural impact videos accomplished much more than advertising, making arguments about their overt commercialism of small consequence. The music video single-handedly revitalized the slumping recording industry, revolutionized television, expanded radio formatting, ignited the careers of dozens of unknown music performers, breathed new life into dance and choreography, and opened avenues of potential in the movie industry. It also changed marketing and audience demographics by creating a new interconnection and interdependence among television, movies, and music.

Pioneers. The earliest videos were primitive but often vital exercises for their creators and, in the long run, for the entire industry. Many pioneering videos were simply concert clips, but several artists, particularly in Europe, were experimenting with surrealistic and narrative forms by the late 1970s. In Europe the shortage of radio stations motivated many young musicians to seek alternative types of exposure. Their promotional videotapes were played at discos and on television. In England David Bowie became a forerunner in the new form with his energetic promo video for his song "DJ" (1979) and his Fellini-esque fantasy "Ashes to Ashes" (1980), in which a stone-faced Bowie, dressed as a harlequin, walks along a postapocalyptic beach while being lectured by an old woman. New-wave bands of the late 1970s and early 1980s embraced the video form, even on nonexistent budgets. Devo and The Residents mixed camp with alienation in their clips, while The Pretenders contributed cinematic style with "Brass in Pocket" (1980). By late 1980 videos were appearing frequently on late-night music programs and in urban dance clubs, which began alternating the promos with avant-garde movie clips and old television footage. Viewers were soon flocking around video screens at clubs such as Hurrah and Danceteria in New York and Lucky Number and Neo in Chicago. The music industry began to take notice.

MTV. The true catalyst of the 1980s video explosion was Music Television (MTV), which began broadcasting in August 1981. MTV was the brainchild of former radio-program director Robert Pittman. With the financial backing of Warner Communications and American Express, Pittman created the cable network to reach what he called "the TV babies," post–baby-boom teenagers and young adults who had grown up with television and rock music. "The set is part of our lives," he said. "We want it to respond to our every need and desire." MTV showed twenty-four hours of nonstop music videos every day, with breaks for rock news, "veejay" chitchat, commercials, and occasional special programming. Record companies supplied their artists' videos for free in return for free airplay. Pittman's market surveying produced demographics that were extremely appealing to advertisers: 85 percent of the viewers were between ages twelve and thirty-four, and 63 percent were under twenty-five. The MTV network vice president in charge of advertising sales noted, "MTV was the most researched channel in television history." After starting with a relatively small playlist — a few hundred clips, mostly rock — and an equally small operating budget, MTV grew rapidly, from 18 advertisers in 1981 to more than 125 by early 1983. By 1983 the company had not yet turned a profit, but its reach was impressive: from 300 cable outlets capable of reaching 2.5 million homes in 1981, it had grown to include 2,000 affiliates received by 17.5 million homes in 1983. John Lack, executive vice president at Warner Amex, summed up the market position of MTV: "We are a company that believes in specialized entertainment, and if you are Budweiser or Kawasaki or Pepsi-Cola, you want our audience." Their audience wanted video; Pittman's new slogan for the burgeoning network was "I want my MTV."

The British Invasion. During the peak years of British punk, the synthesizer had all but disappeared as a rock-band instrument; its artifice was anathema to punk purists. Yet in the late 1970s portable synthesizers became relatively inexpensive, selling for as little as $100. Since they were also easy to master — and provided a full range of sound at the touch of a finger — would-be musicians in Britain began snapping them up. Synthesizer artists such as Gary Numan, excited by David Bowie's early experiments,

began cranking out videos for play in British dance clubs. Programmers at MTV began importing boatloads of these stylish electro-pop videos, whose performers largely shunned live shows in favor of studio productions and sported a carefully crafted "look." The slick electronic sound hit a responsive chord in Americans, whose lives in the early 1980s were already becoming inundated with video games, personal computers, and the synthesized beats of hits such as M's "Pop Muzik" (1980) and Lipps Inc.'s "Funkytown" (1980). As MTV embraced the British "New Romantics," American viewers who would never otherwise have heard, much less seen, these bands were treated to the moody visuals and fashion-plate looks of Soft Cell, Depeche Mode, Orchestral Manoeuvres in the Dark (O.M.D.), Adam and the Ants, Classix Nouveau, ABC, Haircut 100, Thomas Dolby, A Flock of Seagulls, Teardrop Explodes, The Fixx, Talk Talk, The Soft Boys, and others. The high gloss and style-over-substance of these bands was appealing to fashion-conscious America in the early 1980s, and their arty, often quirky, sound was adopted by the new-wave crowd. Not surprising, the "British" look and sound were adopted by American bands such as The Romantics, Oingo Boingo, Romeo Void, and 'Til Tuesday and by the Australian import Men at Work.

The New Romantics. The American chart success of the New Romantics skyrocketed between 1982 and 1987. Howard Jones, Thompson Twins, Simple Minds, Tears for Fears, General Public, Simply Red, and Cutting Crew were among the hit makers. In summer 1982 Human League's "Don't You Want Me" became the first electro-pop song to reach number one in America. Its success was largely the result of the heavy MTV exposure of the accompanying video. Human League's clips, complete with pouty makeup, big spiky hairdos, and complicated fashions, set the standard for video style in the 1980s. Duran Duran raised that standard. In 1983 MTV began playing the highly cinematic videos from Duran Duran's 1982 album *Rio;* it went platinum almost overnight. Nick Rhodes, keyboardist for the band, noted, "Videos are incredibly important for us." A vice president at Warner Communications was perhaps more accurate: "I think Duran Duran owes its life to MTV." By the end of 1985 thousands of adoring teenage girls were packing American stadiums to see Duran Duran, which had racked up nine Top 20 hits, including "Hungry Like the Wolf" (1983). Their success was aided immeasurably by their photogenic good looks, high-tech clothes, and the impeccable coifs of Rhodes and lead singer Simon LeBon. A mock-concert video, "The Reflex" (1984), set Duran Duran's slick 1980s image in stone, from designer jackets, boots, gloves, and "parachute" pants to eyeliner and giant, gelled hairstyles. At the climax of the video a giant wave of water engulfs the enraptured audience.

Instant "Movies." For New Romantic performers one of the appeals of making a music video was the chance to star in an instant "movie." Their video appearances — carefully lit, choreographed, and edited — also enhanced their looks and made them fashion trendsetters. In 1983 and 1984 the American media swarmed over the camera-friendly singer Annie Lennox of the Eurythmics and Culture Club front man Boy George. Both singers were heavily influenced by American soul styles, and both enjoyed tweaking traditional gender roles. George caused a stir with his coy drag look and his surprisingly soulful voice on seven consecutive hits, beginning with the provocative "Do You Really Want to Hurt Me" (1983). Annie Lennox enjoyed playing with traditional images of female beauty and sexuality; she startled many with her androgyny and her powerful vocals in early Eurythmics videos such as "Sweet Dreams (Are Made of This)" (1983) and "Here Comes the Rain Again" (1984). The popularity of Lennox and George only increased after their appearances at the 1984 Grammy Awards. Lennox dressed in Elvis-inspired drag to present an award, while George, accepting the award for Best New Artist, told the American public that "you know a good drag queen when you see one." The gender-bending of these singers dovetailed with an American cinematic preoccupation with the same subject in the 1982 movies *Tootsie* and *Victor/Victoria*. Indeed, the heavy makeup, perfectly styled hair, and pretty-boy looks of many New Romantics, from Soft Cell and O.M.D. to Human League and Duran Duran, hinted at a gay sensibility that was more fully explored by other emerging British video bands during the decade. After the highly visible Boy George, Frankie Goes to Hollywood and Bronski Beat were among the first openly gay artists. Later in the decade Pet Shop Boys, Erasure, and Dead or Alive contributed their own gay-friendly anthems. Yet what seemed liberating and fun to some seemed like mere posturing to others, and there was a predictable backlash against what increasingly came to be called "haircut bands."

New Wave. As the 1980s began, new-wave music, which had been primarily an underground movement during the late 1970s, finally broke through to mainstream America — largely thanks to MTV. Groups such as The Cars, Blondie, Talking Heads, and The Knack had already posted Top 40 hits, and with English electro-pop finding legions of fans through video exposure, quirky new-wave bands suddenly found a ready and willing American audience in the same way. Devo made the charts in 1981 with "Whip It," while The Go-Go's, a smiley Los Angeles girl group, had a string of sunny hits in 1982, including "Our Lips Are Sealed" and "We Got the Beat." " Blondie scored three number-one hits in the early 1980s — "Call Me" (1980), "The Tide Is High" (1981), and the early white rap song "Rapture" (1981) — before singer Debbie Harry left the group for a solo career. Joan Jett, an original member of the all-girl teen-age punk band The Runaways in the late 1970s, went to

number one in 1982 with the street-smart anthem "I Love Rock 'n' Roll." Joining Patty Smyth, Sheena Easton, and a small brigade of other spiky-haired would-be punkers who favored striped leotards and red leather, rocker Pat Benatar scored a string of hits with songs such as "Heartbreaker" (1980), "Hit Me With Your Best Shot" (1981), "Love Is a Battlefield" (1984), and "We Belong" (1985). The videos of these artists tended to be, like many during the early 1980s, fairly primitive exercises. Perhaps the wittiest was "Vacation," which posed the members of The Go-Go's as if they were waterskiing in perfect stacked formation. The Cars moved on to make several influential videos in 1984. The jittery "You Might Think" was animation at its most fun (or most annoying, depending on your viewpoint). "Drive," featuring singer Ric Ocasek's then-girlfriend Paulina Porizkova, was one of the first videos to spotlight a top fashion model.

Demand. MTV created a staggering demand for new music products, video or otherwise. In late 1982 a *Billboard* survey revealed that sales in record stores were increasing by 15–20 percent for acts shown on MTV, especially new acts. "Its impact is phenomenal," commented Bob Krasnow, chairman of Electra/Asylum records. Many artists traditionally unable to get airplay on radio, such as new-wave acts, found new popularity through MTV. The record-breaking sales of Michael Jackson's *Thriller* album (1982) were largely the result of the high visibility of his videos. Sales of the album tripled in late 1983, after only five days of airplay of the single "Thriller." Also in 1982 the rockabilly band Stray Cats watched sales of their debut album mushroom to 2 million after their stylish videos appeared on MTV. Men at Work owed their Best New Artist Grammy to their videos on MTV, and Oingo Boingo began selling out club dates only after regular rotation on MTV. As Les Garland, an MTV vice president, noted, "Groups are chalking up huge sales on songs that have never been played on the radio."

Expansion. Other cable networks quickly jumped on the music broadcast bandwagon. Because MTV largely excluded videos by black artists during its first two years, Black Entertainment Television filled the demand for videos by black artists, while the USA Network show *Night Flight* featured videos by black and white musicians. The Nashville Network featured country videos, and a host of local network stations soon added late-night video programs to their schedules. Radio stations began to feel the influence of video; as ratings for traditional programming sagged, stations started adding to their playlists artists and songs already popular on video programs. In response record companies stepped up production, adding big-budget video departments, hiring directors, and signing new acts largely on their video potential. Electra Records, which made only fifteen videos in 1982, produced forty-three in 1983. Companies also began marketing other video forms, from video jukebox singles to entire video albums. The average amount spent on producing a single video quickly rose from an early range of $6,000 to $10,000 to an average of $35,000 to $45,000 by 1983. Some productions rivaled low-budget movies: Billy Joel's "Allentown" video (1983) cost more than $100,000, and David Bowie's "Let's Dance" (1983) exceeded $150,000. Michael Jackson set a new record and a new industry standard with his high-tech, special-effects-laden video for "Thriller" (1984), which cost more than $1 million for seven minutes of footage.

Clout. The success of Jackson's innovative, cinematic videos heralded the true arrival of video as an art form. His flashy choreography created a new demand for dance in videos, which was heightened by the huge success of Madonna as a video artist in 1984. Several video directors earned reputations for quality work. One of these was Bob Giraldi, who directed "Beat It" (1983) and "Say Say Say" (1984) for Michael Jackson, "Love Is a Battlefield" (1984) for Pat Benatar, and "Running with the Night" (1984) and "Hello" (1984) for Lionel Richie. The new prestige of video directors caught the attention of respected movie directors, such as John Landis and Bob Rafelson, who suddenly wanted to make music videos. In 1984 Bruce Springsteen's "Dancing in the Dark" was directed by Brian De Palma, and the following year John Sayles filmed Springsteen's "I'm on Fire" and "Glory Days." Later in the decade Martin Scorsese gave video a try with Michael Jackson's "Bad" (1987). In turn, successful video directors began graduating to big-budget feature films. Adrian Lyne, who started as a video director, broke through in Hollywood with *Flashdance* (1983), a $100 million smash. The visual style of *Flashdance* evoked rock video, and Jennifer Beals's Danskins, torn jeans, and ripped sweatshirts touched off a fashion craze. The huge success of the soundtrack ($47 million in sales) and its hit singles released a flood of slick, video-inspired, music-oriented movies in 1984, including *Purple Rain, Footloose, Streets of Fire,* and *Reckless.* Other blockbuster films, including the 1984 hits *Beverly Hills Cop* and *Ghostbusters,* were peddled via high-profile videos featuring songs from their soundtrack albums. Video had become the marketing tool of the decade.

Dominance. During the mid 1980s the A. C. Nielsen ratings company estimated that at any one time television sets in some 130,000 homes were tuned to MTV. As Len Epand of Polygram Records noted, "If the video is in power rotation, that's 1.3 million people hearing the record." After several years in the red, MTV earned $8.1 million in profits during the first half of 1984. Two years later Viacom International bought the network from Warner Amex, and that year grossed $111 million and boasted profits of $47 million. By 1986 it tied USA Network and CNN in cable-television ratings. In 1989 it was carried by more than five thousand cable outlets and was seen by more than 46 million viewers. By the end of the decade videos dominated the music industry. With the majority of teens and preteens growing up with MTV, it was hard to imagine American life without music videos and harder still to believe that fewer than ten years earlier the form had barely existed.

Sources:

Fred Bronson, *The Billboard Book of Number One Hits* (New York: Billboard Publications, 1988);

"MTV's Super Market," *Film Comment,* 19 (July/August 1983): 48–50;

"Rock Music Goes Hollywood," *Newsweek,* 105 (11 March 1985): 78;

"Rock 'n' Video," *Film Comment,* 18 (May/June 1982): 39–41;

"Rocking Video," *Newsweek,* 101 (18 April 1983): 96–98;

"Sing a Song of Seeing," *Time,* 122 (26 December 1983): 54–64;

David P. Szatmary, *Rockin' in Time: A Social History of Rock and Roll* (Englewood Cliffs, N.J.: Prentice-Hall, 1987);

Joel Whitburn, *The Billboard Book of Top 40 Hits* (New York: Billboard Publications, 1991);

Whitburn, *Billboard Hot 100 Charts: The Eighties* (Menomonee Falls, Wis.: Record Research, Inc., 1991).

POP-MUSIC STARS

Thriller. In 1983 a single talent redefined the style, course, and possibilities of music videos — Michael Jackson. In making recording history with *Thriller,* the top-selling album of all time, he earned the tag "one-man rescue team for the record business" from *Time* magazine. The success of his album was indeed extraordinary; largely owing to *Thriller,* the recording industry in 1983 had its best year since 1978. The album spent thirty-seven weeks of 1983 at number one on the *Billboard* album chart; by early 1984 30 million copies had been sold, and it was still selling at a rate of more than a million copies a week worldwide. At the height of Jacksonmania, *Thriller* sold a million copies every four days. Jackson released a record-setting seven Top 10 singles from the album, including the number-one hits "Billie Jean" and "Beat It" in 1983. He also became the first artist in history to top the single and album charts in both traditional pop and black categories, and he was the first artist of the decade to have two songs in the Top 5 simultaneously. In 1984 Jackson was given a public-service award by President Ronald Reagan, and the singer won an unprecedented eight Grammys for *Thriller,* which went on to sell more than 40 million copies. Making about two dollars for each album sold in the United States, Jackson earned at least $40 million and pocketed another $50 million from the sale of related products. He also earned royalties from continued sales of his breakout 1979 album *Off the Wall,* which had sold 9 million copies worldwide and spawned four Top 10 singles — including two number-one hits in 1980, "Don't Stop Til You Get Enough" and "Rock with You." By 1984 Jackson was one of the richest men in America and easily one of the most famous.

Michaelmania. In 1983–1984 millions of fans rushed to buy Michael Jackson key chains, duffel bags, pencils, notebooks, caps, posters, T-shirts, and bubblegum cards — all featuring the trademark Jackson image: rhinestone gloves, military jackets, red leather. There was even a Michael Jackson doll. The media had a field day;

in January 1984, when Jackson's hair caught fire during filming of a Pepsi commercial, the accident made headline news around the world. His oddball persona — seemingly half man and half child — was equally newsworthy. Countless tabloid stories detailed his friendships with children (actor Emmanuel Lewis was one companion), his obsession with Diana Ross, his "shrine" to Elizabeth Taylor, his dream of starring as Peter Pan, his Neverland estate (complete with a petting zoo and a private amusement park), his "romance" with Brooke Shields, his habit of sleeping in an air-filtered pod, his ambivalent sexuality, his rumored use of female hormones, and his penchant for plastic surgery, which made his face seem increasingly androgynous and Caucasian. The constant media frenzy over Jackson made it easy to overlook his true significance as the most galvanizing force in popular music since the Beatles.

Style. The real news was Jackson's high-tech pop music and flashy dance moves, which prompted dance legend Fred Astaire to exclaim, "My lord, he's a wonderful mover." Jackson's "moonwalk" number on the Motown Twentieth Anniversary television special in 1983 stopped hearts and traffic. On video he was electrifying. His feline twirls, spins, glides, and poses were perfectly matched by his vocals, with their one-man band of gasps, whoops, moans, squeals, pops, and whispers. The video for "Billie Jean" showed both with style, as Jackson danced along a sidewalk whose squares lit from below when he stepped on them. "Beat It" was harder-edged, with Jackson breaking up a street rumble and leading an aggressive and athletic line dance. "Thriller," which inspired a thirty-minute video on its creation, was the ultimate well-marketed video product. Jackson spent $1 million on its highly choreographed special effects. He was everywhere the next two years, from his brothers' Victory tour, to guest vocals on Rockwell's single "Somebody's Watching Me" (1984), to his "Say Say Say" collaboration with Paul McCartney (1984), to his collaboration with Lionel Richie on the USA for Africa anthem "We Are the World" (1985), one of the biggest media events in music history. While *Bad* (1987), the highly anticipated follow-up album to *Thriller*, did not compare to *Thriller* in sales or impact, the new album launched a record five number-one singles and several memorable videos, including "Dirty Diana" (1988), "Man in the Mirror" (1988), and the title track in 1987. Jackson also appeared in Steven Spielberg's highly publicized short movie *Captain Eo* at Disney World.

In Jackson's Footsteps. Jackson's success opened the door to many other black artists, speeding their crossover success. Lionel Richie was the first to benefit. He had already achieved success as a writer and singer with The Commodores ("Three Times a Lady," 1978), a songwriter for other artists (Kenny Rogers's "Lady," 1981), and as composer-performer of a duet, "Endless Love" (1981), with Diana Ross. Between 1982 and 1986 his career exploded with big solo songs, from "Truly" (1983)

Whitney Houston, who had seven consecutive number-one hit songs between early 1985 and 1988

to "All Night Long" (1984). Richie's videos also attracted attention. "Hello" (1984) was a minimovie featuring Richie as a teacher in love with a blind student, while "Dancing on the Ceiling" (1986) showed a mob of wild partygoers literally going up the wall. In 1985 and 1986 Richie won a Grammy for Album of the Year for *Can't Slow Down*, six American Music Awards, a Writer of the Year award from ASCAP, and an Oscar for "Say You, Say Me" (1986), featured in the movie *White Nights* (1985). In 1984 Richie followed in Jackson's footsteps by signing an $8.5 million deal with Pepsi to write and perform for their television commercials. With Paul McCartney, Stevie Wonder contributed his own feel-good anthem to the decade in 1982, "Ebony and Ivory," the video for which showed the two singers on a giant piano keyboard. Wonder won an Oscar in 1985 for the song "I Just Called to Say I Love You," featured in the movie *The Woman in Red* (1984).

Divas. One of the biggest and brightest new video stars of the decade was Whitney Houston, who catapulted from obscurity in early 1985 to notch seven consecutive number-one hits by 1988, including "Saving All My Love for You" (1985), "Greatest Love of All" (1986), "Didn't We Almost Have It All" (1987), "So Emotional" (1988), and "Where Do Broken Hearts Go" (1988). Her powerful vocals were impressive, but Houston preferred to sing fairly conventional pop ballads and dance numbers on her self-titled debut album and its follow-up, *Whitney* (1987). Her best videos tended also to be conventional, especially the colorful "How Will I Know?" (1986), in which Houston skipped through brightly painted rooms, and the effervescent "I Wanna Dance with Somebody (Who Loves Me)" (1987), which featured the singer in a spirited line dance under showers of balloons. In fall 1988 Houston sang the melodramatic Olympic theme song "One Moment in Time." With her major albums *Control* and *Rhythm Nation 1814* Janet Jackson was almost as successful as Houston. Paula Abdul's choreography helped make Jackson's 1986 videos such as "What Have You Done for Me Lately," "Nasty," and "When I Think of You" electrifying and established Jackson as a funky dance diva. By 1989, with the success of the well-filmed, cutting-edge videos for "Miss You Much" and "Rhythm Nation," Jackson had moved out of the shadow of her famous brother Michael, and her popularity rivaled his.

Black Visibility. Michaelmania created a new demand for funky, flashy material from a wide range of black performers, many of them long established. Rick James found a groove in "Superfreak" (1981) and created one for Eddie Murphy in "Party All the Time" (1986). Kool & The Gang crafted several hot dance videos, most notably "Celebration" (1981) and "Fresh" (1985). Patti LaBelle sported a "New Attitude" (and giant wigs) in 1985, while the Pointer Sisters bubbled over with enthusiasm in "I'm So Excited" (1984) and "Jump (for My Love)" (1984). Tina Turner's career was reborn with her *Private Dancer* album in 1984, a sexy new look (with giant wigs), and the monster hit "What's Love Got to Do with It" (1984). She followed that success by turning down a role in Steven Spielberg's movie *The Color Purple* (1985) to play the part of the sinister, chain-mailed Auntie Entity in *Mad Max Beyond Thunderdome* (1985) and sing the theme song, "We Don't Need Another Hero (Thunderdome)" (1985). Aretha Franklin was similarly resurrected in 1985 with her *Who's Zoomin' Who* release, featuring the liberating song and video "Freeway of Love" (1985), guest-starring Clarence Clemons of the E Street Band. Later in the decade Terence Trent D'Arby released *Introducing the Hard Line* (1988), a mix of funk, soul, pop, and rhythm and blues. The singles from the album, "Wishing Well" (1988) and "Sign Your Name" (1988), spawned videos that spotlighted the singer's exotic, dreadlocked look. In 1988 Bobby Brown, a former member of the quintet New Edition, released a solo album that came to define a hybrid style of music known as "new jack swing." Brown caused a stir with his provocative, highly sexual videos for songs such as "My Prerogative" (1988) and "Roni" (1989). Milli Vanilli ended the black-music craze of the 1980s on an odd note when it was revealed that the dancing duo, featured in the videos to three number-one hits in 1989, were not the vocalists on the original recordings of those songs. It was perhaps the most telling evidence of a decade-long madness for image over reality and style over substance.

A Purple "Reign." Like Madonna and Michael Jackson, Prince was a master of marketing a public image that was at once accessible and enigmatic. In his records and videos he surpassed Jackson and Madonna in overt sexuality. Suggestive early hits such as "Soft and Wet" and "I Wanna Be Your Lover" (1980) established him as a funky sex machine in the style of James Brown and Sly Stone, two of his influences. The album *Dirty Mind,* with the hits "Uptown" and "When You Were Mine," sealed Prince's reputation. He broke through to mainstream success in 1983 with the danceable double album *1999,* which featured the video hit "Little Red Corvette" (1983). In summer 1984 he became a superstar with the album and movie *Purple Rain* and the singles "When Doves Cry," "Let's Go Crazy," and "I Would Die 4 U" — all featuring his band (or entourage) the Revolution, while the videos and the movie showed off his stage pyrotechnics (splits, leaps, bumps, and grinds). By then Prince had captured the wrath of Tipper Gore with his risqué lyrics and the attention of the media for his oddball reclusiveness and penchant for purple in everything from clothing to the walls of his Minneapolis mansion. He had also become known for his "stable" of performers, including Sheila E. and The Time, as well as protégés Vanity, Apollonia, and Lisa and Wendy. After winning an Oscar in 1985 for the *Purple Rain* score (and accepting in a glittering purple cape and hood), Prince formed Paisley Park records and continued his hit factory with songs such as "Pop Life" (1985), "Mountains" (1986), "U Got the Look" (1987), and "I Could Never Take the Place of Your Man" (1988). The cheerfully psychedelic "Raspberry Beret" (1985) and the strikingly sparse "Kiss" (1986) were video standouts. He also wrote songs for other artists — including "Manic Monday" (1986) for The Bangles and "Sugar Walls" (1985) for Sheena Easton — and continued making motion pictures such as the ill-fated *Under the Cherry Moon* (1986) and the concert movie *Sign o' the Times* (1987). In 1989 he contributed the soundtrack to the superhyped *Batman,* and in the 1990s he changed his name to an unpronounceable symbol.

The Boss. Rivaling the success of Prince in 1984 was Bruce Springsteen, long known to a small core of fans as "The Boss." Despite intense media hype in 1975 (including simultaneous cover stories in *Time* and *Newsweek*), Springsteen had failed to generate mass interest in his landmark album *Born to Run,* which many critics considered the best album of the 1970s. Strong follow-up albums — *Darkness on the Edge of Town, The River, Nebraska* — marathon live shows (typically lasting three or four hours), and a public commitment to social causes had built him a fanatical cult following of die-hard fans and the esteem of the rock-music press. Like Jack Kerouac, whose romantic loner spirit he sometimes echoed, Springsteen had a sense of artistic integrity as unshakeable as his material was predictable. A perfectionist, Springsteen kept his audience waiting years between releases and then rewarded them with both exuberant rock songs and moody numbers about romantic loss, broken dreams, and driving all night alone through

Bruce Springsteen singing "Born in the U.S.A." at the Los Angeles Memorial Coliseum, September 1985

paign, President Reagan tried to use the song and the singer to promote restored American pride and "traditional" values, even after Springsteen pointed out that the song was a Vietnam veteran's scream of rage at his betrayal by his country. Many new fans, caught up in media hype and Reagan's Norman Rockwell vision of America, similarly missed the desolate message of "My Hometown" (1985), which addressed factory closings and unemployment. By the end of 1985 *Born in the U.S.A.* had sold almost 10 million copies and had produced seven Top 10 songs. During that year Springsteen proved a strong video presence in the broodingly cinematic "I'm on Fire" and the exuberant "Glory Days." The 1985 leg of his tour coincided with a mania for the jingoistic movie *Rambo*, and by then the pumped-up Springsteen did resemble a movie superhero. An equal part of his appeal for many was the regular-guy heterosexual image he projected, a marked contrast to the often effete and arty images of many British stars of the time. His sound — alternately hard-rocking and quietly poignant — seemed to compress all rock-and-roll history into a single, easy-to-understand package. The brooding bohemian of the 1970s underground had finally caught "the runaway American dream" and had become an icon. He even married a fashion model in 1985. But "Brilliant Disguise" from the haunting 1987 album *Tunnel of Love* revealed that Springsteen was still capable of unflinching honesty in his music.

Regular Guys. Springsteen's success strengthened a growing trend toward lean, straight-ahead American rock in the mid and late 1980s. When songs Springsteen intended for use in the movie *Mask* (1985) were dropped because of a dispute over the rights, Bob Seger numbers were substituted. Seger had been popular since his *Night Moves* album in 1976, but his career really took off in the 1980s, after the song "Old Time Rock and Roll" (1979) was featured in the hit movie *Risky Business* (1983). In 1987 he achieved what even Springsteen was unable to do — a number one hit ("Shakedown," from the soundtrack of *Beverly Hills Cop II*). Tom Petty achieved new popularity with a string of hits and videos, including the sinister "Don't Come Around Here No More" (1985), which depicted Petty as the Mad Hatter from Alice's tea party. Other single releases with his band The Heartbreakers included "Jammin' Me" (1987). Petty toured with Bob Dylan in 1987, and in 1989 he released a strong solo album, *Full Moon Fever,* which included the hits "Runnin' Down a Dream" (1989) and "Free Fallin' " (1989). Other "regular guy" rockers of the 1980s included John Cougar (who later went by his real last name, Mellencamp), with "Jack and Diane" (1982) and "Pink Houses" (1984), and Huey Lewis and the News, who had a long string of Top 20 hits, including "If This is It" (1984) and "The Power of Love" (1985). Another was Canadian Bryan Adams, whose 1985 album, *Reckless,* spawned four Top 10 hits that year, including "Run to You," "Somebody," and "Heaven." Billy Joel was perhaps

the American darkness. Yet he had never tasted true breakthrough success, even with his 1981 hit "Hungry Heart." All that changed in 1984 with the release of the album *Born in the U.S.A.,* a typical Springsteen mix of upbeat car-radio ditties and bleak dirges about dead-end American lives. Previously resistant to video (he did not appear in the 1982 video for his "Atlantic City"), Springsteen plunged into the new form with "Dancing in the Dark" (1984), directed by Brian De Palma. The result was overnight superstardom for the newly muscular, charismatic Springsteen, who was seen in the video in stage makeup and tight jeans boogeying onstage with an excited fan he had pulled from the audience. (The fan was Courteney Cox, who later became a well-known actress.) During his sold-out 1984 tour his gyrating rear end was featured on giant stadium video screens.

All-American. Springsteen had leaped spectacularly into the video era, without compromising his integrity, but more than a few of his new fans misunderstood his message. Many seemed enraptured by his apparent patriotism, especially when "Born in the U.S.A." became a Top 10 hit in 1985. During his 1984 presidential cam-

Cyndi Lauper (right) performing with her band in 1984

the most successful of the all-American pop rockers; like Springsteen, he married a fashion model (Christie Brinkley) and had a long run of successful singles and videos, especially "Uptown Girl" in 1984 (featuring his future wife in the video), "Tell Her About It" in 1983, and "We Didn't Start the Fire" in 1989. The old-fashioned rock spirit caught fire with a host of new bands, including The Georgia Satellites, The Smithereens, and The Fabulous Thunderbirds. The all-American boys loved songs about rock and roll, from "American Girl" (Petty) in 1976 and "Old Time Rock and Roll" (Seger) in 1979 to the 1980s hits "It's Still Rock & Roll to Me" (Joel) in 1980, "The Heart of Rock 'n' Roll" (Lewis) in 1984, "Summer of '69" (Adams) in 1985, and "R.O.C.K. in the U.S.A." (Mellencamp) in 1986.

New Women. Videos also promoted new female performers during the decade. In 1984 Cyndi Lauper's success with the form rivaled and perhaps surpassed Madonna's. Lauper's recording *She's So Unusual* (1984) sold 4 million copies and produced four Top 5 hits — a new record for a debut album and for a female solo artist. The video for "Girls Just Want to Have Fun" (1984) was a classic romp, packed with rocking rows of slumber partyers, cartoonish parents lecturing the wildly costumed Lauper, and even a conga line. Lauper's friend pro wrestler Captain Lou Albano played her father in the video. "Time After Time" (1984) was an abrupt shift to the serious style of a romantic minimovie, with Lauper leaving her trailer-park lover. "She Bop" (1984) was a wacky animation. After the number-one song "True Colors" in 1986, Lauper's career sagged. Bananarama scored

a hit with its "Cruel Summer" single and video in 1984, but the popularity of the female trio crested with the 1986 cover of Shocking Blue's "Venus"; in the video they lip-synched and cavorted madly in overalls. The Bangles, another all-female group, also broke through that year with "Manic Monday," a discarded Prince song that showed off photogenic lead singer Susana Hoffs. The group's biggest hit was "Walk Like an Egyptian" in 1987, which was accompanied by a silly but amusing video in which the band members posed like hieroglyphs. Belinda Carlisle found solo success after leaving The Go-Go's and filming flashy videos for hits such as "Mad About You" (1986), "Heaven Is a Place on Earth" (1988), "I Get Weak" (1988), and "Circle in the Sand" (1988).

Madonna. If the self-promoting and capitalist spirit of the 1980s could be captured and bottled, that product might be called Madonna. As shrewdly adept at packaging her weaknesses as she was her strengths, Madonna became a one-woman conglomerate, largely through her clever use of music video. Her self-titled debut album was a harmless collection of upbeat dance hits, including "Holiday" (1983) and "Burning Up." The video for "Burning Up" — with Madonna panting on a giant steam iron and writhing in the road — established her sexually aggressive image. In 1984 the videos for "Borderline" and "Lucky Star" began a fashion trend imitated by millions of teen and preteen girls: straps, buckles, belts, bootlaces, hair ribbons, and jewelry (especially her trademark crucifixes) worn in complicated layers over junk-store tights, skirts, black bras, and bustiers. After her big hit "Like a Virgin" launched her to superstardom in 1985, Madonna filmed the video for what became her 1980s theme song, "Material Girl." Imitating Marilyn Monroe's performance of "Diamonds Are a Girl's Best Friend," a winking, mink-wearing Madonna chirped that "the boy with the cold hard cash is always Mr. Right." By this time Madonna was catching flak from feminists who claimed that her "boy toy" belt buckles, sexy video come-ons and gold-digging persona were setting the women's movement back twenty years. Madonna shot back that her performances were all meant to be tongue-in-cheek and that her complete control and planning of her image, career, product, and sexuality made her an ideal role model for modern women — and for young girls, who made up the bulk of her fans. Others took issue with Madonna's paper-thin vocals and frivolous dance-pop sound. Most critics realized that her songs were merely a backdrop for her real talent — marketing. Madonna received good reviews in 1985 for her enjoyable performance as a supremely confident urban social climber (herself) in the movie *Desperately Seeking Susan*. She also caused a stir when nude photos, taken in her "hungry art model" days, appeared in *Playboy* and *Penthouse*. Undaunted, Madonna married actor Sean Penn in August 1985, amid a media hysteria that included tabloid reporters circling above the outdoor ceremony in helicopters. The Material Girl seemed to revel in the attention.

Madonna singing at Wembley Stadium in London during her "Who's That Girl?" world tour, August 1987

wisely mixed catchy dance numbers — such as "Dress You Up" and "Into the Groove" in 1985 — with ballads such as "Crazy for You" (1985) and "Live to Tell" (1986). She also disproved those who were eager to see her as a one-year flash in the pan. By constantly manipulating and updating her look, especially in her videos, Madonna was able to remain in the public and the media spotlight for the rest of the decade. She junked her thrift-shop image in 1986 and emerged with a toned dancer's body and sleek blonde looks for "Papa Don't Preach," a well-filmed minimovie that caused another media furor in seeming to advocate unwed teenage pregnancy. In 1987 the video for "Open Your Heart," in which the singer danced in a peep show and kissed a small boy, set more tongues wagging. So did her questionable acting skills in the laughable movie bombs *Shanghai Surprise* (1986) and *Who's That Girl!* (1987). In 1988 Madonna took a break from making albums and videos to appear on Broadway in David Mamet's play *Speed-the-Plow,* for which she received mixed reviews. At this time she also caused a stir by frequenting gay bars with friend Sandra Bernhard. Her carefully timed absence from music created an audience and media demand that paid off handsomely with the release of *Like a Prayer* in 1989. The title video featured a raven-haired Madonna kissing a black Jesus, dancing on a hillside amid burning crosses, and finding stigmata on her hands. After protests from outraged Catholics, Pepsi-Cola withdrew a commercial using the song in a different context, which the company had made as part of a $5 million deal with the singer. Madonna kept the money. Her follow-up, "Express Yourself" (1989), was equally provocative — a monocled Madonna in a tailored suit overseeing an underground slave colony (based on the 1926 silent movie *Metropolis*) and later submitting to bondage from one of her slaves. With typical aplomb and business sense Madonna shrugged off cries from the media and feminists about the subjugation of women. Indeed, by the end of the decade it was hard to accuse Madonna of anything except being the master of her own incredible wealth and fame.

The Dance Craze. American video was a godsend to professional dancers in the 1980s, from Michael Jackson's electrifying moves to Madonna's modern dance poses. Jackson set the standard for choreography with his synchronized finale in "Beat It" (1983) and continued to innovate in later videos such as "Bad" (1987) and "Smooth Criminal" (1989). Madonna made dance the center of her best videos, from "Lucky Star" to "Open Your Heart." By middecade hot dance numbers were taken for granted in new videos: Whitney Houston's "I Wanna Dance with Somebody (Who Loves Me)" (1987) whooped it up with a colorful line dance, while Lionel Richie's raucous "Dancing on the Ceiling" (1986) featured just that. The impact of dance in music video was so great that, for perhaps the first time, a choreographer broke through to solo stardom as a pop singer. At the end of the decade Paula Abdul seemed poised to challenge

Image Master. In just five years Madonna racked up a staggering and record-shattering number of consecutive Top 5 hits: sixteen, including seven number ones. She

Madonna's reign as the queen of baby-voiced dance hits. Abdul, formerly a choreographer for the Los Angeles Lakers cheerleading squad, began to receive serious attention for the tough, street-smart dances she designed for Janet Jackson videos such as "Nasty" (1986), "The Pleasure Principal," and "Control" (1987). In 1988 Abdul began releasing her own material and creating her own videos. "Straight Up" (1989), filmed in high-contrast black and white, was a sharply choreographed dance package, as was the chipper follow-up, "Forever Your Girl" (1989). The decadent "Cold Hearted" (1989) was an homage to choreographer-director Bob Fosse. Abdul scored four Top 5 hits and three consecutive number ones from her *Forever Your Girl* debut album in 1989, tying records already set by Cyndi Lauper and Whitney Houston. Another former cheerleader, Toni Basil, also became a video choreographer, working with Bette Midler, Tina Turner, and Linda Ronstadt.

Charisma. Sting, George Michael, Bono of U2, and Michael Hutchence of INXS all owed much of their success in the 1980s to their camera-ready images. Sting helped propel The Police to arena-sized popularity in the early 1980s. *Synchronicity* (1983) featured four Top 10 hits, including "Every Breath You Take" (1983). The charismatic Sting was one of several 1980s video performers to attempt roles in feature films, and his solo career after leaving The Police produced more favorites, most notably "If You Love Somebody Set Them Free" (1985). George Michael's career after leaving Wham! was even more successful. Wham! had languished in obscurity in England for several years until the videos from their *Make It Big* album (including "Wake Me Up Before You Go-Go," 1985 and "Careless Whisper," 1985) received heavy rotation on in 1984 and 1985. In 1987 Michael released *Faith,* which produced four consecutive number-one hits and became one of the top-selling albums of the decade. The Australian group INXS broke through to mainstream America with their fifth LP, *Listen Like Thieves* (1986), including the single "What You Need." With photogenic lead singer Michael Hutchence as the centerpiece, the group made several well-received videos from their follow-up effort, *Kick* (1988), including "Need You Tonight" and "Never Tear Us Apart." The most successful foreign newcomer, the Irish group U2, started as a new-wave band, with club hits such as "I Will Follow." Their albums *Boy* and *War* took on an increasingly political bent; "Sunday Bloody Sunday" eerily evoked the political and religious upheaval of Ireland. Their U.S. breakthrough, *The Unforgettable Fire* (1984), featured Bono's scorching, stadium-filling vocals on the song "Pride (in the Name of Love)." Their follow-up album, *The Joshua Tree* (1987), established U2 as one of the most popular bands of the decade, spawning giant hits such as "With or Without You" and "I Still Haven't Found What I'm Looking For," and atmospheric videos that traded on Bono's on-camera charisma. *Rattle and Hum,* the group's 1988 live album, likewise sold in the millions.

Comebacks. Throughout the 1980s popular music videos helped established musicians revive sagging careers. Former Eagles Glenn Frey and Don Henley both found solo success, Frey with his television and movie themes (for *Miami Vice* and *Beverly Hills Cop*) and Henley with his haunting video "The Boys of Summer" (1985). Fleetwood Mac also took to the new form, although singer Stevie Nicks's fondness for wind machines, giant hair, and gypsy garb tended to date her solo videos. Other aging, big-haired rockers such as Heart, Starship, Foreigner, Journey, Boston, and REO Speedwagon all had video hits, and by the end of the decade unexpected comebacks were becoming almost commonplace. Diehard rockers, the Grateful Dead achieved their first Top 10 song in 1987. Former new wavers Cheap Trick resurfaced in 1988 with their first number one, while Aerosmith rode the crest of metal mania in the late 1980s with several big singles. Former heartthrobs Donny Osmond and Tom Jones scored their biggest hits in years; Jones was amusingly funky in the stark video for "Kiss" (1989), a Prince remake recorded with the Art of Noise. Cher used her new popularity in movies to rebuild the ashes of her recording career and emerged triumphant with big hair and even bigger video numbers such as "If I Could Turn Back Time" (1989) and "I Found Someone" (1988). Daryl Hall and John Oates had helped define early videos with catchy soul-pop numbers such as "Private Eyes" (1982), "Maneater" (1983), and "Out of Touch" (1984). They faltered with solo efforts in the mid 1980s and had reunited by the end of the decade to make more chart singles and videos. The resurgence of older acts in the late 1980s reflected the aging of the baby-boom generation, who found themselves suddenly nostalgic for the music of their youth.

Veterans. Even older, established, and respected British acts benefited from the video explosion, taking to the new form with aplomb. David Bowie, whose early videos inspired many of the younger electro-pop artists, found himself repaid when his *Let's Dance* album (1983) spawned several big videos on MTV. Bryan Ferry and Roxy Music found new life on video, selling millions of copies of *Avalon* (1982) on the strength of ethereal videos such as "More Than This." Robert Palmer's "Addicted to Love" video (1986), featuring a line of robotic, look-alike glamour girls, earned him legions of American fans. Elton John's career was revitalized in 1983 and 1984 with the videos for "I'm Still Standing" and "I Guess That's Why They Call It the Blues." Rod Stewart did well with the video form throughout the decade, from "Young Turks" in 1981 through "My Heart Can't Tell You No" in 1989. Peter Gabriel's videos, from the alienating "Shock the Monkey" (1983) to "Sledgehammer" (1986) and "Big Time" (1987) from his *So* album, were among the most discussed and acclaimed of the decade. Gabriel's award-winning "Sledgehammer" featured a mad swarm of animated objects from bees to steam engines flying around his head. Gabriel's former bandmate in Genesis,

Bon Jovi performing in 1989

Phil Collins, had a string of hits during the decade, including seven number-one singles — including "Against All Odds (Take a Look at Me Now)" (1984), "One More Night" (1985), and "Sussudio" (1985). His best video was probably the animated "Land of Confusion" (1987) with Genesis, which used puppetlike versions of famous politicians. Steve Winwood, veteran of The Spencer Davis Group, Traffic, and Blind Faith, achieved his biggest popularity to date with the big video hits "Higher Love" (1986) and "Roll with It" (1988). Dire Straits had achieved minor success with *Making Movies* (1980) and its "Skateaway" video. They broke through to American superstardom in 1985 with *Brothers in Arms* (1985), which spun off the animated "Money for Nothing" video.

Metal Stars. The heavy-metal bands of the early 1980s — including Dokken, Quiet Riot, and The Scorpions — all benefited from the hard-rock format of MTV during its first three years. The archetype for the slick, California sound of 1980s metal was the group Van Halen, whose six albums all sold in the millions. Their sly, tongue-in-cheek attitude translated well to video, and *1984* was a huge crossover success, with the anthemic "Jump" (1984) and its follow-up videos "Panama" (in which band members swung over the stage on wires), "I'll Wait," and "Hot for Teacher." In 1983 videos from Def Leppard's *Pyromania* helped the pop-metal band sell more than 9 million copies of the album. Kiss-influenced "glam rockers" Motley Crüe also went into heavy rotation

on in 1983 with clips from their album *Shout at the Devil.* The same year Ratt sold more than 2 million copies of their debut album *Out of the Cellar* with the help of saturation play on MTV. But amid demand for airplay of British electro-pop and American dance stars, metal began to rust. Van Halen's lead singer David Lee Roth left the band for a solo career and was replaced by Sammy Hagar. In 1985 Roth's videos, including "California Girls" (featuring Roth's open-mouthed reaction to bikini-clad models) and the hilarious "Just a Gigolo" (featuring Roth's open-mouthed reaction to imitators of Cyndi Lauper, Willie Nelson, and Boy George), were among the best of the decade, but his career faded with later efforts. So did the popularity of Twisted Sister, whose fist-clenching video "We're Not Gonna Take It" (1984) prompted one viewer to note, "If that had been around when I was in high school, I would've killed my parents." ZZ Top, easily the least photogenic band working in video, kept things interesting with leeringly amusing clips such as "Legs" (1984) and "Sleeping Bag" (1986). By middecade the metal mania seemed to have died down. The charts and playlists were filled with the "safe" pop-rock sounds of Survivor, Night Ranger, and Mr. Mister and resurrected versions of old bands such as Heart, Starship, Boston, Chicago, REO Speedwagon, Foreigner, and Journey.

Bon Jovi Opens the Floodgates. Bon Jovi's unexpected and meteoric success in 1986 almost single-

ARTS

93

handedly resurrected the 1980s metal craze. By the end of 1987, videos for the megahits "You Give Love a Bad Name" (1986) and "Livin' on a Prayer" (1987) had boosted sales of the group's *Slippery When Wet* album to more than 12 million. Billboard columnist Paul Grein said, "They opened the floodgates the same way Michael Jackson did in 1983 for Prince, Lionel Richie and others." Marketer Bob Chiappardi agreed: "The majors are now going nuts. Everyone's out there trying to sign up a metal band." MTV helped out by starting to rotate heavy-metal videos again, especially during its weekly program *Headbanger's Ball*. By late 1987 pop-metal singles and power ballads from Cinderella, Poison, Whitesnake, and Stryper were all regularly climbing the Top 40, and Motley Crüe and Def Leppard were resurging as well. In June 1987 five of the six top-selling albums in the United States were metal oriented, and in November 1988 six of the Top 40 American singles were by metal bands. The next two years saw hits from White Lion, Vixen, Winger, and other new bands. Def Leppard's *Hysteria* sold more than 5 million copies in 1988 and 1989. Even the metal warhorses Aerosmith posted a series of hits. Bon Jovi continued their chart success in 1988 and 1989 with "Bad Medicine," "Born to Be My Baby," and other songs, but by then they had been dethroned as the new kings of metal by a band of arrogant upstarts: Guns N' Roses. Fronted by the flamboyant Axl Rose, Guns N' Roses struck a raw nerve with its "Sweet Child O' Mine" single and video from its debut album *Appetite for Destruction* during summer 1988. The group followed up with the hits "Welcome to the Jungle" and "Paradise City," and by the end of 1989 *Appetite for Destruction* had sold more than 12 million copies. With metal groups such as Metallica, Anthrax, Megadeth, Slayer, Metal Church, and Queensryche also mushrooming in popularity, heavy metal dominated American record sales by the end of the decade.

Sources:

Fred Bronson, *The Billboard Book of Number One Hits* (New York: Billboard Publications, 1988);

"The Heavy Metal Frenzy," *Newsweek,* 110 (10 August 1987): 59;

"He's on Fire," *Newsweek,* 106 (5 August 1985): 48–54;

"Making It in Metal Mecca," *Newsweek,* 114 (7 August 1989): 56–58;

"The Peter Pan of Pop," *Newsweek,* 101 (10 January 1983): 52–54;

"Rock Music Goes Hollywood," *Newsweek,* 105 (11 March 1985): 78;

"Rock's New Women," *Newsweek,* 105 (4 March 1985): 48–57;

David P. Szatmary, *Rockin' in Time: A Social History of Rock and Roll* (Englewood Cliffs, N.J.: Prentice-Hall, 1987);

Joel Whitburn, *The Billboard Book of Top 40 Hits* (New York: Billboard Publications, 1991);

Whitburn, *Billboard Hot 100 Charts: The Eighties* (Menomonee Falls, Wis.: Record Research, Inc., 1991);

"Why He's a Thriller," *Time,* 123 (19 March 1984): 54–60.

ROCK-MUSIC CAUSES

Band Aid. British pop performer Bob Geldof of the 1970s group Boomtown Rats single-handedly started a craze for "charity rock" in the mid 1980s. In 1984 Geldof became concerned about the plight of famine-ravaged Africa and decided to organize a relief project. Under the umbrella name of Band Aid, a group of well-known performers — including Bono of U2, Sting, George Michael, Boy George, Paul Young, and Simon LeBon — recorded "Do They Know It's Christmas?" Released during the 1984 holiday season, the song struck chords of sympathy and guilt with its chilling lyrics describing a draught-ravaged continent "where nothing ever grows" and "no rain or rivers flow." As Bono screamed, "Tonight thank God it's them instead of you," British and American Christmas shoppers dug into their pockets. The song went to number one in England and climbed as high as number thirteen in America, selling 3 million copies. The Band Aid single and a subsequent album raised $11 million in relief funds, but Geldof also achieved something bigger: he raised awareness of the crisis among millions of pop-music fans.

"We Are the World." Aware of Geldof's efforts across the Atlantic, Harry Belafonte became more concerned about conditions in Africa in early 1985, while watching a television special that showed an Australian doctor working in Ethiopia. Belafonte called Ken Kragen, president of the United Support of Artists for Africa foundation, with the idea of organizing a benefit concert featuring black artists. Kragen thought a recording might be more successful than a concert and enlisted his client Lionel Richie to write a song and asked Quincy Jones to produce it. Jones, in turn, asked Michael Jackson to collaborate with Richie. Just a few days later Richie and Jackson produced "We Are the World." Kragen's next step was recruiting forty-five vocalists from the full spectrum of pop and rock music. To ensure maximum participation the taping was scheduled for directly after the American Music Awards ceremony on 29 January 1985. Initial hesitation on the part of some artists disappeared after Bruce Springsteen, long known for his altruism and integrity, agreed to take part. At the recording session a sign warned everyone to "check your ego at the door." After the chorus was taped, vocal solos — by Jackson, Richie, Springsteen, Diana Ross, Bob Dylan, Ray Charles, Willie Nelson, Stevie Wonder, Paul Simon, Kenny Rogers, Tina Turner, Daryl Hall, Cyndi Lauper, Huey Lewis, and others — were recorded. A video was shot during the recording, which finally wrapped at 8 A.M.

USA for Africa. The song was released under the name of Belafonte's nonprofit relief organization USA for Africa. With advance publicity and airplay generating interest, eight hundred thousand copies of "We Are the World" were shipped to stores on 7 March. The reaction was overwhelming; after the first shipment sold out in six days, a million more copies were pressed. At Tower Records in West Hollywood, one thousand copies sold in just two days. "We Are the World" reached number one on the Billboard chart in just four weeks, making it the fastest-climbing single of the 1980s. It also became the

The Live Aid concert at John F. Kennedy Stadium in Philadelphia, 13 July 1985

biggest seller in the history of Columbia Records, with sales totaling 7.3 million for the single and 4.4 million for the album. The video proved to be just as popular, with endless rotation on MTV. On Good Friday came the ultimate gesture of the cause-rock era: five thousand radio stations around the globe played "We Are the World" simultaneously, including stations in East Germany and the People's Republic of China. By July 1985 USA for Africa had earned $55 million, which was to be distributed through established relief agencies. A year later estimated sales of "We Are the World" products, from T-shirts to posters, totaled $44 million.

Live Aid. Even as "We Are the World" was dominating radio and MTV, Geldof was organizing the rock-concert event of the decade: Live Aid. Before the first of some sixty acts ever took the stage on 13 July 1985, he had already raised $7 million in ticket sales and an equal amount for the broadcasting rights. The concert was the most complicated live broadcast ever attempted: two simultaneous events were planned, one at Wembley Stadium in London and one at JFK Stadium in Philadelphia. At a cost of $4 million, the sixteen-hour concert was beamed live via fourteen satellites to 150 countries and an estimated billion and a half people. MTV aired the entire event, and ABC devoted three prime-time hours to it. Prince Charles and Princess Diana were among the seventy-two thousand fans who mobbed Wembley Stadium for performances by George Michael, Elton John, Elvis Costello, Paul Young, and other top acts. Rumors of a Beatles reunion (with Julian Lennon replacing his late

father) turned out to be false, but The Who took the stage for the first time since 1982. At JFK one hundred thousand fans rocked to the music of Hall and Oates, Madonna, Bryan Adams, and a spirited duet by Mick Jagger and Tina Turner. The history-making spirit of the event was infectious: after doing a number with Sting in London, Phil Collins flew to Philadelphia to perform again. The London show ended first, after dozens of stars had taken the stage. In Philadelphia the concert ended with Keith Richards and Ron Wood joining Bob Dylan to sing "Blowin' in the Wind," perhaps the best-known "social cause" song in America.

Logjams. Michael Mitchell, who produced and marketed the television broadcast of Live Aid, thought much of its appeal was that rock fans could participate collectively in a good cause: "The point is not problems. The point is, we can become winners." Yet viewers were in no danger of forgetting the real purpose of the event: between acts they were treated to testimonials from well-known figures (including Coretta Scott King, Pele, and Linus Pauling), documentary pieces on the African crisis, and hotline numbers for phone-in pledges. Thirty countries, including Japan, West Germany, and Canada, held special telethons in conjunction with the Live Aid broadcast. The effort paid off in a virtual logjam of pledge calls — twenty-two thousand every five minutes during the final hours of the JFK concert. The final take for the event was close to $70 million. Despite this success Geldof and his fellow organizers soon faced a massive problem: how to spend the money. By the end of

The Farm Aid concert at the University of Illinois football stadium, Champaign, Illinois, 22 September 1985

July, after spending $2.7 million on trucks and trailers to transport grain, they hit another logjam: outmoded railways and roads as well as lack of cooperation from the Marxist regime in Ethiopia stranded 608,000 tons of grain in African ports. Robert McCluskey, vice president of Catholic Relief Services, chalked it up to lack of knowledge and planning in Geldof's organization: "They don't have the experience of doing the grunt work."

Farm Aid. Despite the bad publicity Geldof was receiving for his impractical idealism, Willie Nelson was determined to push ahead with his own relief project in 1985. Bob Dylan's comments during Live Aid — that a portion of the money raised would be well spent helping impoverished American farmers — had given Nelson the idea for a Farm Aid concert. He asked his golfing buddy, Illinois governor Jim Thompson, to help out. Thompson volunteered the University of Illinois football stadium in Champaign as a site, and Nelson swiftly set about lining up acts, starting with fellow Highwaymen members Waylon Jennings and Johnny Cash. Although critics complained that even the $70 million Nelson hoped to raise would barely pay one day's interest on the $213 billion national farm debt, Thompson responded that "the main point of Farm Aid is to bring the plight of the American farmer to the attention of the nation." The

event started well: seventy-eight thousand tickets were sold in fifty-one hours. And fans enjoyed the variety of performers, who included Lou Reed, Loretta Lynn, Bob Dylan, Bon Jovi, X, and Lone Justice. A highlight was John Fogerty's first live appearance since 1972. Yet the concert, held on a rainy Saturday in September, fell far short of its monetary goal, raising only about $10 million. Nelson then met with farmers to solve the same problem Bob Geldof had faced: how to spend the money. Some felt that out-of-work farmers needed retraining programs. Others favored using the cash for legal aid. Despite the arguments, Farm Aid was a big enough success to encourage two sequels, both organized by John Cougar Mellencamp.

Protests. Mellencamp might have taken a note from Bruce Springsteen, who had already garnered acclaim in 1979 for his participation in the No Nukes concert to protest the spread of nuclear-power plants. Springsteen had also documented a concern for the plight of the common American on four successive albums between 1978 and 1984. With his appearance at Farm Aid and the release of his 1985 album *Scarecrow*, Mellencamp started to shake off the frivolous image he had earned with hits such as "Jack and Diane" (1982) and "Hurts So Good" (1982). Singing about the concerns of farmers in "Rain on the Scarecrow" on his 1985 album and about modern-day "Hard Times for an Honest Man" on his next, *The Lonesome Jubilee* (1987), Mellencamp earned new respect from the media and the public. Between touring and recording hits such as "Lonely Ol' Night" (1985), "Small Town" (1986), "Paper in Fire" (1987), "Check It Out" (1988), and "Cherry Bomb" (1988), Mellencamp helped to mount Farm Aid benefits. In 1989 he dropped the stage name "Cougar" and released an album as John Mellencamp. Part of a miniature folk boom in the late 1980s, Suzanne Vega protested child abuse in her song and disturbing video "Luka" (1987), while in 1988 Tracy Chapman sang about dead-end lives in "Fast Car" and anarchy in "Talkin' About a Revolution." The Australian band Midnight Oil featured nuclear-protest songs on their first two albums. After releasing *Diesel and Dust* (1986), which lashed out at white oppressors of Australian aborigines, the band toured the outback as a show of solidarity.

Challenging Apartheid. In the late 1980s Paul Simon followed the lead of artists Talking Heads, Peter Gabriel, and Sting by using African musicians and sounds on his recordings, but Simon had a broader agenda. He saw his 1986 release *Graceland* as a "powerful form of politics." By using South African musicians, including the choir Ladysmith Black Mambazo, Simon hoped to alert listeners to the realities of apartheid — discriminatory racial separation in all aspects of life in the Union of South Africa. Guitarist Steve Van Zandt, who had left Bruce Springsteen's E Street Band in 1982 to record his own material as Little Steven and the Disciples of Soul, decided in 1985 that his next project would be an artistic protest of South African apartheid. Calling his project Artists United Against Apartheid, Van Zandt wrote the driving, danceable anthem "Sun City." The chorus — "I ain't gonna play Sun City" — encouraged performers to boycott the popular South African resort town. Many artists took part in the recording and the accompanying video — including Miles Davis, Keith Richards, Jackson Browne, Bonnie Raitt, Jimmy Cliff, Daryl Hall, Pete Townshend, Ringo Starr, Lou Reed, Ruben Blades, and Bruce Springsteen. All the musicians worked free, and the studio time was donated. "Sun City" failed to become a major hit, but the album helped raise awareness of apartheid and brought about an organized boycott of South African entertainment venues. Van Zandt donated almost $500,000 to antiapartheid causes.

Cause Mania. In the mid 1980s many rock musicians jumped on the bandwagons for various causes. The Grateful Dead organized a benefit concert to increase awareness of the world's shrinking rain forests. Pete Townshend, who had become partially deaf from years of playing loud rock music, made a large donation to Hearing Education and Awareness for Rockers (HEAR). Springsteen toured with Peter Gabriel in support of Amnesty International, an organization dedicated to freeing political prisoners, and donated more than $200,000 to

the cause. Bob Dylan and Bono seemed to be everywhere: Live Aid, Band Aid, the recording of "We Are the World," an antiapartheid benefit, an Amnesty International tour, and a concert in honor of the first Martin Luther King Day. Most rock altruists of the 1980s focused on African famine relief. A group of Latin artists recorded *Cantare Cantaras*, with the hope of scaring up $15 million, and a gospel contingent cut a benefit album called *Do Something Now*. Not to be outdone, several heavy-metal acts planned a project known as Hear 'n' Aid. Meanwhile, high-profile designers organized Fashion Aid, a benefit show of their work. As rumors circulated that he might be a contender for a Nobel Peace Prize, Geldof announced the School Aid program — British schoolchildren collecting money for famine relief. The generous spirit of rockers in the 1980s set the stage for 1990s cause-rock projects such as *Red, Hot and Blue* (for AIDS research) and the star-studded recording "Voices That Care." Some critics pointed out the potential for self-promotion and the trendiness of these undertakings; rock writer Greil Marcus dismissed them all as "a craze for charity."

Sources:

"Banding Together for Africa," *Newsweek*, 106 (15 July 1985): 52;

Fred Bronson, *The Billboard Book of Number One Hits* (New York: Billboard Publications, 1988);

"The Deadly Politics of African Aid Efforts," *Newsweek*, 105 (3 June 1985): 37–38;

"Forty-Five Voices as One," *Time*, 125 (25 March 1985): 68;

"Harvest Song," *Time*, 126 (23 September 1985): 32;

"Next: We Are the Farm," *Newsweek*, 106 (23 September 1985);

"Rock Around the World," *Newsweek*, 106 (22 July 1985): 56–58;

"Rocking the Global Village," *Time*, 126 (22 July 1985): 66–67;

"Songs from the High Ground," *Time*, 126 (7 October 1985): 78–79;

"Strike Up the Bandwagon," *Time*, 125 (22 April 1985): 66;

David P. Szatmary, *Rockin' in Time: A Social History of Rock and Roll* (Englewood Cliffs, N.J.: Prentice-Hall, 1987);

"Will 'Live Aid' Really Reach the Hungry?," *U.S. News and World Report*, 99 (29 July 1985): 8.

THE THEATER BOOM

Big Productions. After lackluster performances in the 1970s, Broadway rebounded in the 1980s with bigger shows and bigger stars than it had boasted in years. Production budgets and ticket prices were also bigger. In 1980 the typical cost for mounting a big show was about $1 million. By the end of the decade the cost had mushroomed to four or five times that amount. The $4 million production cost for the Andrew Lloyd Webber musical *Cats* in 1982 set a Broadway record; only six years later his *Phantom of the Opera* cost $8 million. Theatergoers, who paid about ten dollars for a seat in the mid 1970s, found themselves spending between twenty-five and forty-five dollars a ticket for a comparable show by 1983. Because it was shrewdly marketed as a theatrical "event," the nine-hour, two-part staging of *The Life and Adventures of Nicholas Nickleby* (1981), David Edgar's adaptation of Charles Dickens's 1838–1839 novel, had people lining up at the box office to shell out a record $100 per ticket. Such high prices were partly attributable to the fact that, like the rest of America, theater audiences had more disposable income by the mid 1980s. Yet the greatest single reason for escalating production budgets was skyrocketing labor costs. As ticket prices went up, theater audiences began expecting bigger and better shows for their bigger cash outlay. Producers, in turn, scurried to find surefire box office hits, packing their productions with elaborate special effects and eye-popping scenery and costumes. Often, as with Claude Michel Schonberg and Edward Behr's musical *Les Miserables* (1987), the results were spectacular. Just as often, as with the musical version of *Carrie* (1988), they were not. Too often, the attempt to create an "event" was transparent. In 1983, when Elizabeth Taylor and Richard Burton starred in a revival of Noel Coward's *Private Lives* (for a reported $70,000 a week apiece), *Time* commented, "Midas cast this revival." *The New York Times* concurred, noting that the show had "all the gaiety of a tax audit" and "never even pretends to be anything other than a calculated business venture."

Big Stars. Throughout the 1980s Broadway attracted slews of movie and television stars. Glenn Close and Jeremy Irons won Tonys for their roles in Tom Stoppard's *The Real Thing* (1984), while William Hurt, Sigourney Weaver, Christopher Walken, and Harvey Keitel headed the cast of David Rabe's *Hurlyburly* (1984). Susan Sarandon starred in William Mastrosimone's *Extremities* (1982), and Jack Lemmon played in the 1985 production of Eugene O'Neill's *A Long Day's Journey Into Night.* Dustin Hoffman and John Malkovich appeared in the 1983 production of Arthur Miller's *Death of a Salesman,* which was later filmed for television. Al Pacino returned to Broadway — and received outstanding reviews — in the 1983 production of David Mamet's *American Buffalo.* Mamet also provided a vehicle for Madonna, who made her stage debut in his *Speed-the-Plow* (1988). Cher made her first-ever Broadway appearance in Ed Graczyk's *Come Back to the Five and Dime, Jimmy Dean, Jimmy Dean* (1982). Elizabeth Taylor braved the footlights for the first time in a 1981 revival of Lillian Hellman's *The Little Foxes.* Mary Tyler Moore tackled Brian Clark's *Whose Life Is It, Anyway?* (1980); Linda Lavin took on the role of the stage mother in Neil Simon's *Broadway Bound* (1986); and Tyne Daly played another stage mother in the 1989 revival of *Gypsy,* by Jule Styne, Arthur Laurents, and Stephen Sondheim. Rita Moreno and Sally Struthers starred in a female version of Neil Simon's *The Odd Couple* (1985). Polly Holliday and Jean Stapleton were in a 1986 revival of Joseph Kesserling's *Arsenic and Old Lace,* and Ed Asner appeared with Madeline Kahn in a 1989 revival of Garson Kanin's *Born Yesterday.* A few vehicles seemed a bit self-serving: Shirley MacLaine carried her Oscar onstage during her one-woman show, and Linda Ronstadt tried a pop version of Giacomo Puccini's *La Boheme.* Others were naturals: Lily

Tomlin won a Tony for her comic versatility in *The Search for Signs of Intelligent Life in the Universe* (1986), written and directed by Jane Wagner. Robert Morse stunned audiences with Jay Presson Allen's *Tru* (1989), based on the life of author Truman Capote. Lauren Bacall triumphed in John Kander's *Woman of the Year* (1981). Richard Burton (1980) and Richard Harris (1981) both returned to Alan Jay Lerner and Frederick Loewe's *Camelot.* Rex Harrison reprised Lerner and Loewe's *My Fair Lady* in 1981; Anthony Quinn resurrected Kander's *Zorba* in 1983; and Yul Brynner remounted Richard Rodgers and Oscar Hammerstein's *The King and I* (1984). And stars rushed to sign up for the popular two-character showcase *Love Letters* (1989), by A. R. Gurney.

Big Musicals. The Broadway musical found itself revitalized in the 1980s, with lavish productions of new works and old favorites. Revivals of the Cole Porter musical *Anything Goes* with a revised book by Howard Lindsay and Russell Crouse (1987), *42nd Street* by Al Dubin and Harry Warren (1980), and *Grand Hotel* (1989) by Luther Davis, Robert Wright, and George Forrest were all hits. Stephen Sondheim shared a Pulitzer Prize and a New York Drama Critics Circle Award with James Lapine for the innovative *Sunday in the Park with George* (1984), which used clever lighting, staging, costumes, and music to re-create Georges Seurat's famous painting *Un Dimanche à la Grande Jatte* (1886). Sondheim's follow-up, *Into the Woods* (1987), ingeniously combined characters from classic fairy tales and received a Drama Critics Circle Award. *Big River* (1985), by Roger Miller and William Hauptman, set the story of Huck Finn to music. Michael Bennett's *Dreamgirls* (1981), loosely based on the story of the Supremes, created a powerful new star in Jennifer Holliday. The flashy costumes and glossy set design, however, caused *The New York Times* to comment that *Dreamgirls* was little more than "a fashion show set to music." A similar charge of "spectacle without a subject" was leveled against *Nine* (1982), Arthur Kopit and Maury Yeston's musical adaptation of the Federico Fellini movie *8 1/2* (1963). *Time* carped, "the clothes have no emperor." Occasionally spectacle paid off, even with the critics. With advance ticket sales of $12 million, *Les Miserables* (1987) became one of the biggest musical hits of the 1980s and won eight Tony Awards. A melodramatic, big-budget adaptation of the classic Victor Hugo novel, *Les Miserables* was directed by Trevor Nunn, who also guided *Nicholas Nickleby* and *Cats.* Its revolving stage and breathtaking sets brought down the house, especially during a climactic number, when two giant towers merged to form a barricade heaped with the bodies of rebel students. The sets were a problem when the show was performed in Washington, D.C.; a bridge had to be closed so that the massive scenery could be transported to the Kennedy Center.

Catalyst. If any single force can be credited with revitalizing the Broadway musical in the 1980s, that catalyst would be Andrew Lloyd Webber. Lloyd Webber started

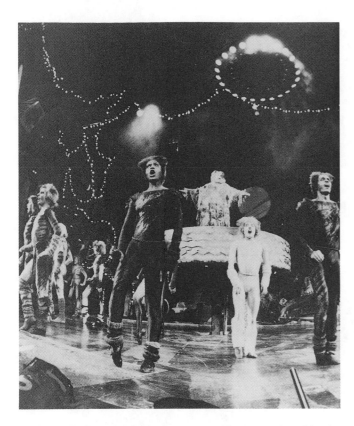

A scene from the Broadway production of the Andrew Lloyd Webber musical *Cats*

set design, including an underground lake and a giant tumbling chandelier that swooped over the audience to the stage.

Megahits. The marketing genius behind *Cats, Les Miserables,* and *The Phantom of the Opera,* all hits in London before they were imported to Broadway, was producer Cameron Mackintosh. Mackintosh attributed his uncanny intuition for picking hits to his admitted middlebrow tastes. The shows he produced were conventional, accessible, and "safe," but Mackintosh cleverly packaged each with a high-tech gloss and effects-laden razzle-dazzle that transformed each into a theatrical "event." Because of his commercial instincts and childlike love of entertainment (not to mention his string of hits), he reminded some people of Steven Spielberg. *Les Miserables* composer Claude Michel Schonberg commented, "He may have a computer-like mind for business matters, but artistically he has the heart of a child." Mackintosh himself said, "We are re-creating a style of theater that went bankrupt." To do so, he revolutionized theater marketing. While producing *Cats* he raised capital by inviting the public to invest in the show. His successful merchandising blitz for *Cats* was dwarfed by his efforts for *Les Miserables,* which included full-page newspaper advertisements ten months before it opened and a logo (a Parisian waif) that decorated T-shirts, coffee mugs, towels, posters, albums, buttons, and other "Les Miserabilia." In 1989 Mackintosh produced yet another megahit, *Miss Saigon.* A variation on the classic Madame Butterfly story set in Vietnam, the musical was written by the *Les Miserables* team. The show-stopping effect this time was a helicopter, which descended onto the stage during a scene depicting the American evacuation of Saigon. *Miss Saigon* was a smash hit in London, with a preopening ticket sale of $8 million. Mackintosh helped create public interest by sending eye-catching posters to ticket agents as early as 1987 — two years ahead of the opening — and continued to spend heavily on advertising ($450,000) even after six months of performances were completely sold out. "There's no better time to beat the drum than when people can't buy tickets," he explained. "You have to let them know they can't buy a ticket. That's what the difference between a hit and a megahit is all about."

Dramas. Despite their appetite for spectacle, audiences in the 1980s also developed a taste for "well-made" plays with serious and challenging themes. Mark Medoff's *Children of a Lesser God* (1980) depicted the confrontations between a fiercely independent deaf woman and the teacher who falls in love with her. John Pielmeier's *Agnes of God* (1982) pitted a psychologist's reason against a Mother Superior's faith when a young nun is accused of murdering her baby. Marsha Norman won the Pulitzer Prize in 1983 for her dark and disturbing drama *'Night, Mother,* which placed a desperate woman in an all-night battle with a daughter determined to commit suicide. Two important plays of 1985 — William Hoffman's *As Is* and Larry Kramer's *The Normal Heart* — dealt with the

out on Broadway with *Evita* (1978), which he wrote with Tim Rice. An imported smash from London, *Evita* was eclipsed in 1982 when Lloyd Webber's British stage hit *Cats* opened in New York. *Cats* set a Broadway record with a preopening advance-ticket sale of $6 million. The musical, a splashy fantasy about the lives of cats, adapted from T. S. Eliot's *Old Possum's Book of Practical Cats,* had American audiences howling with delight. Critics were less kind; one said that "spectacle is the substance" and that the show stressed "motion over emotion." Nevertheless, *Cats* became the most successful musical of the 1980s and, indeed, was still running on Broadway well into the next decade. Heavy on costumes (glowing cats' eyes), effects (actors catapulting onto the stage, a giant tire ascending like a UFO), and scenery design (burning junkyards and oversize garbage), *Cats* was the epitome of Broadway spectacle in the 1980s. By the end of the decade the show had grossed almost $700 million. For a follow-up, Webber concocted *Starlight Express* (1984), a pop musical on roller skates. Far more crowd-pleasing was yet another London import, his *The Phantom of the Opera* (1988), which made a Broadway star of Michael Crawford and, like *Cats,* won every Tony Award for which it was eligible. *The New York Times* called *The Phantom of the Opera* "a triumph of marketing." Effective media hype caused advance-ticket sales to top $18 million. By 1989 the wait for tickets was as long as eight months. The show itself thrilled crowds with its stunning

Marsha Norman with Tom Moore, director of her Pulitzer Prize–winning play 'Night, Mother

growing AIDS crisis. *Amadeus* (1981), by Peter Shaffer, was a chilling character study of Mozart's rival Salieri, who is driven to madness by envy of the young composer's genius. Lee Blessing's *A Walk in the Woods* (1987) was a battle of wits between two powerful world leaders. David Hare's *A Map of the World* (1985) depicted an international incident as it affects a group of travelers, and his *Plenty* (1982) traced the growing madness of a society woman who cannot accept a life without risk. In 1982 Charles Fuller won a Pulitzer Prize and the New York Drama Critics Circle Award for *A Soldier's Play*, which centered on a racially motivated murder at an army base. Alfred Uhry's *Driving Miss Daisy* (1987) tackled racial themes in its examination of a thirty-year friendship between a benevolent black chauffeur and his bigoted Jewish employer. David Henry Hwang's *M Butterfly* (1988) traced the delicate romance between a French diplomat and the male Chinese opera performer he believes is a woman. The title of *Steel Magnolias* (1987), by Robert Harling, refers to the strength of six small-town southern women whose friendship is cemented by tragedy.

Mamet. David Mamet had startled theater audiences during the 1970s by mixing the profane and the poetic in widely acclaimed plays such as *American Buffalo* (1977).

He had even greater success in the 1980s, when his gallery of cynical opportunists and con artists seemed perfectly in tune with the martketplace mentality of the decade. *Glengarry Glen Ross* (1983), which won him a Pulitzer Prize and a New York Drama Critics Circle Award, focused on a group of cutthroat real-estate men who will do anything to make a sale, including sell each other out. *Speed-the-Plow* (1988), heavily publicized because of Madonna's Broadway debut in the role of a conniving secretary, was a brutal but comic story of two Hollywood hustlers out to make a quick buck by producing "the thing everyone made last year." Both plays were characterized by Mamet's trademark syncopated rhythms and overlapping, rapid-fire dialogue. He also made his mark in Hollywood, contributing scripts for *The Postman Always Rings Twice* (1981), *The Verdict* (1982), and *The Untouchables* (1987). He also wrote the screenplay for *House of Games* (1987), which marked his debut as a film director. The movie is classic Mamet, an ever-escalating mind game in which a driven workaholic allows her unleashed passion to draw her into a psychological trap sprung by a consummate chiseler. Mamet's most reliable actor was Joe Mantegna, who appeared in *Glengarry Glen Ross, Speed-the-Plow, House of Games,* and Mamet's 1988 movie *Things Change.*

David Mamet during the Broadway run of his Pulitzer Prize–winning play, *Glengarry Glen Ross*

Matthew Broderick and Penelope Ann Miller in the Broadway production of Neil Simon's *Biloxi Blues*

Shepard. Like Mamet, Sam Shepard had earned a reputation in the 1970s for boldly original dramas such as *Buried Child* (1978), baroque mixtures of violence, humor, and lyricism. Unlike Mamet, however, Shepard often focused on thorny family problems and the no-win relationship between the sexes. He was also preoccupied with the erosion and corruption of American society. The popular *True West* (1980) depicted two brothers locked in an often violent love-hate relationship. *Fool for Love* (1983) explored the volatile, on-again off-again affair between a rodeo cowboy and his half-sister lover. In 1986 Shepard won the New York Drama Critics Circle Award for *A Lie of the Mind*, a challenging three-and-a-half-hour epic seething with American madness and desolation. By that time Shepard had become a movie star in a series of rugged, sexy roles (often opposite his long-time lover, Jessica Lange) that gave him the stature of a modern Gary Cooper. After an Oscar nomination for his strong but silent depiction of Chuck Yeager in *The Right Stuff* (1983), Shepard made his directorial debut with a movie version of his *Fool for Love* (1985), in which he starred as the crazed cowboy. He also wrote the screenplay for the cult movie *Paris, Texas* (1984).

Comedies. The 1980s marked the breakthrough of several female playwrights to major Broadway success. In 1981 Beth Henley won a Pulitzer Prize for her highly acclaimed Gothic comedy *Crimes of the Heart,* about three sisters having a "really bad day." Henley also collaborated with musician David Byrne on the movie projects *True Stories* and *Nobody's Fool* (both 1986). Wendy Wasserstein hit the theatrical jackpot with her comic drama *The Heidi Chronicles* (1989), winning a New York Drama Critics Circle Award, a Pulitzer Prize, and a Tony for Best Play. *The Heidi Chronicles* traced twenty-three years of expectations and frustrations in the life of a feminist art scholar, from late 1960s radicalism to late 1980s yuppiedom. Harvey Fierstein was the first homosexual playwright to score a mainstream Broadway hit about gay life; the success of his highly comic *Torch Song Trilogy* (1982) led to Fierstein's Tony-winning musical adaptation of the drag comedy *La Cage aux Folles* (1983). Terence McNally, another popular gay playwright, contributed the book for the Chita Rivera–Liza Minnelli musical *The Rink* (1984). He also wrote *Frankie and Johnny at the Clair de Lune* (1987) and the opening-night farce *It's Only a Play* (1982). A similar farce, *Lend Me a Tenor,* by Ken Ludwig was a hit in 1989. During the 1980s perennial hitmaker Neil Simon wrote a trilogy of comic but bittersweet memory plays — *Brighton Beach Memoirs* (1982), *Biloxi Blues* (1984), and *Broadway Bound* (1986) — that many critics felt represented the best work of his career.

Wilson. August Wilson emerged as the most highly acclaimed new playwright of the 1980s. He was also a theatrical record breaker. His first three Broadway productions — *Ma Rainey's Black Bottom* (1984), *Fences*

Loretta Lynn, Hal Holbrook, and Luciano Pavarotti on the 1980 ABC-television *Omnibus Special*

(1986), and *Joe Turner's Come and Gone* (1988) — won New York Drama Critics Circle Awards. *Fences* won not only a Drama Critics Circle Award but also a Pulitzer Prize and a Tony. It also set a new box-office record for nonmusicals, grossing a staggering $11 million in its first year. By the end of the decade, Wilson's fourth major drama, *The Piano Lesson,* had opened Off-Broadway to more critical acclaim. *The New York Times* called him "the theater's most astonishing writing discovery this decade" — not bad for a playwright who had modestly set about transforming his memories of The Hill, a poor black neighborhood in Pittsburgh, into a cycle of dramas. In Wilson's plays personal family history becomes a universal celebration of humanity, with all its humor, sadness, and mundane joys. Audiences and critics were charmed and intrigued by the playwright's keen instinct for character, dialogue, and blues music. They also responded to his subtle handling of racial and political issues. *Ma Rainey's Black Bottom* depicted racial segregation as experienced by a 1920s blues singer, while *Fences* focused on the bitterness of a former baseball player who was too old to play by the time blacks were allowed into the major leagues in the late 1940s.

Sources:

"Beth's Beauties," *Film Comment,* 25 (May–June 1989): 9–12;

"The Chutzpah of *Miss Saigon,*" *Newsweek,* 114 (2 October 1989): 68–69;

"Exorcising the Demons of Memory," *Time,* 131 (11 April 1988): 77–78;

"The Light in August," *Esquire,* 107 (April 1989): 116–117;

1995 People Entertainment Almanac (New York: Little, Brown, 1994);

"Portrait of a Lady," *New Yorker,* 64 (26 December 1988): 81–82;

"The Terrors of Tinseltown," *Newsweek,* 111 (16 May 1988): 82–83;

"Who's That Tall, Dark Stranger?," *Newsweek,* 106 (11 November 1985): 68–74.

TRENDS IN CLASSICAL MUSIC

Opera Stars. During the 1970s tenor Luciano Pavarotti became a darling of the American public, the best-known and best-loved opera performer since Enrico Caruso. As the celebrity frenzy escalated in the 1980s, careful marketing made Pavarotti more popular than ever, as familiar to most Americans as any movie or pop star. He appeared on talk shows and television specials and in commercials for American Express and his album *Pavarotti's Greatest Hits!* (1980). With his outsize charm, talent, and girth, he became the best-selling classical artist of the decade. In 1980 alone four of the top-selling classical albums were by Pavarotti. As a stage performer he found joy playing himself, and even a disastrous acting debut in the 1982 movie *Yes, Giorgio!* (critics cried, "No, Luciano!") could not tarnish his superstar status. His immediate successor as "tenor of the moment," Placido Domingo, seemed to follow in Pavarotti's footsteps, doing advertisements for Rolex watches, recording pop albums with John Denver, releasing tango collections, and considering movie offers. Yet he was also a mesmerizing and emotional singer who was less interested in projecting his own personality than in mastering the great tenor roles, including Alfredo, Don Jose, Otello, and Hoffman. *Newsweek* commented that "his modesty, in a world of swollen egos, is staggering." After 1982 Domingo's recordings began outselling Pavarotti's; Domingo was the top classical-music recording artist in 1983 and 1985. He also appeared in Franco Zeffirelli's acclaimed screen adaptation of *La Traviata* (1982).

Met Comeback. The New York Metropolitan Opera had spent the 1970s in serious financial trouble; by the 1974–1975 season, ticket sales had fallen from their traditional 95 percent of the house or better to 85 percent of capacity, and because of escalating prices subscriptions had fallen by more than 10 percent. Meanwhile, production costs had skyrocketed to $74 million per year by 1983, higher than those of its ten largest competitors combined. Anthony Bliss, who became the executive director of the Metropolitan Opera in 1974, and Metropolitan Opera Association president and chief executive officer Frank Taplin decided to reverse their heavy debts with an aggressive new marketing scheme. Starting with newspaper advertisements and an army of phone volunteers, the Met began promoting its operas to the public for the first time. They also increased their fund-raising efforts, offering incentives and privileges to patrons. By 1983 private donations had reached $5 million, and the Metropolitan Opera Guild contributed more than $3 million in 1982. Taplin also began a $100 million endowment fund to guard against losses in "risky" years, including $18 million in corporate gifts raised by the chairman of U.S. Steel. The chairman of Texaco made a $5 million "leadership grant" to encourage other contributions, and Texaco also sponsored *Live from the Met* broadcasts of Saturday matinees on radio and telecasts on PBS, generating more revenue through sales of telecasts to Europe and video producers. The broadcasts helped increase the number of Met contributors from sixty thousand in the late 1970s to one hundred thousand by 1983. By the middle of the decade the Met was back in the black, riding a national wave of enthusiasm for opera made possible by stars such as Pavarotti and Domingo.

Unlikely Heroes. The personality-hungry media created a few more unlikely classical stars during the 1980s, including New York Philharmonic conductor Zubin Mehta and Sir Georg Solti, the popular septuagenarian conductor of the Chicago Symphony. To demonstrate their appreciation for the distinctive sound he stamped on their symphony, Chicagoans threw Solti a seventy-fifth birthday gala at their Orchestra Hall in October 1987. Solti repaid the gesture that night by making his American debut as a soloist in a Mozart piano concerto, leading to speculation that he might tour as a pianist after he retired as a conductor. Solti won twelve Grammy Awards during the 1980s. Pianist Vladimir Horowitz also discovered that life, or at least superstardom, begins at seventy. Horowitz ended his career on a series of high notes. For three straight years (1986–1988) before his death in early 1989, Horowitz had the best-selling classical recordings in America — *The Last Romantic, Horowitz in Moscow,* and *Horowitz Plays Mozart* — and he was the overall top-selling classical artist in 1987 and 1988. The Russian-born Horowitz, who specialized in playing the romantic compositions of Frédéric Chopin and Pyotr Tchaikovsky, also triumphed with a 1982 London performance that marked his first European appearance in thirty years. He followed that in 1983 with a much-heralded tour of Japan.

Violinists. Itzhak Perlman experienced a new level of celebrity in the early 1980s. Already established as one of the premier violinists in the world, along with Pinchas Zukerman and Isaac Stern, Perlman had an ebullient personality that marked him for stardom. He soon became a favorite guest of President Ronald Reagan at the White House and demonstrated a keen show-business savvy in his many television talk-show appearances. He was also one of the highest-paid (five-figure fees), busiest (one hundred concerts a year), and biggest-selling classical artists of the decade. Though a handicap resulting from a childhood battle with polio initially made him something of a media curiosity, it was Perlman's virtuosity on the violin that made his name in America. *60th Anniversary Gala,* the recording of Perlman's 1982 concert with Zukerman, Stern, conductor Zubin Mehta, and the New York Philharmonic, was among the top-selling classical albums of that year. Both Zukerman and Perlman were born in Israel and were protégés of Stern. Zukerman's skill and reputation rivaled Perlman's (one orchestra member likened Zukerman's playing to "the Second Coming"), but, unlike Perlman, he seemed unimpressed by the idea of touring and personal appearances. Instead, he branched into conducting by taking on the directorship of the St. Paul Chamber Orchestra in 1980. He also continued his newfound mastery of the viola. In 1980 Zukerman and Perlman teamed up to record *Music for Two Violins,* a Grammy winner the following year.

Sources:
"The Big Business of Grand Opera," *Fortune,* 108 (17 October 1983): 146–160;

"Bravissimo, Domingo!," *Newsweek,* 99 (8 March 1982): 56–63;

"The Exuberant Solti at 75," *Newsweek,* 110 (19 October 1987): 93;

"The Fiddling Maestro," *Newsweek,* 96 (20 October 1980): 101;

"Itzhak Perlman, Top Fiddle," *Newsweek,* 95 (14 April 1980): 62–71;

1995 People Entertainment Almanac (New York: Little, Brown, 1994).

TRENDS IN COUNTRY MUSIC

Traditionalists. During the early 1980s Nashville was dominated by popular, glossy performers such as Kenny Rogers, Dolly Parton, Barbara Mandrell, and the award-winning Alabama. The gospel quartet Oak Ridge Boys were enjoying chart success with songs such as "Elvira" (1981), while Lee Greenwood became a conservative hero with "God Bless the U.S.A.," the unofficial theme song of Ronald Reagan's 1984 reelection campaign. (Greenwood even sang the song at the Republican National Convention.) Nashville was certainly in tune with the times, but the pop-music sound and television-friendly images of these artists were anathema to country music purists, who welcomed a new breed of country-music performers who labeled themselves traditionalists. Ricky Skaggs, a former blue-grass musician who played with Emmylou Harris, led the rebellion with his 1981

Wynonna and Naomi Judd in 1984, from the cover of their first LP

age twenty-seven Travis already had a voice with the easy authority and world-weariness of a veteran such as George Jones or Merle Haggard. Dwight Yoakam had less success on the charts or with the Nashville establishment, but he won fans in 1986 with his twangy covers of country standards such as "Honky Tonk Man" and "Heartaches by the Number." These songs were featured on his first album, *Guitars, Cadillacs, etc. etc.* (1986), a showcase for his hard-core country sound (created by pedal steel guitars, fiddles, harmonicas, and mandolins) and instant classics such as "It Won't Hurt." In 1988 Yoakam teamed up with country legend Buck Owens on a rousing remake of "Streets of Bakersfield," featured on the album *Buenas Noches from a Lonely Room.*

Country Ladies. Reba McEntire burst onto the Nashville scene in 1982 with a gutsy, spirited country sound that she perfected on her 1984 release *My Kind of Country.* That year she won the Country Music Association award for female vocalist of the year; from 1985 through 1989 she was the top female country artist, with hits such as "What Am I Gonna Do About You" (1987) and "Whoever's in New England" (1986). Fast in McEntire's footsteps were Kathy Mattea, Patti Loveless, and Sweethearts of the Rodeo. Rosanne Cash, daughter of Johnny Cash, was a spiky-haired rebel favorite with a string of big hits, including "Seven Year Ache" (1981), "Never Be You" (1986), and "If You Change Your Mind" (1988). The most popular country duo of the 1980s was The Judds, a mother and daughter singing team who made it big in 1984 with "Mama He's Crazy" and followed up with consistent hits such as "Have Mercy" (1986) and "Cry Myself to Sleep" (1987). K. T. Oslin's theme song, "80s Ladies" (1987), became her biggest hit and an anthem for Nashville's new breed of independent, career-minded female artists.

Originals. Country's tough new women might have used Emmylou Harris as a blueprint; she had already been recording her uncompromising rock- and folk-influenced country music outside the Nashville system for years. In 1987 she teamed with Dolly Parton and Linda Ronstadt for *Trio,* an album that proved the clout of the new country purists. Even more original was K. D. Lang, who caused a stir with her androgynous, Elvis-style looks and stunning vocal range. Her first album, *Angel with a Lariat,* seemed almost a novelty recording, but the follow-up, *Shadowland,* silenced doubters with its strong versions of classics such as "Western Stars" and "Black Coffee." Loretta Lynn and Kitty Wells contributed guest vocals. *Absolute Torch and Twang* (1989) was Lang's strongest effort to date, with numbers such as "Pulling Back the Reins" and "Big Boned Gal." Other notable artists working in more or less traditional country styles during the 1980s included Vince Gill, Ricky Van Shelton, and, at the end of the decade, Clint Black and Garth Brooks. Their popularity meant a surge in airplay and sales for veteran country performers such as George

album *Waitin' for the Sun to Shine.* Skaggs's sparse, hard-core instrumentals and Kentucky vocals opened Nashville ears. By 1982 John Anderson and George Strait had jumped on the new country bandwagon, Anderson with wrenching songs such as "Call on Me" and Strait with his smooth crooning on "If You're Thinking You Want a Stranger." Strait went on to become one of the most popular country performers of the 1980s, consistently recording hits such as "Does Fort Worth Ever Cross Your Mind," "All My Exes Live in Texas," and "Ocean Front Property."

Honky Tonk Heroes. Randy Travis became a star with his first album, *Storms of Life* (1986). With a rich, deep voice and classic country arrangements, Travis became the new hero of the honky-tonk movement. Hit songs such as "On the Other Hand" (1986) were refreshing returns to the old well of bad puns, while others, including "1982" (1986) and "Diggin Up Bones," displayed a more modern edge. His 1987 follow-up album, *Always and Forever,* included his biggest hit, "Forever and Ever, Amen" (1987). Fans and critics marveled that at

Jones, Conway Twitty, Johnny Cash, and Merle Haggard.

Hybrids. As the honky-tonk sound reigned in the 1980s, some artists adapted the sound to create a hybrid style. In 1988 Johnny Cash joined Roy Orbison, Bob Dylan, Tom Petty, George Harrison, and Jeff Lynne to form a country-folk-rock hybrid group, The Traveling Wilburys. On *Guitar Town* (1986) Steve Earle mixed rockabilly with straight-ahead rock and roll. Joe Ely, Lyle Lovett, and Chris Isaak were among the pop and rockabilly performers whose careers benefited during the 1980s from the resurgence in traditional country. The Tail Gators won fans with relentlessly amiable but spirited rockabilly songs such as "Pick Up the Deck" (1985), "Mumbo Jumbo" (1986), and "Chase the Devil" (1986). The LeRoi Brothers adopted a slightly more sinister, bayou-tinged sound, while The Blasters mixed rockabilly and punk. The postpunk band X recorded a rockabilly and country album in 1985 under the name The Knitters. It featured the goofy anthems "Love Shack" and "Poor Little Critter in the Road." On their first album (1985) Lone Justice combined an anthemic pop sound with a country twang in songs such as "After the Flood" and "He's Working Late." Asleep at the Wheel specialized in winsome numbers such as "Miles and Miles of Texas," and Highway 101's hybrid sound won as many fans among urban hipsters as it did in the rural South. The most curious hybrid was perhaps Jon Wayne, a raspy singer with wizened asides that evoked Walter Brennan and rambling, minimalist songs, such as "Texas Wine" and "Texas Cyclone," that added a demented country appeal to the album *Texas Funeral* (1986).

Sources:
"Country Purists Fight Back," *Newsweek,* 103 (9 January 1984): 93;
"Nashville's New Class," *Newsweek,* 106 (12 August 1985): 58–61;
"A New Honky Tonk Hero," *Newsweek,* 108 (27 October 1986): 102.

TRENDS IN JAZZ

New Blood. The 1970s had been a sluggish decade for jazz, producing few "name" performers and notable only for experiments in jazz-rock "fusion." Jazz in the early 1980s offered more of the same, with pop-minded artists such as Spyro Gyra, Pat Metheny, The Crusaders, Al Jarreau, George Benson, Herbie Hancock, Chuck Mangione, Angela Bofill, George Winston, David Sanborn, and Grover Washington Jr. dominating jazz sales and airplay. That trend changed abruptly at middecade as record buyers and jazz enthusiasts began discovering new jazz artists and returning to old favorites. Stanley Jordan and George Howard made a splash in 1985, as did Sade, who attracted a large jazz following with her cool, exotic vocals. Perhaps the most popular jazz performer of the late 1980s was Kenny G, whose albums *Duotones* (1987) and *Silhouette* (1989) were exemplars of the "fusion" sound. The most welcome trend was the resurgence on the charts in the late 1980s of jazz masters such as Ella

Wynton Marsalis, Juilliard-trained jazz trumpeter and historian

Fitzgerald, Ornette Coleman, and Count Basie. The movie *Round Midnight* (1986) quickened record sales for Dexter Gordon, while the movie *Bird* (1988) helped make the late Charlie Parker the biggest-selling jazz artist of 1989.

Marsalis. Trumpeter Wynton Marsalis caught the jazz world by surprise in the early 1980s with a mastery of technique astonishing for such a young performer. At fourteen he played with the New Orleans Philharmonic. At seventeen he was admitted to the Berkshire Music Center to study classical music, and at eighteen he was attending the Julliard School of Music and performing with the Brooklyn Philharmonia. At nineteen he played with Art Blakey's Jazz Messengers and Herbie Hancock. That same year Marsalis signed a major-label recording contract; Hancock produced Marsalis's first album, which sold 125,000 copies. In 1982, at twenty, Marsalis beat Miles Davis as best trumpet player in a *Down Beat* readers' poll and played at the Kool Jazz Festival in New York. At twenty-two he performed in a concert at Lincoln Center that featured the music of Bach and Duke Ellington. Marsalis was rare in being skilled in both jazz and classical music, and in 1984 he became the first artist

New Age music slipped into the American consciousness in the 1980s, an era of hype and hysteria for anything new, and managed to keep a low profile for the rest of the decade — in part because of its elusiveness as a category. No one seemed able to define precisely what made a particular piece of music New Age. Some New Agers, such as harpist Andreas Vollenweider, disavowed the term altogether. Yet most did agree about the effect New Age music had on listeners, describing it as creating sensations such as "a pastoral utopia of peace and centeredness," or "a magic carpet ride for the listener's imagination," or "a pilgrimage through the cosmos."

The enthusiasm for New Age music bridged two separate phenomena. The first was a lingering fondness among many Americans, generally aging baby boomers, for the counterculture of the 1960s. The second was excitement, in largely the same demographic group, about the new digital-sound technology made possible by compact discs. The result was a small underground of mostly white, college-educated professionals (some of them hippies-turned-yuppies) "tuning in" and "turning on" again through the mainstream cultural avenue of New Age music.

The New Age sound originated with acoustic musicians such as pianist George Winston and guitarist William Ackerman, who founded the New Age record label Windham Hill. As jazz and classical musicians picked up the style, it became more complex in texture. New Age music resembles improvisational jazz and jazz "fusion," but it also borrows from the ambient, "pillowy" synthesizer music of artists such as Philip Glass and Brian Eno and the ethnic influences of world music. Ethereal, almost patternless melodies and harmonic washes create a "visual" sound that is best described by New Age song titles such as "The Garden of Ecstasy," "Islands of Paradise," and "Sea of Light."

While some New Age artists went for purely pastoral effects, others had a style close to opera. Their inspiration ranged from mythology and Nordic lore to modern religion, and their mood from serious to playful. Some tried to be innovative; Montreaux included every style from calypso to bluegrass. A lot of first-time listeners griped that New Age music was just high-tech Muzak, elevator music for yuppies — and hospitals and airlines often used it to soothe the fears of patients and passengers. But Vollenweider defended the New Age sound: "With the music, you can build a bridge between the conscious and the subconscious. We have to somehow excite our spirituality."

A few New Age performers, including Enya, Yanni, and Vangelis, broke through to mainstream success with New Age "hits." By 1985 Vollenweider had sold 2.1 million recordings worldwide, The Windham Hill label, started in the mid 1970s, had retail sales of $20 million in 1984, and by the late 1980s New Age stations such as "The Wave" in Los Angeles were springing up across the country. By then New Age music had invaded television, including news programs, soap operas, and the 1988 Winter Olympics. On Independence Day in 1986, the new music received a lot of free exposure when the spectacular Parade of Tall Ships in New York Harbor performed impressively with a New Age "curtain of sound" as a backdrop.

Sources: "Muzak for a New Age," *Newsweek*, 105 (13 May 1985): 68;

Helfried C. Zrzavy, "Issues of Incoherence and Cohesion in New Age Music," *Journal of Popular Culture*, 24 (Fall 1990): 33–54.

ever to win Grammys in jazz and classical in the same year. In 1985 he was the top-selling jazz artist in the United States, with *Hot House Flowers*. In 1988 *Standard Time* put him in the top spot again.

Purist. Marsalis felt that jazz was more difficult than classical music because it required great versatility, creativity, personal style, and emotion, which many critics felt he lacked. Marsalis himself admitted, "I have a lot to learn. My playing isn't spontaneous enough." But few disputed his talent, his ambition, and his seriousness about his art. "I do not entertain and I will not entertain," he said. "I'm a musician." Classical trumpet master Maurice Andre said Marsalis had the potential to be the greatest trumpeter in history. A jazz purist, Marsalis scoffed at the style of jazz "fusion" popular throughout the 1970s and 1980s: "I don't like it when pop is sold as jazz. That's the record companies trying to redefine jazz." His older brother Branford, who developed his own reputation as a tenor saxophonist, was less of a purist. Although he recorded several top-selling albums of sophisticated jazz, Branford Marsalis also dabbled in pop. In 1985 he backed Sting on his solo-debut album and went on to tour stadiums with the former Police idol. He also appeared in several feature films.

Connick. Among Wynton Marsalis's best friends was another boy wonder of jazz, New Orleans–style pianist and vocalist Harry Connick Jr. Only twenty when he achieved stardom in 1988 with his first recording, the debonair Connick struck many listeners and critics as a cocky brat and, worse still, a poseur. "Recycled Sinatra" was a common description. Others sniffed that he was just a jazz version of Michael Feinstein, the cabaret crooner-pianist who specialized in classic show tunes. But Connick had already paid his dues, growing up in New Orleans and sitting in on Bourbon Street gigs. Like Marsalis, Connick excelled in both jazz and classical styles; he even studied piano with Marsalis's father, Ellis. As a teenager he had also played with Eubie Blake, Buddy Rich, and Al Hirt. Most audiences were less interested in Connick's keyboard virtuosity than in his retro style, from his 1940s suits and slicked-back hair to his drawling vocals that suggested an earlier, more glamorous era. Connick was a genuine talent shrewdly marketed to a public that liked their culture packaged, processed, and homogenized.

Sources:

"The Bourbon Street Kid Hits His Stride," *Newsweek,* 113 (20 February 1989): 67;

"Branford's Two Worlds," *Newsweek,* 111 (4 January 1988): 54;

"Kid Zipper's High Horn," *Time,* 122 (7 November 1983): 94;

"Whiz Kid," *New Yorker,* 59 (20 June 1983): 78–80.

TRENDS IN UNDERGROUND MUSIC

Fallout. The British punk-rock movement, which peaked in the late 1970s with the success of the Sex Pistols and other fast and loud bands, fragmented and then regrouped in the early 1980s. Many of these bands specialized in postpunk gloom and doom, the angry nihilism of 1970s punk soured into resigned alienation. After the death of Sid Vicious in 1979, the Sex Pistols' Johnny Rotten reemerged as John Lydon with a dirge-prone ensemble called Public Image, Ltd. (PIL). Other brooding bands included Joy Division (later reformed as New Order), The Cure, Bow Wow Wow, The Smiths, Echo and the Bunnymen, The Psychedelic Furs, and Bauhaus. Several reggae-influenced new-wave bands — including Selecter, English Beat, Madness, The Police, The Specials, UB40 — continued to attract a following on both sides of the Atlantic amid a short-lived ska craze. Other punk and new-wave groups continued on into the new decade, oblivious to the gloom-and-doom movement. The Clash hit the pop charts with singles such as "Train in Vain" (1980) and "Rock the Casbah" (1982). Gang of Four released their seminal *Entertainment* album in 1980. Elvis Costello became increasingly successful with a series of witty and well-crafted albums. Generation X recorded the classic "Dancing with Myself" (1981) before Billy Idol departed for a solo and video career. After several early 1980s albums with The Jam, front man Paul Weller left to form The Style Council. Siouxsie and the Banshees, Squeeze, and XTC continued to gain popularity in the early 1980s.

Postpunks. The originators of the American punk-rock scene began to disperse and lose energy in 1979. Patti Smith retired; The Ramones turned to Phil Spector

Henry Rollins of Black Flag

for inspiration. But punk itself was far from over. While Blondie, Talking Heads, and other seminal bands were basking somewhere in the Top 40, many of the groups they had inspired were busy reinventing punk for themselves. In Los Angeles bands such as X and Black Flag helped define the sound of the postpunk era. X, featuring the husband-wife team of guitarist-singer John Doe and vocalist Exene Cervenka, mixed tumble-down, off-kilter rhythms with darkly humorous lyrics of alienation and despair on their first album, *Los Angeles* (1980). *Under the Big Black Sun* (1982) was their most compelling work, full of deadpan numbers such as "The Hungry Wolf" and "Real Child of Hell" that celebrated the romantic insanity of a decaying world. The members of Black Flag, also from Los Angeles, were early exemplars of what came to be known as "hardcore" — a stripped-down, revved-up attack of guitars, drums, and vocals. In 1981 the band created its own label, SST, to release *Damaged.* Their early 1980s anthems of rage and pain include "Rise Above," "TV Party," "Depression," "Dead Inside," and "Life of Pain." "Pain is my girlfriend," singer Henry Rollins said. "When you see me perform, it's that pain you're seeing coming out."

Hardcore. After the election of Ronald Reagan in 1980, political hardcore was born. New hardcore bands embraced leftist politics, leaving behind the rebellion of late 1970s American punk, which unlike British punk targeted the blandness of mainstream culture and tended to celebrate subversion for its own sake. In Washington, D.C., a local hardcore scene grew up around the independent record manufacturer Discord, founded by Minor Threat singer Ian MacKaye. In the song "Out of Step" and in hardcore fanzines such as *Maximum Rock 'n' Roll,* MacKaye promoted "straightedge," a no-drugs, no-sex, no-alcohol philosophy that encouraged fans to stay sharp, aware, and focused on political and social issues. The

On 2 April 1988, for the first time, all the albums on the Billboard Hot 200 Albums chart were available on CD (compact disc) — marking the end of a scratchy old era and the birth of a shiny new one. The recording industry had started saying good-bye to its forty-year staple — the vinyl LP (long-playing record). In 1988 CD sales surpassed vinyl sales for the first time, increasing 31 percent from the previous year, while LP sales declined 33 percent. The first six months of 1989 were even bleaker for the twelve-inch records; vinyl sales slipped from 15 percent of the total market to just 6 percent, while CDs rose another 38 percent over the previous year. With an increasing number of new releases available only on CD or cassette tape, record stores began dropping LPs and vinyl 45s from their inventories; audio manufacturers trimmed their lines of turntables and cartridges; and vinyl-record pressing plants closed their doors for good.

The change had happened so quickly — in just six years — that it left many music performers, industry leaders, and fans shaking their heads in bewilderment. Yet in an era of stunning technological advancements, from movie special effects and music video to home computers and VCRs, it was change or die, and the technology was hard to resist: compact discs were more resistant to warping and scratching, had better sound quality, and held more music than their vinyl predecessors. When CDs were introduced in late 1982 the cost of a disc player was a prohibitively high $900, and a typical CD sold for $20, but by 1987 their prices were competitive with cassette and LP formats. A CD player cost as little as $150, and CD prices were around $12. Early CD buyers, mostly classical-music enthusiasts, were soon joined by young pop and rock fans who liked their music "mobile."

Huge numbers of these young consumers, comfortable with video-age technology, boom boxes, and the Walkman portable cassette player, began buying CDs. The number of CDs sold mushroomed from just 16.4 million in 1985 to 390 million in 1988, an increase of almost 2,500 percent. Meanwhile, between 1978 and 1988 the number of vinyl units shipped dropped an alarming 80 percent, from 341 million to 72 million. During that period CD sales helped the sagging record industry rebound from a disappointing $3.67 billion in sales in 1979 to $6.46 billion in 1989.

Many vinyl fans, however, adamantly refused to make the switch to CDs. With some justification they found the new discs cold and sterile, devoid of the friendly appeal and creative packaging of LPs. They missed the liner notes, posters, foldouts, inner sleeves, and other marketing gimmicks that came with LPs. Their resistance, and pockets of other consumers who relied on vinyl — including scratch-rappers, jazz collectors, and oldies radio stations — helped keep the LP alive for several more years. Other markets, most notably country, rhythm and blues, folk, blues, and alternative music, continued to have strong LP sales and thus remained loyal to vinyl. In 1987 Rhino Records even started a "Save the LP" campaign, but it was a losing battle. By the 1990s LPs had become as anachronistic as the eight-track tapes and 78s of earlier eras. "A lot of people grew up with vinyl," said Don Radcliffe, president of Justin Entertainment. "To take it away, you take away part of their history. It's more than music . . . it's an era."

Sources: George Plasketes, "Romancing the Record: The Vinyl De-Evolution and Subcultural Evolution," *Journal of Popular Culture,* 26 (Summer 1992): 109–122;

David P. Szatmary, *Rockin' in Time: A Social History of Rock and Roll* (Englewood Cliffs, N.J.: Prentice-Hall, 1987).

sound of Washington, D.C., bands such as Scream and GI — hyperspeed drums, white-noise guitars, screaming vocals — influenced hardcore bands across the country, including the Dead Kennedys in San Francisco. Typical Dead Kennedys songs of the early 1980s include "Terminal Preppie," which sneered at materialism and conformism, "Holiday in Cambodia," which raged over U.S. involvement in Southeast Asia, and "Moral Majority," which took aim at Reagan's conservative administration. Angry over policies that increased military spending, escalated the Cold War, and cut education and social programs, many other hardcore bands including DOA, Government Issue, and Circle Jerks, whose "Stars and Stripes" attacked the president's patriotic, promilitary rhetoric, performed anti-Reagan songs in the early 1980s. In 1983 Rock Against Reagan, a tour organized to benefit leftist causes, climaxed with a hardcore show on the Mall in Washington, D.C., less than a mile from the White House.

Midwest. Among the Dead Kennedys' many musical targets were hardcore fans themselves, particularly fringe extremists such as the ever-present Nazi skinheads. Most of the hardcore audience, however, was made up of restless, young, white, middle-class males; for them the movement was a way of rebelling against the perceived complacency, conformism, and oppressiveness of Ameri-

"The author of the *Satanic Verses* book, which is against Islam, the Prophet, and the Koran, and all those involved in its publication who were aware of its content, are sentenced to death." With these words the Ayatollah Ruholla Khomeini of Iran ordered the assassination of novelist Salman Rushdie, a British subject born in India, in February 1989. For any Muslim who was not provoked to murder simply by the "blasphemy" of the novel, Khomeini's followers offered a reward of more than $1 million.

On its publication in Great Britain in fall 1988 *The Satanic Verses* provoked outcries from Islamic leaders. Rushdie, who was born to a Muslim family but no longer practiced the religion, had skewered the central belief of Islam, that the archangel Gabriel revealed the word of God, the Koran, to the prophet Muhammad. In *The Satanic Verses* a businessman named Mahound claims access to a rule-making archangel, Gibreel, in order to pass his own laws. The angel's "revelations" are little more than a profitable scam for Mahound, whose subjugation of women is among Rushdie's satiric targets.

Khomeini's threat and the fury felt by many Muslims worldwide forced Rushdie into hiding. He issued a statement apologizing for the distress that the book caused to followers of Islam, but Islamic leaders, including Iranian president Ali Khamenei, rejected the apology as inadequate, insisting that Rushdie repent and that the book be withdrawn. The furor was not limited to Iran. Riots in India and Pakistan caused deaths, and an anonymous phone caller in Bombay threatened to murder Indians who criticized Khomeini. British officials claimed that the novel had prevented the release of three British hostages in Beirut, even after Britain agreed that *The Satanic Verses* was offensive to Muslims. Most Islamic countries banned the book; publication was postponed or canceled in France, West Germany, Greece, and Turkey. In Britain protesters burned it. One Muslim in London shouted, "I think we should kill Salman Rushdie's whole family. His body should be chopped into little pieces and sent to all Islamic countries as a warning to those who insult our religion." Another devout Londoner declared proudly, "If I see him, I will kill him straight away." A third Muslim commented, "Salman Rushdie is a dead man. There is no way to protect him. He will be followed for the rest of his life."

In the West, particularly in America, there was a different kind of outrage. Government leaders contemplated sanctions against Iran. Britain put its diplomatic efforts on hold, while the Dutch foreign minister decried Khomeini's "totally unacceptable call for international terrorism." Early in March diplomats from twelve European countries were recalled from Iran. President Bush declared that "inciting murder and offering rewards for its perpetration are deeply offensive to the norms of civilized behavior." Most political experts agreed that Khomeini was using the Rushdie incident as a means of rallying his forces against the West. Meanwhile, American writers joined forces to protest Khomeini's actions, signing petitions and organizing speeches, demonstrations, and readings of Rushdie's novel. Among those at a public protest in New York were Susan Sontag, Norman Mailer, Larry McMurtry, and Joan Didion.

These authors were also railing against several American booksellers who, out of fear of terrorist actions, had removed *The Satanic Verses* from their shelves. One reason for the paranoia was the news that Rushdie's American publisher, Viking Penguin, had to close its offices temporarily after receiving bomb threats. "We've fought long and hard against censorship," said the executive vice president of the Waldenbooks chain, "but when it comes to the safety of our employees, one sometimes has to compromise." B. Dalton also knuckled under to Muslim demands and pulled the novel. The National Writers Union, after picketing the Iranian mission to the United Nations, marched to a nearby B. Dalton store, shouting "one, two, three, four, get that book back in the store!" After a public meeting and at the urging of its employees, B. Dalton decided to carry the novel.

Though sales of *The Satanic Verses* had been sluggish at first, the publicity generated by Khomeini's death threat catapulted it onto the best-seller lists. Within a few weeks after the ayatollah's threat was announced, the first American printing had sold out, and bookstores had received advance orders for two hundred thousand more copies. As for the man who had inadvertently started the controversy, Salman Rushdie continued to hide from terrorists and to insist that his work was not blasphemous. Complaining about the Islamic "thought police," Rushdie defended *The Satanic Verses* as a work of the imagination. Appearing on the news program *Nightline*, Rushdie said, "The idea that this is somehow an attack on religion shows an absolute failure to understand what fiction is."

Sources: "A 'Satanic' Fury," *Newsweek*, 113 (27 February 1989): 34–39;

"The West Gets Tough With Iran, Sort of," *Newsweek*, 113 (6 March 1989): 32–33.

can life in the early 1980s. Sporting military haircuts and layers of disheveled clothing, audience members became experts at slam dancing (slamming into other dancers) and stage diving (diving off the stage into the crowd). Mosh pit aficionados were also fond of loping simian style in a circle in front of the stage. Midwestern hardcore bands such as Articles of Faith, The Subverts, Savage Beliefs, Rights of the Accused, Out of Order, Toxic Reasons, Zero Boys, Big Black, Naked Raygun, and Die Kreuzen soon discovered that the heartland was seething with bored teens and former teens fed up with preppies, suburbia, fraternity boys, and parents. These kids were eager and ready to slam, dive, crowd surf, limbo, skateboard, sleep on bare floors, carry equipment, watch the movie *Taxi Driver* (1976), drink cheap beer, eat generic macaroni and cheese, go to cookouts, and hang around for days on end. Savage Beliefs kept Chicago youths twitching with songs such as "Way of the World" (1983) and "I Will Eat What's Left in the Fridge" (1983), while the Subverts kicked in the hardcore "hits" "Radiation Nation" and "TV Personality." Articles of Faith had a darker, more personal repertoire, chainsawing through numbers such as "Five O'Clock," "Bad Attitude," "Everyday," "My Father's Dreams," and "Cambridge."

Minneapolis. The Twin Cities were home to three of the most influential postpunk bands: Hüsker Dü, The Replacements, and Soul Asylum. All three groups started in the early 1980s as hardcore bands. Hüsker Dü established their trademark sound — buzzing guitars under Bob Mould's wailing vocals — with *Land Speed Record* (1981) and *Metal Circus* (1983). After a cover version of "Eight Miles High," Hüsker Dü released the double album *Zen Arcade* (1984). This recording marked a new direction: amid the howls and revved-up tempos was more mature songwriting from Mould and drummer Grant Hart, which continued to develop on *New Day Rising* and *Flip Your Wig* (both 1985). Songs on *Flip Your Wig* include "Green Eyes," "Hate Paper Doll," "Games," and "Makes No Sense at All," which was released as a single and backed with "Love Is All Around," the theme from Mary Tyler Moore's 1970s sitcom. The Replacements, with their tear-it-up live shows, earned a reputation as lovable drunks, but their records belied that image. *Stink* (1982) was full of cheerfully subversive songs such as "White and Lazy," "Dope Smokin' Moron," and "Gimme Noise." *Let It Be* (1984), with the gorgeous "Unsatisfied," hinted at a new depth to the songwriting of front man Paul Westerberg. The crazed rhythms of Soul Asylum (originally known as Fast Loud Rules) on their first album (1985) marked them as true originals, even if Dave Pirner's play-on-words lyrics were at times reminiscent of Westerberg's. The delirious single "Tied to the Tracks" and their *Made to Be Broken* album (both 1986) defined Soul Asylum's sound.

Growth. In 1985 the Replacements signed with the Warner Bros. Sire label and released *Tim,* one of their best efforts. Strong Westerberg songwriting on songs such as "Left of the Dial," "Hold My Life," and "Here Comes a Regular" landed the Replacements an appearance on *Saturday Night Live* in 1986. Their follow-up album, *Pleased to Meet Me* (1987), which includes "Can't Hardly Wait" and "Alex Chilton," received major critical acclaim. After two more albums the band split up and Westerberg embarked on a solo career. Hüsker Dü also signed with Sire and released *Candy Apple Grey* (1986) and the impressive double album *Warehouse: Songs and Stories* (1987), featuring "Bed of Nails," "Could You Be the One," and "Visionary." After an appearance on Joan Rivers's talk show and a farewell tour in late 1987, the members of Hüsker Dü went their separate ways. Mould recorded a well-received solo album in 1989, and in the 1990s he formed the popular band Sugar. Soul Asylum signed with A & M to record their best effort, *Hang Time* (1988). A triumph of flailing energy and unpredictable rhythms, the album includes "Sometime to Return," "Marionette," "Standing in the Doorway," and "Cartoon." The 1990s brought them unexpected mainstream success with magazine covers, a hit single ("Runaway Train," 1993), a visit to the White House, and singer Dave Pirner's appearance at the Academy Awards with actress girlfriend Winona Ryder.

Regional Originals. Brothers Cris and Curt Kirkwood of The Meat Puppets hailed from Arizona. In songs such as "Swimming Ground" on their *Up on the Sun* album (1985), the Kirkwoods perfected a sunny minimalism that verged on goofiness. Their sparse, vaguely off-key sound and humorous lyrics became almost standard for other mid-1980s postpunk bands such as The Dead Milkmen ("Bitchin' Camaro," 1985). Austin, Texas, was home to a burgeoning postpunk scene, including Zeitgeist and the Big Boys ("We Got Your Money"). The San Antonio band Butthole Surfers became known for their crazed live shows, featuring two onstage drummers, and for creepy delights such as "Mexican Caravan" and "Gary Floyd." R.E.M., from Athens, Georgia, won attention with their 1983 release *Murmur,* featuring "Pilgrimage" and "Talk About the Passion." Their arty sound, notable for strong melodies and Michael Stipe's unintelligible vocals, was perfected on *Reckoning* (1984). The Dream Syndicate, fronted by Steve Wynn, mixed postpunk sensibilities with more standard rock in songs such as "Tell Me When It's Over" (1983). The Minutemen, from San Pedro, California, patented a hilarious and refreshing approach to postpunk songwriting: most of their songs lasted no more than thirty seconds to a minute, just long enough to complete the main musical idea. *Double Nickels on the Dime* (1984) is a smorgasbord of songwriter D. Boon's witty lyrics and Watusi vocals backed by Mike Watt's twangy guitar. The Minutemen reformed as fIREHOSE after D. Boon was killed in a car accident in late 1985.

Mainstream Success. By the mid 1980s the postpunk scene had shifted dramatically. Many bands, like Corrosion of Conformity, had started as hardcore but had altered their sounds toward high-speed metal or thrash. As the audience for heavy metal broadened in the late 1980s, hardcore-influenced metal bands such as Metallica, Anthrax, and Megadeath began to experience mainstream success. Even Black Flag was experimenting with a more metal sound on its 1984 releases. After a court battle involving cover art for their *Frankenchrist* album (1985), the Dead Kennedys called it a day. After releasing *Give Thanks* (1984), Articles of Faith disbanded in 1985. Aggressively political hardcore began giving way to more personal songwriting, exemplified by the increasing mainstream popularity of the Minneapolis bands. X split up after their poignant 1987 effort *See How We Are.* Meanwhile, major labels, encouraged by airplay given to postpunk bands on college radio stations, began signing droves of so-called "alternative" bands (The Lemonheads, The Del Fuegos, The Smithereens, The BoDeans). R.E.M found Top 40 success with songs such as "The One I Love" (1987), "Orange Crush" (1989), and "Stand" (1989). By the end of the decade the original energy of hardcore had been wed with the sound of metal to form the basis for the "grunge" sound first popularized in Seattle. The increasingly melodic, almost mainstream sound of the original postpunk groups had become, in the media at least, a whole new category of music — "alternative rock."

Sources:
"Rock Around the U.S.A.," *Newsweek,* 107 (16 June 1986): 70–71;

David P. Szatmary, *Rockin' in Time: A Social History of Rock and Roll* (Englewood Cliffs, N.J.: Prentice-Hall, 1987).

HEADLINE MAKERS

ROBERT DE NIRO

1943-

ACTOR

MARTIN SCORSESE

1942-

MOVIE DIRECTOR

Outsiders. Frequent collaborators with an instinctive affinity for one another's ideas, Robert De Niro and Martin Scorsese both grew up feeling alienated from their childhood worlds in New York City. Scorsese was born in Queens, but his family moved to Little Italy on the Lower East Side of Manhattan when he was eight years old. Poor health kept Scorsese from participating in the macho world of street fights and sports. Instead, he frequented the cinema with his father, especially the films noirs of the late 1940s and early 1950s. The boy originally intended to become a Roman Catholic priest and even entered a junior seminary, but he failed his entrance examination for a college divinity program and instead entered New York University, where he decided filmmaking was his true vocation and earned a B.S. in 1964 and an M.A. in 1966. De Niro's parents, both artists, separated when he was young, but he continued to see his father and often went to the movies with him. A frail, shy boy, De Niro felt different from other boys in Greenwich Village. Discovering his interest in acting, he attended the High School of Music and Arts and studied acting with Stella Adler and with Lee Strasberg at Actors Studio.

First Movies. Scorsese's first movie to attract attention was the extremely bloody six-minute *The Big Shave* (1967–1968). He went on to film *Who's That Knocking at My Door?* (1968) with Harvey Keitel and served as a supervising editor and assistant director on the documentary *Woodstock* (1970). After working on several more documentaries, Scorsese was approached by producer Roger Corman to work on *Boxcar Bertha* (1972), an exploitation flick that revealed Scorsese's flair for depicting violence. In the mid 1960s De Niro began working for young director Brian De Palma on a series of low-budget counterculture productions, including *Greetings* (1968) and *Hi, Mom!* (1970). A friend, Sally Kirkland, introduced De Niro to Shelley Winters, who picked him to play her morphine-addicted son in the film *Bloody Mama* (1970). To look sufficiently emaciated, De Niro insisted on losing an alarming amount of weight for the role. He also attracted attention for his convincing Sicilian accent in *The Gang That Couldn't Shoot Straight* (1971). He had paid his own way to Sicily to study the dialect.

Collaboration. Soon after they met in 1971, De Niro and Scorsese realized they had known each other on the streets of Little Italy fifteen years earlier. Scorsese asked De Niro to appear in his upcoming movie *Mean Streets* (1973), based on a script he had developed seven years earlier. It was to be the beginning of a long and fruitful artistic collaboration. Set in the macho world of the mafia in Little Italy, *Mean Streets* perfectly merged the alienated urban sensibilities of the director and his actors. De Niro played Johnny Boy, a hotheaded young punk, opposite Harvey Keitel as a small-time hood. The movie received rave reviews, established Scorsese as an important young director, and won De Niro the New York Film Critics Circle Award for best supporting actor. Also in 1973 De Niro captured the attention of critics as a dying baseball player in *Bang the Drum Slowly*. The following year he was cast as the young Vito Corleone in Francis Ford Coppola's eagerly awaited *The Godfather, Part II*. Speaking entirely in Sicilian, De Niro delivered a quiet but stunningly effective performance that meshed well with Marlon Brando's portrayal of the older don in the original movie. De Niro won an Oscar for best supporting actor and was established as a major movie presence. The same year Scorsese departed from his trademark urban violence to direct Ellen Burstyn in *Alice Doesn't Live Here Anymore*, a role for which she won an Oscar.

Siamese Twins. From 1976 through 1983 De Niro and Scorsese made four memorable, highly personal movies together. Scorsese later commented that he and De Niro became "as close as Siamese twins emotionally." They were able to communicate and to understand one another's ideas almost without words. *Taxi Driver* (1976) is a harrowing study of an alienated urban man who goes on a violent rampage hoping to rid the New York streets of the scum he believes are corrupting a twelve-year-old prostitute. De Niro's chilling, often repellent portrayal of Travis Bickle earned him an Oscar nomination, and the movie was nominated for best picture. In *New York, New York* (1977), a highly stylized homage to the 1940s and 1950s, De Niro played loutish saxophonist Jimmy Doyle. Much of the dialogue was improvised by Scorsese, De Niro, and costar Liza Minnelli. Many critics have judged Scorsese's next effort, *Raging Bull* (1980), the best American movie of the 1980s. De Niro played prizefighter Jake LaMotta, who bullies his way to the top only to wind up embittered, imprisoned, and alone. Scorsese's eerily realistic, almost documentary style found its perfect counterpart in De Niro's utterly believable slob; the actor gained

sixty pounds for the role and was rewarded with an Academy Award. Scorsese and the film were also nominated for Oscars. Two years of preparation on the part of both actor and director showed in *The King of Comedy* (1983), an almost painful study of the deranged fan of a television comedian. The movie was less successful with critics and the public than Scorsese and De Niro's other collaborations, but De Niro's portrayal of the slimy Rupert Pupkin was in many ways as terrifying as his Travis Bickle, and Scorsese's ability to create an aura of underlying violence helped make the movie a cult favorite.

Independents. In his work with Scorsese, De Niro gave many of his finest performances of the 1970s and 1980s, but there were other highlights. He earned another Oscar nomination for *The Deer Hunter* (1978), in which he portrayed a loner amid a group of small-town friends who are drafted to fight in Vietnam. By the 1980s De Niro's reputation as one of the top American movie actors allowed him to experiment. He appeared as priests in a murder story (*True Confessions*, 1981), a lush period piece (*The Mission*, 1986), and a comedy (*We're No Angels*, 1989). He was a small-time mobster in Sergio Leone's beautiful urban epic *Once Upon a Time in America* (1984), and he had a big impact in a ten-minute cameo as Al Capone in De Palma's *The Untouchables* (1987). *Midnight Run* (1988) was an enjoyable stab at action comedy. Scorsese's career was no less distinguished; his documentary about The Band, *The Last Waltz* (1978), was considered one of the best of its kind. During the 1980s Scorsese was the most respected movie director working in America, continuing to challenge audiences with unusual subjects. *After Hours* (1985) was a comic study of urban angst. In *The Color of Money* (1986), the sequel to *The Hustler* (1960), Scorsese directed Paul Newman to an Oscar as the aging pool shark Eddie Felson. *The Last Temptation of Christ* (1988) raised protests from fundamentalist groups who thought the movie blasphemous. Critics agreed that "Life Lessons," Scorsese's segment in the three-part movie *New York Stories* (1989), was the best one.

Maturity. *GoodFellas* (1990) was Scorsese and De Niro's first movie together since *The King Comedy*. The darkly comic story of mob informant Henry Hyde, *GoodFellas* was hailed by critics as Scorsese's best movie since *Raging Bull*. He was nominated for Oscars for his direction and his screenplay (with Nicholas Pileggi), and the movie was nominated for best picture. Joe Pesci won as Best Supporting Actor for his portrayal of a trigger-happy thug. After his own nominated performance as a mental patient in *Awakenings* (1990), De Niro starred as a deranged ex-con in Scorsese's chilling remake of *Cape Fear* (1991) and received another nomination. In 1993 De Niro directed his first movie, *A Bronx Tale*, and met with mixed notices. Scorsese received an equally divided response to his lush adaptation of Edith Wharton's *The Age of Innocence* (1993); some critics thought it among his best works, while others dismissed it as rambling and stuffy. Anticipation was high for De Niro and Scorsese's eighth collaboration, *Casino* (1995).

Sources:

Douglas Brode, *The Films of Robert De Niro* (Secaucus, N.J.: Carol Publishing Group, 1993);

Lee Lourdeaux, "Martin Scorsese in Little Italy and Greater Manhattan," in his *Italian and Irish Filmmakers in America* (Philadelphia: Temple University Press, 1990), pp. 217–266;

Martin Scorsese, *Scorsese on Scorsese* (London & Boston: Faber & Faber, 1990).

KEITH HARING

1958-1990

ARTIST

Influences. A lover of cartoons and science-fiction television shows, young Keith Haring responded to encouragement from his artistic father by creating his own vividly original stories and illustrations. He moved to New York in the late 1970s and studied abstract expressionist painting at the School of Visual Arts, where he befriended fellow artist Kenny Scharf. Frustrated with the insistence on artistic tradition at the school, Haring began to work on a different scale, often drawing on giant rolls of paper he spread on studio floors. By 1979 Haring had become captivated by subway graffiti. Its raw energy and sense of color and life pleased his growing pop sensibilities, and its visibility in a public space appealed to his desire to reach everyone with his art. Using chalk instead of the typical graffiti artist's spray paint, Haring began leaving drawings on the rectangles of black paper that covered unused subway advertising space.

Village Days. In 1979 Haring, Scharf, and artist friends such as Ann Magnuson began to organize group shows at Club 57, their new East Village hangout. Their "art parties" were a mixture of performance pieces, comic skits, videos, and visual art, including Haring's graffiti images. Having touched off a vogue for "club art," Scharf and Haring became the leading proponents of "fun art," a form that borrowed freely from the images of popular culture (especially cartoons). Haring arranged an "exhibit" of graffiti art at the Mudd Club in the East Village that turned into a free-for-all; he and hundreds of others covered the club and the surrounding area with colorful tags. In 1981 he began working for gallery owner Tony Shafrazi, who started showing the young artist's work. The following year Haring attracted the attention of critics and the press with a show at the Rotterdam Arts Council and with his contributions to a group exhibition at the trendsetting P.S. 1 Gallery on Long Island. In 1983 he participated in the Whitney Museum of American Art Biennial. Arrested for "criminal mischief" while decorating a subway space in June 1982, the undaunted

Haring continued the practice long after his gallery work began to sell — and sell it did!

Exposure. Haring's distinctive images, which often resembled thickly outlined hieroglyphics or cave drawings, became perhaps the most pervasive, influential, and popular art of the 1980s. While his gallery works sold to collectors for as much as $350,000, the images themselves seemed to belong to the world. While some of his paintings were being displayed at museums, Haring also created murals for schoolyards or on the sides of inner-city buildings. In 1982 one of his drawings was displayed for an entire month on the Spectacolor billboard over Times Square. In 1985 he created a giant canvas of Aztec-inspired figures for the dance floor at the New York club The Palladium and a giant painting to be auctioned off at the Live Aid concert in Philadelphia. He painted clothing for Madonna and Grace Jones, sets for a 1985 MTV concert, sets and props in 1984 for dance works by Bill T. Jones and Arnie Zane, and a curtain for a Roland Petit ballet presented in 1985. That year, in what became an international event, he spent three days creating an epic mural illustrating the Ten Commandments for a French museum. In 1986 three Haring works were placed in the sculpture garden at the United Nations headquarters in New York.

Images. Though the media helped to popularize Haring's "radiant" children, winged television sets, and alligator-headed dogs, Haring was his own best publicist. To reach the largest audience possible, he began marketing a line of products featuring his most popular images, and in 1986 he opened his own store, The Pop Shop, to sell his wristwatches, magnets, coffee cups, tote bags, coloring books, and T-shirts. Haring was as committed to charities and social causes as he was to his brilliant self-marketing, and his seemingly naive, childlike images often had a political subtext. *Radiant Child* carried a warning about the perils of the nuclear age, while Haring's television sets spoke of a technological society out of control. Other seemingly innocuous drawings included messages about social violence or indifference, racism, and approaching apocalypse. "I have strong feelings about the world," he said. "I want my art to make people think." In 1986, as a "humanistic gesture," he painted a giant mural on the Berlin Wall in the colors of the East German and West German flags. He called it "a political and subversive act — an attempt to psychologically destroy the wall by painting it." Haring also enjoyed creating art for children, including a set of permanent murals for the children's division of Mount Sinai Hospital in New York in 1986.

Last Years. Several of Haring's most political works dealt with the indifference of the U.S. government to the AIDS crisis. After learning that he himself had the AIDS virus, Haring took the same energetic, life-affirming attitude toward his illness that he had toward his art. He was open about his condition and met with groups of children to help educate them about AIDS. "The hardest thing is just knowing that there's so much more stuff to do," he said. "I'm so scared that one day I'll wake up and I won't be able to do it." Haring continued to work until just a few weeks before his death on 16 February 1990, painting murals, making giant sculptures for public spaces and playgrounds, and teaching art to disadvantaged youths. Major shows of his work were held in Vienna, London, Los Angeles, and Helsinki, at the Corcoran Gallery in Washington, D.C., and at the Spectrum Gallery in New York City. In 1988 the Museum of Modern Art featured works by Haring in an exhibit titled *Committed to Print*, and in June of that year Haring contributed two giant banners to a seventieth birthday tribute to Nelson Mandela at Wembley Stadium in London; seventy-two thousand people attended the event, and an estimated 500 million worldwide watched it on television — helping to fulfill Haring's desire to reach the largest possible audience. "You can't just stay in your studio and paint," he said. "That's not the most effective way to communicate."

Sources:
Germano Celant, ed., *Keith Haring* (Munich: Prestel, 1992);

Bruce K. Kurtz, ed., *Keith Haring, Andy Warhol, and Walt Disney* (Munich: Prestel / Phoenix: Phoenix Art Museum, 1992).

MICHAEL JACKSON

1958-

SINGER, DANCER, SONGWRITER

The Jackson Five. From birth, Michael Jackson and his five brothers and three sisters were surrounded by music. In the Jackson home in Gary, Indiana, their mother taught them folk songs and their father played the guitar. When the five oldest boys — Jackie, Tito, Jermaine, Marlon, and Michael — displayed a talent for singing, their father, Joe Jackson, encouraged them to form a group and turn professional. A series of local talent contests and their first professional gig, at a Gary nightclub in 1964, made it clear that five-year-old Michael was destined to be the group's leader. By the time he was seven, Michael Jackson was already doing the choreography for the quintet. The group began traveling, doing shows at venues such as the Apollo Theater in New York and the Regal Club in Chicago, where The Jackson Five opened for Motown acts such as The Temptations and The Miracles. Gladys Knight saw them perform at the Apollo and told Motown producer Berry Gordy about the group, and after Diana Ross performed with them at a "Soul Weekend" in 1968, she also recommended the Jacksons — especially young Michael — to Gordy. "He won me over the first time I saw him," Ross said later. "I saw so much of myself as a child in Michael. He was performing all the time. That's the way I was. He could be my son."

Child Star. Gordy signed the group and moved them to California. In 1970 The Jackson Five helped revitalize the faltering Motown label with a series of explosive hits: "I Want You Back," "ABC," "The Love You Save," and "I'll Be There" all went to number one. Michael sang lead on all the Jackson Five hits, and in concert and television performances he emerged as an electrifying dancer. His singing love songs and emulating James Brown's dance moves seemed incongruous for a boy his age — eleven — but it actually added to the appeal of the group. Michael was beginning to emerge as a superstar in his own right, just as his mentor Ross had done with The Supremes. His solo numbers "Got to Be There," "Rockin' Robin," and "Ben" were hits while the group continued to have hits as well with "Never Can Say Goodbye," "Mama's Pearl," and "Sugar Daddy." Soon after reaching the charts with "Dancing Machine" in 1974, the Jacksons decided to leave Motown for Epic Records. Amid continuing hits such as "Enjoy Yourself" and "Shake Your Body (Down to the Ground)," Michael Jackson costarred with his idol Diana Ross in the ill-fated movie version of *The Wiz* (1978). At twenty he felt he was outgrowing his role as a teen idol in his brothers' group. It was time to go solo.

Off the Wall. "He wasn't at all sure that he could make a name for himself on his own," producer Quincy Jones has commented. "And me, too. I had my doubts." Jackson had met Jones on the set of *The Wiz*, and the two had begun to share musical ideas. The result of their collaboration was Jackson's first "adult" solo album, *Off the Wall* (1979). Released during a recession in the music industry, the dance-oriented record sold 9 million copies worldwide and spawned four Top 10 singles, a record for a solo album. Jackson's flashy, eccentric vocal style (including gasps, hiccups, and squeals) helped win him a Grammy in 1980. Jones's dynamic, high-tech production job helped propel "Don't Stop Til You Get Enough" (written by Jackson) and "Rock With You" to number one. Other hits from the album included the title track, "She's Out of My Life," and "Working Day and Night." The album also features the first of several Jackson collaborations with Paul McCartney. After the success of *Off the Wall*, Jackson once again toured with his brothers, then contributed narration and vocals to the storybook album *E.T.: The Extra-Terrestrial* for his friend Steven Spielberg. He also wrote and produced the song "Muscles" for Diana Ross.

Thriller. It is impossible to overestimate the impact of Jackson's next album, *Thriller* (1982), on the music industry and the culture at large. The album became the biggest phenomenon in the history of recorded music. Produced by Jones and featuring a dazzling array of high-tech aural effects, *Thriller* sold more than 40 million copies, yielded a record seven Top 10 singles, won a record eight Grammys, and launched a nationwide hysteria not approached since the eras of Elvis Presley and The Beatles. Part of Michaelmania was attributable to Jackson's uncanny instinct for and mastery of the other biggest musical phenomenon of the 1980s: video. The music videos Jackson produced for *Thriller*, most notably "Billie Jean," "Beat It," and the title track, set the standards for the decade in video choreography and cinematic storytelling. The success of the album helped break down barriers on MTV and radio for other black artists, who began to experience surges in sales and airplay. Dubbed a "one-man rescue team for the record business," Jackson seemed to be everywhere in 1983 and 1984, singing guest vocals on a Rockwell song and a chart-topping duet with Paul McCartney ("Say Say Say"), giving a show-stopping performance at the Motown twenty-fifth anniversary celebration, and going a world tour with his brothers. The demand for Jackson paraphernalia, including dolls, clothing, and videocassettes, almost single-handedly redefined the pop music marketplace.

Aftermath. In 1985 Jackson and Lionel Richie wrote what became the fastest-selling single of the decade, USA for Africa's "We Are the World." He also contributed vocals to the song, one that only polished his superstar credentials. Yet as his sister Janet began to have success with her own recording career in 1986, fans and members of the music industry were beginning to grow restless waiting for Jackson's follow-up to *Thriller*. When it finally appeared in 1987, *Bad* seemed almost anticlimactic. The success of *Thriller* was impossible to live up to, much less top, but *Bad* did produce five consecutive number-one singles, a considerable accomplishment for any artist. The album also sold an impressive 20 million copies worldwide, and its videos — "The Man in the Mirror," "Dirty Diana," and "Bad" — proved popular. Yet neither the singles nor the videos seemed as fresh, innovative, or dynamic as their predecessors from *Thriller*. Jackson projects continued, most notably an appearance in the movie *Captain Eo*, which was shown at the Epcot Center at Disney World. In 1991 Jackson split with Jones and released *Dangerous*. The album yielded "Black or White," a hit with an interracial theme that became the fastest rising single in more than twenty years, but *Dangerous* sold far less briskly than *Bad*; Michaelmania had subsided.

Backlash. In the 1990s a seemingly inevitable Jackson backlash began to gather steam. Jackson's androgynous appearance, shyness, and man-child persona had long been part of his appeal, but his many eccentricities had become common knowledge thanks to a steady stream of tabloid-newspaper reports. As he grew older his tastes and behavior often seemed bizarre. Americans heard of his fondness for children as playmates, his private petting zoo, his private amusement park, his shrines to Elizabeth Taylor, his obsession with Diana Ross, his penchant for sleeping in a germ-free capsule, his lack of romantic or sexual relationships, his dream of playing Peter Pan, and the plastic surgery that lent his features an increasingly Caucasian look. In 1993 the father of a young boy who had spent time at Jackson's estate charged Jackson with sexually molesting his son. Though the charges were later dropped, Jackson paid the boy's parents $14 million in an out-of-court settlement, and his public image was damaged by the scandal. In a move that many viewed as an attempt to quell rumors and rejuvenate his career Jackson married Elvis Presley's daughter, Lisa Marie, in 1994 and moved on by releasing the album *HIStory* in 1995. The album did not meet sales expectations, but the song "You Are Not Alone" became the first single in pop-music history to enter the *Billboard* chart at number one.

Sources:

Paul Honeyford, *The Thrill of Michael Jackson* (New York: Quill, 1984);

Michael Jackson, *Moonwalk* (New York: Doubleday, 1988).

BARBARA KRUGER

1945-

ARTIST

Potential. Barbara Kruger later admitted that she left Syracuse University after one year because she "felt like a Martian." From a middle-class neighborhood in Newark, New Jersey, Kruger could not relate to her more privileged classmates. "I was the only woman on my dorm floor who hadn't had facial surgery and who knew words other than Pappagallo and Evan Picone." She transferred to Parsons School of Design in New York City and began studying photography under Diane Arbus and graphic design under Marvin Israel, art director of *Harper's Bazaar*. While Arbus served as Kruger's first female role model, the demanding Israel told the young artist she was "capable of anything" and encouraged her to put together a graphic-arts portfolio. In 1967 she presented her page designs to the head of the art department at Condé Nast Publications and was hired to work on the magazines *Seventeen* and *Mademoiselle*. By age twenty-two she was chief designer of *Mademoiselle*. During the next ten years she also worked as a teacher, a freelance photography editor, and a designer for book jackets.

Early Work. Kruger was alienated by the macho posturing of the male-dominated New York art scene, describing the art hangout Max's Kansas City, circa 1969, as "a zoo of retching and male hysteria." She turned toward feminist art forms, and during the early 1970s she created fabric wall pieces whose shapes, colors, and designs were "highly sexualized." By middecade she had started writing, an invigorating experience that made her view her earlier work as something akin to arts and crafts. "I felt like I was giving my mind Demerol," she said. Inspired by punk poet Patti Smith, Kruger began giving readings of her poetry in 1974. She also found a group of young artists, including Eric Fischl and David Salle, who treated female artists as equals. In 1977, with the help of an art grant, Kruger began a disquieting new series of works that combined photographs and cryptic bits of text. By 1979 she had found the form she would use for her work throughout the next decade: superimposing pieces of type directly on top of photographs she had appropriated from magazines. Kruger first attracted serious attention in a 1981 group show that also featured works by Keith Haring and fellow word artist Jenny Holzer.

Style. Like Holzer, whose *Truisms* were ominously worded mock-quotations such as "Money created taste" and "Murder has its sexual side," Kruger used words in a way that evoked both advertising and clichés. While Holzer used contradictory statements to create ambiguity, however, Kruger's visuals and word choices made her work confrontational and political. Her juxtaposition of text and image — such as "You are an experiment in terror" with a hand holding an exploding firecracker — was often jarring merely from a graphic standpoint, and the accusatory tone of her words added to the disturbing effect. Her choice of black-and-white photographs overlaid with bold-face red type and surrounded by brilliant red frames suggested the "power" look of old Russian or German political posters. Much of Kruger's best work has feminist messages. She emblazoned an image of a seated woman with giant needles embedded along the outline of her spine and legs with the declaration "We have received orders not to move." The work became a subtle commentary on society's attempts to control women. In 1983 a text piece she created for the Spectacolor billboard in Times Square wryly commented on masculine obsession with sex and war. It was discontinued after two weeks because "it had no Christmas spirit." Later in the decade she created a prochoice poster that declared "Your body is a battleground" over the divided image of a woman's face.

Commodity. Kruger's art proved popular and easy to sell in the graphic-hungry 1980s, and it was easily adapted to postcards, T-shirts, and posters. Many critics grumbled that her work made more sense as advertisement or poster art than as expensive gallery pieces. "These were objects," she responded. "I wasn't going to stick them on the wall with pushpins. That's what the frames were about: how to commodify them. It was the most effective packaging device." In 1987 her work appeared on canvas shopping bags that read "I shop therefore I am." Kruger freely admitted her interest in the commercial culture and enjoyed the feeling of creating a commodity. "Outside of the market there is nothing — not a piece of lint, a cardigan, a coffee table, a human being," she commented. In 1986 she began exploring the use of color photographs and silk screens, and in the late 1980s she began to create in-your-face billboards in large cities with messages such as "Surveillance is your busywork" and "Your money or your life." She also continued to write. The movie critic for *Artforum* since 1982, she became television critic for the magazine in 1987. Her work in the 1990s continued to be political, from AIDS posters to magazine covers for *Ms.* ("Women + Rage = Power") and *Newsweek.*. (For a 1992 story on family values she created a cover that asked, "Whose values?")

Sources:

Barbara Kruger, *Love for Sale,* with text by Kate Linker (New York: Abrams, 1990);

Kruger, *Remote Control: Power, Culture, and the World of Appearance* (Cambridge, Mass.: MIT Press, 1993).

MADONNA

1958-

SINGER, DANCER, SONGWRITER

Michigan Girl. Even as a youngster in the Detroit suburb of Bay City, Madonna Louise Veronica Ciccone was determined to stand out from the crowd. After the death of her mother when Madonna was six years old (an event that would haunt her and help shape her life and music), her father remarried. Disliking her new stepmother and tired of taking care of her five siblings, Madonna escaped into the world of dance, studying ballet with private tutor Christopher Flynn. A dance scholarship took Madonna to Ann Arbor, where she studied at the University of Michigan. After she spent two years there, Flynn encouraged her to try her luck in New York.

Club Girl. With just the clothes on her back and thirty-seven dollars in cash, Madonna arrived in Manhattan in summer 1978. She relied on work as an artist's model and on various boyfriends to make ends meet and won a tryout with the third company of the Alvin Ailey Dance Theater. Restless, Madonna soon quit to study with a choreographer who had once worked with Martha Graham's dance troupe. She also wanted to explore other interests, primarily music. A boyfriend taught her to play guitar and drums; she sang backup for a disco singer in Paris and also performed in several rock bands. A bandmate, former boyfriend Steve Bray, accompanied Madonna on her all-night partying in New York dance clubs and encouraged her to move their band away from rock and toward funk. Madonna agreed, cut a dance demo, and gave it to new boyfriend Mark Kamins, DJ at the nightclub Danceteria. The song was "Everybody." The crowd loved it, and Kamins used his industry connections to introduce Madonna to Sire Records.

Video Girl. Madonna's self-titled first album, a collection of percolating dance numbers, was released in summer 1983. Although the catchy "Holiday" hit the Top 20 late that year, Madonna attracted little press attention until her videos started receiving airplay on MTV. "Borderline" established her first "look": teased, bleached-blonde hair, heavy makeup, and layers of mismatched leggings, buckles, laces, straps, bracelets, ribbons, belts, bows, and junk jewelry. The follow-up, "Lucky Star," perfected her early style; in a complicated mixture of underwear, outerwear, and hardware (especially cruci-fixes), Madonna strutted, kicked, whirled, and wiggled her bare midriff. Madonna's sexy video come-ons and supremely catchy dance sound found their perfect marriage in "Like a Virgin" (1984), the title track from her second album. The song became her breakthrough hit, topping the charts for six weeks and opening the floodgates of wealth and fame Madonna had long dreamed of.

Material Girl. In 1985 Madonna seemed to be everywhere. There were radio hits ("Crazy for You," "Angel," "Dress You Up"), her first tour (the "Virgin" tour), magazine cover stories (*Time* offered opinions on "Why She's Hot"), a well-received movie role (*Desperately Seeking Susan*), and an appearance at the Live Aid concert. There were also hordes of Madonna imitators, teenage and pre-teen girls trying to emulate her sexy ragtag look. Yet many feminists were outraged at the singer's image, which they claimed set the women's movement back by decades. They pointed to her "Boy Toy" belt buckles and her "Material Girl" video, in which she impersonated 1950s icon Marilyn Monroe, swooned over rich men, and crooned about "cold hard cash." Madonna responded to such criticism by claiming that the song was clearly tongue-in-cheek and that, as a woman utterly in control of her image, material, sexuality, and career, she was an excellent role model for young women. In the same year she became embroiled in another controversy: that summer nude photographs of Madonna, taken in her "starving artist" days, were published in *Penthouse* and *Playboy*. With typical aplomb, Madonna shrugged off the scandal and married actor Sean Penn in a ceremony that became a virtual media circus.

Multimedia Girl. After blockbuster success on the pop charts (sixteen consecutive Top 5 hits) and in music videos, Madonna wanted an acting career as well, but her attempts were less than promising. *Shanghai Surprise* (1986), with Penn, met with terrible reviews (she played a Christian missionary), and *Who's That Girl* (1987) and *Bloodhounds of Broadway* (1988) also flopped. In 1988 she received mixed notices for her Broadway debut in David Mamet's *Speed-the-Plow*. At the same time her music and video career soared, causing plenty of controversy along the way. "Papa Don't Preach" caused a stir with its seemingly antiabortion, prolife lyrics, while the "Open Your Heart" video raised eyebrows for Madonna's appearance as an erotic dancer who kisses a small boy. Madonna's $5 million deal with Pepsi collapsed after her "Like a Prayer" video showed her dancing amid burning crosses, kissing a black Jesus, and finding stigmata on her hands, causing a firestorm of protest from Catholics. (She kept the money.) Feminists were angered by the "Express Yourself" video, in which Madonna submitted to bondage. Her other video hits in the 1980s included "True Blue," "Live to Tell," "La Isla Bonita," "Causing a Commotion," "Oh Father," and "Cherish."

Media Girl. In the 1980s Madonna set the standard for manipulating the media and marketing her image to the public. She continued to do so, brilliantly, well into the 1990s. She understood how to keep the world's attention; her seemingly annual, always unpredictable changes in look and style were a model of trend setting. In 1989 she changed direction, divorcing Sean Penn, splitting with her hit-making collaborators Steve Bray and Patrick Leonard, and making the movie *Dick Tracy* (1990) with new boyfriend Warren Beatty. Their relationship and Madonna's nonstop need for attention were exposed, rather uneasily, in Madonna's "documentary" *Truth or Dare* (1991), filmed on her 1990 "Blond Ambition" tour. Both movies and the tour were successful, as was her appearance in the movie *A League of Their Own* (1992). Pop and video hits continued ("Vogue" was a standout), and so did the controversy: the video for "Justify My Love" (1990) was banned from MTV for its explicit sexuality. In the "kinder, gentler" 1990s, the public seemed to be tiring of Madonna's in-your-face self-promotion. *Sex,* a book of photographs illustrating Madonna's sex fantasies, caused a Madonna backlash in 1992 and 1993. Her *Erotica* album failed to generate the expected hits; her movies *Body of Evidence* and *Dangerous Game* bombed; and her use of foul language on David Letterman's talk show backfired. Ever the chameleon, however, Madonna rebounded in 1995 with her biggest hit in years ("Take a Bow") and a series of provocative videos. Though "Bedtime Story" became her first-ever single not to make the Top 40, Madonna's endless drive and ambition finally won the singer her dream role: the lead in the long-delayed film version of *Evita*.

Sources:

Christopher Andersen, *Madonna: Unauthorized* (New York: Simon & Schuster, 1991);

Adam Sexton, *Desperately Seeking Madonna: In Search of the Meaning of the World's Most Famous Woman* (New York: Delta, 1993).

DAVID MAMET

1947-

PLAYWRIGHT, SCREENWRITER, DIRECTOR

Ambition. David Mamet later attributed his uncanny ear for naturalistic dialogue to several influences during his youth. His father, a lawyer, was something of a semanticist, and years of piano lessons gave Mamet a feeling for the rhythms and musicality of speech. His childhood, spent in a Jewish neighborhood on the south side of Chicago, was relatively uneventful until high school, when Mamet became interested in drama while working as a volunteer at a small local theater. A job at the well-known Second City comedy club in Chicago reinforced that desire, and Mamet rejected his father's suggestion that he become a lawyer. He wrote his first play, *Camel,* while at Goddard

College in Vermont (B.A., 1969). During his junior year Mamet studied acting in New York, quitting when he realized that he had no real acting talent. In 1970 Mamet bluffed his way into a drama-teaching job in Vermont by claiming he had written a new play. After getting the job, he quickly wrote *Lakeboat* and staged it as a student production. Mamet continued to write short plays after he began teaching at his alma mater in 1971.

Reputation. Mamet began to circulate his plays. A one-act, *Duck Variations,* was produced at Goddard in 1972, and in 1974 the Organic Theater of Chicago produced *Sexual Perversity in Chicago,* which won the coveted Joseph Jefferson Award for best new play. He followed it with *Squirrels,* which he produced with his own theater company, the St. Nicholas Players. By this time, despite some pans from local critics, Mamet was beginning to develop a reputation as well as a distinctive voice as a playwright. *American Buffalo,* a character study of three small-time hoods, broke box-office records in a run at the Goodman Theater in late 1975. After its Off-Broadway premiere a few months later, Mamet won an Obie Award as best new playwright of the year. In 1976 *Sexual Perversity* and *Duck Variations* were also produced Off-Broadway; both became hits, and *Time* listed both plays as among the ten best of the year. Critics were already noting Mamet's trademarks: a flair for staccato, overlapping dialogue that was both violent and poetic; and a fascination with mind games, con artists, moral corruptibility, and machismo. After a Broadway run of 150 performances, *American Buffalo* won the 1977 New York Drama Critics Circle Award.

Stage and Screen. Established as an important playwright, Mamet continued to develop plays in Chicago with the St. Nicholas Players and then move them to Off-Broadway and Broadway stages. Reviewers were enthusiastic about *A Life in the Theater* (1977), a series of scenes about actors preparing for roles, and *The Water Engine* (1978), which was performed on Broadway as a radio drama. In 1978 Mamet moved to New York with his wife, actress Lindsay Crouse, and soon found himself in demand as a screenwriter. His first effort, a modern revision of *The Postman Always Rings Twice* (1981), reached a limited audience, but *The Verdict* (1982) earned Mamet an Oscar nomination. His next play, *Glengarry Glen Ross* (1983), became his most acclaimed effort and won him both a New York Drama Critics Circle Award and a Pulitzer Prize. Centering on a group of corrupt salesmen all trying to outcon each other, the play is vintage Mamet. In 1983 Al Pacino also revived *American Buffalo* on Broadway with great success. *Sexual Perversity* was filmed as *About Last Night . . .* in 1986. In 1987, after writing the screenplay for Brian De Palma's *The Untouchables,* Mamet directed his first movie, *House of Games,* a critical success and another Mamet classic. In it Crouse plays a psychiatrist embroiled in a murder that turns out to be a high-stakes con game.

Cynicism. Mamet's experience as a screenwriter directly informed his next Broadway success, *Speed-the-Plow* (1988). "The movies," he commented, "are a momentary and beautiful aberration of a technological society in the last stages of decay." *Speed-the-Plow* focused on two corrupt Hollywood producers, one of whom is almost conned into choosing artistic integrity over commerce. As in *Glengarry Glen Ross* and *House of Games,* Mamet's characters' cynicism and corruption whenever there's money to be made became an apt comment on the worship of success and power in the 1980s. Although Madonna's performance as a secretary generated most of the media hype, Ron Silver won a Tony for his performance as Charlie Fox. Mamet's second movie as a director, *Things Change* (1988), was well received; Joe Mantegna (a favorite Mamet actor along with Crouse and Silver) starred as the perpetrator of a mob scam. Mamet continued to write screenplays, most notably *Homicide* (1991) and *Hoffa* (1992). *Glengarry Glen Ross,* with Al Pacino, was filmed in 1992; *American Buffalo,* with Dustin Hoffman, was released in 1995. *Oleanna* (1992), which Mamet later filmed, became one of his most controversial works. The play presents a charge of sexual harassment as an escalating game between accuser and accused.

Sources:

Dennis Carroll, *David Mamet* (New York: St. Martin's Press, 1987);

Anne Dean, *David Mamet: Language as Dramatic Act* (Rutherford, N.J.: Fairleigh Dickinson University Press, 1990);

Leslie Kane, *David Mamet: A Casebook* (New York & London: Garland, 1992).

STEVEN SPIELBERG

1947-

MOVIE DIRECTOR AND PRODUCER

Boy Wonder. Growing up in the suburbs of Phoenix, Steven Spielberg took part in all the typical activities of boyhood, but he was also making movies. He used an 8-mm camera to record family events, such as birthdays and vacations, and also to film dramas (especially horror stories) starring his three younger sisters. Sheltered by his parents, Spielberg was not allowed to see many movies beyond Disney films, but the first theatrical feature he ever saw was Cecil B. DeMille's circus extravaganza *The Greatest Show on Earth.* In high school Spielberg shot dozens of short movies. His first full-length attempt was *Firelight,* a science-fiction movie focusing on a group of scientists puzzled by mysterious lights in the sky that turn out to be unfriendly aliens. By this time all Spielberg wanted was to make movies, but his poor grades kept him out of California's major film schools. He settled for California

State College and tried to learn more about filmmaking by sneaking onto movie sets at major studios. While in school Spielberg shot *Amblin'*, a twenty-two-minute short that won awards at the Venice and Atlanta film festivals. Sidney Sheinberg, head of Universal Pictures' television division, was sufficiently impressed to sign Spielberg to a seven-year contract.

Television Movies. Spielberg's official beginning as a commercial director was an auspicious one: directing Joan Crawford in the pilot for the television series *Night Gallery*. Episodes of series such as *Marcus Welby, M.D.*, *Columbo*, and *The Name of the Game* followed, each shot with Spielberg's brand of perfectionism and care. In 1971 he was assigned to direct a routine movie-of-the-week thriller with Dennis Weaver. The result was *Duel*, a masterpiece of low-budget suspense that many critics considered the finest television movie ever made. *Duel* has almost no dialogue and relies on skillful cutting. Spielberg's instinctive film craft made the movie a theatrical hit in Europe, where it won several awards. He went on to direct several other television movies, including the occult thriller *Something Evil* with Sandy Dennis. Meanwhile, he was sifting through the dozens of feature film offers that had come his way after the success of *Duel*. Not liking any of them, Spielberg instead developed *The Sugarland Express* (1974), a caper comedy starring Goldie Hawn. In this movie, which earned high praise from reviewers, the young director showed a sure touch with action scenes. One critic noted that in the car-chase sequences "the cars are as eloquent as the characters."

Blockbusters. The producers of *The Sugarland Express*, Richard Zanuck and David Brown, ignored its poor box-office performance and decided that their next project needed the Spielberg touch. That movie was *Jaws*, based on Peter Benchley's best-seller about a giant shark terrorizing a resort community. Spielberg was almost fired when increasing technical and labor problems doubled the budget and the shooting schedule, but the additional cost was recouped spectacularly. Released in summer 1975, *Jaws* grossed $60 million in its first month, was nominated for an Oscar for best picture, and went on to become the highest-grossing Hollywood film to date. The unprecedented success of *Jaws* enabled Spielberg to make whatever movie he desired; he chose *Close Encounters of the Third Kind* (1977), a textbook example of Spielberg's childlike, Disneyesque sense of wonder and magic and also of the sort of expensive, high-tech special effects for which he would become famous. Exploring a series of mystical encounters between humans and extraterrestrial visitors, *Close Encounters* earned Spielberg an Oscar nomination for best director and made an impressive $70 million at the box office. Its success that year was somewhat overshadowed by the staggering impact of George Lucas's *Star Wars*, another science-fiction epic that had already surpassed *Jaws* as the top-grossing movie in history. Spielberg followed up with *1941* (1979), a box-office disappointment that nonetheless established the director's love of the movies and images of World War II.

Megadirector. The success of Spielberg and his friend Lucas in the 1970s set the stage for Hollywood's obsession with blockbuster filmmaking throughout the 1980s. Bigger box office meant bigger budgets, bigger special effects, bigger thrills, and bigger media hype. Spielberg, ever the showman, was happy to oblige the studios' and the public's rediscovered thirst for spectacle. With Lucas producing, he directed his thrill-a-minute homage to 1930s movie serials, *Raiders of the Lost Ark* (1981). Starring Harrison Ford, the movie immediately shot onto the list of Top 10 box-office successes ($242 million) and earned both Lucas and Spielberg Oscar nominations. Spielberg's follow-up was an even bigger blockbuster, a Disney-like fantasy that would become one of the best-loved movies of all time: *E.T.: The Extra-Terrestrial* (1982). It also became the top-grossing American movie in history, a position it still retained in 1995, after thirteen years of big-budget challengers. The sweet fable of a lonely boy and his alien friend, *E.T.* earned $367 million in the United States and an Oscar nomination for best picture; Spielberg was once again nominated for best director. By this time Spielberg had formed his own production company; he developed *Amazing Stories* for television and was producer or executive producer on some of the biggest movies of the 1980s, including *Poltergeist, Gremlins, The Goonies, Back to the Future*, and *Who Framed Roger Rabbit?* He also directed the *Raiders of the Lost Ark* sequel *Indiana Jones and the Temple of Doom* (1984). "I want people to love my movies," Spielberg said. They did, but some critics were beginning to grumble that his movies were all style and no substance.

New Directions. In 1985 Spielberg surprised many critics and fans by directing *The Color Purple*, an adaptation of Alice Walker's Pulitzer Prize–winning novel about the struggles of an African American woman in the rural South. The reactions to his first truly adult movie were mixed; some found it beautiful and moving, while others carped that Spielberg oversimplified the subject and covered it with Hollywood gloss. *The Color Purple* won eleven Oscar nominations, and Spielberg won the Director's Guild prize. He was passed over by the Academy for a best director nomination, leading some to conclude that Hollywood admired his moneymaking more than his serious filmmaking ambitions. His next movie, *Empire of the Sun* (1987), received similarly mixed reviews. Yet he could afford to take risks; runaway hits such as *E.T.* had made him the film industry's highest-paid producer and director, earning more than $1 million per project plus large percentages of the box-office receipts. Though *Always* (1989) flopped, *Indiana Jones and the Last Crusade* (1989) was another blockbuster smash, earning more than $150 million. In 1986 the Academy of Motion Picture Arts and Sciences gave Spielberg the Irving Thalberg Award for his achievements as a producer. In his acceptance speech Spielberg encouraged blockbuster-crazed Hollywood to return to the written word — to good screenplays.

Acclaim. The most important director-producer of the 1980s faltered in his first project of the 1990s. His multimillion-dollar movie *Hook* (1991) was a critical and box-office disaster, but in 1993 Spielberg rebounded with two of the most notable movies in Hollywood history. *Jurassic Park,* about dinosaurs re-created by modern science and running amok, is a special-effects thriller in the classic Spielberg form. It also proved to be one of his biggest blockbusters, outgrossing *E.T.* in worldwide receipts and placing second behind *E.T.* in American box-office totals. Later that year Spielberg directed *Schindler's List* and stunned the world. Even many of his harshest critics were moved by the true-story drama of Oskar Schindler, a German businessman and opportunist who ended up craftily saving the lives of more than a thousand Jews during the Holocaust. For the first time Spielberg had made a movie that was both highly personal (addressing his own Jewish roots) and mature in content. He also earned praise for his gritty, documentary-style visual approach, a radical departure from his earlier movies. Amazed that he could deliver two such different (and successful) motion pictures in a single year, the Academy voted *Schindler's List* best picture and at last honored Spielberg as best director.

Source:
Donald R. Mott and Cheryl McAllster Saunders, *Steven Spielberg* (Boston: Twayne, 1986).

BRUCE SPRINGSTEEN

1949-

SINGER, SONGWRITER, GUITARIST

Jersey. From the moment he stood in his New Jersey bedroom with his first guitar in hand, thirteen-year-old Bruce Springsteen was obsessed with rock 'n' roll. Born in Long Branch, New Jersey, Springsteen grew up in a lower-class section of Freehold, near the fading beach resort of Asbury Park. While his father struggled to support his family with a series of blue-collar jobs and his mother worked as a legal secretary to help the family finances, Springsteen grew up feeling insecure and alienated, chafing at the restrictions of school and constantly at odds with his father, who did not approve of his son's musical ambitions. By listening endlessly to his favorite rock and roll songs from the 1950s, Springsteen taught himself to play the guitar and began playing with bands — first the Rogues in 1963 and by 1965 the Castiles — when he was in high school. In 1967 he met fellow rocker Steve Van Zandt, who would join his band in 1970. When his

family moved to California in 1969, Springsteen stayed behind, living along the beaches and boardwalks of Asbury Park and playing in local bands. During gigs at venues such as the Stone Pony, he met John Lyons, who played briefly with Springsteen's band and later recorded as Southside Johnny. At shows in Greenwich Village in New York City in 1972, Springsteen attracted attention for his straight-ahead rock-and-roll sound and the unusual storytelling style of Springsteen's original songs. Mike Appel thought the young musician showed promise and became Springsteen's business manager. That same year Appel finagled an audition with John Hammond, the Columbia Records executive credited with discovering Bob Dylan. Hammond later said that he reacted to Springsteen's talent "with a force I've felt maybe three times in my life." Springsteen was signed to a multialbum recording contract with Columbia.

Early Records. Springsteen's first two albums benefited from his exuberant energy and songwriting ability; they suffered from misguided production and promotion. Columbia executives, believing they had the new Bob Dylan on their hands, sold him like a folk singer. Both albums sold poorly despite some excellent material. *Greetings From Asbury Park* (1973) established Springsteen's penchant for playful but wordy epics such as "Blinded by the Light," later covered by Manfred Mann, and "Spirit in the Night," which introduced a wacky assortment of characters — Killer Joe, Wild Billy, and Crazy Janey — typical of early Springsteen songs. The follow-up album, *The Wild, the Innocent, and the E Street Shuffle* (1973) featured several classic tracks — including "Rosalita" and "Sandy" — that would become staples of his live shows with the E Street Band as well as another collection of romantic, restless urban misfits who often made his songs seem like the aural equivalent of Edward Hopper's paintings. *Rolling Stone* named *The Wild, the Innocent, and the E Street Shuffle* one of the best albums of the year. Also in 1973 rock critic Jon Landau saw Springsteen's live show for the first time and wrote, "I have seen rock and roll's future and its name is Bruce Springsteen."

Hype. Columbia executives picked up Landau's comment and began trying to promote Springsteen as "the future of rock and roll." Pressured from all sides to succeed with his third album, Springsteen was determined to make the greatest rock album ever recorded. With the assistance of Landau and "Miami" Steve Van Zandt, he was able to achieve a Phil Spector–influenced "wall of sound" on *Born to Run,* which was released in fall 1975. The album was a watershed; songs such as "Thunder Road," "Backstreets," and "Jungleland" seethed with pent-up energy and urban drama and seemed to encompass the entire history of rock 'n' roll in a single operatic arc. The media seized the moment, and Springsteen became the first entertainer ever featured on the covers of both *Time* and *Newsweek* in the same week. Album sales were encouraging enough to save Springsteen's contract at Columbia, and the singer asked Landau to produce his next album. Appel, feeling he was being phased out of Springsteen's career, rejected this plan, leading to a legal battle that kept Springsteen from recording for two years. In the meanwhile he toured extensively, gaining a following for his marathon live shows, which often lasted up to four hours. Springsteen and Appel eventually settled out of court, and Landau became his manager and producer.

Darkness. The legal battle with Appel seemed to have aged and even embittered Springsteen. His eventual follow-up to *Born to Run, Darkness on the Edge of Town* (1978), revealed a more mature, less exuberant spirit. Themes of loss, betrayal, heartbreak, and loneliness were common in songs such as "Badlands," "Candy's Room," and "Prove It All Night" and on Springsteen's two subsequent releases, *The River* (1980) and *Nebraska* (1982). The three albums form a trilogy that explores the darker side of the "runaway American dream." Springsteen's tone was still often romantic and even simplistic. Like Beat novelist Jack Kerouac he glorified the street, the night, the elusive girl, the car on the open road. His new albums also had an increasingly rural feeling, seeming to leave behind the wilder urban experiences of his youth. Although *The River*, a double album, produced his first Top 10 hit ("Hungry Heart") and many of its more upbeat numbers (such as "Cadillac Ranch") received heavy FM airplay, it remained too moody and gritty for mainstream success. *Nebraska*, an acoustic album Springsteen recorded at home with just guitar, harmonica, and vocals, spawned an unsuccessful single ("Open All Night") and his first video, "Atlantic City," in which Springsteen did not appear. Judged by many critics to be his finest work, the stark *Nebraska* sold poorly. Other artists struck gold with his material, however. The Pointer Sisters recorded a hit version of Springsteen's "Fire"; Patti Smith had a Top 20 hit with his "Because the Night"; Greg Kihn made the charts with the sunny "Rendezvous"; Gary "U.S." Bonds enjoyed a comeback with Springsteen's ditty "This Little Girl"; and Springsteen's old friend Southside Johnny increased his own album sales by covering Springsteen's songs.

Born in the USA. Despite Springsteen's popularity with critics, his cult following as a live performer, and his reputation as an artist of political integrity (he participated in the No Nukes concert in 1979), no one was prepared for the blockbuster success of *Born in the USA* (1984). The album spawned seven Top 10 hits and sold 15 million copies; the accompanying world tour took Springsteen to stadium-size venues usually reserved for superstar acts such as The Rolling Stones. Shows typically sold out in minutes. Springsteen once again made the cover of *Newsweek*, and for the first time (he had long resisted the trend) he agreed to appear in videos, two of which were filmed by Brian De Palma. "Dancing in the Dark" became his biggest hit to date; others included the exuberant "Glory Days" and the haunting "I'm on Fire." Somehow Springsteen had tapped the zeitgeist; his newly pumped physique and heterosexual, regular guy image proved popular in the age of Ronald Reagan and Sylvester Stallone's action hero *Rambo*. Reagan and many of Springsteen's own fans mistook songs such as "Born in the USA" and the bleak "My Hometown" for their own brand of conservative patriotism. In reality Springsteen was a political independent deeply committed to writing about the plight of downtrodden Americans who faced problems such as farm foreclosures and factory shutdowns. No matter; Springsteen became a superstar and a millionaire. In 1985 Springsteen participated in the all-star recordings of "We Are the World" and "Sun City" and married fashion model and actress Julianne Phillips. His long-anticipated live-performance album set went multi-platinum in 1986.

Follow-up. Subsequent recordings and performances for political causes such as Amnesty International often had the effect of making the 1984–1985 Springsteen juggernaut seem like a dream. The haunting *Tunnel of Love* (1987) and its singles ("Brilliant Disguise," "One Step Up") examined the frailty of relationships, foreshadowing the breakup of Springsteen's own marriage. His affair with newest band member Patti Scialfa became tabloid fodder in 1988. After his divorce the following year, Springsteen married Scialfa in 1991 and started a family. The most soul-searching loner of rock 'n' roll seemed to be settling down. He even dissolved the E Street Band, which included popular performers such as saxophonist Clarence Clemons and drummer Max Weinberg. (Van Zandt had left to pursue a solo career as Little Steven in 1983.) When his two 1992 releases, *Human Touch* and *Lucky Town*, failed to generate the anticipated sales, critics and industry wags speculated that Springsteen's romantic, straight-ahead American sound was out of step in the era of heavy metal, grunge rock, rap, and world music. Indeed, on these two albums Springsteen attempted to confront the dilemma of being simultaneously a blue-collar, working-class hero and a multimillionaire superstar as well as the problems facing the man who has both a family and a rock band. Springsteen released a greatest hits package in 1995.

Sources:
Charles R. Cross and the editors of *Backstreets Magazine, Backstreets: Springsteen, The Man and His Music* (New York: Harmony Books, 1989);

Mark Eliot, with Mike Appel, *Down Thunder Road: The Making of Bruce Springsteen* (New York: Simon & Schuster, 1992);

Dave Marsh, *Born to Run: The Bruce Springsteen Story* (Garden City, N.Y.: Dolphin/Doubleday, 1979);

Marsh, *Glory Days: Bruce Springsteen in the 1980s* (New York: Pantheon, 1987).

MERYL STREEP

1949-

ACTRESS

Early Years. Born Mary Louise Streep in New Jersey, Meryl Streep often felt unpopular and out of step with many of the other children in her neighborhood, especially when she began singing at age twelve and spent four subsequent years in rigorous voice training in New York. During her teen years Streep was a cheerleader, acted in high-school plays, and became homecoming queen, but she was obsessed with improving her self-described "ugly" looks. Competition for and with boys disappeared when Streep entered the all-female Vassar College (A.B., 1971) in 1967: "I remember feeling, 'I can have a thought. I can do anything, because everything is allowed.' Oh, it was a great relief." Streep's reading of some lines from *A Streetcar Named Desire* in a drama class led her instructor, Clint Atkinson, to cast her in the title role of *Miss Julie* at Vassar. Struck by her instinctive acting talent, Atkinson directed Streep the following year in her Off-Broadway debut. She remained reluctant to commit herself to acting, however, because of its "absurdity" as a career choice.

Stage Success. After a semester at Dartmouth College and work with a summer stock company in 1971, Streep entered the prestigious Yale Drama School on a three-year scholarship. By this time she had realized that acting was her one true passion. At Yale she excelled in a variety of classical roles, from Strindberg to Shakespeare. By the time she earned an M.F.A. in 1975, Streep had acquired a sterling reputation as an actress and had generated an unusual amount of "buzz." Joseph Papp of the New York Shakespeare Festival gave her a small part in one of his 1975 productions, and Streep followed that with two roles with the Phoenix Theater; one of them, Tennessee Williams's *27 Wagons Full of Cotton,* earned her nominations for 1976 Drama Desk and Tony Awards. Streep then turned in strong, much-lauded performances in a Broadway staging of *The Cherry Orchard* and two more of Papp's Shakespeare productions. During one of these, *Measure for Measure,* Streep entered a serious relationship with one of her costars, actor John Cazale.

Early Movies. Early in 1977 Streep made her television debut in *The Deadliest Season,* playing the troubled wife of a hockey star. Later that year she attracted attention for a brief but memorable scene as a flighty socialite opposite Jane Fonda in *Julia.* Streep won an Emmy for best actress for her role in *Holocaust* (1978), a harrowing nine-hour television miniseries about a Jewish family torn apart by Hitler's Third Reich. She received her first Oscar nomination for her performance as a sweet, vulnerable, small-town girl in *The Deer Hunter* (1978), which

also starred Cazale. In September 1978, six months after Cazale's death from cancer, Streep married sculptor Don Gummer. Although she continued to act in stage productions (*The Taming of the Shrew* for Papp and a musical adaptation of *Alice in Wonderland* were highlights), by 1978 Streep was increasingly in demand for movies. In 1979 three excellent supporting roles — in *Manhattan, The Seduction of Joe Tynan,* and *Kramer vs. Kramer* — won Streep honors from the National Board of Review; the New York Film Critics recognized her for both *The Seduction of Joe Tynan* and *Kramer vs. Kramer,* and her role in *Kramer vs. Kramer* also won her first Academy Award. At thirty Streep had arrived at the summit of her generation of actresses. *New Republic* critic Stanley Kauffmann expressed a typical opinion of her abilities: "I have been waiting for some years now . . . for Streep to make a false move on stage or screen. I'm still waiting."

Acclaim. Throughout the 1980s Streep had her pick of the best women's roles in Hollywood, which earned her almost annual Oscar nominations. Audiences and critics were often awed by her chameleon-like acting talents, but others began to carp about Streep's "accent mongering," pointing to her eerie ability to take on a different look, nationality, or dialect for almost every role. With the release of *The French Lieutenant's Woman* (1981), in which she played a mysterious British free spirit, a *Time* cover story called "Magic Meryl" proclaimed her the best actress of her generation. She also received her first Oscar nomination for best actress. She won the following year for *Sophie's Choice* (1982), in which she played a tragic and haunted survivor of a Nazi concentration camp. For the role Streep lost weight, shaved her head, and mastered Polish and German. She portrayed an American southerner, the real-life nuclear-energy martyr Karen Silkwood, in *Silkwood* (1983) and was again nominated for an Oscar for best actress. After pairing with Robert De Niro in the innocuous romance *Falling in Love* (1984), Streep tackled back-to back accents — British for *Plenty* and Danish for *Out of Africa* (both 1985). She received her fourth best actress nomination for *Out of Africa,* in which she played coffee-plantation owner and writer Isak Dinesen. Reviews were mixed for *Heartburn* (1986), Streep's first movie with Jack Nicholson; but when she played a mentally disturbed vagabond opposite Nicholson in *Ironweed* (1987), she earned high praise and another Oscar nomination. In *A Cry in the Dark* (1988) she was Lindy Chamberlain, an Australian woman falsely accused of murdering her baby, mastering another accent and earning another Oscar nomination. By this time, despite Streep's acknowledged excellence, audiences and critics were beginning to tire of her rather studied technique and her choice of downbeat roles.

Later Roles. Because of her prestigious reputation, Streep was able to take long breaks to raise a family with Gummer. In 1989 she spoke out publicly against the use of pesticides in the agricultural industry. She also became openly critical of Hollywood's exploitation of women and its refusal to pay female stars the megamillions that male stars typically received. Her movie roles seemed to take a less serious direction, starting with the 1989 comedy *She-Devil*, in which Streep costarred with television star Roseanne. Reviews were mixed. Most critics were kinder to *Postcards From the Edge* (1990), for which Streep, playing a neurotic, chemically dependent actress, received her seventh Oscar nomination for best actress in ten years, a record for a single decade. She next appeared in the lighthearted Albert Brooks movie *Defending Your Life* (1991) and in the high-tech special-effects comedy *Death Becomes Her* (1992). By then fans and critics who had bemoaned her seriousness and constant accent changes only a few years before were wondering what had happened to the "real" Meryl Streep. They continued to wonder: *The House of the Spirits* (1994), despite its all-star cast, was a disaster, and *The River Wild* (1994), despite decent reviews and box office attendance, attempted to present Streep as an action hero. She returned to her classic 1980s form as a lonely farm wife in *The Bridges of Madison County* (1995), complete with a dowdy look and Italian accent. Critics and audiences cheered, and Oscar talk was once again in the air.

Source:
Diana Maychick, *Meryl Streep: The Reluctant Superstar* (New York: St. Martin's Press, 1984).

AUGUST WILSON

1945-

PLAYWRIGHT

Pittsburgh. Growing up in "The Hill," an African American slum community in Pittsburgh, August Wilson was a voracious reader who was fascinated with words — with their sound, form, and meaning. Wilson's biological father, a white man, deserted the family when Wilson was young, and he was raised by his black mother and stepfather. When his family moved to the mostly white community of Hazelwood, they became targets of racial animosity. White classmates at a Roman Catholic academy harassed Wilson for being black, and a teacher accused him of cheating on a term paper about Napoleon. By the time Wilson quit school at age fifteen, he was educating himself, soaking up the works of black writers such as Langston Hughes, Ralph Ellison, and Richard Wright. In 1965 he bought his first typewriter and started writing poetry, recording the rhythms of black speech he had picked up in his neighborhood. Some of Wilson's early poetry, which was also influenced by Dylan Thomas, was published in small black literary journals during the early 1970s. Much of this work was political and militant, reflecting the racism Wilson had suffered growing up and his increasing involvement in the Black Nationalist movement.

Dramatist. During the 1960s Wilson founded Black Horizon, a black-activist theater company, with teacher and playwright Rob Penny. Among their productions were the confrontational works of LeRoi Jones. His early plays tended to be propaganda, written to "politicize the community and raise consciousness." Gradually, though, his drama began to focus on internal rather than external struggles. Moving to Saint Paul in 1978, Wilson supported himself by writing short theatrical pieces for exhibits at the Science Museum of Minnesota. Meanwhile, encouraged by his friend Claude Purdy, Wilson continued to write plays. *Jitney*, produced in Pittsburgh in 1982, established his feeling for the lyrical, metaphoric speech of black characters and reflected his belief that "black Americans have the most dramatic story of all mankind to tell." A follow-up effort, *Fullerton Street*, continued this exploration. By that time Wilson was envisioning a series of ten plays about black life, each set in a different decade of the twentieth century and each focusing on a different issue.

Attention. In 1982 Wilson submitted *Ma Rainey's Black Bottom* to the National Playwrights Conference. Lloyd Richards, artistic director of the conference and dean of the Yale School of Drama, gave *Ma Rainey's Black Bottom* a staged reading at the Eugene O'Neill Theater Center in Connecticut and then produced the play at Yale in 1984. The reaction was tremendous, leading to a staging in Philadelphia and then a Broadway production, directed by Richards, in fall 1984. Set in Harlem during the 1920s and inspired by Wilson's interest in the life of blues singer Gertrude "Ma" Rainey, the play ran for 275 performances and earned lavish praise from reviewers. Frank Rich of *The New York Times* called it "a searing inside account of what white racism does to its victims" and heaped it with superlatives: "funny, salty, carnal, lyrical." Other critics agreed, noting Wilson's sure touch with characterization and dialogue. Both a celebration of blues music and an indictment of racism in the music business, *Ma Rainey's Black Bottom* went on to win several Tony nominations and the New York Drama Critics Circle Award for Best Drama.

Fences. Established as one of the most promising new playwrights in America, Wilson scored again with *Fences*. After a staged reading at the National Playwrights Conference in 1983, *Fences* was refined and revised through productions at the Yale Repertory Theater, the Goodman Theater in Chicago, and theaters in Seattle and San Francisco. *Fences* opened on Broadway early in 1987 and by that summer had won the New York Drama Critics Circle Award, the Tony Award, and the Pulitzer Prize for best drama. In the Broadway production James Earl Jones played an aging garbageman embittered by a lost opportunity for true American success; a former baseball player in the Negro Leagues, he was too old to play in the major leagues when the color bar finally fell. *Fences*, set in the 1950s, is considered by many to be Wilson's finest work. The play won Tonys for Jones and director Richards and also set a Broadway record for a nonmusical production, grossing $11 million in its first year. Wilson sold the movie rights for $500,000.

Follow-up. When Wilson's next play, *Joe Turner's Come and Gone,* opened on Broadway in spring 1988, *The New York Times* reviewer declared him "the theater's most astonishing writing discovery in this decade." Like its predecessors, *Joe Turner's Come and Gone* was developed at Yale in collaboration with Richards, and, like them, it also deals with racial prejudice, missed opportunities, and self-actualization. An ensemble piece set in a boarding-house in 1911, this play won Wilson his third consecutive New York Drama Critics Circle Award, an unprecedented achievement in commercial theater. His follow-up garnered even more acclaim. Produced at Yale in fall 1987, *The Piano Lesson* focused on a Depression-era family forced to choose between an old life in the rural South and a new one in the urban North. *The Piano Lesson* opened on Broadway to critical raves early in 1990; Wilson went on to win yet another Drama Critics Circle Award and another Pulitzer Prize. When the next play in the cycle, *Two Trains Running,* also won the Drama Critics Circle Award in 1992, Wilson was five for five: every one of his Broadway productions had taken the award.

Accessibility. Wilson has attributed the success of his plays to their universality. Although they center on black characters and racial issues, audiences of all races can identify with Wilson's themes: family, life choices, history, regret, hope, and religious faith. In short Wilson studies and celebrates humanity in all its varied forms. Critics lauded the originality of his theatrical voice, but Wilson replied that "style ain't nothing but keeping the same idea from beginning to end." Even so, his strong feeling for language and blues music made his work all the more appealing to a wide audience. "I see the blues as a book of literature and it influences everything I do," Wilson has said. "Blacks' cultural response to the world is contained in blues." Or, as he had Ma Rainey express it, the blues is "life's way of talking. You sing 'cause that's a way of understanding life."

Source:
Samuel G. Freedman, "A Voice from the Streets," *New York Times Magazine,* 15 March 1987, pp. 36, 38–40, 49, 70.

PEOPLE IN THE NEWS

On 12 May 1987 actor-director **Woody Allen** testified before a Senate subcommittee to protest the computerized colorization of classic black-and-white movies.

On 23 May 1983 bandleader **Count Basie** and tenor saxophonist **Sonny Rollins** were both awarded the Jazz Master Awards by the National Endowment for the Arts.

In 1989 movie actress **Kim Basinger** bought the near-bankrupt town of Braselton, Georgia, for $20 million.

On 25–28 August 1988 the Vienna Philharmonic and Boston Symphony were among the participants in a celebration of **Leonard Bernstein**'s seventieth birthday and the forty-fifth anniversary of his conducting debut with the New York Philharmonic.

On 23 January 1986 **Chuck Berry, James Brown, Fats Domino, Ray Charles, Little Richard,** and **Jerry Lee Lewis** were among the first inductees into the Rock and Roll Hall of Fame.

On 7 February more than fifteen hundred friends and fans of composer **Eubie Blake** honored him on his one hundredth birthday at a gala in New York City. Blake, hospitalized with pneumonia, was unable to attend and died on 12 February.

In 1988 **Sonny Bono** was elected mayor of Palm Springs, California.

Yul Brynner gave his final Broadway performance in *The King and I* on 30 June 1985; he died several months later.

On 22 November 1988 writer **Art Buchwald** and producer **Alain Bernheim** filed a $5 million lawsuit against Paramount Pictures, claiming that the movie *Coming to America* was based on a screen treatment they sold to the studio in 1983.

On 26 March 1981 **Carol Burnett** won $1.6 million in a libel suit against the *National Enquirer* after it printed a story claiming that Burnett, a teetotaler, was drunk in a Washington, D.C., restaurant.

On 19 June 1989, after an eleven-year absence from performing, pianist **Van Cliburn** made a successful comeback with concerts in Dallas and Philadelphia.

In November 1980 **Aaron Copland** conducted his *Appalachian Spring* during a fourteen-hour celebration of his eightieth birthday.

On 23 January 1981 **Francis Ford Coppola** presented a restored version of director **Abel Gance**'s four-hour, seventeen-reel silent movie epic *Napoleon* at Radio City Music Hall, with Gance, age ninety-one, in attendance.

In 1981 **Rodney Dangerfield** won a Grammy for his comedy album *No Respect*.

In 1989 artist **Willem de Kooning** and architect **I. M. Pei** were the American winners of the new $100,000 Japanese Imperial Prize for lifetime achievement in the arts.

On 8 November 1983 **Brian De Palma** succeeded in convincing the Motion Picture Association of America to change its X rating of his movie *Scarface* to an R.

Poet **James Dickey** and novelist **William Styron** were elected to the American Academy of Arts and Letters on 4 December 1987.

In April 1986 actor **Clint Eastwood** was elected mayor of Carmel, California.

On 14 June 1989 **Zsa Zsa Gabor** was arrested for slapping a police officer and for driving without a valid license and with an open liquor container in her car. On 29 June she was convicted on all charges and sentenced to 72 hours in jail and 120 hours of community service; she was also fined $3,000 and ordered by the court to reveal her true age.

Freelance violinist **Helen Hagnes** was found murdered at the Metropolitan Opera House in New York during a performance by the Berlin Ballet on 24 July 1980; she had disappeared from the orchestra during intermission.

On 12 December 1980 American oil magnate **Armand Hammer** bought a Leonardo da Vinci notebook of sketches and writings for $5.28 million.

On 24 February 1985 **George Harrison** and **Yoko Ono** filed an $8.6 million lawsuit against **Paul McCartney,** claiming that he had received a disproportionate share of royalties from Beatles recordings.

On 20 April 1986 pianist **Vladimir Horowitz,** a naturalized U.S. citizen, returned to his native Russia for the first time in sixty-one years to give two televised concerts in Moscow.

In 1984, while filming a Pepsi commercial for which he earned $1.5 million, **Michael Jackson** was injured when his hair caught fire.

In 1983 Bolshoi Ballet dancers **Leonid and Valentina Kozlova** joined the New York City Ballet as soloists.

On 29 May 1987 director **John Landis** and four associates were found innocent on manslaughter charges stemming from an accident in which actor **Vic Morrow** and two children were killed by the blades of a crashing helicopter on the set of Landis's segment of *Twilight Zone — The Movie* in 1982.

Sherry Lansing, a thirty-five-year-old former model, was named president of 20th Century-Fox on 1 January 1980, becoming the first woman to head production at a major movie studio.

In 1985 **James Levine** was named artistic director of the New York Metropolitan Opera.

On 12 May 1989 actor **Rob Lowe** was sued for using his "celebrity status" to lure a sixteen-year-old girl into appearing with him in a sexually explicit videotape.

On 2 August 1983 **Norman Mailer** signed a $4 million contract with Random House for the hardcover and paperback rights to his next four books.

Ballet star **Natalia Makarova** suffered a broken shoulder and lacerated scalp on 18 December 1982 when she was struck by a falling piece of scenery during a performance of *On Your Toes* at the Kennedy Center in Washington, D.C.

In 1984 country singer **Barbara Mandrell** survived a near-fatal car accident.

In 1984 conductor **Zubin Mehta** renewed his contract with the New York Philharmonic, giving him the longest tenure of any musical director in the history of that organization. He announced his retirement on 2 November 1988.

In 1983 movie actor **Paul Newman** started marketing his own brand of spaghetti sauce.

Unpublished manuscripts by the late American composers **Cole Porter, George Gershwin,** and **Richard Rodgers** were discovered in a Warner Bros. warehouse on 19 November 1982.

Leontyne Price gave her farewell performance with the Metropolitan Opera on 3 January 1985, in Giuseppe Verdi's *Aida*.

On 10 June 1980 actor-comedian **Richard Pryor** was badly burned while freebasing cocaine.

On 15 March 1981 President **Ronald Reagan** and **Nancy Reagan** attended a benefit performance of the Joffrey Ballet that featured their son **Ronald Reagan Jr.** dancing with the Joffrey II dancers.

On 11 April 1982, after pro-Israeli protests and anti-Palestinian threats, the Boston Pops Orchestra canceled performances that were to be narrated by **Vanessa Redgrave,** an outspoken supporter of the Palestinian cause.

On 5 November 1989 **Jerome Robbins** resigned as codirector of the New York City Ballet.

Julian Schnabel's 1979 painting *Notre Dame* was auctioned for $93,000 at Sotheby's in New York City on 20 May 1983.

On 5 June 1984 **Peter Sellars** was named artistic director and chief executive officer for plays produced jointly by the Kennedy Center for the Performing Arts and the American National Theater in Washington, D.C.

In 1989 **Beverly Sills** retired as director of the New York City Opera.

On 19 September 1981, at a Central Park concert in New York attended by four hundred thousand fans, **Paul Simon** and **Art Garfunkel** performed together for the first time in more than a decade.

On 26 October 1982 singer **Kate Smith** received the Medal of Freedom from President Ronald Reagan for inspiring the nation over the years with her rendition of Irving Berlin's song "God Bless America."

Elizabeth Taylor made her Broadway debut in Lillian Hellman's play *The Little Foxes* on 7 May 1981. The following September she was legally separated from Sen. John Warner, her seventh husband. They were divorced on 5 November 1982.

In 1988 choreographer **Twyla Tharp** retired from dancing, disbanded her dance troupe, and joined the American Ballet Theater as artistic associate.

On 14 November 1981, to honor **Virgil Thomson** on his eighty-fifth birthday, his opera *Four Saints in Three Acts* was revived at Carnegie Hall in New York City, the first full-length production in more than a decade.

Scott Thorson filed a $113 million "palimony" suit against pianist **Liberace** on 14 October 1982.

On 24 January 1988 *The New York Review of Books* published a statement signed by **Alice Walker, Maya Angelou,** and forty-six other African American writers and critics protesting **Toni Morrison**'s failure to win a National Book Award for her novel *Beloved*.

In 1981 **Andy Warhol** designed a series of advertisements for fashion designer Halston.

In 1989 Christie's auction house in New York sold ninety-four works from the collection of movie director **Billy Wilder.**

Stevie Wonder was awarded a special citation by the UN General Assembly Special Committee Against Apartheid on 13 May 1985.

On 5 August 1986 **Andrew Wyeth** sold 240 paintings and drawings to the owner of a publishing firm, who lent them to the National Gallery of Art in Washington, D.C., for display. This previously unknown series of nudes and other portraits of a single woman, dubbed the "Helga" paintings by the media, caused a stir in the art world.

AWARDS

PULITZER PRIZES

1980

Fiction: *The Executioner's Song*, by **Norman Mailer**

Drama: *Talley's Folly*, by **Lanford Wilson**

Poetry: *Selected Poems*, by **Donald Rodney Justice**

Music: *In Memory of a Summer Day*, by **David Del Tredici**

1981

Fiction: *A Confederacy of Dunces*, by **John Kennedy Toole**

Drama: *Crimes of the Heart*, by **Beth Henley**

Poetry: *The Morning of the Poem*, by **James Schuyler**

Music: no award given

1982

Fiction: *Rabbit Is Rich*, by **John Updike**

Drama: *A Soldier's Play*, by **Charles Fuller**

Poetry: *The Collected Poems*, by **Sylvia Plath**

Music: *Concerto for Orchestra*, by **Roger Sessions**

1983

Fiction: *The Color Purple*, by **Alice Walker**

Drama: *'Night, Mother*, by **Marsha Norman**

Poetry: *Selected Poems*, by **Galway Kinnell**

Music: *Three Movements for Orchestra*, by **Ellen T. Zwilich**

1984

Fiction: *Ironweed*, by **William Kennedy**

Drama: *Glengarry Glen Ross*, by **David Mamet**

Poetry: *American Primitive*, by **Mary Oliver**

Music: *Canti del Sole*, by **Bernard Rands**

1985

Fiction: *Foreign Affairs*, by **Alison Lurie**

Drama: *Sunday in the Park with George*, by **Stephen Sondheim** and **James Lapine**

Poetry: *Yin*, by **Carolyn Kizer**

Music: *Symphony RiverRun*, by **Stephen Albert**

1986

Fiction: *Lonesome Dove*, by **Larry McMurtry**

Drama: no award given

Poetry: *The Flying Change*, by **Henry Taylor**

Music: *Wind Quintet IV*, by **George Perle**

1987

Fiction: *A Summons to Memphis*, by **Peter Taylor**

Drama: *Fences*, by **August Wilson**

Poetry: *Thomas and Beulah*, by **Rita Dove**

Music: *The Flight into Egypt*, by **John Harbison**

1988

Fiction: *Beloved*, by **Toni Morrison**

Drama: *Driving Miss Daisy*, by **Alfred Uhry**

Poetry: *Partial Accounts: New and Selected Poems*, by **William Meredith**

Music: *12 New Etudes for Piano*, by **William Bolcom**

1989

Fiction: *Breathing Lessons*, by **Anne Tyler**

Drama: *The Heidi Chronicles*, by **Wendy Wasserstein**

Poetry: *New and Collected Poems*, by **Richard Wilbur**

Music: *Whispers Out of Time*, by **Roger Reynolds**

ANTOINETTE PERRY AWARDS (TONYS)

1980

Play: *Children of a Lesser God*, **Mark Medoff**

Actor, Dramatic Star: **John Rubinstein**, *Children of a Lesser God*

Actress, Dramatic Star: **Phyllis Frelich**, *Children of a Lesser God*

Musical: *Evita*, **Andrew Lloyd Webber** and **Tim Rice**

Actor, Musical Star: **Jim Dale**, *Barnum*

Actress, Musical Star: **Patti LuPone**, *Evita*

1981

Play: *Amadeus*, **Peter Shaffer**

Actor, Dramatic Star: **Ian McKellan**, *Amadeus*

Actress, Dramatic Star: **Jane Lapotaire**, *Piaf*

Musical: *42nd Street*

Actor, Musical Star: **Kevin Kline**, *The Pirates of Penzance*

Actress, Musical Star: **Lauren Bacall**, *Woman of the Year*

1982

Play: *The Life and Adventures of Nicholas Nickleby*, **David Edgar**

Actor, Dramatic Star: **Roger Rees**, *The Life and Adventures of Nicholas Nickleby*

Actress, Dramatic Star: **Zoe Caldwell**, *Medea*

Musical: *Nine*, **Maury Yeston** and **Arthur Kopit**

Actor, Musical Star: **Adam Harney**, *Dreamgirls*

Actress, Musical Star: **Jennifer Holliday**, *Dreamgirls*

1983

Play: *Torch Song Trilogy*, **Harvey Fierstein**

Actor, Dramatic Star: **Harvey Fierstein**, *Torch Song Trilogy*

Actress, Dramatic Star: **Jessica Tandy**, *Foxfire*

Musical: *Cats*, **T. S. Eliot** and **Andrew Lloyd Webber**

Actor, Musical Star: **Tommy Tune**, *My One and Only*

Actress, Musical Star: **Natalia Makarova**, *On Your Toes*

1984

Play: *The Real Thing*, **Tom Stoppard**

Actor, Dramatic Star: **Jeremy Irons**, *The Real Thing*

Actress, Dramatic Star: **Glenn Close**, *The Real Thing*

Musical: *La Cage aux Folles*, **Harvey Fierstein** and **Jerry Herman**

Actor, Musical Star: **George Hearn**, *La Cage aux Folles*

Actress, Musical Star: **Chita Rivera**, *The Rink*

1985

Play: *Biloxi Blues*, **Neil Simon**

Actor, Dramatic Star: **Derek Jacobi,** *Much Ado About Nothing*

Actress, Dramatic Star: **Stockard Channing,** *The Egg*

Musical: *Big River,* **Roger Miller** and **William Hauptman**

Actor, Musical Star: no award given

Actress, Musical Star: no award given

1986

Play: *I'm Not Rappaport,* **Herb Gardner**

Actor, Dramatic Star: **Judd Hirsch,** *I'm Not Rappaport*

Actress, Dramatic Star: **Lily Tomlin,** *The Search for Signs of Intelligent Life in the Universe*

Musical: *The Mystery of Edwin Drood,* **Rupert Holmes**

Actor, Musical Star: **George Rose,** *The Mystery of Edwin Drood*

Actress, Musical Star: **Bernadette Peters,** *Song and Dance*

1987

Play: *Fences,* **August Wilson**

Actor, Dramatic Star: **James Earl Jones,** *Fences*

Actress, Dramatic Star: **Linda Lavin,** *Broadway Bound*

Musical: *Les Miserables,* **Claude-Michel Schonberg, Alain Boublil,** and **Herbert Kretzmer**

Actor, Musical Star: **Robert Lindsey,** *Me and My Girl*

Actress, Musical Star: **Maryann Plunkett,** *Me and My Girl*

1988

Play: *M Butterfly,* **David Henry Hwang**

Actor, Dramatic Star: **Ron Silver,** *Speed-the-Plow*

Actress, Dramatic Star: **Joan Allen,** *Burn This*

Musical: *The Phantom of the Opera,* **Andrew Lloyd Webber** and **Charles Hart**

Actor, Musical Star: **Michael Crawford,** *The Phantom of the Opera*

Actress, Musical Star: **Joanna Gleason,** *Into the Woods*

1989

Play: *The Heidi Chronicles,* **Wendy Wasserstein**

Actor, Dramatic Star: **Philip Bosco,** *Lend Me a Tenor*

Actress, Dramatic Star: **Pauline Collins,** *Shirley Valentine*

Musical: *Jerome Robbins' Broadway*

Actor, Musical Star: **Jason Alexander,** *Jerome Robbins' Broadway*

Actress, Musical Star: **Ruth Brown,** *Black and Blue*

ACADEMY OF MOTION PICTURE ARTS AND SCIENCES AWARDS (THE OSCARS)

1980

Actor: **Robert De Niro,** *Raging Bull*

Actress: **Sissy Spacek,** *Coal Miner's Daughter*

Picture: *Ordinary People,* Paramount

1981

Actor: **Henry Fonda,** *On Golden Pond*

Actress: **Katharine Hepburn,** *On Golden Pond*

Picture: *Chariots of Fire,* Warner Bros.

1982

Actor: **Ben Kingsley,** *Gandhi*

Actress: **Meryl Streep,** *Sophie's Choice*

Picture: *Gandhi,* Columbia

1983

Actor: **Robert Duvall,** *Tender Mercies*

Actress: **Shirley MacLaine,** *Terms of Endearment*

Picture: *Terms of Endearment,* Paramount

1984

Actor: **F. Murray Abraham,** *Amadeus*

Actress: **Sally Field,** *Places in the Heart*

Picture: *Amadeus,* Orion

1985

Actor: **William Hurt,** *Kiss of the Spider Woman*

Actress: **Geraldine Page,** *The Trip to Bountiful*

Picture: *Out of Africa,* Universal

1986

Actor: **Paul Newman,** *The Color of Money*

Actress: **Marlee Matlin,** *Children of a Lesser God*

Picture: *Platoon,* Orion

1987

Actor: **Michael Douglas,** *Wall Street*

Actress: **Cher,** *Moonstruck*

Picture: *The Last Emperor,* Columbia

1988

Actor: **Dustin Hoffman,** *Rain Man*

Actress: **Jodie Foster,** *The Accused*
Picture: *Rain Man,* United Artists

Actress: **Jessica Tandy,** *Driving Miss Daisy*
Picture: *Driving Miss Daisy,* Warner Bros.

1989

Actor: **Daniel Day-Lewis,** *My Left Foot*

DEATHS

Ansel Adams, 82, photographer known for his sharply detailed landscapes, which helped to establish photography as an art form, 22 April 1984.

Kurt Adler, 82, conductor and opera director, 9 February 1988.

Alvin Ailey, 58, modern-dance choreographer, founder, and director of an integrated dance company, 1 December 1989.

Jack Albertson, 71, stage, movie, and television actor, who won a Tony and an Oscar for his roles in the stage (1964) and movie (1968) versions of *The Subject Was Roses,* 25 November 1981.

Ivan Albright, 86, painter, 18 November 1983.

Robert Aldrich, 65, director of movie melodramas such as *Kiss Me Deadly* (1955), *Whatever Happened to Baby Jane?* (1962), and *The Dirty Dozen* (1967), 5 December 1983.

Nelson Algren, 72, author of novels of the urban underground — including *The Man With the Golden Arm* (1949) and *Walk on the Wild Side* (1956), 9 May 1981.

Harold Arlen, 81, composer of music for popular songs such as "Get Happy," "Somewhere Over the Rainbow," "It's Only a Paper Moon," and "Stormy Weather," 23 April 1986.

Hal Ashby, 59, director whose movies include *Harold and Maude* (1972), *The Last Detail* (1973), *Shampoo* (1975), *Bound for Glory* (1976), *Coming Home* (1978), and *Being There* (1979), 27 December 1988.

Fred Astaire, 88, legendary dancer, actor, singer, and choreographer who personified onscreen elegance in the 1930s in movies such as *The Gay Divorcee* (1934) and *Top Hat* (1935), 22 June 1987.

Mary Astor, 81, movie actress well-known for her role in *The Maltese Falcon* (1941) and winner of an Oscar for

best supporting actress for *The Great Lie* (1941), 25 September 1987.

Brooks Atkinson, 89, theater critic for *The New York Times* (1925–1942, 1946–1960), who reviewed more than three thousand opening-night performances, and winner of a Pulitzer Prize for his series of reports on life in the Soviet Union (1947), 13 January 1984.

Chet Baker, 58, jazz trumpeter and vocalist, 14 May 1988.

George Balanchine, 79, Russian-born cofounder of the New York City Ballet (1934) and one of the most influential choreographers of the twentieth century, 30 April 1983.

James Baldwin, 63, African American novelist, playwright, and essayist who influenced the course of the American civil rights movement with works such as *Go Tell It on the Mountain* (1953), *The Amen Corner* (1955), *Notes of a Native Son* (1955), and *Another Country* (1962), 1 December 1987.

Lucille Ball, 77, legendary comedienne, star of *I Love Lucy* (1951–1961), one of the most popular American television shows of all time, 26 April 1989.

Samuel Barber, 70, Pulitzer Prize–winning composer, 23 January 1981.

Alfred Barr, 79, art historian who served as the first director of the Museum of Modern Art in New York, 15 August 1981.

Donald Barthelme, 58, novelist and short-story writer, 23 July 1989.

Count Basie, 77, bandleader who revolutionized jazz with his rhythmic keyboard style, 26 April 1984.

Anne Baxter, 62, Oscar-winning screen actress, whose movie credits include *The Magnificent Ambersons* (1942), *The Razor's Edge* (1946), *All About Eve* (1950), and *The Ten Commandments* (1956), 12 December 1985.

John Belushi, 32, comedian who starred on the television program *Saturday Night Live* and in movies such as *National Lampoon's Animal House* (1978) and *The Blues Brothers* (1980), from an overdose of cocaine and heroin, 5 March 1982.

Nathaniel Benchley, 66, novelist and author of children's books, 14 December 1981.

Michael Bennett, 44, Tony- and Pulitzer Prize–winning director, dancer, and choreographer best known for his creation of *A Chorus Line* (1975), 2 July 1987.

Robert Russell Bennett, 87, composer, arranger, and conductor, who wrote the scores for some three hundred movies and Broadway shows, 11 December 1980.

Ingrid Bergman, 67, Oscar-winning movie actress best known for her roles in *Casablanca* (1942), *For Whom the Bell Tolls* (1943), *Gaslight* (1944), and *Anastasia* (1956), 29 August 1982.

Irving Berlin, 101, prolific composer of popular songs, including "God Bless America," "Cheek to Cheek," "Always," and "Alexander's Ragtime Band"; movie scores, including *Top Hat* (1935) and *Holiday Inn* (1942; for which he wrote the songs "Easter Parade" and "White Christmas"); and stage musicals such as *Annie Get Your Gun* (1936) and *Call Me Madam* (1950), 22 September 1989.

Valerie Bettis, 62, dancer and choreographer, 26 September 1982.

Eubie Blake, 100, popular songwriter and pianist, a pioneer of ragtime music, 12 February 1983.

Mel Blanc, 81, who supplied the voices of Bugs Bunny, Daffy Duck, Porky Pig, Elmer Fudd, and Woody Woodpecker in Warner Bros. cartoons, 10 July 1989.

Ray Bolger, 83, dancer and actor best known as the Scarecrow in *The Wizard of Oz* (1939), 15 January 1987.

Ilya Bolotowsky, 74, a Soviet-born painter and sculptor, who founded the American Abstract Artists group, 21 November 1981.

Richard Brautigan, 49, novelist known for his *Trout Fishing in America* (1967), 25 October 1984.

Bricktop, 89, American expatriate nightclub singer and hostess whose Paris club was a gathering place for café society in the 1920s and 1930s, 31 January 1984.

Louise Brooks, 78, silent movie actress known for her portrayal of Lulu in *Pandora's Box* (1928), 8 August 1985.

Clarence Brown, 97, director whose movies include *Anna Christie* (1930) and *Anna Karenina* (1935), 17 August 1987.

Shirley Brown, 88, poet and critic active in the Harlem Renaissance of the 1920s and 1930s, 13 January 1989.

Yul Brynner, 65, Tony- and Oscar-winning actor best known for playing the king of Siam in stage (1951, 1985) and movie (1956) versions of *The King and I,* 10 October 1985.

Abe Burrows, 74, Pulitzer Prize–winning director, producer, comedian, and writer, 17 May 1985.

Richard Burton, 58, Welsh-born stage and movie actor who starred in the Broadway musical *Camelot* (1960) and whose movies include *Becket* (1963) and *Who's Afraid of Virginia Woolf?* (1966), Elizabeth Taylor's fifth and sixth husband, 5 August 1984.

James Cagney, 81, Oscar-winning movie actor and dancer known for his cocky personality and energy in movies such as *The Public Enemy* (1931), *Footlight Parade* (1933), *Angels with Dirty Faces* (1938), *Yankee Doodle Dandy* (1942), and *White Heat* (1949), 30 March 1986.

Erskine Caldwell, 83, novelist, author of *Tobacco Road* (1932) and *God's Little Acre* (1933), 11 April 1987.

Truman Capote, 59, writer best-known for the novella *Breakfast at Tiffany's* (1958) and for his pioneering "nonfiction novel," *In Cold Blood* (1966), 26 August 1984.

Hoagy Carmichael, 82, composer of fifty hit songs, including "Georgia on My Mind" and "Stardust," 27 December 1981.

Karen Carpenter, 32, singer in the popular 1970s pop duo The Carpenters, 2 February 1983.

John Carradine, 82, character actor in movies such as *Stagecoach* (1936) and *The Grapes of Wrath* (1941), 27 November 1988.

Raymond Carver, 50, poet and short-story writer, 2 August 1988.

Vera Caspary, 83, novelist, playwright, and screenwriter whose movie credits include *Laura* (1944), 6 June 1987.

John Cassavetes, 59, actor, director, and screenwriter who wrote and directed *Faces* (1968), *Husbands* (1970), *A Woman Under the Influence* (1974), *Gloria* (1980), and *Love Streams* (1983), 3 February 1989.

Gower Champion, 59, choreographer, dancer, and director who died hours before the premiere of the Broadway revival of *42nd Street,* which he was directing, 25 August 1980.

Mary Chase, 74, playwright who won a Pulitzer Prize for *Harvey* (1944), 23 October 1981.

Paddy Chayefsky, 58, award-winning playwright and screenwriter who excelled in social commentary and satire; his plays include *Middle of the Night* (1956) and *The Tenth Man* (1959), and his screen credits include

Marty (1955), *The Hospital* (1971), and *Network* (1976), 1 August 1981.

John Cheever, 70, Pulitzer Prize–winning short-story writer and novelist, author of *The Whapshot Chronicle* (1957) and *Bullet Park* (1969), 18 June 1982.

Ina Claire, 92, stage comedienne who specialized in sophisticated wit, 21 February 1985.

Harold Clurman, 78, director, critic, and founder of the Group Theater, which introduced the Stanislavsky "method" to the American stage, 9 September 1980.

James Coco, 57, comic actor known for roles in Neil Simon and Terence McNally comedies, 25 February 1987.

Marc Connelly, 90, Pulitzer Prize–winning playwright, author, producer, and director who collaborated with George Kaufman on popular comedies of the 1920s, 21 December 1980.

Jackie Coogan, 69, child star of silent movies such as *The Kid* (1921), 1 March 1984.

Buster Crabbe, 75, former athlete who played Buck Rogers and Flash Gordon in 1930s movie serials, 23 April 1983.

Broderick Crawford, 74, Oscar-winning actor remembered for his roles in *All the King's Men* (1949) and *Born Yesterday* (1950), 26 April 1986.

Cheryl Crawford, 84, theatrical producer and cofounder of The Actors' Studio, 7 October 1986.

Scatman Crothers, 76, character actor in movies such as *The Shining* (1980), 22 November 1986.

Bosley Crowther, 75, movie critic for *The New York Times* (1940–1967), 7 March 1981.

George Cukor, 83, director known for his skill with actors; his movies include *Dinner at Eight* (1933), *Little Women* (1933), *David Copperfield* (1935), *Camille* (1937), *Holiday* (1938), *The Women* (1939), *The Philadelphia Story* (1940), *Gaslight* (1944), *Adam's Rib* (1949), *Born Yesterday* (1950), and *My Fair Lady* (1964), 24 January 1983.

Frederic Dannay, 76, co-author of Ellery Queen detective novels, 3 September 1982.

Bette Davis, 81, movie actress known for the spirited, independent characters she played in movies such as *Of Human Bondage* (1934), *Jezebel* (1938), *Dark Victory* (1939), *The Letter* (1940), *The Little Foxes* (1941), *Now Voyager* (1942), *All About Eve* (1950), and *What ever Happened to Baby Jane?* (1962), 6 October 1989.

I. A. L. Diamond, 67, screenwriter known for his collaborations with Billy Wilder on movies such as *Some Like It Hot* (1959), *The Apartment* (1960), and *One Two Three* (1961), 21 April 1988.

Howard Dietz, 86, who collaborated with Arthur Schwartz on Broadway musicals such as *Stars in Your Eyes* (1939), *Park Avenue* (1946), *A Tree Grows in Brooklyn* (1951), and *That's Entertainment* (1972), 30 July 1983.

Divine (Harris Glenn Milstead), 42, drag star of John Waters movies such as *Polyester* (1981) and *Hairspray* (1988), 7 March 1988.

Melvyn Douglas, 80, actor who won Oscars for his roles in the movies *Hud* (1963) and *Being There* (1979) and a Tony for his acting in the 1960 Broadway production of *The Best Man* (1960), 4 August 1981.

Morton Downey, 82, singer and composer of the 1930s, 25 October 1985.

Jimmy Durante, 86, vaudeville comedian and radio, television, and nightclub performer remembered for his outsized nose and raspy voice, 29 January 1980.

Florence Eldridge, 86, stage and movie actress, 1 August 1988.

Roy Eldridge, 78, jazz trumpeter, bandleader, conductor, and singer, 26 February 1989.

Faye Emerson, 65, movie and television actress, 9 March 1983.

Walter Farley, 73, author of *The Black Stallion* (1941) and other popular horse novels, 17 October 1989.

Henry Fonda, 77, actor who played men of integrity in more than one hundred stage and screen roles, including *Young Mr. Lincoln* (1939), *The Grapes of Wrath* (1940), *The Lady Eve* (1941), *The Ox-Bow Incident* (1943), *Mister Roberts* (1955), *12 Angry Men* (1957), and *On Golden Pond* (1981), 12 August 1982.

Lynn Fontanne, 85, who with Alfred Lunt made up one of the legendary husband-wife acting teams in theater history, 30 July 1983.

Bob Fosse, 60, dancer, choreographer, and director of Broadway shows such as *How to Succeed in Business without Really Trying* (1962), *Sweet Charity* (1966), and *Pippin* (1972) and movies such as *Sweet Charity* (1969), *Cabaret* (1972), *Lenny* (1974), and *All That Jazz* (1979), 23 September 1987.

Carol Fox, 55, cofounder and manager of the Lyric Opera of Chicago, 21 July 1981.

Ketti Frings, 61, screenwriter and playwright, winner of a Pulitzer Prize and a New York Drama Critics Circle Award for his stage adaptation of *Look Homeward Angel* (1957), 11 February 1981.

Red Garland, 60, jazz pianist of the 1950s, accompanist to Charlie Parker and Miles Davis, 23 April 1984.

Marvin Gaye, singer, shot and killed by his father, 1 April 1984.

Ira Gershwin, 86, Pulitzer Prize–winning lyricist, who wrote dozens of classic songs with his brother George, including "The Man I Love," "Strike Up the Band," and "I Got Rhythm," 17 August 1983.

Jackie Gleason, 71, legendary television actor-comedian who made occasional movies, including *The Hustler* (1961), 24 June 87.

Benny Goodman, 87, orchestra leader and clarinetist, legendary "King of Swing" in the big band era of the 1930s and 1940s, 13 June 1986.

Frances Goodrich, 92, screenwriter and playwright, who collaborated with her husband, Albert Hackett, on movies such as *The Thin Man* (1934) and *It's a Wonderful Life* (1946) and Broadway plays, including the stage version of *The Diary of Anne Frank*, for which they won a Tony Award, a Pulitzer Prize, and a New York Drama Critics Circle Award, 29 January 1984.

Ruth Gordon, 88, Oscar-winning stage and screen actress, who played character roles in movies such as *Rosemary's Baby* (1968) and *Harold and Maude* (1971), and screenwriter, who worked with her husband, Garson Kanin, on scripts for movies such as *A Double Life* (1947) and *Adam's Rib* (1949), 28 August 1985.

Glen Gould, 50, eclectic pianist and composer, 4 October 1982.

Sheilah Graham, 80, Hollywood gossip columnist for three decades, well known for her memoirs of her love affair with novelist F. Scott Fitzgerald, 17 November 1980.

Cary Grant, 82, wry, witty, and debonair movie actor who specialized in comic and romantic roles in movies such as *Topper* (1937), *The Awful Truth* (1937), *Bringing Up Baby* (1938), *Holiday* (1938), *The Philadelphia Story* (1940), *His Girl Friday* (1940), *Suspicion* (1941), *Notorious* (1946), *North by Northwest* (1959), and *Charade* (1963), 29 November 1986.

Philip Guston, 66, painter who mixed abstract expressionist, pop art, and representational styles, 7 June 1980.

Bill Haley, 55, singer with The Comets whose early 1950s hits "Rock Around the Clock" and "Shake Rattle and Roll" helped to popularize rock 'n' roll, 11 May 1981.

Margaret Hamilton, 82, character actress best known for playing the Wicked Witch of the West in *The Wizard of Oz* (1939), 16 May 1985.

John Henry Hammond, 76, record producer, music critic, and jazz and blues impresario, known for discovering young talent, including Count Basie, Billie Holiday, Bob Dylan, Aretha Franklin, and Bruce Springsteen, 10 July 1987.

Nancy Hanks, 57, head of the National Endowment for the Arts and National Council for the Arts during the 1970s, 7 January 1983.

Howard Hanson, 84, Pulitzer Prize–winning composer and conductor, 26 February 1981.

Sterling Hayden, 70, movie actor whose screen credits include *The Asphalt Jungle* (1950) and *Dr. Strangelove* (1964), 23 May 1986.

Stanley Hayter, 86, graphic artist, 4 May 1988.

Rita Hayworth, 68, love goddess of 1940s movies such as *Gilda* (1946) and *The Lady from Shanghai* (1948), 14 May 1987.

Edith Head, 82, Hollywood costume designer who won a record eight Oscars for her wardrobe designs, 24 October 1981.

Jascha Heifetz, 86, virtuoso violinist, 10 December 1987.

Robert A. Heinlein, 80, science-fiction writer best known for his novel *Stranger in a Strange Land* (1961), 8 May 1988.

Woody Herman, 74, composer, bandleader, and clarinetist, 29 October 1987.

Earl Hines, 77, jazz pianist who played with Louis Armstrong and helped to influence bebop style, 22 April 1983.

Joseph Hirschhorn, 82, founder and benefactor of the Hirschhorn Museum in Washington, D.C., owner of one of the world's largest private art collections, 31 August 1981.

Alfred Hitchcock, 80, movie director known as the "Master of Suspense," notable for movies such as *Shadow of a Doubt* (1943), *Notorious* (1946), *Strangers on a Train* (1951), *Rear Window* (1954), *Vertigo* (1958), *North by Northwest* (1959), *Psycho* (1960), *The Birds* (1963), and *Marnie* (1964), 29 April 1980.

Laura Z. Hobson, 85, author of novels such as *Gentleman's Agreement* (1947) and *Consenting Adult* (1975), 28 February 1986.

William Holden, 63, Oscar-winning movie actor whose screen credits include *Sunset Boulevard* (1950), *Stalag 17* (1953), *The Bridge on the River Kwai* (1957), and *Network* (1976), 12 November 1981.

Vladimir Horowitz, 86, Russian-born pianist, 5 November 1989.

John Houseman, 86, director, writer, and actor who won an Oscar for his role in *The Paper Chase* (1973), 31 October 1988.

Rock Hudson, 59, actor in movies such as *Giant* (1956) and *Pillow Talk* (1959), the first celebrity to die of an AIDS-related illness, 2 October 1985.

Alberta Hunter, 89, blues singer and songwriter, 17 October 1984.

John Huston, 81, director of classic movies such as *Treasure of the Sierra Madre* (1948), *The Maltese Falcon* (1941), *The Asphalt Jungle* (1950), *The African Queen* (1951), and *Prizzi's Honor* (1985), 28 August 1987.

Harry James, 67, bandleader who won fame as a trumpet player in Benny Goodman's orchestra and later employed Frank Sinatra and Buddy Rich, 5 July 1983.

Sidney Janis, 93, leading New York art dealer and promoter of Abstract Expressionism, 23 November 1989.

George Jessel, 83, showman, comedian, and inventor of celebrity "roasts," 24 May 1981.

Robert Joffrey, 57, choreographer, dancer, and founder of the Joffrey Ballet, 25 March 1988.

Carolyn Jones, 50, movie and television actress, 3 August 1983.

Danny Kaye, 74, comic actor who appeared in movies such as *The Secret Life of Walter Mitty* (1947), *White Christmas* (1954), and *The Double* (1961), 3 March 1987.

Nora Kaye, 67, ballet star of the 1940s and 1950s, 30 April 1987.

Grace Kelly, 53, princess of Monaco and former actress whose screen credits include *High Noon* (1952), *The Country Girl* (1954), *Dial M for Murder* (1954), *Rear Window* (1954), and *To Catch a Thief* (1955), 14 September 1982.

Iva Kitchell, 75, dancer well known for comic and satiric routines, 19 November 1983.

Alfred A. Knopf, 91, book publisher whose firm published works by sixteen Nobel laureates and twenty-six Pulitzer Prize winners, 11 August 1984.

Andre Kostelanetz, 78, conductor of the New York Philharmonic (1952–1979), 13 January 1980.

Lee Krasner, 75, Abstract Expressionist painter and widow of artist Jackson Pollock, 19 June 1984.

Kay Kyser, 79, bandleader, 23 July 1985.

Louis L'Amour, 80, author of popular western novels, 10 June 1988.

Peter Lawford, 61, movie actor and in-law to the Kennedy family, 24 December 1984.

John Lennon, 40, singer and songwriter, member of The Beatles and later a solo performer, 8 December 1980.

Alan Jay Lerner, 67, lyricist and librettist known for his collaborations with Frederick Loewe on the Broadway musicals *Brigadoon* (1947), *Paint Your Wagon* (1951), *My Fair Lady* (1956), *Gigi* (1958), and *Camelot* (1960), 14 June 1986.

Joseph Levine, 81, producer and distributor of foreign films, 31 July 1987.

Liberace, 69, flamboyant pianist and entertainer, 4 February 1987.

Frederick Loewe, 83, pianist and composer known for the musicals he wrote with Alan Jay Lerner, 14 February 1988.

Joshua Logan, 79, stage director, producer, and playwright, best known as co-author and director of the plays *Mister Roberts* (1948) and *South Pacific* (1949), 12 July 1988.

George London, 63, opera singer, 24 March 1985.

Anita Loos, 88, actress, novelist, and screenwriter, best-known for her novel *Gentlemen Prefer Blondes* (1925), 18 August 1981.

Eugene Lorring, 68, Broadway and Hollywood dancer and choreographer, 30 August 1982.

Joseph Losey, 75, movie director blacklisted in Hollywood during the 1950s because of his alleged communist sympathies, 22 June 1984.

Clare Boothe Luce, 84, dramatist whose plays include *The Women* (1937) and *Kiss the Boys Goodbye* (1937), 9 October 1987.

Charles Ludlam, 44, playwright, director, and cofounder of the Ridiculous Theater Company, 28 May 1987.

John D. MacDonald, 70, novelist and creator of detective Travis McGee, 28 December 1986.

Ross Macdonald (Kenneth Millar), 67, author of hard-boiled detective fiction, who introduced detective Lew Archer in *The Moving Target* (1949), 11 July 1983.

Helen MacInnes, 77, author of suspense fiction, 30 September 1985.

Archibald MacLeish, 89, poet who won Pulitzer Prizes for his long poem *Conquistador* (1932), his *Collected Poems 1917–1952* (1952), and his verseplay *J.B.*, 20 April 1982.

Bernard Malamud, 71, novelist and short-story writer whose novels include *The Natural* (1952) and *The Fixer* (1966), for which he won a Pulitzer Prize, 18 March 1986.

Albert Maltz, 76, screenwriter, novelist, and playwright, one of the "Hollywood Ten" jailed in 1950 and blacklisted for alleged communist sympathies, 26 April 1985.

Rouben Mamoulian, 90, director of Broadway productions such as *Oklahoma!* (1943) and *Carousel* (1945) and movies such as *Dr. Jekyll and Mr. Hyde* (1931) and *Blood and Sand* (1941), 22 July 1988.

Robert Mapplethorpe, 42, photographer noted for his erotic and controversial subject matter, 9 March 1989.

Lee Marvin, 63, Oscar-winning movie actor whose screen credits include *Cat Ballou* (1965) and *The Dirty Dozen* (1967), 29 August 1987.

Raymond Massey, 86, stage and movie actor, 19 July 1983.

Mary McCarthy, 77, novelist and short-story writer best known for her novel *The Group* (1963), 25 October 1989.

Steve McQueen, 50, actor best known for his action-hero roles in movies such as *The Magnificent Seven* (1960), *The Great Escape* (1963), *The Sand Pebbles* (1966), and *Bullitt* (1969), 7 November 1980.

Ethel Merman, 75, singer and actress who helped to make hits of the stage musicals *Anything Goes* (1934), *Annie Get Your Gun* (1946, 1966), and *Gypsy* (1959), 17 February 1984.

Ray Milland, 79, movie actor who won an Oscar for his role in *The Lost Weekend* (1945), 10 March 1986.

Henry Miller, 88, writer whose controversial novel *Tropic of Cancer* (1934) was banned in the United States until 1961, 7 June 1980.

Vincente Minnelli, 73, director of classic M-G-M musical movies such as *Meet Me in St. Louis* (1944), *An American in Paris* (1951), and *Gigi* (1958), 25 July 1986.

Howard Mitchell, 77, conductor, cellist, and music director of the National Symphony Orchestra, 22 June 1988.

Thelonious Monk, 64, jazz pianist and composer, one of the originators of bebop style, 17 February 1982.

Robert Montgomery, 77, actor whose movies include *Night Must Fall* (1937) and *Here Comes Mr. Jordan* (1941), 27 September 1981.

Alice Neel, 84, painter whose unconventional lifestyle earned her the tag "quintessential bohemian," 13 October 1984.

Pola Negri, 87, silent movie actress, 1 August 1987.

Rick Nelson, 45, pop singer and teen idol during the late 1950s, 31 December 1985.

Louise Nevelson, 87, exponent of environmental sculpture, 17 April 1988.

David Niven, 73, Oscar-winning actor best known for playing debonair bachelors in movies such as *Around the World in 80 Days* (1956), *Separate Tables* (1958), and *The Pink Panther* (1964), 29 July 1983.

Isamo Noguchi, 83, sculptor whose abstract style fused Eastern and Western traditions, 30 December 1988.

Lloyd Nolan, 83, movie actor whose credits include *Peyton Place* (1957) and *A Tree Grows in Brooklyn* (1974), 27 September 1985.

Pat O'Brien, 83, actor known for portrayals of Irishmen in movies such as *Angels with Dirty Faces* (1938) and *Fighting Father Dunne* (1948), 15 October 1983.

Mary O'Hara, 95, screenwriter and author of popular horse novels, including *My Friend Flicka* (1941), 15 October 1980.

Georgia O'Keeffe, 98, painter well-known for her imagery of the American Southwest, 6 March 1986.

Roy Orbison, 52, falsetto-voiced rock 'n' roll singer, 6 December 1988.

Geraldine Page, 62, Oscar-winning stage and screen actress, best-known for her roles in *Sweet Bird of Youth* (1962), *Summer and Smoke* (1961), and *The Trip to Bountiful* (1985), 13 June 1987.

Sam Peckinpah, 59, director known for his balletic staging of violence in movies such as *The Wild Bunch* (1969) and *Straw Dogs* (1971), 28 December 1984.

Slim Pickens, 64, character actor who played comic roles in movies such as *Dr. Strangelove* (1964), *Blazing Saddles* (1974), and *The Apple Dumpling Gang* (1975), 8 December 1983.

Walter Pidgeon, 86, actor usually cast as a man of integrity in movies such as *Mrs. Miniver* (1942), *Executive Suite* (1954), and *The Bad and the Beautiful* (1952), 24 September 1984.

Miguel Pincro, 41, playwright and poet, winner of Obie and New York Drama Critics Circle Awards for *Short Eyes* (1974), 17 June 1988.

Katherine Anne Porter, 90, fiction writer whose books include the short-story collection *Flowering Judas* (1930) and the novel *Ship of Fools* (1962), 18 September 1980.

William Powell, 91, actor best known for playing witty, sophisticated characters such as Nick Charles in *The Thin Man* (1934), *After the Thin Man* (1936), *Another Thin Man* (1939), *Shadow of the Thin Man* (1941), *The Thin Man Goes Home* (1944), and *Song of the Thin Man* (1947), 5 March 1984.

Otto Preminger, 79, Austrian-born producer and director whose movies include *Laura* (1944), *The Man with the Golden Arm* (1955), and *Anatomy of a Murder* (1959), 23 April 1986.

Robert Preston, 68, stage actor who won a Tony for his starring role in the Broadway musical *The Music Man* (1957) and also acted in movies, including *Victor/Victoria* (1982), 21 March 1987.

William Primrose, 77, musician often hailed as best violinist of the 1930s and 1940s, 1 May 1982.

Ayn Rand, 77, novelist whose books, including *The Fountainhead* (1943) and *Atlas Shrugged* (1957), promote the theory of "objectivism," a kind of rationalized selfishness and individualism, 6 March 1982.

Donna Reed, 64, Oscar-winning movie and television actress whose movies include *It's a Wonderful Life* (1946) and *From Here to Eternity* (1953), 14 January 1986.

Kenneth Rexroth, 76, poet, playwright, and novelist who associated with and helped to publicize the Beat Generation of the 1950s, 6 June 1982.

Buddy Rich, 69, drummer and orchestra leader who played with Artie Shaw, Tommy Dorsey, and Harry James during the swing era, 2 April 1987.

George Rose, 68, actor who won a Tony for his performance of Alfred P. Doolittle in the 1975 Broadway revival of *My Fair Lady,* 5 May 1988.

Arthur Rubinstein, 95, one of the greatest pianists of the twentieth century, 20 December 1982.

Waldo Salt, 72, screenwriter who won Oscars for *Midnight Cowboy* (1969) and *Coming Home* (1978), 7 March 1987.

Helen Hooven Santmyer, 90, writer who became well known in her eighties with the novel *". . . And Ladies of the Club"* (1984), 21 February 1986.

William Saroyan, 74, novelist, short-story writer, and playwright who refused the Pulitzer Prize he won for his play *The Time of Your Life* (1939), 18 May 1981.

Dore Schary, 74, movie producer and head of the M-G-M movie studio after the death of Louis B. Mayer, 7 July 1980.

Alan Schneider, 66, Russian-born stage director known for his productions of plays by Edward Albee, Harold Pinter, and Bertolt Brecht, 3 May 1984.

Romy Schneider, 43, Austrian-born movie actress whose screen credits include *What's New Pussycat?* (1965) and *Swimming Pool* (1970), 29 May 1982.

Arthur Schwartz, 83, composer who collaborated with Howard Dietz on Broadway musicals such as *Stars in Your Eyes* (1939), *Park Avenue* (1946), *A Tree Grows in Brooklyn* (1951), and *That's Entertainment* (1972), 4 September 1984.

Hazel Scott, 61, jazz pianist and singer, 2 October 1981.

Randolph Scott, 89, movie actor best known for his roles in westerns such as *Badman's Territory* (1946) and *Hangman's Knot* (1952), 2 March 1987.

Roger Sessions, 88, Pulitzer Prize–winning composer, 16 March 1985.

Irwin Shaw, 71, novelist/playwright whose works include the World War I play *Bury the Dead* (1938) and the World War II novel *The Young Lions* (1948), 16 May 1984.

Norma Shearer, 82, actress who was known as the "queen of M-G-M" during the 1930s and played regal, sophisticated women in movies such as *Private Lives* (1931), *Marie Antoinette* (1938), and *The Women* (1939), 12 June 1983.

Max Shulman, 69, comic writer best known for novels such as *The Many Loves of Dobie Gillis* (1953), on which he based a screenplay (1953) and a television series (1959–1963), and *Rally Round the Flag, Boys* (1957), also the basis for a movie (1958); and the play *The Tender Trap* (1954), 28 August 1988.

Phil Silvers, 73, Tony-winning comic actor of stage and television, 1 November 1985.

Douglas Sirk, 86, director of movie melodramas such as *Magnificent Obsession* (1954), *Written on the Wind* (1956), and *Imitation of Life* (1959), 14 January 1987.

Walter Slezak, 80, stage actor and singer who won a Tony for his portrayal of Panisse in *Fanny* (1954), 22 April 1983.

Kate Smith, 77, robust singer best known for her rendition of "God Bless America," 17 June 1986.

Robert Stevenson, 81, director of Walt Disney movies such as *The Absent-Minded Professor* (1961), *Mary Poppins* (1964), *The Love Bug* (1968), and *Bedknobs and Broomsticks* (1971), 30 April 1986.

Donald Ogden Stewart, 85, author of humorous fiction, such as *A Parody Outline of History* (1921) and *Mr. and Mrs. Haddock Abroad* (1924), and of screenplays, including *The Philadelphia Story* (1940), for which he won an Academy Award; he was blacklisted in Hollywood during the McCarthy era of the early 1950s, 2 August 1980.

Clyfford Still, 75, abstract painter who five months earlier was the subject of the largest one-man exhibit of a living artist's work ever held at the Metropolitan Museum of Art in New York City, 23 June 1980.

Irving Stone, 86, author of biographical novels such as *Lust for Life* (1934), about Vincent van Gogh, and *The Agony and the Ecstasy* (1961), about Michelangelo, 26 August 1989.

Lee Strasberg, 80, a founder of the Group Theater and teacher at the well-known Actors' Studio in New York, and a proponent of Stanislavsky "method acting," 17 February 1982.

Gloria Swanson, 84, silent movie star best known for her comeback role as Norma Desmond in the "talkie *"Sunset Blvd.* (1950), 4 April 1983.

Blanche Sweet, 90, silent movie actress, 6 September 1986.

Virgil Thomson, 92, Pulitzer Prize–winning composer and conductor, 30 September 1989.

Ernest Tubb, 70, country-music singer, songwriter, and musician who introduced the honky-tonk sound, 6 September 1984.

Rudy Vallee, 84, popular crooner of the 1930s, 3 July 1986.

Vera-Ellen, 55, dancer and actress whose screen credits include *On the Town* (1949) and *White Christmas* (1954), 30 August 1981.

King Vidor, 88, director whose movies include *The Crowd* (1928), *The Champ* (1931), *The Fountainhead* (1949), and *Beyond the Forest* (1949), 1 November 1982.

Alfred Wallenstein, 84, orchestra conductor and cellist, 8 February 1983.

Andy Warhol, 58, pop artist well known in the 1960s for silk screens of celebrities such as Marilyn Monroe and Elizabeth Taylor and for his party-filled New York studio The Factory, filmmaker whose movies include *Trash* and *Flesh,* and publisher of *Interview* magazine, 22 February 1987.

Harry Warren, 87, composer of more than three hundred popular songs, including "Lullaby of Broadway" and "42nd Street," 22 September 1981.

Robert Penn Warren, 84, poet and novelist who won a Pulitzer Prize for *All the King's Men* (1946) and served as the first poet laureate of the United States, 15 September 1989.

Muddy Waters, 68, blues singer who influenced the Chicago blues style and the sound of rock and roll, 30 April 1983.

Orson Welles, 70, movie director and actor famous for a 1938 radio performance of his *War of the Worlds* and for *Citizen Kane* (1941), often called the "greatest movie ever made," 10 October 1985.

Oskar Werner, 61, German-born movie actor whose screen credits include *Jules and Jim* (1962) and *Ship of Fools* (1965), 23 October 1984.

Jessamyn West, 81, author best known for her novel *Friendly Persuasion* (1945), 23 February 1984.

Mae West, 87, buxom star of stage and screen known for her bawdy double entendres whose movies include *She Done Him Wrong* (1933), *My Little Chickadee* (1940), and *Myra Breckinridge* (1970), 22 November 1980.

E. B. White, 86, humorist and essayist, an early writer for *The New Yorker* and author of the children's classics *Stuart Little* (1945) and *Charlotte's Web* (1952), 1 October 1985.

Alec Wilder, 73, composer of popular songs, 24 December 1980.

Tennessee Williams, 73, playwright noted for the poetic dialogue in classic modern plays such as *The Glass Menagerie* (1945), *A Streetcar Named Desire* (1947), *Cat on a Hot Tin Roof* (1955; for which he won a Pulitzer Prize), *Sweet Bird of Youth* (1959), and *The Night of the Iguana* (1961), 25 February 1983.

Meredith Willson, 82, composer and lyricist who wrote the book music and lyrics for *The Music Man* (1957) and *Here's Love* (1963), and the music and lyrics for *The Unsinkable Molly Brown* (1960), 15 June 1984.

Dennis Wilson, 39, drummer, keyboardist, and singer for the Beach Boys, 28 December 1983.

Natalie Wood, 43, screen actress for more than three decades whose movies include *Miracle on 34th Street* (1947), *Rebel Without a Cause* (1955), *West Side Story* (1961), and *Bob & Carol & Ted & Alice* (1969), 29 November 1981.

William Wyler, 79, Oscar-winning director of movies such as *Jezebel* (1938), *Wuthering Heights* (1939), *The Letter* (1940), *The Little Foxes* (1941), *Mrs. Miniver* (1942), *The Best Years of Our Lives* (1946), *Roman Holiday* (1953), *Ben-Hur* (1959), and *Funny Girl* (1968), 28 July 1981.

Efrem Zimbalist, 95, Russian-born violinist and composer, 22 February 1985.

PUBLICATIONS

Leonard Bernstein, *Findings* (New York: Simon & Schuster, 1982);

Douglas Brode, *The Films of the Eighties* (New York: Citadel Press, 1990);

Edward D. C. Campbell, *The Celluloid South: Hollywood and the Southern Myth* (Knoxville: University of Tennessee Press, 1981);

Francis Davis, *In the Moment: Jazz in the 1980s* (New York: Oxford University Press, 1986);

David Evans, *Big Road Blues: Tradition and Creativity in the Folk Blues* (Berkeley: University of California Press, 1982);

Jonathan Fineburg, *Art Since 1940: Strategies of Being* (New York: Abrams, 1995);

Peter Frank and Michael McKenzie, *New, Used & Improved: Art for the '80s* (New York: Abbeville Press, 1987);

Deborah R. Geis, *Postmodern Theatric(k)s: Monologue in Contemporary American Drama* (Ann Arbor: University of Michigan Press, 1993);

Gary Giddins, *Rhythm-a-ning: Jazz Tradition and Innovation in the '80s* (New York: Oxford University Press, 1986);

Giddins, *Riding on a Blue Note: Jazz and American Pop* (New York: Oxford University Press, 1981);

Tony Godfrey, *The New Image: Painting in the 1980s* (Oxford: Phaidon, 1986);

Donald J. Greiner, *Women Without Men: Female Bonding and the American Novel of the 1980s* (Columbia: University of South Carolina Press, 1993);

Richard Grenier, *Capturing the Culture: Film, Art, and Politics* (Washington, D.C.: Ethics and Public Policy Center, 1991);

Lawrence Grossberg, *We Gotta Get Out of This Place: Popular Conservatism and Postmodern Culture* (New York: Routledge, 1992);

Molly Haskell, *From Reverence to Rape: The Treatment of Women in the Movies* (Chicago: University of Chicago Press, 1987);

Pauline Kael, *When the Lights Go Down* (New York: Holt, Rinehart & Winston, 1980);

Annette Kuhn, *Women's Pictures: Feminism and Cinema* (London & Boston: Routledge & Kegan Paul, 1982);

Marco Livingstone, *Pop Art: A Continuing History* (New York: Abrams, 1990);

Dave Marsh, *Glory Days: Bruce Springsteen in the 1980s* (New York: Pantheon, 1987);

David McClintick, *Indecent Exposure: A True Story of Hollywood and Wall Street* (New York: Morrow, 1982);

Michael Medved, *Hollywood vs. America: Popular Culture and the War on Traditional Values* (New York: HarperCollins, 1992);

Mark Crispin Miller, ed., *Seeing Through Movies* (New York: Pantheon, 1990);

MacDonald Smith Moore, *Yankee Blues: Musical Culture and American Identity* (Bloomington: Indiana University Press, 1985);

George Nelson, *Buppies, B-boys, Baps & Bohos: Notes on Post-Soul Black Culture* (New York: HarperCollins, 1992):

Tom O'Brien, *The Screening of America: Movies and Values from Rocky to Rain Man* (New York: Continuum, 1990);

Andreas Papadakis, Clare Farrow, and Nicola Hodges, eds., *New Art: An International Survey* (New York: Rizzoli, 1991);

Science Fiction Filmmaking in the 1980s: Interviews with Actors, Directors, Producers, and Writers (Jefferson, N.C.: McFarland, 1995);

David P. Szatmary, *Rockin' in Time: A Social History of Rock and Roll* (Englewood Cliffs, N.J.: Prentice-Hall, 1987);

Kirk Varnedoe and Adam Gopnik, *High and Low: Modern Art and Popular Culture* (New York: Abrams, 1990);

Steve Vineberg, *No Surprises, Please: Movies in the Reagan Decade* (New York: Schirmer, 1993);

Art in America, periodical;

ARTnews, periodical;

Billboard, periodical;

Film Comment, periodical;

Films in Review, periodical;

Publishers Weekly, periodical;

Rolling Stone, periodical;

Spin, periodical;

Variety, periodical.

BUSINESS AND THE ECONOMY

by PHILLIP L. PAYNE and PENNY MESSINGER

CONTENTS

1980

- The prime interest rate averages 15.26 percent for the year.

- Inflation averages 12.5 percent for the year, the highest inflation level reached in thirty-three years.

- Civilian unemployment averages 7.1 percent for the year.

- Japanese interests operate some 225 U.S. manufacturing firms.

- The average car costs $7,574.

- Congress removes ceilings on the interest rates that savings and loans can pay to depositors.

- President Jimmy Carter announces plans to cut federal spending by $13 million. His popularity plummets, however, as inflation continues to rise.

- The price of gold rises to a high of $802 on the New York market, rising by $159 in one week.

Mar. Brothers Nelson Bunker Hunt and William Herbert Hunt fail to corner the silver market as the value of silver drops.

The banking industry is deregulated.

AT&T is convicted of antitrust violations and fined $1.8 billion.

June The Motor Carrier Act deregulates the trucking industry.

United Steelworkers and big steel manufacturers attempt to revitalize the steel industry by creating labor-management participation teams.

AT&T begins a telephone 900 service.

Low-fare People Express Airline, founded by Donald Barr, begins providing no-frills service in the Northeast.

Henry Ford II retires from the chairmanship of Ford Motor Company and is succeeded by President Philip Caldwell.

Ted Turner creates Cable News Network (CNN) to offer nationally televised round-the-clock news. Beginning with three hundred employees, CNN grows to fifteen hundred employees by 1985, with 38.5 million subscribers and a $100 million budget.

The Dow-Jones Industrial average reaches the 1,000 level.

Clothing manufacturer Calvin Klein introduces advertisements that feature Brooke Shields, launching a designer jeans fad.

14 July The United States announces that petroleum imports have declined — the United States imported 14 percent less crude oil during the first six months of 1980 than during the same period in 1979.

23 Oct. A ninety-four-day strike by the Screen Actors Guild and the American Federation of Television and Radio Artists (the longest strike in the unions' history) ends with the acceptance of a new contract.

4 Nov. After campaigning on what his running mate George Bush had called "voodoo economics" (based on supply-side ideology) and promising to reduce the size of government, Ronald Reagan is elected president.

19 Dec.   The United States prime interest rate reaches an all-time high of 21.5 percent.

1981

- U.S. agricultural exports reach an all-time high of $43.8 billion.

- The United Automobile Workers (UAW) union reaffiliates with the American Federation of Labor and Congress of Industrial Organizations (AFL-CIO) after thirteen years apart.

- U.S. Steel buys Marathon Oil for $6.3 billion.

- Deficit spending by the national government increases dramatically.

- Inflation rate falls to 10.4 percent.

- Roger B. Smith becomes chairman of General Motors.

20 Jan.   Ronald Reagan takes the oath of office to become the fortieth president of the United States.

5 Feb.   President Reagan makes his first television address as president, asking for cuts in the income tax and in government spending.

18 Feb.   Reagan reveals a program for economic recovery calling for $41.4 billion less than President Carter's budget, asking for cuts in eighty-three federal programs.

Mar.   Reagan discusses plans to link welfare benefits with requirements for work.

Reagan announces plans to cut taxes and the budget by $130.5 billion.

6 Mar.   Reagan announces plans for major cuts in federal employment.

27 Mar.   The United Mine Workers of America (UMWA) contract expires, and coal miners in the eastern states go on strike.

28 Mar.   After reaching a high of $40 per ounce in January, and a low of $4, the price of silver stabilizes at $12 per ounce.

30 Mar.   Reagan is wounded after being shot by John W. Hinckley Jr. in an assassination attempt.

12 Apr.   The space shuttle *Columbia* is launched, promising to provide routine access to outer space.

24 Apr.   Reagan ends a fifteen-month grain embargo on the USSR.

1 May   Japan announces plans to limit exports of its passenger cars to the United States after American officials threaten to impose quotas limiting Japanese imports.

13 May   Reagan proposes to cut Social Security by 10 percent, but the proposal is quickly defeated.

26 May   OPEC (Organization of Petroleum Exporting Countries) freezes oil prices at $32 per barrel and announces plans to cut production by some 10 percent.

12 June   Baseball players begin to strike.

3 Aug.   Rejecting the terms of a government contract, thirteen thousand members of the Professional Air Traffic Controllers Organization (PATCO) go on strike.

1982

- Congress deregulates the savings-and-loan industry, allowing speculative investments.

- Congress raises the amount of federal insurance of each individual savings and loan depositor from $40,000 to $100,000.

- The Japanese companies of Hitachi and Mitsubishi admit to buying secrets illegally from IBM in California's Silicon Valley. Later, in a settlement ending the long antimonopoly court battle brought by the U.S. Justice Department, IBM agrees to terms that make the computer industry more competitive.

- The UAW and American Motors reach an agreement in which workers will give up $150 million in raises to finance investments in new product development.

- The U.S. unemployment rate hits 9.4 percent, the highest level since 1941, with 10.3 million unemployed.

- Female business leaders create the Committee of 200 to promote the national visibility of women in business.

- Secretary of the Interior James Watt opens one billion acres of American coast-line to oil and gas drilling.

- *USA Today*, a colorful, national daily newspaper, is launched by the Gannett Publishing Company.

- The EPCOT Center (Experimental Prototype Community of Tomorrow), which had been visualized by Walt Disney in 1966 as a self-sustaining utopian community, opens at Disney World.

- The Japanese auto manufacturer Honda begins making cars at Marysville, Ohio. Other Japanese firms follow suit and begin production in the United States: Nissan (1983), Toyota (1984), Mazda (1987), Mitsubishi (1988), and Subaru-Isuzu (1989).

- Congress approves a three-year, 25 percent reduction in personal and business income taxes.

Jan. Telecommunications giant American Telephone and Telegraph (AT&T) is broken up.

July The poverty rate is reported at 14 percent, the highest rate since 1967.

Aug. A bull market begins on Wall Street.

The inflation rate falls to 6.1 percent.

19 Oct. Automaker John Z. DeLorean is arrested in California on drug charges.

McDonald's passes Sears as the largest owner of real estate in the world.

1983

- The inflation rate falls to 3.2 percent.

- The worst government failure in U.S. history occurs when the Public Power Supply System of Washington State defaults on more than $2 billion in municipal bonds.

Jan.	Unemployment figures show more than 11.5 million people unemployed. By the end of the year that estimate triples.
20 Apr.	President Reagan signs Social Security legislation that is designed to keep the system out of debt for the next seventy-five years.
Nov.	Drexel Burnham Lambert executive Michael Milken develops the idea of using high-yield "junk" bonds that are repaid by pledging assests of the target company to facilitate company takeovers and corporate buying of public stock. Many insurance and savings-and-loan associations begin buying the junk bonds.
23 Dec.	Two leading U.S. railroads merge to create Santa Fe Southern Pacific.

1984

- General Motors acquires Texnowledge and Electronic Data Systems from H. Ross Perot for $2.5 billion.

- The Hewlett-Packard Company introduces the laptop computer.

- The computer language MS-DOS, developed by Microsoft for IBM, is used in two million computers and in more than 90 percent of IBM personal computers and compatible equipment.

- The Economic Recovery Tax Act passes Congress.

- The inflation rate rises to 4.3 percent.

25 Jan.	In his State of the Union address, President Reagan announces plans to simplify the tax code (genesis of the 1986 Tax Reform Act).
1 Feb.	The Senate confirms Elizabeth Hanford Dole as secretary of transportation.
6 Nov.	President Reagan is reelected with 59 percent of the popular vote, defeating Walter Mondale.

1985

- The inflation rate falls to 3.6 percent.

- A record 43,000 farms go bankrupt as land prices fall and interest rates soar.

- Many banks and savings-and-loan institutions go bankrupt in Texas, Oklahoma, and other oil states that are pressured by collapsing world oil prices.

- As high-yield "junk" bonds are used to finance company takeovers, the number of U.S. corporate mergers and buyouts increases — with twenty-four involving more than $1 billion each.

6 Feb.	In his State of the Union address, President Reagan calls for tax reform and economic growth. Two days earlier he had asked Congress to reduce the budget.
16 Sept.	The Department of Commerce announces that the United States has become a debtor nation for the first time since 1914.
12 Dec.	President Reagan signs the Gramm-Rudman-Hollings Act, limiting congressional spending in an effort to eliminate the federal deficit by 1991.

1986

- The Tax Reform Act is passed.

- Business entrepreneur Rupert Murdoch launches a major noncable network, Fox.

1987

- Microsoft Corporation, led by William Henry Gates's ingenuity in software programming and development, goes public.

- The total value of farmland in the United States drops to $392 billion — approximately half its estimated value in 1980.

14 Nov. Wall Street businessman Ivan Boesky plea bargains with government officials, admitting that he had bought stock after receiving tips about forthcoming merger bids. The day becomes known as "Boesky Day" among inside traders.

Dec. U.S. international indebtedness reaches $269 billion.

The average weekly wage for all U.S. workers is $171.07.

- In early January the Commerce Department predicts that technology companies will produce more than other manufacturing companies.

6 Jan. The Reagan administration, the Federal Reserve Board, and some private economists predict the economy will continue to expand for the fifth straight year.

10 Jan. The government announces that consumer prices rose only 2.5 percent in 1986, the best performance in thirty-seven years, in large part because of low oil prices.

11 Jan. Representatives from business, academia, and labor form the Competitiveness Council to promote the competitive spirit as a means to attack the trade deficit.

17 Jan. The Federal Reserve Board reports that industrial production rose 0.5 percent in November, a solid increase over past reports.

23 Jan. The Commerce Department reports that the economy grew at a substantially slower rate than the Reagan administration had expected.

25 Jan. Treasury Secretary James A. Baker tells Reagan that the two-year fall of the dollar has been good for the economy.

27 Jan. Reagan stresses economic competitiveness in his State of the Union address.

18 Feb. Low interest rates and low oil prices combine with a weak dollar to boost corporate profits. Some American companies start bringing overseas production home because of the weak dollar.

20 Feb. The Commerce Department announces that the economy grew at 1.3 percent after inflation, a lower rate of growth than had been predicted.

27 Feb. The Commerce Department reports that orders to factories for durable goods fell 7.5 percent in January, the biggest drop in seven years, despite a 51 percent increase in military orders.

15 Mar. Evidence suggests that American consumers are ending their four-year buying spree because of high levels of debt.

23 Mar. An independent study suggests that outmoded accounting methods may explain the failure of American companies to modernize their production methods.

7 Apr. The Commerce Department reports to Congress that Japanese companies are increasing their investments in the United States despite the fear that the steady decline of the dollar against the yen might prompt Japanese investors to pull out of the United States.

1988

2 June	Paul Volcker resigns as chairman of the U.S. Federal Reserve Board.
3 Aug.	Alan Greenspan becomes the new chairman of the U.S. Federal Reserve Board.
10 Aug.	In one of the largest leveraged buyouts of the decade, TLS Group L.S. acquires Beatrice International Foods for $985 million, making TLS the largest black-owned firm in America.
19 Oct.	The stock market crashes, dropping 500 points.
Dec.	The U.S. international debt reaches $368 billion.

- The number of millionaires living in the United States rises from 574,000 in 1980 to 1.3 million — and this number includes at least fifty billionaires.

- As the number of cable-television channels and subscribers increase, profits of the Big Three networks (NBC, ABC, and CBS) decrease to $400 million — half the profits gained only four years earlier.

- Prices of farmland begin to rise, aiding a recovery in Midwest economy. Large farms are replacing smaller, family-owned farms.

- As savings-and-loan institutions overextend their credits, experts estimate that $100 billion to $200 billion is needed to bail them out.

- Some 198,000 striking workers return to work at General Electric.

23 Aug.	An omnibus trade bill is signed into law.
23 Sept.	Michael Deaver, President Reagan's former deputy chief of staff, is sentenced for perjury ($100,000 fine, suspended three-year sentence) for lying to a federal grand jury about his lobbying activities after leaving the White House staff.
27 Sept.	A welfare-reform bill is approved and provides more education and training programs for welfare recipients while initiating new work requirements.
11 Oct.	Bank of Credit and Commerce International (BCCI) executives and top employees are indicted on charges of money laundering for cocaine traffickers.
12 Oct.	The Sunstrang Corporation, a military contractor, pleads guilty and is fined $115 million for overbilling the government for millions of dollars on military contracts between 1980 and 1986.
8 Nov.	George Bush is elected president, defeating Democrat Michael Dukakis.

1989

- By the end of the year the prime interest rate reaches 21.5 percent.

20 Jan.	George Bush takes oath of office as president. The national debt stands at $2.6844 trillion — more than twenty-six times the figure reported in 1980.
25 May	The United States accuses Brazil, India, and Japan of unfair trade practices and demands concessions.
10 June	Federal investigators reveal financial scandal at the Department of Housing and Urban Development (HUD) involving embezzlement, mismanagement, and influence peddling.
31 Oct.	The first increase in the minimum wage since 1981 is announced. The wage is to rise from $3.35 per hour to $3.80 beginning 1 April 1990.

OVERVIEW

Economic Malaise. Many Americans perceived the 1980s as a prosperous and pleasant decade, especially in contrast to the 1970s. As the 1980s unfolded, however, others argued that the ailments of the nation had not been cured but instead were being pasted over and ignored. The 1970s had been filled with tumultuous events such as oil shocks, the Watergate affair, and the Iran hostage crisis. President Jimmy Carter's suggestion that the country suffered from a national malaise only seemed to prove America's weakness and decline both at home and abroad. Stagflation, a term referring to an economy suffering from both inflation and stagnation (a combination that was thought impossible before the 1970s), was a matter of great concern. Perhaps no other circumstance better symbolized the perceived decline of American business than the near collapse of the Chrysler Corporation, the third of the Big Three automobile makers and a bulwark of the American economy. In 1979 Chrysler had assets of $13.6 billion and thousands of employees, but it was also on the verge of bankruptcy. To save the faltering giant, Lee Iacocca, Chrysler's new chairman of the board, asked Congress for a $1 billion loan, special tax concessions, and relief from environmental regulations. Iacocca pointed out that Congress had recently aided the troubled Lockheed Corporation and that the government regularly aided small businesses. Near the end of 1979 Congress agreed to a $1 billion loan if Chrysler raised $2 billion on its own.

Recession. The economic recession that began in 1979 and lasted into 1982 was the low point of the economic malaise. In the late 1970s Carter cut federal programs to reduce deficit spending, which contributed to the economy's moving into the recession. In the two years after Ronald Reagan assumed the presidency in 1980, the unemployment rate increased from 5.6–7.8 percent, where it had hovered in the Carter administration, to 10.8 percent by 1982. More than 12 million Americans were out of work. Business bankruptcies rose 50 percent between 1981 and 1982, resulting in 584 business failures in June 1982, nearing the record of 612 business failures in one month set in 1932 at the height of the Great Depression. Some segments of the population fared less well than others. Black Americans, for example, suffered from an unemployment rate of more than 20 percent. Industrial workers also faced hard times, particularly those who lived in the area stretching in a broad band from Pennsylvania to Michigan. This area, the center of America's industrial heartland, was described as the "rust belt" by observers who were struck by the declining status of American industry. The Youngstown, Ohio, area lost five steel mills and twenty-five thousand jobs in the recession. Nearly a third of the nation's industrial capacity lay idle, leading to the popularization in the early 1980s of the new term *deindustrialization.*

Standing Tall. The economy and the national malaise dominated the presidential election of 1980 that pitted Republican Ronald Reagan against incumbent Democrat Jimmy Carter. Making the economy a central issue, Reagan asked voters, "Are you better off today than you were four years ago?" Reagan assured the nation that the best course of action to bring economic recovery was to have the federal government take no decisive action. Reagan proposed reducing the size of the federal government (a course that Carter was already following), reducing taxes, and letting market forces correct economic problems. While many of the underlying problems of the 1970s did not go away, public confidence did begin to improve during the 1980s with Reagan's election. The new president tried to restore public confidence by emphasizing the virtues of American business and stressing the importance of the private sector over that of the public sector.

Business First. Reagan, who had served as the host for General Electric Television Theater in the 1950s, was not the only prominent spokesperson for business. Many company presidents and chief executive officers moved into public view as representatives of their companies. Corporate leaders such as Lee Iacocca of Chrysler and Dave Thomas of Wendy's regularly promoted their companies and in the process achieved celebrity status.

Government Seen as the Problem. Disciples of the Reagan revolution, as the election of 1980 was called, fundamentally challenged the assumption by which the United States had been governed since World War II. Believing in the power of the free market and the private sector, Reagan and his followers worked to remove the federal government from people's lives, "to get government off their backs." This effort took many forms, from deregulation to tax cuts to diminished social spending.

Changing Priorities. Although the trend toward larger government did not change markedly, Reagan did change the spending priorities of the government dramatically. A cornerstone of the prosperity of the 1980s was Reagan's support for increased military spending. While Reagan praised the virtues of the private sector, he condemned the Soviet Union as the "Evil Empire" and argued that the United States must have a strong national defense. He fondly quoted the Preamble of the Constitution, which called for the national government to provide for the common defense, to justify the largest peacetime military buildup in American history. Federal spending on human resources fell during the Reagan administration from 28 percent of the budget to 22 percent while defense spending increased from 23 percent to 28 percent by 1987. Such dramatic shifts in spending had strong effects on the American economy.

Bush Closes out the Decade. George Bush, who faithfully served as Reagan's vice president for eight years, won the Republican nomination and election to the presidency in 1988. Despite Bush's position as one of Reagan's leading critics when the two vied for the 1980 Republican nomination, Bush steadfastly supported Reagan's policies as his vice president and continued many of them as his successor. Bush not only benefited from Reagan's popularity, but he also suffered from many of the problems that had developed during the Reagan years. Against his better political judgment, Bush raised taxes in an attempt to deal with the massive national debt.

Scandals. The business-first attitude of the government perhaps inevitably led to some of the economic excesses of the 1980s. Early in Bush's presidency it was discovered that during the Reagan administration highly placed Republicans had received large fees from developers in return for helping wealthy clients win Department of Housing and Urban Development (HUD) contracts. In part a product of the climate of deregulation, the savings and loan crisis cost taxpayers billions of dollars as the government bailed out failed savings and loan associations throughout the country. The deregulation, and the lack of enforcement of existing regulations, of high finance also led to disastrous results on Wall Street. The nation was rocked by a series of scandals marked by insider trading (where financiers make use of illegally obtained information that grants them an unfair advantage over competitors) as some of the most successful businessmen of the 1980s were proven to be criminals. In some instances stockbrokers and investment bankers were breaking into the offices of coworkers and rivals to gain information. By the end of the decade polls showed that such revelations were causing many Americans to reassess the direction the nation had taken.

TOPICS IN THE NEWS

AMERICA IN THE GLOBAL ECONOMY

Corporate Champions. The United States had been a leading industrial power since the late nineteenth century, when industrialists and entrepreneurs such as Andrew Carnegie and J. D. Rockefeller made the names of their companies synonymous with American prestige. However, by the 1980s the American economy was changing. The emergence of the service economy brought into question the accuracy of labeling the twentieth century as the American Century, a term coined by Henry Luce to emphasize the powerful status of the United States in relation to that of other nations. Indeed, some began to refer to the 1980s as the end of the American century. U.S. involvement in World War II had helped to strengthen the position of the United States as the American economy emerged from the war at the height of its power while other industrial rivals, especially Japan and Germany, lay in ruins. In 1946 the United States produced 60 percent of the steel in the world, but by 1978 the United States provided only 16 percent of the world's steel. After 1973 and the first oil shock, American economic productivity slowed, averaging about 2.3 percent annually (compared with 3.2 percent in the 1950s). To make matters worse, from 1979 to 1982 the United States experienced the most severe economic downturn since the Great Depression. During this recession, economic growth came to a virtual halt as real gross national product dropped by 0.2 percent in 1980 and rose by only 1.9 percent in 1981.

The Japanese Miracle. By the end of the 1980s, imported Japanese cars captured 20 percent of the domestic car market and Japanese-owned auto plants controlled another 8 percent. American business leaders offered a variety of explanations for the success of the Japanese. Among the common explanations offered were government support of business, cooperative workplace arrangements like quality circles, just-in-time delivery systems, robotics and other forms of computer-driven manufacturing, workers who let themselves be underpaid, and even the superiority of the Japanese mind.

Free Trade. While the 1980s began in much the same way the 1970s ended, with economic stagnation, the 1980s went out with a boom. Fueled by government spending, mergers, and speculation, an economic recovery began in the 1980s that lasted until 1990. However, even during the years of prosperity, the underlying trends of deindustrialization did not go away. During the Reagan years private investment in real plants and equipment rose so little that by the end of the 1980s domestic investment was down to 5.7 percent. Funding the deficit, and the resulting debt, required a strong dollar to attract foreign money. As a result, between 1980 and early 1985 the dollar exchange rates increased an average of 74 percent. The issues of America's future were directly tied to international competition and foreign investment. In 1988 Japanese investment in California reached $5.3 billion, $2.5 billion in New York, $1.9 billion in Michigan, $1.5 billion in Hawaii, $1.4 billion in Illinois, $1.2 billion in Ohio, $1 billion in Texas and Tennessee, and $0.7 billion in New Jersey and Washington. Even as members of the Reagan administration confirmed the national commitment to free trade, mounting trade deficits undermined American confidence. Asian and European companies won increasingly large shares of American markets.

Sources:

Paul M. Kennedy, *The Rise and Fall of the Great Powers: Economic Change and Military Conflict from 1500 to 2000* (New York: Random House, 1987);

Clyde V. Prestowitz, *Trading Places: How We Allowed Japan to Take the Lead* (New York: Basic Books, 1988);

Robert Reich, *The Work of Nations: Preparing Ourselves for 21st Century Capitalism* (New York: Knopf, 1991);

Steven Schlosstein, *The End of the American Century* (New York: Congdon & Weed, 1989);

Daniel Seligman, "Looking Backward: The System Worked," *Fortune* (26 March 1990): 183.

DEINDUSTRIALIZATION: HEAVY INDUSTRY IN TROUBLE

Investment. Heavy industry had long been one of the hallmarks of the American economy. However, during the 1980s, heavy industries and those sections of the country that relied on those industries did not fare well. Long-term trends offer a partial explanation for the downward trend, while other causes were more immediate. From the 1950s to the 1970s Americans invested no less than 3.3 percent of the nation's total income in new industrial plants and equipment regardless of the business

cycle. This pattern came to an end during the 1980s; at no time during the 1980s did American investment in new plants reach 3 percent of the national income. The trend can also be seen in the amount of plant and equipment supporting the average nonagricultural American worker. Between 1950 and 1980 the figure rose from $26,000 to $43,000 (in 1980 dollars). Again during the 1980s another major trend came to an end as the growth of the workforce slowed along with an even greater slowing in capital stock investment. In 1987 the average American worker had just $45,900 of plant and equipment behind him, barely more than in 1980. America's investment rate in plants and equipment had been cut in half.

Steel. Once upon a time the American steel industry dominated global markets by size, modern equipment and techniques, and efficiency. The post–World War II world economy had brought much foreign competition into the market. By the mid 1970s a decreased demand for its products, the loss of market share at home, falling production and employment, and low or negative earnings had caused the U.S. steel industry to decline. By 1985 the American steel industry had hit bottom. The groundwork for steel's decline had been laid in the decades following World War II, when the largest and most integrated of the steel companies had gradually lost their technological lead. The large companies failed to adopt such innovations as the oxygen furnace, continuous casting, and computer controls as these became available, even when the advantages of the new technologies became apparent in other countries. Among the largest of the American steel companies, the ranks of upper management were characterized by inertia, the lack of an international perspective, an inflexible organizational structure, and unwillingness to fight constrictive unions. The investments that were made often ended up being ineffective and costly. During the 1980s an American company needed between four and five years to plan, design, and build a new blast furnace, while a Japanese company typically took three years and a Korean company took only two years. In the United States the cost of that new furnace was, on average, $1,700 per ton of finished capacity, compared with $700 to $1,500 in other countries. Until 1982, labor unions won major concessions from the steel industry in wages, benefits, and work rules, increasing the burden on an industry that was not otherwise doing well. The smaller American steel companies that managed to retain technological leadership also retained economic leadership. In 1986 Inland Steel was the world's lowest-cost producer of cold-rolled steel coils, and Armco Steel produced a superior product at a lower cost with a vacuum degassing system.

Textiles. Traditionally, the American textile industry has searched for low wages. The first major industry in the United States in the nineteenth century, the textile industry moved first from New England to the Southeast and then went overseas in a search for cheaper labor. In

Picketing steelworkers at the Wheeling-Pittsburgh plant in Allenport, Pennsylvania. Their walkout, which lasted from July to October 1985, was the first major steel-industry strike since 1959.

the 1970s and the 1980s lower wages did not produce success, and apparel imports had risen from 2 percent of the domestic market in 1963 to 50 percent in the late 1980s. The American textile industry has tended to focus on the mass production of standardized goods, ignoring niche markets that foreign competitors eventually filled. For example, Germany's decision to invest in new technologies, labor-saving machinery, and new plants resulted in a modern textile sector and increased productivity (24 percent in six years). By the late 1980s some American producers had begun to change. Milliken, a major fabric manufacturer, reduced the size of its fabric lots from twenty thousand yards to four thousand yards and began concentrating on research and development and proprietary technology.

Automobiles. Henry Ford and other Americans had been pioneers in the mass production of cars. In the post–World War II era the automobile industry was the largest in the United States and the symbol of American prosperity. By the late 1970s the Big Three American producers, Chrysler, General Motors, and the Ford Motor Company, were suffering from declining revenues and loss of markets to Japanese manufacturers. Chrysler lost $1.71 billion in 1980, the largest loss for an American company that year. General Motors lost $763 million, the company's largest loss since 1921. Ford lost $1.5 billion. From 1981 to 1989, under the leadership of Roger B. Smith, General Motors' market share dropped from 45 percent to 36 percent. In contrast, the sale of

imported cars rose from less than 1 percent of the sales in 1955 to more than 31 percent of domestic sales in 1987. The result of this decline in American automobile manufacturing is that the United States now has an automobile import deficit of $60 billion, the largest single element in the overall trade deficit. By the end of the decade, America was third in automobile production, behind both Europe (Europeans both buy and build more cars than Americans) and Japan. Traditionally the Big Three have concentrated on building cars in the middle price range, assuming that if a consumer wanted a high-end car he or she would buy an expensive import like a Mercedes Benz. During the 1980s foreign producers squeezed the American companies from both ends of the price range. Korean and Japanese imports dominated the low end of the market, and European imports dominated the high end. The recovery of the Asian and European economies after World War II was a main reason for the competitiveness of their automobile industries, but the decline of the American automobile industry also came from weaknesses in the domestic industry.

Technological Lag. The last major innovation that was first installed in an American car was the automatic transmission in the 1940s. Four-wheel steering and four-wheel drive, turbocharging, and antilock braking systems were all first adopted by foreign manufacturers. In 1985 the three leading Japanese producers recorded more than twice as many new patents in the United States as the three American producers. The American automobile in-

DEMING'S FOURTEEN POINTS:

1. Create constancy of purpose.

2. Adopt the new philosophy.

3. Cease dependence on mass inspection to achieve quality.

4. End the practice of awarding business on price tag alone. Instead, minimize total cost, often accomplished by working with a single supplier.

5. Improve constantly the system of production.

6. Institute training on the job.

7. Institute leadership.

8. Drive out fear.

9. Break down barriers between departments.

10. Eliminate slogans, exhortations, and numerical targets.

11. Eliminate work standards (quotas) and management by objective.

12. Remove barriers that rob workers, engineers, and managers of their right to pride of workmanship.

13. Institute a vigorous program of education and self-improvement.

14. Put everyone in the company to work to accomplish the transformation.

Source: Mary Walton, *The Deming Management Method* (New York: Dodd, Mead, 1986).

---

dustry was built upon a system of production and a marketing strategy that dated back to the 1920s. Automobile executives assumed that designs could last for years since they believed that consumers wanted variety only as long as it did not cost much. Laborers could be hired and fired readily and supplies were tangential to the success of the business. Automobile industries kept large inventories on hand to deal with bottlenecks or strikes. Quality was an afterthought; poor workmanship or design could be fixed by reworking the product. After forty years this system failed as the international markets reasserted themselves. While the American automobile industry stood still, Japanese industrialists pioneered flexible manufacturing, allowing a plant to shift from the production of one model to another in minutes, accomplishing changes in five minutes that took from eight to twenty-four hours in American plants. Japanese industrialists set first-time

quality as a major company goal, thus eliminating waste in inventories, defects, excess plant space, and unnecessary human effort. Japanese companies made continuous incremental improvements part of every worker's job. This efficiency and flexibility allowed the Japanese industry to work on a cycle of seven and a half years from initial conception until the last vehicle rolled off the assembly line, compared with the American product cycle of thirteen to fifteen years. Japanese manufacturers responded quicker to consumer preferences; this was the primary advantage they had over their American competitors.

Sources:
Barry Bluestone and Bennett Harrison, *The Deindustrialization of America: Plant Closings, Community Abandonment, and the Dismantling of Basic Industry* (New York: Basic Books, 1982);

Michael L. Dertouzos, Richard K. Lester, and Robert M. Solow, *Made in America: Regaining the Productive Edge* (New York: Harper & Row Perennial Library, 1989);

Paul A. Tiffany, *The Decline of American Steel: How Management, Labor, and Government Went Wrong* (New York: Oxford University Press, 1988).

DEREGULATION

Origins. Deregulation, reducing the restraint placed by government on economic activity, gathered momentum in the late 1970s. The movement grew out of the antibureaucratic rhetoric that was popular in the late 1960s, especially around the presidential campaign of conservative Democrat George Wallace. By the 1970s some liberals had also endorsed deregulation as a way to protect consumers against legally sanctioned monopolies, such as the telephone company, AT&T. President Carter brought several of these trends together when he promised to free the American people from the burden of overregulation. By 1980 Carter had begun deregulating airlines, trucking, railroads, and interest rates. However, Carter did increase environmental regulation.

Acceleration. When Ronald Reagan assumed the presidency in 1980 the basic framework of deregulation was already in place. Indeed, Murray Weidenbaum, Reagan's chairman of the Council of Economic Advisors, described Reagan as extraordinarily timid in taking leadership on deregulation. By 1985 the Reagan administration had taken action in bus deregulation, oil price control, and piecemeal dealings with telephone, electric, and gas utilities. Airline deregulation was saving the public $6 billion a year in airfares. Reagan also expanded the scope of the Carter administration's deregulation efforts. The Reagan administration focused on agencies such as the Environmental Protection Agency, the Consumer Product Safety Commission, and the Occupational Safety and Health Administration. The Republican administration argued that regulations pertaining to the consumer, the workplace, and the environment were inefficient, paternalistic, and excessively expensive. Reagan appointed people like James Watt, his first secretary of the interior, who systematically relaxed enforcement of existing environmental rules and made national land available for de-

Workers painting the Northwest Airlines logo on a Republic Airlines plane after Northwest took over the smaller carrier in August 1986. The merger was one of many that resulted from deregulation in the mid 1980s.

velopment in order to accommodate businesses. Watt was a lawyer who had worked for the Mountain States Legal Defense Foundation, an organization that used legal challenges to fight environmental regulations in the West. At the Department of the Interior, Watt reduced or eliminated restrictions on private development of federal lands. Watt put an end to the practice of the federal government preempting state water rights, leased a billion acres of federal land for offshore oil and gas exploration, and eased restrictions on strip-mining. Perhaps his most controversial move was to open four California offshore oil tracts for exploration. Watt was generally opposed by environmentalists, but the California move drew howls of protest even from leading California Republicans.

Doubts. By 1985 doubts were rising about the wisdom of deregulation. The movement fostered reckless financial speculation. Higher interest rates deepened the recession of 1979–1982. When the economy finally came out of the 1982 recession, the recovery took place with minimal regulatory inhibition applied to interest rates, something that had not occurred since the Harding-Coolidge days of the 1920s. Estimates put the expense of deregulation at several hundred billion dollars in additional interest payments between 1980 and 1988. While the banking industry initially did well in a deregulated

economy, marginal sectors of the economy did not do as well. The housing industry, which is dependent on borrowing, suffered. Deregulation also influenced air travel. During the four years following deregulation in 1978, weekly departures from large cities had risen 5 percent, but weekly departures from small towns dropped 12 percent. By 1988, 140 small towns had lost all air service. Still, air fares were markedly lower throughout the world because of U.S. deregulation.

Labor. From the Reagan administration's point of view, organized labor was another drag on business development. Labor unions had enjoyed the right to organize workers since the New Deal legislation of the 1930s, and in the intervening decades organized labor had accumulated a good amount of political and economic power. Reagan signaled a new less-idealistic attitude toward organized labor when he confronted the Professional Air Traffic Controllers Organization (PATCO) in 1981. PATCO president Robert E. Poli had supported Reagan during the 1980 presidential election. When PATCO workers illegally went on strike Reagan followed the advice of Secretary of Transportation Drew Lewis and fired all of the striking workers. With no sympathy in the administration, organized workers found their position slipping in the face of foreign competition and the antiinflationary policies of Federal Reserve chairman

INFLATION RATES UNDER REAGANOMICS:	
1980	13.5 percent (Carter)
1981	10.4%
1982	6.1%
1983	3.2%
1984	4.3%
1985	3.6%

ANNUAL FEDERAL EXPENDITURES ON INTEREST	
1981	$96 billion
1983	$129 billion
1985	$178 billion
1988	$216 billion

Paul Volcker. By the end of the decade, only about 12 percent of American workers in private industry belonged to unions. Workers in regulated industries had often received 30 percent to 100 percent higher wages than people with comparable skills in the economy at large. Federal and state regulation had allowed these costs to be passed on to consumers, but when competition replaced regulation companies began to drive down the cost of labor.

Sources:
Lou Cannon, *President Reagan: The Role of a Lifetime* (New York: Simon & Schuster, 1991);

Kevin Phillips, *The Politics of Rich and Poor: Wealth and the American Electorate in the Reagan Aftermath* (New York: Harper & Row, 1990).

THE ECONOMY IN TRANSITION

Service Economy. The 1980s saw the culmination of a long-standing trend in the American economy. Throughout most of the twentieth century, most workers had earned their living producing items in factories or working in other jobs related to manufacturing. By the mid 1980s, however, three-fourths of America's 113 million workers earned their living providing services. They were part of the growing service sector and a symptom of the transformation of the economy from an industrial economy to a service economy. Instead of manufacturing products such as automobiles, service workers provided information or performed tasks for customers. Occupations in the service sector varied widely, ranging from work in the fast-food industry, derided as "McJobs," to careers in such fields as computer programming, law, and medicine.

The Rich. The decade saw the reversal of another long-term trend in the American economy. Since World War II the prosperity of the middle class had become the hallmark of the American dream and the gaps between the wealthy, the middle class, and the poor had been lessening. During the 1980s, though, the well-heeled began to leave the middle class and the poor behind. The chief economic beneficiaries in the 1980s were the wealthiest 20 percent of the population, with the greatest benefits going to the top half of the top 1 percent. In 1980 the United States had 574,000 millionaires; by 1988 the number had grown to 1.3 million, including more than fifty billionaires. Adjusted for inflation the country had 180,000 millionaires in 1972 and just 27,000 in 1953.

"Unearned Incomes." The emerging global economy brought accompanying changes in trade, finance, and technology that restructured the U.S. economy. Although the new economic reality favored people with skill, enterprise, and imagination, the United States invested little in the type of education and training that developed those traits — lack of investment that is held by many to be an important contributary factor in the stagnation of wages, the main source of middle-class and lower-class income. Government policy ignored the stagnation in wages but encouraged a high return on capital through disinflation and deregulation. While wages rose slowly — as they normally do in times recovering from damagingly high inflation rates, such as those in the Carter years — incomes from rents, dividends, capital gains, and interest did well.

New Industries. While the 1980s was a period of transition in most of the economy, the transformation seemed the most dynamic in businesses that dealt with information and communication. Since the early years when television became part of American culture the business had been dominated by three networks, ABC, CBS, and NBC. These companies could trace their corporate lineage back to the days of radio. During the 1980s all three of these industries lost market shares. In the mid 1970s the Big Three networks claimed more than 90 percent of the nightly television viewers, but by 1990 they had lost more than a third of the market share, or about 10 million viewers each night. As a result, their profits shrank from $800 million in 1984 to $400 million in 1988. Part of the explanation for this drop came in the explosion of television channels available on cable. In 1991 the average home had thirty-three channels to choose from, while in 1976 they had only the three networks and a small number of independent channels. Entrepreneurs such as Ted Turner launched cable networks. Turner's empire included such networks as Turner Network Television (TNT) and Cable News Network (CNN). Rupert Murdoch spearheaded the launch of a

Farmers standing on a huge pile of surplus grain at a government storage facility in 1983

fourth major network, Fox, in 1986. The breakup of AT&T eventually resulted in an explosion of new long-distance telephone carriers such as Sprint and MCI.

Sources:

Ken Auletta, *Three Blind Mice: How the TV Networks Lost Their Way* (New York: Random House, 1991);

Kevin Phillips, *The Politics of Rich and Poor: Wealth and the American Electorate in the Reagan Aftermath* (New York: Harper & Row, 1990);

Robert Reich, *The Work of Nations: Preparing Ourselves for 21st Century Capitalism* (New York: Knopf, 1991).

FARM CRISIS

The Family Farm. Farming has always held a special, and unusual, place in America. Thomas Jefferson's perhaps naive view of the farmer as a virtuous citizen who served as the cornerstone of the republic has been preserved in the American national culture. The romantic image of the farm family working the soil is not the only reason for the prominence of farming in American society. Taken as a whole, agriculture is the nation's largest industry. More people work in businesses related to agriculture than in steel and automobile manufacturing combined. During the 1980s agriculture accounted for 20 percent of the gross national product but also faced a serious crisis.

Boom and Bust. The history of American agriculture during the 1970s and 1980s is the reverse of what is typically expected. The 1970s were boom times for farmers, while in the 1980s farmers faced a severe bust. During the 1970s Secretary of Agriculture Earl Butz urged farmers to plant from fencerow to fencerow to meet the increasing demands in sales, domestic and abroad. To increase productivity farmers bought new farm equipment and more land. Low interest rates made these loans seem like sound investments since farmers expected increased revenues. However, as the new decade emerged the bottom began to drop out of American agriculture. Part of the explanation lies in foreign markets. The Third World nations that had purchased so much American food exports had overextended their borrowing credit and had begun to reduce their imports, and this included American crops. During the 1980s farmers produced more crops than they could sell. To make matters even more difficult for the indebted farmers, land prices fell sharply. Low land prices lowered the amount of collateral for loans, making additional loans more expensive, with soaring interest rates further complicating the matter for farmers. Family farms went bankrupt, and the lands were foreclosed. Between 1981 and 1986 some 150,000 farms went bankrupt, nearly 43,000 in 1985 alone. The farm belt collapse of 1981–1987 brought on by a collapse in commodity and land prices was the worst in the century, topping even the disaster of the 1920s. In contrast to the huge fortunes being created in the financial markets, wealth vanished in the farm states. The farm collapse slowed only when the Reagan administration decided in the mid 1980s to support farm incomes through expansion of the money-supply and currency devaluation and unprecedented federal spending on farm programs. Federal support represented slightly more than 25 percent of farmers' net cash income in 1981, but by 1986 it rose to almost 60 percent. Even with these subsidies, the value of farmland in states such as Illinois, Iowa, and Minnesota bottomed out in early 1987.

Suburban Farmers. Even massive federal aid did not compensate farmers for their enormous losses. In Minnesota the per-acre price of average land fell from $1,947 in 1981 to $628 in 1987. Because Minnesota had 30 million acres in farm land, the drop in land prices meant a $20–$40 billion loss in wealth. Minnesota was not alone in such losses, as a similar trend also took place in Illinois and Iowa. In North and South Dakota, farmland lost $10 billion to $15 billion in value, a tremendous drop in per capita terms. Estimates placed the total decline in the value of land in the United States from $712 billion in 1980 to $392 billion in 1986. By 1988 prices were starting to reinflate. Even with the recovery of 1988, there were still fewer farmers in the nation as many people had left their farms during the decade. In the early 1980s, 6 million farmers lived in the United States; by 1987 the farm population had dropped to less than 5 million. This was a continuation of a long-term trend, as the farm population was almost 9 million in 1975. With this decrease in population, prosperous larger farms replaced poor smaller ones. By 1987 absentee investors accounted for about 31 percent of farm ownership, up from 23 percent in 1983.

Sources:

Robert Emmet Long, ed., *The Farm Crisis* (New York: H. W. Wilson, 1987);

Kevin Phillips, *The Politics of Rich and Poor: Wealth and the American Electorate in the Reagan Aftermath* (New York: Harper & Row, 1990).

HIGH FINANCE

Corporate Champion. During the early years of the 1980s, the financial institutions of the United States in effect became the chosen industry and corporate champion of the nation. The secretary of the treasury, Donald Regan, who was also the former president of Merrill Lynch, dreamed of the day when American banks would dominate the world. The American finance system had emerged from the 1970s in relatively good shape, and members of the Reagan administration wanted to unleash the potential of the business. The hallmark of free market theory, the doctrine of comparative advantage, holds that in a global economy nations should specialize in doing what they do best. This would maximize the positive effects of competition. In the United States the

Wall Street brokers celebrating on 8 January 1987, the day the Dow Jones Industrial Average closed over 2,000 for the first time in the history of the New York Stock Exchange. Later that year, on 19 October, the market fell 500 points.

theory provided a way to explain why heavy industry was doing so poorly while banks and computer industries were doing so well.

Speculation. Support for the banking industry reached high levels during the 1980s. Corporate raiders and speculative buyouts were tolerated and, to some extent, encouraged by the administration, whose belief in the power of market forces to direct the economy helped to provide rationalization and support for speculative activities. The 1981 Recovery Tax Act had added fuel to the speculative impulse. Intended to spur economic growth by cutting taxes and government spending, the act had also allowed businesses to claim depreciation allowances sooner than had previously been the case. As a result, cash flow grew faster than reported earnings, and companies retained large amounts of cash on hand rather than channeling the money into stock dividends. Companies were able to borrow more money, and they also became attractive targets for speculators, who could then use the assets of a conquered company to pay off debts accrued in its takeover. Other ties between the speculative financiers and the Republican administrations were more direct. Many of the most prominent and successful raiders and speculators, including T. Boone Pickens, Ivan Boesky, leveraged buyout (LBO) magnate Henry Kravis, and Sir

COLA WARS

During the 1980s the soft-drink industry became much more competitive. A Cuban refugee, Robert C. Goizueta, who arrived in the United States in 1959 with $20, became the head of Coca-Cola. In 1983, under his leadership, Coca-Cola released Caffeine Free Coke and Tab; in 1985 New Coke and Cherry Coke were released. The unpopularity of New Coke forced the company to bring back the original formula as Coca-Cola Classic. Also in 1985 independent bottlers and Pepsi Cola brought an antitrust suit against Coca-Cola. Both sides enlisted a variety of celebrities in the Cola Wars, including Michael Jackson and Max Headroom, an animated computerized talking head.

James Goldsmith, supported the Republican Party through fund-raisers.

Credit Card Economy. Debt and borrowing were not just limited to the federal government during the 1980s but were also practiced extensively by businesses, financiers, and private individuals. Many Americans financed major purchases — and minor ones as well — with credit cards, which sometimes had interest rates approaching 20 percent.

The LBO. Leveraged buyouts of corporations also marked 1980s business. In a leveraged buyout, a group of investors pooled resources, including borrowed money, to buy out a resistant company in a hostile takeover. Small investors often used borrowed money to make investments and told themselves that even with sky-high interest rates they could use the cash flow from companies acquired in a corporate takeover, together with profits gained by breaking up a conquered company, to cover their interest payments and to achieve a profit. Leveraged buyouts received much press coverage during the 1980s, including the leveraged buyout of Beatrice (for $8.2 billion) and RJR Nabisco (for $24.7 billion). By the end of the decade many Americans associated the LBO phenomenon with greed and scandal such as that following the 1987 conviction of Ivan Boesky for insider trading. Analysts have also pointed out that LBOs were generally financially unsound. While some corporate raids were successful, many other deals were disastrous. Companies that had been successful and stable were often driven into financial ruin by their new owners, who were generally more interested in squeezing out profit than making sure that newly acquired businesses remained stable and successful. Some of the conquests turned into disaster, including the Federated and Allied retail store chains, which were driven into bankruptcy after being taken over by Robert Campeau. One of the major firms that pro-

moted LBOs and junk bond financing, Drexel Burnham Lambert, itself collapsed as the LBO phenomenon began to fade. Both the firms that were taken over and those that resisted takeovers (often by borrowing money to keep from being taken over) were left with high levels of debt as they entered the 1990s.

Sources:

Connie Bruck, *The Predators' Ball: The Junk Bond Raiders and the Man who Staked Them* (New York: American Lawyer/Simon & Schuster, 1988);

Daniel Seligman, "Looking Backward: The System Worked," *Fortune* (26 March 1990): 183.

MICROELECTRONICS: SEMICONDUCTORS, COMPUTERS, AND COPIERS

Innovation. The microelectronics industries demonstrate several of the defining characteristics of the American economy during the 1980s. One segment of the economy would prosper while other businesses suffered. Innovation and entrepreneurship marked the origins of industries and fortunes, some of which then proved uncompetitive in the global economy. Americans were behind the scientific advances that created the industry: the transistor, the semiconductor chip, and computers large and small. Microelectronic industries such as IBM, Digital Equipment, Intel, Apple, and Xerox led American business.

Competition. Yet America's share of the microelectronics market fell during the decade. The U.S. share of semiconductor production fell from 60 percent to 40 percent during the 1980s. By the end of the 1980s three Japanese companies, NEC, Toshiba, and Hitachi, were the leading semiconductor companies in the world. Underlying this trend was the American pattern of early innovative technological success followed by a failure to establish the company, secure investment, and continue the innovation that would lead to future growth. Typically, in such companies skilled employees left to pursue their own businesses and proprietary knowledge was sold to the highest bidder, often to a foreign company. In contrast to the premium Americans placed on innovation and early entrepreneurship, Japanese firms stressed vertical integration and stability. Japanese companies often made more chips than they used internally and sold the excess. American companies such as IBM and AT&T relied on the outside suppliers to provide chips since they manufactured fewer chips than they needed. Japanese firms in the past prepared for up cycles in demand by investing in production facilities during down cycles. American firms generally invested during good times. The Department of Defense, which relies heavily on microchips for modern weapons, created Sematech, a research consortium of chip makers to deal with the problem. Related to microprocessors is the story of the photocopier. Xerox invented the photocopier and for many years dominated the industry. But by 1979 Xerox's manufacturing costs were twice those of Japanese companies,

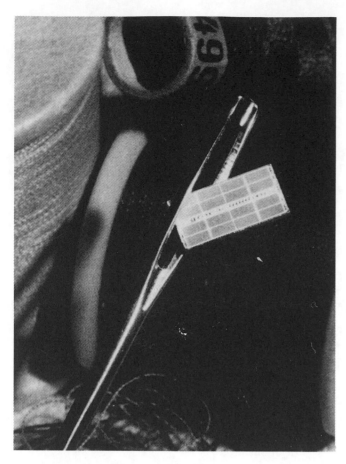

A computer chip introduced by IBM in January 1987. It stored one million bits of data in two-thirds the area of the chip it replaced.

its production-development time was twice as long, and its product-development teams required twice as many people. During the 1980s Xerox lost ground to its competitors, especially to Japanese competitors.

Source:

Michael L. Dertouzos, Richard K. Lester, and Robert M. Solow, *Made in America: Regaining the Productive Edge* (New York: Harper & Row Perennial Library, 1990).

REAGANOMICS

Rejecting Keynes. When Ronald Reagan ran for president in 1980 he rejected the prevailing economic theory that had dominated American economic policy since World War II. Reagan affirmed his belief in free markets and rejected the idea that the federal government should influence the business cycles with its fiscal policies. Indeed, one of the favored targets for Reagan's wrath was the deficit spending that Keynesian economists called for, and the ensuing debt. Upon election, Reagan inherited, as he put it, a runaway deficit of nearly $80 billion in 1981, leading Reagan to proclaim that the federal budget was out of control. Reagan promised to balance the budget and to bring a new type of economics to Washington.

Supply-Side Economics. Reagan desired to change the nation's economic path. During the 1980 presidential primaries Republican presidential hopeful George Bush labeled Reagan's plan as "voodoo economics," although after the election Bush upheld Reagan's economic policies both as his vice president and after his own election to the presidency in 1988. At the heart of supply-side economics was Reagan's belief in incentives. Proclaiming that government was the problem, not the solution, Reagan argued that across-the-board cuts in the personal tax rates would provide enough economic stimulation so that lower tax rates would deliver higher tax revenues. Reagan believed that lower tax rates, with lower government spending, would in fact balance the federal budget, not increase deficit spending. Reagan and his budget director, David Stockman, spoke of reducing federal spending by $67 billion. However, Reagan had also promised to restore America's military might after a losing effort in the Vietnam War and a failed attempt to rescue hostages held by Iran. Fulfilling this promise resulted in the largest increase in peacetime military spending in the history of the United States. Reagan found it politically difficult to counter Democratic opposition to cutting popular nondefense programs. In 1981 Congress overwhemingly passed the Kemp–Roth tax cuts to put Reagan theory into practice. Congress cut the projected federal spending by $35.1 billion, as opposed to the $67 billion that Reagan first proposed, in 1982 and approved a three-year, 25 percent reduction in personal and business income taxes. Following the 1978 capital gains tax cut and the new 1981 tax rates, the combined federal income taxes paid by the top 1 percent of the population on earned income dropped from 50 percent in 1981 to 37.5 percent in 1983. The tax cuts were combined with Democrat-forced modest cuts in nondefense spending and a massive increase in military spending. Americans enjoyed both continued government spending and lower tax rates. According to Reagan's original plan, such policies would produce a balanced budget by 1984.

Debt. Deficit spending was a key issue in presidential politics in the late 1970s. While campaigning for the presidency, Reagan promised to balance the budget by 1983. Deficit spending is the gap between what the federal government takes in as income (mostly but not exclusively from taxes) and what it spends. To make up the difference between expenditures and income, the federal government borrows money from the private sector or from other governments, sometimes in the form of bonds. Therefore, every year that the government runs a deficit it adds to the national debt. Some economists believe that deficit spending can be good in that it will stimulate the economy, as was the case when spending on World War II ended the Great Depression, but others believe that long-term deficit spending makes it harder for people in the private sector to borrow money. When those people borrow money to buy a house or start a business, they end up competing with the government for the available capital. From 1981 to 1987 the federal deficit ranged from a low of $128 billion in 1982 to a high of $221 billion in 1986. The accumulated debt of the six years of deficit spending was more than $1.1 trillion. When Reagan left office in 1988 the national debt was $2.6 trillion, compared with the $914 billion debt he inherited from Carter. In 1986 the United States became a debtor nation, the largest in the world.

Sources:

Lou Cannon, *President Reagan: The Role of a Lifetime* (New York: Simon & Schuster, 1991);

Benjamin M. Friedman, *Day of Reckoning: The Consequences of American Economic Policy Under Reagan and After* (New York: Random House, 1988);

Kevin Phillips, *The Politics of Rich and Poor: Wealth and the American Electorate in the Reagan Aftermath* (New York: Harper & Row Perennial Library, 1990).

THE SAVINGS AND LOAN CRISIS

Background. Historically, savings and loan associations (S and Ls) have served a different body of customers than banks. S and Ls made most of their money by providing services to working-class and middle-class people rather than to large businesses or other financial institutions. In 1903 journalist D. A. Tomkins wrote that the building and loan association gave a solution to the problem of financing people's homes that is most essentially advancement by self-help. According to two authorities on banking systems, with the turn of the century the American banking system rested on three legs: (1) deposit-owned mutual savings banks, (2) stock-chartered savings banks that profited investors rather than depositors, and (3) building and loan associations, later known as savings and loans associations. In 1928 the first great banking crisis of the twentieth century began as the American financial system began collapsing in one of the early symptoms of the Great Depression. The result was an extensive set of regulations put in place by New Deal reformers to prevent a similar collapse in the future and to restore the public's confidence in the banking system.

Bailout. Ed Gray, as chairman of the Federal Home Loan Bank Board, was one of the first people to deal with the impending crisis in the savings and loan industry. The Financial Corporation of America (FCA) and its subsidiaries, located in California, experienced a run on its deposits by worried customers. FCA had participated in the merger mania of the 1980s, and for a period it had grown at nearly $1 billion a month. A run on the institution by depositors endangered the bank, and if FCA collapsed it could create a domino effect among other financial institutions that would lead to disaster. The entire Federal Savings and Loan Corporation could have been bankrupted by the collapse of this one large savings and loan. This scenario became a familiar one in the 1980s. By 1988 the savings and loan crisis was rapidly emerging with the projection that $100 billion to $200 billion or more would be needed to bail out hundreds of overextended institutions. As part of the New Deal regu-

lations, federally chartered S and Ls were required to place almost all of their loans in the relatively safe investment in home mortgages. The high interest rates of the late 1970s and early 1980s made low-interest mortgages unprofitable, so new federal laws passed in 1982 gave S and Ls the liberty to invest their funds more freely. S and Ls could invest 100 percent in commercial real estate ventures; before they would have required 10 or 20 percent down from the developer. Like banks in the 1920s, many S and Ls gambled with their federally guaranteed deposits, often charging large fees for their services. Eventually bad investments and poor loan choices took their toll on the industry. By 1990 the estimated cost to the taxpayers for the savings and loans bailout had reached $500 billion.

Sources:

Martin Lowy, *High Rollers: Inside the Savings and Loan Debacle* (New York: Praeger, 1991);

Paul Zane Pilzer and Robert Deitz, *Other People's Money: How Bad Luck, Worse Judgment, and Flagrant Corruption Made a Shambles of a $900 Billion Industry* (New York: Simon & Schuster, 1989);

Michael A. Robinson, *Overdrawn: The Bailout of American Savings: The Inside Story of the $2 Billion S & L Debacle* (New York: Dutton/Penguin Books, 1990).

SILICON VALLEY: THE COMPUTER REVOLUTIONIZES AMERICA

A New Day. During the 1970s and 1980s, many people made fortunes in the computer business. Beyond the importance of individual fortunes, the computer and the various industries that produced computers and related materials dramatically changed American society. The desktop and the laptop computers made it possible for individuals working a wide variety of environments to accomplish tasks that before required substantially more resources.

Mainframe. The computer industry in the United States is only about forty years old. Originally the computer industry was dominated by IBM, or International Business Machines. During the 1960s the phrase "IBM and the seven dwarfs" was used to describe the computer industry because of IBM's dominance. During the 1960s both RCA and General Electric tried to enter the computer business only to fail. RCA finally wrote off $300 million in losses in 1970. IBM specialized in manufacturing mainframe computers, the computers that were as big as a room — sometimes larger — and required specially trained employees to program and enter data into the computers through punch cards. Indeed, IBM intended for those computers to last for decades and to make most of the profit not through the initial sale but through servicing the mainframe. To escape from IBM's virtual monopoly, many American companies, such as Honeywell, began buying Japanese systems. The government frowned upon IBM's dominance of the market and the Justice Department brought an antimonopoly suit against IBM to promote competitiveness in the industry. The Justice Department intended to break IBM up into a set

Customers lining up at an Ohio savings and loan that had been closed for eight days to prevent depositors from withdrawing their money, March 1985

of little IBMs. The suit, costing millions of dollars, dragged on for more than a decade before it was settled in 1982. Under the agreement IBM ended its practice of discouraging customers from buying competitive systems. IBM also agreed to provide competitors with technical specifications since IBM products often set the standard in the industry. Significantly, IBM also agreed to unbundle its software, that is, IBM would sell software as separate items rather than making software part of the price of the computer. This opened the door for dramatic growth in the software business. The agreement was reached after the computer industry had undergone revolutionary changes. The Defense Department also funded research and development in the industry, resulting in some significant breakthroughs in computer speed.

Microcomputers. During the 1980s there was an explosion in the sale and development of microcomputers. These personal computers, based on microprocessors, eventually made the mainframe all but obsolete and caught IBM off guard. Apple first introduced the easy-to-use personal computer in the 1970s and was soon followed into the business by start-up companies. IBM was slow to follow the market. When IBM did enter the market the company did so in a big way, using the corporation's vast resources and name recognition to dominate the personal computer market temporarily. Initially, IBM did not manufacture computers but bought computers from other manufacturers and then applied

the IBM name to them. It was this temporary dominance that led to the term *IBM clone* to describe computers that operated from IBM's Disk Operating System (DOS) rather than the Apple and Macintosh operating systems.

The Personal Computer. IBM made record profits during the early 1980s but failed to lay the groundwork for future success. IBM managers, who were reluctant to enter the microcomputer business in the first place, turned their attention to personal computers and ignored the $4-billion per-year mainframe business. When IBM began losing market share in the personal computer business IBM found itself in considerable trouble by the late 1980s. For the most part IBM slippage was the result of poor planning. The selling of software is a prime example of IBM not planning well. IBM spent millions of dollars developing bad software even as the upstart Microsoft Corporation sold its DOS system on IBM computers. Eventually Microsoft would dominate the software business. By the early 1990s IBM had lost $75 billion in assets.

The Soul of the New Machine. During the 1980s the entrepreneurial spirit was still alive in the computer industry. Many of the upstarts of the late 1960s and 1970s faced the same problems that IBM did as the companies matured and took on more bureaucrats. Apple, the company that had done so much to pioneer the field of personal computers, was also in trouble. Although Apple had introduced the technically innovative Macintosh, Steve Jobs and Steve Wozniak, the founders of Apple, found themselves on the opposite side of office politics. Wozniak left the company and eventually Jobs also left the company, leaving Apple under the control of John Scully, a business executive brought into Apple's management to improve the company's management structure. Jobs then founded NEXT, a company that built sophisticated scholar workstations that were marketed to universities. Often people with brilliant technical vision lacked the skills, or the interest, to build a company that would last for generations or even for years. Still, the American computer industry did well — despite IBM's troubles — both at home and in international markets. Throughout the 1980s the United States ran a balance of trade surplus in computers, although it declined from $7 billion in 1981 to $3 billion in 1987. In the 1980s people founded both hardware and software companies. Fred Gibbons founded the Software Publishing Corporation in 1981, and by 1985 he had 6 percent of the $400 billion software business. The Intel Corporation, founded in 1968 by Andrew Grove, Gordon Moore, and Robert Noyce, remained a leading developer and manufacturer of microprocessors throughout the decade. J. Reid

Anderson's Verbatim Corporation did well selling magnetic storage media, including floppy disks. The Hewlett-Packard Company, founded in 1939, proved it could still be innovative when it introduced the laptop computer in 1984. Two factors have helped to defend computer markets against assault. The American computer industry is well balanced between entrepreneurs with vision and technological dreams who start companies with a big splash and large well-financed firms such as IBM, Digital Equipment, and Hewlett-Packard. These companies had the staying power and the size needed to exert influence over the structure of the industry.

Sources:

Paul Carroll, *Big Blues: The Unmaking of IBM* (New York: Crown, 1993);

Michael L. Dertouzos, Richard K. Lester, and Robert M. Solow, *Made in America: Regaining the Productive Edge* (New York: Harper & Row Perennial Library, 1989);

Irvin Farman, *Tandy's Money Machine: How Charles Tandy Built Radio Shack Into the World's Largest Electronics Chain* (Chicago: Mobium Press, 1992);

Robert Slater, *Portraits in Silicon* (Cambridge: Massachusetts Institute of Technology Press, 1987).

HEADLINE MAKERS

IVAN BOESKY

1937-

DEAL MAKER AND INSIDE TRADER

Symbol. Ivan Boesky became one of the most famous, and notorious, deal makers of the 1980s. By the middle of the decade Boesky was one of the leading figures on Wall Street and a leading symbol of the prosperity and the corruption of the decade. Boesky was a restless, driven man who found success on Wall Street.

Restless. Ivan's father, William, an immigrant from Russia who owned a chain of bars that featured topless dancing and strippers, became a source of embarrassment for his son as Boesky matured. Boesky never seemed to be accepted by the right crowd. During his teen years Boesky briefly attended the exclusive Cranbrook preparatory school where he had an average academic record,

eventually transferring to the public Mumford High School. Boesky attended a variety of colleges and universities before going to Iran with a high-school friend. Boesky's years in Iran are a mystery, but upon returning to the United States he attended law school. Boesky spent five years getting his law degree because he dropped out twice. Upon graduation he went to work in his father's business. Boesky's success came when he moved to New York and entered into the arbitrage business. In 1975, backed by his wife's money, Boesky founded the Ivan F. Boesky Company. Boesky's new business was speculating on corporate takeovers, a fortunate decision that placed him well for the frenzy of mergers and acquisitions that was about to consume Wall Street.

Boesky Day. On 14 November 1986 government investigators announced that Boesky had pleaded guilty to insider trading and had agreed to pay a $100 million fine, the largest fine ever levied for the offense. Even as Boesky was becoming one of the most successful deal makers on Wall Street it was a poorly kept secret that he participated in insider trading. Boesky would use illegally obtained confidential information to gain unfair advantage in stock trading. Still, the news of Boesky's deal with governmental officials shocked Wall Street insiders and the day became known as "Boesky Day." It was even more unsettling to learn that Boesky had agreed to cooperate with further investigations of insider trading. With the news of Boesky's plea bargain the Securities and Exchange Commission, the federal agency that regulates stock trading, issued subpoenas seeking information about the business transactions of Michael Milken, Carl Icahn, Victor Posner, and Boyd Jefferies — all prominent figures on Wall Street during the 1980s. Boesky's business dealings with Milken dated back to mid 1983, and since then Boesky had relied heavily on Milken's firm, Drexel Burnham Lambert, for funds. The government investigators and prosecutors focused on a $5.3 million payment made by Boesky during March 1986. The payment had long seemed suspicious and was even questioned by Boesky's own auditors. Boesky eventually produced a letter from Milken's firm, signed by top executives, supporting his story that the money was for consulting. In reality, Boesky was parking his assets with Drexel, thereby hiding his real worth. Boesky eventually testified against Michael Milken and Drexel.

The Root of All Evil. Boesky went to prison in 1988, and before entering he separated from Seema Boesky, his wife of more than thirty years. In 1991 she formally filed for divorce, and Ivan Boesky sued his wife for $1 million a year in temporary alimony. Although Seema's money had financed much of Ivan's early business ventures, she claimed she did not know of her husband's illegal dealings. Eventually Ivan Boesky received $180,000 a year in alimony. As of 1993 the Boeskys were arguing over how to divide Seema's estimated wealth of $100 million. Boesky's rise and fall demonstrated the potential and the dangers of unregulated capitalism. Traders like Boesky and Michael Milken raised unprecedented sums of money in creative ways, but in doing so they damaged the credibility of Wall Street; Wall Street firms trade not only in stocks and bonds but also in trust.

Sources:

Connie Bruck, *The Predators' Ball: The Junk Bond Raiders and the Man Who Staked Them* (New York: American Lawyer/Simon & Schuster, 1988);

James B. Stewart, *Den of Thieves* (New York: Simon & Schuster, 1991).

W. EDWARDS DEMING

1900-1993

QUALITY EXPERT

Statistician. Deming grew up in Wyoming when the horse and buggy was still a common means of transportation. Deming began graduate school at Yale University in 1924 and received a Ph.D. in physics. Upon graduating he pursued a career with the Department of Agriculture. In 1940 Deming took charge of the census bureau's new program to use statistical methods to sample the population, but it was his experiences in the late 1940s and early 1950s that would eventually change his life, and the economic direction of two countries.

Teacher. During World War II Deming, like many other Americans, put his skills to work in the war effort. Deming taught statistical control methods to engineers, inspectors, and other people engaged in war production. In 1947 Deming worked in Japan even as Gen. Douglas MacArthur and the Supreme Command Allied Powers (SCAP) decided Japan's fate. American policy during the occupation of Japan was to transform Japan into a democratic and capitalistic nation that could be an ally instead of an enemy. To this end American policymakers decided to restore Japan, and in the process, to transform the nation. Deming was part of this process. Deming and a group of young academics and engineers were separately given the task of making Japan's industries once again functional. Deming and the others began preaching quality as the first priority of production. Deming's efforts were so successful that in the decades following the occupation of Japan the highest award a Japanese company could receive was the Deming Award for Quality.

Expert. Deming's influence in Japan was not matched in the United States. In the 1950s and 1960s the philosophy and techniques of Deming and the other quality experts were not in the mainstream of American business philosophy. Because of the heavy investment in factories made during World War II and the destruction of other national economies, American businesses dominated the global economy. Demand for American manufactured goods was so high in the boom times following the war that quantity rather than quality became the goal of production. American business schools began teaching that quality was an afterthought to be addressed by inspectors and that manufacturing quality goods would increase the price of the product.

Consultant. American businesses, looking for a way to survive and flourish in the global economy, began to notice the teachings of Deming and his colleagues during the 1980s. Deming became a highly sought-after quality consultant. His clients included Ford Motor Company, General Motors, Hughes Aircraft, and Dow Chemicals of Canada. Quality consulting became a cottage industry in its own right as engineers and academics, many of whom had worked in Japan during the occupation, began advising companies on the steps needed to make quality products. Deming, a blunt man, would begin by telling his clients that management, not labor, was the problem, and that quality would improve if workers were given power over production (through input and control). Deming argued that quality was the first job of every worker, from the janitors to the president, and that quality products, not profits, would make a company prosper. Deming continued his teaching and consulting work into the 1990s.

Sources:

W. Edwards Deming, *Out of the Crisis* (Cambridge: Massachusetts Institute of Technology Press, 1982);

Lloyd Dobyns and Clare Crawford-Mason, *Quality or Else: The Revolution in World Business* (Boston: Houghton Mifflin, 1991);

Mary Walton, *The Deming Management Method* (New York: Perigee, 1986).

WILLIAM HENRY GATES

1955-

SOFTWARE DEVELOPER

Entrepreneur. William Henry Gates is a study in contrasts. He has shaped one of the most successful American companies of the last few years, but in many ways he seems atypical of the successful businessman of the 1980s. In an era when pinstriped suits and power ties were signs of success, Gates has often been characterized as a nerd, and at times he seems to epitomize the stereotype of the computer nerd with great technical skills but little in the way of social skills.

An Early Start. Gates, the son of a successful Seattle lawyer, dropped out of Harvard University after his junior year to form Microsoft with Paul Allen and Ric Wieland. Gates and Allen grew up together in Seattle, and both shared an interest in computers. While still in high school, Gates and Allen formed a small programming company called Traf-O-Data that analyzed traffic patterns. They met with some success, and the software company TRW offered Gates and Allen $20,000 a year to work in software development. Gates took a year off from high school to pursue the work and then, at the age of seventeen, he entered Harvard University.

Ambition. Gates believed that the future of computers lay in desktop computers and, in particular, he saw the future in the software that those computers would need to function. In January 1975 Bill Gates read the cover story of *Popular Electronics* that featured the Altair microcomputer that sold for $350. Gates and Allen used the Harvard computers to write a version of BASIC that would operate the Altair since the Altairs were not yet available. Allen sold the BASIC version to Ed Robert, the MITS founder who built the Altair. In 1975 Gates dropped out of Harvard to form the Microsoft Corporation with Allen. Within a few months Gates and Allen were writing programs for Apple and Commodore. Microsoft did well for the first five years, selling the original BASIC and a variety of other computer languages. The truly big break came in 1980 when IBM involved Microsoft in its Project Chess, the IBM effort that produced the IBM Personal Computer. IBM asked Gates to design an operating system for the new computer since no existing system would work on the new computer. After the company went public in 1986, Gates's estimated wealth was $390 million. Initially Microsoft provided IBM with DOS, which IBM sold under the IBM label. In 1984 MS-DOS was being used in 2 million computers and in more than 90 percent of the IBM personal computers and IBM compatible equipment. Gates also helped design software for Apple and for Radio Shack. Microsoft doubled in size every year during its first nine years.

Windows of Opportunity. Despite Gate's unwillingness to dress and act the part in public, he has proven to be one of the most aggressive and competent businessmen of the 1980s. An even bigger success for Bill Gates and the Microsoft Corporation came with the development of Windows. Windows is a graphical interface that allows computer users to operate a DOS-driven machine without using the DOS programming commands. The Windows software is modeled after Apple's Macintosh operating system, with the key difference being that the Apple system is a graphically based operating system and the Windows software is simply a covering for the DOS operating system. Nonetheless, the Windows system made personal computers easier to use and cleared the way for the IBM-style computer to dominate the market.

Sources:

Paul Carroll, *Big Blues: The Unmaking of IBM* (New York: Crown, 1993);

Tracy Kidder, *The Soul of the New Machine* (Boston: Little, Brown, 1981);

Robert Slater, *Portraits in Silicon* (Cambridge: Massachusetts Institute of Technology Press, 1987);

James Wallace, *Hard Drive: Bill Gates and the Making of the Microsoft Empire* (New York: Harper Business, 1993).

(NELSON) BUNKER HUNT

1926-

(WILLIAM) HERBERT HUNT

1929-

SILVER SPECULATORS

Silver Speculators. One of the most spectacular and unsuccessful financial schemes of the early 1980s was the attempt of brothers Nelson Bunker Hunt and William Herbert Hunt to corner the world market for silver. Although the brothers failed to corner the silver market, they did manage to wreak havoc in the international market for precious metals and to lose much of one of the largest fortunes in the world.

Arizona Slim. Nelson Bunker Hunt and William Herbert Hunt were born to one of the wealthiest families in America. Their father, Haroldson Lafayette (known as H. L. or Arizona Slim) Hunt, accumulated a fortune in the Texas oil business during the 1920s and 1930s and then invested his oil profits into a range of enterprises that made his family one of the richest families in America. When H. L. Hunt died in 1974, he left behind a family that was ranked highly among the wealthiest families in the world. Bunker and Herbert Hunt were also shaped by their father's outspoken conservative political views and by his unorthodox private life. The Hunt family was a large one: H. L. Hunt had fathered fourteen children by three women, including six with his legal wife, four in a bigamous marriage, and four more with his mistress. Bunker and Herbert were full brothers, the second and third sons born to H. L. and his first wife, Lyda Bunker Hunt. Overshadowed by their father during his lifetime, they came into a considerable fortune when he died. Bunker also assumed his father's role as head of the family's enterprises. When Bunker and Herbert began their efforts to corner the silver market, in the 1970s, their net worth was valued at around $13 billion.

Oil. H. L. Hunt's chosen successor as head of the family business was his oldest son, Hassie. His plans were thwarted when Hassie developed psychiatric problems in his twenties and failed to respond to any of a wide variety of treatments, including a prefrontal lobotomy. H. L. Hunt reluctantly shifted his attention to his second son, Bunker, who seemed to lack the gift that H. L. had shared with Hassie for locating new sources of oil. Bunker lost millions of dollars in unfruitful efforts to locate oil, including the $250 million in his trust fund, before hitting pay dirt. But when Bunker did locate oil, in Libya, he did so in a big way: the Sarir field was one of the largest oil fields ever tapped. Bunker's big strike more than made up for his previous big failures. Although Bunker had a different approach than his father, he and Herbert had assumed control of the family's businesses by the early 1970s.

The Silver Bug. By the mid 1970s Bunker Hunt was becoming increasingly interested in silver. Looking for a source of stability in a world he saw as unstable and susceptible to inflation and the forces of international communism, he became convinced that silver was the solution. He also came to believe that silver was highly undervalued and that its value was bound to increase. Acting on the advice of financial advisers affiliated with the Bache investment house, Bunker and Herbert Hunt began to speculate in silver futures. By the mid 1970s, the Hunts had quietly accumulated almost 10 percent of the known world supply of silver. As the pace of their buying increased, they drove up the price of silver from around $2 per ounce to more than $6 per ounce. While they invested most of their available capital in silver, they set out to increase the value of their holdings further by attempting to convert others to their cause, focusing on Arab investors who had the money to buy massive amounts of silver and drive up its value. They finally succeeding in converting several wealthy Saudi Arabians. As the Hunts and their Arab partners bought more and more silver, the price of silver increased, driving up the value of the Hunts' holdings and allowing them to borrow more money that was then used to buy more silver. As long as silver appreciated in value, the Hunts were able simultaneously to drive up the cost of the metal and acquire more silver in the process. And the plan seemed as though it would succeed. Throughout 1979 the price of silver kept rising, reaching $35 per ounce by the year's end. As investors recognized the potential for profit from buying silver, they joined in the buying scheme, further driving up the price. As the 1980s began, it seemed that the Hunts would be able to corner the market, to acquire control of all remaining silver reserves. In less than a decade, they had helped to drive the price of silver from around $2 per ounce to $50 per ounce in January 1980. Bunker Hunt believed the price would go higher yet — to $200 or $300 an ounce, or perhaps higher.

The Fall. The price of silver did not go up but down. Silver had peaked and its value soon began to fall, along with the price of gold, which had also reached an all-time high, as investors turned from precious metals to treasury bills and bank certificates offering high interest rates. As the value of precious metals fell, the fortunes of the Hunt brothers also took a sharp downward turn. They had borrowed heavily from brokerage firms including Bache, A. G. Edwards, Merrill Lynch, and others, and the borrowed money had to be repaid as the value of silver fell. The Hunts had to meet margin calls as silver fell lower and lower, finally dropping to $20 per ounce by mid March. When their broker asked for a $100 million payment, the largest margin call yet, the Hunts were unable to meet the call. Instead, Bunker Hunt announced that he and his Arab partners would issue paper bonds backed by their 200 million ounces of silver. In effect, he was attempting to create an international currency, backed by the silver standard. But his plan backfired. Instead of stabilizing the price of silver and rescuing the Hunts and their partners, the news revealed the Hunts' unstable position and drove the price of silver down still further. When the stock market opened on 27 March 1980, a day later known as Bloody Thursday, rumors hinted that the investment house of Bache would collapse, and that other firms might follow suit. But Bache did not fall: Bache covered the Hunts' margin call with its own money and was able to recoup the money by selling the Hunts' holdings. Silver had plunged still lower, however, reaching a low of $10.80 per ounce.

The Aftermath. After hearings held by the House Subcommittee on Commerce, Consumer, and Monetary Affairs, the chairman of the Federal Reserve, Paul Volcker, suggested that the government should help the Hunts to restructure their debt so as to stabilize the nation's financial markets. In the plan that was drawn up, the Hunts were required to liquidate their silver holdings in exchange for a loan secured by a large percentage of their wealth.

Source:
Jerome Tucille, *Kingdom: The Story of the Hunt Family of Texas* (New York: Paperjacks, 1987).

REGINALD F. LEWIS

1942-1993

CORPORATE HEAD

Black Entrepreneur. Reginald F. Lewis grew up in a middle-class neighborhood in Baltimore, Maryland. He had five brothers and sisters, and his mother and father divorced when he was young. As a result of the divorce, Lewis and his mother lived with his grandparents for a period. Lewis's mother was a postal worker who eventually remarried an elementary school teacher. Growing up, Lewis had a paper route and, following his grandfather's advice, saved most of the money. At Dunbar High School Lewis was the captain of the baseball, football, and basketball teams. Lewis went on to play quarterback his first year at Virginia State University. After a shoulder injury ended his football career, Lewis became even more dedicated to his studies. He described economics as "love at first sight." From college Lewis went to Harvard Law School and specialized in securities. Lewis wrote his third-year paper on takeovers. After law school Lewis joined Rifkind Wharton and Garrison but left to become a partner in Murphy, Thorp and Lewis, the first African American law firm on Wall Street. In 1973 Lewis started his own company, Lewis and Clarkson, and specialized in venture capital.

Beatrice Buyout. In 1987 Lewis stunned Wall Street by completing the largest offshore leveraged buyout in business history. Lewis was an African American attorney and a small deal maker. Lewis's TLC group sold its share of the McCall Pattern Company at a 90 to 1 return over the original investment. Lewis used this money to finance the $985 million purchase of Beatrice International Foods. With revenues of $250 million TLC was the largest firm owned by an African American group. In 1986 TLC Group was the sixth-ranked African American-owned company with revenues of $63 million; the leading African American–owned firm was Johnson Publishing Company (publisher of *Ebony, Jet,* and other magazines).

Source:
John N. Ingham and Lynne B. Feldman, *African-American Business Leaders: A Biographical Dictionary* (Westport, Conn.: Greenwood Press, 1994), pp. 434-440.

MICHAEL MILKEN

1946-

JUNK BOND KING

Outsider. Michael Milken rivaled Ivan Boesky as the predominant symbol of 1980s-style capitalism, a fitting comparison since the two men worked together and eventually fell together. Milken, like Boesky, was an outsider on Wall Street, a business arena that has been traditionally dominated by upper-crust Ivy League–educated men from a WASP background. What Milken brought to finance was a creative understanding of how to raise money and a single-minded obsession with doing just that.

Obsession. Michael Milken came from a middle-class Jewish family living in the San Fernando Valley of Los Angeles. He attended the University of California at Berkeley and graduated in 1968 majoring in business administration, a continuation of his childhood fascination with financial issues. After receiving an MBA from the Wharton School of Business, Milken went to work for Drexel Burnham Lambert. Drexel, if not the largest Wall Street firm, was respected. Through its various incarnations the company could trace its lineage back to J. P. Morgan. Milken was smart, energetic, and often described as arrogant. Despite his success Milken was oblivious to the normal signs of Wall Street success — he paid little attention to his clothes or the type of car he drove, and he wore a bad toupee. Milken often hired people whom he believed to be committed to their families and then made them work so many hours that they rarely saw them. In the late 1970s Milken began promoting the use of a diversified portfolio of high-yield bonds (known as junk bonds). The Wall Street establishment frowned upon investing in those bonds since the companies floating the bonds often lacked a credit rating. Milken stressed diversified investments as a way to overcome the risks associated with such investments and to bring substantial profits.

Junk Bonds. In 1985 fifteen hundred people attended the annual Drexel High-Yield Bond Conference in Beverly Hills to pay tribute to Michael Milken. In 1979 only about sixty people had attended the invitation-only conference. They were typical of Milken's clients with Drexel Burnham Lambert. Milken's clients tended to be small and medium-sized companies that were run by entrepreneurs. Milken had begun approaching them in the late 1970s and early 1980s. Because of their small size, lack of credit history, or their leveraged capital structure (they owed a lot of money), these companies had not made investment grade by the rating agencies and thus could not raise money by issuing bonds. In order to raise money, these companies had to resort to short-term loans from banks. Banks placed severe restrictions on the companies as part of the price of the loan. Drexel and Milken served these people by underwriting their bonds for the public marketplace. Michael Milken's firm used junk bonds to raise millions of dollars in relatively restriction-free capital for these companies. By 1985 the junk bond market had reached $100 billion. Milken's clients included people who managed thrift institutions, insurance companies, public and private pension funds, and college endowments, not just the reckless or the desperate. Milken argued that "investors obtained better returns on the same amount of money invested in low-grade issued than on high-grades." That, however, proved not to be true when investments in junk bonds were compared with investments in stocks during the course of a decade.

Outlaw. In September 1988 the Securities and Exchange Commission filed a lawsuit against Drexel, naming Milken in two counts of insider trading, charges stemming from its investigation of Ivan Boesky. As a result of the highly publicized trial Milken was asked to leave the firm. The trial was of such a public nature that Milken began a public-relations campaign to recruit black support in case his jury had black members, even gaining some support from Jesse Jackson. Milken was eventually indicted on ninety-eight charges, including some racketeering charges. In November 1990 Milken received a ten-year prison sentence. In 1991 he began serving his sentence in a federal penitentiary, where he earned forty cents a day. By 1992, lawyers working for Milken announced that Milken had paid $500 million in cash to settle civil claims against him; this represented 80 percent of Milken's remaining wealth. When he completed his prison term, Milken's wealth was estimated at around $125 million.

Philanthropist. In 1993 Milken was released from prison, but on the very day that he was released he was diagnosed with prostate cancer. By 1994 Milken and his family had formed the Association for the Cure of Cancer of the Prostate, to which the Milken family pledged $5 million per year for five years. Milken received praise from President Bill Clinton for his foundation.

Sources:

Connie Bruck, *The Predators' Ball: The Junk Bond Raiders and the Man Who Staked Them* (New York: American Lawyer/Simon & Schuster, 1988);

James B. Stewart, *Den of Thieves* (New York: Simon & Schuster, 1991).

H. ROSS PEROT

1930-

BILLIONAIRE POPULIST

Fame. H. Ross Perot gained quite a bit of notoriety in the 1980s and personified the sometimes conflicting trends of the decade. On one hand, Perot was a self-made billionaire who proved that the capitalist system worked; on the other hand, Perot gave voice to the feelings of many Americans who were dissatisfied with the national direction. Perot became famous for his can-do attitude.

Billionaire. H. Ross Perot was a billionaire by the age of thirty-eight. After serving in the U.S. Navy and working for IBM, he founded Electronic Data Systems Corporation (EDS). Perot ran the company like a combination of the FBI and the marines. EDS employees followed their charismatic boss, and if their loyalty wavered Perot reinforced it legally. EDS employees could not quit without losing their highly valuable stock awards, nor could they go to work for a competitor without violating noncompetition agreements. EDS fit Perot's background as a graduate of the U.S. Naval Academy. In an industry noted for its casual dress codes (with the exception of IBM), EDS was one of the few start-up computer companies that required employees to wear suits. Perot built a reputation as a maverick. In 1969 he televised town-hall meetings in support of Richard Nixon's Silent Majority. Later that same year he alienated the Nixon administration by attempting to deliver Christmas gifts, food, and medicine to American prisoners of war in Vietnam. Servicemen missing in Vietnam became an important cause for Perot throughout the 1970s and 1980s. His 1978 commando mission to free EDS executives held captive in Iran became the subject of the television movie *On Wings of Eagles.*

Populist. Even when things apparently went against Perot, he still seemed to possess the golden touch. In 1988 EDS sued H. Ross Perot, the company's founder. In 1984 the troubled General Motors (GM) had purchased EDS in part to enlist Perot in GM's efforts to revitalize the car maker. The chairman of General Motors, Roger B. Smith, did not get along well with Perot. In fact, they got along so poorly that GM paid Perot $700 million to leave and quit criticizing GM. Although Perot was not friendly toward labor unions, during that period his vocal criticism of Smith and General Motors management made him popular among the rank-and-file workers. Perot took on the role of the populist billionaire. On the first day that he was legally permitted to do so, Perot created Perot Systems Corporation and began hiring executives away from EDS. *Forbes* magazine estimated Perot's wealth at $3 billion and ranked him as the fourth richest man in the United States.

Politician. The 1990s found Perot continuing to act the part of the maverick and the billionaire populist. An independent political movement, United We Stand, rode the crest of Perot's popularity. Perot ran a reluctant, on-again, off-again, third-party campaign spending his own money in the 1992 presidential election. Following the election, many of those who had backed and supported Perot became critical of his power over the former grassroots organization.

Source:

Todd Mason, *Perot: An Unauthorized Biography* (Homewood, Ill.: Business One Irwin, 1990).

DAVID A. STOCKMAN

1946-

REAGAN REVOLUTIONARY

Boy Wonder. Since Ronald Reagan left office in 1989, it has become popular to characterize Reagan as not understanding the intricacies of government or the policies his administration pursued. David A. Stockman, however, was the man within the Reagan administration who understood the policies. An archconservative, Stockman, as Reagan's director of the Office of Management and Budget, became famous for his encyclopedic knowledge of the federal budget and his zeal for cutting it.

Ideologue. David Stockman was born in Texas, but when he was five weeks of age his family moved to southwestern Michigan, the location of his family's farm. Young David Stockman developed an early penchant for books, a fascination that he carried into his adult years. According to one biographer, David's wife, Jennifer, readily admits Stockman is much more fascinated by ideas than by his fellow human beings. Human behavior, motivations, and emotions do not interest him except to the extent that they have a direct effect on political issues. In college Stockman studied theology and philosophy and found himself radicalized by the Vietnam War. Stockman spent his college years as a liberal. After college Stockman rediscovered the conservative ideology with which he grew up. Pursuing a family passion, Stockman entered politics and was elected to the House of Representatives in 1976.

The Smartest Man in Washington. During the 1980 presidential election David Stockman helped Ronald Reagan prepare for debates by impersonating John Anderson and Jimmy Carter. Stockman's performance impressed Reagan, who appointed him to be director of the Office of Management and Budget, despite the reservations of some advisers that Stockman was too young for the job. Stockman soon took the lead in attacking the federal government and implementing Reagan's economic agenda. Indeed, Stockman seemed determined to convince the nation that he was the brains in the administration and the expert on the budget. However, Stockman's critics could have been right about his inexperience. In the December 1981 issue of *Atlantic Monthly* Stockman acknowledged the shortcomings of Reaganomics, including the serious miscalculations that eventually led to massive deficit spending. Stockman's other mistake was to link Reaganomics with the "trickle down" policies of the 1920s, policies that are often blamed for causing the Great Depression. Stockman told the

reporter that the $35 billion budget cut was artificial and that the Kemp–Roth Act, which was the cornerstone of Reaganomics, was always a Trojan horse to bring down the top (income-tax) rate. Supply-side economics was the only way to get a tax policy that was really trickle-down. Stockman also veered from the party line in that he considered the supply-side notion that tax cuts were desirable under any condition to be foolish. By 1986, after Stockman had left the administration, he acknowledged his overestimation of the Reagan revolution in his book, *The Triumph of Politics*. He also acknowledged that his acceptance of overly optimistic economic forecasts contributed to his disillusionment. "We were not headed toward a brave new world, as I had thought," he wrote. "Where we were headed was toward a fiscal catastrophe." In 1986 Stockman could compare the original Reagan economic plan, which projected a budget surplus of $28 billion by 1986, to the actual results of $1.93 trillion in accumulated deficits over the five-year period. The miscalculations forced Reagan to make reductions in the defense buildup his administration undertook and led the administration to implement disguised tax increases that raised $80 billion a year by 1986.

Purist. David Stockman left the Reagan administration during Reagan's second term in a White House shake-up. Stockman took a position in the private sector and began writing his book, *The Triumph of Politics*, in which he denounced the Reagan administration for compromising conservative goals.

Sources:
Lou Cannon, *President Reagan: The Role of a Lifetime* (New York: Simon & Schuster, 1991);

Owen Ullman, *Stockman: The Man, the Myth, the Future* (New York: Donald I. Fine, 1986).

DONALD TRUMP

1946-

REAL ESTATE BARON

Fame. In a decade in which businessmen received a great deal of publicity and public adulation, perhaps no businessman received more than Donald Trump. At one point Trump was regularly called "The Donald," reaching the point where he was the easy target for humorists such as Gary Trudeau of the "Doonesbury" comic strip to lampoon.

His Father's Son. Donald Trump was the third child of Fred Trump, a Brooklyn housing developer. A bright and energetic child, Trump bordered on being a brat. Following the seventh grade, Trump was sent by his father to the New York Military Academy to straighten out. While attending the academy, Donald spent his spare time at construction sites and renovating old houses. After college Trump did graduate work at the Wharton School of Business and subsequently went to work in his father's business. Donald immediately began to encourage his father to be less conservative in his business practices. Eventually Trump, bypassing his older brother, became the president of his father's company. Fred Trump had concentrated on building houses and apartments, but Donald Trump wanted to make his name by making a mark on the Manhattan skyline.

Manhattan. In 1973 Donald Trump convinced his father to enter the Manhattan real estate market. At this time the Trump Company was worth $200 million, up from the $40 million that the company had been worth five years previously when Donald had started working for his father. In moving into the Manhattan real estate business, Trump cultivated political connections and hired Roy Cohn as his attorney, valuing his political connections. Trump developed a plan of buying dilapidated properties during economic recessions when prices were cheap. In 1975 he purchased a run-down tract of land owned by the Penn Central Railroad along the Hudson River for $62 million to build a housing development.

Baron. Eventually Trump would built Trump Tower, Trump Plaza, and the Grand Hyatt Hotel. By 1983 Trump had the Trump Plaza under construction; the Trump Tower was near completion; and Harrahs at Trump Plaza in Atlantic City, New Jersey, was well under way. To accomplish his goals, Trump became an important figure in New York City politics, constantly clashing with elected officials and zoning boards. Trump made himself a household name throughout the 1980s through grandstanding and self-promotion. Trump released two books that held up his life as a model to follow to achieve business success. His life also provided the model for a board game titled *Trump*.

Slump. The 1990s were not as kind to Trump as he faced difficulties with banks and other financial institutions. He had overextended himself on many of his deals and had trouble paying the bills. His name also lost some of its luster as his business woes became public. Additionally, Trump went through a messy and public divorce from his wife Ivana that further tarnished his reputation.

Sources:
John R. O'Donnell, with James Rutherford, *Trumped: The Inside Story of the Real Donald Trump — His Cunning Rise and Spectacular Fall* (New York: Simon & Schuster, 1991);

Jerome Tucille, *Trump: The Saga of America's Most Powerful Real Estate Baron* (New York: Donald I. Fine, 1985).

SAM WALTON

1918-1992

RETAIL MAGNATE

Empire. During the 1980s Sam Walton became America's richest man, combining innovation, business savvy, and a down-home style to achieve his success. Walton built his chain of discount stores into the largest in the country, surpassing even K-Mart, while promoting them with small-town values.

Growing Up. Walton grew up during the Great Depression of the 1930s. Despite the dismal climate of the Depression, Walton enjoyed success in his hometown of Columbia, Missouri, as an adolescent. In 1936 *The Crescent,* the Hickman High School annual, proclaimed him to be the Most Versatile Boy. In fall 1936 Walton began studying business administration at the University of Missouri. Working his way through college, Walton began to demonstrate his entrepreneurial skills. Upon graduating from college in 1940, Walton entered the army reserves as a second lieutenant. While in the reserves Walton decided on retail as his career and took his first job with J. C. Penney for eighty-five dollars per month. Sam received crucial training while working at J. C. Penney, some of it from the company's founder, John Cash Penney, before entering the military full-time to serve in World War II. Because of a nerve problem Sam was rejected for overseas duty.

Discount Chains. Following the war Walton purchased the franchise of a Ben Franklin five-and-dime store in Newport, Arkansas. For the next several years he lived in Newport and other small towns in Arkansas as he worked to advance his retail businesses. In the 1950s Walton began thinking of owning a chain of stores, in part enticed by the availability of airplanes to cut traveling time. The Ben Franklin stores specialized in rural markets, and after some success at running several franchises, Walton proposed that the Ben Franklin stores enter the urban market as a discount chain. The Ben Franklin company rejected Walton's proposal, but Walton was determined to piggyback the success of such rising chains as K-Mart, the discount version of Kresge. In the early 1960s Walton left the Ben Franklin stores behind and began his own discount store, named Wal-Mart.

Number One. Walton might have entered the discount chain store business with the idea of imitating the success of other franchises, but, in a pattern that was characteristic of the rest of his life, Walton and Wal-Mart eventually became leaders of the field. Relying on volume sales and direct purchasing from manufacturers,

Wal-Mart undersold the competition. Walton combined old-fashioned P. T. Barnum–style promotion with down-home charm, charisma, good business sense, and competitiveness to build his new chain. David Dayne Glass, a financial officer whom Walton was trying to hire away from another company, described his first visit to the second Wal-Mart store: "It was the worst retail store I had ever seen. Sam had brought a couple of trucks of watermelons in and stacked them on the sidewalk. He had a donkey ride out in the parking lot. It was 115 degrees, and the watermelons began to pop, and the donkey began to do what donkeys do, and it all mixed together and ran all over the place." Despite his initial exposure to Wal-Mart, however, Glass eventually became Wal-Mart's chief executive and credited Walton's success to his willingness to improve each and every day. By 1985 Wal-Mart had more than 750 stores and more than 80,000 employees; by 1990 the company had more than 250,000 associates. Walton stressed input from his associates to further high productivity and encouraged change. By the end of the 1980s Sears and K-Mart both had more stores in operation and led Wal-Mart in total dollar volume in sales. However, Wal-Mart had a faster rate of growth and in 1988 and 1989 passed both of its competitors in profits earned. Wal-Mart was clearly on the rise while K-Mart and Sears struggled. Walton also introduced a new chain called Sam's Wholesale Club that brought in $96 billion in annual sales by the end of the decade. In 1990 Walton's personal fortune was estimated to be between $9 billion and $13 billion.

Bad Luck. Walton had built his business with his family. His brother Bud had always been an important element in Sam's success and he relied heavily on other family members. His daughter Alice was involved in several car accidents in the late 1980s, and Sam himself was diagnosed as having multiple myeloma, a bone disease. In 1982 he was diagnosed with leukemia. Walton died in 1992, the head of the dominant retail chain in the United States.

Sources:
Vance H. Trimble, *Sam Walton: The Inside Story of America's Richest Man* (New York: Dutton, 1990);

Sam Walton with John Huey, *Sam Walton, Made in America: My Story* (Garden City, N.Y.: Doubleday, 1992).

PEOPLE IN THE NEWS

During the recession of the early 1980s Sen. **Howard Baker** from Tennessee threatened to take away the Federal Reserve Board's monetary powers and place the power in the hands of Congress. Baker and other Republicans in Congress were unhappy with the FRB's tight money policies.

James Baker III was a wealthy Texas lawyer who was known for representing oil companies. He entered politics and managed **George Bush**'s 1980 presidential bid. When Bush became vice president, Baker became a key figure in the Reagan administration, serving first as chief of staff and later as secretary of the treasury (switching places with **Donald Regan**).

As a young Washington economist, **Lauri Bassi** discovered that during the 1980s women's share of poverty was rising along with women's share of employment because divorce was forcing women into low-paying jobs.

President **Jimmy Carter** appointed **Paul Volcker** as chairman of the Federal Reserve Board in 1979, a position he held until replaced by **Alan Greenspan** in 1987. Volcker had been an undersecretary for monetary affairs in the Nixon administration and was chairman of the New York Federal Reserve Bank when Carter made the appointment. Volcker described himself as a pragmatic monetarist and made his chief concern the lessening of inflation.

A prominent Chicago legal scholar, **Richard A. Epstein,** argued that most government regulations are unconstitutional. In 1987 he said, "I oppose most of the legislation written in this century."

Leona Helmsley, president of the Helmsley Hotels chain, was indicted for tax evasion in 1988 (with her husband, Harry) and, after a 1989 conviction, sentenced to a four-year prison term and ordered to pay more than $8 million in back taxes, fines, and related costs.

In 1979 **Lee Iacocca** became president of the Chrysler Corporation. That same year the federal government bailed out Chrysler with a $1 billion loan and other concessions, including tax breaks. Until 1978 Iacocca had been at Ford, where he had been president of the company since 1970. When **Henry Ford III** stepped down as chairman of the board in 1978, Iacocca was expected to replace Ford but was passed over because of personal animosities between Iacocca and Ford. Iacocca revitalized the Chrysler Corporation during the 1980s and became a leading spokesman for business, eventually becoming something of a celebrity.

Steve Jobs, the cofounder of Apple Computer in 1975, resigned as chairman of the company in September 1985.

University of Chicago law professor **Richard Posner**'s *Economic Analysis of the Law* became a standard textbook by the mid 1980s. Posner, a disciple of the free market, briefly suggested making adoption easier by creating markets for babies.

Donald Regan served as Secretary of the Treasury during Ronald Reagan's first term in office, and as his chief of staff from 1985 until forced to resign in 1987 in the midst of the Iran-Contra affair. Regan was a major Wall Street player who had headed Merrill Lynch and Company, the largest securities and brokerage firm in the country, before joining Reagan's Cabinet, and his policies as secretary of the treasury favored financial institutions over heavy industry. Regan was also known as a critic of **David Stockman,** director of the Office of Management and Budget.

As secretary of the interior from 1981 through 1983, **James Watt** drew the wrath of environmentalists when he opened millions of acres of U.S. governmental land, including coastal holdings, to strip mining and oil and gas drilling. Watt resigned after further alienating public opinion by his description of the coal-leasing panel he had appointed: "a black, a woman, two Jews, and a cripple."

DEATHS

I(orwith) W(ilbur) Abel, 78, steelworker and former president of the United Steelworkers of America (1965–1977), 10 August 1987.

Chester Bliss Bowles, 85, advertising executive who also served in a variety of high-ranking positions in the federal government in the administrations of Franklin D. Roosevelt, Harry S Truman, and John F. Kennedy, as well as a member of the U.S. House of Representatives, 25 May 1986.

William Anthony "Tony" Boyle 83, labor leader who headed the United Mine Workers (1963–1972) and was later convicted for his involvement in the murders of democratic challenger Joseph A. Yablonski and his family, 31 May 1985.

August Anheuser Busch Jr., 90, businessman who served as chairman (1946-1975) of the business, the Anheuser-Busch Company, founded by his grandfather and helped to build it into the largest beer brewery in the world, 29 September 1989.

James Casey, 95, cofounder of the American Messenger Company, which later became United Parcel Service, 6 June 1983.

David Dubinsky, 90, labor leader who headed the International Ladies Garment Workers Union from 1932 until 1966 and helped to form the Committee for Industrial Organization (later the Congress of Industrial Organizations) in 1935. Dubinsky was also a American Federation of Labor leader and active in labor politics, 17 September 1982.

Henry Ford II, 70, third-generation automaker (his father, Edsel, was founder Henry Ford's only son) and chairman of the Ford Motor Company (1945–1978), who had revived the family business with cars like the Thunderbird and Mustang, and who parlayed part of his fortune into the philanthropic Ford Foundation, 29 September 1987.

S. B. Fuller, 83, black entrepreneur and cosmetics manufacturer who was the power behind the largest black-owned company in the 1950s, the Fuller Products Company, 24 October 1988.

George Horace Gallup, 82, the dean of American pollsters, who used public opinion polls to measure and forecast U.S. political and economic developments through the Gallup poll, 26 July 1984.

Edward F. Gibbons, 63, executive who directed the Woolworth Company (1978–1982), 26 October 1982.

Joyce Clyde Hall, 90, founder and president (1910–1966) of the Hallmark greeting card company, which became the largest such company in the world under his leadership, 29 October 1982.

Michael Harrington, 61, socialist writer whose book *The Other America* helped generate the war on poverty in the 1960s, 31 July 1989.

Edgar Fosburgh Kaiser, 73, industrialist who directed Kaiser Industry Corporation (founded by his father, Henry J. Kaiser), 11 December 1981.

William Jesse Kennedy Jr., 96, black entrepreneur who had served as president and board chairman of North Carolina Mutual Insurance Company, 8 July 1985.

John S. Knight, 86, founder and former director (until his 1976 retirement) of Knight-Ridder Newspapers, the publishing and broadcasting dynasty, 16 June 1981.

Alfred A. Knopf, 91, publisher and founder of the Alfred A. Knopf publishing house, 11 August 1984.

Ray Albert Kroc, 81, business entrepreneur who franchised the McDonald's chain of restaurants, beginning in 15 April 1955, in the Chicago suburb of Des Plaines, Illinois. Although the McDonald brothers contributed their name and idea (of speedy, efficient hamburger production), Kroc built the chain into a worldwide fast-food empire, 14 January 1984.

Simon Kuznets, 84, economist who won the 1971 Nobel Prize for economics, 8 July 1985.

Herman W. Lay, 73, businessman who developed Lay's potato chips and later merged his company with the Frito Company (1961) and the Pepsi Cola Company (1965), 6 December 1982.

J. Willard Marriott, 84, founder of the Marriott Corporation, 13 August 1985.

Lloyd McBride, 67, labor leader in the steel industry who presided over the United Steelworkers of America (1977–1983), during the years of its most rapid decline in union membership and depression in the steel industry, 6 November 1983.

George Meany, 85, the blunt U.S. labor leader who rose from Bronx plumber to the presidency of the AFL-CIO, a position he held from the federation's merger in 1955 until 1979, two months before his death, 10 January 1980.

Arnold Ray Miller, 62, labor leader who served as president of the United Mine Workers Union (1972–1979), 12 July 1985.

Arthur Charles Nielsen, 82, business executive and market researcher, who founded and led the A. C. Nielsen Company, best known for its system of rating television shows, 1 June 1980.

John Knudsen Northrop, 85, aviation designer and founder of the Northrop Corporation, well known for aircraft designs during and after World War II, 18 February 1981.

James Elias Olson, 62, businessman who headed the American Telephone and Telegraph Company (AT&T) (1986–1988), 18 April 1988.

Jackie Presser, 61, labor leader who presided over the International Brotherhood of Teamsters (1983–1988) amid charges of corruption and support from organized crime, 9 July 1988.

Abram Nicholas Pritzker, 90, founder and owner of the Hyatt hotel chain and a consortium of other business investments including *McCall's* and Braniff Airlines whose estimated value was some $1.5 billion, 8 February 1986.

John A. Roosevelt, 65, investment banker and son of former president Franklin D. Roosevelt, 27 April 1981.

Col. Harland Sanders, 90, founder of the Kentucky Fried Chicken restaurant franchise, 16 December 1980.

Patricia Walker Shaw, 46, banker and president of the Universal Life Insurance Company, an African American company that served the African American community. Shaw was the first woman to head a major American life insurance organization, which she did for the two years before her death of cancer, 30 June 1985.

Jake Simmons Jr., 80, the most successful African American in the oil industry, who arranged oil deals between multinational oil companies and African countries such as Ghana, Nigeria, Liberia, and the Ivory Coast in the 1960s and 1970s, 26 March 1981.

Max Stern, 83, founder of Hartz Mountain Products Corporation, the largest pet food and pet products company in the world, 20 May 1982.

Earl S. Tupper, 76, inventor and producer of Tupperware, the line of plastic storage containers (and related plastic products) marketed to housewives through parties held in their homes, 3 October 1983.

Roy Lee Williams, 74, labor leader who presided over the International Brotherhood of Teamsters (1981–1983) and whose tenure was ended by his conviction on conspiracy charges and subsequent imprisonment, 28 April 1989.

Robert Winship Woodruff, 95, president of the Coca-Cola Company (1923–1955), who was responsible for reviving the declining company and turning it into the leading producer of soft drinks in the world, 7 March 1985.

PUBLICATIONS

Barry Bluestone and Bennett Harrison, *The Deindustrialization of America: Plant Closings, Community Abandonment, and the Dismantling of Basic Industry* (New York: Basic Books, 1982);

Samuel Bowles, David M. Gordon, and Thomas E. Weisskopf, *Beyond the Waste Land* (Garden City, N.Y.: Doubleday, 1983);

W. Edward Deming, *Out of the Crisis* (Cambridge: Massachusetts Institute of Technology Press, 1982);

Michael L. Dertouzos, Richard K. Lester, and Robert M. Solow, *Made in America: Regaining the Productive Edge* (New York: Harper & Row Perennial Library, 1989);

Benjamin M. Friedman, *Day of Reckoning: The Consequences of American Economic Policy Under Reagan and After* (New York: Random House, 1988);

Alice Hanson Jones, *The Wealth of the Nation To Be* (New York: Columbia University Press, 1980);

Paul M. Kennedy, *The Rise and Fall of the Great Powers: Economic Change and Military Conflict from 1500 to 2000* (New York: Random House, 1987);

Katherine S. Newman, *Falling From Grace: The Experience of Downward Mobility in the American Middle Class* (New York: Free Press, 1988);

Michael Novak, *The Spirit of Democratic Capitalism* (New York: Simon & Schuster, 1982);

Tom Peters, *Thriving on Chaos: Handbook for a Management Revolution* (New York: Harper & Row Perennial Library, 1987);

Nathan Rosenberg, *Inside the Black Box: Technology and Economics* (Cambridge: Cambridge University Press, 1982);

Emily Rosenburg, *Spreading the American Dream: American Economic and Cultural Expansion, 1890–1945* (New York: Hill & Wang, 1982);

William W. Scherkenbach, *The Deming Route to Quality Productivity, Road Maps and Roadblocks* (Milwaukee: Ceep Press Books, 1986);

Steven Schlosstein, *The End of the American Century* (New York: Congdon & Weed, 1989);

Alvin Toffler, *The Third Wave* (New York: Morrow, 1980);

Paul Tsongas, *The Road From Here: Liberalism and Realities in the 1980s* (New York: Knopf, 1981);

Jerome Tucille, *Kingdom: The Story of the Hunt Family of Texas* (New York: Paperjacks, 1987);

Tucille, *Trump: The Saga of America's Most Powerful Real Estate Baron* (New York: Donald I. Fine, 1985);

Owen Ullman, *Stockman: The Man, The Myth, The Future* (New York: Donald I. Fine, 1986);

Mary Walton, *The Deming Management Method* (New York: Perigee, 1986);

Jeffery G. Williamson and Peter H. Lindert, *American Inequality: A Macroeconomic History* (New York: Academic Press, 1980).

EDUCATION

by HARRIETT WILLIAMS

CONTENTS

Sidebars and tables are listed in italics.

1980

- Gallup poll shows parents believe that the top three problems in the nation's schools are 1) discipline; 2) drug use; and 3) poor curriculum and low standards.

- Poll results show blacks from the Northeast give public schools a "D."

- Seventy-nine percent of respondents favor instruction dealing with morals and moral behavior.

- A federal judge strikes down a Texas law excluding most illegal alien children from public schools, saying "the rights of man are not a function of immigration status."

- Dade County, Florida, School District decides not to provide special programs for the new wave of twenty thousand refugees inundating the Miami area.

- New Reagan administration rules regarding the school-lunch program sharply downgrades the nutritional requirements of lunches and defines ketchup and pickle relish as vegetables.

- Rand-McNally Corporation, publishers of junior-high chemistry textbooks, is ordered to pay $155,000 to two eighth graders injured while conducting an experiment outlined in their text.

4 July   The National Education Association (NEA) votes to endorse Jimmy Carter for president.

17 July   A U.S. Circuit Court of Appeals upholds a decision ordering New York school districts to provide sign interpreters for deaf children.

Aug.   The Republican presidential platform in New York supports an end to busing and abolition of the Department of Education.

Sept.   One million fewer children begin kindergarten than in 1979.

2 Sept.   Franklin Military School, authorized by the Richmond, Virginia, Board of Education, opens as one of few public military academies. Known as a "miniature West Point," the school is hailed as a balance to the "open" schools elsewhere in Richmond.

1 Oct.   Science teachers publish the Mount St. Helens Curriculum Materials Project, materials that convert the explosive event into lessons.

Nov.   A Rand Corporation study claims that schools that desegregate voluntarily offer a better quality of education than those that desegregate under court order.

1981

Jan.   A U.S. Circuit Court of Appeals rules that the First Amendment "does not require — or even allow" public school officials to permit student prayer meetings in classrooms before school.

13 Jan.   A federal judge orders Texas school district to provide catheterization for a five-year-old girl at school under the provisions of the Education for All Handicapped Children Act.

19 Jan.   On the last day of the Carter administration, the Department of Education publishes a new, stricter interpretation of Title I regulations.

1982

20 Jan. The Heritage Foundation, a conservative think tank, publishes "Agenda for Progress," recommending "the eventual goal of complete elimination of federal funding" for schools.

Mar. New York City schools, having identified an extra twenty thousand handicapped students to comply with court order, find themselves with seven thousand identified handicapped students with no teachers. The schools hope to hire one thousand special-education teachers.

5 Mar. Parents of six public-school students sue the Philadelphia Board of Education for more than $20 million, claiming the students had been exposed to harmful levels of asbestos, a cancer-causing agent.

1 Apr. Jesse Helms, senator from North Carolina, introduces a bill that would leave to state courts challenges to state laws relating to "voluntary prayers in public schools and public buildings." The bill is defeated.

5 Apr. The District of Columbia announces that more than six thousand children in grades one through three will not be promoted under the schools' new competency-based curriculum.

10 Aug. A federal judge throws out a Louisiana creationism suit saying it had no place in federal court; the 1981 Louisiana law required balanced treatment to creation science and evolution science.

Sept. The National Assessment of Educational Progress announces that in five years Hispanic nine-year-olds have made improvements in their reading skills, twice as much as the average for children that age.

Nov. Teacher unions in fourteen states declare Democratic gubernatorial victories to be "victories for education."

1 Nov. The College Board reports that the SAT for college-bound seniors in 1982 rose for the first time in nineteen years. The average verbal score was 425, average math score 467; when the decline began, in 1963, the average verbal score was 478, average math score, 502.

1983

• Chicago school officials announce they are investigating charges that school-bus drivers smoke marijuana and drink alcohol on the job.

• An Education Department survey of fifteen thousand kids reveals that children of working mothers scored lower on reading and math tests than those students with mothers who stay home.

• The U.S. Supreme Court upholds a lower court approval of New York's state aid to education despite the disparity it leaves between wealthy and poor districts. The reasoning is that "no substantial federal question" is involved in the lawsuit.

Jan. A federal appeals court strikes down sweeping sex bias rules of the Department of Education, ruling that the department can regulate only those school programs that receive direct federal funds.

24 Jan. A U.S. Circuit Court of Appeals rules in a Peoria, Illinois, case that handicapped students have to pass minimum competency tests for a diploma if their state mandates passing the test for all students.

7 Feb. A U.S. district judge in Philadelphia rules that once racial integration of faculty has been achieved, districts do not have to maintain racial balance on each faculty by constantly reshuffling teachers' assignments.

21 Feb. School finance experts tell school officials that little attention to equalizing funding will be given in the next decade because of high unemployment and revenue shortfalls.

5 Mar. The director of curriculum in New York announces that all students will be assigned a minimum amount of homework each night.

7 Mar. Two psychologists in *TV Guide* claim video games are good for kids: playing games siphons off money that could be spent for drugs and encourages problem solving, they report.

21 Mar. The U.S. Supreme Court hears a case of an unmarried teacher fired when she gave birth; she insists a married teacher would have been treated differently. The district counters that she was fired for failure to give notice, not merely for immorality.

4 Apr. An American Association of School Administrators' survey finds that Chapter II block grant funds are being spent on equipment, not staff.

18 Apr. School security directors say most districts' computer files are vulnerable to hackers; so far students' favorite target is to change grades in data banks.

16 May A federal judge in Florida upholds denial of diplomas to seniors failing that state's minimum competency exam. That blacks make up 57 percent of the failures but only 20 percent of the student body is not considered evidence that the test is racially biased.

30 May Only 50 percent of pupils in Coalinga, California, return to their elementary schools a week and a half after the town was hit by an earthquake measuring 6.5 on the Richter scale.

11 July The U.S. Supreme Court upholds a ban on sweep searches of students by dogs.

26 Sept. School district officials from five areas sue the U.S. Department of Agriculture in hopes of suspending the USDA's required verification procedure for free or reduced-price lunches. The suit charges that each verification costs the district $18.

10 Oct. A long-range study finds that low pay given to teachers in Catholic schools (top pay of $18,000) compared to pay in the public schools (top of about $30,000) contributes to the 20 percent turnover in Catholic schools.

21 Nov. In the first Wisconsin case of a teacher taking a student to court for battery, a Wisconsin teacher is awarded $23,000 in punitive damages from a student who hit him three times in the face.

19 Dec. A Vatican research group urges parochial schools to augment children's sexual education.

1984

- A new congressional bill authorizes $425 million in fiscal 1984 for new programs in math, science, and foreign languages over the next five years.

2 Jan. A University of Texas study shows that undocumented aliens paid $157 million in state taxes, while using $97 million in services, including education.

16 Jan.   The Pasadena, Maryland, school board rejects a request from a fundamentalist Christian parent who wants teachers to tell the "truth" about Santa to first graders.

27 Feb.   In Alabama a state superintendent–appointed committee finds that teacher time is too valuable to sell class rings, caps, gowns, yearbooks, and the other paraphernalia desired by high-school seniors.

28 Feb.   The Cincinnati, Ohio, school district becomes the latest to end many years of struggles over desegregation by designing a voluntary choice system involving extensive use of magnet schools.

26 Mar.   Dr. Robert Graham, a member of Reagan's Task Force on Food Assistance, suggests a universal school-lunch program that taxes parents for the value of kids' meals as income.

7 May   Texas repeals its textbook restriction, passed in 1974, requiring evolution to be presented as "only one of several explanations" of how the universe began.

4 June   A Hicksville, New York, school district approves a referendum reinstating a period of silent meditation at the beginning of the school day. A parent vows to sue with the help of the New York Civil Liberties Union if the period exists when her daughter begins school in September.

9 July   Arlington, Virginia, high schools see a 45 percent reduction in cutting class, because of the installation of a computer system capable of phoning parents of everyone absent without permission (and speaking in English, Spanish, and Vietnamese).

11 Sept.   Los Angeles officials report that students are now required to maintain a C average with no failures in order to participate in extracurricular activities.

Oct.   A judge in Schuylkill County, Pennsylvania, upholds Catholic school officials who kicked a sixteen-year-old football player off the team for getting another student pregnant. The parents had sued, claiming that suspension for the season would cause irreparable harm.

8 Oct.   The Supreme Court agrees to hear an Oklahoma City rule that affirms firing homosexual teachers if they openly espouse homosexuality. Gay teachers say that espousal is a constitutionally protected activity.

17 Dec.   Ten Arkansas teachers sue to block the state from requiring them to take a literacy test and a competency exam in their subject areas.

18 Dec.   The National Council for Better Education, a conservative group, announces plans for a recruitment drive for teachers who want an alternative to the National Education Association.

1985

- A study reveals that one-third of the nation's teachers report they are uncomfortable using computers; nearly all want more training, however.

- U.S. Gypsum is forced to pay $675,000 to School District Five of Lexington and Richland Counties in South Carolina for asbestos removal from Irmo High School after the jury learns that the company's safety director knew of dangers as early as 1955.

- The nation's 2.1 million teachers receive an average 7.3 percent pay boost this academic year, for a 1984–1985 salary of $23,546.

- The annual Gallup poll on education shows a split among teachers, principals, and the public on the number one problem facing education: Principals claim lack of money; teachers claim too much paperwork; the public claims discipline.

- The Senate confirms William Bennett as education secretary by a vote of 93–0 after Reagan assures Orrin Hatch, R–Utah, that he would not demand that Bennett dismantle the department.

3 Jan. Survey released by Secretary of Education Terrel H. Bell shows that none of the states with top-achieving SAT students — Wisconsin, New Hampshire, Iowa, and Minnesota — were top-spending states.

7 Jan. The Chicago school board reaches an agreement with twenty thousand striking teachers out for two weeks by offering a 4.5 percent salary increase.

Feb. A random sampling of student achievement before and after five Colorado school districts went to a four-day week shows student achievement unaffected.

4 Feb. The Supreme Court affirms "reasonable" searches of students — upholding a New Jersey vice principal who searched the purse of a fourteen-year-old drug dealer.

5 Feb. Montgomery County, Maryland, announces plans to send school information such as report cards and newsletters to both divorced parents, not just custodial parent.

May Johns Hopkins researchers are giving students at Pimlico Middle School in Baltimore tokens worth thirty-five cents for attending classes; the tokens may be used at the school store or cafeteria.

7 May *Science* magazine publishes the result of two researchers' study of more than one thousand scientific and technical journals during a three-year period to determine if evidence of creationism was being suppressed. Of the more than 135,000 articles submitted, only eighteen concerned creationism, and none was written by an author skilled in the scientific method. "It is inappropriate to invoke censorship," said the researchers.

June The ACT announces that trade and technology jobs have replaced social-services occupations as the most popular career choices among eighth and eleventh graders.

10 June The Agriculture Department scraps its rule barring the sale of junk food at public schools. Junk-food sales are still not allowed in the cafeteria or at lunchtimes.

July A study by the Southern Regional Education Board finds that education majors take less-demanding courses than most students.

8 July Research by the Youth Suicide Center says the last person a teen contemplating suicide would confide in is a school counselor — and that 11 percent of the nation's high-school seniors have made a suicide attempt sometime in their lives.

5 Aug. Sixty years after John Scopes went to trial in Tennessee for teaching the theory of evolution in high-school biology, a federal appeals court strikes down a four-year-old Louisiana law mandating the teaching of creationism.

Sept. Ohio University professor Myron Lieberman's 1959 article calling for an independent national board to certify superior teachers modeled on similar bodies that exist for lawyers and doctors is reprinted in the journal *Phi Delta Kappan*.

23 Sept.   A Metropolitan Life Insurance poll claims that by 1990 one of every four teachers will have left the job because of low pay and poor work conditions. Only 36 percent of teachers rate merit pay and teacher bonuses as a good thing for education.

7 Oct.   A new Georgia state law mandates that all newly elected or appointed school-board members must undergo training in Georgia's new reform bill as well as in school finance.

8 Oct.   The National Center for Education Statistics announces that high-school students in 1982 did less homework than peers in 1972, but more than students in 1980.

15 Oct.   Fitness expert Bonnie Prudden tells a Senate subcommittee that today's sixteen-year-olds did worse on fitness tests than students did thirty years previously. Fifty-eight percent of American students (but only 8 percent of Europeans) failed a standard fitness test.

13 Dec.   The American Medical Association journal publishes a research study showing that students and teachers run unusually high risks of contracting hepatitis B virus from mentally retarded children mainstreamed into classrooms. (Hepatitis B strikes Down's Syndrome children at extremely high rates.) The researchers urge immunization programs.

1986

- In the first federal study of the nation's teachers in fifteen years, the Department of Education announces that most put in long workweeks, are quite likely to have advanced degrees, and earn $22,701. One-third of male teachers have a supplementary job; one-fifth of females do.

- Parents, in the annual Gallup poll of education, say for the first time that drugs are the number one problem in schools, replacing the perennial favorite, discipline.

Jan.   For the first time since records began to be kept twelve years previously, a principal's salary tops the $70,000 mark; the principal, unnamed, leads a senior-high school with a population between 2,500 and 9,999, according to the American Association of School Administrators.

Feb.   For the fifth time in five years, President Reagan requests a reduction in the amount of federal spending for education. This year, for fiscal year 1987, the total is $15.2 billion, down $3.2 billion from fiscal year 1986.

24 Feb.   The Council for Basic Education publishes a study claiming that minimum competency tests for students are at best a "waste of time, at worst, a form of consumer fraud."

10 Mar.   The American Association of School Administrators releases a study of the nation's 154 best high schools. The factors they have in common are "the hardest to pin down": a positive climate, strong administrative leadership, and excellent teachers. "It's the people who run the school who make the difference," researchers conclude.

24 Mar.   A study shows that women are steadily increasing their representation on the nation's school boards: from 12 percent in 1972 to 38 percent in 1985.

Apr.   Broughton High School in Raleigh, North Carolina, is the first public school in the nation to establish a privately funded endowment. This endowment, of $100,000, provides for two $5,000 awards for the school's two best teachers in 1986.

5 May   The National Council on Year-Round Education estimates that more than two hundred students in some three hundred schools now are involved in year-round schooling. Most common is the 45/15 plan, in which students spend forty-five days in class, then fifteen days on vacation.

16 June   A test given in March to two hundred thousand Texas teachers is formally challenged by teachers' union charging racial bias. One percent of white teachers failed the test; 18 percent of black teachers and 6 percent of Hispanic teachers failed.

28 Aug.   Nobel laureates speak out at a news conference against creationism, claiming that to "teach that the statements of Genesis are scientific truths is to deny all the evidence."

9 Sept.   The National Education Association says that social ills of kids are schools' biggest problems; that suicide, teen pregnancy, and teen drug use are problems teachers simply cannot solve.

14 Sept.   The Department of Education announces that the per-pupil expenditure for this school year has reached a high of $4,263.

22 Sept.   A University of Minnesota study finds that 80 percent of latchkey children like being home alone, and that nearly 30 percent of children in K–3 go home to a situation with no adult custodian.

6 Oct.   A National Assessment of Educational Progress survey shows that of 3,600 adults ages 21–25, only 40 percent could understand a newspaper editorial; only 20 percent could use a bus schedule to plan a trip; and only 10 percent could interpret a four-line poem by Emily Dickinson.

20 Oct.   The Education Department's budget for fiscal year 1987 is set at $19.2 billion by a House-Senate committee, more than 25 percent above Reagan's proposed $15.2 billion budget.

30 Oct.   William Bennett and Caspar Weinberger, defense secretary, hold a press conference to promote military retirees as excellent candidates for teaching positions. They present a new brochure, "A Second Career for You," published by the Department of Education to military retirees.

3 Nov.   U.S. Surgeon General C. Everett Koop calls on nation's schools to launch programs at the "lowest grade possible" alerting children to the dangers of Acquired Immune Deficiency Syndrome.

17 Nov.   In the first case of its kind, a student athlete at the University of Colorado challenges a school-run drug testing program as a violation of the Fourth Amendment's ban on unreasonable search and seizure.

1 Dec.   In a completed study of teacher evaluations nationwide, the Rand Corporation concludes that most schools do not put the necessary resources into the program, and that "even fewer put the results into action."

1987

Feb.   William Bennett's fourth annual "wall chart" of state education statistics shows no improvement on SAT scores. Also, graduation rates have dropped in thirty-three states.

9 Feb.   The U.S. Supreme Court announces it will consider legality of a New Jersey law allowing one minute of "silent contemplation" at the start of the school day; the case is *Karcher* v. *May*.

23 Feb.   A Kent State University researcher creates an interactive video simulation of violence in schools for teacher training purposes.

23 Mar.   New Jersey officials promise to find ten thousand new jobs for ten thousand high-school graduates by 1992.

4 May   The New Jersey Supreme Court, in a 7–0 decision, requires schools to admit students with AIDS.

15 June   A survey shows that graduates of vocational education programs in Ohio earn 21 percent more than comparable students with no vocational training.

17 Aug.   Setting what could be a mandate for textbook publishing nationwide, the California Board of Education unanimously passes a measure requiring more facts on religion in history textbooks.

1 Sept.   The Department of Education notifies nearly a million student-loan defaulters that they must pay by 1 October or be held responsible for collection costs and repayment loans, adding up to 45 percent to their bills.

28 Sept.   U.S. secondary-school students know less about science than their predecessors did in 1970; they lag behind students in England and Japan, a Teachers College study finds.

9 Nov.   A group of twelve conservative historians and education writers attacks American history text publishers, accusing them of filling student texts with "cowardice, commercialism, condescension, and crassness" and serving as "cheerleaders for minorities at the expense of central stories that mark the nation's development."

7 Dec.   A coalition of urban school superintendents releases a plan to curb the nation's dropout rate; it includes early intervention, a positive school climate, high expectations for students, and strong teachers.

1988

- The Department of Education announces that this year will be marked by more students, more teachers, and more spending compared to last year.

18 Jan.   The Education Commission of the States releases a survey on illiteracy that claims that the majority of illiterates in America are white.

1 Feb.   A U.S. Supreme Court ruling gives school administrators wide latitude over student newspapers in *Hazelwood* v. *Kuhlmeier.* In the 5–3 decision, the majority writes, "A school need not tolerate student speech that is inconsistent with its mission, even though government could not censor similar speech outside school."

12 Feb.   Public-school administrators, mostly male, white, and well paid, have higher opinions of schools than the public, says a survey by the National Center for Educational Information.

14 Mar.   The fifth annual Department of Education "wall chart" comparing state educational statistics shows SAT scores unchanged. "Substantial and ever-increasing dollars have not given us the results our children deserve," claims William Bennett.

16 May   William Bennett announces he will resign as secretary of the Department of Education in the fall to speak and write.

23 May   The National Endowment for the Arts reports that American education produces "artistic and cultural illiterates."

28 June   Most states will need a tax hike to carry out educational reforms, a new report of the National Council of State Legislatures warns.

10 July   A catastrophic-health-care bill signed by President Reagan provides Medicaid for some special-education services, such as speech pathology and audiology, psychological services, and physical and occupational therapy.

Sept.   New Education Department secretary Lauro Cavazos takes over from William Bennett.

12 Sept.   A Rand Corporation report recommends recruiting homemakers and career switchers to fill the gap of qualified math and science teachers.

26 Sept.   An Education Department study finds that special education costs less in the mainstream — the cost to educate a student in special-ed classes is $8,649 per year; mainstreamed into regular classes, $3,847.

Nov.   During the month seven thousand schools receive a series of ten videos designed to sway children from drug use funded by the Drug-Free Schools and Communities Act.

7 Nov.   A Lehigh University professor who has studied the role of the courts in public education announces that "It seems the pendulum is shifting in favor of school authorities."

19 Dec.   Principals from several districts report that use of student uniforms has improved their school climates and have been welcomed by 97 percent of parents.

1989

- The Texas Supreme Court rules 9–0 that the state's school-finance system is unconstitutional because it offers poor children a poor education. Texas must devise a new funding formula by May 1990.

Jan.   A NAACP Defense Fund survey says chronically poor blacks are increasingly relying on education to catapult their children from poverty.

27 Feb.   Three of four American students do not master enough math to cope in college or on the job, reports the National Research Council.

13 Mar.   Principals' salaries outpace inflation, with the average principal earning $52,987, according to a report from the American Association of School Administrators (AASA).

10 Apr.   The flood of innovations emerging from 1983's "A Nation at Risk" has left middle schools largely unscathed, researchers claim at AASA conference.

24 Apr.   A quarter of the nation's eighty-eight thousand school buildings are threats to children's safety, says a study by the Education Writers Association.

8 May   The EPA finds radon levels high in schools in sixteen states. Twenty-two percent of the three thousand classrooms tested exceeded safety standards for radon gas.

17 July   The U.S. Supreme Court rules that states are immune from parents' suits for tuition reimbursement for private-school special education. Local school districts must continue bearing the burden alone.

11 Sept.   A research study shows that children from small families far outstrip their classmates from large families in educational attainment.

25 Sept.   The Women's Sports Foundation analyzed data on thirteen thousand students and found that female high-school athletes are more likely to enter college than nonathletes.

23 Oct.   An annual survey reveals that fewer students are drinking alcohol and using drugs than two years ago, but more are smoking cigarettes.

Dec.   The American Institute for Research announces that forty-four states are now requiring teachers to pass competency tests, up from just ten in 1980.

4 Dec.   The Virginia State Board of Education declares that parents need not tell school official if their child has AIDS.

18 Dec.   The U.S. Supreme Court refuses to review a ruling that no child is too handicapped to receive services from school districts.

OVERVIEW

Expanded Opportunity. In the early 1980s the educational policy catchword changed from *equity* to *excellence*. Battles had raged during the 1960s and 1970s over expanding educational equity and opportunity, and many Americans who had been excluded from the mainstream emerged as winners. The percentage of Americans graduating from high school rose from 50 percent in 1950 to 75 percent in 1980. In the 1970s the Education for All Handicapped Children Act had assured young Americans with disabilities of access to educational opportunities. From 1968 to 1978 the percentage of black student enrollment in colleges grew from 6.4 percent to more than 10 percent; for women, the numbers went from 39 percent to 48 percent. By the early 1980s access to higher education was nearly universal. A College Board study found in 1982 that one-third of all postsecondary institutions were "open door" (meaning any high-school graduate could attend), significantly fewer were "selective" (taking only those who qualified), and only 8 percent of colleges were "competitive" (accepting only a portion of those qualified).

The Pendulum Swings. Having successfully pursued goals of increased participation, educators in the late 1970s were vilified for neglecting the quality of education. By the late 1970s a groundswell of criticism emerged as Americans, who now assumed mass education as a given, focused on exactly how well the masses were being educated. The problems were multidimensional, but most critics agreed that when colleges lowered their entrance requirements in the 1970s, and most high schools abolished strict course requirements, the quality of education suffered. The common curriculum was lost when appeals to relevance brought an array of minicourses and electives, considered "soft" fare, replaced more-academic courses in science, math, and English. The curriculum, packed with courses such as values education, moral education, death education, consumer education, drug education, and driver education, failed to emphasize fundamental academic skills.

Early Alarm Bells. Bad news erupted by the early 1980s: Scholastic Aptitude Test (SAT) scores (the measure by which most colleges evaluated applicants) went on a downward spiral from 1962 through 1982, and the

National Assessment of Educational Progress reported that 8 percent of seventeen-year-old American whites and 42 percent of the same age blacks were functionally illiterate. The report argued that automatic promotion had contributed to the problem and that the high-school diploma no longer represented any measurable level of proficiency. As a result of the report, many school districts adopted minimum competency testing for graduation. Between 1976 and 1980, thirty-eight states adopted these tests, a spontaneous national movement with no single spokesperson nor any one organization's promotion. On 22 October 1980, just weeks before Ronald Reagan's landslide presidential victory, the Department of Education and the National Science Foundation, on orders from President Jimmy Carter, announced that America was headed toward "virtual scientific and technological illiteracy." Warning the citizenry that the United States was behind the Soviet Union, Japan, and West Germany in elementary and secondary science and math, the announcement claimed that the United States was in danger of losing its competitive edge; that while "the best seem to be learning as much as they ever did — the majority is learning less and less."

Assessments. Evidence was clear that students were learning less. In 1982 the California Roundtable investigating the situation in that state found that the school day and the school year had been shortened. Fewer than one-fifth of the students did a single homework assignment per week, and more than one-half of the students entering the California college and university system were placed in remedial math and English courses despite having good grades in those subjects in secondary schools. The National Center for Educational Statistics, the data analysts for the Department of Education, reported in 1982 that only 2.6 percent of the 1982 high-school graduates actually met the College Board's newly proposed graduation requirements. By 1980 the percentage of students studying foreign languages was down to 15, from more than 24 percent in 1964. In the early 1980s Ernest Boyer chaired the National Science Board's Commission on Precollege Education in Math, Science and Technology, and recommended federal spending of more than $1 billion to offer courses most secondary students were not taking. In 1980, when the Gannett newspaper chain sent investigative reporting teams into twenty-four high schools, they found that the average public school had only about three hours of instructional time per day. Citing a "pervasive dilution of the secondary curriculum," the report catalogued high-school credit awarded for astrology, marriage simulation, cheerleading, child care, student government, and a host of other electives. And it was not just curriculum that presented problems. Absenteeism, formerly considered intolerable, was condoned, and parents nationwide reported in a Gallup poll that violence and discipline problems were their number one concern.

Pointing the Finger of Blame. Liberals and conservatives agreed that America's schools were not delivering a quality education, and ironically, they tended to agree as to the causes of mediocrity. Most conservatives were convinced that the increased federal presence in education had been a starting point for decay. Some more-liberal thinkers were also critical of federal intervention. For example, Democratic governor of Arizona Bruce Babbitt commented on the television show *Meet the Press* in 1982 that "Federal involvement in education has been counterproductive. I believe it's responsible for some of the decline in quality." Other liberals tended to disagree with Babbitt, citing integration and access for bilingual and handicapped students as positive results of federal intervention. Liberal and conservative thinkers both blamed the counterculture of the 1960s and 1970s for the sorry state of education. Jay Sommer, the 1981 National Teacher of the Year, summarized the conservative viewpoint: "A period like the Sixties can have a devastating effect on learning and schooling." Too much student choice in curriculum was one of these effects, many argued. Christopher Lasch, a leftist critic, agreed with this assessment, asserting in *The Culture of Narcissism* (1979) that democratization of education had eroded critical thought and intellectual standards without raising popular culture or equalizing wealth. Lasch ridiculed the widespread notion during the 1970s of abolishing grades: "Although defended on grounds of high pedagogical principle, this practice reflected a desire for less work and a wish to avoid judgment on its quality." Both camps agreed that teachers were facing more difficult and perilous times than ever before in American history, but conservatives were more likely to attack teachers as part of the problem. Ronald Reagan summed up this attitude in 1982 when he said, "Although America boasts thousands of fine teachers, in too many cases teaching has become a resting place for the unmotivated and unqualified. We should give teachers more honor and respect, and we should pay and promote on merit, but no hard-earned tax dollars should go to reward mediocrity." Also in 1982 Ernest Boyer, a more centrist thinker, suggested that the teaching profession had been "caught in a vicious cycle, spiraling downward. The rewards are few, morale is low, the best teachers are bailing out and the supply of good recruits is drying up." Other explanations shifted blame away from school personnel. *Newsweek* weighed in with the explanation that the 1960s and 1970s had brought a shift away from expository writing and real reading toward more "creative" modes of expression such as film, video, and photography — a shift that eroded basic intellectual skills. Conservatives agreed readily, condemning the schools for abandoning the "basics" while glorifying self-expression and free choice.

An Economic Explanation. Liberal thinkers such as Ira Shor, author of *The Culture Wars: School and Society in the Conservative Restoration 1969–84* (1986), laid the blame at the feet of economic conditions. He attacked the "careerism" emphasis in education during the Nixon administration as particularly ill-timed. Just as baby boomers swamped the higher-education arena in the late 1960s and early 1970s, they swamped the job market in the late 1970s. Jokes abounded about how many Ph.D.'s were driving taxis, and aspiring graduates were as problematic as dropouts: what would society do with them all? Shor saw the educational problems of the 1980s as merely a mirror of economic frustration: "In too many corners of life there was unemployment, low wages, menial work, high rent, crime, drugs and the spectacle of the rich and powerful spending their way from midnight to dawn. The vast military machine dragged the economy down, and it took more to get less." The damage to schooling, Shor explained, was that education no longer facilitated social mobility. Surrounded by a depressed job market, shabby schools, and a base curriculum, average students ceased to believe that education mattered. Shor concluded that the decay in education was caused by the combination of the "culture of narcissism" and the career education debacle of the 1970s.

A Nation at Risk. If conservatives and liberals were not wholly in agreement on causes of the problem, they were united in recognizing the extent of the educational crisis after 1983. It was during this "year of wonder" in education that President Reagan's bipartisan National Commission on Excellence in Education produced the document *A Nation at Risk,* the indictment of the educational status quo that launched a sweeping reform movement. The tone of the foreword of *A Nation at Risk* epitomized the sense of urgency about reforming education in the 1980s: "If an unfriendly foreign power had been responsible for the state of education, it would be considered an act of war." A score of other studies came fast on the heels of this effort. Nationally more than one hundred commissions set up shop to work on school reform. These commissions were populated in the majority by powerful business and political leaders. The task force for the Reagan Commission on Excellence, for example, consisted of one classroom teacher, fourteen heads of major corporations, thirteen governors, one union leader, and various college presidents, school superintendents, and principals. The effect of these collaborations was powerful: well-meaning but limited reform efforts lead solely by educators were displaced by general, well-publicized programs for "excellence," the new key word in educational circles. Dozens of these community-wide efforts, led by teams of educators, business professionals, and politicians, identified three key areas for reform: 1) a comprehensive overhaul of curriculum, including proposed extensive new requirements for graduation and new testing regimes for students to assess that curriculum; 2) new management regimes for teachers, including such concepts as merit pay and teacher-competency testing; and 3) new business-education partnerships allowing business to have a greater force in shaping curriculum.

Colleges Face Dilemma. Although the vast majority of the reform efforts in the 1980s were aimed at elementary and secondary education, colleges suffered from the access-versus-excellence conundrum as well. The Carnegie Council on Policy in Higher Education in 1980 called the time "a golden age" for students because of declining enrollments and the increased competition for students. Former University of California chancellor Clark Kerr, the chair of this commission, said that 1980s college students would be "recruited more actively, admitted more readily, retained more assiduously, counseled more attentively, graded more considerately, financed more adequately, taught more conscientiously, and placed in jobs more insistently than ever before." Richard Berendzen, president of American University, predicted that the decade would be a "remarkably transitional time" for colleges. "We have never been worse off," he said. "Yet we've never had greater opportunities. There is no right age to go to school. We are open to all races. We have learned the importance of blending theory with the practical." Boyer's later Carnegie report in 1986 emphasized the continuing problems that resulted from colleges' attempts to retain their traditional and nontraditional constituencies. American higher education was "unmatched, but troubled," the report claimed. At the same time, the study predicted that colleges would become less selective and that a downward drift in quality was likely. This prediction, too, came to pass as many schools lost their sense of mission while scrambling for students. As Russell Jacoby reports in *Dogmatic Wisdom* (1994), his critique of postmodern American higher education, the college experience was altered in the 1980s by virtue of the influx of underprepared students: "A revamped higher education has elicited many reports of students not learning; teachers not teaching; college presidents not presiding."

A Shift in Emphasis for Higher Education. Many analysts blamed the problems in higher education on administrators who slighted the liberal arts as they attempted to satisfy student demands for career training. By 1984, for example, more than 50 percent of the nation's undergraduates chose to major in vocational or occupational fields. Clifford Adelman surveyed the courses taken by a representative sample of twenty-two thousand college students' transcripts, a source more reliable than queries to administrators as to educational requirements, and published his results in a 1992 book, *Tourists in Our Own Land*. In his longitudinal study he discovered that the total credits of the humanities and social sciences amounted to less than a third of the credits the students took. This emphasis on applied and vocational courses inevitably affected higher education in the 1980s. Too many schools were credentialing students rather than educating them. And college students seemed pleased to grab those credentials and get out into the business world. The hottest degree was the master of business administration, the MBA, while majors in philosophy decreased 65 percent, history by 50 percent, and English by 45 percent. "The pendulum has swung too far," said Williams Banowsky, president of the University of Oklahoma. The mercenary bent of college students in the 1980s was undeniable. According to a national survey in 1980, 62.7 percent of freshmen felt that status and money were their most important goals. As Jacoby laments in *Dogmatic Wisdom,* "An unbridled desire for practical knowledge and good money recasts higher education. . . . An exclusively commercial and instrumental vision degrades the enterprise."

The National Will to Change. American educational policy is typically pulled from extreme to extreme every ten years or so, according to educational historian Dianne Ravitch. The decade of the 1980s was unique in that nonpartisan coalitions of those from outside the educational establishment tended to establish goals that were much more centrist in nature. Why was the nation suddenly so willing to cooperate and attack problems they had formerly ceded to educators? The answer probably lies in economic conditions. According to Secretary of Labor William Brock in *Nation's Business* in 1985, the overwhelming majority of new jobs created in the United States would require postsecondary education, and America was not preparing the populace for this revolution. As Lamar Alexander, who earlier served as education secretary under Reagan, explained in 1986, "What has suddenly riveted everyone's attention on our education system is that our standard of living is threatened. We're not going to have the jobs and good incomes in America if we don't have the good skills." When the pocketbooks of Americans felt the effect of poor schooling, America became interested in improving the problems.

The Role of Business in Reform. The education policy developments of the 1980s strongly reflected the interest of business in education reform, according to Michael Timpane in *Business Impact on Education and Child Development Reform* (1991), his research study prepared for the Committee on Economic Development. Business interests produced three distinct types of initiatives consistent with the business agenda: 1) improving educational quality by raising standards for students, teachers, and schools and focusing on accountability; 2) restructuring schools as places of work and teaching as a profession; 3) focusing on the educational and social-service needs of at-risk children. Frank Doyle, senior vice president for public relations at General Electric, reiterated in 1984 the business community's concern about the last goal: "A competitive America — let alone a compassionate America — will need every trained mind and every pair of skilled hands. . . . When the GEs and GMs and AT&Ts and USXs of America no longer have low-skill, low-value-added jobs — because they have adjusted to a higher skill competitive world — those left out will be locked out of the great American middle class," Doyle warned. "And every time that happens, it is a tragedy for America." Reporter and writer William Greider takes a more skeptical view of the public-spirited rhetoric of the corporations, however. He argues in his book *Who Will Tell the People?* (1988) that like other multinational corporations, General Electric wants maximum freedom to do as it chooses in the global economy — shifting production and jobs wherever seems efficient. And it wants minimal responsibility, Greider claims, for the economic consequences created by the steady loss of high-wage industrial jobs. Timpane's report also tempers his assessment of the effectiveness of business in creating reform. His research study asserts that despite good intentions, business interests and involvement in school, reform did not solve educational problems in the 1980s. These projects in the local schools varied widely in scope and effect. Often the reforms "barely addressed, let alone provided, needed improvements in the larger educational system," he says.

The Political Climate. Nonpartisan commissions advocated reform, and conservatives and liberals found a great deal of common ground in recommending changes. However, their efforts were played out in a fiercely partisan Congress. Reagan's New Federalism marked a concrete and dramatic shift from the Great Society programs of the 1960s and 1970s, which targeted minority groups. Under Reagan's leadership congressional conservatives claimed a mandate to reduce the size of the federal government, restoring autonomy to the states by shifting federal financing into block grants. The 1980s marked the culmination of twelve years of effort under four presidents to undo what conservatives felt were the excesses of the previous administrations. For the prior two decades the Senate Committee on Labor and Human Resources had been the originating source for much liberal legislation, including all major education laws known as hallmarks of the Great Society: the Elementary and Secondary Education Act of 1965, the Higher Education Act, and the Education for All Handicapped Children Act. Leading Democrats historically associated with this committee included John F. Kennedy, Robert F. Kennedy, Edward Kennedy, Claiborne Pell, Jacob Javits, and Thomas Eagleton. In 1981 the committee majority shifted to Republicans, with Orrin Hatch as chairman overseeing several freshman conservative senators, including Dan Quayle. These conservatives favored none of the reforms of the Great Society and even demanded the abolition of the Department of Education.

A Distaste for Federal Spending. Although the Reagan administration claimed to support strong educational reform, financial support was not forthcoming. The administration pursued a fiscal strategy in the early 1980s that had direct educational impact: by cutting taxes before being able to cut spending, conservatives set the stage for cutting educational programs later in the name of fiscal austerity. Supporters of education bemoaned the lack of fiscal support for the reforms that nonpartisan groups had recommended. Sen. Ernest Hollings (D–South Carolina) complained on the Senate floor in 1986 that "Since release of *A Nation at Risk,* ten other reports which censure our nation's educational system have been released. They all agree on the dire need for reform. But the response to the plethora of demands has been to decrease the amount of available funding to education." As early as 1983, the budget for Title I programs (designed for helping disadvantaged children) was down 38 percent from 1981. By 1986 the percentage of the federal budget allotted to education was down to 1.6, from 2.3 percent in 1980. In 1987 House of Representatives Majority Leader Jim Wright (D–Texas) railed against "misplaced priorities" in the presidential budget that zeroed out the GI Bill for Vietnam veterans and cut student college loans and work-study grants. These skirmishes illustrate the contradictions of the politics of education in the 1980s: the mood of the country reflected dissatisfaction with the status quo, yet the public refused to support increased money to fund reform. Although every reform commission recommended more spending on education, new leaders in Congress, reluctant to finance Great Society programs, were equally unenthusiastic about new federal spending.

Spending at the State Level. Unfortunately, during the 1980s an unprecedented decline in the fiscal health of the states, especially in the Northeast and Midwest, all but guaranteed that state funding levels would not rise. At the state level the problems were compounded by the fact that an aging population tended to resent school taxes for something they perceived as having little benefit to them, according to Michael Schaller's analysis in his book, *Reckoning with Reagan* (1992). Meanwhile, a growing portion of the middle class, especially in cities, abandoned public schools, leaving public schools to educate a larger proportion of poor, minority, or otherwise disadvantaged children. Middle-class flight further reduced the school districts' ability to raise needed revenues. Working-class parents had less faith in the value of education, Schaller argues, and they saw school-tax increases as just another financial burden. These divisions accentuated the decline of faith in public education that characterized the 1980s. Because of these economic realities, dramatic educational reforms got more press attention than financial support.

TOPICS IN THE NEWS

ACADEMIC AND ATHLETIC REFORM

"No Pass, No Play" Initiative. Prominent Texas business executive H. Ross Perot led a 1984–1985 campaign in his admittedly football-obsessed state to enact strictures barring failing high-school students from participating in sports. Perot's reform efforts were successful, and in 1985 a Texas law, which was emulated around the country, officially made achievement of a 70 average in every course for six weeks a prerequisite for playing a sport. A research study conducted three years later concluded that the Texas law was succeeding even beyond Perot's expectations. The percentage of students failing dropped from 15.5 in 1984–1985 to 12.8 in 1987–1988. Although opponents had predicted that students would opt for the easiest courses in the curriculum to assure sports eligibility, the number of athletes enrolled in honors courses remained constant. Also, most students interviewed for the study said the rule encouraged them to achieve.

Proposition 48. The National Collegiate Athletic Association (NCAA) voted on 13 and 14 January 1986 to instigate minimum eligibility requirements for college athletes based on standardized test scores and to implement drug testing at championship events. By fall 1988 athletes at Division I schools had to score 700 on the Scholastic Aptitude Test or 15 on the American College Test and maintain a 2.0 (a "C" average) or better in their high school's core curriculum. These new NCAA rules were called Proposition 48. One of the most outspoken opponents of this new rule was John Thompson, Georgetown University's black basketball coach. Complaining bitterly that the new rules would adversely affect minority youth, Thompson admitted that some athletes were unprepared for college, but he maintained, "It wasn't a coach who passed these kids from grades one through six when they weren't able to read." Indiana University basketball coach Bobby Knight had a different opinion. He believed that the strengthening of the rules would benefit all student athletes by forcing high schools to pay more attention to academics. "College isn't for everyone," Knight argued. "College isn't for you if you aren't a pretty good reader and a pretty good writer. In athletics, we really haven't understood that over the years."

Actor Bill Cosby promoting reading on a poster celebrating National Library Week in 1985

Unfair to Blacks? Those who agreed with Thompson criticized the rule on the grounds that minority achievement on standardized tests was required. Some educators believed that such tests were culturally biased against blacks, 41 percent of whom were enrolled in some of America's most troubled urban schools. Statistics from the SAT in 1987 show that the average score was 906 of a potential 1600; the average for blacks was 728, just above the 700 level required by Proposition 48. An Associated Press (AP) study in 1988 suggested that the Proposition 48's new freshman eligibility rule was primarily penalizing black athletes. The AP found that 274 college football players had been disqualified in 1988, and of the

213 athletes whose race could be determined, 86 percent were black. John Thompson's protests of these seeming inequities failed to change Proposition 48, and in protest he announced on 13 January 1989 that "I will not be on the bench in an NCAA-sanctioned Georgetown basketball game until something is done to provide student-athletes with opportunities and hope for access to college education." Thompson's protest soon ended, and Proposition 48 remained in effect, setting a clear threshold for high-school student-athlete academic achievement.

Source:
"Athletics and Academics," *Nation's Schools Report,* 14 August 1989, p. 5.

AIDS: CATALYST FOR CHANGE IN THE SCHOOLS

A Glass Booth. By the late 1980s the AIDS epidemic was significantly affecting school policy. When a Florida school district mandated that a seven-year-old girl infected with HIV be educated in a glass booth, the case made it to the federal courts. In *Martinez* v. *School Board of Hillsborough County* a federal judge reversed this decision in 1989, arguing that the child's presence in class posed "no significant risk" to the school. A 1987 survey on laws affecting students with AIDS concluded that the courts were using the antidiscrimination provisions of the Rehabilitation Act to protect infected students' rights.

AIDS Booklet. Education Secretary William Bennett, bowing to intense pressures from the scientific community, published three hundred thousand copies (one for every parent group and school board in the nation) of *AIDS and the Education of Our Children: A Guide for Parents and Teachers* on 26 October 1987. Another two hundred thousand copies of the twenty-eight-page document were made available, free of charge, to anyone requesting it. The tone of the booklet was highly moralistic, emphasizing the value of deferring sexual activity until adulthood and then choosing between abstinence or monogamy. One carefully written page mentioned condoms, but emphasized that their use was no guarantee of safety. Defending the message as "scientifically accurate and morally cogent," Bennett claimed, "When it comes to AIDS, science and morality walk the same path, teach the same thing." However, Ted Weiss, chair of the Senate Human Resources Committee, pronounced the guide "grossly inadequate" because, he said, it failed to clarify Centers for Disease Control (CDC) guidelines for containing the disease. "It's fine to have a moral message," he countered, "but that just does not deal with the real world. Seventy-five percent of singles are sexually active by age twenty." Although the Reagan administration response was to emphasize abstinence, a March 1987 U.S. Conference of Mayors' survey of seventy-three large school districts showed that the majority were taking a much more direct approach. In forty-eight of the school districts, programs defining safe sexual practices including condom use were in effect, and similar programs were

planned in twenty-four more. In teaching students how to avoid infection, 78 percent of the programs emphasized abstinence, but also provided direct information about condom use and avoidance of high-risk behaviors.

Dealing with Openly Gay and Lesbian Students. In the 1980s a new assertiveness by the gay and lesbian population forced schools and districts to grapple with the fact that, as the larger gay pride movement put it, "They're here and they're not going away." After a young man in Cumberland, Rhode Island, threatened legal action in the early 1980s if he were denied the right to bring a male date to the prom, high schools in diverse parts of the nation were confronted with informal networks and formal groups of students "coming out" to teachers. The immediate need for AIDS-prevention education for the male part of this high-risk population was a catalyst for a significant amount of national attention to this heretofore invisible population. AIDS experts warned that gay youths were most at risk for a "third wave" of infection, following adult gays and intravenous drug users.

A New Look at Teen Sexual Preference. For years researchers had believed that sexual preferences expressed during youth were merely a phase, that true sexual orientation was not solidified until age twenty or so. However, during the 1980s previous opinions about this issue were challenged. A December 1988 Seattle Commission on Children and Youth, after extensive public hearings, issued recommendations for schools in that area to address the "special needs" of lesbian and gay youth. A survey of all public high schools in Illinois resulted in huge numbers of requests by teachers for information on counseling gay students, and in Minnesota teachers and AIDS educators were encouraged to show "positive images of gays." However, in several other states laws forbade any positive discussion of homosexuality. California served as a microcosm of the conflict generated by the new openness about teen sexuality. Project 10, a special unit of the Los Angeles Unified School District, was established in 1985 to provide general counseling and education about homosexuality for all students and to establish a speakers bureau and library as resources for all district high schools. While the California Democratic Party resolved that "every school district in the state should provide counseling for those struggling with sexual orientation, based on the Project 10 model," conservatives organized to sponsor a bill to kill Project 10. Furthermore, their bill would require verified parental consent even to discuss the issues of homosexuality or AIDS. Both sides failed in their efforts. But the debate continued throughout the 1980s, as some believed that gay youths were merely "stuck in some immature phase of social development" and should, therefore, be ignored, while others bemoaned the fact that "at the period of life when one should find one's identity, how sad that gay youth must be mired in shame, denial and self hatred."

Sources:
"AIDS and School Policy," *Nation's Schools Report,* 22 May 1989, p. 65;

"AIDS Booklet Issued," *Nation's Schools Report,* 26 October 1987, p. 187;

Eric Rofes, "Opening Up the Classroom Closet," *Harvard Educational Review,* 59 (November 1989): 444–453.

APARTHEID SPURS CAMPUS PROTESTS

Antiapartheid Rallies. In 1985 the Reagan administration defended its refusal to apply economic sanctions to South Africa as a means of ending that country's official policy of apartheid. Demonstrations on campuses all across the United States on 4 April 1985 marked the seventeenth anniversary of the assassination of Rev. Martin Luther King Jr. with protests against racism in general and South Africa's apartheid system in particular. Amy Carter, daughter of former president Jimmy Carter and a Brown University student, was one of the more-prominent personalities arrested in a four-thousand-person demonstration led by Washington, D.C., mayor Marion Barry at that city's South African embassy.

Divestiture Demands. Also coinciding with the 4 April King anniversary, several hundred students at Columbia University in New York City began a blockade of a campus building to demand that the university divest itself of $32.5 million in stock of companies doing business in South Africa. Although the demonstrators padlocked the front door and camped out around it, another entrance to the building remained open and classes continued without interruption. On 25 April, when Columbia had given no concessions on the divestment issue, the students called off the protest, claiming it was time to "move on to new tactics." Simultaneously, another sit-in protest began at the University of California, Berkeley, drawing more than four thousand students and residents to denounce that university's holdings in companies doing business with South Africa. However, the regents refused to advance their June meeting, at which plans had been made to discuss possible action regarding the school's $1.8 billion investment in firms operating in South Africa. Despite this lack of success, other pro-divestment sit-ins began at Rutgers and Cornell Universities. On 24 April 1985 thousands of students around the country took part in what organizers named National Antiapartheid Protest Day and A Day of National Solidarity. The activities, including rallies, marches, teach-ins, and acts of civil disobedience, were concerned with U.S. policies on nuclear disarmament and Central America as well as investments in South Africa.

Some Universities Divest. Some universities did agree to divest themselves of holdings connected with South Africa. In 1985 Stanford University trustees voted to sell the university's $5 million stock investment in Motorola if the company resumed sales of electronic gear to the South African military or police. Harvard University that same year announced it had sold its stock holdings in Baker International Corporation after the company refused to provide evidence that it followed "reasonably ethical standards" in its South African operations. Al-though Harvard had taken an official stand against the apartheid system, this sale was the first time that the university had divested itself of part of its stock portfolio to back up its position.

BILINGUAL EDUCATION

Native Culture or Larger Culture? The Supreme Court case of *Lau* v. *Nichols* in 1974 affirmed the concept of language rights when a group of Chinese students in San Francisco demanded, and won, instruction in their native language. This case marked an official recognition of multilingualism in the United States. Schools were required to offer the curriculum in a manner understandable to the non-English-speaking child. The federal Bi-Lingual Education Act, which had been in effect since 1967, had as its primary goals "cultivating ancestral pride, reinforcing native languages, and cultivating inherent strengths of students." However, during the decades following the Lau decision, two competing philosophies of bilingual instruction emerged. In the early days, the goal was successful integration of the students into the culture

---

"STEREO DIVESTITURE"

On his first week on the job as education secretary in 1985, William Bennett was asked by CBS news about the possible effects of the Reagan administration's proposed student-aid reductions. In outlining how the well-to-do might cope, Bennett warned, "For some it may require divestiture of certain sorts — stereo divestiture. Tightening the belt can have the function of focusing the mind."

That year 77 percent of Americans surveyed in a Harris poll felt that too many well-off families had received loans, and 62 percent felt that student loans had to be included in budget cuts. College presidents, however, were livid. The University of the Pacific canceled Bennett as its proposed graduation speaker, and dozens of other universities expressed outrage. Students, however, did not appear to be intimidated by their government; indeed, they showered Bennett with cards and letters written in reply from spring break in Florida. Typical was the card postmarked Fort Lauderdale: "Dear Mr. Secretary Bennett: Wish you were here. Sun is great. Send money, preferably not one of those things that takes six months from your department. Stereo broke; would appreciate your sending bureaucrat down with a Walkman."

Source: William J. Bennett, "The Great University Debates," in *The De-Valuing of America* (New York: Summit Books, 1992).

---

188 **AMERICAN DECADES: 1980-1989**

A bilingual elementary-school class

as a whole; the competing view that emerged during the 1970s was promotion of cultural differences as a valid educational goal. Advocates of the first philosophy believed students should be taught English in immersion programs as quickly as possible so that they may better succeed in other subjects that are taught in English; the other advocates believed students should be taught all of their subject-matter classes in their native language.

Politics and Bilingual Instruction. During the 1980s a furor erupted over funding instruction in native languages when the Reagan administration expressed real concern that some bilingual programs based on the cultural-difference model were failing to help students enter the larger culture. President Reagan's education secretary, William J. Bennett, denounced the cultural-difference model and suggested that all bilingual education change to conform to the short-term immersion program. Because Reagan proposed amendments to the federal Bi-Lingual Education Act, the National Advisory and Coordinating Council on Bi-Lingual Education undertook a comprehensive study of programs nationwide. Their report, which was not issued to Congress until 1988, stated that the instructional quality and comprehensiveness in meeting student needs was significantly more important that any particular method or philosophy. In some settings one approach was successful but the same approach elsewhere was not effective. The best programs were judged to be those taught by teachers linguistically and culturally sensitive who maintained high expectations of the students. Bennett's successor in the Bush administration, Lauro Cavazos, a native speaker of Spanish himself, similarly supported the immediate teaching of English. However, he emphasized that the children should also be encouraged to maintain their native language and culture.

Spanish as First Language. The debate on bilingual instruction took on greater significance in the 1980s as the percentage of households with Spanish as a spoken language grew. By 1982, 7.5 million Mexican Americans and 16 million Hispanics made up the largest American ethnolinguistic group: 30 percent of the population in New York City, 32 percent in Miami, 35 percent in both Hartford and Denver, 50 percent in Los Angeles, and 60 percent in both San Antonio and El Paso. The number of Hispanics judged in need of spoken-language assistance in school was estimated to be 3.6 million in 1981. These students progressed through school at an average of two to three levels behind their peers; Hispanic unemployment was more than double that of the rate for whites; and annual income of Hispanics averaged $12,600 in the late 1970s whereas that of whites averaged $17,600. Clearly, improvements in education for this segment of the population were needed. Additionally, there was a big demand for bilingual instruction for the estimated 1.7 million immigrant Hispanics attempting to fulfill the second stage of immigration legalization. In order to receive citizenship, applicants must present to the Immigration and Naturalization Service a certificate of satisfactory pursuit of English language acquisition. The state or local school districts were obligated to provide classes for these non-native speakers as well as for enrolled students. Thus, if for no other reason than to facilitate immigration, funding for bilingual programs in the 1980s remained steady, despite Reagan administration efforts to cut expenditures.

Sources:
"Bilingual Education," *Education Digest* (September 1982): 4–8;

Hugh Davis Graham, *The Uncertain Triumph: Federal Education Policy in the Kennedy and Johnson Years* (Chapel Hill: University of North Carolina Press, 1984).

BLACK EDUCATIONAL PROGRESS SLOWS

Black Enrollment Declines. Although black Americans made major economic and social gains in the mid twentieth century, that progress stagnated by the 1980s. "Many blacks remain separated from the mainstream of national life under conditions of great inequality in education, housing and health care," concluded the National Research Council in *A Common Destiny: Blacks and American Society* in 1989. Certainly progress in higher education had slowed. Blacks remained underrepresented in graduate and professional degree attainment and were actually losing ground in undergraduate education compared to the momentum of the 1970s. By 1989 the number of black men enrolled in universities and colleges in the United States had declined to 436,000 from the high point in 1976 of 470,000, according to an American Council on Higher Education study. Although the num-

Students taking the Scholastic Aptitude Test, which some educators consider culturally biased against black students

ber of black women rose from 563,000 in 1976 to 645,000 in 1989, the overall percentage of black students in higher education fell during the decade from 9.4 to 8.6. Some black leaders attributed this drop to federal educational policies that had shifted financial aid away from college grants. Other explanations include a tightening of the open admissions policies of the 1970s. Even though the scores of blacks on the SAT continued to improve into the 1980s, on the average the scores lagged behind those of whites. At some schools this widespread change in academic standards disproportionately affected minority applicants. The University of California, Berkeley, attempted to avoid this inequity when in May 1989 officials announced that academic entrance standards would be raised for some students. Fifty percent of the 1989 freshman class would be admitted only on academic credentials. The remainder would be divided into separate categories and would compete for admission based on the following categories: 1) socio-economic disadvantage; 2) underrepresented minorities; 3) older students; 4) the disabled; and 5) rural students.

Racially Charged College Campuses. Some college campuses provided a hostile atmosphere for minority students who did enroll. Racist graffiti, jokes, brawls, and anonymous hate letters were reported at 175 colleges across the country, according to *The New York Times* in

May 1989. Ground zero of collegiate racial conflict was Dartmouth College, where in 1986 on the Martin Luther King holiday twelve students used sledgehammers and crowbars to wreck shantytowns erected to protest the South African policy of apartheid. All but two of the students were staffers of the *Dartmouth Review*, a weekly publication with a right-wing perspective that had previously waged a campaign against a black professor. All twelve students were suspended by a panel of students, faculty, and administrators, and classes were canceled for a day to hold a forum on "racism, violence, and disrespect for minority opinion." Following this incident, racist letters were sent to black women students at Smith College in Massachusetts. At the University of Wisconsin a fraternity skit used various African effigies as objects of ridicule, and racist jokes were broadcast on the student radio station at the University of Michigan. Explanations for this outbreak of racist acts were varied. Some administrators suggested that white resentment of distinctive educational opportunities for minorities, such as black cultural centers and affirmative action, fueled the hostilities. Others felt the lack of emphasis on civil rights during the Reagan administration had undermined the public's support for affirmative action and given rise to racist attitudes.

City Public Schools Still Unequal. Race was a factor in many problems in the public schools as well. Despite the thirty-year effort to improve equal educational access since the Supreme Court's 1954 *Brown* v. *Board of Education* decision that separate schooling is inherently unequal, many black children in cities were still not a part of the educational mainstream. Although black students made up 16 percent of the population, 41 percent of these black students were enrolled in urban, predominantly minority schools in low-income areas. Six such cities — Chicago, Cleveland, Houston, Los Angeles, New Orleans, and New York — whose schools were disproportionately minority, were studied by the Carnegie Foundation, and the resulting report, "An Imperiled Generation: Saving Urban Schools," concluded that many of these city schools had been written off as "human storehouses to keep young people off the streets." Suggesting that no other crisis would be as calmly accepted by the American public, the 1988 report determined that, for these cities at least, the "reform movement largely by-passed our most deeply troubled schools." Data from yet another study, this one by the Office of Civil Rights in 1988, revealed that in the 3,378 school districts examined, blacks were twice as likely as whites to be suspended, receive corporal punishment, or to be placed in special-education classes. An Office of Civil Rights analyst suggested that the inability of teachers and administrators to handle students with backgrounds different from their own was the reason for the inequities. Mary Hatwood Futrell, president of the National Education Association, agreed, saying that teachers often deal with students of a different race in a discriminatory way because of their own biases and backgrounds. When the National Association for the Advancement of Colored People commissioned a Louis Harris poll in January 1989, whites and blacks surveyed disagreed about the severity of racial problems. However, both races agreed on one key point — that more money and effort should be used to improve education for the underclasses. At the end of the decade, it appeared that schools with primarily minority populations were badly in need of improvement.

Reform and Inner-City Schools. The national reform movement bypassed most inner-city, predominantly minority schools for several reasons. The essential underlying factor was economic. City schools, relying on local property taxes for their funding for public education, drew on a considerably smaller tax base in proportion to their student populations than did those in nearby wealthy suburbs. In Chicago, for example, annual spending for city secondary-school students in 1989 was about $5,500, compared to about $9,000 per student in nearby Winnetka. Children enrolled in cash-poor city schools suffered from teacher shortages (hiring permanent substitutes was much cheaper than hiring qualified teachers), reduced curriculum offerings (few foreign languages, no advanced math or science lab courses), desperate short-

---

REPLACING THE CANON

In spring 1986 a small but vocal group of students called on Stanford University to abolish a required freshman course called Western Culture, one of the remaining core courses of the school. In its place they proposed a course that would "emphasize the contribution of cultures disregarded and/or distorted by the present program." This charge marked the beginning of a steady stream of charges against the Western Culture program — charges of racism, sexism, imperialism, elitism, and ethnocentrism.

Students campaigning for the change used the tactics of 1960s activists: a student group occupied President Donald Kennedy's office for five hours and released a set of ten demands; on the birthday of Dr. Martin Luther King Jr. in 1987 Jesse Jackson visited the campus and led a group of students chanting, "Hey, hey, ho, ho, Western Culture's got to go." Editorials in the student newspapers summed up the debate by saying, "We're tired of reading books by dead white guys."

In 1988 the Stanford faculty senate replaced the Western Culture program with a new course called Cultures, Ideas, and Values. Under the old system the course content had consisted of fifteen required books of Western philosophy and literature. With the new course individual instructors would decide year by year the new content — to include works by women, minorities, and persons of color. Additionally, instructors were to assign at least one work per quarter that explicitly addressed issues of race, gender, or class. Stanford, "the Harvard of the West," was one of hundreds of colleges and universities to reconsider the "canon" and to replace traditional curricula with formerly underrepresented thinkers and writers.

Source: William J. Bennett, "The Great University Debate," in *The De-Valuing of America* (New York: Summit Books, 1992).

---

ages of materials, and health-threatening physical facilities. Many teachers and administrators in nearly totally segregated city schools were perplexed when their reform-minded legislators "mandated" that students score higher on standardized tests. Principal Ruthie Green-Brown of Camden High, located in Camden, New Jersey, the fourth-poorest city of more than 50,000 in America, pointed out the unfair practice of comparing Camden students' progress with those in nearby suburbs: "If they first had given Head Start to our children and prekindergarten, and material and classes of fifteen or eighteen children in the elementary grades, and computers and attractive buildings and enough books and supplies and teacher salaries sufficient to compete with the suburban schools, and then come in a few years later with their tests and test demands, it might have been fair play." As it was, however, some state legislators seemed confident that reform could be enacted through mandating proficiency testing alone.

Sources:

A Common Destiny: Blacks and American Society (Washington, D.C.: National Research Council, 1989);

Jonathan Kozol, *Savage Inequalities: Children in America's Schools* (New York: Crown, 1991);

"Racial Incidents Reported at 175 Campuses," *New York Times,* 22 May 1989, p. 1A;

Gail Thomas, "Black Students in U.S. Graduate and Professional Schools in the 1980s: A National Assessment," *Harvard Educational Review,* 57 (August 1987): 261–265.

Secretary of Education Shirley M. Hufstedler unveiling the sign for the newly established cabinet-level Department of Education, May 1980

FEDERAL EDUCATION INTERVENTION: HARMFUL OR HELPFUL?

The Federal Role. Both before and after his election, Ronald Reagan never made a secret of his desire to reduce or even eliminate the role of the federal government in education. He consistently asserted that "the greatest public school system the world has ever seen" began to deteriorate when federal intervention started, primarily in the 1960s. His oft-stated agenda on education included the following: 1) Do away with the Department of Education; 2) Encourage prayer in the schools; 3) Enact tuition tax credits and family educational allowances or vouchers to help parents finance private-school education or choice of public schools; 4) Weaken federal regulations, including those aimed at civil rights for disadvantaged and handicapped children; and 5) Enact massive cuts in the education budget.

Rhetoric versus Reality. Reagan argued that the federal influence had grown so massive that it had usurped the role of state and local governments. However, in 1983, of the $230 billion expended on all education from all sources, the federal share was only 9 percent. The rest of the funding came from state sources (39 percent), local sources (24 percent), and tuition, fees, endowments, and gifts. A second argument was that federal assistance was simply not needed. Evidence from the reports of all the task forces and commissions, including President Reagan's own Commission on Excellence in Education, contradicted this contention. The next argument was that any federal money brought with it onerous and expensive rules and regulations that distort the proper balance of responsibilities of state and local entities. A 1983 study by the independent Educational Testing Service of eight states' federal/state policies, however, concluded that federal involvement had not "imposed harsh burdens; on the contrary, it had strengthened state educational agencies." Finally, and to many voters most importantly, Reagan asserted that federal involvement had simply wasted money, that federal programs had failed. Many families whose children had been granted access by virtue of such programs as Head Start, the Higher Education Act, and the Education for All Handicapped Children Act, disagreed. Numerous studies supported the claim that these programs had raised the level of achievement for many Americans, who for reasons of poverty, disability, or discrimination had in the past been denied educational opportunity.

Head Start. As early as 1979, Yale University professor Edward Ziglar, previously director of President Richard Nixon's Office of Child Development, summarized the studies to date that assessed effectiveness of the Head Start program. The Head Start children, he reported, repeatedly scored better on preschool achievement tests than their peers without Head Start experience. They also scored higher on a "social competence" scale, which included variables such as a healthy self-image, motivation, curiosity, and independence. But do these improvements last? skeptics asked. A landmark longitudinal study, begun in 1964 and published in 1984, suggested the answer was an unequivocal yes. These results, reported in *Changed Lives: The Effects of the Perry Preschool Program on Youths Through Age Nineteen,* concluded that black children who sixteen years earlier had entered Head Start at age three had grown up more successfully, academically and socially, than had a comparable group without such training. The employment rate and/or the college or vocational school enrollment of the Head Start youth was more than double that of the other group at age nineteen. Teenage pregnancies were slightly more than half of the non–Head Start group, and 20 percent

THE COALITION OF ESSENTIAL SCHOOLS: PRINCIPLES FOR SECONDARY REFORM

In 1984 the Coalition of Essential Schools, an association of school people who agreed on a set of ideas that should inform all good schools, arose from research conducted primarily by Theodore R. Sizer at Brown University on secondary-school reform. Schools joining this reform movement agreed to incorporate nine common principles into their individualized local reform plans:

1. Schools should focus on helping adolescents learn to use their minds well. Intellectual growth is the central purpose. 2. Schools' goals should be simple: each student should master a number of essential skills and be competent in certain areas of knowledge. The aphorism "less is more" should dominate: curricular decisions are to be directed toward students' attempts to gain mastery rather than by teachers' efforts to cover content. 3. Goals should apply to all students, but the means to these goals will vary as these students themselves vary. 4. Teaching and learning should be personalized to the maximum feasible extent. No teacher should have direct responsibility for more than eighty students. 5. The governing metaphor of the school should be student as worker, rather than the more familiar metaphor of teacher as deliverer of instructional services. Teachers coach, not lecture. 6. Students embarking on secondary studies must show competence in language and elementary mathematics. Students of traditional age without this competence must be provided with intensive remedial work so they can quickly meet those standards. Diplomas should be awarded on a successful final demonstration of master for graduation — an Exhibition. This Exhibition must display his or her grasp of the central skills and knowledge of the school's program. 7. The tone of the school should explicitly stress the values of unanxious expectations, of trust, and of decency. Parents should be treated as essential collaborators. 8. The principal and teachers should perceive of themselves first as generalists and next as specialists. 9. Administrative and budget targets should include substantial time for collective planning by teachers, competitive salaries for staff, and an ultimate per-pupil cost not more than 10 percent higher than that at traditional schools. Administrative plans may have to show the reduction or elimination of some services now provided for students in many traditional comprehensive secondary schools.

By the end of the 1980s nearly two hundred schools, both public and private, in twenty-three states were involved with the coalition.

Source: Theodore R. Sizer, *Horace's School: Redesigning the American High School* (Boston: Houghton Mifflin, 1992).

---

fewer of the experimental group had been arrested or dropped out of school.

Fate of Reagan Education Goals. Although Reagan had clearly delineated goals for revamping public education, many of his attempted reforms failed. Terrel H. Bell, the first-term secretary of education, wrote after leaving office that his battles with "the lunatic fringe of ideological political thought" and "zealots pressing radical and off-the-wall ideas" had distracted his attention from his appointed purpose of closing down the Department of Education. Bell also admitted that Title I of the Elementary and Secondary Education Act (renamed Chapter One in 1981 and the recipient of 34 percent of all federal spending for elementary and secondary education at the federal level) had been effective and that its funding should continue. Other developments thwarted the Reagan agenda as well. In 1984 the Omnibus Education bill was actually increased by $250 million from the previous year, and a House amendment on silent prayer was dropped. Spending continued for bilingual, adult, immigrant, Indian, women's, disadvantaged, and handicapped education. New policy on bilingual education was set — allowing all English "immersion" instruction as well as the former practice of teaching academic courses in native languages. And Reagan himself set into motion a new federal intervention program, created in November 1984. This new spending initiative was the drug-education package, headed by FBI director William Webster. The plan, using professional and amateur athletes, coaches, and schools banding together, had the goal of reducing drug use among youth by 50 percent to 75 percent during the next five years. Although forty drug-prevention organizations were involved, the coordination was the responsibility of the federal government. With much federal intervention still in place when a more moderate President Bush took over from Reagan in 1989, many advocates of ending federal involvement in education saw their best opportunities for change ended.

Sources:
John Brademas, *The Politics of Education: Conflict and Consensus on Capitol Hill* (Norman: University of Oklahoma Press, 1987);

John Clements, *Changed Lives: The Effects of the Perry Preschool Program on Youths Through Age Nineteen* (Ypsilanti, Mich.: High Scope Press, 1984).

GUNS, DRUGS, AND SUICIDE

Escalation of Troubles. Newspaper headlines from a single week in April 1987 demonstrate an alarming esca-

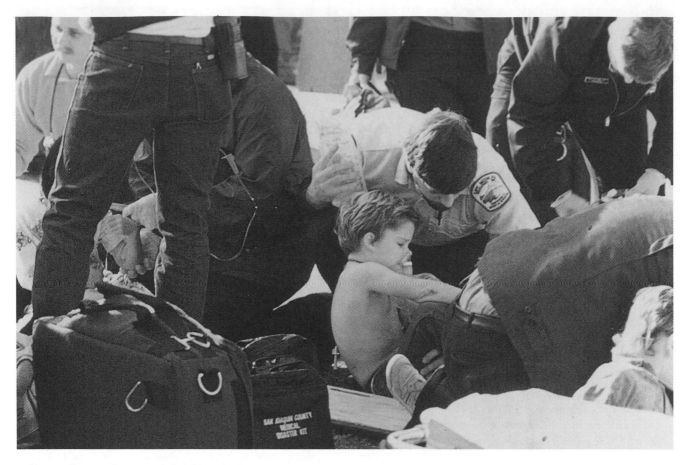

Paramedics treating wounded children in Stockton, California, after a gunman opened fire in the playground at Cleveland Elementary School, killing five children and wounding twenty-nine others, 17 January 1989

lation of violence, drug use, and abuse in the nation's schools: "Tennessee Teacher Shot By Special Ed Student in Class," "Reported Abuse Deaths up 29%," "Boy Shot Outside Detroit High School," "NYC Board Sued in Rape Incident at Local School," "Tighter Security Urged after Attack on NYC Principal," "LA Student Shoots Self in Principal's Office," "Cal Student's Parents Sued After Attack on Teacher," "Kentucky Boy Shot at Football Game," "GA Student Fatally Stabs Elementary Principal," "Three Alabama Students Charged With Rape of Classmate," "Boy Kills Classmate, Self in Missouri," "Four NJ Teens Die in Apparent 'Suicide Pact,'" and " 'Copy Cat' Suicide Pacts and Attempts in Three States."

Drug Use and the Schools. Many of the problems with violence, abuse, and suicidal impulses were associated with illegal drugs. In 1979 surveys of student drug use indicated that 54 percent had tried drugs at least once, so it is not surprising that parents consistently listed drug use as their greatest worry about their children's schools in annual surveys from 1980 to 1987. First Lady Nancy Reagan's "Just Say No" campaign in the early 1980s targeted youngsters in elementary schools with the hope of making abstaining the popular choice. The "Just Say No" program replaced the usual lectures about the dangers of drugs with sports, games, and programs aimed at helping

children develop the ability to rebuff drug dealers' and users' overtures. During his administration George Bush appropriated more than $250 million of his National Drug Control Strategy (of a total $6.9 billion) for programs in the schools. Former education secretary William Bennett, who left that job to become President Bush's coordinator of drug policy, warned that no schools without valid drug-use policies would receive federal funding. By the late 1980s drug use among students appeared to be declining. A University of Michigan Institute for Social Research study of 16,000 high-school seniors at 130 schools in 1988 revealed that 39 percent of them had tried drugs, down from 42 percent in 1987 and the 54 percent high in 1979. For the first time since its appearance in 1985, use of the powerful cocaine derivative crack declined, as did alcohol, marijuana, cocaine, and PCP. Only cigarette smoking remained constant, with 29 percent of students reporting regular usage. The study attributed these findings to the growing perception of the dangers of illegal drugs.

Guns in the Classroom. Although drug use appeared to wane in the 1980s, violent episodes in the schools — especially involving guns — increased dramatically. Violence may not have been the norm, but it was also not an isolated problem. In 1989 in New York City metal detectors in only five high schools uncovered more than two hundred guns. At Lindbergh Middle School in Long Beach, California, a ten-foot-high, nine-hundred-foot-long concrete wall was erected between the school and a nearby housing project to protect students from flying bullets. The American Federation of Teachers in 1989 reported that 66 percent of member teachers surveyed were scared of violence and gang activity and more than 70 percent knew colleagues who had been victimized by teens. Teachers attributed the problems to the easy access to guns and drugs, a lack of parental supervision, and the influence of violence in the media. Reactions to the violence inevitably pitted students' rights against group safety. One California school, Bassett High in La Puente, began using parent patrols in 1981. After banning baggy clothes, closing all but one entrance (staffed by a full-time guard), removing lockers, and teaching the entire student body a course in conflict resolution, authorities reported that in-school crime had been reduced 50 percent.

Suicide Prevention in the Curriculum. In this culture of frequent drug use and prevalent violence, suicide attempts by teenagers became all too frequent. Schools reacted to this escalation by incorporating suicide prevention information into the curriculum. Teachers' continuing education training at in-service workshops frequently centered on ways to detect potential problems and possible referral options for suicidal students. As early as 1982 California became the first state to mandate a state task force to train teachers to counsel students in the aftermath of suicide attempts by peers. Several state departments of education added a college course in suicide prevention to certification requirements. Suicide prevention became a popular subject in educational research, and a consensus emerged as to the components of successful programs: 1) preventive efforts that address children at risk for physical, sexual, or psychological abuse; 2) intervention programs involving cooperation among parents, schools, and students; and 3) both long-term and crisis intervention.

Sources:
Eleanor Guetzloe, "School Prevention of Suicide, Violence and Abuse," *Education Digest* (February 1989): 46–49;

"Violence in the Schools," *Nation's Schools Report*, 3 December 1989, p. 3.

1983: "THE HINGE OF HISTORY" FOR REFORM

The First Call: *A Nation at Risk.* The catalyst for the serious reform movements during the 1980s was the Reagan administration's National Commission on Excellence in Education (NCEE), a bipartisan group of business, political, and education leaders who addressed what they referred to as a "rising tide of mediocrity." Their report, *A Nation at Risk: The Imperative for Educational Reform,* published in May 1983, called for reform which would address the twin goals of equity and high-quality schooling. Commission members insisted that both goals have profound and practical meaning for society and the economy; that the United States could not permit one to yield to the other in principle or in practice. It was imperative, they said, that our educational system develop the talents of all students to the fullest extent. This commission was particularly distressed that the number of

David Gardner, chairman of the National Commission on Excellence in Education, and Secretary of Education Terrel H. Bell briefing reporters on the commission's findings, April 1983

students taking the general (nonacademic) track in high school had grown from 12 percent in 1964 to 42 percent in 1980, a pattern that had resulted when graduation standards had been relaxed in every state. The report bemoaned widespread easy grading, easy admissions to college, too little homework, watered-down textbooks, too little writing and reading, poor teaching, and few incentives for excellence among teachers. Commission members suggested there was a legitimate, if unproven, concern that the observed declines in educational performance were being translated into lower productivity in the workplace. Recommending a massive federal effort to create national standards for teaching and learning, the commission also called for a significant increase in federal spending for education. Ernest Boyer, a strong voice for educational reform, foresaw that these recommendations for national standards could be resisted by some local authorities. The central dilemma of reform, he warned, was that "Americans want local control but national results. They like the idea of localism, but how do they know their schools are doing a good job unless they have a national yardstick to measure by?"

The Next Wave of Reform Proposals. In June 1983 a group of the nation's governors, the Education Commission of the States, issued their plan for reform, titled *Action for Excellence: A Comprehensive Plan to Improve Our Nation's Schools*. This report, sometimes called the Hunt Report, after Gov. James B. Hunt of North Carolina

(who chaired the group), suggested the same reforms at the state level that the NCEE had proposed at the federal level. In September of that year the National Science Board issued "Educational Aims for the 21st Century." This effort hit the math/science crisis head-on with estimated costs for reviving technology in the schools at $1.5 billion the first year alone. The panel suggested that $5 billion more would be needed in the coming decade to train teachers, buy hardware, and revamp curricula to keep up with the burgeoning technology field. The Reagan administration, which had set aside only $50 million for science programs in 1983, was silent in response. One important finding of this group was that the basics in the 1980s now included communication skills, higher problem-solving skills, and scientific and technological literacy. The National Science Board warned that defining basics in the sense of merely reading, writing, and math would assure Americans of falling further and further behind developing industrial nations. Within months, the College Board issued a key (though somewhat misnamed) report, "Academic Preparation for College," which echoed these findings. They cited six basic academic subjects, including computer competencies, which all students should take during high school: English, math, arts, science, social studies, and foreign languages. Arguing that leaders in business want workers with academic training, the College Board recommended an academic experi-

LOW-TECH EDUCATION IN THE HIGH-TECH WORLD OF THE 1980S

Two of the economic boom corridors of the 1980s, the famed Route 128 of Boston's bedroom communities and California's "Silicon Valley" of Santa Clara, were home to the burgeoning micro-electronics industry. The annual wage of workers in these two regions was approximately $20,500, tying for the fifth highest in all of the U.S. metropolitan areas. But the indifference that high-tech businesses displayed toward the low-tech educational realities of their communities was startling. In the seven school districts in Boston and the eight in Silicon Valley, terrible deterioration of the educational systems — characterized by declining enrollment and financial support as well as demoralized faculties — existed in the shadow of booming new businesses. In California, districts in Silicon Valley paid less per pupil than the national average, and the San Jose Unified School District actually declared bankruptcy. "Nowhere in America is there a greater disparity between private affluence and declining public services," claimed the *Washington Post* in 1982. Budget reductions because of property tax cuts from California's Proposition 13 and Massachusetts's Proposition 2 1/2 had a particularly disastrous effect on industrial arts and vocational education programs in each state. Another serious problem was the decline in new teachers trained in science and math; in the Pacific Coast states, an incredible 84 percent of science and math teachers hired in 1982 were unqualified in their fields. Conditions in these states — larger classes, shorter school days, fewer teachers, sharply reduced budgets for science equipment, tests and facilities — made it even more difficult to prepare students for the challenges and opportunities of the new information society. After President Reagan declared 1983–1984 as "National Year of Partnerships in Education," boards of regents in both California and Massachusetts had leaders of high-tech industries appointed as members. Also, by the mid 1980s, many Adopt-a-School programs, partnerships between businesses and schools, focused on upgrading the secondary schools.

Sources: Edward Morgan, "The Effects of Proposition 2 1/2 in Massachusetts," *Phi Delta Kappan* (December 1982): 252–258;

Elizabeth Useem, *Low Tech Education in a High Tech World: Corporations and Classrooms in the New Information Society* (New York: Free Press, 1986).

More Alarms. By fall 1983 the Carnegie Foundation–sponsored study "The Condition of Teaching," by Emily Feistritzer, presented a state-by-state analysis of the teaching profession and its shortcomings. Her conclusions were grim. "Far fewer persons are choosing teaching as a career, and the academic caliber of those who are is decreasing. . . . Over half the teachers in a 1981 survey said they certainly would not become a teacher again," Feistritzer reported. In December John Brademas, chair of a National Commission on Graduate Education, issued the committee's report on graduate education in the United States as a "warning to all who care about America's future: our graduate enterprise is in trouble; so is our national capacity to face and master change, to chart and define the future, and to enjoy the rich blessings of democracy secure in the knowledge that others will create the future for us." Brademas ended his report agreeing with the Business–Higher Education Forum's claim that "We stand at the hinge of history, requiring the kinds of sacrifices a nation makes in wartime." As the year came to an end, the American public had ample information about the sad state of education and no shortage of dire predictions about the future. The stage was set for reform.

Convergence of Opinions. There was a remarkable convergence of opinions about ways to institute reform — a consistently moderate, centrist agenda. From the many 1983 documents and those that followed, nine general recommendations emerged: 1) Raise academic requirements for high-school graduation so that students read and write more. Replace electives with math and science courses and replace the general, vocational track with academic requirements for all students; 2) Provide computer education for all students. This basic literacy must be taught from K to 12; 3) Provide more opportunities for development of higher-order reasoning skill. Students must have more problem-solving practice to adjust to the new work demands; 4) Students must spend more time on learning tasks. The school year should be 200–220 days, and the day should go from 6.5 hours to 8 hours as teachers are freed from noninstructional duties to concentrate only on teaching; 5) Enforce stricter discipline. Unruly students must be expelled or separated from the general population; 6) Colleges must make it more difficult to enter. They must send an academic message to the high schools that more academics are neccessary to succeed in higher education; 7) Explore the concepts of merit pay for teaching excellence and a master-teacher career ladder for those who succeed in the classroom but do not want to move into administration; 8) Improve teacher quality, first through changing teacher training, requiring fewer education courses and more in subject matter, next through competency testing for new teachers, and finally through crash programs to train science, math, and engineering teachers; 9) Target state and federal funds to programs committed to increasing student

ence for every student, whether he or she attended college or chose to go into technical training.

performance in academics, so that federal aid focuses on quality, not just equity.

Reality versus Rhetoric. The year 1983 was a landmark in educational reform. Because of the significant number of calls for change in the system — coming simultaneously from the established education community, the business world, liberal and conservative politicians, as well as parents and taxpayers — a national consensus for reform emerged. As New Jersey governor Thomas Kean summarized the process, the nation began a process to "reinvent the school for modern times." Unfortunately, during the decade changes resulting from the reforms enacted were not nearly as dramatic as the rhetoric of 1983. However, every state did enact some form of educational reform, ranging from modest changes in attendance requirements to sweeping administrative and curricular changes.

Sources:

Hendrick Gideonse, "The Necessary Revolution in Teacher Education," *Phi Delta Kappan* (September 1982): 15–19;

Dianne Ravitch, *The Schools We Deserve: Reflections on the Educational Crises of Our Time* (New York: Basic Books, 1985);

Ira Shor, *Culture Wars: School and Society in the Conservative Restoration* (Boston: Routledge & Kegan Paul, 1986);

Gary Sykes, "A Contemporary Account of the Status of Teaching," *Phi Delta Kappan* (October 1983): 87–94;

Michael Timpane and Laurie Millar McNeill, *Business Impact on Education and Child Development Reform* (New York: Committee for Economic Development, 1991).

RISE IN CENSORSHIP

Reagan and the First Amendment. Ronald Reagan spoke to a religious group in Dallas on 22 August 1980 during the presidential campaign: "When I hear the First Amendment used as a reason to keep traditional moral values away from policy-making, I am shocked. The First Amendment was written not to protect the people and their laws from religious values, but to protect those values from government tyranny." Before this group candidate Reagan also claimed there were "great flaws" in the theory of evolution, and he suggested that along with the scientific version of creation, public schools should teach the biblical story of creation. Not surprisingly, after the election a significant rise in the number of objections to textbooks and curriculum occurred nationwide, evenly distributed across both city and rural areas. By the year 1985–1986 the organization People for the American Way recorded 130 attempts to censor classes, texts, and library books — a 33 percent increase from the previous year. Literature classes were the most frequent targets, then science, health, sex education, and drug education classes. These censorship attempts were primarily from the religious Right, but there were also significant censorship efforts from the Left, primarily in California.

"Secular Humanist" Theology. *Mozert* v. *Board of Education,* a censorship suit in Tennessee, was representative of the overall climate of attacks on school readers in the 1980s. A group of self-identified "born-again" fami-

CHANNEL ONE BRINGS TV TO NATION'S CLASSROOMS

In 1989 Christopher Whittle, head of Whittle Communications Educational Network, unveiled plans to bring his Channel One to about eight thousand schools. Whittle's company, half owned by Time, delivered a twelve-minute news and information show ("like a Today show for teenagers") via free equipment, including a satellite dish, a videocassette recorder and color television monitors — all paid for by four thirty-second commercial spots sold to Channel One sponsors eager to reach an audience of seven million teenagers, twice that of any prime-time show. William Rukeyser, Whittle's editor in chief, explained that the commercials were required to finance this new use of television as an educational resource. Whittle claimed his programming addressed two serious problems: the ignorance of the kids and the poverty of the schools. In addition to the Channel One program, the company promised to provide one thousand hours of free satellite time and $500,000 annually to make instructional programs accessible to participating schools.

Test audiences in six schools reacted favorably to Channel One during spring 1989. Principal Stanley Jasinskas of Eisenhower Middle School in Kansas City, Kansas, reported that students who viewed the shows became "much more knowledgeable" and they "took positions on issues." Many educators, however, objected to children being made captive to corporate America, and Channel One was denounced by national associations of school boards, principals, and teachers. As Peggy Charen, president of Action for Children's Television put it, "When television first started, there was a huge debate about whether you should advertise to children at all. Now it's stuck right in the middle of the curriculum." At the close of the 1980s educational leaders and school personnel were divided over the merits of Channel One.

Sources: "Teacher or Trojan Horse?" *Time* (19 June 1989): 56;

"Today, Class, We'll Learn About Soap," *Newsweek* (20 March 1989): 82–83.

lies, led by lay minister Bob Mozert, protested their children's exposure to Holt publishing company's fifth-grade readers. More than 1,117 pages of depositions cited the plaintiff's more than 400 separate objections to the Holt series; among their complaints were that the stories did not "confine themselves to the domain of knowledge and facts educationwise" and instead encouraged the process of imagination, which "distracts people from the Word of God." "Once the mind is open to imagination," plaintiffs testified, "all kinds of alien thoughts may enter and a soul may be lost." Jack London's story "To Build a Fire," one of the selections in the Holt reader, was offered as a perfect example of indoctrination into "secular humanism," defined as the belief that man has the power to save himself. In London's story a man trapped in the wilderness freezes to death, and plaintiffs insisted that the story taught that survival depends on what people do rather than on God's will.

The Legal Arguments. The defendants in the *Mozert* case argued that there was a difference between indoctrination and mere educational exposure, that the lawsuit failed to distinguish between mentioning an idea and teaching it as truth. The topics covered in the Holt readers, they said, were common in U.S. society, and they challenged the plaintiffs' rights to pressure the public schools into avoiding subjects that all children encounter outside of school. The plaintiffs countered by saying that the act of reading this objectionable material — the opening of the book, the moving of their eyes across the page — was forbidden by their religion. They could not, they argued, be forced to forfeit their government benefit of a free public education as a consequence of their refusal to commit an act forbidden by their religion.

The Ruling. Although the Tennessee judge ruled for the plaintiffs, in 1987 the Sixth Circuit Court of Appeals overturned that ruling 3–0. This panel cited the following principles in overturning *Mozert*: 1) freedom of religion is no protection against mere exposure to opposing ideas; 2) the state has a compelling interest in promoting religious and social tolerance; and 3) school boards have the authority to determine curriculum within broad parameters. In many of the censorship suits filed against reading materials for elementary children during the 1980s, these general principles were upheld.

The *Smith* Case. Another representative case of censorship against secular humanism gathered national attention in the 1980s. However, in this lawsuit, *Smith* v. *Board of School Commissioners of Mobile County (Alabama)*, the plaintiffs wanted the court to declare that secular humanism was actually a religion and should be either removed from schools entirely or balanced by inclusion of Christian teachings in the curriculum. Also, unlike *Mozert*, this case challenged not one textbook series, but forty-five different texts used in social studies, history, and home-economics courses. The National Legal Foundation, affiliated with the Christian Broadcasting Network owned by Pat Robertson, funded the plaintiffs in this effort to prove that "every topic is in some way religious — any view which contradicts biblical absolutism is part of the religion of secular humanism." On numerous occasions Robertson preached about the *Smith* case on the *700 Club*, his television show, and by 1985 the American Civil Liberties Union and People for the American Way joined in funding the *Smith* defense.

Smith Case Accusations. A sample specific objection listed in the *Smith* case included the "family life" chapter found in a home-economics course that promoted a positive self-image, decision making, and personal responsibility. The National Legal Foundation supplied as an expert witness psychologist Dr. Williams Coulsen, who testified for five days. His testimony included the argument that this chapter could encourage delinquency in those "who do not deserve to have self-esteem." He testified that encouraging teens (whom he referred to as "little children") to think independently violates parents' rights, and also submitted that the implication in one home-economics chapter that teens would grow up and choose their own careers was a violation of parents' rights. It is wrong, he said in later testimony, to tell a student he can decide between right and wrong. Asked whether teens who are offered drugs have to make a choice, he answered, "No, they can fall back on the commandments." When a defense lawyer asked whether teens who fall back on the commandments are making a choice, he asserted, "No, not if they are well trained. If they're well trained, they have no choice. They cannot but do the right thing."

Ruling on *Smith*. Although a lower court ruled in favor of *Smith*, an appeals court reversed that decision. The reasoning was that mere exposure to instruction is not unconstitutional simply because it happens to coincide with ideas the plaintiffs call humanistic. The court ruled that "appropriate secular effects" of teaching included independent thought, tolerance, self-respect, self-reliance, and logical decision making. The case ended there. By this time Pat Robertson had become a national presidential candidate, and he was trying to build up his image as a political, as opposed to a religious, figure. The publicity engendered by appealing this case to the Supreme Court would have focused national attention on his *700 Club* statements and the testimony of the trials.

Publishers' Responses to *Smith* and *Mozert*. Although these cases failed to end the precedent that public schools may set their own curriculum, the *Smith* and *Mozert* arguments had significant effects on schoolchildren nationally. The passages the *Mozert* plaintiffs had highlighted in court were removed from the Holt readers, and the other major textbook publishers made so many changes that Mel Gabler, the most famous Texas textbook censorship leader, deemed the 1987 texts "much more balanced." The publishers' responses illustrated the two realities of protracted textbooks lawsuits: 1) regardless of legal outcomes, a nationally publicized case can have direct effects on text content; and 2) litigation, combined with market forces, encourages publishers to produce texts that will satisfy buyers in the two largest, highly lucrative state contract areas of California and Texas. Because California is generally liberal, whereas Texas is generally conservative, publishers eager to offend no one produced texts that were bland and unfocused. Market decisions, not academic standards, drove text publishing in the 1980s, and therefore children in every state received texts that were essentially censored by lobbyists in California and Texas.

Social Content Standards. By the early 1980s textbook publishers had begun to adjust to California's new "social content standards": materials in that state's texts were required to show men and women in all types of roles; demonstrate the contributions of numerous ethnic groups to the development of the nation; show the necessity of protecting the environment; and demonstrate the ill effects on humans of tobacco, alcohol, and drugs. Another provision, known informally as the "junk-food law," emphasized the importance of a balanced diet. Because of California's disproportionate share of the lucrative textbook market, these standards became national by default. An example of the standards in use is illustrated by the adaptation of Patricia Zeltner's short story "A Perfect Day for Ice Cream," originally published in *Seventeen* magazine, for a junior-high-school anthology of literature. Because of the junk-food law, publishers deleted references to burgers, pizza, and ice cream. They also changed the title to "A Perfect Day," removed the expression *kamikaze ball,* and deleted an argument between siblings and a reference to Gloria Steinem. When the author protested the changes, she was informed by the publishers that they had been made in anticipation of California's complaints about junk food and ethnic stereotyping, as well as Texas's complaints about family conflicts and feminism.

Censorship in Science. California was also a battleground for science-textbook censorship during the 1980s as conservatives argued that offering the theory of evolution as fact violated their religious rights. The creationism-evolution controversy reached California state courts in 1981 when the Creationist-Science Research Center joined other plaintiffs in a lawsuit, *Seagraves* v. *California,* over educational policy. As a result of this suit, the court ruled that science teachers must offer alternatives to Darwin's evolutionary theory: "Dogmatism must be changed to conditional statements where speculation is offered as an explanation for the origins of man." In California this ruling was followed by a blizzard of protests about the teaching of evolution; this storm of protest from both sides lasted from 1981 to 1989.

Scientists Weigh In. At California's public hearings sponsored by the state board of instruction in 1985, creationists blamed the general decline in academia and morals on the teaching of evolution in the schools. California scientists, who attended the hearings in record numbers, argued that the protesters did not grasp the scientific process, particularly the word *theory.* A scientific theory, they explained, is not just any unproven idea; it is a hypothesis that has withstood empirical testing and is subject to further testing. Evolution, they said, has withstood so many tests that virtually the entire scientific community accepts it. Creationism, on the other hand, is a religious belief that is not subject to testing. Therefore,

they argued, giving equal weight to each in textbooks would be misleading. The compromise that was reached produced textbooks that satisfied nobody. Finally, in 1989, California put an end to the wars by adopting textbook guidelines requiring that evolution would be taught as the only scientific theory of human origins. Ironically, the Texas Board of Education had voted unanimously in 1984 to repeal a ten-year rule restricting the teaching of the theory of evolution. Because Texas spent approximately $65 million per year on texts (more than 10 percent of the market) publishers had hurried to fit the new Texas standards. By the end of the 1980s science books more explicitly and persuasively outlined evolutionary theory. This nine-year struggle effectively illustrated the fact that the scientific community does not decide how science is taught in elementary and secondary schools — publishers do.

Huckleberry Finn. In 1985, the one hundredth anniversary year of publication of *Huckleberry Finn,* Mark Twain's classic narrative about the friendship between runaway Huck and runaway slave Jim became the subject of intense controversy over perceived racism in the novel. Led by Chicago black educator John H. Wallace, the first censorship case occurred when black parents in Waukegan, Illinois, succeeded in having the book taken off the required reading list. A significant number of school officials followed suit, banning *Huckleberry Finn* from their required curriculum (though not from their library collections) because it "serves to legitimate the word 'nigger' and humiliate students who are forced to read it aloud." Wallace, who concluded that "the novel is the most grotesque piece of racist trash ever written," cited the fact that characters in the book casually utter racist remarks and frequently use the word *nigger* as evidence of the fact that Twain's novel is unfit for teaching in the schools. Literary scholars promptly jumped to Twain's defense. Typical was Shelley Fisher Fishkin of Yale University, who cited a recently discovered letter in which Twain agreed to pay a black student's law school tuition. "We have ground the manhood out of black men and the shame is ours, not theirs," Twain wrote, lending credence to those who view the climax of the novel as clearly antiracist. In this scene Huck rejects the conventional morality of the day and decides not to turn in Jim, the runaway slave. This debate was not confined to the educational community. Wallace appeared often on national television to denounce the novel (though he did not often mention that he had printed his own version of the novel, which was for sale to the schools), and prominent columnist James J. Kilpatrick was one of numerous columnists who commented on the controversy, writing in his column that "A school superintendent in Kinston, North Carolina, last month threw Huck Finn out of his classrooms. I think the gentleman acted properly." The debate raged on into the 1990s, and, as Huck Finn himself said, "It shows how a body can see and don't see at the same time."

Sources:

Dudley Barlow, "Why We Still Need Huckleberry Finn," *Education Digest* (September 1992): 31–35;

Ben Brodinsky, "The Religious Right: The Movement and Its Impact," *Phi Delta Kappan* (October 1982): 289–294;

Joan Delfattore, *What Johnny Shouldn't Read: Censorship In America* (New Haven: Yale University Press, 1992);

Rev. Gary Dixon, "The Deliberate Sabotage of Public Education by Liberal Elitists," *Phi Delta Kappan* (October 1982): 297–298;

David Heim, "Further Adventures of Huckleberry Finn," *Christian Century* (20 November 1985): 1052–1053;

Charles Nicol, "One Hundred Years on a Raft," *Harper's* (January 1986): 65–70.

TEACHERS UNDER FIRE

Assessing Teacher Training. By 1984 four studies of the teaching profession all concurred that the profession was troubled. "It's a mess," said Emily Feistritzer, author of "The Condition of Teaching," produced in 1983 for the National Center for Educational Information and the most far-reaching study to that point. Feistritzer, whose research delved into conditions in every state, blamed a significant part of the problem on the chaotic certification procedures at state departments of education. A drastically reduced pool of students going into the field exacerbated the situation; in 1973, 200,000 graduates planned to go into teaching, but by 1981, only 108,000 students studied to become teachers. Of those students, 35 percent were in elementary education; 17 percent were in physical education; 13 percent in special education. Although less than 3 percent planned to go into secondary teaching, this abnormally low figure could reflect the fact that some secondary teachers majored in their subject-area field and planned to go to graduate school to become credentialed. The salary advantages teachers had enjoyed in the 1970s disappeared: in 1983 starting teachers could expect only $13,000 annually while starting accountants made $17,000. Students in colleges of education consistently had lower SAT scores (SAT verbal of 394, compared to the group's average of 426 in 1982) than their counterparts in other majors, as newly opened opportunities in business for the women who traditionally dominated the teaching field siphoned off the best and the brightest for more-lucrative careers. Teacher education programs at some major institutions were called "intellectual ghettos," and "higher education's dirty little secret," according to a report published in *Phi Delta Kappan*, a journal for educational professionals.

The Status of the Profession. Feistritzer's study also addressed conditions for teachers already in the field. In all of the states, incompetent teachers were rarely fired because of administrators' fears of lawsuits. Teacher-evaluation methods in most districts were found to be "perfunctory," and inadequate to make decisions about merit pay. Most alarming was the prediction of dire teacher shortages by 1988 unless the teaching field became more professional. Dianne Ravitch, a historian of education, echoed this fear when she warned that good

THE PAIDEIA PROPOSAL

Written by philosopher Mortimer Adler on behalf of a group of academicians calling themselves the Paideia Group, *The Paideia Proposal: An Educational Manifesto* contributed to the great debate of the 1980s: How can we achieve equity and excellence? The proposed twelve-year curriculum would be the same for all students — eliminating tracking, vocational ed, and all specialized courses and electives. A greater emphasis on homework would accompany the three required modes of teaching: first, acquisition of organized knowledge by didactic instruction; next, development of intellectual skills by coaching and supervised practice; last, the enlarged understanding of ideas and values through Socratic dialogue. Teachers would be trained in graduate programs after earning a liberal arts degree. The role of the principal is redefined as that of a dedicated teacher who has increased authority over the hiring, firing, and assignment of teachers as well as over disciplinary standards of the school. Proponents of this approach argued that it would prepare students for citizenship in a democratic society, encourage lifelong learning and personal development, and provide skills for earning a living. Opponents tended to criticize the plan as difficult, if not impossible, to implement, and few schools were influenced by Adler's philosophy.

Sources: Mortimer Adler, *The Paideia Proposal: An Educational Manifesto* (New York: Macmillan, 1982);

"The Paideia Proposal: A Symposium," *Harvard Educational Review*, 53 (November 1983): 356–367.

teachers were abandoning the profession in record numbers. Ravitch reported that many teachers particularly resented a 1982 New Jersey Supreme Court decision that invalidated evidence seized from a student's purse in a junior-high-school drug deal. Ruling that the student's right to privacy nullified the school's obligation to serve in loco parentis, the court undermined school officials' authority. Ravitch also interviewed teachers who felt the 1980s trend of testing teachers for basic academic competency changed the profession into "a civil service job" with diminished prestige. The implicit message of many public policies directed at teachers sent a clear message: "We don't trust you."

Competency Testing. The public demanded accountability from their teachers. Since competency testing had been instituted for many high-school students as a standard for graduation, many legislatures decided that teachers should be tested also. Although teacher groups vigorously opposed instituting tests for practicing teachers, there was professional support for testing candidates in basic competencies. "Let us tell America that just as no law graduate can practice without the bar exam," said National Education Association Mary Futrell in 1985, "no teaching graduate should be allowed to instruct American children without first passing a valid exam." Bill Clinton, governor of Arkansas, expressed what many politicians believed about the efficacy of these tests: "They won't measure abilities to maintain order, inspire students, or communicate effectively. A person could achieve a perfect score and still not be a good teacher. But anyone who makes that argument opposing the test should get an F in logic, because it does not follow that someone can be a good teacher and fail this test." In 1983 teacher-competency tests given in thirty-six states produced some embarrassing results. In Houston where practicing teachers were tested, 62 percent of teachers tested failed the reading segment, 46 percent failed math, and some tests had to be declared invalid because of cheating. By 1986 forty-two states required competency testing of future teachers.

Revitalizing Teacher Training. Nearly every educational professional offered suggestions for reinvigorating the teaching profession. There was widespread agreement that students in teacher training should take more courses in their subject areas and fewer in education. In a 1982 *Phi Delta Kappan* article, "The Necessary Revolution in Teacher Education," Hendrick Gideonse recommended that teacher candidates spend six years in training: four in studying subject matter, then two learning professional competencies such as different instructional approaches, media usage, curricular models and theories, and assessment and management strategies. This "revolutionary" idea was widely accepted by the end of the decade as this basic model (often reduced to five years) was adopted by many universities.

Merit Pay and Master Teachers. One popular idea for professionalizing teaching was that of designating superior teachers as "master teachers," a new category of employment that would financially reward excellence, not merely experience. Plans for master teachers and/or merit pay increases were considered by a majority of the states. In Tennessee, under Gov. Lamar Alexander (who would become secretary of education under President George Bush), the proposed 1986–1987 plan was typical: it offered annual salary increases of $1,000 to $7,000 based on evaluation of performance. Teachers would work three years before being allowed to apply to become "senior teachers." That designation would be accompanied by a five-year certification and an additional $2,000 salary for ten-month employees; senior teachers willing to sign eleven-month contracts would receive an extra $4,000. After the five years as a senior teacher, applicants could attempt to become master teachers, with $3,000 and $5,000 extra compensation for the ten- and eleven-month employees, respectively. Master teachers could also commit to a twelve-month contract, a move that would guarantee an additional $7,000 annually. This

THE CLOSING OF THE AMERICAN MIND

In 1987 Allan Bloom, a professor at the University of Chicago, published what he called "an essay — a meditation on the state of our souls, particularly those of the young, and their education — written from the perspective of a teacher." The book was titled *The Closing of the American Mind: How Higher Education Has Failed Democracy and Impoverished the Souls of Today's Students*, and to Professor Bloom's great surprise, the serious, scholarly work zoomed to the number-one spot among American best-sellers. Both a fundamental critique of higher education and a series of insights into the national state, the volume "hit with the approximate force and effect of what electric-shock therapy must be like," asserted *New York Times* reviewer Christopher Lehmann-Haupt. Writer Saul Bellow, in the book's introduction, summed up Bloom's argument this way: "The university was to have been an island of intellectual freedom where all views were investigated without restriction. Liberal democracy in its generosity made this possible, but by consenting to play an 'active, participatory' role in society, the university has become inundated and saturated with the backflow of society's problems: Health, Sex, Race, and War. Academics have made their reputations and their fortunes and the university has become society's conceptual warehouse of often harmful influences." In his text Bloom criticized the 1980s "multiversity smorgasbords" that resulted in "multi-life style multi-disciplines" and bemoaned the fact that the "diversity of perversity was added to the diversity of specialization." The result of the specialization of curriculum (the adding of women's studies and black-studies departments and the splitting off of deconstructionists from comparative-literature departments, for example) had shown that "the demand for greater community had ended in greater isolation." Bloom's defense of higher education in the face of what he called its "decomposition" generated a vociferous debate that spanned the rest of the decade.

Source: Allan Bloom, *The Closing of the American Mind* (New York: Simon & Schuster, 1987).

plan, and others much like it in other states, was hailed as both ideal and impossible. The Tennessee legislature was told to set aside $116 million in 1987 for the supplements needed if the anticipated 87 percent of the state's teachers upgraded their skills and contracts. Unfortunately, the 1980s were financially tight times for most states, and this amount simply was not available. The next seemingly insurmountable problem was the inability of administration and teachers to agree on criteria for the required evaluations. Although some states instituted career ladder moves for teachers, the vast majority of merit pay schemes were abandoned by the end of the 1980s.

Sources:

Hendrick Gideonse, "The Necessary Revolution in Teacher Education," *Phi Delta Kappan* (September 1982): 15–19;

John Parish, "Excellence in Education: Tennessee's Master Teacher Plan," *Phi Delta Kappan* (June 1983): 722–724;

Diane Ravitch, *The Schools We Deserve: Reflections on the Educational Crises of Our Time* (New York: Basic Books, 1985).

WOMEN'S ISSUES IN EDUCATION

Qualified Women Shun Teaching Profession. During the 1980s the teaching profession suffered as many qualified women entered other fields formerly closed to them. Women who in prior decades might have become teachers deserted the field for business, medicine, and law. The other professions' gain was education's loss, said Carol Gilligan, a prominent feminist researcher in women's development at Harvard University. According to Gilligan's research, women respond more readily to people than to principle; they are guided not so much by broad perceptions of right and wrong as by the moral logic of care. It is impossible, she said, for most women to consider an action or moral dilemma without considering its effects on the people involved. Therefore, women have special gifts for teaching, and she and others expressed concern that teaching may become a "nesting ground for those who can't do anything else."

Women in Administration. By middecade 70 percent of elementary and secondary teachers were women whose median age was thirty-six. When the education journal *Phi Delta Kappan* commissioned a survey of the attitudes of these teachers toward their careers, two-thirds of the women reported a career crisis of sorts, defined by fatigue, anger, anxiety, and depression. Most cited frustration about the fact that a teaching career reaches a plateau, with no opportunity for advancement except going into administration. Administration was still clearly the province of males. Only 1.8 percent of the superintendents' jobs and only 16 percent of the principalships were held by women. Twenty-three percent of elementary principals were women while only 7 percent of secondary schools were headed by women. By 1987, however, significantly more women had entered administration.

Research on Women in Administration. Researchers who studied the effects of this influx of women into leadership positions found that staffs and faculties rated women leaders higher than male colleagues and reported better morale. Women administrators were given high marks for encouraging innovation in teaching. Women's greater knowledge of teaching techniques and methods was suggested as the reason for their sharpened, and therefore more successful, focus on teaching and learning. Several studies also showed that women appeared to be more successful at building community. From their speech patterns to their more inclusive decision-making styles, women administrators operated more democratically than men. Chester Finn, a noted reform expert, remarked on the necessity of reform being instigated from the inside out, or as he put it, from a "homegrown ethos, a team spirit that cannot be mandated from outside." It appeared from these studies that many of the new influx of women administrators were successfully building the climate for participatory reform.

Sources:

Mary Lynn Crow, "The Female Educator at Midlife," *Phi Delta Kappan* (December 1985): 281–284;

Debra Martorelli, "Is Teaching a Female Ghetto?" *Instructor*, 92 (September 1982): 30–32;

Carol Shakeshaft, "The Female World of School Administrators," *Education Digest*, 52 (September 1987): 234–340.

HEADLINE MAKERS

WILLIAM J. BENNETT

1943-

SECRETARY OF EDUCATION, 1985-1989, CHAIRMAN OF THE NATIONAL ENDOWMENT FOR THE HUMANITIES, 1981-1984

No Stranger to Controversy. William J. Bennett began his public education career at the University of Texas and Boston University; later he became president of the National Humanities Center near Raleigh, North Carolina. From 1981 to 1984 he was chairman of the National Endowment for the Humanities. His outspoken attacks on spending for cultural events that were "damaging to America's well-being" earned him recognition by conservatives. In 1985 Secretary of Education Terrel Bell resigned because of frustrations in trying to implement President Reagan's plans to shut down the Department of Education, and Bennett was tapped to take his place. Whereas Bell's demeanor was conciliatory, Bennett's was combative. He sought opportunities to debate issues rather than merely conduct department business, and soon Bennett became a familiar figure on the nightly news, arguing for his version of educational reforms.

Bennett's 3 C's. Although the 3 R's were important, Bennett argued, the 3 C's — content, character, and choice — were in desperate need of attention in the 1980s. In explaining the need for more content in curriculum, Education Secretary Bennett issued this often-quoted directive:

Every student should know how mountains are made, and that for every action there is an equal and opposite reaction. They should know who said 'I am the state' and who said 'I have a dream.' They should know about subjects and predicates, about isosceles triangles and ellipses. They should know where the Amazon flows, and what the First Amendment means. They should know about the Donner party and slavery, and Shylock,

Hercules, and Abigail Adams, where Ethiopia is, and why there is a Berlin Wall. They should know a little of how a poem works, how a plant works, and what it means to remark 'If wishes were horses, beggars would ride.' They should know the place of the Milky Way and DNA in the unfolding of the universe. They should know something about the Constitutional Convention of 1787 and about the conventions of good behavior. They should know a little of what the Sistine Chapel looks like and what great music sounds like.

Bennett emphasized that these were things that all students should know; he often complained that schools held some students to lesser goals, pushing them into "educational backwaters while everyone else is advancing upstream." He appealed to teachers to adapt good material to the level of the student and to vary the pedagogy for lower students without losing the substance.

The Second C: Character. Bennett thought that Americans have always believed that in education the development of intellect and character go hand in hand. He defined character as "strength of mind, individuality, independence, thoughtfulness, fidelity, kindness, honesty, respect for law and standards of right and wrong, diligence, fairness and self-discipline." He castigated educators for overintellectualizing moral development while underintellectualizing the rest of the curriculum. He dismissed the "values education" movement as a trend that would accomplish nothing. "It is habit which develops virtues, habit shaped by precept and example," he argued. "You cannot teach morality without being committed to morality yourself," Bennett said, and "you cannot be committed to morality yourself without holding that some things are right and others wrong." Bennett insisted that America must have principals and teachers who know the difference between right and wrong, good and bad, and who themselves exemplify high moral purpose.

The Third C: Choice. Bennett reasoned that if children are to be taught challenging material, and if children are to benefit from strong moral examples set by their teachers, then parents must have the choice to send their children to the school that they trust will provide this education. Since parents are ultimately responsible for their children's learning, they must have instruments of choice within public education and between public and private education. All parents, not only the affluent, Bennett vowed, must be able to exercise greater choice in what, where, and how their children learn.

Bennett's Agenda. Although Bennett campaigned widely on other issues, including curtailing both student drug use and student loans, it was his tireless advocacy on behalf of the three C's that was his most lasting effect on the education agenda in the 1980s. As one of the most controversial figures of the decade, he invigorated the national debate about curriculum and values education. Much of Bennett's agenda became popular with many Americans. The 1987 Gallup poll of the public's attitudes toward the public schools reflected widespread support for increased parental choice; for greater accountability; for higher and more rigorous academic standards; for schools' role in the formation of character; and for emphasis on the basic subjects of math, English, history, and science.

Source:
William J. Bennett, *Our Children and Our Country: Improving America's Schools and Affirming the Common Culture* (New York: Simon & Schuster, 1988).

ERNEST L. BOYER

1928-

CHANCELLOR OF STATE UNIVERSITY OF NEW YORK; U.S. COMMISSIONER OF EDUCATION; PRESIDENT OF CARNEGIE FOUNDATION FOR THE ADVANCEMENT OF TEACHING

From Teacher to Administrator. Ernest L. Boyer was one of the most influential voices in the calls for educational reform in the 1980s. As the head of the Carnegie Foundation for the Advancement of Teaching, beginning in 1980, the issues he addressed received national attention. Born in Dayton, Ohio, Boyer moved west to receive his doctoral degree in audiology at the University of Southern California in 1957. He became a professor of speech pathology and audiology and academic dean at Upland College, but in 1960 he reached what he called a "crucial crossroad" in his life when he switched from teaching to administration. When he accepted a position with the Western College Association, the California Board of Education had ordered all public schoolteachers to obtain a degree in an academic discipline, and Boyer was appointed director of the commission charged with carrying out the directive. In 1962 he assumed the director-ship of The University of California's Center for Coordinated Education, where he administered projects to improve the quality of education from kindergarten through college. At this early point in his career he began to develop an understanding of the needs of the entire system of public education.

Dealing with Cutbacks in Funding. From 1970 to 1977 Boyer was chancellor of the State University of New York, a complex system of sixty-four campuses, hundreds of thousands of students, and fifteen thousand faculty members. He assumed his duties during a period of crisis in state and federal support of higher education. In 1976 declining government support forced Boyer to take rigorous economizing measures, including halting construction on partly finished buildings and freezing enrollment. Although he was criticized by teachers and students, his proponents argued that he had wisely taken on the burden of cutting costs himself rather than leaving it to the legislature to make even deeper cuts. These political experiences in educational financing served him well later in his career.

From Government to the Carnegie Foundation. During a stint as President Carter's federal commissioner of education, responsible for administering education programs involving billions of dollars, Boyer was frustrated by the failure of Congress to pass a bill creating a new, cabinet-level Department of Education. In 1980 he became president of the Carnegie Foundation for the Advancement of Teaching, an organization that held income-producing assets worth more than $35 million. There, he said, his first priority would be efforts to reshape the American high school. "I am convinced that the high school is the nation's most urgent education problem," he told an interviewer.

High School: A Report. In 1983 Boyer released the result of a fifteen-month study of the nation's high schools that was conducted by twenty-eight prominent educators. The results suggested that although 15 percent of American high-school students were getting "the finest education in the world," about twice that number were merely passing time. The study recommended development of a core curriculum for all students; designated mastery of the English language, including writing, as the central curriculum objective for all students; and a gradual increase in teachers' pay of 25 percent, after making up for inflation. Boyer felt that a lack of creative teaching was crippling the high schools; as he said, "To my mind, teaching is the nub of the whole problem. . . . All other issues are secondary." This massive study contributed significantly to the reform debate of the 1980s, and its recommendation for core curriculum and higher standards became key issues in policy struggles.

Boyer Tackles the Colleges. In 1986 Boyer released *College: The Undergraduate Experience in America,* "the most systematic study ever done of four-year colleges," a project which involved surveys of forty-five hundred undergraduates, five thousand faculty members, and more than one thousand college administrators on twenty-nine campuses. This report found that colleges, like the high schools, were "troubled." Boyer wrote that American higher education was "driven by careerism" and was more successful in "credentialing than in providing a quality education." Boyer contributed to the national movement toward strengthening curriculum. After he issued his report, many colleges accepted the recommendations to require a core curriculum embracing language, the arts, history, social and governmental institutions, and the natural sciences. The book form of this report, *College: The Undergraduate Experience in America,* has been called "the most thorough look at undergraduate colleges ever taken. . . . the best book to read for the student preparing to get the most out of his or her undergraduate experience."

Boyer's Effect on Education. In 1987 Boyer trained his sights on the earliest years of a child's education. Noting that much of the reform efforts of the late 1980s were bypassing many impoverished children, Boyer proposed improvements in nutrition, prenatal care for teen mothers, more-effective day care including summer programs, and preschool education. During the decade Boyer influenced educational policy in numerous ways: he championed academic credentialing of secondary teachers; he demonstrated tough-minded coping with financial cutbacks; and he advocated a more rigorous, coherent curriculum at the high-school and college level. His clear-minded willingness to seek consensus rather than conflict did much to advance these issues.

Sources:
Ernest Boyer, *College: The Undergraduate Experience in America* (New York: Harper & Row, 1987);

Boyer, *High School: A Report on Secondary Education in America* (New York: Harper & Row, 1983).

JOE LOUIS CLARK

1939-

HIGH-SCHOOL PRINCIPAL

National Folk Hero. Joe Louis Clark, principal of inner-city Eastside High School in Paterson, New Jersey, gained a wide reputation as a folk hero when national news reports showed him patrolling his halls with a bullhorn and baseball bat in hand. After six years of Clark's leadership at a school where 90 percent of the students were black or Hispanic and most came from poor families, Eastside boasted order and some improvement in test scores. Parents and students praised him for restoring order and instruction to a school once called a "caldron of terror and violence," and Education Secretary William Bennett held him up as an example of what strong leadership can accomplish in the nation's most troubled urban schools. Clark exhibited that leadership by working the halls and corridors like a consummate politician, shouting through his bullhorn at students, but usually addressing them by name and inquiring about their progress. "A lot of students here have it bad at home," said a junior who supported Clark's approach. "But they can come in here and say: 'This man wants something for me. I can do better.'"

A Man of Extremes. However, Clark's critics, among them some school board members, raised serious questions about his methods. He ran into trouble in 1988 with the Board of Education for expelling failing students who he said did not deserve a diploma. In 1982, his first year, he threw out three hundred of the three thousand students at Eastside, the state's second largest school. More followed. From 1983 to 1986 the total of students who dropped out or were forced out was 1,904. In 1988, when he banned some sixty students who he said were "all leeches, miscreants and hoodlums," he was ordered to take the students back. In New Jersey principals cannot expel students, only school boards can. Circumstances had changed: while earlier boards tolerated the expulsions, in the late 1980s three new members argued that legally, the state was responsible for providing free public education to students until they are twenty-one. "We have to uphold the law," one new member asserted.

Teacher Charges. Some teachers at Eastside High felt intimidated by Clark. His memos indicated that their perception was warranted. Three teachers who were Paterson Education Association delegates received memos titled "Denunciation of Your Anarchistic Activities," which ended, "I invite you to purge yourselves of the demons that make you so dangerous to the very institutions and ideologies to which you should be dedicating your professional lives or to purge the Paterson school system by leaving it."

Microcosm of Reform Problems. The students still in school wholeheartedly supported Clark and threatened to march on the school board if Clark were replaced. "If Mr. Clark goes, we all go," said a junior. Paterson Education Association's superintendent, Dr. Frank Napier, staunchly supported Clark's efforts to remove problem students, maintaining that lower schools had already failed them and they could not be educated. And Clark's approach did yield some positive results. At Eastside under Clark's leadership, scores on a statewide proficiency test given at the end of the freshman year rose, and scores on the Scholastic Aptitude Test (SAT) also improved. In both cases, however, scores were still significantly below the national averages. Reforming Paterson's inner-city schools presented the same problems other reform-minded high-school administrators faced: were individual student rights more important than the good of the whole? While William Bennett called Clark "a national folk hero," his own employers, the school board, charged him with insubordination.

Source:
"Joe Clark: A Man of Extremes," *New York Times Biographical Service* (January 1988): 75–77.

MARVA COLLINS

1936-

EDUCATOR

Miracle Worker. Marva Collins, an inner-city elementary-school teacher from Chicago, became a national celebrity in the late 1970s and early 1980s when she founded Westside Preparatory School in Chicago. Under Collins's guidance, supposedly "unteachable" ghetto children turned into avid readers quoting Shakespeare and Socrates to media visitors, who quickly deemed her a "miracle worker" and "a national treasure."

Background. Collins's own education began in rural Alabama, in all-black schools where "teachers were strict and strong; there was no foolishness." When she was denied access to her local library because of her race, she read the *Farmer's Almanac*, Bible stories, and any books her father could buy in Mobile. She graduated from the all-black Escambia County Training School and obtained her B.A. degree in secretarial sciences in 1957 from Clark College in Atlanta.

From Secretary to Teacher to Critic. Collins moved to Chicago to work as a medical secretary, and although she claimed she "never wanted to be a teacher," she decided in 1961 to enter the teaching profession. Because she lacked teaching credentials, she went to work for the Chicago school system as a full-time substitute, with no seniority or permanent placement. Working in inner-city schools for the next fourteen years, Collins developed a reputation as a caring, though demanding, teacher whose criticism of ineffective teachers was loud and unrepentant. She complained that many teachers came to school unprepared, had no respect for the children, and merely created "more welfare recipients."

Founding Westside Prep. Collins became so disillusioned with the public schools of inner-city Chicago that she quit her job in 1975 and with $5,000 in retirement money began the school that would soon be famous. First called the Daniel Hale Williams Westside Preparatory School and housed in the basement of Daniel Hale Williams University, the school's first class consisted of Collins's daughter and three neighborhood children. Soon it moved to Collins's own home. Within three years twenty-eight children were enrolled, and there was a waiting list of 175 applicants willing to pay the requested $80-a-month tuition. Collins insisted that "all you really need for teaching is a blackboard, books, and a good pair of legs that will last through the day," and she claimed she would refuse all federal aid because, she said, "I don't want any experts telling me what's good for these kids or telling me how to teach." Instead, she accepted funds from churches and the community. Chicago insurance magnate W. Clement Stone, for example, gave her a $50,000 grant after he learned of her methods and her success.

Old-Fashioned Curriculum. The curriculum at Westside Prep emphasized the basics of reading and language, but there were no specifically designated subjects or periods. From 9 A.M. until 2:30 P.M., with no recess or gym and only twenty minutes for lunch, students read works of literature, wrote daily compositions, and memorized a quotation of their own choosing each day. When studying mathematics, they simultaneously learned ancient history and language roots by talking about the life and times of Pythagoras and discussing Latin and Greek roots of mathematical concepts.

Fame Brings Opportunity, Questions. In 1980 members of the Ronald Reagan transition team promoted Collins as a prospect for the post of secretary of education. She declined to be considered, citing a desire to remain in teaching. She also declined a seat on the Chicago school board and the post of superintendent of the Los Angeles county school system. When a Hallmark Hall of Fame CBS television special, "The Marva Collins Story," starring Cicely Tyson, aired in 1981, her reputation grew exponentially. She moved the school to an expanded facility with the fees from the special and from her many speaking engagements. Westside Prep in 1982 had five teachers, two hundred students, and a waiting list of nearly one thousand. In 1982, however, George Schmidt, a Chicago teacher who had lost his job as a result of budget cuts, released an "investigation" into Collins's accomplishments that labeled her story of success as a "hoax aimed at crippling public education" in Chicago and throughout the United States. Furthermore, he charged that Collins's claims about students' accomplishments were exaggerated. Most Westside Prep parents expressed support for Collins, and Harvey Gross, admissions director at Chicago's prestigious Providence–St. Mel private high school, revealed that he had tested eleven of the Westside students and they did, indeed, average more than one year's growth academically during the school year.

Collins's Legacy. Marva Collins's ability to create an effective school in which impoverished children succeeded coupled with her severe critiques of the Chicago public school system helped to focus national attention on the best ways to educate poor children. Her work highlighted the abilities of motivated children to learn, and her demanding curriculum demonstrated that sometimes asking more, rather than expecting less, of children is the best way to teach.

JAIME ESCALANTE

1930-

CALCULUS TEACHER

From Trade School to Academics. Jaime Escalante, a native of La Paz, Bolivia, and the son of two elementary-school teachers, inspired a movie in the 1980s by raising the aspirations of Hispanic students in one of Los Angeles's most decaying urban high schools. Shortly after Escalante came to Garfield High, its reputation had sunk so low that its accreditation was threatened. Instead of gearing classes to poorly performing students, Escalante offered AP (advanced placement) calculus. He had already earned the criticism of an administrator who disapproved of his requiring students to answer a homework question before being allowed into the classroom. "He told me to just get them inside," Escalante reported, "but I said, there is no teaching, no learning going on." Determined to change the status quo, Escalante had to persuade the first few students who would listen to him that they could control their futures with the right education. He promised them that the jobs would be in engineering, electronics, and computers, but they would have to learn math to succeed. He told his first five calculus students in 1978 that "I'll teach you math and that's your language. With that you're going to make it. You're going to college and sit in the first row, not the back, because you're going to know more than anybody." The student body at Garfield High, more than 90 percent Mexican American, had been told by teachers for years that to be Mexican American was to be unintelligent, but many of them rose to his challenge.

Public Acclaim. Within three years of instituting the calculus class, some of Escalante's students were scoring the highest possible grade, five, on the extremely difficult AP test, which entitles a student to credit at most colleges and universities. Almost all his students were receiving at least the passing grade on the test. In 1982, however, the College Board, which supervises the AP courses and testing, challenged the scores of eighteen of the Garfield students, citing irregularities in answers. The College Board accused the students of cheating. Escalante protested and convinced the students to redeem themselves by taking another test. They all passed. This event established the academic reputation of the program, and soon thereafter the 1987 film *Stand and Deliver*, starring Edward James Olmos, introduced the nation to the dramatic story of a teacher who, through igniting a love of learning in his barrio students, changed their lives.

Program Continues. In 1980 there were thirty-two calculus students in AP courses at Garfield; by 1988, 443 students took the AP exams and 266 passed. Because of state-granted waivers and a school-sponsored corporate fund raiser, only a few of the students had to pay the seventy-one-dollar fee to take the exams. Besides calcu-

lus, Garfield added sixteen AP courses in other fields, and many of the teachers in the program feel that the intellectual ability in their school could have remained untapped had Escalante not served as a catalyst. The changes at Garfield were not only among the elite students, however; the dropout rate, which was 55 percent in 1978, dropped to only 14 percent by 1988. Fully 75 percent of Garfield's 1987 graduating seniors planned to go on to some type of postsecondary instruction. Escalante emerged from the 1980s as a national figure — praised by President Reagan on a special visit to the White House, and singled out by Vice President Bush as a personal hero during one of his presidential campaign debates. During a decade with seemingly conflicting educational goals — excellence and inclusion — Escalante served as a model of a teacher who could achieve both.

Source:
New York Times Biographical Service (January 1988): 75–78.

JOHN I. GOODLAD

1920-

DEAN, GRADUATE SCHOOL OF EDUCATION, UNIVERSITY OF CALIFORNIA, LOS ANGELES

A Teacher's Teacher. John Goodlad, author of a landmark 1980s study of American education titled *A Place Called School*, began his teaching career in a rural one-room school. Since that time he has taught at every grade level from first grade through advanced graduate work. During the quarter-century preceding the 1980s, he inquired into the nature of schooling at all levels in more than ten countries. As dean of the Graduate School of Education at the University of California, Los Angeles, he read the numerous reports published in the late 1970s that contended that American education had gone seriously wrong. Dissatisfied with their alarmist tone and simplistic suggestions, Goodlad set out to write a study of schooling that identified what was actually going on in American schools. Because he believed that most school improvement efforts "founder on reefs of ignorance" and therefore inspire reforms that are merely cosmetic, he insisted on gathering "thick descriptions" of schools — composites of observations by students, teachers, parents, principals, and trained observers.

Scope of the Study. Goodlad directed more than twenty trained investigators who went to communities all over the country to collect information on every aspect of schooling. The sample of schools studied was enormously diverse in regard to size, family income, and racial composition of the student bodies. Although only thirty-eight schools were examined, the data came from 8,624 parents, 1,350 teachers, and 17,163 students. For the first time ever, researchers examined and made detailed observations of more than one thousand classrooms. The descriptions raised questions about schooling and suggested many patterns of teaching and learning common to most schools.

What Were Schoolrooms Like? The picture was not particularly rosy. Researchers learned that classes, at all levels, "tended NOT to be marked with exuberance, joy, laughter, praise and corrective support of individual student performance." Although the elements commonly regarded as positive were observed in early elementary grades, a decline set in by the upper elementary grades and continued through the secondary years, with a sharp drop at the junior-high-school level. Students at all levels were passive, listening to their teachers and spending a good deal of time just waiting for the teacher to hand out materials or to tell them what to do.

Different Approaches. Effective instructional practices were found more often in high-tracked classes (those with more-advanced students); indeed, students in the lower tracks were the least likely to experience the types of instruction most highly associated with achievement. For example, in high-track classes teachers were much more likely to express clearly their expectations for students, and they were perceived by students to be more enthusiastic in their teaching. Students in high-track classes also saw their teachers as more concerned about them and less punitive toward them. In general, profound similarities existed: students in the high tracks in schools all over the country were experiencing quite similar curricular content, instructional practices and human relationships in their classes; the same was true for the low tracks.

Conclusions. Goodlad concluded that the thirty-eight schools in the study "received children differentially ready for learning, educated them differentially in their classrooms, and graduated them differentially prepared for further education, employment, and, presumably, vocational and social mobility." The 17,163 students in the study had quite different opportunities to gain access to knowledge during their years of schooling. At least some of these differences, it appears, were "differentially associated with economic status and racial identification." The schools reflected the surrounding social and economic order; therefore, "the home advantaged or disadvantaged the child in enormously significant ways — especially in the acquisition of language, attitudes toward others, and social and economic values."

Reform Suggestions. Goodlad saw that the schools in the 1980s were "reproducing and perpetuating in practice inequalities of the surrounding society." Teaching practices reflected the well-established notion that there are winners and losers in learning and that teachers require only common sense and not much professional preparation. If these conditions were to be changed, Goodlad suggested, teachers must begin with the optimistic pedagogical assumption that nearly all children can learn — given appropriate support, corrective feedback, and time. Teachers must be trained to display their excellence, he

said, not by failing a third of the class but by bringing an overwhelming percentage of children to mastery of the material. Real reform, according to Goodlad, must begin with teacher reform: they must first be convinced that all students can learn, then they must receive from their districts full support for staff development.

Goodlad's Influence. Goodlad's picture of schooling in America was clear: pedagogy and curriculum were worlds apart, and only joining schools of education with schools of liberal arts was likely to remedy the situation. Indeed, Goodlad's study motivated many teacher-training institutions to rethink their requirements. By the end of the 1980s many schools demanded that future teachers get a degree in their subject matter first, then be trained in pedagogy. Also, Goodlad observed that many teachers were frustrated, burned out, uncertain as to what was expected of them, and suffering from low morale. He gave impetus to another major reform movement of the 1980s when he suggested eliminating the "flatness" of the teaching profession — the situation in which the motivated teacher who is better prepared intellectually and academically is paid the same salary as a less effective teacher. He advocated providing differentiated salaries based upon differentiated roles and preparation, not merely on seniority. He called for opening up new career paths for teachers and creating new staffing patterns. These changes helped pave the way for the idea of "master teachers" who could advance in salary without having to leave the classroom for administrative duties.

Source:
John I. Goodlad, *A Place Called School* (New York: McGraw-Hill, 1984).

MADELINE HUNTER

PROFESSOR

Research into Practice. In 1985 Ron Brandt, executive director of the Association for Supervision and Curriculum Development, said that Madeline Hunter "has had more influence on U.S. teachers in the last ten years than any other person." Hunter's popularity was based on her instructional-theory-into-practice (ITIP) model for effective teaching, which was designed to "teach more faster" in all disciplines and to all grade levels. Her training first as a practicing psychologist and later as a school psychologist served as the foundation for her ITIP model. This model translated her research in behavioral and social psychology into eight sequential steps for every teacher to follow in any given lesson.

ITIP Model. To follow the Hunter ITIP model, the teacher initiates an anticipatory set, determines objectives, gives input, models the task, checks for understanding, guides practice, assigns independent practice, then offers closure. According to Hunter, the ITIP model enables teachers to make appropriate decisions in three major aspects of teaching: content, learner style and behavior, and teacher behavior. Key learning principles on which Hunter based her model are motivation, retention, reinforcement, and transfer. Hunter published several programmed books, most notably *Teach More — Faster* (1986), that promised teachers who followed her model that "psychological theory will be more meaningful to you."

Widespread Popularity. Hunter, a researcher who treated the classroom like a clinical field test, was widely popular in the reform-minded early 1980s. Her "learn more faster" promise seemed like the ideal cure for the teachers and students who had been told that they had failed miserably on measure after measure. Hunter won the trust and admiration of many administrators nationally who viewed her model as a means by which teachers could be evaluated. Department chairs and principals could simply monitor lessons and assess whether all eight parts of the model were in evidence. Teachers would be diagnosticians of their students' learning needs and administrators would be diagnosticians of their employees — the teachers. The notion was orderly, manageable, and easily measured. Teachers who inculcated Hunter's model into their every lesson became, in some school districts, "master teachers." By the end of the 1980s dozens of states had instituted assessment procedures, both for student teachers and experienced teachers, based on Hunter's model.

Sources:

Madeline Hunter, *Mastery Teaching* (El Segundo, Cal.: TIP, 1986);

Hunter, *Teach More — Faster* (El Segundo, Cal.: TIP, 1986);

Joan Naomi Steiner, *A Comparative Study of the Educational Stances of Madeline Hunter and James Britton* (Urbana, Ill.: National Council of Teachers of English, 1993).

CHRISTA MCAULIFFE

1950-1986

TEACHER; ASTRONAUT

A Representative Teacher: A Woman, A Mother. Christa McAuliffe, a thirty-seven-year-old social-studies teacher at Concord (New Hampshire) High School was chosen from eleven thousand candidates to be a pioneer: the nation's first ordinary citizen in space. Her life ended when the space shuttle *Challenger* exploded ninety seconds after liftoff in February 1986. McAuliffe left her mark on the decade and on the nation as a model teacher, a woman who combined the idealism of the 1960s and the feminist ideas of the 1970s and 1980s.

Background. All of the important decisions of her life, her friends said, were as a result of her essentially solid values. She attended a Roman Catholic college-preparatory school in Framingham, Massachusetts, her hometown, with a solid academic reputation and a strict code of behavior. She decided before graduation that her life's work would be teaching, to her mind a noble profession because, as a high-school classmate remembered, "You could be a wife and mother as well." At Framingham State College where she studied to be a teacher, she was particularly interested in the diaries of pioneer women, recalled Carolla Haglund, a former professor and dean of women. Years later she would stress to her students the importance of ordinary people in history. Her project for the National Aeronautics and Space Administration (NASA) was to keep a three-part diary on the *Challenger* mission: preparation, flight, and postflight.

Teaching Career. Her career in teaching reflected that of thousands of other young women of the 1970s and 1980s. She married just out of college, to Steven McAuliffe, who immediately entered Georgetown Law School. She taught school, worked part-time as a waitress at a Howard Johnson's, and earned a master's degree in teaching administration from Bowie State College in Maryland. Her thesis was on the acceptance of handicapped children by other children in a regular classroom. The chair of her department remembered that McAuliffe was "eager to do things with her students, taking them on field trips and conducting mock trials." She gave birth to her son, Scott, in 1976, and to a second child, Caroline, a few years later after a move to New Hampshire. A month later, McAuliffe went to work as a social-studies teacher in Concord and soon became president of the local fifty-member teachers' union. Her role as a wife and mother came first. She often did not start on her schoolwork until ten in the evening, when the children were in bed, and she could grade her students' papers in relative quiet. She applied for a job as an assistant principal, but she was not hired. A friend later recalled that McAuliffe believed she had not been chosen because "the administration just wasn't ready for a woman."

Training as an Astronaut. When NASA invited teachers to apply for the shuttle mission, she wrote in her application, "As a woman, I have been envious of those men who could participate in the space program and who were encouraged to excel in the areas of math and science. I felt that women had indeed been left outside of one of the most exciting careers available. When Sally Ride and other women began to train as astronauts, I could look among my students and see ahead of them an ever-increasing list of opportunities." She endured the training with admirable stamina and good humor and was enthusiastic and excited about her adventure as the teacher in space. By the time of the launching, she had made her mark on NASA and had been accepted by the crew. At a portrait session in Houston, the regular crew wore mortarboards and held plastic lunch boxes and apples in her honor. McAuliffe's career as a wife, mother, and teacher was unusual only in its dramatic, tragic end. She was recognized by the nation as a true pioneer in space whose work in the classroom was representative of millions of other dedicated, enthusiastic teachers.

Source:
New York Times Biography Service (10 February 1986): 177–180.

ALBERT SHANKER

1928-

UNION OFFICIAL

Militancy Gone Straight. Albert Shanker was president of the American Federation of Teachers (AFT) from 1974 through the 1980s. During the 1980s the dues-paying membership of the AFT hovered at slightly more than six hundred thousand, only one-third that of the National Education Association (NEA). However, the organization represented a powerful force of mostly urban, mostly northeastern teachers. Shanker earned a reputation in the late 1960s and 1970s as something of a loose cannon, a radical whose involvement in a dramatic black-white confrontation in the Brownsville–Ocean Hill section of New York City helped to stamp him as a major force for militant teacher unionism. By 1987, though, he decided not to run for reelection to the presidency of the AFT's pugnacious New York affiliate, the United Federation of Teachers. In the late 1980s Shanker, his rhetoric toned down, became much more statesmanlike.

Education is Politics. Although Shanker was actively anticommunist and prodefense, he was staunchly committed to federal intervention in matters of social and economic justice. Although he was a lifelong Democrat, he enjoyed cordial relations with the Reagan administration. One of his AFT aides, Linda Chavez, became a senior White House staffer, and he warmly supported the choice of William Bennett as secretary of education. Later, however, he wavered in his support of Bennett, telling United Press International in 1985 that "He has made a lot of headlines, and almost all have been blunders." From the first ripples of reform in the early 1980s, Shanker broke dramatically with the traditional, slow-paced approach to change of the education establishment and the teachers' unions. Recognizing that the role, responsibilities, and performance of teachers would inevitably be the centerpiece of a move toward excellence, Shanker aligned himself with measures that would "professionalize" the status of teachers. He launched a national campaign for a professional examination to credential teachers, insisting that teachers, like lawyers and doctors, should control their profession. Shanker's espousal of the national examination implied that the AFT was a statesmanlike body capable of rising above the narrow, entrenched interests of teachers; conversely, many citizens viewed the rival NEA as a union whose sole interest was that of teachers.

"Where We Stand." Shanker's all-out effort to "enrich, enhance, and empower the role and status of teachers" grew stronger during the 1980s thanks to his weekly op-ed column (published as a paid advertisement) in *The New York Times*. With its clear, concise style completely purged of educationese, his column, titled "Where We Stand," consistently anticipated major reform movements in education and in society: national exams to credential teachers, general strengthening of standards for teachers, and a modified voucher system for students. Shanker emerged during the 1980s as a voice for teachers, yet he spoke louder than some other union leaders because he was also a realistic political operator who knew how to compromise.

Source:
"Four Leading Lights in Education Reform," *Phi Delta Kappan*, (October 1984): 114–118.

PEOPLE IN THE NEWS

Mortimer Adler, educational philosopher, announced in 1986 that the American educational system was "absolutely inadequate for purposes of democracy."

In 1986 **Lamar Alexander,** Republican governor of Tennessee, said that "What has finally riveted our attention on our education system is that our standard of living is threatened. We're not going to have the jobs and good incomes in America if we don't have the good skills."

Bruce Babbitt, Democratic governor of Arizona, said in 1982 on *Meet the Press* that "Federal involvement in education has been counterproductive. I believe it's responsible for some of the decline in quality."

Reagan administration Secretary of Education **Terrel H. Bell** said in 1981 that the nation's schools had been too preoccupied with the laudable aim of "bringing up the bottom"— concentrating on raising the performance of the less talented and the handicapped. The time had come, he said, to focus more on "challenging those on the outer limits of talent and ability."

Camilla Benbow of Johns Hopkins University studied ten thousand gifted and talented seventh and eighth graders and concluded in *Science* magazine in 1981 that "boys outscore girls on math tests because they have more aptitude for math, not just because they take more advanced courses."

In 1982 **Wendy Borcherdt,** a campaign fund-raiser for **Ronald Reagan,** was nominated for the highest-ranking post at the Education Department held by a woman; however, several women's groups, including the American Association of University Women, successfully blocked her appointment.

In 1987 Labor Secretary **William Brock** said in *Nation's Business* that "Twenty-three million Americans are illiterate and another 40 million are marginally illiterate. Yet the overwhelming majority of new jobs created in the U.S. will require post-secondary education."

Chief Justice **Warren Burger** blamed schools for contributing to the crime problem in 1981 because, he said, they had "virtually eliminated any effort to teach the values of integrity, truth, accountability, or respect for others' rights."

In 1987 Harvard professor **Jeanne Chall** explained that phonics isn't a cure-all for reading problems. Students experience a "reading slump" in fourth grade, she said, when they begin to use reading as a tool for gaining more knowledge; only more context and content will give them the vocabulary and understanding to gain in comprehension.

University of Georgia professor **James Dinnan** was taken to jail in his academic robe and hood on 3 July 1980 to begin serving a ninety-day sentence for contempt of court after he refused to reveal how he voted on a tenure committee ballot.

Abandoned as a child in Vietnam and adopted by an American serviceman, **Terry Dozier,** a history teacher at Irmo High School near Columbia, South Carolina, was named National Teacher of the Year in 1985.

Rebecca Fisher, lobbyist for the national PTA, asked Education Department officials in 1983 to track how $451 million in Chapter II block grants had been spent. The department admitted that with the new block grants, their ability to track the funds depended upon each of the states' accountings.

University of Houston educational psychology professor **Barbara Foorman** criticized the idea of "cooperative learning" in 1989: "In utopia, that's wonderful. But education should prepare kids for life in a particular culture; in reality, the name of the game is dog eat dog. Kids have to learn to get by on their own smarts."

Ellen Fulter, president of Barnard College, gave birth to a baby girl in 1981; the only previous president to become pregnant was **Emily Jane Putnam,** who was dismissed in 1901 when she informed the board of her condition.

Bartlett Giamatti, Yale University president, told the freshman class of 1981 that members of the Moral Majority were "peddlers of coercion."

U.S. District Court Judge **John Grady** ruled in 1980 that Chicago schools may use I.Q. tests for student placement in special education classes, that the tests are not "culturally unfair or suspect."

Barry Grove, head of Alexander Dawson, a private school in Colorado, created a curriculum based on "the real world in miniature." Students who created a government, a peer judicial system, and a real shopping mall with seven retail stores all had jobs on campus.

Gary Hart, candidate for the Democratic nomination for president, said to the Democratic Convention in 1982 that "If this administration thinks education is too expensive, wait till they find out how much ignorance costs."

Georgetown University president Rev. **Timothy Healy** likened the Moral Majority to the Ku Klux Klan, saying "Its voice is the voice of hatred."

Republican Sen. **John Heinz,** who worked in his family business, gave expert testimony in 1982 when the Agriculture Department attempted to classify ketchup served with school lunches as a vegetable: "It's a condiment," he said, "not a vegetable."

E. D. Hirsch Jr., University of Virginia professor, argued in 1989 that it was imperative that Americans agree on a definite core of knowledge that each child in the nation should master in each grade.

Joe Hogan, the first male admitted to the Mississippi University for Women, entered on 29 August 1981.

Economist **Pearl Kamer** reported conclusions of her 1980 study: If women "continue to cling to traditional, female-intensive professions like education, the gap between their earnings and males' will remain wide." In 1980 women earned 60 percent of what men with comparable educations earned.

Jonathan Kozol, writer and literacy advocate, argued in *The New York Times* in 1986 that "Illiteracy is one of the few problems in America that you can solve by throwing more money at it."

Luis Laosa, senior research scientist at the Educational Testing Service (ETS), claimed in 1981 that "Chicano children may have higher failure rates in school because their mothers use different teaching techniques at home than non-minority mothers." Their teaching by demonstrating an action and having children copy it rather than explaining the action verbally creates a "discontinuity in learning at school," he explained.

In 1985 **Walter Mondale** said of Reagan administration cuts in aid to education: "There's a whole generation of my age that are doctors and lawyers and dentists and nurses and business leaders who come from families with no money." Mondale argued that these advances would cease if scholarship funds were cut.

Stanley Moore, dismissed from Reed College after his refusal in 1954 to testify before the House Un-American Activities Committee, was given a formal apology and reinstated 30 May 1981.

National School Boards Association attorney **Edward Remsburg** warned his association in 1980 to expect a rise in educational malpractice suits during the next decade.

Lottie Riekehof, chair of the department of sign communication at Gallaudet, the nation's only liberal arts college for the deaf, announced that high-school students in Texas would be able to earn foreign language credit after 1981 for American Sign Language.

Albert Shanker, American Federation of Teachers president, told a 1980 Senate hearing that IEP's (Individual Education Plans, required for handicapped children) are "basically unproductive, even detrimental" to the education of handicapped children because their results in no way justify the time and paperwork required by federal guidelines.

Barry Singer, California State University professor who offered homework credit to students for reporting on homosexual, extramarital, and group-sex experiences, resigned his position in the psychology department in 1982.

Warner Slack, Harvard Medical School professor, published a study in 1980 asserting that coaching substantially improves scores on the SAT and discriminates against students who cannot afford such private preparation.

Thomas Sowell, black economist and adviser to the Reagan administration, said in 1981 that the fifteen-point I.Q. gap between black and white students was not unusual and segregated schools were not the cause of it. He based his findings on his study of seventy thousand I.Q. records dating back to the early 1900s.

Ernest Sternglass, professor of radiological physics at the University of Pittsburgh School of Medicine, published a study in 1983 claiming that the drop in SAT performance, and the beginnings of a rise in 1982, were linked to exposure to radioactive fallout from nuclear-weapons testing.

In 1983 House Majority Leader **Jim Wright** questioned our level of investment in education, noting that while the United States graduated 34,000 students in engineering and science in 1982, Japan (with half the population) graduated 77,000 and Russia, 330,000.

DEATHS

Ernest Arbuckle, 73, dean of Stanford's business school from 1958 to 1968 when it became known as one of the best U.S. institutions of its kind, 17 January 1986.

Frederik Barry Bang, 78, biologist and teacher since 1948 at Johns Hopkins University who developed a test to detect potentially lethal infections caused by toxic bacteria, 3 October 1981.

Edward Barrett, 79, dean of Columbia University's Graduate School of Journalism from 1956 to 1968 and founder of the Columbia Journalism Review in 1962, 23 October 1989.

Sarah Gibson Blanding, 86, sixth president and first female president of Vassar College from 1946 to 1964, 6 March 1985.

Kingman Brewster, 69, former president of Yale from 1963 to 1977 during a turbulent time of student protests over minority enrollment, student rights, and admission of women, 8 November 1988.

Fawn McKay Brodie, 65, history teacher best known for her controversial biography of Thomas Jefferson, which focused on the alleged thirty-four-year affair Jefferson conducted with mulatto slave Sally Hennings, 10 January 1981.

Sterling Allen Brown, 69, poet and former teacher of black American literature and the creator of the first black American literature course at Howard University and credited with laying the foundation for university studies in black literature; among his students were Toni Morrison, Amiri Baraka, and Ossie Davis, 13 January 1989.

Glenn Dumke, 72, chancellor of California State University system which, during his tenure, grew from sixteen separate campuses into the nation's largest unified system of higher education, 29 June 1989.

Milton Stover Eisenhower, 85, educator and adviser to every president from Franklin Roosevelt to Richard Nixon (including his brother, Dwight Eisenhower); served as president of Kansas State College (later University), Pennsylvania State University, and Johns Hopkins University, 2 May 1985.

Rudolf Flesch, 75, author of many books on reading and leading advocate of phonics instruction whose best-selling 1955 book, *Why Johnny Can't Read*, popularized his theories, 5 October 1986.

Bartlett Giamatti, 51, scholar who at age forty was the youngest man in two hundred years to become president of Yale University where he confronted debts, strikes, and great unrest; later named commissioner of Major League Baseball, 1 September 1989.

Richard Green, 52, first black chancellor of the New York City public schools whose greatest challenge was confronting widespread student violence and drug use, 10 May 1989.

Frederick Douglass Holliday, 58, Cleveland's first black superintendent of schools who was found dead 28 January 1985 of a self-inflicted gunshot wound; a note was found bearing his signature bemoaning the "petty politics" of the city's racially divided school board.

John Holt, 62, educational reformer whose books *How Children Fail* and *How Children Learn* touched off a national debate on the quality of American education in the 1960s; in 1977 he started *Growing Without Schooling*, a magazine for home schooling, 1 March 1986.

Sidney Hook, 86, philosopher and prolific writer on education and public policy who, as a self-proclaimed "secular humanist," believed that morality is linked to human nature and not to religious beliefs, 12 July 1989.

Elizabeth Duncan Koontz, 69, the first black woman head of the National Education Association who resigned in 1969 when President Richard Nixon named her the head of the Women's Bureau in the U.S. Labor Department, 6 July 1989.

Margaret McNamara, 64, founder in 1966 of Reading Is Fundamental, a nationwide reading program designed to motivate underprivileged children by giving them books of their choice, 3 February 1981.

Marion Monroe, 85, child psychologist and co-author with Dr. William Gray of the Dick and Jane series early readers used from the 1940s through the 1970s to teach millions of children to read; the readers, perceived by some to be racist and sexist, were removed from schools in the late 1970s, 25 June 1983.

Frederick Douglass Patterson, 86, president from 1935 to 1953 of Tuskegee Institute of Alabama and founder of the United Negro College Fund in 1944, which grew to be the largest source of money for private, historically black colleges and universities in the United States, 26 August 1988.

Katherine Towle, 87, first woman dean of students at the University of California, Berkeley, from 1961 to 1965; in 1964 she signed the order that touched off the Free Speech Movement, 1 March 1986.

Sidney Weintraub, 69, professor of economics at the Wharton School of the University of Pennsylvania who, in 1970, proposed "TIP," the federal income-tax-based policy to hold down wage and price inflation without causing recession, 19 June 1983.

Jack Williams, 61, first commissioner of the unified Texas college and university system in 1966, and founder of the Texas Medical Center in Houston, 28 September 1981.

PUBLICATIONS

Mortimer Adler, *The Paideia Proposal: An Educational Manifesto* (New York: Macmillan, 1982);

Bruno Bettelheim and Karen Zelan, *On Learning to Read: The Child's Fascination With Meaning* (New York: Knopf, 1982);

Ruth Bleier, *Science and Gender* (London & New York: Pergamon Press, 1984);

Allan Bloom, *The Closing of the American Mind: How Higher Education Has Failed Democracy and Impoverished the Souls of Today's Students* (New York: Simon & Schuster, 1987);

Godfrey Brandt, *The Realization of Anti-Racist Teaching* (Philadelphia: Falmer Press, 1986);

Philip Cusick, *The Egalitarian Ideal and the American High School* (New York: Longman, 1983);

Thersa Escobedo, ed., *Early Childhood Bilingual Education: A Hispanic Perspective* (New York: Teachers College Press, 1982);

Rudolf Flesch, *Why Johnny Still Can't Read* (New York: Harper & Row, 1981);

Douglas Franzosa and Karen Mazza, compilers, *Integrating Women's Studies into the Curriculum: An Annotated Bibliography* (Westport, Conn.: Greenwood Press, 1984);

Howard Gardner, *Frames of Mind: The Theory of Multiple Intelligences* (New York: Basic Books, 1983);

Carol Gilligan, *In a Different Voice: Psychological Theory and Women's Development* (Cambridge, Mass.: Harvard University Press, 1982);

Kenneth Goodman, *Language and Literacy* (Boston: Routledge & Kegan Paul, 1982);

Shirley Brice Heath, *Ways With Words* (Cambridge: Cambridge University Press, 1983);

Karen Klein and Deborah Strother, eds., *Planning for Microcomputers in the Curriculum* (Bloomington, Ind.: Phi Delta Kappa, 1984);

Herbert Kohl, *Basic Skills: A Plan for Your Child, A Program for All Children* (Boston: Little, Brown, 1982);

Jonathan Kozol, *Savage Inequalities: Children in America's Schools* (New York: Crown, 1991);

Ken Macrorie, *Twenty Teachers* (New York: Oxford University Press, 1984);

Jeannie Oakes, *Keeping Track: How Schools Structure Inequality* (New Haven: Yale University Press, 1985);

David Owen, *None of the Above: Behind the Myth of Scholastic Aptitude* (Boston: Houghton Mifflin, 1985);

Arthur G. Powell, Eleanor Farrar, and David Cohen, *The Shopping Mall High School: Winners and Losers in the Educational Marketplace* (Boston: Houghton Mifflin, 1985);

Stanley Sharp, *The REAL Reason Johnny Still Can't Read* (Smithtown, N.Y.: Exposition Press, 1983);

Larry Silver, *The Misunderstood Child: A Guide for Parents of Learning Disabled Children* (New York: McGraw-Hill, 1984);

Sherry Turkle, *The Second Self: Computers and the Human Spirit* (New York: Simon & Schuster, 1984).

FASHION

by JULIA TAYLOR

Sidebars and tables are listed in italics.

1980

- American designers abandon synthetics for natural fabrics and more-expensive weaves.

- Skirts become shorter and shorter.

- Knits in a wide variety of textures, and colors take a significant place in fashion — even as dress-up clothes.

- Norma Kamali shows her successful collection of cotton fleece-sweats separates modeled after exercise-dance clothes.

- *The Official Preppy Handbook,* edited by Lisa Birnbach, is published.

21 Nov. An estimated eighty-three million Americans watch an episode of the television series *Dallas* to find out "Who shot J. R.?" T-shirts printed with the question had been appearing in stores all over the country.

1981

- Postmodernist slogan "Less is a Bore" replaces modernism's "Less is More."

- Tom Wolfe's *From Bauhaus to Our House* is published; the book criticizes the architectural profession for creating abstract buildings that do not properly celebrate American capitalism.

- Ralph Lauren introduces "retro cowgirl" look that becomes a fad: petticoats and denim skirts worn with boots.

- Sailor-theme clothes are shown by Chloe, Geoffrey Beene, Yves Saint Laurent, and others.

20 Jan. Ronald Reagan is inaugurated as president; his wife, Nancy, wears a white, one-shouldered inaugural-ball gown designed by James Galanos; her complete inaugural wardrobe reportedly costs $25,000.

1982

- Perry Ellis shows a new silhouette for women's clothing: boxy jacket with long, pleated skirt; this theme — long and full or short and lean — would continue to be popular for the rest of the decade.

- White, cream, and pastels are popular colors for the summer.

- The Vietnam Veterans Memorial is built in Washington, D.C.

1983

- According to *The World Almanac,* young Americans' "top hero" is Michael Jackson; his look is widely copied.

- A study by the Society of Podiatrists reports that one in every ten women now wears a size ten or larger shoe as a result of increased participation in dancing, aerobics, or jogging.

- Ray-Ban sunglasses, worn by Tom Cruise in the movie *Risky Business,* are popular.

- The oversized coat becomes a trend.

- The pop singer Madonna shows her navel and wears underwear as outerwear.

- The designers Kamali and Ellis show narrow, midi-length skirts that flare slightly at the hem.
- The High Museum of Art, designed by Richard Meier and Partners, is built in Atlanta.
- The Transco Tower is built in Houston; the architects are Philip Johnson and John Burgee.

1984

- The "men's skirt" — pants with wide legs, one of which folds over the other — is introduced; despite heavy press coverage, it fails to become popular.
- The movie *Flashdance* inspires an off-the-shoulder sweatshirts fad.
- Michael Jackson travels the country on his Victory tour, and his album *Thriller* sells thirty-eight million copies, inspiring youths to wear one glove, mock military jackets, and black patent leather shoes.
- 1950s-inspired bustiers are worn with contemporary minis, boxer shorts, or gathered skirts.
- The television shows *Dallas* and *Dynasty* inspire shoulder pads and short skirts — the bold and alluring look.
- The television series *Miami Vice* influences men's styles: unconstructed sport coats worn over T-shirts, both in pastel colors.

1985

- The female silhouette is softer and ultrafeminine, with full skirts and scooped necklines.
- Curvier, more athletic-looking models replace the malnourished "Twiggy look" in fashion magazines.
- Lingerie — from garter belts to one-piece body suits with lace inserts — becomes popular.
- *Dynasty* costumer Nolan Miller launches a commercial collection of extravagant clothes.
- Anne Klein shows a pale pink cashmere blazer with classic but strong lines that becomes a quintessential garment of the mid 1980s and will still be copied late in the decade.
- Linen, popularized by Giorgio Armani, is chic for men.
- Street style, the deliberately underdressed look of youth, is the height of fashion.

1986

- *American Vogue* shows sweater twin sets with Grace Kelly–inspired scarves and bags.
- The T-shirt dress, in plain matte colors, is popular.
- The movie *Out of Africa*, starring Robert Redford and Meryl Streep, inspires safari jackets.

1987

- For men the conservative preppy look still dominates.

- The fashion industry attempts to revive the short skirt and fails.
- The average woman spends $569 on clothes this year.
- Men's suits return to favor.
- The punk-rock influence in fashion is waning.
- Video presentations, using computer graphics, are a standard requirement for architectural competitions.

19 Oct. The stock market crashes; the fashion industry attempts to recover by raising prices.

1988

- The fashion industry experiences a lull as career women refuse to pay top prices for impractical, trendy clothes.
- *Modern Classicism,* by Robert Stern and Ramon Gastil, is published.

8 Nov. George Bush is elected president; his wife, Barbara, will influence women's fashions with such accoutrements as her three-strand fake-pearl necklace.

1989

- Increasingly, models of diverse ethnic backgrounds are seen in fashion magazines as the Caucasian "all-American" face wanes in popularity.
- Brocade is popular with women's casual clothes.
- The sarong shape is seen in women's pants, skirts, and bathing suits.
- Big, beaded necklaces are piled one on top of the other, often in vivid colors and geometric shapes.
- Rockefeller Plaza West, designed by Kohn Pederson Fox Associates, is completed in New York City; it evokes the 1920s-style skyscraper.
- The World Financial Center and Winter Garden, designed by Cesar Pelli, are completed in New York City.
- Peter Eisenman's Wexler Center for the Arts is built in Columbus, Ohio.
- Frank Gehry and Associates win the commission to design the Walt Disney Concert Hall in Los Angeles.
- *Progressive Architecture* magazine reports that diversity is the only common thread in contemporary American architecture.
- A computer-operated camera that calculates the buyer's measurements and prints out a custom-made bathing suit is used in eighteen stores.

OVERVIEW

Conservatism and Luxury. The turbulent, self-expressive era of the 1960s and 1970s evolved into the 1980s — in fashion, a decade marked by traditionalism, luxury, and consumerism. Many Americans were yearning for better times as the new decade began; they were wary of the new gender roles brought on by the women's movement and weary of the political unrest of the past two decades, and they longed for the safe familiarity of the past. The Reagan administration, announcing itself in 1981 with the most expensive inaugural celebration in history, gave Americans not only the sense of security they were seeking but also an excuse to indulge themselves after the fear and constraints brought on by the energy shortages of the 1970s. Ronald and Nancy Reagan, with their Hollywood associations and 1950s social outlook, satisfied Americans' hunger for glamour and wealth, as well as their longing for traditional values. America's conservative, nostalgic mood was reflected in the realm of fashion, in which borrowing from the past was the dominant form of expression. Although the wealthy prospered, the 1980s were not an easy time for the middle and lower classes. The sharp division in America's distribution of wealth was displayed in fashion as ostentatious classic styles played against cheap, casual, and innovative styles from the street. Although Americans seemed to lose interest in political protests, stylistic rebellion, or street fashion, thrived.

From Hippie to Yuppie. The predominant fashion figure of the 1960s and 1970s was the hippie, and the 1980s saw its antithesis: the young urban professional, or yuppie. In the 1980s the culturally influential baby boomers were rising to executive positions and starting families, and their wardrobe reflected their rising social status and affluent lifestyle. "Dressing for success" and displaying newfound wealth through material possessions became characteristic of the decade. Whereas the hippie was self-expressive, sensual, and innovative, the yuppie borrowed his or her style from the sterile, neat look of the 1950s. The wide-lapelled polyester suits and wide ties of the 1970s were replaced by conservative business suits in fine wool or cotton. As more women entered the workforce they, along with the men, became corporate clones clad in dark-colored "power" suits — for men, white dress shirts, narrow ties, classically tailored jackets, and leather wing-tipped shoes; for women, knee-covering skirts, white blouses tied with bows, and, again, tailored jackets. Such accessories as Rolex watches, Sony Walkmans, and Filofax organizers and cellular phones in expensive leather briefcases were as important to the yuppie wardrobe as the suits themselves. By the late 1980s some women felt confident enough to vary and personalize their yuppie "uniform" with pants, or with curvier dresses with wide belts. Reflecting an athletic trend, women commuters sported cross-trainer sneakers and socks on the train, their low-heeled pumps stuffed into their briefcases for the office.

Preppy Leisure Wear. The sensual, expressive, disco-style leisure wear and synthetic fabrics of the 1970s were passé in the 1980s. Instead, a style that emphasized professionalism, status, and wealth became popular: the "preppy look" evoked images of elite private schools and sports of the affluent, such as tennis and sailing; classic tan khakis paired with tennis or polo shirts, cable-knit sweaters, and cotton turtlenecks were staples for the preppy dresser. Leather boat shoes or 1950s-inspired penny loafers were worn by both men and women, sometimes without socks. Preppy prints were classic and conservative plaids or narrow stripes. The preppy style was the casual-wear look of the yuppie generation, whose favorite status symbol became the polo shirt with an insignia on the left chest — initially the polo player by the designer Ralph Lauren. Labels — from the Lacoste alligator (which succeeded the polo player) to Calvin Klein underwear were important to a generation that valued social status.

Trickle-down Style. The 1980s also saw a "trickling down" of elite styles to the masses. Luxurious status symbols, such as Hermes scarves, gold chains with pearls, and Chanel suits made their way into less-expensive clothing lines that were accessible to the middle classes in the proliferating shopping malls. Similarly, Ralph Lauren's preppy clothes — from expensive polo shirts to lace and velvet dresses — were made available in catalogues, such as those of L. L. Bean, and in chain stores, such as The Gap. The labels were different — instead of Lauren's polo player there was J.C. Penney's fox, for example — but the style was the same. American designers supplied yuppie consumers with elaborately crafted clothes in cotton, silk, and rayon but were willing to make the same designs available in cheaper fabrics and crafting to gain the business of those with smaller bank accounts. For instance, Perry Ellis and Halston expanded their businesses with less-expensive lines that were sold in department stores rather than their exclusive Seventh Avenue stores. Their careers were not aided by this move to the malls; it was as if the designs lost their value for the affluent by touching the racks of department stores.

Rebel Fashion. Although top-scale designers made their mark on the middle class, the world of fashion was tremendously affected by styles of the street — primarily clothes worn by those younger than twenty-five. With less money and darker politics, youth looked to the British antiestablishment punk movement of the 1970s, black urban culture, or pop musicians for their styles. "Street fashion" — secondhand clothes, deliberately torn T-shirts and jeans, multiple earrings, black leather — collided with and eventually infiltrated the luxury and formality of the yuppie wardrobe, so that by the end of the decade a woman could be dressed in faded jeans and a preppy wool blazer, while wearing several earrings and carrying a sophisticated leather bag. On a slightly different front, styles derived from the clothing of urban breakdancers and rappers — baggy pants, heavy gold chains, and name-brand sneakers — echoed the informality of 1970s disco culture and also held its own status symbols. Rap styles originated from African American musicians in urban areas such as New York City, but in a decade of frenzied profit-making schemes the rebellious fashion statements were soon watered down into trendy commodities for suburban teenagers to buy at malls across the country.

Revivals and Rejections. Seemingly at a loss for new fashion ideas for women and feeling nostalgic, designers relied heavily on the past. The 1980s were a decade of revivals, during which everything from nineteenth-century bustles and crinolines to the 1970s smiley-face motif were retrieved. Still feeling the fashion freedom of the 1970s, women chose from the fads they liked, such as large shoulder pads, and rejected some that they detested, such as, in the late 1980s, an ultrafeminine look: miniskirts, ruffles, low necklines, and breast-raising bras. This look was spurned by the majority of career women because of its high prices and impracticality. In general, the chasm between what was seen on fashion runways and what women actually wore widened in the 1980s. After the stock-market crash in 1987 there was a lull in the fashion industry that was a result both of the general economy and of women's dissatisfaction with designers' impractical clothes.

Knitwear. Among the few well-received innovations were clothes that began as exercise gear. Ironically, as women gained entrance and respect in the professional world, emphasis on their physical appearance only became more intense. In the 1970s, as a result of the women's movement, cosmetics and perfume sales went down. By the 1980s advertisers were intent on making women feel unattractive and physically inadequate so that they would buy more beauty products. An exercise and body-improvement trend was partially a result of these tactics. As women toiled on exercise machines and enrolled in aerobic dance classes, fashion designers met their clothing needs with skintight bike shorts, bodysuits, spandex leggings, and leg warmers. The polyester of the 1970s had been replaced not only by natural fabrics, such as cotton, but also by the "fabrics of fitness": synthetic spandex, such as Lycra. The exercise obsession led to casual clothes of wrinkle-proof, stretchy fabrics, featuring oversized T-shirts and short skirts. More-refined knit pants, skirts, and sweaters crossed over as evening wear. Like the preppy style, this fad permeated all levels of designers and therefore, consumers. Knit items, such as leggings, could be found at prices as high as $100 or as low as $20. It was an influential and popular style that would continue into the 1990s.

Postmodernism Makes Its Sweep. The revivals in clothing styles were paralleled by the rapid growth of an architectural movement that reveled in the past — postmodernism, which had been born in the late 1970s as a reaction against modernism. The abstract, impersonal style of the long-reigning modernist movement was increasingly rejected in favor of the contextual, historicist postmodernist style. In office buildings the change in style reflected a shift in corporate ethos: modernist office buildings were towering, mirrored, flat-topped high-rises that seemed to express the rigidity and indifference of the huge corporations within; postmodernist buildings were often low-rises and used warm pastel colors and historical ornaments, such as arches and columns, that reflected a more personal, creative, and decentralized corporation. This change was first demonstrated in Philip Johnson and John Burgee's pink granite AT&T Building in New York City (1978), which continued to inspire architects throughout the 1980s. It was soon followed by the equally innovative Portland Building in Oregon. This building's architect, Michael Graves, with his distinct style that replays history in whimsical ways, became the hero of postmodernism in the decade.

Innovators versus Corporate Architects. The architectural world is generally divided between design-oriented architects and those of a more practical bent; the latter usually work within large corporate firms. In the 1980s the design-oriented innovators were led by such postmodernists as Michael Graves, Robert Venturi, and Frank O. Gehry. With buildings such as Gehry's Aerospace Hall in Los Angeles and Graves's Humana Building in Louisville, Kentucky, the goal was to create interesting buildings that blended with their surroundings. The corporate leaders, such as Paul Kennon's firm, CRS, often adopted the postmodernist style but were willing to sacrifice innovation and simplify ideas to meet a client's needs, resulting in unimaginative postmodernist duplicates. I. M. Pei, however, fused a concern for design and a commitment to corporate practice. Pei's firm won major commissions during the 1980s, including the Arco Tower (1983) and the Allied Bank Tower (1986), both in Dallas.

Pluralism in Interiors. A wide range of possibilities and styles existed in the homes of the 1980s. Interior design, like architecture and clothes, relied heavily on the past, and the diverse borrowings resulted in a mix of styles. Stylistic revivals, as well as an overall interest in preservation rather than renovation, reflected the country's sense of nostalgia and respect for the past. Ralph Lauren created popular home furnishings that, like his clothes, seemed to be relics from the past. The British designer Laura Ashley's floral country look was also prevalent. There was a renewed interest in color, influenced by postmodernism, and Graves's "ice cream" pastels were favorites among interior designers. Home furnishings designed by postmodernist architects (such as Graves's tea kettle) quickly became trendy among status-seeking yuppies. Like their wardrobes, yuppies' homes — large, ornamented houses containing expensive, elegant possessions — were opportunities to display their wealth. In the meantime, students and struggling urban dwellers chose increasingly popular futons and other convertible, space-saving items. As in clothing, there was an alternative punk style: milk crates for storage and throwaway couches, for example. Milk-crate shelves caught on, and department stores began to sell them in bright colors.

Computer Revolution. As computers became indispensable at home and in the office, designers created workstations, desks, and chairs specifically for them and for other electronic equipment. And whereas downsizing cars had been the goal in the 1970s, upscaling was the 1980s ideal. High-tech cars featured computerized rearview mirrors, power steering, touch-sensitive dashboards, and antilock brakes. Computers also oversaw the operation of the engine and transmission. Like yuppie fashions, these cars were designed and priced with the appetites and budgets of the affluent in mind.

The Party's Over. By the decade's end Americans had experienced the October 1987 stock-market crash and the Iran-Contra scandal, which revealed disdain for the law within the federal government. Despite the discovery of a drug (AZT) to slow the progress of AIDS, no cure or vaccine was in sight, and the epidemic was spreading from the cities into upper-class suburbs and small towns. Companies were downsizing, a recession had set in, and the national debt continued to grow. The Cold War was coming to an end, but soon Americans would be involved in a war with Iraq over Kuwait. Americans had not been able to pacify their fears by making money, nor to reestablish traditional values by mimicking the past. By 1990 the yuppie lifestyle was no longer a goal but something to disdain and ridicule as self-centered and wasteful. The rebellious youth and underground fashion that had established itself in the 1980s took off in the 1990s, replacing the ostentatious yuppie style. Postmodernism, a movement that had begun as a call for innovation, had become a trendy formula used by design-illiterate developers to attract business; the cheerful facades of office buildings often masked the greedy old-style corporations within. The new architecture would reflect a concern for ecology, small communities and businesses, and cities. Fashion, architecture, and design in the 1980s reflected an era in which Americans lived with an illusion of prosperity and longed for a return to the past. The 1990s called for a return to reality.

TOPICS IN THE NEWS

ATTIRE FOR WOMEN

Eclecticism Led by Individuality and History. After a decade of fashion freedom in the 1970s, women had become accustomed to creating an individual look from many options rather than conforming to the dictates of the fashion runways of Paris and New York. And in the 1980s women were practically forced to call on their individuality, rather than try to keep up with the quickly changing fads: in a decade that reveled in the past, stylistic revivals formed a dizzying parade. Each fashion season designers brought out styles that borrowed from a different historical period, modernizing them with new fabrics and colors. Among the revived styles were nineteenth-century bustles and crinolines, turn-of-the-century camisoles and petticoats, 1920s drop-waisted chemises, 1940s large shoulders and shirring, 1950s toreador pants and off-the-shoulder stoles, and 1960s and 1970s Day-Glo minis and ethnic fabrics. An eclectic style resulted when designers mixed decades: a contemporary miniskirt with a 1950s-inspired bustier, for example. But women themselves also created variety by combining and modifying trends, mixing them with longtime personal favorites — for example, a trendy flippy skirt with a T-shirt and a worn denim jacket decorated with antique pins. Another example of the freedom women felt from fashion authorities was the lengths of skirts. No single length dominated in the 1980s, and when the miniskirt attempted a comeback late in the decade many women held fast to their mid-length or long skirts, forcing designers to pay heed to their needs and tastes.

Elaboration and Decoration. By the 1980s many women were in the workforce, holding or striving for powerful positions in the professional world and making enough money to spend on luxuries. Their wardrobes reflected their new status, growing salaries, the 1980s emphasis on wealth and ostentation, and a return to traditional femininity after the 1970s unadorned, "natural" woman. Women's styles intensified as their tastes became more-expensive and elaborate: simple 1970s cotton became more expensive 1980s linen, glossy leather became alligator or lizard, crepe de chine became silk jacquard. In general, plain became ornamental: fabric prints were bold and colorful rather than, as in the previous decade, sub-

NANCY REAGAN

Not since Jackie Kennedy in the 1960s was there a more style-conscious first lady. Well acquainted with elite fashion designers before the 1981 inauguration of her husband, former actress Nancy Reagan's expensive taste and conservative style made fashion headlines throughout the decade. She was known for her trim suits, simple linear gowns, and her signature color, red. While some were outraged by the extravagance of her $25,000 inaugural-ball wardrobe (a price she denies), she had fans among American fashion designers and the fashion industry. Designers for whom Nancy Reagan showed enthusiasm, such as Bill Blass and James Galanos, were keenly aware of her valuable fashion influence, and they offered her expensive dresses and suits free of charge. In an era of haves and have-nots, this practice caused disapproval among those who were accustomed to paying for their wardrobes. (In 1982 she promised not to accept the designers' gifts, but she had gone back on this vow by 1988.) She was also criticized for her concern with clothes and china over more-political issues. During a decade in which women were gaining a powerful voice in the political and professional worlds, Nancy Reagan, like the ultra-feminine style that designers pushed on women, seemed to represent a relic of the past: the traditional woman's role as decoration to flaunt her husband's wealth and power.

Sources: "The Best in Fashion: Nancy Reagan Salutes American Fashion," *Harper's Bazaar*, no. 3277 (December 1984): 162–165;

Coco Chanel advertisement, *Vogue*, 177 (September 1987): 205;

Haynes Johnson, *Sleepwalking through History: America in the Reagan Years* (New York: Norton, 1991);

Chris Wallace, *The First Lady: A Portrait of Nancy Reagan* (New York: St. Martin's Press, 1986).

dued and earthy. Women in the 1980s wore ribbons, ruffles, bows, and feathers on their dresses, a trend unseen in the 1970s. Hair and makeup even became more

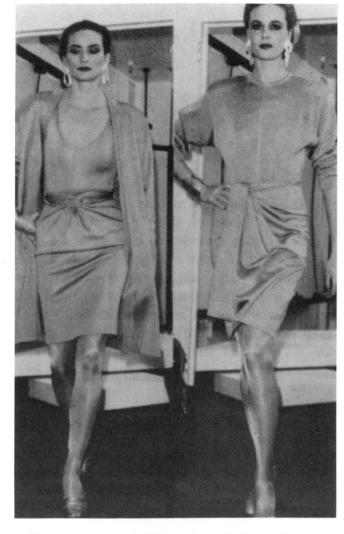

Evening separates of silk jersey shown by Donna Karan in 1985, the year she left Anne Klein and Company to launch her own line

elaborate: the 1970s just-blown-dry look was replaced with deliberately tousled hair, held in place with mousse and gel, or with new, diverse hair ornaments such as bows or fabric-covered elastic.

Makeup and Traditional Femininity. After a decade in which makeup was seen as unnatural or antifeminist, in the 1980s women began shadowing their eyes, outlining their lips, and slathering themselves with the newest sun-protective/moisturizing/wrinkle-erasing makeup. Self-improvement techniques did not stop at the surface of the skin: plastic surgery, silicone-enlarged lips and breasts, and aerobic exercise became more common. Ironically, as women gained entrance into and respect in the professional world they worked even harder at maintaining their physical appearance; their efforts to decorate and beautify themselves were throwbacks to traditional femininity.

Dress for Success. But women's fashion was not all luxury and adornment. In the previous two decades women had increasingly entered the traditionally male professional world, and by the 1980s they made up a significant segment of it. In this decade they grappled with how to dress practically and stylishly without sacrificing their professionalism — or, simply, with how to dress like women in a male world. In the late 1970s and early 1980s women subscribed to the idea that a traditional masculine business suit would assure them respect and authority in the professional world. Anything that was sexy or that called attention to their femaleness was seen as a threat to their professional status. Accordingly, they wore standardized suits that came to be known as the "dress for success" style: a conservative navy or black blazer and knee-covering skirt with an unadorned white shirt closed at the neck with a tied bow, conservative low heels (changed into at work after a commute in cross-trainer sneakers made by companies such as Nike, Etonic, or Adidas), and a loose, androgynous trench coat. Even aside from the business suit, women's styles borrowed from masculine prints such as pinstripes, and women wore ties and pants inspired by menswear. If not dressing like men, they were hiding their femininity in loose, boxy, Japanese-designer-inspired clothes. This androgynous style was, however, waning by 1985 and was soon to be replaced by curvier, softer, more-feminine silhouettes.

Bolder, More-Feminine Suits. By middecade a shift was seen in the dress-for-success suit and in the theory that inspired it. Gradually, the suit's tailoring became bolder, the shoulders wider, and the colors brighter. The new theory was that the dress-for-success suit only demonstrated a woman's lack of status by reflecting a lack of freedom in dress. So, women rising up the corporate ladder became confident enough to wear more-individualized and creative suits. They chose from a wider range of colors and from options such as pants or short skirts. Women in conservative fields such as law, and those who were still struggling to gain status in the corporate world, however, did not feel comfortable with these style options and stayed with their inconspicuous suits throughout the decade. For those who dared, designers such as Donna Karan created work clothes that included shaped dresses with wide belts; short skirts; colorful scarves; higher heels; and chunky jewelry. Launching her own line in 1985, after leaving Anne Klein and Company, Karan introduced the kind of clothing that she felt was missing from her own career wardrobe. With comfort and practicality in mind, she created shirts that stayed neatly tucked (bodysuits and then body blouses) and knit clothes that traveled well and matched everything. By the end of the decade power dressing was still the goal, but women had a few more options.

Fitness. The jogging trend of the 1970s evolved into a fitness craze in the 1980s. A healthy escape from the demands of a busy professional life, exercise became the new pastime for both men and women. Women, in particular, were trying to prove their competence in the professional world, and they transferred this sense of

Got the knit knack?
What it takes: a svelte

Clinging knit dress, a figure-revealing style that was popular
during the fitness and body-improvement craze of the 1980s

The return of elegance: evening gowns from James Galanos's
1987 collection

competition into improving their appearance. They became immersed in body improvements that began with aerobic dance classes and sometimes led to surgical changes such as cellulite removal, tummy tucks, and face peels. Clothes of the decade were greatly influenced by this obsession. The exercise gear that women (and men) wore to aerobics classes was soon seen on the street as well. The new fabrics were comfortable, breathable knits — cotton fleece and shimmering spandex that hugged the skin, showing off newly formed arm muscles and lean legs. The fabrics were used in everything from stirrup pants, leggings, tights, tank tops, midriff-baring tops, bicycle shorts, and jogging suits. One-piece bodysuits or other body-hugging items were layered with loose sweatshirts or T-shirts ripped to reveal a shoulder, as seen in the movie *Flashdance*. The layered look continued into fall and winter with bulky, oversized sweaters worn over short skirts or leggings and flat, ankle-length boots. Confident with their newly toned bodies, at night women wore textured or patterned stockings with whimsical shoes, cotton or Lycra short skirts, short chemise or tight

T-shirt dresses, and, underneath it all, lingerie from bustiers to garters. Tidy and masculine in their suits all day, women were happy to flaunt their new bodies in the evening and on weekends.

Formality. Whereas leisure looks had dominated in the 1970s, in the 1980s dressing up — elegance — came back in style. The return of formality and ostentation was partly an effect of the presence in the White House of Ronald Reagan and the fashion-conscious first lady. Nancy Reagan's fitted, linear dresses without fussy detail contrasted with another trend: elaborate dresses with bows, feathers, or ruffles, in lively fabrics from floral or animal prints to polka dots and wide stripes. But women had many other options; they dressed up in billowing taffeta ball gowns or short black dresses. Television characters, such as Sue Ellen on *Dallas* and Alexis on *Dynasty*, inspired beaded or sequined dresses with big shoulder pads, alluring costume jewelry, furs, and high heels.

The Country Look. The Laura Ashley country look — dresses, skirts, and home furnishings in cabbage-rose prints — was also fashionable. The British designer Ashley and the American designer Ralph Lauren provided women with classic velvet, lace, and linen in the form of long skirts and traditionally feminine blouses. Lauren prided himself on making clothes that were not trendy but classics; he said, "These clothes have a heritage, they're not frivolous, but things to treasure even when they get old."

Sources:

Susan Faludi, *Backlash: The Undeclared War against Women* (New York: Crown, 1991), pp. 169–214;

Caroline Rennolds Milbank, *New York Fashion: The Evolution of American Fashion* (New York: Abrams, 1989), pp. 264–294;

Jane Mulvagh, *Vogue History of 20th Century Fashion* (London & New York: Viking, 1988);

Blanche Payne, *The History of Costume* (New York: HarperCollins, 1992);

Lynn Schurnberger, *Let There Be Clothes* (New York: Workman, 1991), pp. 396–410;

Doreen Yarwood, *Fashion in the Western World: 1500–1990* (New York: Drama Books, 1992).

CLOTHING FOR MEN

Bye-Bye, Leisure Suit. In the 1970s the emphasis for men, as for women, was on leisure; but the 1980s man returned to work. The open-necked shirt and wide-lapelled, loosely tailored suit of the previous decade reflected a leisurely lifestyle and relaxation of roles for men. In the 1980s gender roles for men and women were changing as more women contributed financially to their families and gained power in the professional world; the traditional housewife and male provider were relics of the 1950s. But rather than reflect these changes, 1980s menswear suggested a reaffirmation of traditional values and gender roles. The 1980s suit meant business: suit lapels and obligatory ties were narrower; trousers were straighter; and colors were subdued blacks, grays, and blues. The style reflected a return to 1950s masculinity — a conservative, professional man with no time for leisure. Even men's hairstyles became more conservatively short after the longer, more androgynous hair of the previous two decades. Neat and clean shaven — unmistakably masculine — was the desired look.

Hello, Power Suit. By 1980 the quintessential 1970s leisure suit had nearly disappeared. In 1975 John T. Molloy had written in his book *Dress for Success* that the suit is "the central power garment." In the 1980s yuppies applied this idea, and the "power suit" became both a fashion statement and a value statement. Work shirts and cardigan sweaters were associated not only with former president Jimmy Carter's relaxed wardrobe but with his liberal politics and working-class associations as well; the 1980s male style, represented by President Reagan's expensive morning suit at the 1981 inaugural, paralleled a new esteem for corporate life, the upper class, and tradition. Even Reagan's jeans and plaid shirt — his ranch clothes — echoed the traditional masculinity of the cowboy and the good old days of the West. There were deviations from the standard suit, but these borrowed

The preppy look in casual wear

from history as well: for instance, high-waisted pants worn with suspenders were revived, as were the easy-fitting suits of the late 1930s. By the mid 1980s the suspenders were being produced in colorful striped and jacquard patterns, but overall, the mood was still conservatively classic.

Preppy Style. Men (and women and teenagers) dressed on the weekends in what was called a "preppy" style, which, like their business clothes, reflected the 1980s conservative values and the importance of appearing to be wealthy. With classically styled jeans, khakis, or long shorts, they sported the quintessential preppy shirt: the polo shirt (also called a tennis shirt), with a three-button placket, ribbed collar, and a small logo — polo player, alligator, or royal crest — on the left breast. The ubiquitous logo — which altered depending on what brand shirt a man bought and, therefore, how much he spent on it — became one of the many status symbols of Americans, who were so concerned with emblems of their financial success that a plain shirt was difficult to find. The preppy style, which also included the popular tennis sweater (a white V-neck with blue-and-burgundy trim on the waist and neck) and leather moccasins called dockside shoes, echoed pastimes of the upper class such as sailing, golf, and tennis. The style also recalled collegiate or preparatory-school clothes: tan khakis; rugby shirts; turtlenecks; white, pink, or pale blue button-down oxford shirts; navy blue blazers; and penny loafers, perhaps worn without socks as *The Official Preppy Handbook*

(1980) suggested. But though the preppy look suggested affluence, because it was accessible to almost any consumer in mall stores such as J. C. Penney or The Gap, it lost some of its impact. Shopping by mail was common in the 1980s, and catalogues such as those of J. Crew and L. L. Bean also stocked the preppy staples for those who could not or did not want to spend the money on an "authentic" polo shirt from Ralph Lauren's collection.

Sportswear Influence. In the midst of the 1980s conservative wave, 1970s-originated sportswear and fashion from the street in general still influenced menswear. For instance, the jogging suits of the 1970s were still worn in the early 1980s, and men wore sheepskin jackets, flight jackets, and duffel coats, as well. The 1970s trend of unstructured clothes, such as looser jackets with lower buttons, became standard. The permissive, relaxed spirit of the 1970s led to a creative black-tie style that gave men the option to go to semiformal parties without a tuxedo jacket, or to accessorize with colorful cummerbunds, vests, bow ties, and socks. (Women at such parties were also less dressed up than in earlier decades, often wearing costumy outfits designed by Calvin Klein or Yves Saint Laurent.) Instead of formal leather shoes, men and women could wear cowboy boots or tennis shoes.

Mix of Styles. Some men's styles blended the sensuality and expressiveness of the 1970s with the elegance of the 1980s. Despite the conservative trend, the growing gay-rights movement and an emphasis on youth allowed for a new freedom to experiment with style. As one fashion writer put it, men could "flirt with fashion without encountering disapproval." The Italian designer Giorgio Armani's popular double-breasted, slightly droopy suits were an example. Reflecting changing social roles of the sexes, Armani was less gender-specific in his choice of fabrics and styles, using, for instance, fabrics such as wool crepe, which had previously been associated with women's attire, for his men's suits. The double-breasted suits, which hearkened back to the styles of the 1930s, were seen as a mark of success, especially among the wealthy; the suits signified the confidence and power to rise above the constraints of the typical, single-breasted yuppie suit. Double-breasted suits, after all, held associations with the elegance of stars from old movies, such as Clark Gable and Cary Grant, and more recently with the television star Don Johnson. Johnson and his *Miami Vice* costar Philip Michael Thomas reinforced this trend, though Johnson preferred a Versace suit paired with a T-shirt — his fashion statement from the street. Armani borrowed from the street as well, pairing the rough, urban rapper look of hooded sweatshirts with suits.

Sources:
Farid Chenoune, *A History of Men's Fashion* (Paris: Flammarion, 1993);

Richard Martin and Harold Koda, *Jocks and Nerds: Men's Style in the Twentieth Century* (New York: Rizzoli, 1989);

Jane Mulvagh, *Vogue History of 20th Century Fashion* (London & New York: Viking, 1988);

Blanche Payne, *The History of Costume* (New York: HarperCollins, 1992);

Norma Kamali outfit inspired by youthful street fashion

Doreen Yarwood, *Fashion in the Western World: 1500–1990* (New York: Drama Books, 1992).

CLOTHING FOR YOUTH

Rebel Clothes — Street Fashion. The 1980s saw the mainstreaming of fashion from the street, that is, the gradual permeation of adult chic by youthful rage. The evolution began in the 1970s with the breakdown of the traditional divisions of fashion. It continued into the 1980s as high-end designers and wealthy pop stars appropriated street fashion, thereby defeating the style's original purpose: inexpensive, functional clothing. Whether Americanized punk, urban rap, or Madonnaesque sleazy,

Faded denim jacket and jeans, a youth-inspired style that became chic in the late 1980s

and T-shirts at thrift stores and flea markets. The look did not enter the mainstream of American fashion until the 1980s. American punks wore black clothing, leather accessories and jackets, ripped jeans, unisex earrings (several in one ear, the nose, and so on), and spiked and/or brightly dyed hair. The "Mohawk" hairstyle was a drastic form of the spiked look, with shaved sides and long spikes held up with gel or glue in the middle. Whereas in Britain the style carried an overt antiestablishment political message, in America it became more of a fashion statement: "weekend punks" wore a safety pin or two stuck in a jacket, or tore holes in the knees of their jeans. By the late 1980s, however, the look was waning, and it evolved into the "hobo" or flea-market style — equally rebellious but not as antagonistic or sexual (no more studded leather chokers).

Secondhand Clothes. Oversized clothes were part of the trend that also included old jeans, men's undershirts, thrift-shop overcoats, and dark sunglasses. Youth purposely tore their shirts or treated their jeans with bleach or acid to give them a lived-in or old look. The objective was to look as if one did not have money to spend on clothes or just did not care how one looked. It was a style that was in direct opposition to the older generation, who, in an effort to show off their wealth, were sporting Rolex watches, flashy jewelry, and expensive leather bags. But eventually this ragged, low-cost look caught on and entered the mainstream, as in the manufacturing of acid-washed jeans. These worn-looking jeans sold in catalogues and mall stores for as much or more than new-looking jeans. Faded denim in pants, skirts, and jackets became stylish and even chic. American designers also caught on to the marketability of youth fashion. One example was the young designer Stephen Sprouse, who made clothes for pop musicians such as Debbie Harry: he turned the secondhand look into a slicker, more urban style by using Day-Glo colors of the 1960s. Although he went out of business twice, he enjoyed a great deal of positive attention from the fashion runways. The other trend in high fashion inspired by youth fashion's second-hand look was quirky tailoring — pants too short, sleeves too long, collar too large, and so on.

Breaking and Rapping. Another fad came from urban African American break-dancers and rap singers. Both trends began on the streets of city neighborhoods as expressions of urban teenagers' experience; street music and the corresponding fashion were gritty, sexual, and aggressive — a kind of aural graffiti. In the 1980s their audience broadened as performers were seen in subway stations and in shows in New York's Times Square area. Eventually, rap groups such as Run-DMC and the Fat Boys received countrywide attention on MTV, Arsenio Hall's talk show, and Swatch Watch commercials. Their clothing, which was in opposition to the contained, clean-cut yuppie style, became as stylish as their music. In the early 1980s dancers wore nylon jogging suits decorated with zippers, along with gloves to break their falls when danc-

these styles made a lasting mark on the way Americans dressed; street fashion became high fashion. Oversized clothing, worn jeans, T-shirts, leather, and multiple ear piercings, once limited to youth, were in the mainstream of adult fashion by the end of the decade. Women with ripped jeans or gel-spiked hair, combined with the more elegant yuppie style of a blazer and Chanel bag — or other such combinations — represented the merging of the styles.

Punk Style Comes to the United States. The punk influence had its roots in England in the mid 1970s. A style that was conceived when teenage unemployment first began to rise drastically, it carried the message of being on the outside looking in, of being rejected. What began as an aggressive and even sadomasochistic style worn by alienated youth became a tremendous fad, led by the British designer Vivienne Westwood. It spread with the help of punk bands, such as the Sex Pistols. It was the first style of which teenagers had complete control, and, therefore, the look was created with limited funds. Youths found their tight jeans, studded leather jackets,

ing or spinning. Bandannas or punk-inspired leather bands around the wrists and high-tops or other sneakers were part of the look. Sleeveless muscle shirts or chest-revealing jackets showing off heavy gold chains were reminiscent of the machismo look of the 1950s as well as the sexual expressiveness of 1970s disco. By the late 1980s rap was overtaking break dancing in popularity, and the look became less macho but just as aggressive in its status symbols and deliberate sloppiness: the typical rapper wore laceless brand-name sneakers with huge gold rope chains and a sideways baseball cap, along with the established sweatsuit or, later, baggy tops with jeans.

Urban Street Fashion Appropriated and Sold. The media, specifically television, disseminated the aggressive, sensual styles of black urban culture into the mainstream. The cable channel Music Television — MTV — made its rise in the 1980s, gaining 24.2 million viewers by 1984 with its continuous showing of music videos: three- to five-minute narratives accompanying the musicians' performances. The impact on fashion was immense: the oversized look, inspired by rappers, permeated all aspects of clothing, from huge T-shirts worn with jeans or leggings to the large flea-market-style coat. First, rap music was popularized through music videos and performances on the African American host Arsenio Hall's talk show. Then, pop musicians, such as Michael Jackson and Madonna, appropriated dance moves and clothing from break-dancing and rap culture. Finally, MTV aired the pop musicians' latest videos twenty-four hours a day. Avid television viewers, suburban teenagers soon filled the malls, clamoring for oversized "rap" clothes, Nike brand sneakers (to be worn untied), inspired by break dancing and Michael Jackson gloves, and punk/Madonna-like lace stockings and miniskirts. Punk, break-dancing, and rap cultures had inspired pop musicians, who then made the styles safe for suburban mall fashion. The music video had become the fashion industry's and retailers' favorite advertising tool.

Sexual Identity and Gender Play. As conservative adult fashion tried to reaffirm traditional gender roles and push sex (along with AIDS and homosexuality) into the background, youth fashion grappled with these issues through androgynous clothes and sexually expressive styles. Rectangular-shaped, androgynous clothes created by Japanese designers were copied in America. The British singer George Michael updated the sexy, rugged look with his punk/street version: one earring, stubble, and black leather jacket. In contrast, another British musician, Boy George, inspired an androgynous look with long hair and makeup. In their dress and behavior Michael Jackson, Madonna, and Prince (who wore black panties on stage) drew attention to social issues such as gender and racial identity; part of their success can be attributed to their ability to do so without offending the still-conservative mainstream — to water down radical styles into safe commodities.

Madonna. This closely watched star borrowed from innovative street fashion such items as gloves (from break-dancers) and black miniskirts and lacy stockings (from punk). Her sexual, predatory-woman look was inspired by the female punk's miniskirts and ripped lace, but Madonna softened and glamorized the look with movie-star makeup, neon colors, and lace left intact. Her "material girl" look was highly popular; girls as young as eleven tied rags in their hair and wore fingerless gloves and rows of bangle bracelets. Madonna's look was always changing, but remnants of her earlier styles, especially the "sleaze look," permeated young women's wardrobes; Madonna-inspired crucifix necklaces were a fad that continued into the 1990s. She also took part in the exercise trend, transforming her body from soft and curvy to lean and muscular by the end of the decade.

Michael Jackson. Jackson was young Americans' top hero, according to the 1983 *World Almanac,* and his influence on youth fashion was, accordingly, substantial. His costume — mock-military jacket, single glove, ankle-length pants, low-cut white socks worn with black patent leather slippers — crossed gender lines and mocked tradition at a time when tradition was receiving new respect from the older generation. Jackson had teenagers across the country (as well as abroad), including those who had never seen a break-dancer, wearing one glove and doing the "moon walk."

Authenticity. For teenagers the label fad seen in adult preppy fashion evolved into an authenticity trend. As they became aware of the status associated with a label, teenagers wanted only the accepted — and usually most expensive — brand of jeans, shirts, and shoes. Shopping malls, with the same chain stores in each, made it possible for teenagers from all parts of the country to buy trendy products, resulting in conformity throughout the high schools of America. The logos proving the items' authenticity came to mean status and wealth. Students had created their own system to prove "success": their yuppie suit was a pair of authentic 501 Levis with an oversized T-shirt or rugby shirt, *real* dockside shoes, and maybe a Swatch Watch: a flimsy, clear-plastic timepiece with colorful, playful designs instead of numbers on the face.

Sources:

Craig Brown, "The Rock and Roll of Fashion," *Harper's Bazaar,* 120 (July 1986): 128–137;

Farid Chenoune, *A History of Men's Fashion* (Paris: Flammarion, 1993);

Nelson George, *Buppies, B-Boys, Baps, and Bohos: Notes on Post Soul Black Culture* (New York: HarperCollins, 1992);

MaryBeth Kerrigan, "Punk Passion, Fashion," *Daily News Record* (New York), 3 October 1986;

Richard Maltby, *Passing Parade: A History of Popular Culture in the 20th Century* (Oxford: Oxford University Press, 1989);

Jane Mulvagh, *Vogue History of 20th Century Fashion* (London & New York: Viking, 1988);

Blanche Payne, *The History of Costume* (New York: HarperCollins, 1992).

DESIGNERS OF APPAREL

Design for Design's Sake. In the 1980s, as American designers abandoned synthetics in favor of natural fabrics and gained new respect from their European counterparts, their designs were becoming increasingly expensive and impractical — much to the dissatisfaction of the people who were supposed to buy and wear the clothes. Despite fashion-industry growth, especially in menswear, and retail success (until 1987) as shopping became a national pastime, the design industry became more distanced from the populace. Fashion shows became stages rather than places to find styles, and a disparity developed between the clothes that were featured on the runways or in the press and the clothes that women actually wore. The editor of *Vogue* magazine during the 1980s, Grace Mirabella, recalls the decade: "Clothes were about labels, designers were about celebrities, and it was all . . . about money." Indeed, designers seemed to be designing for design's sake rather than for wearability; many women were rejecting the fashions and prices of the elite designers and, instead, buying their conservative suits and classics from catalogues or discount department stores. Mirabella observes: "At the very same time that women were really emerging as a potent economical and political force in America, there were no clothes for them at all." Mirabella is referring, in particular, to the lack of suitable clothes for professional women in the 1980s.

Women Revolt against Fashion. In 1987 sales of women's clothes dipped considerably for the first time since 1974, which was a recession year. The stock-market crash in October was partially to blame, but given that menswear sales were still up, the lack of sales must have had more to do with women's dissatisfaction with the clothes available to them. The 1987 slump corresponded with a push by the fashion industry for ultrafemininity, based partly on looks of the 1950s such as the "babydoll" dress (a loose, above-the-knee dress with no waistline). The fashion industry's Intimate Apparel Council worked to sell ultrasexy looks, such as miniskirts and blouses with plunging necklines intended to be worn with push-up bras. The Intimate Apparel Council tried to convince women that "cleavage is back." But women were not buying the notion. Not only did women's purchases of lingerie go down in 1987, but between 1986 and 1987 dress sales declined while suit sales rose, reflecting the many women who needed work clothes rather than impractical girlish dresses and garter belts. Designers were not listening: they showed clothes that looked good only on the tall, slim, twenty-year-old models on runways and in magazine ads. The median age of the American woman in 1986 was thirty-three, and the median height was five feet, three inches. And these women did not want to wear short skirts to the office: a *New York Times* poll indicated that only one quarter of adult women had worn a skirt above the knee even once in 1988. The fashion trends were associated with youth, but women wanted clothes that reflected their rising status. Even

Calvin Klein minidress, 1986: an example of the ultrasexy look that the fashion industry failed to sell to women in the late 1980s

though stores in the 1980s tried at first to cater to professional women, by 1987 many, such as Alcott and Andrews, which began as a store for affluent professional women, did not even bother with suits, stocking only dresses. Alcott and Andrews was convinced by the fashion press's message that women could proclaim their femininity at the office. The fact that this store went out of business in 1989 indicates that women disagreed with the fashion press.

More-Expensive Clothes. Many consumers also reacted against higher prices. American designers produced clothes with expensive fabrics and intricate crafting that fed the 1980s appetite for luxurious and elaborate possessions. Many designers moved their manufacturing operations to other countries, where they could pay lower wages than American union workers received. To sell their clothes, designers had several strategies. First, they advertised with full spreads in fashion magazines. They wanted a specific look to sell the image that would sell their clothes; as a result, models (as well as the designers

Advertisement for mascara: the "natural" look of the 1970s was replaced in the 1980s by traditional ideas of feminine glamour.

themselves) became celebrities; Brooke Shields, Elle Macpherson, and Christie Brinkley became household names. The fashion industry also tried to promote "investment dressing," the notion that expensive clothes would last much longer than cheaper ones and were, therefore, more economical in the long run. Finally, as consumers — frustrated by time constraints, crowded malls, or the new antitheft devices that made trying on clothes less convenient — discovered the convenience of shopping by telephone, many department stores began putting out catalogues that became more and more like fashion magazines, with editorial comment and some of the same well-known models.

Less Expensive Collections. Designers with dresses that cost as much as $10,000 tried to reach lower-income shoppers by using cheaper fabrics or less elaborate crafting to make similarly styled clothes that could be sold in the ubiquitous malls of America. In 1988 Donna Karan launched her DKNY (Donna Karan New York) line, aimed at women's weekend needs and selling for half the price of her deluxe line. The prices of these items ranged from $100 to $700 — still not down to the level of

middle-income women's budgets. For this group Halston (known for his expensive minimalistic clothes) designed a reasonably priced line for J. C. Penney department stores in 1982, but sales of his expensive line were hurt by this expansion. In the same year Anne Klein and Company, whose clothes were often made of luxurious fabrics such as satin and cashmere, started its A. Klein II line, which featured similar styles with cheaper materials and crafting.

The Winning Styles. Designers who created clothes inspired by the America of the past did well in this decade of nostalgia, but many women put together less-expensive versions of these styles. Early in the decade Ralph Lauren and Perry Ellis showed romantic styles reminiscent of pioneer women: voluminous skirts in Madras checks, complete with tousled hair tied with (Madonnaesque) silk and lace "rags." Lauren's cowgirl look — big bulky sweaters, cotton blouses with high collars, and calf-length blanket skirts worn with boots — was popular and easily copied. Women also dressed as sailors, with stylistic ideas from Geoffrey Beene, Sonia Rykiel, or Yves Saint Laurent, and more androgynously in kimono-inspired outfits in shades of blue, gray, and black. Rei Kawakubo of Commes des Garçon (meaning "like the boys") was influential in spreading the latter style, which was widely copied by American designers who created more-accessible clothes with the dark, boxy look. The boxy jacket was seen throughout the decade; Ellis paired it at first with long, pleated skirts and later with shorter, narrower ones.

Sources:

Farid Chenoune, *A History of Men's Fashion* (Paris: Flammarion, 1993);

Moira Hodgson, Review of *In and Out of Vogue,* by Grace Mirabella, *New York Times Book Review,* 24 September 1995, p. 13;

Barbara Kantrowitz, "A Fashion Revolt," *Newsweek,* 112 (5 December 1988): 60–65;

Caroline Rennolds Milbank, *New York Fashion: The Evolution of American Fashion* (New York: Abrams, 1989);

Jane Mulvagh, *Vogue History of 20th Century Fashion* (London & New York: Viking, 1988);

Anne Stegemeyer, *Who's Who in Fashion* (New York: Fairchild, 1988).

DESIGNERS OF BUILDINGS: POSTMODERNISM IN ARCHITECTURE

What Would Happen to Postmodernism? In the late 1970s the postmodernist movement had made a tremendous impact on American architecture. Observers wondered whether the postmodernist architectural upstarts of the 1970s, such as Frank Gehry and Robert Venturi, would effect a wholesale architectural revolution in the 1980s. A hint of what was to come in the 1980s could be discerned in Philip Johnson and John Burgee's postmodernist design for the AT&T Building in New York City (1978). A white neoclassical skyscraper capped by a cornice borrowed from eighteenth-century furniture, Johnson's "Chippendale skyscraper" portended a shift from the modernist ethos of austere, sterile, form-follows-function minimalism to a new postmodernist eclectic, playful, and accessible style. Johnson's shift to postmodernism signaled a sea change; he had been among the most influential architects in introducing modernism to America in the 1930s and 1940s. In the 1980s almost the entire profession followed suit.

Postmodernism Eclipses Modernism. In the 1980s the founding leaders of postmodernism — Venturi, Denise Scott, Charles Moore, and Michael Graves — continued to design, integrating historical forms with new decorative and functional designs. They had established the movement that brought ornamentation, history, and contextuality back into American architecture. Even firms that received much attention in the decade and preferred exploring abstract styles, such as the Miami-based Arquitectonica, were influenced by postmodernism, as seen in their site-sensitive buildings and their playful use of color. In 1982 Paul Goldberger, an architectural critic, wrote that there was at this point in the decade "no clear sense of style at all." During the rest of the decade postmodernism clarified American architectural style, triumphing over modernism.

Michael Graves and the Portland Building. Not until the AT&T and Portland Buildings did postmodernists venture into designing commercial or government struc-

The postmodernist Portland Building, designed by Michael Graves

tures; during the 1970s they had worked on private homes. The award-winning Portland Building, finished in 1982, was one of the most influential buildings of the 1980s and helped to establish Graves as one of the most inventive designers of the day. Like the AT&T Building, it was a rejection of the cool, unadorned style of modernism. Also like the AT&T Building, it was controversial: the public was still warming to postmodernism early in the decade. Graves won the commission in a competition held by the city of Portland, Oregon. His design was a fifteen-story building containing office, rental, and commercial space. Because it would be flanked on one side by the city hall and on the other by the county courthouse, both in the neoclassical style, one of Graves's challenges was to create a building that suited the surroundings while also possessing its own distinct character. His solution was to use classical references but to give them a new, fresh look that relied on warm colors both inside and out. The building is classically arranged in three tiers, in equally traditional rectangular shapes; the unexpected comes in Graves's use of color — blue and ivory on the facade and green ceramic tiles on the base, widely spaced windows on the facade framed in red, and blue-ribbon garlands to balance the geometric shapes. The interior is equally colorful, with ample views. With complexity, wit, and warmth, Graves evoked past styles from eighteenth-century French to Art Deco. Graves later designed the Humana Building (1985) in Louisville, Kentucky, in which he continued to use historical allusions, ornamentation, and conspicuous colors.

Historical Allusions and Decadence. As it became evident that historical allusions, such as arches, columns, and cornices — the darlings of postmodernist style — were the trend of the decade, developers decided to cash in on the fad. Gerald Hines, who built high-rises — such as the Transco Tower (1983) in Houston — from coast to coast, hired the hip architects of the AT&T Building, Johnson and Burgee, to design buildings with borrowings from periods such as Art Deco and the 1930s. Der Scutt's $93 million Trump Tower in New York City, the talk of the town early in the decade, is one of the lavish buildings that combined America's shopping frenzy and extravagant tastes with the historical quality that characterized postmodernism. Here people could shop in expensive boutiques in surroundings — from the marble atrium to the live piano player in a tuxedo — that recalled another corporate heyday, the Jazz Age. They could then ascend to an equally opulent apartment, with Mr. and Mrs. Donald Trump as their upstairs neighbors. Georgetown Park was the equivalent in Washington, D.C., with its elite stores and condominium apartments catering to the rich in mock-Victorian surroundings.

Environmentalism. Another influence of postmodernism was a renewed respect for the place that surrounds the building. Whereas modernists boasted that their functional glass-box buildings could be built anywhere, postmodernism was concerned with creating distinctively shaped buildings that were expressive of their locale. One example of this concern was Antoine Predock's Nelson Fine Arts Center in Tempe, Arizona (1989), a lavender stucco building that resembles the structures built by the Pueblo Indians. Similarly inspired by the environmental consciousness of Native Americans, Steven Holl created in Martha's Vineyard a private home that recalls not only seafaring legends but also the shorelines and shrubland that surround it. The skeletal look of the wood evokes images of local Native Americans who built their houses by stretching skins around skeletons of beached whales, and the weathered gray color blends with the surroundings and conforms to local laws concerning color of homes that were developed to preserve the look of Martha's Vineyard's serene, noncommercial environment.

Revitalizing American Downtowns. The postmodernist emphasis on locale and regional character also lent itself to the preservation and urban-planning revolution in America. Whereas in the previous two decades the trend was slum removal, or tearing down of buildings and neighborhoods, the 1980s humanistic goal was neighborhood renewal. Architects were hired to investigate, in collaboration with the members of the community, ways to revitalize their neighborhood or town. These revitalization projects often led to the use of environmental

Frank O. Gehry's California Aerospace Hall in Los Angeles, which features an F-104 jet fighter attached to its facade

assets such as bodies of water or unique regional characteristics. This trend also meant a preservation of historic sites and old buildings. For instance, by the mid 1980s approximately one hundred old hotels had been restored from coast to coast. Architect Graham Gund's Church Court Apartments in Boston were another example of preservation.

Edge Cities. In the meantime, outside the cities and in competition with these struggling downtowns, a new urban landscape called edge cities was rapidly developing. These newly populated areas shaped Americans' lifestyles and also determined the kind of building that was done. During the 1960s and 1970s Americans increasingly moved away from small towns or from noisy, crime-ridden cities. This transformation was gradual, taking place in three stages: first, suburbs were built increasingly after World War II; second, malls sprang up to provide convenient shopping for the people living in the suburbs; finally, in the 1980s, these areas that had been only places to live and shop were also becoming places to work — creating a whole new urban center, the edge city. Office parks, megamalls, hotels, parking garages, and planned communities made up the edge cities that became as common in the West as on the East Coast.

Mainstreamed Postmodernism. Edge-city buildings featured postmodernist qualities: imposing facades that recalled Greek or Victorian architecture were used for middle-class shopping centers, medical office parks, and even chain drugstores. Office parks, like postmodernist office buildings, reflected the new corporate ethos of the decade. Many buildings — such as the General Foods Corporation headquarters (1984) in Rye, New York, designed by Kevin Roche, John Dinkerloo and Associates of Hamden, Connecticut — that were meant to be "corporate homes" were given a residential quality by the use

In 1981, when Chinese American Maya Ying Lin's plan was selected from 1,421 nationwide contest entries for a memorial in Washington, D.C., commemorating the soldiers who had served in the Vietnam War, she was still a twenty-one-year-old architecture student at Yale. Her design, meant to be a pensive place where people could contemplate the war, consisted of two two-hundred-foot-long black granite walls carved with names of the more than fifty-eight thousand Americans who had died in the war (a required feature). Lin lent even more meaning by listing the names in the order they were killed, rather than alphabetically. The black granite creates a mirrorlike surface, and the walls form a "V" with a gently sloping plot of ground in between, so that visitors have the sensation of walking down into the earth.

Her seemingly simple design resulted in a politically and emotionally driven two-year battle between Lin and the committee of the American Institute of Architects who had chosen her plan, on one side, and Vietnam veterans, who saw the design as too cool and abstract, on the other. Supporters of the design considered it moving and fitting, given the controversy surrounding the war, but the veterans thought the funereal black color (the veterans wanted a white monument) and sloping earth were disrespectful and degrading. The design was initially regarded as apolitical, but by the climax of the dispute one decorated marine was calling it a "wailing wall for antidraft demonstrators" that was meant to symbolize a "black spot in American history." The Texas businessman H. Ross Perot personally paid to fly in veterans to lobby against the design. The battle between the veterans and the supporters of the design became representative of the conflicting feelings Americans had about the war itself.

Finally, the sculptor Frederick Hart was commissioned to create a realistic sculpture to add to the existing plan. His larger-than-life-size statue of three rifle-carrying soldiers, one black and two white, to be placed 120 feet from the walls, came to represent the military establishment, and Lin's design the antiwar movement. Lin called the addition a "trite" illustration that "destroy[ed]" the meaning of her original design. In 1983, almost three years after Lin's design won the contest, the statue and a fifty-foot flagpole were added to the original design. In 1984 Lin and Cooper-Lecky Partnership won an AIA award for the memorial. Since its opening in November 1982, thousands of people have visited it, leaving personal mementos of the soldiers on the ground near the names. Lin went on to design a memorial to the civil rights movement in Montgomery, Alabama (1989).

Sources: Paul Goldberg, *On the Rise: Architecture and Design in a Postmodern Age* (New York: Penguin, 1983);

Elizabeth Hess, "A Tale of Two Memorials," *Art in America*, 71 (April 1983): 120–126.

---

of plants and natural lighting. Office buildings became known as "corporate campuses," with low-rise structures linked by a circular path. They were more personal and worker-friendly than the previous modern high-rises, in which workers met only in elevators on the way to their cubicles. The postmodernist, worker-friendly office buildings did not, however, result in user-friendly corporations: by the end of the 1980s many firms had increased in size because of mergers, alienating their workers in the process.

From Innovation to Repetition. A prominent feature of edge cities were huge shopping malls with megaplex movie theaters. These malls were built with such references to history as pastel-colored facades, pediments, and colonnades. By the end of the decade such facades had become repetitive rather than contextual, lending nothing to the surroundings but a front for yet another place to shop. This tendency, and the general excess of unimaginative postmodernist design, led some critics to condemn the movement for failing to keep innovation alive and for being too preoccupied with surfaces. One critic said that postmodernism had become an "exercise in image-making, in promotion, in decoration." With its glitzy exteriors and emphasis on flashy facades, some felt, it had become a design for large businesses, greedy developers, and the rich yuppies who worked and shopped in the buildings.

Sources:
Peter Blake, "The Case against Postmodernism," *Interior Design*, 58 (October 1986): 324–325; (November 1986): 276–277; (December 1986): 276–277;

Douglas Davis, "Raiders of the Lost Arch," *Newsweek*, 107 (20 January 1986): 66–68;

Joel Garreau, *Edge City* (New York: Doubleday, 1991);

Paul Goldberg, *On the Rise: Architecture and Design in a Postmodern Age* (New York: Penguin, 1983), pp. 20–36, 161–162;

William Dudley Hunt Jr., *Encyclopedia of American Architecture* (New York: McGraw-Hill, 1990);

Spiro Kostof, *History of Architecture: Settings and Rituals* (Oxford: Oxford University Press, 1995);

Sydney LeBlanc, *20th Century American Architecture* (New York: Watson-Guptill, 1993);

Ann Lee Morgan and Colin Naylor, eds., *Contemporary Architecture* (Chicago: St. James Press, 1987);

Beverly Russell, *Architecture and Design 1970–1990: New Ideas in America* (New York: Abrams, 1989), pp. 30–60.

DIGITAL DESIGN

Computer Revolution. By the 1980s a computer revolution had taken hold of America. Its influence on fashion and design was tremendous. From clothes to cars, computers were changing the kinds of designs produced, how they were produced, and how newly computer-literate Americans interacted with one another.

The Fashion Industry. Increasing mechanization and advances in computer technology were major influences on the direction taken by fashion in the 1980s. For instance, clothing stores began to use computers for customer services, such as answering questions about merchandise. Computers were used to analyze buying trends and determine marketing strategies, which — to the relief of some customers and the annoyance of others — resulted in fewer salespeople on the floor. Salespeople began to use computers to allow potential customers to see themselves with a makeover, a new hairdo, or even a facelift.

Shift in Design. In 1988 approximately nine million Americans worked at home, hooked up to a computer. Throughout the decade, as more and more homes and offices became equipped with computers and other electronic gadgets, designers worked to accommodate the devices. In what were called "intelligent buildings" designers created workstations, desks, and chairs with the needs of computer users specifically in mind. The popular computer chair was designed to prevent the back and neck strains inherent in long hours at a keyboard. With the use of vertical panels, interior designers accommodated not only computers but also wide-screen television sets, fax machines, and other electronic devices.

Intelligent Offices. Possibly because the geometric shapes of modernist and postmodernist design are easily handled by computers, computers and new design software quickly made their way into architects' and interior designers' offices, where they increased speed, accuracy, and efficiency (after the initial learning stage). Computer drafting made the T-square and triangle obsolete. Computers also allowed architects and interior designers to work on various parts of a building simultaneously by linking their computers together in networks and viewing each other's work on their monitors. This process, called "workgroup" computing, became practical for both large and small firms.

Hotel Technology. Hotels took advantage of the new computer technology by introducing a variety of guest-friendly features. In some hotels a guest could unlock the door of his or her room by inserting a credit card into a slot. With computers, hotels could easily keep records of guests' preferences; thus, a guest's room could be stocked with his or her favorite magazines, or the guest could be served coffee each morning as he or she likes it, without the hotel having to ask the guest more than once. At the deluxe Riverparc in Miami, guests using their televisions and touch-sensitive control panels, could shop, play interactive video games with someone in the next room, research travel options, and send electronic mail to their families or employers without leaving their rooms.

An Electronic World. During the 1980s Americans were becoming increasingly engaged with electronic and computerized equipment. On the train professionals in business suits plugged their ears with earphones connected to Walkmans or gazed at the screens of their portable computers. Communication at the office, in hotels, and in stores was done more and more through computers or fax machines, making face-to-face contact less common. This technology facilitated work but also left people in isolation from one another. The stress that this lonely lifestyle will have on Americans has yet to be seen.

Sources:
"High-Tech Hotels of the Future," *Futurist*, 23 (July–August 1989): 55;

Haynes Johnson, *Sleepwalking through History: America in the Reagan Years* (New York: Norton, 1991).

DWELLING PLACES: AMERICAN HOMES

Yuppie Homes. The understated interior style of the 1970s was replaced in the 1980s by the decadent tastes of the yuppies. While the town house early in the decade reflected the largely single status of the baby boomers in the 1970s, in the 1980s many detached homes were built to house affluent professionals who were starting families — or increasing existing ones as a result of divorce and remarriage. The yuppies tended to build two-story Georgian homes that dwarfed existing houses in their neighborhoods; much to the annoyance of academic architects, the exteriors were embellished with historical references, such as arches and dormers, purely for decorative reasons. Inside, homeowners filled their rooms with expensive tokens of their wealth, such as teakettles designed by the architect Michael Graves and overstuffed couches with Laura Ashley floral or Ralph Lauren classic patterns. To attract yuppie buyers, the homes included features such as kitchen islands, cathedral ceilings, and master-bedroom suites with whirlpool baths. The 1970s open-space concept continued its influence: to encourage family unity in a time when computers and other technological advances were promoting isolation, the kitchen and family room were linked and called a "great room."

Safe, Isolated Neighborhoods. The new houses were built in suburbs, edge cities, or the redesigned suburbs called "planned communities." These planned projects, which grew in popularity in the late 1980s, were meant to assure homeowners pleasant living space, secure property values, and personal safety. Rather like feudal lords, developers controlled architectural style, building materials, size of street signs, and tree planting. They surrounded the community with brick walls and hired security guards to patrol them. The new suburbs, in direct opposition to the 1970s communal-living ideal, reflected a growing sense of insecurity and fear of the street.

Postmodernist Influence. The postmodernist movement and clothing fashions influenced interior designers: variety prevailed. Attention to history was a postmodernist characteristic, as was the renewed interest in color. Designers used Michael Graves's "ice cream" pastels, such as pale apricot, raspberry, and vanilla, or the bold reds, blacks, pinks, and turquoise seen in the clothes of the decade. A prevailing idea was that designs should be expressive and personal, reflecting the owners' interests and backgrounds. Avant-garde furniture designers followed the postmodernist architects by embellishing contemporary pieces with historical references, integrating old with new in interesting, playful ways. Furniture, wall coverings, upholstery fabrics, and dinnerware echoed history.

Office Interiors. As worker-friendly suburban office parks and "corporate campuses" were built, their interiors were designed to be both functional and expressive. The offices became worker-friendly, as well as places to show off new corporate wealth, with elaborately designed cafeterias, athletic facilities, and even museums. One striking example is the General Foods Corporation headquarters in Rye, New York, with its centrally located museum of one thousand historical objects used in the storage, preparation, cooking, and serving of food. The communal area includes a cafeteria illuminated by natural light from a ninety-five-foot atrium. The atrium, with skylight and indoor trees, also became a popular style for central spaces and food courts in malls and other indoor shopping areas.

Alternative Interiors. As in fashion, a counterculture existed in interior design. This minimalistic style — old furniture, wall posters, Chinese paper lamp shades — seen in dormitory rooms and in students' and other struggling urban dwellers' apartments, began as functional and inexpensive. It evolved into a popular Bohemian style that could be manufactured and sold. For instance, the mattress on the floor in place of a bed became the Japanese-inspired futon, a foldable cotton mattress with a frame that could convert into a chair or sofa. Manufacturers refined and multiplied the designs, with frames in wood or metal. Soon futons with elegant covers and matching unfinished furniture were being sold in mainstream stores. Also, in the absence of bookshelves or bureaus,

students used milk crates. This innovation caught on, and soon department stores were selling brightly colored crates as back-to-school furniture. In the 1980s anything could become a commodity.

Sources:

Joel Warren Barna, *The See-Through Years: Creation and Destruction in Texas Architecture and Real Estate 1981–1991* (Houston: Rice University Press, 1992);

Thomas Cowan, *Living Details: More than 500 Ways to Make a House a Home* (New York: Whitney Library of Design, 1986);

Jim Kemp, *American Vernacular: Regional Influences in Architecture and Interior Design* (New York: Viking, 1987);

Mildred F. Schmertz, "Corporate Image," *Architectural Record,* 172 (September 1984): 140–143;

Ray Smith, *Interior Design in 20th Century America: A History* (New York: Harper & Row, 1987).

ELECTRONIC CARS

High-Tech Automobiles. As a result of the Arab-induced oil crisis and rising gasoline prices, cars in the 1970s were built with conservation and moderation in mind. In the 1980s car manufacturers wanted to sell to affluent yuppies, and upscaling became the trend. With the 1980s focus on work, it was no surprise that Americans began equipping their cars with cellular phones. Portable computers and fax machines were popular by the end of the decade, allowing cars to become minioffices. But the focus was also on making cars more fun, comfortable, and luxurious. Oldsmobile offered a $225 dashboard option that included colored bar charts and a zoom-in display to inform the driver of fuel level; Buick offered a screen that let the driver control radio, interior temperature, and trip computer with the touch of a finger. Safety features were also improved with computers; antilock brakes became a popular feature in expensive cars, and Cadillac designed a computerized rearview mirror that diminished nighttime headlight glare. Many automakers began introducing computerized power steering. Of course, with these high-tech improvements came higher prices and a need for more-specialized mechanics; an automotive analyst suggested that "mechanics will have to be trained like doctors." On the other hand, with computers under the car hood to monitor performance and remind the driver of proper maintenance, perhaps mechanics will become less necessary.

Sources:

Jeffrey Kluger, "Working on the Highway," *Discover,* 10 (April 1989): 34, 37;

Peter Petre, "The High-Tech Car Hits the Road," *Fortune,* 111 (29 April 1985): 204–224.

HEADLINE MAKERS

ARQUITECTONICA

1977-

ARCHITECTURAL FIRM

Quick Success. Arquitectonica — the name means "architectural" in Spanish — was responsible for placing Miami on the contemporary architectural map. In 1982, when the firm was only five years old, its row of fashionable condominium towers was completed on Brickell Avenue, and the people who could afford the $400,000 per unit could not move in fast enough. One of these towers, the Atlantis, became an icon — Miami's answer to an Eiffel Tower — partly due to its weekly appearance on the popular television show *Miami Vice*. This $11 million project was preceded by townhouses in Houston, a theater in Key West, an art gallery in Philadelphia, and an amusement park in Nigeria. Arquitectonica had its origins in the collaboration on the Pink House of Laurinda Spear and Bernardo Fort-Brescia, who would later become founding members of the firm, as well as husband and wife. As a student Spear, with the Dutch architect Ren Koolhaas, had received a *Progressive Architecture* award for the Pink House design in 1975; after Spear and Fort-Brescia's revisions, it was built in 1978 and received worldwide attention. The firm was overwhelmed with commissions by 1982.

Young Firm. The original firm was made up of a group of architects from Ivy League schools who were either friends or spouses. Spear, Fort-Brescia, and the other founder, Hervin Romney, were all in their thirties when they established the firm. They established a base in Miami, but to achieve their goal of becoming an international firm they put satellite offices in Lima, Peru; Paris; and Hong Kong.

Flamboyant Style. Arquitectonica, and its lead designers Spear and Fort-Brescia, rejected some themes of the day, especially the historical eclecticism of postmodernism. Like the modernists, they preferred unprecedented, innovative structure, shocking viewers with bright primary colors, mirrors, and abstract geometric shapes with no references to the past. Their style has been called flashy and fantasylike. The prominent architect Philip Johnson described the firm as "the gutsiest team in the business."

Atlantis on Brickell. The Atlantis on Brickell is an arresting sight, with a thirty-seven-foot hole cut out of the middle of the mirrored rectangular building. The cut-out box frames a bright red spiral staircase, yellow walls, and a huge palm tree. Each side of the building is different, but they are all balanced visually with a red triangular roof on one side and yellow triangular balconies on the opposite side. The building holds ninety apartments and six duplexes on twenty floors. Four of the floors open to the cut-out space, which contains a whirlpool, a hot tub, and a tremendous view. The bold, fun building set a new style for Miami Beach.

Courthouse. In Dade County, Florida, in 1988 Arquitectonica redefined American courthouse architecture with its first public building. Not wavering from its modernist stance, the firm designed the courthouse in an abstract style, with skylights, checkerboard floors, trapezoidal windows, and colors such as turquoise and purple. In an unmistakable nod to the Miami Moon motel a mile to the south, the firm placed three crescent-shaped windows in the roadside elevation. Local materials — stucco and tile — were used. Unlike the postmodernists, however, Arquitectonica refused to make regional context a prominent feature of its buildings, instead striving for a classicism that could be repeated in any locale. Fort-Brescia describes the firm's idea of regional architecture: "We do want to create buildings that belong to Miami, but we don't want to imitate past architecture to be contextual. Our buildings try to capture a more intangible spirit of the place. That's what makes them timeless." In 1995 the firm competed against the postmodernist architect Michael Graves in a design competition for a $330 million skyscraper in Times Square in New York City; Arquitectonica won with a forty-seven-story glass tower.

Sources:

Charles Gandee, "Plunging Ahead," *Vogue*, 185 (August 1995): 226–231, 272;

Sidney Le Blanc, *20th Century Architecture* (New York: Watson-Guptill, 1993);

Paul M. Sachner, "Miami Virtue," *Architectural Record*, 176 (May 1988): 122–129.

CHRISTIE BRINKLEY

1953-

SUPERMODEL

1980s Ideal. Athletic, blond, blue-eyed, and classically stylish, Christie Brinkley embodied not only the all-American look of the 1980s but also the fantasy life of many 1980s women. Brinkley had it all: successful career, wealthy husband, and beautiful child. As a supermodel, her life was well publicized: her swimsuit covers and $5–6 million a year salary, her marriage in 1983 to pop musician Billy Joel, and the birth of their daughter, Alexa Ray, in 1985. She became the envy of many professional women, who admired her ability to juggle family and career. Her repeated *Sports Illustrated* covers made her the object of many men's affections, as well. By the end of the decade Brinkley's wide smile and blue eyes had appeared on more than two hundred magazine covers. She held contracts with Noxell and with the Simplicity sewing catalogue, and she had acted in a movie (*National Lampoon's Vacation,* 1983) and a music video (husband Joel's pop hit "Uptown Girl," 1983 — a song he had written for her). Her classic good looks and "regular life" as spouse and mother made her an accessible celebrity and, therefore, one whom people watched for style.

Life. As the daughter of a television producer, Brinkley was primed for a life of luxury and spotlights. She grew up in Malibu, California, but dreamed of living the life of a poor artist in France. In 1972, at age eighteen, she moved to Paris and enrolled in art school. After marrying and working as an illustrator for three years — living the bohemian life of which she had dreamed — she was spotted on the street by an American photographer. She was soon off to Morocco for her first modeling assignment, which she accepted only because she was broke. Despite her hesitancy to join the modeling profession, she would become the only model to have three consecutive *Sports Illustrated* swimsuit edition covers and would make millions of dollars a year. Until their separation in November 1993, Joel and Brinkley lived on Long Island; they also had an apartment on Manhattan's Upper West Side. In April 1994 she survived a helicopter crash while on a skiing trip in Colorado with real-estate developer Ricky Taubman; she and Joel were divorced in August of that year, and in December she married Taubman. They separated seven weeks after the birth of their son, Jack Paris.

Clothes. When Brinkley was pregnant with Alexa Ray in 1985, she was featured in the fashion magazine *Harper's Bazaar* to demonstrate how women could be stylish and attractive in maternity clothes. She became a trendsetter for the growing number of "thirtysomething" women who had begun to have babies in the midst of a busy career. In 1985 *Glamour* featured her in clothes she had helped design and that had her name on the labels. Wearing an oversized pale blue blazer with a T-shirt, khakis, and Perry Ellis loafers, or a miniskirt with loosely cut jacket, she was the picture of American style in the 1980s — comfortable but sexy in menswear-inspired classics. Another outfit — a big shirt worn loosely over cropped pants, with a bandanna tied in her hair — echoed street fashion.

Supermodels. In the 1980s supermodels, once only faces and bodies in magazine advertisements, became personalities in their own right. With their glamorous clothes, perfect bodies, jet-set lifestyles, and $25,000-a-day salaries, they had joined movie stars as celebrities. Designers used them to sell clothes, but in the 1980s the models branched out into music videos, television commercials, and movies. From Lauren Hutton, the successful 1970s gap-toothed model, to Linda Evangelista and Cindy Crawford of the late 1980s, a supermodel could set a trend with a new haircut or even a facial mole. In the 1980s, as a result of the exercise fad and the push for feminine clothes, a more "voluptuous" female shape came into fashion, replacing the ultrathin "Twiggy" models of the previous two decades. By 1989 Brinkley's all-American face was increasingly being replaced in fashion magazines by more ethnically diverse models — the trend of the 1990s.

Sources:

"Christie Brinkley Designs Clothes for You," *Glamour,* 83 (February 1985): 184–187;

Sherry Suib Cohen, "Billion Dollar Beauties," *Ladies' Home Journal,* 105 (August 1988): 136, 158;

Gabé Doppelt, ed., "Talking Fashion," *Vogue,* 181 (August 1991): 309–312;

Bruce Newman, "Rich and Famous," *Sports Illustrated,* 70 (February 1989): 167–169;

"Pretty and Pregnant," *Harper's Bazaar,* no. 3287 (October 1985): 235, 288.

PETER EISENMAN

1932-

ARCHITECT

Rebel Turned Success. Peter Eisenman, long known by his peers as the incomprehensible rebel of architecture, flourished in the late 1980s. He is recognized as a member of the postmodernist group called the "New York Five," who collaborated on an influential 1972 publication. Eisenman had not been as productive as his peers, creating four houses in two decades, but in 1989 he designed (with Richard Trott of Columbus) the Wexner Center for the Visual Arts on the campus of Ohio State University, which resulted in more major commissions. Not only an architect but also an educator and theoretician, he is the leader of the deconstructivism movement in architecture.

Life. Eisenman was born in Newark, New Jersey, in 1932. After completing a bachelor's degree in architecture at Cornell University, he received advanced degrees at Columbia University and Cambridge University. His early influences included the unconventional dean of architecture at the Cooper Union School, who led Eisenman to study other disciplines such as philosophy and literature. In reading the works of the philosopher Jacques Derrida, Eisenman became intrigued by the theories of deconstruction that he would translate into architecture.

Work. Eisenman's early houses, which he designated by Roman numerals, were known for their unexpected and purposeless features, such as stairways leading into a wall, or columns that obstructed furniture. He often designed in the abstract with no clear connection to the sites. Gradually, he began to design more-practical structures; this change can be seen especially in his public buildings. The later buildings, usually designed in collaboration with other architects, were more site-specific, less abstract, and generally more comprehensible.

Wexner Center. The Wexner Center is an example of such a building. Built in Columbus, a city increasingly known for its architecture, the building is actually an addition placed between two existing auditoriums. It is a large building containing four galleries, a film and video theater, performing and exhibition spaces, and an arts library. Most of the structure is underground, but the entranceway is unmistakably announced by a long, white steel framework that recalls scaffolding. And unlike Eisenman's former work, this building was designed with its site in mind: Eisenman paid tribute to the armory that formerly existed in the space by marking the entrance with fragments of its brick tower, and he used grids in his design that seem to extend the street grids of the city and the university, which seem to collide within the arts center.

Deconstructivism. Deconstruction was originally a technique of literary criticism; Eisenman took the theory's main concept — the need to illuminate and break down traditional oppositions to show that there are no dualities — and translated it into architecture and design. His designs, such as the staircase leading into a blank wall, challenged one of the basic assumptions of architecture, that building is intended to be purposeful. In his book *House of Cards* (1987) Eisenman posited that recent buildings had been built only to perpetuate established conventions. His goal was to disrupt these conventions by building architectural contradictions.

Sources:
Kurt Andersen, "A Crazy Building in Columbus," *Time*, 134 (20 November 1989): 84, 89;

Herbert Muschamp, "Art," *Vogue*, 179 (October 1989): 272–275;

Beverly Russell, *Architecture and Design 1970–1990: New Ideas in America* (New York: Abrams, 1989), pp. 75–79.

PERRY ELLIS

1940-1986

FASHION DESIGNER

Styles. Perry Ellis, often grouped with other classic sportswear designers such as Calvin Klein and Ralph Lauren, designed for both men and women. Eternally antitrendy, he refused to join the label fad of the 1980s. He showed much talent in carrying out a theme, whether inspired by an artist such as Sonia Delauney (winter 1986 collection) or by Chinese export ceramics (spring 1986 collection). He was particularly known in the 1980s for his popular female silhouette: an oversized, boxy jacket worn, first, with long pleated skirts and, later in the decade, with shorter, narrower skirts. He borrowed from the 1920s, showing pleated straight linen skirts, loose linen jackets, and jumpers with puffed sleeves, all in white, cream, or pastels. Ellis's clothes captured a young, adventurous spirit, and he was known for the use of natural fabrics and painterly colors. Ellis's loafers and his trademark hand-knitted sweaters in cotton, silk, and cashmere were coveted in the 1980s. He received many Coty American Fashion Critics' awards, including several Return awards. He entered the Hall of Fame for his women's lines in 1981 and for menswear in 1984. He was also recognized by the Menswear Fashion Association of America as Outstanding U.S. Designer in 1983 and 1984.

Life. Ellis was born in Portsmouth, Virginia, in 1940. He earned a B.A. at William and Mary College and an M.A. in retailing from New York University. He began as a sportswear buyer for several companies, learning sketching, pattern making, and fabric selection along the way. In 1975 he expanded his career by designing with the Portfolio Division of Vera Companies, and three years later he established Perry Ellis Sportswear. His menswear company began in 1980.

Expansion. In his years as president of his own company Ellis designed furs, shearling coats, a successful sportswear line for export to Japan, and a less-successful line of children's clothes. He eventually expanded his business to include shoes, leg wear, scarves, and Vogue patterns. His sheets, towels, and blankets for Martex were classically designed, like his clothes. His handmade sweaters and other articles made with fine fabrics and intricate crafting were expensive, but in 1984, like many other designers during the decade, he launched a moderately priced line. He paired with the jeans company Levi Strauss to make the "American Line," which included items such as sixty-dollar sweatshirts. This venture was not as successful as his more-expensive sportswear lines. In May 1986 Ellis, who was too frail to walk down the runway, was given a dramatic standing ovation on receiving an achievement award at a New York fashion show. He died later that month, at age forty-six. It was quietly understood, especially after his last public appearance, that he had suffered from AIDS. Because of the stigma attached to the disease, Ellis never disclosed his illness publicly. His company is now headed by his former design assistant, Patricia Pastor. In 1988 a respected young designer, Marc Jacobs, was selected as head designer.

Sources:

Jennet Conant, "A Designer's Death: AIDS and the Fashion Industry," *Newsweek*, 107 (9 June 1986): 25–26;

Jonathan Moor, *Perry Ellis: A Biography* (New York: St. Martin's Press, 1988).

JAMES GALANOS

1925-

FASHION DESIGNER

Luxury, Endurance. James Galanos, known as "Jimmy," is considered one of the finest American designers working today. Galanos's clothes are known for their luxurious quality, flawless crafting, and imported fabrics. He prides himself on creating clothes that endure: "I have women tell me that they still wear dresses that are fifteen, twenty years old. Women who wear my clothes year after year wait for me." Galanos sells his expensive lines in specialty shops around the world, making personal appearances with his assistant and their stainless steel standup trunks to show gowns that range from $1,500 to $15,000; these appearances can result in $500,000 in sales. His clients include Diana Ross and Nancy Reagan.

Galanos and Nancy Reagan. Although Galanos had been well known in the fashion world since the 1950s, his name became more familiar when Nancy Reagan became first lady. His elegant, elaborately made clothes were in great demand by wealthy fashion enthusiasts in the decade of opulence, and Nancy Reagan was no exception. But Mrs. Reagan and Jimmy Galanos were acquainted long before she wore his gowns to the balls at both of her husband's inaugurations, as is evident from the signed photograph of the Reagans in Galanos's office. She chose a white satin one-shouldered gown for the first ball and a straight, jeweled dress with a bolero top four years later.

Life. Born in Philadelphia in 1925, Galanos was the son of Greek immigrants. His mother and his father, a frustrated artist, ran a restaurant in southern New Jersey, where Galanos had his first glimpses of well-dressed women. A shy boy in a family of three sisters, by the age of ten Galanos had decided to become a designer. After a few months at Taphagan School of Fashion in New York, he began selling his sketches at five dollars apiece to Seventh Avenue manufacturers. He worked for a time in Los Angeles, starting his own business in 1951. His lines include hats, shoes, hosiery, and accessories, all designed by Galanos. In 1980 he launched a perfume that cost $100 an ounce. In 1984 the Council of Fashion Designers of America recognized his many years of producing high-quality fashion with a Lifetime Achievement Award.

The 1980s. Galanos is wary of fashion trends, preferring to design classic, enduring clothes for women. In the 1980s his styles reflected some of the choices and paradoxes that dominated the decade. At middecade he combined youthful long and short denim skirts with elegant ivory satin shirts. He said in 1985, "Today women want inventive clothes that transcend trends, clothes that will last." He watches trendy street fashion with interest but at a distance: "Today many designers make clothes that are extreme, clothes that are simply statements of fashion news [but] I am happy making understated clothes or dazzling embroidered dresses, whichever it takes to make a woman beautiful."

Source:

Andre Leon Talley, "A Certain Quality: Galanos," *Vogue*, 175 (June 1985): 130–133.

FRANK O. GEHRY

1929-

ARCHITECT

Cheapscape Architect. Frank Gehry's radical and unusual style is not easily defined, although he has long referred to the past, borrowing from both Eastern and Western architectural traditions, and is usually ranked as a postmodernist. His ties to minimalist and conceptual art are apparent, as well. He blends architecture with qualities of art and sculpture, creating playful homes and buildings that push the limits of design. He is especially known for his use of inexpensive and unusual building materials, coining his own term for this style: "cheapscape architecture." One of his goals is to create a look of incompletion. This unfinished, minimalist quality, coupled with materials such as metal panels, plywood, and chain-link fences, often gives his buildings the look of industrial structures rather than the homes and museums that they in fact are. Although Gehry works in an avant-garde, and even antiarchitectural manner, he has increasingly designed major public buildings and has received international recognition and respect. His steady work in the 1980s is reflected in his receipt of the prestigious international Pritzker Prize in 1987.

His Business. Gehry established his own practice in 1962 in Santa Monica, California. His interest in industrial building materials began when he was a GI at Fort Benning, Georgia. There, assigned to put up temporary buildings, he became familiar with the materials he would use to create his distinct unfinished, industrial look. In the 1960s and 1970s his work appealed to the antiestablishment/antiarchitecture mood, but by the 1980s he was receiving commissions that indicated that he had been accepted by the mainstream. His inexpensive materials and focus on minimal construction may have appealed to people concerned with conservation, recycling, and other environmental trends of the decade.

Understanding Gehry. The usual notions of beauty and design rarely apply to Gehry's buildings. As Gehry explained his style: "I prefer the sketch quality . . . the appearance of 'in progress' rather than the presumption of total resolution and finality." He also approaches each building "as a sculptural object," inviting the viewers' interpretations of and interaction with the work. Gehry made a statement about his seriousness and devotion to art as well as to cheapness when he refused to allow some of his cardboard furniture to be sold as expensive pop-art objects in upscale galleries.

1980s Work. In the 1980s Gehry designed diverse types of buildings, including artists' studios, a bank office, homes, and an amphitheater, but his most popular buildings include the California Aerospace Hall (1984) and Loyola Law School (1984), both in Los Angeles. The Aerospace Hall arrests the viewer with an unexpected airplane — a Lockheed F-104 Starfighter — attached to an outside wall, angled as if in flight. Gehry's design consists of two parts: the larger is a seven-sided hangar covered with angling riveted sheet metal; the other is a more traditional museum building in white stucco, but the Starfighter breaks up this traditional look and gives the building a dramatic appearance. For the law school Gehry designed six buildings: three lecture halls, an administrative office building, a classroom building, and a bookstore. The style is typically Gehry, inventive yet unfinished looking, with exposed construction and the use of plywood. A greenhouse in the style of a Romanesque temple rests above the classrooms, with jagged stairs leading to it; thus, a historical reference appropriate to a site for legal education is integrated with Gehry's long-standing concern with the environment. Such innovative fusions made Gehry one of the most respected architects of the decade.

Sources:
Beverly Russell, *Architecture and Design 1970–1990: New Ideas in America* (New York: Abrams, 1989), pp. 72–74;

Stamm Shapiro, "A Minimalist Architecture of Allusion: Current Projects of Frank Gehry," *Architectural Record,* 171 (June 1983): 114–125.

NORMA KAMALI

1945-

FASHION DESIGNER

Cotton Fleece Line. In 1980 Norma Kamali became a household name as a result of her collection of cotton fleece coordinates inspired by dance and exercise clothes. Her line reflected the essence of 1980s clothes for women: comfortable, body-conscious, and affordable. The separates, made of sweat-clothes material, included minis, leggings, and big-shouldered tops in unassuming gray, pink, or striped fleece. They were widely copied. Kamali became particularly well known for her giant removable shoulder pads, a fad that lasted for the whole decade.

Life and Business. Of Basque and Lebanese descent, Kamali was born Norma Arraez in New York City on 27 June 1945 and grew up on the Upper East Side, where her father owned a candy store. She studied fashion illustration at the Fashion Institute of Technology, graduating in 1964. With her husband, Eddie Kamali, she opened a small shop in 1969, selling European imports and her own funky designs. In 1974 they moved to a larger store on Madison Avenue; by then Kamali's designs were less funky and more delicate, featuring suits and lace dresses. Following her divorce in 1977 she established her own retail boutique and wholesale firm, OMO (On My Own). By 1983 she was doing so well that she moved the store into a multilevel building with a ninety-nine-year lease.

Self-Sufficient. She continued to design clothes for her fleece line, produced by Jones Apparel Group, until 1986, when a dispute with the International Ladies' Garment Workers' Union erupted. Accused of using illegal aliens at five dollars an hour, Kamali insisted that "All my contractors . . . are legal contractors, and my sample makers earn $400–$500 a week." Rather than agree to the union's demand to hire only its contractors, she opted to terminate her affiliation with Jones Apparel and take control of all of her production. Union members began picketing her stores the day she refused their demands, and some persisted until 1987. To stay in business, Kamali decided to design only what she could produce and sell in her Fifty-sixth Street store, with the exception of a licensed line of bathing suits that she would produce in Italy. That meant terminating the fleece line.

Revivals. Although her fleece coordinate line was contemporary-looking and reflected the 1980s exercise trend, Kamali was also inspired by the past. Her favorite decade was the 1940s, as seen in her shirred, draped siren dresses and bathing suits with snoods and platform shoes. But she also evoked the 1930s with long, slinky dresses and the 1950s with her popular shirtwaist dress in diverse fabrics — eyelet, printed rayon, and crushed velvet. She is also known for her quilted down coats and has created lingerie and children's clothes.

Awards. Kamali's work was well recognized in the 1980s. In 1981 she was awarded the Coty American Fashion Critics' "Winnie," followed by its Return award in 1982. She entered the Hall of Fame in 1983. In 1982 and 1985 she received awards from the Council of Fashion Designers of America, and in 1984 and 1986 she was recognized by the Fashion Institute of Design and Merchandising and by the Fashion Group.

Sources:

"ILGWU vows to keep picketing Kamali," *Women's Wear Daily*, 18 May 1987, p. 15;

Irene Daria, *Women's Wear Daily*, 5 December 1986, p. 15;

Caroline Rennolds Milbank, *New York Fashion: The Evolution of American Fashion* (New York: Abrams, 1989);

Anne Stegemeyer, *Who's Who in Fashion* (New York: Fairchild, 1988).

PEOPLE IN THE NEWS

In 1988 and 1989 **Barbara Bush** and **Ivana Trump** were referred to by the fashion commentator Mr. Blackwell as "Fabulous Fashion Independents."

In 1984 **Cher,** known for her bold, alluring Bob Mackie–designed dresses and her overall fashion individuality, was featured in an article in *Glamour* in which she expressed her desire to be taken seriously: "I'm not what I wear," she said.

By 1986 supermodel **Cindy Crawford,** 20, had made curvier, "voluptuous" bodies and facial moles acceptable, even sexy.

In 1987 **James Ingo Freed** of I. M. Pei and Associates unveiled his design for the U.S. Holocaust Museum.

In 1982 **Halston** designed a line of reasonably priced clothes for J. C. Penney. The clothes sold, but Halston's top-scale lines suffered as a result.

In 1981 internationally known beauty **Carolyn Herrara** started a couture-caliber clothing business in New York. She designed Caroline Kennedy's wedding dress.

French fashion designer **Jean Paul Gaultier** shocked American critics with his theatrical clothes that explore the myths of masculinity.

In 1989 architect **Michael Graves** unveiled his third proposal for an addition to the Whitney Museum in New York City. Graves's previous designs would have doubled the height and extended an ornamental pink granite facade to both buildings. Those designs were thought to detract from the main building.

In 1987 **Marc Jacobs** received first Perry Award given by Council of Fashion of America in remembrance of designer Perry Ellis, who had died the previous year. The following year Jacobs was hired as head designer for the Perry Ellis firm.

Throughout the decade **Betsy Johnson** showed continued success with outlandish and opulent clothes made of spandex blends and stretch lace with striking floral, striped, or fish patterns. Her clothes inspired many copies during the decade.

In 1985 **Donna Karan** (formerly of Anne Klein and Company) presented her first independent clothing collection based on the bodysuit and clothes that travel well. Her collection established her as a new star, and in 1988 she launched the DKNY line of less expensive clothing aimed at women's leisure needs. Her clothes were described as "sexy wearability with minimum fuss."

In 1982 high-quality clothing company **Anne Klein** initiated A. Klein II, a less expensive line.

Calvin Klein created provocative, sexually explicit, and controversial advertisements for his underwear line, jeans, and perfume, Obsession.

In 1983 designer **Karl Lagerfeld** left Chloe to launch his own label, KL, and to become chief designer of Chanel couture.

In 1989 **Kenneth Jay Lane,** designer of Barbara Bush's signature pearls, produced a new collection of necklaces for dogs and cats.

Clothing designer **Ralph Lauren** introduced his first housewares collection in 1983, including sheets, towels, blankets, tableware, and accessories.

In 1982 **Bob Mackie** launched his own ready-to-wear fashion company, having spent the last two decades primarily designing costumes for television shows such as *The Carol Burnett Show* and *The Sonny and Cher Comedy Hour*. He helped Cher dazzle the public with beaded, boldly baring dresses.

In 1986 architect **Robert Stern** hosted Public Broadcasting System's *Pride of Place: Building the American Dream,* a survey of American architecture.

In 1985 **Diana Vreeland,** former editor of *Vogue* magazine, was recognized for her contributions to fashion with an award given by the Council of Fashion Designers of America (CDFA).

In 1987 American designer **Zoran** premiered his ten-piece line that will fit into a small suitcase. His clothes attracted the fashion world (which quickly copied them) with their efficiency and unobtrusive quality but outraged others because of their high prices.

AWARDS

COTY AMERICAN FASHION CRITICS' AWARD

(The "Winnie" — to an individual selected as the leading designer of American women's fashions; award was discontinued in 1985)

1980 — Michaele Volbracht
1981 — Norma Kamali
　　　　Ronaldus Shamask
1982 — Adri
1983 — Willi Smith
1984 — Adrienne Vittadini

RETURN AWARD

(Award to a designer whose work merits a top award for a second time)

1980 — Perry Ellis
1981 — Donna Karan and Dell'Olio for Anne Klein
1982 — Norma Kamali
　　　　Sal Cesarani
1983 — Perry Ellis*
1984 — Jhane Barnes*

* for Menswear

HALL OF FAME

("Winnie" designer chosen three separate times as the best of the year)

1980 — Alexander Julian
1981 — Perry Ellis
1982 — Donna Karan and Louis Dell'Olio for Anne Klein
1983 — Norma Kamali
1984 — Perry Ellis*

* for Hall of Fame for Menswear

MENSWEAR

1980 — Jhane Barnes
1981 — Perry Ellis
1982 — Jeffrey Banks
1983 — Alan Flusser
1984 — Andrew Fezza

SPECIAL AWARDS

(Honoring noteworthy contributions to fashion)

1980 — Jeffrey Aronoff
　　　　Ron Chereskin
　　　　Alex Mate and Lee Brooks
　　　　Stewart Richer for Free Spirited Fashions
1981 — Fabrice
　　　　Hot Sox
　　　　Robert Lee Morris
　　　　Laura Pearson of Tijuca
1982 — Jackson Allen and Tim Veness
　　　　Susan Bennis and Warren Edwards
　　　　Robert Cornstock
　　　　Jay Lord Hatters
　　　　Ted Muehling
　　　　Patricia Underwood
1983 — Carlos Falchi
　　　　Susan Horton
　　　　Selma Weiser, Barbara Weiser, and Jon Weiser for Chivirari Workshop
1984 — Milena Canonero
　　　　Robin Kahn

Barry Kieselstein

M and J Savitt

* for Special Awards in Menswear

AMERICAN INSTITUTE OF ARCHITECTS (AIA)

AIA Gold Medal (Awarded annually to an individual for distinguished service to the architectural profession or to the institute. It is the institute's highest honor.)

1980 — No Award

1981 — Josep Lluis Sert

1982 — Romaldo Giurgola

1983 — Nathaniel A. Owings

1984 — No Award

1985 — William Caudill

1986 — Arthur C. Erickson

1987 — No Award

1988 — No Award

1989 — Joseph Esherick

AMERICAN SOCIETY OF INTERIOR DESIGNERS

ASID Designer of Distinction Award

1980 — Everett Brown

1981 — Barbara D'Arcy

1982 — Edward J. Wormley

1983 — Edward J. Perrault

1984 — Michael Taylor

1985 — Norma DeHaan

1986 — Rita St. Clair

1987 — James Merrick Smith

1988 — Louis Tregre

1989 — Joseph Braswell

NATIONAL ACADEMY OF DESIGN FOR INTERIOR DESIGN

Thomas B. Clarke Prize

1980 — Jeffrey Kronsnoble

1981 — Mary Beth McKenzie

1982 — Jack Kramer

1983 — No Award

1984 — Alan Feltus

1985 — No Award

1986 — Alinor Schnurr

1987 — No Award

1988 — Audrey A. Ushenko

1989 — No Award

DEATHS

Laura Ashley, 60, English designer and distributor of interior design products and women's clothing, 17 September 1985.

Pierre Balmaine, 68, French designer of quietly elegant clothes for women, 29 June 1982.

Cecil Beaton, 76, English artist and costume and set designer who created sets for many productions, winning Academy Awards in 1965 for costumes and sets for the film *My Fair Lady,* 18 January 1980.

Aldo Cipullo, 48, Italian-born jewelry designer who, while working at Cartier, designed the gold "love bracelet," 31 January 1984.

Enzo Ferrari, 90, Italian sports-car manufacturer, 4 August 1988.

Anne Fogarty, 62, fashion designer best known for her crinoline petticoats under full-skirted shirtdresses with tiny waists, and lounging overalls, 15 January 1981.

R. Buckminster Fuller, 88, industrial designer and futurist who held more than two thousand patents for inventions meant to be solutions to social problems, 1 July 1983.

Rudi Gernreich, 63, Austrian-born fashion designer known as one of the most original American designers of the 1950s and 1960s, whose daring clothes — such as the topless bathing suit — were often controversial, 21 April 1985.

Philippe Guibourge, 55, French designer for Chanel and Christian Dior, 7 March 1986.

Harry Russell Hitchcock, 83, architectural historian and teacher who, with Philip Johnson, coined the term *International Style,* 19 February 1987.

Tina Leser, 76, fashion designer known for her use of exotic fabrics from the Orient and Hawaii, 24 January 1986.

Raymond Fernand Loewy, 93, French-born U.S. industrial designer who established his field as a profession with designs for refrigerators, cars, buses, and spacecraft, 14 July 1986.

Jean Schlumberger, 80, award-winning jewelry designer whose imaginative designs attracted clients such as the Duchess of Windsor, 29 August 1987.

Josep Lluis Sert, 81, international city and housing pioneer who established urban design program at Harvard University, 15 March 1983.

Willi Smith, 39, fashion designer whose company, Williwear, created classic clothes for women and men that were fun and functional, 17 April 1987.

Chester Weinberg, 55, fashion designer who was known for simple, sophisticated designs, 24 April 1985.

Minoru Yamasaki, 74, architect who designed New York City's twin-towered World Trade Center, the world's second-tallest building, 2 February 1986.

PUBLICATIONS

Charles Boyce, *Dictionary of Furniture* (New York: Facts On File/Holt, 1985);

Lois Fenton, *Dress for Excellence* (New York: Rawson Associates, 1986);

Paul Goldberg, *On the Rise: Architecture and Design in a Postmodern Age* (New York: Penguin, 1983);

Simon Jervis, *The Penguin Dictionary of Design and Designers* (London: Penguin, 1984);

Jim Kemp, *American Vernacular: Regional Influence in Architecture and Interior Design* (New York: Viking, 1987);

Diane Maddex, ed., *Master Builders: A Guide to Famous American Architects* (Washington, D.C.: Preservation Press, 1985);

Richard Martin and Harold Koda, *Jocks and Nerds: Men's Style in the Twentieth Century* (New York: Rizzoli, 1989);

Colin McDowell, *McDowell's Dictionary of Twentieth Century Fashion* (London: Muller, 1984);

Caroline Rennolds Milbank, *Couture: The Great Designers* (New York: Stewart, Tabouri & Chang, 1985);

Milbank, *New York Fashion: The Evolution of American Fashion* (New York: Abrams, 1989);

Jane Mulvagh, *Vogue History of 20th Century Fashion* (London & New York: Viking, 1988);

Lisa Phillips and others, *High Style: Twentieth Century American Design* (New York: Whitney Museum of American Art, 1985);

Ray Smith, *Interior Design in 20th Century America: A History* (New York: Harper & Row, 1987);

Anne Stegemeyer, *Who's Who in Fashion* (New York: Fairchild, 1988);

Architectural Forum, periodical;

Architectural Record, periodical;

Art in America, periodical;

Art News, periodical;

Glamour, periodical;

Global Architecture, periodical;

Harper's Bazaar, periodical;

House and Garden, periodical;

Ladies' Home Journal, periodical;

Mademoiselle, periodical;

Newsweek, periodical;

People, periodical;

Progressive Architecture, periodical;

Time, periodical;

Vogue, periodical.

GOVERNMENT AND POLITICS

by ROBERT M. ROOD and KAREN L. ROOD

CONTENTS

Sidebars and tables are listed in italics.

1980

4 Jan. President Jimmy Carter reacts to the Soviet invasion of Afghanistan on 29 December 1979 by withdrawing the SALT II arms-control treaty from consideration by the U.S. Senate. He also places an embargo on the sale of grain and some types of electronic equipment to the Soviet Union.

7 Jan. President Carter signs a bill guaranteeing loans to bail out the Chrysler Corporation.

2 Feb. The news media report the results of a two-year sting operation (code name: Abscam) in which an FBI agent posing as a wealthy Arab offered bribes to elected officials. Among those arrested and eventually convicted on bribery or related charges are Sen. Harrison Williams Jr. (D–N.J.) and Representatives John W. Jenrette Jr. (D–S.C.), Richard Kelly (R–Fla.), Raymond Lederer (D–Pa.), John M. Murphy (D–N.Y.), Michael Myers (D–Pa.), and Frank Thompson Jr. (D–N.J.).

2 Apr. President Carter signs the Crude Oil Windfall Profits Tax Act of 1980.

12 Apr. At the urging of President Carter, the U.S. Olympic Committee votes to boycott the 1980 summer games in Moscow to protest the Soviet invasion of Afghanistan.

24–25 Apr. A U.S. strike force fails to rescue fifty-three Americans held hostage since Iranian militants seized the U.S. embassy in Tehran on 4 November 1979.

1 July President Carter signs a bill deregulating the trucking industry.

20 Aug. The Defense Department announces the development of the Stealth aircraft, which can elude detection by radar.

14 Oct. President Carter signs a bill deregulating the railroads.

4 Nov. Republican Ronald Reagan is elected president of the United States with 51.6 percent of the popular vote to 41.7 percent for incumbent president Jimmy Carter and 6.7 percent for third-party candidate John Anderson.

1981

20 Jan. The Iran hostages are freed.

Ronald Reagan is inaugurated president of the United States. In his first official act he freezes all government hiring.

28 Jan. President Reagan lifts most oil price controls.

29 Jan. President Reagan orders a sixty-day freeze on all pending federal regulations.

18 Feb. In his State of the Union Address President Reagan calls for tax reduction and budget cuts of $41.4 billion.

Mar. President Reagan directs the CIA to assist "Contra" guerrilla forces opposed to the Marxist Sandinista government of Nicaragua.

6 Mar. President Reagan announces the cutting of thirty-seven thousand government jobs.

30 Mar. John W. Hinckley Jr. shoots President Reagan in the chest as he walks to his limousine after delivering a speech at the Washington Hilton Hotel. Press Secretary James S. Brady receives a serious but nonfatal head wound, and two law-enforcement officers are also shot.

11 Apr.   President Reagan returns to the White House and a restricted work schedule after surgery and eleven days of hospitalization resulting from the 30 March assassination attempt.

24 Apr.   President Reagan lifts the Soviet grain embargo.

7 July   President Reagan nominates Sandra Day O'Connor to be the first woman justice on the U.S. Supreme Court.

19 Aug.   Libyan and U.S. jets clash over the Gulf of Sidra, and two Libyan planes are shot down. The United States considers the gulf to be in international waters, but Libya claims it as territorial waters.

29 Sept.   President Reagan orders the U.S. Coast Guard to turn back boatloads of Haitian refugees fleeing their country without proper immigration papers.

6 Nov.   President Reagan says that the federal budget cannot be balanced by 1994 as he had hoped.

18 Nov.   President Reagan proposes that the United States and the Soviet Union reduce the number of intermediate-range missiles they have in Europe.

23 Nov.   President Reagan vetoes a bill to pay for the current operation of the federal government. Congress votes to continue funding at present levels until 15 December.

1982

- The United States adopts a Defense Guidance Plan, which outlines a $1.6 trillion increase in defense expenditures over a five-year period.

26 Jan.   In his State of the Union Address President Reagan proposes a "New Federalism," a transfer of social programs to the states.

6 Apr.   Secretary of State Alexander M. Haig Jr. says the United States will not rule out the first use of nuclear weapons.

9 May   President Reagan suggests that the United States and the Soviet Union begin Strategic Arms Reduction Talks (START) to negotiate the reduction of each nation's nuclear warheads by one-third.

June   President Reagan proposes that NATO and the Warsaw Pact each reduce their conventional forces to nine hundred thousand.

25 June   Haig resigns as secretary of state, and the president names George P. Shultz to replace him.

29 June   START talks begin in Geneva.

5 Aug.   The House of Representatives votes down a nuclear-freeze resolution.

19 Aug.   Congress approves a tax increase of $98.3 billion.

25 Aug.   U.S. Marines land in Lebanon to help multinational forces enforce a peace agreement reached after an Israeli invasion of that nation in June.

9–10 Sept.   Congress overrides President Reagan's veto of a $14.1 billion appropriations bill.

1 Oct.   The House of Representatives votes down a proposed constitutional amendment requiring a balanced federal budget.

1 Dec.   Unemployment reaches 10.7 percent, the highest rate since 1940.

8 Dec.	Congressman Edward Boland (D–Mass.) successfully sponsors an amendment making it illegal to use U.S. funds to overthrow the Sandinista government of Nicaragua. Congress renews the amendment in 1983, 1984, and 1985, extending it through the 1986 fiscal year.
23 Dec.	Congress approves a five-cent-per-gallon gasoline tax increase.

1983

21 Jan.	President Reagan tells Congress that El Salvador has made progress in reducing human rights abuses and is therefore entitled to military aid.
3 Mar.	The State Department announces that the number of military advisers in El Salvador will be increased from thirty-five to fifty-five.
21 Mar.	William D. Ruckelshaus is named to head to Environmental Protection Agency, replacing Anne Gorsuch Burford, who resigned on 9 March.
23 Mar.	President Reagan proposes the development of a defense shield — at least partly based in space — to intercept incoming missiles. Formally called the Strategic Defense Initiative (SDI), this proposal becomes popularly known as "Star Wars."
25 Mar.	Congress passes legislation to prevent the Social Security system from going bankrupt.
Apr.	The American public learns that the CIA assisted a Contra attack on Nicaraguan oil terminals.
18 Apr.	A terrorist bombing severely damages the U.S. embassy in Beirut, Lebanon, and kills sixty-three people.
8 July	Congress repeals the 10 percent withholding tax on dividend and interest income.
28 July	The United States and the Soviet Union agree on terms for a five-year Soviet purchase of American grain.
6 Aug.	The United States sends military aircraft to the government of Chad, which is fighting rebels backed by Libya.
29 Aug.	Two U.S. Marines are killed during heavy fighting in Beirut. They are the first American casualties in Lebanon.
23 Oct.	A suicide bombing at the U.S. Marine Corps compound in Beirut kills 241 marines and sailors.
25 Oct.	U.S. troops invade Grenada after the assassination of Grenadan prime minister Maurice Bishop during a coup led by militant leftist Gen. Hudson Austin.
23 Nov.	Soviet representatives walk out of ongoing arms-control talks in Geneva, Switzerland, to protest U.S. deployment of cruise missiles in Europe.

1984

Jan.	The CIA helps to mine Nicaraguan harbors.
11 Jan.	A blue-ribbon presidential commission headed by former secretary of state Henry Kissinger recommends an $8 billion increase in economic assistance and further military aid for El Salvador.

22 Jan.	Attorney General William French Smith resigns pending congressional approval of his successor, Edwin Meese III, whose confirmation hearings are suspended in March pending an inquiry into his financial dealings.
7 Feb.	President Reagan orders the withdrawal of U.S. Marines from Lebanon.
20 Mar.	The Senate blocks a constitutional amendment requiring prayer in public schools. Proponents garner a majority of the votes cast (56–44), but they fall eleven votes short of the necessary two-thirds margin.
9 Apr.	Nicaragua asks the International Court of Justice to rule that U.S. aid to the Contra rebels and its role in mining Nicaraguan harbors is illegal. On 10 May the court orders the United States to pay reparations to Nicaragua and to refrain from further involvement with the Contras. The United States contends that the court has no jurisdiction on the matter.
10 Apr.	By a vote of 84–12 the Senate passes a nonbinding resolution opposing the use of federal funds to mine Nicaraguan harbors. Two days later the House approves it by 281–111.
17 July	Congress passes a bill that will cut federal highway funding for states that fail to raise their minimum drinking age to twenty-one.
20 Sept.	The new U.S. embassy building in Beirut is destroyed in a terrorist bombing. Two Americans are among the twenty-three people killed.
	Edwin Meese III is cleared of charges of financial misdealings.
26 Sept.	Congress passes a law requiring tougher health warnings on cigarette packs.
1 Oct.	Secretary of Labor Raymond J. Donovan is indicted on charges of grand larceny and keeping false records.
6 Nov.	President Reagan is elected to a second term in a landslide victory over Democrat Walter Mondale, who wins only the District of Columbia and his home state of Minnesota.
26 Nov.	The United States and Iraq resume diplomatic ties severed since 1967.
	The International Court of Justice rules that, despite U.S. claims to the contrary, it does have jurisdiction over the case Nicaragua has brought against the United States.
5 Dec.	The House Intelligence Committee charges that the CIA violated federal law in some of its aid to Contra rebels.

1985

7–8 Jan.	Secretary of State George P. Shultz and Soviet foreign minister Andrey A. Gromyko hold preliminary arms talks in Geneva. The meeting is the first U.S.–Soviet arms discussion in thirteen months.
8 Jan.	President Reagan announces that White House Chief of Staff James A. Baker III and Treasury Secretary Donald T. Regan will trade jobs.
18 Jan.	President Reagan announces that the United States will boycott further International Court of Justice proceedings regarding the Nicaraguan suit against the United States.

20 Jan. President Reagan takes the oath of office marking the beginning of his second term. Because of the bitter cold, public ceremonies are postponed until 21 January.

6 Feb. In his State of the Union Address President Reagan calls for cuts in domestic spending and more military spending.

23 Feb. The Senate confirms Meese's appointment as attorney general more than a year after his nomination.

12 Mar. The United States and the Soviet Union reopen formal arms-control talks in Geneva.

25 Mar. A Soviet sentry shoots and kills Maj. Arthur D. Nicholson Jr., an American army officer on a reconnaissance mission in Potsdam, East Germany. The United States condemns the shooting as "totally unjustified."

Spring Israeli intelligence tells the United States that Shiite Muslims will exchange western hostages for arms for Iran.

26 Apr. The Soviet Union and east European nations renew the Warsaw Pact treaty for twenty years.

1 May The United States bans trade with Nicaragua.

July At the urging of the Reagan administration, Congress repeals the Clark Amendment of 1975, which has prevented the United States from aiding either side in the Angolan civil war. The Reagan administration begins sending aid to the UNITA faction, which is also backed by France, Saudi Arabia, and South Africa.

Aug. President Reagan agrees to ship antitank missiles to Iran, with the hope of winning the release of American hostages. After the missiles are delivered only one hostage, Rev. Benjamin Weir, is released.

29 Aug. President Reagan orders a fifteen-month freeze on the pay of federal civil servants.

Nov. At the urging of Lt. Col. Oliver North and with the covert assistance of the CIA, a shipment of Hawk missiles is delivered to Iran.

19–21 Nov. At a summit in Geneva, President Reagan and Soviet premier Mikhail Gorbachev agree to meet again but reach no agreements on arms control because of a failure to resolve differences over Star Wars.

11 Dec. Congress passes the Gramm-Rudman Act requiring a balanced federal budget.

1986

1 Jan. President Reagan and Premier Gorbachev deliver televised New Year's messages to one another's nations.

7 Jan. President Reagan declares a state of emergency between the United States and Libya, ordering U.S. oil companies out of Libya and ending trade and transportation between the two nations.

25 Feb. The United States recognizes the Philippine government of Corazon Aquino after the Reagan administration at first refused to acknowledge that outgoing president Ferdinand Marcos has attempted to prevent her election victory through vote fraud.

24–25 Mar.	Libya fires two missiles at U.S. ships on maneuvers in the Gulf of Sidra; the United States retaliates by sinking three Libyan patrol boats and destroying a coastal radar installation.
5 Apr.	A bomb explodes in a West Berlin nightclub, killing an American army sergeant and injuring fifty other American servicemen and 230 civilians. The CIA charges that the Libyan government was behind the attack.
14–15 Apr.	American planes bomb Libya.
25 June	The House approves $100 million in humanitarian and economic aid to the Contras.
27 June	The International Court of Justice rules that U.S. aid to the Contras is illegal and again orders payment of reparations. The United States ignores the ruling.
7 July	The Supreme Court declares unconstitutional a key provision of the Gramm-Rudman Act that would allow the comptroller general to decide precise spending cuts in each federal department.
15 July	U.S. troops are sent to Bolivia to help in operations against cocaine smugglers.
15 Sept.	President Reagan orders drug testing for federal employees in sensitive jobs.
27 Sept.	Congress passes the most sweeping tax-reform bill since the 1940s.
2 Oct.	Congress overrides President Reagan's veto of the Comprehensive Anti-Apartheid Act, which condemns racial separation in South Africa, institutes an embargo on most South African imports, and bans most American investment in that nation.
11–12 Oct.	President Reagan and Premier Gorbachev meet in Reykjavík, Iceland, to discuss reactivating stalled arms-control talks in Geneva and to draw up an agenda for a 1987 meeting in Washington, D.C.
3 Nov.	A Lebanese newspaper with ties to Iran reveals that contrary to its stated policy of not negotiating with terrorists, the United States has been trading arms for hostages.
6 Nov.	President Reagan signs a sweeping immigration-law reform bill that prohibits the hiring of illegal aliens and offers amnesty to those already in the United States.
13 Nov.	President Reagan says the United States has sent Iran a few defensive weapons and spare parts, but he denies any attempt to exchange weapons for hostages.
19 Nov.	President Reagan acknowledges missile sales to Iran and asks Attorney General Edwin Meese to investigate.
23 Nov.	Meese announces that he has discovered that proceeds from the sale of arms to Iran have been diverted to the Contras.
26 Nov.	President Reagan appoints former senator John Tower, former secretary of state Edmund Muskie, and former national security adviser Brent Scowcroft as a commission to investigate what has become know as the Iran-Contra affair.
7 Dec.	U.S. Army helicopters carry Honduran troops into battle against Nicaraguan military forces that pursued Contra rebels into Honduras.

1987

4 Feb.	Congress overrides President Reagan's veto of a $20 billion Clean Water Act. It is identical to an act he vetoed successfully in 1986.
26 Feb.	The Tower Commission report places chief blame for the Iran-Contra affair on National Security Council director Robert McFarlane, Lt. Col. Oliver North, Adm. John Poindexter, and former CIA director William Casey. It also criticizes the president for remaining too remote from the planning process.
27 Feb.	White House Chief of Staff Donald Regan resigns and is replaced by former Senate majority leader Howard Baker of Tennessee.
4 Mar.	In a televised speech President Reagan accepts "full responsibility" for the Iran-Contra affair. At a 19 March news conference he denies knowing that profits from Iranian arms sales went to the Contras.
2 Apr.	Congress overrides President Reagan's veto of an $87.5 billion highway and transit bill that also allows states to raise speed limits to 65 MPH on interstate highways in sparsely populated areas.
17 Apr.	President Reagan imposes a 100 percent import tariff on personal computers, television sets, and power tools from Japan in response to allegations that Japan violated an export agreement on computer chips.
5 May–3 Aug.	Congress holds public hearings on the Iran-Contra affair.
15 May	President Reagan says he was aware of private efforts to help the Contras.
17 May	An Iraqi jet mistakenly fires a missile at the USS *Stark,* one of the ships escorting Iraqi oil tankers through the Persian Gulf, which has been mined by Iran during the Iran-Iraq War. Thirty-seven American sailors are killed.
8 June	Reagan lifts 17 percent of the tariff imposed on the Japanese in April.
16 Oct.	An Iranian missile strikes a Kuwaiti oil tanker sailing under the American flag in the Persian Gulf. The navy retaliates three days later by destroying an Iranian oil rig.
23 Oct.	The Senate rejects the nomination of Robert Bork to the U.S. Supreme Court.
11 Nov.	President Reagan nominates Anthony M. Kennedy to the Supreme Court. He is confirmed on 2 February 1988.
18 Nov.	In its final report on the Iran-Contra hearings Congress criticizes those involved in the operation for "secrecy, deception and disdain for the law."
8–10 Dec.	During a summit meeting in Washington, D.C., President Reagan and Premier Gorbachev sign the Intermediate Nuclear Forces (INF) Treaty, agreeing to eliminate intermediate-range weapons from their nuclear arsenals.

1988

4 Feb.	Two federal grand juries in Florida indict Panamanian dictator Manuel Noriega on drug-trafficking charges.
11 Mar.	McFarlane pleads guilty on four counts of illegally withholding information from Congress in connection with the Iran-Contra affair. On 3 March 1989 he is sentenced to two years' probation and fined $20,000.
16 Mar.	A federal grand jury in Washington, D.C., indicts Poindexter, North, and two others on charges relating to their involvement in the Iran-Contra affair.

22 Mar.	Congress overrides President Reagan's veto of the Civil Rights Restoration Act, which extends federal antibias laws to an entire school or other organization if any of its programs receive federal funding.
29 Mar.	Six top Justice Department officials resign over concerns with the investigation into alleged legal violations committed by Attorney General Meese.
8 Apr.	President Reagan freezes all Panamanian assets in the United States.
27 May	The Senate ratifies the INF Treaty.
29 May – 2 June	President Reagan visits the Soviet Union for a summit conference with Gorbachev.
8 June	Congress passes a bill providing extra Medicare coverage for catastrophic illness.
3 July	The USS *Vincennes* mistakenly shoots down an Iranian airliner, killing 290 passengers.
5 July	Attorney General Meese resigns, claiming that although he has been "completely exonerated" by James C. McKay, the independent prosecutor investigating his finances, the lengthy investigation has undermined his support on Capitol Hill.
13 July	Congress passes a bill requiring a sixty-day notice to employees of plant closings or large layoffs.
18 July	Independent prosecutor McKay issues a report stating that Meese "probably" violated the law four times while in office by allowing a false income-tax return to be filed for him, late payment of capital gains taxes, and twice violating conflict-of-interest laws.
13 Sept.	President Reagan signs a bill extending the Fair Housing Act of 1968 to protect the disabled and families with children.
22 Oct.	Congress passes a Taxpayer's Bill of Rights
8 Nov.	Republican George Bush is elected president, defeating Democrat Michael Dukakis by a margin of 53.4 to 45.6 percent.
14 Dec.	President Reagan authorizes talks with the Palestine Liberation Organization (PLO), after its leader, Yassir Arafat, renounces terrorism.

1989

4 Jan.	U.S. jets shoot down two Libyan planes over the Mediterranean.
20 Jan.	George Bush is inaugurated president of the United States.
9 Mar.	The Senate rejects John Tower's nomination as secretary of defense by a margin of 53–47.
17 Apr.	House Speaker James C. Wright Jr. is charged by the House Ethics Committee with accepting improper gifts and violating rules that limit outside income.
4 May	Oliver North is found guilty on three felony charges: obstructing a congressional inquiry, destroying documents, and accepting an illegal gift. On 5 July he is fined $20,000, given a three-year suspended prison sentence, placed on probation for two years, and ordered to perform twelve hundred hours of community service. Poindexter's trial is set to begin in January 1990.

13 June	President Bush successfully vetoes a bill that would raise the minimum wage to $4.55 a hour.
17 July	The B-2 Stealth bomber makes its first flight.
5 Aug.	Congress passes a bill to bail out failing savings-and-loan banks.
8 Nov.	Congress passes a compromise minimum wage bill, raising it to $4.25 by 1991.
2–3 Dec.	President Bush and Premier Gorbachev hold their first summit meeting, informal shipboard talks at Malta.
20 Dec.	U.S. troops invade Panama and overthrow the government of Manuel Noriega, who surrenders on 3 January 1990 and is extradited to the United States, where he is tried and found guilty on drug-trafficking charges in 1992.

OVERVIEW

The Reagan Decade. In American politics the 1980s were the decade of Ronald Reagan, who was elected president in 1980 and succeeded by his vice president, George Bush, in 1989. Reagan's vision of the nation — and to a somewhat lesser extent his conservative agenda — shaped the economic and political fortunes of the United States for most of the 1980s.

Malaise. As the decade began, Americans were struggling with an image of a country that was no longer the most powerful and prosperous nation in the world. Trust in politicians had been eroded by a series of political scandals that began in 1974 with the spectacle of an administration disgraced, as Richard Nixon resigned the presidency in the wake of Watergate, and continued into the 1980s with revelations about bribery of elected officials in the FBI Abscam sting. Social problems such as drug abuse, teen pregnancy, and violent crime were on the rise. The American economy exhibited a conjunction of high inflation, rising unemployment, and little growth. Americans were losing well-paying manufacturing jobs and taking low-paying service jobs in their place. Japan and Germany were challenging American dominance in world trade, and the United States was incurring larger and larger trade imbalances. As the major oil-producing countries raised the price of oil higher and higher, Americans were spending more and more of their incomes for gasoline and heating fuels.

Insecurity. The cost of human lives and international prestige incurred by a losing military effort in Vietnam had Congress shying away from Third World conflicts. Yet the Soviet Union seemed more aggressive than ever in expanding its sphere of influence. When student radicals seized the American embassy in Tehran, Iran, in late 1979 and held its staff hostage over the next fourteen months, Americans learned a frustrating lesson that was repeated again and again during the 1980s: even the finest, best-equipped military force in the world could not protect American citizens from political terrorism.

Reagan's Campaign. During the 1980 presidential campaign Ronald Reagan projected an optimistic, "can-do" persona and offered an appealing vision of an America restored to its former glory and prosperity through the good-old Puritan virtues of hard work, self-reliance, and faith in God. He promised to right the economy by reducing taxes, cutting government waste and bureaucracy, balancing the budget, and eliminating the deficit. He appealed to Americans' deep-seated patriotism with his vow to restore the prestige and power of the United States in foreign policy. Americans liked what they heard. Reagan defeated incumbent president Jimmy Carter, in large measure because of the votes of "Reagan Democrats," traditionally Democratic voters who bolted their party to vote for Reagan. Many of them were blue-collar workers dissatisfied with the Democrats' embrace of civil rights and so-called cultural liberalism. Setting aside their traditional suspicions that the Republicans were the party of the rich, they embraced Reagan's populist rhetoric. He promised them a new "supply-side" economic program that would ostensibly support their entrepreneurial spirit.

The Economy. Democrats charged that Reagan's economic program took from the poor to enrich the wealthy and that the nation he envisioned left out minorities, the disadvantaged, and the disabled. Echoing Calvin Coolidge's pronouncement in the 1920s that the "business of the United States is business," Reagan and his supporters replied that economic incentives to the wealthy stimulated investment in American companies, creating a "trickle-down" of prosperity to the American worker through jobs and raises.

Deficits and Economic Growth. Reagan's economic program never actually worked as planned. Tax-reform bills passed in 1981 and 1986 substantially reduced rates for personal and corporate income taxes, but the economy did not grow quickly enough to offset the loss of revenue. Owing in part to the reluctance of Congress to cut programs such as Social Security as much as the administration wanted, but primarily to major increases in military spending, the federal deficit had grown enormously by the end of the decade. While Reagan could take credit for strengthening the economy and curbing inflation, the huge deficit and an alarming trade imbalance offset his economic accomplishments.

The Reagan Doctrine. From the beginning the Reagan administration conducted foreign policy according to the maxim that an enemy of Communism was a friend to the United States. Money, arms, and military assistance were provided to regimes fighting Communist insurgencies and to guerrilla forces fighting Marxist governments — regardless of human-rights violations or authoritarian practices on the part of those regimes. Furthermore, Reagan sometimes used military force, sending the Marines to Lebanon to assist in peacekeeping, bombing Libya in retaliation for its support of Arab terrorists, and invading Grenada to topple a Marxist regime. He nearly scrapped President Richard Nixon's policy of détente with the Soviet Union, authorizing a massive arms buildup and creating a strategic policy based on the supposition that a nuclear war in Europe was winnable.

The End of the Cold War. With Mikhail Gorbachev's accession to power in the Soviet Union in 1985, tensions between the two superpowers were eased, and real progress was made in arms control. Gorbachev's willingness to cut Soviet aid to Third World countries and his withdrawal of Soviet troops from eastern Europe ushered in a major transformation in world politics by the end of the decade. During 1989 nearly every Communist government in eastern Europe collapsed and was replaced by a new, democratically elected government. The Berlin Wall was torn down, and in 1990 Germany was reunified. The Cold War, which had dominated global politics since the end of World War II, was over.

Scandal. Ronald Reagan began his presidency in a spirit of optimism, and for most of his eight years in office his enormous personal popularity seemed unscathed by the ethical and legal misdeeds of various members of his administration. By the middle of his second term journalists were keeping score of the number of Reagan administration officials who had been indicted — a tally that ended up with the largest number in U.S. history. Reagan, who was nearly seventy when he took office in January 1981, was the oldest man ever to serve as chief executive, and throughout his presidency there were frequent jokes about his tendency to fall asleep during cabinet meetings and his apparent ignorance about actions his administration took in his name. The laughter stopped in late 1986, when news of the Iran-Contra scandal began to break. Members of the administration had been illegally selling arms to Iran in return for the Iranians' promise of help in securing the release of Americans held hostage by Shiite radicals in Beirut. The scandal deepened when it was revealed that profits from the arms sales were diverted to aid the Contra rebels in Nicaragua — contrary to congressional prohibitions against such assistance. The scandal seriously undermined Reagan's image and the effectiveness of his administration.

The Reagan Legacy. During the eight years Reagan was in office the Republican Party became markedly more conservative, owing in large part to the rise of the religious Right, which had been a major force in his winning the Republican nomination in 1980. While Reagan gave lip service to their conservative social agenda, which included constitutional amendments requiring school prayer and banning abortion, he did little to implement their programs during his presidency. Instead he concentrated his administration's efforts on his conservative economic and foreign-policy agendas — areas in which he had a much higher degree of public approval than on issues such as prayer and abortion. By the end of his second term it was clear that the nation as a whole was far less conservative than the president's party, but it was equally clear that, for better or worse, the Reagan administration had shaped the terms of political debate for the foreseeable future. Democrats as well as Republicans were equally concerned with the mounting federal deficit. Political discourse, which since the New Deal era of the 1930s had focused on social justice and the fine-tuning of social programs to help the needy, shifted to a debate over how to reduce government spending and bureaucracy — both of which Reagan had increased vastly, despite campaign promises to the contrary.

Need for Vision. As George Bush took office in the last year of the 1980s, Democrats and Republicans alike were not only faced with serious and mounting deficits that required innovative spending cuts, they were also confronted with a world in which the Cold War would no longer serve as an organizing principle for American foreign policy. After 1945 the conservative agenda had become prioritized in a set order: anticommunism, fiscal responsibility, and social conservatism. With anticommunism no longer relevant, the conservative movement and the Republican Party in particular were faced with the growing debate between traditional fiscal conservatives, who wanted to focus on economic reform, and the religious right, who sought to focus on social issues. The search for a new world order and a fresh American political agenda was set to begin.

TOPICS IN THE NEWS

THE COLD WAR

New Tensions. Soviet-American relations, which had relaxed in the mid 1960s and most of the 1970s, intensified in the late 1970s, as the Soviets became more adventuresome in Latin America and Africa. President Jimmy Carter's conservative critics harped on the Soviets' attempt to extend their sphere of influence to the Third World and decried Soviet intransigence regarding the immigration of Soviet Jews to Israel. By 1978 Carter was calling for massive increases in defense spending, and by 1979 he had authorized the Trident submarine program, as well as the development of a new nuclear-powered aircraft carrier and the MX missile. He reinstituted draft registration and announced the deployment of new intermediate-range missiles and cruise missiles to Europe. With a longer range than the missiles they were replacing, these new missiles were capable of hitting targets in the western part of the Soviet Union. Also in 1979 the United States formally recognized the People's Republic of China, an action troublesome to the Soviet Union, which feared that the United States and China might ally themselves against the Soviets.

SALT II. Despite the increasingly hostile tone in U.S.–Soviet relations, the two nations were able to conclude negotiations on a new arms-control agreement, SALT II, which was signed on 18 June 1979. This treaty placed a ceiling on the number of strategic launchers — intercontinental ballistic missiles (ICBMs), submarine-launched ballistic missiles (SLBMs), and bombers. A ceiling was also placed on launchers for multiple-warhead missiles (MIRVs). Each side was allowed to develop new launch vehicles, but the numbers of launch vehicles and warheads each missile could carry was limited.

The Afghanistan Invasion. On 29 December 1979 the Soviet Union invaded Afghanistan, ostensibly in response to a plea for assistance from the government of Babrak Karmal. Many conservatives in the United States called the Soviets' action an example of naked aggression and part of their traditional drive toward acquisition of a warm-water port. The proximity of Afghanistan to the Persian Gulf supported the claim that by expanding into the Middle East, the Soviets could threaten western sources of oil. The United States and many other nations roundly condemned the Soviet action. In January 1980 President Carter responded by withdrawing the SALT II treaty from consideration by the U.S. Senate and by placing a embargo on the sale of grain and some types of electronic equipment to the Soviets. He also convinced the U.S. Olympic Committee to cancel U.S. participation in the 1980 Summer Olympics, which were to be held in Moscow, and he issued a directive that made possible an American first strike against the Soviet Union. He also enunciated the Carter doctrine, which declared that it was in the interest of the United States to defend the Persian Gulf area. Throughout the 1980 presidential campaign Republican nominee Ronald Reagan pledged that he would confront the Soviets and vigorously oppose communism and terrorism anywhere. To many Reagan seemed tougher than Carter.

Reagan's Hard Line. After winning the 1980 presidential election Reagan continued his anti-Soviet rhetoric. Early in his presidency he charged that Soviet leaders were capable of lying, cheating, and stealing to further their cause. Speaking to a group of religious broadcasters in March 1983, the president referred to the Soviet Union as the "evil empire." Public perception of the Soviet Union as dangerous was heightened in September 1983, when the Soviets shot down a South Korean airliner that had gone off course and strayed into Soviet airspace.

Military Buildup. Reagan backed his rhetoric with deeds. During his first term as president the military underwent the biggest peacetime buildup since 1940. A five-year Defense Guidance Plan adopted in 1982 outlined plans for $1.2 trillion in new defense spending. The B-1 bomber program was resurrected, and a six-hundred-ship navy was projected. When American cruise missiles were deployed in Europe in 1983 (Carter's decision), the Soviets walked out of ongoing arms talks in Geneva in protest.

Star Wars. On 23 March 1983 President Reagan startled Americans and the world with a speech in which he proposed that the United States should develop and deploy a shield, at least partially based in space, to intercept incoming strategic missiles. With a cost estimated in the hundreds of billions, the project was called the Strategic

THE REAGAN ASSASSINATION ATTEMPT

During the afternoon of 30 March 1981 President Ronald Reagan gave a speech to the AFL-CIO convention at the Washington Hilton Hotel. As he and his party left the hotel and walked toward his motorcade, six shots were fired from the midst of a group of bystanders who had mingled with the press. The president suffered a bullet wound to the chest from a shot that ricocheted off the armored presidential limousine. Press Secretary James Brady was critically wounded by a shot to the head. Also wounded were Washington policeman Thomas Delehanty and Secret Service agent Timothy McCarthy.

The Secret Service pushed Reagan into the limousine and — not realizing at first that he had been shot — ordered the motorcade to rush him to the White House. It was not until the president coughed up blood that the Secret Service realized he had been wounded and turned the motorcade around to take him to George Washington University Hospital. During the delay Reagan lost a dangerous amount of blood, but he was able to joke with aides as he was wheeled to an operating room, where he underwent two hours of surgery to remove the bullet and repair damage. He recovered quickly.

The gunman, John W. Hinckley Jr., was quickly subdued and taken into custody. Hinckley was a twenty-five-year-old loner and drifter who had grown up in Texas as the youngest of three children of a wealthy oilman. He had spent seven years as an average student at Texas Tech but never earned a degree. He flirted with right-wing causes and in the late 1970s was briefly a member of the National Socialist Party of America. A gun fancier who had been arrested at the Nashville airport in October 1980 for carrying three guns, Hinckley was also enamored of eighteen-year-old actress Jodie Foster, then a freshman at Yale, and had sent her letters. On the day he attempted to assassinate the president he wrote her a letter explaining his action as an attempt to impress her. While in custody he attempted to commit suicide several times, and on 21 June 1982 he was found not guilty by reason of insanity and committed to St. Elizabeths Hospital for the Criminally Insane in Washington, D.C., for an indefinite term.

At the White House the initial response of Reagan's staff to the assassination attempt was confusion. At first they did not know the president had been shot, and then they were unsure of how badly he had been wounded. White House Chief of Staff James Baker had to make a quick determination of whether the president's condition was serious enough to invoke the provisions of the Twenty-fifth Amendment that would temporarily transfer power to the vice president. After Baker, Deputy Chief of Staff Michael Deaver, and White House Counsel Edwin Meese talked to Reagan at the hospital just before his operation, they decided not to make the transfer.

Meanwhile, at the White House, Secretary of State Alexander Haig rushed up a flight of stairs and broke into a press briefing being conducted by Deputy Press Secretary Larry Speakes. Disheveled, winded, and with his voice quavering, Haig announced that the appropriate cabinet members had gathered at the White House, that Vice President George Bush and allied nations had been notified, and that there was no military alert. (In fact Defense Secretary Caspar Weinberger had ordered a low-level alert.) Haig also announced that since he was next in line of succession to the vice president, he was in charge until Bush returned from Texas. Actually the speaker of the House and the president pro tempore of the Senate were ahead of Haig in the line of succession. Other cabinet members and Congress were dismayed at Haig's performance, and his gaffe did little to improve his standing in an administration where he had already engaged in several power struggles over control of the foreign-policy agenda.

Source: *Newsweek*, 97 (13 April 1981): 31–46.

Defense Initiative (SDI), but it soon had the popular nickname "Star Wars." Although Edward Teller, one of the nuclear physicists prominent in the initial development of U.S. nuclear weapons, promoted the project, many questioned whether such a program was technically workable. Critics also said SDI would violate provisions of the 1972 Antiballistic Missile (ABM) Treaty, a charge the Soviets also made.

MAD. Other critics also pointed to the cost of Star Wars and its impact on nuclear deterrence. Since the late 1960s the United States and the Soviet Union had approached parity in numbers and types of nuclear weapons. According to conventional wisdom, the fact that each side could destroy the other produced stability because neither side would risk attacking the other. This strategic doctrine was labeled Mutual Assured Destruc-

On 1 September 1983 Korean Airlines flight 007 (KAL007) began its regular, five-nights-a-week flight from the United States to Seoul, South Korea. After the normal stopover in Alaska, the flight proceeded on its way over the northern Pacific where its path crossed that of an American RC-135 reconnaissance aircraft. During a part of its trip when it was out of the reach of civilian air traffic controllers and their radar, the flight strayed off course into Soviet airspace. For some two hours the plane was tracked by Soviet air defense and aircraft as it continued over the Kamchatka Peninsula, the Sea of Okhotsk, and Sakhalin Island. Finally, as it passed over the Sea of Japan and approached the limit of Soviet airspace, a Soviet fighter jet shot down the airliner, killing all 269 passengers and crew members.

As the world condemned the action, which President Ronald Reagan labeled a massacre, the Soviets initially said only that they had shot down a spy plane. They then stonewalled for six days before admitting that their target had in fact been a civilian airliner, but they still insisted that the plane was on a spy mission for the United States. They claimed that the airliner had been flying with its navigation lights turned off and had ignored all of the attempts to contact it through radio, wing signals, and firing warning shots.

According to messages between Soviet air defense ground commanders and interceptor aircraft (which were intercepted by western intelligence), the Soviets at first thought they were tracking the RC-135, which had already returned to its base in Alaska. The messages recorded attempts to contact the airliner through military channels, which the civilian aircraft was unable to use, but no efforts to reach it through civilian channels. Furthermore, the transcripts indicate that the plane's navigation lights were on.

The best explanation for this tragic incident is Soviet paranoia over violations of its borders. Article 36 of the Soviet Border Law authorized the use of force to stop any such violation of its borders, and the general feeling among Soviet defense forces was that it was better to be safe than sorry. After a 1978 incident — in which a Korean airliner flew hundreds of miles into Soviet territory before it was shot at and forced to land — careers were ruined and at least one Soviet air defense commander was rumored to have been executed for not bringing the airliner down quickly enough. After this incident the Soviets added to the firepower of their air defense system and gave regional commanders greater power to act independently in such situations.

The tragedy of KAL007 lent credence to President Ronald Reagan's characterization of the Soviet Union as "the evil empire" and dampened several promising openings in arms-control negotiations.

Source: *Newsweek*, 102 (19 September 1983): 18–35.

---

tion (MAD). By providing a defense against the Soviets' strategic weapons, SDI would place the United States in a position from which it could threaten the Soviet Union with nuclear weapons without risking a successful Soviet counterattack. Reagan wanted to get a jump on the Soviet Union in the development of SDI because he feared that the Soviets might try to develop and deploy their own system. Many critics feared that, should either side gain such an advantage over the other, deterrence would be unstable. The position of the United States would be even further advanced with the deployment of the more accurate warheads on the new MX missile.

Strong Rhetoric. Many thought that the Reagan program was designed to win a nuclear war with the Soviet Union. Formulation of plans to bolster civil defense and to deliver mail in the aftermath of a nuclear war did little to dispel such a notion. In fact the Defense Guidance Plan of 1982 suggested that a nuclear war might be winnable. The administration sent contradictory signals on this subject. During spring 1982 Reagan declared that a nuclear war was unwinnable, a position Secretary of Defense Caspar Weinberger reiterated in a June 1982 speech at the U.S. Army War College.

Mixed Signals. As its rhetoric regarding the Soviet Union grew more hostile and the administration committed more and more resources to a military buildup, it also sent contradictory signals regarding arms control. In a November 1981 speech before the National Press Club in Washington, D.C., Reagan proposed reducing U.S. and Soviet intermediate-range missiles in Europe. The following April he suggested that he wanted to push strategic-arms control and to discuss a freeze on nuclear weapons. In a May 1982 graduation speech at Eureka College (his alma mater), Reagan proposed that the United States and the Soviet Union should begin Strategic Arms Reduction Talks (START) designed to reduce one another's warheads by one-third. He again suggested that it might be possible to eliminate intermediate-range weapons in Eu-

A 1981 cabinet meeting: (at table, clockwise from lower left) Vice President George Bush, Attorney General William French Smith, Treasury Secretary Donald Regan, Interior Secretary James Watt, Secretary of State Alexander Haig, President Ronald Reagan, and Defense Secretary Caspar Weinberger. The large jar on the table contains the president's favorite snack: jelly beans.

rope. He further expounded on these themes during a June trip to NATO countries, where in separate addresses before the British and West German parliaments he reiterated the dangers of nuclear war and suggested that NATO and the Warsaw Pact countries could reduce their conventional forces to nine hundred thousand apiece. Reagan's anti-Soviet rhetoric and his enormous commitment of resources to the military stood in apparent contrast to these public expressions on arms control, sending mixed signals to the rest of the world and helping to make the Soviets more suspicious of American intentions. At the same time, widespread public perception of the danger posed by the Soviet Union ensured fairly broad-based support for Reagan's policies and rhetoric in the early 1980s.

Sources:

William H. Chafe, *The Unfinished Journey: America Since World War II*, second edition (New York: Oxford University Press, 1991);

Robert Dallek, *Ronald Reagan: The Politics of Symbolism* (Cambridge, Mass.: Harvard University Press, 1984);

Robert D. Schulzinger, *American Diplomacy in the Twentieth Century*, third edition (New York: Oxford University Press, 1994).

THE COLD WAR: THAW

A New Generation of Soviet Leadership. The early 1980s were characterized by rapid changes in the leader-

ship of the Soviet Union. Leonid Brezhnev, who had led the Soviet Union since 1964, died in 1982 and was succeeded by Yuri Andropov, a former head of the KGB. Andropov died in 1984 and was succeeded by Konstantin Chernenko. These leaders had their political roots in the Stalin era and the Cold War period that followed World War II. When Chernenko died in 1985, he was succeeded by Mikhail Gorbachev, who at fifty-four years of age was part of a new generation of Soviet leaders whose political experiences were forged during the leadership of the reform-minded Nikita Khrushchev. Gorbachev and many of his generation of leaders were better educated, more widely traveled, and more cosmopolitan than their predecessors.

Soviet Reforms. Gorbachev unleashed revolutionary reforms in Soviet politics and economics. He instituted a policy of *glasnost* (openness) in Soviet society, increasing freedom of speech and assembly and introducing new rights for consumers, employees, and managers. Greater competition in the political sphere, as well as reforms in the legal system, were included in the policy of *demokratizatsiia* (democratization). In the economic sector *perestroika* (restructuring) was designed to decentralize economic decision making, provide greater incentives and rewards for workers and managers, modernize technology, introduce free-market discipline, and open the

After Mikhail Gorbachev took over as Soviet premier in 1985, his wife, Raisa, began appearing regularly with her husband in public. Spouses of Soviet leaders had generally been relegated to the sidelines, and in the west Gorbachev's move was widely viewed as a means of humanizing his government. While Muscovites joked that she was the first wife of a Soviet leader to weigh less than her husband, the western media became fascinated by the attractive fifty-three-year-old with a doctorate in sociology.

At the Geneva summit in 1985 Raisa Gorbachev thoroughly upstaged First Lady Nancy Reagan. After a dinner party hosted by the Reagans, where Mrs. Gorbachev regaled the president with an extensive explanation of Soviet philosophy, White House Chief of Staff Donald Regan overheard Mrs. Reagan commenting, "Who does that dame think she is?" Though the first lady later denied the statement, the relationship between the two women was clearly tense from that point onward.

When the Gorbachevs visited Washington, D.C., in December 1987, Raisa Gorbachev stole the spotlight again during a tour of the White House, where she embarrassed the first lady by asking questions Mrs. Reagan could not answer (such as the age of the house) and annoyed her by stopping frequently to talk at length with reporters. Mrs. Reagan politely described her guest as "very nice, bright, intelligent," but the first lady's friends were quick to point out that Mrs. Gorbachev had committed the wardrobe faux pas of wearing a "cocktail" dress for an afternoon visit — a fact that did nothing to dampen the media's enthusiasm for her.

When the Reagans visited the Soviet Union in May and June 1988, Nancy Reagan seemed determined not to be upstaged again. The White House arranged for her to be shown around Leningrad by Soviet president Andrei Gromyko's wife, Lidiya, a woman older and less attractive than Mrs. Gorbachev, who hosted the first lady in Moscow. There, while the two women were visiting an art gallery, Mrs. Reagan interrupted Mrs. Gorbachev's explanation of the artistry of some icons with, "I want to say something. I want to say something now, okay?" Then she added, "I don't know how you can neglect the religious elements. I mean, they're there for everyone to see." Mrs. Gorbachev looked at her watch and did not respond. Mrs. Reagan "wanted to pay her back for what happened in Washington," a senior aide said later. "She knew exactly what she wanted to say and had a little scrap of paper to remind her."

Sources: Howard G. Chua-Eoan, " 'My Wife Is a Very Independent Lady': Educated, Attractive and Opinionated, Mikhail Gorbachev's Closest Adviser Is a One-Woman Revolution," *Time*, 131 (6 June 1988): 38–43;

"Raisa and Nancy: Superpower Struggle," *Newsweek*, 110 (21 December 1987): 18–19;

Donald T. Regan, *For the Record: From Wall Street to Washington* (San Diego, New York & London: Harcourt Brace Jovanovich, 1988);

Russell Watson, "Reagan's 'Moscow Spring,'" *Newsweek*, 111 (13 June 1988): 16–22.

Soviet Union to world trade and foreign investment. In foreign policy Gorbachev wanted to be more conciliatory to the West, to see further reductions in conventional and strategic arms, and to downscale or eliminate Soviet influence in Third World conflicts. In part Gorbachev was motivated by the notion that money saved from a reduction of military spending for costly efforts supporting liberation movements abroad could stimulate the Soviet domestic economy. Politically he could justify such cuts only by persuading the West to agree to similar cuts in strategic and conventional forces and by resolving some of the ongoing conflicts in the Third World.

Further Tensions. During 1985 U.S.–Soviet relations were still tense. In March a Soviet sentry shot and killed an American officer on a reconnaissance mission in Potsdam, East Germany. In April the Warsaw Pact nations extended their alliance for twenty years. In June the U.S. Senate voted to repeal the Clark Amendment, thereby freeing the United States to aid rebels fighting the Soviet-backed government in Angola. Western distrust of the Soviets was hardly ameliorated when Great Britain and the Soviet Union each expelled twenty-five of one another's diplomats and leveled charges of espionage against one another.

Favorable Impressions of Gorbachev. British prime minister Margaret Thatcher had met with Gorbachev in mid December 1984, just weeks before he succeeded Chernenko. As stridently conservative and anti-communist as Reagan, Thatcher had nonetheless formed a favorable impression of Gorbachev and publicly declared that the West would be able to negotiate in good faith with him. When Reagan and Gorbachev met in Geneva, Switzerland, on 19–21 November 1985, no substantive agreements were reached, but each leader came away believing that he could work with the other. For much of 1986 tensions continued. Little progress was made in any of the three sets of arms-control talks going on between the United States and the Soviet Union in

President Reagan, Nancy Reagan, Premier Mikhail Gorbachev, and Raisa Gorbachev during the Washington Summit, December 1987

Geneva — talks on reducing or eliminating intermediate-range missiles, on reducing in strategic arms, and on issues related to space and defense. Furthermore, the Reagan administration was deeply suspicious of what it termed Gorbachev's "peace offensive," his willingness to lessen tensions with western Europe, which many in the administration considered a ruse to destroy NATO. Reagan persisted in his SDI program despite Russian protests. After the United States arrested a Soviet diplomat and charged him with espionage in August 1987, the Soviets retaliated by arresting an American journalist, Nicholas Daniloff, and charging him with the same crime. After some months the two were exchanged.

The Reykjavík Summit. President Reagan and Premier Gorbachev met in Reykjavík, Iceland, on 11–12 October 1986 to discuss ways to reinvigorate the three sets of talks in Geneva and to set the stage for another meeting in Washington, D.C., in 1987. Gorbachev had proposed the Reykjavík meeting in a September letter to Reagan, in which he appeared to suggest that he was willing to reach an accord on intermediate missiles without an accompanying agreement placing limits on SDI. The American delegation came expecting to negotiate an intermediate nuclear forces (INF) treaty and to explore ways of getting the strategic arms control talks moving. Reagan had periodically floated the idea of reducing or even eliminating strategic missiles, but the Americans and the world were stunned when Gorbachev offered a specific proposal that each side should reduce its strategic missiles by up to 50 percent and that the Soviets would also cut their most powerful missiles. He asked only that the United States agree to continue for ten years the provisions of the ABM Treaty, which placed the most restrictions on the development and deployment of an American SDI program. On the second day of the meeting Gorbachev further shocked the participants and the world when he proposed that the two countries eliminate all nuclear weapons over a period of ten years. During weekend talks the two sides expressed a willingness to discuss limiting strategic weapons, if not eliminating them entirely, but the talks foundered on a single issue: the failure of the two governments to find a mutually satisfactory solution to differences over SDI. Both leaders were obviously and publicly disappointed, but subgroups were able to make substantial progress in getting the three sets of talks in Geneva going again.

The Washington Summit. Reagan and Gorbachev met again in Washington, D.C., on 8–10 December

1987. Despite the disappointment of Reykjavík, enough progress had been made on smaller issues that over the intervening year the two countries had been able to negotiate an agreement on intermediate-range missiles, and Reagan and Gorbachev were able to sign the INF Treaty on the first day of the summit. In the INF Treaty the two countries agreed not just to remove intermediate-range nuclear weapons from Europe but to eliminate them from their arsenals entirely. Each side was to withdraw its missiles and to destroy them. The treaty provided for rigorous on-site verification through inspection by teams based in one another's territories. The treaty was ratified by the U.S. Senate on 27 May 1988. After their success in concluding the INF agreement the two countries were able to reinvigorate the START negotiations, and a successful START agreement was completed in June 1991.

Third World Pullback. In 1988 Gorbachev began implementing a Soviet pullback from confrontation with the United States in Third World countries. On 8 February 1988 he announced that the Soviet Union would withdraw from Afghanistan, and on 14 April 1988 the Soviets signed an accord in which they agreed to withdraw half their forces from Afghanistan by August and the remaining half by the following February. On 22 December the Soviet Union, South Africa, and Cuba signed an agreement that had been brokered by U.S. Assistant Secretary of State for African Affairs Chester Crocker. Cuba agreed to withdraw its troops from Angola, and South Africa said it would withdraw its troops from adjacent Namibia.

Eastern Europe. In a speech at the United Nations on 6 December 1988 Gorbachev announced that the Soviet Union would unilaterally withdraw five hundred thousand troops and ten thousand tanks from eastern Europe. While ostensibly stationed in Europe to confront NATO, these troops had also ensured the stability of pro-Soviet Communist regimes in the region. Without the promise of Soviet support, Communist regimes in eastern Europe began to collapse. In Poland the Solidarity movement was recognized as a legal entity in January 1988 and had begun to take political control of the country by August 1989. At the Warsaw Pact meeting in July Gorbachev informed leaders of eastern European states that the Soviets no longer wished to control their economic and political affairs. On 25 October 1989 he repudiated the Brezhnev Doctrine. Articulated by Soviet premier Leonid Brezhnev on 13 November 1968, the doctrine had justified the use of armed force against any socialist country deemed to be in danger of deviating from the ideals of communism. The doctrine had been used to justify the 1968 Warsaw Pact invasion of Czechoslovakia, when liberalization in that country appeared to be moving too fast. With the announced withdrawal of Soviet troops and the repudiation of a right to intervene in their politics, Communist governments in eastern Europe began to collapse rapidly. The governments of Hungary, Czechoslovakia, and Bulgaria all fell

East Germans surging through a new opening in the Berlin Wall, November 1989

quickly and relatively peacefully. The regime of Romanian Communist dictator Nicolae Ceausescu gave way in a bloody coup in which Ceausescu and his wife were executed.

East Germany. The East German regime tried to resist, but when the government of Erich Honecker ordered the army to fire on demonstrators, he was overruled and deposed. Throughout 1989 the Hungarians provided an avenue for East Germans to escape to the West. Finally, on 9 November, East Germany opened its borders. The following day citizens on both sides started tearing down the Berlin Wall. The following year the two Germanies were reunified. Inaugurated in January 1989, President George Bush had the good fortune to be in office during the breakup of the Soviet empire in eastern Europe and the collapse of Communism — and to profit politically from events not of his making.

China. At the same time massive changes were going on in eastern Europe and the Soviet Union, students launched prodemocracy protests in the People's Republic of China. The Chinese government used the military to suppress the protests. On 3–4 June 1989 the world watched aghast as the military moved with force against the Tiananmen Square demonstrators in Beijing. The Bush administration mildly protested the massacres and temporarily stopped contact with the Chinese government, but it resisted congressional attempts to sanction the Chinese further. During summer 1989 Bush sent

Hostages from the U.S. embassy in Tehran returning home after nearly fifteen months of captivity, 20 January 1981

National Security Adviser Brent Scowcroft on a secret mission to reestablish contact with the Chinese government and to reassure it that the United States remained friendly with China. While Bush had the good fortune to oversee the beginnings of democratization in eastern Europe, he did little to promote a similar process in China.

Sources:
Wilbur Edel, *The Reagan Presidency: An Actor's Finest Performance* (New York: Hippocrene Books, 1992);

Robert D. Schulzinger, *American Diplomacy in the Twentieth Century*, third edition (New York: Oxford University Press, 1994);

Geoffrey Smith, *Reagan and Thatcher* (New York: Norton, 1991);

Strobe Talbott, *The Master of the Game: Paul Nitze and the Nuclear Peace* (New York: Knopf, 1988).

THE COLD WAR: THIRD WORLD WOES

Afghanistan and Iran. In 1980 U.S. policy toward the Third World was dominated by two ongoing events that had begun in late 1979: the Soviet invasion of Afghanistan and the seizure of the U.S. embassy in Iran by militants who held the embassy staff hostage. The Soviets' move into Afghanistan was especially trouble-some to the United States because of the proximity of Afghanistan to the Persian Gulf, from which mideastern oil is shipped to the west, and because of political instability in neighboring Iran. Since 1953 the United States had been closely allied with the Iranian government of Shah Mohammed Reza Pahlavi, and in 1978 there were some fifty thousand Americans in Iran helping to train the military and operate the oil fields and other industries. Opposition to the shah's government began to grow in early 1978 and eventually became unified under the leadership of the Ayatollah Ruholla Khomeini, a nearly eighty-year-old religious leader living in exile in Paris. Throughout 1978 the shah's regime became shakier and shakier; he finally stepped down and went into exile in January 1979. He was replaced by a militant Islamic fundamentalist government dominated by the ayatollahs, leaders of the Shiite branch of Islam. The U.S. ambassador to Iran, William Sullivan, urged the United States to accommodate the new government.

The Iran Hostage Situation. After the deposed shah entered the United States on 22 October for treatment of cancer, relations between the United States and the new

Iranian government deteriorated rapidly. Following large street demonstrations outside the American embassy on 1 November, militant Iranian revolutionaries stormed the embassy on 4 November, taking the sixty-nine Americans there hostage. The Khomeini government declared that these Americans would be held until the shah and his fortune were returned to Iran. President Carter responded by refusing the Iranian demands and freezing Iranian assets in the United States. In December the Iranians released sixteen black and female hostages but otherwise refused to yield. The two countries found themselves in a standoff as U.S. presidential primary campaigns heated up in spring 1980.

A Failed Rescue Mission. Carter eventually decided to attempt a military assault on the embassy to free the hostages. On 24–25 April 1980, eight helicopters carrying a special strike force left the aircraft carrier *Nimitz*. Hampered by a dust storm, the mission had to be aborted after two of the helicopters had to turn back and crashed. In the aftermath the militants dispersed some of the hostages to locations away from the embassy, making another rescue attempt futile.

Hostage Release. During summer 1980 a new government took office in Iran, with Abdul Hassan Bani-Sadr as prime minister, and on 11 July another hostage, who was ill with multiple sclerosis, was released. The shah died of cancer on 27 July, making the Iranian demands for his return superfluous. In August talks began with a focus on freeing the fifty-two remaining hostages in exchange for unfreezing Iranian assets. The talks continued through the fall election campaign and into January 1981. The hostages were eventually released on 20 January 1981, Carter's final day in office and inauguration day for newly elected President Ronald Reagan.

The Reagan Doctrine. Throughout the 1980 presidential campaign Republican nominee Ronald Reagan had denounced Soviet aggression and promised to fight Soviet expansionism aggressively, as well as to restore U.S. prestige abroad. Reagan's views were influenced by a thesis developed by conservative academician Jeane J. Kirkpatrick, whom he subsequently named U.S. ambassador to the United Nations. Kirkpatrick elaborated a distinction between totalitarian and authoritarian regimes. According to Kirkpatrick, totalitarian regimes are incapable of evolution toward democracy and should be resolutely opposed. In contrast, she said, authoritarian regimes, which can change peacefully and become democratic, should be supported, especially if they are anticommunist. This thesis provided much of the rationale for Reagan administration policies toward the Third World, culminating in 1985 with the enunciation of the Reagan doctrine, a policy designed to combat Soviet influence in the Third World. The Reagan doctrine promised aid and counterinsurgency assistance for governments fighting communist movements and support for guerrilla movements opposing governments linked to the Soviet Union. The Reagan doctrine was used to justify aid to guerrillas in Angola, Nicaragua, and Afghanistan.

Afghanistan. Over the next several years the Reagan administration supported the mujahideen, guerrillas fighting the Marxist regime and Soviet troops in Afghanistan. Millions in aid and arms were funneled through the neighboring country of Pakistan. At one point the Soviets had 115,000 troops fighting in Afghanistan, but after years of fighting an increasingly expensive and deadly war against the Afghan guerrillas, the Soviet Union shifted its focus to domestic issues and withdrew its troops in 1988.

Angola. By 1975 Angola had won its independence from Portugal after a long civil war, and the three groups that had fought the Portuguese began fighting each other for control of the country. Throughout the war with Portugal the Soviets had provided some minimal backing for the Popular Movement for the Liberation of Angola (MPLA) and the United States had backed the National Front for the Liberation of Angola (FNLA). The National Union for the Total Independence of Angola (UNITA), the movement that represented the largest population group in Angola, had backing from the People's Republic of China and the Republic of South Africa. As the FNLA and MPLA battled for control of the capital, Luanda, the American CIA and the Soviet Union rapidly escalated their aid to their respective sides. Cuban troops were sent to Angola to back the MPLA. When a South African force — collaborating with elements of UNITA and the FNLA — entered Angolan territory on 23 October 1975, the Cubans, with Soviet support, became actively involved in the civil war. The South African government, which controlled neighboring Namibia, preferred that Angolan territory along the border of Namibia continue be in the hands of friendly UNITA rather than falling to the MPLA. The South Africans feared that the Soviets, the Cubans, and the MPLA would be able to provide assistance to the South West African People's Organization (SWAPO), which was involved in a guerrilla war with the South Africans in Namibia.

The Clark Amendment. With these events occurring in the immediate aftermath of U.S. withdrawal from Vietnam, Congress sought to avoid entanglement in an African civil war. On 19 December 1975 it passed an amendment to a defense-appropriations bill, prohibiting the CIA from supplying covert aid to any side in the Angolan civil war. For the next several years the Clark Amendment — named after its sponsor, Sen. Dick Clark (D-Iowa), effectively limited the United States to diplomatic efforts.

Repealing the Clark Amendment. By the early 1980s UNITA was in a military stalemate with the Cuban-backed MPLA forces and was receiving aid from the French as well as the Saudi Arabians and South Africans. Pursuant to the Reagan doctrine, the Reagan administration successfully persuaded Congress to repeal the Clark

Amendment in July 1985. The Reagan administration quickly began to supply UNITA with covert aid, and by the last year of Reagan's presidency the United States was providing some $60 million to UNITA.

Diplomatic Efforts. At the same time, the United States continued diplomatic initiatives to find a settlement to the Angolan civil war, seeking to remove Cuban troops from Angola, resolve the status of Namibia, and get the South African troops out of Angola and Namibia. Assistant Secretary of State Chester A. Crocker led U.S. efforts to broker what eventually culminated in the Alvor Agreements, signed on 22 December 1988. In October South Africa agreed to withdraw its troops and grant Namibia its independence. At the same time, Cuba and Angola announced the withdrawal of Cuban troops. Although the United States continued providing assistance to UNITA, the Cubans withdrew, and the Soviets began leaving as Gorbachev substantially reduced the Soviet presence overseas. The civil war between UNITA and the MPLA continued into the 1990s.

South Africa. South Africa provided a different problem for the Reagan administration, which considered the Republic of South Africa an important ally because of its important geopolitical location, its reserves of strategic minerals, and its role in opposing the Soviets and Cubans in Angola. Despite South Africa's morally repugnant policy of racial segregation, or apartheid, the Reagan administration thought that South Africa fit in the category of an authoritarian state capable of change, one that could eventually evolve into a more just society, and was thus supportable under the Reagan doctrine. More and more countries were condemning South African apartheid, embargoing trade and imposing economic sanctions on that nation, but the Reagan administration resisted the diplomatic and economic efforts to get South Africa to change.

Constructive Engagement. In a 1984 address to the UN Reagan supported a peaceful evolution away from apartheid but was unwilling to pressure South Africa to change. When black South African Anglican bishop Desmond Tutu won the Nobel Peace Prize for his efforts to eliminate apartheid, Reagan congratulated him but supported the U.S. policy of constructive engagement, which urged the South African government to engage in dialogue with its black citizens over a possible end to apartheid. Reagan reiterated this stance when Tutu visited the White House in December 1984.

Congress Takes on Apartheid. As Reagan began his second term, opposition to apartheid among blacks in South Africa grew increasingly militant and occasionally violent. The Reagan administration faced pressure from other countries and at home to take a more proactive stance against South Africa. In summer 1985 Democratic senators and representatives began pushing for economic sanctions. To counter this effort Reagan issued an executive order prohibiting some kinds of bank loans to the

Prime Minister Margaret Thatcher of Great Britain and President Reagan at Camp David, November 1986

South African government, sales of certain types of equipment to the South African military and security forces, and the importation of military equipment made in South Africa. Reagan's attempts to preempt congressional action were short-lived. In September 1986 Congress passed the Comprehensive Anti-Apartheid Act. Republican senators Robert Dole of Kansas and Richard Lugar of Indiana joined Democrat Edward Kennedy of Massachusetts in supporting the bill and helped to override Reagan's veto of it on 2 October. The problem of apartheid in South Africa vexed the Reagan administration through its last year and continued to be a problem during the first year of the new Bush administration. Between 1989 and 1992 South African President F. W. de Klerk led a series of reforms that began dismantling the system of apartheid.

The Philippines. Reagan had similar problems in dealings with the Philippines, a longtime Pacific ally of the United States and the site of several key U.S. military bases. The United States had governed the Philippines from the end of the Spanish-American War in 1898 until 1946. Reagan repeatedly stood by Philippine strongman President Ferdinand Marcos, despite the uproar over the assassination of Marcos's chief political rival, Sen. Benigno Aquino Jr., on 21 August 1983. After a Marcos-appointed investigatory commission blamed the assassination on a plot among Aquino's military bodyguards, a court appointed by Marcos exonerated the accused. Despite continued charges that the Marcos regime was corrupt and repressive, Reagan continued to stress the close links that existed between the Marcos government and the United States. In the February 1986 presidential election Corazon Aquino, the widow of Senator Aquino, ran against Marcos. The United States and Great Britain sent official delegations to monitor the election. There were widespread charges of election fraud and violence, but despite reports from his own appointed observers that the Marcos campaign was deeply involved in these violations, Reagan turned a blind eye and declared the United States neutral. Senator Lugar, who had been one of Reagan's election observers, reported that the Marcos government was trying to juggle the vote count to deny an Aquino victory. Along with senators Dole and Sam Nunn (D–Ga.), Lugar protested Reagan's indifference. Aquino eventually took office after thousands of Philippine citizens took to the streets, and military and government leaders abandoned Marcos. The United States recognized the new Aquino government on 25 February 1986. Reagan's stubborn defense of the Marcos government put a strain on relations with the Philippines, which affected negotiations over renewal of U.S. leases on its Philippine bases. The United States had to make several concessions and promise substantial increases in economic and military aid before the Philippines would renew the lease arrangements.

Grenada. In addition to supporting anti-Communist insurgencies and aiding anti-Communist governments, the Reagan administration was also willing to use military force to oust Marxist governments. On 25 October 1983 Americans awoke to early-morning newscasts announcing that the United States was in the process of invading the Caribbean island nation of Grenada. Since 1979 Grenada had been led by Prime Minister Maurice Bishop, head of the New Jewel political movement and an avowed Marxist who had good relations with the Cuban regime of Fidel Castro. The Reagan administration had cut off aid for Grenada and sought to isolate the country diplomatically. In summer 1983 Bishop distanced himself from Cuba and signaled a desire to return to a good working relationship with the United States, but on 12 October 1983 he was killed during a successful coup led by Gen. Hudson Austin, leader of a militant faction of the New Jewel movement. The United States used concern for the safety of five hundred Americans studying at Saint George's University School of Medicine as a pretext for the invasion. After three days of sporadic fighting, the nineteen hundred American troops defeated a force made up of the Grenadan army and Cuban workers. While there was some initial criticism and even ridicule of the U.S. giant taking on the diminutive island nation, the furor died quickly. Most Americans quickly forgot about the incident.

Sources:

William H. Chafe, *The Unfinished Journey: America Since World War II*, second edition (New York: Oxford University Press, 1991);

Wilbur Edel, *The Reagan Presidency: An Actor's Finest Performance* (New York: Hippocrene Books, 1992);

Robert D. Schulzinger, *American Diplomacy in the Twentieth Century*, third edition (New York: Oxford University Press, 1994).

THE MIDDLE EAST

The Reagan Doctrine. The Reagan administration's policies toward the Middle East were at least partially informed by the Reagan doctrine, which pledged U.S. support to nations faced with a perceived Communist threat and promised to assist guerrilla groups that sought to displace Marxist governments.

Lebanon. The crown jewel of President Jimmy Carter's Middle East policy was the 1978 Camp David peace accords between Israel and Egypt, a positive contribution toward peace in the region that was later overshadowed in the court of public opinion by the debacle of the hostage crisis in Tehran. The Reagan administration fumbled its way through Middle East policy making. A crucial problem was the civil war in Lebanon. Palestinian refugees from the Israeli-occupied West Bank and Jordan radically altered the delicate political balance in Lebanon. The Palestinians used bases in southern Lebanon to challenge the Israelis. Other parties to the Lebanese civil war were armed militias representing the Maronite Christian community, the Druse Muslims, the Amal, and the Shiite Muslims — as well as the forces of the official Lebanese government and Syrian troops.

The Palestinian Problem. The Reagan administration tended to view the Palestinians' demands for their own homeland in the West Bank region of Israel through Cold War lenses. The Palestine Liberation Organization (PLO) got some support from the Soviets, and Israel was perceived as the bastion of western democracy in the Middle East. The Israelis invaded Lebanon in June 1982 with what they believed was tacit permission from the United States. When the Israelis fought their way into Muslim sections of western Beirut, the United States helped to broker a plan whereby PLO fighters would leave Lebanon. A multinational force consisting of French and Italian troops and U.S. Marines landed in Lebanon on 25 August 1982 to enforce the shaky peace and to help evacuate the PLO fighters. After the PLO had been evacuated, the marines withdrew. On 14 September the leader of the Christian group, Bashir Gemayel, was assassinated. In retaliation Christian forces rampaged through Palestinian camps, killing men, women, and children while the Israelis stood by. The multinational forces, including the marines, were sent back to Beirut. The situation deteriorated, and the peacekeeping forces became the targets of sniper attacks. The rules of engagement were changed to allow peacekeepers to fire back when fired upon. Occasionally air support and bombardment from U.S. warships were used to retaliate for attacks on the peacekeepers. On 18 April 1983 a vanload of explosives blew up at the U.S. embassy in Beirut, severely damaging the building and killing sixty-three people. On 23 October Shiite fighters drove a

During the last two years of Ronald Reagan's presidency several White House staffers published memoirs that called into question the president's grasp on the workings of his administration. Perhaps the most alarming of these books was *For the Record* (1988), by Donald Regan, who had been treasury secretary during Reagan's first term (1981–1984) and White House chief of staff for part of the second (1985–1987). Regan revealed that First Lady Nancy Reagan dictated her husband's schedule according to the advice she received from a San Francisco astrologer whom she called every Saturday, usually from Camp David. Although Regan never knew the astrologer's name, she was later identified as San Francisco heiress Joan Quigley.

Before Regan arrived at the White House the job of squaring the president's schedule with Quigley's predictions belonged to longtime Reagan aide Michael Deaver, who told Regan that Nancy Reagan had been consulting astrologers at least since her husband was governor of California. Her faith in her current astrologer had been reinforced after Quigley had predicted that "something bad" would happen on 30 March 1981, the day John Hinckley Jr. tried to assassinate the president.

For part of the time he headed the White House staff, Regan kept a color-coded calendar — with dates highlighted in green for "good" days, in red for "bad" days, and yellow for "iffy" days — "as an aid to remembering when it was propitious to move the president of the United States from one place to another, or schedule him to speak in public, or commence negotiations with a foreign power." He reported frequent last-minute changes and cancellations in the president's schedule, made because of Nancy Reagan's consultations with Quigley.

Before the Geneva summit in 1985, the president's first meeting with Soviet premier Mikhail Gorbachev, Mrs. Reagan not only talked to Quigley about "auspicious moments for meetings" between the two world leaders but also had her draw up a horoscope for Gorbachev to provide information about his "character and probable behavior."

According to Regan, Nancy Reagan's insistence on following her astrologer's advice especially hurt the president during the Iran-Contra scandal. Believing that Reagan's national security advisers acted without the president's knowledge or consent, Regan emphasized the need for him to get his explanation of what he knew about the arms-for-hostages deals before the public quickly and to speak to the press on a regular basis thereafter, but Mrs. Reagan vetoed the plan. Based on Quigley's predictions of "good" and "bad" days for the president, Reagan was not allowed to talk publicly about the scandal until 12 November, nine days after the news had broken, when he spoke to a delegation from Congress, and — although he delivered a televised address on the subject the next evening — he did not answer reporters' questions until the nineteenth — a date Quigley identified as "good." Furthermore, because Quigley said the early months of 1987 were mostly "bad" for the president, he did not hold another press conference until 19 March. During that period he made few public appearances, and on some occasions he was not allowed to leave the White House.

As Regan predicted, the president's lack of communication with the public and the media reinforced the perception that he had something to hide. By the time of the March press conference, Regan had resigned — forced out, he (and many others) believed, by Nancy Reagan.

When news of the first lady's consultations with an astrologer broke in May 1988, the president stated emphatically that he had never consulted an astrologer about policy decisions, but Nancy Reagan made it clear that she would continue to consult Quigley.

Sources: George Hackett and Eleanor Clift, "Of Planets and the Presidency: Ron and Nancy Look to the Stars for Guidance," *Newsweek*, 111 (16 May 1988): 20;

Donald T. Regan, *For the Record: From Wall Street to Washington* (San Diego, New York & London: Harcourt Brace Jovanovich, 1988).

---

truck loaded with dynamite into the headquarters compound of the U.S. Marine contingent, killing 241 marines and sailors. The following February the marines were withdrawn from Lebanon. On 20 September 1984 the new U.S. embassy in Beirut was bombed and destroyed. For the rest of Reagan's presidency, his administration relied on halting diplomacy in the region. In 1988, when PLO leader Yassir Arafat renounced terror-ism and called on all parties including Israel to begin negotiations toward a settlement, Reagan authorized the State Department to begin talks with the PLO.

Hijackings and Kidnappings. Lebanon and the Palestinian question dogged the Reagan administration throughout the 1980s, especially because of terrorist actions by groups sympathetic to the Palestinians, including airplane hijackings and bombings. These incidents

U.S. Marines going ashore in Beirut, Lebanon, September 1982

brought increasing frustration in the West, especially in the United States, because there appeared to be little that could be done to stop them. The most frustrating and frightening form of terrorism was the practice of Shiite groups in Beirut of kidnapping western residents of the city, including Americans, and demanding to exchange them for prisoners held by the Israelis.

The Libyan Connection. There was also increasing tension between the Reagan administration and the Libyan regime of Col. Mu'ammar al-Gadhafi. Gadhafi, a demagogic and charismatic leader, used some of Libya's oil wealth to finance terrorists operating in Europe and the Middle East. Moreover, there was evidence that Libyan diplomats had used their diplomatic status to move weapons and explosives across borders for the terrorists, as well as providing communications links for them. The United States specifically considered the Libyans responsible for the hijacking of TWA flight 847 in 1985. For some time Libya had claimed the Gulf of Sidra as part of its territorial waters, while the United States took the position that the gulf was international waters and periodically sent U.S. naval vessels into the gulf to emphasize that position. U.S. vessels entered the gulf some sixteen times between 1981 and March 1986. Periodically the Libyans sent jets, which were turned back without incident, but on 19 August 1981 there was an aerial dogfight

between U.S. and Libyan jets, and two Libyan planes were shot down.

Retaliation. On 7 January 1986 Reagan signed an executive order declaring a state of emergency between the United States and Libya. The order ended trade and transportation between the United States and Libya and ordered U.S. oil companies to end their Libyan operations. On 24 March missiles were fired at U.S. planes flying over the gulf. In retaliation the U.S. Navy fired missiles at the Libyan launch sites and fired on Libyan patrol boats that approached U.S. vessels, sinking three of them and damaging a fourth. On 5 April a bomb detonated in a West Berlin nightclub killed a U.S. Army sergeant and injured fifty other American servicemen, as well as 230 civilians. U.S. intelligence linked the bomb to Libya. On the night of 14–15 April aircraft from carriers in the Mediterranean and long-range bombers based in Great Britain attacked Libya. Gadhafi's command post was targeted, but he escaped harm. His young daughter was killed, and other members of his family were wounded. In 1989 U.S. and Libyan planes engaged in further aerial combat, and two Libyan planes were shot down.

The Iran-Iraq War. On 22 September 1980 Iraqi aircraft attacked Iran. Iraqi ground forces invaded the next day. The two countries had long disputed ownership of the Shatt al Arab waterway on their border. Furthermore,

Rescue workers removing an injured marine from the wreckage of the marine compound in Beirut after a terrorist bombing on 23 October 1983

the Iranians had provided support for Kurdish rebels in northern Iraq, and Iraq opposed the spread of radical fundamentalist Shiism from Iran. Many of Iraq's Persian Gulf neighbors provided funds and logistical support to Iraq, which also received military equipment from the Soviet Union. Seeing the two countries as effective counterweights to one another, the United States did little to assist either side — other than imposing an arms embargo on Iran in the early years of the war, which dragged on for eight years with neither side gaining a decided advantage. In addition to the arms embargo, it was contrary to U.S. law to sell arms to any country designated as a source of international terrorism. Iran had been identified as having a role in the Beirut bombings and kidnappings and thus fell within this prohibition.

The Arms-for-Hostages Deal. In 1984 American intelligence became concerned about growing Soviet influence in Iran, and the National Security Council (NSC), under the direction of Robert C. McFarlane, began seeking ways to counter that influence. They also hoped that the Iranians might be able to persuade Shiite groups in Beirut to release Americans they were holding hostage. In spring 1985 Israeli intelligence reported to their American contacts that the Israelis could provide Ameri-

can arms to Iran, in return for which Iranians would work to release the hostages. The Americans would then replace the arms that Israel shipped to Iran. McFarlane circulated a draft proposing this exchange, which was severely criticized by Secretary of State George Shultz and Secretary of Defense Caspar Weinberger. Despite the opposition of these two cabinet members, McFarlane and the NSC staff persuaded Reagan in August 1985 to go ahead with the delivery of five hundred TOW (tube-launched, optically tracked, wire-guided) antitank missiles to Iran. After the delivery of this shipment, a single hostage, Rev. Benjamin Weir, was released. Lt. Col. Oliver North, a marine attached to the NSC staff, then proposed the sale of eighty Hawk missiles to Iran, a proposal McFarlane accepted. Some of the Hawks were delivered in November, with the covert assistance of the CIA. During these arms transfers both North and McFarlane met with Iranian officials, even making secret trips to Iran to do so.

Presidential Approval. North continued to press the sale of arms in exchange for the release of hostages to an increasingly skeptical McFarlane. He got a more receptive audience when McFarlane was replaced as NSC director by Adm. John Poindexter in December 1985. In meetings throughout December 1985 and January 1986 the Reagan administration wrestled with the proposal, which Shultz and Weinberger continued to oppose, while Poindexter, North, and CIA director William Casey pressed for approval. Reagan sided with the latter group and signed a presidential finding authorizing the ongoing covert operation on 17 January 1986.

Operation Rescue. Starting with the January presidential finding, the United States began directly but covertly selling arms to Iran, in violation of the arms embargo and of the statutes prohibiting the sale of arms to any nation involved in international terrorism. These covert activities were also carried on without required statutory reporting to congressional oversight committees. This operation, which North called Operation Rescue, went on until early summer 1986. Three hostages were released, instead of the five or six for which the administration had hoped, and since the Shiite groups soon took additional hostages, the net effect was zero. The operation then got mixed in with U.S. Central American policy, when the administration began diverting the proceeds from the arms sales to support covert activities in El Salvador and Nicaragua.

Sources:

William H. Chafe, *The Unfinished Journey: America Since World War II,* second edition (New York: Oxford University Press, 1991);

Wilbur Edel, *The Reagan Presidency: An Actor's Finest Performance* (New York: Hippocrene Books, 1992);

Robert D. Schulzinger, *American Diplomacy in the Twentieth Century,* third edition (New York: Oxford University Press, 1994);

John Tower, Edmund Muskie, and Brent Scowcroft, *The Tower Commission Report: The Full Text of the President's Special Review Board* (New York: Bantam Books, 1987).

Lt. Col. Oliver North testifying before a joint session of the Senate and House committees investigating covert aid to Iran and the Contras in Nicaragua, 7 July 1987

THE MIDDLE EAST, CENTRAL AMERICA, AND THE IRAN-CONTRA SCANDAL

The Sandinistas. On 20 July 1979 the Sandinista guerrillas, a Marxist group led by Daniel Ortega, won a civil war they had been fighting against the Nicaraguan government of right-wing dictator Anastasio Somoza and proclaimed a new revolutionary government. Although the new government was made up of a coalition of anti-Somoza groups, the real power was held by the Marxist elements. Relations with the United States deteriorated. By the end of 1980 the Carter administration was planning to suspend economic aid to Nicaragua, and the CIA was covertly building an anti-Sandinista force. Even before Reagan took office, the Sandinistas began assisting leftist guerrillas in neighboring El Salvador.

El Salvador. The Reagan administration enthusiastically began providing economic assistance and military advisers to assist the government of El Salvador in fighting the leftist insurgency within its own borders. In March 1981 Reagan signed a directive to the CIA authorizing the covert recruiting, training, arming, and paying of an anti-Sandinista force in Nicaragua. By mid 1982 the force, which became known as the Contras, was

only eight hundred strong, but by 1985 it had some twenty thousand fighters. These actions fit well within the Reagan doctrine.

Human Rights Abuses. In El Salvador, Christian Democratic President José Napoleon Duarte had to deal with insurgency from the left and pressure from the right. The extreme right won control of the legislature in 1982, and right-wing death squads associated with the military indiscriminately killed people they considered inimical to their interests, including American nuns. Concerned over the human-rights abuses in El Salvador, Congress passed requirements that improvement in the Salvadoran human-rights record had to be certified by the president before additional aid could be given to that nation. Military advisers to the El Salvador armed forces were also scornful of their tendency to fight a "nine to five" war against the guerrillas.

The Boland Amendment. The secret war against the Sandinista government in Nicaragua became public knowledge within a year, and late in 1982 Rep. Edward Boland (D-Mass.) sponsored a successful amendment to the Defense Appropriations Bill for the 1983 fiscal year, prohibiting the use of U.S. funds to overthrow the Nicaraguan government. Reagan tried to get around this pro-

As president, Ronald Reagan practiced a "hands-off" style of management and decision making. Delegating substantial authority and relying on his appointees to recommend a set of options or even a single option, Reagan tended to endorse, rather than originate, decisions. He made policies in meetings with a few close confidants and then announced them at cabinet meetings. The president usually arrived at the Oval Office around 9:00 A.M. He would watch the squirrels in the Rose Garden, then receive a national-security briefing, and spend from 10 to 11 A.M. answering mail. After lunch he would nap and then work in the office until 5 P.M He spent most evenings exercising, eating dinner, and watching television. He was usually in his pajamas by 6 P.M.

Reagan was able to maintain such a light schedule because he followed a policy he expressed as "Surround yourself with the best people you can find, delegate authority, and don't interfere." Also, most information came to him in condensed form. A typical decision memorandum was a single page. Sometimes these memoranda were too condensed, and he would subsequently be embarrassed when he failed to show full awareness of the details or ramifications of a policy. After he issued a directive ordering unlimited use of polygraphs for all personnel in the national security field, he was surprised when Secretary of State George Shultz publicly threatened to resign rather than submit to a lie-detector test. When pressed by a businessman about his tax plan, he had to refer him to Secretary of the Treasury Donald Regan for the details. The press was also occasionally amused during press conferences, when Reagan would apparently get confused if he was asked to depart from his prepared script. Usually an aide (or Nancy Reagan) would whisper the answer in his ear, and he would dutifully repeat it.

Despite his dependence on the members of his administration, Reagan was remarkably passive and detached when appointing them. When he named Alexander Haig as his secretary of state, he had talked to him only once, and that was before his 1980 campaign. In that conversation the two men had discussed the show-business career of recently deceased Edgar Bergen. Wall Street banker Donald Regan was appointed secretary of the treasury after a brief phone conversation. Regan reports in his memoir of the Reagan administration that he and the president never privately discussed economic policy or the direction of the administration prior to the appointment or, in fact, during the entire four-year period Regan was in the cabinet. Terrel Bell reported a similar lack of direction when he was appointed secretary of education. At a meeting of mayors, Reagan failed to recognize Samuel Pierce, an African American he had made secretary of housing and urban development, and asked him how things were going in his city.

Reagan's detachment from his appointees led many of them to divine policy direction by extrapolating from the broad generalizations included in the president's public policy pronouncements, a process that gave them enormous freedom of action. During two major international incidents that took place while the president was asleep — the shooting down of two Libyan jet by the U.S. Navy in August 1981 and the Soviet downing of a Korean airliner in September 1983 — members of the administration saw no need to wake the president for instructions. This freedom of action contributed significantly to the Iran-Contra scandal. National Security Adviser John Poindexter testified that he acted without specifically informing the president because the National Security Council knew the president's wishes and thought they had the authority to act independently.

By 1987 members of the Reagan administration and Congress were beginning to wonder openly about Reagan's inattention to governing. Complaints began to circulate that the president seemed unable to respond to policy proposals made in private meetings and that he would interrupt policy discussions to engage in personal reminiscences with no relevance to the topic at hand. The administration was embarrassed in 1988, when former secretary of the treasury and White House chief of staff Donald Regan revealed in his memoir that Nancy Reagan sought advice from an astrologer and made him adjust the president's schedule according to the astrologer's predictions about which days were propitious and which were not.

In 1994 former president Reagan announced that he was suffering from Alzheimer's disease, which had developed since he left office. Future historians will likely speculate about the extent to which he may have been suffering from the disease during his last years as president.

Sources: William H. Chafe, *The Unfinished Journey: America Since World War II,* second edition (New York: Oxford University Press, 1991);

Wilbur Edel, *The Reagan Presidency: An Actor's Finest Performance* (New York: Hippocrene Books, 1992);

Donald T. Regan, *For the Record: From Wall Street to Washington* (San Diego, New York & London: Harcourt Brace Jovanovich, 1988).

vision by issuing a finding that authorized support for the Contras to "put pressure" on the Sandinista government — a phrasing that split legal hairs with the Boland Amendment prohibition against funding the "overthrow" of the Sandinistas. Congressional opponents of the effort to arm the Contras renewed the Boland Amendment in 1983, 1984, and 1985, keeping it in effect through the 1986 fiscal year. The political furor in the United States over Reagan's policy toward Nicaragua heated up after news broke in April 1983 that the CIA had helped to plan and execute Contra attacks on oil terminals in several Nicaraguan locations.

Diplomatic Efforts. Starting with a January 1983 meeting on the island of Contadora, off the coast of Panama, the Central American nations of Colombia, Mexico, Panama, and Venezuela began several years of efforts to find a diplomatic solution to the conflict in Nicaragua. Other Latin American countries were also becoming increasingly critical of the American effort to overthrow the Sandinista government.

Advice from Kissinger. Facing increased pressure from Congress and critics of his policy toward Central America, Reagan appointed a blue-ribbon commission headed by former national security adviser and secretary of state Henry Kissinger to advise him on Central America. Beginning its work in June 1983, the commission reported early the following year. They viewed the turmoil in Central America as stemming from social inequities rather than a Marxist plot for global domination. The commission urged additional U.S. economic assistance and recommended continued support for the efforts in El Salvador and Nicaragua.

Mining Harbors. The furor over U.S. efforts in El Salvador and Nicaragua was fueled further when it was learned that the CIA had helped to mine Nicaraguan harbors in January 1984. Dutch, Panamanian, and Soviet ships were among those damaged when they struck the mines.

The International Court of Justice. Nicaragua sought relief by appealing to the International Court of Justice, claiming that U.S. attacks on its oil facilities, mining of its harbors, and support for the Contras violated the UN charter and the provisions of a 1956 treaty between the United States and Nicaragua. The Reagan administration took the position that the court did not have jurisdiction in the case. When the court ruled unanimously that it did have jurisdiction, the United States refused to participate in further proceedings and unilaterally abrogated a 1946 agreement that the United States would accept the court's jurisdiction in cases of this sort. In June 1986 the court ruled against the United States and declared that Nicaragua was entitled to reparations, a decision that the United States ignored.

Funding the Contras. Congress continued its prohibition against U.S. funding of the military efforts against the Sandinista government through fiscal year 1986, but they did approve some humanitarian assistance in late 1985. Although the Reagan administration tried several public-relations efforts designed to win public support for their backing of the Contras, they were never able to generate more than a lukewarm response. They then began to look for other ways to continue funding for the Contras.

A Secret Bank Account. Members of the NSC staff set up a secret Swiss bank account for funds to support the Contras. They then began actively soliciting funds from other nations, especially the oil-rich states of the Persian Gulf. Lieutenant Colonel North was among those staffers most active in these efforts, which were kept secret to bypass congressional scrutiny. Beginning in 1985 North, who was also involved in the secret arms-for-hostages deals with Iran, proposed that the proceeds from direct arms sales to the Iranians be deposited in the secret Contra bank account.

Press Investigations. On 3 November 1986 *Al Shiraa*, a small Lebanese weekly with ties to the Iranian government, published a story in which it stated that McFarlane and other Americans had visited Tehran the previous spring to negotiate a release of the hostages in exchange for American arms. Over the next week reporters began investigating the story and questioning American officials. Initially the administration declined to comment, and then it denied the story. The head of the Iranian parliament then announced that McFarlane and others had indeed visited Tehran as part of a secret initiative. Reporters began pressing harder, and members of Congress began to demand answers. Information leaks from the American intelligence community fueled public curiosity. On 13 November Reagan gave a televised address in which he admitted to a secret diplomatic initiative designed to end the Iran-Iraq War, reduce terrorism, and free the hostages in Beirut. He also admitted to sending Iran small numbers of defensive weapons and spare parts, but he denied a swap for hostages. In the aftermath of his speech, more and more information came to light, including Reagan's signed directives authorizing the arms transfers and proof that he had instructed the CIA to avoid reporting these actions to the relevant congressional committees. At a 19 November news conference Reagan admitted the transfer of TOW missiles to Iran. He directed Attorney General Edwin Meese to investigate his administration's involvement, and on 23 November Meese announced his discovery that proceeds from arms sales had been diverted to the Contras. Both North and Poindexter were relieved of their positions at the NSC. Critics demanded an impartial investigation and even suggested the appointment of a special prosecutor to look into possible violations of law.

Investigation. The pressure on the administration to account for the arms deals and the secret Contra fund built rapidly. Reagan responded on 26 November 1986 by naming conservative senator John Tower (R-Tex.), former secretary of state and former Democratic presi-

American forces taking prisoners during the U.S. invasion of Panama, December 1989

dential candidate Edmund Muskie, and retired general and former national security adviser Brent Scowcroft as a review board to investigate the so-called Iran-Contra affair and to make recommendations to the president. Reagan pledged the full cooperation of his administration with the group, which became known as the Tower Commission. A day later Reagan authorized the attorney general to seek the appointment of a special prosecutor to investigate whether criminal prosecution was warranted. Lawrence Walsh was appointed as special prosecutor. In January 1987 Congress decided to hold hearings before joint sessions of the House Select Committee to Investigate Covert Arms Transactions with Iran and the Senate Select Committee on Secret Military Assistance to Iran and the Nicaraguan Opposition. The committees and their staffs conducted closed-session interviews with many of the principals in the transactions and then conducted televised hearings in May, June, and July.

The Tower Commission. The Tower Commission began work in December 1986 and issued its report on 26 February 1987. North and Poindexter refused to cooperate with the inquiry. The commission placed blame for the affair on McFarlane, North, former CIA director William Casey, and some former intelligence officials, as well as several Israelis and Iranians. The commission was also critical of White House Chief of Staff Donald Regan, Secretary of State Shultz, and Secretary of Defense Weinberger for failing to oppose the scheme more vigorously. The commission portrayed President Reagan as too detached from the process and too little aware of what his subordinates were doing. Rather than suggesting that the NSC process had failed, they concluded that it had been bypassed.

Congressional Hearings. The congressional hearings uncovered information that not only had the arms embargo been subverted, but the law prohibiting the selling of arms to nations that supported terrorism had been violated, and public funds had been diverted to supporting the Contras in violation of the Boland Amendment. Furthermore, some of the participants had lied to Congress; key documents had been shredded; and some funds from the arms sales had been diverted to some of the principals for personal use. There was also evidence that some of them had tried to cover up the incident by planting false stories, doctoring the chronology of events, and otherwise seeking to keep secret the full dimensions of the arms-for-hostages deal and the diversion of funds to the Contras. North and Poindexter vigorously defended their actions by claiming that they were carrying out the expressed policy preferences of the president and that once given direction they saw themselves free to implement policy by whatever means necessary. In his testimony North revealed that consideration was being given to funding other covert activities in a similar manner, again bypassing congressional oversight. Critics suggested that the affair was a subversion of the Constitution and the rule of law and thus a challenge to the foundations of American democracy. Others tended to view North and Poindexter as patriots standing up against Communism in Central America. Like the Tower Commission, the congressional committee report tended to show Reagan as too detached from the policy process. They found no evidence that Vice President George Bush or his staff had more than a vague awareness of the Contra operation.

Indictments. Lawrence Walsh, the special prosecutor, brought indictments for perjury and misuse of public funds against North, Poindexter, McFarlane, and some of the arms dealers who acted as middlemen. McFarlane pleaded guilty. The others were convicted; North and Poindexter later appealed and won reversals of their convictions.

Public Opinion. Through all of 1987 the furor surrounding the Iran-Contra investigations seriously undermined Reagan's reputation and generally hindered the conduct of foreign policy. There was also a public-opinion backlash. Memories of the 1980 Iran hostage crisis were still clear, and many Americans had difficulty reconciling the administration's public condemnation of Iran as an outlaw nation responsible for sponsoring terrorism and the hostages held in Beirut with that same administration's secret and illegal arms transfers to Iran.

Helping Iraq. With the war between Iran and Iraq continuing, the Reagan administration then tilted toward Iraq, giving the Iraqis intelligence information on Iran's armed forces and providing credit guarantees, loans, and technical assistance for weapons production, including missiles. When Iran started releasing antiship mines in the Persian Gulf, hampering the shipping of oil from Iraq and other nations, the United States and other western countries sent naval vessels to escort tankers in the Persian Gulf and to clear mines from the shipping lanes. The presence of American naval vessels in the gulf also served to hamper the Iranian war effort.

Casualties. During the escort in May 1987, thirty-seven sailors on the USS *Stark*, a destroyer, were killed when an Iraqi jet mistakenly fired an Exocet missile at the ship. On 3 July 1988 the USS *Vincennes* mistook an Iranian passenger plane for a warplane and shot it down. The United States took responsibility for the error and compensated the families of the victims. Exhausted by their war, Iran and Iraq negotiated and signed a cease-fire in August 1988 with the help of UN Secretary General Javier Perez de Cuellar.

Nicaragua and El Salvador. The fighting between the Contras and the Sandinista government in Nicaragua went on haltingly in 1987 and 1988, as did the guerrilla war against the government of El Salvador. In February

1989, with the assistance of the other Central American countries, the two sides in the Nicaraguan conflict agreed to stop fighting and to hold free elections before 25 February 1990. Newly elected President Bush was able to persuade Congress to provide humanitarian assistance to the Contras through the 1990 elections. The war in El Salvador also sputtered to a halt in 1989.

The Panama Invasion. During the 1988 presidential campaign, the Republican administration was embarrassed by the revelation that Panamanian dictator Gen. Manuel Noriega, an ally of the United States with long-standing connections to the CIA, was involved in the drug trade and had been indicted by a federal grand jury for his role in smuggling cocaine into the United States. When the United States threatened economic sanctions, Noriega called for elections, which were held in May 1989. Surprisingly he lost, but he refused to step down. In October a CIA-sponsored coup failed to dislodge him. On 20 December, as the decade ended, U.S. troops invaded Panama, quickly taking over the country. Noriega hid in the Vatican embassy but finally surrendered to U.S. troops on 3 January 1990. The new Panamanian government extradited him to the United States, where he was tried and convicted in 1992 for conspiracy to smuggle cocaine into the United States.

Sources:
William H. Chafe, *The Unfinished Journey: America Since World War II*, second edition (New York: Oxford University Press, 1991);

Wilbur Edel, *The Reagan Presidency: An Actor's Finest Performance* (New York: Hippocrene Books, 1992);

Robert D. Schulzinger, *American Diplomacy in the Twentieth Century*, third edition (New York: Oxford University Press, 1994);

John Tower, Edmund Muskie, and Brent Scowcroft, *The Tower Commission Report: The Full Text of the President's Special Review Board* (New York: Bantam Books, 1987).

NATIONAL POLITICS: REPUBLICAN NOMINATION RACE 1980

Reagan Emerges Early. Former California governor Ronald Reagan quickly became the front-runner in a crowded pack of Republican presidential hopefuls that also included Sen. Howard H. Baker Jr. of Tennessee, former UN ambassador and CIA head George Bush of Texas, Congressman John B. Anderson of Illinois, former Texas governor John B. Connally, and Sen. Robert J. Dole of Kansas. After beating Reagan by 33,530 to 31,348 votes in the Iowa precinct caucuses on 21 January 1980, Bush claimed to have the "Big Mo" (momentum) in his favor, but his campaign stalled in New Hampshire. He hurt his image when he supported the *Nashua Telegraph* plan to limit the debate it sponsored to the two front-runners, believing quite rightly that it was not to his advantage to split his targets and appear to be at odds with other moderates. Also realizing the problems such a debate would cause Bush, Reagan invited the others to join in the debate, creating the image of Bush as an elitist and of himself as a man of the people. Reagan beat Bush by a 2–1 margin in the 26 February primary. Bush's

George Bush during his 1980 campaign for the Republican presidential nomination

subsequent victories over Reagan in Massachusetts (4 March), Connecticut (25 March), Pennsylvania (22 April), and Michigan (20 May) were overshadowed by Reagan wins in twenty-eight of the thirty-two primaries he entered. (Bush also won in the District of Columbia and Puerto Rico, where Reagan's name was not on the ballot.) By 20 May Reagan had more than enough delegates to win the Republican nomination.

Reagan's Preparations for Victory. In 1976, after failing for a second time to win his party's presidential nomination, conservative Republican Ronald Reagan had begun almost immediately to plan for 1980. From 1977 until he announced his candidacy in November 1979, he earned more than $100,000 a year from taped radio editorials and newspaper columns while delivering speeches all across the United States. He also established a political action committee (PAC), Citizens for the Republic, which contributed more that $600,000 to Republican candidates in the 1978 elections. Other Republicans had PACs as well, but Reagan's PAC spent more money, offering support to 234 House candidates, 25 Senate candidates, and 19 gubernatorial hopefuls — as well as 122 other Republicans running for state and local offices. In 1980 Reagan was able to call in a large number of political IOUs, thereby demonstrating a far broader base of support than he had in his two earlier tries for the presidential nomination.

Moderates Cancel Each Other Out. The crowded field of would-be nominees hurt Bush, who found himself competing with Anderson and Baker for the votes of Republican moderates. Many Republicans did not share Reagan's conservative social views, nor were they sure about his faith in supply-side economics: the theory that substantial tax cuts will result in increased economic activity that will generate sufficient revenue to replace the money lost by the tax cuts. Bush labeled this theory "voodoo economics" and charged (as President Jimmy Carter would later) that a massive tax cut would stimulate inflation not reduce it. Yet because moderate voting was split, Reagan forged ahead in the Republican nomination race and stayed there — even after Baker dropped out of the race on 5 March, after four quick defeats.

Ford Considers Running. As Reagan gained momentum, former president Gerald R. Ford toyed with the idea of challenging him, asserting on 2 March that "a very conservative Republican can't win a national election." A CBS News/*New York Times* poll for 12–15 March showed that Republicans preferred Ford to Reagan by 52 to 27 percent and that Ford was the only Republican all voters favored over President Jimmy Carter (47 to 42 percent). Yet on 15 March Ford withdrew from the race.

Reagan's Conservative Opponents Falter. Meanwhile Reagan's fellow conservatives were falling by the wayside. Connally of Texas had stayed out of the New England primaries to concentrate on South Carolina, where he hoped for strong support from fellow southerners, but he came in a distant second when that state held its primary on 8 March, earning less than 30 percent of the vote to 54.7 percent for Reagan. Connally dropped out the race the next day. Dole, who had never managed to capture Republican voters' imaginations, announced his departure from the race on 15 March.

The Illinois Primary. The 18 March primary in Anderson's home state was a crucial test for Reagan. Anderson, considered a liberal Republican because he favored abortion rights and opposed increased defense spending, hoped to attract crossover votes from liberal Democrats. Yet Reagan's appeal among conservative Democrats and independents was also strong. He benefited from their support, defeating Anderson by a 4–3 margin. Bush finished third.

The Field Narrows to One. After coming in second to Reagan again in Wisconsin (1 April), Anderson announced on 24 April that he would withdraw from the Republican nomination race and become an independent candidate for president. On 20 May Reagan won the Oregon primary, gaining the votes he needed for the nomination. In addition to coming in first in twenty-eight of thirty-two primaries, he won nearly 400 of the 478 delegates elected by party caucuses. Bush officially dropped out of the race on 26 May.

The Republican National Convention. When the Republicans met in Detroit on 14–17 July, Reagan won 1,939 of 1,994 votes (97 percent) on the first ballot. Anderson was a distant second with 37 votes, while 13 of the 18 remaining votes went to Bush. Moderate and conservative Republicans compromised to give Reagan a party platform he and they could live with, though no one was entirely happy with it. It took Reagan's position against renewing the peacetime military draft (though many delegates favored it), and it took no stand on the Equal Rights Amendment (which Reagan opposed), becoming the first Republican platform since 1940 not to favor such an amendment. The platform also included planks calling for tax cuts and less governmental regulation — policy statements on which most of the party agreed. At the same time it took Reagan's hard-line, conservative positions on two major issues, calling for a constitutional amendment to outlaw abortion and for a massive increase in defense spending.

The Vice Presidential Candidate. The only suspense at the convention was over Reagan's choice of a running mate. Many Republicans wanted Ford, who had suggested in two television interviews that he would accept if Reagan met certain unspecified conditions. It later became known that the former president wanted clearly defined responsibilities that would make him virtually a copresident. Although the two men nearly reached an agreement, Reagan finally decided that he could not accede to all Ford's demands. He offered Ford the second spot on the ticket anyway, but Ford refused it. Reagan then turned to Bush, who offered political and geographical balance to the ticket. Bush accepted despite clear differences of opinion with Reagan. Unlike his running mate, Bush supported the Equal Rights Amendment and opposed a constitutional amendment outlawing abortion (while sharing Reagan's stand against publicly funded abortions). Bush was also less doctrinaire than Reagan on issues involving the Soviet Union, and he had called Reagan's tax-cut proposal inflationary, while favoring a smaller cut. Emphasizing his "common ground" with Reagan, Bush vowed, "I'm not going to get nickeled and dimed to death" over differences. In his acceptance speech Reagan reached out to mainstream Republicans, as well as deliberately appealing to Democratic voters such as blacks and union members.

NATIONAL POLITICS: DEMOCRATIC NOMINATION RACE 1980

Carter's Public Opinion Ratings. In July 1979 President Jimmy Carter's approval rating reached a low point of 26 percent, with the American public particularly unhappy with his handling of domestic issues such as inflation, unemployment, high interest rates, and a major oil shortage. After a ten-day conference at Camp David, Carter managed to cloak a good energy proposal in a speech that preached to the American people about a national "crisis in confidence" and offered a personal mea culpa for his concerns having "become increasingly narrow, focused more and more on what the isolated world of Washington thinks is important." His subsequent reshuffling of his cabinet and the forced resignations of five advisers only deepened the impression among many Americans that the true "crisis of confidence" belonged to

their president, whose administration seemed incompetent to govern the nation. Democrats overwhelmingly favored Sen. Edward M. Kennedy as their candidate in the 1980 presidential election, and there was speculation that the president was incapable of winning renomination.

Rallying Round the Flag. By October Carter's popularity had climbed to a meager 33 percent, and his party still favored Kennedy by a margin of 2–1. Then, on 4 November 1979 — exactly one year before the 1980 elections — Iranian militants seized the American embassy in Tehran and held more than sixty Americans hostage, Public-opinion polls began to exhibit the "rally round the flag" phenomenon that historically has followed any sort of American foreign-policy crisis: no matter how the president acts, or how successful or unsuccessful his response, his popularity increases. Carter's overall approval rating began climbing, reaching 53 percent by February 1980. Yet in the same month — with approval of his Iran policy at 63 percent — only 48 percent approved of his handling of foreign policy in general, and only 26 percent liked his economic policy.

Democratic Challengers. Gov. Edmund G. "Jerry" Brown Jr. of California was the first Democrat to challenge the president. Having made an impressive showing after entering the 1976 presidential race late and having easily won reelection in the 1978 California gubernatorial race, Brown entered the 1980 nomination contest with high hopes. After polls repeatedly showed him the Democrat most likely to win the election, Kennedy also decided to run and scheduled the formal announcement of his candidacy for 8 November 1979 — a date that turned out to be four days after the seizure of the American embassy in Tehran.

Carter Surges Forward. Riding the crest of his popularity — fueled by the Soviet invasion of Afghanistan in late December 1979 as well as the hostage crisis — Carter employed the "rose garden" strategy of most incumbent chief executives: he stayed in the White House and acted presidential. By refusing to debate Kennedy and Brown on television he created the impression that he was too involved in crucial decision making to engage in "mere politics," and he deprived his opponents of free media exposure. Many of his public responses to crises were timed to have optimal impact on the nomination process. On the Sunday before the Iowa caucuses (21 January 1980) he proposed a boycott of the summer 1980 Olympic Games in Moscow. Just before the Illinois primary (18 March), in which Kennedy was expected to make a strong showing, the president threatened to cancel the Strategic Arms Limitation Treaty (SALT II) unless the Soviet Union withdrew its troops from Afghanistan. On the day before the crucial 1 April Wisconsin primary, the United States set a deadline for the release of the hostages in Iran, and just as the polls opened the next morning Carter went on television to announce what appeared to be a breakthrough in hostage negotiations. While many of the president's decisions later hurt his chances for reelection, during the early months of 1980 a combination of luck and good timing enhanced his image as an experienced, level-headed decision maker.

Kennedy and the Character Issue. Having decided to wait until late 1979 to announce his candidacy, Kennedy inadvertently found himself challenging an incumbent president just as a major foreign-policy crisis had created the usual calls for solidarity behind the chief executive. At this point in the hostage situation criticism of Carter was widely viewed as a threat to national unity. As Carter's approval rating rose, Kennedy's popularity declined. In February 1980, 58 percent of the respondents to a CBS News/*New York Times* poll said they had a favorable opinion of Carter while 32 percent had an unfavorable opinion. Kennedy's numbers were reversed: 25 percent favorable, 56 percent unfavorable. The reason for his decline in the polls was not just the "rally round the flag" phenomenon. Before Kennedy announced his candidacy the majority of the American public seemed to have forgotten or to no longer be concerned about a fatal automobile accident in summer 1969 that had called into question the senator's morality, honesty, and ability to handle crises. After his announcement, however, the incident once again became an issue.

The Chappaquiddick Incident. In July 1969 Kennedy and a young aide, Mary Jo Kopechne, left a party on Chappaquiddick Island, Massachusetts, in Kennedy's car, which Kennedy then accidentally drove off a bridge. He managed to escape, but he was unable to free Kopechne, who drowned. Kennedy's indecisive actions in seeking help for her and his failure to report the accident until the next morning led to charges that he had been more concerned about his political image than saving a human life, to suggestions that he lacked the character and emotional stability to deal with the pressures of the presidency, and to speculation about where the married senator and his pretty, young assistant had been headed.

Issues Take Second Place. As the primary season began, Kennedy offered liberal alternatives to the president's largely unsuccessful attempts to improve the economy, attempting to portray himself as a Democrat in the tradition of Franklin D. Roosevelt and John F. Kennedy. The Massachusetts senator proposed wage and price controls, national health insurance, and a jobs program while opposing Carter's plan to end price controls on oil and natural gas. Polls taken during the Democratic primaries showed that voters who said they cast their ballots based on the candidates' stands on the issues tended to prefer Kennedy, but those who based their choices on their perceptions of the candidates' personal integrity overwhelmingly voted for Carter. In February 1980 one out of every ten Democrats said they disliked Kennedy because of the Chappaquiddick incident. The Carter campaign played on this sentiment by running a television advertisement in which people interviewed "on the street" in Philadelphia made statements such as "I don't think he [Kennedy] can deal with a crisis," and "I trust Carter more than Kennedy."

The Search for Delegates. Carter won 58 percent of the delegates in the Iowa caucuses while 30 percent supported Kennedy, and Brown ran a distant third. Carter came in first in New Hampshire, though with less than half of the total Democratic votes cast (47.1), and he went on to win in Vermont (4 March); Alabama, Florida, and Georgia (11 March); and Puerto Rico (16 March), while preparing for a big showdown with Kennedy in Illinois (18 March). The Massachusetts senator won the primary in his home state (4 March) and arrived in Illinois with the endorsement of Mayor Jane Byrne of Chicago and the support of the powerful Chicago Democratic "machine." Given Kennedy's popularity with urban, industrial, ethnic, and Catholic voters, he should have done well in Illinois, but Carter's victory there was overwhelming. After this primary he had a quarter of the votes he needed to win the nomination. The media predicted that the president's renomination was assured, even after Kennedy upset him in New York and Connecticut on 25 March. The next big test was in Wisconsin (1 April), where Carter stopped Kennedy's momentum by winning with 56.2 percent of the vote. Brown, who had won only 10 percent of the vote in New Hampshire, had lost federal campaign funding because of his low standing and had limited his campaigning to one last attempt in Wisconsin. After coming in a distant third in that primary, he dropped out of the race.

A Flip-Flop in Public Opinion. Just as the president had the nomination nearly wrapped up, public opinion began to turn against him. In March 49 percent of Democrats and 48 percent of the public overall had a favorable opinion of Carter. In April those numbers stood at 52 percent and 43 percent, and by June they had dropped to 43 percent and 33 percent. Carter's handling of the economy had never been popular, and in this three-month period the public began questioning his foreign-policy decisions as well. The Soviets showed no sign of leaving Afghanistan, despite Carter's cancellation of grain sales to the Soviet Union, which hurt American farmers, and his threats to renounce SALT II, which worsened U.S.–Soviet relations just as the Cold War had seemed ready to thaw. In April the U.S. Olympic Committee, under pressure from the White House, voted to boycott the Moscow Olympics, but many allies of the United States refused to follow suit, and the boycott irritated the American people far more than it hurt the Russians. The focal point for the public's negative perception of the president was the Iran hostage situation. On 12 February Carter had vowed to the world, "I am not going to resume business-as-usual as a partisan campaigner out on the campaign trail until our hostages are back here — free and at home." At the time this stand bolstered his image as a statesman, but by late April — after negotiations and diplomatic maneuvering had come to naught and an armed attempt to free the hostages had failed miserably — the president began to seem like a prisoner in his own house, an inept statesman held hostage by his own promise.

Kennedy Wins Too Little Too Late. During the same three-month period, as Carter's popularity was waning, Kennedy's favorable rating with the public overall improved from 25 percent in March to 29 percent in June, and among Democrats it climbed from 36 percent to 40 percent, bringing him almost even with the president. Kennedy scored upset victories in the Pennsylvania primary (22 April) and the Michigan party caucuses, and he won five of the eight primaries held on 3 June, including those in the delegate-rich states of California and New Jersey. Yet a quarter of the Democrats in New Jersey and 40 percent in California said they voted for "the lesser of the evils." When Kennedy won he won narrowly, and Carter had continued winning primaries in big states such as Texas (3 May) and Ohio (3 June) as well as in many smaller states, especially in the South. In general he had also fared better than Kennedy in states where delegates were chosen in party caucuses.

Fallout from "Billygate." With more than enough votes to win the nomination, Carter still had to contend with his slipping approval rating. During the month before the Democratic National Convention, the president's prestige took another blow. It was revealed that his brother, Billy Carter, who had been acting as an intermediary between the United States and Libya in an effort to gain the release of the Iran hostages, had taken a $220,000 loan from the Libyan government. The president told the Senate subcommittee formed to investigate his brother's dealings that Billy Carter had not influenced governmental policy toward Libya, and the subcommittee agreed, while also concluding that Billy Carter had done nothing illegal. Yet the senators also faulted the president — along with some members of his cabinet, family, and staff — for using poor judgment.

A Divided Convention. When the Democratic National Convention opened in New York City on 11 August, 1,981.1 delegates were pledged to President Carter, 315 more than he needed for the nomination; 1,225.8 were pledged to Senator Kennedy, while 122.1 were uncommitted and 2 were committed to other candidates. Amid widespread speculation that voters in the early primaries would have voted differently if they had cast their ballots in June or July, Kennedy launched a last-ditch effort to win the nomination. Backed by as many as fifty Democratic congressmen, he and other Carter opponents tried to change the convention rule that bound delegates on the first ballot to vote for the candidate to whom they were pledged when they were elected. The day before the convention opened, Kennedy strategists believed they were within fifty to one hundred votes of success, but when the convention voted on 11 August, they lost by 545.84. (Only about 165 Carter delegates voted with them.) Bowing to the inevitable, Kennedy announced

that he would not allow his name to be placed in nomination, but, he vowed, "the efforts for Democratic principles must and will continue."

The Platform Wars. The Kennedy and Carter camps proceeded to face off on writing the party platform, carrying more than twenty unresolved issues to the convention floor, where heated debates illustrated deep divisions in the party. After the delegates had voted, the president found himself running on a platform that was more liberal than his own views. For example, the platform called for federal abortion funding, which Carter opposed while supporting legal abortion. He also favored ratification of the Equal Rights Amendment but stopped short of agreeing with the plank denying party support to candidates who opposed it. Kennedy forces also did well on issues related to the economy, winning three of four challenges to Carter platform proposals. They succeeded in gaining approval for a plank calling for a $12 billion jobs program, which Carter accepted in principle without committing himself to budgeting a specific amount of money for it. For many delegates and television viewers Kennedy's 12 August speech in support of his economic proposals was the most exciting event of the convention.

Carter's Hollow Victory. The next night Carter was renominated, winning 2,123 votes to 1,150.5 for Kennedy. In his acceptance speech the president appealed directly for Kennedy's support and called for party unity, but the delegates' thunderous applause was interrupted by loud boos when he mentioned his call for reinstating the military draft (a policy given only tepid support in the platform). Vice President Walter Mondale, accepting his renomination, was nearly alone in expressing unequivocal admiration for the president's record.

NATIONAL POLITICS: 1980 ELECTIONS

A Nation in Turmoil. The 1980 presidential campaign was waged against a backdrop of national insecurity. The United States had emerged from World War II as the most prosperous and powerful nation on earth. Three and a half decades later the United States no longer dominated the world economy, nor did it have a military edge on the Soviet Union, whose conventional forces were superior in number and whose stockpile of strategic nuclear weapons had grown to at least equal that of the United States. Despite fears created by the erosion of their country's international standing, Americans were most concerned with pocketbook issues: high unemployment, soaring interest rates, and double-digit inflation.

The Energy Debate: Carter. After the severe gasoline shortage of 1979 Americans had become painfully aware of how closely their economic woes were connected the their nation's dependence on foreign oil. They were also beginning to realize that any possible solution to the problem would cost them money. By the time the 1980 presidential campaign got underway, part of President Carter's energy plan was already in place and working. In

April 1979 he had announced a gradual phasing out of government controls on the price of domestic crude oil, a measure designed to limit consumption by raising consumer prices. The following July he proposed a windfall-profits tax to fund research on alternative energy sources such as solar power and synthetic fuels, which passed Congress and reached the president's desk in April 1980. A separate bill proposed the creation of the Energy Security Corporation (ESC) to allocate the income from this tax. This bill passed in June 1980, after heavy opposition from Ronald Reagan and congressional Republicans, who saw the ESC as a major extension of federal power into yet another area previously reserved for private enterprise. Another element of Carter's plan — an Energy Mobilization Board (EMB) to cut through red tape blocking "construction of needed energy facilities" — failed to pass Congress, in part because Reagan and his congressional allies opposed it as still more encroachment of "big government" and in part because many environmentalists feared that the "red tape" the board was intended to cut through would include important environmental protection laws. By mid 1980 Carter could point to several successful results of his program: the United States had cut its importation of foreign oil by one million barrels a day; there was more exploration for domestic oil than ever before in the nation's history; and the use of solar energy had soared. Yet some critics questioned the long-term effectiveness of the program, and Carter had managed to anger both the environmentalists and the conservatives.

The Energy Debate: Reagan. While Carter stressed the limits of the world's resources of fossil fuels, his Republican opponent refused to acknowledge that such limits existed. Reagan called for "more domestic production of oil and gas" and "greater use of nuclear power within strict safety standards." While Carter sought cooperation between the private and public sectors, Reagan believed that the American oil companies could solve the energy crisis essentially by themselves. Instead of creating new agencies, he proposed to eliminate the Department of Energy. At the same time he said he would rapidly decontrol oil and natural gas prices, ease environmental regulations, and use federal funds for oil exploration. While rejecting "unequivocally punitive gasoline and other energy taxes designed to artificially suppress domestic consumption," he called for higher oil and natural gas prices, with the resulting oil company profits to be spent on exploration for new natural resources.

The Energy Debate: Anderson. Independent candidate John Anderson, who made the energy issue the major thrust of his campaign, offered a plan that also meant higher gasoline prices. He argued that a fifty-cent per gallon tax could reduce gasoline consumption by more than one million barrels a day. Unlike his opponents he called for returning the extra money spent on gasoline directly to the American people, by using the proceeds from this tax to decrease payroll taxes and raise Social Security benefits.

Inflation. The Republican platform called inflation "the greatest domestic threat facing our nation today," and most Americans agreed. The GOP blamed the problem on big government, high taxation, and ever-increasing government spending. The solution — according to Reagan — was a downsizing of the federal government, elimination of government regulations that limited the growth of private industry, balancing the budget, and cutting taxes, both for individuals and businesses. These proposals, more populist than Republican, cast Reagan as the classic outsider waging battle against the Washington establishment — the tactic Carter had used in 1976. The Democrats borrowed Bush's label, "voodoo economics," to denigrate Reagan's economic plan. Carter preached austerity as the only way out of the wage-price spiral, offering only a small tax cut to offset a 1981 Social Security tax increase. He blamed much of the increase in inflation on the Organization of Petroleum Exporting Countries (OPEC) and promised that reducing American oil imports would lower inflation as well. He reiterated his party's stand against a constitutional amendment requiring a balanced budget (which the Republicans favored), while supporting fiscally responsible spending to get the federal government gradually out of debt. At the same time, he distanced himself from Democratic liberals who called for more federal programs to control the wage-price spiral.

Voting for Change. In autumn 1980 most American voters found themselves trying to choose among candidates for whom they felt little enthusiasm. During primary season Reagan's opposition to the ERA and his call for a constitutional ban on abortion had solidified his support from the religious Right and other conservatives. In the fall he could afford to appeal to a broader range of voters with slogans such as "Together, A New Beginning" and "For a Change." (In fact he did little to fulfill his abortion-amendment promise during his eight-year presidency, and the ERA failed without any concerted effort on his part.) Reagan concentrated on attacking Carter's handling of the economy and his foreign-policy failures. From his self-imposed imprisonment in the White House, Carter found himself waging a negative and defensive campaign — attacking Reagan as "simplistic" and "not equipped to be President," while defending himself against Reagan's charges. The president's campaign staff did little to focus public attention on their candidate's accomplishments in human rights and energy policy, or his foreign-policy successes, which included the Camp David accords between Egypt and Israel, the Panama Canal treaty, and the normalization of relations with mainland China.

The Public-Relations Seesaw. In the early weeks of the presidential campaign Carter forged ahead. In mid September a CBS News/*New York Times* poll asked Americans if each of the two major candidates "under-

President Jimmy Carter addressing well-wishers on election day in Plains, Georgia, 4 November 1980

stands the complicated problems a President has to deal with." Sixty-eight percent thought Carter did, while only 48 percent could say the same for Reagan. Yet by late September Reagan's rating on the same question had risen to 62 percent while Carter's remained the same. The main reason for the increase in Reagan's rating was his 21 September televised debate with Anderson. Because Anderson was in direct competition with Carter for liberal votes, the Carter campaign realized that their candidate had more to lose than to gain from a three-way debate with Reagan and Anderson, and they refused to have Carter participate, hoping his absence would make the debate seem unimportant. While ratings were undoubtedly lower than they would have been if Carter had taken part, Reagan was able to use the occasion to his advantage. Displaying the style that would earn him the sobriquet "The Great Communicator," Reagan presented his views in a moderate manner, dispelling many doubts about competence and accusations of extremism. Before the debate he was 4 percent behind Carter in opinion polls. Afterward he was 5 percentage points ahead. The Democrats intensified their attacks on Reagan, charging that he was not to be trusted with nuclear weapons and a threat to the social fabric of the United States. Carter called the election "a choice between peace and war" and said Reagan might well separate the American people into black versus white, Jew versus Gentile, North versus

South, and rural versus urban. Reagan countered such attacks calmly, and the press called them "vindictive." Yet while to some extent they backfired, Reagan's competence rating dropped to 51 percent in mid October while Carter's rose to 70 percent. During the same period the president had been working hard and with apparent success at putting together the traditional Democratic coalition of liberals, labor, blacks, Catholics, Jews, and southerners — and he seemed to be making headway toward a deal to bring the hostages home from Iran. As election day neared he had a narrow lead. Then he agreed to debate Reagan.

The Debate. Although his advisers believed that a debate at that point in the campaign "could only hurt us," Carter agreed to face Reagan on national television a week before the election. Carter presented his views well but failed to make Reagan look like a dangerous extremist, and the Republican nominee once again used his superior communication skills to convey an image of competency and reasonableness. Overall the debate was judged a draw. Few voters shifted their allegiance as a result of the debate, but Reagan convinced many undecided voters that he was capable of handling the presidency, and he moved ahead in the polls. The final blow for Carter came the weekend before the election, when the Iranians issued a new set of demands in the hostage negotiations, ending Democratic hopes for having them

Senate	96th Congress	97th Congress	Net Gain/Loss
Democrats	58	46*	-12
Republicans	41	53	+12
Independents	1	1	0

*By the 1982 elections there were 45 Democrats and 54 Republicans in the Senate.

House	96th Congress	97th Congress	Net Gain/Loss
Democrats	276	242*	-34
Republicans	159	192	+33
Independents	0	1	+1

*By the 1982 elections there were 241 Democrats and 192 Republicans in the House with two seats vacant.

Governors	1978	1980	Net Gain/Loss
Democrats	32	27	-4
Republicans	18*	23	+4
Independents	0	0	0

*Republicans gained one governorship in 1979.

free by election day. Instead of spending the last days before the election campaigning, Carter rushed back to the White House to deal with the crisis.

Election Results. Reagan won the 4 November election in a landslide, with 51.6 percent of the popular vote to 41.7 for Carter and 6.7 for Anderson. Reagan won forty-four of fifty states for 489 electoral votes to 49 for Carter and none for Anderson. Voter turnout, which had been progressively declining since 1960, was 52.6 percent, the lowest turnout since 1948. Many voters had expressed their dislike for all the candidates by staying home; more of them were potential Carter voters than possible voters for Reagan, proving once again the traditional rule that Democrats win elections with large voter turnouts and that Republicans win those with small turnouts. Early analysis suggested that by taking 9 percent of the vote in the East — to 43 percent for Carter and 47 percent for Reagan — Anderson allowed Reagan to sweep the region, where Carter might otherwise have taken vote-rich states such as New York, with 41 electoral votes, and Massachusetts, with 14. Yet subsequent surveys of Anderson voters showed that they were essentially voting against Carter. If Anderson had not been in the race, they would have been as likely to have stayed home or voted for Reagan as they would have voted for Carter. In fact much of the electorate voted against one candidate or the other, and on election day nearly two-fifths of those who voted for Reagan did so only because they believed "it was time for a change."

No Conservative Mandate. Reagan cut heavily into the Democratic coalition, especially among labor and Jews, where Carter won, but just barely, and in the South, where all but Carter's home state of Georgia voted for Reagan. Carter got 80 percent of the black vote, but fewer blacks voted than in 1976, and the liberal vote was also down from that election. Overall the Reagan landslide was much more an expression of voter dissatisfaction than a sign of an emerging conservative coalition in American politics.

The Republicans Gain Control of the Senate. Reagan's coattails carried in sixteen new Republican senators, giving the GOP a 53–47 majority in the Senate, the largest Republican majority since the Seventy-first Congress of 1929–1931, when the party had 56 seats. (Sen. Harry F. Byrd Jr. of Virginia, an Independent, is here counted as a Democrat because he chose to caucus with that party.) Among the Republican newcomers elected to replace Democratic incumbents were Steven D. Symms of Idaho, who defeated Vietnam War opponent Frank Church; J. Danforth Quayle of Indiana, who triumphed over liberal Birch Bayh; Warren Rudman of New Hampshire, whose opponent, John A. Durkin, had strong labor backing; James Abdnor of South Dakota, who won over the liberal 1972 Democratic presidential candidate George McGovern by a wide margin; Slade Gorton of Washington State, who ousted New Deal Democrat Warren G. Magnuson; and Robert W. Kasten Jr. of Wisconsin, who beat another liberal stalwart, Gaylord Nelson. Another liberal who would be missing from the Ninety-seventh Congress was Republican Jacob Javits, defeated in his party primary by conservative Alfonse M. D'Amato, who went on to easily defeat his Democratic opponent. Another new Republican face was Arlen Specter of Pennsylvania, elected to replace retiring Republican Richard S. Schweiker.

Democrats Hold on to the House. The Democrats suffered a net loss of 33 seats in the House of Representatives, but ended up with a 51-seat edge on the Republicans. Prognosticators wondered how real this slim Democratic majority would be on issues where conservative Democrats tended to vote with Republicans. Thirty-one of 392 incumbents running for reelection were defeated; 27 of the losers were Democrats, including 5 of 6 House members awaiting trial in the Abscam bribery scandal.

Governorships. While the Democrats maintained a lead in governorships, with twenty-seven statehouses in the Democratic column, the Republicans picked up the governorships of Arkansas, Missouri, North Dakota, and Washington State — for a total of twenty-three. One Democratic governor considered a future presidential contender, John D. Rockefeller IV of West Virginia, was reelected, but another, Bill Clinton of Arkansas, was defeated by Republican Frank D. White.

Sources:
Congressional Quarterly Almanac, 36 (1980);

Gerald M. Pomper, Ross K. Baker, Kathleen A. Frankovic, Charles E. Jacob, Wilson Carey McWilliams, and Henry Plotkin, *The Election of 1980: Reports and Interpretations* (Chatham, N.J.: Chatham House, 1981).

NATIONAL POLITICS: 1982 ELECTIONS

The Ninety-seventh Congress. The Republicans' margin in the Senate was unchanged after the 1982 congressional elections, with the GOP holding onto its majority, owing in large part to a nationally financed campaign that tipped the balance in favor of the Republicans in every close contest. Only five new senators were sworn in at the opening of the Ninety-eighth Congress. Big changes took place in the House of Representatives, where redistricting and fallout from the recession of the early 1980s resulted in the election of 81 new congressmen, 57 of them Democrats, increasing their edge in the House to 103 seats. The majority of the new Democrats campaigned on promises to defend the social programs the Reagan administration was trying to cut back, while promising to hold down the creation of new ones. Most of them also called themselves fiscal conservatives and blamed the recession on Reagan's supply-side economic measures. Several Republican incumbents from districts hurt badly by the economic downturn lost their seats because they allowed themselves to become too closely associated with Reagan's economic programs. When reapportionment had shifted 17 House seats to the Sun Belt, many had predicted that the House would become more conservative. The Republicans had hoped to take a dozen of these new districts in the South and Southwest, but Democrats, most of them moderates, won in 10. The Democrats also managed to withstand the losses of districts in the Northeast and Midwest. In the ten northern states that lost seats in the reapportionment, Republicans ended up with 18 fewer seats than they had after the 1980 elections. Their losses were a setback for the Republicans but not a major upset. Hereafter the Reagan administration would have to compromise with liberal and moderate Democrats rather than counting on a coalition of Republicans and conservative Democrats to push through its programs relatively intact.

Governorships. The Democrats also gained seven governorships, while suffering the defeat of only one Democratic incumbent. Among the Democratic victors were Bill Clinton of Arkansas, who won back the governorship he lost in 1980; Bruce Babbitt, reelected as governor of Arizona; Richard Riley, elected to a second term in South Carolina; George C. Wallace of Alabama, a onetime segregationist who won a fourth term by putting together a coalition of blacks and working-class whites; and newcomers Michael Dukakis of Massachusetts, Robert Kerrey of Nebraska, and Mario Cuomo of New York.

Source:
Congressional Quarterly Almanac, 38 (1982).

Senate	97th Congress	98th Congress	Net Gain/Loss
Democrats	45	46*	+1
Republicans	54	54	0
Independents	1	0	-1

*By the 1984 elections there were 45 Democrats and 55 Republicans in the Senate.

House	97th Congress	98th Congress	Net Gain/Loss
Democrats	241	269*	+26
Republicans	192	166	-26
Independents	0	0	0

*By the 1984 elections there were 267 Democrats and 168 Republicans in the House.

Governors	1980	1982	Net Gain/Loss
Democrats	27	34	+7
Republicans	23	16	-7
Independents	0	0	0

NATIONAL POLITICS: REPUBLICAN NOMINATION RACE 1984

The Great Communicator's Vision of America. During his campaign in 1980 Ronald Reagan borrowed his image of America from a sermon delivered on shipboard by the great colonial leader John Winthrop in 1630 as he and fellow Puritans were sailing toward the New World. Their settlement, Winthrop said, would be a "City upon a Hill" watched by "the eyes of all the people." Therefore, he asserted, "we are commanded this day to love the Lord our God, and to love one another, to walk in his ways and to keep his Commandments. . . ." This vision of America is the one Reagan offered Americans throughout his first term in office, as he returned repeatedly to the image of the "City upon a Hill" in advocating a return to traditional patriotic, moral, and religious values. As Theodore H. White summed it up, Reagan "saw the future in the lost summertime of the nation's past, when neighborhoods were safe, when families held together . . . when U.S. power bestrode the world. He wrapped both past and future in the American flag" (*Time*, 19 November 1984). To the nearly 55 million people who voted for Reagan in 1984 it did not seem to matter that the past he evoked so skillfully was one made beautiful by selective memory. Nor did it seem to matter that Reagan, who spoke so often of religion, was the first divorced president, seldom attended church himself, and so far had done little to obtain the constitutional

"QUEEN NANCY"

After Ronald Reagan was elected president in November 1980, it quickly became apparent that the new first lady, Nancy Reagan, would be markedly different from First Lady Rosalynn Carter, who dressed plainly, did her own hair, and devoted her energies to humanitarian causes. Nancy Reagan got off to a bad start almost immediately by hinting that the Carters should move out of the White House early so she could begin redecorating. Before long Mrs. Reagan and her staff were devoting an unusual amount of time and energy trying to answer charges that she was extravagant and autocratic.

In September 1981 when asked why — in the midst of a recession — she chose to spend $209,508 from funds donated for White House redecoration on a 4,732-piece set of china, she explained, "The White House really badly, badly needs china." On 14 December 1981 *Newsweek* reported the results of a poll showing that 62 percent of Americans thought that the first lady "puts too much emphasis on style and elegance" at a time when many of her fellow citizens were in need, and 61 percent considered her "less sympathetic to the problems of the poor and underprivileged" than her predecessors.

The following January, after Mrs. Reagan was criticized for wearing expensive clothing for which she did not pay, her press secretary was compelled to issue a statement explaining that the first lady "derived no personal benefit" from clothing "lent" to her by American designers, that she wore it only to publicize the American fashion industry. Although her "Just Say No to Drugs" campaign helped to rehabilitate her public image, Nancy Reagan was never as popular as her successor, the grandmotherly Barbara Bush, and was periodically the subject of negative press throughout her husband's eight years in office.

Mrs. Reagan was stung by such criticisms, but she was also capable of seeing humor in them. A couple of months after the flap over her designer clothing, she attended the annual Washington Gridiron dinner dressed as a bag lady and sang "Secondhand Clothes." On another occasion, when shown a satiric postcard portraying her as "Queen Nancy," she joked, "Now that's silly. I'd never wear a crown. It messes up your hair."

Source: Paul Slansky, *The Clothes Have No Emperor: A Chronicle of the American '80s* (New York: Simon & Schuster, 1989).

amendment requiring school prayer for which he had promised to fight in 1980. "I think I'll put in an amendment to build a chapel at Camp David so he could go to church," House Speaker Thomas P. "Tip" O'Neill (D-Mass.) quipped in March 1984.

The President's Popularity and the Economy. Despite his personal popularity, the president's poll ratings were not consistently high. In late 1982, with unemployment reaching 10.7 percent (the highest point since the Depression), Reagan's approval rating declined, reaching a low of slightly better than 40 percent in January 1983. After the Democrats handed the Republicans a significant, but not major, setback in the 1982 elections, Republicans began to position themselves to replace the president should he decide not to seek a second term. Senate majority leader Howard Baker decided not to seek reelection to the Senate in 1984 and began planning for a national presidential campaign — in 1988, if not 1984. Vice President George Bush did some fence-mending with right-wing groups that had opposed him in 1980, beginning a gradual slide to the right.

An Economic Upswing. Then the economy started to get better. The Democrats were able to pass some quick-fix legislation to rescue Social Security from bankruptcy, ease unemployment, and reduce the huge federal deficit somewhat. There were still signs that the economy was in trouble: high interest rates and a fast-growing federal deficit. Yet, ironically, the Democrats had eased the president's political problems, and as unemployment declined his approval rating climbed, reaching 57 percent in January 1984 and remaining high throughout the year. By the time primary season opened in early 1984 all thoughts of opposing the president for the Republican nomination had evaporated. In 1984, when Reagan asked "Are you better off than you were four years ago?," most Americans said yes, and it was difficult for the Democrats to convince them otherwise. In a poll taken on election day 57 percent of voters said the economy was better than it had been four years ago, and they overwhelmingly gave the president credit for the improvement.

The "Teflon" President. While the majority of the American public was expressing approval for Reagan the man and crediting him for an economic recovery that was largely not of his making, a surprising number of his supporters did not agree with his policy positions. A Harris poll taken on 24 July 1984 revealed that 32 percent of the respondents favored Reagan and approved of his opposition to the Equal Rights Amendment, while 27 percent favored him but disagreed with his stand on the issue. In that same poll only 10 percent favored the president and agreed with his administration's relaxation of federal pollution controls, while 42 percent said they favored the man but opposed his policies on this issue. The numbers in regard to Reagan's position against an immediate nuclear freeze are closer together but also surprising: 23 percent favored him and his policy; 29 percent favored him and opposed his policy. On the issue of

President Reagan accepting his nomination for reelection beneath a large-screen television image of himself at the Republican National Convention in Dallas, 23 August 1984

favored Reagan and his stand against abortion, while 31 percent favored him but opposed his position on that issue. Similar poll results throughout Reagan's first term had Democrats wondering why the president never seemed to be blamed for his mistakes or unpopular policies. Congresswoman Pat Schroeder (D-Colo.) said in August 1984 that Reagan was "perfecting the Teflon-coated Presidency . . . nothing sticks to him. He is responsible for nothing — civil rights, Central America, the Middle East, the economy, the environment. He is just master of ceremonies at someone else's dinner."

The Republican National Convention. Whatever policy differences existed among Reagan supporters in the nation as a whole, few were apparent among the Republicans who met in Dallas on 20–23 August. Major American political parties have historically embraced individuals with a wide spectrum of political views, and to some extent the Democratic Party has continued to exhibit such diversity into the 1990s. Yet by 1984 the Republicans had become an ideologically coherent, truly conservative party. Only 1 percent of the delegates at the convention called themselves liberals, while only 25 percent labeled themselves moderates. Billed as a moderate in 1980, Vice President Bush continued to redefine his political orientation. At one point during the convention he came up with "I'm conservative, but I'm not a nut about it."

Platform. Conservatives kept tight control over the platform, rejecting not only support for the ERA but also a moderate proposal for a plank favoring "equal rights and equal responsibilities for women." In fact they were sometimes more conservative than their party's standard-bearer, opposing all tax increases and calling for an end to progressive tax rates. The platform also restated the strong antiabortion stand it took in 1980. Congressman Jim Leach, a moderate Republican from Iowa, warned, "The country is a progressive, moderate nation. Yet our party is becoming ideologically narrow." Sen. Lowell Weicker of Connecticut, one of the small minority of liberal Republicans at the convention, described the platform in terms more graphic than Leach's: "It's a pain in the ass to explain. . . . No ERA and no exception for rape or incest. On women's issues, it's a stinkeroo." Convention speaker Sen. Barry Goldwater met with approval when he asserted, "Extremism in defense of liberty is no vice" — a statement that had contributed heavily to his defeat in the 1964 presidential election.

Inching Back toward the Middle. Yet Reagan's campaign staff knew that regardless of the views of party stalwarts, their candidate had to appear middle of the road to win the election. The climax of events at the convention — a film biography of Reagan and his acceptance speech — stressed a return to prosperity and patriotism, the maintenance of peace, and Reagan's personal popularity. Most important was the economy. In his acceptance speech the president said:

Reagan's cuts in aid to the poor, however, there was considerable agreement: 34 percent favored him and his policy; only 14 percent favored him and opposed his policy. Results of a *New York Times* poll, reported on 11 August 1984, revealed that 28 percent of respondents

Democratic presidential contenders Walter Mondale, Jesse Jackson, and Gary Hart at a debate moderated by CBS newsman Dan Rather (back to camera) in March 1984

In 1980, the people decided with us that the economic crisis was not caused by the fact that they lived too well. Government lived too well. It was time for tax increases to be an act of last resort, not of first resort. . . . America is on the move again, and expanding toward new eras of opportunity for everyone. . . . Our opponents are openly committed to increasing your tax burden. We are committed to stopping them, and we will.

NATIONAL POLITICS: DEMOCRATIC NOMINATION RACE 1984

Reforming the Nomination Process — Again. While President Ronald Reagan sat unopposed in the White House, enjoying the incumbent's privilege of acting statesmanlike and above the fray of mere politics, the Democrats took potshots at each other along the primary trail. Having reformed the nomination process to give representation to all its various minorities and interest groups, the party had discovered unforeseen snags in 1980 and subsequently tinkered with the rules again. Among the reforms was a requirement that all delegate selection, whether by primary or caucus or open meeting, take place within a three-month period — an attempt to reduce the cost of drawn-out primary-season campaigns and lessen the impact of media reporting on later contests. The states were also given more flexibility in the methods by which they selected delegates. To avoid dividing up delegates among many candidates with only limited support, a new rule required that an individual receive a minimum percentage of the vote (usually 20 percent) in a caucus or primary before he or she could win any delegates. Another rules change reserved 14 percent of the total number of delegate places as special seats for Democratic senators, representatives, governors, mayors, and top national and party officials. These "super-delegates" would be officially uncommitted, a move designed to give the party some of the maneuverability in candidate selection that it had lacked in 1980.

The New Rules Favor Mondale. Whatever the intention of these rules changes, they favored the well-known, well-financed, well-organized candidate. In 1984 that candidate was former vice president Walter "Fritz" Mondale, who was not only well connected within the party but had begun in November 1980 to build what became widely recognized as "the nation's most elaborate presidential campaign organization" (*New York Times,* 26 September 1983). Once Sen. Edward Kennedy announced in 1982 that he would not run for president in 1984, Mondale was widely acknowledged to be the Democratic front-runner. He was also helped by the AFL-CIO, which endorsed his candidacy in October 1983 — breaking with its tradition of waiting until after a candidate was officially nominated to announce its endorsement of him.

Match-ups with Reagan. Neither Mondale nor any other Democrat did well when matched against Reagan in public-opinion polls. In a series of sixteen Gallup polls conducted between April 1982 and February 1984 Mondale led the president by margins of 5 to 12 percent in six of the first eight and beat him again in November and December 1983, but by February 1984 — with the improving economy — Reagan had pulled ahead of Mondale by ten percentage points and stayed ahead for the duration — usually by margins of 15 to 20 percent. Early on only 14 percent of Democrats liked Mondale, while 10 percent preferred Kennedy. By January 1984 a majority of Democrats expressed a preference for Mondale, but support for him dipped during the primary season — only to return to the level of January after the final primaries. In general Democrats did not dislike Mondale, but their enthusiasm for him was limited.

A Democrat with the "Right Stuff." In 1982 and 1983 Sen. John Glenn of Ohio was considered Reagan's toughest challenger. He beat the president in the first eight of the Gallup polls mentioned above by margins of 4 to 17 percent. As a former astronaut, Glenn had the right image. He was widely perceived as the patriotic hero who could counter Reagan's attempt to preempt patriotism for the Republicans. A new movie about the astronauts, *The Right Stuff,* released in November 1983, was expected to help Glenn win votes. Yet by February 1984, with Reagan ahead of him by fifteen percentage points, Glenn was losing supporters among Democrats as well. British journalist Peter Preston summed up the problem: calling the Ohio senator "a solid, able, tolerably modest fellow, . . . a hero and celebrity," Preston added, "The legend of heroism carries charisma but Glenn himself — apart from an odd resemblance to the Pope — has no charisma" (*Manchester Guardian Weekly,* 4 December 1983).

The Rest of the Field. Sen. Alan Cranston of California, former governor Reuben Askew of Florida, and Sen. Ernest "Fritz" Hollings of South Carolina showed regional support. George McGovern, the antiwar candidate who had been so resoundingly defeated by Richard Nixon in 1972, came in third in one Gallup poll. Yet Mondale's most serious challengers were Sen. Gary Hart of Colorado, whose association with Robert F. Kennedy's 1968 presidential campaign seemed to lend him some of the Kennedy charisma, and civil rights activist Rev. Jesse Jackson, the first African American to launch a full-scale campaign for a major-party presidential nomination.

Campaign Issues. Mondale, Hart, and Jackson were all from the liberal wing of the party and in basic agreement on the major issues. All three called for cuts in defense spending, higher taxes on the rich, a freeze on nuclear testing, expansion of civil rights, increased spending on social programs, and creation of more job and affirmative-action programs. They also supported the ERA and freedom of choice on the abortion issue.

Jackson. Jackson's main emphasis was on social issues, as he called for a "rainbow coalition" of blacks, other racial and ethnic minorities, poor people, women, homosexuals, and others left out of the Reagan vision of America. With his sympathy for Third World radical liberation movements such as the Palestine Liberation Organization and the Sandinistas in Nicaragua, Jackson's foreign policy, while not clearly defined, frightened some Democrats, who believed it would alienate the Jews, conservative Catholics, and moderates whose loyalty the party needed to keep if it wanted to win the election. Jews were in fact alienated when the press reported that Jackson had privately referred to Jews as "Hymies" and when he refused to repudiate anti-Semitic Nation of Islam leader Louis Farrakhan until June 1984, after Mondale's nomination had become a certainty. In the end Jackson's support came mainly from African Americans, but he brought so many new — especially young — black voters into the electoral process that he established a formidable power base. Almost 20 percent of the voters in the 1984 primaries were African Americans. To maintain the loyalty of these voters the Democratic Party knew it had to accommodate Jackson. Yet it also feared alienating two other important groups in its New Deal coalition, Jews and white southerners.

Hart and the Yuppies. The core of Hart's support came from affluent members of the "baby boom" generation — many of then drawn by Hart's association with Robert Kennedy's antiwar campaign of 1968. Hart's staff called these young urban professionals *yuppies,* a play on the antiwar Yippies of the 1960s, and once the media picked up the term, it became part of the American language. (A more accurate acronym used by political analysts, *yumpies,* for "young upwardly mobile professionals," never caught on.) Hart appealed to this group with his call for "a new generation of leadership" with "new ideas." Yet many of his supporters were uncertain what his ideas were. Hart was a stronger advocate than Mondale of environmental protection, an immediate nuclear freeze, and defense spending cuts. Yet his campaign tended to blur his stands on the issues in order to attract as many followers as possible to his camp, a situation that caused Mondale to quote a popular hamburger-chain commercial by asking, "Where's the beef?" Hart's greatest appeal to his supporters came from his attacks on the "Establishment," which included Mondale with his support from the labor unions — for which yuppies had little sympathy. By late April Hart was attacking Mondale for taking "hundreds of thousands of dollars" from union PACs and implying that he would be under the thumb of organized labor. Though the union contributions were legal, Hart called on Mondale to return them, and soon he had crowds at his campaign rallies chanting, "Give the money back, Walter!" (On 17 May Mondale announced that he would return $400,000 of the PAC contributions. Hart called the amount "not enough.")

Mondale Gets a Head Start — and Fades. Even before the Iowa caucuses on 20 February 1984, Mondale was ahead in the delegate count. House Democrats had already selected their 164 superdelegates, and though superdelegates were officially uncommitted, virtually all favored Mondale. The front-runner won easily in Iowa with 48.9 percent of the vote and picked up thirty-four delegates. Hart came in second with 16.5 percent and eighteen delegates, while Glenn — then considered Mondale's strongest rival — came in sixth with 5.3 percent of the vote and no delegates. Looking for news in an election year when both major-party nominations already seemed sewn up in February, the media began talking about Hart's surprisingly "strong" showing as proof that Democrats were unhappy with Mondale. This interpretation seemed borne out in New Hampshire (28 February), where Hart won with 37.2 percent of the vote to 27.9 percent for Mondale and 5.3 percent for Jackson. Columnist Murray Kempton quipped that New Hampshire Democrats "were tired of Mondale, who is the husband type, and they turned in their weariness to Hart, who seemed the boyfriend type." Though Hart's victory seemed significant percentagewise and gave him momentum for later contests, in real numbers and actual delegates won it was less impressive. In the small, heavily Republican state of New Hampshire slightly more than one hundred thousand people had voted in the Democratic primary, and Hart's margin of victory was only about nine thousand votes. More important, because delegates were selected district by district rather than statewide, Mondale ended up with eleven delegates while Hart got ten. The third-place winner, Jackson, got none because he was below the percentage threshold set by the party in that state. New Hampshire was not the only state in which Hart came in first with impressive percentages of the popular vote but came away with fewer delegates than Mondale. On 13 March he beat Mondale by 40 percent to 32.4 percent in Florida but came away with fifty-one delegates to Mondale's seventy-seven; and in other cases, such as Rhode Island (13 March) and delegate-rich Ohio (8 May), he came out ahead of Mondale percentagewise but ran even with him in numbers of delegates. There were also cases in which one of the three major candidates scored under the percentage threshold but would have won delegates if it were not for the threshold rule.

Mondale Regroups. Once Hart became the front-runner in the eyes of the media, he found himself in their spotlight, as they created a character issue from questions about his shaky marriage, why he had changed his name from Hartpence to Hart, and why his campaign literature subtracted a year from his age. Mondale recovered to win significant victories in the Michigan caucuses (17 March) and primaries in Illinois (20 March), New York (3 April), and Pennsylvania (24 April). From this point on he also led in the polls as his party's first-choice candidate. Hart's sweep of the western primaries and caucuses — which included a big 41.2 percent, 207-delegate win over Mondale (37.4 percent, 91 delegates) in California — could not prevent Mondale from ending the primary season with a commanding lead.

The Democratic National Convention. Two-thirds of the Democratic delegates who met in San Francisco on 16–19 July called themselves liberals, in contrast to the one-third of Democratic voters who gave themselves that label. In a conciliatory mood, Mondale supported the formation of a committee to rewrite the rules for delegate selection in 1988 in light of Jackson's and Hart's complaints about inequity in the process.

Congresswoman Geraldine Ferraro and Democratic front-runner Walter Mondale in Saint Paul, Minnesota, after Mondale's announcement that Ferraro would be his running mate, July 1984

Keynote. In one of the most memorable keynote speeches of the 1980s Gov. Mario Cuomo of New York attacked Reagan's vision of America as a "City upon a Hill," saying that "the hard truth is that not every one is sharing in this city's splendor and glory" and adding: "There is despair, Mr. President, in the faces that you don't see, in the places that you don't visit in your shining city." For him the idea of family values, much touted by the Republicans, meant "Mutuality. The sharing of benefits and burdens for the good of all." The speech fueled speculation that Cuomo might be the next Democratic candidate.

Platform. The platform committee, dominated by Mondale supporters, was so eager to accommodate the viewpoints of Hart and Jackson supporters that the platform mushroomed to an unheard of thirty-five thousand words. Only five items were left to be decided on the floor of the convention. The delegates accepted Hart's proposal to restrict the authority of the president to employ military forces abroad and Jackson's call for omitting opposition to racial quotas in affirmative-action programs. Following the lead of Mondale supporters, who hoped to appeal to moderate voters, they voted down Jackson's proposals to reject first use of nuclear weapons, to cut defense spending below current levels, and to eliminate runoffs in southern primaries (which tended to favor white candidates). In his acceptance speech Mondale spoke of a "new realism," promising: "By the end of my first term, I will reduce the Reagan budget deficit by two-thirds. Let's tell the truth. . . . Mr. Reagan will raise taxes, and so will I. He won't tell you. I just did." That statement alone may have cost Mondale the election.

Madam Vice President? Before the convention Mondale had begun interviewing potential running mates, accepting input from all factions of the party. Feminists were especially vocal, announcing that they would take their cause to the convention floor if Mondale did not select a woman. Conservative columnist George Will observed, "Mondale bought his own paint and then painted himself into a corner. . . . He has no choice but to pick a woman, and he must not do it. If he does not, he will have got half of the population up on its tiptoes and then not kissed it. If he does, he will be the wimp who was bullied by the National Organization for Women" (*Newsweek,* 16 July 1984). Yet when Mondale tapped Congresswoman Geraldine Ferraro of New York to be his running mate, many felt that he had made an excellent choice. Ferraro, who had chaired the platform committee, was seen as a vibrant, feisty campaigner who could make up for the stolid Mondale's lack of charisma. The Mondale-Ferraro ticket moved slightly ahead of Reagan and Bush in the days just after the convention, but instead of taking advantage of their momentum, Mondale went fishing, and questions about the financial dealings of Ferraro's husband, real-estate developer John Zaccaro, soon began to cloud the image of what had seemed a dream ticket.

NATIONAL POLITICS: 1984 ELECTIONS

Conservative versus Liberal. The 1984 presidential election was unusual in the annals of American politics because the two major-party candidates represented diametrically opposing ideologies. American voters have traditionally preferred middle-of-the-road candidates, and not since Lyndon B. Johnson's landslide victory over Barry Goldwater exactly twenty years earlier had a liberal, New Deal Democrat gone up against a truly conservative Republican. In 1984 the results were reversed, with Ronald Reagan winning a second term by decisively defeating Walter Mondale. Reagan had clearly moved the nation to the right during his first term, but his election was widely interpreted as a victory for Reagan the man rather than his conservative policies.

Blurring Political Distinctions. During the campaign each candidate tried to appeal to the broadest possible range of voters by portraying himself as a moderate and his opponent as a dangerous extremist. Despite jokes about his inability to discuss important issues without cue cards and stories about his nodding off during cabinet meetings, Reagan was helped by his likable personality and his ability to project an image of leadership. Even his supporters conceded that Mondale was boring. According to one campaign joke, Reagan might fall asleep during his cabinet meetings, but if Mondale were elected he would put the whole cabinet to sleep.

The Debates. Reagan led Mondale in most polls for all 1984, with the Democratic challenger making significant inroads in the incumbent's level of support only twice: immediately after the Democratic National Convention and after the first televised debate (7 October). In that debate Mondale politely and effectively attacked the president's policy decisions and raised the issue of his competence. Reagan's statements seemed increasingly muddled, and in his closing comments he admitted to being "confused." The media was immediately flooded with questions about whether the oldest president in U.S. history was in fact too old to hold that office. Even the conservative *Wall Street Journal* observed that his "debate performance invites open speculation on his ability to serve" (9 October). Mondale performed ably, though less spectacularly, in the second debate (21 October), but Reagan came back strong, managing to convince most viewers that he was indeed of sound mind and competent to be president. He also cracked a joke: "I will not make age an issue in this campaign. I am not going to exploit for political purposes my opponent's youth and inexperience." While 75 percent of the people who said they made up their minds on the basis of the debates chose Mondale, only 10 percent of those who cast votes on election day picked their candidate in that way. Most people had made up their minds months ago. Those undecided voters who joined the Mondale camp after the first debate would have probably ended up there by election day anyway. The second debate shored up Reagan's commanding lead.

Election Results. On 6 November Reagan won 58.8 percent of the votes cast by nearly 93 million Americans, 55.3 percent of eligible voters. The turnout was disappointing to Democrats, who had hoped for 100 million on the long-held theory that the bigger the turnout the more votes for Democrats, but the vote was big enough to end a twenty-year decline in voter turnout, which had dropped to 52.6 percent in 1980. Mondale, who got 40.6 percent of the popular vote, won only the District of Columbia and his home state of Minnesota. He wound up with 13 electoral votes to 525 for Reagan. There was widespread speculation about the demise of the New Deal Democratic coalition and the emergence of a new conservative Republican coalition, but later analysis proved both predictions premature. Parts of the New Deal coalition were still evident: Mondale had won the majority of votes cast by unemployed, low-income, and union families. He had also beaten Reagan among African American, Hispanic, Jewish, and urban voters. Yet Reagan had once again attracted away two key elements of that coalition: Catholics and white southerners. He won 55 percent of the Catholic vote and 72 percent of the votes cast by white southerners, taking that region with 63 percent — his largest percentage in any region. He also benefited significantly from an eight-year drift of

Senate	98th Congress	99th Congress	Net Gain/Loss
Democrats	45	47	+2
Republicans	55	53	-2
Independents	0	0	0

House	98th Congress	99th Congress	Net Gain/Loss
Democrats	267	253	-14
Republicans	168	182	+14
Independents	0	0	0

Governors	1982	1984	Net Gain/Loss
Democrats	34*	34	-1
Republicans	16	16	+1
Independents	0	0	0

*Democrats gained one governorship in the 1985 elections.

so-called middle Americans — people of moderate income, blue-collar workers, and high-school graduates — toward the Republican camp, where they joined its traditional coalition of white Protestants, high-income people, and individuals with high-status employment. Yet, as the polls indicated, Reagan had won the election on the basis of personality, not political philosophy. It was also apparent that the nation was entering an era of declining party loyalty. Two out of five voters in 1984 were members of the "baby boom" generation or younger. They were far more likely than their parents to call themselves independents, and they represented a considerable challenge, and promise, to both parties.

Congressional Elections. The results of House and Senate elections were disappointing to both parties. Republicans, who discovered that Reagan had short coattails, lost two seats but maintained control in the Senate, which the Democrats had hoped to take away from them. At the same time the Republicans failed to regain control of the House but chipped away part of the Democratic majority there for a net gain of fourteen seats. Of the fourteen Democratic senators up for reelection, thirteen were reelected, and three Democratic House members won Senate seats formerly held by powerful Republicans: In Illinois Rep. Paul Simon edged out Sen. Charles H. Percy, chairman of the Senate Foreign Relations Committee; in Iowa Rep. Tom Harkin defeated Sen. Roger W. Jepsen; and in Tennessee Rep. Albert Gore Jr. won the seat vacated by Senate Majority Leader Howard Baker. Yet the Democrats failed to upset Republicans in five other states where Republicans had seemed beatable, including North Carolina, where Sen. Jesse Helms nar-

rowly won reelection in a bitter, expensive contest against Gov. James B. Hunt, and Texas, where Phil Gramm, who had resigned his House seat after losing his Democratic committee assignments for voting too often with the Republicans, ran for the Senate as a Republican and won. Other Senate newcomers included Democrat John D. "Jay" Rockefeller IV of West Virginia, Democrat John F. Kerry of Massachusetts, and Mitch McConnell of Kentucky, the only Republican to defeat a Democratic incumbent.

Sources:

Congressional Quarterly Almanac, 40 (1984);

Gerald M. Pomper, Ross K. Baker, Charles E. Jacobs, Scott Keeter, Wilson Carey McWilliams, and Henry A. Plotkin, *The Election of 1984: Reports and Interpretations* (Chatham, N.J.: Chatham House, 1984);

Austin Ranney, ed., *The American Elections of 1984* (Durham, N.C.: Duke University Press, 1985).

NATIONAL POLITICS: 1986 ELECTIONS

Democrats Regain the Senate. Two years after handing the Democrats a stunning defeat in the 1984 presidential election, American voters on 4 November 1986 gave that party a majority in the Senate, which had been controlled by the Republicans since their sweep of the senatorial elections in 1980. In fact six of the Senate newcomers of 1980 were among the nine GOP senators defeated in 1986 by Democrats, who lost only one of their own incumbents, for a net gain of eight seats. Of the thirty-four seats at stake in 1986, Democrats won twenty. Eleven of the thirteen new faces in the Senate were Democrats. These results were achieved despite a Republican campaign chest eight times the size of the Democrats'.

Democratic Wins in the South. After Reagan's 63 percent victory in the South in 1984, the region had appeared to be a Republican stronghold for the foreseeable future. But southern voters shocked the pundits by electing Democrats to all five of the southern seats up for election in 1986. Democratic wins in the South illustrated a pattern that party candidates used successfully nationwide. While the GOP spent much of its money on television advertising and a national campaign to mobilize Republican voters, Democrats stressed local issues, accusing their opponents of being "national Republicans" with little concern for what was happening back home. The Democrats also relied on old-fashioned grassroots organizing, and — especially in the South — they rebuilt traditional Democratic alliances and renewed ties with local party officials. Moderate Terry Sanford won in North Carolina by securing the backing of conservative Democrats. They helped him attract voters who might otherwise have voted for Republican incumbent James T. Broyhill (as they had for Republican Jesse Helms in 1984). In Alabama Rep. Richard C. Shelby, a conservative Democrat, beat GOP incumbent Jeremiah Denton by developing links to the Democrats' black and labor-union supporters. Democrat Wyche Fowler Jr., an

Senate	99th Congress	100th Congress	Net Gain/Loss
Democrats	47	55*	+8
Republicans	53	45	-8
Independents	0	0	0

*By the 1988 election there were 54 Democrats and 46 Republicans in the Senate.

House	99th Congress	100th Congress	Net Gain/Loss
Democrats	253	258*	+5
Republicans	182	177	-5
Independents	0	0	0

*By the 1988 elections there were 257 Democrats and 178 Republicans in the House.

Governors	1984	1986	Net Gain/Loss
Democrats	34	26	-8
Republicans	16	24	+8
Independents	0	0	0

Atlanta congressman, also enlisted the support of local party officials, who helped him overcome rural Georgians' doubts about his urban roots and defeat Republican incumbent Mack Mattingly.

House Seats. Democrats increased their majority in the House of Representatives by five, but Republican losses were below average for a president's party in an off-year election. In general voters seemed to be saying that they liked the status quo in the House. Only five Republican incumbents and one Democratic incumbent were defeated. One noteworthy newcomer was Democrat Mike Espy, the first black Mississippian in the House since 1883.

Governorships. Any attempt to interpret the Democrats' victories in the national elections of 1986 as a swing in voter sentiment toward the Democratic Party was cut short by the results in the governors' races. The GOP ended up with a net gain of eight, for twenty-four governorships — their highest count since 1970.

Source:
Congressional Quarterly Almanac, 42 (1986).

NATIONAL POLITICS: DEMOCRATIC NOMINATION RACE 1988

Dropping Out Early. In early 1987 Gary Hart, runner-up to Walter Mondale in 1984, led in preference polls of Democratic voters, but he dropped out of the race on 8 May 1987, after press reports about his affair with model Donna Rice. Hart, who was married, announced on 15 December that he would reenter the nomination contest, but he was never able to garner much support in the 1988 primaries and caucuses. Many Democrats also liked Gov. Mario Cuomo, who had delivered an inspiring keynote address at their 1984 national convention, but in February 1987 Cuomo announced that he would not run, clearing the way for Michael Dukakis. Dukakis ran on his record as governor of Massachusetts, pointing to the improved economy and balanced budget of his state as proof of his managerial abilities. He began to pick up support from northeastern Democrats who might otherwise have backed Cuomo or Sen. Edward M. Kennedy of Massachusetts, who had said in December 1985 that he would not seek his party's presidential nomination in 1988. Another attractive candidate, Sen. Joseph R. Biden Jr. of Delaware, dropped out on 23 September 1987, after media reports that he had used without attribution words and ideas from an autobiographical campaign speech by Neil Kinnock, head of the British Labour Party, and that he had plagiarized a paper when he was in law school. By the end of 1987 other well-known Democrats who had announced plans not to run included Gov. Bill Clinton of Arkansas, Sen. Bill Bradley of New Jersey, Rep. Pat Schroeder of Colorado, and former governor Charles S. Robb of Virginia.

The "Seven Dwarfs." The seven Democrats who started in the 1988 nomination race were often called the "seven dwarfs." Only one, Rev. Jesse Jackson, who had campaigned extensively in 1984, had any sort of national reputation. In addition to Dukakis and Hart the other candidates were Gov. Bruce Babbitt of Arizona, Rep. Richard Gephardt of Missouri, Sen. Albert A. Gore Jr. of Tennessee, and Sen. Paul Simon of Illinois. In the first contest of the year, the Iowa caucuses on 8 February, Gephardt came in first (31.3 percent), followed closely by Simon (26.7 percent). They were followed by Dukakis (22.1 percent) and Jackson (8.8 percent). Dukakis won easily in his neighboring state of New Hampshire (16 February), taking 35.8 percent of the vote to 19.8 percent for Gephardt, 17.1 percent for Simon, and 7.8 percent for Jackson. Gore, who had not campaigned in New Hampshire, got 6.8 percent.

Super Tuesday. Although the early contests helped the candidates to win press coverage and increased voter recognition, the first big test came on Super Tuesday, 8 March, when twenty states — including fourteen southern and border states — held caucuses or primaries. Gore, who had bypassed the early races to concentrate on the areas where he had the strongest support, won in six states — including the primaries in Arkansas, Kentucky, North Carolina, Oklahoma, and Tennessee — and came second in five others. Jackson also did well, winning six states — including primaries in Alabama, Georgia, Louisiana, Mississippi, and Virginia — and coming in second in eleven other states. Yet Dukakis was the big winner. He came in first in seven states, including the two with

Michael and Kitty Dukakis, Jackie and Jesse Jackson, and B. A. and Lloyd Bentsen at the conclusion of the Democratic National Convention, 21 July 1988

the most delegates, Florida and Texas. Although Gephardt won in his home state of Missouri, the race had become a three-way contest among Dukakis, Gore, and Jackson, with only Dukakis demonstrating strength outside his home region.

Jackson Expands His Base. Jackson had been working hard to create a coalition of lower-class blacks and whites, deemphasizing the foreign-policy positions that had limited his appeal in 1984, and the press began to recognize him as a viable candidate after his impressive second-place showing (32.3 percent) behind Simon (42.3 percent) in Illinois on 15 March. When Jackson trounced Dukakis in the Michigan primary on 26 March with 53.5 percent of the vote to only 29 percent for Dukakis, it seemed briefly that he might be able to win the nomination. In addition to his core of black supporters he was attracting white voters, not from the lower and working classes as he had hoped, but from middle- and upper-middle-class, college-educated, liberal whites. He also did well with voters in the 18–29 age group. His support dropped off among median-income ($30,000), moderate, high-school-educated white Democrats — a large and influential demographic group in the party's candidate-selection process — and even among the groups of whites who did support him, Dukakis as a rule did better. Subsequent analysis showed that Jackson did best in states with

lower voter turnouts, as was the case in Michigan. In those states his devoted and enthusiastic black supporters came out to vote while whites unmotivated by any of the candidates stayed home.

The Field Narrows. After Michigan Gephardt dropped out of the race. Dukakis went on to beat Jackson 58.1 to 28.3 percent in Connecticut (29 March). Simon withdrew on 7 April after coming in a distant third (4.8 percent) to Dukakis (47.6 percent) and Jackson (28.2 percent) in Wisconsin on 5 April. Gore held on for the next big test, the 19 April primary in New York. A full 25 percent of the Democratic voters in that state were black, the largest number in any nonsouthern state — a fact expected to favor Jackson. Yet another quarter of New York Democrats were Jews, many of whom continued to suspect Jackson of anti-Semitism because of statements he had made in the 1984 campaign. Gore had the endorsement of Mayor Edward Koch of New York City, but with virtually no chance of winning the nomination he seemed irrelevant to many voters. Gore dropped out of the race on 7 April, after winning only 10 percent of the vote in New York, where Dukakis garnered 50.9 percent to 37.1 percent for Jackson. Dukakis won a plurality of the vote in every demographic and ideological group of New York Democrats except African Americans, who voted for Jackson by a margin of twenty to one, and

Hispanic Americans, who favored Jackson 3 to 2. With Jackson in the race to stay, Dukakis won twelve of the last thirteen primaries, clinching the nomination on 7 June with victories in California, Montana, New Jersey, and New Mexico. Carrying the delegate-rich state of California with 60.8 percent of the vote (to 35.2 percent for Jackson), Dukakis became the first Democratic frontrunner to win that state's primary since 1964.

Choosing a Vice President. To win the election Dukakis, a moderate, had both to consolidate his Democratic base by attracting enthusiastic support from those blacks and liberals who had supported Jackson and to expand his base by bringing back into the fold those conservative Democrats who had abandoned the party to vote for Reagan in 1984 and 1988. Jackson's name on the ticket would likely ensure a large turnout of blacks and liberals for the Democrats, but their votes alone could not win the election. A *Los Angeles Times* poll (18 July) revealed that two-thirds of the so-called Reagan Democrats — a group equal in size to African Americans in the total electorate — opposed the nomination of Jackson for the vice presidency. With Jackson campaigning openly for the job, Dukakis found himself in a difficult position. His choice of Sen. Lloyd Bentsen of Texas, designed to appeal to southerners and westerners as well as ideological moderates and conservatives, angered Jackson and his supporters, in part because Jackson learned about Dukakis's choice from reporters rather than Dukakis himself.

The Democratic National Convention. In a meeting on the eve of the convention in Atlanta (18–21 July), Dukakis and Bentsen managed to mend fences with Jackson. At a news conference the next morning Dukakis asserted, "I want Jesse Jackson to play a major role in this campaign." Jackson announced that he was no longer seeking the vice presidency but was still going to have his name placed in nomination for the presidency. Dukakis made concessions as well — among them new modifications in delegate-selection rules that would benefit Jackson if he should choose to run again and the addition of seats for Jackson supporters on the Democratic National Committee.

Platform Agreements. Jackson was clearly the more liberal of the two candidates. Yet Jackson and Dukakis supporters came to substantial agreement on most platform issues. Dukakis accepted nine platform amendments proposed by the Jackson camp, including strengthening the wording of the plank denouncing apartheid in South Africa, a condemnation of U.S. aid to "irregular" forces in Central America, a call for a national-health program, and a promise to end in-flight missile testing. They compromised on other issues. For example, Jackson wanted to double education spending but ended up accepting a plank that promised to "significantly increase" those funds. Only three of Jackson's proposals went to the convention floor. A call for increased taxes on the rich was voted down by Dukakis supporters

afraid that Republicans would use such a plank to once again call the Democrats the "tax and spend" party. Jackson's renewed call for no first use of nuclear weapons was voted down, just as it had been in 1984. After they had had their say in favor of a plank calling for Palestinian self-determination, Jackson supporters withdrew the potentially divisive proposal before it was brought to a vote. The final platform was only five thousand words. Considerably shorter and vaguer, but also less controversial, than the 1984 platform, it was designed to stress the basic issues on which all facets of the party could agree. (For example, it talked about "reproductive freedom" but did not include the word *abortion*.)

Rallying the Faithful. While future Texas governor Ann Richards's keynote address was not as ideologically eloquent as Cuomo's four years earlier, she was frequently applauded for her humorous assertions of the Republicans' lack of concern for working Americans. The crowd was especially responsive to her jokes about Vice President Bush, a New England–born patrician who had made Texas his home. "After listening to George Bush all these years," she said in her introduction, "I figured you needed to know what a real Texan accent sounds like." Later she feigned sympathy for the Republican candidate: "Poor George. . . . he was born with a silver foot in his mouth." The next night John F. Kennedy Jr. introduced his uncle, Sen. Edward Kennedy, who accused Bush of "burying his head in his hands and hiding from the record of Reagan-Bush mistakes." He soon had the delegates chanting "Where was George?" as he listed those "mistakes" — including the Iran-Contra dealings, of which Bush claimed to have no knowledge. Jackson followers were considerably mollified by the major part their candidate and his family played in the convention. All five Jackson children spoke to the convention before delegates were shown a video biography of the candidate. Even Dukakis supporters carried Jackson signs during the inspirational speech by Jackson that followed. He called on liberal and conservative Democrats to find common ground. Speaking of Dukakis, and pointing to his own poverty-stricken origins, he exhorted Americans suffering from hunger, disease, inequality, or physical handicaps not to give in to despair or drugs. "You must not surrender. . . . We must not surrender," he concluded. "America will get better and better. Keep hope alive." The next night seemed anticlimactic. Gov. Bill Clinton of Arkansas nominated Dukakis in a speech twice the length anticipated. The restive crowd cheered noisily when they heard the words "And in closing . . ." and went on to nominate Dukakis with 2,876.5 votes to 1,218.5 for Jackson. Many feared that the candidate's acceptance speech would be also be overshadowed by Jackson's eloquent oratory, but though he was well known for his humorless, lackluster speaking style, Dukakis rose to the occasion, talking about his own family's "rags to riches" fulfillment of the American dream, calling for "an economic future that will provide good jobs at good wages for every citizen of this land."

Promising "to exchange voodoo economics for can-do economics," he asserted, "This election isn't about ideology. It's about competence." Having avoided potentially contentious liberal issues such as abortion and taxation and stressing popular Democratic issues such as education and health care, Dukakis had successfully portrayed himself as a mainstream politician. A few days later a Gallup poll showed him leading Bush by 55 to 38 percent. (A CBS News/*New York Times* poll had him ahead by 50 to 33 percent.)

NATIONAL POLITICS: REPUBLICAN NOMINATION RACE 1988

Conservative Candidates. By 1988 the old Republican split between conservative midwesterners and moderate/liberal easterners was a thing of the past. Each of the candidates for the GOP presidential nomination presented himself as the true conservative heir to the legacy of President Ronald Reagan, while emphasizing different aspects of that legacy. Congressman Jack F. Kemp of New York talked about lower taxes, while offering unqualified support for the "Star Wars" strategic defense system and aid to the Contras in Nicaragua. Gov. Pierre S. "Pete" du Pont IV of Delaware proposed a private savings option to Social Security and giving parents "education vouchers" that could be used at either public or private schools. Sen. Robert J. Dole of Kansas, the party leader in the Senate, stressed his service and experience, promising to balance the budget through spending cuts that would not hurt the most vulnerable Americans. Televangelist Marion G. "Pat" Robertson sought a return to "fundamental moral values," opposing abortion and supporting school prayer and a balanced federal budget. A retired army general who had served as White House chief of staff under Presidents Richard Nixon and Gerald Ford, a former supreme commander of NATO forces, and Reagan's first secretary of state, Alexander M. Haig Jr. was the most critical of the Reagan administration, calling its foreign policy ineffective. In contrast Vice President George Bush ran on the Reagan record across the board. Completing the gradual slide to the right that he had begun in 1980, he now concurred with Reagan's opposition to abortion and accepted the "Reaganomic" theories he had once dismissed as "voodoo economics."

Bush Overcomes Adversity. Widely considered the front-runner, Bush came in third in the first test of 1988, the Iowa caucuses (8 February), in which he won only 18.6 percent of the vote to 37.3 for Dole and 24.6 for Robertson. Haig, who came in last, dropped out of the race, throwing his support to Dole. Bush staged a comeback in New Hampshire, coming in first with 37.6 percent of the vote to 28.4 percent for Dole. Du Pont, who finished in fourth place, withdrew from the race. Kemp, who finished third, and Robertson, who had come in last, remained in the contest, but it had essentially become a

two-way race between Bush and Dole. That point was underlined in South Carolina (5 March), where Robertson was expected to do well. Attractive to evangelical Protestants, many of whom were participating in the electoral process for the first time, Robertson was expected to mobilize a "secret army" of conservative Christians, especially in the South, but he proved unable to broaden his narrow base of support. Bush won big in South Carolina, with 48.5 percent of the vote, trailed by Dole (20.6 percent) and Robertson (19.1 percent).

Super Tuesday. The vice president did even better on Super Tuesday (8 March). He won all sixteen primaries, collecting 577 delegates. Dole came away with about one hundred, while Kemp won only 4 and quit the race two days later. Robertson, who won the Super Tuesday caucuses in Washington State, hung on until the day after the Illinois primary (15 March), where he finished with a disappointing 6.8 percent of the vote, well behind Bush (54.7 percent) and Dole (26 percent). Dole bowed to the inevitable on 29 March. Even before Republicans voted in big states such as Pennsylvania, Ohio, New York, and California, Bush had the nomination sewn up, and he swept the remaining primaries.

Bush's Image Problem. The favorite candidate of most Republicans who approved of Reagan's performance as president (a vast majority of the party), Bush was not widely liked or admired by the American public as a whole. In May 1988, when pollsters matched him up with Michael Dukakis for the first time, registered voters preferred Dukakis by a margin of 49 to 39 percent. By the end of the Democratic National Convention the Democratic candidate had widened his margin to seventeen percent. Despite his heroism in World War II, Bush was widely regarded as a wimp. Liberal PBS commentator Michael Kinsley called him "the national twit," while Congresswoman Pat Schroeder, who had pinned the "Teflon" label on Reagan, said Bush would not choose a woman as his running mate because "people would say, 'We need a man on the ticket.'" Even Republicans had their doubts. Primary opponent Al Haig called him "a do-nothing lackluster wherever he sat." One source of Bush's image problem may have been his voice, which often sounded whiny, and he often had difficulty expressing himself. As the vice president's sister, Nancy Ellis, commented during the campaign, "Poor George is hopelessly inarticulate. He never finishes a sentence or puts in a verb." Bush and his campaign staff arrived at the Republican National Convention determined to rehabilitate his image and take the offensive against Dukakis once and for all.

The Republican National Convention. The first day of the Republican National Convention, held in New Orleans on 15–18 August, was devoted to celebrating the presidency of Ronald Reagan, the first two-term chief executive since Dwight D. Eisenhower. The day before, Reagan had told a group of fellow Republicans that Bush's campaign would reveal his Democratic opponent

President Reagan (center) meeting with the two leading contenders for the 1988 Republican presidential nomination, Sen. Robert Dole of Kansas and Vice President George Bush, July 1987

to be "liberal, liberal, liberal," and in his opening night speech the president defended Bush against charges that the vice president was taking credit for policies and decisions that he had not helped to make. Reagan listed Bush's accomplishments as vice president and soon had delegates responding the Democrats' "Where was George?" with the chant of "George was there!"

Choosing a Vice President. The next day Bush surprised the nation with his choice of running mate. Bypassing the apparent front-runners — Dole, Kemp, Sen. Alan Simpson of Wyoming, and Sen. Pete Domenici of New Mexico — Bush picked Sen. J. Danforth Quayle of Indiana, a little-known conservative who was best known for the long hours he had spent on the golf course during his four years in the House of Representatives and eight years in the Senate. It was believed that the young, photogenic Quayle would not only solidify Bush's standing with the conservative majority of his own party but also help attract Reagan Democrats of the baby-boom generation. Yet within days there were allegations that Quayle's wealthy family had pulled strings so that he could avoid serving in Vietnam by enlisting in the Indiana National Guard, and Quayle soon proved himself a political — and intellectual — lightweight. (At one point in the campaign he referred to the Holocaust as "an obscene period in our nation's history," and when asked

to clarify the statement, he responded, "We all live in this century. I didn't live in this century.") Quayle found himself campaigning in small towns where he would get limited media exposure.

Pinning the Liberal Label on Dukakis. On the evening of 16 August keynote speaker Thomas Kean, governor of New Jersey, warned the convention that the Democrats' economic program added up to one thing: "More Taxes!" He was followed by Pat Robertson, who sounded the theme of the Republicans' fall campaign in charging that the Democrats' vision of America was a nation in which "criminals are turned loose . . . disease carriers are protected . . . [and] welfare dependency flourishes." The last speaker of the evening was former president Gerald R. Ford, who reviewed Bush's record of government service and — to chants of "George was there!" — concluded, "I'll be damned if I will stand and let anyone with a smirk and a sneer discredit the honor, service, accountability, and competence of George Bush." The next night, amid further allegations that Dukakis would be soft on crime, Bush won the Republican nomination easily on the first ballot. In his acceptance speech Bush referred to polls that showed him trailing Dukakis and announced, "There are a lot of great stories in politics about the underdog winning — and this in going to be one of them." He charged that Dukakis was yet another liberal big spender who would not rule out a tax increase and said that he would tell anyone who proposed added taxation, "Read my lips. 'NO NEW TAXES.'" (These words were used against him in the 1992 election, after he had in fact raised federal income taxes.) Bush also stressed law-and-order issues and followed Reagan's practice of wrapping himself in the flag by ending his speech by leading the delegates in reciting the Pledge of Allegiance. He left the convention with a 46 percent to 40 percent lead over Dukakis and stayed ahead for the remainder of the campaign.

NATIONAL POLITICS: 1988 ELECTIONS

The Willie Horton Issue. When they first heard that George Bush was planning to go after Dukakis on the crime issue, the Dukakis campaign was incredulous. The crime rate in Massachusetts had gone down markedly during Dukakis's governorship, and they believed that the Republicans' strategy would have little effect on their candidate's chances. They severely underestimated the abilities of Republican strategist Lee Atwater, who created in the minds of the public such a strong association between Dukakis and a convicted murder named Willie Horton that the crime issue became the single biggest factor in Dukakis's loss of the election. Under Dukakis's predecessor Massachusetts prisons had begun giving weekend furloughs to prison inmates with records of good behavior. Most states had similar programs (including California during Reagan's governorship), as did the federal prisons, and Dukakis allowed the Massachusetts prisoner furloughs to continue. Unfortunately a black man named Willie Horton, who had been convicted of first-degree murder, was given a weekend furlough and escaped to Maryland, where he raped a white woman and stabbed her fiancé. Dukakis immediately made first-degree murderers ineligible for the program, but the Republicans already had all the ammunition they needed.

Negative Campaigning. Speech after speech at the Republican National Convention used Horton's name or the Massachusetts furlough program as symbols of Dukakis's softness on criminals, with Sen. Pete Wilson charging that Dukakis's challenge to prisoners was not "'Make my day,' but 'Have a nice weekend.'" But the real damage was inflicted during the election campaign, with a series of Bush adds attacking Dukakis on the prison furlough issue. One showed prisoners going in and out revolving prison doors while a voice-over said Dukakis allowed even murderers sentenced to life without parole to take part in the furlough program and that many prisoners had escaped while free on weekend passes. Later groups not officially connected to the Bush campaign also ran television ads focusing on this issue. One such ad featured Horton's Maryland victims. Critics called the ads unfair and distortions of the truth and charged the Bush campaign of pandering to the deepest racist sentiments of white Americans. Dukakis and his advisers

Senate	100th Congress	101st Congress	Net Gain/Loss
Democrats	54	55	+1
Republicans	46	45	-1
Independents	0	0	0

House	100th Congress	101st Congress	Net Gain/Loss
Democrats	257	260	+3
Republicans	178	175	-3
Independents	0	0	0

Governors	1986	1988	Net Gain/Loss
Democrats	26*	28	+1
Republicans	24	22	-1
Independents	0	0	0

* Democrats gained one governorship in the 1987 elections.

failed to realize until too late how much damage the so-called Horton ads had done. Dukakis was a cautious, seemingly unemotional man who vowed at the start to avoid negative campaigning. Faced with hostile attacks from the opposing camp, his first response was to ignore them as beneath notice — despite warnings from Democrats who had been subjects of Republican negative campaigning in 1980 and 1982 that voters tended to believe accusations that were not aggressively refuted.

The Pledge of Allegiance. While pinning Horton on Dukakis, Republican campaign strategists also managed to pin to their own candidate one of the most powerful symbols of American patriotism: the Pledge of Allegiance. As governor of Massachusetts Dukakis had vetoed a bill that required teachers to lead their students in reciting the pledge, explaining that the bill was unconstitutional because it violated teachers' first amendment guarantees of freedom of expression. Implying that Dukakis had banned the pledge outright, Bush frequently told campaign audiences, "I believe that our schoolchildren should have the right to say the Pledge of Allegiance. . . . I don't know what his problem is." Thinking like the lawyer that he is, Dukakis looked at this issue from a strictly legal standpoint and suggested that if Bush did not recognize the unconstitutionality of the bill Dukakis had vetoed, the Republican candidate would not be a good president. Again Dukakis failed to recognize the emotional subtext of Bush's accusation. In poll after poll, reciting the Pledge of Allegiance, a powerful symbol of patriotism and national unity, has repeatedly achieved high approval ratings. Republican campaign strategists so successfully identified their candidate with the "right" side of that issue and so adeptly tied Dukakis to a convicted murderer and rapist that by election day large numbers of voters were choosing not between Dukakis and Bush but between Willie Horton and the Pledge of Allegiance. As Robert Strauss, former Democratic national chairman, commented, "Dukakis made a major mistake." By getting into a constitutional debate involving the Pledge of Allegiance, "He captured the hearts of seventeen lawyers and lost three million voters" (*Christian Science Monitor,* 21 September 1988).

The Debates. Dukakis had similar problems in the presidential debates, which he tackled with all the skill of a formal debater and none of the emotion of a partisan politician. He went into the first debate on 25 September determined to reclaim his image as a moderate and scored points by proposing specific programs to attack drug abuse, shortages of adequate housing, rising health-care costs, and the difficulty of obtaining affordable health insurance — all issues that concerned Americans deeply. Bush called a Dukakis plan to require employers to provide health insurance for their employees too expensive for businesses and stressed law-and-order issues, while charging Dukakis with liberalism. Most commentators agreed that Dukakis won the debate on points, but as in previous presidential elections, few voters actually chose their candidate on the basis of the issues discussed in debates, and he had come across as too serious, his face frequently wearing an expression that reporters had started to call his "eat your peas" look. With the Republicans fully in possession of the momentum, waging a tough, effective, focused campaign while Dukakis's inexperienced staff floundered in an uncoordinated effort to provide a coherent package for their candidate's message, Dukakis needed not just a decisive victory in the second debate (13 October) but a victory in which he managed to reach voters on an emotional level, to reveal something about his character. He lost the debate on the first question. When asked if he would still oppose the death penalty if his own wife were raped and murdered, Dukakis calmly answered that, yes, he would still be against it — passing up the opportunity to express the sort of revulsion for violent crime that the Republicans had been using to their advantage, while also speaking of the moral issue of grounding the rule of law in humanity rather than vengeance. He tried hard to seem warmer in this debate, but by the end of the evening the media had decided the election race was over. The main question seemed to be Bush's margin of victory.

Another Republican Victory. On 8 November Bush won forty states with 53.4 percent of the popular vote to 45.6 percent for Dukakis, who had the small consolation of having done better against Bush than his two immediate predecessors had done against Reagan. Bush swept the South, much of the Farm Belt, the Rocky Mountain states, and every heavily populated state except New York, ending up with 426 electoral votes to 112 for Dukakis. Voter turnout dropped to 50.1 percent, a de-

George and Barbara Bush celebrating his election as president of the United States, 8 November 1988

cline attributed in part to lack of charisma in either candidate and in part to a disaffection for the political process caused by the negativity of the campaigns. Democrats could take heart that Dukakis had won back from the Republicans blue-collar workers, individuals without college educations, and people who earned less than the median family income of $30,000 a year — essential elements of the Democratic coalition that Reagan had won in 1984. In fact more than half of the Reagan Democrats returned to the party in 1988, and Bush ran about five percentage points lower than Reagan in every demographic group. Yet the election also taught the Democrats an important lesson: with declining union membership, the defection of white southerners to the Republicans, and the slow erosion of the working-class Catholic vote, the Democrats had to find a way to attract new voters to replace their losses from the New Deal coalition forged by Franklin D. Roosevelt in the 1930s. While no one was ready to declare that coalition dead, politicians of the 1980s had witnessed the gradual dissolution of the glue that held it together.

Congressional Elections. Despite Bush's decisive victory, Democrats maintained their majorities in the Senate and the House of Representatives. Yet with no significant gains in either house and the loss of the presidential election for the third time in a row, there was little celebration among Democrats. Voters continued to favor incumbents. In the Senate only one Democratic and three Republican incumbents were defeated. In the House the Republicans lost four incumbents, and the Democrats lost two. The election of Republican Trent Lott in Mississippi and Connie Mack in Florida to fill Senate seats vacated by the retirements of two powerful Democrats, John C. Stennis and Lawton Chiles, was interpreted as evidence of the GOP's increasing hold on the South. Democratic newcomers to the Senate included Charles S. Robb of Virginia and Robert Kerrey of Nebraska, both considered possible presidential candidates for the 1990s.

Governorships. Twelve gubernatorial elections were held in 1988, and eight of nine incumbents were reelected. The one exception was Republican Arch A. Moore Jr. of West Virginia, who was replaced by Democrat Gaston Caperton. Democrats were also pleased by the election of Evan Bayh in Vice President Dan Quayle's home state of Indiana, ending twenty years of Republican control of the governorship in that state. Republicans celebrated the election of Stan Stephens to replace a retiring Democrat in Montana and Judd Gregg's victory in New Hampshire, where he replaced fellow Republican John Sununu, who became President George Bush's chief of staff.

Sources:

Sidney Blumenthal, *Pledging Allegiance: The Last Campaign of the Cold War* (New York: HarperCollins, 1990);

Congressional Quarterly Almanac, 44 (1988);

Gerald M. Pomper, Ross K. Baker, Walter Dean Burnha, Barbara G. Farah, Marjorie Randon Hershey, Ethel Klien, and Wilson Carey McWilliams, *The Election of 1988: Reports and Interpretations* (Chatham, N.J.: Chatham House, 1988);

THE NEW RIGHT

Resurgence of Conservatism. Conservatism went into a temporary decline after Lyndon B. Johnson's landslide victory over conservative Republican Barry Goldwater in the presidential election of 1964 and the accompanying defeat of many conservative senators and House members, but a "New Right" emerged as a potent force in American politics during the late 1970s and early 1980s, reenergized by the increasing hostility of U.S.–Soviet relations in the late 1970s. Conservatism was also bolstered by a reaction to the social upheavals that accompanied the civil rights and antiwar movements of the late 1960s and early 1970s. The New Right pointed to the sexual revolution and the hippie drug culture as proof of the breakdown in traditional social values. They decried the rapid expansion of government power that began in the mid 1960s, labeling federal initiatives such as busing for school desegregation, affirmative-action programs, the proposed Equal Rights Amendment, sex education in the schools, and increasing environmental regulation as intrusions on individual freedoms. Furthermore, they blamed the decline of the U.S. economy throughout the 1970s on overspending for the Great Society social programs instituted by President Johnson in the 1960s.

The Old "New Right." The term *New Right* is really a misnomer. Many of the leaders of the resurgent conservative movement had been part of conservative efforts in the 1960s. Howard Phillips, Patrick Buchanan, Richard Viguerie, and John Terry Dolan had been among the founding members of the right-wing Young Americans

THE TRASHING OF JOHN TOWER

Newly elected President George Bush tapped former Texas senator John Tower to be his secretary of defense on 16 December 1988. A conservative Republican, Tower had served in the Senate from 1961 to 1985, and from 1981 to 1985 he had chaired the Senate Armed Services Committee. He had also been President Ronald Reagan's chief negotiator for the Strategic Arms Reduction Talks (START) in 1985–1986, and in 1987 he had chaired the special presidential commission that investigated the Iran-Contra affair. In 1986–1987 he had also been a consultant to four major defense contractors.

After Tower's nomination rumors of alcohol abuse and womanizing began to surface. At a 31 January Senate hearing Paul Weyrich, a longtime conservative activist with close ties to the religious right, questioned Tower's moral character and fitness for the appointment. Other critics questioned Tower's close ties to the defense industry and suggested that he might have conflict-of-interest problems if he had to make decisions regarding contracts with his former employers. Tower responded that he would avoid such conflicts by delegating any decisions about contracts with those companies.

In early February suggestions that Tower had leaked information about the START talks to interested defense contractors and questions about defense-industry campaign contributions made to Tower while he chaired the Senate Armed Services Committee resulted in an FBI probe. After President Bush excluded Democratic committee members when he briefed their Republican counterparts on the results of the FBI investigation, the deliberations over Tower's nomination took a decidedly partisan turn. On 23 February the Armed Services Committee voted 11 to 9 along party lines against the nomination.

The Bush administration decided to stand by the Tower nomination and took the battle to the full Senate, where the debate became rancorous and increasingly partisan. On 9 March 1989 the Senate voted 47 to 53 against Tower with only three Democrats supporting him and only one Republican opposing him. It was the first rejection of a president's initial nomination for a cabinet post in history. Despite the fact that the earliest attacks on Tower had come from the religious right, his defeat was largely blamed on the Democrats.

Source: "Tower Nomination Spurned By Senate," *Congressional Quarterly Almanac*, 45 (1989): 403–411.

for Freedom (YAF) in the 1960s. Along with other conservative activists of the 1980s — including Phyllis Schlafly, Robert Weyrich, and Phillip Crane — they had helped to secure the Republican nomination for Goldwater in 1964 and then worked in his presidential campaign. Moreover, the political message of the "New Right" was little different from that of the "Old Right" of the 1950s and 1960s. Both were militantly anticommunist. Both were libertarian in their approach to the relationship between the government and the economy; that is, they opposed taxation, government spending, and government social programs. Both emphasized traditional morality and maintenance of the community.

Supply-Side Economics. While conservatives have always favored cuts in programs and spending, as well as a balanced budget, they found these policies difficult to sell to the American people, many of whom considered the economic consequences to be painful. What the New Right brought to the traditional perspective was the theory of supply-side economics, which suggested that tax cuts would stimulate the economy sufficiently to offset the loss of tax revenues with increased federal income generated by economic growth. According to this theory, traditional conservative policies such as balancing the budget might be accomplished much less painfully than previously expected. Thus, supply-side economics made fiscal conservatism seem politically palatable to many voters.

Opposing "Secular" Values. The New Right placed much greater emphasis on moral and social issues than conservatives had in the 1960s. During the 1980s their emphasis on personal morality issues had political resonance with a public concerned with issues such as the Equal Rights Amendment and abortion. Conservatives charged that a liberal elite dominated government and threatened the authority and influence of parents by promoting "secular values" such as abortion, sex education, and distribution of birth control information (and condoms) in the schools.

The New Religious Right. The conservatives' new emphasis on social issues provided a powerful means to attract and politicize traditionally apolitical evangelical Christians, leading to the emergence of the new religious right. Demographically, evangelical Christians constituted a larger and larger portion of the American religious framework over the years between 1960 and 1980. In 1963, 23 percent of Americans identified themselves as "born-again" Christians. By 1978 that number had grown to 40 percent. By the end of the 1970s some 50 million Americans had links to evangelical religious organizations, constituting a large base with the potential to be mobilized in support of conservative positions in politics.

Political Televangelism. Throughout the first six decades of the twentieth century the evangelical churches had stressed the separation of church and state and la-

beled the political order as corrupt. In the 1970s they reverted to the nineteenth-century view that the church should provide leadership in infusing the political realm with Christian values. Longtime right-wing activists Howard Phillips and Robert Weyrich turned to the televangelists and to the pastors of so-called superchurches (individual churches with more than twenty thousand members) for help in recruiting and training the new religious right. Helped by a Federal Communications Commission (FCC) rule that allowed broadcasting stations to count paid religious broadcasts as part of their public service programming, televangelists reached millions of people. By the 1980s they had almost a monopoly on religious airtime. The most political of these televangelists were Rev. Jerry Falwell with his *Old Time Gospel Hour* and Rev. Marion G. "Pat" Robertson with his *700 Club*. Robertson's Christian Broadcasting Network was the fifth largest cable network.

Grassroots Activism. Under the tutelage of Weyrich and Phillips, Falwell founded the Moral Majority; Robertson started the Christian Voice; and another televangelist, James Robison, established the Religious Roundtable as organizations designed to provide a political outlet for evangelical Christianity. In contrast to the politically conservative religious leaders of the 1960s, the new religious right used its television access and mailing lists of donors to found and finance grassroots political organizations that mobilized a new cadre of highly dedicated voters.

RAVCO and the Computerized Mailing List. The use of computerized mailing lists to raise funds and mobilize support for specific conservative causes was perfected by Richard Viguerie. The computer allowed him to tailor appeals to different subgroups on a mailing list and thus to generate the maximum desired response to a mailing. Viguerie built his company, RAVCO, into a multimillion-dollar business that generated millions of dollars and mobilized substantial support for conservative groups and causes.

Corporate Conservatism. Another factor in the emergence of the New Right was the development during the 1970s of a conscious and organized corporate conservatism. While corporate America had long been fiscally conservative, big business had been supporting think tanks and research organizations across the political spectrum. Moreover, corporate contributions to politicians had been primarily pragmatic rather than ideological, tending to support incumbents regardless of their party affiliation.

The Business Roundtable. A strong voice for deregulation and fiscal conservatism during the 1980s was the Business Roundtable, founded in 1972–1973. Especially effective in the political arena, the Roundtable organized the chief executives of large corporations to lobby congressmen and senators directly rather than relying solely on paid lobbyists. The group established task forces that

President Reagan delivering the speech in which he called the Soviet Union an "evil empire," at the forty-first annual convention of the National Association of Evangelicals in Orlando, Florida, 8 March 1983

generated research reports and publicity on economic-policy positions, and it also developed and promoted pro–Big Business teaching materials for use by elementary- and secondary-school teachers.

Business PACs. During the 1970s a change in the campaign-finance laws limited the size of individual donations to particular campaigns but did not place such limitations on the political action committees (PACs). The result was a dramatic increase in the number of business PACs. In the early 1970s labor PACs were more numerous than business PACs, but by the early 1980s business PACs outnumbered labor PACs by 2 to 1. Business PACs such as the Business Roundtable helped to coordinate the flow of money to business-oriented PACs, which increasingly applied a conservative litmus test for the candidates to whom they gave their money.

Conservative Think Tanks. By the 1980s corporate donors were shifting away from liberal and moderate think tanks to support more conservative ones. When beer maker Joseph Coors helped to found the Heritage Foundation in 1973, it was worth a few hundred thousand dollars; by 1983 it was operating with a budget of $10.6 million. The American Enterprise Institute, which had promoted conservative ideas since the 1940s, had its budget grow from $0.9 million in 1970 to $10.6 million

in 1983. The Hoover Institute, a conservative think tank at Stanford University, almost had to close its doors in the 1960s, but by 1983 it was operating with an annual budget of $8.4 million. Foundations such as the John M. Olin Foundation, the Scaife Foundation, and the Smith Richardson Foundation poured financial support into conservative academic research, especially the projects of supply-side economists. All these efforts helped to push conservative ideas into the mainstream political debate, as they provided a steady flow of policy papers. Many of the top appointees of the Reagan administration came from conservative think tanks.

The Eclipse of the New Right. A potent force in Ronald Reagan's victory in the 1980 presidential election and an important source of ideas and conservative personnel for his administration, the New Right was nonetheless in disarray by the end of the 1980s. In its later years — with the Iran-Contra scandal and an investigation into questionable ethical practices of Attorney General Edwin Meese, among the most ideologically conservative of Reagan's appointees — the Reagan administration was troubled. Republicans had lost control of the Senate in 1986. Many of the leading New Right groups were in debt, and Viguerie's company was in financial difficulty. The Reagan administration's failure to win congressional confirmation for Supreme Court nominee Robert Bork in 1987 and congressional rejection of President George Bush's appointment of conservative former senator John Tower as secretary of defense in 1989 were evidence of a loss of power on the New Right.

The East-West Thaw. The demise of communism and the freeing of eastern Europe in the late 1980s made the militant anticommunism of the New Right seem anachronistic. They were left with their economic agenda and with their emphasis on those social issues that had a particular resonance with the religious right. The continuing organizational strength of the new religious right was evident in Pat Robertson's ability to mobilize evangelical Christians on his behalf as he challenged George Bush for the Republican presidential nomination in 1988. Yet his failure to take control of the Republican Party machinery in several key states illustrated his inability to mobilize a substantial following outside his core group of supporters. In 1989 Robertson helped to found the Christian Coalition to articulate concerns of the religious right in the political arena and to mobilize supporters for political campaigns. They continued to be a potent force in Republican politics into the 1990s.

Sources:

David H. Bennett, *The Party of Fear: From Nativist Movements to the New Right in American History* (Chapel Hill: University of North Carolina Press, 1988);

William H. Chafe, *The Unfinished Journey: America Since World War II*, second edition (New York: Oxford University Press, 1991);

Jerome L. Himmelstein, *To the Right: The Transformation of American Conservatism* (Berkeley: University of California Press, 1990).

REAGANOMICS

Inflation. As the 1980 presidential campaign began, the U.S. economy was in a shambles. The inflationary trend that began in the late 1960s, as Lyndon Johnson tried to fund both the Vietnam War and his Great Society social programs, had continued unabated through the 1970s. The inflation rate hit double-digit levels by 1975 and stayed high. Real wages had peaked in 1973. Then inflation began taking a heavy toll, and they declined 18 percent between the early 1970s and the early 1980s. In 1979 a temporary stop in the flow of Iranian oil, coupled with an OPEC price hike, caused a major oil shortage. That year gasoline prices went up 52 percent; heating oil prices increased by 73 percent; and there were long lines at gas stations. The price increases added to inflationary pressures in the United States and most western countries. They also contributed to higher balance-of-payments deficits for the United States, as did growing imports of automobiles and electronics, especially from Japan and West Germany. To fight the escalating inflation rate, the Federal Reserve Board, headed by Paul Volcker, instituted a tight-money policy in October 1979 and continued it through 1982.

Low-End Jobs. The economy was restructuring itself. High-wage, high-skill manufacturing jobs were disap-

pearing. The auto industry alone lost 250,000 jobs between 1979 and 1982. These jobs were being replaced with low-wage, low-skill service jobs. From 1963 to 1973, 40 percent of all new jobs in the United States were high paying, and only 20 percent were at the bottom of the scale. From 1979 to 1985 low-paying jobs accounted for 40 percent of the job growth, with high-paying jobs constituting only 10 percent.

Government Spending. Moreover, the government was absorbing a larger and larger percentage of the country's financial resources. In 1980 government spending was 35 percent of the gross national product (GNP) whereas it had been only 24 percent in 1950 and 29 percent in 1960.

Stagflation. Unemployment reached double-digit percentages by the late 1970s and continued at that level into the early 1980s. According to classical economic theory, it was impossible to have both high inflation and high unemployment; yet it was occurring in the United States. Economic growth came to a halt, and the American standard of living dropped to fifth in the world. The combination of economic stagnation, high unemployment, and high inflation was called *stagflation*.

Reagan's Economic Proposals. Throughout the 1980 presidential campaign, Republican candidate Ronald Reagan attacked the incumbent, Jimmy Carter, for the performance of the economy. He railed against the $40 billion deficit the Carter administration was running and promised to balance the budget if elected. Reagan blamed government red tape and overregulation for stifling economic growth and promised deregulation. His views were a loose amalgam of some features of economic libertarianism, supply-side economics, and tax theory propounded by William Laffer. Supply-siders considered the conventional prescription of stimulating the economy by increasing government spending to be potentially wasteful. Instead, they said, taxes should be cut and incentives created to encourage savings and investment. To this view Reagan added an adaptation of Laffer's theory that economic growth resulting from such a tax policy would generate new revenues, which would offset those lost through tax reduction.

"Voodoo Economics." Even some conservative Republicans were skeptical of the mixture of theoretical perspectives that were the basis of Reagan's ideas on economics. George Bush, his opponent for the Republican nomination and eventual running mate, referred to Reagan's economic plan as "voodoo economics." Many supply-siders did not accept Laffer's views either. The public was less interested in theoretical fine points and wanted changes in economic policy. Reagan's message of cutting taxes, balancing the budget, reducing government spending, cutting bureaucracy, and deregulation appealed to many constituencies and helped lead to his election.

Stockman. Reagan chose David Stockman as director of the Office of Management and Budget (OMB). As a

In June 1981 the Professional Air Traffic Controller's Organization (PATCO) rejected an offer of a new three-year contract with $105 million in raises to be paid in 11.4 percent increases over the next three years, a raise more than twice that being given to other federal employees. Because of their frustrating and highly stressful working conditions, however, the air traffic controllers also wanted shorter workweeks and earlier retirement.

On 3 August 1981, after Secretary of Transportation Drew Lewis and PATCO president Robert Poli were unable to reach a compromise, PATCO members walked off their jobs, even though strikes by federal employees were and are illegal. PATCO was banking on the perception that its members were indispensable to the safe operation of the air transportation system and that air travel would be severely crippled by their strike. PATCO also expected support from other unions and the public, neither of which was forthcoming.

The Reagan administration was determined to maintain the traditional position of all past administrations, regardless of party, that strikes by federal employees would not be tolerated. They also wished to demonstrate to other federal employees' unions that the administration was capable of standing tough in negotiations. After PATCO disobeyed a federal court injunction ordering the air traffic controllers to end the strike and return to work, union leaders were fined and jailed for contempt of court. President Reagan then issued an ultimatum demanding that the strikers be back on the job within forty-eight hours or be fired with no possibility of an amnesty. He further stated that negotiations on a contract would not resume until the strikers were working again.

The administration miscalculated the strikers' resolve. Most defied the ultimatum, and two days later Reagan ordered their dismissal, while prohibiting the Federal Aviation Administration from ever rehiring them. More than twelve thousand PATCO members lost their jobs, and attempts to regain them through the courts proved futile. Furthermore, PATCO was decertified as the legal bargaining agent for federal air traffic controllers.

A Gallup poll showed that 57 percent of Americans applauded President Reagan's decisiveness and toughness, but prounion groups deplored the demonstration of a general antiunion ethic in this strong message to other public employees' unions that the administration would not tolerate strikes.

Source: "Who Controls the Air?," *Newsweek*, 98 (17 August 1981): 18–24.

---

member of the House of Representatives, Stockman had been an ally of Jack Kemp in the losing 1978 fight over the Kemp-Roth tax bill, which had proposed a substantial 30 percent tax cut. While in Congress, he had developed a reputation for his expertise in fiscal matters. At the OMB Stockman put together a package that combined proposals for $64 billion in budget cuts and the 30 percent tax-cut plan from Kemp-Roth. The budget cuts in the plan Reagan introduced in February 1981 targeted social programs. The tax cuts Stockman had in mind could be made only by cutting Social Security benefits for early retirees and reducing the rates of automatic cost-of-living adjustments for those receiving Social Security.

Congressional Reaction. At first the House and the Senate appeared ready to accept both aspects of Reagan's plan, but as the legislative process wore on the plan was weakened. Budget cuts did not go as far as Stockman wanted. In fact, no cuts in Social Security benefits survived congressional consideration. Substantial progress was made in reducing the tax rates, however. When the tax reform process was through, taxes for those in the highest income brackets — those paying 50 percent on earned income (wages and salaries) and 70 percent on unearned income (from sources such as investments) under the old tax plan — were reduced to 37.5 percent on all income by 1983, a substantial flattening of the rate of progression in tax rates. Those in lower brackets saw smaller reductions. Critics pointed out that the new tax bill included substantial loopholes, creating inequities and new tax breaks for special interests.

Contradictory Policies. At the same time the Reagan administration was cutting taxes to stimulate economic growth, the Federal Reserve Board was continuing its tight-money policy. The two policies contradicted one another, and the GNP declined in 1982. The inflation rate was beginning to slow, but unemployment increased substantially. The economy continued sliding into a recession, which bottomed out in December 1982. As a result the tax reductions did not generate the growth needed to keep revenues up, and the size of the deficit grew. Reagan's 1982 deficit was about three times the size of the $40 billion Carter deficit he had criticized during the campaign.

Defense Spending. While Stockman preached cuts in social programs, the Reagan administration unveiled a plan in 1982 to increase defense spending by $1.2 trillion

President Reagan meeting with Budget Director David Stockman and Treasury Secretary Donald Regan

over the next five years. Without growth in revenue, this level of military spending was projected to increase the deficit substantially. Concerned over the deficit, Senators Robert Dole (R–Kan.) and Jesse Helms (R–N.C.) helped to persuade the president to accept changes in tax reform that eliminated some of the concessions. They also convinced him to support increases in gasoline taxes and Social Security taxes in 1982. These increases in taxes rendered the earlier tax reforms somewhat illusory because they offset the aggregate effect of reducing tax rates.

Increasing the Deficit. By 1983 the inflation rate had been brought down to 6 percent, and the GNP had grown by 4 percent. Unemployment was still high, at 11 percent. Even though the economy started to grow again, revenues lagged behind estimates. With cuts in social spending and the reduction in costs that occurred as the rate of inflation slowed, Reagan's policies managed to reduce the rate of government spending, which had been increasing by 15–17 percent from 1979 to 1981. Over the three years from 1981 to 1984, the rate of increase slowed to 10 percent, 8 percent, and 5 percent. Despite this reduction the deficit continued to grow — running around $200 billion a year from 1983 to 1985 — because revenues were not coming in at the expected rate. By the time the deficit reached $277 billion in 1986, the United States had become a debtor nation.

Gramm-Rudman. In August 1985 senators Phil Gramm (R–Texas) and Warren Rudman (R–N.H.) introduced legislation requiring that the federal deficit be cut by specific amounts over a several-year period or that across-the-board cuts be made in all programs. The proposal got the support of most Republicans and enough

key Democrats to pass in December. While the bill was well intentioned, it exempted spending for Social Security, interest on the national debt, and existing government contracts (purchases of equipment, buildings, military equipment) from cuts, thereby removing a substantial proportion of annual federal expenditures from its provisions. In 1986 the Gramm-Rudman Act was further weakened when the Supreme Court found some of its provisions unconstitutional. Nevertheless, Congress made an attempt to live up to its provisions in 1986 and 1987. Reagan's ambitious military-spending program — especially the controversial Star Wars program — came under the knife, making the 1987 defense-budget increase the smallest since 1981.

Tax Reform. As soon as the 1981 tax-reform bill passed, Democrats in Congress began to call for reforms to eliminate some of the inequities produced by that bill. In spring 1982 Sen. Bill Bradley (D–N.J.) and Congressman Richard Gephardt (D–Mo.) sponsored a tax-reform proposal designed to eliminate most preferences and deductions. Their bill was set up to cut rates slightly but to keep revenues the same and to ease the tax burden of the urban poor. The Reagan administration slowly backed parts of the proposal. Eventually, in December 1984, Secretary of the Treasury Donald Regan announced a new administration plan that incorporated many features of the Bradley plan but was more generous to corporations. Regan's successor, James Baker, expanded on this plan during spring 1985, and the president introduced the new tax proposal on television in May 1985. Congress passed it in September 1986. This tax-reform bill reduced the top tax rate to 25 percent for personal income and eliminated many personal deductions. It kept revenues from personal income taxes at roughly the same level, but it reduced the corporate share of the income-tax structure substantially — a provision that added still more fuel to the deficit.

Deregulation. While campaigning in 1980, Reagan had not only called for reductions in taxes and government spending, he had also charged that government regulations were a disincentive to innovation and a drag on the economy. He thus pledged to eliminate or simplify federal regulations. Within two days of his inauguration, he appointed a committee, chaired by Vice President George Bush, to find ways of reducing economic and social regulation. In February 1981 the president issued an executive order requiring that all proposed regulations had to be reviewed by the OMB and subjected to cost-benefit analysis before they could be approved and implemented. By 1983 the new regulations proposed each year were down by one-third from previous numbers.

Airline Deregulation. Deregulation had begun during the Carter administration. The Reagan administration carried out the Air Transportation Act of 1978, first deregulating route allocations and fare setting. In 1984 it implemented the final stage of the act by eliminating the Civil Aeronautics Board (CAB), which had been responsible for routes and fares.

Deregulating the Regulators. President Reagan also used his appointment power to name to regulatory boards individuals who shared his views on government regulation and who tended to be sympathetic toward the groups and industries being regulated. For example, Anne Gorsuch Burford, whom he made head of the Environmental Protection Agency (EPA), personally opposed many environmental regulations and actively ensured that implementation of regulations was delayed and enforcement curtailed. By 1983 EPA enforcement actions had been reduced by 84 percent, and suits against persistent violators had decreased by 78 percent. Burford resigned in March 1983, during an inquiry into her mismanagement of environmental-cleanup funds. Secretary of the Interior James Watt was also controversial. His role in the giveaway of mineral rights on public lands to mining interests, his opposition to increased fees for the use of public lands for grazing, and his anticonservation stance brought him criticism from conservation and environmental groups. Watt resigned under pressure in October 1983, after his public use of ethnic slurs further swelled the ranks of his critics.

Reduced Enforcement Levels. The Reagan administration also crippled the enforcement ability of agencies by cutting budgets and personnel. The Interstate Commerce Commission (ICC) had its budget cut by 25 percent, and the Federal Trade Commission (FTC) suffered a cut of 5 percent, with a 9 percent cut in staff. Agencies adjusted by reducing enforcement levels. The Occupational Safety and Health Administration (OSHA), charged with protecting workers on the job, decreased

Congressman Dan Rostenkowski and Sen. Robert Packwood promising to "go to the trenches" for tax reform, June 1986

the number of citations it issued by 90 percent. Agencies also moved away from long-established positions. The National Highway Traffic Safety Administration (NHTSA) gave up its campaign for automobile airbags, which were favored by the insurance industry, and instead promoted seatbelts, which were favored by the automobile industry. The Food and Drug Administration (FDA) stopped advocating a no-risk policy regarding traces of carcinogens in foods and adopted one that espoused minimum risk.

Good News/Bad News. The GNP increased by a robust 7 percent in 1984, and unemployment declined rapidly. At 11 percent in early 1983, it was at 7.55 percent in 1984 and 5 percent in 1988. Real personal income, which had declined in the 1970s, was rising again by the late 1980s. Toward the end of the decade, however, interest rates began to rise, slowing the rate of economic growth. In 1987 the Federal Reserve Board and major banks raised the prime interest rate from 7.5 percent to 8.75 percent in six months. By December 1988 the prime rate was up to 10.55 percent, making borrowing more expensive and cooling economic growth. The stock market had a major jolt on 19 October 1987, when there was a drop of 508 points on the New York Stock Exchange. At 23 percent in a single day, this drop was the largest in history, exceeding that of the stock-market crash of 1929 that ushered in the Great Depression. Analysts blamed the sharp decline on investors' worries over trade imbalances and the Reagan administration's deficits.

The Bush Administration. While the economy slowed a little in 1988 and 1989, there was a general return to prosperity that helped George Bush's campaign to succeed Ronald Reagan as president. In April 1989 Bush and the Democratic Congress surprised many commentators by reaching an accord on budget priorities and deficit reduction measures. A new budget had yet to pass, however, by the end of the fiscal year on 30 September. When no agreement was reached by 15 October, the automatic budget-reduction provisions of the Gramm-Rudman Act went into effect. The budget passed on 22 November kept spending at the Gramm-Rudman level until 1 February 1990, when the regular budget became operative. By spending at reduced levels and delaying new spending for four months, the government reduced the deficit by some $14.7 billion. The new budget cut military spending, especially the Star Wars program, which had 25 percent cut from the funding initially proposed in Bush's first budget message.

Reforms. As the decade ended, economists and sociologists pointed to the strengths and weaknesses of the economy and society of the Reagan years. Reagan's policies had been partially responsible for a reduction in the rate of government spending. The rise in inflation that began in the late 1960s and continued through the 1970s had been eliminated (though much of the credit for this improvement can be traced to the tight-money policies of Paul Volcker and the Federal Reserve Board). Substantial reform had been made in the income-tax structure, reducing the highest tax rates and theoretically freeing up money for savings and investment.

Deficit. Economists worried as the public debt rose during the Reagan years. By the time he had finished his two terms as president, an additional $1.7 trillion had been added to the $907 billion federal deficit that had existed in 1981. Reagan's addition to the national debt was 2.5 times greater than the total accumulated debts of all previous presidents. As a result deficit reduction became a major theme in political debate. Economists also worried about the trade deficits the United States was incurring annually.

Economic Restructuring. At the end of the decade economists and sociologists were also expressing concern about the restructuring of the American economy. High-pay, high-skill manufacturing jobs continued to be replaced by low-paying service jobs, and the income structure of the United States was changing accordingly. For most of the post–World War II period, the United States had a robust middle class whose disposable income rose substantially in the 1960s. As the 1980s ended, observers pointed to a shrinking size of the middle class and an increasingly large percentage of the population under the poverty level. Economists and sociologists were worried by the implications of a future class and income structure that looked more like the America of the 1920s than that of the 1950s and 1960s.

Sources:

Michael Barone, *Our Country: The Shaping of America from Roosevelt to Reagan* (New York: Free Press, 1990);

William H. Chafe, *The Unfinished Journey: America Since World War II,* second edition (New York: Oxford University Press, 1991);

Wilbur Edel, *The Reagan Presidency: An Actor's Finest Performance* (New York: Hippocrene Books, 1992);

Larry N. Gerston, Cynthia Fraleigh, and Robert Schwab, *The Deregulated Society* (Pacific Grove, Cal.: Brooks/Cole Publishing, 1988);

Garry Wills, *Reagan's America: Innocents at Home* (Garden City, N.Y.: Doubleday, 1987).

HEADLINE MAKERS

JAMES A. BAKER III

1930-

WHITE HOUSE CHIEF OF STAFF, 1981-1985

SECRETARY OF THE TREASURY, 1985-1988

Background. Scion of a wealthy, established Houston family, Jim Baker attended eastern preparatory schools and graduated from Princeton University in 1952 and the University of Texas Law School in 1957. He spent his early career in business and corporate law, showing little interest in politics until he was nearly in his forties. (Some friends have suggested that he rarely voted.)

Political Friendship. Yet both his first wife, who died in 1970, and his second wife were deeply involved in grassroots Republican politics in Texas and are considered to have sparked his interest in politics, as did his close friendship with George Bush, who was involved in the same Houston social and business circles as Baker. During the 1960s both joined the same Episcopal Church and became vestrymen. They were both tennis players and won the doubles championship at the Houston Country Club in 1966 and 1967. Both men suffered family tragedies, and their lives became closely intertwined. Their pastor at that time has said that the two men were "closer than brothers, and each is smart enough to listen to the other." By the late 1960s Baker had become involved in Republican politics, and he served as Harris County chairman of Bush's losing campaign for the U.S. Senate in 1970.

Government Service. In 1975 Bush persuaded Secretary of Commerce Rogers Morton to appoint Baker as an undersecretary in the Commerce Department. Within a year Baker was acting secretary. Then he was asked to take over the directorship of Gerald Ford's campaign for

the presidency (1976). Ford trailed badly in early polls. Baker is widely considered to be responsible for reorganizing the campaign and narrowing the distance between Ford and his opponent, Democrat Jimmy Carter, to the point that Ford lost the election by only a narrow margin instead of a landslide.

Campaign Manager. In 1980, after running for attorney general of Texas in 1978 and losing, Baker ran George Bush's campaign for the Republican presidential nomination. He is credited with convincing Bush to tone down his attacks on Ronald Reagan — especially his description of Reagan's "voodoo economics" — and getting Bush to drop out of the contest earlier than he would have liked. Because of these actions, Baker is often credited with having maneuvered Bush into position for the vice-presidential nomination. Baker subsequently became a senior adviser to the Reagan campaign and was put in charge of negotiations with Carter's aides over television debates.

Political Tactician. By the time Reagan won the election Baker had developed a reputation as a superb political tactician with an impeccable sense of political timing. He has been described as a hard worker, a superior organizer, and a quick study who is action-oriented but risk-averse. He rarely got involved in political projects that went sour and was extremely sensitive to relationships with Congress and the press. He has also been called nonideological and the ultimate pragmatist, with the ability to remove himself from his formal role and analyze a situation objectively. His pragmatism is said to be so fundamental to his character that he is rarely involved in long-term planning; instead he immerses himself in the immediate problem and its short-term solution.

White House Staffer. A surprise pick for White House chief of staff, Baker recruited non-Reaganites for staff positions and maintained tight control over the president's schedule and the flow of paper in the Oval Office. Together with Michael Deaver, he muted the influence of conservative ideologues and is considered to have been a steadying and moderating influence on the Reagan White House during the president's first term. Baker has been given partial credit for Reagan's "Teflon" image, which enabled him to remain personally popular in the midst of political adversity.

Treasury Secretary. Unlike Baker's tightly run staff, the National Security Council (NSC), which was outside his jurisdiction, was near chaos. In 1983 Baker was involved in a losing attempt to bring national-security affairs and the NSC staff under his direction. He retrenched, and in early 1985 he engineered a deal whereby he and Secretary of the Treasury Donald Regan switched positions. At the Treasury Department Baker was deeply involved in the tax reforms and deficit-cutting measures of Reagan's second term. In fall 1985 he met secretly with the finance ministers and the heads of the central banks of Great Britain, West Germany, France, and Japan at the Plaza Hotel in New York to discuss methods of dealing with joint economic problems resulting from an inflated value of the dollar. They agreed to devalue the dollar, let other currencies rise, and coordinate regulation of interest rates. Canada and Italy subsequently agreed to the same measures. The following spring this ad hoc process was formalized, and it has subsequently evolved into the regularized efforts of the "Group of Seven" to coordinate economic policy and discuss other political matters.

Secretary of State. In 1988 Baker directed George Bush's successful presidential campaign and was named secretary of state. At the State Department his early priorities were arms-control talks with the Soviet Union, pushing for a Middle East Peace Conference, and redefining NATO after the collapse of Communism in Eastern Europe.

Sources:
Maureen Dowd and Thomas L. Friedman, "The Fabulous Bush & Baker Boys," *New York Times Magazine,* 6 May 1990, pp. 34–36, 58, 62–64, 67;

John Newhouse, "The Tactician," *New Yorker,* 66 (7 May 1990): 50–82.

GEORGE BUSH

1924-

VICE PRESIDENT OF THE UNITED STATES, 1981-1989

PRESIDENT OF THE UNITED STATES, 1989-1993

In Reagan's Shadow. Serving as vice president under one of the most personally popular presidents of the twentieth century, George Bush seemed colorless and ineffectual next to the charismatic former actor Ronald Reagan. Though he won election to the presidency as the heir to the Reagan legacy and had his image enhanced by interna-

tional events largely not of his making, Bush ultimately took the blame for domestic woes that had their roots in his predecessor's economic policies and lost his reelection bid in 1992.

Background. Born in Milton, Massachusetts, and brought up in Greenwich, Connecticut, George Herbert Walker Bush was the second of the five children of Prescott Sheldon Bush and Dorothy Walker Bush. Prescott Bush became managing partner of the investment banking house of Brown Brothers, Harriman and Company before leaving Wall Street to serve as a Republican senator from Connecticut (1952–1968). In 1942 George Bush graduated from the prestigious Phillips Academy in Andover, Massachusetts. Although he had been accepted at Yale University, he instead enlisted in the U.S. Naval Reserve for service in World War II, and by the end of 1943 Ensign Bush was the youngest fighter pilot in the navy. He was awarded the Distinguished Flying Cross for his actions on a 2 September 1944 mission in the South Pacific, during which his plane was shot down. Rotated stateside by Christmas, Bush married Barbara Pierce, daughter of the publisher of *McCall's* and *Redbook* magazines, on 6 January 1945. They eventually had six children, one of whom died of leukemia in 1953.

A Yale Man. Bush entered Yale that fall and graduated three and a half years later with a B.A. in economics and a Phi Beta Kappa key. He was also a member of the Skull and Bones society and captain of the baseball team during his senior year.

The Oil Business. Though he could have had a job in his father's firm, Bush decided to move to Texas and go into the oil business. By 1954 he was president of the Zapata Offshore Company, and drilling for oil in the Gulf of Mexico made him wealthy.

Politics. In 1962 Bush was elected chairman of the Harris County Republican Party. Two years later he ran for the Senate and lost, but in 1966 he was elected to the House of Representatives. During his two terms in Congress he compiled a mostly conservative voting record but supported several liberal social measures, including lowering the voting age to eighteen, abolition of the military draft, and an open-housing bill. Encouraged by President Richard M. Nixon, Bush ran for the Senate in 1970 and lost to Democrat Lloyd Bentsen.

Political Appointments. In December 1970 Nixon named Bush U.S. ambassador to the United Nations, where he negotiated a reduction in U.S. financial support to that body and unsuccessfully defended a plan to seat UN representatives from both Taiwan and mainland China. In January 1973 Bush became chairman of the Republican National Committee, presiding over the party at the height of the Watergate scandal over illegal activities surrounding Nixon's election the previous year. On 7 August, after Nixon's personal involvement in the scandal became known, Bush urged the president to resign, and he did so two days later. In October 1974

Nixon's successor, Gerald Ford, made Bush head of the U.S. Liaison Office in the People's Republic of China, and in December 1975 Ford called Bush home to head the Central Intelligence Agency (CIA), which was under fire from Congress for engaging in covert activities that overstepped the bounds of its legal mandate. Bush helped to draft an executive order designed to prevent such abuses in the future and won high marks for improving agency morale. He turned in his resignation after the election of Democrat Jimmy Carter in November 1976.

Vice President Bush. Bush sought the Republican presidential nomination in 1980 and was widely viewed as an attractive moderate alternative to conservative Ronald Reagan. After a strong start, however, Bush fell behind in the primary vote tally and dropped out of the race. He accepted Reagan's offer of the vice-presidential slot despite their differences of opinion on several key issues, and — seeing his party's swing to the right — Bush began a gradual slide in that direction himself. During his two terms as Reagan's vice president, whatever influence Bush may have exerted on policy decisions took place behind the scenes. In public he loyally supported the Reagan agenda, and one anonymous administration official has called the vice president a "neutral political functionary." Bush is believed to have contributed to softening Reagan's view of the Soviet Union as the "evil empire," and Bush's aides have reported that in 1985 and 1986 their boss interceded with the president to prevent Attorney General Edwin Meese's plan to eliminate an executive order applying certain affirmative-action standards to government hiring.

Heading Task Forces. Bush received mixed reviews for his chairmanships of several special task forces. While his staff claimed that his Task Force on Regulatory Reform would save the government $150 billion over ten years, conservative critics said it had done little more than report the costs of regulation. The South Florida Task Force, established in 1982 to deal with an increase in drug trafficking in that region, was successful in getting the various government agencies charged with drug interdiction to work together, but cocaine imports actually increased while marijuana smugglers switched to growing it in Florida. The Vice President's Task Force on Combating Terrorism came up with no better ideas than the conventional assertion that the United States "will make no concessions to terrorists" — a rule the Reagan administration proceeded to break in the arms-for-hostages trade that was part of the Iran-Contra scandal.

President Bush. In 1988 Bush was elected president, overcoming his image as a wimp and allegations that he had known more than he claimed about Iran-Contra. As chief executive he was widely viewed as a foreign-policy president with little interest in domestic issues. During the first year of his term he had the good fortune to be in office while the Communist governments of the Soviet Union and eastern Europe self-destructed. He worked with Congress to continue whittling away at the federal budget deficit. Yet he also suffered a defeat when Congress refused to confirm his nomination of former Texas senator John Tower for secretary of defense, and he inherited a scandal in the Department of Housing and Urban Development (HUD). It was revealed that Reagan's HUD secretary, Samuel R. Pierce Jr., had engaged in influence peddling and favoritism toward prominent Republicans and wasted millions, perhaps billions, of dollars through mismanagement of agency funds. The "rally-round-the-flag" phenomenon during American involvement in the Persian Gulf War of 1990 boosted Bush's popularity to the point where many believed he would be unbeatable in the next presidential election. Yet by 1992, with the nation in the midst of a recession, he lost a three-way race to Democrat Bill Clinton.

Sources:

Barbara Bush, *Barbara Bush: A Memoir* (New York: Scribners, 1994);

George Bush, *Looking Forward* (Garden City, N.Y.: Doubleday, 1987);

Michael Duffy, *Marching in Place: The Status Quo Presidency of George Bush* (New York: Simon & Schuster, 1992);

Randall Rothenberg, "In Search of George Bush," *New York Times Magazine,* 6 March 1988, pp. 28–30, 44, 46, 48–49, 61.

GERALDINE FERRARO

1935-

DEMOCRATIC NOMINEE FOR VICE PRESIDENT, 1984

Trail-Blazing Politician. When Walter Mondale announced on 12 July 1984 that Geraldine Ferraro would be his running mate, the Democratic congresswoman from Queens, New York, became the first woman ever to seek the vice presidency as the candidate of a major national political party. Little known outside her district before that day, Ferraro stepped into a spotlight of intense media scrutiny that ultimately derailed what had seemed to be a promising political career.

Background. Geraldine Anne Ferraro was born in Newburgh, New York, to an Italian immigrant and his Italian American wife. After earning a B.A. in 1956 from Marymount College in Tarrytown, New York, Ferraro taught grade school in the Queens public school system while attending Fordham University School of Law at night, earning a J.D. in 1960. On 16 July 1960 — about a week after passing the New York State bar exam — she married John Zaccaro, a Manhattan real-estate developer, and spent the next fourteen years raising their three children while practicing civil law part-time and becoming involved in local Democratic politics.

The Queens District Attorney's Office. In 1974 Ferraro became an assistant district attorney in Queens, working in the Investigations Bureau. The next year she helped to create and was reassigned to the new Special

Victims Bureau for cases involving domestic violence, child abuse, and rape. She earned a reputation as a tough but fair prosecutor and was named head of the bureau in 1977. During these years she became convinced that the root causes of many of the crimes she encountered were poverty and social injustice, and her political views evolved from what she called "small 'c' conservative" to "progressive" or liberal.

Running for Congress. In 1978 Ferraro ran for Congress in the Ninth Congressional District, a conservative, predominantly white, working-class section of Queens. Her Italian American heritage, her husband's ability to finance an expensive campaign, and the backing of her cousin Nicholas Ferraro, a popular state senator, all stood Ferraro in good stead, as she surprised political pundits by beating her conservative Republican opponent by ten percentage points. She was reelected by even larger margins in 1980 and 1982.

Team Player. In Congress Ferraro tended to vote with her fellow Democrats. Over her three terms she earned a 76 percent approval rating from the liberal Americans for Democratic Action and 91 percent from the AFL-CIO Committee on Political Education. She sometimes crossed party lines on issues of concern to her conservative district — as when she voted against mandatory busing and for tuition tax credits for parents with children in private or parochial schools. Yet she also took stands that were unpopular with her constituents, following the dictates of her conscience in supporting federal funding for abortions, especially in the case of rape or incest. She tended to be stronger on defense issues than some other liberal Democrats, but she stopped short of backing funding for nerve-gas research and the development of the B-1 bomber or Reagan's "Star Wars" system.

Support from the Speaker. Early in her first term Ferraro won the respect of House Speaker Thomas P. "Tip" O'Neill, whose backing helped her win election as secretary of the House Democratic caucus in 1980 and 1982. In that capacity she sat on the House Steering and Policy Committee, which handles committee assignments. In 1981 she represented the House on the commission that revised the Democratic Party delegate-selection process. Ferraro is credited with devising the plan by which uncommitted "superdelegate" slots were reserved at the convention for Democratic office holders and party officials. In 1983 O'Neill appointed her to the powerful Budget Committee.

Chairing the 1984 Platform Committee. By 1984 many political insiders viewed Ferraro as a rising star in the Democratic Party. In that year, as the first woman to chair the Democratic platform committee, she won positive media attention for her deft handling of opposing special-interest groups. The resulting platform had something for everybody and pleased most delegates, but it was criticized as overly long and unwieldy.

Vice Presidential Candidate. When Mondale announced his choice of Ferraro as his running mate, Democrats hailed his decision, believing that the enthusiastic Ferraro would help to enliven Mondale's stolid, somber image. Yet media scrutiny of her husband's finances soon tarnished Ferraro's image. (Despite innuendoes of mafia connections and major financial wrongdoing, only one irregularity was proved. After the election Zaccaro pleaded guilty to the misdemeanor charge of overvaluing property in a real-estate transaction.) Other critics pointed to her lack of experience in foreign affairs. Ferraro's stand on abortion hurt her as well. When asked how she could be a devout Roman Catholic and still favor federal funding for abortions, Ferraro responded that she was personally opposed to abortion but could not in good conscience impose her moral views on others. That stand earned her repeated attacks from Archbishop John J. O'Connor of New York, Bishop James C. Tiflin of Scranton, Pennsylvania, and other Catholic clerics — and lost her support among the conservative, working-class Catholic constituencies that Democrats had hoped she would attract back to their party. No analyst has ever suggested, however, that Ferraro's campaign liabilities had any significant influence on Ronald Reagan's landslide defeat of Mondale in the presidential election.

Aftermath. After the election, rumors continued to plague Ferraro. Her attempts to reenter politics were met with continuing allegations of mob friendships and financial irregularities. Ferraro denied these charges and decried those who "smear by innuendo" and judge "guilt by association." Yet so far negative opinion ratings have blocked her return to elected office.

Sources:
"The Child Star's New Role," *U.S. News & World Report*, 113 (14 September 1992): 35, 38;

Jane Perlez, "Ferraro the Campaigner," *New York Times Magazine*, 30 September 1984, pp. 22–26, 84, 90–93;

Perlez, "Liberal Democrat From Queens: Geraldine Anne Ferraro," *New York Times*, 13 July 1984, I: 1, 9.

JESSE HELMS

1921-

SENATOR FROM NORTH CAROLINA, 1973-

Background. Born in Monroe, North Carolina, Jesse Helms studied at Wingate Junior College and Wake Forest University before serving in the navy during World War II. He became active in politics while working as a journalist in Raleigh, North Carolina, and served as an adviser to Willis Smith during his campaign for the U.S. Senate in 1950. After Smith's victory in what is regarded as the most virulently racist election in North Carolina history, Helms worked in Washington as an administrative assistant for Smith (1951–1953) and then briefly for Sen. Alton Lennon (1953). Returning to North Carolina in 1953, he worked as a television commentator and as a lobbyist for the banking industry before his election to the Senate as a Republican in 1972. He has been re-elected by close margins in 1978, 1984, and 1990. In 1972 and 1984, presidential election years, he ran behind the Republican presidential nominee.

Ideological Purity. Helms has developed a reputation as an ideological purist. His record in the Senate has been consistently anti–United Nations, anti-Communist, anti–government spending, antiwelfare, anti–arms control, anti–foreign aid, and promilitary. His only major political about-face was his 1985 switch from an anti-Israeli position to one that is pro-Israel — one said to have been prompted in part by the narrowness of his 1984 victory over an opponent who received substantial contributions from pro-Israel individuals and groups outside North Carolina.

Support from the Religious Right. Helms is known for his derisive treatment of those he opposes — from Martin Luther King to the Soviet Union to homosexuals — and he has an old-time southern politician's visceral appeal for conservative, mostly rural, white North Carolinians. Said to have an Old Testament sense of good and evil, he has had close ties to the religious right throughout his career, and during his campaigns he has made frequent appearances on the shows of the televangelists Jim Bakker and Pat Robertson. Leaders of Jerry Falwell's Moral Majority have spoken on his behalf at political rallies.

Pushing Conservative Causes. Helms has not often been successful in getting his own legislation passed. In 1982 he failed to implement measures that would have stripped the Supreme Court of jurisdiction over cases involving abortion, school prayer, and school busing. He has cast dozens of votes to outlaw or restrict abortion, to eliminate busing for school integration, and to do away with food stamps. In 1989 — after he became enraged over the inclusion of homoerotic photographs by Robert Mapplethorpe and Andres Serrano's photograph of a crucifix in a glass of urine in exhibits funded by the National Endowment for the Arts (NEA) — he tried unsuccessfully to convince the Senate to pass a bill that banned the funding of "obscene" art by the NEA or any other federal agency.

The Foreign Relations Committee. Throughout the 1980s Helms was consistently a thorn in the sides of Democratic and Republican administrations as he tried to promote his own ultraconservative foreign-policy agenda. As a member of the Senate Foreign Relations Committee and the ranking Republican since 1987, he has developed a network that gives him inside information on world affairs. His staff includes former intelligence personnel who have retained ties within their agencies, and he promotes the hiring of his staffers and aides for key positions in the various national security agencies. It has been reported that sometimes he gets reports on events before the White House. He has opposed all arms control regardless of whether a Republican or Democratic president has submitted them, and he led the 1984 fight that blocked U.S. ratification of the UN Treaty Against Genocide.

Blocking Nominations. Helms has also used his position on the committee to block or hold up nominations regardless of which party controlled the White House. He opposed Republican Gerald Ford's nominations of Nelson Rockefeller for vice president and Donald Rumsfeld for secretary of defense. Many of Democrat Jimmy Carter's nominees faced the same treatment, as did Caspar Weinberger, whom Republican Ronald Reagan nominated for secretary of defense. In 1981 Helms stalled Senate approval of several Reagan appointees as undersecretaries of state, including Lawrence Eagleburger, Chester Crocker, Robert Hormats, and Thomas Enders. In 1985 Helms held up the confirmation of Thomas Pickering as ambassador to Israel at a time of crucial discussions over possible exchanges of western hostages in Beirut for Arabs in Israeli prisons.

Right-Wing Ties. The animosity between Helms and Pickering stemmed from Pickering's service as ambassador to El Salvador, where he was actively trying to work with the Duarte government while Helms had close ties to Duarte's ultraright-wing opponent, Roberto D'Aubuisson. Helms has been closely tied to various right-wing governments, including the regime of Augusto Pinochet in Chile. Beginning in 1986 Helms served as chairman of the editorial advisory board of the International Freedom Foundation, a front organization for the South African Defense Fund, which set up and funded the foundation to conduct political warfare against opponents of apartheid in the United States. Other prominent conservative Republicans connected to the foundation included representatives Dan Burton and Robert Dornan of California and African American political activist Alan Keyes. In 1988 Helms led the fight to pass legislation that required the United States to maintain two embassies in Israel, one in Tel Aviv, the secular capital, and one in Jerusalem, in the contested West Bank region.

Sources:

Peter Applebone, "Pit-Bull Politician," *New York Times Magazine*, 28 October 1990, pp. 34–35, 46–50;

Eric Bates, "What you Need to Know about Jesse Helms," *Mother Jones* (May/June 1995): 57–68;

Sidney Blumenthal, "Republican of Fear," *New Republic*, 203 (12 November 1990): 15–17;

Ernest B. Furgurson, *Hard Right: The Rise of Jesse Helms* (New York: Norton, 1986);

Donald Neff, "Jesse Helms at the Helm," *Middle East International*, 488 (18 November 1994): 7–8.

JESSE JACKSON

1941-

Breaking New Ground. The Reverend Jesse Jackson made history in 1984, when he campaigned to be the Democratic candidate for the presidency of the United States. Though Democratic congresswoman Shirley Chisholm became the first black to seek the presidential nomination of a large, national party when she entered some Democratic primaries in 1972, Jackson was the first African American to wage a full-scale campaign to head a major-party ticket.

Background. An illegitimate child born to an impoverished family in Greenville, South Carolina, Jackson graduated from North Carolina Agricultural and Technical State University in 1963. He went on to study at the Chicago Theological Seminary, dropping out in spring 1965, six months before his expected graduation, to become active in the civil rights movement. In 1967 Dr. Martin Luther King made Jackson head of Operation Breadbasket, a group that used boycotts and other sorts of economic pressure to convince businesses to hire black workers.

Operation PUSH. Jackson was ordained a Baptist minister in 1968, and in 1971 he founded Operation PUSH (People United to Save Humanity; later People United to Serve Humanity), which continued the campaign for hiring of black workers, organized the underpaid, and helped minority businesses. In 1975 Jackson expanded PUSH to include PUSH for Excellence (PUSH/Excel), a self-help program for African Americans students living in urban slums. By 1978, with the help of funding from the Department of Health, Education, and Welfare (HEW) under the Carter administration, PUSH/Excel had established programs in several major cities. During the Reagan administration federal funding for PUSH/Excel was cut off as of February 1982, and the program went into a gradual decline. Administration officials pointed to several unfavorable evaluations of PUSH/Excel and vigorously pursued an audit of its finances, which turned up no evidence of illegal activity but faulted the program for inadequate record keeping. Those involved in PUSH/Excel perceived it as an inspirational program designed to motivate parents, students, and educators to work together in defining the needs and goals of individual schools. In contrast federal evaluators had expected national program administrators to define goals and devise specific procedures to implement them. Evaluations of the program were doubtless also colored by the views of the chief investigator, Charles Murray, future author of *Losing Ground* (1984), in which he argued that the social programs of the 1960s had done poor blacks more harm than good. Jackson took a leave of absence from Operation PUSH when he decided to run for president in 1984 and later resigned.

Running for President. He announced his candidacy on 3 November 1983, criticizing Reagan administration cutbacks in funding for programs that helped minorities and the poor and calling on all Americans who had been victims of discrimination or economic oppression to join his "rainbow coalition." He described his campaign as "growing out of the black experience" but "not for blacks only" and went on to explain: "I can empathize with the plight of Appalachia because I have known poverty. I know the pain of anti-Semitism because I have felt the pain of discrimination." In a candidate profile aired on 9 December 1983 CBS newsman Dan Rather called Jackson one of the most spellbinding orators of our time, "whose appeal to voters goes across racial lines to the young and to those who he says are stuck at the bottom." Jackson, he concluded, "can lay legitimate claim to the King legacy." Jackson's candidacy did not cross racial lines as successfully as Rather predicted — doubtless in part because of his race. Yet some voters were uncertain if Jackson, who had never held political office and had been labeled a sloppy administrator of his poverty programs, was qualified to be president.

Policy Proposals. Jackson put forth a range of proposals that aligned him with the liberal wing of the party, including a major public employment program, a renewal of federal spending on social services, a reduction in defense spending, a nuclear freeze, direct aid for Native Americans, and help for small farmers.

Foreign Policy. On 3 January 1984 Jackson earned positive press when he successfully negotiated the release of black navy pilot Robert Goodman, a resident of New Hampshire who had been shot down over Syria. While Jackson's domestic policy was for the most part in line with the standard liberal Democrat call for compassion and aid for the disadvantaged and needy, his foreign policy, never clearly defined, made many Democrats uneasy. Jackson was open in his support for Third World radical liberation groups such as the Sandinistas in Nicaragua — who, he said, were "on the right side of history" — and the Palestine Liberation Organization (PLO). In June 1984, with the nomination already decided, Jackson underlined his Third World sympathies by visiting Cuba, where Fidel Castro expressed his appreciation of Jackson's vocal opposition to the U.S. invasion of Grenada by releasing twenty-two Americans held in Cuban prisons. At the same time Jackson reinforced his radical image by visiting Nicaragua. His controversial policy stands, as well as his race, made him the target of more death threats than any other candidate. Geraldine Ferraro, the Democratic vice-presidential candidate, reportedly told her children not to stand too close to Jackson at public gatherings lest they be hit by stray bullets.

Charges of Anti-Semitism. Unpopular with Jewish voters ever since his literal embrace of PLO leader Yassir Arafat on a visit to the Middle East in 1979, Jackson was openly accused of anti-Semitism just two weeks before the New Hampshire primary, when the *Washington Post* revealed that in a private conversation that included one of its reporters, black journalist Milton Coleman, Jackson had called Jews "Hymies" and referred to New York City as "Hymietown." Jackson first denied using the words, then said he did not remember uttering them, and finally said he recalled using them, but it was "not done in a spirit of meanness." The flap might have ended there if it were not for Jackson's association with Nation of Islam leader Louis Farrakhan, an avowed anti-Semite who often traveled with Jackson's entourage and who provided the candidate's bodyguards. Farrakhan fueled the controversy with anti-Semitic remarks on several occasions, and he publicly warned Coleman, "One day we will punish you with death." Jackson disavowed the remark, but, fearing a split in his large and essential black constituency, he did not repudiate Farrakhan. Finally, on 28 June, after Farrakhan was quoted as calling Judaism a "gutter religion," Jackson broke with the Nation of Islam leader, calling his remarks "reprehensible and morally indefensible."

Jackson's Constituency. In 1984 Jackson earned only 5 percent of the white primary vote, a statistic more impressive than it seems at first glance; of the 3.4 million people who voted for him 22 percent (about 788,000) were nonblacks, including significant numbers of Hispanics, Asians, and white liberals, independents, and college graduates. He won 21 percent of the total primary and caucus votes, but because of selection rules he ended up with only 11 percent of the delegates. Most important, however, was his ability to effectively mobilize a large core group of African American supporters, who turned out in record numbers for party caucuses and primaries. The third-place finisher, he arrived at the Democratic National Convention with the backing of a powerful bloc of voters. To maintain their loyalty the party had to accommodate Jackson, whose speech to the convention made it clear that he was ready to broaden his voter appeal and begin again. He reached out to Jewish voters in particular, and he painted a picture of a nation unified in its diversity:

> America is not like a blanket. . . . It is more like a quilt — many patches, many pieces, many colors, many sizes, all woven and held together by a common thread. The white, the Hispanic, the black, the Arab, the Jew, the woman, the Native American, the small farmer, the businessperson, the environmentalist, the peace activist, the young, the old, the lesbian, the gay and the disabled make up America's quilt. . . .

> . . .We are much too intelligent, much too bound by our Judeo-Christian heritage . . . to go on divided from one another.

Although some of his black supporters were unhappy that Jackson had not taken on the white party establishment for perceived rebuffs to their cause, the speech moved many white delegates to tears.

Running Again. After 1984 Jackson continued campaigning, formally establishing a National Rainbow Coalition and building a grassroots organization. His 1984 campaign staff had been enthusiastic, naive, and disorganized. By 1988 he had aides who could make more efficient use of his time and campaign funds. On his second run for the nomination he emphasized the theme of unity that had proved so effective at the 1984 convention and deemphasized foreign policy, while offering a strong antidrug proposal that appealed to Americans of all races and a wide range of political persuasions. Journalists began reporting that Jackson had "matured."

Finishing Second. Though he still could not attract the working-class whites who make up the backbone of the party, Jackson increased his appeal to white liberals and other nonblacks and ended up in second place. Nearly seven million people voted for him nationwide (to about ten million for Michael Dukakis). As second-place finisher, Jackson felt he had a strong claim on the vice presidential nomination. He was angry when he was passed over for Lloyd Bentsen — and learned about it from the news media rather than Dukakis himself. Dukakis and Jackson patched over their differences for the short term, and Jackson agreed to campaign for the Democratic ticket in the fall, but within weeks of the convention he had become a self-proclaimed "free agent," focusing his speeches on his own political agenda.

Impact. Without ever holding public office Jackson had a profound impact on the Democratic Party in the 1980s while also serving as a constant inspiration and example to the poor and disadvantaged. He has been variously described as egotistical and charismatic, morally committed to social justice but humanly flawed. As his eldest son, Jesse Jr., said at the 1988 Democratic National Convention, he taught his children that the greatest tragedy in life is "not failure but a low aim."

Sources:

Lucius J. Barker and Ronald W. Walters, eds., *Jesse Jackson's 1984 Presidential Campaign: Challenge and Change in American Politics* (Urbana & Chicago: University of Illinois Press, 1989);

Elizabeth O. Colton, *The Jackson Phenomenon: The Man, The Power, The Message* (New York: Doubleday, 1989);

Bob Faw, *Thunder in America: The Improbable Presidential Campaign of Jesse Jackson* (Austin: Texas Monthly Press, 1986);

Ernest R. House, *Jesse Jackson & the Politics of Charisma: The Rise and Fall of the PUSH/Excel Program* (Boulder: Westview Press, 1988).

RONALD REAGAN

1911-

PRESIDENT OF THE UNITED STATES, 1981-1989

"The Great Communicator." Promising to cut taxes, reduce government regulation and bureaucracy, shrink the federal deficit, and combat Soviet influence anywhere in the world, conservative Republican Ronald Reagan won a landslide victory in the 1980 presidential election and was reelected by an even larger margin in 1984. His appeal to voters was based less on specific policies than on his ability to communicate a vision of an America where a return to "old-fashioned" values such as patriotism, religion, hard work, self-reliance, and family togetherness would miraculously eradicate the nation's pressing economic and social woes and bolster its sagging reputation abroad. He so successfully wrapped himself in the flag that he co-opted "patriotism" for himself and his party, leaving the Democrats to sputter ineffectually about the large number of Americans who were left out of the idealized "City upon a Hill" Reagan described in speech after speech.

Background. Born in Tampico, Illinois, and a graduate of Eureka College in 1932, Reagan went from radio announcer to movie actor and president of the Screen Actors Guild (SAG) in 1947. Active politically as head of SAG and nominally a Democrat, Reagan switched to the Republican Party in 1962 and helped Richard Nixon in his unsuccessful campaign for the California governorship. In 1964 he gave a speech on behalf of Barry Goldwater at the Republican National Convention that was considered even more conservative than Goldwater's acceptance speech. Running for governor of California in 1966, Reagan was elected handily and reelected in 1970. While governor he endeared himself to conservatives by vetoing spending measures, reforming the welfare system, and providing property tax relief (while increasing sales and income taxes). He also enhanced his reputation among conservatives by vigorously confronting student radicals at the University of California, Berkeley. He was narrowly defeated by incumbent Gerald Ford in a 1976 bid for the Republican presidential nomination, and he spent the next four years building the grassroots organization and solid financial backing that won him the nomination, and the election, in 1980.

Assassination Attempt. On 30 March 1981, within three months of his inauguration, Reagan was shot by a would-be assassin as he left a Washington hotel where he had just delivered a speech. After surgery to remove a bullet from his left lung, he remained hospitalized until 11 April. Although White House reports at the time tended to deemphasize the seriousness of his wound, information released in 1995 revealed that he nearly died.

The Reagan Doctrine. During his first term Reagan vigorously pursued an anti-Communist foreign-policy agenda announcing at the start a five-year program to increase defense spending by $1.2 trillion. In March 1983 he proposed the Strategic Defense Initiative (SDI, or "Star Wars"), which was intended to protect the United States against a Soviet strategic-missile attack. Calling the Soviet Union "the evil empire," he employed anti-Soviet rhetoric that was more reminiscent of the 1950s than the late 1960s and the 1970s. He also enunciated a policy that was subsequently dubbed the "Reagan doctrine," promising American help for friendly nations threatened by Communist insurgencies and for insurgency movements seeking to topple Marxist regimes. During his presidency the United States supported insurgent movements in Angola, Nicaragua, and Afghanistan and anti-Communist governments in the Philippines and El Salvador. He also committed U.S. troops to assist peacekeeping efforts in Lebanon, ordered the bombing of Libya in retaliation for its support of terrorist activities, and launched an invasion of Grenada to oust a Marxist government friendly to Fidel Castro's government in Cuba.

Domestic Issues. Reagan won the Republican nomination in 1980 by appealing to the religious right and other social conservatives with his support for right-wing initiatives such as the drives for constitutional amendments requiring school prayer and banning abortion. During the election campaign, however, he projected a more moderate image to attract the broader range of voters he needed to win the presidency. Although he continued to give lip support to school prayer and banning abortion during his presidency, Reagan focused his energies on trying to enact his conservative, pro-business economic agenda, based on the notion that tax breaks and other incentives would stimulate business investment and create a new prosperity that would "trickle down" to the middle and working classes through new jobs and pay increases. Thus, despite lower tax rates, government revenues would actually increase. Shortly after his inauguration in 1981, Reagan proposed a tax-reform package and a budget-cutting program designed to reduce the deficit. The tax cuts passed easily, but Congress refused to reduce spending for many social programs and regulatory agencies as deeply as the administration desired. Nor did the tax cuts generate enough additional revenues to match Reagan's radical increases in defense spending. Consequently, the federal deficit continued to grow at an alarming rate, and the economy plunged further into a recession that it did not begin pulling out of until 1983.

Cold War Thaw. During Reagan's second term as president, relations between the Soviet Union and the United States improved dramatically as Premier Mikhail Gorbachev sought to reduce tensions with the West in the hope of attracting the western investment necessary to revitalize the Soviet economy. Reagan and Gorbachev successfully negotiated major arms-control agreements as the Soviet Union withdrew its troops from Afghanistan and ended its support for Communist regimes in Angola and Nicaragua, allowing negotiated solutions to those civil wars. As tensions between the United States and the Soviet Union became virtually nonexistent, military spending was decreased and the Star Wars budget was cut. Yet the Reagan administration continued to accumulate deficits at an alarming rate as the economy grew stronger but still did not create revenues at the levels the administration had anticipated.

The Iran-Contra Scandal. Reagan suffered a major embarrassment after the Iran-Contra arms-for-hostages trading came to light in late 1986. Although inquiries by a special presidential commission, a congressional investigation committee, and a special prosecutor found that Reagan knew little about the details of those complex operations, he was criticized for his failure to supervise the actions of his subordinates. The criminal prosecution of several administration officials and questions about his management style led to negative political fallout for Reagan.

Record. An assessment of Reagan's presidency yields mixed results. His ability to stimulate the economy and to foster major tax reforms must be weighed against his responsibility for an astronomical increase in the federal deficit. The public scandal of the Iran-Contra affair must be balanced against his real achievements in arms control and ending the Cold War.

Sources:
Wilbur Edel, *The Reagan Presidency: An Actor's Finest Performance* (New York: Hippocrene Books, 1992);

Ronald Reagan, *An American Life: The Autobiography* (New York: Simon & Schuster, 1990);

Garry Wills, *Reagan's America: Innocents at Home* (Garden City, N.Y.: Doubleday, 1987).

PEOPLE IN THE NEWS

On 3 September 1983 **David Bergland,** a lawyer from California, won the Libertarian Party nomination for president. He opposed taxes, domestic spending, and involvement in foreign affairs and pledged to sell the national parks.

William Buckley, first secretary of the political section of the U.S. embassy in Beirut, Lebanon, was kidnapped by Arab extremists on March 1984. He was the third American abducted in Beirut in three weeks. On 20 January 1987 it was revealed that Buckley, who was alleged to have been chief of CIA operations in Lebanon, had been slain by his captors.

On 12 April 1988 Sen. **Robert Byrd** (D–W.Va.) announced that he would step down as head Senate Democrat after eleven years as majority or minority leader.

In February 1982 **Juanita Castro,** sister of Cuban president Fidel Castro, became a citizen of the United States, underscoring her political differences with her brother.

Edward Clark, the Libertarian candidate for president in 1980, won a place on the ballot in all fifty states and the District of Columbia. Clark and his running mate, David Koch of New York City, received 880,000 votes in the election, stressing that the sole purpose of government should be to protect individual freedoms.

Barry Commoner, a professor of environmental science at Washington University in Saint Louis, organized the Citizens' Party in April 1980 and ran as its candidate for president, charging that the Democrats and Republicans could not solve the nation's problems. He and his running mate, LaDonna Harris, got 220,000 votes in the election.

Richard M. Daley was elected mayor of Chicago on 4 April 1989. His father, Richard J. Daley, held the same office from 1955 to 1976.

On 16 May 1989 City Councilman **George Darden** of Nashville, Tennessee, failed to convince fellow council members to build a landing pad for unidentified flying objects (UFOs). One councilman suggested he might support the idea if the pad were built in Darden's district, but an opponent pointed out that the area had "too much traffic already."

On 5 January 1983 **Elizabeth Dole,** wife of Sen. **Robert Dole** (R–Kan.), was nominated as secretary of transportation. She was the first woman named to President Ronald Reagan's cabinet.

In April 1986 actor **Clint Eastwood** was elected mayor of Carmel-by-the-Sea, California, running as an opponent of political bureaucracy. When asked if he had aspirations for higher office, Eastwood replied, "This is where it stops."

On 2 April 1984 Congressman **George Hansen,** a Republican from Idaho, became the first congressman convicted under the Ethics in Government Act (1978) when he was found guilty of filing false financial statements.

On 12 January 1983 President Reagan added a second woman to his cabinet: **Margaret Heckler,** a former congresswoman from Massachusetts, who was appointed secretary of health and human services.

Yippie leader **Abbie Hoffman** emerged from hiding in September 1980, just in time to publicize his new book, *Soon to Be a Major Motion Picture.* The radical political activist had gone underground in 1974 after jumping bail on a drug charge in New York City. Changing his appearance through plastic surgery and taking the name Barry Freed, he had become an environmental activist, even testifying before a U.S. Senate subcommittee without having his true identity discovered.

In August 1984 **Sonia Johnson** of Virginia became the Citizens' Party candidate for president. Johnson, a feminist, had first made the news in 1979, when the Church of Jesus Christ of Latter-day Saints (the Mormons) excommunicated her for supporting the Equal Rights Amendment.

On 24 February 1989 Gov. **John R. McKernan Jr.** of Maine married Congresswoman **Olympia J. Snowe,** also of Maine. The wedding is believed to be the first between a governor and a member of Congress to take place while the bride and groom were both in office.

On 17 March 1989 six English springer spaniel puppies were born at the White House to **Millie,** pet to President and Mrs. George Bush.

Ron Paul, the Libertarian candidate for president in 1988, won 431,616 votes in the November election, 0.5 percent of the total votes cast.

On 10 August 1989 Gen. **Colin L. Powell** became the first African American chairman of the Joint Chiefs of Staff.

Maureen Reagan, daughter of President Ronald Reagan, was hired by the Republican National Committee on 23 August 1983 to help improve her father's image with women. The appointment came several days after her father had commented, "If it wasn't for women, us men would still be walking around in skin suits and carrying clubs."

On 31 January 1982 Adm. **Hyman G. Rickover** retired as head of the U.S. Navy Nuclear Propulsion Program. He used the occasion to speak out in favor of disarmament. Appearing before the Joint Economic Committee of the U.S. Congress, Rickover, widely known as the father of the nuclear navy, criticized defense contractors and the nuclear arms race and asked the committee to put him in charge of an international disarmament conference.

In April 1988 former deputy presidential secretary **Larry Speakes** published a memoir, *Speaking Out,* in which he revealed that during the 1985 Geneva summit meeting he had made up some of the statements he had attributed to President Ronald Reagan because he believed the president was being outshone by Soviet premier Mikhail Gorbachev. Speakes also admitted that in 1983, when the Soviets shot down a Korean airliner, he had attributed to his boss some statements actually made by Secretary of State George P. Shultz. According to *Newsweek* (25 April 1995), the president said, "I wasn't aware of that and just learned it recently." A few weeks after the book was published, Speakes was forced to resign from a job as a vice president and chief spokesman for Merrill Lynch.

Sen. **John C. Stennis** (D–Miss.) retired on 3 January 1989, after forty-one years, one month, and twenty-one days in the U.S. Senate. The only senator in office longer was Sen. Carl Hayden (R–Ariz.), who retired in 1969, after forty-one years and ten months of ser-vice. At the time of his retirement Stennis was president pro tempore of the Senate and chairman of the Appropriations Committee. The last of the powerful Southern Democrats who dominated the Conservative Coalition of the 1950s and 1960s, he was a strong supporter of military spending and played a dominant role in policy decisions as chairman of the Armed Services Committee at the height of the Vietnam War.

On 4 February 1988 **Philip Stevens,** great-grandson of Chief Standing Bear, became the first war chief elected by the Sioux Indians of the United States in one hundred years. Stevens, the head of an engineering firm, was charged with leading the fight to recover unoccupied government-owned land in South Dakota that was taken from the Sioux 110 years earlier.

The November 1981 issue of *The Atlantic Monthly* quoted Budget Director **David Stockman** as saying President Ronald Reagan's "trickle-down" economic program would not work. On 12 November the president delivered an angry reprimand to Stockman but did not demand Stockman's resignation. As he emerged from the White House, Stockman compared the meeting to a "visit to the woodshed." He remained in his post until 9 July 1985.

Sixty-year-old **Matt Urban,** a retired U.S. Army lieutenant colonel, was awarded the Medal of Honor by President Jimmy Carter on 19 July 1980. Urban was given the medal, the highest military award for valor, for his actions in France in 1944, during World War II. A soldier who fought under Urban had recommended him for the Medal of Honor, but the letter was lost and did not come to light until a search was begun for it in 1978.

On 2 April 1986 Alabama governor **George Wallace** announced his retirement from politics.

On 5 October 1981 President Ronald Reagan made Swedish diplomat **Raoul Wallenberg** an honorary citizen of the United States, praising Wallenberg for saving some one hundred thousand Hungarians from Nazi death camps during World War II. Wallenberg disappeared in 1945, after agents of the Soviet Union seized him in Hungary.

On 12 April 1983 Democrat **Harold Washington** was elected the first black mayor of Chicago.

DEATHS

Edwin R. Adair, 75, representative (R) from Indiana (1951–1971), 7 May 1983.

Sherman Adams, 87, Republican representative (1945–1947) and governor of New Hampshire (1949–1953), White House chief of staff (1953–1958), 27 October 1986.

Joseph P. Addabbo, 61, representative (D) from New York (1961–1986), 10 April 1986.

Hugh J. Addonizio, 67, representative (D) from New Jersey (1949–1962) and mayor of Newark (1962–1970), 2 February 1981.

George D. Aiken, 92, senator (R) from Vermont (1941–1975), 19 November 1984.

Gordon L. Allott, 82, senator (R) from Colorado (1955–1973), 17 January 1989.

J. Lindsay Almond Jr., 87, Democratic representative (1945–1948) and governor (1958–1962) of Virginia, 14 April 1986.

Joseph Alsop, 78, influential conservative political columnist, 28 August 1989.

John Z. "Jack" Anderson, 76, representative (R) from California (1939–1953), 9 February 1981.

Robert B. Anderson, 79, secretary of the navy (1953–1954), deputy secretary of defense (1954–1955), secretary of the treasury (1957–1961), 14 August 1989.

Leslie C. Arends, 89, representative (R) from Illinois (1935–1975), 16 July 1985.

Orland Kay Armstrong, 92, representative (R) from Missouri (1951–1953), 15 April 1987.

John M. Ashbrook, 54, representative (R) from Ohio (1961–1982), 24 April 1982.

Robert T. Ashmore, 85, representative (D) from South Carolina (1953–1969), 4 October 1989.

Wayne N. Aspinall, 87, representative (D) from Colorado (1959–1983), 9 October 1983.

Malcolm Baldridge, 64, secretary of commerce (1981–1987), 25 July 1987.

Raymond E. Baldwin, 93, Republican governor (1939–1941, 1943–1946) and senator (1946–1949) from Connecticut, 4 October 1986.

Ross R. Barnett, 89, governor (D) of Mississippi (1960–1964), defiantly opposed desegregation at the University of Mississippi, 6 November 1987.

Robert R. Barry, 73, representative (R) from New York (1959–1965), 14 June 1988.

Page Belcher, 81, representative (R) from Oklahoma (1950–1972), 2 August 1980.

Adam Benjamin Jr., 47, representative (D) from Indiana (1977–1982), 7 September 1982.

Alan H. Bible, 78, senator (D) from Nevada (1954–1975), 12 September 1988.

Jonathan B. Bingham, 72, representative (D) from New York (1965–1982), 3 July 1986.

Ray C. Bliss, 73, chairman of the Republican National Committee (1965–1969), 6 August 1981.

William F. Bolger, 66, postmaster general of the United States (1978–1984), 21 August 1989.

Reva Z. B. Bosone, 88, representative (D) from Utah (1949–1953), 21 July 1983.

Chester B. Bowles, 85, Democratic governor (1949–1951) and representative (1959–1961) from Connecticut, ambassador to India (1951–1953, 1963–1969), 25 May 1986.

John W. Bricker, 92, Republican governor (1939–1945) and senator (1947–1959) from Ohio, 22 March 1986.

Charles B. Brownson, 74, representative (R) from Indiana (1951–1959), 4 August 1988.

Ellsworth Bunker, 90, ambassador to Vietnam (1967–1973) during the Vietnam War, 27 September 1984.

Arthur F. Burns, 83, economist, chairman of Federal Reserve Board (1970–1978), 26 June 1987.

Phillip Burton, 57, representative (D) from California (1964–1983), 10 April 1983.

Sala Burton, 62, representative (D) from California (1983–1987), 1 February 1987.

John W. Byrnes, 71, representative (R) from Wisconsin (1945–1973), 12 January 1985.

Millard F. Caldwell, 87, Democratic representative (1933–1941) and governor of Florida (1945–1949), 23 October 1984.

Frank Carlson, 94, Republican representative (1935–1947), governor (1947–1950), and senator (1950–1969), from Kansas, 30 May 1987.

Charles J. Carney, 74, representative (D) from Ohio (1970–1979), 7 October 1987.

John A. Carroll, 82, Democratic representative (1947–1951) and senator (1957–1963) from Colorado, 31 August 1983.

Tim Lee Carter, 76, representative (R) from Kentucky (1965–1980), 27 March 1987.

William A. "Billy" Carter III, 51, brother of President Jimmy Carter, involved in "Billygate," 25 September 1988.

Clifford P. Case, 77, Republican representative (1945–1953) and senator (1955–1979) from New Jersey, champion of civil rights legislation, 5 March 1982.

William J. Casey, 74, director of the Central Intelligence Agency (1981–1987), 6 May 1987.

Emanuel Celler, 92, representative (D) from New York (1923–1972), 15 January 1981.

William V. Chappell Jr., 67, representative (D) from Florida (1969–1989), 30 March 1989.

J. Edgar Chenoweth, 88, representative (R) from Colorado (1941–1949, 1951–1965), 2 January 1986.

Frank F. Church, 59, senator (D) from Idaho (1957–1980), 25 August 1984.

Earle C. Clements, 88, representative (1945–1947), governor (1947– 1950), and senator (1950–1957) from Kentucky, 12 March 1985.

Wilbur J. Cohen, 73, secretary of health, education, and welfare (1968–1969), 18 May 1987.

Roy M. Cohn, 59, attorney who helped Sen. Joseph McCarthy (R-Wisc.) in his investigations of communist influence in the U.S. government, 2 August 1986.

W. Sterling Cole, 82, representative (R) from New York (1935-1957), 15 March 1987.

James M. Collins, 72, representative (R) from Texas (1968-1983), 16 April 1989.

William R. Cotter, 55, representative (D) from Connecticut (1971-1981), 8 September 1981.

Norris Cotton, 88, Republican representative (1947–1954) and senator (1954–1975) from New Hampshire, 24 February 1989.

Shephard J. Crumpacker Jr., 69, representative (R) from Indiana (1951–1957), 14 October 1986.

Laurence Curtis, 95, representative (R) from Massachusetts (1953–1963), 11 July 1989.

Price M. Daniel, 77, Democratic senator (1953–1957) and governor (1957–1963) of Texas, 25 August 1988.

Wilbur Clarence "Dan" Daniel, 74, representative (D) from Virginia (1969–1988), 24 January 1988.

Dominick V. Daniels, 78, representative (D) from New Jersey (1959–1977), 17 July 1987.

Glenn R. Davis, 73, representative (R) from Wisconsin (1954–1957, 1965–1975), 21 September 1988.

James J. Delaney, 86, representative (D) from New York (1945–1947, 1949–1979), 24 May 1987.

John N. Dempsey, 74, governor (D) of Connecticut (1961–1971), 16 July 1989.

John H. Dent, 80, representative (D) from Pennsylvania (1958–1979), 9 April 1988.

James P. S. Devereux, 85, representative (R) from Maryland (1951–1959), 5 August 1988.

Michael V. DiSalle, 73, governor (D) of Ohio (1959–1963), 5 September 1981.

Peter H. Dominick, 65, Republican representative (1960–1962) and senator (1962–1974) from Colorado, 18 March 1981.

Francis E. Dorn, 76, representative (R) from New York (1953–1961), 17 September 1987.

Helen Gahagan Douglas, 79, representative (D) from California (1945–1951), defeated by Richard M. Nixon in 1950 after a hard-fought campaign for a seat in the U.S. Senate, 28 June 1980.

Thaddeus J. Dulski, 73, representative (D) from New York (1959–1975), 11 October 1988.

John J. Duncan, 69, representative (R) from Tennessee (1965–1988), 21 June 1988.

John P. East, 55, senator (R) from North Carolina (1981–1986), 29 June 1986.

James O. Eastland, 81, senator (D) from Mississippi (1941, 1943–1979), 19 February 1986.

Milton S. Eisenhower, 85, adviser to six presidents, brother of President Dwight D. Eisenhower, 2 May 1985.

M. Harris Ellsworth, 86, representative (R) from Oregon (1943–1957), 7 February 1986.

Sam J. Ervin Jr., 88, senator (D) from North Carolina (1954–1975), chaired the Senate committee that investigated Watergate, 23 April 1985.

Joe L. Evins, 73, representative (D) from Tennessee (1947–1977), 31 March 1984.

George Fallon, 77, representative (D) from Maryland (1945–1971), 21 March 1980.

Walter Flowers, 51, representative (D) from Alabama (1969–1977), 12 April 1984.

James E. Folsom, 79, governor (D) of Alabama (1947–1951, 1955–1959), 21 November 1987.

Edwin B. Forsyth, 68, representative (R) from New Jersey (1970–1984), 29 March 1984.

George H. Gallup, 82, statistician and founder of the Gallup Poll, 26 July 1984.

Ray D. Garrett Jr., 59, chairman of the Securities and Exchange Commission (1973–1975), 3 February 1980.

James H. Gildea, 97, representative (D) from Pennsylvania (1935–1939), 5 June 1988.

Charles E. Goodell, 60, senator (R) (1968–1971) and representative (1959–1968) from New York, 21 January 1987.

Ella T. Grasso, 61, Democratic representative (1971–1975) and governor (1975–1980) of Connecticut, first woman elected to a governorship without succeeding her husband, 5 February 1981.

Edith S. Green, 77, representative (D) from Oregon (1955–1975), 21 April 1987.

Harold Royce Gross, 88, representative (R) from Iowa (1949–1975), 22 September 1987.

John E. Grotberg, 61, representative (R) from Illinois (1985–1986), 15 November 1986.

Tennyson Guyer, 68, representative (R) from Ohio (1973–1981), 12 April 1981.

James C. Hagerty, 71, White House press secretary (1953–1961), 11 April 1981.

James A. Haley, 82, representative (D) from Florida (1953–1977), 6 August 1981.

Charles A. Halleck, 86, representative (R) from Indiana (1935–1969), 3 March 1986.

Cecil Murray Harden, 90, representative (R) from Indiana (1949–1959), 5 December 1984.

Bryce N. Harlow, 70, White House aide for Presidents Dwight D. Eisenhower and Richard M. Nixon, 17 February 1987.

W. Averell Harriman, 94, ambassador to the Soviet Union (1943–1946), ambassador to Great Britain (1946), administrator of the Marshall Plan (1948), special adviser to President Harry S Truman on Far Eastern affairs (1950–1951), governor (D) of New York (1955–1959), assistant secretary of state for Far Eastern affairs and special adviser to President John F. Kennedy (1961–1963), chief negotiator for the Limited Nuclear Test Ban Treaty (1963), undersecretary of state for political affairs (1963–1968), head of the U.S. delegation to the Paris peace talks with Vietnam, 26 July 1986.

Patricia R. Harris, 60, secretary of housing and urban development (1977–1979) and secretary of health, education, and welfare (1979–1981), first black woman to hold a cabinet post, 23 March 1985.

Clement F. Haynsworth Jr., 77, federal appeals court judge whose nomination by Richard Nixon to the U.S. Supreme Court was rejected by the Senate in 1969, 22 November 1989.

Brooks Hays, 83, representative (D) from Arkansas (1942–1958), 12 October 1981.

Wayne L. Hays, 87, representative (D) from Ohio (1949–1976), resigned his seat after revelations about his affair with staff member Elizabeth Ray, 10 February 1989.

Walter W. Heller, 71, economist, charman of the Council of Economic Advisers (1961–1964), 15 June 1987.

Lister Hill, 89, senator (D) from Alabama (1938–1969), wrote the bill that established the Tennessee Valley Authority, 20 December 1984.

Charles B. Hoeven, 85, representative (R) from Iowa (1943–1965), 10 November 1980.

Abbie Hoffman, 52, radical antiwar protester and a founder of the Yippie Party in 1968, 12 April 1989.

James J. Howard, 61, representative (D) from New Jersey (1965–1988), 25 March 1988.

John E. Hunt, 80, representative (R) from New Jersey (1967–1975), 22 September 1989.

Edward Hutchinson, 70, representative (R) from Michigan (1963–1977), 22 July 1985.

Henry M. "Scoop" Jackson, 71, Democratic representative (1941–1953) and senator (1953–1983) from Washington State, 1 September 1983.

John Jarman, 66, representative from Oklahoma (1951–1977), who switched from the Republican Party to the Democratic Party in 1975, 15 January 1982.

Jacob K. Javits, 81, senator (R) from New York (1947–1954, 1957–1981), 7 March 1986.

Leon Jaworski, 77, Watergate special prosecutor whose investigation precipitated the resignation of President Richard M. Nixon in 1974, 9 December 1982.

William E. Jenner, 76, senator (R) from Indiana (1944–1945, 1947–1959), 9 March 1985.

Harold T. Johnson, 80, representative (D) from California (1959–1981), 16 March 1988.

Thomas F. Johnson, 78, representative (D) from Maryland (1959–1963), 1 February 1988.

Charles R. Jonas, 83, representative (R) from North Carolina (1953–1973), 28 September 1988.

Len B. Jordan, 84, Republican governor (1951–1955) and senator (1962–1973) from Idaho, 30 June 1983.

Abraham Kazen Jr., 68, representative (D) from Texas (1967–1985), 29 November 1987.

James Kee, 61, representative (D) from Virginia (1965–1973), 11 March 1989.

Eugene J. Keogh, 82, representative (D) from New York (1937–1967), principal sponsor of the Keogh Pension-Plan legislation, 9 October 1989.

Earl F. Landgrebe, 70, representative (R) from Indiana (1969–1975), 29 June 1986.

Alfred M. Landon, 100, Republican nominee for president (1936) and governor of Kansas (1933–1937), 12 October 1987.

George Thomas "Mickey" Leland, 45, representative (D) from Texas (1979–1989), 7 August 1989.

Henry Cabot Lodge Jr., 82, Republican senator from Massachusetts (1937–1944, 1947–1953) and vice presidential nominee on the ticket with Richard M. Nixon (1960), ambassador to the United Nations (1953–1960), ambassador to Vietnam (1963–1964, 1965–1967), ambassador to Germany (1968–1969), and envoy to the Paris peace talks (1969), 27 February 1985.

John D. Lodge, 87, Republican representative (1947–1951) and governor of Connecticut (1951–1955), brother of Henry Cabot Lodge Jr., 29 October 1985.

Gillis W. Long, 62, representative (D) from Louisiana (1963–1965, 1973–1985), 20 January 1985.

Alice Roosevelt Longworth, 96, last surviving child of President Theodore Roosevelt and prominent Washington hostess, 20 February 1980.

Robert A. Lovett, 90, secretary of defense (1951–1953), 7 May 1986.

Allard K. Lowenstein, 51, representative (D) from New York (1969–1971), leading critic of the Vietnam War, special U.S. envoy to United Nations human-rights meetings during the Carter administration, 14 March 1980.

Wingate H. Lucas, 81, representative (D) from Texas (1947–1955), 26 May 1989.

Clare Boothe Luce, 84, playwright, jounalist, and politician, representative (R) from Connecticut (1943–1947), ambassador to Italy (1953–1956) and Brazil (1959), widow of *Time* magazine founder Henry Luce, 9 October 1987.

Warren G. Magnuson, 84, Democratic representative (1937–1944) and senator (1944–1981) from Washington State, 20 May 1989.

Fred Marshall, 79, representative (D) from Minnesota (1949–1963), 5 June 1985.

Robert N. McClory, 80, representative (R) from Illinois (1963–1983), 24 July 1988.

John W. McCormack, 88, representative (D) from Massachusetts (1928–1971) and Speaker of the House (1962–1971), 22 November 1980.

Floyd J. McCree Sr., 65, mayor of Flint, Michigan (1966–1968), one of the first African American mayors of a U.S. city, 16 June 1988.

Lawrence Patton "Larry" McDonald, 48, representative (D) from Georgia (1975–1983) and chairman of the John Birch Society, 1 September 1983.

Ernest W. McFarland, 89, Democratic senator (1941–1959) and governor (1955–1959) of Arizona, 8 June 1984.

William D. McFarlane, 85, representative (D) from Texas (1933–1939), 18 February 1980.

Stewart B. McKinney, 56, representative (R) from Connecticut (1971–1987), 7 May 1987.

Gregory McMahon, 74, representative (R) from New York (1947–1949), 27 June 1989.

William E. Miller, 69, representative (R) from New York (1951–1965) and vice presidential candidate on the ticket with Barry Goldwater in 1964, 24 June 1983.

William M. "Fishbait" Miller, 80, doorkeeper of the U.S. House of Representatives (1949–1953, 1955–1974), 12 September 1989.

John N. Mitchell, 75, attorney general (1969–1972), implicated in the Watergate scandal, the only attorney general convicted of a felony, 9 November 1988.

A. S. "Mike" Monroney, 77, Democratic representative (1939–1950) and senator (1950–1968) from Oklahoma, 13 February 1980.

William S. Moorhead, 64, representative (D) from Pennsylvania (1959–1981), 3 August 1987.

Albert P. Morano, 79, representative (R) from Connecticut (1951–1959), 16 December 1987.

Ernest N. Morial, 60, first African American mayor of New Orleans (1978–1986), 24 December 1989.

Thurston B. Morton, 74, Republican representative (1947–1953) and senator (1957–1969) from Tennessee, chairman of the Republican National Committee (1959–1961), 14 August 1982.

Robert Moses, 92, city planner, chief of staff for the New York State Reconstruction Commission (1919–1921), chairman of the New York State Council of Parks and president of the Long Island State Park Commission (1924–1963), chairman of the Metropolitan Conference on Parks (1926–1930), secretary of state for New York State (1927–1928), chairman of Jones Beach State Parkway Authority and Bethpage Park Authority (1933–1963), sole member of the Henry Hudson Parkway Authority and Marine Parkway Authority (1934–1938), New York City park commissioner (1934–1960), executive officer of the World's Fair Commission (1936–1940), member of the New York

City Planning Commission (1942–1960), New York City construction coordinator (1946–1960), chairman of the Triborough Bridge Authority and the consolidated Triborough Bridge and New York City Tunnel Authority (1946–1968), chairman of the New York City Mayor's Slum Clearance Committee (1948–1960), chairman of the New York State Power Authority (1954–1963), president of the New York World's Fair Corporation (1960–1967), director of the Lincoln Center for the Performing Arts (1960–1969), 29 July 1981.

Frederick A. Muhlenberg, 92, representative (R) from Pennsylvania (1946–1948), 19 January 1980.

Abraham J. Multer, 66, representative (D) from New York (1947–1967), 4 November 1967.

Huey P. Newton, 47, a founder of the Black Panther Party (1967), 22 August 1989.

William Flynt "Bill" Nichols, 70, representative (D) from Alabama (1967–1988), 13 December 1988.

Robert N. C. Nix Sr., 81, first African American representative (D) from Pennsylvania (1958–1979), 22 June 1987.

George M. O'Brien, 69, representative (R) from Illinois (1973–1986), 17 July 1986.

Leo O'Brien, 81, representative (D) from New York (1952–1967), 4 May 1982.

James G. O'Hara, 63, representative (D) from Michigan (1959–1977), 13 March 1989.

Alvin E. O'Konski, 83, representative (R) from Wisconsin (1943–1973), 8 July 1987.

Otto E. Passman, 88, representative (D) from Louisiana (1947–1977), 13 August 1988.

James T. Patterson, 80, reprsentative (R) from Massachusetts (1947–1959), 7 February 1989.

Clarence M. Pendleton Jr., 57, first black chairman of the U.S. Commission on Civil Rights (1981–1988), 5 June 1988.

Claude D. Pepper, 89, senator (D) from Florida (1936–1951), representative (D) from Florida (1963–1989), 30 May 1989.

Carl D. Perkins, 72, representative (D) from Kentucky (1949–1984), 3 August 1984.

William R. "Bob" Poage, 87, representative (D) from Texas (1937–1978), 3 January 1987.

C. Norris Poulson, 87, representative (R) from California (1943–1945, 1947–1953), mayor of Los Angeles (1953–1961), 25 September 1982.

Charles Melvin Price, 83, representative (D) from Illinois (1945–1988), 22 April 1988.

Adm. Hyman George Rickover, 86, director of Nuclear Propulsion, U.S. Navy Bureau of Ships (1953–1982), responsible for building the nuclear submarine fleet, 8 July 1986.

Kenneth A. Roberts, 76, representative (D) from Alabama (1951–1965), 9 May 1989.

Franklin D. Roosevelt Jr., 74, son of President Franklin D. Roosevelt and representative (D) from New York (1949–1955), 17 August 1988.

Benjamin S. Rosenthal, 60, representative (D) from New York (1962–1983), 4 January 1983.

Harold Runnels, 56, representative (D) from New Mexico (1971–1980), 5 August 1980.

Charles H. Russell, 85, Republican representative (1947–1949) and governor (1951–1959) of Nevada, 13 September 1989.

Bayard Rustin, 77, civil rights leader, chief organizer of the 1963 march on Washington, 24 August 1987.

Charles W. Sandman Jr., 63, representative (R) from New Jersey (1967–1975), 26 August 1985.

David E. Satterfield III, 67, representative (D) from Virginia (1965–1981), 30 September 1988.

Gordon H. Scherer, 81, representative (R) from Ohio (1953–1963), 13 August 1988.

Keith G. Sebelius, 65, representative (R) from Kansas (1969–1981), 5 September 1982.

John M. Slack, 65, representative (D) from West Virginia (1959–1980), 17 March 1980.

Larkin Smith, 45, representative (R) from Mississippi (1989), 13 August 1989.

John J. Sparkman, 85, senator (D) from Alabama (1947–1979), 16 November 1985.

Thomas J. Steed, 79, representative (D) from Oklahoma (1949–1980), 8 June 1983.

Robert T. Stevens, 83, secretary of the army (1953–1955), a major witness in the hearings that led to the condemnation of Sen. Joseph R. McCarthy, 30 January 1983.

Bennett M. Stewart, 75, representative (D) from Illinois (1979–1981), 26 April 1988.

Leonor K. Sullivan, 86, representative (D) from Missouri (1953–1977), 1 September 1988.

Jack Swigert, 51, astronaut, elected as a representative (R) from Colorado (1982), died before taking office, 27 December 1982.

Stuart Symington, 87, senator (D) from Missouri (1953–1977), 14 December 1988.

Glen H. Taylor, 80, senator (D) from Idaho (1945–1951) and vice presidential candidate on the Progressive ticket (1948), 28 April 1984.

Gen. Maxwell D. Taylor, 85, chairman of the Joint Chiefs of Staff (1962–1964), ambassador to Vietnam (1964–1965), 19 April 1987.

Olin E. Teague, 70, representative (D) from Texas (1946–1977), 23 January 1981.

Frank Thompson Jr., 70, representative (D) from New Jersey (1955–1981), convicted in 1980 of bribery charges stemming from the Abscam scandal, 22 July 1989.

Vernon W. Thomson, 82, Democratic governor (1957–1959) and representative (1961–1975) from Wisconsin, 2 April 1988.

Elizabeth Virginia "Bess" Wallace Truman, 97, widow of President Harry S Truman, 18 October 1982.

William M. Tuck, 86, Democratic governor (1946–1950) and representative (1953–1969) from Virginia, 9 June 1983.

Al Ullman, 72, representative (D) from Oregon (1957–1981), chairman of House Ways and Means Committee (1975–1981), 11 October 1986.

James E. Van Zandt, 87, representative (R) from Pennsylvania (1939–1943, 1947–1963), 6 January 1986.

Carl Vinson, 97, representative (D) from Georgia (1914–1964), 1 June 1981.

Jerry Voorhis, 83, representative (D) from California (1937–1947), 11 September 1984.

Harold Washington, 65, representative (D) from Illinois (1981–1983) and first African American mayor of Chicago (1983–1987), 25 November 1987.

Barbara M. Watson, 64, first woman and first African American to serve as assistant secretary of state (1968–1974), 17 February 1983.

Phillip H. Weaver, 70, representative (R) from Nebraska (1955–1963), 16 April 1989.

Robert H. W. Welch, 85, founder of the John Birch Society (1958), 6 January 1985.

Victor E. Wickersham, 82, representative (D) from Oklahoma (1941–1947, 1949–1965), 15 March 1988.

William B. Widnall, 77, representative (R) from New Jersey (1950–1975), 28 December 1983.

Roy Wilkins, 80, head of the NAACP (1955–1977), 8 September 1981.

G. Mennen "Soapy" Williams, 76, governor (D) of Michigan (1949–1960) and assistant secretary of state for African affairs (1961–1966), 2 February 1988.

John Bell Williams, 64, Democratic representative (1947–1968) and governor (1968–1972) of Mississippi, 26 March 1983.

John J. Williams, 83, senator (R) from Delaware (1947–1971), 11 January 1988.

Charles H. Wilson, 67, representative (D) from California (1963–1980), 21 July 1984.

Henry Winston, 75, chairman of the Communist Party USA (1966–1986), 12 December 1986.

John W. Wydler, 63, representative (R) from New York (1963–1981), 4 August 1987.

Milton R. Young, 95, senator (R) from North Dakota, 4 September 1983.

Stephen M. Young, 95, senator (D) from Ohio (1959–1971), 1 December 1984.

Clement J. Zablocki, 71, representative (D) from Wisconsin (1949–1983), 3 December 1983.

Edward Zorinsky, 59, senator (D) from Nebraska (1976–1987), 6 March 1987.

PUBLICATIONS

Ken Auletta, *The Underclass* (New York: Random House, 1982);

Terrel Bell, *The Thirteenth Man: A Reagan Cabinet Memoir* (New York: Free Press, 1988);

Sidney Blumenthal, *Our Long National Daydream: A Political Pageant of the Reagan Era* (New York: Harper & Row, 1988);

Blumenthal, *Pledging Allegiance: The Last Campaign of the Cold War* (New York: HarperCollins, 1990);

Walter Dean Burnham, *The Current Crisis in American Politics* (New York: Oxford University Press, 1982);

Lou Cannon, *Reagan* (New York: Putnam, 1982);

Leslie Cockburn, *Out of Control: The Story of the Reagan Administration's Secret War in Nicaragua, the Illegal Arms Pipeline, and the Contra Drug Connection* (New York: Atlantic Monthly Press, 1987);

Elizabeth O. Colton, *The Jackson Phenomenon: The Man, The Power, The Message* (New York: Doubleday, 1989);

Michael Deaver, with Mickey Hershkovits, *Behind the Scenes* (New York: Morrow, 1987);

Bob Faw, *Thunder in America: The Improbable Presidential Campaign of Jesse Jackson* (Austin: Texas Monthly Press, 1986);

John Kenneth Galbraith, *Reaganonomics: Meaning, Means, and Ends* (New York: Free Press, 1983);

Jack W. Germond and Jules Witcover, *Wake Us When It's Over: Presidential Politics of 1984* (New York: Macmillan, 1985);

Roy Gutman, *Banana Diplomacy: The Making of American Policy in Nicaragua, 1981–1987* (New York: Simon & Schuster, 1988);

Alexander M. Haig, *Caveat: Reaganism, Realism, and Foreign Policy* (New York: Macmillan, 1984);

Jesse Jackson, *Straight from the Heart* (Philadelphia: Fortress Press, 1987);

Hamilton Jordan, *Crisis: The Last Year of the Carter Presidency* (New York: Putnam, 1982);

Paul Kennedy, *The Rise and Fall of the Great Powers: Economic Change and Military Conflict from 1500 to 2000* (New York: Random House, 1987);

Jeane J. Kirkpatrick, *The Reagan Phenomenon, and Other Speeches on Foreign Policy* (Washington, D.C.: American Enterprise Institute, 1983);

Jane Mayer and Doyle McManus, *Landslide: The Unmaking of the President, 1984–1988* (Boston: Houghton Mifflin, 1988);

Thomas P. O'Neill, *Man of the House: The Life and Memoirs of Speaker Tip O'Neill* (New York: Random House, 1987);

Kevin P. Phillips, *The Politics of Rich and Poor: Wealth and the American Electorate in the Reagan Aftermath* (New York: Random House, 1990);

Phillips, *Post-Conservative America: People, Politics and Ideology in a Time of Crisis* (New York: Random House, 1982);

Nancy Reagan, with William Novak, *My Turn: The Memoirs of Nancy Reagan* (New York: Random House, 1989);

Ronald Reagan, *An American Life: The Autobiography* (New York: Simon & Schuster, 1990);

Donald T. Regan, *For the Record: From Wall Street to Washington* (San Diego, New York & London: Harcourt Brace Jovanovich, 1988);

Robert Reich, *The Next American Frontier* (New York: Times Books, 1983);

Gary Sick, *All Fall Down: America's Tragic Encounter With Iran* (New York: Random House, 1985);

Paul Slansky, *The Clothes Have No Emperor: A Chronicle of the American '80s* (New York: Simon & Schuster, 1989);

Larry Speakes, with Robert Pack, *Speaking Out: The Reagan Presidency from Inside the White House* (New York: Scribners, 1988);

David A. Stockman, *The Triumph of Politics: Why the Reagan Revolution Failed* (New York: Harper & Row, 1986);

Strobe Talbott, *Deadly Gambits: The Reagan Administration and the Stalemate in Nuclear Arms Control* (New York: Knopf, 1988);

Talbott, *The Master of the Game: Paul Nitze and the Nuclear Peace* (New York: Knopf, 1988);

Lester Thurow, *The Zero-sum Solution: Building a World-Class American Economy* (New York: Simon & Schuster, 1985);

John Tower, Edmund Muskie, and Brent Scowcroft, *The Tower Commission Report: The Full Text of The President's Special Review Board* (New York: Bantam Books, 1987);

Caspar W. Weinberger, *Fighting For Peace: Seven Critical Years in the Pentagon* (New York: Warner, 1990);

Theodore H. White, *America in Search of Itself: The Making of the President, 1956–1980* (New York: Harper & Row, 1982);

Garry Wills, *Reagan's America: Innocents at Home* (Garden City, N.Y.: Doubleday, 1987).

LAW AND JUSTICE

by PAUL L. ATWOOD and MICHAEL PIERCE

CONTENTS

Sidebars and tables are listed in italics.

1980

21 Jan. The Supreme Court votes 6–2 that prisoners who do not turn themselves in immediately following their escape are not entitled to an opportunity to persuade a jury that harsh prison conditions justified their escape.

3 Feb. Initial reports surface of an FBI investigation into corruption in high offices, code-named Abscam.

8 Feb. News sources report an FBI undercover sting operation named Brilab (for bribery labor) involving southwestern labor leaders and politicians.

14 Feb. Indictments against fifty-five persons in ten states are handed down in an undercover FBI investigation into child pornography distribution called Miporn.

15 Mar. Terrorists of the Puerto Rican proindependence group FALN (Armed Forces of National Liberation) invade Carter-Mondale and Bush political headquarters, tie up staff members, and spray paint the walls of the offices with antistatehood slogans. No injuries are reported.

27 June President Carter signs a bill permitting the imposition of peacetime draft registration.

17 Nov. The Supreme Court, voting 5–4, overturns a Kentucky law requiring the display of the Ten Commandments in every public school classroom in the state.

1981

26 Jan. The Supreme Court rules 8–0 that states may allow cameras into courtrooms if they so choose.

9 Mar. The Supreme Court decides 8–1 that a defendant who remains silent in a criminal case is entitled to have the judge instruct a jury that no inference of guilt may be drawn from his decision not to testify in his own behalf.

30 Mar. President Ronald Reagan is severely wounded in an assassination attempt. Press Secretary James Brady, a Secret Service agent, and a Washington, D.C., police officer are also wounded. All recover, but Brady suffers permanent brain damage.

16 June Supreme Court associate justice Potter Stewart announces his retirement effective 3 July after twenty-three years on the bench.

6 Nov. Former FBI officials Mark Felt and Edward Miller are convicted of conspiring to violate the rights of Americans during searches they authorized for bombing suspects in 1972 and 1973. They are later pardoned by President Reagan.

25 Nov. Ford Motor Company agrees with the Equal Employment Opportunity Commission to pay $23 million in damages and other benefits to women and minorities as a result of complaints of discriminatory employment practices.

1982

23 Jan. Federal district court judge Prentice Marshall enjoins the U.S. Immigration and Naturalization Service from surrounding or invading homes or factories and questioning Hispanic Americans as to their citizenship status.

24 Mar. The Supreme Court rules 5–4 that states must have "clear and convincing" proof of child abuse or neglect before removing children from the custody of their natural parents.

18 June   The Supreme Court rules unanimously that mentally retarded people in state institutions are guaranteed all of the constitutional rights afforded to citizens under the Fourteenth Amendment due-process clause.

23 June   The Supreme Court rules 5–4 that a confession of a suspected criminal, even if obtained through legitimate interrogation, cannot be used as evidence if the subject had been arrested without probable cause to believe that a crime had been committed.

24 June   Leaders of the fight to amend the Constitution to add an Equal Rights Amendment for women admit defeat in their ten-year battle. The proposed amendment fell three states short of the required number (thirty-eight) needed for ratification.

15 Oct.   Reagan announces a new plan to combat organized crime in the distribution of narcotics.

7 Dec.   First person executed by lethal injection dies in Huntsville, Texas.

1983

2 Mar.   The Supreme Court rules 5–4 that state employees are covered by the federal law that prohibits discrimination on the basis of age.

20 Apr.   Reagan signs a Social Security reform bill intended to ensure the solvency of the system for as many as seventy-five years.

2 May   The Supreme Court rules 7–2 that the state cannot authorize police to arrest pedestrians who fail to produce proper identification when demanded.

6 July   The Supreme Court rules 5–4 that an employer-sponsored retirement plan cannot pay women a lower monthly benefit based on the fact that women statistically live longer than men.

2 Nov.   Reagan signs bill designating the third Monday in January as Martin Luther King Day.

1984

17 Jan.   The Supreme Court rules 8–1 that there is no time limit on the collection of taxes owed on a fraudulent or false tax return, even if the taxpayer had subsequently filed a true tax return.

10 May   A federal district court judge in Salt Lake City, Utah, holds that the U.S. government had been negligent in above-ground testing of nuclear weapons in Nevada between 1951 and 1962 and awards $6.2 million in damages to nine victims or their families.

11 June   The Supreme Court rules unanimously that evidence obtained illegally was admissible if the police could prove that the evidence would have been inevitably discovered by lawful means.

17 July   Reagan signs a bill that will penalize those states that do not move to raise the legal drinking age to twenty-one by cutting off highway funding.

19 Dec.   The United States formally withdraws from UNESCO (United Nations Educational, Scientific, and Cultural Organization) as demanded reforms had not been instituted.

1985

15 Jan. The Supreme Court rules 6–3 that public school officials can legally search public school students if they reasonably believe this would result in evidence of a violation of school rules or the law.

19 Mar. The Supreme Court rules 8–1 to uphold the right of public employees to a hearing before being terminated from their jobs.

27 Mar. The Supreme Court rules 6–3 that police do not have the right to shoot fleeing suspects who are not armed or dangerous.

1986

19 Feb. The U.S. Senate, by a vote of 83–11, ratifies the United Nations treaty outlawing genocide.

3 Mar. The President's Commission on Organized Crime issues a report stating that drug trafficking is the most serious problem presented by organized crime. The government estimates twenty million Americans used marijuana at least once per month and five million to six million used cocaine in any given month.

19 May The Supreme Court rules 5–4 that an affirmative action plan under which black schoolteachers in Jackson, Michigan, retained their jobs while some white teachers who had more seniority were laid off violated the Fourteenth Amendment right to equal protection of the law.

4 July Hundredth anniversary of the unveiling of the Statue of Liberty. In ceremonies on Ellis Island and around the country, thirty-eight thousand immigrants took the oath of citizenship. Chief Justice Warren Burger conducted the Ellis Island ceremony.

14 Aug. A U.S. Senate Judiciary Committee approves Associate Justice William Rehnquist as the new chief justice and Antonin Scalia as a new associate justice of the Supreme Court.

1987

31 Mar. A New Jersey court awards custody of "Baby M" to the natural father and his wife. Mary Beth Whitehead, the baby's mother, was artificially inseminated with the father's sperm as the result of a contract entered into with the father. After giving birth, Whitehead decided to keep the baby. A New Jersey appellate court later granted Whitehead visitation rights to the child.

20 Apr. The United States, for the first time, deports an accused war criminal against his will for trial in another country.

27 Apr. For the first time, the United States bars a head of state of a friendly nation from entering the United States. Barred is Kurt Waldheim, former secretary general of the United Nations and president of Austria, who had been linked to war crimes committed while a member of the Nazi Party.

1 June Reagan signs a bill making the new G.I. Bill permanent.

7 Nov. Judge Douglas Ginsburg withdraws from consideration for a spot on the Supreme Court after admitting that he used marijuana several times in the 1970s while a professor at Harvard University Law School.

1988

18 Feb. U.S. Appeals Court judge Anthony Kennedy is sworn into office as an associate justice of the Supreme Court.

4 May Almost 1.4 million illegal aliens meet a deadline to file for legal status under an amnesty program.

13 June A New Jersey jury finds a tobacco company partly responsible for the death of a women who had used their product in the past.

5 July Attorney General Edwin Meese announces that he will resign from his position after a report by an independent counsel had found that he had probably violated criminal law four times while in office but recommended no further action, as there was no financial gain or corrupt intention.

12 Aug. Former Pennsylvania governor Richard Thornburgh is sworn in as attorney general.

1989

3 Apr. The Supreme Court rules 7–2 that it is constitutional for drug agents to detain briefly airline passengers who fit the profile of a drug courier.

3 Nov. U.S. district court judge Walter Nixon Jr. of Biloxi, Mississippi, is impeached and removed from the bench because of his conviction in 1986 of lying to a grand jury.

16 Dec. Judge Robert Vance of the U.S. Court of Appeals for the Eleventh Circuit is killed at his home in Birmingham, Alabama, by a pipe bomb that had been mailed to him.

OVERVIEW

The Reagan Revolution. With the election of former California governor Ronald Reagan to the presidency, the country was entering a decade of change that was soon to become known as the Reagan revolution. During the period between 1981 and 1989 President Reagan and his administration had a profound influence on the way Americans thought about themselves and the world at large. While the so-called Reagan revolution promised great things, and delivered many of them, it also had a downside. Not more than a year and a half into his presidency, Reagan was being criticized by civil rights leaders for his lack of motivation in ensuring that the rights of minorities continued to be diligently protected. Early in his administration he replaced the well-regarded head of the U.S. Civil Rights Commission with another person who was thought by many leaders of the civil rights movement as something of an "Uncle Tom," due to his conservative views including negative feelings about such things as affirmative action. On the other hand, Reagan was quick to appoint the first female Supreme Court justice in American history. And despite fears of many liberals that his picks to fill vacancies on the Supreme Court would be right-wing archconservatives, they turned out to be more middle of the road in their decision making. This is not to say that they have not tended to be more conservative than previous members of the Burger court. As one example, during the 1980s, the Court ruled that evidence illegally obtained by police could be used against the suspect if it could be shown that such evidence would have been inevitably discovered at some other point. Prior to this decision, such evidence could not be used under a doctrine called the Exclusionary Rule. The general feeling of people in America in response to such rulings was one of hope that the judicial system was finally going to crack down on criminals.

Crime in the 1980s. While crime in this decade climbed ever upward, it took some strange twists as well. While mass murders and serial killers had always existed, it was during the 1980s that the public came to realize just how dangerous and unpredictable these types of criminals were. Media attention focused on reports of murders committed with chilling similarity either in small areas or, in some cases, across the country. The FBI's little-known Behavioral Science Unit gained wide-spread renown when its psychological profiles of unknown suspects in serial-killing cases led to the solution of more and more of these kinds of cases. Often, the profile fit the killer almost identically. The 1980s were also called the "me" decade. Examples of greed and white-collar crime abounded and included the Abscam scandal and the sale of worthless junk bonds as prudent investments, leading to charges of investor fraud. Presidents Reagan and Bush declared a war on drugs that helped educate the public and cut down on certain types of drug abuse, but did little to stem the flow of illegal drugs into the country. The stress of attempting to lead the good life during the "me decade," proved too much for some to bear, and several highly publicized examples of mass murders occurred, sometimes for no discernible reason. Prison populations reached an all-time high, and the burden became so great that states and counties began experimenting with the privatization of prisons in an effort to save taxpayer dollars. Increasingly violent gang warfare reached new heights, with several Los Angeles and New York street gangs becoming organized more along the lines of the Mafia and beginning to reach across America in their efforts to expand their territories.

American Justice. In an effort to fight what seemed a never-ending onslaught of crime, the Supreme Court loosened rules that police had to follow in order to assist in apprehending criminal suspects. New case law allowed illegally obtained evidence to be used in certain circumstances; the Court ruled that the FBI could apprehend citizens of other countries who were wanted for crimes against Americans (this was done when a terrorist was captured off of the coast of Italy by an FBI sting operation); and limited military interdiction was authorized for the first time to assist South American countries in their efforts to eradicate drug crops. Several television shows became popular in publicizing the fight against crime, including *COPS*, *Unsolved Mysteries*, and *America's Most Wanted*, which was hosted by the father of a murdered youngster. Block patrols sprang up in cities and towns all over the country, and the establishment of private security forces occurred in certain high-income areas such as Beverly Hills. McGruff the Crime Dog commercials urged children and adults to "Take A Bite Out of Crime," and the DARE program (Drug Abuse Resistance Education) became popular in elementary and junior high schools and, more important, showed results in the battle against crime and drugs. As the decade ended, the war may not have been won, but the victories appeared to have outweighed the losses.

TOPICS IN THE NEWS

ABSCAM

Abdul Scam. "Everybody was laughing at what was happening. It was like guys coming out of the bush, saying, 'Hey, give me some of the money.' They'd pay one guy and the next day five guys would be calling them, guys they didn't even know. The tapes are hilarious." This was how a reporter described a statement by a former federal prosecutor in an undercover operation known as Abdul scam, or Abscam, named after a fictional sheikh named Kambir Abdul Rahman. During the course of twenty-three months, about one hundred Federal Bureau of Investigation (FBI) agents became involved in a series of undercover operations targeting public officials, including members of Congress. By the time the sting operation was over, two dozen state and local officials, one U.S. senator, and seven U.S. representatives were implicated in offering services for cash.

Swindled by a Swindler. Prior to Abscam the FBI had been involved in a series of sting operations as a result of its increasing emphasis on white-collar crime. The FBI approached convicted swindler Mel Weinberg for his assistance in setting up fake fencing operations to get high-level art and securities thieves to sell their stolen property to the fake fence. During the course of this operation, Weinberg named two associates who had allegedly bribed Angelo Errichetti, the mayor of Camden, New Jersey. With the approval of FBI director William Webster, the FBI began in March 1978 laying the groundwork to help Weinberg lure public officials into engaging in criminal behavior. The irony was that the officials caught in the web were set up by a convicted, although admittedly expert, swindler.

The Operation. The first quarry was Mayor Errichetti, who was informed that Sheikh Abdul Rahman was interested in investing money in Camden and might want to open a casino as well. Errichetti was videotaped saying that he would help the sheikh for a fee of $400,000 and accepting a $25,000 down payment for his services. Errichetti later showed up at a meeting with Rahman with U.S. senator Harrison Williams (D–N.J.).

Williams agreed to help Rahman with his attempts to invest in the United States and his wish to open a casino. The senator was provided with shares of stock in a titanium mine for his assistance. This was also filmed for later courtroom use. Errichetti also introduced the sheikh's aides to Howard Criden, a lawyer from Philadelphia who was involved in real estate. Criden passed the word of available cash to several members of Congress, who were filmed accepting cash or otherwise acknowledging on tape receipt of the funds through intermediaries. One congressman, Rep. Richard Kelly (R–Fla.), was filmed stuffing $25,000 in cash into his suit, pants, and coat pockets and then asking, "Does it show?" He later stated that he took the money (most of which was later returned to the FBI) as part of his own investigation into what was obviously something "crooked" going on.

The Fallout. One of the problems with the sting operation was that it tested the thin line between entrapment and legally capturing those who were already disposed to commit the crime of bribery. While the U.S. Supreme Court held in 1973 that sting operations were legal only as the means to capture certain kinds of criminals, the Court has also held that law enforcement agencies may not pressure or induce the victim of the sting to commit the crime. To do so would be entrapment, and the criminal defendant would probably go free. Although all of those caught in the Abscam sting pleaded entrapment, they did so to no avail as the videotapes spoke volumes about the greed of which some public officials were capable. Six congressmen and numerous other state and local officials were subsequently convicted on bribery charges. Weinberg has since stated that when the operation was shut down because of possible news leaks, he had at least nine more congressmen lined up whom he believes would have taken the bait.

Source:
United States Congress, *Final Report of the Select Committee to Study Undercover Activities of Components of the Department of Justice, to the U.S. Senate* (Washington, D.C.: GPO, 1983).

ABSCAM FALLOUT

The end of the Abscam scandal, which resulted in convictions of a U.S. senator and several congressmen, also brought calls for the regulation of undercover operations by the Federal Bureau of Investigation. On 6 January 1981 the Justice Department issued guidelines to govern such operations.

AUTHORIZATION OF THE CREATION OF OPPORTUNITIES FOR ILLEGAL ACTIVITY

(1) Entrapment should be scrupulously avoided. Entrapment is the inducement or encouragement of an individual to engage in illegal activity in which he would otherwise not be disposed to engage.

(2) In addition to complying with any other requirements, before approving an undercover operation involving an invitation to engage in illegal activity, the approving authority should be satisfied that:

(a) The corrupt nature of the activity is reasonably clear to potential subjects;

(b) There is a reasonable indication that the undercover operation will reveal illegal activities; and

(c) The nature of any inducement is not unjustifiable in view of the character of the illegal transaction in which the individual is invited to engage.

(3) Under the law of entrapment, inducements may be offered to an individual even though there is no reasonable indication that the particular individual has engaged, or is engaging in the illegal activity that is properly under investigation.

Nonetheless, no such undercover operation shall be approved without the specific written authorization of the Director, unless an Undercover Operations Review Committee determines . . . that either:

(a) there is a reasonable indication based on information developed through informants or other means that the subject is engaging, has engaged, or is likely to engage in illegal activity of a similar type; or

(b) the opportunity for illegal activity has been structured so that there is reason for believing that persons drawn to the opportunity, or brought to it, are predisposed to engage in the contemplated illegal activity.

(4) In any undercover operation, the decision to offer an inducement to an individual, or to otherwise invite an individual to engage in illegal activity, shall be based solely on law enforcement considerations.

THE BORK NOMINATION

A Public Fight. During the failed Supreme Court confirmation of Robert H. Bork in 1986, what had previously been a largely behind-the-scenes process moved suddenly into a public forum, a daytime news show. The unprecedented television proceedings in the Senate Judiciary Committee emerged from President Ronald Reagan's announced intention to change the philosophical orientation of the nation's highest court and from the liberal establishment's determination to prevent this. In the aftermath, the Supreme Court nomination process was changed forever, as four more nominees were subjected to similar scrutiny, culminating in the Clarence Thomas confirmation spectacle of 1991. Many critics of the changed process have decried confirmation "by sound bite" and the role of media spin doctors, but the televised hearings also made clear to the viewing public how much power is wielded in the Supreme Court and therefore how important it is that citizens know who nominees are and what they represent. Bork probably would have won confirmation had he been subjected to the old closed-hearing system, and he castigated the proceedings as a circus and witch-hunt. While many commentators say that the new, more public process ensures the court will never become simply the mouthpiece of the president who nominates the justices, others assert that it moves confirmation from the intellectual and narrowly political basis on which it had formerly rested to the uninformed and politically populist tool of the sound bite, the fax machine, and the telephone.

A Distinguished Judge. Bork was a distinguished jurist, much respected by the right wing of the Republican Party. Educated at the University of Chicago, he later became a professor of law at Yale University. Bork had written and spoken widely about constitutional matters, and had ruled favorably (from the conservative perspective) on key issues. He said that freedom of the press and freedom of speech had been taken too far. In one speech he said that the High Court had illegitimately created a woman's right to an abortion (an opinion shared by many abortion rights supporters). He attacked as intellectually sloppy previous High Court decisions such as a 1966 case that had outlawed racially discriminatory poll taxes.

Political Dues. Politically he had paid his dues as well, having written position papers for Barry Goldwater in 1964 and by supporting President Richard Nixon's decision to send troops into Cambodia in 1970. He also fired the special prosecutor in the Watergate scandal, Archibald Cox, in the infamous "Saturday Night Massacre." As Nixon's solicitor general, Bork had become acting attorney general after Elliot Richardson and William Ruckelshaus both resigned rather than carry out the task of sacking Cox, who had demanded that the president turn over his secret White House tapes. He remained solicitor general — often a stepping-stone to the Supreme Court — during Gerald Ford's presidency, but was passed over for nomination to the high bench in 1975

Robert H. Bork

upon the retirement of William O. Douglas in favor of Justice John Paul Stevens. Bork's role in Watergate was still too prominent and controversial.

Court of Appeals. After a brief return to Yale, Bork became a partner in a prestigious Washington, D.C., law firm and in 1981 was appointed to the Second District Federal Court of Appeals. There his rulings drew considerable notice and controversy. By now the intellectual leader of conservative jurisprudence, Bork was passed over once again when Reagan nominated Sandra Day O'Connor to the High Court and was especially crushed when the younger, and less well known, Antonin Scalia was nominated to fill the vacancy created by Justice William Rehnquist's elevation to chief justice. Reagan strategists believed that the combination of Rehnquist and Bork would prove too great a target for liberals.

Powell's Replacement. Yet Reagan had not forgotten Bork. When Lewis Powell retired in 1987, Reagan finally nominated Bork to the nation's highest court. At this stage the high bench was seen as evenly balanced between liberals and conservatives. Bork would therefore provide the much sought-after "swing" vote that would finally reorient the Supreme Court. Because Bork was known as the most incisive and acerbic critic of the court's direction

during the previous thirty years, his nomination sent civil rights and abortion rights activists scrambling.

A Media Confirmation. At first Bork's White House handlers sought to play down his opinions and to emphasize his qualifications as law professor, corporate attorney, judge, and government official. But no one could ignore the fact that Reagan had nominated the man for reasons far more portentous than his record. By the time the Senate Judiciary Committee convened, Bork's nomination was already in trouble, and the unprecedented television broadcast of the hearings, which had previously always taken place behind closed doors, probably served to undo him. Subject to the highly focused camera, Bork made no attempt to make himself telegenic and came across to the viewing public as an unfeeling thinker with a scowling visage, and as intellectually arrogant.

Judicial Restraint. Bork was a strict constructionist who believed he was hewing to the original intent of the framers of the Constitution. Judicial restraint was Bork's watchword. In other words, courts should leave lawmaking to the legislators, not the courts, and should refrain from overturning local statutes. On civil rights Bork had opposed new laws, made necessary by striking old ones, giving blacks the right to be served in public accommodations such as restaurants and hotels. He also believed that pre-1966 laws allowing discrimination in housing against blacks and Jews were constitutional and that actions by the Supreme Court to strike them had deprived property owners of their rights to dispose of their holdings as they saw fit. Bork was also critical of *Regents of the University of California* v. *Bakke* (1978), which overturned racial and gender quotas but upheld racial preferences. Bork argued that any admissions preferences for blacks, other minorities, and women discriminated against citizens not members of those minorities and deprived them of Fourteenth Amendment guarantees. In his philosophy, individual liberties not expressly mentioned in the Constitution were not to be created by the Supreme Court but rather by the normal political process. On the Ninth Amendment in the Bill of Rights, for example, which since the *Roe* v. *Wade* decision is said to construe the citizen's right to privacy, Bork contended that the founders had never intended the Constitution to create a privacy right outside those explicitly mentioned in other amendments, let alone one covering the right to abortion.

Political Judgment. In his 1990 book *The Tempting of America*, Bork argued that his nomination had been derailed by a liberal witch-hunt. Yet it was Bork's opposition to abortion that killed his nomination. Under questioning in the Judiciary Committee he stated baldly that the Constitution provided no such guarantee of privacy. Then the mail began to pour into the Senate. When the moderate Arlen Specter (R–Pa.) announced his intention to vote against Bork, thereby leading a defection of key Republicans, and when black voters began to pressure southern Democrats, there was little hope for Bork's success. Nevertheless, he refused to withdraw his name, and in the end the Senate voted 58–42 against his appointment to the Supreme Court, the largest margin of defeat of a Supreme Court nominee in U.S. history.

Media Circus. Critics on both sides of Bork's nomination questioned the ethics and efficacy of the media circus accompanying the televised proceedings. The integrity of the process had been sacrificed, they said. The Court was intended to be above partisanship. Yet the Senate's perquisite and obligation under the Constitution — to provide advice and consent to the president in such matters — necessarily required an adversarial process given the party system. The key issues of our time today are in the national consciousness, in part because of the mass media, and citizens no longer accept measures bearing on matters of such importance being settled behind closed doors. While Chief Justice Rehnquist has vetoed televised Supreme Court hearings, all future nomination procedures (for all important offices, not only judicial) before the Senate will apparently continue to be televised, thereby complicating the debate over the extent to which the nomination process has been further politicized. Nonetheless, one of the seemingly lasting effects of the Bork confirmation fight is that nominees will not be as honest and forthcoming in their testimony as was Bork.

Sources:

Robert H. Bork, *The Tempting of America: The Political Seduction of the Law* (New York: Free Press, 1990);

Paul Simon, *Advice & Consent: Clarence Thomas, Robert Bork and the Intriguing History of the Supreme Court's Nomination Battles* (Washington, D.C.: National Press Books, 1992).

THE CHANGING AMERICAN PRISON

Beginning the Decade with a Bang. The New Mexico State Penitentiary, near Santa Fe, was lauded as one of the "most advanced correctional institutions in the world" when it opened in 1954. During the next twenty-six years it became one of the worst. By 1980, 1,136 inmates were packed into cells designed for 800, and young inmates with little criminal experience were being housed with some of the worst offenders. Inmates complained about substandard food and medical care. The correctional officers were underpaid and undertrained. In February 1980 the conditions proved too much for the inmates, and a riot lasting thirty-six hours occurred. Remarkably, no shots were fired and no officers were killed, but the brutality committed by inmate against inmate was the worst in U.S. history. Thirty-three inmates were killed before the riot was over. Many of the dead were believed to be informants to prison authorities. Inmates used acetylene torches to break into other inmates' cells, dragged the men out, and tortured them to death with the flames. Another had a steel rod shoved in one ear and out the other. Several were slashed to death, and at least one was hanged. The killing and beating was so bad that a group of eighty-four inmates cut themselves out of a cellblock in order to surrender to authorities. By the time it was over, the main questions in everyone's mind were, "What

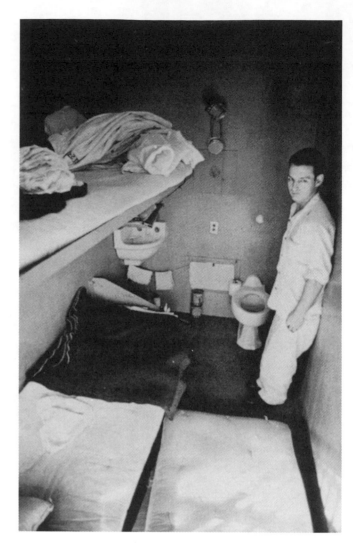

A convict standing in one of the cells that housed three men in a Texas prison. In 1982 thirty-five states were under federal court order to relieve overcrowding in their correctional facilities.

went wrong and how can we keep it from happening again?"

What Are Prisons For? In 1790 a group of Quakers began an experiment in penology with noble aims but with mixed results. They wished to create a prison system that would engage in "such degrees and modes of punishment . . . as may . . . become the means of restoring our fellow creatures to virtue and happiness." Certainly, few would disagree with the concept of making an offender serve his debt to society and at the same time succeed in turning him into a useful member of society. Other Americans had their own ideas about their prison stays, and for the most part during the ensuing two hundred years have not conformed to this Quaker ideal. Neither of course have our prisons. Prisons do punish offenders by depriving them of their rights and their dignity, but by doing so, appear to have turned many inmates into more-hardened criminals. Throughout the 1970s and 1980s prison reform along the lines of thinking of the early

GIMME SOME TRUTH

On 8 December 1980 a twenty-five-year-old former mental patient who had recently worked in the hospital where he had once been a patient struck out at what he saw as the phoniness of the world. He assassinated John Lennon. Mark David Chapman was a music fan who had been attracted to John Lennon in a most unusual way for years. He held that Lennon was the most talented of the Beatles, and for a period of some twelve years he was obsessed with Lennon's music and his writing. Perhaps as a result of his LSD use, patterned after Lennon's, or more likely because of a personality disorder that caused him to rely on others for his identity, Chapman found himself in a mental hospital in 1977, after attempting suicide. A year later, when he worked at the same hospital in Hawaii, he taped the name John Lennon over his identification tag. "I'm going nuts," Chapman wrote a correspondent in September 1980, and his fragile mental state worsened when he read an article in the November 1980 *Esquire* that questioned John Lennon's adherence to the ideals expressed in his music, calling him a phony. Upon reading the article Chapman bought a gun, left Hawaii for New York City, and took a room half a block from the Dakota Hotel, where Lennon lived. After struggling for a month with his demons, Chapman acted. He shot John Lennon dead, and told arresting officers they could find the reason for his action in the book *The Catcher in the Rye* by J. D. Salinger, which Chapman carried with him when he committed the murder.

Source: John Wiener, *Come Together: John Lennon in his Time* (New York: Random House, 1984).

EVOLUTION AND CREATIONISM AGAIN

In a conflict reminiscent of the 1925 Scopes "Monkey Trial" in Tennessee, on 19 June 1987 the U.S. Supreme Court ruled that a Louisiana state law requiring the teaching of creationism alongside evolutionary theory was unconstitutional. "The Balanced Treatment for Creation-Science and Evolution-Science in Public School Instruction Act" had been passed by the Louisiana House of Representatives in 1981 by a vote of 71 to 17, and it passed in the Louisiana State Senate by 26 to 12. The act never went into effect, however, because it was almost immediately challenged in the courts. In a 7–2 decision the United States Supreme Court's majority ruled that the Louisiana law's "primary purpose was to change the science curriculum of the public schools in order to provide persuasive advantage to a particular religious doctrine that rejects the factual basis of evolution in its entirety." Justice William Brennan, writing for the majority, noted that the law "advances a religious doctrine by requiring either the banishment of the theory of evolution from public school classrooms or the presentation of a religious viewpoint that rejects evolution in its entirety." The Louisiana law ran afoul of the First Amendment prohibition on laws "respecting an establishment of religion."

Sources: "High Court Rejects Creationism Law," *Science News*, 131 (27 June 1987): 404;

"High Court: The Day God and Darwin Collided," *U.S. News and World Report*, 102 (29 June 1987): 12;

"Memories of the Monkey Trial," *Time*, 129 (29 June 1987): 54.

Quakers was tried but failed miserably. Given less discipline, prisoners took more advantage of the system, and an increase in inmate riots and disturbances occurred. Gradually modern penologists have learned that prisons punish but cannot rehabilitate unless the inmate wishes to be rehabilitated. Of more concern in the 1980s was the cost of housing an increasing population of offenders, as more and more states pass mandatory minimum sentencing statutes. In 1982 the price of a cell in a new prison in Nevada was reported to be $37,000. The nationwide annual cost of housing inmates in 1982 was $15,000 per inmate. State officials were facing increasing costs on one hand and an increase in inmates on the other and were beginning to explore possible alternatives to the growing problem of prison overcrowding.

The Corporate Warden. A new concept in prison administration appeared in the mid 1980s. The Corrections Corporation of America and other corporate entities began urging state and local officials to allow them to run for-profit prisons. The concept would theoretically allow businesses to help alleviate the overcrowding problem to some degree by charging the state a fee to house an inmate for a year. Most Americans believe that when successful, a business tends to run more efficiently and economically than does the government, and that was the main attraction to this new idea. The keys to success were that these companies could build prisons quicker and more cheaply by using nonunion labor and obtaining tax credits for construction. Critics argued that abuses might occur once strict state supervison was removed, but this would not stop the inmates' right to go to court to correct any such abuses. In 1984 nearly twenty states were negotiating to use private jails in some circumstances, and the proliferation has continued since then. Only time will tell how successful the effort will be. And the lawsuits arising from the first riot at a privately held prison will be the make-or-break test. Will the business absorb the loss, or will it go bankrupt? Regardless of the outcome, some form of private correctional business seems sure to survive in the future.

Source:
Are Prison's Any Better? Twenty Years of Correctional Reform (Newbury Park, Cal.: Sage, 1990).

ESPIONAGE SCANDALS

Increase in Vigilance. One of Ronald Reagan's primary messages in the 1980 presidential election was that America had become soft on communism, and that as president he would renew the crusade against the Soviet Union and its communist allies. Four decades of the Cold War had resulted in massive spying campaigns on the part of each superpower against the other. Reagan renewed campaigns against espionage. Beginning as soon as he took office in 1981, the U.S. Justice Department and the director of the Central Intelligence Agency (CIA) doubled the nation's counterintelligence forces, with a resultant increase in espionage cases prosecuted throughout the 1980s. In 1983 the government tried five such cases, and fourteen in 1984. Defense Secretary Caspar Weinberger dubbed 1985 "the year of the spy," when so many arrests for espionage were made that the Department of Justice could not offer reporters an accurate count. Indeed, extremely serious separate spy charges were brought by federal prosecutors within a space of four days in that year, all involving civilian personnel working in sensitive government posts.

Ronald William Pelton. In a case involving breaches at the National Security Administration, the nation's electronic spying hub, Ronald William Pelton sold surveillance secrets to the Soviet KGB. At the CIA translator Larry Wu-tai Chin was charged with spying for China for more than thirty years. The U.S. Navy was compromised by two major scandals, the first involving Jonathan Jay Pollard, a civilian analyst who revealed key secrets about U.S. Middle East strategies to Israel, the second exposing the activities of three members of the John Anthony Walker family in selling nuclear submarine secrets to the Soviet Union.

China and the Soviet Union. The latter two cases received the most exposure, particularly that of the Walkers, because of the unusual circumstances involved in both, but the government claimed that Pelton had done more damage to national security between 1980 and 1985 than had the Walkers in eighteen years. Pelton provided the Soviets with top-secret anti-code-breaking methods, thereby enabling them to keep one step ahead in the espionage game of cat and mouse. The Soviets were able to use these secrets to spread disinformation, or false information, keeping U.S. surveillance experts off balance and confused. Chin's case received the least attention though his decades-long leaks involved enormous security breaches. At a time when the Reagan administration was turning on the pressure against the Soviets, it was decompressing the Chinese side of the Cold War, making use of information that had been available for years — that the Chinese feared the Soviets more than the United States.

Jonathan Pollard. The Pollard case was unique because it involved spying for an ostensible ally, Israel. The close connection between Washington and Tel Aviv had led some analysts to believe that most information was shared between the CIA and the Israeli Mossad. This view failed to take into consideration the fact that the United States also cultivated relations — and secrets — with Arab regimes, like Saudi Arabia and Iraq, which were deeply hostile to Israel. Jonathan Jay Pollard was a young midwesterner of Jewish descent who early in life had become, by his own account, a committed Zionist. He believed profoundly that the future security of world Jewry was intimately bound up with the fate of Israel. He dreamed of one day immigrating to the Holy Land, taking up Israeli citizenship, and serving in Israel's armed forces. He remained in the United States, however, studying at Stanford University, where he claimed to fellow undergraduates to be a Mossad agent. Pollard subsequently attended the prestigious Fletcher School of Law and Diplomacy at Tufts University where he came under the influence of Israeli scholar and Sovietologist Uri Ra'anan. In 1977 he applied for a job with the CIA but was rejected because of his propensity to fabricate stories about his supposed exploits. Nevertheless, Pollard was accepted as a civilian employee of the U.S. Navy's Operational Surveillance and Intelligence Center, and then in the Naval Intelligence Service.

Spying for an Ally. In 1982 Pollard read top-secret orders from Defense Secretary Weinberger intended to pressure Israel to withdraw from Lebanon, which it had invaded illegally, according to the United Nations. At that moment Pollard made his decision to help Israel. In 1984 he met a high-level Israeli Air Force officer working not for Mossad but for an agency named Lakam, so secret that even the CIA did not know of its its existence. Lakam's purpose was to obtain secrets about U.S. Middle East policies that the United States would not openly provide. Of course, the CIA was doing exactly the same thing in Israel. With his top-secret clearance Pollard soon began providing information on terrorism, Soviet arms shipments to Arab nations, electronic communications intercepts, and, most important, secrets about weapons systems provided to Israel's Arab enemies. Information provided by Pollard allowed Israel successfully to target and destroy the Palestine Liberation Organization's headquarters in Tunisia in 1985.

Running to the Embassy. Pollard was caught because he kept requesting copies of documents that were not related to his specific assignments. At one point his commanding officer requested an FBI investigation of Pollard but was refused because the bureau was too busy with other cases. Naval counterintelligence began questioning him. Panicking, both Pollard and his wife phoned their

Lakam contact, who told them to shake their followers and seek asylum in the Israeli Embassy in Washington, D.C. When the Pollards arrived they were denied entry and arrested by U.S. agents outside the embassy compound.

Israeli–U.S. Relations. Relations between Israel and the United States suffered some minor setbacks as a result of the Pollard affair, and some American Jews began to question their absolutist faith in Israel's policies. William Safire, the *New York Times* columnist, wrote that the affair encouraged and abetted anti-Semitism in America. But the incident was effectively buried in both countries and later overshadowed by allegations about Israeli arms brokering in the Iran-Contra scandal. Both the Pollards had been promised reduced sentences for cooperating in the investigation of their activities and because they did not act primarily for money. However, Weinberger wrote a personal letter to Judge Aubrey Robinson of the U.S. District Court in Washington to say that it was difficult for him to see greater harm than that caused by the defendants. He added that Jonathan Pollard "deserved to be hanged or shot." At the age of thirty-two, Pollard was sentenced to life in prison, while his wife received five years.

Walker Fallout. The Walker spy case involved far more serious damage to national security. John Anthony Walker was a retired naval petty officer who had a "top secret crypto clearance" when on active duty. His knowledge of naval communications led to jobs with civilian military contractors, whose secrets he sold. He was caught after being witnessed placing a bag full of documents under a tree on a rural Maryland road. Some of those documents seemed to come directly from the aircraft carrier U.S.S. *Nimitz*, a trail that led to Walker's son, seaman Michael L. Walker. Before long Arthur J. Walker, John's brother, also a navy veteran and submarine specialist, and a longtime family friend were implicated, too. John Walker had a reputation in Norfolk, Virginia, a navy town, as a "staunch Reaganite." His friends and associates said he was a "patriot bordering on a jingo." Reporters soon discovered he had been in the John Birch Society, an ultraright-wing organization devoted to unmasking those whom it called traitors, and had flirted with the Ku Klux Klan in his early years of military service.

Nuclear Weakness. The Walkers' espionage severely compromised the third, and strongest, leg of the U.S. nuclear triad. Most analysts believed that the air force's B-52 squadrons and intercontinental ballistic missile (ICBM) sites were already vulnerable to Soviet attack. The navy's submarine force stood as the best deterrent to surprise attack because of its ability to retaliate without suffering a first, potentially knockout, blow. Locating submarines under water was a difficult and often impossible task, especially for the Soviets, whose technology always lagged behind that of the United States. Information provided by the Walkers enabled the Soviets to learn

how the United States heard and located Soviet submarines and how it silenced its own against Soviet detection efforts. For selling the secrets of the most sensitive force of the United States, John and Arthur Walker were sentenced to life in prison. Michael L. Walker was held to have come early under his father's influence and so was given a relatively light sentence with eligibility for parole.

Diplomatic Problems. In the midst of the bad feelings generated between the superpowers because of these espionage scandals, a bizarre incident was created that exacerbated tensions, threatened to collapse pending arms-control talks, and even threatened to derail the 1986 summit meeting between President Reagan and Soviet Premier Mikhail Gorbachev. In 1986 a Russian agent named Gennady Zakharov, a member of the Soviet Union's UN staff, was arrested on a Queens, New York, subway platform shortly after accepting a folder full of "secrets" from an FBI double agent. The result was the arrest in Moscow of Nicholas Daniloff, an American newsman. Daniloff had been the Moscow bureau chief for *U.S. News and World Report* but was heading home to a new assignment. Just before he was to leave the Soviet Union, a friend handed him what he took to be a folder of commonplace news clippings from Russian newspapers. The Soviet government charged, however, that Daniloff was spying for the U.S. government and so arrested and imprisoned him. Obviously trumped up, the charges were designed to enable a tit-for-tat trade for the Soviet spy Zakharov, which took place after a few weeks of bargaining. Republican conservatives were outraged, believing that Reagan was being made to look foolish. Zbigniew Brzezinski, former national security adviser to President Carter, thought that Zakharov should be tried and imprisoned as an example, but that clearly would have left the innocent Daniloff to languish in the far harsher Soviet prison system. So to much consternation the trade went off. Yet the summit meeting took place as scheduled, setting the stage for greater arms-limitations agreements.

Marines Arrested. Tensions over spying continued, however, in the spring 1987 with the arrest in Moscow of four U.S. Marines by the U.S. government on charges of having provided U.S. Embassy secrets to female Soviet agents in exchange for sexual favors. All twenty-eight of the embassy guards were returned to the United States to face lie-detector tests. Little valuable information was thought to have been given away by the enlisted men, but the case showed that the U.S. Embassy building was latticed with more bugs than had previously been thought. It was soon discovered that the new embassy under construction in Moscow was so compromised by electronic eavesdropping devices that it would probably never even be occupied by the U.S. government. The Marine Corps suffered a black eye as a result of the case, since these were the first embassy guards in Marine Corps history to betray their duty. Said Marine Commandant Gen. P. X. Kelley, the scandal was "like a dagger in our heart." The incident also highlighted the difficulties of stationing lonely and single young men in such isolated posts and, in one positive result, led to changes in the way the government identified and trained its embassy guards.

Source:

Nigel West, *Games of Intelligence: The Classified Conflict of International Espionage* (New York: Crown, 1990).

THE FORD PINTO CASE

A Dangerous Product. On 10 August 1978 Judy Ann Ulrich, eighteen, was driving a 1973 Ford Pinto to volleyball practice in Goshen, Indiana. Inside the car with her were her sister Lynn Marie, sixteen, and their cousin Donna Ulrich, eighteen. As they were heading north on U.S. Route 33, their car was struck from behind by a 1972 Chevrolet van. The Pinto collapsed like an accordion; the fuel tank ruptured; and the car exploded in flames. Lynn Marie and Donna burned to death in the car. Judy Ann was pulled from the wreckage but died from her injuries several hours later at a hospital. Two months earlier, Ford had recalled all Pintos produced from 1971 to 1976 to repair their defective gas tanks. The recall effort by Ford only came after it was revealed that more than fifty people had died in Pinto-related accidents.

What Was Wrong? The recall of Ford Pintos only came about after news reports of the cars' propensity to explode in flames after rear-end accidents had caused sales of the car to take a dramatic nosedive. That, when combined with the verdicts that were starting to be handed down against Ford, finally turned the company's attention to its bottom line: profitability. Prior to the crash that killed the Ulrichs, a California judge had awarded $6.3 million to a youth who suffered burns in a Pinto crash. Fifty or so other lawsuits were pending as well. In a pending criminal action filed in relation to the Ulrich accident, prosecutor Michael Consentino hoped to prove that Ford officials knew of the likelihood that early Pinto gas tanks may rupture after a rear-end collision. Rather than install a part costing $6.65 to help prevent such an occurrence, Consentino believed that company officials performed a cost-benefit analysis of the situation and determined that a higher profit would be achieved from not installing the part in relation to any foreseeable harm that might be caused.

What Worried Ford. After paying out millions of dollars in settlements and jury verdicts, Ford faced a maximum penalty of $30,000 in fines if convicted of criminal charges of reckless homicide in the deaths of the Ulrich girls. So why did it budget $1 million to defend itself? Prior to the filing of criminal charges, Ford was at risk for actual damages suffered by those killed or injured by using its products. Examples of such injuries would be lost wages, permanent disability, pain and suffering, or loss of consortium (losing the companionship of an in-

jured or killed parent or spouse). If, however, the Ford Motor Company was found guilty of reckless homicide in knowingly introducing a product into the marketplace, where it could reasonably be foreseen that great harm or death might result, then the company would be opening itself up to judges or juries assessing punitive damages against it in the nearly forty Pinto cases still pending at that time. Punitive damages, legally speaking, are the court's way of punishing a person or company for knowingly engaging in behavior that is foreseeably dangerous to another. By allowing punitive damages to be assessed in future cases, the courts would be sending a message to Ford that they had better not engage in such conduct in the future. What worried the company was that punitive damages can be in any amount a jury might feel necessary to send such a message. Conceivably, the message sent could be in the tens or even hundreds of millions of dollars.

Victory — But for Whom? The prosecution produced witnesses at trial who testified that the Ulrich Pinto had been moving at between 15–35 MPH when struck from behind. At that speed a fuel tank should not rupture. The defense produced two witnesses who testified that before she died, Judy Ann Ulrich had said her car was not moving when it was struck at about 50 MPH, an impact that no subcompact could withstand. The jury took twenty-five hours to conclude that Ford should be exonerated of the charges. While Ford officials celebrated the victory and the defense counsel said that he hoped the verdict, "would discourage prosecutions like this in the future," many legal experts thought it would not. In fact, in the years since, it has not. In many states corporations or their directors have been held criminally responsible for actions that their corporations took that resulted in foreseeable harm to the public. Ford may have won the battle, but it woke corporate America up to the fact that it could lose the war if it did not begin acting more responsibly.

Source:

The Ford Pinto Case: A Study in Applied Ethics, Business, and Technology (Albany: State University of New York Press, 1994).

THE IRAN-CONTRA SCANDAL

Secret Deals. In the fall of 1986 two seemingly disparate and secret arms deals were revealed to the nation, and during the next six years the American public would become transfixed by even more revelations that would become known as the Iran-Contra scandal. In a series of highly publicized hearings, special investigations, and prosecutions of high Reagan and Bush administration officials, a clandestine government operating within the official one was revealed to have taken charge of U.S. foreign policy. The Iran-Contra scandal threatened to result in impeachment proceedings against the president of the United States and to cause the utter collapse of public confidence in the integrity of government. Caught flatfooted in late 1986, the Reagan administration sought

President Ronald Reagan formally accepting the report of the Tower Commission from members Edmund Muskie, John Tower, and Brent Scowcroft

to investigate itself through the Department of Justice and succeeded in making matters worse by making it seem as though it was engaging in a cover-up. As a result it had to endure the prolonged public scrutiny of a joint congressional investigation and efforts by a specially appointed prosecutor to probe the allegations that lawbreaking reached into the highest offices in the land. In the end, however, Congress settled on the proposition that only a handful of rogue junior players in the Reagan administration had fomented wrongdoing, and that while the president himself was negligent in the oversight of his appointees, neither he nor Vice President Bush was guilty of any crimes personally. In all, fourteen men were prosecuted for various charges, and none were penalized with anything more than fines. Though the special prosecutor in the affair ultimately sought criminal charges against Secretary of Defense Caspar Weinberger and a top-ranking Central Intelligence Agency official, President Bush pardoned these men in 1992 shortly before leaving office, thus obviating a public trial and the likelihood of even more damaging revelations. While several minor players, such as Lt. Col. Oliver North, Adm. John Poindexter, and retired Gen. Richard Secord, received light sentences, most of these were overturned on appeal on the grounds that they had been granted immunity to testify before Congress and thus could not be incriminated by any statements they made in the Iran-Contra hearings, despite their admission of lawbreaking.

Hasenfus. The scandal began on 5 October 1986 when Eugene Hasenfus, piloting a clandestine CIA aircraft, was shot down over Nicaragua. His cargo bay was full of weapons intended for Nicaraguan rebels, known as Contras, for use against the Nicaraguan government. Since in 1982 and 1984 Congress had passed laws, known as the Boland Amendments I and II, expressly forbidding attempts both to overthrow the government of Nicaragua and secret efforts to arm the Contras, the captured Hasenfus revealed evidence that the Reagan administration had broken the law. Initially Reagan said his administration had no connection to this flight, but subsequent revelations proved this to be false. Less than five weeks later an obscure Lebanese newspaper revealed that Reagan's special assistant for national security, Robert McFarlane, had engaged in secret arms-for-hostages deals with the Iranian government of the Ayatollah Khomeini. In the aftermath of the ordeal of fifty-two American hostages taken by Iran in 1979 and held for more than a year, the official policy of the U.S. government was never to make such trades with terrorist governments. In fact such arms deals had been ongoing for years in order, as officials would subsequently testify, to appeal to "moderates" in Iran. But the more shocking revelation, announced by Attorney General Edwin Meese, was the fact that money obtained in secret arms movements to Iran was being channeled back to the Nicaraguan Contras to arm them in direct contravention of the law. Meese's revelation on 25 November 1986 was an effort to avoid another Watergate-type scandal. He hoped to persuade the public, Congress, and the news media that the administration had found lawbreakers at lower levels and was going to punish them. Efforts to provide arms to Iran, he said, were intended to cultivate more-reasonable politicians in that nation's government and to win release of hostages held by pro-Iranian terrorists throughout the Middle East. As for what was done with money paid for the arms, that was Israel's responsibility, said Meese, and was orchestrated through the renegade actions of a single National Security Council (NSC) staffer, Lt. Col. Oliver North.

Evolving Stories. Holes in the official story soon surfaced. On 6 November Reagan had said that reports about arms sales had "no foundation." On 13 November he admitted the sales but denied they were for hostages. On 19 November Reagan declared that such sales were, in fact, legal. Under controversial powers granted by Section 501 of the National Security Act, the president is sometimes able to circumvent the law (legally) by issuing what is called a "finding," in which national security issues are claimed to override lawful constraints. Meese said that Reagan had signed such a finding in order to override the Arms Export Control Act, but it surfaced that Reagan did so only after the fact. Moreover, Reagan failed to inform Congress of this finding in a timely manner as the law stipulates and did so only when the scandal broke. North later testified that he had altered official NSC chronologies to cover for the president, and Admiral Poindexter later revealed he had destroyed the original of this finding in order that it not be "politically embarassing" to the president. North also later admitted to shredding thousands of documents that would have incriminated him, and presumably many others, up to and including Reagan. The need to conceal this illegal activity and to protect the president from an impeachable offense led Meese to focus on the activities of North as a diversion from the president's troubles. Subsequently, with the exception of North, numerous administration officials shouldered the burden of providing, in Poindexter's phrase, "plausible deniability" to President Reagan and sought to exculpate themselves. Testifying under congressional immunity granted in the Iran-Contra hearings, North, McFarlane, and Poindexter admitted some of their illegal activities. North, understanding that he was being scapegoated, claimed that he believed Reagan knew and approved of his actions, but his immediate supervisor, Poindexter, denied this. North went so far as to insist that CIA director William Casey had personally approved his clandestine operations, but since Casey died during this period, he could not be questioned personally (though famed Watergate reporter Robert Woodward claimed in his book *Veil: The Secret Wars of the CIA, 1981–1987* [1988] that Casey had confessed to him on his deathbed). Numerous other officials of the executive branch, including Vice President Bush; Secretary of De-

THE LAW AND THE IRAN-CONTRA SCANDAL

The Iran-Contra scandal in many ways centered on the differing interpretations of the two Boland Amendments, which governed the use of U.S. funds against the government of Nicaragua. The text of the second Boland Amendment, known as Boland II, seriously constrained Reagan administration efforts to support the Contra rebels:

No appropriations or funds made available pursuant to this joint resolution to the Central Intelligence Agency, the Department of Defense, or any other agency or entity of the United States involved in intelligence activities may be obligated or expended for the purpose of which would have the effect of supporting, directly or indirectly, military or paramilitary operations in Nicaragua by any nation, group, organization, movement or individual.

While the prohibition seems clear, it was not so clear to many in the administration. That the Boland amendment was in direct contradiction with the stated goal of President Ronald Reagan was either unimportant or ignored by the intelligence staff. As Lt. Col. Oliver North said, "My understanding was that first of all, we were to comply with with Boland and that we were to work to keep alive the Nicaraguan Resistance." Years of trials and congressional hearings never fully resolved how far up the political ladder the willful ignorance traveled.

Source: Theodore Draper, *A Very Thin Line: The Iran-Contra Affairs* (New York: Hill & Wang, 1991).

fense Weinberger; his aide, Gen. Colin Powell; Elliott Abrams, an assistant secretary of state; Duane Clarridge of the CIA; and others, also testified in one fashion or another that they "were out of the loop" and had no knowledge of any arms or cash transfers, or hostage deals.

Tower Commission. Several investigations were mounted in the wake of the Iran-Contra revelations. The first was the Tower Commission, named after its chair, former senator John Tower (R–Tex.). Appointed by Reagan to conduct a "comprehensive review" of the NSC's role, the Tower Commission issued its report on 26 February 1987 and blamed the NSC's "rogue staff," concluding the affair was the result of Reagan's notoriously poor management skills. Public furor demanded a better accounting, however, and each house of Congress set up its own investigative committee and then took the unprecedented step of merging them to conduct publicly televised hearings in the summer of 1987. Though their final report repudiated the Tower Commission's conclusions and said that "It was the President's policy — not an isolated decision by North or Poindexter — to sell arms secretly to Iran and to maintain the 'body and soul' " of the Contras, the select congressional committees avoided investigating numerous areas of concern that emerged from testimony, including numerous other "off the shelf" operations in Latin America and relations with narcotics runners and their connections to Central American governments. Members of the Senate committee put matters most succinctly when they concluded in January 1987 that "the country didn't need another Watergate."

Lawrence Walsh. The most important and far-reaching investigation was carried out by Special Prosecutor Lawrence E. Walsh. At first the Reagan administration tried to avoid sponsoring an independent investigation but realized this seemed an obstruction of justice. Attorney General Meese thus asked the U.S. Court of Appeals in the District of Columbia to investigate and prosecute any criminal activities uncovered. Walsh, a noted former government prosecutor and longtime liberal Republican Party stalwart, seemed a safe enough choice from the administration standpoint, but the special prosecutor immediately showed his intent to be independent and thorough. Fighting an uphill battle, in many cases against former friends who labeled him a turncoat, Walsh doggedly pursued as many leads as his staff could support. His final report concludes unequivocally that the Iran-Contra policies at the heart of the matter were developed at the "highest levels" of the Reagan administration, with the knowledge of every senior cabinet member involved in foreign policy, many of whom lied to cover up their and the president's knowledge. The special prosecutor's report also affirms that following the initial Iran-Contra revelations, these officials "deliberately deceived the Congress and the public" about their support for illegal operations.

Court Proceedings. Walsh charged fourteen individuals with criminal violations. North and Poindexter were tried and found guilty of various charges, but their convictions were overturned on appeal largely on the basis that their self-incriminating testimony before the congressional committees, which had granted them immunity from criminal prosecution, could not be used against them. McFarlane and Secord pleaded guilty to witholding information and to lying before Congress but received short sentences. As Walsh said in his final report, most of the best evidence of cover-up was found in his final year of active investigation, too late, under statutory limitations, for more prosecutions. However, of the remaining individuals two — Weinberger and Clarridge — were scheduled to be tried for perjury but were pardoned by President Bush on Christmas Eve 1992.

Vague Impact. It is difficult to assess the long-term impact of Iran-Contra on the American public. Certainly, after six years of intense scrutiny by congressional and legal panels, the public saw that little was accomplished in terms of punishing those responsible, while tens of millions of taxpayer dollars were expended. Public cynicism about politics plummeted to new depths. Belief that those in power charged with crimes were held to different standards than ordinary citizens and subject to less than full punishment under the law if convicted probably helped further to erode general standards of honesty and public comity. Most revealing was the post-Iran-Contra elevation of Oliver North from scapegoat to hero, and his candidacy in Virginia for the U.S. Senate in 1992. His relative political success — receiving approximately 40 percent of the vote in Virginia and enjoying widespread national fund-raising — signaled that significant numbers of citizens see the justice and political systems as corrupt almost beyond repair and that the Iran-Contra scandal was more a question of partisan politics rather than constitutional fidelity.

Sources:

Peter Kornbluh and Malcolm Byrne, *The Iran-Contra Scandal: The Declassified History* (New York: New Press, 1993);

100th Congress, *Report of the Congressional Committees Investigating the Iran-Contra Affair* (Washington, D.C.: GPO, 1987);

Lawrence E. Walsh, *Iran-Contra: The Final Report* (New York: Times Books, 1994).

THE MIAMI RACE RIOTS

Act of Retribution. "It was real bad, I hadn't seen anything like it since I left Vietnam." So went the description by Miami police officer Manny Lopez of a scene of mob violence in the black neighborhood of Liberty City following the acquittal of four white former police officers of charges that they had beaten black businessman Arthur McDuffie to death. Lopez was describing what he found when he arrived on the scene of black mob violence against three young white people, attacked for no reason other than the color of their skin. Michael Kulp, eighteen, was driving a car containing two passengers — his brother Jeffrey, twenty-two, and their friend Debra Getman, twenty-three — through the Liberty City area when the car was struck by bricks and bottles. Michael Kulp lost control of his car and struck Shanreka Perry, an eleven-year-old black girl, then smashed into a building. The crowd pulled the three from the car and began beating them. Michael suffered a fractured skull; Jeffrey was shot in the back, stabbed, beaten, and repeatedly run over by a car. When police found the still-living victims, a red flower had been inserted in Jeffrey Kulp's mouth. Debra Getman was taken to safety by a black man.

Arthur McDuffie. Arthur McDuffie, thirty-three, was a former marine and an insurance agent. He had just won a free trip to Hawaii as a bonus for selling so much insurance and was in the process of remarrying his former wife. On 17 December 1979 things were definitely looking rosy for him. On that night however, he was riding his cousin's motorcycle at about 2 A.M. when he drove through a red light in north Miami. His driver's license had been suspended because of a bounced check written

Burned-out row houses in Philadelphia after the battle between MOVE and city police in May 1985

to pay for another traffic offense. When Dade County Metro police pursued him for running the light, he attempted to escape and, according to police, ran more than twenty-five more red lights at speeds up to 100 MPH before being apprehended by a dozen Miami and Metro police. Initial police reports indicated that he had crashed and hit his head on the ground, then resisted arrest so that police had to use force to arrest him.

Conflicting Stories. Rumors and stories began to swirl around the police stations after McDuffie's death from head injuries four days later. Police officials notified Dade County's state attorney (and future U.S. attorney general), Janet Reno, of the situation. After a four-day investigation, prosecutor Henry Adorno filed charges against six Metro police officers on charges ranging from participating in a cover-up to second-degree murder. Eventually four officers, Alex Marrero, Ira Diggs, Michael Watts, and Herbert Evans Jr. went on trial. Because of what a judge called the "time-bomb" nature of the incident, the trial was moved to Tampa. The defense was successful in obtaining a jury of six white males. After

hearing conflicting versions of who did what from officers, some of whom received immunity in exchange for their testimony, the jury acquitted the four men. After the verdict the prosecution came under attack for not taking more time to investigate the incident, for granting immunity to some officers on the scene, and for not protesting the all-white jury more forcefully.

The Aftermath of the Verdict. The aftermath to the trial was predicted by the judge who moved the trial to another part of the state. Following what many thought was an unjust verdict, especially since several officers had testified that McDuffie had been beaten as he lay handcuffed and defenseless on the ground, rioting broke out in Tampa and Miami on 17 May 1980. The rioting was worse in Miami and resulted in the first large-scale urban riot in the United States in more than a decade. The Justice Building was broken into and vandalized; dozens of cars were overturned or burned; and many people, mainly white, were pulled from their cars and beaten or killed. The governor called out thirty-six hundred National Guardsmen to help restore order. By the time the rioting had ended three days later, sixteen people were dead and four hundred had been injured.

Source:
U.S. Commission on Civil Rights, *Confronting Racial Isolation in Miami* (Washington, D.C.: U.S. Commission on Civil Rights, 1982).

PHILADELPHIA AND THE MOVE BOMBING

MOVE. Founded in the early 1970s, the MOVE organization was the brainchild of an idealistic social worker named Donald Glassey and a man named Vincent Leaphart. The name of the organization actually stood for nothing, and Leaphart and his followers espoused a back-to-nature retreat from the technology that they believed was ruining civilization. MOVE members were not known for much prior to 1977. During that year and into 1978, its members confronted the administration of former mayor Frank Rizzo. After six hundred police surrounded a MOVE commune, shots were exchanged between the police and commune members. One officer was killed and several others wounded. A dozen MOVE members were arrested on weapons and murder charges, and the movement spread out to other communes in the city. The group living at the Osage Avenue commune allegedly engaged in drug dealing, using the profits to purchase guns and explosives. Many of the members living there were children of the MOVE members imprisoned after the 1978 shootout. The stage for a second confrontation of authorities was set in the eighteen months prior to May 1985, when MOVE members in the Osage Avenue commune fortified the house and threatened the neighbors.

Confrontation. Because of their previous experience with MOVE in 1978, city officials took a vastly different approach in their efforts to evict the cult members from Osage Avenue. They evacuated more than five hundred people from a three-block area surrounding the cult house. When a last-minute appeal by boyhood friends of "defense minister" Conrad Africa failed to draw the MOVE members out, police began their siege. First, high-pressure water jets were used in an unsuccessful attempt to dislodge a steel-reinforced bunker on the roof of the building that allowed the cult members a clear field of fire over Osage Avenue. MOVE members and police then engaged in a ninety-minute gunfight. An attempt to enter the building by breaking through a cellar wall failed when MOVE members became aware of the attempt and set up an ambush, successfully fighting off the Special Weapons and Tactics (SWAT) team.

Air Attack. A decision was finally made to attack the roof bunker with explosives. A police helicopter dropped two pounds of DuPont Tovex TR-2, a nonincendiary blasting agent, onto the bunker. About twenty minutes later, flames were visible on the roof. Rather than once again turning on the water cannons, a decision was apparently reached to allow the fire to burn in an attempt to force the MOVE members out. By the time firefighters eventually responded, the roof collapsed and the entire building was in flames. This tragic decision was only the beginning of what turned out to be a monumental misjudgment by city officials.

Conflagration. Firefighters soon learned that the fire was spreading in the neighborhood of row houses. Attempts to halt the fire were initially unsuccessful. Only two MOVE members were able to escape the flames, Ramona Africa and a thirteen-year-old boy, Birdie Africa. By the time that the fire was brought under control, 11 people were killed, 250 people were left homeless, and 61 houses were destroyed. The eleven dead included six adults and five children. After months of hearings into the tragedy, Philadelphia mayor Wilson Goode admitted that he and city officials made a mistake in handling the situation.

Source:
Michael Boyette, *"Let it Burn!": The Philadelphia Tragedy* (Chicago: Contemporary Books, 1989).

SERIAL KILLERS AND MASS MURDERERS

Cultural Obsession and Reality. While serial killers and mass murderers have existed at all times in human history, the reporting of their crimes seemed to have reached an all-time high during the 1980s. A series of incidents that came to light during this decade as well as increasing success by the FBI in predicting the behavior of serial killers led to a greater public awareness of their existence. The decade also saw some horrible incidents of mass murder, explained in some cases as retribution by fired or harassed employees. In other cases motives were unavailable.

Ted Bundy. While many serial killers are less-educated drifters who may in some instances travel across wide areas killing their victims, in some cases the serial killer is a highly intelligent, seemingly socially respectable person. Ted Bundy was of this type. As one noted expert on serial killers, Robert Keppel, states, "He taught us that a serial killer can appear to be absolutely normal, the guy next door." Bundy had been a law student at one time and had appeared to be a pillar of the community as well. He had even been the assistant director of the Seattle Crime Prevention Advisory Commission. Bundy was born on 24 November 1946 and never knew the identity of his biological father. By the time he finished high school, he knew that he was somehow different. He looked upon others as objects, not people to be loved or hated, just objects. What he did not know was that this is the hallmark of the psychopathic personality. By 1974 Ted Bundy began to murder. He began abducting, raping, and torturing college students in Oregon and Washington. By August of that year, police knew of at least twelve killings presumably committed by a mysterious man known only as "Ted," the name he gave to one intended victim who chose not to accompany him. In September 1974 Bundy moved to Utah. A month after his arrival, he began killing again. He killed at least eleven women in Utah and Colorado. As often happens in law enforcement, a chance encounter with a police officer who pulled him over marked the beginning of the end for Bundy. The officer noticed a crowbar, a ski mask, handcuffs, and rope in Bundy's vehicle and arrested Bundy for possession of burglary tools. In describing Bundy to other officers, a homicide detective noted the similarity to a man who had kidnapped a woman a year earlier. When checks of his credit card receipts placed Bundy near the scene of several murders in Colorado, the circumstantial evidence grew. At a police lineup the kidnap victim and two other witnesses picked Bundy out, and he was charged and later found guilty of aggravated kidnapping and sent to Utah State Prison on a one-to-fifteen-year sentence. In the meantime police continued investigating him and linked him to three murder victims in Colorado. In 1977, while awaiting trial for the murder of Caryn Campbell, he escaped by jumping from the second floor of the Pitkin County courthouse library. He was captured in a stolen vehicle several days later. In December 1977 he escaped once again from his prison cell through a small trapdoor he had cut in the ceiling and headed for Florida. Only a week after arriving in Florida, on the night of 14 January 1978, he attacked several coeds at the Chi Omega sorority on the campus of Florida State University, killing two and viciously wounding two others. On 12 February 1978 he was once again pulled over, by a suspicious police officer who saw Bundy's car leave an alleyway late at night. Bundy fought the officer but was finally subdued and arrested. He refused to identify himself. Several days later, a fingerprint check with the FBI, who had just placed him on their Most Wanted list, established his identity. On 23 July 1979 he was convicted of killing the two students at FSU. One of the key pieces of evidence used against him were dental impressions made of his teeth, which perfectly matched several bite marks found on the body of one of the young women. He was sentenced to death by electrocution. For nearly the next decade he tried every method of appeal he could to escape the executioner. He even started listing where additional bodies of victims could be found as a bargaining chip to stay alive a little longer. But he ran out of appeals and schemes to remain alive. On 24 January 1989 Ted Bundy, admitted killer of at least thirty women (and perhaps, investigators believe, more than one hundred) was electrocuted by a female executioner.

The Hillside Strangler. The Hillside Strangler actually turned out to be two men, cousins Angelo Buono and Kenneth Bianchi. As many serial killers often do, they copied the technique of another well-known criminal (Caryl Chessman, a kidnapper and rapist, executed in 1960) by impersonating undercover police officers to ensnare women into entering a "police car." Their killing spree began in 1977, and during the next several years they killed at least ten women. The fact that there were two killers working together held the police off for awhile as this was a somewhat unusual method for serial killers to use. Buono also took precautions to minimize the ability of the authorities to identify the killers by washing the bodies of the victims before disposing of them so that clues such as hairs or semen would be washed away. One early intended victim who later testified at the Buono trial got lucky because of a photograph she carried in her wallet. Catherine Lorre was stopped by the two men, and upon handing over her license, Bianchi noticed that she had a picture of herself as a girl sitting on the lap of her father, the actor Peter Lorre. The duo's fear of the publicity that would surround her death is all that kept her from becoming a victim. After several murders in California, Bianchi moved to Washington State, where he was eventually connected to two murders and was linked as a possible suspect to the Hillside Strangler killings in California. Bianchi offered Washington authorities a deal to escape the death penalty in that state by identifying the "real" strangler. As a result, Buono was convicted of nine murders in 1983. Buono received nine life sentences without the possibility of parole, and Bianchi received a life sentence in Washington. Bianchi will be eligible for parole in 2005.

John Wayne Gacy, Bisexual Serial Killer. Gacy was born on 17 March 1942, the second child of Marion and John Gacy's three children. Over the years the young boy suffered under the stern discipline and verbal abuse of an authoritarian father. As he entered his teens, Gacy was caught on more than one occasion wearing women's underwear, and he feared that his father thought him less of a man as a result. No matter what Gacy did in an effort to impress his hardworking father, it didn't seem to be enough. He abruptly left home at age nineteen after another disagreement with his father and went to work in a mortuary. He left that job after his supervisor began finding bodies undressed for no reason. In 1964, at age twenty-two, Gacy had his first homosexual encounter with an acquaintance who managed to take advantage of Gacy after getting him intoxicated. During the 1960s Gacy enjoyed increasing business success, but during a run for president of the Jaycees in Waterloo, Iowa, he was charged with assaulting a fifteen-year-old son of another Jaycee. He bowed out of the race and eventually pleaded guilty to sodomy in the hope that he would get probation. To his surprise, Judge Peter Van Metre sentenced him to ten years at the Iowa State Reformatory. His wife, Marilyn, filed for divorce and later remarried.

Murder Spree. When Gacy left prison, he moved to Chicago to live with his mother, his father having died. Gacy married for a second time in 1972, despite having admitted to his prospective wife that he was bisexual. What he hadn't told his new wife was that he had started killing young men earlier that year and burying them in the crawl space of his house. By 1975 it became apparent to both Gacy and his wife that their marriage was essentially over. He and his wife were divorced amicably in 1976. During 1975 and 1976 John Gacy, or, as he would later put it, his "alter ego, bad Jack," began a killing spree. In 1977 he tortured, raped, and killed nine young men and buried them under his house. Unfortunately, the authorities did not believe several potential victims who were able to escape from Gacy during this period. The killings continued until 11 December 1978. Police arrested him on unrelated marijuana charges on 21 December and obtained a warrant to search his house as a result. They eventually dug up twenty-nine bodies on the property. Gacy's trial began 6 February 1980 and lasted nearly six weeks. On 12 March 1980, after deliberating for only one hour and fifty minutes, the jury found him guilty of thirty-three counts of murder. The next day the same jury took two hours to decide that he deserved the death penalty. For the next fourteen years he successfully fought off the executioner through appeals of his sentence. In June 1994 John Wayne Gacy was executed in the Illinois gas chamber.

James Huberty, Mass Murderer. While history has no shortage of criminals who kill for no apparent reason, James Huberty ranks right at the top for sheer viciousness. Huberty was born on 11 October 1942 in Canton, Ohio. When he was three he contracted polio and had to wear braces on his legs for several years. During that time other children made fun of the way he walked. When he was seven, his mother abandoned the family to become a Pentecostal missionary to Indian reservations, leaving her son devastated. An introvert, his one passion was guns, and he became very good with them. He became a welder and prospered for several years with his wife, Etna, and his two daughters. Coworkers, friends, and even the pastor who performed the marriage of Huberty and Etna noticed that he was a man who clearly suffered from inner demons and pent-up hostility. The beginning of the end started in late 1982, when Huberty was laid off from his position because of the economic recession. He became increasingly paranoid and blamed his misfortune on a massive conspiracy involving government figures, the Trilateral Commission, and practically anyone else he could think of. He began to hear voices that urged him toward suicide. After a short attempt to live in Mexico, he moved to San Ysidro, California, into an apartment complex where his family were the only Anglo-Americans in a largely Hispanic facility. Things began to look more promising when he successfully completed a security-guard training course and obtained a part-time job. However, the voices got worse and worse. He became delusional and in one instance approached a police car, claiming to be a war criminal. After checking with the FBI, who found no record of him, police sent him home. On 10 July 1984 he was fired from his job as a security guard because his superiors were worried about his nervousness and mental state for the job. On 17 July his wife was able to convince him to contact a mental health clinic, but the clinic did not get back to him right away. On 18 July, when he had not heard from the clinic, he apparently reached a decision to end it all. On that afternoon he told his wife that he wanted to kiss her good-bye. As to the mental health clinic's failure to return his call he stated, "Well, society had their chance." Shortly before 4 P.M., Huberty walked into a McDonald's restaurant and opened fire with a shotgun, a 9-mm pistol, and an Uzi submachine gun. He indiscriminately shot men, women, children, and even infants. As police arrived, Huberty walked around inside the restaurant shooting the wounded to death. Because of the broken glass from the shotgun pellets, the police had trouble seeing inside the restaurant to get a clear shot at the gunman. Meanwhile, Huberty's wife had heard of the shooting on the television, and her daughter had reported that her father's car was at the McDonald's. Etna contacted police and gave them as much information as possible to assist them, pointing out that her husband owned armor-piercing ammunition and was an excellent shot with either hand. At 5:17 P.M. SWAT sniper officer Charles Foster obtained a clear view of Huberty from the neck down and killed him. The final toll from what was at that time America's worst mass murder: twenty-one dead and nineteen wounded. This grim record stood until 16 October 1991, when a man named George Hennard killed twenty-two and wounded twenty-three at Luby's Cafeteria in Killeen, Texas.

Source:
Joel Norris, *Serial Killers: The Growing Menace* (Garden City, N.Y.: Doubleday, 1988).

THE SUPREME COURT TURNS RIGHT

Historical Analogues. When President Franklin Delano Roosevelt sought to "pack" the Supreme Court in 1937 by increasing the number of justices and appointing men favorable to his social interventionist philosophy, he was roundly condemned by members of both political parties for attempting to destroy the independence of the Court. As taught in civics texts, the Supreme Court is the third branch of government. Its membership is supposed to represent the wide range of judicial philosophies to be found across the nation, and to be the arbiter of disputes between the executive and legislative branches and the ultimate interpreter of the Constitution. Roosevelt's attempt to rewrite the Constitution to overplay his own power in order to fill the Court with political allies was viewed as an illegitimate effort to overpoliticize the Court. Since judicial appointments are proposed by the president and confirmed (or denied) by the Senate, however, the process is always fraught with political intrigue. Though Roosevelt failed in his attempt to increase the number of justices, he did, by the end of his tenure as president, succeed in creating a liberal court that held sway until the Reagan administration. Among Reagan's major campaign promises was the vow to appoint as many new justices to the Supreme Court as possible, to insist on an ideological litmus test for all such appoint-

The Supreme Court in 1981: Harry A. Blackmun, Thurgood Marshall, John Paul Stevens III, Chief Justice Warren E. Burger, Sandra Day O'Connor, Byron R. White, Lewis F. Powell Jr., William H. Rehnquist, and William J. Brennan Jr.

ments, and particularly to nominate judges who would overturn *Roe* v. *Wade,* the 1973 abortion rights decision. Though Republicans were in office more than half the time between the elections of 1952 and 1980, they could not turn the liberal majority out because Supreme Court justices serve for life. President Eisenhower had seized a golden opportunity to change the court's direction in 1953 by appointing Earl Warren as chief justice, believing the longtime Republican would change the Court's Democratic bent. Instead, Warren came to preside over the most socially active Court in U.S. history. The retirement of Warren in 1969 allowed the recently elected President Richard Nixon to appoint Warren Burger as chief justice, and Republicans had another opportunity. Yet, even the appointment of three more Nixon nominees failed to shift the Court significantly rightward. The 1970s saw landmark victories for liberals in which the Supreme Court allowed busing for school desegregation, struck down the death penalty, legalized abortion, and upheld affirmative action. Justices who had been appointed to fill a conservative role failed to live up to expectations, and the liberal "old guard" clung to their positions despite advancing age. Thus hopes were high among conservatives when Ronald Reagan was swept into office. Within six months of his inauguration he was able to appoint Sandra Day O'Connor as the first woman to sit on the Court — thereby undercutting feminists while seating a conservative. O'Connor, however, voted

for affirmative action, against school prayer, and waffled on the abortion issue. Conservatives chafed, and by 1986 it seemed time was running out for Reagan to finish off 1960s-style liberalism on the Court. That year Chief Justice Burger announced his retirement. Reagan's legal advisers understood they could achieve a "double steal" by promoting Associate Justice William Rehnquist to chief justice, and then by appointing someone philosophically like him to fill the vacancy left by his promotion. Antonin Scalia, the son of an Italian immigrant, a federal appeals judge, and former law professor, filled the bill. Though Democrats struggled to foil Rehnquist's appointment, having "left no stone unthrown," in the words of Sen. Orrin Hatch (R–Utah), the Republican majority in the Senate confirmed him by a vote of 65–33, the most votes ever cast against a chief justice. After this bitter fight the Senate was no longer in a mood for ugly infighting and so confirmed Scalia without dissent. A photograph taken shortly afterward on the Supreme Court's steps, showing a smiling Rehnquist and Scalia shaking hands, spoke volumes. A new era was beginning.

The Brennan Court. Rehnquist had decried what he saw as the dangerous leftward course of the Court. Believing the high bench to be a "boat keeling over in one direction," he saw his job as to "lean the other way." There were still problems, though. Justice John Paul Stevens, who had been appointed by President Gerald Ford, continued to be unpredictable and quirky in his opinions, and Justices Harry Blackmun and Lewis Powell, though law-and-order judges, tended to vote with liberals on civil rights cases. Thus, key efforts to overturn affirmative action, opposition to the death penalty, and *Roe* v. *Wade* were lost in 1986–1987, the first year of Rehnquist's tenure. On the key issues of concern to conservatives, the liberals still held sway in the highest legal chamber, leading many to dub it "Brennan's Court," after its oldest and most influential member. For the "rule of five" to have meaning on the Rehnquist court, a reliable fifth conservative would have to be found.

Powell's Resignation. In summer 1987 the announcement of Powell's retirement sent a surge of anticipation through the Department of Justice. What followed, however, was a political backlash and media circus the likes of which had rarely attended Supreme Court nominations. Reagan's term was almost up, and Iran-Contra had severely damaged public faith in his integrity. When Reagan nominated Robert Bork, a former professor of law at Yale University with a reputation as a leading constitutional scholar and outspoken conservative theorist, alarm bells rang all over liberal Washington.

The Bork Affair. Bork came to the nomination process with much the same problems as had Rehnquist and Scalia. Both would have been pilloried in the changed circumstances after Iran-Contra. But the chief justice had the advantage of already sitting on the Court, while Scalia benefitted from an exhausted Senate after the Rehnquist fight. Bork also suffered from his role as Nixon's solicitor general in the aftermath of the infamous "Saturday Night Massacre" during the Watergate scandal. After his two predecessors had resigned rather than fire the special prosecutor appointed to investigate the affair, Bork did as the president instructed and fired Archibald Cox. His clear ideological positions on freedom of speech, privacy rights, civil rights (he had condemned the legal reasoning behind some key desegregation decisions) were anathema to liberals, but Scalia's had been much the same. His opposition to abortion also frightened those Republicans who did not wish to buck public opinion. In the end, the key to the process that rejected Bork's nomination lay in widespread public opposition to Bork and the clear-cut intention of Reagan to shift the balance in the Court. Having regained control of the Senate in the 1986 midterm elections, the Democrats locked arms against him. The final vote, 58–42 against, was the largest margin of defeat ever for a Supreme Court nominee.

Ginsburg is Smoked. Reagan's next nomination, a another federal appeals judge, Douglas H. Ginsburg, fared no better. Having written and spoken little, he was Bork "without the record," said his Department of Justice advocates. A former member of that very Justice Department, he was considered "one of us" by insiders. The attempt to promote Ginsburg lasted about one week, however, completely falling apart when it was learned

---

JUDICIAL AUTHORITY

The following statement is an excerpt from the introductory remarks of Robert H. Bork at the Senate Judiciary Committee hearing on 15 September 1987 to consider his nomination as an associate justice of the United States Supreme Court. Judge Bork's nomination was rejected by the committee. The judge's authority derives entirely from the fact that he is applying the law and not his personal values. That is why the American public accepts the decisions of its courts, accepts even decisions that nullify the laws a majority of the electorate or their representatives voted for. The judge, to deserve that trust and that authority, must be every bit as governed by law as is the Congress, the president, the state governors and legislatures, and the American people. No one, including a judge, can be above the law. Only in that way will justice be done and the freedom of Americans assured.

How should a judge go about finding the law? The only legitimate way, in my opinion, is by attempting to discern what those who made the law intended. . . .

If a judge abandons intention as his guide, there is no law available to him and he begins to legislate a social agenda for the American people. That goes beyond his legitimate power.

He or she then diminishes liberty instead of enhancing it. . . . [W]hen a judge goes beyond [his proper function] and reads entirely new values into the Constitution, values the framers and the ratifiers did not put there, he deprives the people of their liberty. That liberty, which the Constitution clearly envisions, is the liberty of the people to set their own social agenda through the processes of democracy. . . .

My philosophy of judging, Mr. Chairman, as you pointed out is neither liberal nor conservative. It is simply a philosophy of judging which gives the Constitution a full and fair interpretation but, where the constitution is silent, leaves the policy struggles to the Congress, the President, the legislatures and executives of the 50 states, and to the American people.

Source: Robert H. Bork, *The Tempting of America: The Political Seduction of the Law* (New York: Free Press, 1990).

---

that he had smoked marijuana as a student and as a professor. Initially the Reagan administration tried to write this off as a harmless peccadillo, but the president's wife, Nancy, had promoted her "Just Say No" approach to drug use, and this had found widespread appeal in the conservative hinterland. Attorney General Meese, moreover, had just initiated mandatory drug testing for all Department of Justice employees. The press seized the issue with glee, making such political capital of it that virtually every seeker of public office since — whether elective or appointive — has had to answer the "Ginsburg question."

A Right Kennedy. That left "Mr. Clean," Judge Anthony Kennedy of the U.S. Ninth District Court of Appeals in California, whose friends claimed that he was so enamored of law and order that he would not jaywalk. Those in the Department of Justice who knew him swore he would vote to overturn *Roe* v. *Wade.* Though he would never have the impact that the Reagan team had hoped for with Bork, his appellate decisions rejecting the doctrine of "comparable worth" in wages for women and against black complainants in discrimination cases, made him seem the ideal candidate to cast the much sought after "swing" vote. Moving swiftly, the Senate compared him to his predecessors and reasoned that he had to be better, and so unanimously confirmed this so-called "stealth" candidate with a record too thin to be held against him.

Affirmative Questions. Opposition to Bork had centered on fears that he might roll back precedents, but Kennedy wasted no time in demonstrating that he could be as useful as Bork. In a landmark decision, *Patterson* v. *McLean Credit* (1988), the Supreme Court set aside key precedents against racial discrimination set during the Warren court. The ruling jolted much of the legal community. The Patterson case portended that the very stability of seemingly settled law was in jeopardy. In late fall 1988 the Court ruled in *Richmond* v. *Croson* that a Richmond, Virginia, ordinance that set aside 30 percent of city contracts for minority-owned businesses violated the Fourteenth Amendment by discriminating against whites. The Rehnquist court was sending a clear signal that it would not look upon affirmative action by local and state governments as benign efforts on behalf of racial equality. Henceforth, affirmative action might be considered racial discrimination against white males, unless clear racial discrimination against minorities was present. In one of the last two, and most important, cases of the 1988–1989 session, the Court voted 5–4 in each case to uphold death penalties in Texas and Kentucky for juvenile and mentally retarded murderers. Justice Scalia wrote the majority opinion in the case. He rejected the arguments that such executions represented cruel and unusual punishment. Since 126 such youngsters had been put to death in the nation's history, there was nothing unusual about it at all, said Scalia.

Abortion. The key legal issue of concern to the conservatives remained *Roe* v. *Wade,* and Ronald Reagan's promise to overturn it by appointing Supreme Court jus-

tices whom he felt certain would vote to do so. By summer 1989 a case pending before the Court seemed to provide the opportunity to weaken or nullify the extremely controversial decision originally made in 1973. The attorney general of the state of Missouri, William L. Webster, had asked the Supreme Court to revive a 1986 law that banned abortions at publicly funded hospitals. At stake in this case was not the right to abortion but rather whether the states were legally required to pay for such procedures. A federal appeals court in Saint Louis had struck down Missouri's law, and in *Webster* v. *Reproductive Health Services* conservatives saw their chance, if not to overrule *Roe* entirely, then to let it survive only as a weakened precedent. Indeed, Chief Justice Rehnquist had already prepared a draft opinion as the case came before the entire Court. Rehnquist's language gave greater power to the states to regulate abortion. Thus, antiabortionists would get a new opening to enact more-stringent regulations in the future. He had carefully crafted his language precisely to appeal to Justice Sandra Day O'Connor, but she surprised everyone by writing that "When a constitutional invalidity of a state's abortion statute actually turns on the constitutional validity of *Roe* v. *Wade,* there will be time enough to reexamine *Roe.* And do so carefully." With a few broad strokes she had denied Rehnquist his majority in the ruling. Seething, Scalia wrote in his scathing dissent: "It thus appears that the mansion of constitutionalized abortion-law, constructed overnight in *Roe* v. *Wade,* must be disassembled door-jamb by door-jamb, and never entirely brought down, no matter how wrong that may be." Even so, the consitutional "right" to abortion still hung by only a thread. Conservatives consoled themselves by reasoning that the addition of more votes, and a better case, could easily finish it off.

A Rightward Shift. By decade's end the Supreme Court had undergone a decisive and rapid transformation. President Reagan had delivered on his campaign promises to reorient the Court. Despite the ideal notion that the Supreme Court should be above politics, the Court during the 1980s followed politics the way it almost always had. The change in the court's philosophy was profound. Whereas the Warren court had committed to the notion that rights held by one citizen must be held by all, the Rehnquist court had reverted to an earlier conception that held that each separate community, or state, could judge the extent of individual rights on its own. Nevertheless the new Supreme Court has not embraced the atavistic probusiness conservatism that characterized the early 1930s. The New Deal insistence that government may regulate the marketplace has not been swept away, as high punitive-damage verdicts against corporations have been upheld, as antiracketeering judgments have been sustained against business leaders, and as city rent-control laws remain on the books. The extent to which the marketplace will be regulated for producers over consumers or capital over labor remains to be seen.

Source:
David G. Savage, *Turning Right: The Making of the Rehnquist Supreme Court* (New York: John Wiley, 1992).

THE WAR ON DRUGS

On 30 January 1982, to much publicity and acclaim, President Ronald Reagan announced the war on drugs and took the unprecedented step of appointing his vice president, George Bush, as chief coordinator of drug policy. As a former head of the Central Intelligence Agency, Bush seemed both a logical choice and a strong indication of the administration's resolve to extirpate this growing cancer from the body politic. With stirring speeches the vice president announced that the American people had had enough and that his office would coordinate all of the chief law enforcement agencies of the federal government "to stop the storm surge of cocaine" and other drugs "drowning" the citizens of the United States "in a sea of murders, violence, and blood-drenched narcodollars." Targeting the seedbed of narcotics distribution, south Florida, Bush declared that the U.S. Attorney's Office; the Drug Enforcement Agency; the U.S. Customs Service; the Federal Bureau of Investigation; the Bureau of Alcohol, Tobacco and Firearms; the Internal Revenue Service; the U.S. Border Patrol; and the army, navy, and Coast Guard would pool resources, share information, and coordinate a strategic assault to rid America of the drug plague and the crime, social dislocation, and demoralization that accompanied it. Given this panoply of forces, optimism seemed the order of the day. For six months or so the mass media reported impressive results. President Reagan was photographed standing before tons of seized drugs and weapons proclaiming such successes "a brilliant example of working federalism." During the first year of the war, the U.S. Attorney's Office reported a 64 percent increase in drug prosecutions. In 1983 six tons of cocaine were seized in south Florida; by 1985 such seizures snared twenty-five tons; in 1986, thirty tons. According to the DEA, this represented more cocaine than the Medellín and Cali drug cartels in Colombia had been producing in 1980. Therefore, while these arrests and seizures were touted as successes, they also indicated a growing drug problem and a need to escalate the war on drugs. More people were using cocaine and heroin and other drugs than ever before. Even in south Florida, the primary theater of combat, illicit drugs were as easily available as over-the-counter varieties, and were often sold in the same places — openly, without fear of the law. Something was profoundly wrong, and many drug agents on the streets were highly critical and pointed to an absence of the will to win in Washington and deep corruption from top to bottom.

Legacy of the 1960s. Widespread concern about the pervasive, destructive social effects of such corruption, and recognition that it enabled the narcotics traffic to emerge in the first place, had led to public demands for

Federal agents guarding twenty tons of cocaine (worth at least $2 billion) after a major drug bust in Los Angeles, on 29 September 1989

action. Prior to the late 1960s the problem of drug abuse in the United States had been relatively minor. Opium and cocaine had been problems in the late nineteenth and early twentieth centuries when they had been legal and their addictive effects little understood. The Pure Food and Drug Act of 1906 had banned them (for example, preventing Coca-Cola from adding its most potent ingredient). Thereafter, numerous laws prohibited the possession and distribution of many substances. Though organized crime had always managed to break such laws, the use of illegal drugs was minuscule by today's standards and confined largely to the margins of society. This changed suddenly in the late 1960s and early 1970s, as the rampant drug use by the young and a "tidal wave" of heroin inundated the United States from southeast Asia. As many studies have shown, and as congressional committees have verified, this was made possible, in part, by military and political alliances between the CIA and warlords it recruited to fight covert anticommunist campaigns in Laos, Cambodia, Thailand, and Burma during the Vietnam War. Congress had granted authority to President Lyndon Johnson to wage limited war in Vietnam — but to do so nowhere else. Thus, to extend the anticommunist crusade into the rest of southeast Asia, the CIA had to make an "end run" around Congress. In order to generate funds to organize covert warfare, the CIA allowed its right-wing partners to sell large quantities of drugs, a good deal of which made its way into the United States, owing to corruption among individual agents, Saigon government officials, and actions taken by the Corsican mafia (the "French Connection") in Marseilles, France, to profit from this glut of heroin. Simultaneously, the Sicilian mafia, facing competition, stepped up its own drug operations, smuggling heroin from anticommunist guerrillas in Afghanistan, who were also backed by the CIA. By the late 1980s heroin had again become popular, and much of this product was generated by the Mujahideen to fund their CIA-supported war against the communist government of Afghanistan. Anticommunist warlords needed money to fund their operations, and the CIA was willing, in the words of Victor Marchetti (a high-ranking CIA operative), "to look the other way" when they grew and sold prodigious quantities of drugs. The problem was that these banner crops needed outlets, and this resulted in organized crime pushing drugs on an unprecedented scale in the streets of America.

Cocaine. By the late 1970s, as the market for heroin seemed to become saturated, new organized crime rings from Latin America began to step up production and distribution of a different, but equally addictive and destructive, drug — cocaine. By the mid 1980s new, more potent methods of ingestion (freebasing) and forms (crack) appeared. As the street price plummeted, more citizens tried the novelty items and quickly became dependent. Cocaine was the "drug of choice" of the 1980s, said *Time* magazine, with few of the drawbacks of heroin, thus appealing to middle-class consumers. As it turned out, long-term cocaine abuse had its own attendant set of medical horrors, but this was not to be realized until later, when millions of Americans were addicted.

Drugs and Foreign Policy. Simultaneously as the new cocaine cartels were growing in power, the Reagan administration undertook to wage a covert war against the Sandinista government of Nicaragua and to oppose all Marxist and communist influence throughout Latin America. Congress had expressly forbidden the overt overthrow of the Sandinistas and covert operations paid for by public funds. Essentially the same scenario that had emerged in southeast Asia was repeated in Central America. The Iran-Contra hearings showed that the Reagan administration circumvented the will of Congress by violating at least the spirit, if not the letter, of the law. One of the sensitive issues all but ignored by this congressional inquest was that of connections between the sale of illicit drugs and arms purveyed to the Contras. Responding to public pressure, the Senate Foreign Relations Committee set up a special Subcommittee on Terrorism, Narcotics, and International Operations, chaired by Sen. John Kerry (D–Mass.) to conduct its own hearings into these matters. Its conclusion was clear: at the very least the CIA (and other U.S. agencies) had again looked the other way as the Medellín and Cali drug cartels had provided millions of dollars earned from the sale of drugs to arm the Contras. The Kerry Committee also found numerous other instances of illegal drug activities throughout the region, the most important of which was that of Gen. Manuel Noriega of Panama, who had

been known to U.S. drug enforcement since at least 1971 as a drug trafficker, cooperating with the cartel of Medellín. The CIA had also used Noriega to funnel secret arms to the Contras. As evidence uncovered by the Kerry committee showed, Noriega had been on the payroll of the CIA beginning in 1976 (the year George Bush took over as head of the CIA), when he collected $110,000 dollars a year. By 1985 he was collecting $200,000 per year, all in secret cash deposits in the Bank of Credit and Commerce International (BCCI — which would figure prominently in new scandals in the early 1990s, including drug-money laundering). Ostensibly Noriega was "our man" in Central America serving in the war against communism. Yet in 1986 when the DEA proposed an undercover plan to unravel the mysteries of a multibillion-dollar drug laundering scam in Panamanian banks, it had to seek CIA approval. The go-ahead was given, but with the proviso that any information that exposed Panamanian government officials would have to be dropped. Nevertheless, the Kerry Committee's revelations could not be ignored. In 1988 the U.S. District Court in Miami issued an indictment against Noriega and a warrant for his arrest. George Bush claimed that his subordinates kept him in the dark about Noriega's drug operations, and he was sufficiently embarrassed by the Kerry Committee's revelations that in 1989 as president, he ordered the invasion of Panama by U.S. troops, ostensibly to safeguard U.S. bases and personnel, but also to remove Noriega from power. Eventually Noriega was tried. His planned defense included calling for secret government documents that his lawyers said would prove that Noriega had done nothing not approved by his Washington contacts. Both the CIA and NSC refused to hand over files on Noriega, saying that to do so would compromise national security. Noriega was duly convicted and imprisoned.

Drugs and Corruption. The dismal revelations brought to light both by the Iran-Contra hearings and the Kerry Committee cast grave doubts upon the war on drugs — both about its efficacy and the competency and integrity of the generals. There is little doubt that CIA alliances with organized crime rings in the late 1940s, intended as anticommunist measures, also opened avenues of opportunity for criminal drug smugglers. Later, political alliances with right-wing regimes in small countries fighting communism also promoted drug trafficking. This history of toleration and/or complicity in the drug trade suggests strongly that corruption in Washington, D.C., should become a main focus of combat in the war on drugs.

Sources:

Alfred McCoy, *The Politics of Heroin in Southeast Asia* (New York: Harper & Row, 1972);

Peter Dale Scott and Jonathan Marshall, *Cocaine Politics: Drugs, Armies, and the CIA in Central America* (Berkeley: University of California Press, 1991);

Senate Committee on Foreign Relations, Subcommittee on Terrorism, Narcotics, and International Operations, *Drugs, Law Enforcement and Foreign Policy* (Washington, D.C.: GPO, 1989).

HEADLINE MAKERS

TAWANA BRAWLEY

1972-

ALLEGED RAPE VICTIM

First Report. On Sunday, 29 November 1987, the 1.2 million viewers of New York City's channel 2 first heard of an incident that would make their skin crawl. A teenage black girl named Tawana Brawley had been found partially naked, wrapped in plastic, with human feces smeared over her body and in her hair. The letters *KKK* were scratched onto her chest, over her breasts, and the words *nigger, nigger* were written onto her stomach. Initial reports were that she had been kidnapped by a white man who had flashed a police badge and then taken her to a wooded area on the previous Tuesday, where she had been held captive for four days, raped, and sodomized by six white men, some or all of whom may have been law enforcement officers. Early reports were that the Federal Bureau of Investigation was investigating.

Questions. Following the first reports of the apparently racially based attack, the investigation soon stalled. Brawley and her mother refused to cooperate with investigators, and several self-appointed advisers stepped in to assist the family. The three main advisers were the well-known Rev. Al Sharpton and attorneys Alton Maddox and C. Vernon Mason. The three advisers quickly placed themselves squarely into the middle of the fray and conducted numerous press conferences and interviews to share their version of what Brawley went through. The initial inclination of some reporters was to tend to ignore any event in which the publicity-hungry Sharpton was

involved, but other events served to keep the focus on the case. On 21 January 1988 Duchess County district attorney William Grady suddenly dropped out of the investigation and asked supervising justice Judith Hillery to appoint special prosecutors because of a potential conflict of interest. The two special prosecutors dropped out twenty-four hours later for the same reason. On 26 January Gov. Mario Cuomo appointed Attorney General Robert Abrams as special prosecutor. Sharpton, Maddox, and Mason claimed that there was a cover-up under way to protect the law enforcement personnel who were involved in the assault; the recusal by the district attorney served to give their argument some credibility.

Bits and Pieces. During the next few months, charges and countercharges flew between the advisers and law enforcement personnel. The charges included allegations (false) that news reporters had bribed some students to state that Tawana had been seen at a dance during the period that she had claimed to have been abducted. A break in the story finally came when WCBS news reporter Mike Taibbi and producer Anna Sims-Phillips obtained a statement from Perry McKinnon, a former aide of the Brawley team. McKinnon indicated that the advisers had been consciously playing the matter for publicity and political gain. Worse still, he stated on tape that the advisers had been soliciting and receiving large sums of money for the Brawley family during the course of the stymied investigation. To be on the safe side, the reporters had McKinnon take a polygraph test, which he passed.

The Grand Jury Report. On 6 October 1988 Judge Angelo Ingrassia accepted the report of the grand jury that had been convened to ascertain the facts of the alleged assault. While the grand jury had failed conclusively to learn that Tawana was in Newburgh, New York, during part of the time she had claimed to have been kidnapped, they had nevertheless concluded that the forensic and medical evidence proved that Tawana Brawley had fabricated the story. The one law enforcement officer publically identified as an attacker, Assistant District Attorney Stephen Pagones, had a solid alibi. Later reports indicated a suspicion that Brawley had fabricated the story to escape punishment for several days' absence from her home. The fact remains that only she knows for sure what actually transpired.

Source:
Outrage: The Story Behind the Tawana Brawley Hoax (New York: Bantam, 1990).

BERNHARD GOETZ

1947-

SUBWAY GUNMAN

A Vigilante in the Making. Bernhard Hugo Goetz Jr. was born on 7 November 1947 in New York City. He enjoyed a seemingly carefree existence as a child, but behind the veneer he suffered at the hands of a dictatorial father, a "real Prussian disciplinarian," according to an aunt. Various people and former classmates who knew him over the years related the impression that he was a bookworm, but one who at times seemed to be under a lot of pressure. As an adult in New York City, he had been the victim of a mugging by three black youths in 1981 in which he was injured. This appears to have been the impetus for his later actions.

Mister, Can I Have $5? Those are the words that Troy Canty states he said to Goetz on a subway train on 22 December 1984. Goetz's response reportedly was, "Sure, I've got five dollars for each of you." Instead, he pulled out a gun and started firing. After the fact, the four black youths shot by Goetz admitted that they were "fooling around on the train when this white dude came in and sat down next to us." Canty was the first one shot, in the chest, the bullet just missing his heart. Barry Allen was shot next, in the back of his neck as he turned to try to escape. James Ramseur was shot next, by one of two hollow-point bullets that Goetz had in the revolver. Hollow-point bullets, also known as dum dums, are designed to cause the maximum damage possible to human flesh by expanding as they enter their target. The one that hit Ramseur went through his arm, into his chest, and destroyed his spleen. The last person shot, Darrell Cabey, also suffered a shot by a hollow-point bullet. It pierced both of his lungs and severed his spinal cord, paralyzing him from the waist down.

Concord Confession. On 31 December 1984, nine days after the shooting, Goetz walked into police headquarters in Concord, New Hampshire, and informed the officer on duty that he was the gunman that the New York City authorities were searching for. During the course of a rambling statement to Concord police officer Warren Foote, he admitted to the shooting and informed the police of his activities afterward. Goetz's description of the shooting was that he entered the subway car and took a seat at one end of the car, near where the four black youths were sitting. He then stated that two of the youths got up to stand next to him and asked him for five dollars. When Goetz got up, he claimed that one of the black males put his hand in his pocket and "made like he had a weapon of some type there." Goetz went on to explain that by that time, he had already laid down his pattern of fire. He admitted shooting all four of the victims.

Verdict. For nearly three years following the shooting, the defense and the prosecution played cat and mouse, with the prosecution calling first one and then a second grand jury in an effort to indict Goetz and with the defense filing a series of motions for dismissal. The prosecution wanted to try Goetz for assault, attempted murder, illegal weapons possession, and reckless endangerment. The defense succeeded in having the lower courts drop the assault and attempted murder charges based on the prosecution's error in relating the law of self-defense to the grand jury. The New York Court of Appeals reinstated the charges, and Goetz was finally going to trial. In June 1987, nearly three and a half years after shooting the four men, Goetz received the jury verdict — not guilty on all counts except illegal possession of a handgun.

Source:
George P. Fletcher, *A Crime of Self-Defense: Bernhard Goetz and the Law on Trial* (New York: Free Press, 1988).

JEAN HARRIS

1923-

MURDERER

Early Years. Jean Harris was born Jean Struven on 27 April 1923 in Chicago, Illinois. Her father was a successful but bigoted engineer who was verbally abusive to those who disagreed with him. Despite his attitude, she enjoyed a privileged upper-middle-class lifestyle and did well in school. She married James Harris and they led a happy existence, with Jim working at a carburetor manufacturer and Jean working as a teacher. However, a silent growing discontent was awakening in Jean. In 1964 she finally decided to end the marriage, and she obtained a divorce the next year. She later left the teaching field to enter the academic administration arena for the increased income it provided. But the nonstop work was beginning to take its toll and her social life was virtually nonexistent until December 1966.

Introduction. A friend invited Harris to a dinner party in an attempt to fix her up. It was there that she met Dr. Herman Tarnower. Like Jean, Tarnower was also something of a social climber, and over the years he had established a large practice for himself and had founded the Scarsdale Medical Center in Scarsdale, New York. Hi, as he liked to be called, and Harris hit it off from the start. Correspondence followed, and they first dated in March 1967. The affair between the two continued off and on throughout the 1970s. During this time Hi once proposed to Jean but later backed out, citing the fact that he was a confirmed bachelor. As the decade wore on, Tarnower openly dated other women, including his secretary, Lynne Tryforos. While Harris appeared to be happy and did not seem to mind the other women, in fact she was under increasing pressure. Tension between her and Tryforos increased, and Harris began receiving anonymous telephone calls suggesting that she take sex lessons or calling her old and pathetic.

The Scarsdale Diet. In January 1979 Tarnower published *The Complete Scarsdale Medical Diet*, and it immediately became a best-seller, earning Tarnower millions of dollars. Tarnower went on a book tour and took Tryforos with him, effectively shutting Harris out of a large part of his life. Harris was suffering from depression and exhaustion from trying to compete with the younger Tryforos for Tarnower's attention. On 10 March 1980, suffering from withdrawal from an antidepressant that Tarnower had prescribed for her and that she had run out of, she decided to commit suicide at Tarnower's house.

Fact or Fiction? According to her testimony, Harris pulled into the driveway of Tarnower's house. The house was dark and she was disappointed that Tarnower had not left a light on for her. He was already asleep when she went upstairs to the bedroom. She wanted to talk to him but he abruptly told her to be quiet and go to sleep. She entered the bathroom, saw a nightgown and hair curlers that were not hers, and threw the curlers at the dresser, breaking the glass. Tarnower appeared at the bathroom door and, for the first time ever, struck her across the face and told her to get out. She took a gun out of her purse, placed it against her head, and pulled the trigger. At that moment Tarnower jumped for it from behind her and was shot in the hand. A struggle for the gun ensued and he was shot in the torso. Harris then tried to shoot herself again only to realize that the gun was empty. The police arrived shortly thereafter and she admitted that she had shot Tarnower. Later that night he was pronounced dead, and Harris was charged with murder. After a trial that many thought might have resulted in her acquittal were it not for her insistence to take the stand in her own defense, she was found guilty of intentional murder. She was sentenced to fifteen years to life in prison. A model inmate, she suffered two heart attacks in prison, and as she was awaiting quadruple-bypass heart surgery, Gov. Mario Cuomo pardoned her on 29 December 1992.

Source:
Diana Trilling, *Mrs. Harris: The Death of the Scarsdale Diet Doctor* (New York: Harcourt Brace Jovanovich, 1981).

EDWIN MEESE III

1931-

ATTORNEY GENERAL OF THE UNITED STATES, 1985-1988

Scandal. No other member of the Reagan administration, with the exception of Oliver North, was as tainted by scandal as Edwin Meese III. Certainly, no other Reagan official was more disliked, both within the administration and on Capitol Hill, though Reagan himself called Meese his "alter ego." At one point in his tenure as attorney general Meese was under investigation by three special prosecutors, each inquiring into separate allegations of influence peddling, bribery, and cover-up in the Iran-Contra affair. Though Meese was never charged with any crime, the last of the special investigators said that Meese "had probably broken conflict of interest and income-tax laws, though none of the indictments were worthy of prosecution." This statement provoked outrage and derision among congressional staffers who had helped to build cases against Meese, for its logic supposed that the nation's chief law enforcement officer was to be held to a lower standard of conduct than ordinary citizens. Though Meese had figured in virtually every imbroglio of the Reagan administration, like the president himself he was able to shed charges of personal culpability. Nevertheless, the "sleaze factor" emerging from the Reagan presidency jeopardized, but did not undermine, the election campaign of Vice President George Bush in 1988, which feared the political capital to be gained by Democratic candidate Michael Dukakis. So when Reagan accepted Meese's resignation in late 1988, before the end of the president's second term, the Bush campaign was relieved. Though officially exonerated of all charges, Meese departed under a cloud; he breezily dismissed all critics as cynical ideologues with an ax to grind.

Growing Up. Born in Oakland, California, to a family that had resided in the state since the Gold Rush days, Meese earned an academic scholarship to Yale University and subsequently earned a J.D. from the University of California, Berkeley. He later served two years on active duty in army intelligence as a lieutenant. Known as a law-and-order man, Meese became a deputy district attorney in his native Alameda County, where he spent his free time riding with patrol officers on their beats. He supervised the mass arrests of seven hundred students during the Berkeley Free Speech Movement in 1964 and was especially tough with members of the Black Panther Party. Coming to the attention of Ronald Reagan, Meese was appointed the governor's special secretary and given broad authority. In 1969 Meese relieved the president of beleaguered San Francisco State University when students occupied administration buildings, overseeing the arrest of their leaders. That same year Meese influenced Governor Reagan to declare a state of emergency in the community conflict over use of land known as People's Park in Berkeley, which led to pitched battles between police and protesters. Campus unrest in the 1960s particularly offended Meese because he believed that demonstrations gave "aid and comfort" to the North Vietnamese, and in 1966 he testified before the House Un-American Activities Committee that antiwar demonstrations should be made a crime. "Basically, those demonstrations prolonged the war," said Meese, "and cost a lot of American lives. The demonstrations encouraged them (North Vietnamese) . . . and prevented our elected officials from taking the necessary steps to win the war."

Reagan. During Reagan's second gubernatorial term Meese became his chief of staff and, according to some, the "deputy governor." In 1978 he was appointed a law professor at the University of California, San Diego, where he remained until Reagan's presidential campaign in 1980. Joining as an adviser at first, Meese quickly replaced the first campaign manager, John Sears, and served as the architect of the successful effort to portray Reagan as a tough-talking, law-and-order candidate. When Reagan took office in 1981, Meese became chief of transition, and after other Reagan staffers blocked his appointment as chief of staff, he accepted the newly created cabinet position of counselor to the president and became, according to his enemies within the administration, effectively the "surrogate president."

Counselor to the President. As counselor to the president Meese took highly public and controversial positions, including asserting that evidence gathered in violation of guidelines established by the Supreme Court should be used in a court of law, and he then defended the president's pardon of two FBI agents who had illegally conducted break-ins. He argued that certain persons identified by the government as dangerous, but charged with no crime, could be held in "preventive detention." He attacked the American Civil Liberties Union (ACLU), calling it a nationwide "criminals' lobby," and declared himself in favor of abolishing the Legal Services Corporation, saying that legal aid for the poor could be provided by local bar associations instead.

Attorney General. Law-and-order conservatives were enamored of Meese, and, disenchanted with Reagan's first attorney general, William French Smith, they were convinced that the former would far better serve the president as the nation's chief law enforcer. When Smith resigned at the end of Reagan's first term, Meese was nominated, but he ran headlong into polit-

ical objections to his public positions and questions about unethical behavior. The Office of Government Ethics had found Meese in violation of the minimum standards expected of public officials. During lengthy and charged hearings before the Senate Judiciary Committee, Meese was grilled about many things, including his claim to have inadvertently failed to list a $15,000 interest-free loan provided to him by a former business associate. His response was that "it never occurred to me that an interest-free loan was a thing of value." Sen. Joseph Biden (D–Del.), chairman of the Judiciary Committee, said that Meese appeared to him to be "beneath the office." Nevertheless, Meese promised that his days of playing loosely with ethical standards were over and so won confirmation as attorney general. Controversy and allegations of corruption were to dog him, however, and these intensified as his role in the Iran Contra affair was scrutinized.

Iran-Contra. The report of the congressional committees investigating Iran-Contra, issued in November 1987, stopped short of accusing the attorney general of criminal acts. But the report raised serious doubts about Meese's credibility on the matter of the controversial "finding" at the heart of the scandal. Technically, arms shipments to Iran violated the Arms Control Export Act. However, under certain circumstances, in the name of national security, the president may override the law by issuing a signed finding. The Iran-Contra committees discovered evidence, however, that Reagan had done so ten days after the arms were actually shipped. Could the nation be expected to believe, asked committee members, that the top law enforcement official of the U.S. government had never been asked to render an opinion as to the legality of these measures? Meese insisted he was never consulted. Other issues were raised as well. In 1986 the assistant U.S. attorney for Miami, Florida, uncovered evidence of Oliver North's secret arms-for-the-Contras network, but suddenly found his investigation blocked from above. Information surfaced that Meese had visited the head of the Miami office at that time, who suddenly caused all further inquiries into the matter to languish. Iran-Contra investigators wanted to know why Meese had not dispatched FBI agents instead. Since Meese himself informed the nation of illegal activity on the part of Oliver North in November 1986, committee members also asked why federal agents had not immediately sealed all offices and records in the case. Meese had warned Adm. John Poindexter, Reagan's national security adviser and North's boss, that Department of Justice agents would be visiting him, thereby giving him, and North, time to destroy incriminating documents, a felony that North freely admitted. The Iran-Contra Committee's final report indicated that at the least Meese had bungled badly, though clear questions remained as to the extent of active cover-up. The Iran-Contra special prosecutor, Lawrence E. Walsh, in his final report stated that

Meese had indeed given a legal opinion on arms-for-hostages and that former White House chief of staff Donald Regan had testified under oath that Meese's assertion he was not consulted was false. Walsh believed that Meese was part of a conspiracy both to violate the law and subsequently to disguise that fact, but said that the five-year passage of time since his investigation had begun had rendered proof impossible.

More Investigators. Other independent counsels were named to investigate different matters. At his confirmation hearings in 1984 Meese had promised to sell stock he owned in so-called "Baby Bells," or subsidiaries of American Telephone and Telegraph. Later he was shown to have participated in regulatory meetings that affected the value of the stock from which he continued to draw dividends. In 1986 Meese failed to declare $21,000 in capital gains, calling it an oversight, but some Meese associates said that the attorney general kept meticulous financial records and doubted his self-styled image as a bungler. In 1987 several indictments against various Meese business associates were handed down in the Wedtech scandal. Meese himself was accused of intervening personally to win lucrative defense contracts for his friends. Meese had also placed his investment holdings in a blind trust managed by a Wedtech partner, who subsequently had invested for Meese more money than was in the trust, in effect extending the attorney general an illegal loan. Finally, in what came to be called the Iraqi Pipeline scandal, Meese was investigated for violating the Foreign Corrupt Practices Act after failing to disclose an attempt at bribing a key Israeli official, as detailed to him in a personal memorandum from E. Robert Wallach, who had also figured in the related Wedtech scandal. Meese's response was that he had been so busy he had never gotten around to reading the memo.

Resignation. By 1988, while President Reagan continued to insist that Meese was "a public servant of dedication and integrity," the number two and three men immediately below Meese resigned, saying that their boss had compromised the credibility of the Department of Justice. Other prominent members of the administration urged him to resign for the good of the government, including White House chief of staff Howard Baker, who as a senator had investigated Watergate, and Charles Fried, the solicitor general. Members of the Republican National Committee expressed fears that Meese would jeopardize the party's prospects in November. Even James J. Kilpatrick, the noted conservative journalist and friend of Meese, wrote that the attorney general should resign. Bowing to such pressures, Meese finally did resign, claiming that the special prosecutors had "completely vindicated" him, and returned to California.

Source:
Edwin Meese, *With Reagan: The Inside Story* (Washington, D.C.: Regnery Gateway, 1992).

OLIVER NORTH

1943-

MARINE OFFICER, NATIONAL SECURITY COUNCIL STAFFPERSON

Iran-Contra. Of all the individuals charged in the Iran-Contra scandal none gained more notoriety or prominence than Oliver North, a career marine officer who had been detailed as a staff assistant to the National Security Council (NSC), ironically against his wishes, at the beginning of the first Reagan administration. Fearing at first that this assignment would harm his career, North came to see his work in the NSC as an opportunity to become a central figure in the crusade against communism revived by Reagan. He envisaged a once-in-a-lifetime chance to help set his nation's course straight again in the wake of what he perceived as the erosion of the American creed after Vietnam and Watergate. A former Catholic altar boy, North epitomized the patriot of the "my country right or wrong" variety in opposition to the flabby liberalism he believed responsible for America's decay. As such he was lionized by conservatives, and the image he projected at the Iran-Contra hearings catapulted him into folk-hero status. Yet he was subsequently charged with felonies and came also to symbolize the dangers of ideological zealotry wedded to the considerable power of the presidency. Because he was more than willing to put his — and the president's — personal crusade ahead of the U.S. Constitution, his name became synonymous to many with power's legendary propensity to corrupt. Owing to the legal finesse of his lawyer, however, coupled with his popular support, and the unwillingness of liberals and conservatives either to crucify or to martyr him, North was able to have all charges dropped and to become a wealthy and potent force in the new Christian right.

Background. North was a product of middle-class, small-town America, spending his formative years in the village of Philmont, New York, just south of Albany in the Hudson Valley. The son of a World War II veteran and a strict, religious mother, North has been described as an exceptionally dutiful son and straight-arrow youngster. After spending a year at a state teachers college in 1962, the young North enrolled in a special summer program run by the Marine Corps at Camp Lejeune, North Carolina, after which he applied to and was accepted at the U.S. Naval Academy. Six months into his first, or "plebe," year he was seriously injured in an automobile accident which very nearly derailed his career plans. Placed on probation during his recuperative period, North demonstrated the drive, discipline, and single-mindedness to repair his injuries that would later characterize his work in the NSC. Against great odds North was readmitted to Annapolis where, once back on track for his commission, he drove himself beyond the demanding and stressful pace expected of all midshipmen. "Ollie was all blood, sweat and tears," said one of his classmates, in no small measure because the Naval Academy class of 1968, and especially those opting to become marines, fully expected to go to war.

Vietnam. Graduates of the Naval Academy during the Vietnam War years had more occasion, perhaps, to view themselves as a separate breed than had earlier classes, quite apart from the military traditions and rituals designed for that purpose. As their contemporaries at civilian colleges were taking to the streets to condemn the war and oppose the draft, the professional military underwent a dramatic plunge in prestige unprecedented in American history, and the military found its values under siege. Like many who responded by forming tighter bonds with their comrades-in-arms, North tended to tar all war protest with the brush of disloyalty and anti-Americanism. Feeling unjustly scapegoated for the war, bridling that his patriotism was equated with jingoism, North viewed the antiwar movement as deeply disloyal and symptomatic of a profound political and social malaise. Blaming liberals for this wrong turn, North and many others in the professional military deepened their commitment to what they saw as traditional conservative values and determined that their tours in Vietnam would reflect their devotion to God, country, and duty. In the process they hoped to shame those they labeled "peaceniks" by example.

NSC. North served with distinction in Vietnam, being decorated for valor under fire with the Silver Star, the Bronze Star, and two Purple Hearts. He returned to an America where the military's prestige had all but collapsed, and where the public mood all but negated any future overseas deployments. A warrior without a war, he settled in for barracks life. In the late 1970s he was chosen to attend the Naval War College, where he earned the notice that would cause him to be assigned to the NSC. North resisted this posting at first because he knew that the Marine Corps general staff looked down upon officers who spent too much time in the company of civilian politicians, and he feared the NSC assignment would dim his hopes for further promotion. At the same time, he had been heartened by the election of Ronald Reagan in 1980, who promised to "turn America around." When shortly after his election Reagan declared Vietnam a "noble cause" betrayed by disloyal Americans who had all but made the world safe for communism, North came to believe that he could play some role in returning America to what he believed was her time-honored course. When Reagan indicated that he would do all in his power to overthrow the Marxist Sandinista government in Nicaragua and to stop the leftist insurgency in El Salvador, North threw himself into his new duties with all the enthusiasm of the past.

Secret Work. A workhorse, North initially did much of the scut work in the NSC avoided by others. By dint of long hours and devotion to detail, North made himself the de facto executive of the president's cabinet-level advisory council. The master of all details, North became chief expediter of a covert operation involving the NSC, CIA, Department of Defense, and a private enterprise for profit, the aim of which was to circumvent the will and laws of Congress forbidding the expenditure of public funds to overthrow Nicaragua's government. Two separate amendments to omnibus spending bills (named after their author, Rep. Edward Boland [D–Mass.]) to this effect had been passed and signed, though reluctantly, by President Reagan. Believing their desire to rid the Western Hemisphere of Marxists a better measure of their patriotism than rigid adherence to the law, North and his coconspirators created an "off-the-shelf" program to sell arms to Iran, which the United States had labeled a "terrorist state," and used the proceeds secretly to fund the Nicaraguan Contras. This is what Iran-Contra special prosecutor Lawrence E. Walsh called the "operational conspiracy" not only to violate the Boland Amendments but to defraud the government of the United States as well.

North's Responsibility. When the Iran-Contra scandal broke in the fall of 1986, North was prepared to shoulder the burden of responsibility, because, he said, he believed himself to have been carrying out orders legitimized by presidential authority. But after the infamous press conference of 25 November 1986 wherein Attorney General Edwin Meese declared the affair a "rogue" operation run illegally, North took the Fifth Amendment at every legal proceeding until Congress granted him immunity to testify before its joint special committee investigating the scandal. At the nationally televised hearings North, resplendent in his dress green uniform, combat ribbons prominent, proved himself to be a media superstar. Though his testimony indicated both widespread conspiracy and lawbreaking at the highest levels, North cast himself as a loyal foot soldier serving his commander in chief. Said the colonel, "I'm not in the habit of questioning my superiors . . . if the commander-in-chief tells this lieutenant colonel to go stand in the corner and stand on his head, I will do so." While North's performance was given stellar ratings by the television critics, who immediately dubbed the widespread adulation of North as "Olliemania," this statement was particularly galling to many career military officers who believed they owed their allegiance first to the Constitution, as their oaths of office dictated. As Sen. Daniel Inouye (D–Hawaii), chairman of the Senate committee, said in his final remarks, "members of the military have an obligation to disobey unlawful orders." If North's testimony was true — that both Reagan and Casey had approved the operations, then they, and North, had knowingly violated at least the spirit of the law and the Constitution. North did not deny breaking the law but said he had done so in the name of promoting democracy abroad. Even so, Rep. Henry Hyde, a conservative Republican from Illinois, was moved to say that North's performance was the most stirring patriotic display "since the first time I saw Jimmy Cagney singing 'Yankee Doodle Dandy.'" Syndicated columnist Patrick Buchanan said that North was "a patriotic son of the republic," who, faced with a choice of betraying his cause or lying to Congress, chose the "path of honor."

Bad? or Merely Bad? Was North an overzealous patriot or a Machiavellian plotter? There was much in the public record to cast doubt about his character. While he admitted to lying before Congress and to shredding and falsifying documents to achieve a "higher purpose," his career seems to have been checkered with other untruths as well. Among other things, he failed in his NSC application to disclose a hospitalization for psychiatric reasons shortly after his return from Vietnam. NSC officials said that had they known this they would have denied clearance for North to serve. Many public statements that North made about his service in Vietnam, about his personal relationship with Reagan, about missions and exploits supposedly carried out in Central America, the Falklands, and the Middle East, have been flatly denied by Reagan administration officials and his military superiors. Either North's clandestine operations had a longer history than the Iran-Contra affair or he invented them to bolster his public persona. There is little doubt that North chafed at the debacle of Vietnam. As an anticommunist zealot, he wished to refight that war and recoup on new battlefields the honor lost in Indochina. Blaming liberal lawmakers for abandoning American troops and allies, North rationalized that Congress was the enemy, against whom any maneuver was justified.

On Trial. Shortly after the Iran-Contra hearings ended, North (as well as Adm. John Poindexter, Gen. Richard Secord, and Albert Hakim) was indicted by a federal grand jury in Washington, D.C., charged with sixteen felonies. North was ultimately found guilty on three and ordered to pay heavy fines, which were easily payable given the huge fees he was commanding on the lecture circuit. For a time his Marine Corps pension was jeopardized (he had resigned his commission after being indicted), but that was saved when a federal appeals judge overturned his, and the others', convictions on the grounds that their immunized testimony before Congress could not be used against them in court. No longer bearing the burden of felony convictions, North immediately entered the world of politics, where he set his sights on becoming a United States senator from Virginia.

Sources:

Ben Bradlee Jr., *Guts and Glory: The Rise and Fall of Oliver North* (New York: Donald I. Fine, 1988);

Peter Meyer, *Defiant Patriot: The Life and Exploits of Lt. Colonel Oliver L. North* (New York: St. Martin's Press, 1987);

Oliver L. North, with William L. Novack, *Under Fire: An American Story* (New York: HarperCollins, 1991).

SANDRA DAY O'CONNOR

1930-

SUPREME COURT JUSTICE

Fate Can Be a Strange Thing. Attorney Sandra Day O'Connor, third in her law school class of 102 students, graduated in 1952 from Stanford Law School. That year, as law firm after law firm turned her down since she was a woman, she was finally offered a position as a legal secretary at a firm where a lawyer named William French Smith was a partner. She turned it down. Nearly thirty years later, U.S. Attorney General William French Smith had a hand in recommending her appointment as the first female Supreme Court justice.

A Solid Beginning. Sandra Day was born on 26 March 1930 in El Paso, Texas. Her parents, Harry Day and Ada Mae Wilkey Day, owned a ranch comprising nearly two hundred thousand acres of land on which they raised two thousand cattle. Their home was a simple four-room building made of adobe that did not even have running water until 1937. Sandra learned to be independent early as she was an only child on a remote ranch until the births of her sister, Ann, and brother, Alan, in 1938 and 1939, respectively. She reportedly spent much of her time reading and having her mother read to her from sources such as the *Saturday Evening Post* and the *Wall Street Journal.* When she was five years old, she began living with her maternal grandmother, Mamie Wilkey in El Paso. While school was in session, she attended a private school for most of the next eleven years until graduating from high school at age sixteen. She went on to Stanford University and earned a magna cum laude degree in economics in 1950. Later, while studying at the Stanford Law School, she was inducted into the Order of the Coif and served as a member of the *Stanford Law Review.*

Career Years. Rather than accept a position as a legal secretary, Day went to work as a deputy county attorney in San Mateo, California. The same year that she graduated from Stanford Law School, she married John O'Connor III. When her husband graduated from law school in 1953, he joined the U.S. Army Judge Advocate General Corps and served in Germany for three years. During that time, Sandra Day O'Connor worked as a civilian attorney for the army's quartermaster corps. Upon their return to the United States in 1957, the O'Connors moved to Maricopa County, Arizona. During the next six years they had three sons, and Sandra divided her time between being a full-time mother, going into partnership with another attorney for a short period, and engaging in volunteer work. From 1960 through 1965 she worked in a variety of activities ranging from writing some of the questions for the Arizona bar exam to serving as a member of the Maricopa County Board of Adjustment and Appeals. She also became increasingly involved in local Republican politics. She returned to work in 1965 as an assistant attorney general and in 1969 was appointed to fill an Arizona senate seat being vacated by the incumbent. She thereafter won reelection to two successive terms and in 1972 was elected majority leader of the state senate, the first woman to hold such a position anywhere in the country.

The Call of the Judiciary. In 1974 O'Connor ran for and won an election as a judge on the Maricopa County Superior Court. Although Republican leaders urged her in 1978 to run for governor, she declined and continued to serve as a judge. In 1979 Bruce Babbitt, the Democratic governor, appointed her as a judge on the Arizona Court of Appeals, where she worked on a wide range of legal matters for the next twenty-one months. On 19 August 1981 President Ronald Reagan nominated her to the U.S. Supreme Court seat being vacated by retiring Justice Potter Stewart. On 26 September 1981 the U.S. Senate confirmed her nomination by a vote of 99–0. Although initially thought to be a conservative vote on the court, Justice O'Connor has come to be regarded as more of a swing vote and has in fact voted with both the conservative and the liberal justices on various 5–4 margins during the years. No one, however, questions her commitment. In 1988 she was diagnosed with breast cancer, had surgery, and returned to the bench only ten days later, without missing any work.

Source:
Peter W. Huber, *Sandra Day O'Connor* (New York: Chelsea House, 1990).

SAMUEL RILEY PIERCE JR.

1922-

SECRETARY OF HOUSING AND URBAN DEVELOPMENT, 1981-1989

A Lone Black. Samuel Pierce was the only black cabinet member during the Reagan presidency, and the only one to serve the full eight years. Chosen because of his race, strong civil rights credentials, and his prior government experience, Pierce expected to improve management at the Department of Housing and Urban Development while also working to retain housing projects of vital importance to the nation's poor against Reagan's fiscal cuts. Instead, Pierce's tenure ended with his competency and integrity in question and with the department engulfed in scandal.

Background. Born on 8 September 1922 in Glen Cove, New York, Pierce was the oldest of three sons born to a groundskeeper at the upper-class Nassau Country Club on Long Island. His father used the connections he had developed to establish a valet service for the club's members and eventually earned enough to invest successfully in real estate. Prior to the New Deal the majority of black Americans were Republicans, loyal to the party of Lincoln. Their father's success in business drove home the virtues of self-reliance, ambition, and political awareness among the Pierce sons. A star athlete, Pierce won an academic scholarship to Cornell University but dropped out in 1943 to serve in the U.S. Army, where he became one of the few blacks to be trained as an officer. Leaving the military at the end of the war with the rank of first lieutenant, he finished his undergraduate degree and attended Cornell's law school. He subsequently earned an LL.M from New York University and was a Ford Foundation Fellow at Yale University Law School. After serving as Manhattan district attorney and as U.S. attorney in New York, Pierce entered the Eisenhower administration as the first black to hold the post of assistant to the undersecretary of labor. He then became an associate counsel to the House Judiciary Committee. During the 1960s Pierce became the first black partner in a major New York law firm and the first black to serve on the board of a Fortune 500 company. He joined a team of lawyers assisting Martin Luther King Jr. and later was a principal founder of the Freedom National Bank, the first black-owned bank in New York State.

Treasury Department. Though most civil rights activists were Democrats, Pierce remained loyal to the Republican Party of his upbringing, becoming a leading member of the Committee of Black Americans for Nixon-Agnew in 1968. For that he was rewarded with the post of general counsel to the Department of the Treasury, helping to draw up the Nixon administration's wage-price freeze. When Ronald Reagan was looking for a member of a minority group for secretary of the Department of Housing and Urban Development (HUD), he turned to Pierce. Knowing that Reagan had campaigned to cut social programs, he preferred to be secretary of labor or attorney general, but was persuaded by Reagan personally to take the HUD position. At his confirmation hearings he promised that those programs of most importance to the poor would not be cut, only the most egregious waste. But Pierce also echoed Reagan's "trickle-down" rhetoric when he said that "the fact is that reliance on government hasn't worked and it's time to try something new. The fact is that revitalizing the economy will help everyone . . . and the poor have the most to gain." Within months Pierce backed severe cuts in the Section 8 basic housing program, while also proposing to make such residents pay more of their limited income in rent. He nevertheless succeeded in blocking cuts in the Urban Development Action Programs, keeping $500 million available to stimulate private investmentin downtown rehabilitation projects. Criticizing previous HUD secretaries, Pierce claimed that there was little administrative efficiency at the department and launched a massive collection program to reduce the $1.8 billion in debts owed to HUD.

Silent Sam. Unlike other cabinet members, Pierce remained in the background of the Reagan administration, and was dubbed "silent Sam" for his relative invisibility. By the end of his tenure, however, this moniker had acquired new meaning when, his department engulfed in scandal, Pierce pleaded the Fifth Amendment when called before Congress to testify about corruption, influence peddling, and kickbacks that had been previously uncovered in HUD. As government lawyers sought to make sense of the widening scandal, the key question was whether Pierce was a lax administrator despite his promises to improve efficiency or at the heart of a giant conspiracy to defraud taxpayers and reward Republican Party contributors.

Stockman's Warning. The first revelations of abuse came as early as 1981 when former budget director David Stockman warned that the "hogs were really feeding" throughout the Reagan administration. By the mid 1980s HUD's own general counsel began to indicate that something was amiss, yet he was ignored. It was not until late 1987 that the press began to close in on the story, which consisted at first of fairly commonplace allegations of kickbacks in HUD, but before long an avalanche of charges came forth from every corner of the nation, indicating a clear pattern suggestive of conspiracy. By 1989 more than 630 separate criminal investigations would be opened against HUD. In an agency ostensibly founded to assist the poorest Americans, government lawyers uncovered numerous instances where tax monies benefited the wealthiest. While the Federal Housing Administration and its mortgage-guarantee agents suffered more than $90 million in defaulted loans on projects intended to house the poor, it was found to be subsidizing luxury condominiums and golf courses. All across the country, Republican insiders were provided with loans and rent subsidies for projects not needed, and when those projects failed, the American taxpayers were stuck with the default bill. HUD spent more than $3 billion to build eighty thousand houses that ultimately had to be foreclosed upon and sold by agents who were supposed to deduct their fees and submit the remainder to HUD. Most fees were shown to be hyperinflated, and in some cases agents pocketed the principal as well. One notorious agent dubbed "Robin HUD" by the press walked off with $5.5 million. With a budget of $20 billion designed to be awarded in contracts, HUD had always been open to corruption, but the scandals unearthed in the late 1980s were so extensive that the press spoke of a "feeding frenzy" on the part of connected Republicans to cash in at the trough. James Watt, the disgraced former secretary of the interior, collected $400,000 in one fee simply for picking up the telephone and making a connection for a friend. By last accounting the total damage to taxpayers was estimated at $8 billion, rivaling the losses in the savings-and-loan scandals.

Despair. All of this was laid at the feet of Samuel Pierce. Rep. Tom Lantos (D–Cal.) said that while Pierce claimed to be fighting bureaucratic inefficiency, he realized early on that this was a hopeless cause and so instead "milked" the system for himself, his cronies, and connected Republicans. Pierce retorted by claiming that he was unaware of what was happening, yet one columnist answered that the secretary would have to have been "an embalmed corpse" not to know. Some of Pierce's immediate subordinates in HUD testified that all was known at the top. Deborah Gore Dean, Pierce's administrative assistant, who was found guilty of fraud and conspiracy and sentenced to five years in prison, declared that HUD was a "system of spoils and favoritism," while Dubois Gilliam, one of HUD's highest administrators, also jailed and testifying before Congress on furlough from prison, said that orders had come down from above. In the end, investigations into possible criminal activity on the part of Pierce found that while the secretary had allowed loans to projects not meeting guidelines, approved administrative pay raises and jobs for political favorites, and allowed tax breaks for the wealthy and fat fees to influential Republicans, there was "no proof" of outright theft or intent to defraud.

Inefficiency. Despite being the only member of Reagan's cabinet to serve for two full presidential terms, Samuel Pierce left office under a cloud, his reputation in question. At the least, HUD's record during Pierce's tenure undermined the Republicans' creed and their claim to be rigorously efficient in their efforts to curb what they called the waste and profligacy of previous Democratic administrations.

CLAUS VON BULOW

1926–

MAN ACCUSED OF MURDER

A Privileged Life. Claus von Bulow began life as Claus Cecil Borberg in Copenhagen, Denmark. His father was a playwright, and his mother was a descendant of a prominent and wealthy German family, the von Bulows. His parents were divorced when he was four, and Claus was raised by his mother. Claus, who took his mother's name as his surname, entered Cambridge University at the age of sixteen and graduated after World War II with a degree in law. Von Bulow apprenticed with British barrister (an English attorney) Quintin Hogg. He later worked for billionaire J. Paul Getty, rising to become one of Getty's chief assistants. In 1966 he married Sunny von Auersperg after her divorce from Prince Alfred Eduard Friedrich Vincenz Martin Maria von Auersperg. In 1967 they had a daughter, Cosima, who was their only child. This idyllic existence continued until after Cosima's birth, when Sunny apparently became no longer interested in sex. As a result, von Bulow sought affection elsewhere. In 1978 he began an affair with a soap-opera actress named Alexandra Isles who insisted in mid 1979 that he divorce his wife and marry her. The events that followed led to what at the time was known as the trial of the decade.

The Comas. Sunny von Bulow nearly died on 27 December 1979. Her husband's actions during the time that Sunny was unconcious and apparently in a coma made Sunny's maid and loyal friend, Maria Schrallhammer, suspicious. When Maria could not wake Sunny, normally a light sleeper, Claus shrugged it off as a case of his wife imbibing too much alcohol the night before. Claus initially refused to call a doctor or Sunny's mother as the maid requested. Later that day, Maria saw Claus rushing to the telephone to call the doctor, who got to the house just in time to perform cardiopulmonary resuscitation and save Sunny's life. During 1980 Sunny had several more episodes of illness that the maid found to be suspicious, but none turned out to be serious. Sunny was eventually diagnosed as suffering from severe reactive hypoglycemia, a condition that causes low blood sugar after eating sugary substances. During this period the maid also stumbled across a mysterious black bag that contained insulin, Valium paste, and a powder that turned out to be secobarbital, a barbiturate. Just before Christmas 1980, the von Bulows traveled to the family home, but Claus instructed the maid to stay in New York because she might get tired and catch the flu. The maid once again saw the black bag but said nothing of her suspicions that Claus was poisoning Sunny. After arriving at the estate and having something to eat, Sunny appeared to be weak and was assisted into bed by her son from her first marriage, Alex. The next morning Sunny was found on the floor in the bathroom and an ambu-

lance was called. A few minutes after arriving at the hospital she went into cardiac arrest and needed to be revived. She never awoke from the coma. Tests at the hospital showed that Sunny had an extremely high concentration of insulin in her blood. Her children by her first marriage, Alex and Ala, now suspected Claus of having attempted to kill their mother in order to inherit her fortune and be free to see other women. They obtained the black bag, which contained an insulin-encrusted needle, and went to the authorities.

Trials and Tribulations. On 6 July 1981 von Bulow was indicted by a grand jury and charged with two counts of assault with intent to commit murder for the two times his wife had lapsed into a coma. On 16 March 1982 a jury found him guilty of both counts, mainly because of the testimony of the maid as well as the doctor who almost literally wrote the book on blood sugar and insulin's effect on it. On 7 May 1982 he was sentenced to thirty years in prison but posted a $1 million bail, pending an appeal. After the defense, led by well-known attorney and Harvard law professor Alan Dershowitz, and the prosecution each filed their one-hundred-page briefs, the state supreme court reversed the convictions based upon new or undisclosed evidence that might tend to show von Bulow's innocence. The court also declared that the police should have obtained a search warrant prior to sending pills from the black bag to the state police lab for testing. On 5 January 1985 the state of Rhode Island announced that it would try von Bulow once again. His second trial began on 25 April 1985 and lasted until 10 June. Based in large part upon new evidence that the insulin found on the needle could not have been residue from an injection (the human skin acts as a swab and wipes a needle clean as it is withdrawn from the body) and evidence that a bottle of insulin was not initially found in the black bag as the first jury had been told, von Bulow was acquitted on both counts of attempted murder.

Source:
Alan Dershowitz, *Reversal of Fortune: Inside the Von Bulow Case* (New York: Random House, 1986).

PEOPLE IN THE NEWS

In January 1987 **Hector Escudero Aponte,** a maintenance worker at the Dupont Plaza Hotel in San Juan, Puerto Rico, was arraigned on ninety-six counts of murder as the result of a deadly fire at the hotel. The fire was apparently started as the result of an ongoing labor dispute. On 22 June 1987 Aponte and two accomplices were sentenced to terms ranging from seventy-five to ninety-nine years in prison for these homicides.

In October 1989 televangelist **Jim Bakker** was convicted of fraud and conspiracy in federal district court in Charlotte, North Carolina.

In November 1984 **Margie Velma Barfield** became the first woman put to death in the United States in twenty-two years. She had been convicted of murdering her fiancé and three other people, including her mother.

In August 1988 U.S. Rep. **Mario Biaggi** of New York was found guilty of racketeering, conspiracy, and extortion in what had become known as the Wedtech scandal. Biaggi had received Wedtech stock worth about $1.8 million in return for lobbying on the company's behalf.

In June 1986 star basketball player **Len Bias,** who had recently been drafted by the world champion Boston Celtics, collapsed and died in his dormitory in College Park, Maryland, as the result of a physical condition brought on by the use of cocaine.

In June 1981 former Tennessee governor **Ray Blanton** was found guilty of extortion, conspiracy, and mail fraud for accepting over $23,000 in bribes in a plan to sell liquor licenses to friends.

In August 1981 **Christopher John Boyce,** a convicted spy and prison escapee, was captured near Seattle, Washington, after a nineteen-month manhunt.

In June 1986 President Ronald Reagan announced that Chief Justice **Warren Burger** would be retiring from the Supreme Court, which he had served on for the previous seventeen years.

In June 1981 former secretary of agriculture **Earl Butz** was sentenced to thirty days in jail and a $10,000 fine for filing a false federal income tax return.

In December 1985 **Paul Castellano,** age seventy and reputed to be one of the main leaders of organized crime in the United States, was shot to death in New York City. He and an associate were slain as they were preparing to enter a restaurant in midtown Manhattan.

In March 1988 **Robert Chambers Jr.,** who had been charged in the death of **Jennifer Levin** in New York City, changed his plea during the ninth day of jury deliberations and pleaded guilty to first-degree manslaughter. He admitted that he had intended to injure Levin and had caused her death during what was termed "rough sex." Under the plea-bargain arrangement, he would serve at least five years in prison.

In March 1981 **Joseph William Coyle,** age twenty-six, was arrested at New York's Kennedy Airport for stealing money that had fallen from an armored truck a week before. The amount that fell off of the truck was $1.2 million dollars.

In July 1980 **Charles Dederich,** the founder of Synanon, the drug-rehabilitation organization, and two of its members pleaded no contest to charges that they had conspired to commit murder by planting a rattlesnake in the mailbox of a lawyer who had sued Synanon on behalf of former members of the group who had contended that they were kept in the group against their will.

In August 1984 **John DeLorean,** developer of the DeLorean automobile, was found not guilty of charges that he conspired to distribute cocaine worth $24 million dollars. Some jurors later stated that they felt he had been entrapped by government agents disguised as drug dealers during a period when he was trying to save his failing automobile company in Ireland.

In April 1985 convicted rapist **Gary Dodson** was briefly freed on bail from his twenty-five-to-fifty-year sentence when his accuser recanted her testimony. His accuser, **Kathleen Webb,** stated in an affidavit that she had made up the story in 1977 because she had become pregnant by her boyfriend at the time. She claimed to have simply picked Dodson's photograph from a file of mug shots. The judge chose not to believe Webb and sent Dodson back to jail; however, he was later freed when the governor of Illinois commuted his sentence on 12 May.

In December 1980 **Bernadette Dohrn,** age thirty-eight, surrendered to authorities ten years after going underground to escape riot charges resulting from Chicago's "Days of Rage" demonstration in 1969. She received three years probation and a $1,500 fine.

In August 1987 thirty-five-year-old hospital worker **Donald Harvey** pleaded guilty to killing twenty-four people by poisoning, twenty-one of them at the Daniel Drake Memorial Hospital in Middletown, Ohio. An investigation occurred when an autopsy showed that one patient died of a lethal dose of cyanide. Harvey was sentenced to three consecutive life terms in prison.

In July 1981 **Joseph George Helmich** was arrested by the FBI and charged with selling sophisticated encoding equipment to Soviet officials.

In April 1981 former Yippie and counterculture leader **Abbie Hoffman** was sentenced to up to three years in prison for selling $36,000 in cocaine to undercover policemen in 1973. He surrendered in 1980 after spending six years underground.

In August 1986 the Soviet press agency TASS reported that former CIA agent **Edward Howard** had been granted political asylum in the Soviet Union. Howard had been dismissed from the CIA in 1983 after failing a lie-detector test.

In May 1980 White House Chief of Staff **Hamilton Jordan** was cleared of cocaine-use charges when a special grand jury concluded that there was insufficient evidence to sustain an indictment.

In May 1980 **Vernon Jordan Jr.,** president of the National Urban League and a respected black civil rights leader, was shot and critically injured but survived an assassination attempt in Fort Wayne, Indiana.

In April 1980 former United States budget director **Bert Lance** was acquitted after a sixteen-week trial of nine counts of bank fraud.

In May 1987 Hollywood director **John Landis** and four others were found not guilty of criminal charges resulting from the deaths in 1982 of actor **Vic Morrow** and two children during the filming of the movie "Twilight Zone." The deaths occurred when an explosive caused the crash of a helicopter, which struck and killed the three people.

In December 1988 perennial fringe presidential candidate **Lyndon LaRouche** was convicted of conspiracy and mail fraud. He and six others were found guilty of charges related to improper solicitation of loans by his organization. He was sentenced to fifteen years in prison.

In December 1983 former EPA official **Rita Lavelle** was found guilty of committing perjury and of obstructing a congressional investigation regarding her knowledge that a former employer had dumped hazardous waste at a California disposal site.

In December 1980 **John Lennon,** a founding member of the Beatles, was shot dead outside his New York apartment by **Mark David Chapman,** a deranged fan.

In March 1980 former U.S. representative **Allard Lowenstein** was shot and killed in his New York City law office. He had been the main architect of the 1968 antiwar movement to block the renomination of President **Lyndon Johnson** for a second term. The gunman was later identified as **Dennis Sweeney,** a former associate of Lowenstein's in the civil rights movement. Sweeney was later found not responsible for the killing due to mental illness.

In June 1985 it was announced that the search for **Dr. Josef Mengele,** the Nazi war criminal known as the "Angel of Death," who had been wanted for the torture and murder of inmates at the Auschwitz concentration camp, had come to a conclusion. Forensic scientists declared that his remains had been found in a grave in São Paulo, Brazil, and had been positively identified as being his remains. Mengele reportedly drowned in 1979 and was buried under the name of Wolfgang Gerhard.

In October 1984 FBI agent **Richard Miller,** an agent for twenty years, was arrested on espionage charges, the first FBI agent ever to be so charged. He was convicted on bribery and espionage charges on 19 June 1986.

In June 1986 **Jonathan J. Pollard** pleaded guilty to his involvement in an espionage conspiracy on behalf of Israel. His wife, Ann Henderson Pollard, also pleaded guilty to conspiring to receive embezzled government property and possession of national defense documents.

In January 1989 **Patrick Edward Purdy,** a former student at the Cleveland Elementary School in Stockton, California, returned to the school grounds, killing five students and wounding twenty-nine others and a teacher. He then committed suicide with a pistol.

In September 1989 **Richard Ramirez,** the so-called California "Night Stalker," was convicted of the serial-killing murders of several of his victims.

In August 1989 baseball legend **Pete Rose** was banned from the game for life. Commissioner **A. Bartlett Giamatti** had concluded that Rose had gambled on baseball games, including games involving the Cincinnati Reds while Rose had been the manager of the team.

In August 1986 postal worker **Patrick Sherrill** killed fourteen coworkers at the Edmund, Oklahoma, post office and wounded seven others. He reportedly had received a verbal reprimand the previous day from a supervisor. He then committed suicide.

In January 1989 former criminal lawyer **Joel Steinberg** was found guilty in New York City of the first-degree manslaughter death by beating of his six-year-old, illegally adopted daughter, Lisa. The details of the case drew nationwide attention to the ongoing problems of child abuse.

In October 1980 **Cathlyn Platt Wilkerson,** age thirty-five, was sentenced in New York for illegal possession of dynamite as the result of a Greenwich Village explosion in 1970 that killed three persons. She was sentenced to nine months for her part in the 1969 "Days of Rage" disturbances.

In June 1981 **Wayne B. Williams** was arrested in Atlanta, Georgia, for the serial murders of twenty black children and young adults. He was later convicted on several counts of murder in connection with these deaths.

DEATHS

Emile Z. Berman, 78, trial lawyer who defended Sirhan Sirhan, who murdered Robert F. Kennedy, 3 July 1981.

William Anthony Boyle, 81, United Mine Workers president from 1963 to 1972 who was convicted in 1974 of ordering the murder of union rival Joseph A. Yablonski and members of his family, 31 May 1985.

Roy M. Cohn, 59, socialite lawyer who served as an aide to Sen. Joseph McCarthy during his Senate subcommittee investigations in the early 1950s into communist subversion, 2 August 1986.

Earl B. Dickerson, 95, lawyer and civil rights leader, 1 September 1986.

William O. Douglas, 80, longest-serving United States Supreme Court justice, 19 January 1980.

Clinton T. Duffy, 84, warden of San Quentin Prison from 1940 to 1952, 11 October 1982.

Sam J. Ervin Jr., 88, Democratic senator from North Carolina from 1954 to 1975 who directed the Senate Watergate investigation, 23 April 1985.

Abe Fortas, 71, associate justice of the United States Supreme Court from 1965 to 1969 who resigned in the wake of allegations about his association with financiers of questionable reputation, 5 April 1982.

Clement F. Haynsworth Jr., 77, federal judge whose nomination to the United States Supreme Court in 1969 was rejected by the Senate, 22 November 1989.

Julius J. Hoffman, 88, federal judge who presided over the trial of the Chicago Seven, the radicals who were accused of inciting riots at the 1968 Democratic National Convention, 1 July 1983.

Leon Jaworski, 77, special Watergate prosecutor who led the investigation that led to the resignation of President Richard M. Nixon, 9 December 1982.

Albert E. Jenner Jr., 72, lawyer who participated in the investigation of John F. Kennedy's assassination and in the Watergate investigation of Richard M. Nixon, 18 September 1988.

Clarence Mitchell, 72, lobbyist for the National Association for the Advancement of Colored People from 1950 to 1978, 18 March 1984.

John N. Mitchell, 75, United States attorney general in the Nixon administration who was the only man in this office ever to be convicted of a felony, 9 November 1988.

Clarence Norris, 76, last surviving of the Scottsboro Boys, who became symbols of civil rights violations in the South after they were, many said, falsely accused of rape in 1931, 23 January 1989.

Jackie Presser, 62, Teamsters union president, 9 July 1988.

Anthony Provenzano, 71, mafia leader, 12 December 1988.

James H. Rowe, 65, attorney and adviser to President Franklin Roosevelt, 17 June 1984.

Willie Sutton, 79, notorious bank robber who stole some $2 million in his thirty-five-year career and spent thirty-three years in jail, 2 November 1980.

PUBLICATIONS

David Abramsen, *Confessions of Son of Sam* (New York: Columbia University Press, 1985);

Shana Alexander, *Very Much a Lady* (Boston: Little, Brown, 1983);

Tim Cahill, *Buried Dreams: Inside the Mind of a Serial Killer* (New York: Bantam, 1989);

Deborah Cameron and Elizabeth Frazer, *The Lust to Kill* (New York: New York University Press, 1987);

Alan Dershowitz, *Reversal of Fortune: Inside the Von Bulow Case* (New York: Random House, 1986);

Dominick J. Di Maio and Vincent J. Di Maio, *Forensic Pathology* (New York: Elsevier/Nelson, 1989);

J. H. H. Gaute and Robin Odell, *The New Murderers' Who's Who* (New York: International Polygonics, 1989);

Robert W. Greene, *The Sting Man: Inside ABSCAM* (New York: Dutton, 1981);

Jean Harris, *Stranger in Two Worlds* (New York: Zebra Books, 1986);

Ronald Holmes and James De Burger, *Serial Murder* (Newbury Park, Cal.: Sage, 1988);

Elizabeth Kendall, *The Phantom Prince: My Life with Ted Bundy* (Seattle: Madrona, 1981);

Jack Levin and James Alan Fox, *Mass Murder: America's Growing Menace* (New York: Plenum, 1988);

Elliott Leyton, *Hunting Humans: Inside the Minds of Mass Murderers* (New York: Pocket Books, 1986);

Lillian B. Rubin, *Quiet Rage: Bernie Goetz in a Time of Madness* (New York: Farrar, Straus & Giroux, 1986);

Ted Schwarz, *The Hillside Strangler: A Murderer's Mind* (Garden City, N.Y.: Doubleday, 1981);

Carl Sifakis, *The Encyclopedia of American Crime* (New York: Facts On File, 1982);

Terry Sullivan and Peter Maiken, *Killer Clown* (New York: Grosset & Dunlap, 1983);

Mike Taibbi and Anna Sims-Phillips, *Unholy Alliances: Working the Tawana Brawley Story* (New York: Harcourt Brace Jovanovich, 1989);

Maury Terry, *The Ultimate Evil: An Investigation into a Dangerous Satanic Cult* (New York: Bantam, 1989);

Ronald Tobias, *They Shoot To Kill* (Boulder, Colo.: Paladin Press, 1981);

Colin Wilson and Donald Seaman, *Encyclopedia of Modern Murder* (New York: Arlington House, 1988).

CHAPTER EIGHT

LIFESTYLES AND SOCIAL TRENDS

by KENNETH GRAHAM and DARREN HARRIS-FAIN

CONTENTS

Sidebars and tables are listed in italics.

1980

- An estimated 1.1 million Americans live together out of wedlock, and an estimated 25 percent of these households include children.

- A survey finds that although smoking has dropped among men, women, and teenage boys during the last ten years, smoking among teenage girls has increased by more than 50 percent.

- Rum outsells vodka in the United States and outsells whiskey for the first time since the nineteenth century.

- Opposition to President Jimmy Carter grows as inflation continues to rise. Ronald Reagan and George Bush win the presidential and vice-presidential elections on 4 November after basing their campaign on supply-side economics and a promise to reduce the size of government.

4 Jan.   Bert Parks is relieved of his duties as master of ceremonies for the Miss America pageant after twenty-five years.

22 Jan.   The National Urban League issues a report saying that the 1970s were a time of "retreat, retrenchment and lost opportunities" for black Americans.

4 Feb.   A Census Bureau study estimates that there are between 3.5 million and 4 million illegal aliens living in the United States.

1 Mar.   More than a thousand people attend a national Conference on a Black Agenda for the 1980s in Richmond, Virginia, and call for the election of more black public officials.

7 May   Rioting breaks out in black neighborhoods in Miami after an all-white jury acquits four police officers who had been charged with beating an African American insurance executive to death. In the wake of the rioting Miami is declared a disaster area.

22 July   Racial strife erupts in Chattanooga, Tennessee, after two Ku Klux Klansmen are acquitted in the random shootings of four black women.

25 Sept.   The thirty-story, fourteen-hundred-room Grand Hyatt Hotel opens in New York City. Owned by thirty-four-year-old Queens developer Donald Trump, the hotel features a mirrored glass facade and an atrium four stories high.

21 Nov.   An estimated 83 million Americans — the largest audience for a television program in history — tune in to the CBS prime-time soap opera *Dallas* to find out the answer to the question "Who Shot J. R.?"

A fire sweeps through the M-G-M Grand Hotel in Las Vegas, killing eighty-four people and injuring hundreds of others.

1981

- AIDS (acquired immunodeficiency syndrome) begins to take a worldwide toll and is found to be more widely spread among homosexual males and drug addicts who share needles.

- Kellogg introduces Nutri-Grain wheat cereal, one of its many healthy breakfast foods to be marketed during the decade. Later introductions include Just Right (1987) and Common Sense Oat Bran (1988).

30 Jan.   Millions of New Yorkers attend a ticker-tape parade to honor the American hostages released by Iran.

1982

23 Feb. The 1980 U.S. census reports that the black and Hispanic population grew at a faster rate than the overall U.S. population during the 1970s.

23 May The U.S. Census Bureau reports that the number of Americans older than sixty-five grew by 28 percent compared to an 11 percent general population growth during the 1970s.

17 July Two aerial walkways collapse in the Hyatt Regency Hotel in Kansas City, Missouri, killing eleven people and injuring nearly two hundred.

22 Aug. The Kinsey Institute releases a major study announcing that homosexuality is a deep-rooted predisposition, perhaps inborn.

1 Sept. A study released by the Equal Employment Opportunity Commission finds that women's earnings remain about 60 percent of men's earnings in comparable jobs.

21 Sept. Appointed by President Reagan, Sandra Day O'Connor is the first woman confirmed to the U.S. Supreme Court.

- Reebok aerobic shoes, introduced in fashion colors, overtake Nike running shoes in sales.

- Rubik's Cube, a puzzle for which the solution proves frustrating and even obsessive for many, sells wildly in the United States and in other countries.

- Unemployment reaches its highest rate in more than forty years, and the number of Americans living below the poverty line is the highest in seventeen years.

6 Jan. Thirty-nine thousand supporters of the Equal Rights Amendment demonstrate in four states that are key to the amendment's passage in an attempt to beat the 30 June ratification deadline.

13 Jan. After taking off from National Airport in Washington, D.C., a Boeing 737 crashes into the city's 14th Street bridge. Only five of the seventy-nine passengers are rescued.

15 Mar. The city of Kennesaw, Georgia, passes an ordinance that requires the head of every household to "maintain a firearm and ammunition."

12 June A peace rally in New York City that coincides with a United Nations special session on disarmament draws between 500,000 and 750,000 participants.

30 June The Equal Rights Amendment misses the deadline for ratification after it fails to get the support of three more states; thirty-five state legislatures had already voted in favor of the amendment.

5 Oct. After seven people die in the Chicago area in late September from taking Extra-Strength Tylenol capsules laced with cyanide, Johnson & Johnson recalls the product. Tylenol is reintroduced in triple-safety-sealed packages and within a year regains most of its consumer sales.

14 Oct. President Reagan announces a war on drugs. A report estimates that more than 25 million Americans smoke marijuana, spending about $24 billion on the substance.

13 Nov. In Washington, D.C., 150,000 observers witness the dedication of the Vietnam Veterans Memorial.

1983

- First Lady Nancy Reagan begins a nationwide program to combat drug abuse and uses the slogan "Just Say No."

- U.S. soft-drink companies begin using NutraSweet artificial sweetener in diet beverages.

1 Jan. The Census Bureau reports that the U.S. population numbers well over 200 million at the start of the new year.

24 Feb. A congressional committee concludes that the World War II internment of more than one hundred thousand Japanese Americans was an injustice caused by a "long and ugly history of racism" and "failure of political leadership."

15 June In three decisions, the U.S. Supreme Court limits the power of state and local governments to restrict access to legal abortions.

8 Aug. A federal jury awards $500,000 to female newscaster Christine Craft, who claimed that the owners of KMBC in Kansas City considered her "too old, unattractive, and not deferential enough to men."

27 Aug. More than 250,000 participants rally in Washington, D.C., to commemorate the twentieth anniversary of the March on Washington for civil rights, at which Martin Luther King Jr. made his famous "I Have a Dream" speech.

17 Oct. *The New York Times* announces that the video-game craze of the early 1980s is over.

Nov. Cabbage Patch Kids are the year's must-have Christmas toys, prompting long lines and short tempers at stores around the country.

20 Nov. Approximately 100 million people view *The Day After,* an ABC television movie about the aftermath of nuclear war.

Dec. After the Federal Communications Commission (FCC) authorizes placement of low-power transmitters throughout the city, Chicago motorists talk on cellular telephones available for $3,000 plus $150-per-month service fees.

1984

- U.S. economic growth rises to a rate of 6.8 percent, the highest rate since 1951.

- The board game Trivial Pursuit is introduced into U.S. stores by a Canadian entrepreneur and revitalizes the board-game industry.

17 Jan. The U.S. Commission on Civil Rights renounces the use of numerical quotas for promotion of black workers and executives, releasing a statement saying that "such racial preferences merely constitute another form of unjustified discrimination" that "offends the constitutional principle of equal protection of the law for all citizens."

15 Mar. A jury awards a woman $390,000 when she sues a Church of Christ congregation that publicly condemned her for the sin of "fornication."

7 Apr. Los Angeles surpasses Chicago as the second most populous city in the United States. New York City remains first.

9 Apr. San Francisco public-health director Mervyn Silverman announces a controversial plan to curb sexual activity in the city's bath houses, which are popular meeting places for homosexuals.

16 Apr.   A two-year study of religious television reports that more than 13 million Americans watch religious television programming on a regular basis.

1 May   A report by the Department of Housing and Urban Development estimates the nation's homeless population as numbering between 250,000 and 350,000. Many other national organizations claim that there are actually ten times that many homeless Americans.

10 May   The United Methodist Church passes legislation barring practicing homosexuals from the ministry.

7 June   The House of Representatives passes legislation to cut federal highway funds to any state with an alcoholic-beverage drinking age below twenty-one.

11 July   The Olympic committees of six Asian and African nations report that their athletes received death threats from the Ku Klux Klan in the United States. The Summer Olympic Games open in Los Angeles on 28 July.

23 July   Vanessa Williams becomes the first Miss America to resign in the sixty-three-year history of the pageant when *Penthouse* magazine announces that it will publish nude pictures of her.

17 Aug.   The U.S. Court of Appeals holds that "private, consensual homosexual conduct is not constitutionally protected," thus affirming the U.S. Navy's right to dismiss homosexuals automatically.

25 Sept.   Texas billionaire Ross Perot buys a seven-hundred-year-old copy of the Magna Carta — one of only seventeen copies in existence — for $1.5 million and donates it to the National Archives in Washington, D.C.

11 Oct.   Brown University undergraduates vote to request that the campus health service "stockpile suicide pills for optional student use exclusively in the event of nuclear war."

22 Nov.   About one-third of homosexual men in San Francisco respond in a survey that they continue to practice unsafe sex despite the danger of AIDS.

1985

- After noting that more than 80 percent of athletic shoes are bought for fashionable attire as opposed to strict athletic use, Robert Greenberg closes his L.A. Gear athletic apparel store and begins importing Korean-made fashion sneakers to sell under the L.A. Gear name.

- A group of American rock and pop stars organize under the name U.S.A. for Africa to record "We Are the World." Sales of the single raise approximately $50 million for African famine relief.

- Crack — crystallized cocaine that can be smoked to produce a short but intense high — is introduced into the United States. Abuse of the drug is blamed for criminal and violent offenses, especially in urban areas, during the next years.

11 Jan.   Meeting in Reno, Nevada, a council of Native American leaders overwhelmingly votes to reject a White House commission's proposed program for increasing private enterprise on Native American reservations.

14 Jan.   In an effort to slow the influx of illegal aliens into the United States, the Justice Department announces that more than sixty immigrants have been arrested in roundups across the nation.

16 Jan.   The National Urban League reports that the Reagan administration's record on black concerns is "deplorable."

17 Jan.   A U.S. district court orders the Central Intelligence Agency (CIA) to reinstate an employee who was fired "as a security risk" because of his homosexuality.

22 Jan.   President Reagan speaks to antiabortion marchers in Washington, D.C., telling them, "I feel a great solidarity with all of you."

15 Feb.   According to an Electronic Industries Association report, 98 percent of U.S. households have at least one television, 24 percent have video games, and 13 percent have videocassette recorders.

26 Feb.   A panel of doctors and public-health officials concludes that hunger has reached epidemic proportions in the United States. Twenty million Americans go hungry at least two days a month, and the problem is worsening because of cuts in federal food programs.

23 Apr.   Coca-Cola announces that it is replacing its ninety-nine-year-old formula with a sweeter-tasting formula. Protests induce the company into reintroducing the old formula under the name Coca-Cola Classic later in the year.

13 May   More than two blocks of homes in Philadelphia burn to the ground, killing eleven people and leaving approximately two hundred homeless, when police firebomb a house in an attempt to dislodge armed members of the radical African American group MOVE.

15 May   According to a U.S. Census Bureau report, a March 1984 survey finds that one-fourth of all U.S. families with children have only one parent present.

4 June   The U.S. Supreme Court affirms a federal appellate ruling against an Alabama law authorizing a one-minute period of silence in public schools "for meditation or voluntary prayer."

11 June   The Presbyterian Church (U.S.A.) approves a statement that abortion is in some cases a "responsible choice within a Christian ethical framework."

13 July   Live Aid, an all-star concert telethon held simultaneously in Philadelphia and London to benefit African famine victims, becomes the most-watched television program in history when it is televised in more than one hundred countries, attracts approximately 1.5 billion viewers, and raises more than $40 million in pledges.

5 Aug.   The Recording Industry Association of America announces that nineteen leading record companies will begin using a parental advisory label on popular music albums and cassettes that contain "blatant explicit lyric content."

14 Aug.   Reports surface that White House aides have drafted an executive order that would free federal contractors from meeting numerical quotas for the hiring of women and minorities.

9 Sept.   Approximately twelve thousand New York City children are kept home by their parents when the city permits an AIDS-infected seven-year-old girl to attend public-school classes. The school is following guidelines issued on 29 August by the U.S. Centers for Disease Control that "casual person-to-person contact appears to pose no risk" of AIDS infection.

22 Sept.   Farm Aid, an all-star concert telethon inspired by Live Aid, is held in Champaign, Illinois, to raise funds for American farmers. Dubbed as a "Concert for America," the concert is televised nationwide on cable television, attracts approximately 20 million viewers, and raises approximately $10 million.

2 Oct. When movie actor Rock Hudson, 59, dies of AIDS in Beverly Hills, Americans are shocked into an awareness of the disease and its growing number of victims.

28 Oct. In Oregon, U.S. authorities arrest Indian guru Bhagwan Shree Rajneesh, whose wealthy followers have given him funds that he has used to buy a fleet of Rolls-Royce automobiles.

11 Nov. According to the U.S. Centers for Disease Control, 14,739 AIDS cases have been reported in the United States and 7,418 of these patients have died.

14 Dec. Wilma Mankiller is the first woman in history to lead a major American tribe when she is sworn in as principal chief of the Cherokee Nation of Oklahoma, the largest Native American tribe in the United States after the Navajos.

23 Dec. President Reagan signs a farm bill that favors large producers as small-farm producers continue to go bankrupt.

1986

- Nintendo video games, featuring high-tech, sophisticated graphics, debut in the United States and reach $300 million in U.S. sales.

- More than sixty thousand U.S. farms are sold or foreclosed as depression continues in the rural West and Midwest.

- The Immigration Control and Reform Act is passed to grant amnesty to immigrants who have resided within U.S. borders since 1 January 1982. The act will expire in 1988.

3 Jan. Rev. Jerry Falwell announces that he is forming a new political group to rally support for conservative causes on many domestic and foreign issues.

14 Jan. Because the defendant was indicted by a grand jury from which members of his own race had been unconstitutionally excluded, the U.S. Supreme Court overturns a twenty-three-year-old murder conviction.

15 Jan. A U.S. National Institutes of Health report links smokeless tobacco to "increased risk of oral cancer."

23 Jan. The National Urban League reports that during 1985 the United States came closer to becoming "permanently divided between the haves and have-nots."

6 Feb. Two members of the neo-Nazi group Order are sentenced in Seattle for crimes including racketeering and murder.

8 Feb. A New York woman dies after ingesting a cyanide-laced Tylenol capsule. Nine days later Johnson & Johnson ends production of nonprescription capsule medicines.

13 Feb. Fourteen-year-old Ryan White, who is infected with AIDS, wins a county medical ruling that he poses no health threat to his classmates and should be allowed to attend classes at his middle school in Indiana.

9 Mar. In what is purported to be the largest rally ever staged by the National Organization of Women, abortion rights demonstrators gather in Washington, D.C.

1 May The black community of Indianola, Mississippi, calls off a five-week boycott of local white-owned businesses after the town's school district board appoints the protesters' candidate as school superintendent.

25 May More than 5 million people form a human chain from New York City to Long Beach, California, in Hands Across America, a project organized by U.S.A. for Africa to call attention to poverty, hunger, and homelessness in the United States.

2 July The U.S. Supreme Court upholds affirmative action and the use of numerical quotas as a remedy for past job discrimination.

3 July President Reagan ceremonially relights the torch of the Statue of Liberty to mark the beginning of a four-day international centennial celebration of the newly restored statue.

8 July A Johns Hopkins University study finds that teen participants in an experimental public-school sex-education program that includes free contraceptives and open discussions about sex are more likely to seek contraceptives, less likely to become pregnant, and refrain longer from sex.

9 July The U.S. Attorney General's Commission on Pornography releases a report stating that violent pornography probably leads to sexual violence. The report calls for a crackdown on obscenity by federal, state, and local authorities.

10 July The National Institute on Drug Abuse reports that the number of Americans killed each year in cocaine-related deaths rose from 185 in 1981 to at least 563 in 1985.

14 July Reports surface that white supremacists and anti-Semites gathered in Hayden Lake, Idaho, for a two-day meeting of the Aryan Nations World Congress.

4 Oct. CBS News anchorman Dan Rather is attacked on the street in New York City. According to Rather, a man asked him, "Kenneth, what is the frequency?" Rather replied, "You have the wrong guy." The man punched Rather in the face, knocking him on the pavement.

7 Oct. President Reagan signs into law a measure designating the rose as the national floral emblem of the United States.

1987

- Environmentalists fear that humanity is threatened by a "greenhouse effect" of rising global temperatures and sea levels that is partly being caused by Latin American landowners' burning of the Amazonian rain forest.

- U.S. sales of microwave ovens reach a record 12.6 million.

- U.S. spending on health care rises almost 10 percent from 1986.

2 Feb. The Children's Defense Fund, a nonprofit Washington, D.C.–based organization, releases a report showing that the U.S. infant mortality rate is one of the highest in the industrialized world.

10 Feb. Surgeon General C. Everett Koop tells a House subcommittee that condom commercials should be allowed on television to fight the AIDS epidemic.

3 Mar. Many well-known actors and politicians take part in the "Grate American Sleep-Out" by sleeping on heating grates in Washington, D.C., to draw attention to the plight of U.S. homelessness.

10 Mar. The Vatican condemns all forms of artificial fertilization, including any medical or scientific interference.

19 Mar. PTL televangelist Jim Bakker resigns after his cheating on his wife, Tammy Faye, by having a sexual encounter with church secretary Jessica Hahn is made public. The Reverend Jerry Falwell takes over the PTL ministry.

31 Mar. A Bergen County, New Jersey, superior court rules that a surrogate mother contract is "constitutionally protected," awarding custody of "Baby M" to her biological father, William Stern, and terminating all parental rights for surrogate mother Mary Beth Whitehead.

4 May The U.S. Supreme Court rules that Rotary clubs must admit women.

7 June The Ku Klux Klan stages its first march and rally in Greensboro, North Carolina, since 1979, when five Communist anti-Klan demonstrators were shot to death at a rally.

19 June The U.S. Supreme Court strikes down a Louisiana law that requires public schools teaching evolution to teach "creation science" as well.

28 Aug. A fire suspected as arson destroys the Arcadia, Florida, home of a couple whose three hemophiliac sons carry HIV, the virus that causes AIDS. The boys recently had returned to public school.

1 Sept. Lovastatin, a cholesterol-lowering drug, is approved by the U.S. Food and Drug Administration (FDA). High blood-cholesterol levels have been linked with arterial disease and heart attacks, and an estimated 20 million Americans have cholesterol levels that put them at risk of heart attacks. Previously the U.S. surgeon general has warned that obesity also poses a serious health risk to Americans.

16 Sept. The United States joins other nations meeting at Montreal, Canada, to agree on measures to protect the environment, including a gradual ban on chlorofluorocarbons that deplete the earth's ozone layer and increase incidence of skin cancer.

11 Oct. Homosexuals and their advocates demonstrate in Washington, D.C., to demand an end to discrimination and more federal funds for AIDS research. Six hundred people are arrested when they try to enter the Supreme Court to protest a sodomy decision.

7 Nov. Following a disclosure that he had smoked marijuana in the past, U.S. Appeals Court judge Douglas H. Ginsburg withdraws as President Reagan's nominee to the U.S. Supreme Court.

11 Nov. Vincent van Gogh's *Irises* (1889) is purchased for a record $53.9 million at an auction at Sotheby's in New York City.

28 Nov. Fifteen-year-old Tawana Brawley of Wappingers Falls, New York, is found half naked with the letters "KKK" and "Nigger" smeared with dog feces on her body. She claims six white men kidnapped her four days earlier and repeatedly raped her. On 6 October 1988 a grand jury finds that she staged her condition to avoid punishment from her stepfather.

Dec. *Time* magazine's Man of the Year is Soviet leader Mikhail S. Gorbachev.

1988

- Bob Barker, longtime host for the Miss USA pageant, resigns his position because one of the prizes included is a mink coat. Barker is a crusader for animal rights.

21 Jan. Occidental Petroleum Corporation chairman Armand Hammer announces plans to build a $30 million private museum to house his extensive art collection, valued at $250 million.

25 Jan.	In a live interview, Vice President George Bush and CBS news anchor Dan Rather begin shouting at each other over Bush's involvement in the Iran-Contra affair.
	Reza Eslaminia and Arben Dosti, two members of former Los Angeles business and social organization the Billionaire Boys Club, are convicted in California of kidnapping and murdering Eslaminia's father.
29 Jan.	The U.S. Department of Health and Human Services bars federally funded family-planning clinics from providing abortion services. The Reagan administration suspends this effort on 3 March after a federal judge in Boston prohibits enforcement.
5 Feb.	President Reagan signs the first major housing legislation since his administration began, providing $15 billion for housing and community development in fiscal year 1988 and $15.3 billion in fiscal year 1989.
17 Feb.	After university administrators agree to address a list of racial grievances, a group of minority students at the University of Massachusetts at Amherst ends a peaceful six-day occupation of a school building.
21 Feb.	Speaking to a crowd of six thousand at his ministry's Family Worship Center in Baton Rouge, Louisiana, televangelist Jimmy Swaggart tearfully confesses to an unspecified sin. Swaggart loses 69 percent of his viewers and is defrocked by the Assemblies of God on 8 April after it is discovered that he has had sex with a prostitute.
Apr.	U.S. unemployment falls to 5.4 percent, the lowest percentage since 1974.
4 May	As the 1986 Immigration Control and Reform Act expires, more than a hundred thousand applicants jam U.S. immigration offices.
23 May	The FDA approves cervical cap contraceptives long available in Europe.
26 May	The U.S. government begins a nationwide mailout of approximately 114 million copies of an eight-page brochure on AIDS that has been prepared by Surgeon General C. Everett Koop.
1 July	President Reagan signs legislation passed by Congress expanding the Medicare program to protect the elderly and disabled against "catastrophic" medical costs.
12 Aug.	The movie *The Last Temptation of Christ,* based on the novel by Nikos Kazantzakis, which traces the life of a more human, less godlike Jesus plagued by fears and desires, opens to street protests in seven U.S. cities.
2 Sept.	Many American performers take part in a world rock tour to benefit the human rights organization Amnesty International as the tour opens at London's Wembley Stadium.

1989

- Fear of flying is further boosted by two U.S. commercial airplane accidents, including a 24 February accident in which a cargo door rips away from a United Airlines Boeing 747 over the Pacific Ocean and 9 people are sucked out, and a 19 July crash in which a United Airlines DC-10 plows into a cornfield near Sioux City, Iowa, killing 112 of 296 passengers and flight crew.

23 Jan. The U.S. Supreme Court invalidates a Richmond, Virginia, program requiring that 30 percent of the city's public works funds be set aside for minority-owned construction firms; the court calls it reverse discrimination.

8 Mar. A *Harvard Business Review* article sparks controversy by proposing that women in managerial positions must choose between a "career-primary" and a "career-and-family" (or "mommy track") career path.

24 Mar. The U.S. tanker *Exxon Valdez* runs aground on a reef in Prince William Sound, Alaska, and spills 240,000 barrels of crude oil.

Disbarred lawyer Joel B. Steinberg is given the maximum sentence of eight and one-third to twenty-five years in prison for the beating death of his six-year-old adopted daughter.

27 Mar. The Bush administration reportedly plans to make Washington, D.C., the showpiece of its war on drugs and drug-related crime after reports stating that the city had the highest murder rate of any U.S. city during 1988 are publicized.

9 May Pablo Picasso's 1901 self-portrait, *Yo Picasso,* is sold to an unidentified bidder for $47.85 million, the highest price yet paid for a twentieth-century artwork.

12 June Corcoran Gallery in Washington cancels an exhibition of work by photographer Robert Mapplethorpe, who died of AIDS on 8 March, because the show includes homoerotic pictures. Sen. Jesse Helms of North Carolina introduces legislation that would bar the National Endowment for the Arts from funding "obscene" works.

21 June The U.S. Supreme Court rules 5–4 that burning the U.S. flag in public is a right protected by the First Amendment. President Bush asks for a constitutional amendment to prohibit flag-burning.

3 July The U.S. Supreme Court upholds a Missouri abortion law when it rules 5–4 that states can limit access to abortion.

23 Aug. Racial tensions are inflamed throughout New York City when one black teen is fatally shot after he and three black friends respond to a used-car advertisement in a Brooklyn neighborhood and are attacked by seven white youths.

30 Aug. Millionaire New York hotel owner Leona Helmsley, 69, is convicted on thirty-three counts of income tax evasion and massive tax fraud and is sentenced to four years in prison and fined $7.1 million. A former housekeeper has testified that Mrs. Helmsley told her, "Only the little people pay taxes."

21–22 Sept. Hurricane Hugo hits the Carolinas, killing more than seventy people, leaving thousands homeless, and causing damages estimated at $4 billion.

5 Oct. Former PTL televangelist Jim Bakker is convicted of twenty-four counts of fraud and conspiracy and sentenced to forty-five years in prison and a $500,000 fine because he has misused at least $4 million in donations and pledges to his ministry to buy himself expensive and extravagant luxury items.

17 Oct. Registering 7.1 on the Richter scale, the most destructive earthquake in North America since 1906 hits San Francisco, buckling highways and the Bay Bridge, killing at least ninety people, and causing an estimated $6 billion in property damage.

21 Oct.   President Bush vetoes a bill that includes a provision allowing the use of Medicaid funds to pay for abortions for poor women who are victims of rape or incest.

Nov.   President Bush signs the Internment Compensation Act to award $20,000 to each Japanese American surviving victim of imprisonment during World War II.

8 Nov.   National Endowment for the Arts chairman John E. Frohnmayer suspends a $10,000 federal grant for an art exhibit about AIDS but reverses his decision on 16 November after being pressured by the arts community.

20 Nov.   Genetic tests show that ten-year-old Kimberly Michelle Mays is the biological daughter of Ernest and Regina Twigg, who maintain that the girl was switched at birth for a baby whom they raised as their own until the child died last year.

OVERVIEW

Conservatism Ascendant. In the 1980s American culture was defined by a triumphant political and social conservatism. The election of Republican Ronald Reagan to the presidency in 1980 was the high-water mark of twentieth-century American conservatism, and his two terms as chief executive marked a true sea change in American life, a definitive redirection of political energy, purpose, and perspective. Reagan and his resurgent conservative ideology set forces in motion that some Americans cheered while many others looked on in astonishment. The conservative political agenda in the 1980s focused on undoing the liberal consensus that had prevailed since the 1930s and had reached its high point in President Lyndon B. Johnson's Great Society of the 1960s. Reagan and his supporters vowed to revoke the so-called welfare state and reduce the size of the federal government. "Government is not the answer to our problems," they declared; "government *is* the problem." They believed that abolishing federal bureaucracy and regulations would allow American business to return to doing what it did best: producing mountains of goods for a mass-consumption society. In foreign policy these conservatives were staunchly anticommunist, returning the nation to a 1950s-style Cold War mentality. At the same time, social conservatives worked to dislodge the residual impact of the 1960s counterculture, calling for a return from "liberal permissiveness" to "traditional" moral and social values. For the conservative orthodoxy the 1960s were politically and socially bad; the 1950s provided the models for political purpose and for codes of individual and family behavior. After the political, economic, and social upheavals of the 1960s and 1970s, Reagan's nostalgic appeal for a return to traditional values found a receptive audience — especially among middle-class Americans of the baby-boom generation, who were children in the 1950s period that Reagan celebrated. In that decade Americans were masters of the world, and — in retrospect, at least — life was exponentially simpler than in the 1980s.

Conservatism on the Offensive. The public mood fostered by Reagan's conservative triumph did not easily accommodate activism; indeed, the conservatives' victory created a backlash grounded in their conviction that earlier social justice and civil rights movements had gone too far and that it was time to draw the line against them, even reverse their momentum where possible. The feminist movement was caught in this vortex. The gains women had made in the 1960s and 1970s increasingly came under attack from the New Right. After the Equal Rights Amendment failed to be ratified in 1982, the feminist movement entered a period of disarray and disagreement, with some leaders and supporters turning against it. As the movement struggled to redefine itself and its agenda in the new conservative climate, antiabortion groups grew increasingly powerful, and reproductive rights were narrowed by state and federal laws. Civil rights leaders were unable to mount effective defenses against the Reagan administration's large cuts in social programs, and affirmative action programs were attacked. Advocates for the homeless struggled with little success to gain public support for corrective measures. Those who sought to raise public awareness of the AIDS crisis, to evoke a serious governmental response, and to elicit funding for AIDS research fought an uphill battle. On a different front the antinuclear movement, which challenged President Reagan's fast-forward of the arms race, gained wide support in the first years of the 1980s, but then it lost momentum as well. Protests against the U.S. policy regarding Central America grew in strength and, polls showed, found widespread support. Yet voices critical of the use of American military force were drowned out by cheers for U.S. military actions against Grenada, Libya, and Panama. The American news media, so engaged in the later 1960s and 1970s, were widely criticized for yielding before Reagan's conservative juggernaut and the mood of complacency it seemed to favor.

The Domination of Self-Interest. Reaganomics, with its tax-cutting fervor and probusiness bias, helped to promote a noticeable rise in self-interest. During his election campaign in 1980 Reagan promised to balance the federal budget, make the U.S. economy strong again, and let American capitalism regain strength in an ecomomic climate that encouraged free enterprise and free markets. In its simplest model the "free market" was supposed to operate on the assumption that each individual pursuing his or her own self-interest provided the mechanism by which everyone ultimately benefited. Government regulations were eliminated or purposely underenforced, allowing entrepreneurs and businesspeople to pursue their self-interests more freely. The government defended cuts in social spending by noting that it was trying to undo the damage of Great Society programs, which had fostered a "culture of dependency." George Gilder, a favored economic theorist of the New Right, declared that low-income people needed "the spur of poverty" to give them the incentive to realize the benefits of their presently diminished impulses to create their own destinies in accordance with enlightened self-interest; to ignore a homeless person begging for a quarter was to do that person a favor. With this emphasis on self-interest came a rediscovered American infatuation with wealth and success, a newfound pleasure in material possessions, which promoted the consumerist boom of the 1980s. Americans had felt their economic security slipping in the 1970s. Following self-interest was the newly celebrated American virtue, the dominating ethic for a nation bent on restoring its stature in the world. Partly on the theory that consumer optimism is a prerequisite for an expanding economy, Americans in the 1980s were encouraged to spend and spend again. From taking over a corporation to buying a gold Rolex or a large-screen home entertainment center or a $100 pair of running shoes, spending money was treated as a guilt-free process. Even when government spending sent the national debt skyrocketing to previously unthinkable levels, breaking the implied contract between generations that Americans had traditionally honored — that the next generation would be left with the potential for a higher standard of living — few people blinked their eyes.

The Giant Shadow of AIDS. Few things changed people's lifestyles in the 1980s more radically or pervasively than the calamity of AIDS (acquired immunodeficiency syndrome). This disease entered the public awareness early in the decade, but it did not become the cause of national concern until the death of actor Rock Hudson from an AIDS-related illness in 1985. As building statistical evidence showed the rapid, seemingly relentless spread of the disease, it came close to creating mass national hysteria in the late 1980s. It is hard to overestimate the impact of AIDS on American society in the 1980s. AIDS became a topic of daily conversation and banner headlines, generating tremendous

fear and uncertainty as the public, as well as the medical and scientific communities, struggled to understand a virus that slowly devastated the human body before it became fatal and for which there was no known treatment. Because the virus was spread primarily through sexual contact, the sexual revolution of the previous decades came under attack on medical as well as moral grounds. Health officials warned loudly against the dangers of unprotected sex, and because an infected individual might not experience AIDS symptoms until years after contracting the virus, many people wondered if perhaps they had already been infected. In the beginning AIDS struck with particular ferocity at the homosexual community, reversing much of the increased tolerance toward that lifestyle that had grown up during the previous two decades. Some members of the religious Right even charged that AIDS was God's way of punishing homosexuals for "perversion." Because another principal means of transmitting the AIDS virus was through the sharing of unsterile needles, many drug abusers also fell victim to AIDS. The plague of AIDS redefined conventions of behavior throughout society, from the wealthiest neighborhoods to the streets of the inner cities.

Social Problems. Cocaine use, homelessness, and child abuse affected large numbers of Americans in the 1980. In the early 1980s cocaine was expensive and consequently was abused mainly by upper-income people, frequently celebrities and often yuppies (young urban professionals). Robin Williams once said that cocaine was "God's way of showing you were making too much money." Later when the price of cocaine dropped and a smokable, highly addictive form, "crack," became widely available, the drug became a scourge on inner cities, where abuse became rampant and drug-related homicides soared. Homelessness was also a dominant social ill in the 1980s, as increasing numbers of unemployed Americans lost their homes and found their society had neither means nor will to help them in times of crisis. Reports of child abuse soared through the decade, overwhelming social-service agencies and eventually leading officials to declare the problem of child abuse "a national emergency." As with cocaine abuse and homelessness, society's attempts to address child abuse were inadequate.

TOPICS IN THE NEWS

AIDS

The New Reality. Identified in 1981, the incurable disease known as AIDS (acquired immunodeficiency syndrome) has had a major impact on American society. As ignorance and misunderstanding of the inevitably fatal disease — most commonly transmitted by intravenous drug use and sexual activity — gradually gave way to fuller knowledge, the number of reported cases in the United States rose from 225 in 1981 to 40,000 in 1987. By the end of the decade hundreds of thousands of Americans were known to be infected; it looked as if the nation were in the midst of an epidemic; and thousands of people began to transform their lifestyles in accordance with the new reality.

Discovering AIDS. In 1980 doctors in cities such as New York, Los Angeles, and San Francisco began noticing patients who were dying because their immune systems had been rendered inoperative, making them susceptible to opportunistic infections. Researchers eventually learned that the human immunodeficiency virus (HIV), which was recognized in 1984 as the cause of AIDS, could infect a person years before that individual developed AIDS. They also learned that carriers of HIV could infect others while the virus was incubating within their own bodies, and they determined that HIV was transmitted through body fluids, in particular blood and semen. This discovery accounted for the fact that most AIDS victims in the early 1980s were homosexuals and intravenous drug users who shared needles. The relatively good news that AIDS was infectious rather than contagious meant that spread of the disease could be controlled more easily than if one could get it from simply being near someone with HIV.

Public Reaction. Americans' responses to this information varied widely, but two reactions dominated. Many were judgmental, with some religious leaders and other spokespersons for mainstream morality believing that AIDS victims deserved their fates. Many other people were merely indifferent, feeling that it was not their problem. The federal government was also slow to respond. Even as awareness of the disease grew, the Reagan administration did not offer much support for AIDS

research. Funding for AIDS research did increase substantially during the Bush administration.

The Fundamentalist Response. Religious conservatives tended to be even less caring in their responses. Many Christian fundamentalists, whose political power grew during the 1980s, were quick to label AIDS as God's retribution against those who had defied divine authority. America, they believed, had gone astray during the 1960s and the 1970s, violating moral conduct by condoning widespread drug use and promoting gay and lesbian lifestyles, as well as promiscuity, in the name of the Sexual Revolution. These behaviors, they claimed, were justly punished by AIDS, which Moral Majority leader Jerry Falwell called a "gay plague." Nor were such people swayed from their belief in AIDS as divine punishment as statistics gradually revealed that victims of AIDS were to be found not only among homosexuals and drug users but among heterosexuals as well. If anything, this fact confirmed their opinion that AIDS was an indictment of those who flouted biblical morality.

Growing Awareness. It took much of the decade for health officials to convince the American public that the threat of AIDS was not restricted to homosexuals and intravenous drug users. Eventually, though, the message began to reach most Americans that anyone who was exposed to the bodily fluids of someone already infected with HIV could get AIDS. Despite this improvement in public knowledge about the disease, some continued to fear that AIDS was contagious, not just infectious. Moreover, the common perception about AIDS being transmitted through bodily fluids created its own share of problems. Fears grew among many in the population that the disease could be contracted through the air; through touch, kissing, or being sneezed on; through using a toilet seat previously used by someone with HIV; or even through mosquitoes. Although researchers tried to dismiss such misconceptions about the disease, myths and fears persisted for many. In addition, many Americans considered AIDS an urban problem, with the result that some people in the suburbs or in rural areas felt less risk, and therefore took more risks, in their sexual lives.

Precautions. The fact that AIDS could be transmitted through contaminated blood led to preventive measures

AIDS quilt in Central Park, New York City, 1988. Composed of squares made by friends and family in memory of AIDS victims, the AIDS quilt is a nationwide project.

that were adopted with astonishing speed. Blood-collection agencies such as the Red Cross began screening blood for HIV in 1985, after a test became available; they also added questions to their interview forms aimed at identifying high-risk donors, with professed homosexuals being denied the chance to donate blood. Doctors and dentists, and eventually police officers, began donning rubber gloves for routine jobs, and schoolteachers added rubber gloves to their supplies — all to avoid the possibility of accidental infection. The case of a Florida dentist who had infected a handful of his patients was a rare instance of AIDS being transmitted by a health-care worker, but public fears about AIDS were such that cautionary measures were deemed essential.

Outcasts. Because of fears and misconceptions about the disease, many AIDS patients found themselves pariahs, the modern equivalent of lepers or plague victims. Even those who acquired the disease through blood transfusions or other medical procedures were frequently shunned. A notable case was that of Ryan White, a young hemophiliac who acquired HIV through a routine blood transfusion. The decision of a school to deny him admission received nationwide attention, and White, whose family won a legal battle to force his admission, was befriended and defended by celebrities such as singer Michael Jackson. As a consequence of such public responses, many AIDS patients decided to hide the fact that they had the disease for fear of discrimination or persecution. Such a situation was dramatized in the movie *Philadelphia* (1993), for which Tom Hanks received an Academy Award for his sensitive portrayal of a gay man dying of AIDS. Ryan White died on 8 April 1990 at age eighteen.

Safe Sex. AIDS had a significant impact on the sexual practices of thousands of Americans. The phrase "safe sex" was added to Americans' vocabulary as public-health representatives tried to teach people that the best way to avoid catching the disease was either to be in a monogamous relationship with someone who did not have HIV or to abstain from sex altogether. People were told that when they went to bed with someone, they were going to bed with everyone their partner had ever had sex with. If one were unsure of one's partner's sexual history, public-health officials said, one should at least refrain from sexual acts involving the transmission of semen. Sales of condoms, which went from being a drugstore commodity to a product advertised in magazines and on television, soared. Local communities stirred controversy by giving away condoms and hypodermic needles in an effort to cut down on dangerous practices. Some high schools made condoms available to students, and condom vending machines appeared on college campuses. Though not everyone got the message, thousands of Americans changed their sexual practices in response to the threat of AIDS. For those who feared they might have been exposed to the disease, AIDS testing became widely available.

Media Attention. Public-health officials spread the word about AIDS through public-service announcements on television and articles in magazines and newspapers. Once it was clear that the epidemic was not limited to a small segment of the population, media attention grew rapidly. The AIDS-related death of popular actor Rock Hudson in 1985 shocked many people and brought home to them the seriousness of the epidemic. Hudson was only the first of a string of celebrities who would die of AIDS: he was followed by popular pianist Liberace in 1987, photographer Robert Mapplethorpe in 1989, and artist Keith Haring in 1990, to name only a few artists and entertainers who succumbed to the disease.

Popular Responses. Inevitably American popular culture dealt with such a serious issue through indirection or by making light of it. Jokes about condoms, safe sex, and the possible consequence of having multiple sexual partners proliferated in movies and television shows of the decade. Only a handful confronted the issue directly. Many artists dealt with the disease in their work, as did playwrights such as Harvey Fierstein, Larry Kramer, and Tony Kushner. Celebrities such as Madonna and Elizabeth Taylor performed for AIDS-research benefits, and red ribbons, indicating support for those with AIDS, appeared on lapels, evening gowns, and eventually postage stamps.

Gay Support. In addition, the gay community rallied to the challenge of AIDS. In the face of increased homophobia resulting from the public's association of the disease with the gay lifestyle, homosexuals, their friends, and their families participated in parades and demonstrations calling for increased AIDS research. Besides red ribbons, one especially visible sign of support and sympathy emerged with the NAMES Project, in which victims of AIDS were commemorated by having panels with their names sewn into quilts that were displayed across the country as a striking visual representation of the impact of the disease.

A Continuing Problem. The effects of AIDS continued to be felt worldwide into the 1990s. Many individu-

als failed to modify their behavior, and a sense of fatalism set in for many people. Nonetheless, scientists continued to struggle to find a cure for the disease and to educate people about how they could avoid it.

Sources:

James Kinsella, *Covering the Plague: AIDS and the American Media* (New Brunswick, N.J.: Rutgers University Press, 1989);

Nancy F. McKenzie, ed., *The AIDS Reader: Social, Political, and Ethical Issues* (New York: Meridian, 1991);

Dorothy Nelkin, David P. Willis, and Scott V. Parris, eds., *A Disease of Society: Cultural and Institutional Responses to AIDS* (Cambridge, New York, Port Chester, Melbourne & Sydney: Cambridge University Press, 1991).

AMERICAN CONSUMERISM

The New Consumerist Chic. In 1981 President Ronald Reagan set the tone for an upsurge in American consumerism by celebrating his inauguration with $11 million worth of pageantry and balls, signaling to the nation that glitter was back in style. First Lady Nancy Reagan was soon overseeing expensive renovations at the White House and ordering a new set of White House china that cost more than $200,000. Although none of these expensive undertakings was financed with public funds, the Reagans were criticized for displaying an ostentatious extravagance that seemed inappropriate during the economic recession than plagued the early 1980s. Yet the "small is beautiful" philosophy that had charmed some in the 1970s was put aside for good. "America is back," the president declared, and the subtext of that declaration seemed to be "shop till you drop."

Consumer Culture as New Wave. All across the United States there was a huge assortment of goods and services to buy; and, as the president reminded Americans, the only limits they had were those they imposed on themselves. "We are living in a material world, and I am a material girl," Madonna sang; "Greed is good," declared the character Gordon Gekko in the movie *Wall Street* (1987). Supply-side economists, such as George Gilder in his *Wealth and Poverty* (1981), promoted the idea that free markets were the antidote to American economic problems, that if American businessmen were allowed to pursue their own self-interests, the profits they made would "trickle down" to all Americans in the form of raises and jobs, creating prosperity for all. It was a message that many Americans seemed ready to hear. Even the baby boomers who had been so idealistically anticapitalist in the 1960s rapidly began to sign on to the nouveau chic of unabashed materialism. "Money is the long hair of the eighties," said actress Elizabeth Ashley. Everything necessary for the good life appeared to be for sale. The boomers, their parents, and their children had thousands of malls, supermarkets, and restaurants to visit. With inflation and interest rates falling, why not spend money? One timely wall poster, which showed a well-heeled young man standing smugly in front of a polished Bentley, was captioned "Poverty sucks."

Cabbage Patch Kids, the most popular dolls of the 1980s. In December 1983 the demand for them was so great that parents stood in line at toy stores for hours hoping to get one of the scarce dolls.

The "Greening" of America. *Money* magazine and a host of other glossy periodicals for the money-minded filled the newsstands. Financial planning became a craze. The popular media celebrated the big moneymakers, instantly conferring celebrity on Steven Jobs, the yuppie multimillionaire entrepreneur who founded Apple Computer; on super real-estate dealmaker Donald Trump; and on Wall Street financiers Michael Milken and Ivan Boesky, who made more in a few hours than most people made in a lifetime — and eventually ended up in jail for illegal insider trading. The mid 1980s became a time of multi-billion-dollar mergers and leveraged buyouts of multinational corporations. Former chief executive officers routinely bailed out in multimillion-dollar "golden parachutes." Teen stars, such as Molly Ringwald, made $1 million a movie and became teen producers. Vincent van Gogh's *Irises* sold for $53.9 million. *Dynasty* and *Dallas,* prime-time television shows about millionaires, were hugely popular. Later in the evening millions watched *Lifestyles of the Rich and Famous,* a series that took viewers into the sumptuous living rooms of the kings and queens of American enterprise. Millionaire Malcolm Forbes declared, "He who dies with the most toys wins."

The Changing Market. Marketers intensively studied the baby-boom generation — which by its sheer size (roughly 70 million) decisively imprinted each decade it passed through — trying to understand what its needs and buying habits would be. "What The Baby-Boomers Will Buy Next," a 1984 article in *Fortune,* noted,

> With the oldest boomers now approaching 40 and the youngest just leaving college, the generation is entering its prime years of earning — and spending.... The boomers are a mouthwatering market ... because they're maturing into the most affluent generation the U.S. has ever seen. Not only will they be rich, but the boomers will also spend a greater proportion of their wealth than any previous generation. It all adds up to the hugest consumer market ever.

The article also observed that in 1983 households headed by people aged twenty-five to thirty-four (the center of the baby boom) had a median income of $21,746, already higher than the national median for all age groups; it projected that by 1995 that same group would be making more than $50,000 (in constant 1982 dollars). Business and Madison Avenue took note. Clearasil antiacne medication followed the boomers as they aged. With its research showing that a growing number of adults had skin problems, the company introduced Clearasil Adult Care. In late 1985 *Business Week* ran an article titled "Consumers Are Spending The Economy To Health," and an article in *Ad Age* was headed "Young Adults Power Economic Engine." Yuppies became a favored market, their upscale trendiness sometimes referred to as "Cuisinart culture," after the popular and high-priced food processor found in more and more "well-furnished" kitchens, as yuppies happily

By the end of the 1980s popular magazines were filled with articles about compulsive shoppers. In her self-help book *Women Who Shop Too Much: Overcoming the Urge to Splurge* (1990), Carol Wesson pointed out that many men were subject to the same compulsion but specifically focused on women caught in the cycle of irresistible consumption. Discussing "shopaholics" in "the shopping explosion," she noted that, according to a study of American attitudes about shopping commissioned by Nieman Marcus and American Express, Americans "enjoy shopping as much or more than watching TV or going to the movies. Seventeen percent of Americans, and four times as many women as men, said they prefer shopping to sex." In another study by a psychologist, nearly one-fourth of all the women questioned — single, married, and divorced — said they use shopping as a "quick fix" for problems. Divorced women, the psychologist found, shop more than single and married women. According to Wesson, if the figures in this survey are extrapolated to all women in the United States, "it means that fifty-nine million women use shopping as a way of dealing with psychological problems or anxieties."

Source: Carol Wesson, *Women Who Shop Too Much: Overcoming the Urge to Splurge* (New York: St. Martin's Press, 1990).

embraced the notion that the latest high-tech creature-comfort gadgets were defining signs of their rising status.

The New Great American Pastime. During the 1980s various observers began to assert that shopping had become Americans' favorite leisure-time activity. In a five-year period at middecade the 91 million U.S. households purchased 62 million microwave ovens, 63 million VCRs, 57 million washers and dryers, 88 million cars and light trucks, 105 million color television sets, 31 million cordless phones, and 30 million telephone answering machines. Americans engaged in the greatest spending spree since the boom that followed World War II, causing journalist Tom Wolfe to refer to Americans in the 1980s as "the splurge generation." Surveys showed that Americans were spending more time in malls than anywhere else except home, job, or school; they made 7 billion trips in and out of shopping centers every year. By middecade there were more than twenty-six thousand shopping centers, and they accounted for 45 percent of retail sales, with annual purchases reaching $1 trillion. In his *The Malling of America* (1985) William Severini Kowinski called the American mall "the cathedral of the postwar culture, the Garden of Eden in a box." Indeed, in the 1980s shopping malls, which had been primarily subur-

ban in the 1970s, not only continued to grow in number but expanded their reach both to small towns and, contrary to most predictions, even into the cities, hoping to capitalize on the yuppies living and working in cities such as Los Angeles, Chicago, Washington, D.C., Atlanta, Saint Louis, and Philadelphia. Surveys reported that most Americans could easily travel from their residences to at least two shopping malls. In the 1980s mall planners and managers began to reconceive their consumer paradises, adding more restaurants, cafeterias, movie theaters, arcades, concerts, and special events. Kowinski describes the malls as a symbol of security, "a controlled environment that eliminates any suggestion of unpleasant realities, any reminders of war, terrorism, random murder, senseless death, toxicity in the biosphere, or of stupidity, mendacity, and psychosis in places high and low. . . ." "Especially since the advent of the nuclear-tipped intercontinental missile," he adds, "Americans have lived in sublimated terror of the 'bolt from the blue,' the instant and unwarned rain of annihilation. When we feel helpless, we hide. An entire society may have tried to find shelter, first in suburbia and then in the psychological bomb shelter of the shopping mall."

The Mall in the Home. During the 1980s the shopping mall was challenged by an unexpected competitor. More and more shopping could be done without leaving one's home or apartment — in fact, without leaving one's chair. Businesses both large and small moved into the American home, a new, not always invited, guest. Telemarketing reached millions of potential buyers by telephone. Continuing a trend that began in the late 1960s, more and more new mail-order outlets — as well as department stores, art museums, and various nonprofit charitable groups — began competing with old-time mail-order companies such as Sears, Montgomery Ward, and L. L. Bean. Another complement to home shopping was the home computer, which provided links to hundreds of markets through videotex systems such as CompuServe or, later, the IBM/Sears service, Prodigy. Through such on-line services customers could bank and shop. Finally, there was the new phenomenon of television channels such as the Home Shopping Network, and QVC Network. According to *Fortune* magazine, the home-shopping industry grew from sales of $1 million in 1982 to sales of $1.4 billion by 1989. Home shopping was facilitated especially by credit cards, the "plastic money" that was responsible for an explosion in consumer debt during the decade. By the mid 1980s the average credit card holder carried seven cards; the number of Mastercard and Visa charge cards held by American consumers was estimated to be 125 million.

Defining Upscale Markets. In the 1980s, trying to define the markets and attract the biggest chunks of discretionary spending or disposable income, marketers chased other demographic groups in addition to the baby boomers. Realizing that senior Americans were relatively better off than previous generations of the elderly, marketers began exploring the newly identified "Gray Market." Reaganomics was slowly but surely redistributing income, and marketers knew where the income was going. Television and magazine advertisements catered to upscale markets, creating lustrous images to appeal to the resurgent materialism of the 1980s consumer: fine luxury cars, futuristic multifunctional computers with color graphics, designer jeans and underwear, even an "upscale" mustard, Grey Poupon. In ad after ad people clustered in fashionable bars or restaurants, stepped out of Rolls Royces or BMWs, or swept effortlessly across marble parquet floors past gorgeous furnishings, enjoying the 1980s fantasy of the good life. Other ads featured yuppie business executives wrestling with problems of competitiveness in sleek corporate environments.

Signs for Beginning Marketers. Meanwhile, sales and research gurus told enterprising sellers how not to mistake their targets. In *Why They Buy: American Consumers Inside and Out* (1986) Robert B. Settle and Pamela L. Alreck pointed out, "Social class distinctions are vital to consumer goods marketers. Social classes differ not only in their power, prestige, and wealth, but also in their *values, attitudes, lifestyles, and behaviour patterns.*" The authors measured such things as the average amount of money spent on decorating living rooms, and spoke unabashedly of identifying clientele by "The Great Absolutely Infallible Living Room Test." "Upscale social strivers," they observe, "have homes with white walls and textured fabric drapes in plain, solid colors. Prints, paintings, tapestry, or hanging sculpture may decorate the walls." By contrast, "downscale homemakers paint walls in various colors or use wallpaper. Print curtains and patterned drapes are popular.... Religious pictures and icons, figurines and knick-knacks, family photographs, and handcraft items decorate the rooms." In another section of their book the authors list as "upscale products and brands" Stouffer, Lean Cuisine, Le Menu, Dannon yogurt, and Haagen-Dazs ice cream; "downscale products and brands" include Banquet, Swanson frozen TV dinners, Hamburger Helper, Kraft Macaroni and Cheese casseroles, and Jell-O Pudding. In another book designed to help marketers capture customers, demographers study "purchase behavior by cluster" to discover chief indicators of highest-income households (8 percent of U.S. households in 1988). Consumers in this group tend to travel frequently and prefer tennis and golf as leisure activities. Indicators of those at the lowest income level (about 6 percent of U.S. households) include heavy consumption of liquor and cigarettes and frequent purchase of insecticides.

Criticisms of the Culture of Consumption. Many people, it appeared, were having a good time spending money in the mid 1980s. Even after the stock-market crash of 1987, a popular song lyric advised, "Don't worry, be happy!" Yet cautionary and critical voices were heard throughout the decade. Sociologists, cultural critics, social historians, and theologians argued about the

meaning of the triumphant commercialism in contemporary society. Some progressives argued that the phenomenon of rampant consumerism could be explained as a mass reaction to and compensation for the political powerlessness many individuals felt, either consciously or subconsciously. In *The Poverty of Affluence: A Psychological Portrait of the American Way of Life* (1983) Paul L. Wachtel argued,

> Our restless desire for more and more has been a major dynamic for economic growth, but it has made the achievement of that growth largely a hollow victory.... in America, we keep upping the ante.... It is not what we have that determines whether we think we are doing well; it is whether we have *more* — more than our parents, more than we had ten years ago. Our entire economic system is based on human desire's being inexhaustible, on there being a potential market for almost anything we can produce. Without always recognizing what we are doing, we have established a pattern in which we continually create discontent.

For some worried economists national economic policy throughout the decade both encouraged and exemplified irresponsible overconsumption. In his *Day of Reckoning: The Consequences of American Economic Policy under Reagan and After* (1988) Benjamin Friedman criticized Reaganomics as a collective national folly of overconsumption. Decrying the fiscal policies that transformed the United States from the largest creditor nation in 1980 to the largest debtor in the world by 1986, Friedman claimed that the U.S. government had shifted from a tax-and-spend policy to a spend-and-borrow policy. Commenting on the perception of good times that many Americans shared in middecade, he wrote, "But it is clear that this sense of economic well-being was an illusion, an illusion based on borrowed time and borrowed money. Jobs are plentiful and profits are high because we are spending amply, but more than ever what we are spending for is consumption.... We are living well by running up our debt and selling off our assets. America has thrown itself a party and billed the tab to the future." The costs, he predicted, would include "a lower standard of living for individual Americans and reduced American influence and importance in world affairs." The consumerism of the 1980s also became a subject of satire. One cartoon featured a yuppie couple standing in a gourmet delicatessen, gazing at a floor-to-ceiling array of cheeses, breads, croissants, wines, and mineral waters as the husband asked his wife, "See anything?"

Sources:

Margaret K. Ambry, *Consumer Power: How Americans Spend Their Money* (Ithaca, N.Y.: New Strategists Publications, 1991);

Peter Francese and Rebecca Piirto, *Capturing Customers: How To Target The Hottest Markets of the 90's* (Ithaca, N.Y.: American Demographics Press, 1990);

Benjamin Friedman, *Day of Reckoning: The Consequences of American Economic Policy under Reagan and After* (New York: Random House, 1988);

George Gilder, *Wealth and Poverty* (New York: Basic Books, 1981);

William Severini Kowinski, *The Malling of America: An Inside Look at the Great Consumer Paradise* (New York: Morrow, 1985);

Dedication of the Vietnam Veterans Memorial in Washington, D.C., November 1982

Christopher Lasch, "The Culture of Consumption," in *Encyclopedia of American Social History*, 3 volumes, edited by Mary Kupiec Cayton, Elliott J. Gorn, and Peter W. Williams (New York: Scribners, 1993), II: 1381–1390;

Kevin Phillips, *The Politics of Rich and Poor: Wealth and the American Electorate in the Reagan Aftermath* (New York: Random House, 1990);

Robert B. Settle and Pamela L. Alreck, *Why They Buy: American Consumers Inside and Out* (New York: Wiley, 1986);

Paul L. Wachtel, *The Poverty of Affluence: A Psychological Portrait of the American Way of Life* (New York: Free Press, 1988).

AMERICANISM RETURNS

Patriotism Rekindled. During the 1970s the loss of the war in Vietnam sank deeply into the national consciousness, but in the 1980s President Ronald Reagan and the New Right brought back into fashion the traditional virtue of patriotism. President Reagan called for renewed pride in the United States and its military might, announcing that "America is back and standing tall" as Republicans celebrated "Morning in America." The newly elected president connected to a mood in the country in which many were clearly ready to demonstrate their old-fashioned pride in being Americans. One of the first national events to unleash this new patriotic fervor was the release of the U.S. embassy hostages in Iran, minutes after the inauguration of President Reagan in January 1981. Their homecoming was cause for great national celebration, and Congress passed a joint resolution naming the first week in February "National Patriotism Week." The new mood was unmistakable, as articles with titles such as "What's Right with America" began appearing in popular magazines. In July 1981 *Newsweek* reported that enlistments in the military were increasing, flag sales were booming, and people were again gustily singing "The Star-Spangled Banner." This renewed patriotism was not limited to older and middle-aged citizens. A Gallup poll found that 81 percent of teenagers surveyed were "very proud" to be Americans. At the Pentagon an official noted, "Patriotism is back. Once again people like to wear a uniform. We're kind of over the Vietnam blahs." A flag seller in New York City said exultantly, "My father, who founded this business in 1947, said he never dreamed in a thousand years he would see this much business." A Rutgers University political scientist who warned against the dangers of excessive patriotism nevertheless observed, "People are tired — and rightly so — of defeatism, negativism, of powerlessness, and are anxious to regain control of America's destiny." This powerful new Americanism was captured in Lee Greenwood's immensely popular song "God Bless the USA," which he sang at the 1984 Republican National Convention.

Vietnam Revisited. In his final televised appeal to the nation before his election in 1980, Reagan declared that the Vietnam War, which had caused such profound divisions among Americans, was in fact "a noble cause." Following this lead, the conflict that had caused such a wound in the national psyche was reexamined by some and newly defended or gradually rehabilitated by others.

THE VIETNAM VETERANS MEMORIAL

On 13 November 1982, 150,000 Vietnam veterans and their families gathered in Washington, D.C., for the dedication of the Vietnam Veterans Memorial. Funded through private contributions, the memorial had been conceived, planned, and established by Vietnam veterans. Like the war to which it bore testimony, the memorial was surrounded by controversy at each stage of planning and construction. Many suggested America was still trying to ignore or forget the conflict that caused so much impassioned division and then ended in defeat. Criticism was especially heated regarding the design that won the competition for the memorial, submitted by Maya Ying Lin, a twenty-one-year-old undergraduate architecture student at Yale University. She envisioned a black granite wall, positioned in the shape of a stretching, open wedge, with the names of the Americans killed in Southeast Asia carved in the polished granite surface. (Eventually there were more than 58,000 names on the wall.) Many veterans expressed dismay at the simplicity of the design; journalist Tom Wolfe ridiculed the plan; the *National Review*, a leading conservative magazine, called Lin's design "Orwellian glop," an "outrage." But other veterans liked it, and in the end, after approval by the National Parks Commission, the Vietnam Veterans Memorial was situated on the National Mall near the Lincoln Memorial. At the dedication a writer observed the veterans and families who came to view the new memorial: "They looked for the names of loved ones, old comrades, someone from home. They laid little tributes at the base of the wall, touched the incised letters of the names, and they saw themselves reflected, like shadows of history, in the dark and shining stone." One veteran said of the dedication ceremonies, "It's the first time in 12 years that I haven't felt like an alien." The Vietnam Veterans Memorial soon became one of the most visited memorials in Washington, attracting more than 5 million visitors in its first two years.

Sources: Tom Morganthau, "Honoring Vietnam Veterans — At Last," *Newsweek*, 100 (22 November 1982): 81–82;

Jan C. Scruggs and Joel L. Swerdlow, *To Heal a Nation: The Vietnam Veterans Memorial* (New York: Harper & Row, 1985).

In the revived debate about Vietnam, perceptions tended to shift in favor of those who had fought the war and — in the view of many Americans — never been sufficiently recognized for their sacrifices. Even many of those who had been deeply critical of the war observed that their argument had been with U.S. policy, not the men and women of the armed services. The Vietnam Veterans Memorial in Washington, D.C., dedicated in November 1982, helped to foster a sense of national healing. In May 1985, ten years after the U.S. withdrawal from Vietnam, a huge ticker-tape parade for twenty-five thousand Vietnam veterans in New York City drew one million spectators, some with signs saying "Welcome Home!" Movies about the war became popular: Sylvester Stallone starred in two phenomenally successful *Rambo* films (1985, 1988), sequels to the less-popular *First Blood* (1982). Other Vietnam movies, new books, articles, and television documentaries explored the tangled history of the war. In the eyes of many, being a Vietnam veteran became a badge of honor. Candidates for public office proudly cited their wartime service; editorial cartoons suggested that a politician who had not served in Vietnam could not be elected.

Platoon. Into this new climate of reexamination stepped filmmaker and Vietnam veteran Oliver Stone, whose 1986 movie *Platoon* mesmerized audiences, renewed fierce controversy over the war, earned critical raves, won four Academy Awards (including the award for best picture), and grossed $160 million at the box office. The unflinching portrayal of the war in *Platoon* raised profound moral questions about the exercise of American power in Southeast Asia and about the actions of some U.S. soldiers in that conflict. Some veterans claimed the movie was filled with misconceptions, while others claimed it was the first to show what the war was "really like." One veteran told a *Time* correspondent it was a relief for him to be able to share the nightmare he had lived and still not shaken. Whatever their political persuasions, audiences across the country were moved and sobered by the movie, which did not, however, reverse the gradually increasing acceptance of the Vietnam War as "a noble cause." Patriotism remained strong throughout the decade, proving that conservative Republicans had indeed tapped into a deeply nationalistic mood that had been searching for expression. In 1986 another highly visible sign of the nation's patriotic leanings was seen in the extravagant celebration for the centennial of the Statue of Liberty in New York Harbor.

The Iran-Contra Debate. Patriotism also figured in the debate that surrounded the testimony of Lt. Col. Oliver North in congressional hearings about the unlawful use of funds and resources to ransom hostages and to aid the Contra forces opposing the Marxist government of Nicaragua. Many Americans praised North's actions in support of what he believed was right as true patriotism, while others suggested his actions were a subversion of the democratic process on which the nation was founded and represented a shallow or even false patriotism.

Pledging Allegiance. During the 1988 presidential campaign, Republican candidate George Bush proved that the rekindled Americanism of the decade was still a potent force. In May, after the Democratic and Republican nominations were virtually sewn up, Bush criticized his opponent, Michael Dukakis, governor of Massachusetts, for vetoing a state bill that would require teachers to lead their students in recitation of the Pledge of Allegiance. The bill did not forbid students to recite the pledge, and Dukakis had vetoed it because it was clearly an unconstitutional violation of the teachers' right to free speech; but Bush gained considerable mileage from claiming that Dukakis was against the Pledge of Allegiance and thus was unpatriotic. The Bush campaign orchestrated photo opportunities at flag factories, and at the Republican National Convention the candidate finished his address by asking everyone to join him in the Pledge of Allegiance. Some critics snickered at the Republican Party attempt to "wrap itself in the flag," but flag-waving proved a potent campaign issue and was one of the chief factors in Bush's come-from-behind victory over Dukakis. After the election Republican leaders in Congress passed a resolution to begin every session of Congress with the Pledge of Allegiance. Sales of the American flag soared again as the fall of Communist governments in Eastern Europe and democratic reforms in the Soviet Union suggested to many that the United States was on the verge of becoming a major leader in a new world order.

A Tradition of Dissent. The renewed patriotic fervor of the 1980s did not preclude strong dissent from some Americans who judged themselves as patriotic as any other citizens but opposed many Reagan administration policies. For them genuine patriotism did not mean uncritical, unquestioning support for the government. Through the 1980s many citizens protested cutbacks in domestic social programs under the so-called Reagan revolution, and there was also sustained and vocal protest of the reacceleration of the arms race and the vast increase in the defense budget, as well as the Reagan administration's involvement in the Iran-Contra scandal and its policies toward Central America in general, which, critics charged, favored right-wing, reactionary governments.

Sources:

David L. Bender and Bruno Leone, eds., *Opposing Viewpoints, Sources: Foreign Policy,* volume 1 (Saint Paul, Minn.: Greenhaven Press, 1984);

Richard Corliss, "Platoon: Vietnam, The Way It Really Was, On Film," *Time,* 129 (26 January 1987): 54–61;

Morris Janowitz, *The Reconstruction of Patriotism: Education for Civic Consciousness* (Chicago: University of Chicago Press, 1983);

Neal Karlen, "Welcome Home," *Newsweek,* 105 (20 May 1985): 34;

John S. Lang, "Patriotism — It's Back in Style," *Newsweek,* 91 (6 July 1981): 41–43;

Richard A. Melanson, *Reconstructing Consensus: American Foreign Policy Since the Vietnam War* (New York: St. Martin's Press, 1991).

THE ANTINUCLEAR MOVEMENT

Countdown to Doomsday. In the early 1980s the specter of a nuclear war with the Soviet Union began to haunt the public consciousness more forcefully than at any time since the Cuban Missile Crisis of 1962. Warning of "the Soviet military threat," and calling the Soviet Union "the focus of evil in the world," President Ronald Reagan presided over a $1.5 trillion military buildup that pointedly included new generations of nuclear weapons. At the same time, the Soviet Union continued to add aggressively to its own nuclear arsenal. In the United States defense officials spoke of fighting a "protracted" nuclear war, while military strategists suggested nuclear war was "winnable." Periodically during these years, *The Bulletin of Atomic Scientists* moved the hands of its "Doomsday Clock," which represents the statistical probability of nuclear war, closer and closer to midnight. In a 1983 Gallup poll 40 percent of the respondents thought it likely a nuclear war would occur within ten years. In November of the same year, when ABC broadcast *The Day After,* a fictional dramatization of a nuclear attack on Kansas City, 100 million Americans tuned in.

The Freeze Movement. Appalled by the accelerating arms race in a world where fifty thousand nuclear warheads already existed, many people began to protest the military policies of the Reagan administration and the Soviet leadership. Spearheaded by existing groups such as the Committee for a Sane Nuclear Policy (SANE), the growing antinuclear movement assimilated new peace organizations at local and state levels. Fundamentally a grassroots phenomenon, it embraced secular and religious groups, winning the support of activists and volunteers from all walks of life and in all areas of the country. One popular proposal of these groups called for an immediate halt to the arms race — a "freeze" on all nuclear weapons testing, production, and deployment. Once the freezing of arms levels was achieved by both superpowers, proponents called for determined arms-control negotiations. In 1982 polls showed that a weapons freeze was supported by 70 percent of the American public. The idea of a nuclear freeze is usually credited to Randall Forsberg, a woman who headed the antinuclear group FREEZE and worked long and hard to win public support for the plan. Freeze propositions were placed on many state ballots and approved in some states. The freeze movement also won the support of Sen. Edward M. Kennedy and others in Congress, as well as the distinguished diplomat George F. Kennan, who said in an address accepting the Albert Einstein Peace Prize in 1981, "We have gone on piling weapon upon weapon, missile upon missile, new levels of destructiveness upon old ones. We have done this helplessly, almost involuntarily: like the victims of some sort of hypnotism, like men in a dream, like lemmings headed for the sea, like the children of Hamlin marching blindly along behind their Pied Piper. And the result is that today we have achieved, we and the Russians together, in the creation of these devices and their means of delivery, levels of redundancy of such grotesque dimensions as to defy rational understanding."

GROUND ZERO ON THE DAY AFTER

On a Sunday night in November 1983 the ABC television network broadcast *The Day After,* a made-for-television movie dramatizing a nuclear attack on the United States. Set in Kansas City in the near future, the story followed the main characters from the day before the attack until the day after, focusing on the individual human consequences of a nuclear apocalypse — the devastation to ordinary people. Filmmaker Nicholas Meyer used special-effects wizardry to show nuclear weapons exploding in black clouds over the Kansas countryside and people with their skeletons showing through their flesh in the instant irradiation from the thermonuclear flash. The week before it was broadcast, the movie was featured in a *Newsweek* cover story that generated a wave of publicity and debate. Supporters of the nuclear-freeze movement praised the network and the filmmaker for having the courage to bring the effects of nuclear warfare into American living rooms. Critics called the movie "freezenik" propaganda, a disservice to President Reagan's nuclear-arms policies. The impending broadcast inspired national debate about how to talk to children about nuclear warfare and whether or not children should be allowed to see the movie. Many educators advised parents not to permit young children to watch *The Day After* and urged that great discretion be exercised in letting older children see it. Fearing that the violence and bleakness of *The Day After* would not attract a major audience, or, if it did, would not provide the proper upbeat atmosphere in which to present products, many sponsors were wary of buying commercial time during the movie. To alleviate sponsor concerns, ABC aired four-fifths of the advertisements before the missiles fell. The two-hour movie was seen by 100 million Americans.

Source: Harry F. Waters, "TV's Nuclear Nightmare," *Newsweek,* 102 (21 November 1983): 66–70.

The Fate of the Earth. Although members of the antinuclear movement sometimes disagreed on the methods of achieving disarmament, they were united by an urgent conviction that continuing the present course of escalation and confrontation was an invitation to disaster. Many writers warned that the fate of the planet was literally hanging in the balance, but in the early 1980s one book in particular was widely read and gave eloquent expression to the fundamental concerns of antinuclear activists. The book was *The Fate of the Earth* (1982) by Jonathan Schell, who argued that the horrors of a nuclear war must be avoided at all costs, not only to save the present human race but to save the unborn millions of future generations. Reviewing the book for *The New York Times,* Kai Erikson said that *The Fate of the Earth* "accomplishes what no other work has managed to do in 37 years of the nuclear age. It compels us — and compels *is* the right word — to confront head on the nuclear peril in which we all find ourselves." Many readers said reading *The Fate of the Earth* marked a turning point in their thinking about the nuclear threat. Toward the end of his book Schell wrote:

> The task is nothing less than to reinvent politics: to reinvent the world. However, extinction will not wait for us to reinvent the world. Evolution was slow to produce us, but our extinction will be swift; it will literally be over before we know it. We have to match swiftness with swiftness. Because everything we do and everything we are is in jeopardy, and because the peril is immediate and unremitting, every person is the right person to act and every moment is the right moment to begin, starting with the present moment. For nothing underscores our common humanity as strongly as the peril of extinction.

The Demonstration in New York. In June 1982 the strength of the antinuclear movement was made vividly clear when more than a half million people gathered in New York City to advocate world nuclear disarmament. This massive peace rally, held in conjunction with the opening of the United Nations Special Session on Disarmament, was one of the largest political gatherings in American history. The immediate concern to many at this gathering was the projected deployment of new U.S. intermediate-range nuclear missiles in Western Europe. The Reagan administration argued that such an action was necessary to counter the Soviets' deployment of SS-20 missiles in Eastern Europe. Antinuclear activists feared the introduction of U.S. missiles in Europe would make serious arms negotiations less likely and a nuclear confrontation more probable. Their concerns about this "Euromissile" crisis were shared by a strong antinuclear movement in Western Europe. Following the great outpouring in New York City, activists continued to lobby Congress, to support profreeze candidates for public office, to sponsor public symposia, to publish books and articles, and to speak on television and radio. Prominent in the movement were such well-known peace activists as pediatrician Benjamin Spock, physicist Linus Pauling, and Rev. William Sloane Coffin. Members of the antinuclear movement also opposed the building of new nuclear power plants in the United States.

The Reagan Reaction. The Reagan administration paid little attention to the antinuclear movement, except to suggest its wrongheadedness, and it never supported the idea of a nuclear freeze, arguing that it would lock the Soviet Union in a position of nuclear superiority. The administration believed the only way to achieve serious arms control with the Soviet Union was to show an unwavering resolve to continue the U.S. nuclear buildup. In March 1983 President Reagan surprised almost everyone by proposing the Strategic Defense Initiative (SDI), soon popularly known as "Star Wars." Under this plan the United States would construct an enormous shield in space to protect itself against incoming Soviet missiles. The president claimed that the successful deployment of such a shield would render nuclear weapons "impotent and obsolete." Antinuclear activists were among the many Americans who were skeptical about the proposal, judging it merely another high-tech, exorbitantly expensive acceleration of the arms race. Nevertheless, SDI undercut, at least rhetorically, some of the power of the antinuclear movement's arguments and allowed President Reagan, in a sense, to present himself as the biggest antinuclear activist in the country.

Later Years. In 1986, four years after the huge New York rally, the antinuclear movement made headlines again with the Great Peace March for Global Nuclear Disarmament. Climaxing an eight-month, cross-country march, demonstrators carried their disarmament message to the gates of the White House. The number of participants in this event disappointed many in the movement, and the 1982 outpouring in New York was not equaled by any subsequent event either. While activists continued to campaign throughout the 1980s, disagreements about tactics slowed their earlier momentum; moreover, their agenda seemed to many to become somewhat less urgent. After Mikhail Gorbachev came to power in the Soviet Union in 1985, it soon became apparent that he was working to lessen tension between his nation and the United States, especially after he proposed at the Reykjavík summit meeting in October 1986 that the two nations eliminate all nuclear weapons over a period of ten years. In the Intermediate Nuclear Forces (INF) Treaty they signed in December 1987, Reagan and Gorbachev agreed that both powers would remove their intermediate-range nuclear weapons from Europe, thus ending the Euromissile crisis. Serious negotiations for the reduction of intercontinental ballistic missiles (ICBMs) followed.

Assessment. As the decade drew near its close, critics of the antinuclear movement claimed that progress in reducing the threat of nuclear war was achieved despite the efforts of the "freezeniks." Yet peace activists argued that their grassroots advocacy had been instrumental in pressuring government leaders to alter disastrous policies. Whatever the extent of their influence, the freeze movement kept public attention focused on the horrors of nuclear warfare and the profoundly human costs of the arms race.

Sources:

Alan Geyer, *The Idea of Disarmament: Rethinking the Unthinkable* (Elgin, Ill.: Brethren Press, 1982);

Patrick Glynn, *Closing Pandora's Box: Arms Races, Arms Control, and the History of the Cold War* (New York: Basic Books, 1992);

Milton S. Katz, *Ban the Bomb: A History of SANE, the Committee for a Sane Nuclear Policy, 1957–1985* (Westport, Conn.: Greenwood Press, 1986);

Paul Rogat Loeb, *Hope in Hard Times: America's Peace Movement and the Reagan Era* (Lexington, Mass.: Lexington Books, 1987);

Robert Scheer, *With Enough Shovels: Reagan, Bush, and Nuclear War* (New York: Random House, 1982);

Jonathan Schell, *The Fate of the Earth* (New York: Knopf, 1982).

BABY BOOMERS BECOME "YUPPIES"

The Rise of the Young Urban Professionals. At the end of the 1970s Jerry Rubin, onetime radical antiwar activist, began working on Wall Street, a surprising event that the media saw as symbolic of a change taking place in the baby-boom generation: the radicals of the 1960s counterculture were growing proestablishment. Meanwhile, with less publicity than Rubin, other members of the huge baby-boom generation were also revising their antiestablishment views. Faced with the energy crisis and the runaway inflation of the 1970s, many former student activists were deciding financial power and economic security were goals not to decry but to emulate. Distrust and disdain of corporate America dissipated. Careers in business, once loudly derided, grew increasingly respectable. As the recession of the early 1980s gave way to economic boom times, success American style began to occupy the pedestal baby boomers had once reserved for social justice. Raised during the great period of American prosperity and influenced by the turning inward of the "Me Decade" of the 1970s, many baby boomers responded enthusiastically in the 1980s to Republican calls for reinvigorating the U.S. economy. Gary Hart's presidential campaign in 1984 labeled these baby boomers "yuppies" (young urban professionals), and the name stuck. Frankly and unapologetically materialistic, they focused on careers and the good life promised by the American Dream. Defined by one research group as people between the ages of twenty-five and thirty-nine, with incomes of at least $40,000 from a professional or management job, yuppies were estimated in 1984 to be 4 million strong — and three times more likely than other Americans to have an American Express card. By less restrictive definitions, estimates of the number of yuppies in the United States reached 20 million. Whatever their number, they became highly visible and much discussed, considered by many to be the trendsetters of their generation. Celebrating their increasingly high profile in American life, *Newsweek* dubbed 1984 "The Year of the Yuppie."

M.B.A. Fever. During the 1980s many yuppies pursued law and medical degrees, believing they could have lucrative careers in those fields. At the same time, the number of students studying for liberal arts degrees steadily declined, while enrollment in business schools boomed. The M.B.A. (master of business administration) began to be touted as the yuppie degree, a passport to high pay and rapid advancement in corporate America. Hearing stories about twenty-six-year-old investment bankers making six-figure incomes at Wall Street firms, would-be yuppies in droves mailed their applications to Harvard Business School and the Wharton School of

Business. If they were not accepted by the most prestigious schools, they could earn the degree at many other business schools throughout the country. Enrollment in business schools, having doubled in the 1970s, increased dramatically in each year in the 1980s. In 1980, 55,000 graduate business and management degrees were awarded. In 1985 there were 67,000, and by 1990 the number had risen to 77,000. Moreover, only 3 percent of these degrees were awarded to women in 1971; by 1989 one third of all business graduates were women. During the 1980s the M.B.A. was said to have "sex appeal." Some joked its letters stood for "Making it Big in America." In 1984 alone, according to *Forbes* magazine, 200,000 students were pursuing M.B.A.'s. Karen Seigler, a student at Columbia University, noted, "In New York there are so many M.B.A.'s on the market that the degree no longer gives you a competitive edge." Yet even while business leaders began to complain about an M.B.A. glut, many yuppies considered the degree a prerequisite to success, and the M.B.A. boom continued. In March 1987 *Business Week* reported that M.B.A.'s were "hotter than ever." In fact business courses of all kinds became hugely popular. According to *The Encyclopedia of Educational Research*, the number of business students enrolled in bachelor's, master's, and doctoral degree programs in 1989 totaled 1.3 million.

The Yuppie Lifestyle. Not all yuppies earned M.B.A.'s, but they did tend to share a fairly identifiable lifestyle, sometimes celebrated and often satirized. Most yuppies lived and worked in metropolitan areas, the centers for the high-paying jobs they usually sought. They seemed to be hard-driving overachievers who thought little of working late at the office, bringing work home, and working weekends if necessary. Yuppies placed high importance on appearance; abiding by the maxim "dress for success," they were frequently identified by their shiny leather briefcases, business suits from upscale stores such as Brooks Brothers, Rolex watches, and, in inclement weather, Burberry raincoats. For more-relaxed occasions yuppies wore trendily fashionable Nike running shoes and bought clothing from stores such as Banana Republic or catalogues such as L. L. Bean's — tending to dress as though they were off on a great outdoor adventure even while running errands around the city. At the same time their favorite sources for home decorating were stores such as Laura Ashley, which allowed them to re-create their urban apartments as ersatz English country houses. One frequent source of humor was the way in which yuppies — with the help of advertisers pitching their products to aging baby boomers — seemed to make even the most mundane activities seem trendy and chic. Though they were snobbish about having the finest foods and wines, yuppies were also health conscious, creating a rage for low-fat dishes, herbal teas, natural fruit juices, and bottled waters such as Perrier. Many were joggers and patrons of health spas. The typical yuppie seemed to thrive on upscale city life, especially the availability of

THE YUPPIE PREACHER

In the early 1980s many yuppies were fans of the Reverend Terry Cole-Whittaker, author of the best-selling book *How To Have More in a Have-Not World* (1983). Based in San Diego, "Reverend Terry," as she was known to her followers, broadcast her message each Sunday on a syndicated television program that reached millions. Stressing that "You can have it all — now!," she encouraged her listeners week after week to seek prosperity, power, and abundance. In her book she wrote, "You can have exactly what you want, when you want it, all the time. . . . Affluence is your right." Blending New Age spirituality, science of mind, and pop and motivational psychology, she provided her followers with newsletters and instructional tapes. In 1985, for reasons not entirely clear, she ended her ministry.

Sources: Ronald Enroth, "Self-Styled Evangelist Stretches God's Truth," *Christianity Today*, 28 (21 September 1984): 73–75;

D. Keith Mano, "Terry Cole-Whittaker," *People*, 22 (26 November 1984): 99–106.

fashionable restaurants, sushi bars, singles bars, theaters, and multiplex cinemas. One trend among yuppies was to move into lower-income or declining neighborhoods, renovate and refurbish the apartments, and attract new yuppie-oriented businesses into the area. Inside their well-appointed apartments and condominiums, yuppies tended to have the latest high-tech gadgets: CD players, VCRs, personal computers, pocket calculators, cordless phones, answering machines, Cuisinart food processors, and microwave ovens. For leisure time their favorite television shows included *Hill Street Blues, Dynasty,* and *L.A. Law.* Many yuppies aspired to incomes that would allow them to take regular vacations in Europe, and some succeeded.

Relationships versus Careers. Being intensely career-oriented, many yuppies seemed to regard personal relationships as secondary to career goals. Men and women alike decided to defer relationships, marriage, and children until they had established themselves in their careers. Married yuppies with no children became known as *dinks* (double-income, no kids). Married yuppies with children frequently employed nannies to look after the children while both parents worked. For single yuppies, dating services such as Great Expectations became extremely popular, partly because they were seen as an efficient way to meet people when one's schedule allowed limited time for socializing. As twenty-eight-year-old Rob Lewis, a yuppie profiled in *Newsweek*, noted, yuppies were often willing to sacrifice "marriage, families, free time, relaxation." He added, "Our marriages seem like mergers, our divorces like divestitures."

A Generation in a Hurry. Since time was a precious commodity to yuppies, most kept their appointment books filled and used the new technologies of fax machines, personal computers, car phones, and answering machines to stay connected to their business and social networks. Carrie Cook, another yuppie profiled in *Newsweek*, remarked, "I don't think earlier generations of young people were as consumed by time as we are. We seem to be moving every minute. If we lose our appointment books, we're through." Because of their hectic paces, yuppies were regular take-out patrons and restaurantgoers. Indeed, dinners out became a major source of yuppie entertainment. After work they often sought out the latest and trendiest restaurants, creating fads for Tex-Mex cooking, Japanese sushi, and other ethnic cuisines. After they finished reading *The Wall Street Journal, Forbes, The Economist,* and other financial periodicals, yuppies favored self-help books on time management and how-to business books offering techniques for becoming more productive. Popular phrases such as "A.S.A.P." (as soon as possible), "what's the bottom line?," and "cut to the chase" communicated the yuppies' sense of urgency. Many yuppies were fans of the New Age preacher Rev. Terry Cole-Whittaker, whose upbeat message was "You can have it all — now!" Her phrase, loudly echoed in a Miller Light commercial, was sometimes called, only half facetiously, "the battle cry of the yuppies."

Media Reflections. The yuppie phenomenon waned in the later 1980s, particularly after "Black Monday," the stock-market crash of 1987. Layoffs in the financial industry hit many yuppies hard, and their way of life seemed suddenly less assured. Yet yuppies continued to attract much media attention. To many, their lifestyle easily lent itself to caricature and parody, as in the *Doonesbury* comic strips that poked fun at yuppie materialism and career obsession. At the same time, the lifestyle was taken seriously by Madison Avenue market researchers vying for the yuppies' disposable dollars. Television, newspaper, radio, and magazine advertisements were filled with products for the good life, 1980s style. Yuppies were the subject of Hollywood movies, including *The Big Chill* (1983), *Baby Boom* (1987), and *When Harry Met Sally* (1989). Oliver Stone explored the dark side of yuppie aspirations in *Wall Street* (1987). Yuppies were also chronicled and satirized in fiction such as Jay McInerney's *Bright Lights, Big City* (1984), Louis Auchincloss's *The Yuppie Diary* (1986), and Tom Wolfe's *The Bonfire of the Vanities* (1987). There was even *The Yuppie Handbook* (1984), by Marissa Piesman and Marilee Hartley, a tongue-in-cheek guide to achieving ultimate yuppiedom.

Sources:
Jerry Adler and others, "The Year of the Yuppie," *Newsweek,* 104 (31 December 1984): 14–24;

Barbara Ehrenreich, *The Worst Years of Our Lives: Irreverent Notes from a Decade of Greed* (New York: Pantheon, 1990).

CHILD ABUSE

A Nationwide Concern. Child abuse became a powerful social issue in the 1980s, generating intense media attention, heightened public concern, congressional hearings, numerous books and articles, and increased workloads for child-protective-service (CPS) agencies. The first national studies to determine the prevalence of child abuse were conducted in 1974, and in 1979–1980 periodic National Incidence Reports were mandated by the federal Child Abuse Prevention and Treatment Act. In 1984 the American Humane Association (AHA) estimated that there were 1.7 million abused or neglected children in the United States. Although the methods employed in this and other studies provoked debate among experts, producing disagreement about the total numbers of abused children, there was broad agreement among professionals that the problem in America was widespread and probably growing. By 1980 nearly all states required social-service professionals who had contact with children to report any case of suspected child abuse — one factor that helped to account for the increase in reported cases. The 1988 Study of National Incidence and Prevalence of Child Abuse and Neglect estimated that in 1986, 1.5 million children nationwide had experienced abuse or neglect. Although this estimate was slightly lower than the 1984 AHA estimate, the report emphasized that its definitions for "countable" abuse cases were strict and thus its conclusions should be regarded as minimum estimates. Among its other findings, the report estimated that 1,100 children died in 1986 as a direct result of maltreatment. Among cases of child maltreatment, neglect was found to be the largest problem, representing 63 percent of all cases. The report broke abuse into three categories — physical, sexual, and emotional. Of these, physical abuse was found to be the most frequent — representing 53 percent of all cases and involving 358,000 children in 1986. In addition, the study found an increase from 1980, when it did its first survey, in the rates of physical and sexual abuse. Physical abuse had risen by 58 percent; sexual abuse had more than tripled.

Sexual Abuse Cases. Meanwhile, public concern about the issue of child abuse was fired by several highly publicized cases, including the McMartin Preschool sexual-abuse case, which raised nationwide concern about the safety of nursery schools and day-care centers. News of sexual-abuse charges against adults in the Boy Scouts of America organization and against the clergy of various religious groups fueled parents' fears. One consequence of this heightened concern was a rash of new children's books, such as Rick Chacaon's *You Can Say "No!,"* board games such as Strangers and Dangers and Safe City, U.S.A., as well as various flashcards and coloring books. Saturday-morning cartoon shows featured public service announcements warning children not to get into strangers' cars. At some schools children attended classes instructing them what to do if someone tried to fondle them sexually. Some psychologists thought these methods were useful to educate children and their parents about important issues. Some disagreed. Psychologist Lee Salk protested, "We are terrifying our children."

Abuse in the Home. At the same time, child sexual abuse within the family became an increasingly frequent charge in custody battles between divorcing parents. Then, in 1986, national attention focused on the case of Lisa Steinberg, a six-year-old who died from injuries inflicted by her adoptive father. Lisa Steinberg's troubled face, in a picture taken shortly before her death, stared from the covers of newsmagazines. Her tragedy provoked a wave of compassion for the young victim, and outrage toward the perpetrator. In 1982 a Harris poll found that nine out of ten people thought child abuse was a serious social problem. In 1989 a Gallup poll found that 25 million Americans claimed to know children whom they suspected had been physically or sexually abused. After studying the national data on child abuse, the U.S. Advisory Board on Child Abuse and Neglect, established in 1988, declared in its first report (1990) that "child abuse and neglect now represents a national emergency."

National Reports. Basing its conclusions on data gathered mainly in the 1980s, the report stated that the increase in the number of reports of child abuse in recent years had been "astronomical." "In 1974," the board observed, "there were about 60,000 cases reported, a number that rose to 1.1 million in 1980 and more than doubled during the 1980s to 2.4 million." The report acknowledged an important debate among experts about the issue of substantiation, the process by which CPS agencies determined whether child-abuse charges were supported by evidence. After investigation, many reports were dismissed. Some professionals believed the dramatic rise in child-abuse reports proved a greater public sensitivity to the issue of abuse, not that the rate of abuse was actually increasing. According to the board, however, "the absolute number of substantiated cases has increased at a rate as shocking as the increase in the number of reported cases." Of the 2.4 million cases reported in 1989, it noted, more than 900,000 were officially substantiated; and "there are reasons to believe that even that number is just a fraction of the actual incidence of child abuse and neglect." Indeed, it noted, "Surveys consistently show that large proportions of cases of suspected child maltreatment remain unreported." Furthermore, some cases unsubstantiated for lack of evidence were later confirmed.

The Child-Abuse Emergency. In concluding that child abuse "now represents a national emergency," the U.S. Advisory Board cited three findings. First, "each year, hundreds of thousands of children are being starved and abandoned, burned and severely beaten, raped and sodomized, berated and belittled." Second, the system

designed to protect these children was failing; and, third, the United States was spending billions of dollars on programs that dealt with the results of child abuse, not on programs to prevent it — a failure the board called "a moral disaster." Another part of the study laid out the many factors that contributed to child abuse, especially "poverty, ethnicity, neighborhood dysfunction, mental health problems, substance abuse, and the presence of children with special needs." Regarding substance abuse, the report noted that "the extraordinary increase in the number of parents using cocaine and crack . . . and the severity of the injuries to children resulting from such use, has caught all parts of the system unprepared." In its final recommendations the board urged Congress and all state and local governments to view the prevention of child abuse and neglect "as a matter of national security" and urged these bodies "to increase their support for basic necessities, such as housing, child care, education, and prenatal care for low income families including the working poor."

The McMartin Preschool Case. In 1984 a case in California instantly attracted national attention and continued to preoccupy the media and much of the public with a trial that lasted six years. Investigations began after teachers at the McMartin Preschool — a well-known, highly respected fixture in the upscale community of Manhattan Beach, not far from Los Angeles — were accused of sexually abusing children in their care. According to the criminal charges brought against seven teachers

Photographs of missing children on milk cartons, a practice begun in many cities in the mid 1980s. In 1985 more than one million American children were reported missing; about six thousand of them were abducted by strangers.

at the school, during a period of years hundreds of three-, four-, and five-year-old children who had attended the preschool had been sexually abused, sometimes in bizarre rituals. Shortly after these allegations became public, claims surfaced that similar abuse had occurred at other preschools in the area. Local officials became overwhelmed by the scope of the investigations, and the district attorney's office called in the Los Angeles County Sheriff's Task Force on Child Abuse. The McMartin Preschool closed its doors in January 1984, and the preliminary hearing for the seven McMartin teachers began that summer. Meanwhile, six other preschools in the South Bay area closed because of sexual-abuse allegations. The shocking charges in the McMartin trial made national headlines. As the trial plodded slowly through stage after stage of complex, confusing legal proceedings, the case became a national obsession.

Shock Wave. The McMartin case sent a shock wave through the nation. At the time, there was little information to provide a scientific context for the case. Child sexual abuse had generally been supposed to afflict older children, not preschoolers. In studies that did exist, such abuse had rarely been associated with preschools or day-care centers. As a result, psychologists, psychiatrists, doctors, and social workers often provided conflicting views. Experts who testified at the trial rendered professional

judgments that exactly contradicted those of other professionals. Furthermore, with more and more women entering the workforce and becoming dependent on preschools and day-care centers for their children, the allegations in the McMartin case and other similar cases were so frightening that mothers and fathers nationwide began to wonder if their own children were in danger of the same kind of abuse.

McMartin Aftermath. Seven years after it started, the McMartin trial, the longest in U.S. history, ended with the acquittal of all the defendants. Even so, many people believed the legal system had failed, that sexual abuse had in fact occurred at the preschool. During these years convictions were obtained in sex-abuse cases regarding other day-care centers; but in many other cases charges were later dropped or trials ended in acquittals. By the end of the decade the issue of the safety of child-care centers was not resolved in the public mind. Dr. Richard Gardner, a well-known child psychiatrist associated with Columbia University, reviewed much of the evidence from such abuse cases in the 1980s and concluded that most likely the "vast majority of allegations" were false. Many of these cases, he wrote in 1991, had "all the hallmarks of mass hysteria similar to that which took place at the time of the Salem witch trials in 1692." He did not deny that sexual abuse of children was a tragically frequent occurrence, but he believed the majority of actual abuses took place either in the victim's home or in orphanages or boarding schools. Yet in 1988 the only national study to report on incidents of sexual abuse in day-care facilities reported 270 substantiated cases of preschool sexual abuse, involving 1,639 victims.

Sources:

David Bender and Bruno Leone, eds., *Child Abuse: Opposing Viewpoints* (San Diego: Greenhaven Press, 1994);

Robin E. Clark and Judith Freeman Clark, *The Encyclopedia of Child Abuse* (New York: Facts On File, 1989);

David Finkelhor, Linda Meyer Williams, and Nanci Burns, *Nursery Crimes: Sexual Abuse in Day Care* (Newbury Park, Cal.: SAGE Publications, 1988);

Richard A. Gardner, *Sex Abuse Hysteria: Salem Witch Trials Revisited* (Cresskill, N.J.: Creative Therapeutics, 1991);

Richard Layman, *Child Abuse* (Detroit: Omnigraphics, 1990).

National Center on Child Abuse and Neglect, *Study Findings — Study of National Incidence and Prevalence of Child Abuse and Neglect: 1988* (Washington, D.C.: Children's Bureau, Administration for Children, Youth and Families, Office of Human Development Services, U.S. Department of Health and Human Services, 1988);

U.S. Advisory Board on Child Abuse and Neglect, *Child Abuse and Neglect: Critical First Steps in Response to a National Emergency* (Washington, D.C.: Department of Health and Human Services, Office of Human Development Series, 1990);

Jill Waterman, Robert J. Kelly, Mary Kay Oliveri, and Jane McCord, *Behind the Playground Walls: Sexual Abuse in Preschools* (New York: Guilford Press, 1993).

THE COCAINE CRISIS

A Drug Epidemic. During the 1980s few subjects were in the news as consistently as the widespread and increasing use of cocaine in the United States. There were two main stages in this growing problem. In the first stage, during the early 1980s, many considered cocaine a harmless, even glamorous, "recreational" drug; it was the drug of choice of the famous and successful — professional athletes, celebrities in the arts and entertainment, lawyers, university professors, and Wall Street brokers — who were among the few who could afford the high black-market price of cocaine. In 1982 the National Survey on Drug Abuse found that 22 million Americans had used cocaine at one time or another. Experts debated the significance of this number; but none disputed that cocaine use was spreading rapidly, and health officials began to speak openly about a cocaine "epidemic." Even the cocaine-related death of the comedian John Belushi in 1982 failed to dim many users' enthusiasm for the drug, and cocaine use, which had risen dramatically since the late 1970s, continued to increase. Because of its high price, it was sometimes called the "champagne of drugs," and the white powder became a sort of status symbol at yuppie parties. Such users persisted in the misconception that cocaine was nonaddictive. At this stage cocaine use seemed to be an adjunct to the "life-in-the-fast-lane" syndrome prevalent among the yuppies.

Growing Public Alarm. The sense of a crisis built steadily in the public mind. In the early 1980s medical experts produced study after study that countered what

COCAINE ANONYMOUS

Modeled on the twelve-step program of Alcoholics Anonymous, Cocaine Anonymous (CA) is dedicated to helping people overcome their dependence on cocaine, perhaps the most seductively pleasurable drug available. According to a 1984 study, "Laboratory animals will give up both food and sex for self-administered doses of cocaine and will even starve to death to continue receiving cocaine instead of food." Most CA members say that they started using cocaine "recreationally" but quickly lost control to the power of the drug. CA members talk about the euphoria they experienced in the first stages of cocaine use and the later spiral downward into depression, lying, hiding, and manipulating others. One member noted, "Most of us were brought down by a medley of financial, physical, social, and spiritual problems."

Source: Harrison M. Trice, "Cocaine Anonymous," in *The Encyclopedia of Drugs and Alcohol*, edited by Jerome H. Jaffe (New York: Macmillan, 1995).

they called the "myth" that cocaine was harmless and nonaddictive. A growing body of scientific literature demonstrated the destructive, addictive, and potentially fatal effects of cocaine use. Yuppies' casual cocaine use — and their subsequent serious drug abuse and addiction — were portrayed in Jay McInerney's highly successful 1984 novel *Bright Lights, Big City,* and in the 1985 movie *St. Elmo's Fire.* Even as treatment centers for cocaine problems grew in number, however, there were reports of increasing cocaine use in American high schools. Meanwhile, reports from law-enforcement authorities showed not only that the availability of cocaine was growing but also that the retail price of the drug was falling. If these trends continued, the National Institute on Drug Abuse warned in 1985, "this society may experience an epidemic of cocaine use without historical equal in terms of magnitude and coverage. . . . the tentacles of the cocaine epidemic in the United States may have considerably more capacity for expansion." Such reports fueled public alarm — as did other reports about the power of the Colombian drug cartels, the source of most cocaine in the United States — and the unsuccessful efforts of law enforcement to keep drug dealers from smuggling cocaine into the country. In 1983 the first cocaine hotline, 1-800-CO-CAINE, was started, and it soon became a twenty-four-hour service, gathering clinical data and making referrals for professional help. The first survey of its callers showed that most users were well educated, had good incomes, and had been using cocaine for about five years; the average user was spending $640 per week on cocaine. By 1985, 12 million people in the United States were estimated to be frequent cocaine users.

The First Peak. Also alarming were statistics showing that large cities were experiencing dramatically rising crime rates, which were attributed to the drug gangs, or "posses," that sold cocaine on the streets. Most cocaine trafficking inside the United States was controlled by these gangs, whose members were from the inner cities. As more cocaine flowed into the country and profits from its distribution soared, the drug gangs fought each other for control of territories: drug-related homicides skyrocketed, and the emergency rooms of urban hospitals were filled with the maimed victims of the drug wars. Then, on 21 June 1986, University of Maryland basketball star Len Bias died suddenly after taking cocaine. His death made national headlines, shocking the public not only because it was caused by cocaine but also because the reports indicated that he had died from his first use of the drug. Bias's tragic death raised public awareness to new heights. By middecade polls showed that many Americans regarded drug abuse as the most serious problem facing the nation. Responding to the growing sense of urgency, President Reagan called for a "national crusade" against drugs, and Congress began considering new, comprehensive antidrug laws.

The Crisis Spreads. Even as public concern about drug abuse was building to its first peak, the cocaine crisis of the 1980s was entering a sinister new stage that built on and engulfed the first and seized national attention through the end of the decade. In 1985 "crack" — an easily made, smokable form of cocaine that was far more addictive than powder cocaine and much cheaper — suddenly appeared on the streets of American cities. Crack could be purchased in small vials for two or three dollars but was still highly profitable for dealers because of huge increases in the cocaine supply and the resulting fall in the market price. Crack spread quickly and disastrously through inner-city neighborhoods as young, poor minority males saw dealing the drug as a means to escape the ghetto. A severe escalation in drug-related violence followed as rival gangs fought for territory, and new crimes, such as drive-by shootings, entered the national vocabulary. From New York to Detroit, from Chicago to Los Angeles, from Philadelphia to Atlanta, inner-city neighborhoods were ravaged by the spread of crack cocaine. Washington, D.C., was especially hard hit: drug-related deaths in its predominantly black neighborhoods escalated so dramatically that in the late 1980s Washington began to be called the "murder capital of the world." The New York City police commissioner called 1986 "The Year of Crack," and the first elite anticrack police task force began sweeping through the city's neighborhoods, arresting thousands of street dealers. Other cities followed New York City's lead. Meanwhile, as crack devastated inner-city neighborhoods, it was seen as an aggravating cause in the rise of domestic violence, child abuse, homelessness, violence in schools, and dropout rates. Whole neighborhoods became battle zones in which people were afraid to leave their homes; innocent bystanders were killed in the crossfire of gang wars, sometimes inside their own homes. Communities acquired new nicknames, such as "The Graveyard." Pregnant mothers addicted to crack gave birth to "crack babies," infants with damaged central nervous systems. Cocaine addiction fueled the spread of the AIDS virus, because a major means of transmission was the sharing of unsterile needles used for intravenous injection. Treatment centers for addicts were frequently so overloaded and understaffed that help for many addicts was unavailable. At the end of the decade *The New York Times* called the crack epidemic a new form of genocide.

New Trends in the Late 1980s. Studies indicating that the use of cocaine in powder form was leveling off in the mid 1980s led some observers to conclude that abuse of the drug had reached a saturation point among the middle and upper-middle classes and that the epidemic was afflicting primarily the inner cities in the form of crack. Yet there was mounting evidence that crack cocaine was spreading to higher-income city neighborhoods, middle-class suburbs, and even the small towns and rural areas that had been thought of as havens from the drug crisis. Drug experts began to estimate that the number of crack users in the middle and upper-middle classes might exceed those in the inner cities. William Hopkins, a leading narcotics expert, estimated in 1989 that 70 percent of the crack users in New York City were upper-income professionals. Dr. Arnold Washton, director of a New York treatment clinic, estimated that by the late 1980s there were more crack addicts among white, middle-class people than among any other population group. He told *The New York Times* that these new addicts were "business executives and house painters and doctors and receptionists. And if you met them on the street, you wouldn't have a clue they're smoking their brains out on crack back home in the basement."

The Drug Czar. In 1988 President Reagan established the Office of National Drug Control Policy; its director, William Bennett, quickly became known as the nation's "drug czar." Nationwide, the "war on drugs" became a principal topic of discussion and concern. In the budget-cutting climate of the time, people debated how much the federal government should spend on fighting drug abuse. A survey conducted by *Newsweek* in August 1988 revealed that Americans were more supportive of government spending to fight drugs than of spending for the "Star Wars" defense program. The 1986 Anti-Drug Abuse Act was a major legislative effort to respond to the crisis; the 1988 Anti-Drug Abuse Act was even stronger, though critics objected to its emphasis on increased law enforcement at the expense of education and drug-treatment programs. Concern about drugs in the workplace grew; controversies arose about whether employers should have the right to test employees for possible drug use. As politicians and editorial writers called for a crackdown on drugs, federal, state, and local governments continued to step up their law-enforcement efforts, imposing stiffer penalties for the sale or purchase of powdered cocaine or crack and putting more police on the streets. The federal government tried harder to prevent the smuggling of cocaine into the country while also looking for ways to destroy the Colombian cocaine cartels; eventually U.S. military forces were employed to capture "drug lords" and to destroy the coca crop in the Colombian fields. With some justification, commentators began to speak of a "drug frenzy" in America. Inheriting the war on drugs from President Reagan, President George Bush told the nation in his inaugural address: "When that first cocaine was smuggled in on a ship, it may as well have been a deadly bacteria, so much has it hurt the body, the soul of our country. There is much to be done and much to be said, but take my word for it: This scourge will stop."

Sources:

David F. Allen and James F. Jekel, *Crack: The Broken Promise* (New York: St. Martin's Press, 1991);

Steven R. Belenko, *Crack and the Evolution of Anti-Drug Policy,* Contributions in Criminology and Penology, no. 42 (Westport, Conn.: Greenwood Press, 1993);

Jonathan Harris, *Drugged America* (New York: Four Winds Press, 1991);

Jerome H. Jaffe, ed., *Encyclopedia of Drugs and Alcohol* (New York: Macmillan, 1995);

Nicholas J. Kozel and Edgar H. Adams, eds., *Cocaine Use In America: Epidemiologic and Clinical Perspectives,* National Institute on Drug Abuse Research Monograph 61 (1985), U.S. Department of Health and Human Services Publication no. (ADM) 85–1414 (Washington, D.C.: U.S. Government Printing Office, 1985);

Geraldine Woods, *Drug Abuse In Society: A Reference Handbook,* Contemporary World Issues Series (Santa Barbara, Cal.: ABC-Clio, 1993);

FEMINISM FLOUNDERS

Backlash. In the early 1980s the initial agenda of the women's movement was carried over from the 1970s, but there was renewed opposition to that agenda, not only from traditionalist men but from antifeminist women, an opposition more influential as the decade progressed. The two triumphs of the women's liberation movement in the 1970s were the 1973 Supreme Court decision in *Roe* v. *Wade,* protecting a woman's right to choose abortion, and the congressional approval of the Equal Rights Amendment (ERA) in 1972. Both these victories came under heated attack in the resurgent political and social conservatism of the Reagan era. A decisive sign of the power of the backlash against the women's movement was the defeat of the ERA in 1982.

The Defeat of the ERA. The ERA, which stated, "Equality of rights under the law shall not be denied or abridged by the United States or by any State on account of sex," needed the approval of two-thirds of the states before it could become an amendment to the Constitution. The deadline for ratification was June 1982. Its supporters argued there were many forms of discrimination against women, which could be stopped only by an explicit Constitutional guarantee of women's equality. In

"THE GREAT AMERICAN MAN SHORTAGE"

In June 1986, in the midst of public discussions of "family values," at a time when young women were urged to reconsider the virtues and blessings of married life, a *Newsweek* cover ominously reported "The Marriage Crunch" and added, "If You're A Single Women, Here Are Your Chances Of Getting Married." A full-cover chart dramatized the probability for marriage as female college graduates progressed from age twenty to fifty. At twenty, such a woman's chance of marriage was well above 70 percent; by thirty, her chance had plummeted to 20 percent; and by thirty-five, it was about 10 percent. Inside, in an article titled "Too Late for Prince Charming?," *Newsweek* writers detailed the results of the Yale University study that had set off the alarm. The media seized on the "man shortage" theme, and the grim statistics were promulgated in formal and informal discussions around the country. Three months after the *Newsweek* article, *Mademoiselle* magazine noted that "women across the country have been thrown into shock by the widely reported but misleading" demographic study. According to this article, the Yale study was seriously flawed; women of any age who wanted to marry should not be worried; there were plenty of men to go around. Yet one critical article was not sufficient to kill the story of the "man shortage," and the subject continued to generate intense discussion. In succeeding years other researchers attacked the Yale study, and it became reasonably certain that its numbers and conclusions were indeed unreliable. For the most part, however, the exposés of the original study did not stir much media interest, and the notion of a "man shortage" for educated women persisted through most of the decade.

Source: Eloise Salholz and others, "Too Late for Prince Charming?," *Newsweek,* 107 (2 June 1986): 54–61.

1980 and 1981 there were many reasons to expect that the ERA would be ratified. Public-opinion polls showed that the majority of women and men favored the measure, and by 1977 thirty-five states of the thirty-eight required for its ratification had already given their approval. Yet in the late 1970s the ERA campaign had lost momentum, and partly because a determined opposition had arisen. Facing a rapidly approaching deadline, the National Organization for Women (NOW) and other women's rights groups lobbied aggressively for the passage of the ERA. Declaring a state of emergency, NOW stated that "The ERA is the last best hope in this century of committing this country to the principle of human equality — regardless of sex." Opponents of the amendment argued that women were already protected by statute and that adding a federal guarantee for equality of rights "regardless of sex" would create numerous undesirable consequences. For one thing, they argued, the ERA would give far too much power to the federal government; for another it would further to serve blur gender roles already challenged by the feminist movement. In the end, despite the intense efforts of advocates and its broad public support, the ERA failed to gain approval in the three more legislatures necessary for final ratification.

Reaction to Defeat. What did the defeat of the ERA mean? Pundits and opinion makers, politicians, and the clergy tackled the question with enthusiasm. Because the ERA had been of such paramount importance to feminists, some saw its defeat as the end of the women's movement. Opponents such as Phyllis Schlafly argued that women's rights activists did not represent the majority opinion in the nation, that they were out of touch with the concerns and values of most women in their everyday lives. Advocates of the ERA maintained they were foiled by special interests, especially businesses that believed passage of the amendment would threaten their economic interests. In any case, the failure of the ERA was a profound blow to feminists' morale. Nevertheless, ERA advocates such as Gloria Steinem urged their colleagues not to despair. After all, she noted, "It took a Civil War plus nearly a century to get racial equality into the Constitution."

The Rise of the Antiabortion Movement. At the same time, the other great feminist advance of the 1970s, freedom of choice, came under fire from a growing antiabortion movement, often called the "pro-life" movement by those sympathetic to its aims. Members of this group believed that human life began at conception and argued that abortion was a deliberate taking of that life, not to be condoned under any circumstances. Indeed, most simply referred to abortion as "murder." Antiabortionists were predominantly conservative Catholics and Protestant fundamentalists. Politically, they were frequently Republicans and were viewed by the Republican Party as an increasingly important constituency. Most of them strongly advocated a constitutional ban on all abortions, a proposed amendment known as the Human Life Amendment (HLA). Two of the movement's prominent spokespersons were Phyllis Schlafly, leader of the antifeminist Eagle Forum, and Rev. Jerry Falwell, head of the Moral Majority. Many Catholic clergymen also reasserted the Catholic Church's long-standing opposition to abortion. Moreover, the antiabortion movement included numerous smaller grassroots organizations. Throughout the decade opponents of abortion waged a fervent campaign to convert public opinion to their position, and the ensuing public debate gained wide attention in the media. In 1985 an antiabortion documentary, *The Silent Scream,* provoked much controversy and apparently brought some converts into the antiabortion camp.

Antiabortion Activism. The more radical members of the antiabortion movement increasingly chose to picket and sometimes block the entrances to clinics where abortions were performed. In many cases such demonstrators tried to dissuade medical personnel or patients from entering the clinics. The language of the antiabortion campaign grew more and more strident, more fervent in calling for direct action. A 1984 book was called *Ninety-Nine Ways to Close the Abortion Clinics.* One antiabortion group called itself the "Army of God." In this increasingly militant atmosphere, clinics around the country were invaded by demonstrators; some were even burned and bombed. In 1983 alone reported incidents of violence or harassment at abortion clinics totaled 123. These extremist tactics were denounced by many in the antiabortion movement. Nevertheless, such incidents continued through the decade.

Defending Reproductive Rights. Women's rights advocates believed the 1973 Supreme Court decision was a landmark ruling, one that saved the lives of many pregnant women who, before *Roe* v. *Wade,* might have resorted to unsterile, backroom abortions. These activists, often referred to as the "pro-choice" movement, believed the right to a safe, legal abortion should be protected vigilantly and that the critical decision whether or not to abort a pregnancy should be a private decision, one to be made by the woman in consultation with her doctor, her family, and her conscience. Seeing this fundamental right increasingly challenged by the antiabortion movement, whose basic position was publicly supported by President Reagan and later President Bush, pro-choice activists hurried to defend their position. Polls supported their belief that their stand on a woman's right to choose abortion represented the majority opinion in the United States. Yet as early as 1976 they had encountered opposition when the Hyde Amendment denied Medicaid benefits to pay for abortions, and state and local ordinances that aimed to restrict access to abortion followed. To counter the increasingly vocal and mobilized opposition, pro-choice advocates, like their opponents, courted the media and supported public officials in agreement with their position. They also staged marches and public demonstrations. The largest such rally was held in 1989, when more than six hundred thousand abortion rights supporters marched in Washington, D.C., in what was billed as the largest single march in Washington's history.

Definitions and Redefinitions. The defeat of the ERA, the rising influence of antiabortion groups, and a growing criticism of feminism in general convinced some observers that the women's movement was on the decline in the 1980s. Indeed, some veteran feminists began to engage in soul-searching and reevaluation. Some, such as Sylvia Ann Hewlett in her *A Lesser Life: The Myth of Women's Liberation in America* (1986), denounced feminism outright. Others claimed that the women's movement had become too radical, that it needed to move toward a more centrist position. In *The Second Stage* (1981) Betty Friedan, the "founding mother" of the women's liberation movement, declared that the movement needed to achieve a better balance between the goals of feminism and the traditional concerns of women. Many women, inspired and mobilized by Friedan's groundbreaking book *The Feminine Mystique* (1963), felt betrayed.

Renewed Traditionalism. Even as some feminists experienced self-doubts, other women called for a renewed traditionalism. These women, like the tireless antifeminist Phyllis Schlafly, celebrated homemaking and child rearing and urged a renewed focus on family life. They argued that the women's movement had confused and misled women by urging them to deny their natural identities. It had also, they maintained, created terrible disruptions in American society, contributing to the rising divorce rate and the multiplying troubles plaguing the nation's young. This theme of a return to more-traditional sex roles became prominent in political speeches, sermons, television programs, and women's magazines. Across the country working women were reportedly yearning for more time at home, more time with their children and spouses. With some success, conservatives portrayed feminists as being insensitive to mainstream values, extremists who were advancing false notions of gender equality and the right to abortion. Nevertheless, at the end of the decade feminists could point to some singular facts. Polls showed that large majorities of Americans still supported the principles of equal rights for women and of a woman's right to choose abortion. At the same time, most women believed that the women's movement had significantly improved their lives.

Women in the Workforce. Despite calls for women to return to traditional roles, the number of working women rose dramatically in the 1980s. Many worked out of necessity; more and more were single mothers supporting their children on their own. As Cynthia Taeuber reported, "Among women with infants, nearly two million, or over one-half of all new mothers were in the labor force in 1988 compared with less than one-third in 1976." This increase in working mothers put a strain on already inadequate child-care facilities. Cuts in federal funding for child care in the early 1980s profoundly affected the availability of safe child care for lower-income workers. As baby boomers began to have children of their own, the demand for child-care increased still further. By 1988 politicians had recognized this new concern among their constituents, as polls showed that most Americans favored the investment of their tax money to create viable child-care options for working parents.

Sources:

Toni Carabillo, Judith Meuli, and June Bundy Csida, *Feminist Chronicles: 1953–1993* (Los Angeles: Women's Graphics, 1993);

Barbara Ehrenreich, *The Worst Years of Our Lives* (New York: Pantheon, 1991);

Susan Faludi, *Backlash: The Undeclared War against American Women* (New York: Crown, 1991);

Homeless people getting a free Thanksgiving dinner at a soup kitchen in Lafayette Square, across the street from the White House in Washington, D.C., November 1989.

Sylvia Ann Hewlett, *A Lesser Life: The Myth of Women's Liberation in America* (New York: Morrow, 1986);

Fern Marx and Michelle Seligson, "Child Care in the United States," in *The American Woman: 1990–1991: A Status Report,* edited by Sara E. Rix (New York: Norton, 1991);

Cynthia Taeuber, ed., *Statistical Handbook on Women in America* (Phoenix: Oryx Press, 1991).

THE HOMELESS CRISIS

Homelessness in America. After the New Deal of the 1930s and the Great Society programs of the 1960s, many Americans believed that homelessness was no longer a serious problem in the United States; but in the 1980s the number of homeless Americans grew dramatically, and their plight came to be recognized as one of the leading social problems of the decade. Starting in the early 1980s homeless people — often called "street people" — became an increasingly frequent sight in New York; Los Angeles; Chicago; Washington, D.C.; Saint Louis; and most other major cities, as well as many smaller cities. Men and women of all ages, individuals and families from varied backgrounds and circumstances — shabbily dressed and inadequately nourished — began roaming city streets, sleeping on benches in summer and on heating grates or in crowded public shelters in winter. The sight of people who for one reason or another had "slipped between the cracks" of the system, fallen through the social safety nets designed to help those in crisis, tore at the conscience of what was still the richest country in the world, even in the recession-plagued early years of the 1980s. Estimates of the number of homeless people ranged from three hundred thousand or five hundred thousand to as many as 2 million or 3 million. Because, by definition, the homeless had no permanent addresses at which they could be contacted and counted, statistics were never reliable, but as the decade continued most observers believed that the number of homeless individuals was closer to the high range of 2 million to 3 million, and that the numbers were growing by something like 25 percent per year.

Public Awareness. As the crisis built, the issue of homelessness gained wide coverage in the media: television networks produced special reports and made-for-television movies; newspapers printed numerous stories and editorials; articles began to fill magazines and scholarly journals; academic studies were conducted and Congressional hearings held. One of the most important books on the subject was Michael Harrington's *The New American Poverty* (1984). Meanwhile, the issue of homelessness began to be framed by the growing affluence and conspicuous consumption of many more-fortunate Americans.

Families with Children. According to the National Low-Income Housing Coalition, families with children, mostly women caring for children alone, were "the fastest growing segment of the homeless." The coalition estimated that the proportion of homeless people in families varied from 25 percent in some cities to 70 percent in others. Many homeless families were turned away from emergency shelters because of lack of space. According to a Providence, Rhode Island, official reporting in 1988 to the U.S. Conference of Mayors, the emotional impact of homelessness on families included "fighting, fear, depression (acute or chronic), feelings of failure, and lack of stability. . . . These families are so beaten, it's almost to the point of self-abuse." In the same year a study of twenty-seven cities by the U.S. Conference of Mayors estimated that one in every four homeless people was under nineteen years of age. In his *Rachel and Her Children: Homeless Families in America* (1988), Jonathan Kozol wrote that if all the homeless children in the country "were gathered in one city, they would represent a larger population than that of Atlanta, Denver, or St. Louis. Because they are scattered in a thousand cities, they are easily unseen."

Causes of Homelessness. Homelessness has been a problem throughout American history, particularly after the rise of urbanization and industrialization; but experts and officials who grappled with the problem in the early 1980s labored to explain why the homeless population in America had grown so large — and why it had grown so suddenly. The debate about the causes of this homelessness was politically charged and never fully resolved. Almost all participants agreed, however, that no single cause lay behind the crisis. Most advocates for the homeless were fierce critics of the Reagan administration, pointing to Republican economic and social policies as a principal agent in precipitating and aggravating the crisis. They blamed Republican-inspired cuts in social-welfare programs such as Aid to Families with Dependent Children (AFDC) for pushing many individuals into the situation of being unable to make rent payments. Critics of the Republicans also decried dramatic cuts in federal assistance for subsidized low-income housing. Under the

---

HANDS ACROSS AMERICA

In a human chain stretching from New York City to Long Beach, California, more than 5 million people grasped hands on 25 May 1986 to raise money and focus the nation's attention on poverty, hunger, and homelessness. Hands Across America stretched more than four thousand miles across sixteen states and through five hundred cities. Celebrities such as Bill Cosby, Steven Spielberg, Lily Tomlin, and Frank Sinatra took part in the event as both planners and participants. Although organizers hoped to raise $50 million, only $33 million came in, and after expenses only $16 million remained for distribution to groups aiding the poor and the homeless.

Sources: Melinda Beck, "A New Spirit of Giving," *Newsweek*, 107 (22 June 1986): 18–20;

Coleen O'Connor, "A $50 Million Handshake," *Newsweek*, 107 (19 May 1986): 25.

Reagan administration, the budget for the Department of Housing and Urban Development (HUD) was reduced from $36 billion in 1980, the last year of the Carter administration, to $14 billion in 1987.

Multiple Factors. At the same time, most people agreed that other economic forces also contributed to the homeless problem. For example, some of the homeless were working people whose low wages, frequently from minimum-wage jobs, did not allow them to keep up with the rising cost of living, much less the rising price of housing. Experts also pointed to a continuing nationwide decline in manufacturing jobs, which in many cases forced displaced workers to take lower-wage positions. Another factor compounding the homeless problem was the urban renewal and development projects that destroyed many old buildings, including the single-room-occupancy hotels (SROs) that had been subsidized by cities to provide housing for low-income people, particularly the elderly. Furthermore, there was gentrification, the process whereby old buildings and neighborhoods that provided low-income housing were converted to condominiums and cooperatives, frequently for the young urban professionals who were moving in increasing numbers into the cities, reversing an earlier trend of suburbanization. In rural areas the farm crisis of the 1980s, in which thousands of farmers lost their farms and their homes, contributed to the stream of the homeless heading for cities in search of work. The homeless population was certainly increased by the "deinstitutionalization" of mental patients that began in 1960s and 1970s. Well-intentioned laws designed to guard mentally ill people from involuntary commitment to institutions except under clearly defined conditions resulted in the release of many patients who, unable to care for themselves, often ended

CHILDREN AND POVERTY IN A SMALL CITY

Critics of conservative politics and rampant materialism during the 1980s pointed to what they perceived as a growing disparity between social classes during the decade. The rich were getting richer, they noted, but the poor were getting poorer. In 1989 *Life* highlighted those at the bottom of the economic spectrum in a heartrending story about children growing up in poverty. Focusing on the residents of a dilapidated building in Portsmouth, a city in south-central Ohio in one of the poorest of the state's counties, the story and accompanying photographs used the wide-eyed, bleak stares of poor children and their stunted dreams to dramatize the fact that 13 million children, one in five, were living in poverty in the United States — the highest number and percentage since the 1960s, when President Lyndon Johnson launched his War on Poverty. While many citizens of Portsmouth were indignant at the city's being featured in such an article, the larger point was that such poverty could be found anywhere. In a country proud of its wealth and support of progress, *Life* said, many children were growing up learning poverty as a way of life.

Source: Peter Meyer, "Children of Poverty: Growing up at 215 Washington Street, Portsmouth, Ohio," *Life*, 12 (September 1989): 56–66.

up living in the streets. Some officials claimed deinstitutionalization was possibly the leading cause of homelessness; this claim was hotly contested by others, who viewed it as a means of shrugging off responsibility for the situation.

Activism. As homelessness grew through the 1980s, many homeless advocacy groups lobbied city, state, and federal officials, urging both short- and long-term measures to meet the burgeoning problems of the homeless. The most prominent of these groups was the Community for Creative Non-Violence (CCNV), headed by Mitch Snyder, a former advertising executive who campaigned throughout the 1980s on behalf of the homeless. Abandoning his own family and taking up residence in a homeless shelter, he led many nonviolent protests aimed at increasing public awareness and ameliorating the conditions of homeless people. In 1984 he engaged in a hunger strike to secure an abandoned federal building in Washington, D.C., for use as a homeless shelter. President Reagan acceded to his demands. In 1989 Snyder led the "Housing Now!" march on Washington, in which 250,000 people participated. His activities were the subject of a 1985 made-for-television movie, *Samaritan*, starring Martin Sheen. Snyder committed suicide in 1990.

Other Responses. On the front lines of the homeless crisis, most cities, to meet at least the minimum daily needs for food and housing, worked hard to maintain and even expand their systems of emergency public shelters. Existing shelters, which had met the needs of the homeless for years, were inadequate to the demands of the 1980s dilemma. Cities also contracted with commercial hotels, sometimes called "welfare hotels," to provide temporary accommodations for homeless families. At the same time many churches and synagogues set up "soup kitchens" and sometimes provided limited shelter. Volunteer organizations joined the effort to provide assistance, and charitable organizations such as the Salvation Army and the Robert Wood Johnson Foundation, and relief organizations such as the American Red Cross, Catholic Charities USA, and the Children's Defense Fund also helped.

Federal Responses. As for the federal government, President Reagan seldom publicly addressed the issue of homelessness. In a remark reported by *The New York Times* in December 1988 Reagan said that many of the homeless "are homeless . . . you might say, by choice," a remark that seemed to typify his response to the issue through his two terms in office. For its part, Congress held hearings about the homeless crisis and passed several pieces of legislation, the most significant of which was the Stewart B. McKinney Homeless Assistance Act, reluctantly signed into law by President Reagan in 1987. The McKinney Act, the first comprehensive federal legislation designed to combat homelessness, authorized the spending of $1 billion in 1987 and 1988 (only $600 million was actually appropriated) and included twenty provisions for homeless aid, including emergency-shelter funds, health care, job training, and the establishing of the Interagency Council on the Homeless to coordinate federal programs assisting the homeless.

No Simple Solutions. As the decade progressed, so did the crisis. In a 1989 poll reported in *The New York Times*, 65 percent of those responding favored greater federal spending on homelessness. But despite increased national awareness of the crisis and various legislative and charitable efforts to alleviate its severity, the numbers of homeless people remained large. While the nature of the problem and its solutions continued to be debated, public attention to the issue began to wane. A front-page *New York Times* article in 1990 reported, "A decade after the vast numbers of homeless people began to be seen on New York City's streets, officials and advocates fear that homelessness has become embedded in the city's life for the foreseeable future."

Sources:

Rick Fantasia and Maurice Isserman, *Homelessness: A Sourcebook* (New York: Facts On File, 1994);

Michael Harrington, *The New American Poverty* (New York: Holt, Rinehart & Winston, 1984);

Nintendo Power Pad, introduced in the United States in 1989, allowed children to control the action in a video game by jumping on a vinyl mat. In the second half of the 1980s Nintendo games were so popular that they hurt sales of traditional toys.

Mary Ellen Hombs, *American Homelessness: A Reference Handbook* (Santa Barbara, Cal.: ABC-Clio, 1990).

LEISURE TIME

The Cost of Recreation in the 1980s. In the 1980s Americans continued to find new means of escape from their work schedules and to consider these means an important investment. In 1980 total personal expenditures for recreation were $149 billion; by 1989 the figure had risen to $250 billion. In 1980 sales of sporting goods totaled nearly $17 billion; by 1989 that total had risen to $45 billion. In 1980 Broadway shows took in $143 million; by 1989 their receipts totaled $262 million. Total motion-picture receipts in 1980 were $2.7 billion; by 1989 they had risen to more than $5 billion. In 1980 Americans spent $9 billion on books; by the end of the decade they were spending more than $19 billion. The leisure and entertainment industries were bigger businesses than ever before during the 1980s. According to Margaret Ambry, in 1988 American households spent $126 billion for entertainment, and the average household devoted 5 percent of its total spending to entertainment costs. Middle-aged householders accounted for 72 percent of the entertainment market. Among people ages thirty-five to forty-four, overall spending for entertainment was nearly 50 percent above average. Those in the age group forty-five to fifty-four spent 80 percent more than the average household on sporting events. Householders younger than twenty-five spent almost four times more than the average household on tape recorders and players.

Trends. Of the $126 billion Americans spent on entertainment, $50 billion was spent on sports. According to a 1988 report in *Sports, Inc.*, that amount equaled "the sum of the output of goods and services generated by the sports industry." In the 1980s professional football teams received 60 percent of their revenues from television. The three major networks earned $1.6 billion in sports advertising in 1986. At the same time, cable television increasingly gave viewers more choices in channels: by 1989 cable television was found in 60 percent of all homes with television sets. Sales of VCRs were at 475,000 at the beginning of the 1980s and soared to 11 million by the end of the decade. Rentals of movies on video became so popular that by 1985 income from video rentals for home viewing equaled the income studios made from movies shown in theaters. Another leisure activity that grew to popularity was attending professional wrestling matches featuring such muscle-bound giants as Hulk Hogan. As for games, Trivial Pursuit become a national craze in the early 1980s. Video games became another leisure-time favorite. Nintendo video games were played in 20 percent of all American homes, and one business publication reported that in the latter part of the 1980s Nintendo "stymied the growth of the traditional toy industry." During the decade more and more Americans were eating out. By 1986, 40 percent of the average household food budget was spent anywhere from McDonald's to the finest restaurants. Among yuppies, dining out became an especially noticeable trend. They favored restaurants featuring ethnic or natural foods. And Americans continued to travel in large numbers, both domestically and abroad. In 1987, 13 million Americans traveled outside the United States.

The Health Club Craze. The health clubs popular in the 1970s boomed in the 1980s, and more and more featured shiny upscale facilities marketed to attract yuppies — who were about the only ones who could afford memberships in the poshest of these clubs, which could cost as much as $2,000 per year. Yuppies as a group tended to be health conscious, and the fitness buzzword of the 1980s was "wellness," defined by Frank Rosato in his 1982 book, *Fitness and Wellness: The Physical Connection,* as "a global concept that emphasizes self-responsibility for achieving an optimal state of health and well-being." The wellness concept included such factors as "stress management, nonuse of tobacco, nutritional awareness, alcohol and drug awareness, mental and emotional health, and physical fitness." Capitalizing on the yuppies' interest in wellness, as well as their tendency to be attentive to physical appearance, the upscale health clubs offered high-tech, computerized equipment and all the latest exercise machinery, as well as personal trainers, aerobics classes, racquetball courts, squash courts, swimming pools, steam rooms, saunas, and masseurs and masseuses. Many featured fresh juice bars as well, capitalizing on the yuppies' interest in natural foods and nutrition; and, since many clubs were coed, the management often played up the social possibilities of membership. Indeed, for many yuppies, health clubs seemed nearly to replace singles' bars as prime places to meet members of the opposite sex. Some of the best-known clubs were the Sports Club in Los Angeles and the Health and Racquet Club in (HRC) New York City. In 1986 a *New York Times* advertisement for the New York Health and Racquet Club featured a picture of Olympic gold medal winner Peggy Fleming, who was quoted as saying, "I strive for perfection, so when I'm in New York, I go straight to the place where I can challenge my body, the place where I can use the facilities and get the professional help that keeps me fit." The ad boasted that the HRC "offers over 100 exercise classes every week . . . , karate, nutritional and quitsmoke programs and spas that sparkle with style and luxury . . . and individualized nautilus and professional one-to-one training." What one wore in such upscale clubs was considered important, and many patrons made sure to bring the right sneakers, sweatpants, leggings, tanktops, and leotards. For such people L. L Bean offered a fitness/fashion catalogue, *The L. L. Bean Guide to Fitness.* Articles in magazines such as *Vogue* and *Harper's Bazaar* advised their readers how to shop for the

THE DECLINE OF LEISURE?

In *The Overworked American: The Unexpected Decline of Leisure* (1991) Juliet B. Schor disagrees with researchers who claim that Americans had more leisure time in the 1980s than they had in earlier decades. According to Schor, Americans enjoyed less leisure in the 1980s than at any other period since the end of World War II. She says that a gradual but definite increase in working hours has hit most sections of the workforce, from professionals to low-paid service workers, creating "a profound structural crisis of time." According to Schor, "the media provide mounting evidence of 'time poverty,' overwork, and a squeeze on time. . . . Stress-related diseases have exploded, especially among women. Workers' compensation claims related to stress tripled during just the first half of the 1980s." The fast-paced corporate world of the 1980s emphasized commitment and initiative. Schor quotes one aggressive CEO as saying, "People who work for me should have phones in their bathrooms." She adds that complaints about a hectic lifestyle are particularly noticeable among the baby-boom generation. As for women, Schor's thesis is supported by the *Statistical Handbook on Women in America,* which notes that, although the majority of women work outside the home, "there was no significant reduction in household and family responsibilities in the last decade." These "super Moms" "have little free time and say they are just plain tired." Schor's thesis is also supported by the essayist Barbara Ehrenreich, who wrote whimsically that if yuppies as a group had died, as some reports claimed in 1987, it was because "they never rested, never took time to chew between bites or gaze soulfully past their computer screens." Though yuppies survived the decade, they frequently suffered from a malady that was widely reported in the 1980s: chronic fatigue syndrome, often called the "yuppie flu."

Sources: Barbara Ehrenreich, *The Worst Years of Our Lives: Irreverent Notes from a Decade of Greed* (New York: Pantheon, 1990);

Juliet B. Schor, *The Overworked American: The Unexpected Decline of Leisure* (New York: Basic Books, 1991);

Cynthia Taeuber, ed., *Statistical Handbook on Women in America* (Phoenix: Oryx Press, 1991).

right health club and how to choose the right exercise programs. In 1986 a *New York Times Magazine* article quoted John McCarthy, executive director of a health club trade group, who noted, "In every major city there are large clubs and small exercise studios that weren't there five years ago." Chicago had so many health clubs that it tried to levy what was dubbed a "yuppie tax" on

RUBIK'S CUBE

Invented in the 1970s by a Hungarian professor of design, Ernö Rubik, the toy that was sold in the United States as the Rubik's Cube became a popular phenomenon in the early 1980s. The Rubik's Cube was the most challenging — and for many people, infuriating — puzzle ever to achieve mass-market success. Composed of twenty-six smaller cubes, or "cubies," the cube presented nine colored squares on each of its six faces. When the cube was purchased, each face was of a uniform color, different from that of any of the other faces; after the faces were rotated randomly, the cube would end up a jumble of colors — and most people had no idea how to restore it to its original state. People spent hours, if not days, rearranging the cube in dozens of the 43,252,003,274,489,855,999 (43 quintillion) positions other than the one correct position before achieving success or giving up.

The puzzle could be solved, of course, as Rubik and many others demonstrated. People who had figured out a system for solving the puzzle wrote best-selling books on how to do it, and some held contests with lubricated cubes to see who could solve it the fastest. (In a world championship contest in Budapest in 1982, a high-school student from Los Angeles solved the puzzle in 22.95 seconds.)

In the United States the Rubik's Cube was the 1980s equivalent of the hula hoop of the 1950s. Millions of cubes were sold, as was a Cube Smasher designed "to beat it into 43 quintillion pieces." A fake commercial on the television show *Saturday Night Live* featured a Rubik's Grenade, which had to be solved in ten seconds or it would explode. Mathematics professors used the cube in classes to illustrate the finer points of group theory.

Rubik, who became the richest individual in Hungary from international sales of the cube, devised other puzzles that were even more difficult than the Rubik's Cube. While sales were respectable, nothing matched the incredible success of his first invention.

Sources: Anne Steacy, "Rubik's Newest Twist," *Maclean's*, 99 (29 September 1986): 52;

John Tierney, "The Perplexing Life of Erno Rubik," *Discover*, 7 (March 1986): 81–88.

membership fees, so the city could increase its tax base. (The attempt was unsuccessful.) Estimates of the numbers of health clubs throughout the nation in the mid 1980s ranged from four thousand to thirteen thousand.

Break Dancing. At the same time that fashion and leisure trends were filtering down from the upper classes, the hip-hop culture of African American neighborhoods of the Bronx and Brooklyn was having a major influence on teen culture. Break dancing and rap music became popular nationwide. According to a 1986 article in *Rolling Stone*, break dancing reflected the multicultural influence of blacks from Barbados, Jamaica, Cuba, Puerto Rico, and North America. Break dancing was most often accompanied by rap lyrics and music. It involved improvised, highly athletic, acrobatic dance movements, and the dancers, almost always male, often competed to see who could make the best moves. The baggy shorts and shirts and backwards caps worn by break-dancers and rap musicians became as popular with teens nationwide as the hip-hop culture's music and dancing.

Sources:
Margaret Ambry, *Consumer Power: How Americans Spend Their Money* (Ithaca, N.Y.: New Strategist Publications, 1991);

A. Bartlett Giamatti, *Take Time for Paradise: Americans and Their Games* (New York: Summit Books, 1989);

William R. Greer, "Finding the Right Health Club," *New York Times Magazine*, 28 September 1986, pp. 102, 103, 107;

Charles Panati, *Panati's Parade of Fads, Follies, and Manias: The Origins of Our Most Cherished Obsessions* (New York: Harper & Row Perennial Library, 1991);

Robert Farris Thompson, "Hip-Hop 101," *Rolling Stone*, no. 470 (27 March 1986): 95–100.

THE MEESE COMMISSION ON PORNOGRAPHY

A Conservative Look at Pornography. On 9 July 1986 the report of the Attorney General's Commission on Pornography was released. For those who had followed the proceedings of the commission, the report held no surprises: the two-volume, 1,960-page document advocated stricter enforcement of existing obscenity laws and the expansion of definitions of obscenity to make more types of pornography illegal. While conservatives praised the commission's report as a step toward restoring what they perceived as the lost moral tenor of American life, publishers denounced it as an effort to undermine the First Amendment, and social scientists found fault with its use of research. Some stores pulled magazines censured by the commission from their shelves, and local communities increased efforts to crack down on sellers of pornography — even if sales clerks, rather than the owners of the stores, were the ones who were arrested.

Procedures. U.S. attorney general Edwin Meese created the commission in May 1985 with the goal of finding "new ways to control the problem of pornography" — showing a conservative bias from the start, since the very perception that there *was* a "problem with pornography" contradicted the findings of the 1970 President's Commission on Obscenity and Pornography. Indeed, the constitution of the committee indicated that it would begin with certain assumptions and incline toward certain interpretations: seven of its eleven members had publicly

Attorney General Edwin Meese with the 1,950-page report of his Commission on Pornography, 9 July 1986

spoken out against pornography before being named to the commission. Nor were its procedures reassuring to those who desired a fair examination of the issue, since most of the people the commission interviewed about the effects of pornography favored control of its production and distribution. In addition, the commission made a show of drawing on social-science findings on pornography, but many social scientists criticized the commission's conclusions as unsupported by existing research. Likewise, the commission drew on the ideas of feminist antipornography advocates while ignoring their calls for increased sex education.

The Report. After examining 2,375 magazines, 725 books, and 2,370 movies, the majority of the commission members decided, over the objections of the more moderate members, that pornography led to violence against women and children and "debased" women. The report, which had the full support of Attorney General Meese, encouraged the abolition of sexually explicit materials.

The Reaction. While hardly anyone objected to such recommendations as the banning of child pornography, many Americans found the report an unwarranted intrusion into the private lives of citizens. Mainstream men's magazines such as *Playboy* and *Penthouse* went on the defensive, particularly after the 7-Eleven chain of convenience stores pulled the magazines from their shelves in response to threatened boycotts by antipornography ac-

tivists such as the Reverend Donald Wildmon's National Federation for Decency. Some writers ridiculed the commission as a kangaroo court putting pornography on trial as part of a conservative agenda to reshape the American cultural landscape.

Aftermath. While conservatives did make some progress in limiting pornography during the late 1980s, America had come too far in its notions of sexual expression to revert to the attitudes of the 1950s. Magazine publishers and filmmakers, though concerned about increased scrutiny, for the most part went about their business, and they did not have to search far for customers. A few years after the report was released it was largely seen as much ado about very little.

Sources:

F. M. Christensen, *Pornography: The Other Side* (New York, Westport, Conn. & London: Praeger, 1990);

John D'Emilio and Estelle B. Freedman, *Intimate Matters: A History of Sexuality in America* (New York: Harper & Row, 1988);

Susan Gubar and Joan Hoff, eds., *For Adult Users Only: The Dilemma of Violent Pornography* (Bloomington & Indianapolis: Indiana University Press, 1989).

RACE RELATIONS

The New Conservative Climate. Although civil rights leaders had believed that the movement toward social and racial equality for minorities was slowing in the 1970s, the determined conservatism of the 1980s Reagan era caught them unprepared. The conservative mood that settled across some sections of the American public in this decade seemed to be a backlash against the civil rights movement that had been building since the landmark victories of the 1960s. Many white middle-class voters found Reagan's conservatism appealing because they feared that social change in America had been too rapid and too extensive. As a candidate, Ronald Reagan had criticized school busing and affirmative action programs; as president he continued to exhibit a distaste for civil rights activism and for some of the gains that activism had achieved. During his two terms in office he met only once with the Congressional Black Caucus, and black leaders realized that, for the first time in many years, they had no real allies in the White House. Meanwhile, cuts in federal spending for such programs as food stamps and Medicaid proceeded without effective opposition, fueling the perception that the president and his administration were insensitive to issues affecting low-income and minority Americans. As the decade progressed, and civil rights policies and legislation from previous years were attacked and sometimes reversed by the Reagan administration, many blacks became increasingly discouraged. In a 1988 *Newsweek* poll, 71 percent of blacks surveyed said that the federal government was doing "too little" to help blacks. A year earlier Justice Thurgood Marshall, a legendary civil rights activist and the only black ever to serve on the U.S. Supreme Court, said he believed that President Reagan ranked at "the bottom" of U.S. presidents in terms of rights for blacks. "Honestly," he said, "I think he's down with Hoover and that group . . . when we really didn't have a chance."

Another Troubled Decade. The 1980s were riddled with racial incidents, many of which made the local news where they occurred and some of which made national headlines. The decade began with the 1980 Miami riots that followed the acquittal of four white police officers in the beating death of a black man, riots that left 9 dead and 163 injured. The decade ended with the 1989 fatal shooting in Bensonhurst, New York, of a sixteen-year-old black youth by young white men. In the years between, there were highly publicized events involving hate groups such as neo-Nazis and the Ku Klux Klan, which in 1987 attacked civil rights marchers in Forsyth County, Georgia, who were celebrating the recently established Martin Luther King Jr. holiday. In addition to other violent incidents — such as that in the Howard Beach section of New York City, in which three white teenagers attacked three black youths, one of whom died — the decade also saw a rise in racially motivated incidents on college campuses, incidents watched closely because colleges had traditionally been considered havens of tolerance. In the two academic years between 1986 and 1988, the National Institute Against Prejudice and Violence listed 163 incidents on campuses across the country. Throughout the United States many blacks felt that the social climate had turned against them, that there was both greater hostility from some white groups and greater indifference from others. *Newsweek* magazine's special report, "Black and White in America," described the general attitude as "less caring" than in the 1960s. District of Columbia representative Walter Fauntroy, a veteran civil rights activist, detected "a new meanness" in human relations. At the same time, older leaders such as Roy Wilkins of the National Association for the Advancement of Colored People (NAACP), had died, and some major civil rights organizations that flourished earlier, such as the Southern Christian Leadership Conference (SCLC), had declined. At the beginning of the decade, with the triumph of Republican conservatives in national politics, black leaders looked grimly at the troubles ahead. Vernon Jordan, head of the National Urban League, who had been shot and seriously wounded in 1980, said in a 1981 speech to the organization, "The complexities of today's racial, economic and political issues are such that there is no one grand strategy or leader to deliver us. We will have to draw on our immense resources of survival skills to get us through these hard times."

Jesse Jackson. The Reverend Jesse Jackson, a youthful black leader during the civil rights battles of the 1960s and 1970s and considered by some blacks the successor to Martin Luther King Jr., became a pivotal figure in race relations and civil rights in the 1980s. In 1983, charging that Democratic leaders had been too passive in the face of Republican cutbacks in programs for the poor and minorities, he became a Democratic presidential candi-

date; he also announced his intention to build a coalition of dispossessed minorities, including African Americans, Native Americans, Hispanic Americans, and Asian Americans — what he called a "rainbow coalition" of those who were "rejected and despised" and "left naked before the Lord in wintertime." This presidential campaign, and another in 1988, not only made him a hero to many blacks but also proved something that had appeared unlikely if not impossible before: that a black could be taken seriously as a presidential candidate. Indeed, in the 1988 primaries Jackson gained the support of a significant number of white voters; although he did not win the Democratic nomination, he was a major force by the time of the party's national convention in Atlanta, where his eloquent plea for racial harmony in America drew admiration from Americans of all races. After 1988 the idea that Jackson, or some other African American, could become president in the reasonably near future did not seem unreasonable.

Louis Farrakhan. Black leader Louis Farrakhan, head of the Nation of Islam, was a stirring orator who exerted a profound influence on his followers, many of whom were young black men from inner cities who were lured away from drugs, violence, and the casual siring of illegitimate children to a new lifestyle based on pride, self-discipline, education, and the avoidance of drugs (including alcohol and tobacco) and promiscuity. But, although he was closely associated with Jesse Jackson and a strong supporter of Jackson in both his presidential campaigns, Farrakhan was widely viewed outside the black community — and by some blacks, as well — as an anti-Semite, a demagogue, and an extremist in his view of race relations. Acknowledging these widespread perceptions, Jackson was forced to distance himself publicly from Farrakhan, although he refused to break completely with him. The principal disagreement between Farrakhan and Jackson concerned their views of race relations: while Jackson advocated the integration and harmony of all racial groups in American society, Farrakhan preached racial antagonism and separatism. In speaking tours across the United States, Farrakhan was greeted by large and enthusiastic crowds. At Madison Square Garden in New York City in 1985, for example, he addressed twenty-five thousand listeners. At this meeting, according to a reporter for *The Economist*, Farrakhan attacked "established Black leaders, white folk in general, and Jews in particular." Five years later, in an interview in *People* magazine, Farrakhan stated his view that the United States should pay reparations to blacks for the oppression they have suffered. "Blacks are separate," he said. "If America does not have the will to bring about a change within a permanent underclass, then . . . what does America owe us? Reparations must include the freeing of all blacks from state and federal penitentiaries. Then let us ask our brothers and sisters in Africa to set aside a separate territory for us, and let us take the money that

America is spending to maintain these convicts and [invest it in] a new reality on the African continent."

Former KKK Member Wins Political Office. Although small in number at the beginning of the 1980s, the white supremacists in the Ku Klux Klan attracted extensive media coverage and won new converts to their ranks as the decade proceeded. While the KKK began to change its image somewhat, presenting itself as an organization of paramilitary guerrillas fighting for racial survival, it continued its terrorist cross burnings: from 1985 to 1987 the Klanwatch Project of the Southern Poverty Law Center reported forty-five cases of arson and cross burnings, as well as hundreds of acts of vandalism. Then, in 1989, in an event that symbolized the troubled race relations in the decade, David Duke, a former grand wizard of the Klan, won a seat in the Louisiana legislature. Elected by a virtually all-white suburb of New Orleans, Duke took pains to dismiss his earlier leadership role in the KKK, attributing it to youthful indiscretion; but most outside observers were unconvinced, believing that his campaign demonstrated racist views carefully couched in language designed to obscure them. To the great embarrassment of the national Republican Party, Duke had been elected as a Republican. Although both President Reagan and President Bush had denounced Duke, many people felt that Republican policies had promoted the climate in which people like Duke could thrive. Critics pointed to the allegedly race-baiting "Willie Horton" television ad that, the year before Duke's election, Republicans had used against Bush's opponent, Michael Dukakis. Duke's election gave him nationwide media attention; he later ran for the U.S. Senate but was defeated, to the relief of those who hoped for improved race relations in the next decade.

Sources:

"Black Power, Foul and Fragrant," *Economist,* 292 (12 October 1985): 25–26;

David Gelman and others, "Black and White in America," *Newsweek,* 11 (7 March 1988): 18–23;

Harry A. Ploski and James Williams, eds., *The Negro Almanac: A Reference Work on the African American,* fifth edition (Detroit: Gale Research, 1989);

"Predicting Disaster for a Racist America, Louis Farrakhan Envisions an African Homeland," *People,* 34 (7 September 1990): 111–116.

SENIOR CITIZENS' ISSUES

The Graying of America. In 1980 26 million Americans were sixty-five or older; by the end of the decade their number had reached 31 million. Because of medical advances and a relatively high standard of living, Americans were living longer than previous generations. Indeed, by 1985 the average life expectancy had increased nearly twenty-five years beyond what it had been in 1900, giving older Americans, in effect, a quarter century more than their grandparents had in which to be elderly. Being predominantly middle-class and generally more affluent than previous elderly populations, retired Americans in the 1980s contradicted many stereotypes about the later

AGE WARS

The Social Security crisis of the early 1980s brought into focus the concept of intergenerational conflict, frequently referred to in the media as "age wars" or "the war between the generations." The 1960s had popularized the idea of a "generation gap," referring to the difference in values between the parents and children of that era. The 1980s took the seed of this idea and cultivated it into something markedly different. The idea gained increasing currency that the relationship between the older and the younger generations was being transformed by economic and demographic trends, trends that would continue to impact with rising urgency for at least the next fifty years. Specifically, older Americans in the 1980s were charged with claiming an unduly large share of federal resources through the Social Security system. Not only were Baby Boomers paying high taxes to support benefits for the elderly, but they were doing it at a time when they should be saving for their own retirements. Projections showed that when the 75 million-strong Baby Boom generation entered retirement in the early decades of the twenty-first century, the generation behind it, being much smaller — and saddled with paying interest on the huge deficits run up in the 1980s — would be unable to fund the tremendous costs of the baby boomers' Social Security and Medicare benefits. The idea of generational conflict, therefore, referred first to the conflict between adult baby boomers and their elders, the notion being that the elderly should forgo some of their excessive benefits in the interest of "generational equity." The idea of generational conflict also referred to the future, when elderly baby boomers would be competing with their children's generation for diminishing resources. In 1982, according to polls taken by many organizations, from Gallup to NBC News, the idea that there was a marked conflict between the generations was not supported. Skeptics claimed that the concept of "age wars" was a creation of the media. In 1985, however, Americans for Generational Equity (AGE) was organized "to promote greater public understanding of the problems arising from the aging of the U.S. population and to foster public support for policies that will serve the economic interests of next century's elderly." Formed by two U.S. senators, AGE became a principal catalyst for keeping public attention focused on what it believed was the growing risk of a serious clash between the generations.

Sources: Jerry Gerber, Janet Wolff, Walter Klores, and Gene Brown, *Lifetrends: The Future of Baby Boomers and Other Aging Americans* (New York: Macmillan, 1989);

Philip Longman, "Age Wars: The Coming Battle between Young and Old," *Futurist,* 20 (January–February 1986): 8–11.

stages of life, living more dynamically than might have been predicted. While well-appointed retirement communities began to flourish across the country, senior citizens traveled the superhighways in recreational vehicles (RVs), ran in marathons, took ocean cruises, formed and joined new organizations, and continued to educate themselves by participating in programs such as Elderhostel and the Shepherd's Center, which provided formal and informal instruction on subjects from computers to international politics. Americans, who had been famously preoccupied with youth for at least twenty years, began to focus on "the graying of America." In the media, as well as among politicians, social scientists, and economists, attempts were made to describe and understand the phenomenon of increasing — and increasingly visible — aging Americans. While businesses began to court the dollars of retirees, even teen-fixated Hollywood began to notice their older audience. *On Golden Pond* (1981), starring the elderly Henry Fonda and Katharine Hepburn as a couple facing their last years, was a surprise box-office hit and won several Academy Awards. After long absences from the screen other older actors, including Jessica Tandy, Hume Cronyn, and Don Ameche, began appearing in major films, and *The Golden Girls*, a comedy about three middle-aged women — and the mother of one of them — living together, became a hit television series.

Another Dimension. Of course, not all senior citizens were on golf courses or cruises. During the decade special problems of the elderly, such as Alzheimer's disease, received increasing attention, generating their own array of books, articles, and television movies and documentaries. Nursing homes multiplied to accommodate the multiple and complex needs of older Americans, many of the most elderly of whom suffered from chronic, incurable illnesses. Advances in medical technology that enabled some older Americans to enjoy healthier lives also provided the means to keep severely ill elderly persons alive indefinitely on "life support" systems. "Living wills," specifying in advance an individual's wishes regarding medical treatment should he or she become incapacitated, became more and more common. Medical schools began to offer increased education in geriatric medicine, a previously neglected specialty. At the same time, lawyers became aware that the problems of the elderly required new legal specialists. All in all, whether focusing on the brighter side of "the golden years" or the darker side of old age (loneliness, depression, bereavement, fears of impoverishment by catastrophic illness), people discussed the themes of aging and later life more frequently and openly than they had in previous decades, as if a taboo had been lifted. (It should be added that the "graying of America" most often referred to the increase in, and increased visibility of, the currently retired population. In some discussions, however, it referred to the Baby Boom generation of 1945 to 1965, especially re-

garding questions of what their retirement circumstances would be in the early decades of the next century.)

Gray Power. Correctly or incorrectly, senior citizens were increasingly perceived as a distinct segment of American society, a cohesive group with its own special perspectives and agenda. The Gray Panthers, formed in the 1970s, signaled the beginning of a remarkable growth in the number of organizations dedicated to seniors' concerns. In the 1980s the Gray Panthers were overshadowed by the American Association of Retired Persons (AARP), which, with 20 million members, became one of the largest mass-membership organizations in the United States — second only to the Catholic Church. From its headquarters in Washington, D.C., the AARP was a forceful lobbyist and advocate for older Americans. Because of its influence and that of other groups such as the National Council on the Aging and the National Council of Senior Citizens, the perception grew that senior Americans were a new single-interest group capable of exerting tremendous power on the electoral process and influencing government policies. Phrases such as *gray power* and *the gray lobby* became popular; politicians referred to the senior lobby as "the eight-hundred-pound gorilla" (who can sit wherever he wants). As statistics showed older Americans were among the most active voters, officials and candidates for public office increasingly showed up at retirement communities and even at nursing homes. Some observers, arguing that the political clout of older Americans was exaggerated, pointed out that older citizens, like every other segment of the population, were a diverse group with diverse values and interests. Nevertheless, it was commonly recognized that certain issues, such as Social Security, united most senior citizens. Indeed, those citizens were extremely visible when this highly charged issue came into sharp focus in 1981.

Social Security Crisis. For several years in the early 1980s an intense debate focused on Social Security, a debate stirred by the highly publicized claim and growing perception that the Social Security system was facing a crisis. This hugely important program, the foundation of federal social insurance since the Great Depression, paid all senior citizens monthly cash benefits from a trust fund financed by payroll taxes on workers and their employers. Social Security also provided health insurance to senior citizens through its Medicare component. Suddenly, after it had been widely accepted that the fiscal problems of Social Security had been resolved in the 1970s by huge tax increases, officials in the newly elected Reagan administration charged that Old Age, Survivors, Disability, and Health Insurance, the part of Social Security that paid retirement benefits, was threatened with imminent bankruptcy. Reagan officials claimed further that even if this problem were resolved, the system faced serious deficits for the remainder of the decade; moreover, the long-term solvency of Social Security was also in jeopardy. In twenty to thirty years, they argued, when the baby boomers would be eligible for benefits, deficits would be so huge that the system would collapse. There simply would not be enough workers in the labor force to finance the benefits.

Reactions. Such reports alarmed both senior citizens and younger Americans concerned about their own retirement years. Their fears were exacerbated by the economic troubles of the early 1980s — inflation, recession, high unemployment, federal budget deficits — and by the budget-cutting zeal of the Reagan administration. Many senior citizens feared that financing for Social Security, which one congressman called "the lifeblood of millions," would be slashed. When the Reagan administration confirmed these fears in 1981 by proposing significant cuts in the program, Democrats charged that the president was trying "to balance the budget on the backs of the elderly." Around the country senior citizens demonstrated with signs warning, "Hands Off Social Security." The administration proposal met such a storm of protest that the Senate rejected it by a vote of 96–0, and the issue was quickly dropped. Nevertheless, there was a deficit in the retirement trust fund, forcing Congress to make unprecedented provisions to borrow from other funds in the system. By this means the short-term crisis was averted: monthly checks continued to be mailed to beneficiaries. But, for the first time since the program began in 1935, public confidence in Social Security had been severely shaken; and the apocalyptic projections about the program's future remained. In 1982 a *Washington Post*–ABC News poll found that 66 percent of Americans younger than forty-five believed Social Security would not exist by the time they retired.

Social Security "Saved." Under the pressure of public concern about a program Americans had long taken for granted, President Reagan appointed the bipartisan National Commission on Social Security Reform. The commission included important Republicans such as Sen. Robert Dole of Kansas, chair of the Senate Finance Committee, and influential Democrats such as Sen. Daniel Patrick Moynihan of New York and Rep. Claude Pepper of Florida — the eighty-year-old Pepper was known as "Mr. Senior Citizen" and "the Champion of the Elderly" because of his passionate advocacy on behalf of older Americans. In the highly charged political atmosphere, the mandate of the commission was to propose reforms that would ensure both the short-term and long-term financial health of Social Security. Generally, Democrats believed there was a short-term problem in funding but that the Social Security system was basically sound. They claimed Reagan officials were exaggerating both short- and long-term problems so that the administration could justify cutting this widely supported domestic spending program. Republicans generally favored cutting benefits, which would allow them to cut payroll taxes, thus helping President Reagan fulfill his pledge to cut taxes and reduce the size of government. After deliberating for a year, the National Commission on Social

NURSING HOMES

As Americans lived longer in the 1980s, increasingly reaching ages into the eighties and beyond, the problem of caring for the gravely ill or incapacitated elderly grew into a critical issue for many senior citizens and their families. Many Americans, faced with the loss of spouses or parents to devastating and incurable illnesses like Alzheimer's disease, learned to their dismay that neither Medicare, the government health-insurance for the elderly, nor private medical insurance covered the costs of long-term, catastrophic illness. In fact, neither Medicare nor private insurance benefits covered any nursing-home care beyond several months. After this period, the costs of a nursing home had to be paid by the individual who required it. Unfortunately, the average cost of nursing home care was $2,000 per month, and it was estimated that most people who entered nursing homes for long-term stays would exhaust their entire lifetime incomes in two to three years. When assets were fully exhausted, the individual was then qualified to receive government assistance in the form of Medicaid. In the 1980s the number of nursing homes increased dramatically in the United States, but not dramatically enough to meet the demand. Shortages of nursing-home beds was a serious problem in most states, and, despite the high costs of their services, most nursing homes found themselves with long waiting lists for people needing care. In 1989 it was estimated that 7 million seniors were in need of long-term care, and that number was increasing steadily. Studies showed that 47 percent of families had experienced a long-term care problem within the family. As the decade progressed, the problem of long-term care was increasingly seen as one of the most severe social problems of American society. In response insurance companies began to offer some nursing-home policies, but most of these policies were judged to be seriously inadequate. Congress finally tried to address the problem of catastrophic illness in 1988 by extending Medicare benefits to cover such an emergency. The bill it passed, however, was repealed in 1989.

Sources: David L. Bender and Bruno Leone, eds., *The Elderly: Opposing Viewpoints* (San Diego: Greenhaven Press, 1990);

Elizabeth Vierck, *Fact Book on Aging* (Santa Barbara, Cal.: ABC-Clio, 1990).

Security Reform nearly ended in failure. A dramatic eleventh-hour compromise, however, produced a complex plan that was offered to the president.

The Final Plan. This "rescue" plan attacked the trust-fund deficits by proposing to raise $165 billion in new revenues by 1990 from a combination of accelerated increases in payroll taxes and deferred cost-of-living allowances (COLAs) for beneficiaries. Also, while benefit levels would be maintained, for the first time since Social Security began, a portion of those benefits would be taxed. In addition, the age at which people were eligible for benefits would gradually rise from sixty-five to sixty-seven. To increase the financial base of Social Security, newly hired federal employees — previously excluded — would be added to the system. Finally, cost controls were added to the Medicare part of the system. The package was designed to keep Social Security solvent twenty to thirty years into the next century. Although there had been predictions of intense partisan bickering, Congress quickly approved the plan with only minor amendments. Critics charged that the bill was a "quick fix" that did not sufficiently address long-term structural problems; nevertheless, the bill President Reagan signed in the spring of 1983 was the most serious reform of the Social Security system since its beginning.

Sources:

Andrew Achenbaum, *Social Security: Visions and Revisions* (Cambridge: Cambridge University Press, 1986);

Merton C. Bernstein and Joan Brodshaug Bernstein, *Social Security: The System That Works* (New York: Basic Books, 1988);

Erdman B. Patmore, *Handbook on the Aged in the United States* (Westport, Conn.: Greenwood Press, 1994).

HEADLINE MAKERS

ALLAN BLOOM

1930-1993

PROFESSOR

Prophet of Doom. Each era has its prophets of doom, critics who diagnose the ills of their society in apocalyptic terms. During the 1980s Allan Bloom emerged from academic obscurity to become America's best-known advocate of a return to a classical model of higher education, a back-to-the-basics approach that saw many of the changes that had occurred in the universities since the 1960s as misguided. His critique, *The Closing of the American Mind: How Higher Education Has Failed Democracy and Impoverished the Souls of Today's Students* (1987), was a surprise best-seller that generated a storm of controversy about such issues as cultural literacy and political correctness.

Scholarly Career. No one could have been more surprised by the success of the book than Bloom himself. His previous publications had been translations of works by Plato and Jean-Jacques Rousseau and *Shakespeare's Politics* (1964), written with Harry V. Jaffa. Though he had been a professor of political philosophy since 1955 at the University of Chicago, Yale University, Cornell University, the University of Toronto, and again at the University of Chicago, before the 1980s he was hardly known as a scholar, let alone as a major social critic.

Protest. Popular with students, Bloom was known by his colleagues as a classical humanist — a stance that, as political theory evolved during the 1960s, cast him in the minds of many of those colleagues as a political conservative. One of the key events in his career occurred in 1969, when administrators at Cornell submitted to the demands of armed students that the curriculum be expanded to include programs of study reflecting current social concerns. Bloom resigned in protest and taught for nine years in Toronto before joining the Committee on Social Thought at the University of Chicago, where he had earned his Ph.D. twenty-four years earlier.

Best-Seller. At Chicago he met and became friends with the Nobel Prize–winning novelist Saul Bellow, who was also on the faculty. In 1982 Bloom wrote an article for the conservative journal *National Review* in which he critiqued American universities; Bellow encouraged him to expand it into a book and helped him to get it published by Simon and Schuster. *The Closing of the American Mind* was widely reviewed and became a best-seller, igniting a controversy about higher education that lasted for months. Bloom had touched a nerve.

What Is Wrong with Higher Education? To be sure, *The Closing of the American Mind* was not a typical best-seller; filled with erudite arguments drawing on such thinkers as Plato and Friedrich Nietzsche, it was hardly beach reading. Its main points were simple enough, however. Bloom claimed that higher education had abandoned its traditional devotion to reason and the free marketplace of ideas in favor of programs that catered to the demands of women and minorities and that reflected trendy ideas rather than a grounding in great books and timeless issues. As a result, he wrote, students learned more about themselves than about the world around them and saw "truth" as an ideological construction based on race, gender, or economic status rather than as a universal and immutable ideal that one aspired to attain through study and debate. Today's students, he said, are "practical nihilists" whose minds have been closed rather than opened by their educations.

Reaction. The initial reviews, in the mainstream media, praised the forcefulness of Bloom's argument, even if the reviewers did not agree with him on every point. Academic criticism of the book, however, was vitriolic, attacking Bloom as an educational fundamentalist who failed to see anything good in curricula that did not praise the accomplishments of "dead white males." Many professors and administrators dismissed the book as nostalgia for an outmoded and misguided ideal. On the other hand, some sided with Bloom, decrying what they perceived as an appalling lack of basic knowledge on the part of contemporary college students and calling for an emphasis on the importance of "cultural literacy."

Other Voices. Bloom eventually returned to his previous obscurity as the battle in academe shifted to such related issues as the nature of the literary canon, multiculturalism, and political correctness and as other voices entered the arena. He completed two more books — the essay collection *Giants and Dwarfs* (1990) and *Love and Friendship* (1993), an exploration of the treatment of these ideas in canonical literary and philosophical works — before his death in 1993.

Sources:

Allan Bloom, *The Closing of the American Mind: How Higher Education Has Failed Democracy and Impoverished the Souls of Today's Students*, foreword by Saul Bellow (New York: Simon & Schuster, 1987);

William McWhirter, "A Most Uncommon Scold," *Time*, 132 (17 October 1988): 74–76;

Clifford Orwin, "Remembering Allan Bloom," *American Scholar*, 62 (Summer 1993): 423–430.

BOB GUCCIONE JR.

1956?-

MAGAZINE PUBLISHER

A New *Spin* on Things. In 1985 Bob Guccione Jr. introduced a new magazine to the American public. While it was centered around popular music, *Spin* gained greater attention for its irreverent take on American culture. In this respect it was more similar to edgy, youth-oriented 1980s magazines such as *Spy* than to its direct competitor, *Rolling Stone*. "Let the Baby Boomers read *Rolling Stone*," Guccione seemed to be saying; "this is a magazine for Generation X."

You Can't Keep Me in Your Penthouse. The son of the publisher of *Penthouse* and *Omni*, Guccione came into magazine publishing naturally. His parents separated in 1965, and he lived with his mother in her native England until they moved to New Jersey when he was fifteen. A high-school dropout, Guccione worked in magazine circulation and marketing before launching *Spin* under the *Penthouse* aegis with $500,000 from his father. It was a bold venture: in sharp contrast to *Rolling Stone*, the magazine covered unknown performers and criticized major names in the music business. At first it failed to attract enough subscribers and advertisers to turn a profit, and Guccione Sr. announced in 1987 that the magazine would cease publication. But Guccione Jr. decided to separate *Spin* from *Penthouse* and publish it with support from independent investors — a move that created a rift between father and son.

Success. *Spin* would remain unprofitable until 1992. It was able to hang on because young music fans found its irreverence appealing, and because the alternative rock it championed went to the top of the charts in the early 1990s. *Spin* was more current than many magazines of the late 1980s: for instance, it featured a monthly column on AIDS long before the mainstream media devoted much attention to the disease. It also featured offbeat journalism and satire.

Sources:

Eric Konigsberg, " 'Dad Always Liked You Best!' " *GQ*, 65 (June 1995): 101–106;

Patrick Reilly, " 'Spin' Whirls with Guccione Jr.," *Advertising Age*, 59 (13 June 1988): 57;

"The 'Spin' Doctor," *Forbes*, 156 (17 July 1995): 98.

MAGGIE KUHN

1905-1995

ACTIVIST

Founder of the Gray Panthers. In 1970, when Maggie Kuhn turned sixty-five, her employer forced her to retire from a job she loved. Kuhn could have gotten mad. Instead, she got busy, organizing what became known as the Gray Panthers to protest not only mandatory retirement policies but also American involvement in the Vietnam War. One of the few protest organizations of the Vietnam era to survive into the 1980s, the Gray Panthers, with Kuhn at the helm, served as a model of grassroots organization for such causes as national health care, job training, and housing for the homeless. The organization was also a model of inclusiveness: though many elderly people belong to the Gray Panthers, and though it lobbies on issues important to the elderly, its members range from college students to people like Kuhn, who remained active in the Gray Panthers until her death at eighty-nine.

The Making of an Activist. Kuhn's parents lived in Memphis, Tennessee, but moved to Buffalo, New York, so that their daughter would not grow up in a segregated society. Besides being influenced by her parents, Kuhn was also influenced as a child by an aunt who was a suffragist at the turn of the century. Kuhn attended college in Cleveland at Case Western Reserve University, where she helped to form a college chapter of the League of Women Voters. She then worked for the Young Women's Christian Association and for the Presbyterian Church, where she helped to promote social change, especially concerning women's roles. Ironically, she was required to give up her job of twenty-five years because of a form of discrimination the church had not addressed — age discrimination.

The Gray Panthers. For the next twenty-five years Kuhn devoted her energies to battling mandatory retirement laws and other forms of injustice through the Gray Panthers, which grew from six members in 1970 to forty thousand by the time of her death. During the 1980s she spoke out against the Reagan administration's efforts to cut back on Social Security and in favor of a national health-care plan similar to that in Canada. Like the American Association of Retired Persons (AARP), Kuhn and the Gray Panthers were powerful advocates for the elderly (she disliked the term *senior citizens,* stressing that there was nothing shameful about growing old). Unlike the AARP, however, the Gray Panthers included members of all ages and did not limit their activities to lobbying for matters of concern to the elderly. Kuhn was thus very much a part of her time in the 1980s and a reminder of an earlier era of political activism.

JOAN QUIGLEY

1927-

WHITE HOUSE ASTROLOGER

Stranger Than Fiction. In Robert A. Heinlein's 1961 science-fiction novel *Stranger in a Strange Land* the president of the world secretly receives advice from an astrologer. In 1988 it was learned that the wife of the president of the United States had, for some years, been consulting an astrologer concerning her husband's schedule. Nancy Reagan's unnamed "friend" was soon revealed to be San Francisco astrologer Joan Quigley. Astonishment and outrage that the leader of the free world was guided in his actions by a woman who saw destiny in the stars provided the Reagan administration with one of its greatest embarrassments.

How to Become a White House Astrologer. Quigley, who was educated at prestigious Vassar College, had been interested in astrology since she was a teenager. After college she began studying with an astrologer and writing about the subject for the magazine *Seventeen.* Born into a prominent San Francisco family, she returned to the city and lived a dual existence as an astrologer and socialite. A regular guest on radio and television programs, she first met Nancy Reagan in 1973 on *The Merv Griffin Show.* Both Reagans possessed an interest in astrology, as Ronald Reagan revealed in his 1965 autobiography *Where's the Rest of Me?,* but Nancy Reagan did not begin consulting Quigley until 1981, when Quigley told her that she had accurately predicted that someone would attempt to assassinate the president. Fearing for her husband's safety, Mrs. Reagan began consulting Quigley regularly about the president's schedule.

All Is Revealed. The American public did not know that the White House had its own astrologer until 1988, when former White House Chief of Staff Donald Regan, who had been ousted from his position in 1986, revealed in his memoir, *For the Record,* that the first lady regularly received advice from an astrologer, whom she called her "Friend," and that on the basis of this advice she manipulated the president's itinerary. *Time* magazine quickly uncovered Quigley's identity, and she stepped into the limelight. Both she and the Reagan administration stressed that she did not offer advice about policy, only about scheduling, but the damage was done, and Mrs. Reagan took Quigley off the payroll.

Contradictions. Furthermore, after Nancy Reagan's memoir *My Turn* (1989), in which the former first lady downplayed Quigley's influence, Quigley responded in her memoir, *"What Does Joan Say?" My Seven Years as White House Astrologer to Nancy and Ronald Reagan* (1990), by quoting Regan's review of Mrs. Reagan's book, where he said that whoever "controls the President's schedule controls the workings of the presidency," thus highlighting her influence in major policy decisions. Her prescience was not complete, however: when the story broke she mentioned that because Ronald Reagan was born with Mercury in Capricorn, his memory was excellent, failing to predict his battle with Alzheimer's disease in the mid 1990s.

Sources:

Joan Quigley, *"What Does Joan Say?" My Seven Years as White House Astrologer to Nancy and Ronald Reagan* (New York: Birch Lane Press–Carol Publishing, 1990);

Donald T. Regan, *For the Record: From Wall Street to Washington* (San Diego, New York & London: Harcourt Brace Jovanovich, 1988);

Barrett Seaman, "Good Heavens!," *Time,* 131 (16 May 1988): 24–25;

Laurence Zuckerman, Wayne Svoboda, and Dennis Wyss, "The First Lady's Astrologer," *Time,* 131 (16 May 1988): 41.

SHELBY STEELE

1946-

PROFESSOR

The Rise of Black Conservatism. Conservatism made impressive gains in the United States during the 1980s, including the presidencies of Ronald Reagan and George Bush, the rise of Protestant fundamentalism, and challenges to multiculturalism and feminism in academe. The decade also saw the rise to prominence of several black intellectuals who questioned liberal orthodoxy on such matters as racial preferences and affirmative action. One of the most articulate of such figures was Shelby Steele, a professor of English at San Jose State University in California.

Opportunity. Steele was born in Chicago and earned a doctorate in English from the University of Utah in 1974. During the late 1980s, however, he became known for his skillfully written articles on race in such periodicals as *Harper's, Commentary, The American Scholar,* and *The New York Times Magazine.* In these articles, and in many interviews, he dealt with such issues as black self-reliance, racism, white guilt, and affirmative action, arguing for black self-determination over preferences and claiming that the acceptance of the position of victims on the part of blacks kept them from seizing opportunities present in American society. While not denying the existence of racism, he downplayed its significance, insisting that blacks needed to return to a sense of self-reliance promoted by the civil rights movement and move beyond the well-intentioned but ultimately harmful policies that followed. Several of his essays were collected in *The Content of Our Character: A New Vision of Race in America* (1990).

Debate. Conservatives, both black and white, readily claimed Steele as one of their own, while black leaders and liberals often dismissed his views and implied that he had sold out to those who did not have the best interests of blacks at heart. In response Steele insisted that he was a liberal in the classic sense of the word, one who believed in individualism and personal freedom. Nevertheless, he identified with black conservatives such as Stanley Crouch and Thomas Sowell and supported the controversial nomination of Clarence Thomas to the U.S. Supreme Court. The presence of such figures as well as his own, he said, was a healthy indication of diversity within the black community, which before the 1980s was often viewed as monolithic.

Sources:

Denise K. Magner, "A New Voice Among Analysts Probing the Nation's Racial Psyche," *Chronicle of Higher Education,* 5 September 1990, p. A3;

Sylvester Monroe, "Nothing Is Ever Simply Black and White," *Time,* 138 (12 August 1991): 6–8;

Monroe, "Up from Obscurity," *Time,* 136 (13 August 1990): 45;

Shelby Steele, *The Content of Our Character: A New Vision of Race in America* (New York: St. Martin's Press, 1990).

MARTHA STEWART

1941-

AUTHORITY ON ENTERTAINING

Authority on the Good Life. The 1980s were a decade of conservatism but also of materialism, if not excess. Yuppies climbed income brackets and social ladders, consumers sought out designer labels and exclusive products, and bumper stickers appeared proclaiming that whoever dies with the most toys wins. Catering to America's growing taste for the good life but injecting an element of breeding and good taste, Martha Stewart emerged during the decade as America's foremost authority on entertaining and decorating.

Early Experiences. Born Martha Kostyra in New Jersey, she began modeling in high school and learned gardening from her father, a salesman. Continuing to model while studying European history and architectural history at Barnard College, in 1960 she met Andrew Stewart, a student at Yale Law School. They married the following year. She continued to model, making as much as $35,000 a year. After the birth of their only child, Alexis, in 1965, Martha Stewart became a stockbroker with a small but successful Wall Street firm, where she remained until 1973. After a brief effort with a take-out food shop, she began working as a caterer — at first with a partner, then on her own as Martha Stewart, Inc.

Becoming Known West of the Hudson. By the mid 1980s Stewart's company was making a million dollars a year serving clients on the East Coast. She also wrote books, beginning with *Entertaining* in 1982 and including such titles as *Martha Stewart's Quick Cook Menus, Martha Stewart Weddings,* and *Martha Stewart's Christmas.* Combining her patrician good looks and next-door-neighbor approachability with a keen marketing sense, Stewart proceeded to build a one-person empire. In her books and television appearances she created impossibly perfect desserts and decorations, often from everyday materials, and made it seem as though anyone could do the same. Many believed her, as evidenced in the hundreds of women who signed up for her lectures and seminars, which often cost hundreds of dollars per person. Her house in Westport, Connecticut, became a mecca for admirers who wanted to emulate her intricate desserts, stylish homemade decorations, and impeccable gardening techniques.

The Empire Spreads Out. Following her 1987 divorce, after which she was a houseguest of writer Kurt Vonnegut Jr. and his wife, photographer Jill Krementz,

Stewart expanded her empire with two ventures. In 1987 she entered into a business relationship with K-Mart, which began marketing Martha Stewart products such as linens and dishes. In 1990 she created a magazine, *Martha Stewart Living,* published by Time Warner. Such enterprises made Stewart the target of critics who ridiculed her relentless self-promotion and considered her attention to fine details of decorating and entertaining bordering on the anal retentive. Nonetheless, she remained popular among a wide spectrum of American women across the country into the 1990s.

Sources:

Elizabeth L. Bland and Janice C. Simpson, "A New Guru of American Taste?," *Time,* 132 (19 December 1988): 92;

Jeanie Kasindorf, "Living with Martha," *New York,* 24 (28 January 1991): 22–30.

VANESSA WILLIAMS

1963-

SINGER, ACTRESS, FORMER MISS AMERICA

From Infamy to Fame. Young, beautiful, and ambitious for an entertainment career, Vanessa Williams made headlines in the 1980s for two "firsts" in American history: she was the first black Miss America and the first Miss America to resign her crown. The resignation took place, under pressure from the Miss America organization, following the 1984 publication in *Penthouse* magazine of steamy photographs taken of Williams when she was nineteen. Williams emerged from the controversy with a great deal of sympathy from the public — many people believed that she had been exploited — and was well on the way to the career she desired. In fact, the publicity surrounding her resignation may have helped her chances more than merely being Miss America could have.

The Girl Next Door. The daughter of two music teachers, Williams grew up in Millwood, New York, with the dream of becoming the first black Rockette. Instead, the summer after her first year at Syracuse University she found work as a receptionist for a freelance photographer, Tom Chiapel, who persuaded her to pose nude for him, both alone and in erotic poses with another woman. Williams later claimed that Chiapel assured her that no one else would ever see the photographs.

Miss America. During her sophomore year at college Williams acted in a play; her cast photo led to suggestions that she could be the next Miss America. She won the Miss Greater Syracuse pageant, became Miss New York State, and, in September 1983, entered the Miss America pageant. She won — the first black woman to do so in the pageant's history. The pageant's organizers could not have asked for a better Miss America: though outspoken — Williams supported the Equal Rights Amendment and was pro-choice on the abortion issue — she was obviously intelligent, as well as beautiful and gracious.

Grace under Pressure. She remained poised when, two months before the end of her year-long reign, *Penthouse* announced that it would be publishing nude photographs of Williams. At the request of the Miss America officials she relinquished her title, but she emerged from the ordeal with much public support. Many people believed that she should not have been required to step down as Miss America; some criticized *Penthouse* publisher Bob Guccione for buying the photographs from Chiapel (*Playboy* had turned them down); and there were those who considered the Miss America officials to be hypocritical for claiming that the pictures violated the sanctity of a contest based largely on women's appearances.

Living Well. Williams disappeared from the public eye, returning in the late 1980s as a pop singer and an actress in television movies and onstage. Her albums have earned her Grammy nominations and have sold millions of copies, and in 1994 she assumed the title role in a Broadway production of *Kiss of the Spider Woman.*

Sources:

Melinda Beck and Renee Michael, "For Want of a Bathing Suit," *Newsweek,* 104 (6 August 1984): 23;

Jay Cocks and Dorothy Ferenhaugh, "There She Goes, Miss America," *Time,* 124 (6 August 1984): 61;

Elizabeth Kaye, "Miss America's Crown of Thorns," *Rolling Stone* (31 January 1985): 32–37, 50, 52;

Jack Kroll, "Success Is the Best Revenge," *Newsweek,* 124 (15 August 1994): 65;

Cathleen McGuigan and Jennifer Boeth, "Miss America: A Title Lost," *Newsweek,* 104 (30 July 1984): 85.

People in the News

In May 1980 **Maxie Anderson** and his son **Kris** became the first balloonists to cross North America nonstop.

In 1989 twenty-year-old cadet **Kristin M. Baker** was selected as brigade commander and first captain of the corps of cadets at the U.S. Military Academy at West Point, New York. Baker was the first woman in West Point history to be chosen for the post, in which she would be overseeing all aspects of life for the academy's mostly male cadet corps.

In 1980 the Mattel toy company celebrated the twenty-first anniversary of its **Barbie** doll by unveiling the first "adult figure" Barbie; more than 115 million dolls had been sold since 1959.

Sharon Batts, a nine-year-old from Texas, became a singing star with her recording of "Dear Mr. Jesus" in 1987. The gospel song about child abuse was played by hundreds of radio stations throughout the country.

In 1981 **Elizabeth Jordan Carr** was the first test-tube baby born in the United States. Delivered by caesarean section in Norfolk, Virginia, Elizabeth weighed five and a half pounds.

In 1983 former television news anchorwoman **Christine Craft** sued Metromedia, Inc., owner of the station in Kansas City at which Craft had worked. In 1983 Craft's male bosses had demoted her from her anchorwoman position because, she charged, they considered her "too old, unattractive, and not deferential enough to men." A federal jury awarded Craft $500,000 in damages.

In the summer of 1980 **Charles Dederich,** founder of the drug-addiction rehabilitation program Synanon, pleaded no contest to a charge that he conspired to murder attorney Paul Morantz by putting a rattlesnake in Morantz's mailbox.

Singer and animal-rights advocate **John Denver** admitted in February 1980 that he had shot BBs at a neighbor's dog who was "hounding" his puppy.

In April 1980 **Craig Evans,** executive director of the American Hiking Society, organized a thirteen-month, four-thousand-mile hike to urge Congress to increase funding for the National Trails System.

Sgt. **Bambi Lin Finney** was honorably, though forcibly, discharged from the United States Marine Corps after appearing nude in the April 1980 issue of *Playboy*.

In January 1980 **Jane Fonda** held a fund-raiser for the Equal Rights Amendment at her Beverly Hills health club, where ERA supporters could participate in the "Jane Fonda Workout" for $100.

Deborah Ann Fountain, Miss New York, was banned from the 1981 Miss America contest when it was discovered that she wore padding in the bosom of her swimsuit during competition.

In summer 1980 **John Gelinas Jr.,** eighteen, earned his 121st Boy Scout merit badge, becoming one of the few scouts to earn every badge possible.

In February 1984 ninety-year-old actress **Lillian Gish,** who made her movie debut in 1912, received the American Film Academy's Lifetime Achievement Award. Gish, who performed in several silent films made by the renowned director D. W. Griffith, had acted in fifty plays and more than one hundred movies by 1984, and a new film was scheduled for release in 1985.

Jean Harris, headmistress of the Madeira School, who in February 1981 was convicted of murdering her boyfriend, **Herman Tarnower,** co-author of *The Complete Scarsdale Medical Diet* (1979), described her minimum-security prison as being similar to a college dormitory.

In June 1981, after tabulating results from 119,000 questionnaires, each of which contained 173 questions, **Shere Hite** published her report on male sexuality; it included the speculation that the only activity that allows men free expression of emotion is sexual intercourse: "for a moment or an hour it overcomes the loneliness and separation of life."

Former antiwar activist **Abbie Hoffman** emerged from six and a half years as a fugitive in September 1980 to face charges of selling $36,000 worth of cocaine and then jumping bail. He pleaded guilty in April 1981 and was sentenced to one-to-three years in prison.

At seventy-nine, Rear Adm. **Grace Murray Hopper** was the navy's oldest officer on active duty before she retired in August 1989. During her career Hopper had been instrumental in the development of computers and had helped to develop the early computer language COBOL. In retirement, she planned to lecture and keep up with her field. "The day I stop learning is the day I die," she said.

In July 1980 investor **Nelson Bunker Hunt** held a sale of racehorses at his Blue Grass Farm in Lexington, Kentucky, raising $10.3 million to help pay his debts in the wake of his attempt to corner the silver market.

In 1985 and 1986 **J. Z. Knight** of Yelm, Washington, became a popular "channel" who supposedly linked her followers, who paid $400 apiece to hear her, to a metaphysical world. In meetings at the Double Tree Inn outside Seattle, Knight seemingly transferred herself to a different state of consciousness to become the voice of "Ramtha," a thirty-five-thousand-year-old male spirit who was once a warrior.

In 1981, after observing videotapes covering three years of fifty families at dinnertime, sociologist **Michael Lewis** concluded that, despite the women's movement, preparing dinner continued to be women's work even when both spouses had jobs. Usually, Lewis observed, the female cooked and served, while "the male [sat] back and [ate]."

On Valentine's Day 1980, working from information gathered by undercover agents **Ray Livingston** and **Bruce Ellevsky,** four hundred FBI agents in ten cities wrapped up "Operation Miporn" by arresting what they claimed was "every major producer and distributor [of pornography] in the country."

Connaught Marshner, chairman of the Pro-Family Coalition, objected to the White House Conference on Families in summer 1980 because, she said, while "they'd like to talk about child care for working mothers, we'd like to talk about why there have to be so many working mothers."

In 1982 Atheneum published **Judith Martin**'s "Miss Manners' Guide to Excruciatingly Correct Behavior." According to Miss Manners, when inviting houseguests who are unmarried but living together, two bedrooms should be prepared for the visiting couple.

In 1987 the plight of eighteen-month-old **Jessica McClure,** who fell into an abandoned well in Midland, Texas, attracted national concern. A large television audience watched as Jessica, after being trapped for fifty-eight hours, was lifted to safety by rescue workers.

On 5 November 1985 **Rev. Patricia Ann McClurg,** a Presbyterian minister from Plainfield, New Jersey, was the first female minister to be elected president of the National Council of Churches.

In April 1980 California vintner **Robert Mondavi** and French wine magnate **Baron Phillipe de Rothschild** announced plans for a $3 million joint venture that would produce a Napa Valley cabernet sauvignon by 1983.

In January 1980 **Dr. George C. Nichopoulos** was convicted of illegally prescribing and dispensing illegal drugs to ten patients — including Elvis Presley, who had died in 1977 of causes that were allegedly related to drug abuse.

"Fatherhood is the new family romance of the '80s," said New York psychiatrist **Avodah K. Offit** in 1981. According to the 1980 census, not only were more fathers involved in child raising in two-parent homes where both parents worked outside the home, but with a rising divorce rate and changes in child custody laws, more than one million children were being raised exclusively by their fathers.

In January 1980 Miss America pageant officials announced that longtime host **Bert Parks** would be replaced by a younger man.

Rosa Parks won the Martin Luther King Jr. Peace Prize in 1980 for her role in "galvaniz[ing] black Americans into the most successful nonviolent protest in our nation's history."

Clara Peller became a celebrity in 1984 when the eighty-year-old Chicago woman appeared in a television commercial for Wendy's hamburgers, in which, after receiving a small hamburger patty on a large bun (from an unnamed Wendy's competitor), she feistily asked, "Where's the beef?" The commercial was a hit, and the question "Where's the beef?" became a popular quote.

On 5 October 1987 **Cheryl Pierson,** eighteen, was sentenced in Riverhead, New York, to five months in prison for hiring a classmate to kill her father. Pierson, arrested when she was sixteen, had for years been sexually abused by her father and wanted to prevent her younger sister from being a victim.

In March 1985 **Libby Riddles** became the first woman to win the 1,137-mile Iditarod Trail Sled Dog Race. After fighting terrible blizzards, Riddles crossed the finish line in Nome, Alaska, and said of her competitors, "I left those guys in the dust."

In 1982, along with growing numbers of churchmen, the **Reverend Miles O'Brien Riley** of the Catholic Archdiocese of San Francisco decided to speak out against the nuclear arms race, saying that nuclear disarmament was "the moral issue of the day. Everything else is a footnote."

In August 1980 former antiwar and anticapitalism activist **Jerry Rubin** took a job as a Wall Street securities analyst.

In 1988 **Sheelah Ryan,** a real-estate broker from Winter Springs, Florida, won $55 million, the largest lottery prize ever awarded to one person. In January 1989 Ryan announced the formation of the Ryan Foundation, a nonprofit organization to benefit the poor, the elderly, and abused women and children.

Noting that she had "worked as hard as I could from day one," model and actress **Brooke Shields** graduated from Princeton University with honors in June 1987.

At a party in New York in 1982 **Gloria Steinem,** a founding editor of *Ms.,* celebrated the feminist magazine's tenth anniversary. Despite predictions of disaster when it started, *Ms.* was still going strong.

Noting the growing trend toward the use of personal computers, **Jack Tramiel,** vice chairman of Commodore International, said that he expected 3 million personal computers to be sold in 1982 and 50 million by 1985.

On 12 October 1987 **Sam Moore Walton,** founder of the Wal-Mart discount stores, was named by *Forbes* magazine as the richest person in America — for the third year in a row. Walton's assets were estimated at $8.5 billion. Ranked second in wealth was media mogul **James Kluge,** worth $3 billion; third was Texas investor **H. Ross Perot,** worth $2.9 billion.

DEATHS

George Adamson, 83, environmentalist whose work was featured in his wife's book *Born Free* (1960), 20 August 1989.

Joy Adamson, 69, naturalist, author of *Born Free,* 3 January 1980.

Roger Baldwin, 97, helped to found the American Civil Liberties Union, 26 August 1981.

James Beard, 81, renowned chef, 23 January 1985.

Billy Carter, 51, well-known brother of President Jimmy Carter, 25 September 1988.

Miles L. Colean, 82, economist who helped to create the Federal Housing Administration, coiner of the term *urban renewal,* 16 September 1980.

Dorothy Day, 83, founder of the Catholic Worker Movement, 29 November 1980.

James F. Fixx, 52, authority on running, 20 July 1984.

R. Buckminster Fuller, 87, inventor and futurist, 1 July 1983.

George H. Gallup, 82, pioneer in opinion polling, 26 July 1984.

Sylvan N. Goldman, 86, inventor of the shopping cart, 25 November 1984.

John Howard Griffin, 60, whose book *Black Like Me* (1961) described his experiences as a white man who masqueraded as a black man to understand prejudice in the South, 9 September 1980.

Gayelord Hauser, 89, health-food advocate, author of *Look Younger, Live Longer* (1950), 26 December 1984.

Eric Hoffer, 80, former longshoreman who became a best-selling nonfiction author, 21 May 1983.

Abbie Hoffman, 52, political activist, founder of the Yippies (Youth International Party) in the 1960s, 12 April 1989.

Rock Hudson, 59, actor whose death from AIDS brought increased attention to the disease, 2 October 1985.

Ruby Hurley, 70, civil rights leader, 9 August 1980.

Walter L. Jacobs, 88, founder of the first car-rental agency (which later became Hertz), 6 February 1985.

Christine Jorgensen, 62, who underwent the first sex-change operation in 1952, 3 May 1989.

Martin Luther King Sr., 84, civil rights leader, 15 November 1984.

Ray A. Kroc, 81, founder of the McDonald's hamburger chain, 14 January 1984.

Susanne K. Langer, 89, philosopher, 17 July 1985.

Benjamin Mays, 89, civil-rights leader, 28 March 1984.

Robert Moses, 92, urban planner, 29 July 1981.

John Needham, 65, national commander of the Salvation Army, 13 April 1983.

Huey P. Newton, 47, one of the founders of the Black Panthers, 22 August 1989.

Arthur C. Nielsen, 83, television ratings pioneer, 1 June 1980.

John Ringling North, 81, head of the Ringling Bros. & Barnum and Bailey Circus, 4 June 1985.

Mary Parkman Peabody, 89, civil rights and antiwar activist, 6 February 1981.

Karen Ann Quinlan, 31, whose parents' successful legal efforts to end her coma by removing her from life support sparked debates about the definition of life and the right to die, 11 June 1985.

John Rock, 94, obstetrician/gynecologist who developed the first oral contraceptive in the 1950s, 4 December 1984.

Carl R. Rogers, 85, psychotherapist active in encounter groups during the 1960s, 4 February 1987.

Col. Harland Sanders, 90, founder of the Kentucky Fried Chicken chain, 16 December 1980.

Zerna Sharp, 91, creator of the Dick and Jane series used in classrooms for decades, 17 June 1981.

Samantha Smith, 13, whose letter to Soviet leader Yuri Andropov led to a brief lessening of Cold War tensions, 26 August 1985.

Vic Tanny, 73, founder of a chain of health clubs, 11 June 1985.

Roy Wilkins, 80, civil rights figure who led the National Association for the Advancement of Colored People (NAACP) for twenty-two years, 8 September 1981.

PUBLICATIONS

Andrew Achenbaum, *Social Security: Visions and Revisions* (Cambridge: Cambridge University Press, 1986);

Merton C. Bernstein and Joan Brodshaug Bernstein, *Social Security: The System That Works* (New York: Basic Books, 1988);

Richard C. Carlson, Willis W. Harman, Peter Schwartz, and others, *Energy Futures, Human Values, and Lifestyles: A New Look at the Energy Crisis* (Boulder, Colo.: Westview, 1982);

Robert E. Clark and Judith Freeman Clark, *The Encyclopedia of Child Abuse* (New York: Facts On File, 1989);

Lee B. Cooper, *Images of American Society in Popular Music: A Guide to Reflective Teaching* (Chicago: Nelson-Hall, 1982);

John D'Emilio and Estelle B. Freedman, *Intimate Matters: A History of Sexuality in America* (New York: Harper & Row, 1988);

Park O. Davidson and Sheena M. Davidson, eds., *Behavioral Medicine: Changing Health Lifestyles* (New York: Brunner/Mazel, 1980);

David Finkelhor, Linda Meyer Williams, and Nanci Burns, *Nursery Crimes: Sexual Abuse in Day Care* (Newbury Park, Cal.: SAGE Publications, 1988);

Benjamin Friedman, *Day of Reckoning: The Consequences of American Economic Policy Under Reagan and After* (New York: Random House, 1988);

Jerry Gerber, Janet Wolff, Walter Klores, and Gene Brown, *Lifetrends: The Future of Baby Boomers and Other Aging Americans* (New York: Macmillan, 1989);

Alan Geyer, *The Idea of Disarmament: Rethinking the Unthinkable* (Elgin, Ill.: Brethren Press, 1982);

A. Bartlett Giamatti, *Take Time for Paradise: Americans and Their Games* (New York: Summit Books, 1989);

George Gilder, *Wealth and Poverty* (New York: Basic Books, 1981);

Susan Gubar and Joan Hoff, eds., *For Adult Users Only: The Dilemma of Violent Pornography* (Bloomington & Indianapolis: Indiana University Press, 1989);

Michael Harrington, *The New American Poverty* (New York: Holt, Rinehart & Winston, 1984);

Sylvia Ann Hewlett, *A Lesser Life: The Myth of Women's Liberation in America* (New York: Morrow, 1986);

Morris Janowitz, *The Reconstruction of Patriotism: Education for Civic Consciousness* (Chicago: University of Chicago Press, 1983);

Michael C. Jaye and Ann Chalmers Watts, eds., *Literature and the Urban Experience: Essays on the City and*

Literature (New Brunswick, N.J.: Rutgers University Press, 1981);

Milton S. Katz, *Ban the Bomb: A History of SANE, the Committee for a Sane Nuclear Policy, 1957–1985* (New York: Greenwood Press, 1986);

Alvin B. Kernan, *The Imaginary Library: An Essay on Literature and Society* (Princeton, N.J.: Princeton University Press, 1982);

James Kinsella, *Covering the Plague: AIDS and the American Media* (New Brunswick, N.J.: Rutgers University Press, 1989);

William Severini Kowinski, *The Malling of America: An Inside Look at the Great Consumer Paradise* (New York: Morrow, 1985);

Judith Langer, *Consumers in Transitions: In-Depth Investigations of Changing Lifestyles* (New York: American Management Association Membership Publications Division, 1982);

Paul Rogat Loeb, *Hope in Hard Times: America's Peace Movement and the Reagan Era* (Lexington, Mass.: Lexington Books, 1987);

Russell Lynes, *The Tastemakers: The Shaping of American Popular Taste* (New York: Dover, 1980);

John B. McLaughlin, *Gypsy Lifestyles* (Lexington, Mass.: Lexington Books, 1980);

Carlton C. Rochell, ed., *An Information Agenda for the 1980s: Proceedings of a Colloquim, June 17–18, 1980* (Chicago: American Library Association, 1981);

Robert Scheer, *With Enough Shovels: Reagan, Bush, and Nuclear War* (New York: Random House, 1982);

Jonathan Schell, *The Fate of the Earth* (New York: Knopf, 1982);

Robert B. Settle and Pamela L. Alreck, *Why They Buy: Wealth and the American Consumers Inside and Out* (New York: Wiley, 1986);

Paul Von Blum, *The Critical Vision: A History of Social and Political Art in the U.S.* (Boston, Mass.: South End Press, 1982);

Paul L. Wachtel, *The Poverty of Affluence: A Psychological Portrait of the American Way of Life* (New York: Free Press, 1988);

Larzer Ziff, *Literary Democracy: The Declaration of Cultural Indepedence in America* (New York: Viking, 1981);

Advertising Age, periodical;

Business Week, periodical;

CSP: Contemporary Social Problems, periodical;

Fortune, periodical;

Money, periodical;

New York Times Magazine, periodical;

Newsweek, periodical;

Rolling Stone, periodical;

Time, periodical.

MEDIA

by CHARLES D. BROWER, JAMES W. HIPP, and KAREN L. ROOD

CONTENTS

Sidebars and tables are listed in italics.

1980

1 June Atlanta entrepreneur Ted Turner debuts the twenty-four-hour news channel, Cable News Network (CNN).

2 July In *Richmond Newspapers* v. *Virginia* the Supreme Court rules that the press and the public have a right to attend criminal trials.

15–19 Sept. NBC's miniseries *Shogun*, starring Richard Chamberlain and Toshiro Mifune, captivates audiences.

14 Oct. President Carter signs a law forbidding the unannounced search of newsrooms, except in special circumstances.

21 Nov. An episode of the television soap opera *Dallas* captures the largest audience for a program in television history. The episode answers the question from the spring season concerning an attempted assassination of the lead character J. R. Ewing, "Who Shot J. R.?"

1981

- Warner Communications, owners of the Superman character, sue the students of Richard J. Daley College in Chicago for trademark infringement when they name their student newspaper *The Daley Planet*.

12 Jan. ABC debuts the prime-time soap opera *Dynasty*.

15 Jan. *Hill Street Blues*, a police drama produced by Steven Bochco, debuts on NBC.

6 Mar. CBS news anchorman Walter Cronkite goes off the air after nineteen years in broadcasting. He is replaced by veteran newsman Dan Rather.

8 Oct. *Cagney and Lacey*, a police drama featuring two female leads, debuts on ABC.

1982

- Technological improvements in facsimile communications make the fax machine a popular business tool.

- Music Television (MTV), a cable channel playing music videos twenty-four hours a day, debuts.

8 Jan. Following an eight-year antitrust suit, American Telephone and Telegraph (AT&T) agrees to divest itself of its twenty-two Baby Bell telephone systems.

29 Jan. The *Philadelphia Bulletin* ceases publication.

16 Aug. The *Saturday Review*, a monthly featuring art and literary criticism, ceases publication.

15 Sept. Gannett's national daily, *USA Today*, begins publication.

29 Sept. NBC debuts the television sitcom *Cheers*, set in a Boston bar.

1983

- The Federal Communications Commission (FCC) authorizes the testing of a cellular telephone system in Chicago.

28 Feb. The farewell episode of the popular sitcom *M*A*S*H* attracts an audience of 125 million, making it the highest-rated show in history.

20 Nov. ABC airs *The Day After*, a controversial movie simulating the effects of a nuclear war on a Kansas town.

1984

17 Jan. In a decision condemned by the film industry, the Supreme Court rules that home videotape recording of movies does not infringe upon copyright law.

4 Mar. A television hall of fame is established. Among its first inductees are comedians Lucille Ball and Milton Berle, playwright Paddy Chayefsky (posthumously), producer Norman Lear, and industry magnates William S. Paley and David Sarnoff.

9 June At Disneyland Donald Duck's fiftieth birthday is celebrated.

16 Sept. The postmodern police drama *Miami Vice*, starring Don Johnson, debuts on NBC.

20 Sept. NBC debuts the television sitcom *The Cosby Show*, starring comedian Bill Cosby.

1985

24 Jan. New York courts acquit *Time* magazine of libel in a suit filed by Israeli politician Ariel Sharon.

18 Feb. Former commander of American forces in Vietnam, Gen. William Westmoreland, drops a $120 million libel suit against CBS.

4 Mar. The avant-garde publisher Grove Press is bought by Britain's Weidenfeld Limited, for $2 million.

8 Mar. *The New Yorker* magazine is bought by Newhouse Publications for $142 million.

18 Mar. Capital Cities Communications buys the American Broadcasting Corporation (ABC) for $3.5 billion.

19 July The U.S. Court of Appeals rules that the FCC's "must carry" provisions, which require cable systems to carry local broadcast stations, are a violation of the First Amendment.

Dec. General Electric buys the Radio Corporation of America (RCA) and the National Broadcasting Company (NBC) for $6.3 billion.

1986

14 Jan. The FCC rules against local laws that forbid the use of backyard satellite dishes as opposed to other types of antennae.

10 Sept. CBS president and chairman Thomas Wyman resigns. He is replaced as president by Laurence Tisch, the company's largest stockholder. Company founder William Paley becomes acting chairman.

15 Sept. The television drama *L.A. Law* debuts on NBC.

29 Sept. American journalist Nicholas Daniloff, arrested by the Soviet Union for spying, is released in a spy exchange.

1987

- Media baron Rupert Murdoch buys Harper and Row for $300 million.

- Experts estimate that 43.2 million households have cable television, an increase of 2 million from the previous year.

- Harcourt Brace Jovanovich successfully repels a $1.7 billion takeover bid by British publishing entrepreneur Robert Maxwell.

1988

- The baby-boomer melodrama *thirty something* debuts on ABC.

13 Mar. On appeal a $2 million libel judgment against the *Washington Post* is overturned.

24 Sept. The A. C. Nielsen Company introduces a new means of measuring television viewing audiences. A new system of push-button "people meters" replaces its old-fashioned television diary system.

24 Feb. The Supreme Court rules that *Hustler* magazine's satires of evangelist Jerry Falwell are constitutionally protected speech.

13 Apr. By purchasing an American publisher, Diamandis Communications, Inc., the French book and magazine publisher Hachette S.A. becomes the largest magazine publisher in world, printing over seventy-five publications in ten countries.

17 May Pepsico Inc. becomes the first American company to buy advertising time on Soviet television.

7 Aug. Media mogul Rupert Murdoch buys Walter Annenberg's Triangle Publications (*TV Guide, Daily Racing Form, Seventeen*) for $3 billion.

1989

- News Corporation Limited buys William Collins and Sons of Great Britain, forming HarperCollins.

- The New York Times Company sells all of its cable television properties for $420 million. CBS buys television station WCIX in Miami, Florida, for $59 million.

OVERVIEW

Consolidation and Change. The 1980s was a decade of consolidation in the media, as huge television networks were bought up by even bigger companies, small publishing firms were cobbled together into multimedia behemoths, and small-town newspapers were bought by nationwide chains and changed into local voices of a national editorial policy. Because almost everyone read newspapers and magazines, listened to the radio, or watched television, the decade's "merger mania" in these businesses received more public attention than in other industries. The money involved in all forms of media — both profits and losses — climbed to astronomical levels. The American public was confronted with a staggering array of new magazines, cable channels, movies, and books, as well as relatively new media such as videotapes and audiocasette recordings of books.

Visual Newspapers. Even the local newspaper familiar to most Americans was changing. The national newspaper *USA Today* hit newsstands in 1982 and within four years had a daily circulation of more than one million readers: not a large enough audience to turn a profit, but enough to concern the owners of its local competitors. To compensate, papers around the country began to emulate *USA Today*'s style, which relied on eye-catching color photographs, charts, and snippets of sports and entertainment news calculated to be of interest mainly to travelers. Production costs climbed, and many of the nation's oldest newspapers, in cities from Philadelphia and Cleveland to Memphis and Los Angeles, closed their doors. The papers that survived were mostly those that had been bought up by large syndicates such as Knight-Ridder and Gannett, the group that started *USA Today*. By the end of the decade there were fewer than four hundred independent dailies left, compared to the 1,228 owned by the publishing conglomerates.

The Blockbuster Syndrome. Book publishing underwent a similar transition during the decade. The country's most recognized publishing names — Macmillan, Simon and Schuster, Prentice-Hall, Harper and Row, to name only a few — changed hands with sometimes dizzying speed. Their new owners, for whom book publishing was only one of a variety of business endeavors, were interested more in profits than literary value or the firm's reputation. Quality, "risky" books were less likely to be published than ever before; increasingly the shelves of bookstores and libraries were dominated by "blockbusters," mediocre bestsellers for which the authors were paid millions in advance.

Paperback Originals. Paperback books gained a new-found respectability in the 1980s as consumers tired of paying the rising cost of hardbacks. Previously mainstream publishing houses had issued a hardcover edition of a book and then sold the reprint rights to a paperback publisher. In the 1980s, however, the publishing conglomerates bought or started their own reprint lines, to retain the rights to their own bestsellers and to reprint older favorites from their lines. In response the softcover publishers turned to paperback originals, mostly inexpensive science fiction and romance novels, while they continued to bid exorbitant sums for the rights to the few hardcover books that remained available to them.

Book Products. Publishers also sought new profit opportunities in other forms of media, including audiocasette versions of popular books, computer software, and self-help books. This led the larger chain bookstores (many of which were owned by the publishing conglomerates) to broaden their inventories beyond books, to the extent that finding a book in some bookstores became an increasingly difficult proposition.

New Magazines. Magazine publishing experienced something of a boom during the decade, with more new titles aimed at increasingly specialized audiences. Shelves of newsstands were crowded with magazines devoted to computing, child-rearing, health and exercise, travel, sports, television, and popular music. Most of these new arrivals folded within a few years, although a few of the new magazines enjoyed considerable success, including the music magazine *Spin*; *EM Ebony Man*, a fashion and lifestyles magazine aimed at young black men; and *Sassy*, targeted at teenage girls. The 1980s also saw the arrival of glossy periodicals such as *Tiffany* and *Veranda* aimed at a more affluent readership, and the revival of *Vanity Fair*, which found its niche after a disastrous few years.

Radio. Perhaps the most common communications medium in the decade continued to be radio, owned by 99 percent of American households and a standard feature in nearly every automobile. In the 1980s there were nine thousand radio stations around the country, with most of their programming originating locally. The differences between AM and FM programming became more pronounced over the decade, as the better sound quality of FM stations made them the preferred choice among music listeners. AM stations, on the other hand, were oriented more toward talk shows, sports, and news. An ideological difference between AM and FM began to develop as well: the nonprofit National Public Radio carried the allegedly liberal news program *All Things Considered* on FM stations around the country; AM stations, on the other hand, began carrying the unabashedly right-wing Rush Limbaugh in national syndication.

The Television Revolution. Like radio, television was in nearly every home in the nation. The explosive growth of the cable industry during the 1980s ended the dominance of the three major networks, which had been responsible for most television programming, news, and sports for the first four decades of the medium. But during the course of the decade, the average number of channels available to the typical viewer had increased from seven to more than thirty, and the major networks' share of viewers dropped by 15 percent. Cable networks were cheaper to operate than the major networks, since they mostly showed syndicated reruns, old movies, sporting events, and inexpensive talk shows; consequently they could be content with a smaller audience share. Many cable channels practiced "narrowcasting," which meant

that their programs were aimed at a specific, specialized target audience. Cable television could direct their programs at a more mature audience, as well: the most successful cable service, Home Box Office, specialized in unedited, commercial-free showings of popular theatrical releases. Thus, network executives extolled television as a medium to bring people together and deplored the vulgarity of cable's programs, while cable owners placed a higher value on diversity, individualism, and free expression.

The Networks Respond. CBS, ABC, and NBC attempted to respond to cable's challenge in various ways. They loosened their programming standards and developed series that were more graphically violent and sexual, as well as adopting a more sensational approach to the news. They extended their programming hours to compete with cable's round-the-clock schedules. In some instances they tried to join the cable boom themselves, as when ABC launched the Satellite News Channel to compete with Ted Turner's Cable News Network in 1992. But for the most part network executives were simply bewildered at the changes to the industry they had once controlled. Their falling earnings made them ripe for takeover in 1985, when all of the "Big Three" were bought by larger corporations in a span of nine months. By 1986 ABC and CBS were being outearned by twelve major cable channels. With more channels added every year, the trend toward cable and away from network television showed no signs of abating.

TOPICS IN THE NEWS

CABLE AND THE DECLINE OF THE BIG THREE

More Channels. Cable television has been around since the 1940s but until recently was used almost exclusively to bring watchable television reception to communities that were separated from broadcasting antennae by distance or physical barriers such as mountains. In the 1970s individuals in a few communities had cable connections to their homes that allowed them to see movies, sports, and special events on a subscription basis. By the 1980s, however, the availability of commercial telecommunications satellites made it economically feasible for independent stations and special-interest channels to broadcast nationwide. As more material became available to the nation's cable providers, the business grew dramatically, gaining subscribers in urban centers around the country. In 1976 the average American home received seven channels on its television set; by the end of the 1980s the average number of channels had climbed to nearly thirty.

New Options. Before the 1980s the "Big Three" networks — ABC, CBS, and NBC — were practically television's sole providers of national news and sporting events, major Hollywood releases (which were edited for content), and original dramatic series. But during the decade ten million viewers defected from the networks to watch what was on cable. There were a variety of reasons for the switch: cable channels offered audiences round-the-clock news (CNN), sports (ESPN), movies (Home Box Office, Showtime, and The Movie Channel, among many others), music videos (MTV, VH1, CMT), and reruns of favorite older series. Unlike the networks, whose success had always depended on appealing to as broad an audience as possible, cable channels practiced "narrowcasting" — targeting a specialized viewership. The programming on cable channels was generally far cheaper to air than network fare; and, since the new networks made money both by selling their programming to cable distributors around the country and by selling advertising revenue, the profits stood to be much greater.

Less Regulation. Cable networks were also less restricted in content than the major networks. The premium movie channels that charged a monthly subscrip-

tion fee, such as Home Box Office (which premiered in 1972) and Showtime (debuted in 1978), could show their movies unedited, without commercials, and at all hours of the day. Even basic-service channels (those that did not require the additional monthly fee) were more liberal in their content standards than the Big Three. In order to compete, ABC, NBC, and CBS tried to spice up their programming, and prime-time television became more titillating and more violent over the course of the decade. "Trash TV" began to dominate the airwaves, especially on the local stations that bought sensational syndicated talk shows and pseudojournalistic "tabloid" shows such as *Inside Edition* and *A Current Affair*.

Consolidation. Weakened by the bewildering variety of new competitors, the major networks were ripe for takeover during the merger mania of the mid 1980s. In less than a year all three networks changed ownership. ABC was first, bought by the Capital City Communications group of affiliate television stations in March 1985. In October of that year CBS was purchased by Laurence Tisch and the Loews Corporation. And in December NBC was swallowed by the corporate giant General Electric. The networks' new owners all had strong ideas about how to reverse their acquisitions' falling profits. Each of the Big Three faced budgetary cutbacks in the latter part of the decade, most notably in their news divisions, which were notorious money losers.

Profits. By 1986 the major networks, with the exception of NBC, were earning fewer profits than several of the most popular cable channels; the second-highest earner that year was HBO. In 1987 cable's ratings jumped by a third, so that 15 percent of television sets were tuned to cable networks every night. Half the homes in America were connected to cable television, and that number would continue to grow. Cable channels continued to claim more programming that had once been the exclusive domain of the networks: ESPN brought national coverage of college basketball and Major League Baseball, and TNT contracted with the National Football League to show Sunday night games. The Cable News Network's coverage of the peace demonstrations in Beijing in 1989 and Operation Desert Storm in 1990–

The cast of *M*A*S*H*. The final episode of this popular, long-running series (1972–1983) aired on 28 February 1983.

Michael Conrad and Daniel J. Travanti on *Hill Street Blues* (1980–1987), a new style of police-drama series that won a record number of Emmy awards.

way network television had been able to. With a growing number of channels aimed at increasingly specialized audiences, it was less likely that a family would sit together and watch the same program. It was becoming less likely, in fact, that anyone would watch an entire program at all. With thirty or more channels to choose from, many viewers were plagued with the fear that there was always something better on. Channel surfing — restlessly flipping through one's available channels with the remote control — became a common pastime for the cable junkie.

Sources:

Ken Auletta, *Three Blind Mice: How the TV Networks Lost Their Way* (New York: Random House, 1991);

Harry P. Waters, "Trash TV," *Newsweek* (14 November 1988): 72–78.

1991 established the all-news network as the channel that even the president watched to stay on top of events.

The Cost of Cable. By the end of the decade, however, many issues relating to cable and broadcast television were unresolved. Although cable's rating continued to improve and the networks' continued to slide, not every television viewer could afford cable's rates. Free television had been an American institution for almost four decades and in some ways was a necessary part of the life of the country. Some observers of the medium wondered if cable were capable of bringing the nation together the

THE CABLE NEWS NETWORK

News Network. The Cable News Network (CNN) was the first television network to devote its entire programming schedule to reporting the news — in the process the network changed the definition of news itself. Previously, the nightly news broadcasts offered by the three major networks were summaries of the day's events, condensed into a half-hour format that allowed little room for detailed coverage or analysis. Live reporting of events that occurred outside the "news hour" of 6:00–7:00 P.M. was unusual. But CNN's round-the-clock dedication to current events gave the network the ability to cover events as they occurred and the time to follow those events, however long they took to develop.

Bill Cosby and Malcolm Jamal-Warner on *The Cosby Show,* the top-rated television show during the second half of the 1980s

Turner's Vision. CNN was the brainchild of Ted Turner, the unconventional entrepreneur who in 1981, when the news network debuted, was known primarily as the owner of the Atlanta Braves baseball team. Turner had also owned Atlanta's independent channel 17 since the early 1970s and was quick to see the possibilities for cable television: in 1976 the SuperStation WTBS (for Turner Broadcasting System) became the first broadcast station to transmit via satellite and thus was one of the cornerstones of cable television. At that time Turner was already considering the possibility of an all-news network, but the conventional wisdom of the television industry was that the public's taste for news was limited to about an hour a day, minus commercials.

Risky Business. Turner gambled most of his holdings on the Cable News Network, to the dismay of his stockholders and employees. But Turner had faith that the public would be lured to the drama of a breaking story, something that the network news usually lacked. In May 1979 he hired Reese Schonfeld to serve as president of his new network. Schonfeld had been a reporter, editor, and executive for the failed UPI Television News and then managing editor for the Independent Television News Association; so he had experienced firsthand the frustrations of an independent news source trying to compete directly with the three major networks. Schonfeld and

Turner went to work assembling their news bureau, which included Daniel Schorr, veteran of CBS's news team, as their senior Washington correspondent. Unlike the polished network news, CNN was intended to be spontaneous and sometimes awkward. Schonfeld and Turner were convinced that any miscues or ragged edges would add to the excitement of watching news as it developed. To add to the sense of viewers being involved in the process of news gathering, the anchors would deliver the news from the newsroom itself, surrounded by reporters, producers, and technicians.

First Broadcast. Cable News Network began broadcasting at 6:00 P.M. on 1 June 1980 with a dedication by Turner from the station's Atlanta headquarters: "To provide information to people when it wasn't available before.... To offer those who want it a choice; For the American people, whose thirst for understanding and a better life has made this venture possible; For the cable industry, whose pioneering spirit caused this great step forward in communication; ... I dedicate the News Channel of America — The Cable News Network." At 6:05 the network began its first news broadcast, anchored by Dave Walker and Lois Hart. CNN's first several hours of broadcast were audacious, but they were also somewhat chaotic. Live reports were aired from Fort Wayne, Indiana, where President Jimmy Carter was making a

Bruce Willis and Cybill Shepherd on *Moonlighting* (1985–1989), a popular television show that blended romantic comedy and detective drama

statement; Jerusalem, where correspondent Ned Bushinsky was waiting to report on Middle East politics; and the Florida Keys, with a live report on an arriving flotilla of Cuban refugees.

Predictions of Failure. Media critics recognized the importance of Turner's great experiment but also predicted it would fail. The expense of maintaining an organization that could supply twenty-four hours of news daily was too great, with little promise of return from advertising revenues. Veterans of broadcast journalism noted that CNN's coverage of the news lacked "focus," but focus implied exactly the set format that the network was trying to avoid. In addition to its newsroom coverage the network featured daily shows dedicated to sports, financial news, and entertainment news, as well as interview and viewer call-in shows. Any of these might be interrupted to cover a breaking story, however. The desire of the producers at CNN to catch a big event as it developed led them sometimes to devote considerable attention to stories that never developed at all.

Early Successes. At the same time, the network had its early successes: after the Shah of Iran died the network brought live coverage of his funeral, and at that summer's national convention of the Republican Party CNN was the first to get former president Richard Nixon's thoughts on the upcoming presidential race. CNN put its own spin on the presidential debates between Jimmy Carter and challenger Ronald Reagan that fall, using tape delay to include independent candidate John Anderson as well. For its live coverage of many news stories CNN relied on reciprocal agreements with stations around the country to provide them with coverage. One such arrangement provided the news network with dramatic material when the M-G-M Grand Hotel in Las Vegas burned in November 1980; using a satellite feed from local station KLAS, CNN broadcast the tragedy to a nationwide audience.

Losing Money. Despite encouraging successes the network was still losing money at an alarming rate. When President Reagan was shot in March 1981, CNN covered the story for twenty-nine continuous hours, and its coverage led directly to a confrontation with the major news networks over the use of "pool" footage from the White House press corps. The three network news divisions had an agreement with the White House in which news released by the White House staff was pooled for use by all of the networks, and CNN had been excluded from that pool. Denied the pool footage of the president's shooting, CNN taped it from ABC and rebroadcast it. In May 1981 the network sued NBC, ABC, and CBS for illegally excluding them from the press pool; the suit also named the Reagan administration, faulting them for limiting CNN's constitutional freedom of the press. Competition between CNN and the "Big Three" remained fierce: when CNN had exclusive pictures of Pope John Paul II's shooting that same month, ABC broadcast the same footage a few minutes later.

Cable Competition. By the end of that year CNN was also facing even more direct competition from the growing cable market. ABC and Westinghouse had joined forces to create two all-news cable networks, the Satellite NewsChannels, which would be offered free to cable operators around the country. Ted Turner decided to respond aggressively by creating CNN-2, which would condense CNN's material into a more traditional half-hour format that would be updated every few hours. To beat the Satellite NewsChannels to the punch Turner proposed that CNN-2 go on the air at midnight, 31 December 1981. The second news network, soon renamed CNN Headline News, debuted on schedule; and as a further assault on the Big Three, Headline News offered its news show in syndication to stations across the country. The first Satellite NewsChannel debuted in June 1982 into the homes of more than twice as many cable subscribers as received Headline News. With ABC's resources at its disposal, the SNC network had the finances and journalistic experience to pose a considerable threat to CNN. While the networks competed to scoop each others' news coverage, Turner waged a legal battle with ABC and Westinghouse, charging that they had made secret deals to exclude his news networks from cable companies. The SNC owners were clearly unwilling to make the same commitment Turner was: in the fall of 1983 they accepted the $25 million he offered them for the network.

Superior News. Having survived the challenge from the SNC, CNN was poised to solidify its status as one of the nation's major news sources. The lawsuit to end the major networks' monopoly of the White House pool had been a success, and CNN's coverage of the national party conventions in the summer of 1984 was considered by many to be superior to that of the giants. By that time the network was also distinguishing itself internationally, broadcasting in twenty-two foreign markets. It was in January 1986, however, that the difference between CNN's news coverage and the Big Three became clear to the nation: due to its routine coverage of space-shuttle launches, only the cable network had live footage of the tragic explosion of the *Challenger*.

Tiananmen Square. In May 1989 the network scored what was possibly the scoop of the decade, when Bernard Shaw and a staff of CNN reporters and technicians were on hand for the student uprising in the streets of Beijing, China. CNN was there to cover Soviet president Mikhail Gorbachev's visit, the first official meeting between the two great communist powers in more than thirty years. On their last day there, the CNN crew recorded the dramatic spectacle of one million Chinese demonstrating for freedom in Beijing's Tiananmen Square as well as the Chinese government's brutal response. As would be the case with later events, CNN's coverage became part of the story itself, as the news team stalled the efforts of Chinese government officials to end their satellite access. American viewers were spellbound, and White House officials issued statements on the crisis based on what they saw on the cable network. Even the Kremlin was reportedly following CNN's coverage. Tensions mounted, and for a time it seemed as if the CNN news crew might be in actual jeopardy before they were finally allowed to return to the United States.

Audience Gains. By the end of the decade, as CNN's tenth anniversary approached, the news network's place as a major player in television journalism had been established. The Nielsen ratings for 1989 indicated that the network's share of the news audience had risen from 16.5 percent to nearly 25 percent, while the three major networks had all lost viewers; CNN's audience share actually exceeded that of *NBC Nightly News*. Turner's gamble had changed the face of the news, ending the monopoly the three major networks had enjoyed for decades.

Sources:
Robert Goldberg and Gerald Jay Goldberg, *Citizen Turner* (New York & San Diego: Harcourt Brace, 1995);

Hank Whittemore, *CNN: The Inside Story* (Boston: Little, Brown, 1990).

COMPUTERS: MACHINES OF THE DECADE

You Say You Want a Revolution. By the middle 1980s the social revolution envisioned twenty years earlier by the pioneers of the small computer was in full swing. In 1981 some 750,000 personal computers were estimated to be in use in American homes; 39.4 million computers were shipped between 1984 and 1988. In 1984 alone Americans bought $37.6 million worth of computer software for home use, about two-thirds of it in the "entertainment" category — that is, computer games. By the end of 1982, 250 different computer games were available, and some $2 billion worth were sold. In the mid 1980s home computers came in three types. For less than $100, one could buy a game-only computer made by Atari or Sega. It hooked up to the family television set, which acted as the monitor, and the programs came as plug-in cartridges or tape cassettes similar to those used in tape recorders. For less than $500, the home user could buy a computer that purported to serve the serious user — a Timex Sinclair 1000, a Commodore VIC-20, or an Atari 400 — but these machines were normally upgraded game computers with simple programs. For $1,000 to $2,000, the more serious home user could buy an Apple II, an IBM Personal Computer, or a Radio Shack TRS-80 with a keyboard, a monitor, and as much as thirty-two kilobytes of RAM (random-access memory). For another $750 or so a printer could be attached, making the computer useful as a word processor. Those adventuresome computer users who were willing to spend $100 for a telephone modem were the trailblazers. They could connect with bulletin board services (BBSs) and acquire information — or, more usually, exchange ideas with other computer users. The BBSs were free (except for the cost of a long-distance call, if the BBS was in a different area) and often allowed pseudonymous subscriptions. Commercial services, such as CompuServe and The Source, charged a monthly fee for a certain number of hours of use and certain services; additional time on-line or more specialized services carried extra charges. In 1981 180,000 modems were in American homes; by 1988 there were 10.9 million.

Machine of the Year. On 3 January 1983 a computer appeared on the cover of *Time* as the Machine of the Year. The magazine was saluting the personal computer's potential rather than its accomplishments. Clearly, the vision of the "cyberpunks" of the late 1960s and early 1970s had captured the attention, if not the imagination, of the average American. The challenge was to find uses for the computer that took advantage of the machines' unique capabilities and could not be accomplished more efficiently by traditional means (such as the typewriter or calculator). As adults struggled to justify their purchase of the devices, their children played computer games and came to regard computing as a routine part of life. Through such popular game programs as Pac-Man and Super Mario Brothers, children developed an interest in computer hardware and in the programming routines that told the computer what to do. *Bit, byte, RAM, ROM* (read-only memory), *CPU* (central processing unit), and *software* were standard words in the vocabulary of elementary-school children that baffled their elders.

Uses. Meanwhile, the older set sought a practical use for computing. The typewriter industry was the first to feel the impact as word-processing programs offered erratic typists an efficient way to correct mistakes. For home finances and record keeping there was VisiCalc, an early spreadsheet program that allowed nearly instant calculation according to formulas determined by the user. Software manufacturers struggled, with mixed success, to provide other practical uses for home computers. Thousands of programs were introduced each year in the mid 1980s, most of uncertain utility. The determined user could store recipes, inventory household items, learn languages, and fill in the blanks on prepared legal forms, such as simple wills and bills of sale, using computer programs, though often it was more efficient to accomplish these tasks using traditional means. The uses that

Arsenio Hall (right) interviewing Jesse Jackson on *The Arsenio Hall Show,* which premiered on Fox in 1988

established the computer among middle-class families as a required household item were basic ones — writing, ciphering, and placating the children, who amused themselves for hours on end with digital games.

Incompatibility. A serious drawback to the computers of the early 1980s was that different brands, or even different models produced by the same company, were often incompatible. Because there was no clear standard of operating software, ambitious computer companies, notably Sharp, marketed computers that would only run software provided by the manufacturer. Thus, if one bought a Sharp computer, one had to buy programs from Sharp, as well — a situation that frustrated experienced users, who may, for example, have had one type of computer at home and another at the office. Software incompatibility also served to add to the confusion of novices, who failed to understand the nuances of hardware architecture. As Microsoft Corporations's MS-DOS and Apple's Macintosh became established as the two major operating systems, customers and software producers insisted that computers be able to run any software written for one or the other. General users were attracted to later-generation machines and software that required only simple typing skills and intuitive responses to "icons" — pictures on the monitor screen that represented sets of complicated instructions to the machine; the instructions could be executed by using a mouse (a small device that sat on the desktop next to the keyboard) to position a cursor (pointer) over the icon and clicking a button. By the end of the 1980s the term *user friendly* had become not only a merchandising slogan but also a basic principle of computer hardware and software design.

Source:
Otto Friedrich, "Machine of the Year: The Computer Moves In," *Time* (3 January 1983): 14–24.

THE COMPUTER REVOLUTION

Computer Literacy. By the mid 1980s computer technology had transformed American life. The watches people wore, the cars they drove, the mail they received, the games they played, the state of their health, and the way they learned were altered by the computer chip. Schools, workplaces, the health industry, government, and the law were all dramatically affected by the computer. Social engineers began to ponder the question of how to prepare the citizens of the future for lives and careers that would require at least a rudimentary understanding of computing. The notion of literacy, the fundamnetal measure of capability for modern life, was expanded to include "computer literacy": a basic familiarity with computers.

Business Uses. Big business had recognized the importance of the computer from the beginning; but by the 1980s, as equipment and the programs to make it useful became affordable, even small business offices relied on computers for word processing, accounting, record keeping, and a variety of specialized uses limited only by the imagination of programmers. Computers changed the way telephone systems operated and were managed. Banking moved swiftly from personal service to computerized automatic teller machines (ATMs). Computer-driven robots reshaped manufacturing processes. Computer-assisted teleconferencing began to be recognized as an efficient alternative to expensive business travel. Even show business was affected as computerized synthesizers were developed that could emulate the sound of any musical instrument, and filmmakers used computers to design and execute special effects.

Health Care Uses. In the hospital and the doctor's office the computer had two important effects: it made diagnosis and treatment more reliable, and it helped to drive health-care costs to soaring heights. Body-imaging techniques refined in the 1980s, such as ultrasound, positron-emission technology (PET scans), magnetic resonance imaging (MRI), and nuclear magnetic resonance (NMR), allowed physicians views of the inside of the body that would have been unimaginable a decade earlier; the machines were extremely expensive, but once the technology was available physicians argued that prudent medical practice necessitated their frequent use. The computerized axial tomography (CAT scan) machine had been introduced in 1973; by the mid 1980s four thousand were in use in American hospitals, which paid more than $1 million each for them, in addition to some thirteen hundred MRI machines costing $2.5 million apiece. Computers operated heart pacemakers, though a 1988 study showed that 20 percent of them were unnecessary and 36 percent were of questionable benefit. Computers offered medical-services personnel an efficient means of record keeping, as well as of sharing patient information and the latest research findings.

Educational Uses. School administrators were awestruck by the educational potential of the computer, but classroom teachers were slow to turn the theory of computer-assisted education to practical use. Bewteen 1980 and 1988 the number of computers in schools from kindergarten to grade twelve increased from 100,000 to more than 2 million; in 1987, 95 percent of elementary schools, 97 percent of junior high schools, and 98 percent of high schools had at least one computer, and by the end of the decade it was estimated that there was one computer for every twenty students in America. Apple led the march of computers into the schools, donating hardware in some areas and making it available at deeply discounted prices in others. As a result, the firm dominated the school market: 77 percent of elementary schools had Apples, as did 47 percent of the nation's high schools. But many of the machines simply collected dust: teachers were sometimes reluctant to alter well-established curricula to incorporate the computer, and there was rarely adequate staff to maintain the machines. The students who were interested in computers often had much better ones available at home, as anxious middle-class parents rationalized that a home computer was a necessary school-related purchase. About half of the available educational software was in the category of skills practice — what teachers referred to as "homework" or "seat work"— and, thus, it offered limited benefit to teachers struggling to manage overcrowded classrooms. Meanwhile, social revolutionists searched for ways to displace the school as the center for education. In the early 1980s Control Data Corporation energetically sought to adapt a program developed in 1959 for home educational use, but people were not yet ready for such a bold departure from traditional practice.

Scientific Uses. Scientific analysis of data was enormously simplified by computers; but scholars were quick to point out that while computers might provide information with unprecedented speed and accuracy, a well-trained scientist was still required to devise the data sets and interpret them. Even the humanities showed the effects of the computer age, as electronic storage made it possible to accumulate, organize, and search huge amounts of information; scholars could, in an afternoon, accumulate data that, in previous generations, would have taken a lifetime to amass.

Governmental Uses. Government, the judiciary, and law enforcement were similarly affected. Tellingly, some said, the U.S. Census Bureau and the Internal Revenue Service, two of the highest profile computer users in the country, struggled with outmoded equipment and awkward programs. The introduction of the computer created a new class of criminal and required regulations as hackers used computers instead of handguns to rob banks and to commit fraud. Meanwhile, law enforcement agencies used computerized storage facilities to store criminal records and profiles. Theoretically, computers had made it harder than ever for malefactors to escape punishment; but computers require users, and law enforcement agencies were as understaffed as they had always been. The copyright laws that had served the nation for a century were found to be inadequate to address the problems related to digitized intellectual property.

The Controllers. Computers had only become commonly available about five years before the beginning of the 1980s, but by the end of the decade it was difficult to imagine a present or a future that did not depend on computer technology. The social revolution imagined in the early 1970s by the young rebels in such groups as the Homebrew Computer Club in San Francisco was in full swing by the mid 1980s, and it proved to be as thorough a reformation as America had ever experienced. Businesses, schools, and home users — mainstream Americans — realized that they needed computers, but they lacked the imagination, the specialized skill, and the creative resources to provide for their needs. For the fulfillment of their digital dreams, they were forced to look to an unusual source: youth. As business and scholarly interests took over the development of the mainframe computer, the personal computer, which grew more powerful by the month, was the domain of the young "chipheads," and few Americans escaped their influence.

Source:
Richard S. Rosenberg, *The Social Impact of Computers* (San Diego: Academic Press, 1992).

FOX: THE FOURTH NETWORK

A New Network. The first four decades of commercial American television were dominated by three huge networks of affiliated stations, known as the "Big Three" — CBS, NBC, and ABC. The Big Three provided virtually all of the programs aired on television stations around the country, particularly between the hours of 8:00 and 11:00 P.M. — "prime time." By the early 1980s, however, it was clear that television was changing in fundamental ways that the executives at the Big Three barely understood, if at all. Cable television was offering alternatives to major-network programming in the form of unedited movies, all-news and all-sports formats, music-video channels, and a variety of other endeavors that were challenging conventional wisdom about how the business of television operated. In 1985 the picture for the Big Three seemed especially bleak: all three networks were purchased by larger companies between March and December of that year.

Murdoch. For Australian entrepreneur Rupert Murdoch this troubled time for the major networks offered the perfect opportunity to launch a fourth network that would comprise independent stations around the country. Murdoch had made his fortune with a variety of newspaper and television holdings around the world, most notoriously the tabloid-style *New York Post*. In 1985, the same year ownership of each of the Big Three changed hands, he purchased 20th Century-Fox, the movie studio, which produced television programs as well, and Metromedia, a chain of major-market indepen-

---

M*A*S*H FAREWELL

The 251st episode of M*A*S*H, the sitcom set during the Korean War, was a media event. CBS decided to terminate the series after eleven successful seasons while the show still drew a large audience. On 28 February 1983 the final episode, "Goodbye, Farewell and Amen," a heavily promoted two-and-a-half-hour special was broadcast. It was about the end of the war and the disbanding of the medical unit that had provided the focus of the series. Seventy-seven percent of the national television audience tuned in. Alan Alda, the series star, called the final show "a long piece . . . in which the people say goodbye to each other and the experience."

---

dent television stations. These new acquisitions would form the foundation for the Fox network.

Talented Team. Murdoch assembled an impressive array of executive talent to run his new network, including Barry Diller, the head of 20th Century-Fox; Jamie Kellner, a producer and former CBS executive who was hired to serve as the network's president; and Garth Ancier and Kevin Wendle, programming executives who had been lured away from NBC. Murdoch had acquired a star for the network as well: Joan Rivers, the popular comedian, who had signed a contract for $15 million to develop and host a late-night talk show for Fox. Rivers's new show would compete directly with NBC's long-running *Tonight Show,* which Rivers guest-hosted when regular star Johnny Carson was on one of his frequent vacations. Murdoch and Diller hoped that Joan Rivers would provide the big-name entertainment that would sell their network to independents around the country.

Doubt of Success. Observers of the industry doubted the new network's potential. Cable and the growing popularity of home videocasette recorders had cut the Big Three's audience share by 25 percent since 1970; consequently, there were simply fewer advertising dollars (the source of a network's profits) out there to compete for. Fox executives claimed that the few stations they had assembled for their network would reach 85 percent of American homes, but competitors suspected that the Fox affiliates — mostly weak UHF stations — more likely would be available to about 55 percent of viewers. Murdoch, however, was willing to commit as much of his considerable resources as were necessary to give the Fox network a real chance. *The Late Show Starring Joan Rivers* made its debut on the new network in October 1986 to encouraging audience numbers, but after its initial few weeks the show settled into a 2 percent audience share, well below the number of viewers Fox executives had promised advertisers. Fox soon found itself in the uncomfortable position of having to give away commercial time on *The Late Show* to make up for what they had overcharged sponsors.

Expansion. Despite the fact that the network was losing money on *The Late Show*, it expanded its schedule to offer prime-time programming on Saturday and Sunday nights by the summer of 1987. Most of those early shows were unmemorable and low-rated sitcoms, but there were also encouraging successes: *21 Jump Street,* a police melodrama about young cops who went undercover as teenagers that launched the career of teen heartthrob Johnny Depp; *Married . . . With Children,* an irreverent, tasteless, and often hilarious send-up of family-style sitcoms; and *America's Most Wanted,* which offered viewers rewards for tips leading to the capture of fugitive criminals. Hosted by John Walsh, a victim's-rights activist whose own son had been murdered, *America's Most Wanted* told each villain's story through lurid dramatizations that most critics considered blatantly exploitative; still, the show was Fox's first bonafide ratings hit and actually was responsible for the capture of many fugitives. The network gambled big that year by buying the rights to telecast the Television Academy's annual Emmy awards show, but their presentation was a resounding failure, earning the lowest ratings ever for the event.

Failure of Rivers. *The Late Show,* meanwhile, self-destructed on the air in front of the few American viewers watching. Joan Rivers and her manager husband had well-publicized disputes with the Fox executives before the show even reached the air, and as the ratings for *The Late Show* continued to decline Fox sought to exercise more control over it. Fearing that affiliates would begin to pull out of the network if *The Late Show* continued to lose them money, Fox finally decided to pay off Rivers's contract and fire her as host of the show. Rivers's bitter departure from the network had a tragic postscript: husband Edgar Rosenberg, depressed over his role in the failure of *The Late Show,* committed suicide a few months after Rivers's firing. Fox kept the talk show on with a different host every night; one of them, Arsenio Hall, hosted his own successful late-night talk show beginning in 1988.

Success. Despite the *Late Show* debacle, Fox was stronger than ever at the end of the decade. On 16 July 1989 *America's Most Wanted* won its time slot over all three of the major networks, and later that week *Married . . . With Children* repeated the feat. Fox executives were understandably triumphant that their shows were beating the Big Three in a little more than two years since the network had signed on. In the early 1990s the network expanded its programming schedule to seven days a week and introduced several of the most popular shows of the decade, including *The Simpsons, Beverly Hills 90210,* and *Melrose Place.*

The first issue of the women's magazine media magnate Rupert Murdoch launched in mid 1989

Sources:

Ken Auletta, *Three Blind Mice: How the TV Networks Lost Their Way* (New York: Random House, 1991);

Alex Ben Block, *Outfoxed: Marvin Davis, Barry Diller, Rupert Murdoch, Joan Rivers, and the Inside Story of America's Fourth Television Network* (New York: St. Martin's Press, 1990).

MTV AND ITS INFLUENCE

Music Video. MTV, or Music Television, a cable television network that devotes most of its programming time to video clips that accompany popular songs, has had a profound influence on young people, and on popular culture in general, since its first broadcast in 1982. Although originally conceived as a promotional tool for the popular music industry, it quickly assumed a life of its own and was embraced by young America as a source of information on the latest trends in music, fashion, and opinion. As a visual companion to rock 'n' roll, the video clips shown on MTV were frequently juvenile, vulgar, tasteless, and violent — which inevitably delighted teenage viewers and offended their parents. Advertisers and studio executives attempted to capitalize on the network's enormous success, and soon commercials, television series, and feature films were being shot in the style of music videos — with glossy visuals, rapid editing, and a throbbing pop-music soundtrack. Most of the biggest musical stars of the decade got their first public exposure on MTV, a circumstance that has led some critics to charge that the video network was instrumental in elevating style and appearance over talent in the music industry.

Start on Nickelodeon. MTV was one of the cornerstones of the cable revolution that transformed television during the 1980s. It began on the Nickelodeon network as a half-hour show called *Pop Clips.* Nickelodeon's shows were mostly aimed at children; but under the guidance of John Lack, a marketing executive for Warner Cable Corporation (which owned Nickelodeon and several other pioneer cable channels), the network went after the teenage audience as well. Teenagers were traditionally considered "low users" by the television industry, and Lack saw visual rock music as a way to reach that vast, untapped audience. Lack commissioned a production studio owned by Michael Nesmith, once a member of the pop group the Monkees, to produce the show. In *Pop Clips* many of the features of MTV were present: the shows were fast-paced mixes of videos set to popular songs, animation, and segments featuring a "veejay," the video equivalent of a disc jockey.

Pittman's Vision. The plan to use *Pop Clips* as the premise for a twenty-four-hour cable channel was originally Lack's, but the real vision for MTV came from twenty-six-year-old Robert Pittman, who despite his youth had already established himself as a radio station manager in some of the country's largest and most competitive markets. Lack hired Pittman to program movies on The Movie Channel, another of Warner Cable's projects, but they both believed that a video channel would reach a huge audience of twelve to twenty-four-year olds. They first had to convince cable and music executives, however, most of whom were openly skeptical about the network's potential. In January 1981 the owners of Warner Communications, Inc., were convinced and committed the necessary $20 million dollars to fund MTV.

Ebb and Flow. MTV debuted at midnight on 1 August 1982; the first video aired, appropriately enough, was the Buggles' "Video Killed the Radio Star." The channel's format was already in place, although it took a little while for the veejays — a mix of actors and former radio talents — to settle into their roles. MTV strove for a carefully crafted air of spontaneity: as a critic for *Rolling Stone* noted, it featured "a well-designed studio that looked like something casually thrown together, scripted patter that sounded like it was made up on the spot, an ironclad format that proceeded like a random chain of events, well-trained actors who came on like folks you'd meet at a campus mixer, and a generally perfectionist attitude in bringing about a what-the-hell, let's-boogie mood." Most unusual about the network's format was the continuous repetition of commercials and videos, what Bob Pittman called "the ebb and flow": "They said to me, when I started MTV, 'You're violating the contract you have with the viewers. . . . People want a beginning, a

---

---

middle and an end to their television.' And I said, 'There is no beginning, middle and end.' "

Contests. MTV was initially unable to penetrate the country's two biggest markets, New York City and Los Angeles, but in the markets it did reach viewers were seeking out the bands they saw. The network featured a contest — contests would become a staple for the channel — after two weeks on the air, flying a lucky winner to New York to see the group Journey. Industry critics began to take notice, but not all of the attention was favorable: in October 1981, at a Video Music Conference sponsored by *Billboard* magazine, panelists wondered why there were no African American performers on the channel. But MTV defended its almost exclusively white "rock" playlist until the enormous success of Michael Jackson's *Thriller* album in 1983 finally compelled the channel to start accepting clips by black pop artists.

Advertisers. By that time MTV was reaching more than ten million homes around the country and was becoming increasingly appealing to advertisers, but it was still operating at a loss. Criticism of the station continued to mount: not only were there ongoing charges of racism, but the network was also being accused of destroying teenage viewers' morality and their attention spans. In the summer of 1983 the network faced direct competition from several fronts, including NBC's *Friday Night Videos* and *Night Tracks,* a weekend offering from Ted Turner's

TBS Superstation. MTV executives protected their product ruthlessly, frequently exacting exclusive rights to a video before they'd show it and refusing to play bands who gave their videos to the competitors. The competition had another effect: MTV soon was having to pay for the rights to the videos they showed. But the network ultimately triumphed: in June 1983 it reached an agreement with four major record labels for thirty-day exclusive rights to selected videos.

Influence. The network was also clearly having an influence on television, music, fashion, and feature films. The movies *Flashdance* and *Footloose* virtually were feature-length music videos, and in fact several videos taken from the movies enjoyed heavy rotation on MTV. In September 1984 NBC premiered *Miami Vice*, a successful police drama that relied on flashy visuals and video-style sequences. The stylish men's suits worn by the cop heroes of the show became one of the fashion hallmarks of the decade; so did new-wave hairstyles and clothes, tattered heavy-metal fashions, and Madonna's underwear-as-outerwear look — all thanks to their visibility on MTV. By 1985 MTV's popularity could be measured by the backlash against it; the network was a frequent target of complaints from the Parents' Music Resource Center (PMRC), a group of senators' and cabinet members' wives who had appointed themselves the foes of "porn rock."

Increasing Budgets. Videos themselves were becoming more sophisticated: budgets for them climbed, so that the average clip cost nearly $100,000. Increasingly "videos" were actually shot on film, and feature-film directors and stars were drawn to collaborate with bands, as when Brian de Palma directed Bruce Springsteen's "Dancin' In the Dark" video. Pop musicians continued to grumble about the medium, complaining that there was entirely too much emphasis placed on their visual appeal as opposed to their musical talent. As Bob Dylan commented, "I know they're thought of as an art form, but I don't think they are." Many of the biggest musical acts of the decade, however, for example Madonna and Michael Jackson, made videos as important an element of their artistic expression as their music.

News. Toward the end of the decade MTV began to modify its format, adding a weekly news broadcast hosted by rock journalist Kurt Loder and experimenting with traditional television formats such as the game show (without much success). The network also hired a younger crop of veejays to replace its original on-air hosts. By the late 1980s, perhaps smarting from the claims that the network had a negative influence on its young viewers, MTV mounted several public-service campaigns, including RAD (Rockers Against Drugs) and Rock the Vote, a voter-registration drive. Several years later, during the 1992 presidential elections, candidate Bill Clinton recognized MTV's influence on its audience and appeared on the network to solidify his support among young voters;

Copies of the last issue of the *Baltimore News-Journal* leaving the loading dock, 27 May 1986

MTV celebrated Clinton's election with its own inaugural ball, at which the new president made an appearance.

Sources:
R. Serge Denisoff, *Inside MTV* (New Brunswick, N.J.: Transaction Books, 1988);

Andrew Goodwin, *Dancing in the Distraction and Factory: Music Television and Its Influence* (Minneapolis: University of Minnesota Press, 1992);

Ron Powers, *The Beast, the Eunuch, and the Glass-eyed Child: Television in the '80s* (San Diego: Harcourt Brace Jovanovich, 1990).

NEW MAGAZINES

Magazines for the Affluent. After the recession of the early 1980s, most of the decade was marked by increased prosperity and a slowdown in the rate of inflation, leaving many Americans with disposable income to spend on magazines that addressed their interests in topics such as fashion, celebrities, children, health, fitness, lifestyle, travel, and new technologies. In a period when style seemed to count for more than substance, the magazines of the 1980s even imparted a new glamour to subjects such as dieting, gardening, and exercising.

Science and Computer Magazines. In 1980 two new magazines were launched to capitalize on Americans' interest in new scientific discoveries. Time, Inc., introduced *Discover*, geared for an educated audience interested in the effects of science on daily life, and the Litton Publishing Group brought out *Next: The Magazine of the Future*, which purported to forecast breakthroughs in science and technology. By 1983 the advent of relatively inexpensive and user-friendly home computers had spawned several new magazines for computer owners, including *Family Computing* (Scholastic, Inc.); *Microkids: The Magazine for Kids Who Love Computers* (Warner Software/Cloverdale); and *Enter: The World of Computers and Electronic Games* (Children's Television Workshop), for ten- to sixteen-year-olds. Of these five magazines, only *Family Computing* was still in existence in 1995.

Magazines on Parenting. By the 1980s many members of the baby-boom generation were beginning belatedly to have children of their own, having postponed childbearing until their careers were well established. Publishers targeted this affluent segment of the population with magazines such as *Families*, introduced in 1980 by the publishers of *Reader's Digest*; *Child* (Taxi Publishing, Inc., 1986); *Parenting* (Time, Inc., 1987); *Fathers* (Fathers, Inc., 1988); and *Baby Times* (Busch Publishing, 1989). Only *Parenting* was still around in the mid 1990s.

Health and Physical Fitness. As trendy fitness clubs, expensive workout clothing, low-fat and organic foods, and "designer" bottled waters captured an ever growing share of Americans' disposable incomes, publishers of another crop of new magazines sought to cash in on the market. In 1982 Rodale Press, publishers of *Prevention* magazine, introduced a physical-fitness magazine, *Spring*, while Oppenheimer and Company spent $5 million to launch another physical-fitness magazine, *American Health*. No publisher had ever spent so much money to start a new magazine, and neither it nor *Spring* was successful. The publishers of *Southern Living* had better luck with *Cooking Light*, which in the 1990s continued to attract readers interested in losing weight and lowering their cholesterol levels.

Targeting Specific Markets. The success of *EM Ebony Man* (Johnson Publishing, 1985), a magazine covering fashion, fitness, and personal finances for the black male, spawned other magazines aimed at minority "yuppies" (young urban professionals). Yet *Emerge* (Emerge Communications), for upwardly mobile African Americans and *Que Pasa* (Edrei Communications), for Hispanics — both founded in 1989 — quickly faded into obscurity. Other magazines targeted readers in specific regions. *New England Monthly* (New England Monthly, Inc., 1984) covered business, politics, sports, food, and gardening for residents of the New England states. Time, Inc., introduced *Southern Travel* (1987), and the publishers of *Southern Living* produced *Southern Living Classics* (1986), which covered art, interior design, and travel for affluent southerners. None of these regional magazines was successful, nor were most other magazines that went after wealthy readers. Of *Millionaire* (Douglas Lambert), *Veranda* (Lisa Newsome), and *Tiffany* (Tiffany Publishing) —

A DECADE OF DOCUMENTARIES

Documentary maker Ken Burns's eleven-hour documentary *The Civil War* (1990) attracted an estimated audience of thirty-nine million viewers, the largest audience ever for a Public Broadcasting System program. The foundation for Burns's remarkable success was laid in the 1980s with six previous PBS documentaries. Burns was twenty-seven when he made his first nationally broadcast film, *The Brooklyn Bridge*. Working with Yale historian David McCullough, who had written a highly regarded book about the structural wonder, Burns developed his technique of moving his camera along still photographs to give them a quality of motion. For his efforts, he was offered membership in the Society of American Historians. In 1985, Burns produced *The Statue of Liberty* for the centennial of the erection of the statue, and *The Shakers: Hands to Work, Hearts to God*, which he followed with a book on the subject, co-authored with his wife. *Huey Long* followed in 1986, featuring dramatic readings by Robert Penn Warren, whose *All the King's Men* was the best known novel about the demagogue from Louisiana. In 1989 Burns worked on two projects, a ninety-minute portrait of painter Thomas Hart Benton commemorating his one hundredth birthday, which featured Burns's camera-sweep technique, and *The Congress*, a history of the legislative body in conjunction with the national bicentennial. The premiere was before a joint session of the House of Representatives and the Senate. By 1990 Burns was ready for his masterwork, and he drew heavily on his work of the 1980s to produce it.

Source: David Marc and Robert J. Thompson, *Prime Time, Prime Movers* (Boston: Little Brown, 1992).

all launched in 1987 — only *Veranda* was still around in 1995. Another travel magazine, *National Geographic Traveler* (1984), with the reputation of its parent magazine to help it get off to a good start, had increased its frequency of publication from quarterly to bimonthly by 1995.

The College Market. Publishers also overestimated the potential magazine readership among college students. *Newsweek on Campus* and *Campus Voice* (Gates Communications) were among several such magazines that failed to get off the ground in 1988. *In View* (Whittle Communications, 1989), for coeds, and *Career Vision* (InterVision, 1989), covering career choices and lifestyle for college students, never garnered much attention, but *Campus Scene* (Stamats Communication, 1989), tailored to individual campuses, attracted enough advertising and a large enough readership to keep it going into the mid 1990s.

Fashion and Lifestyle. New fashion and lifestyle magazines in the 1980s also tended to target specific audiences. *Lear's* (Lear Publishing), a magazine for women over forty, which was launched with much publicity in 1988, was short-lived, as was *It's Me* (Lane Bryant, Inc., 1981), billed as "Not for Little Women." In 1989 Murdoch Magazines, owned by Australian media magnate Rupert Murdoch, launched *Mirabella* with a lavish advertising campaign. Edited by Grace Mirabella, formerly the editor of *Vogue,* the new magazine was aimed at women between the ages of thirty and fifty. By 1995 it had changed hands and was being published bimonthly instead of monthly. *Sassy* (Petersen Publishing, 1988) successfully carved out a niche for itself in the crowded field of magazines for adolescent girls by offering a hip, slightly irreverent approach to teenage life and fashion. *M* (Fairchild, 1983), which covered upscale men's fashions and lifestyle trends, was less successful than its counterpart, *W,* for women.

Sports and Entertainment. Despite ever growing audiences for televised football, *Pro* (National Football League, 1981) was not long-lived, but *Spring Training* (Merle Thorpe, 1988), which covers mainly baseball, continues to find a market. *The Dial* (Public Broadcasting System, 1981), a monthly television magazine and program guide, and *The Record* (1981), a rock-music tabloid launched by the publishers of *Rolling Stone,* were unsuccessful. *Video Digest* (AFI Communications Group), which became *Entertainment Retailing Industry* in 1993, is still in existence.

Big-Budget Promotions. Several publishers risked millions on new magazines in the 1980s. *First for Women,* launched in 1989 with a $1 million television advertising campaign by the Bauer Group of West Germany, continued to appear on newsstands in the mid 1990s. The most spectacular flop of the 1980s was *TV-Cable Week,* a cable-television program guide launched with high expectations by Time, Inc., in April 1983. By the time the company abandoned the project the following September, the magazine had lost $47 million, nearly half of the $100 million Time, Inc., had planned to spend on the magazine over the first four to five years. S. I. Newhouse came close to a similar disaster with *Vanity Fair* (Condé Nast, 1983), developed at the cost of nearly $15 million. During its first eleven months of existence the magazine went through two editors and was widely considered an expensive joke. Then Newhouse hired a third editor, Tina Brown, who turned the magazine around, stirring up controversy by blending gossipy and sometimes outrageous celebrity coverage with articles on serious topics.

NEWSPAPERS IN THE 1980s

Trouble and Change. The traditional view of newspapers — fiercely independent papers run by strong individual personalities with strong local ties and flavors in a competitive local market — continued to be less true in the 1980s. More cities were left with single newspapers, all morning editions, as publishers not facing direct competition in local markets eliminated slowly dying afternoon editions.

Gannett's Influence. The founding of *USA Today* in 1982 by the Gannett group and its chief executive officer, Allan H. Nueharth, was influential in both newspaper content and design, despite Nueharth's stated intention that the paper was a supplement to, rather than a replacement of, local newspapers. But in an era when more and more people chose to get their news and information from television, *USA Today* taught lessons different from those intended by Neuharth.

Splashy Layout. *USA Today* featured a splashy layout with lots of color; short news articles with little analysis; a heavy emphasis on sports; and weather, business, and entertainment snippets for travelers. By 1986 its daily circulation was 1.17 million copies, though Neuharth claimed 4.8 million daily readers. Although the paper was a circulation success, it proved a money loser well into the 1990s. Still, its circulation success put great pressure on daily newspapers throughout the country.

Pressure on Independents. Gannett's success with its flagship paper — in 1990 the company owned eighty-one daily newspapers and sixty-five Sunday papers — focused attention on those newspapers that could afford the investment in technology required to compete with *USA Today* and splashy competitors in the television medium. Increasingly that investment was possible only for large newspaper groups — corporations that owned multiple newspapers in markets throughout the country — and independent daily newspapers came under increasing pressure both financially and editorially.

Power of Conglomeration. By the end of the 1980s there were 135 newspaper publishing groups with 1,228 newspapers. There were only 383 independent daily newspapers. Cost pressures and dwindling circulation caused many independent newspapers to close or sell out to the conglomerates. The Gannett group continued its expansion first begun in 1964. In 1981 it bought *El-Diaro-La Prensa,* the Spanish-language tabloid in New York City. In 1985 and 1986 Gannett spent $635 million to buy papers in Detroit, Des Moines, and Louisville and the *Arkansas Gazette.* The Knight-Ridder group bought the *Columbia* (S.C.) *State* and the *Columbia Record* in 1986. The Hearst Newspaper group bought the *Houston Chronicle* in 1987.

Closures. Many papers, both great and small, closed during the 1980s. In 1982 the *Washington Star,* the *Philadelphia Bulletin,* the *Buffalo Courier-Express,* and the *Cleveland Press* all ceased publication. The *Memphis Press-Scimitar* closed in 1983, and the *Columbus* (Ohio) *Citizen-Journal* closed in 1986. The *St. Louis Globe-Democrat* and the *Baltimore News-American,* both papers

One of the unsung success stories of commercial television was Joe Franklin, who in 1985 entered the *Guinness Book of World Records* when he broadcast episode number 21,050 of his long-running talk show, *The Joe Franklin Show,* on station WOR in New York City. In the thirty-six years his talk show had been on the air, Franklin had hosted thousands of guests, including rising young stars such as Woody Allen and Barbra Striesand. Just as likely to appear on the show, however, were unknown, frankly mediocre performers such as Judi Jourdan of the Shower Singers and pianist Irving Fields, who had appeared on *The Joe Franklin Show* more than four hundred times.

Franklin plied his trade in relative obscurity for years until the 1980s, when WOR made the move to nationwide cable. Soon, as Franklin liked to report, he had grown beyond his limited New York City viewership and become "hot with the campus crowd." Perhaps he gained the most attention when comic Billy Crystal began to do a devastating parody of his schmoozing, product-hawking style on NBC's *Saturday Night Live.* But Franklin was philosophical about Crystal's caricature: "He was doing a satire of a satire. 'Cause I'm putting the world on. That's something only a select few can see."

Source: Ron Powers, *The Beast, the Eunuch, and the Glass-Eyed Child* (San Diego: Harcourt Brace Jovanovich, 1990).

---

more than one hundred years old, closed in 1986. In 1989 the Hearst Corporation closed its Los Angeles paper, the *Herald Examiner.*

Openings. Despite the decline in the number of U.S. newspapers — over the ten-year period from 1981 to 1991 the number of general-circulation dailies declined from 1,745 to 1,611 — there were a handful of start-ups of interest in the 1980s besides *USA Today.* The Long Island, New York, tabloid *Newsday,* founded in 1940 by Alicia Patterson but controlled since 1970 by the Times Mirror group, started *New York Newsday* in 1985. The Manhattan-based evening tabloid featured such writers as Murray Kempton, Jimmy Breslin, and Pete Hammill. Although the paper won awards for its local news coverage and added to competitive pressures facing the *New York Post* and the *New York Daily News,* it was not able to post a profit. Times Mirror closed *New York Newsday* in 1995.

Higher Costs. As they had since the late 1930s, newspaper production costs rose during the 1980s. Ink and newsprint account for 25 percent of the cost of a newspaper. Between 1981 and 1988 the average price of newsprint rose by more than 50 percent, on top of an increase of almost 200 percent between 1973 and 1981. Ink also went up substantially in price. Faced with rising costs and greater competition from radio and television for advertising dollars, newspapers increased both subscription and advertising rates — moves which tended to exacerbate circulation and advertising problems. That higher cost to both readers and advertisers helps to explain the decline in the number of people who read more than one daily newspaper, from 28 percent in 1970 to 15 percent in 1987.

Joint Operating Agreements. The rise in costs and the seeming inability of cities to support more than one newspaper led to a rise in joint operating agreements (JOA), arrangements in which two competing newspapers shared printing and business operations while maintaining separate editorial staffs. One of the more interesting JOAs began in 1989 between the *Detroit Free Press,* owned by Knight-Ridder, and the *Detroit News,* owned by Gannett. Concerns were raised about the nature of the agreements and whether the two papers were truly independent voices.

An Uncertain Future. The continued rapid pace of change in the newspaper industry has led many commentators to predict the end of the traditional newspaper and its replacement by various media products, from facsimile machine news sheets to Internet computer news outlets and global satellite television news channels. Still, newspapers are an integral part of the cultural history of the United States and remain an important source of local, national, and international information. The challenge for the daily newspaper, both those owned by local interests and those owned by large corporations, is to remain profitable while retaining readership and giving their product a community flavor.

Source:
Michael Emery and Edwin Emery, *The Press and America: An Interpretive History of the Mass Media,* seventh edition (Englewood Cliffs, N.J.: Prentice Hall, 1992).

THE NIGHTLY NEWS

Networks under Attack. The news divisions of the Big Three networks were immediately on the defensive as the 1980s began: in June 1980 maverick communications entrepreneur Ted Turner launched his Cable News Network, a twenty-four-hour news channel that posed the first real challenge ever to the major networks' near monopoly on broadcast journalism. Over the next several years CNN scored a number of successes against its larger rivals, for example suing successfully in 1981 for the right to use White House press pool footage that had previously been the exclusive property of the three networks. CNN used young, nonunion employees and small domestic and foreign bureaus to save costs, and it established agreements with local television stations for the rights to use their footage of breaking stories. All of these factors shook an industry that had become complacent in many ways.

SNC. Executives at ABC, deciding that the best defense is a good offense, linked the resources of their news department with Group W, one of the largest partnerships of local stations, to form the Satellite News Channel (SNC) in June 1982. With the experience, personnel, and financial backing behind the SNC, the new network "[should] certainly . . . outgun Turner if they have a mind to," as *Broadcasting* magazine observed at the time. But Turner simply outmaneuvered the media giant with a variety of strategies, most notably by quickly launching a new channel, CNN Headline News, which condensed CNN's reports into a more conventional half-hour format. Faced with lawsuits, significant losses, and grumbling stockholders, ABC/Group W closed the doors on the SNC in 1983 after sixteen months of operation and sold the network to Turner.

Late-Night News. Another response to the success of CNN was to expand the amount of programming time devoted to the news. NBC added *Overnight* to its schedule in 1982 and *NBC News at Sunrise* the next year. CBS debuted *Nightwatch*, which ran from 2:00 to 6:00 A.M. ABC added an early show, *World News This Morning*, before *Good Morning, America* and lengthened its late-night discussion show, *Nightline*. In 1984, however, the authority of the major networks was further shaken by a new cable endeavor, the Cable Satellite Public Affairs Network (C-SPAN), which brought to 40 million cable subscribers unedited coverage of congressional hearings, conferences, speeches by public officials, demonstrations, and almost any other variety of political activity occurring in the nation's capital, as well as British parliamentary debates and the evening news from Moscow. Clearly, cable was offering increasing opportunities for television viewers to bypass the networks in their quest for news.

Jolting the Status Quo. Many industry observers thought that the challenge from cable was good for the Big Three, jolting them out of their complacency as television's sole providers of information on the day's events. The news divisions of the major networks were traditionally financial sinkholes, but they were also shielded from budgetary considerations because of the public trust involved — the networks had a civic responsibility not to hinder their news reporters with mundane matters like cost. CNN's success, however, suggested that the major-network news divisions were overblown, inefficient, and overly expensive, particularly when it came to paying superstar salaries to its anchorpeople. After the major networks were in turn bought up by larger corporations in 1985, this question of civic duty versus fiscal responsibility was argued repeatedly between the network news divisions and their new owners.

Cutting Costs. Some network newspeople welcomed publicly the streamlining efforts of the corporate owners. Tom Brokaw, for example, anchor of *NBC Nightly News*, who earned an annual salary of $1.8 million, praised General Electric's charge to the news division to cut their budget by 5 percent: "I think it's a useful exercise he's [Robert Wright, the GE-appointed president of NBC] putting everyone through." Still, costs in the NBC news department rose every year in the 1980s, even though *Nightly News* was two minutes shorter and aired almost a thousand fewer stories in 1987 compared to the newscasts in 1977. Further, salaries for NBC News personnel had risen astronomically since the beginning of the decade: the average NBC correspondent, for example, was paid $84,000 in 1981 and $174,000 in 1986. The message was inescapable: NBC News was paying much more for less. The realignment effort at NBC involved trimming the news staff from 110 correspondents to 70 and culminated in 1987 with the firing of NBC News president Larry Grossman, reportedly spurred by Brokaw.

CBS. The CBS news division was even more embattled during the decade due to internal conflicts and pressure from its new owner, Loews Corporation president Laurence Tisch. Within the division, anchorman Dan Rather argued for the network's tradition of journalistic excellence, which began with Edward R. Murrow and extended through the years when anchor Walter Cronkite was considered the most trusted man in America. Representing the other pole of the debate was news division president Gordon Van Sauter, whose penchant for "soft" news, some claimed, had ruined the division. Van Sauter lost his position in a series of firings that seemed like a bloodbath compared to NBC's cutbacks: Tisch mandated that CBS News slash its budget by 10 percent and lay off more than two hundred employees. The result was nothing short of mutiny. Popular *60 Minutes* columnist Andy Rooney condemned Tisch in his syndicated newspaper column; anchorman Rather joined the picket lines and wrote an editorial against Tisch in *The New York Times*.

Dan Rather. Dan Rather was indisputably the most powerful man in the CBS news division and therefore arguably the most powerful in network journalism. He was not only the anchorman of the *CBS Evening News* but its managing editor. Yet he also suffered from credibility problems during the decade as well. In 1986 Rather was involved in a bizarre incident when he was violently assaulted on the street by a man who asked him, "Kenneth, what's the frequency?" The mysterious attacker was never caught, and Rather was unable to account for what had happened. In September 1987 the notorious "six-minute gap" occurred when Rather walked off the set to protest the fact that coverage of a tennis match had cut into the *Evening News* time slot. When CBS Sports switched to Miami, where Rather was covering Pope John Paul II's visit, the anchorman was not in front of the camera. The network went completely black for six minutes. A few months later, in January 1988, viewers were surprised by an angry exchange between Rather and Vice President George Bush over the Iran-Contra affair.

A BOMBING NOTICE

Among the most notable moments in broadcasting occurred off the air in 1984 when President Ronald Reagan, preparing for a radio address to the nation, was asked to speak into his microphone to check the sound. Attempting to amuse the technical crew he said, "My fellow Americans, I'm pleased to tell you today that I've signed legislation that will outlaw Russia forever. We begin bombing in five minutes." Reporters, sensing a sensational news story, reported the remark, and Russian leaders missed the president's humor. The Soviet military was placed on special alert, briefly, and *Tass* complained about the "unprecedented hostility" of the president's remark.

Bush, looking to toughen his image for his presidential race that year, snapped his responses to Rather's questions and at one point made reference to the six minutes of dead air.

Diane Sawyer. Another of the stars of CBS's news division was Diane Sawyer, who for much of the decade was an object of bidding wars between the networks for her talents. Sawyer's case is indicative of the generous salaries the Big Three were willing to pay their news stars. ABC news director Roone Arledge finally lured Sawyer away in 1989 by offering her a five-year contract with an annual salary of $1.7 million, considerably more than Peter Jennings, the ABC anchorman, was making. Jennings had first anchored the evening news in the mid 1960s, at age 27 the youngest man to hold that position; his first stint at anchor was a failure, however, and he asked to be reassigned. In the late 1970s he became one of three hosts of *ABC World News Tonight* along with Frank Reynolds and Max Robinson. In 1983, upon Reynolds's death of cancer, Jennings was offered the solo anchor spot. Although hesitant because of his first failed effort, he agreed to take the anchor's desk and soon was fighting hard for control over the evening news. With Jennings as anchor *World News Tonight* began to climb in the ratings. In 1988 he was named Best Anchor by the *Washington Journalism Review,* and that same year a Gallup poll listed his believablity rating among viewers at 90 percent.

Change. For all the pressures from outside and inside, network news actually changed in appearance little during the 1980s. Brokaw, Rather, and Jennings, all of whom became anchors in the first half of the decade, were already familiar to most viewers of the news; the nightly news broadcast was still the cornerstone of the Big Three news divisions. What did change was its content and the expectations of its corporate owners.

Bigger, Not Better. The 1980s was a decade in which publishers' business decisions changed the sorts of works available to readers and markedly altered the format in which those works were presented. The combination of recession and inflation that afflicted the American economy in the late 1970s and early 1980s adversely affected book sales and made publishers easy prey for large conglomerates more concerned with profits than good books. At the same time, independent bookstores, often owned and staffed by book lovers, were giving way to large chain stores that had large advertising budgets and could sell books at lower prices because publishers gave them discounts for buying in large quantities. Even after publishers responded to complaints from independent store owners by offering them discounts as well, the small bookshops had difficulty competing with the chains. The result was a growing standardization of offerings nationwide, with both publishers and bookstores merchandising best-sellers and books by popular authors at the expense of books with acknowledged merit but limited sales potential.

Takeovers and Mergers. The trend of publishing houses being swallowed up by larger and larger conglomerates picked up speed in the 1980s and continued into the 1990s. By 1992 seven giant conglomerates dominated the publishing industry and accounted for 80 percent of all best-sellers. Several of these companies brought together book publishing with other media, including newspaper chains, television networks, and movie studios. In 1980 the Newhouse newspaper chain made news when it paid between $65 million and $70 million for Random House — which had earlier merged with Knopf (1960) and Pantheon (1961), become a subsidiary of RCA (1966), and then bought Ballantine paperbacks (1976). Bertelsmann AG, a German company that became the largest media conglomerate in Europe, bought Bantam paperbacks in 1980 and Doubleday in 1986. The merger news in the late 1980s centered on the actions of two controversial media moguls: Englishman Robert Maxwell and Australian Rupert Murdoch. After an unsuccessful attempt to take over Harcourt Brace Jovanovich, Maxwell acquired a foothold in the United States in 1988, when he bought Science Research Associates from IBM and Macmillan. Murdoch spent several decades creating a newspaper empire before turning to book publishing, buying the British firm William Collins in 1981 and the U.S. publisher Harper and Row in 1987. In 1989 he merged these firms with several other publishers — including Basic Books, T. Y. Crowell, and Scott Foresman — to form HarperCollins. Murdoch's News Corporation also owns 20th Century-Fox movie studios and the Fox Broadcasting television network. Gulf and Western, which had owned Paramount Pictures Corporation since 1966 and book publisher Simon and Schuster since 1975, expanded further into publishing in 1984, when it bought Esquire, Inc., Prentice-Hall, and Glen and Company. By 1989 Gulf and Western had sold its consumer-and-industrial-products and financial-services divisions, becoming exclusively an entertainment and communications company and changing its name to Paramount Communications. In 1991 the company bought Macmillan and moved into pay-per-view television. Three years later Paramount was bought by Viacom, Inc.

Looking for "Blockbusters." In 1980 a Supreme Court decision changed the way publishers accounted for unsold books and had an adverse effect on the availability of books to the public. The court upheld an Internal Revenue Service ruling that the value of unsold merchandise could not be discounted for tax purposes. Faced with having to pay taxes on the full value of books sitting in warehouses, publishers began remaindering or destroying unsold books much sooner than they had in the past. The ruling, combined with the conglomerates' emphasis on profits, made publishers less willing to take chances on quality books that seemed unlikely to become best-sellers immediately. The ruling had a particularly adverse effect on scholarly and technical publishers, who typically expect to sell their books slowly but steadily over several years, but it also hurt commercial publishers committed to maintaining the availability of books of genuine merit regardless of their sales. At the same time, publishers began to gamble on "blockbusters," paying larger sums of money for books by authors with proven track records of best-sellers. For example, in 1980 Bantam Books paid $3.2 million for Judith Krantz's novel *Princess Daisy,* a move widely deplored as proof that publishing had become "a money-mad branch of show business," as John F. Baker said in *Publishers Weekly* (13 March 1981). In 1981 Simon and Schuster paid popular astronomer Carl Sagan a $2 million advance for a novel he had not yet started to write. By the middle of the decade the ante had increased. In 1986 William Morrow and Avon Books paid $5 million for James Clavell's novel *Whirlwind,* and in 1988 Simon and Schuster paid Mary Higgins Clark a $10 million to $11 million advance for her next four novels.

The Paperback Trend. During the runaway inflation of the late 1970s and early 1980s, book costs increased sharply, and consumers began to balk at paying high prices for hardcover books. Bookstores began stocking more and more paperbacks and fewer hardbacks. Mainstream publishers responded to the trend by publishing some books simultaneously in hard and soft cover and by starting their own lines of trade paperbacks, including old, proven moneymakers as well as new books brought out only in paperback. This break with the traditional practice of first publishing a book in hardcover and later selling reprint rights to a mass-market paperback publisher also had an effect on mass-paperback publishers, who began publishing more and more paperback originals. Often these books were genre fiction, such as science-fiction or romance novels, and these publishers continued to bid high for softcover rights to hardcover

"blockbusters." Yet they bought fewer and fewer of the sort of moderate sellers on which they had been willing to take chances in the past. The trend hurt hardcover publishers, who depended heavily on the subsidiary-rights income generated by sales of paperback rights, and it adversely affected readers, whose selection of inexpensive paperbacks became more narrowly limited to books with proven sales records.

The Birth of Desktop Publishing. In general publishers were slow to understand the implications of the computer revolution for their industry. John F. Baker, editor of *Publishers Weekly,* commented in early 1983 that in most publishers' offices only billing and record keeping had been computerized and added, "oddly enough, authors seemed in many cases to be more technically sophisticated than their publishers." The situation soon changed, however, after the resolution of problems arising from the incompatibility of different brands of computer hardware and software. Where once publishers depended on outside typesetters to set type from edited typescripts, by the mid 1980s they could avoid printers' errors by entering editorial changes directly into the version provided by the author and then create their own pages directly from desktop computers.

New Technologies Create New Markets. In 1984, while publishers were finding ways of using new technologies in book production, they also began efforts to bolster sagging profits from book sales by exploiting the markets created by the development of VCRs, small audiocassette players, and home computers. Self-help books and best-sellers on audio tape turned out to be hot marketing news in 1985, catching on faster than the higher-priced videos, which eventually found a niche in the market. Publishers' efforts at creating and marketing computer software were largely unsuccessful. By the end of 1984 they had flooded the market with some four thousand software titles — far exceeding the needs of a still-limited number of home-computer owners. The problem was compounded by the fact that the software was being sold in bookstores, where salespeople lacked the expertise to advise customers about selection and installation. Publishers saw potential in computer software, but the market was not yet established. Even in the early 1990s traditional publishers avoided digital publishing, which was taken over by software entrepreneurs.

Source:
The Bowker Annual of Library & Book Trade Information (New York & London: R. R. Bowker, 1981–1990).

RADIO

Five Radios in Every Home. Radio continued throughout the 1980s to be the most pervasive medium in America. Ninety-nine percent of American households owned radios in the 1980s (compared to 98 percent who owned televisions), and each household had an average of 5.5 radios. Those figures do not take into account automobile radios, which had become standard equipment in most of the 5.5 million passenger cars sold each year. The American radio audience tended to be younger, better educated, and wealthier than the television audience, though *Multimedia Audiences*, a sampling of media choices at specified times, indicated that 91.7 percent of Americans were likely to be watching television as compared to 85.3 percent who were listening to the radio.

Local Origins. Radio and television differed significantly in the origin of their programming. The three major national television networks dominated prime-time programming, and though FCC rules stipulated that a certain amount of the broadcast day had to be reserved for locally originated programs, network shows were the meat of the television schedule. Radio programs almost always originated locally. Radio networks provided some feeds and owned a handful of stations, but radio was a medium of independent stations airing local programs. The radio listener had access to more than nine thousand stations in the United States (as compared to 1,362 television stations in 1988), though most could only be picked up by listeners within about a fifty-mile radius of the broadcast center. Those were about evenly divided between AM and FM broadcasters by 1989.

The Rise of FM. The most significant change in radio during the 1980s was in the rise of FM programming. In 1980 AM stations outnumbered FM broadcasters by about 3–2, and about nine hundred new FM stations were authorized by the FCC during the decade. Quality of signal was the reason. FM broadcasts had greater fidelity, less superfluous noise, and could be easily converted to stereophonic reception with standard equipment. AM broadcasts, on the other hand, had a built-in staticlike noise, and though the FCC authorized the production of AM stereo broadcasts in 1982, there was no standard, and stations were unwilling to commit to the expense of equipment to improve sound quality that might not meet whatever standard emerged. As a result no standard was established, and FM became the medium of choice for listeners who appreciated clearly reproduced music. Slowly AM became the home of talk radio — news, sports, and call-in programs.

Shock Radio. In notable instances FM radio acquired a rebel character. Alternative programming was far more common on FM bands, and rock music calculated to shock adults as presented by irreverent disc jockeys was a staple of progressive stations in most large markets. In 1986 Susan Baker, wife of Secretary of Treasury James A. Baker, led a group called Parents' Music Resource Center (PMRC) to lobby Congress for legislation to prohibit radio broadcast of songs, specifically popular rock 'n' roll music, with sexually explicit lyrics. The issue was broadened when listeners complained about disc jockeys whose programs featured obscene language and explicit sexual content — their programs were called shock radio. In November 1987 the FCC ruled that indecent programming was allowed, but only between the hours of mid-

night and 6:00 A.M. The ruling was in keeping with a general inclination during the decade to avoid unnecessary regulation of broadcasting. In 1981 broadcasters had been freed of the fairness doctrine, which required equal airtime for political opponents; the restriction limiting commercials to no more than twenty minutes an hour had been lifted; and radio broadcasters had been relieved of many FCC reporting requirements

NPR. National Public Radio (NPR), on the other hand, brought the voice of civility to FM radio. *All Things Considered* and its rising-time counterpart *Morning Edition* won awards and attracted record audiences for public broadcasting, but the network also faced a budget crisis. In May 1983 NPR president Frank Mankiewicz announced a surprisingly large debt that had been masked by accounting errors and promptly resigned. The Corporation for Public Broadcasting, the umbrella organization that included NPR, negotiated a multimillion-dollar loan and initiated an aggressive fund-raising campaign. Beginning that year NPR may have been commercial free, but during specified weeks it gave a significant portion of its programming to pleas for donations to support operations. The tactic worked, and by the end of the decade NPR was a significant radio presence, as the most successful nationally based news radio network.

TURNER BROADCASTING SYSTEM

Cable Pioneer. Ted Turner, the unconventional Atlanta-based entrepreneur who was also known as "Captain Outrageous" and the "Mouth of the South," became one of the pioneers of the burgeoning cable-television industry in the 1980s. Beginning in the late 1970s he parlayed an independent Atlanta television station and an idea for a twenty-four-hour news channel into the foundation of the multibillion-dollar Turner Broadcasting System.

Billboard Start. Turner Advertising was a prosperous billboard business in Savannah, Georgia, that Ted Turner inherited under tragic circumstances when his father committed suicide in 1963. Several months earlier, the senior Turner had made a series of business deals that made Turner Advertising the largest outdoor advertising company in the Southeast and gained the company entry into the lucrative market in Atlanta, the capital of the "New South." The company was in financial upheaval after Ed Turner's death, but his son had remarkable success over the next year. He built a clientele made up mostly of local businesses in the Atlanta area and — demonstrating the lack of subtlety that would characterize his career — built a seven-story billboard along the newly constructed Atlanta Freeway. At that same time Turner was establishing himself as a talented yachtsman, winning the first of several national championships in August 1963.

Station Purchases. In 1968 Turner began to expand his business into broadcasting as well, purchasing a radio station in Chattanooga, Tennessee. Other stations in Jacksonville, Florida, and Charleston, South Carolina, soon followed. In 1970, most significant for the future of Turner's cable empire, he purchased WJRJ, a failing independent Atlanta television station whose only distinction was that it had the tallest freestanding transmission tower in the country, and soon renamed it WTCG, for Turner Communications Group. Since Turner was completely lacking in television experience, the venture seemed sure to fail; the entrepreneur compounded his apparent madness by acquiring another independent station, WRET in Charlotte, six months later. Soon the financial situation of the two stations was so dire that WRET resorted to a "begathon," asking for viewer donations and promising to repay them with interest when the station turned a profit.

Programming. WTCG, meanwhile, continued to limp along in Atlanta, offering a steady diet of old situation comedies, wrestling and roller derbies, movies, and Atlanta Braves baseball. About this time Turner had his first experience with cable, when Teleprompter, the largest cable distribution company in the 1970s, wanted to make a deal that would send WTCG's fare of old movies and Braves games to cable subscribers throughout the Southeast. WTCG's association with Teleprompter marked a turning point for the station: by the end of 1973 the station earned its first real profit. A little more than a year later, inspired by the potential of Home Box Office, Turner bought a link to RCA's new telecommunications satellite. The satellite uplink eliminated the need for the costly system of microwave transmitters that had been used to beam WTCG's signal to cable subscribers; once on the satellite the dying station could compete in markets around the nation. As Turner told the House Subcommittee on Communication in 1976, cable alternatives to the Big Three networks would benefit the country as a whole: "They [ABC, CBS, and NBC] have an absolute, a virtual stranglehold, on what Americans see and think, and I think a lot of times they do not operate in the public good, showing overemphasis on murders and violence and so forth." His "SuperStation," he argued, "will be another voice. Perhaps it might be a little more representative of what the average American would like to see."

Satellite Network. Because of its satellite link WTCG was now available to viewers in twenty-seven states, but advertisers were slow to get onboard. The station was still too small for national companies, and Atlanta-based sponsors were not willing to pay extra so that their commercials would be seen in Pennsylvania, Nevada, and Hawaii. Turner would often accompany his sales staff to meet potential clients, but his brash, often vulgar style — which included getting on his hands and knees or climbing on tables and shouting at the top of his voice — hurt more often than it helped.

Baseball. The only WTCG programming that consistently drew advertisers, at least in the Southeast, was its sports coverage, despite the fact that the Braves were a perennial cellar team. By the 1975 season it seemed likely that the Braves would leave Atlanta and deprive the SuperStation of a crucial source of revenue. Turner's solution was typically flamboyant: he bought the team. Still, the move made plenty of business sense: WTCG would no longer have to pay for the rights to show the Braves games and would have hundreds of hours of cheap programming every year. Turner approached owning the Braves with his customary love of showmanship, making singing commercials with the team and on opening night of the 1976 season jumping out onto the field during the game to congratulate Ken Henderson on a home run.

America's Cup. Turner had become a national celebrity, primarily for his antics as the Braves' owner and for his skill as a sailor. In June 1977 he was on the cover of *Sports Illustrated*, the first of several national magazines that would feature "Captain Ted" and his gap-toothed grin. That summer Turner led a yachting crew that successfully qualified to represent the United States in the 1977 America's Cup races. When the crew of the *Courageous* beat Australia to win the cup that fall, Turner was a national hero. Turner returned to Atlanta and the business of running the SuperStation, but he was also distracted by a new idea: a television station devoted exclusively to reporting the news.

All News. Conventional wisdom held that the public taste for news, except in unusual circumstances, was limited to a half-hour summary of the day's events during the customary news hour, 6:00 to 7:00 P.M. Turner was not the first to come up the idea of an all-news channel, but previous efforts had failed to break the monopoly held by the "Big Three." WTCG's journalism was limited to a tongue-in-cheek newscast hosted by an anchorman and a talking German shepherd, so critics were understandably doubtful about Turner's new endeavor. Turner himself was candid about his contempt for most television journalism. "I never watched TV at night. I hated television.... Can I tell you how many hours of TV *news* I watched, before I started my own network when I was forty? I had not watched more than maybe a hundred hours in my whole life." In the late 1970s Turner busily assembled the personnel of his new Cable News Network. As he had in the past, Turner invested a considerable amount of his personal fortune in the effort to get the new network off the ground. CNN debuted in June 1980, and before long the network had transformed broadcast journalism. (See the section on the Cable News Network in this chapter.)

A Growing Empire. Turner's cable operations, for which he had laid the groundwork in the 1970s, took on the proportions of an empire in the 1980s. In 1981, in order to head off competition in the form of the Satellite News Channel, Turner Communications launched CNN-2, soon to become Headline News, which condensed CNN material into the more familiar half-hour news format. CNN lost millions of dollars in its first years of existence; but the SuperStation (renamed WTBS, for Turner Broadcasting System, in 1979) continued to grow, reaching 80 percent of cable subscribers by 1984 — approximately 34 million households, unimaginable when the station ranked a distant fourth in a four-station town. Not all of Turner's ventures were successful, however: in 1984 he launched a video channel, the Cable Music Channel (CMC), which would offer a more wholesome alternative to MTV. For Turner competition with the established music channel took the form of a moral crusade: "You can take a bunch of young people and turn them into Boy Scouts or into Hitler Youth, depending on what you teach them, and MTV's definitely a bad influence. My wife used the word 'satanic' to describe it." But the crusade was short-lived. CMC was only on the air for five weeks in the fall of 1984 before it sold off its assets to MTV.

Aware of Influence. Despite its failure, CMC was indicative of Turner's approach in the 1980s. He was sensitive to his unique and influential position as the owner of two of cable television's most widely viewed networks. As he was fond of telling interviewers, "I want to be the hero of my country. I want to get it back to the principles that made us good. Television has led us, in the last twenty-five years, down the path of destruction. I intend to turn it around before it is too late." He even briefly considered a run for the presidency of the United States in 1984, despite being more or less apolitical all of his life. Turner felt passionately about environmental issues, and he believed in the necessity of overcoming international conflicts — and he had the resources to bring his message to hundreds of millions of Americans. Increasingly, WTBS and CNN devoted programming time to the issues of deforestation, overpopulation, and global warming, until by the end of the decade nearly three hundred hours of programming time on the two networks was devoted annually to environmental issues.

Setbacks. The late 1980s saw a series of setbacks for Turner Communications. In 1985, hoping to join in the corporate takeovers of the Big Three that began when Capital City Communications bought ABC, Turner tried to buy CBS, which was something like a minnow attempting to swallow a whale. Although a complete failure, the CBS takeover attempt helped further Turner's reputation as a major player in the television industry. That same year, Turner sought entry into the world of Hollywood entertainment with the purchase of the Metro-Goldwyn-Mayer entertainment company. Turner soon realized he had overextended himself and was forced to sell off most of M-G-M's holdings, much of it back to its former owner at a significant loss. Turner Communications kept only the M-G-M film library of more than three thousand movies, for which it still owed M-G-M $1 billion. Even Turner's plan for making money with the M-G-M movies, by "colorizing" black-and-white movies through computer animation, turned out to be a public-relations nightmare. Turner had been interested in securing for TBS the rights to the 1988 Summer Olympics in Seoul, South Korea, and he sent an emissary to Moscow to encourage the Soviet Union to attend. When the plan fell through, TBS broadcast its own version of the Olympics, the "Goodwill Games," in 1986. The games sparked little interest among the world's athletic community or television viewers, and TBS lost $26 million on the venture.

TNT. By the end of the decade, however, Turner Communications had added another jewel to its crown: Turner Network Television (TNT), which debuted in October 1988 in nearly 20 million homes. TNT made use of the M-G-M film library (the first movie shown on the channel was Turner's favorite, *Gone With the Wind*) but also lured big-name Hollywood talent and major production studios to make movies for the network. The network also secured the rights to NFL and NBA games, which helped to make it an immediate success. By mid 1989, the four networks of the Turner Broadcasting System — WTBS, CNN, CNN Headline News, and TNT — were in millions of homes in the United States and abroad, watched by approximately one-third of all cable viewers. Less than twenty years after Turner's Charlotte station had to beg viewers to help it stay on the air, Turner Broadcasting held assets of $5 billion.

Sources:

Robert Goldberg and Gerald Jay Goldberg, *Citizen Turner* (New York & San Diego: Harcourt Brace, 1995);

Hank Whittemore, *CNN: The Inside Story* (Boston: Little, Brown, 1990).

HEADLINE MAKERS

STEVEN J. BOCHCO

1943-

TELEVISION PRODUCER

Successful and Respected. Steven J. Bochco was one of the most successful television producers of the 1980s, the creator of two of the decade's most popular and critically lauded series: the police drama *Hill Street Blues* and *L.A. Law*. Between them the two won the Emmy award for best television drama seven times over the course of the decade. Both series followed an original approach to nighttime drama: they featured large ensemble casts; alternated between dramatic and comic scenes; followed multiple story lines over several episodes; and addressed mature, sometimes controversial, subject matter.

Beginnings. Bochco got his start in television in the story department of Universal Studios in 1966. His first real success was as story editor for NBC's popular *Columbo* detective series; two of the teleplays he wrote for *Columbo* earned him Emmy nominations in 1971 and 1972. Throughout the rest of the decade he developed several series, none of which lasted longer than half a season. Bochco was laid off from Universal twice during his tenure there, and his regular clashes with the studio's management helped to establish his reputation as uncompromising and sometimes difficult. In 1978 he was hired by MTM Enterprises, the production studio responsible for *The Mary Tyler Moore Show*.

Hill Street Blues. In 1980 NBC president Fred Silverman encouraged Bochco and fellow screenwriter Michael Kozoll to develop a police drama that would focus on the personal lives of the main characters. Bochco had recently seen a public-television documentary called *The Police Tapes* that followed police officers on their daily rounds, and he wanted his show to have the same gritty realism. It would focus not on mysterious murders or violent action, but on the personalities of the characters. As Bochco told an interviewer from *The New York Times* in

1982, *Hill Street Blues* was envisioned as "a show about people who happen to be cops, as opposed to cops who, in some small corner of their lives, happen to be people."

Realism. Bochco and Kozoll created a large cast of characters to populate the fictional Hill Street precinct of an unnamed metropolis (actually Chicago). They avoided the "supercop" of standard police shows and instead portrayed realistic men and women with flaws and eccentricities. Many of the parts were written for friends of the writers, including the part of Fay Furillo, the former wife of the precinct's commander, who was played by Bochco's wife, Barbara Bosson. *Hill Street Blues* debuted on NBC on 15 January 1981. Critics were immediately impressed by the show's deft blend of comedy, adult sexuality, and harsh urban realism — two of the show's main characters, street officers Andy Renko and Bobby Hill (played by Charles Haid and Michael Warren), were gunned down and left to die at the end of that first episode. *Hill Street Blues* was nominated for twenty-one Emmy awards that year and won eight, a single-season record, even though it debuted as a midseason replacement.

Finding an Audience. Despite its critical acclaim, the show's ratings were dismal — it ranked near the bottom of that season's network offerings, eighty-seventh out of ninety-four shows. By the middle of the next season, however, once the show had settled into a regular time slot, it began to find its audience. The unique style of *Hill Street Blues* influenced other prime-time dramas, including MTM's *St. Elsewhere*, a hospital drama with a large cast and multiple story lines, which debuted on NBC in 1982. Bochco himself tried to recapture the success of his formula with *Bay City Blues*, about the fortunes of a minor-league baseball team, but the show was cancelled after only a month during the 1983 season. In 1985, after years of arguments with Bochco about high production costs on *Hill Street Blues*, MTM Enterprises fired the producer. By that time the police series had won twenty-six Emmy awards, making it the most-honored drama up to that time.

L.A. Law. Bochco was not idle for long: within months he had signed a multimillion-dollar contract with 20th Century-Fox to develop series for them. He struck gold in 1986 with *L.A. Law*, which was set in the successful Los Angeles law firm of MacKenzie, Brackman — on the other end of the spectrum from the blue-collar characters on *Hill Street Blues*. *L.A. Law* also featured an ensemble of characters, controversial subject matter, and a liberal dose of sexuality; but, perhaps having learned his lesson from his conflicts with MTM, Bochco abandoned the gritty realism and expensive location filming of *Hill Street Blues* in favor of soundstages and more conventional videotape. Bochco's partner in creating *L.A. Law* was Terry Louise Fisher, a former deputy district attorney whose experience contributed to the authenticity of the series. Debuting in September 1986 at 10:00 P.M. on Thursday nights (the old time slot of *Hill Street Blues*), the show was an instant critical success and a greater popular hit than its predecessor. *L.A. Law* won the Emmy for best dramatic series in its first season and again in 1989 and 1990.

A Mixed Bag. Bochco established his own production company in 1987 and entered into a new contract with 20th Century-Fox and the ABC network to produce ten new series. His first efforts for ABC were a mixed bag of innovative shows: *Hooperman,* a police comedy-drama starring comedian John Ritter that ran for two seasons beginning in 1987; *Doogie Howser, M.D.,* about a child prodigy who becomes a surgeon at age sixteen, which the critics judged well made despite its questionable premise; and 1990's notorious disaster *Cop Rock,* an attempt to blend the mature drama of *Hill Street Blues* with MTV-style music videos.

Source:
David Marc and Robert J. Thompson, *Prime Time, Prime Movers* (Boston: Little, Brown, 1992).

TINA BROWN

1953–

MAGAZINE EDITOR

A Magazine for the 1980s. One of the most talked about and controversial magazines of the 1980s was *Vanity Fair,* which editor in chief Tina Brown turned into a near-perfect representation of the interests and tastes of the "yuppie" (young urban professional) or "me" generation. She successfully exploited their obsession with wealth, status, and celebrity to create a magazine that became notorious for publishing stories about Soviet premier Mikhail Gorbachev and long intellectual think pieces next to starstruck movie-celebrity profiles or pictures such as Roseanne and Tom Arnold mud wrestling. As Brown told an interviewer in 1989, "My kind of editing comes very much from the tradition of the eclectic magazine which mixes culture, arts, business — all those things —

with an overriding point of view," and, she added, bringing an irreverent viewpoint to "stuffy subjects" can "really make a lot of waves" (*Washington Journalism Review,* November 1989).

Background. Born in Great Britain and a 1974 graduate of Oxford University, Brown came to *Vanity Fair* in 1984 from London, where she had taken over the *Tatler* in 1979 and quadrupled its circulation in five years. Her success came to the attention of S. I. Newhouse, head of the Condé Nast magazine empire and co-owner with his brother Donald of the large media conglomerate Advance Publications. In 1983 Newhouse had attempted to create an updated version of the chic and sophisticated *Vanity Fair* (1913–1936) that had been popular in the 1920s, but despite much media fanfare the magazine had attracted few readers and little advertising, while critics treated it as an expensive joke with no apparent editorial focus.

Editing *Vanity Fair*. Brown brought to *Vanity Fair* an acknowledged talent for writing and editing and an even greater gift for generating publicity. Realizing that free media coverage was more effective than expensive advertising, she was less concerned with what other journalists said about the magazine than with giving them something to write about. Two covers featuring actress Demi Moore in the nude (once in the advanced stages of pregnancy) and another featuring a leather-clad Claus von Bülow, who was charged with the attempted murder of his wealthy socialite wife, attracted a huge amount of free publicity — much of it negative — as did a photograph of President and Mrs. Ronald Reagan kissing and Brown's unflattering story on Princess Diana. Calvin Trillin of *The New Yorker* called the magazine "the house organ of the Eurotrash," and many critics agreed. Yet, as many critics also acknowledged, Brown had discovered Americans' fascination with the rich and famous, and the circulation of *Vanity Fair* more than quadrupled, going from about 200,000 in 1984 to 750,000 in 1989 and reaching nearly a million by the time Brown left the magazine in 1992. Although advertising revenues also mushroomed, the magazine continued to lose money because it was so expensive to produce.

Taking Over *The New Yorker*. Nevertheless, Brown's rescue of *Vanity Fair* from near-certain failure endeared her to Newhouse, who put her in charge of another Condé Nast magazine, *The New Yorker,* in 1992. Brown's changes in that venerable institution, which had admittedly become stodgy and predictable, have at times been controversial, and it remains to be seen if her formula for success can attract the sort of large and loyal readership that the magazine enjoyed in earlier years.

Sources:
Elizabeth Kolbert, "How Tina Brown Moves Magazines," *New York Times Magazine,* 5 December 1993, pp. 68–72, 83, 85, 87, 97;

Charles Leerhsen and Tony Clifton, "A New Editor for Vanity Fair," *Newsweek,* 103 (16 January 1984): 70–71.

BILL COSBY

1937-

TELEVISION STAR

Television Popularity. Actor and comedian Bill Cosby became one of the most popular television personalities of the 1980s with the success of *The Cosby Show,* a situation comedy unprecedented in its portrayal of an affluent African American family. Although *The Cosby Show* occasionally received criticism for ignoring the issues facing the African American community, the series earned some of the highest ratings on television from its debut in the 1984 season.

Stand-up Comic. Cosby had his first success in show business as a stand-up comic in the 1960s. He received national exposure on NBC's *Tonight Show* in the summer of 1963 and released the first of a series of popular comedy albums in 1964. While many comics were using the growing freedom of that decade to explore controversial, sometimes risqué material, Cosby was making his reputation with humorous recollections of his childhood. Many Americans wondered about the absence of race as a topic in Cosby's stories. As Cosby's success grew he had to defend his choice of material regularly; as he argued, "A white person listens to my act and he laughs and he thinks, 'Yeah, that's the way I see it too.' Okay. He's white. I'm Negro. And we both see things the same way. That must mean that we are alike. . . . So I figure I'm doing as much for good race relations as the next guy."

I Spy. In 1965 Cosby achieved a first for African Americans when he costarred with Robert Culp in *I Spy,* an adventure show that reflected cold-war America's seemingly endless appetite for James Bond–style espionage fantasies. But Cosby's presence as the first black star of a dramatic television series made *I Spy* unique; Cosby and NBC executives were concerned that some affiliates might be unwilling to carry the series. At the beginning of the 1965 season, however, only four stations — in Georgia, Florida, and Alabama — declined the show. But the rest of the country was taken with the show's exotic locales and the authentic chemistry of the stars, and it became one of the ratings hits of that television season. *I Spy* finished among the twenty most-watched shows that year, and Cosby was honored with an Emmy award for outstanding actor in a dramatic series, as he would be again for the next two consecutive years. Although ostensibly focused on Culp's character, the show had clearly become a vehicle for his costar.

Questions of Race. Yet throughout the series' three-year run Cosby was repeatedly confronted with the question of race. For him it was enough that *I Spy* portrayed two men who worked as equals despite their different races; but critics took the show to task for not having a black character engage the racial issues that inflamed the country at that time. Cosby was relieved when the series ended, enabling him to concentrate on his family (he and wife Camille had two daughters by this time) and to return to live performing. He still pursued a variety of television projects: as a regular guest host on *The Tonight Show* and the star of an annual special for NBC. He returned with another series in 1969, *The Bill Cosby Show,* a situation comedy that ran for two seasons. Cosby played a physical education teacher at a Los Angeles high school (he had actually majored in physical education at Temple University); while only a modest critical success, the show was a ratings hit, finishing eleventh in its first season.

Education. After *The Bill Cosby Show* left the air Cosby returned to his education, actively pursuing an advanced degree in education from the University of Massachusetts. This professional interest led to his involvement in the PBS series *The Electric Company,* for which he recorded several segments teaching reading skills to young children. During the 1970s he made an attempt at big-screen success, but the movies in which he appeared were modest successes at best. In 1972 he was back in prime time, with a variety series, *The New Bill Cosby Show,* but this time he met with poor ratings, and the show lasted only a season. More successful was a Saturday morning show, *Fat Albert and the Cosby Kids,* hosted by Cosby and based on his own childhood.

Greatest Success. Cosby's greatest television success, however, came in 1984 with the debut of *The Cosby Show.* For Cosby the new situation comedy was a response to the increasingly violent fare the networks usually offered. Cosby insisted on and got total creative control of the series, and he was involved in every aspect of the series. Not surprisingly, the show had parallels to Cosby's actual family life: like the characters Cliff and Claire Huxtable, Cosby and his wife Camille were college educated, financially successful, and had five children. Essentially a throwback to the wholesome family situation comedy, *The Cosby Show* was unprecedented in its portrayal of an intelligent, affluent, nonstereotypical African American family.

Questions of Relevance. The series was an immediate success, debuting near the top of the ratings and staying there for most of its long run. The familiar question of relevance came up again but was more or less drowned out by praise for the series. *People* magazine called the show "revolutionary," and *Newsday* concurred that it was a "real breakthrough." Cosby's formula for success, as had been the case throughout his career, was to appeal to the common humanity of his audience rather than to the racial differences that might divide it.

Source:
Ronald L. Smith, *Cosby* (New York: St. Martin's Press, 1986).

ROBERT CLYVE MAYNARD

1937-1993

NEWSPAPER PUBLISHER

First Black Owner. When Robert Maynard bought the *Oakland Tribune* in 1983, he became the first black in the United States to own a major daily newspaper. But Maynard had a career full of firsts, from being the first black national newspaper correspondent to being the first black newspaper editor in chief.

High-School Dropout. The son of immigrants from Barbados, Maynard grew up in the Bedford-Stuyvesant section of Brooklyn, New York. Interested in writing from an early age, Maynard frequently cut classes at Boys High School in Brooklyn to hang around the editorial offices of the black weekly newspaper the *New York Age*. By the age of sixteen he had dropped out of school to work full-time as a reporter for the *New York Age*. In 1956 he moved to Greenwich Village, where he wrote freelance articles and met writers such as James Baldwin and Langston Hughes.

Niemann Fellowship. Applying for jobs on white-owned newspapers brought no results, and it was 1961 before he found a job on a mainstream paper. Maynard began as a police and urban-affairs reporter for the *York* (Pa.) *Gazette and Daily*. In 1965 Maynard applied for a Niemann Fellowship and won, spending 1966 at Harvard University studying economics, art, and music history. After Harvard, he returned to the *York Gazette and Daily* as night city editor.

Washington Post. In 1967 Maynard was hired by the *Washington Post* as national correspondent, the first black to hold that position on any major newspaper. He was widely praised for his 1967 series on urban blacks. In 1972 he was appointed as ombudsman and associate editor for the *Washington Post* and also began working as senior editor for the new black monthly magazine *Encore*. In 1976 he was chosen to be one of three questioners for the final debate between Jimmy Carter and President Gerald Ford.

California. In 1977 Maynard left the *Washington Post* and moved to the University of California, Berkeley, to found the Institute for Journalism Education, a program for the training of minority journalists. In 1979 he was hired by the mammoth newspaper publisher Gannett as editor of its newly acquired but struggling *Oakland Tribune*. When he became editor of the paper, which was renamed simply the *Tribune,* circulation was at 170,000. By 1982 circulation had plummeted to 110,000, and the paper lost $5 million in 1981.

Owner. In response to the declining readership, Maynard started a morning edition, which was named *Eastbay Today*. Although the morning edition drew only 90,000 readers, in the fall of 1982 Maynard announced the end of the afternoon *Tribune.* The afternoon paper was merged with *Eastbay Today* into a morning *Tribune,* a move that was a prelude to Maynard's purchase of the paper in 1983 from the Gannett Company for $22 million.

Leadership and Illness. By 1985 the paper's circulation had increased to more than 150,000, but expenses still outpaced revenues. Maynard was forced to sell real estate holdings to meet expenses. Despite the losses the *Tribune* and Maynard's leadership garnered much praise and many awards for editorial excellence. In 1992 Maynard was disgnosed with prostate cancer and was forced to sell the *Tribune.* He died on 17 August 1993, an important figure in American journalism and a pathfinder for black journalists.

RUPERT MURDOCH

1931-

MEDIA MAGNATE

Media Giant. Born in Australia but a citizen of the United States since 1985, Rupert Murdoch has become one of the major players in the global media revolution of the 1980s and 1990s. Murdoch is the son of Australian newspaper publisher Sir Keith Murdoch. After graduating from Worcester College, Oxford University, in 1953, Murdoch worked briefly as an editor for Lord Beaverbrook's sensationalist London tabloid the *Daily Express*. After his father's death in 1952, Murdoch inherited in 1954 the Australian newspapers the *Sunday Mail* and *The News*.

Sensationalist Content. Using experience he gained while working on the *Daily Express,* Murdoch converted *The News* into a tabloid emphasizing crime and sex. Circulation soared, and Murdoch instituted similar editorial rationales at newly bought newspapers in Sydney, Perth, Melbourne, and Brisbane. In 1964 he established the *Australian,* a national daily that won respect as a more traditional newspaper. As his control of the Australian newspaper market increased, Murdoch set his sights on England.

The English Market. In 1969 he purchased the *News of the World* and instituted the same sex and sensationalist editorial policy he had used in Australia. In 1970 he purchased *The Sun,* a London daily tabloid that he used as a platform for his editorials supporting the Conservative Party. In 1981 Murdoch shocked the establishment with the purchase of the *Times* of London and the *Sunday Times*, the two most respected names in English journalism. In 1986 and 1987 Murdoch modernized the printing plants of the *Times* and the *Sunday Times*, leading to labor conflict over the cost-cutting implications of the improvements. Murdoch's victory over the British unions foreshadowed the pressure on newspapers to cut costs.

Texas and Beyond. Murdoch bought two small daily newspapers in San Antonio, Texas, in 1973. The afternoon paper, the *San Antonio Express*, was changed into a *Sun*-like tabloid that soon dominated the San Antonio market. Those purchases led Murdoch to gather many holdings in the United States. In 1974 he began a supermarket tabloid weekly, the *Star*. In 1976 he purchased the *New York Post*, the newspaper founded in 1801 by Alexander Hamilton and the oldest newspaper in New York City. In 1982 he purchased the Boston *Herald American* from the Hearst Corporation, changing its name to the *Boston Herald* and turning the paper into a conservative counterpoint to the more liberal *Boston Globe*.

Movies and Television. In the mid and late 1980s Murdoch expanded his holdings into movies and television. In 1985 he purchased 20th Century-Fox Film Corporation. After he purchased several independent television stations from Metromedia, Inc., he merged the studio and the stations into Fox, Inc. This company formed the basis for the Fox Television Network, the first new television network in the United States since the Du Mont network in the 1950s. The expansion into television greatly increased Murdoch's presence in the U.S. media market.

Book Publishing. In 1987 he began his move into book publishing with his purchase of Harper and Row Publishers. In 1988 he bought Zondervan, the religious-book publisher. In 1989 he bought Scott, Foresman, a giant textbook publisher, and William Collins, a venerable British publisher. All these were combined with other publishing properties in HarperCollins Publisher, a global behemoth that influenced other publishers to set up large multinational corporations.

Magazine Flirtations. In 1988, in connection with his television network, Murdoch bought Triangle Publications — holdings that included *TV Guide*, the leading television program–listing publication — from Walter Annenberg for $3 billion. During the 1980s he bought and sold several magazines, including the *Village Voice* and *New York*. In 1995 he underwrote the *Weekly Standard*, a political magazine run by second generation neoconservatives and generally supportive of Republican policies.

A Global Force and Influence. Murdoch's career has been a whirlwind of acquisition and influence, clearly making him the most powerful and influential individual in the global media market. His News Corporation, though heavily laden with debt, is the leader in the rush toward a global presence in the wide-ranging media marketplace.

Sources:

Thomas Kiernan, *Citizen Murdoch* (New York: Dodd, Mead, 1986);

William Shawcross, *Murdoch* (New York: Simon & Schuster, 1992).

S. I. NEWHOUSE

1927-

PUBLISHER

Family-Owned. The cohead of one of the last great family-owned media conglomerates, S. I. Newhouse Jr. runs with his brother Donald a powerful corporation with major holdings in newspaper, book, and magazine publishing as well as cable television.

Brash. The son of the late newspaper publisher S. I. Newhouse Sr., Newhouse oversees the family empire, Advance Publications, with his younger brother Donald. S. I. oversees the magazines and publishing concerns while Donald runs the newspapers. Newhouse's brash manner in dealing with employees and his bottom-line approach to publishing made him one of the most hated bosses in the publishing industry.

Random House. After dropping out of Syracuse University, where his father had endowed a journalism school, Newhouse began working for his father in the newspaper business, where he failed miserably. He joined Condé Nast, the magazine-publishing arm of Advance Publications, and found his niche. But it was not until his father's death in 1979 that Newhouse began to branch out and build up the empire. In February 1980 Advance Publications and Newhouse bought the Random House publishing group, adding a plum to the empire that had eluded his father.

Condé Nast. In 1983 he resurrected *Vanity Fair*, a famous magazine first published by Condé Nast from 1913–1936. After *Vanity Fair* had floundered in the marketplace for two years, Newhouse hired Tina Brown, the British former editor of the *Tatler* magazine, in 1984. By 1989 the magazine had increased its circulation from 200,000 to 750,000, and Brown was hailed as a miracle worker.

The New Yorker. In 1985 Newhouse shocked the magazine and publishing world by purchasing the venerable *New Yorker* magazine for $142 million. In 1987 Newhouse continued his unpredictable methods in personnel matters by firing legendary editor Wallace Shawn, only the second editor in the magazine's history, in 1987. Robert Gottlieb, a longtime editor at Alfred A. Knopf, another of Newhouse's properties, was hired to edit the magazine. Faced with a wide protest from the magazine's staff and its frequent contributors, Newhouse angrily insisted on the prerogative of the owner, and the staff be damned.

Changes at *Vogue*. Newhouse had already cleaned house at *Vogue* magazine in 1971, when he fired Diana Vreeland, the magazine's editor since 1962. In her place he hired Grace Mirabella, who served until 1988. The firing of Mirabella is perhaps the pinnacle of the Newhouse method of personnel relations. Mirabella learned of her sacking from columnist Liz Smith's report on the afternoon news.

More Personnel Tales. In 1989 Newhouse fired Anthea Disney as editor of *Self* magazine, delivering the news personally by stopping by Disney's home while she was on vacation. In 1989 Robert Bernstein, Random House's chief executive, was forced to resign. In addition to the forced resignation, Bernstein was publicly criticized for failing to pay attention to profits. The major problem at Random House, though, was the difficulty in digesting the Crown Publishing Group, another of Newhouse's big purchases. Andre Shiffrin, the publisher at the Random House imprint Pantheon Books, resigned in 1989 after being told to reduce his new books list from 120 titles to 40. More than 350 Random House authors marched and picketed outside Random House headquarters to protest the treatment of Schiffrin.

Power. Despite his bottom-line obsession and his less than kind way of dealing with employees, Newhouse remains one of the most powerful figures in print media. As one of the few remaining privately held giants in publishing, Advance Publications stands as an almost lone figure against the corporate giants of the global media marketplace. Newhouse is the daunting individual among the corporate boards.

Source:
Thomas Maier, *Newhouse: All the Glitter, Power, and Glory of America's Richest Media Empire and the Secretive Man Behind It* (New York: St. Martin's Press, 1994).

Jessica Savitch

1943-1983

Television News Anchor

Recognized Personality. When Jessica Savitch died in 1983 she was one of the most recognized news personalities in America and a frequent anchorwoman for *NBC Nightly News*. Yet few Americans knew of the personal problems that plagued her until reports and biographies began to appear after her death. Her life was a tragic illustration of the stresses that can accompany celebrity in the competitive television industry.

Beginnings. Savitch was raised in New Jersey, the daughter of a clothing merchant whose untimely death

traumatized the girl as a teenager. She began working for a local radio station while a sophomore in high school and majored in communications at Ithaca College in New York. Savitch gained her first television experience on the campus station in the mid 1960s; from the start she showed an affinity for the camera that promised a bright future in the medium. She was also demonstrating a drive to succeed that bordered on unhealthy obsession. A strikingly pretty blonde, Savitch worked as a model and as a disc jockey at a Rochester, New York, pop music station in addition to her studies and her appearances on the campus television broadcasts. Her college years were busy but also lonely: her ambition alienated most of her classmates.

In Front of the Camera. At the time Savitch graduated from Ithaca, on-air jobs for women in television journalism were scarce, especially when it came to reporting "hard" news. Savitch's entry to the profession was as a news copy writer at New York City's WCBS radio station. Savitch was not satisfied, however, until she was in front of the camera; with her characteristic determination, she convinced a local CBS television station to let her make a demo film and sent out letters to hundreds of stations around the country. She got one response, from CBS's Houston affiliate, KHOU, the same station that gave CBS newsman Dan Rather his start. Because of Savitch's liberal values and prickly personality she was considered a Yankee outsider by her new colleagues and found few friends in KHOU's conservative, mostly male newsroom. The young reporter gained much valuable experience in Houston, however; and when she covered the explosion of a railroad oil car in 1971, her report was picked up by the *CBS Evening News*.

Kershaw. While in Houston Savitch began the longest of a series of unhappy romantic relationships with Ron Kershaw, a Houston reporter who later became the news director of WNBC in New York. Savitch and Kershaw were drawn to each other instantly; they had in common strong wills and an aggressive commitment to the news business. Their relationship lasted on and off for most of the rest of Savitch's life, even though they quarreled frequently and sometimes violently. One of the adventures the two had together occurred in July 1972, when Kershaw, trying to cross a police barricade, scuffled with an officer, and Savitch, who was also on the scene, joined the fray. Both Savitch and Kershaw were arrested.

Philadelphia. A little more than a year after her arrival in Houston, Savitch had the opportunity to move back north to a larger market as a reporter and weekend anchorwoman at KYW in Philadelphia. She worked hard in Philadelphia to polish her on-screen persona, taking speech lessons, fixing her teeth and hair, and visiting a makeup consultant. Soon Savitch became a popular on-air personality for KYW, admired by viewers as much for her good looks as for her journalistic edge. She was not above taking advantage of her appearance but also fought hard to avoid being stuck covering only "women's stories." In August 1974 Savitch was made coanchor of KYW's evening news, at a time when a woman newsreader was still an unfamiliar sight to most viewers. The *Eyewitness News* team was popular in Philadelphia, particularly Savitch, whose frequent five-part series were a popular part of the program. Stress haunted her, however, caused by squabbles among the news team and her increasingly painful affair with Ron Kershaw, who had relocated to Baltimore to be near her but now seemed resentful over her success.

Marriage. In June 1975 Savitch met Mel Korn, an advertising executive more than ten years her senior who would become her first husband. Over the next year Korn advised her in negotiations with the major networks, all of whom had expressed interest in Savitch for their news departments. In 1977 she settled on NBC, and in the fall of that year she had her first network assignment, as a correspondent in NBC's Washington bureau. Every weekend she flew up to New York to anchor the Sunday evening newscast. Although Savitch was extremely effective as an anchor, she was less so as the Senate correspondent. Still, by 1978 she was being referred to as "NBC's Golden Girl" and was considered the logical choice for a coanchor to replace the retiring John Chancellor. She was also hosting *Prime Time Sunday*, NBC's latest effort at a successful prime-time news digest.

Network. Savitch married Mel Korn in January 1980, but almost immediately problems surfaced between the two. Savitch's career received another boost later that year, though, when NBC picked her as one of the hosts of its coverage of the national party conventions. As in her stint as Senate correspondent, she seemed out of her league, and her performance earned a lukewarm response. In addition to her quickly disintegrating marriage with Korn, Savitch's recreational use of cocaine was becoming something more serious. She found brief happiness with Donald Payne, a gynecologist whom she married soon after her divorce from Korn became final in 1981; but that relationship soon went sour as well. Worse, Payne was providing Savitch with amphetamines, thus compounding her substance-abuse problems. The marriage ended tragically when Payne committed suicide in July, just four months after the two were married. Savitch was able to find some solace in her work, and when she returned to the weekend edition of the *NBC Nightly News* in August she thanked the viewers for their outpouring of sympathy. Somehow, during the same time, she found a way to finish an autobiography, *Anchorwoman*, which came out in 1982.

Hosting. Savitch also hosted the *Today* show on an irregular substitute basis but lost her coveted weekday anchor position to former *Today* host Tom Brokaw. Meanwhile, her drug use was beginning to have an adverse effect of her professional career. Although in early 1983 she signed on as the host of the PBS documentary series *Frontline*, she was unable to conduct interviews and looked increasingly haggard and ill. In May 1983 NBC News executives gave the weekend anchor position to newcomer Connie Chung. In October of that year Savitch's career hit bottom: during a two-minute Digest segment she appeared dazed and incoherent, mumbling her way through the news in front of millions of viewers. NBC executives deliberated about what to do, and coworkers worried for Savitch's safety, but no one seemed to know the proper way to help her. Three weeks later Savitch was dead, drowned when her companion Martin Fischbein accidentally drove his car into a canal. Apparently neither Savitch nor Fischbein were on drugs at the time of the accident. Savitch had considerable success in her brief career at NBC, although she never received the respect she craved from her fellow journalists.

Sources:
Gwenda Blair, *Almost Golden: Jessica Savitch and the Selling of the American News* (New York: Simon & Schuster, 1988);

Jessica Savitch, *Anchorwoman* (New York: Putnam, 1982).

OPRAH WINFREY

1954-

TELEVISION STAR AND PRODUCER

Changing the Format. Oprah Winfrey changed the format of the daytime television talk show in the 1980s, scoring huge ratings success with frank discussions of sensitive, sometimes controversial topics. Her nationally syndicated *Oprah Winfrey Show* was one of the most popular of the decade, and she earned honors as an actress as well.

Rough Childhood. Winfrey came from a troubled childhood that included sexual abuse and a pregnancy when she was fourteen. Determined to rise above her unhappy circumstances, she entered beauty pageants in Nashville as a teenager and worked part-time at a local radio station. In 1973 she made the jump to television as a newscaster in Nashville; three years later, at age twenty-two, she was hired by ABC's Baltimore affiliate, WJZ-TV, to coanchor the station's local news. Her career in Baltimore initially foundered, but she found her niche in 1977 as the cohost of a local talk show, *People Are Talking*. Winfrey's talent as an interviewer was immediately apparent to WJZ executives and to viewers as well: she prepared for each guest, asked interesting, insightful questions, and was sincerely interested in how the guests responded. Soon *People Are Talking* was winning the ratings in its local market, beating the popular national talk show hosted by Phil Donahue.

Against Donahue. In 1984 Winfrey moved to Donahue's home turf to host *A.M. Chicago*, the local ABC affiliate's morning public-affairs show, which had consistently trailed *Donahue* in the ratings. Winfrey was considered an unlikely candidate for success in Chicago: as she later recalled, "Everybody . . . told me it wouldn't work. They said I was black, female, and overweight. They said Chicago is a racist city and the talk-show formula was on its way out." Her success in the city, however, was dramatic and immediate. Impressed by her warmth and directness, Chicago viewers took Winfrey to heart. As a local television critic reported soon after her arrival: "She is greeted by strangers on the street, recognized in restaurants and once was driven to work by a Chicago policeman when she was late and couldn't get a cab." Within three months she was outscoring Donahue handily in the ratings and by December 1984 was beginning to gain national attention. Early the next year Phil Donahue relocated his show to New York, probably due at least in part to the success of Winfrey's *A.M. Chicago*.

Winfrey's Success. The new success of *A.M. Chicago* was entirely due to Winfrey: her vibrant personality; her frank but good-natured interviewing style; and, most notable, her willingness to share with viewers and guests the painful details of her past. During a show devoted to child abuse, for example, she revealed the abuse that she had suffered. In response viewers telephoned the station, grateful that Winfrey had the courage to speak out on the air. This empathy has been perhaps the most important factor in Winfrey's success on daytime television. Before her show talk shows as exemplified by Phil Donahue's series followed a journalistic format, focusing objectively on social and political issues. Winfrey has made her career by dealing with personal more than public concerns — including sensitive matters such as incest, adultery, obesity (a problem Winfrey herself has battled for her entire adult life), violent children, and sexual relationships — and more significantly by reaching out to the people behind these issues. Emotionally revealing for the guests, the host, and the audience, Winfrey's show tended to resemble a group-therapy session more than a news interview.

Academy Award Nomination. In 1985 Winfrey came to national attention for another accomplishment, her performance in the Steven Spielberg movie *The Color Purple*, based on Alice Walker's novel about the painful lives of women in the rural South. The film received eleven Academy Award nominations, including one for Winfrey for best supporting actress. About that time — taking advantage of Winfrey's national exposure from *The Color Purple* — her talk show changed its name from *A.M. Chicago* to *The Oprah Winfrey Show* and made the move to nationwide syndication. *The Oprah Winfrey Show* was an immediate national success and, thanks to her 25 percent ownership of the show, made Winfrey a wealthy women, earning her $2 million in 1986 and $12 million the year after. She won the first of many Daytime Emmy awards in 1987, beating out former perennial winner Phil Donahue for outstanding talk show, host, and directing honors. Winfrey also became a sought-after public speaker around the country.

Competition. The success of *The Oprah Winfrey Show* ended Phil Donahue's domination of the format and proved that there was room for competition among daytime talk shows. Winfrey was beating Donahue in most of the markets where they were scheduled directly opposite each other, but Donahue's ratings were actually up as well. Hence, there was little professional animosity between the two hosts. Winfrey continued to explore a diverse range of issues with her usual candid style and featured celebrity interviews also. In the late 1980s and early 1990s the floodgates opened, and dozens of new talk shows tried to duplicate Winfrey's success. These shows were frequently sensational and exploitative, however, and the new crop of hosts rarely treated their guests with the same compassion and taste that had made Winfrey's show distinctive.

Money. By the end of the decade Oprah Winfrey was alone at the top of the daytime television ratings and one of the wealthiest women in America. A dramatic series she produced and in which she starred in for ABC, *The Women of Brewster Place*, debuted in 1990 but met with lukewarm response and was quickly cancelled.

Source:
George Mair, *Oprah Winfrey: The Real Story* (New York: Birch Lane Press, 1994).

PEOPLE IN THE NEWS

In September 1980 **John R. Anderson,** publisher of *Runner's World* magazine, was accused by the FTC of accepting cash bribes to give favorable mention to running shoes in the annual shoe-rating survey published by the magazine.

The Official Preppy Handbook by **Lisa Birnbach** sold 165,000 in the first month after it was published in November 1980; by the end of the year there were 550,000 copies in print and the book was among the bestselling paperbacks of the year.

In April 1983 media consultant **John Bowen** reported the results of a National Association of Broadcasters survey. According to Bowen, television viewers were increasingly attracted to alternatives such as shows on cable networks because "much of TV's regular fare is seen as repetitious, boring and juvenile."

In January 1987 television talk-show host **Phil Donahue** became the first Western media representative to visit Chernobyl, site of the disastrous 1986 nuclear-power accident. Donahue visited the Ukrainian town during a ten-day visit to the Soviet Union, during which he gathered material for his syndicated talk show.

On 1 April 1988 **Douglas Edwards,** the first nightly news anchorman in broadcasting, retired. Edwards had been an anchorman at CBS radio since 1942.

Malcolm Forbes, billionaire publisher of *Forbes* magazine celebrated his seventieth birthday on 19 August 1989 by throwing a $2-million party in Tangier, Morocco. Among his guests were television news broadcasters Walter Cronkite and Barbara Walters.

Mark Fowler, a Reagan administration official who favored deregulating the telecommunications and broadcast industries, announced on 16 January 1987 he would resign from the Federal Communications Commission, which he had chaired since 1981.

In November 1981 NBC-TV named sportscaster **Bryant Gumbel,** 33, to replace **Tom Brokaw** as coanchor of the *Today* show. Brokaw moved to the *NBC Nightly News.* Gumbel said he felt a special responsibility in his new position, noting, "I'll be holding the most prominent position for a black in this business."

The 21 November 1980 episode of the television show *Dallas* drew an estimated 250 million viewers who tuned in to find out who shot J. R. Ewing (played by **Larry Hagman**). The culprit turned out to be J. R.'s sister-in-law and former lover Kristin Shepard (played by **Mary Crosby**).

N. S. Hayden, publisher of the 134-year-old *Philadelphia Bulletin,* announced to his reporters and editors in February 1982 that the newspaper was closing. Said Hayden, "This is the kind of day I never wanted to live."

When the *Denver Post* took over the tabloid *Rocky Mountain News* in June 1982, **Michael Howard,** former editor of the *Rocky Mountain News,* wrote a series of stories for the *Denver Post* in which he confessed that before he was fired from his job in 1980, he had a $6,000-a-week cocaine habit.

"Drive-ins are going downhill," observed **Pierre Jelis Jr.** in August 1982. Jelis, for twenty-five years the projectionist for the Copiague Drive-In in a Long Island suburb of New York City, added mournfully, "It's sad. Now you go to sterile movie houses to watch a screen not much bigger than a television set."

On 14 February 1987, humorist **Garrison Keillor** announced he would host his final broadcast of his National Public Radio show, *A Prairie Home Companion,* on 13 June 1987. The popular show, which had been heard throughout the United States since 1980, revolved around a fictional Minnesota community called "Lake Wobegon."

At 9:00 P.M. Eastern Standard Time on 25 January 1985, CBS News aired **Bill Moyers**'s documentary *The Vanishing Family — Crisis In Black America.* The program explored the circumstances surrounding the statistic that nearly 60 percent of all black children in the early 1980s were born out of wedlock.

On 3 July 1980 the *Berkeley Barb,* a well-known and influential underground newspaper of the 1960s and 1970s, ceased publication. While the antiwar and countercultural periodical had enjoyed a circulation of more than 90,000 in 1969, its readership had plummeted to 2,500.

In March 1982 **Ronald Simmons** and **Gary Harris,** television-news cameramen in Jacksonville, Alabama, videotaped Cecil Andrews setting himself on fire after he had asked, "How would you like to see someone burn?" Andrews, an out-of-work roofer protesting unemployment, suffered second- and third-degree burns over more than half his body in the incident. Some journalists charged the two WHMA-TV cameramen, who waited thrity-seven seconds before extinguishing the blaze, were more interested in getting a story than in saving a life.

In November 1981 *Philadelphia Daily News* columnist **Chuck Stone** helped mediate a potentially deadly crisis at Graterford prison in Pennsylvania. Stone met with inmates holding six hostages, and after he persuaded state officials to accept the inmates' demands, the inmates freed their hostages and surrendered.

In fall 1984 **Garry Trudeau**'s cartoon strip, *Doonesbury,* returned to the comics pages of 735 newspapers. Trudeau had taken a sabbatical from the Pulitzer Prize–winning comic strip to write a satiric review on the Reagan administration.

On 15 November 1989 Random House named **Alberto Vitale,** former president of Bantam Doubleday Dell, to replace its long-time chairman, Robert L. Bernstein.

In October 1984 the case of *General William C. Westmoreland* v. *CBS, Inc., et al.* went to trial in U.S. District Court. Westmoreland, former commander of U.S. combat troops in Vietnam, charged that a CBS documentary falsely accused him of distorting estimates of enemy troop strength in the Vietnam War. On 17 February 1985 Westmoreland agreed to drop the suit after CBS agreed to issue a statement expressing respect for the general's patriotism. Westmoreland considered the statement an apology, but the network maintained that it stood by the information included in its documentary.

On 9 February 1987 **Oprah Winfrey,** nationally syndicated television talk-show host, taped her show in Forsyth County, Georgia, an all-white community that had recently been the scene of civil rights marches. Winfrey was the only African American among the 125 local residents who gathered to discuss racial issues.

By fall 1985 **Dr. Ruth Westheimer,** usually called simply "Dr. Ruth," was the best-known sex therapist in America. Her book, *Dr. Ruth's Guide To Good Sex,* had sold 100,000 copies; her NBC radio show aired in sixty-six markets; her cable televion show was seen in 25 million homes.

AWARDS

EMMY AWARDS

1980

Outstanding Dramatic Series: *Lou Grant* (CBS)

Outstanding Comedy Series: *Taxi* (ABC)

Outstanding Variety Program: *IBM Presents Baryshnikov on Broadway* (ABC)

1981

Outstanding Dramatic Series: *Hill Street Blues* (NBC)

Outstanding Comedy Series: *Taxi* (ABC)

Outstanding Variety Program: *Lily: Sold Out* (CBS)

1982

Outstanding Dramatic Series: *Hill Street Blues* (NBC)

Outstanding Comedy Series: *Barney Miller* (ABC)

Outstanding Variety Program: *Night of 100 Stars* (ABC)

1983

Outstanding Dramatic Series: *Hill Street Blues* (NBC)

Outstanding Comedy Series: *Cheers* (NBC)

Outstanding Variety Program: *Motown 25: Yesterday, Today, Forever*

1984

Outstanding Dramatic Series: *Hill Street Blues* (NBC)

Outstanding Comedy Series: *Cheers* (NBC)

Outstanding Variety Program: *The 6th Annual Kennedy Center Honors: A Celebration of the Performing Arts* (CBS)

1985

Outstanding Dramatic Series: *Cagney & Lacey* (CBS)

Outstanding Comedy Series: *The Cosby Show* (NBC)

Outstanding Variety Program: *Motown Returns to the Apollo* (NBC)

1986

Outstanding Dramatic Series: *Cagney & Lacey* (CBS)

Outstanding Comedy Series: *The Golden Girls* (NBC)

Outstanding Variety Program: *The Kennedy Center Honors: A Celebration of the Performing Arts* (CBS)

1987

Outstanding Dramatic Series: *L.A. Law* (NBC)

Outstanding Comedy Series: *The Golden Girls* (NBC)

Outstanding Variety Program: *The 1987 Tony Awards* (CBS)

1988

Outstanding Dramatic Series: *thirtysomething* (ABC)

Outstanding Comedy Series: *The Wonder Years* (ABC)

Outstanding Variety Program: *Irving Berlin's 100th Birthday Celebration* (CBS)

1989

Outstanding Dramatic Series: *L.A. Law* (NBC)

Outstanding Comedy Series: *Cheers* (NBC)

Outstanding Variety Program: *The Tracey Ullman Show* (Fox)

PULITZER PRIZES FOR JOURNALISM

1980

Public Service: *Gannett News Service*

National Reporting: Charles Stafford and Bette Swenson Orsini, St. Petersburg (Fla.) *Times*

International Reporting: Joel Brinkley and Jay Mather, Louisville (Ky.) *Courier-Journal*

Local Reporting: *Philadelphia Inquirer*

Editorial Writing: Robert L. Bartley, *Wall Street Journal*

Editorial Cartoons: Don Wright, *Miami* (Fla.) *News*

1981

Public Service: *Charlotte* (N.C.) *Observer*

National Reporting: John M. Crewdson, *New York Times*

International Reporting: Shirley Christian, *Miami Herald*

Local Reporting: *Longview* (Wash.) *Daily News staff*

Editorial Writing: No award

Editorial Cartoons: Mike Peters, *Dayton* (Ohio) *Daily News*

1982

Public Service: *Detroit News*

National Reporting: Rick Atkinson, *Kansas City Times*

International Reporting: John Damton, *New York Times*

Local Reporting: *Kansas City Star, Kansas City Times*

Editorial Writing: Jack Rosenthal, *New York Times*

Editorial Cartoons: Ben Sargent, *Austin American-Statesman*

1983

Public Service: *Jackson* (Miss.) *Clarion-Ledger*

National Reporting: *Boston Globe*

International Reporting: Thomas L. Friedman, *New York Times*

Local Reporting: *Fort Wayne* (Ind.) *News-Sentinel*

Editorial Writing: Editorial board, *Miami Herald*

Editorial Cartoons: Richard Lochner, *Chicago Tribune*

1984

Public Service: *Los Angeles Times*

National Reporting: John Noble Wilford, *New York Times*

International Reporting: Karen Eliot House, *Wall Street Journal*

Local Reporting: *Newsday* (Long Island, N.Y.)

Editorial Writing: Albert Scardino, *Georgia Gazette*

Editorial Cartoons: Paul Conrad, *Los Angeles Times*

1985

Public Service: *Ft. Worth* (Tex.) *Star-Telegram*

National Reporting: Thomas J. Knudson, *Des Moines* (Iowa) *Register*

International Reporting: Josh Friedman, Dennis Bell, and Ozier Muhammad, *Newsday* (N.Y.)

Local Reporting: Thomas Turcol, *Virginia Pilot* and *Ledger-Star*, Norfolk, Va.

Editorial Writing: Richard Aregood, *Philadelphia Daily News*

Editorial Cartoons: Jeffrey K. MacNelly, *Chicago Tribune*

1986

Public Service: *Denver Post*

National Reporting: Craig Flournoy and George Rodrigue, *Dallas Morning News*

International Reporting: Lewis M. Simons, Pete Carey, and Katherine Ellison, *San Jose* (Cal.) *Mercury News*

Local Reporting: Edna Buchanan, *Miami Herald*

Editorial Writing: Jack Fuller, *Chicago Tribune*

Editorial Cartoons: Jules Feiffer, *Village Voice* (New York City)

1987

Public Service: *Pittsburgh Press*

National Reporting: *Miami Herald*

International Reporting: Michael Parks, *Los Angeles Times*

Local Reporting: *Akron Beacon Journal*

Editorial Writing: Jonathan Freedman, *The Tribune* (San Diego)

Editorial Cartoons: Berke Breathed, *Washington Press*

1988

Public Service: *Charlotte Observer*

National Reporting: Tim Weiner, *Philadelphia Inquirer*

International Reporting: Thomas L. Friedman, *New York Times*

Local Reporting: *Alabama Journal; Lawrence* (Mass.) *Eagle-Tribune*

Editorial Writing: Jane Healy, *Orlando Sentinel*

Editorial Cartoons: Doug Marlette, *Atlanta Constitution, Charlotte Observer*

1989

Public Service: *Anchorage Daily News*

National Reporting: Donald L. Barlett and James B. Steele, *Philadelphia Inquirer*

International Reporting: Glenn Frankel, *Washington Post*

Local Reporting: *Louisville Courier-Journal*

Editorial Writing: Lois Wille, *Chicago Tribune*

Editorial Cartoons: Jack Higgins, *Chicago Sun-Times*

DEATHS

Desi Arnaz, 69, Cuban-born actor, musician and producer, created the television comedy *I Love Lucy* (1951–1956) with wife Lucille Ball, 2 December 1986.

William Bernbach, 71, founder of the Doyle Dane Bernbach advertising firm, 2 October 1982.

Barry Bingham Sr., 82, publisher of the Louisville (Kentucky) *Courier-Journal and Times*, 15 August 1988.

James Burnham, 82, political essayist and founding editor of the *National Review*, 28 July 1987.

Cass Canfield, 88, publisher and author associated with Harper and Row for more than sixty years, 27 March 1986.

Milton A. Caniff, 81, cartoonist and creator of the *Terry and the Pirates* comic strip, 3 April 1988.

Gardner Cowles Jr., 82, head of the Cowles publishing and communications empire, 8 July 1985.

Broderick Crawford, 74, television actor, 26 April 1986.

Dave Garroway, 69, long-time host of the *Today* program on NBC, 21 July 1982.

Jackie Gleason, 71, television comedian best known for his 1950s sitcom *The Honeymooners*, 24 June 1987.

Arthur Godfrey, 79, television and radio host, 16 March 1983.

Chester Gould, 84, cartoonist and originator of the *Dick Tracy* comic strip, 11 May 1985.

Robert A. Heinlein, 80, science-fiction writer, 8 May 1988.

Mary Welsh Hemingway, 78, foreign correspondent and wife of novelist Ernest Hemingway, 26 November 1986.

Frank Herbert, 65, science-fiction author known for his Dune series, 11 February 1986.

James L. Hicks, 70, first black correspondent accredited by the State department and first black sent to cover the Korean War, 19 January 1986.

L. Ron Hubbard, 71, science-fiction writer and founder of Scientology, 24 January 1986.

William Bradford Huie, 76, newspaperman and editor of *The American Mercury*, author of *The Execution of Private Slovik* and *The Americanization of Emily*, 22 November 1986.

Jim Jordan, 91, star of the radio program *Fibber McGee and Molly*, 1 April 1988.

Murray "The K" Kaufman, 60, radio disc jockey, 2 February 1982.

George G. Kirstein, 70, principal owner and publisher of *The Nation* magazine, 3 April 1986.

Donald Klopfer, 84, cofounder of Random House with Bennett Cerf, 30 May 1986.

John S. Knight, 87, founder of the Knight newspaper chain, 16 June 1981.

Ted Knight, 62, television actor best known as the egotistical news anchorman on *The Mary Tyler Moore Show* (1970–1977), 26 August 1986.

Joseph Kraft, 61, journalist and syndicated columnist, 10 January 1986.

John D. MacDonald, 70, mystery novelist, creator of the highly successful Travis McGee series, 28 December 1986.

Don W. Moore, 81, writer of the *Flash Gordon* comic strip, 7 April 1986.

William S. Paley, founder and chief of CBS, 26 October 1989.

Marlin Perkins, 81, zoologist and host of the popular *Wild Kingdom* television series, 14 June 1986.

John A. "Shorty" Powers, 57, the "voice of the astronauts" who broadcast the early U.S. space missions over radio, and coined the term *A-OK*, 1 January 1980.

Donna Reed (Donna Belle Mullenger), 64, "nice girl" television actress famous for *The Donna Reed Show*, 14 January 1986.

Adela Rogers St. John, 94, journalist and author, 22 April 1988.

Max Shulman, 69, screenwriter and creator of "Dobie Gillis" television character, 28 August 1988.

Al Smith, 84, creator of the Mutt and Jeff comic strip, 24 November 1986.

Lowell Thomas, 89, pioneering broadcaster, 30 August 1981.

Theodore White, 71, journalist best known for his Making of the President books, 15 May 1986.

Kim Williams, 62, public-radio broadcaster, 6 August 1986.

William B. Williams, 62, New York radio personality, 3 August 1986.

Vladimir Zworykin, 92, Russian-born inventor often called "the father of television," 29 July 1982.

PUBLICATIONS

Ken Auletta, *Three Blind Mice: How the TV Networks Lost Their Way* (New York: Random House, 1991);

David Armstrong, *A Trumpet to Arms: Alternative Media in America* (Los Angeles: J.P. Tarcher, 1981);

Thomas G. Aylesworth, *Great Moments of Television* (New York: Exeter Books, 1987);

Ben H. Bagdikian, *Media Monopoly* (Boston: Beacon, 1990);

Barnouw, Eric, *Tube of Plenty: The Evolution of American Television*, second edition (New York: Oxford University Press, 1990);

Gwenda Blair, *Almost Golden: Jessica Savitch and the Selling of the American News* (New York: Simon & Schuster, 1988);

Alex Ben Block, *Outfoxed: Marvin Davis, Barry Diller, Rupert Murdoch, Joan Rivers, and the Inside Story of*

America's Fourth Television Network (New York: St. Martin's Press, 1990);

The Bowker Annual of Library & Book Trade Information (New York & London: R.R. Bowker, 1981-1990);

Les Brown, *Les Brown's Encyclopedia of Television* (New York: New York Zoetrope, 1982);

David S. Broder, *Behind the Front Page* (New York: Simon & Schuster, 1987);

Jack Casserly, *Scripps: The Divided Dynasty* (New York: Donald I. Fine, 1993);

Jannette L. Dates and William Barlow, eds., *Split Image: African Americans in the Mass Media* (Washington, D.C.: Howard University Press, 1990);

Edwin Diamond and Stephen Bates, *The Spot: The Rise of Political Advertising on Television* (Cambridge, Mass.: MIT Press, 1988);

R. Serge Denisoff, *Inside MTV* (New Brunswick, N.J.: Transaction Books, 1988);

Michael Emery and Edwin Emery, *The Press and America: An Interpretive History of the Mass Media,* seventh edition (Englewood Cliffs, N.J.: Prentice Hall, 1992);

Martin Esslin, *The Age of Television* (San Francisco: Freeman, 1982);

Todd Gitlin, *Inside Prime Time* (New York: Pantheon, 1983);

Robert Goldberg and Gerald Jay Goldberg, *Citizen Turner* (New York & San Diego: Harcourt Brace, 1995);

Andrew Goodwin, *Dancing in the Distraction and Factory: Music Television and Its Influence* (Minneapolis: University of Minnesota Press, 1992);

Mark Hertsgaard, *On Bended Knee: The Press and the Reagan Presidency* (New York: Farrar, Straus & Giroux, 1989);

David H. Hosley and Gayle K. Yamada, *Hard News: Women In Broadcast Journalism* (Westport, Conn.: Greenwood Press, 1987);

Douglas Kellner, *Media Culture: Cultural studies, identity and politics between the modern and the postmodern* (London & New York: Routledge, 1995);

Thomas Kiernan, *Citizen Murdoch* (New York: Dodd, Mead, 1986);

Richard Kluger, *The Paper: The Life and Death of the New York Herald Tribune* (New York: Knopf, 1986);

J. Fred MacDonald, *Black and White TV: Afro-Americans in Television Since 1948* (Chicago: Nelson-Hall, 1983);

Thomas Maier, Newhouse: *All the Glitter, Power, and Glory of America's Richest Media Empire and the Secretive Man Behind It* (New York: St. Martin's Press, 1994);

George Mair, *Oprah Winfrey: The Real Story* (New York: Birch Lane Press, 1994);

Alvin H. Marrill, *Movies Made For Television: The Telefeature and the Miniseries, 1964-1986* (New York: New York Zoetrope, 1987);

David Marc and Robert J. Thompson, *Prime Time, Prime Movers* (Boston: Little, Brown, 1992);

Barbara Matusow, *The Evening Stars* (Boston: Houghton Mifflin, 1983);

Richard H. Meeker, *Newspaperman: S.I. Newhouse and the Business of News* (New Haven & New York: Ticknor & Fields, 1983);

Kathryn C. Montgomery, *Target Prime Time: Advocacy Groups and the Struggle Over Entertainment Television* (New York: Oxford University Press, 1989);

Ron Powers, *The Beast, the Eunuch, and the Glass-eyed Child: Television In the '80s* (San Diego: Harcourt Brace Jovanovich, 1990);

Carl Rowan, *Breaking Barriers: A Memoir* (Boston: Little, Brown, 1991);

Jessica Savitch, *Anchorwoman* (New York: Putnam, 1982);

Michael Schudson, *The Power of News* (Cambridge, Mass.: Harvard University Press, 1995);

Madelon Golden Schlipp, and Sharon M. Murphy, *Great Women of the Press* (Carbondale, Ill.: Southern Illinois University Press, 1983);

William Shawcross, *Murdoch* (New York: Simon & Schuster, 1992);

Anthony Smith, *Goodbye Gutenberg: The Newspaper Revolution of the 1980s* (New York: Oxford University Press, 1980);

Ronald L. Smith, *Cosby* (New York: St. Martin's Press, 1986);

James D. Squires, *Read All About It: The Corporate Takeover of America's Newspapers* (New York: Times Books, 1993);

Christopher H. Sterling, ed., *Electronic Media: A Guide to Trends in Broadcasting and Newer Technologies, 1920-1983* (New York: Praeger, 1983);

Gerald Stone, *Examining Newspapers: What Research Reveals About America's Newspapers* Vol. 20, The Sage CommText Series (Newbury Park, Cal.: Sage, 1987);

Doug Underwood, *When MBAs Rule The Newsroom: How the Marketers and Managers Are Reshaping Today's Media* (New York: Columbia University Press, 1993);

Hank Whittemore, *CNN: The Inside Story* (Boston: Little, Brown, 1990);

Ana Veciana-Suarez, *Hispanic Media, USA* (Washington, D.C.: Media Institute, 1987);

Michael Winship, *Television* (New York: Random House, 1988).

MEDICINE AND HEALTH

by JOAN LAXSON

CONTENTS

Sidebars and tables are listed in italics.

1980

- The World Health Organization formally announces the worldwide eradication of smallpox under the leadership of the U.S. Centers for Disease Control.

3 Jan. The Food and Drug Administration (FDA) gives tentative approval to the National Cancer Institute for the first clinical study of the effects of the controversial and allegedly ineffective drug, Laetrile, on humans.

8 Jan. Virginia authorities give final approval for the opening of the first "test-tube baby" clinic in the United States.

10 Jan. University of California Medical Center at San Francisco researchers devise a fetal test to predict the skin disease epidermolytic hyperkeratosis in an unborn child.

14 Jan. The U.S. surgeon general reports the appearance of the first signs of an epidemic of smoking-related diseases among women.

15 Jan. A federal judge rules that the Hyde Amendment, restricting federal financing of abortions under Medicaid, is unconstitutional.

16 Jan. Genetic engineering techniques produce human interferon, a natural disease-fighting protein effective in curing some viral diseases and cancers.

25 Jan. Studies report an increased risk of miscarriage or premature births in daughters of women who took the drug DES (diethylstilbestrol) when they were pregnant.

31 Jan. The drug sulfinpyrazone is reported to reduce the incidence of sudden death among heart attack victims in the first seven months after a coronary attack.

2 Feb. A new drug, buprenorphine, is reported to treat heroin addiction successfully.

4 Feb. The Departments of Agriculture and Health, Education, and Welfare issue dietary guidelines aimed at reshaping the American diet and warn against excessive amounts of fat, sugar, cholesterol, salt, and alcohol, provoking opposition from major sectors of the food industry, especially farm and cattle interests.

7 Feb. The FDA upholds the federal ban on the sale of cyclamates, sugar substitutes banned since 1969 as a cancer danger.

14 Feb. Research conducted at the Baylor College of Medicine in Houston, Texas, reports that jogging and running reduces the risk of heart attacks.

15 Feb. A widespread outbreak of influenza B and associated deaths is reported.

28 Feb. A Rutgers Medical School study links SIDS (Sudden Infant Death Syndrome), or "crib death," to hereditary respiratory defects.

6 Mar. National Cancer Institute, U.S. Public Health, and American Health Foundation studies dispute earlier studies linking the artificial sweetener saccharin to cancers of the bladder and urinary tract.

20 Mar. The U.S. Cancer Society announces that it recommends the elimination of such cancer tests as chest X rays and a sharp reduction in the frequency of others such as the annual Pap smear for women to "at least once every three years."

24 Mar. Duke University researchers report the active ingredient in marijuana, THC (tetrahydrocannabinol), could help reduce nausea and vomiting suffered by cancer patients undergoing chemotherapy.

26 Mar.   A report in the *New England Journal of Medicine* reports nonsmoking workers exposed to cigarette smoke suffer deterioration of air tubes and sacs in their lungs.

24 Apr.   The U.S. Drug Enforcement Administration limits production of the active ingredient in Darvon, a mild painkiller that turned out to be addictive and is said to have caused hundreds of accidental deaths and suicides.

6 June   A Senate health subcommittee is told of a baffling, recently discovered disease called toxic shock syndrome that frequently strikes young women and can cause death within a few days.

9 June   The FDA approves a new rabies vaccine requiring only five shots in the arm instead of twenty-three injections in the abdomen.

30 June   The U.S. Supreme Court backs the Hyde Amendment, ruling neither the federal government or states are constitutionally required to fund abortions for poor women.

11 July   The FDA gets manufacturers of Valium, Librium, and other widely used tranquilizers to agree to issue warnings to physicians not to overprescribe these drugs for "everyday" stress.

13 July   The National Center for Health Statistics finds birth control pills to be the most effective form of contraception.

22 July   The American Medical Association adopts a revised code of medical ethics allowing doctors to advertise their fees and services and to refer patients to chiropractors.

19 Aug.   The FDA and U.S. Department of Agriculture reject a ban on the preservative sodium nitrate from food, reporting a 1978 study claiming that nitrate caused cancer in animals is inconclusive.

4 Sept.   The FDA advises pregnant women to stop or reduce consumption of coffee, tea, cola drinks, and other caffeine-containing products because of the danger of birth defects.

7 Sept.   The U.S. National Oceanic and Atmospheric Administration reports 1,265 deaths, mostly among the elderly or poor who did not live in air-conditioned homes, from the 1980 summer heat wave.

22 Sept.   Rely tampons are recalled because federal studies link their use to increased risks of toxic shock syndrome.

1981

- AIDS begins taking a worldwide death toll.

- Scientists find that spirochetes, later named Borrelia burgdorferi, cause Lyme disease.

- Surgeons at the University of Denver insert a valve into the skull of an unborn baby to drain off excess fluid from the brain and prevent hydrocephalus.

8 Jan.   Scientific studies confirm a long-term health advantage in reducing cholesterol and saturated fats in the diet.

13 Jan.   A three-month study links toxic shock to the use of high-absorbency tampons and confirms earlier findings that teenagers have the highest risk of developing toxic shock syndrome.

30 Jan.   A federal court jury in Chicago finds the American Medical Association innocent of civil antitrust charges filed by chiropractors.

26 Feb.   An influenza outbreak begins to decline after reaching epidemic proportions in thirty-one states.

2 Mar.   The New York State Legislature approves a tissue-typing procedure for use as court evidence in paternity cases.

11 Mar.   Harvard University scientists find a statistical link between increased coffee consumption and cancer of the pancreas, the fourth leading type of fatal cancer; but the National Coffee Association notes the scientists did not claim they had found a cause-and-effect relationship.

26 Mar.   A National Cancer Institute study links chewing tobacco and snuff to cancer of the mouth.

30 Apr.   A $500,000 National Cancer Institute study finds Laetrile ineffective as a treatment for cancer, even though advocates of the controversial drug derived from apricot pits continue to defend it as the last hope for terminal patients.

21 May   The Centers for Disease Control announce an influenza mortality toll for 1980–1981 at sixty thousand to seventy thousand, the highest since the 1968–1969 epidemic of Hong Kong flu, and recommend that the strength of flu vaccines be doubled in the future.

June   A new disease that will come to be known as AIDS is first detected among homosexual men and intravenous drug users.

18 June   Genetic engineering technology creates an effective vaccine against foot-and-mouth disease through gene splicing.

   The first successful operation to destroy a defective fetus in a pair of fraternal twins is reported in the *New England Journal of Medicine*.

9 July   The President's Commission for the Study of Ethical Problems in Medicine and Biomedicine and Behavioral Research recommends legislation to standardize the definition of death for every state.

   The *New England Journal of Medicine* reports the successful suppression of the herpes simplex virus with the use of an experimental drug called acyclovir.

15 July   The FDA approves aspartame, a combination of two amino acids for use as an artificial sweetener.

17 July   The surgeon general advises women to abstain entirely from alcohol while pregnant.

20 July   The *New England Journal of Medicine* reports that women who use birth control pills face an increased risk of heart attacks even after stopping their use.

4 Aug.   Doctors and scientists from twenty-five nations issue a joint statement warning of antibiotic overuse and abuse, resulting in the development of many strains of drug-resistant bacteria.

14 Aug.   A *Journal of the American Medical Association* study says heart pacemakers are being implanted more often than necessary.

7 Oct.   American life expectancy drops in 1980 for the first time since 1968, because of an increase in deaths from flu and pneumonia.

29 Oct. National Heart, Lung, and Blood Institute scientists announce that the drug propranolol could reduce the risk of second heart attacks by 26 percent.

16 Nov. The FDA approves the first vaccine against the hepatitis B virus.

1982

- Evidence grows that children living near traffic routes are more affected by lead poisoning.

- The first commercial product of genetic engineering appears when human insulin produced by bacteria is marketed.

- A naturally occurring chemical in the brain is discovered and named tribulin; it is an antitranquilizer that stimulates alertness.

- Combined heart-lung and kidney-pancreas transplants are carried out successfully.

21 Jan. A *New England Journal of Medicine* study contradicts earlier studies suggesting coffee drinking during pregnancy contributes to premature births and birth defects; however, neither the FDA nor the March of Dimes intends to change their advice to pregnant women to reduce their coffee consumption.

22 Jan. The Centers for Disease Control report a penicillin-resistant form of gonorrhea has been identified.

24 Jan. Statistics show the cost of medical care increased 12.5 percent in 1981, the highest increase since the government began reporting medical costs in 1935.

18 Feb. A *New England Journal of Medicine* study indicates that the ability of women to conceive after the age of thirty declines much more sharply than was previously thought.

25 Feb. The American College of Obstetricians and Gynecologists challenges the previously held view that once a woman has a caesarean delivery, all her subsequent deliveries must also be surgical.

30 Mar. The FDA approves the use of the drug acyclovir in the treatment of genital herpes.

21 Apr. A federal jury finds the Proctor & Gamble Company, the makers of Rely tampons, liable for the toxic-shock-syndrome death of a twenty-five-year-old woman and awards $300,000 in damages.

4 June Parents and doctors are warned against using aspirin to treat children suffering from the flu, chicken pox, and other viral infections because of its association with the onset of a rare but often fatal children's disease known as Reye's syndrome.

23 June A weeklong slowdown by surgeons in southern Florida ends when the governor signs a compromise bill on malpractice insurance rates.

1 July The U.S. Supreme Court rules that the nursing school at the Mississippi University for Women cannot refuse to admit a male student.

9 July A report in *Science* challenges early 1970s studies suggesting that alcoholics can be trained to drink in moderation.

15 July The *Journal of the American Medical Association* publishes a study suggesting many apparently "senile" elderly nursing home patients actually suffer from treatable conditions.

17 July	Doctors report they are at a loss to explain the cause of a new disease known as acquired severe immunodeficiency disease (ASID), which almost exclusively affected homosexual males and heavy drug users when it was first detected in June 1981; since then it has spread to women and heterosexual males who were not drug users and is reaching epidemic levels.
12 Aug.	The U.S. Census Bureau reports the continuing aging of the U.S. population; the median age as of July 1981 was 30.3 years.
16–20 Aug.	The U.S. Senate debates abortion issues.
9 Sept.	The Senate Special Committee on Aging reports corrupt financial practices such as kickbacks associated with Medicare pacemaker programs.
29 Sept.	The first of seven people die in Chicago after taking Extra-Strength Tylenol painkilling capsules tainted with cyanide.
1 Oct.	The FDA warns consumers to stop using Extra-Strength Tylenol.
5 Oct.	Following the discovery of Extra-Strength Tylenol laced with strychnine in California, the manufacturer announces a nationwide recall of all Tylenol capsules.
	A federal task force begins meeting to discuss improved packaging of over-the-counter medicines.
7 Oct.	A *New England Journal of Medicine* study warns women against using aspirin during pregnancy because of the danger of fetal bleeding.
15 Oct.	A tourist in Florida reports minor throat burns after using mouthwash tainted with hydrochloric acid.
29 Oct.	The FDA reports more than 270 reports of possible product contamination, with thirty-six cases verified as "true tampering."
	The *Wall Street Journal* reports an 80 percent decline in sales of Tylenol since the Chicago deaths.
4 Nov.	New packaging regulations to protect consumers from product tampering are approved by the secretary of health and human services and the FDA.
13 Nov.	The General Accounting Office makes public a report stating that abuse of prescription drugs results in many more deaths and drug emergencies than the use of illegal drugs.
20 Nov.	The U.S Supreme Court hears arguments on a variety of laws to make it more difficult for women to obtain legal abortions in several states.
2 Dec.	Physicians at the University of Utah Medical Center in Salt Lake City successfully implant a permanent artificial heart, the Jarvik-7, in a sixty-one-year-old retired dentist.
9 Dec.	The Centers for Disease Control in Atlanta announce the disease now known as Acquired Immunodeficiency Syndrome (AIDS) is spreading to infants and children.
15 Dec.	A *New England Journal of Medicine* study suggests the typical U.S. diet — high in meat and low in fiber — may increase the risk of breast cancer in women.
24 Dec.	A California jury awards $10.5 million in damages to a woman who suffered from toxic shock syndrome after using tampons made by Johnson & Johnson.

1983

- The first liposuction surgery to reduce subcutaneous body fat is performed in the United States.

- Chorionic-villi sampling for early prenatal diagnosis is performed in the United States in Chicago.

- The FDA approves the immunosuppressant drug cyclosporine, which is used during organ transplants to prevent the body from rejecting the new organ.

- The U.S. government approves the use of aspartame as an artificial sweetener in soft drinks.

- Scientists identify gene markers that identify Duchenne muscular dystrophy and Huntington's disease.

6 Jan. The annual Department of Health and Human Services health survey announces that death rates have declined for most Americans, except for those aged fifteen to twenty-four, where violent deaths have become increasingly common.

Spending on health care reaches $286.6 billion in 1981, or 9.8 percent of the GNP.

21 Jan. The Bureau of Labor Statistics reports health-care costs outpace inflation.

25 Jan. A study by the Food Resource and Action Center links an eight-state increase in infant mortality to poverty brought on by the economic recession.

18 Feb. A federal district judge in Washington, D.C., blocks the implementation of a Health and Human Services Department rule requiring federally funded birth control clinics to notify parents after providing prescription contraceptives to persons under eighteen.

3 Mar. The Public Health Service urges that several groups, including homosexual men, intravenous drug users, and Haitians, not donate blood because of the possibility of the transmission of AIDS through transfusions after hemophiliacs contract the disease.

4 Mar. The pharmaceutical company Johnson & Johnson withdraws the painkiller Zomax from the market following reports of five deaths from allergic reactions to the drug.

21 Mar. A presidential panel studying ethical problems associated with medicine issues a report recommending that patients be allowed to discontinue life-support treatment if they wish.

22 Mar. The Reagan administration implements the so-called "Baby Doe" rules designed to prevent federally funded hospitals from denying food or medical care to handicapped infants.

25 Mar. A *Journal of the American Medical Association* article concludes that birth control pills do not increase a woman's risk of breast cancer and apparently lower the risk of uterine and ovarian cancer.

6 Apr. The FDA approves a contraceptive sponge that will not require a doctor's prescription.

27 Apr. The *New England Journal of Medicine* publishes a study indicating that in nearly a quarter of studied autopsies of patients who died in hospitals, the patients' illnesses were incorrectly diagnosed.

4 May   The *New England Journal of Medicine* reports the use of interferon, an infection-fighting protein, appears helpful in fighting a rare form of cancer, Kaposi's sarcoma, that often develops in AIDS victims.

19 May   The *New England Journal of Medicine* reports the possibility of AIDS transmission in heterosexual relationships.

24 May   AIDS is called the nation's "number one priority" of the U.S. Public Health Service.

6 June   A Minnesota jury awards $1.5 million to a woman who suffered an infection from a Dalkon Shield intrauterine contraceptive device (IUD).

21 July   A *New England Journal of Medicine* study says supposedly low-nicotine cigarettes deliver about as much nicotine to smokers as regular brands.

25 July   Accutane, an acne drug, is linked to birth defects.

2 Aug.   The American Cancer Society says women older than forty should have regular mammograms to detect breast cancer.

31 Aug.   The Reagan administration imposes standard hospital rates in an attempt to curb increased Medicare spending.

11 Sept.   Tylenol regains most of its leading market share a year after the Chicago-area poisonings scare consumers away from the product.

21 Sept.   The Tennessee Supreme Court orders chemotherapy treatment for a twelve-year-old girl whose fundamentalist parents resisted treatment for her rare form of bone cancer.

26 Oct.   A ten-year national study suggests about 15 percent of patients undergoing heart bypass surgery could safely postpone or avoid the operation.

6 Dec.   The American Medical Association votes a resolution in favor of abolishing the insanity plea in criminal cases.

19 Dec.   The Robert Wood Johnson Foundation reports one American in eight has "serious trouble" getting medical care, and one in nine has no regular source of care.

22 Dec.   The Equitable Life Insurance Society of the United States reports hospital costs rose at about double the rate of inflation.

1984

4 Jan.   The Centers for Disease Control report evidence that AIDS can be spread through heterosexual relations.

10 Jan.   The University of Utah approves revised guidelines for artificial-heart patients permitting the operation at earlier rather than later stages of heart disease.

11 Jan.   The Centers for Disease Control report evidence linking the transmission of AIDS through blood transfusion among hemophiliacs.

12 Jan.   A National Heart, Lung, and Blood Institute study reports reducing cholesterol consumption lowers the risk of heart disease.

3 Feb.   The first baby from a donated embryo is born to an infertile woman.

8 Feb.   A National Institutes of Health panel advises physicians to limit ultrasound use on their pregnant patients.

13–14 Feb.   A six-year-old Texas girl becomes the first dual heart and liver transplant recipient.

16 Feb.   The American Heart Association, American Lung Association, and American Cancer Society denounce cigarette ads.

A National Institutes of Health study links smoking to low birth weights in newborns.

23 Feb.   The American Medical Association asks doctors to freeze their fees for one year to aid the nation's economy.

1 Apr.   The American Cancer Society reports a 7 percent drop in cigarette smoking, the largest recorded in a single year.

9 Apr.   A vitamin E solution linked to the death of premature infants is recalled.

The San Francisco public-health director announces steps to curb sexual activity in the city's homosexual bathhouses to regulate the spread of AIDS.

21 Apr.   The Centers for Disease Control confirm news reports that French researchers have identified a virus thought to be the cause of AIDS.

7 May   A $180 million settlement for Vietnam vets is reached in their suit over injuries suffered from dioxin from the herbicide Agent Orange.

10 May   The FDA approves the new drugs glipizide and glyburide for treatment of diabetes.

18 May   The FDA approves the over-the-counter sale of the pain drug ibuprofen.

23 May   The U.S. surgeon general warns about the dangers to nonsmokers from being exposed to cigarette smoke.

31 May   The *New England Journal of Medicine* reports effective testing of a chicken pox vaccine.

7 June   The *New England Journal of Medicine* reports health maintenance organizations (HMOs) could cut health-care costs 25 percent over the traditional fee-for-service system.

13 June   Wyeth Laboratories announces it has stopped production of pertussis (whooping cough) vaccine because of rising liability problems from rare complications.

16 June   Record numbers of foreign-trained physicians fail medical tests necessary for internship or residency appointments in the United States.

9 July   Minnesota nurses end a five-week strike, the longest in American history.

5 Sept.   Certain human illnesses are linked to drug-resistant germs spread by livestock fed antibiotics.

10 Sept.   The House of Representatives passes a measure to require stronger warnings on cigarette packages and ads.

12 Sept.   The American Psychiatric Association says that the policy of discharging mentally ill patients from institutions into local communities has failed, and that the resulting plight of homelessness is a "major societal tragedy."

24 Sept.   Low-cost generic versions of many widely used prescription drugs will be available to consumers with the signing of legislation.

20 Oct.   The Centers for Disease Control report lung cancer will soon become the leading cause of cancer deaths among women.

26 Oct.   Doctors in Loma Linda, California, replace the defective heart of a newborn baby girl known as "Baby Fae" with the heart of a young baboon, in the first heterograft (cross-species organ transplant) involving a human heart.

5 Nov.   Federal health officials announce that exposure to the AIDS virus is much wider than previously expected.

15 Nov.   The infant who received the baboon heart transplant dies of complications stemming from rejection of the organ.

25 Nov.   Humana Heart Institute doctors perform the second permanent artificial-heart operation, provoking controversy that the technology is a misapplication of medical research funds better spent on preventive health.

28 Nov.   San Francisco gay bathhouses reopen with strict regulations on sexual activity.

11 Dec.   A medical laboratory worker suffering from AIDS is determined to have contracted the disease after accidentally pricking himself with a needle while drawing blood from an infected patient.

13 Dec.   The Centers for Disease Control report the incidence of hepatitis B, a serious viral disease that can lead to cancer, is on the rise and urge a major push to vaccinate high-risk groups.

1985

- Surgeons use lasers to clean out clogged arteries.

3 Jan.   A new finding links the AIDS virus, currently called HTLV-3, to brain damage in AIDS victims.

10 Jan.   The Department of Health and Human Services announces that a new test to detect the AIDS virus will soon be commercially available to reduce the incidence of AIDS transmission through donated blood, although the new test could not predict whether the infected individual would develop AIDS.

16 Jan.   A Mayo Clinic study says vitamin C is ineffective as a cancer treatment.

17 Jan.   The American Medical Association reports malpractice suits have reached a crisis stage.

23 Jan.   Aspirin manufacturers plan to issue warnings to consumers of a possible link between aspirin use and Reye's syndrome, a rare and often fatal disease in children when aspirin is used to treat viral infections.

24 Jan.   A study questions the value and cost of routine chest X rays in symptomless patients.

29 Jan.   The FDA approves the first oral drug, acyclovir, for the treatment of genital herpes.

7 Feb.   The controversy continues between French and American scientists about the discovery of the AIDS virus.

8 Feb.   The American Cancer Society says more women will die of lung cancer than breast cancer.

10 Feb.   The National Center for Health Statistics reports one out of every three American women of reproductive age is infertile.

11 Feb.	U.S. life expectancy rises to 78.2 for women and 70.9 for men.
13 Feb.	A National Institutes of Health panel calls obesity a major killer in the United States.
15 Feb.	A U.S. Census Bureau study reports that 15 percent of Americans lack any type of health-insurance plan.
17 Feb.	A third permanent artificial heart, the Jarvik-7, is implanted at Humana Hospital in Louisville, Kentucky.
19 Feb.	The FDA approves an intravenous form of the drug indomethacin for use in premature infants instead of heart surgery to repair a congenital defect.
21 Feb.	The Office of Technology Assessment calls the Reagan administration's spending on AIDS research too low.
26 Feb.	A private panel of doctors and public-health officials charge that hunger is "epidemic" in the United States because of cuts in federal food programs.
2 Mar.	The Department of Health and Human Services approves the first commercial test to screen donated blood for signs of the AIDS virus.
12 Mar.	An Alan Guttmacher Institute study calls U.S. teen pregnancy rate higher than in other industrial nations.
14 Mar.	A *New England Journal of Medicine* study suggests that simple removal of a malignant breast lump and radiation is as effective as removal of the entire breast in treating early breast cancer.
21 Mar.	A massive outbreak of salmonella food poisoning traced to contaminated milk from a Chicago dairy strikes six midwestern states; at least six die.
2 Apr.	The A. H. Robbins Company sets up a $615 million fund to settle legal claims from women who suffered infections from the company's Dalkon Shield IUD birth control device.
11 Apr.	The *New England Journal of Medicine* reports the use of IUD birth-control devices doubles the risk of infertility.
23 May	A *New England Journal of Medicine* study reports running and other hard exercise contribute to making young women temporarily infertile.
	The *Journal of the American Medical Association* reports a study linking infertility with cigarette smoking by women.
June	The Renfrew Center, the first residential facility devoted exclusively to the treatment of the eating disorders anorexia nervosa and bulimia, is opened in Philadelphia.
28 June	A National Institutes of Health panel gives cautious endorsement to electroconvulsive therapy as a treatment of last resort in severe forms of depression.
July	The American Red Cross and the American Heart Association endorses the Heimlich maneuver for choking victims.
10 July	The *New England Journal of Medicine* reports finding that the AIDS virus selectively destroys T4 helper cells, a key set of blood cells that detect invading infections.
13 Aug.	Cancer researchers at Johns Hopkins University report progress in treating normally fatal liver cancer with radiolabeled antibodies.

29 Aug.   The Centers for Disease Control issue guidelines recommending that AIDS victims be able to attend school since casual person-to-person contact poses no risk of contagion.

A sixth permanent artificial-heart implantation is performed.

9 Sept.   New York City school districts are struck by a boycott when a seven-year-old AIDS victim is given permission to attend school.

26 Sept.   Harvard Medical School scientists announce the discovery of an organ-growth protein.

3 Oct.   The Centers for Disease Control report twenty-five times the risk of fetal malformation in women who used the acne drug accutane in the first three months of pregnancy.

16 Oct.   Baby Fae's death is revealed to be caused by the wrong blood type in the transplanted baboon heart.

7 Nov.   The American Medical Association reports studies indicate no link between saccharin, an artificial sweetener, and bladder cancer in humans.

11 Nov.   A Johns Hopkins study suggests coffee drinking is linked to heart disease.

14 Nov.   The Center for Science in the Public Interest indicts fast-food chains for deep frying with beef fat rather than with oils lower in saturated fats.

4 Dec.   Cancer therapists announce a new cancer treatment by activating the body's own immune system to combat untreatable cancers.

10 Dec.   Health officials announce that taking one aspirin a day can reduce subsequent heart attacks.

1986

- Scientists discover the first gene known to inhibit growth; it inhibits the cancer retinoblastoma.

9 Jan.   The *New England Journal of Medicine* publishes the results of a study reporting the drug interferon alpha 2 shows promise in preventing the spread of cold infections.

A Harvard University study links exercise to a lower risk of breast cancer in women.

17 Jan.   A cyanide-filled Tylenol capsule kills a Yonkers, New York, woman; Johnson & Johnson, the manufacturer, ends production of all its nonprescription capsule medicine.

Massachusetts Institute of Technology scientists announce the production of the first artificial blood vessels from cells grown in the lab.

22 Jan.   A *Wall Street Journal* poll finds 18 percent of unmarried adults have changed their sexual habits for fear of contracting AIDS.

23 Jan.   A *New England Journal of Medicine* study says heredity appears to play the central role in adult body-fat levels.

6 Feb.   A *New England Journal of Medicine* study rules out contracting AIDS through casual contact.

6 Mar.   The *New England Journal of Medicine* reports moderate physical exercise in adulthood can significantly increase life expectancy.

10 Mar. The FDA reports preliminary trial success with a new clot-dissolving drug, TPA, or tissue plasminogen activator, a genetically engineered protein.

13 Mar. Public-health officials warn that the population at a high risk of developing AIDS has a rising incidence of tuberculosis.

20 Mar. A *New England Journal of Medicine* study finds replacing dietary saturated fats with olive oil reduces cholesterol.

25 Mar. Pancreatic cancer is linked to smoking.

6 Apr. A Massachusetts General Hospital study finds evidence linking AIDS transmission from infected women to men.

May An international commission names the AIDS-causing virus the human immunodeficiency virus, or HIV.

20 May A Senate Special Committee on Aging condemns conditions in the nation's nursing homes.

21 May National Institutes of Health experts report patients suffering from pain are likely to be treated with too little or too much pain medication.

22 May Federal officials announce an ongoing nationwide crackdown on illegal steroids used by athletes.

5 June The FDA approves the use of alpha-interferon, a synthetic human hormone, against a rare blood cancer.

6 June A Los Angeles woman gives birth to the first baby in the United States to be born from a frozen embryo.

11 June The army curbs smoking among its personnel, limiting it to designated areas.

National Institutes of Health scientists report that genital herpes, a viral infection, is continuously infectious and spreading throughout the population.

15 June The American Medical Association calls for a curb on the supply of new doctors.

23 June The U.S. Justice Department says federal civil rights laws do not forbid the firing of employees with AIDS.

30 June The federal government announces $100 million in contracts to step up research for a cure for AIDS.

7 July The McDonald's Corporation announces it will make a booklet available listing the ingredients of its fast foods after pressure from consumer groups.

8 July The FDA bans some sulfite preservatives in fresh vegetables and fruits after linking them to deaths, primarily among people with asthma.

10 July The National Institute on Drug Abuse reports cocaine-related deaths are on the rise.

15 July A federal advisory committee urges systemization of the nation's arrangements for organ donors and transplants.

23 July The FDA approves the first genetically engineered vaccine intended to protect against the hepatitis B virus, a major cause of liver disease.

29 July The Department of Health and Human Services reports 1985 health-care costs reached $425 billion.

28 Aug. A 1981 study linking coffee drinking with pancreatic cancer is refuted.

4 Sept. The *New England Journal of Medicine* calls fetal heartbeat monitoring and caesarean sections into question, as increasingly common procedures that do not improve outcomes for most babies.

19 Sept. The federal government announces that an experimental drug, azidothymidine (AZT), prolonged the lives of some AIDS victims.

7 Oct. California surgeons, in a pioneering operation, remove a twenty-three-week-old fetus from his mother's uterus, perform surgery to correct a blocked urinary tract, then return the fetus to the womb.

24 Oct. The Federal Trade Commission issues rules requiring makers of smokeless tobacco to include health warnings in their ads and on packages of the product.

29 Oct. The National Academy of Sciences criticizes the federal effort against AIDS as inadequate.

4 Nov. The National Academy of Sciences calls secondhand smoke a real health risk for children and adults.

28 Nov. Four out of five middle-aged American men have an extensive risk of death from heart disease because of unhealthy levels of cholesterol, according to a *Journal of the American Medical Association* study.

2 Dec. A University of Minnesota study claims the genetic makeup of a child is a stronger influence on its personality than child rearing.

5 Dec. The General Services Administration announces requirements to provide federal workers with a "reasonably smoke-free environment."

9 Dec. The National Academy of Sciences issues a report saying teens should not be forced to seek parental consent for abortion and should have easy access to contraceptives.

1987

- Transparent orthodontic braces are introduced.

- A new plaque-removing mouth rinse is patented.

- A bone-marrow transplant registry is created in Saint Paul, Minnesota, to match donors with patients.

13 Jan. The U.S. Supreme Court upholds a California law requiring employers to give women disability leave for pregnancy and childbirth and to guarantee they can return to their jobs.

16 Jan. San Francisco television station KRON becomes the first major-market station in the United States to lift the long-held ban on advertising condoms on televison because of fear of AIDS.

2 Feb. The Children's Defense Fund reports that U.S. infant mortality is one of the highest in the industrialized world.

6 Feb. A *Journal of the American Medical Association* study shows it is relatively easy for husbands or wives to transmit AIDS to their spouses through sexual intercourse, but not through casual family contact.

2 Mar. The Centers for Disease Control report the chance of developing AIDS rises steadily in the seven years after infection with the HIV virus.

16 Mar. The FDA recommends approval of minoxidil (brand name Rogaine) to treat baldness.

20 Mar.   The FDA approves the marketing of AZT in the United States for treating symptoms of AIDS.

8 Apr.   A National Institutes of Health panel recommends that screening for sickle cell disease be routine for all infants.

17 Apr.   A *Journal of the American Medical Association* study reports the percentage of women who had contracted AIDS via sex with infected men had more than doubled between 1982 and 1986, with the greatest danger for nonwhite women.

31 May   President Reagan refuses entry to the United States of immigrants and aliens with AIDS.

1–5 June   The Third International Conference on AIDS meets in Washington, D.C.

1 June   Washington, D.C., police wear rubber gloves to protect themselves against possible AIDS infection while policing demonstrators protesting Vice President Bush's address to the Third International Conference on AIDS.

19 June   The *Journal of the American Medical Association* reports the first "clear evidence" that a cut in dietary cholesterol can benefit those with symptoms of coronary artery disease.

20 July   Louisiana becomes the first state to make HIV testing and disclosure of results mandatory for marriage-license applicants.

30 July   President Reagan bars federal funding for family-planning programs that offer abortion counseling.

18 Aug.   U.S. health officials announce plans for the first human trials in the United States of an experimental AIDS vaccine.

28 Aug.   A fire of suspicious origin destroys the Arcadia, Florida, home of a couple with three hemophiliac sons known to have been exposed to the AIDS virus from donated blood.

1 Sept.   The FDA approves marketing of lovastatin, described as the most effective drug for lowering cholesterol in the bloodstream.

11 Sept.   The Centers for Disease Control report smoking in the United States is at its lowest level ever, with an all-time low of 26.5 percent of adults.

21 Sept.   Illinois becomes the second state to require AIDS testing for marriage licenses.

11 Oct.   The AIDS quilt is unfurled for the first time on the Mall in Washington, D.C.

2 Nov.   The *Wall Street Journal* reports that the Pap smear, a procedure used to detect cervical cancer, has a failure rate of about one in four cases.

12 Nov.   The American Medical Association issues guidelines informing U.S. physicians that they are under a moral obligation to treat AIDS victims.

13 Nov.   The FDA approves the marketing of TPA, or tissue plasminogen activator (brand name Activase), a genetically engineered blood-clot dissolver, as an emergency heart attack medication.

22 Dec.   Scientists report the discovery of a specific gene that determines whether a fetus develops into a male or female.

1988

- Health-care costs reach $51,926 per person, accounting for 11.1 percent of the GNP.

- Surgeons implant the world's first plutonium-powered pacemaker.

2 Jan. The Centers for Disease Control report a substantial increase in tuberculosis and tie the increase to the AIDS epidemic.

21 Jan. A *New England Journal of Medicine* study suggests that up to half of the heart pacemakers implanted by doctors might be unnecessary.

22 Jan. Retin-A, an acne drug, seems to reverse some of the effects of sun-induced wrinkles.

26 Jan. A study indicates an aspirin taken every other day could cut the rate of heart attacks in men in half.

27 Jan. NutraSweet produces a low-calorie, cholesterol-free fat substitute called Simplesse, made of milk or egg proteins.

31 Jan. New York City health authorities are given permission to distribute free needles to drug addicts to fight the spread of AIDS.

2 Feb. The National Cancer Institute reports cancer cases continue to rise at the rate of 1 percent a year.

23 Feb. A Reagan panel urges a $2 billion increase in spending to expand drug treatment programs and improve health care to fight the spread of AIDS.

10 Mar. A *Journal of the American Medical Association* study questions whether mammograms are worth the expense in women younger than fifty with no risk factors for breast cancer.

17 Mar. A study indicates women who smoke drastically increase their risk of strokes.

22 Mar. A *New England Journal of Medicine* study reports carotid endarterectomy surgery, designed to prevent strokes, carries a 10 percent chance of stroke or death.

15 Apr. The Reagan administration bans research with fetal tissues.

21 Apr. A Massachusetts universal health-care bill guarantees health insurance to all residents.

23 Apr. Smoking is banned on domestic airline flights lasting less than two hours.

5 May A government study reports that chorionic villi sampling is nearly as safe as amniocentesis as a prenatal test for birth defects.

12 May The National Institutes of Health halt funding for artificial-heart programs, citing failures for all five patients who had received them.

21 May The U.S. Cancer Institute urges women who have undergone breast surgery for cancer to follow up with drug or hormone therapy.

23 May The FDA approves prescription marketing to women of the cervical cap, a contraceptive device.

26 May The FDA orders unprecedented curbs against the antiacne prescription drug Accutane to prevent its use by pregnant women because of its potential for serious birth defects.

1 June The National Academy of Sciences criticizes the absence of strong federal leadership and support in the fight against AIDS.

13 June   A federal jury in Newark, New Jersey, finds a tobacco company partly to blame for the death of a cigarette smoker, the first such ruling in more than three hundred liability lawsuits.

14 June   New York's Suffolk County enacts a law regulating use of video display terminals in the workplace because of health hazards related to their use.

21 June   The National Institute of Dental Research reports that nearly half of all schoolchildren in the United States have no tooth decay.

27 June   Michigan becomes the first state to outlaw surrogate-mother contracts.

5 July   The FDA issues a warning against the indiscriminate use of the antiacne drug Retin-A to erase wrinkles.

28 July   A study reports that about 31 percent of all conceptions end in miscarriage, usually in the early months of pregnancy.

17 Aug.   The FDA gives final approval to market minoxidil (Rogaine) as a prescription treatment for baldness.

31 Aug.   A Florida manufacturer pleads guilty to U.S. federal charges that it sold cardiac pacemakers that could suddenly malfunction.

28 Sept.   A Harvard School of Public Health study recommends restructuring of Medicare payments to doctors, with family doctors receiving more money and specialists receiving less.

1 Oct.   A Rand Corporation study says up to 27 percent of hospital patient deaths because of heart attack, stroke, or pneumonia could have been prevented with proper care.

19 Oct.   The FDA adopts a new policy on drug approval designed to speed access to new drugs for patients suffering from life-threatening illnesses such as AIDS or cancer.

1 Nov.   A new Medicare reimbursement policy aimed at reducing hospital stays for Medicare patients is implemented.

11 Nov.   A panel of physicians and medical school faculty recommend the radical revision of medical school training, placing a greater emphasis on physicians' social psychology skills.

14 Nov.   The Department of Transportation announces plans for the first federal anti-drug effort in the private sector — random testing of nearly 4 million transportation workers.

21 Nov.   The FDA approves the use of alpha interferon for treatment of Kaposi's sarcoma, a skin cancer often found in AIDS victims.

25 Nov.   A Harvard Medical School study warns against overmedication with psychoactive, or mood-altering drugs, to nursing-home patients.

1 Dec.   A Department of Health and Human Services study finds flaws in nursing-home drug dispensing and food service.

12 Dec.   A government report warns against a growing nursing shortage and recommends better recruitment, training, and pay for nurses.

22 Dec.   The FDA reports that there is insufficient evidence to justify a ban on silicone breast implants.

30 Dec.   The Department of Health and Human Services announces that the U.S. government will establish a nationwide computer registry of malpractice suits and disciplinary actions against doctors and dentists.

1989

5 Jan. *Journal of the American Medical Association* studies show that cigarette smokers are increasingly likely to be poor, limited in education, and members of a minority group.

11 Jan. The surgeon general reports that smoking has caused more deaths than was previously believed — in 1985, 390,000 deaths, or about one-sixth of all deaths in the country.

1 Feb. The Environmental Protection Agency announces plans to ban daminozide (brand name Alar), a suspected cancer-causing chemical sprayed on apples, but will not do so for at least eighteen months.

6 Feb. The FDA announces that it will widen the availability of an experimental aerosol drug, pentamidine, used to treat Pneumocystis carinii pneumonia, a formerly rare disease that has become more common in AIDS patients.

2 Mar. The National Academy of Sciences calls for a broad change in Americans' eating habits — more fruit, less fat.

5 Mar. The American Academy of Pediatrics reverses it position and states that the circumcision of male infants has medical benefits in protecting against kidney and urinary infections.

8 Mar. The Department of Health and Human Services says it will support programs to supply hypodermic needles to drug addicts to help halt the spread of AIDS.

9 Mar. The *New England Journal of Medicine* reports that prompt treatment of heart attack victims with blood-clot-dissolving drugs is as effective as balloon angioplasty, an expensive procedure increasing in popularity.

16 Mar. The median incubation rate for AIDS is put at 9.8 years.

17 Mar. The FDA quarantines all fruit imported from Chile after government investigators discover traces of cyanide in Chilean grapes.

30 Mar. An eight-year study concludes that a lumpectomy, followed by radiation therapy, is as effective a treatment for breast cancer as a mastectomy.

27 Apr. The FDA grants approval to an implantable contraceptive for women called Norplant.

28 Apr. The Department of Health and Human Services shows that physicians who have a financial interest in clinical laboratories order 45 percent more tests and lab services.

1 May The first U.S. patient to have human fetal cells implanted into his brain as a Parkinson's disease treatment shows slow but steady improvement.

22 May The American College Health Association finds that 0.2 percent of U.S. college students are infected with the AIDS virus, a higher rate than had been expected.

National Institutes of Health scientists inject genetically engineered nonhuman cells into a human patient for the first time.

1 June The FDA approves a genetically engineered drug, epoetin, (brand name Epogen), to treat anemia in kidney patients.

A *New England Journal of Medicine* study finds the AIDS virus can lie dormant for up to three years before it is detected with standard blood tests.

9 June *Science* publishes a study showing that the extent of AIDS among whites and in the Midwest is underestimated.

15 June   The FDA approves the aerosol pentamidine to prevent Pneumocystis carinii pneumonia, which is the leading cause of death in AIDS victims.

28 June   A national survey shows as many as 25 million Americans, or 16 percent of the U.S. population over age fifteen, might be infected with the sexually transmitted herpes simplex II virus.

30 June   Researchers pinpoint a set of genes that seem to cause some families to be unusually susceptible to multiple sclerosis, a debilitating nerve disease.

7 July   The *Journal of the American Medical Association* says more than one-third of all American adults need to lower their blood cholesterol.

10 July   The National Institute of Allergy and Infectious Diseases announces that AZT will be given to pregnant women infected with AIDS to determine whether it can protect newborns from infection.

20 July   The *New England Journal of Medicine* confirms that an aspirin tablet every other day reduces the risk of heart attack in men older than fifty.

28 July   The Centers for Disease Control report sharp increases among women in deaths from lung cancer, up 44 percent from 1979 to 1986, compared to increases of only 7 percent among men.

4 Aug.   A new drug called deprenyl appears to slow the progression of Parkinson's disease, a degenerative brain disorder.

9 Aug.   A *Journal of Pediatrics* study says in vitro babies are as healthy and mentally alert as those conceived normally.

15 Aug.   The Gay Men's Health Crisis of New York City reverses its policy and announces that it will endorse widespread voluntary testing for AIDS.

16 Aug.   The *New England Journal of Medicine* says nursing mothers who drink appear to transfer enough alcohol to their infants to impair their muscle coordination.

18 Aug.   The *Journal of the American Medical Association* estimates that only about 20 percent of the 10 million Americans afflicted with depression get treatment.

24 Aug.   American and Canadian scientists announce the isolating and cloning of the gene causing cystic fibrosis.

6 Sept.   A Harvard School of Public Health study finds no evidence of increased cancer risk among women who started taking birth control pills in their mid twenties.

13 Sept.   The University of Minnesota releases a new version of the Minnesota Multiphasic Personality Inventory, the most widely used psychological assessment test, first published in 1942.

22 Nov.   Simple blood tests are introduced that can detect 60 to 70 percent of the fetuses with Down's syndrome, the main cause of mental retardation.

27 Nov.   The first U.S. liver transplant using a living donor is performed with a mother who gave part of her liver to her twenty-one-month-old daughter.

2 Dec.   A bipartisan report recommends that the government lift its ban on funding research into in vitro fertilization, which is opposed by antiabortion groups.

8 Dec.   Scientists at Tulane University's Delta Regional Primate Research Center develop a vaccine that protects monkeys against a simian version of AIDS.

OVERVIEW

AIDS. A deadly epidemic disease, AIDS, or Acquired Immune Deficiency Syndrome, marked the 1980s for Americans more than any other medical or health news. AIDS, first reported in 1981, is caused by infection with the human immunodeficiency virus (HIV), which attacks selected cells in the immune system, leading to its inability to resist disease-causing organisms and certain cancers. Americans were profoundly shocked by AIDS. The disease at first seemed to affect predominantly homosexual and bisexual men. But the medical community soon found that intravenous drug users, hemophiliacs, and recipients of blood transfusions were also at risk, as were heterosexual sexual partners of AIDS victims. AIDS spread rapidly until 1 million to 1.5 million Americans were estimated to be infected with the virus by the end of the decade. Until AIDS, major killer epidemics seemed to be problems of the past. Americans, with their great faith in scientific technology, assumed medicine would soon provide a "quick fix." But by 1989 no cure or vaccine existed for AIDS. Many of those infected were not even aware that they carried the virus and could spread it through three primary routes: sexual intercourse, either vaginal or anal, with an infected individual; exposure to infected bodily fluids including blood products; and from an infected mother to her child before or during birth. Problems with their immune systems might not be apparent for years because of the long gestation period of the virus. The medical and social costs of the disease were enormous. Because of its early association with "deviant" forms of behavior, AIDS acquired a stigma that further complicated identification and treatment. Its deadly, incurable nature and little-understood transmission complicated the lives of hemophiliacs and others who contracted the disease. Public hysteria led to children who were AIDS patients being banned from schools. Victims were shunned by family, friends, neighbors, and even some medical personnel. In the absence of effective medical technology against AIDS, prevention and education were the only weapons. By 1985 the blood supply was protected by a new test to screen blood directly for HIV antibodies, but many still feared transfusions. In 1988, after years of controversy, the U.S. Public Health Service mailed a comprehensive and straightforward brochure to every American household that emphasized preventive measures against the epidemic. By 1989 the physical, economic, and social tolls of AIDS were still increasing, but scientists, the medical community, and others continued to address the problem, and Americans continued to hope for a solution.

The Three Babies. Technology often races ahead of other aspects of culture, leaving social and ethical considerations to catch up. Many of the technological and social issues in medicine and health in the 1980s came to be symbolized by three small Americans: "Baby Fae," "Baby M," and "Baby Doe." By the 1980s technology had progressed to the point where a physician might try to save a doomed newborn by a xenograft, the transplantation of a heart from a different species into the chest of a "Baby Fae." Reproductive technology gave many infertile couples new hopes, but in the case of "Baby M" and her surrogate mother, it also presented new ethical and legal issues and heartaches. Ethical questions of patients' rights and government intervention in private medical issues also arose with the case of "Baby Doe," a handicapped newborn left to die without the surgery that might have saved him.

Product Tampering and Product Failures. Americans were shaken from their complacent faith in their healthcare products by several cases of product tampering and product failure. In 1982 an unidentified person murdered seven victims in Chicago by refilling Tylenol gelcaps with cyanide. After several other "copycat" episodes of product tampering, the industry was forced to revamp both gelatin capsules and product containers, creating elaborate protective devices. Lawsuits over infection-causing contraceptives, such as the Dalkon Shield, and toxic-shock-causing superabsorbent tampons, forced manufacturers to withdraw such products from the market. The Food and Drug Administration (FDA) was increasingly involved in such product problems as well as in its more usual oversight of new drugs for the U.S. market.

Medical Technology. Medical technology of the 1980s made news with new lasers for surgery and genetic engineering. Genetic engineering technology was exploited to make products such as insulin or to learn more about human biology. The most controversial possibility for genetic engineering was gene therapy — a technology with the potential to change the human organism itself. The most widely publicized medical technology of the 1980s was the artificial heart program. Until the FDA withdrew its approval in 1990, many avidly followed the progress of patients such as Barney Clark and Bill Schroeder as they suffered medical setbacks after receiving a permanent mechanical artificial heart.

Alternative Medicine. Some Americans continued their involvement in alternative approaches to health, particularly for stress-related problems. The medical profession traditionally focused on acute organic diseases and end-stage illnesses. But by the 1980s the great majority of patients instead suffered from chronic or stress-related complaints such as headaches and backaches. As many as one out of three Americans claimed to use the increasingly popular alternative and "holistic" healing methods. These focused on the total person — body, mind, emotions, and environment — instead of relying on the more traditional lab tests, drugs, and surgery. Some observers saw the holistic movement as a reaction to an ever increasing role for expensive and depersonalized medical technology and a high dependence on drugs to diagnose and treat disease. Although most physicians dismissed aspects of holistic "medicine" as pseudoscientific and even downright unscientific, consumers continued to visit practitioners of such therapies as aromatherapy, homeopathy, naturopathy, reflexology, and Rolfing. The holistic/self-care/preventive movement developed and grew during the 1970s. By the 1980s members of the medical profession began to find themselves divided over the value of such alternative forms of treatment as acupuncture, biofeedback, and meditation. Organized medicine would not generally validate most alternative practices. But it did agree that many Americans with chronic health problems were making themselves sick and could benefit from many of the preventive measures and lifestyles suggested by holistic-health advocates that lessen the probability of developing disease. "Prevention," said Surgeon General Julius Richmond in July 1989, "is an idea whose time has come."

The Impact of Health Care as Big Business. Many of the 1970s controversies about health care's soaring costs continued into the decade of the 1980s, as soaring medical costs forced many to realize that health-care was a big business. During the decade unprecedented competition in the health-care industry resulted in major shifts in power as hospitals, physicians, the federal government, and insurers fought for their share of medical business. Concerns with the astounding cost of health care resulted in many new cost-containment measures. Provider practice patterns moved customers away from traditional sources of care, especially hospitals. Insurance companies required second opinions from physicians for surgical procedures and insisted that tests and other procedures, when possible, be performed outside hospitals in less expensive settings. Economy measures affected medical practice. In the past a surgical patient might enter a hospital the day before the scheduled procedure for tests, have the surgery performed the next day, then leave the hospital a day or two later. By the mid 1980s that same patient could arrive at the surgical unit after having had the tests performed on an outpatient basis, have the surgery performed, rest for the appropriate amount of time in a room filled with gurneys lined up next to each other, and then be released the same day. In 1980 only 16 percent of surgeries were done on an outpatient basis, but by 1989 fully 48.7 percent of all surgeries were outpatient. Thus hospitalization for some surgical procedures was reduced from three or four days to none. As a result of government and private changes, there was a dramatic decline in hospital use. Hospitals, faced with decreasing utilization and declining insurance payments for their services, were forced into competition with each other to maintain their shares of the market. The declining occupancy of hospitals led to consolidations within the industry. Some 3 percent of the nation's community hospital beds were eliminated during 1984 and 1985. Growing numbers of Americans without health insurance increased the burden on hospitals and the health-care system. Thirty-five million Americans lacked health insurance in 1985, up from 29 million in 1970. Hospitals were reluctant to treat those who could not pay.

Government Cost-Cutting. Private and government attempts to control costs led to other reorganizations of health-care delivery systems and threatened the traditional practice of the independent physician. U.S. government efforts to contain costs began in 1983 when Congress set flat rates for the hospital care of elderly and disabled Medicare patients based on predetermined "diagnosis-related groups," or DRGs. Patients were classified by diagnosis, and the payment to the hospital was determined by the DRG of the patient, rather than the actual services given. When hospitals provided care for less than the given DRG payment, they could profit from the difference; if not, they had to pay for the difference. In January 1986 federal officials required hospitals to inform Medicare patients that they had the right to challenge what they thought to be a premature discharge through a "peer review organization," which would have to make a decision within three days.

Accounting for Costs. In 1985, according to the U.S. Department of Labor's Bureau of Labor Statistics, the price index of all medical goods and services rose 6.7 percent. This was almost twice as fast as the general consumer-price inflation rate, but was considerably less than the rates of increase in health-care costs in the 1970s and early 1980s. In addition to the government's efforts, much of this decrease was because of the many private employers and insurance companies who cut health-care costs by making changes in their employees' insurance plans. Employees paid higher deductibles and shared more of the health-care costs. The industry was forced to become more accountable for its cost expenditures. During the decade the number of organizations demanding cost accounting procedures increased rapidly. Health-care providers found themselves doing enormous amounts of paperwork to satisfy the demands of regulators, consumer groups, government financing agencies, policy setters, employers, insurance agencies, hospitals, physicians groups and others. The industry had to undergo a radical transformation. Hospitals merged; health maintenance organizations (HMOs) multiplied; doctors joined widening networks; and Americans learned they had to be sophisticated consumers of health care.

Changes in Practice. The shrinking health-care dollar led to more changes in different ways of providing care beyond the traditional individual fee-for-service doctor's office. In 1980 a report issued by the Congressional Office of Technological Assessment reported the United States was rapidly accumulating an oversupply and maldistribution of physicians, perhaps as many as 185,000 more than it needed. As HMOs continued to grow, many physicians joined them, paid by HMO sala-ries rather than their traditional fee-for-service. The HMOs offered medical care for a prepaid fee from provider organizations or groups of physicians and hospitals who provided care at predetermined rates. HMO enrollment rose 24.9 percent between June 1984 and June 1985, paralleling the increase in the number of HMOs, which rose 28.9 percent in the same time period. HMOs decreased health-care costs by practicing more preventive medicine and by restricting inpatient hospital care by delivering many services in physicians' offices or ambulatory-care centers.

Medicine's Future. Although great strides continued to be made in many aspects of medical technology, America's faith in the ability of science to solve heart failure or AIDS was shaken. Concerns about the growing costs of medical care and the new directions of managed care left them with many questions about the future of medicine by the end of the decade.

TOPICS IN THE NEWS

AIDS

A New Disease. About the beginning of the decade, physicians discovered the existence of a "new" illness. This disease burst on the world scene in a terrible way as a new "plague" striking mankind. For a while there was general alarm when Americans discovered that the disease was linked to sex, blood, and drugs. It came to be known as AIDS, an acronym that stood for Acquired Immunodeficiency Syndrome. AIDS is caused by infection with the human immunodeficiency virus (HIV), which attacks certain cells in the immune system, leaving it unable to fight off "opportunistic" infectious diseases and certain unusual cancers. The virus also can invade brain cells, leading to psychological disturbances. The disease is always fatal.

Early Cases. The first warnings came when a Los Angeles physician noticed a cluster of symptoms from young men in California who were members of the growing gay community there. The first official announcement was published on 5 June 1981 by the Centers for Disease Control (CDC), the federal epidemiology agency in Atlanta. The CDC researches health problems and works to prevent and control the spread of disease. In its weekly bulletin the CDC described several severe pneu-

Surgeon General C. Everett Koop telling reporters about *Understanding AIDS,* a pamphlet mailed to every American household in 1988

REPETITIVE STRESS INJURY (RSI)

What do playing video games, typing on computer keyboards, hammering nails, strumming a guitar, doing pushups, and playing tennis have in common? They can be bad for your health. Many aches and severe pains resulting from these activities became known as a syndrome doctors called "repetitive stress injury" (RSI). Tennis players suffered from "tennis elbow," an elbow strain that came from constantly hitting the backhand incorrectly, and "carpal tunnel syndrome," a wrist problem caused by snapping the racket instead of following through on a swing. Video-game fans found themselves with an especially troublesome carpal tunnel injury nicknamed "Space Invader's Wrist" after the popular game. The pain and swelling in the wrist was caused by rapid repetition of button pressing, paddle twisting, joystick pushing, sphere rolling, or combinations of these actions. An estimated 65 percent of all video-game players suffered at some time.

Most publicity went to injuries from computer use. According to the Bureau of Labor Statistics, RSI accounted for nearly half of all 1988 workplace illnesses in private industry, compared to only 18 percent in 1981. Meatpackers and textile workers still suffered, but the big increase came from data processors and journalists who spent long hours at the keyboard. Hours at the computer continuously stressed the wrists, elbows, and shoulders. Tendons in the arm became inflamed, leading to numbness and pain. Unless the injuries were diagnosed and treated, they could develop into serious lifelong disabilities. The science of ergonomics, or how humans adapt to the workplace, came to the rescue with design alterations to minimize problems. Experts said frequent short breaks from work were crucial, but that the real key was to make technology adapt to humans instead of the other way around.

Sources: Susan Block, "Tennis Elbow? Runner's Knee? Golf Toe? Easing the Pain Those Fitness Fads have Wrought," *Los Angeles Magazine* (Nov. 1982): 112+;

Barbara Kantrowitz, "Casualties of the Keyboard: a Push to End Injuries from Computer Use," *Newsweek* (20 August 1990): 57;

" 'Space Invaders' May Be Hazardous to Your Health," *Current Health* (November 1982): 10.

monia cases observed in five patients in three Los Angeles hospitals. All the victims were young gay men, and all had lethal pneumonia called PCP from the *pneumocystis carinii* organism, which usually only causes illness when there is a serious problem in the immune system. Five cases does not seem like many, but this form of pneumo-

nia was so rare that five cases in a single year made it definable as an epidemic. On the East Coast the incidence of PCP was increasing, and rumors were circulating about the unusual appearance of a rare malignant disease (Kaposi's sarcoma) that had appeared in the gay community in New York.

A New Name for a New Disease. The CDC began its work. A Kaposi's Sarcoma and Opportunistic Infections (KSOI) Task Force was formed under the direction of James Curran, then chief of the venereal disease branch. On 4 July 1981 the CDC informed the medical community of the fatal nature of the new illnesses and "highly unusual" spread of the normally rare Kaposi's sarcoma among young homosexual men. Although Kaposi's sarcoma was usually limited to the elderly, there were two key exceptions. It was endemic (an epidemic disease found in a particular locality) across equatorial Africa and was also found among patients receiving immunosuppressive treatment. Since the first cases in the United States seemed to affect only homosexuals, the Public Health Service named the complex of diseases GRID — gay-related immune deficiency. But when heterosexuals began to become victims also, GRID became Acquired Immunodeficiency Syndrome, or AIDS.

A Slow Call to Arms. After 1982 the AIDS epidemic spread rapidly. Ten new cases were diagnosed each week in 1982, one hundred in 1984. At the end of 1988 the total number of AIDS cases reported to the CDC numbered 86,000. Many physicians realized that they were in the throes of a major medical problem. Public fears fueled by media reports led to a kind of collective hysteria; but public health agencies and the federal government moved very slowly against the disease. There were two primary reasons for the government's reluctance to confront the issue. In the first place, the diseases associated with the AIDS virus were rare enough that there were relatively few trained clinicians and researchers who were familiar with them. The second reason was that the first patients with AIDS were primarily homosexual men. AIDS forced a confrontation between the politics of the gay revolution of the 1970s and the politics of the Reagan revolution of the 1980s. The needs of public health — to stop the AIDS virus — got lost in the sexual politics of the early 1980s. White House officials and many public health sources were made uncomfortable by the link between the spread of AIDS and homosexual behavior. They made vague references to "exchanging bodily fluids," which lost them valuable time in helping the public to understand how AIDS could be transmitted and further fueled public panic as well as a backlash against the gay community. In the early years of the crisis the federal government's research teams saw AIDS as a budget problem and did not provide major funding for AIDS research until the epidemic had spread throughout the country.

Those at Risk. Although the syndrome was first observed to be affecting homosexual and bisexual men, soon

Haitians, intravenous drug users, and recipients of blood transfusions, including hemophiliacs, were recognized as being at increased risk. Homosexual and heterosexual sexual partners of victims of the disease could also contract it. Strong evidence from the medical community indicated that HIV was transmitted only through three primary routes: vaginal or anal sexual intercourse with an infected individual; exposure to infected blood or blood products through blood transfusions or in intravenous drug abusers exposed to HIV-infected blood through shared needles; and from an infected mother to her child before or during birth.

The Social Dimension of AIDS. Rejection, fear, and stigmatization of the victims complicated the nation's ability to deal with the deadly disease. Since the earliest victims identified as AIDS sufferers were homosexual males and intravenous drug users whose practices countered many mainstream definitions of morality, the disease was associated in some minds with sin and punishment. "The poor homosexuals — they have declared war upon nature, and now nature is exacting an awful retribution," wrote conservative newspaper columnist Pat Buchanan. Misinformation was common. A *New York Times*/CBS poll revealed in 1985 that about half of all Americans wrongly believed AIDS could be transmitted through casual contact, such as sharing a drinking glass. The fatal nature of the disease also terrified and panicked people. Schoolchildren with AIDS were rejected, and attempts were made to either keep them out of school or isolate them from their classmates. In Queens, New York, parents kept as many as twelve thousand children out of classes after a girl with AIDS received permission from the city to enroll in school. Ryan White, a schoolboy who contracted AIDS from a blood transfusion, became a household name after he was driven from his school and town in Indiana. In Florida the family of three little hemophiliac boys — also infected with HIV through blood transfusions — had their house burned down by fearful arsonists.

Issues. The announcement in July 1985 that film actor Rock Hudson had AIDS (he died on 2 October 1985) dramatically increased public awareness of the crisis. But many problems remained unsolved. Questions of screening and isolating patients led to controversies. Protecting the donated blood supply, for example, became difficult since potential donors feared stigmatization and discrimination if they were identified as HIV-positive. Efforts to protect public health led to discrimination against foreign visitors or potential immigrants. Those testing positive for AIDS were not permitted to enter the country. Some victims of the disease found it difficult to get adequate health insurance coverage because of the high yearly expense of treating patients. The slow process of the Food and Drug Administration (FDA) for approval of new AIDS drugs caused AIDS activists to demand that the government speed up the process by postponing some of the required testing. The activists argued that even

SCHOOL KIDS, NUTRITION, AND THE CONDIMENT WARS

In 1981 the news media had a field day when the Department of Agriculture proposed new rules for the nutritional content of federally subsidized school lunches—rules that reflected the Reagan administration's efforts to cut government support for social services. The new rules cut back from 1 1/2 ounces of meat or meat substitute per day per child to one ounce, and elementary-school kids found their milk ration dropping from eight ounces to six. Government regulations for the school lunch program also required that children be given two vegetables or fruits a day. Under the new regulations ketchup and pickle relish were redefined as vegetables. Sen. Henry J. Heinz (R-Penn.), of the family-owned condiment company H. J. Heinz Co., stated, "Ketchup is a condiment. This is one of the most ridiculous regulations I ever heart of. I suppose I need not add that I do know something about ketchup and relish!" In the face of all the publicity and criticism, the administration quickly shelved the proposals. French fries with ketchup were not defined as an adequate number of veggies in a school lunch.

Source: "Who Deserves a Break Today?," *Newsweek* (24 September 1981): 43.

though earlier approval could lead to unknown side effects, it was more important to provide potentially life-saving drugs to patients who had no other choices.

Treatment. By 1989 there was still no vaccine to protect against HIV infection, nor were there many major therapeutic agents to greatly prolong and ease the lives of victims. AZT (azidothymidine) was one drug licensed by the FDA for AIDS patients. It interfered with virus replication, prolonging life for many years in some patients and delaying the onset of full-blown AIDS in people with no symptoms. But it had harmful and toxic side effects. The nature of the highly variable virus was a primary obstacle to the development of a vaccine. The virus existed in many different strains, and mutated rapidly into others, even within an individual's body. AIDS was difficult to treat because unlike most known disease agents, HIV infected the immune system cells, the same cells that should be leading the attack against invading pathogens. If the virus was killed, the already threatened immune system was endangered.

Prevention. Since no vaccines or lifesaving effective therapies were available, prevention by means of education to reduce the risk of contracting the disease was the only real means to fight it. In March 1983 the major blood banks attempted to reduce the risk of transmitting the disease via transfusion of contaminated blood by asking individuals at risk for the disease not to donate blood. They also expanded their screening procedures to exclude donors at risk for AIDS. By 1985 tests to screen donated blood for HIV antibodies were available to eliminate blood containing the antibody from the donor pool. In 1988 the U.S. Public Health Service issued a candid brochure about HIV infection and AIDS based on the surgeon general's report. Every household in America received it in the mail. "Safe sex," meaning sex using AIDS-preventive measures, became a common phrase even as controversies arose over providing condoms for high-school-age children instead of encouraging sexual abstinence. The question of providing clean needles to drug addicts to prevent the spread of AIDS from infected drug users when needles were used repeatedly also created controversy. Public health officials were concerned to discover that many of the groups at highest risk of contracting AIDS, such as drug users and inner-city populations, were the ones least likely to be affected by the prevention campaigns.

Predictions for the Future. By the end of the decade AIDS was still spreading in the United States and the rest of the world. It continued on its mysterious, debilitating, and fatal course, made even worse by its social stigma. Despite prodigious efforts to create new weapons against AIDS, it still baffled scientists and the medical community. Some infected with HIV were without symptoms, and some AIDS victims lived throughout the decade with the disease, raising hopes that information could be found from their ability to fight off the disease that could help others. By 1989 scientists felt that while they might not be able to cure the disease, they might find some additional therapies that could keep the AIDS virus in check without the toxic side effects of AZT. Perhaps the real answer would lie in some national strategy to create an effective prevention campaign through education that involved all Americans. But millions of people around the world still became gravely ill. Ironically, AIDS became the main cause of death for persons under age fifty, even though in contrast to other deadly epidemics such as influenza or plague, the routes of transmission of AIDS were in large part controllable.

Sources:

Mirko D. Grmek, *History of AIDS. Emergence and Origin of a Modern Pandemic* (Princeton: Princeton University Press, 1990);

C. Everett Koop, *Koop: The Memoirs of America's Family Doctor* (New York: Random House, 1991), pp. 194–239;

Randy Shilts, *And the Band Played On: Politics, People, and the AIDS Epidemic* (New York: St. Martin's Press, 1987).

ALCOHOL-RELATED TEENAGE DEATHS: UNITED STATES, 1980

Alcohol and Premature Death. In 1985, two letter writers to the *Journal of the American Medical Association* used 1980 data from the National Center for Health Statistics to call attention to the premature deaths of American teenagers from the abuse of alcohol. The authors studied the deaths of persons ten to nineteen years of age in 1980 whose death certificates showed alcohol as an underlying or contributing cause of death.

Deaths from Alcohol Abuse. They found eight deaths in persons younger than fifteen years old. The youngest child, a twelve-year-old girl, died of exposure to the weather. From fifteen to nineteen years of age there were 276 deaths. Fifty-two deaths were because of alcohol abuse without trauma, including 9 from aspiration of food, 7 from exposure, and 3 with acute pancreatitis. The remaining deaths from trauma, by cause and number, were: motor vehicle accidents, 126; drowning, 32; shooting, 26; stabbing, 7; carbon monoxide inhalation, 7; hanging, 6; drugs or poisoning by chemicals, 6; falls from heights, 5; fire, 4; and "other," 5.

Alcohol Deaths Underestimated and Underreported. The authors concluded that deaths associated with alcohol abuse were still vastly underestimated and underreported. A study in San Francisco in 1985 showed alcohol blood levels legally defined as intoxicated in 50 percent of persons aged twelve to twenty-four years who died after accidents. In 1980, among persons fifteen to nineteen years of age, there were 10,663 deaths in the United States from motor vehicle accidents alone. If 50 percent were associated with intoxication, one would expect about 5,000 such deaths in comparison with only 126 observed in the study.

Sources:

I. M. Friedman, "Alcohol and Unnatural Deaths in San Francisco Youths," *Pediatrics*, 76 (1985): 191–193;

Robert W. Miller and Frank W. McKay, "Alcohol-Associated Teenage Deaths: United States, 1980," *Journal of the American Medical Association* (20 December 1985): 3308.

ALZHEIMER'S DISEASE

More than Simple Forgetfulness. Do you ever leave the house and wonder if you remembered to turn off the iron or the water? All people experience this occasional absentmindedness, but for some it is the beginning of the loss of their minds — and a long, wasting death. In November 1989 researchers at Boston's Brigham and Women's Hospital found that more than 10 percent of people sixty-five years old and older, and nearly half of those older than eighty-five, suffered from "probable" Alzheimer's disease. This new information almost doubled previous estimates, raising the number to as many as 4 million victims nationwide. With predictions of 14 million victims by the year 2050, Alzheimer's was becoming "one of the biggest public health dilemmas we've ever encountered," according to the National Institute on Aging's deputy director, Gene Cohen. Before 1980 many Americans had never heard of Alzheimer's disease, described by some as "a living death," or "the long goodbye." Although many families watched their loved ones succumb to the disease, it did not become generally fa-

Members of SADD (Students Against Drunk Driving), founded by a high-school teacher in 1981, after two of his students were killed in alcohol-related automobile accidents. Teenagers who join the group sign a "Contract for Life," promising not to drive if they have been drinking and to call their parents for a ride home. Parents of SADD members promise to put off discussions of their children's alcohol use until it can be discussed calmly.

miliar to the public until the news broke that film star Rita Hayworth suffered from Alzheimer's disease.

The Long Good-Bye. Senility was long seen as an inevitable consequence of getting old. But it is not an inescapable aspect of old age; there are many reversible dementias that can be successfully treated. But Alzheimer's, a neurological condition that impairs the brain's functioning, is an irreversible disease. It is diagnosed through a process of elimination of other disorders. Neurofibrillary tangles and senile plaques in the brain characteristic of Alzheimer's disease could only prove the disease in autopsies of victims. It was the fourth leading killer of adults, causing more than one hundred thousand deaths a year. Researchers did not know the cause of the disease, although genetics was thought to play a role. Other theories suggested a slow virus, a disorder in the immune system, or excessive amounts of aluminum in the brain. First recognized in 1906 by the German neurologist Alois Alzheimer, it was marked by early forgetfulness. Within three to ten years the disease progressed through severe losses of intellectual functioning, and painful personality and physical changes. Patients were unable to speak, think, or care for themselves. Death usually occurred within ten years after diagnosis. "The emotional impact of watching a parent or spouse deterio-

rate is devastating," said Johns Hopkins psychiatrist Peter Rabins.

Victims and Their Families. Families bore most of the burden of care, with about 70 percent of Alzheimer's victims remaining at home. In the earlier stages of the disease, some victims were prone to wander or have outbursts of violence and anger; in the later stages they became incontinent and could not dress or feed themselves. The twenty-four-hour needs of the Alzheimer's sufferer often severely taxed the physical and psychological stamina of caregivers and caused breakdowns in their own immune systems. Health concerns for the caregiver could begin to rival those of the patient. Alzheimer's also came to be known as "the survivor's disease." Nursing-home costs of caring for Alzheimer's sufferers ranged from $22,000 to $30,000 a year and were not covered by Medicare or by many private health insurance companies. For families to become eligible for Medicaid funds, they had to run through their savings. Community resources were important since social support was an important way for caregivers to provide for the increasing needs of their loved ones and themselves. Day-care centers for the elderly were few in 1989, and most only took Alzheimer's victims in the early stages. For "difficult" patients who needed constant watching or restraints, there was almost nothing. Neither nursing homes nor day-care centers would take these patients.

Elusive Treatments. Finding treatments were even more elusive than finding the cause. No "wonder drug" existed for the disease, nor even a clear and consistent treatment approach. Researchers found that some drugs helped some of the people some of the time, but there were puzzling inconsistencies in response from one patient to the next. Sadly, even once diagnosed, a person inevitably got worse, and as knowledge of the puzzling disease spread, sufferers had a frantic awareness in the early stages — they had it and could not do anything about it. By 1989 much was known about the symptoms of the disease, but little was known of the causes. Ongoing research attempted to unlock the secrets of the disease, but neither a full scientific understanding nor a cure existed. Before the 1980s Alzheimer's was thought to be a rare disease and few Americans had heard of it. Alzheimer's disease received considerable public attention during the 1980s. The media emphasized the impact the illness had on both its victims and their families. Most communities did not have services or care facilities developed specifically for the long-term needs of Alzheimer's patients, nor did they provide support services for the caregivers. But many communities did have agencies that provided for the various needs of the elderly, and by decade's end many of these agencies often provided support and service to both patients and caregivers. The next decade and the increased aging of America would see an increase in care facilities and other social supports for both Alzheimer's victims and their families.

Sources:

David Gelman, Mary Hager, and Vicki Quade, "The Brain Killer," *Newsweek* (18 December 1989): 54–56;

Howard Gruetzner, *Alzheimer's. A Caregiver's Guide and Sourcebook* (New York: John Wiley & Sons, 1988);

Abigail Trafford and Joseph Carl, "Behind Spreading Fear of Two Modern 'Plagues,'" *U.S. News & World Report* (12 August 1985): 46–47.

ARTIFICIAL HEARTS

At the Heart of the Matter. We think of our hearts as the center of our beings — the source of our deepest feelings. A lost love results in a "broken heart," and disappointments give us "heavy hearts." But to doctors and scientists, the heart is an extraordinary muscle that beats about 40 million times a year to pump our life-giving blood through some 100,000 miles (160,000 km) of blood vessels in every part of our bodies. Heart disease was the nation's number one killer in the 1980s. Surgery could repair some damaged hearts, and in 1967 a South African heart specialist, Dr. Christiaan Barnard, transplanted the world's first human heart from one patient to another. Thousands of human heart transplants followed his historic achievement. But one person has to die for a human heart to be available for another person.

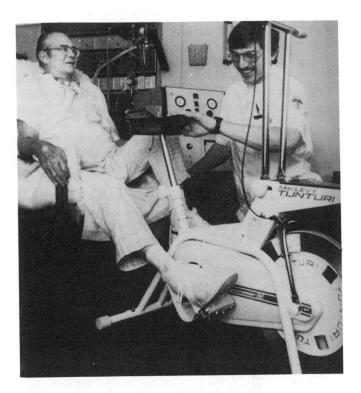

Barney Clark, the first artificial-heart recipient, working out on an exercise bicycle three weeks before his death on 23 March 1983

Mechanical Hearts. For many years scientists and the medical community worked for the day when a mechanical heart would be available. The first successful artificial heart procedure occurred in 1957 when Dr. Willem Kolff and Tetsuzu Akutsu of the Cleveland Clinic developed a heart that kept a dog alive for one and a half hours. Researchers spent the next several decades developing four-chambered hearts for temporary use in humans. Dr. Denton A. Cooley performed the first successful operation to implant the temporary device in 1969. These artificial hearts were originally intended as permanent replacements for a diseased heart. The first artificial heart, the Jarvik-7, was developed by Robert K. Jarvik, working with Kolff in the artificial-organs division of the University of Utah Medical Center. It consisted of compressed-air tubes leading outside the chest to a power source and was first widely tested on animals. Among the more than one hundred calves, sheep, and goats receiving the artificial heart, three had strokes related to infections.

The "Bionic Man": Barney Clark. After the FDA granted approval for human use, the Jarvik-7 was first implanted on 2 December 1982 into the chest of Dr. Barney Clark, a sixty-one-year-old retired dentist suffering from cardiomyopathy, a fatal disease of unknown cause that destroys the heart muscles. After many medical setbacks including subcutaneous emphysema, seizures, pneumonia, and nosebleeds, Clark died on 23 March 1983 of complications from preexisting kidney and lung disease. The Jarvik-7 heart worked until the end, when it was turned off after Clark was "essentially

THE PACEMAKER SCAMS

Colorado ski trips, gold-plated shotguns, and plain old American cash. According to federal investigators, physicians accepted these lures from manufacturers working to convince doctors to implant a particular brand of pacemaker in their patient — including patients who did not need the electronic device that helped to regulate the heartbeat. More than 130,000 Americans underwent surgery in 1982 to get a pacemaker. The device cost from $600 to $900 to make, but hospitals were billed from $2,000 to $5,000 apiece, and then they added a markup of 50 to 150 percent before sending the whole cost on to Medicare or other insurance plans. In a country with too many specialists, unnecessary surgery was a major concern. Senate and Department of Health and Human Services (HHS) investigators estimated that up to 50 percent of the implantations done at some hospitals were unnecessary. They estimated that as much as half of the $2 billion Medicare spent on pacemaker operations each year may have been wasted. Salesmen offered some cardiologists as much as $500 for each of the company's pacemakers that were used. "Criminal prosecutions would be charged," said HHS as it gave its findings to the Justice Department.

Source: Matt Clark and Mary Hager, "Pacemakers: A Scandal at Heart," *Newsweek* (20 September 1982): 86.

dead." The artificial heart and its implantation were considered a success.

Blood Clots and Strokes. Three of the first five human recipients of permanent artificial hearts suffered strokes. Three of the five also died after relatively short periods. Barney Clark lived 112 days after receiving his artificial heart. Murray Haydon lived for sixteen months. William Schroeder survived the longest, living for 620 days, close to two years, when a fourth stroke and lung infection led to his death. It was not a good life for either Schroeder or his family during the months he lived with his artificial heart. His wife, Margaret, said while he was still alive, "At first I thought it was just for Bill so he would be able to get better and come home. And now I see it as more of a research experiment. The longer he lives the more information they get. Only for us it's just hard sometimes." Unlike the three experimental animals whose strokes were related to infections, the human strokes were caused by blood clots that originally formed in the heart and then traveled to the brain. Anticoagulants were given to artificial-heart recipients to prevent the blood from clotting to try to prevent strokes but produced other serious complications.

A New, Temporary Role. After the disturbing strokes, physicians questioned the use of the devices as permanent replacements and began to use them as a temporary "bridge" for people awaiting a human heart transplant. Some patients did not have a suitable donor heart immediately available, or needed time to recover from health conditions that made a transplant inadvisable. The FDA authorized heart surgeon Dr. William C. DeVries to perform seven permanent Jarvik-7 heart transplants, but after the many complications in his early patients, it recommended that DeVries be required to obtain case-by-case clearance for the remainder of the implants. The first FDA-authorized temporary use of an artificial heart as a bridge to a human heart transplant occurred in August 1985 at the University of Arizona Medical Center in Tucson, where a twenty-five-year-old Arizona man suffering from a severe viral heart infection awaited a new donor heart. Seven days after the surgery, he suffered a series of mild strokes, necessitating an urgent human heart transplant. The Jarvik-7 was later found to have blood clots on its left side, where the main pumping chamber joined the aorta.

Cancellation of the Program. This dramatic new medical technology brought problems along with its many potential benefits. Media reports affected public opinion. Patients and their families lost a great deal of their privacy as the curious public demanded its right to know. The procedure was enormously expensive, and many people raised the question whether such money might be better spent on prevention than on a risky and expensive procedure for one patient. Barney Clark had once been a two-pack-a-day smoker. Quality of life became an issue. With all the medical problems he had had after he received his artificial heart, had Clark lived for 112 days or was he dying for 112 days? The artificial heart did prove potentially useful in a way its original designers had not seen. Originally intended as a permanent replacement for a diseased heart, it became used more as a temporary bridge to keep patients alive until a human heart could be found for transplant. It also contributed in a major way to the wider issue of medical ethics and human experimentation, one of the most important issues in medicine of the time. Federal funding for the Jarvik-7 project stopped in 1988, and implantations were restricted to temporary use. On 11 January 1990, after reviewing the ongoing problems with the device, the FDA recalled the Jarvik-7 and forbade its further use in human patients.

Sources:
Melvin Berger, *The Artificial Heart* (New York: Franklin Watts, 1987);

Carnegie Library of Pittsburgh, Science and Technology Department, *The Science and Technology Desk Reference* (Detroit: Gale Research, 1993), pp. 425;

Health & Medical Horizons 1986 (New York: Macmillan, 1986), pp. 287–288.

ZAPPING CORONARY ARTERY DISEASE WITH "STAR WARS" LASERS

Instead of using bypass surgery to repair clogged arteries, surgeons began during the 1980s to vaporize plaque and blood clots in peripheral arteries with lasers. A University of California, Davis, assistant professor of internal medicine, Garrett Lee, designed a special fiber-optic catheter that could be threaded through the body's major arteries to deliver bursts of laser light directly at the fatty plaque deposits obstructing the artery. Another laser developed for the Defense Department at Jet Propulsion Laboratories, the eximer laser, used short pulses of ultraviolet light. First successfully used in November 1988, the eximer laser vaporized plaque without the heat-damage problems of the earlier devices.

The major problems still to be solved were how to manipulate the laser beam inside the artery and how to distinguish normal and diseased segments of an artery before using the laser to vaporize tissue. Physicians in future decades would have access to "smart" systems relying on endoscopic fluorescence to perform the task and prevent blood-vessel perforations. The new laser procedures promised to save thousands of patients from open-heart surgery, but doctors still recommended that people should practice preventive measures to stay out of doctors' offices. "Stop smoking, reduce weight, and get on an exercise plan," advised Dr. Thomas Robertson, chief of the cardiac disease branch of the National Heart, Lung and Blood Institute.

Sources: Teresa Carson, "Now Lasers Are Taking Aim at Heart Disease," *Business Week* (19 December 1989): 98;

Abraham Katzir, "Optical Fibers in Medicine," *Scientific American* (May 1989): 120–125;

Lise Spiegel, "Medical Breakthroughs," *Harper's Bazaar* (April 1983): 199+.

"BABY FAE" AND THE BABOON HEART

A Daring Surgical Procedure. On 15 November 1984 at Loma Linda University Medical Center in southern California, a tiny baby girl died twenty days after she had heart surgery. The hopes of many died with her. For "Baby Fae," as she had come to be known, died with the heart of a baboon pumping blood through her body. The baboon heart experiment offered hope that animal organs could be used in ailing infants for whom transplant organs were difficult to obtain. Baby Fae was born with a fatal congenital deformity known as hypoplastic left heart, which left the entire left side of her heart useless. A successful transplant from a baboon promised a new life for Baby Fae and a revolution in pediatric heart surgery.

Xenografts. Dr. Leonard Bailey, chief of pediatric heart surgery at Loma Linda, had experimented with interspecies transplants for seven years, grafting lamb hearts into baby goats. Many of the goats lived as long as 165 days. Bailey hoped his work could ultimately be used for humans, especially those newborns dying of hypoplastic left heart. For his xenografts ("foreign grafts" between species) he chose baboons because of their biological similarity to humans. Baboons were also more available compared to the much rarer, although genetically closer, chimpanzees. He was also encouraged to perform the surgery on Baby Fae because of the success of a new antirejection drug, cyclosporine, which could suppress the body's reaction to a new heart but not destroy its ability to fight off infections. His experiments with young animals convinced him that their immature immune systems made their bodies more receptive to transplants. He theorized that they might be able eventually to adopt a xenograft organ as their own.

Controversies. After the surgery on 26 October, the medical community, although usually receptive to technological innovation, was sharply divided. Controversy arose from many quarters. Physicians challenged the use of an animal heart when a human heart seemed preferable; and animal rights groups protested the sacrifice of a healthy baboon for what they saw as medical sensationalism. Those concerned with medical morality worried about the ethical questions of consent for an infant in such a risky undertaking; and there were questions about whether Baby Fae's young, unmarried parents were properly advised about the drastic procedure. Questions even arose about her psychological well-being once she was old enough to understand that the heart that beat within her chest was that of a baboon. But hopes ran high. Her progress and setbacks were followed throughout the country, and in a videotape made just four days after surgery, Baby Fae was seen yawning and stretching, looking for all the world like a normal infant.

Kidney Failure. Although her survival was not expected to be easy, her death came as a surprise to those Americans who had avidly followed her every heartbeat. According to her physicians, she had done well until the fourteenth day after surgery when her body began to reject the foreign heart. Doctors increased her dosages of antirejection drugs and put her back on a respirator and intravenous feedings. But her kidneys failed and put her other organs into danger, ultimately leading to her heart failure.

Medical Perspectives. A year later the transplant of the baboon heart into the newborn infant was strongly criticized in an editorial published in the *Journal of the American Medical Association* (*JAMA*) in December 1985. The editorial suggested that Bailey's belief that an infant's immature immune system would protect against the rejection of a foreign organ was "wishful thinking." Bailey himself had admitted that he had made a grave error when he used a heart from a baboon with a different blood type. The editorial concluded that the operation was doomed to failure from the beginning. In an article in the same issue of the *JAMA* and at a news conference after its publication, Bailey defended himself. He noted that human infant donors were extremely scarce and said that in future cases like Baby Fae's he would look for a human donor. But, if none were available, he would transplant an animal heart as a bridge until a human donor was found. The critics from the medical journal agreed that an animal heart transplant could be a way to keep an infant alive until a human donor could be found.

Unanswered Questions. In the end, many questions remained unanswered. Other members of the medical profession saw the doctors of Loma Linda as pioneers, and reminded the country that advances in medicine were only made by trying things that seemed daring. Some people asked if it were right to spend so much time, effort, and money to try to save a baby who had so little chance of survival when many millions of the world's children were dying for simple want of food. Baby Fae brought out defenders of medical experimentation, animal rights activists, and the press. But it was not clear who had defended Baby Fae. What exactly were the ethics of the case? The medical world and other Americans would reflect on the case of Baby Fae for a long time to come.

Sources:

Leonard L. Bailey and others, "Baboon-to-Human Cardiac Xenotransplantation in a Neonate," *Journal of the American Medical Association* (20 December 1985): 3321–3329;

Health & Medical Horizons 1986 (New York: Macmillan, 1986), pp. 315;

Olga Janasson and Mark Hardy, "The Case of Baby Fae," *Journal of the American Medical Association* (20 December 1985): 3358–3359;

Paul O'Neil, "The Heart That Failed," *Discover* (January 1985): 14+;

Claudia Wallis, "Baby Fae Loses Her Battle: The Baboon Heart Fails, But a Doctor Defends the Transplant," *Time* (26 November 1984): 88–89.

THE CASE OF "BABY M" AND THE NEW REPRODUCTIVE TECHNOLOGIES

Gifts of Life. By the 1980s parents who wanted children but were unable to conceive had a bewildering variety of new procreative possibilities available to them. There was in-vitro fertilization (IVF), the results of which are popularly known as "test-tube babies." Scientists retrieved an egg (ovum) from the mother and mixed it with the father's sperm in a glass container called a petri dish so that the ovum could be fertilized. Once the zygote was created, a doctor was able to place it in the woman's uterus to develop, as in a normal pregnancy. In July 1978 the world's first "test-tube baby," Louise Brown, was born in Great Britain. With in-vitro fertilization, excess embryos could even be frozen for later pregnancies. In the GIFT procedure (gamete intrafallopian transfer) zygotes were created when prepared sperm and three to four harvested ova were injected a short distance into the end of the woman's fallopian tube rather

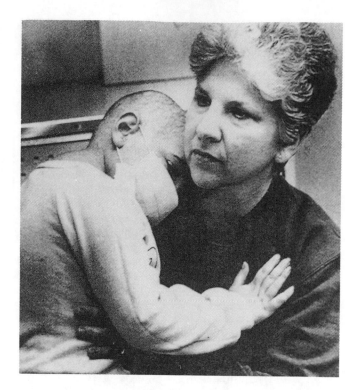

Brooke Ward of Raleigh, North Carolina, in the arms of her mother after becoming the first bone-marrow recipient matched through a national donor program established in March 1988

than united in a petri dish. Surrogate motherhood — bearing a child for another woman, often for payment — also evolved, using technologies related to IVF. Instead of a child having two parents, a mother and a father, there could be as many as five different "parents": two genetic parents who contributed sperm and ova for in vitro fertilization or artificial insemination; the birth mother who accepted the transferred zygote, gestated the fetus, and gave birth; and the social parents who reared the child. All of this became news to most Americans in 1986 when the notorious case of "Baby M" made headlines.

Surrogate Motherhood. The Baby M court case in 1987 was one of the first to generate public debate about the issue of surrogate pregnancy. Typically in the mid 1980s, surrogacy was based on a formal legal agreement between the would-be parents and the woman who agreed to serve as a surrogate. During the pregnancy the usual agreement called for restrictions on the surrogate mother's behavior and authority to make medical decisions about her and the fetus. There were often large sums of money involved, and a growing industry of surrogate-mother brokering began to make the formal practice more common. In other cases surrogacy was a private arrangement with no legal contracts involved. In 1985 Mary Beth Whitehead signed a contract agreeing to act as a surrogate mother for William and Elizabeth Stern for a payment of $10,000. The following year she broke her contract and decided to keep the baby. Her decision led to a widely publicized court battle and many legal and ethical questions. For Whitehead the arrangement required her to undergo artificial insemination, to gestate the fetus, and to give the child up at birth to the genetic father and his wife, who was not biologically the child's mother.

Baby M. When the baby (who came to be known to the public as Baby M) was born, Whitehead felt she had made a terrible mistake. Although she first turned over the baby to her contractual parents, she later asked to have her for a visit. She then fled to Florida with the baby, her other two children, and her husband. The FBI investigated and the child was returned to the Sterns. After a well-publicized and prolonged custody battle, the New Jersey Superior Court upheld the legal contract, giving the child to the Sterns. In 1988 New Jersey's Supreme Court reversed the ruling and banned surrogate contracts for pay. It gave custody to William Stern, invalidated Elizabeth Stern's adoption of Baby M and gave Mary Beth Whitehead broad visitation rights.

Troubling Questions. Most legal problems in the United States fall under state laws, so cases must be resolved in several jurisdictions before legal precedents can be established. Many other state legislatures began to regulate surrogate arrangements because of the large sums involved and the growing industry of surrogate-mother brokering. Legal regulations for the behavior of the surrogate mother, such as requiring her to exercise, seek regular medical attention, or to refrain from drugs, alcohol, and tobacco, created issues of potentially dangerous precedents for regulating all women during pregnancy and standardizing the behavior and medical care of pregnant women. The Baby M case raised other troubling questions. What makes a mother or father suitable to be a parent, and who should decide? Should surrogacy be abolished? Who was qualified to determine a child's "best interest?" Was a surrogate-mother contract baby-selling? Mary Beth Whitehead was not well educated. She and her family lived on a low income and needed the funds paid for her service. The Sterns were well educated and upper middle class. Was surrogacy becoming a blue-collar "occupation?" At the end of the decade the answers were still being explored, and commercialized surrogate brokering had decreased. Commercial surrogacy was banned in some states, while others legalized it, passing laws that made couples who contracted for surrogacy services the legal parents of the children produced. Voluntary arrangements for surrogate mothering did not pose the same threats as the commercial ones and were likely to continue in all their different forms. Still unanswered by 1989 was the question of how the children of these surrogate arrangements and other new reproductive technologies would fare. Most children conceived by the new technologies were not yet adolescents by 1989, and evaluating the psychological costs of surrogacy and other

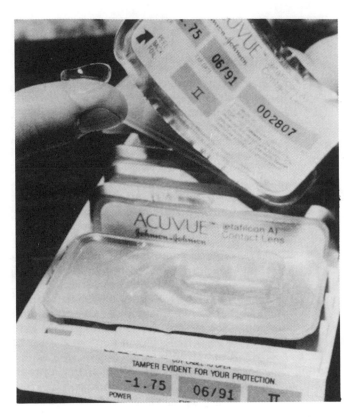

Johnson & Johnson Acuvue, the first disposable contact lens, introduced in July 1987

reproductive technologies on children would have to wait until the next decade.

Sources:
Elaine Hoffman Baruch, Amadeo F. D'Adamo Jr., and Joni Seager, eds., *Embryos, Ethics and Women's Rights. Exploring the New Reproductive Technologies* (New York: Harrington Park Press, 1988);

Phyllis Chesler, *Sacred Bond: The Legacy of Baby M* (New York: Times Books, 1988);

Kathlyn Gay, *Pregnancy: Private Decisions, Public Debates* (New York: Franklin Watts, 1993).

EATING DISORDERS

The "Disease of Abundance." When Karen Carpenter, a member of the popular singing duo The Carpenters, read a review that called her "chubby," she began an eight-year obsession with her weight. By 1983, when she died from heart failure from emetine poisoning brought on by taking ipecac to induce vomiting, anorexia and bulimia had become household words. American society was obsessed with dieting, and these puzzling and frustrating disorders were extreme examples of the national obsession with weight and appearance.

Anorexia Nervosa. Anorexia was a form of extreme self-starvation and distortion of body image. Patients refused food until they reached a point of severe emaciation or even death. Even though looking in a mirror should tell them that they were too thin, they persisted in seeing themselves as too fat and were proud of their control over food. The term *anorexia* which means "lack of appetite,"

Popular singer Karen Carpenter, whose death in 1983 called attention to the serious consequences of anorexia nervosa and bulimia

was first used in England by physician Sir William Gull in 1873. Although anorexia was better defined as an obsession with food, Gull was also the first to note its prevalence in young upper-middle-class girls. In the 1980s it occurred most commonly among adolescent women. As it became more common during the decade, estimates of its incidence among young women in the United States were as high as one in one hundred teenage girls and young women. Unlike other psychological disorders that are more randomly distributed, anorexics had many social traits in common. Anorexia was fifteen times more likely to be found in females than males, typically began in adolescence, and, as Gull noted, was most common in wealthier families.

Bulimia. Little known even by physicians before the 1980s, bulimia was first thought to be an aspect of anorexia nervosa. It was characterized by secretive episodes of uncontrollable eating binges followed by self-induced vomiting to prevent weight gain. Bulimics differed from anorexics in terms of their loss of control over their eating. The anorexic prided herself on her control over food. Bulimics knew they had an eating disorder and were repulsed and frightened by their behavior, while the anorexic denied it. Most bulimics were either normal weight or overweight compared with the emaciated anorexics. Left untreated, the disease caused vitamin deficiency and serious physical ailments such as liver, kidney, and heart disease. Hair loss occurred. Repeated vomiting could rupture the stomach, and the acid in the vomit eroded tooth enamel. About 40 percent of women with bulimia developed irregular menstruation, and, like anorexics, about 20 percent entirely stopped having their periods.

Causes. Theories about these disorders included psychological, biological, and social explanations. Psychological explanations for anorexia focused on the fear of maturing and the fear of loss of control. Bulimia was regarded as a fear of food that created a compulsion, which led to stress and fear around episodes of binge eating and purging. Scientists also thought the disorders might be associated with a disorder of the hypothalamus, which produces hormones and regulates hunger, thirst, and temperature. Since some bulimics improved after treatment with antidepressant drugs, other biological theories linked it to decreased serotonin activity in the brain. Social scientists blamed social pressures. Women were constantly bombarded with advertisements and unrealistic role models suggesting that women's only worth was in their youth and their slim appearances. A *Glamour* magazine survey in 1984 revealed that even 45 percent of underweight respondents thought they were too fat and needed to lose weight. Although the response was not reflective of the population as a whole, the survey revealed a striking number of women who considered themselves overweight even though they were normal or underweight.

Treatment. Hospitalization and lifesaving measures were the first course of treatment for anorexia, with psy-

Health and Human Services Secretary Margaret M. Heckler at a March 1985 news conference where she revealed that lung cancer had passed breast cancer as the leading cause of death in women

chotherapy following as soon as the patient was stabilized. Residential treatment facilities for anorexics were developed during the 1980s that included family therapy, behavior modification, and counseling. Between 15 percent and 25 percent of anorexics relapsed occasionally; and another 15 percent to 20 percent continued to be anorexic. Ten to 20 percent died from self-starvation. Bulimics could be successfully treated outside the hospital since their disorder was not so life threatening. Treatment usually consisted of therapy and antidepressant drugs, but a high rate of treatment failure was reported. As celebrities such as Jane Fonda and Cherry Boone O'Neill, the daughter of singer Pat Boone, publicly admitted their struggles with these eating disorders, other Americans continued their obsession with food and dieting. Almost any diet cookbook could appear rapidly on the best-seller list, but the diseases anorexia and bulimia were still poorly understood, and the treatments for them were far from universally successful.

Source:
John R. Matthews, *Eating Disorders* (New York: Facts On File, 1991).

GENETIC ENGINEERING

A Powerful and Awesome Skill. In 1982 scientists took the gene that produces human insulin and inserted it into E. coli, a microorganism that lives in intestines. Genetic engineering, "the most powerful and awesome

skill acquired by man since the splitting of the atom," had harnessed the hereditary mechanisms of bacteria. Genetic engineers manipulated bacterial genes in an effort to produce new medicines and cures for human diseases. These bacterial microorganisms became capable of manufacturing human insulin for diabetics, human growth hormone for dwarfism, and the antiviral-anticancer drug interferon. Also known as "gene splicing" and "recombinant DNA," genetic engineering showed promise for producing important new vaccines and even safer older vaccines. There were hopes that the quality of life could be improved by manipulating human genes once the complete set of genetic instructions on human DNA (called the human genome) was mapped.

Recombinant DNA and Medicine. DNA (deoxyribonucleic acid) is the blueprint for life in all organisms. Its sequences of paired chemical bases are the hereditary information needed to produce proteins, the building blocks for all life. These proteins are large molecules, so they could not be artificially synthesized in the way the sulfa drugs or vitamins were. Genetic engineering began in the 1970s with the discovery of restriction nuclease enzymes. These "biological scissors" were able to recognize and chemically cut apart specific chemical sites along a DNA molecule. Another enzyme, ligase, permitted a gene snipped from one DNA molecule to be attached to a similar site in the DNA of an unrelated organism, even in another species. It was this hybrid that was called "recombinant DNA." The process of gene therapy got the desired gene into a cell by piggybacking it onto inactivated viruses known for their ability to penetrate cells. The first genetically engineered drug was human insulin, produced when the human gene responsible for insulin production was spliced into a bacterium, which then produced human insulin. In 1985 a more efficient copying procedure was developed. Called polymerase chain reaction (PCR), it could create many copies of a DNA sequence from a few originals. Until the advent of recombinant DNA, vaccination against some diseases involved using killed or weakened microorganisms. Some risks were still involved in using the vaccines, because errors in making them could introduce infectious live pathogens into the vaccinated individual. Recombinant DNA made it possible to transfer the genes that caused the disease to a harmless microorganism and use it as the vaccine instead.

Gene Therapy. Genetic disorders can be caused by chromosomes as in the case with trisomy 21, or Down's syndrome. More than three thousand human diseases can result from a defect in a single gene. Most are very rare, but others, such as cystic fibrosis, are much more common. Some of the most common genetic disorders such as diabetes mellitus and coronary artery disease result from many genes, making them much more complicated to analyze and treat genetically. Certain viruses can cause cancerous tumors by integrating their genetic information into the chromosomes of the human cells they infect. These defective genes cannot be treated by surgery, nor can many of the illnesses they cause be cured. But if their DNA sequences could be altered in some way, the new set of genetic instructions could save or improve a life. Such treatment is known as gene therapy.

The First Step. The first approved experimental transfer of new genes into human beings took place on 22 May 1989. Steven A. Rosenberg and R. Michael Blaese of the National Cancer Institute, and W. French Anderson of the National Heart, Lung, and Blood Institute, used a retrovirus, a special form of virus easily used in the laboratory, to transfer genes safely into the white blood cells of five consenting patients, all with advanced melanoma, a form of skin cancer, who had life expectancies of less than ninety days. The transformed white blood cells, which regularly detect and destroy cancerous cells before they can become established as a deadly tumor, continued to be detectable for several months after being transferred to a human subject. The first major step toward gene therapy was taken.

Controversy. Genetic engineering could be used for humans in two different ways. The technology could be exploited to make products such as insulin, or to learn more about human biology. The most controversial possibility for genetic engineering was gene therapy that had the potential to change the human organism itself. In 1975 famed scientist Paul Berg convened a landmark meeting in California of one hundred scientists from around the world to study the safety and propriety of certain scientific research relating to genetic engineering. It was the first time a group of scientists got together to police themselves and to think of the implications of their research. They declared a moratorium on certain experiments until they knew more about genetic engineering. In 1983 Robert Sinsheimer, a molecular biologist and the chancellor of the University of California, Santa Cruz, urged the world to consider the dark side of genetic engineering. He asked three crucial questions: "Is it safe? Is it wise? Is it moral?" Many people were against interfering with nature. They feared that strange new antibiotic-resistant viruses would be created in genetics laboratories and accidentally released into the world.

Federal Regulation. Since the recombinant DNA technique was first introduced in 1973, genetic material has been transfered thousands of times without accidents. In 1980 the U.S. National Institutes of Health (NIH) relaxed or eliminated most restrictions on work with all but disease-causing bacteria. For genetic therapy, in the fall of 1985 the NIH approved national guidelines for improving transplanted genes into a patient's body cells to correct an otherwise incurable disease. But it excluded any experimental treatment that could be passed on to the patient's children through his or her genes. By 1986 the biotechnology field had grown so rapidly that President Reagan had to update its coordination among many federal agencies. Responsibility for overseeing the multiple aspects of genetic engineering was to be shared by six agencies: the Department of Agriculture, the Environmental Protection Agency, the Food and Drug Administration, the National Science Foundation, the Occupational Safety and Health Administration, and the National Institutes of Health. Some critics of biotechnology feared it could be used unwisely in business and industry. Genetic testing might be used to help employers and health insurance companies predict tendencies of employees to develop certain health problems. This could lead to denying people employment or dismissing them from their jobs. By the end of the decade there were still few laws regulating the use of genetic information. One of the most controversial issues of the new power over biology was human reproductive engineering. In 1987 the Vatican issued a statement against reproductive technology, which it condemned as unnatural. The Roman Catholic Church felt that birth, death, and the lottery of genetic heredity belonged forever in the hands of a superior power and was not for humans to try to change. By 1989 the question of "whether to make perfect humans" was not yet solved by scientists, ethicists, or ordinary Americans.

Sources:

Lawrence Galton, *Med Tech: The Layperson's Guide to Today's Medical Miracles* (New York: Harper & Row, 1985), pp. 237–242;

Thomas F. Lee, *Gene Future: The Promise and Perils of the New Biology* (New York: Plenum Press, 1993);

THE HIGH COST OF GOOD HEALTH

Type of Expenditure	1980 Total (in billions)	1989 Total (in billions)	Percent increase
Health Services and Supplies	$238.9	$583.6	144
Personal health care	219.4	530.9	142
Hospital care	102.4	232.4	127
Physicians' services	41.9	116.1	177
Dental services	14.4	31.6	119
Nursing-home care	20.0	47.5	138
Drugs and drug sundries	21.6	50.5	138
Eyeglasses and appliances	4.6	10.4	126
Other professional services	8.7	27.1	214
Government public health	7.2	18.9	163
Other personal health care	4.6	9.8	113
Private health insurance	12.2	33.8	177
Home health care	1.3	5.6	331
Research and Medical Facilities Construction	11.3	20.7	83
Research	5.4	11.0	104
Construction	5.8	9.7	67

Eve and Albert Stwertka, *Genetic Engineering*, revised edition (New York: Franklin Watts, 1989);

"Whether to Make Perfect Humans," *New York Times*, 22 February 1988, sec. 1, p. 18.

THE HIGH COST OF GOOD HEALTH

Big Business. During the 1980s health care in the United States was big business and was marked by enormous costs. From 1980 through 1989 national health-care expenditures rose 142 percent. In 1989 the nation spent $604.3 billion on health costs compared to $250.1 billion in 1980, $74.7 billion in 1970, and $26.9 billion in 1960. Some expenses rose faster than others, but they all rose.

Hospital Costs. The average cost of a hospital room increased more than 99 percent from 1980 to 1988, outpacing inflation. The average daily charge for a semiprivate room was $127 a day in 1980, $215 in 1985, and $253 in 1988. But the average cost to the hospital was more than the charge to the patient — $250 a day in 1980 and $501 in 1985. The most expensive state if one needed hospitalization was California at $281 a day. Mississippi cost the least at $114 a day. To cut hospital costs, many insurance companies began to insist that more surgeries be done on an outpatient basis. Previously, patients entered a hospital on the day before their surgery for tests, had surgery the following day, and then stayed for several days afterward. Now patients needing certain surgeries could find themselves visiting the hospital for tests, going home again, coming in for surgery, and then leaving on the same day without being admitted to the hospital. Outpatient surgery increased from 16 percent of surgeries in 1980 to 48.7 percent in 1989, although there were many issues raised about quality of care when patients were sent home groggy from anesthesia or still in pain.

Medical Incomes and Costs. In 1980 the average pretax net income of self-employed physicians was $94,000.

By 1989 it had increased to $120,000. But for many, their expenses were rising faster than their incomes. Overhead expenses such as rent for office space, malpractice-insurance premiums, and nurses' salaries rose faster than physician income. The 1980s saw a surplus of physicians, although they were not uniformly distributed throughout the country. Every 10,000 Americans had 24 physicians available to them in 1990 compared to 16 twenty years earlier. The growing number of physicians made it more difficult for a doctor to establish a traditional independent practice. Therefore more sought salaried jobs with hospitals, medical companies, and government agencies. These physicians could expect to make less money than those in independent practice. Salaries also varied by specialty. Surgeons made the most money, and general practitioners and pediatricians were on the lower end of the scale. General practitioners made less income than physicians in any specialty. This increased the reluctance of many medical students to choose general practice. More specialists meant higher medical costs.

Cutting Costs. Businesses limited medical benefits for their employees and encouraged them to seek nonhospital treatment in outpatient clinics and same-day surgical centers. Insurance companies certified hospital admissions. Attempts were also made to control government programs. The creation of Medicare in 1965 greatly improved the medical coverage of the elderly. The federally sponsored program provided medical insurance to almost all older Americans and to the disabled. But it, too, was costly. From 1979 through 1982, national health-care expenditures rose 12.7 percent; while Medicare payments to hospitals grew 25.2 percent. Medicare payments to physicians grew an amazing 30.9 percent. As a result, the program, funded largely out of general tax revenues, became the third largest and fastest-growing single program in the federal budget. The Reagan administration's 1984 Deficit Reduction Act attempted to reform how and how much doctors were paid for Medicare patients. The act froze all fees and required physicians to accept Medicare "assignments" at the government's rate for Medicare payment for their services and to charge no additional fees to their patients. There was a high degree of variation in how much doctors were reimbursed. Physicians in New York received much higher Medicare payments for medical procedures than their counterparts in other states — merely because they historically charged more. Physician participation rates for Medicare varied greatly from state to state. Alabama had the highest physician participation in 1989 with 75.9 percent of its physicians enrolled as Medicare providers, contrasted with Idaho, which had the lowest at 16 percent. The federal government's new prospective-payment system for Medicare patients pressured the nation's hospitals to cut services. Hospitals were paid a set fee per diagnosis. If it actually cost more money than the set fee, the hospital had to pay the difference. To keep from losing money, hospitals cut expenses

WHAT THE DOCTOR EARNED

	Average Net Income*	
Specialty	1985	1988
All	94,000	120,000
GP/Family practioner	70,000	85,000
Internal medicine	90,000	156,000
Surgery	129,000	180,000
Pediatrics	70,000	85,000
OB/GYN	120,000	150,000
Radiology	135,000	158,000
Psychiatry	80,000	97,000
Anesthesiology	133,000	180,000

*Nurse salaries in 1987 ranged from a high of $27,190 in Connecticut to Nebraska's low of $18,968. Malpractice premiums for physicians were high and more than doubled during the decade.

AVERAGE MALPRACTICE PREMIUMS, 1983-1989

1983	$6,900
1984	8,400
1985	10,500
1986	12,500
1987	15,000
1988	15,900
1989	15,500

by reducing hospital stays. Hospitals cut their staffs and some had to close. Even though lobbyists, physicians, and other health-care personnel had many anecdotes about effects of cost-cutting on the quality of the nation's health care, by decade's end there were no clear cost-benefit analyses available. Costs and questions about health care continued to be major issues for the American people and their government.

Sources:
Susan Dentzer, Mary Hager, Vincent Coppola, and Daniel Shapiro, "Taking a Scalpel to Doctors," *Newsweek* (14 January 1985): 58–59;

COSTS TO SEE THE DOCTOR IN 1989

Specialty	Median Office Visit	
	First visit	Return Visit
General Practice	$35	$26
Family Practice	34	26
General Internal Medicine	51	34
Obstetrics/Gynecology	60	30
Pediatrics	40	30
General Surgery	41	29
Orthopedic Surgery	51	31
Cardiovascular Surgery	75	31
Neurosurgery	120	37
Plastic Surgery	46	27
Thoracic Surgery	74	33
Cardiology	101	37
Dermatology	45	31
Gastroenterology	80	35
Neurology	136	45
All Surgical Specialties	51	31
All Nonsurgical Specialties (excludes GPs and Family Practices	51	33

These costs were for the visit itself. They did not include charges for tests, medicines, or treatment at the time of the visit. In 1980 the per-capita American health expenditure was $1,059. By 1990 it rose to $2,566.

Source: Richard K. Thomas, Louis G. Pol, and William F. Sehnet Jr., *Health Care Book of Lists* (Winter Park, Fla.: PMD Publishers Group, 1994), pp. 369, 525.

Health Care Financing Administration, Office of the Actuary; data from Office of National Health Statistics, in *The World Almanac and Book of Facts, 1994* (Mahwah, N.J.: Funk & Wagnalls, 1994), pp. 971;

"Hospital Costs — State by State," *U.S. News and World Report* (28 October 1985): 12;

Richard K. Thomas, Louis G. Pol, and William F. Sehnert Jr., *Health Care Book of Lists* (Winter Park, Fla.: PMD Publishers Group, 1994);

U.S. Bureau of the Census, *Statistical Abstract of the U.S.: 1989* (Washington, D.C.: U.S. Government Printing Office, 1989), pp. 104;

U.S. Bureau of the Census, *Statistical Abstract of the U.S.: 1993* (Washington, D.C.: U.S. Government Printing Office, 1993), pp. 126.

LASER THERAPY

From Science Fiction to Scientific Reality. In the nineteenth century H. G. Wells, in his *War of the Worlds* (1898), wrote of Martians invading with weapons that fired deadly light beams. In the 1930s comic-book hero Buck Rogers used a ray gun. In the 1980s laser therapy came into use for a wide variety of medical problems. Lasers repaired detached retinas in the eye, vaporized abnormal growths and tumors, halted internal bleeding, and erased port-wine birthmarks without scarring.

How It Works. Since the laser's invention in 1960, many different types were created — gas, solid-state, diode, and others. Basically, a laser is a glass rod or tube filled with a gas. When it is stimulated with energy, electrons in the gas are excited into higher energy states. These high-energy electrons are unstable and must return to a lower energy level, but as they lose their energy, it is released as light. The light is amplified by bouncing it between mirrors, and when it emerges the laser beam is a thin line of pure color that shines with tremendous energy. Each laser type shines at a different wavelength. Some pulse on and off; some operate continuously. These differences provide great versatility for use in medical technology.

Lasers in Eye Surgery. One of the earliest applications was in the repair of retina rips or tears. A beam aimed through the front of the eye sealed down the edge of a tear, preventing retinal detachment and vision loss. Excimer lasers, which produce short-pulsed, high-power ultraviolet radiation, became commercially available at the beginning of the decade. Experiments were initially carried out by researchers on the cornea and on the skin. The excimer laser was also potentially useful in the removal of tumorous plaque (found in blood vessels) and of bone.

Lasers and Endoscopes. Improved lasers paired with endoscopes were used for head and neck surgery, especially for destroying tumors. Endoscopes are tiny instruments formed of thin shafts filled with fiber optics. When inserted through a tiny incision or natural opening in the body, the scopes allowed the physician to see inside the body part. Using lasers with operating microscopes connected to endoscopes, physicians removed tumors from areas that were previously inaccessible or difficult to reach except by major surgery, including the larynx, the base of the skull, and the middle and inner ear. Lasers and endoscopes sealed off blood vessels to allow virtually bloodless surgery, often on an outpatient basis. Lasers cleared airways in the lung that became obstructed by cancerous tissue. Lung cancer was not cured, but the treatment eased many of its symptoms. Physicians used a type of laser called a YAG (yttrium aluminum garnet) laser to deliver a beam through a fiber-optic tube. The light vaporized tissue blocking the airways. To get to the target, doctors used another fiber-optic tube, a bronchoscope, to see into the lung.

Other Uses. The port-wine birthmark is disfiguring, especially when it covers several square inches of skin on the face. Composed of abnormally dilated blood vessels, it was treated successfully by the laser. The laser's cell-vaporizing properties were also used to remove precancerous lesions of the mouth such as epithelial dysplasia. Laser mouth surgery, performed under local anesthetic, caused little pain and swelling compared to the conventional surgical removal, which resulted in extensive pain, swelling, and bleeding. Some complications could occur in surgery, both minor and serious. The greatest danger was an accident in which the laser burned through a major blood vessel, causing severe bleeding. Laser techniques were difficult and required experienced and skillful doctors. But they continued to show promise in areas ranging from opening atherosclerotic plaques blocking arteries to cosmetic surgery for infants born with face and skull deformities. By the 1980s Buck Rogers's "ray gun" had been harnessed by science for the good of humankind.

Sources:

Lawrence Galton, *Med Tech: The Layperson's Guide to Today's Medical Miracles* (New York: Harper & Row, 1985), pp. 267–271;

Health & Medical Horizons 1986 (New York: Macmillan, 1986), pp. 229, 263, 271, 319.

MANAGED CARE

The Changing Face of Medicine. Americans in the 1980s were increasingly confronting the relatively new concept of "managed care." The interests of physicians, especially doctors' interests in controlling their own work and setting their own prices, originally shaped medicine in the United States. Traditionally, patients paid their doctors directly on a fee-for-service basis rather than by salary or capitation (that is, per patient per year). Until fairly recently, physicians were one of the few occupational groups able to resist being drawn into industrial and bureaucratic organizations as were other self-employed professionals. Rising health-care costs and the realization that health care was big business forced changes. Unprecedented competition in the health-care industry resulted in major shifts in power in the 1980s as hospitals, physicians, the federal government, and insurers fought for their share of medical business. Concerns with the astounding cost of health care resulted in many new cost-containment measures. Provider-practice patterns moved customers away from traditional sources of care, especially the traditional fee-for-service payment system. Insurance companies became more reluctant to pay automatically for medical care on demand, and econ-

---

DEFENSIVE MEDICINE AND MALPRACTICE

A major cause of rising health costs in the 1980s was the practice of "defensive medicine"—the medical profession's response to increasing malpractice suits. By 1985 the frequency of medical malpractice cases filed against physicians was triple that of 1975, and the average amount awarded to plaintiffs paralleled the increase. In high-risk specialties such as obstetrics, the costs of malpractice suits and insurance rose so high that many physicians abandoned their specialty. Many doctors countered by practicing "defensive medicine." They protected themselves against legal challenges by ordering extra diagnostic tests and procedures—a practice that the American Medical Association (AMA) estimated cost $15 billion to $40 billion annually

Source: *Health & Medical Horizons 1986* (New York: Macmillan, 1986), pp. 286–287.

---

omy measures increasingly affected both patients and physicians.

Managed Care. In the 1980s paying for health care rapidly moved in the direction of "managed care," a form of health insurance that tried to control rising costs. Provider networks were groups of doctors, hospitals, and other health-care providers who treated plan members, often at rates of payment predetermined by the insurance company. Utilization management was done by medical professionals who reviewed potential medical procedures to determine if they were necessary and either gave or withheld insurance payments. The alternative to managed care was a more traditional form of health insurance called indemnity insurance. Under this plan a policyholder paid his doctor for each visit; then his insurer reimbursed him if his policy covered that particular service. But by the late 1980s few companies marketed pure indemnity plans alone. Under indemnity insurance the policyholder and his family could see any doctor they wanted, but under managed care they had to use the providers in the plan's network. His network's primary-care provider decided if and when he could see a specialist or be admitted to a hospital except for emergencies. But a health-insurance policyholder was lucky — in 1985, 35 million Americans had no form of health insurance at all.

The Gatekeepers. Three basic types of managed care existed: health maintenance organizations (HMOs), managed indemnity, or preferred provider organizations (PPOs). An HMO was a prepaid group practice in which a person, or his or her employer, paid a monthly premium for comprehensive health-care services. Each member chose a primary-care physician who guided him through his treatment. HMOs tried to keep costs down by avoid-

THE LEADING CAUSES OF DEATH IN 1981; BY SEX AND RACE

The data in this table are reported as ratios. For example, in the male-to-female column, diseases of the heart has a ratio of 2.00. This means that men died of heart disease at nearly twice the rate as women. For cancer the ratio is 1.50, meaning men were one and a half times as likely as women to die of cancer. Comparing African Americans to whites, the ratio of heart disease was 1.28. Blacks were 1.28 times more likely to die of heart disease than whites. The average American could expect to live 74.5 years in 1983. White women had a life expectancy of 78.7 years compared to white men with 71.4 years. African American women had a life expectancy of 75.2, compared to African American men who could expect to live only 66.5 years.

Rank	Cause of Death	Ratio of Male to Female	Ratio of Black to White
	All causes	1.79	1.47
1	Diseases of the heart	2.00	1.28
2	Cancer	1.50	1.33
3	Cerebrovascular diseases	1.17	1.80
4	Accidents Motor vehicle accidents Other accidents	2.95 2.89 3.02	1.16 0.81 1.64
5	Chronic obstructive pulmonary diseases	2.75	0.75
6	Pneumonia and influenza	1.80	1.52
7	Diabetes mellitus	1.04	2.21
8	Chronic liver disease and cirrhosis	2.16	1.82
9	Atherosclerosis	1.30	1.09
10	Suicide	3.15	0.52
11	Homicide	3.88	5.89
12	Conditions originating before birth	1.25	2.26
13	Nephritis and related disease	1.55	2.92
14	Congenital anomalies	1.09	0.98
15	Septicemia	1.41	2.72

Source: *The World Almanac and Book of Facts, 1986* (New York: Newspaper Enterprise Association, 1986), pp. 782–783.

ing hospitalization and by emphasizing preventive services. Members received doctors' services, laboratory tests, X-rays, and perhaps prescription drugs and other health needs, at little or no additional cost. Hospital coverage was also provided through the HMO's network. Under managed indemnity, a patient could see any medical provider he wished. But he still had to get prior approval from the plan for hospitalizations and some outpatient procedures. Not all preventive services were covered, and the patient had to file claim forms for some services. The PPO borrowed from both traditional indemnity and HMO plans. The PPO, like an HMO, contracted with a network of providers, but a PPO member was not limited to those in the network as he would be with an HMO. However, he had to pay a larger copayment for going out of the network. PPO financial incentives encouraged the use of network providers.

Costs and Benefits. Each plan had many costs and benefits. Managed-care plans, especially the HMO, limited a choice of provider but meant lower out-of-pocket expenses in the form of lower deductibles and lower copayments. HMOs and PPOs provided more preventive care. Traditional indemnity, managed indemnity, and PPOs would mean a patient would have more paperwork to file claim forms to get approval for some services. The managed-care providers, especially the HMO, took more responsibility for assuring the quality of service and care their members received. But traditional-indemnity and managed-indemnity insurers had little or no quality monitoring. Physicians began to find themselves increasingly subject to the hierarchical control and monopolistic power of insurance companies. Many found themselves losing freedom in choosing their hours and their clients. The face of traditional medicine was changing for both health-care consumers and their providers. Managed-care and health-care insurance was as confusing and complicated to many Americans in the 1980s as was health-care technology.

Sources:

Marc. S. Miller, ed., *Health Care Choices for Today's Consumer* (Washington, D.C.: Living Planet Press, 1995);

Paul Starr, *The Social Transformation of American Medicine* (New York: Basic Books, 1982);

Richard K. Thomas, Louis G. Pol, and William F. Sehnert Jr., *Health Care Book of Lists* (Winter Park, Fla.: PMD Publishers Group, 1994);

U.S. Bureau of the Census, *Statistical Abstract of the U.S.: 1993* (Washington, D.C.: U.S. Government Printing Office, 1993), pp. 116.

MEDICINE, THE GOVERNMENT, AND "BABY DOE"

Birth Defects and Decisions about Life. In 1982 an extremely sick baby was born in Bloomington, Indiana. The infant, who came to be known as "Baby Doe," suffered from Down's syndrome and had a surgically correctable abnormality of the throat and esophagus that prevented him from taking food or drink by mouth. It was not certain whether the child suffered the heart defect that occurs in 40 percent of babies with Down's syndrome. With the encouragement of their obstetrician, the parents refused the surgery. Baby Doe died six days later as legal appeals were being filed for treatment against the wishes of his parents. After his death, the government became officially involved in the controversy. When President Reagan learned about the death of the infant, he instructed the Health and Human Services (HHS) secretary to make certain that such a situation could never happen again. HHS passed regulations that were successively challenged in the courts. From Baby Doe's unfortunate situation came a bitter controversy over the question of the government's right or obligation to interfere in a matter affecting a newborn child and overturn the wishes of the parents.

Who Makes the Decisions? Baby Doe's case had multiple sides to every issue: What should the treatment be? Who should make decisions about the treatment? How should these decisions be made? Which procedures should be followed when there was no consensus? Who should make decisions about medical care — the medical profession, a patient's relatives, the courts, or the federal government? The case led to the first efforts by the federal government to intervene in decisions on whether or not to treat seriously ill newborns. It once again raised questions about the role of government regulation in medicine. When President Reagan's administration became involved, the political struggles over the issue resulted in Congress passing of the Child Abuse Amendments of 1984, often called the Baby Doe Amendments, to the Child Abuse Prevention and Treatment Act. In 1985 the U.S. Department of Health and Human Services issued a regulation requiring doctors and hospitals to provide lifesaving treatment for ill newborns unless death seemed inevitable. The rule created a new condition that state agencies had to set up mechanisms for receiving and investigating complaints of alleged cases of "medical neglect" in order to qualify for federal grants directed at preventing child abuse. A key element of the rule was a new category of medical neglect, which included "withholding of medically indicated treatment." State agencies were also required to be able to obtain court-ordered treatment when the agencies decided that the treatment was being wrongfully withheld.

Definitions and Questions. Much of the political fight was over definitions. Right-to-life groups wanted to define phrases such as "medical neglect," "reasonable medical judgment," and "merely prolong dying" so strictly that nearly all parents' and physicians' rights in decision making would have been removed. Pressure from many sources, including the coalition of senators who sponsored the legislation, forced the HHS to issue a final rule leaving more room for choice on the part of parents and the medical profession. American medicine and American government were not able to come to an agreement about the role of government regulation in medicine. But Americans had learned more about the difficult questions surrounding handicapped infants, the decisions doctors and family members have to make, and the role of the government in their lives.

Sources:

Health & Medical Horizons 1986 (New York: Macmillan, 1986), pp. 242–243;

C. Everett Koop, *Koop: The Memoirs of America's Family Doctor* (New York: Random House, 1991), pp. 240–261;

Claudia Wallis, "The Stormy Legacy of Baby Doe; Should the Government Try to Save Severely Afflicted Infants?," *Time* (26 September 1983): 58.

PRODUCT TAMPERING

Poisoned Tylenol. With their chalky consistency, pills are difficult for some people to swallow. Traditional over-the-counter pain relievers in a round shape often seem to stick in the throat and sometimes make taking

Johnson & Johnson employees in Chicago testing safety seals on bottles of Extra-Strength Tylenol, after cyanide-laced Tylenol capsules killed seven area residents in October 1982

the pill seem as unpleasant as the headache. Drug manufacturers thought they had solved the problem with their invention of gelatin capsules — two tubular shapes that fit together, enclosing the medicine, that slipped easily down the throat with a sip of water. But in 1982 disaster struck when seven Chicago-area residents died after taking Extra-Strength Tylenol capsules that an unknown person had laced with cyanide.

Copycat Poisonings. The incident led to a rash of copycat poisonings of other food and drug products, including Extra-Strength Tylenol laced with strychnine in California, mouthwash tainted with hydrochloric acid in Florida, and cold medicines, allergy remedies, and appetite suppressants spiked with rat poison. In response, the Food and Drug Administration mandated tamper-resistant packaging for over-the-counter drugs. Tylenol manufacturer Johnson & Johnson exceeded the FDA packaging requirements with a "triple safety seal." But in early 1986 a twenty-three-year-old woman died of cyanide poisoning in Yonkers, N.Y., after she took two capsules from a freshly opened bottle. The FBI announced in late February that its scientists had found that a determined and skillful individual could open and replace the triple seals of glued end flaps on the cardboard carton, a plastic shrink wrap over the cap, and an inner seal of foil over the mouth of the bottle.

Caplets. Tylenol was pulled from the shelves and Johnson & Johnson announced that it was discontinuing the manufacture and sale of the capsule form of its drugs. Instead, Tylenol would be produced only as tablets and "caplets" — tablets that were capsule-shaped and coated to be more easily swallowed. Both the American people and American corporations had to make new adaptations to face the complexity and uncertainty of the world of the 1980s.

Source:
Health & Medical Horizons 1986 (New York: Macmillan, 1986): 298–299.

SICK-BUILDING SYNDROME

Environmental Medicine. When the carpenter, electrician, and plumber finally packed up their tools and left Joan in her new kitchen, she breathed a sigh of relief. After two months of making do with the microwave oven on the dining-room table and the camp stove on the porch, she was ready to do some real cooking. But this was not to be. As soon as she set foot in the new kitchen, she began to sneeze. An allergy sufferer, Joan recognized the sneezing and watering eyes, but the headaches, dizziness, and sore throat were something new. She was reacting to formaldehyde, a chemical preservative used in many building materials such as adhesives, furnishings, and particleboard. After six weeks of open windows admitting the chilly autumn air, the chemical had "gassed off" and the family could use their new kitchen. Joan was lucky, but others were not. Formaldehyde may have the

AMERICAN HEALTH HABITS

A 1986 Harris survey commissioned by *Prevention* magazine reported only 40 percent of Americans "try a lot" to avoid cholesterol in foods. Sixty-two percent of adults older than twenty-four were overweight, and only 8 percent of all respondents said they exercised strenuously daily, a drop from 12 percent in the 1983 survey. Reflecting an awareness of osteoporosis, 57 percent said they tried to include adequate amounts of calcium in their diets, up from an earlier 50 percent. Safety habits showed a marked change, with 41 percent of respondents saying they always used their seat belts, up from 19 percent in 1983. Observers said the growing number of states with seat belt laws accounted for the difference.

Source: *Facts On File*, 1 August 1986, p. 563.

potential to "sensitize" persons. It might be one of a handful of chemicals that can be a forerunner to "chemical sensitivities" and even cancer. In the early 1980s a new and controversial branch of medicine began to center on the links between health and environmental factors. Pollution-related health hazards were problems for decades, but the 1980s saw a growing concern about air pollution inside the home or workplace.

Indoor Air Pollution. The formaldehyde used in building materials and foam insulation was not the only problem. Many new homes and office buildings were made with many synthetic, chemically treated building materials and finishings. Air breathed in these buildings was contaminated by many things, including death-causing carbon monoxide from incomplete burning of fuel, and nitrogen dioxide, produced during burning of natural gas, which was thought to cause increased respiratory problems in children in winter. The air in tobacco-free homes and buildings could be filled with as many as 150 contaminants — from stove gases, furnaces, solvents, paints, furnishings, mold, and pesticides. Many of these chemicals occurred as ingredients or by-products of common items such as household cleansers, construction materials, and cigarettes. The new buildings were models of energy efficiency, with little outside ventilation. As a result, chemical contaminants were being trapped indoors. Environmental Protection Agency (EPA) studies of American homes found chemical levels that were two to five times higher indoors than outdoors. Officials estimated as many as 30 percent of new office buildings displayed "sick-building syndrome" symptoms, and newspapers and television broadcasts showed workers complaining that working in their new offices made them ill. The EPA ranked indoor air pollution among the nation's top five environmental health problems.

Radon Contamination. Synthetic chemicals were not the only culprits. People in several states found high concentrations of the radioactive gas radon in their homes. Radon is a product of the radioactive breakdown of radium found in certain rock formations. The colorless and odorless gas can enter a building through cracks in the foundation, and can build up to potentially dangerous levels in closed areas. Long exposure to radon can lead to lung cancer. U.S. Centers for Disease Control scientists estimated that high radon levels could cause as many as thirty thousand lung cancer deaths in the country each year. In the fall of 1985 the EPA announced plans to conduct a national survey on radon and present a five-year plan to lessen its health hazard. Pennsylvania became the first state to help home owners to measure radon levels and increase ventilation to disperse the gas.

Public-Health Implications. As the average life expectancy in the United States rose, more Americans died of cancer. Although some cancers were genetically linked, most cases were believed to be related to the environment in some way. Some of the polluting items in the workplace could have accounted for a percentage of the cancers. In 1980 fewer than 4 of every 300,000 Americans died from the respiratory disease asthma. By 1990 the figure increased 46 percent to nearly 6 deaths in 300,000, with some 4,000 asthma deaths a year, according to the CDC. No one knew for sure just why the increase occurred, but some researchers suspected outdoor and indoor air pollution. Statistics showed higher rates among minorities and city dwellers who were more likely to live and work in "sick buildings." Similar trends occurred in traditional allergic disorders that experts said had experienced an unprecedented rise since the 1970s. Federal statistics indicated about 40 million Americans were allergy sufferers. Many in the medical community turned their attention to the role of the environment and to environmental medicine in the nation's public health picture. Prevention, rather than treatment, seemed to be the key. By 1989 there was a body of information on how to reduce human exposures to toxic contaminants. Many sick buildings in the workplace solved their air-quality problems by properly maintaining their HVAC (heating, ventilation, and air-conditioning) systems. Careful selection of building materials, equipment, and cleansing supplies could also limit the level of indoor contaminants. Although there was no single easy cure for sick buildings, indoor pollution was easier to control than outdoor pollution. By 1989 many Americans looked forward to the 1990s as an "environmental decade" that would help to improve the quality of the indoor air they breathed.

Sources:
Health & Medical Horizons 1986 (New York: Macmillan, 1986), pp. 264–265;

Nicholas Tate, *The Sick Building Syndrome* (Far Hills, N.J.: New Horizon Press, 1994).

THE HEIMLICH MANEUVER

Help! Someone's choking! But don't slap her on the back; it might force the foreign object causing the distress deeper into her throat. In July 1985 the American Red Cross and the American Heart Association endorsed the Heimlich maneuver, or "abdominal thrust." Dr. Henry Jay Heimlich, the pioneering chest surgeon who developed the technique in the early 1970s, had the rescuer reach around the choking person and put a fist—thumb side against the abdomen—at the bottom of the victim's rib cage. Grasping the fist with the other hand, the rescuer bent the victim forward, and gave one or more quick upward thrusts into the abdomen, pumping air out of the lungs to expel the foreign material.

In September the U.S. surgeon general also endorsed the maneuver, and in early 1986 the American Academy of Pediatrics recommended a modified form to help children who were choking victims. Millions of people learned the technique, including a five-year-old boy in Lynn, Massachusetts, who saw the maneuver on a television episode of *Benson* and saved a choking playmate.

Sources: Gwenda Blair, "How to Save a Life," *McCall's* (August 1994): 50+;
Health & Medical Horizons 1986 (New York: Macmillan, 1986), pp. 258–259.

TOXIC SHOCK AND PRODUCT SAFETY

A Rare Illness on the Increase. "It even absorbs the worry," proclaimed Procter & Gamble when it first distributed its tampon products. But decades later in 1980, Procter & Gamble had plenty of worries. After 344 cases of a rare and baffling illness were reported in 1980, the Centers for Disease Control linked women's use of tampons to an outbreak of a rare, sometimes fatal, toxic shock syndrome. One study of a group of sufferers discovered that 71 percent of them had used Procter & Gamble's Rely tampons. Procter & Gamble ordered a recall of its tampons and soon found itself in court.

Toxic Shock Syndrome. Toxic shock syndrome (TSS) is a severe, systemic illness associated with infection by the bacterium *Staphylococcus aureus*. The CDC's findings indicated it occurred most commonly in menstruating women who used tampons — about 75 percent of TSS victims — although it also occurred in children, men, and nonmenstruating women. Three to 5 percent of the cases were fatal. The syndrome had a sudden onset with high fever, vomiting, diarrhea, and a sunburn-like red rash that could occur anywhere on the body. Within a day or two, victims could suffer a drop in blood pressure, ranging from mild symptoms of dizziness to fatal shock. Treatment included intensive antibiotic therapy.

Lawsuits. By 1982 hundreds of lawsuits flooded the courts — four hundred against Procter & Gamble and one hundred or so against four other manufacturers. The first verdict on Rely resulted in a strange outcome when a federal jury in Denver returned a finding with bad news for both sides. After nearly twenty hours of deliberation, the jury found that the company was negligent in selling a defective product, but it also concluded that the young plaintiff who brought the case should not be awarded any money. After the first Rely case, a federal jury found Procter & Gamble liable for the TSS death of a twenty-five-year-old woman and awarded $300,000 in damages. On 24 December 1982 a California jury awarded $10.5 million in damages to a woman who had suffered from toxic shock syndrome after using tampons made by Johnson & Johnson.

A Defective Product. Toxic shock was first identified in 1978, and the number of reported cases peaked in 1980, then decreased. Studies of Rely and other tampons indicated that certain types of superabsorbing tampons contained cellulose chips that absorbed magnesium, which acted as a nutrient to encourage the growth of *Staphylococcus aureus*. The bacteria, in turn, generated poisonous waste products, which were circulated by the blood. Complaints were brought on behalf of victims who suffered brain damage, gangrene, partial paralysis, and death. The superabsorbing products were removed from the market, and preventive measures educated menstruating women about the safe use of tampons. But lawsuits against manufacturers continued, leaving consumers to ponder the safety of common products.

Sources:
"Tampon Alarm," *U.S. News & World Report* (6 October 1980): 91;
"A Verdict on Tampons," *Time* (29 March 1982): 73.

HEADLINE MAKERS

WILLIAM CASTLE DEVRIES

1943-

ARTIFICIAL-HEART SURGEON

Medical History and National Headlines. Dr. William DeVries and his surgical team at the University of Utah Medical Center made medical history and national headlines on 2 December 1982, when they replaced the diseased heart of Barney Clark with the Jarvik-7, the first permanent artificial heart ever used for a human patient. DeVries was the only surgeon authorized by the federal Food and Drug Administration (FDA) to implant an artificial heart into a human.

A Fateful Lecture. William DeVries was the son of a physician and a nurse. His widowed mother remarried and brought him up in Ogden, Utah. The young DeVries had an early mechanical bent and excelled in sports and his studies. During his first year in medical school at the University of Utah College of Medicine, he attended a lecture by Dutch-born Dr. Willem Kolff, a pioneer of biomedical engineering. Drawn to Kolff's work, DeVries asked him for a position on his research team. When DeVries introduced himself, Kolff replied, "that's a good Dutch name. You're hired!" In his work for Kolff, DeVries performed experimental surgery on the first animal recipients of the artificial heart. DeVries left Utah to do his internship and residency in cardiovascular surgery at Duke University, but returned to Kolff's team in 1979.

The Jarvik-7. When DeVries rejoined the team, he began to use Dr. Robert K. Jarvik's design for a mechanical heart. The Jarvik-7 replaced the ventricles of the human heart. Its pumping action came from compressed air from an electrical unit located outside the patient's body. After many experiments implanting the mechanism into animals, DeVries began the long and hard process of getting the permission required by the FDA to implant the heart into a human patient. After FDA approval in 1982, a panel of six members at the University of Utah Medical Center began reviewing heart patients. The decision made by DeVries, two cardiologists, a psychiatrist, a nurse, and a social worker had to be unanimous. The first patient they chose was sixty-one-year-old Barney Clark. After suffering a series of medical complications closely followed by the news media, Clark died 112 days after his artificial-heart surgery.

Innovative Therapy or Hard-Core Experimentation? Many people expressed philosophical, religious, and practical objections to the artificial-heart program. DeVries felt these slowed his work in Utah, so he left his post for a new position. The second implantation of the device occurred at DeVries's new appointment at the Humana Human Heart Institute International in Louisville, Kentucky. DeVries's patients at Humana also suffered setbacks widely covered by the media. DeVries and the Humana Institute were criticized for publicity seeking. *Life* magazine referred to "the Bill Schroeder Show" in an article about DeVries's second patient who suffered several strokes following implantation. After critics began to charge that the implant substituted mechanical heart disease for human heart disease, DeVries seemed to concede the dilemma when he said, "People always look at artificial hearts as innovative therapy. But the other part is hard-core experimentation. You may exchange one set of complications for another."

An Unusual Eulogy. Doctors do not usually attend their patients' funerals because of an unwritten code about maintaining professional distance, but DeVries attended the funerals of several of his patients, including Barney Clark and Murray Haydon. At the widow's request, DeVries gave the eulogy at Bill Schroeder's funeral. By March 1987, forty-nine Jarvik-7 hearts were implanted by different surgeons in different parts of the world in dying patients as temporary bridges to transplantation. In January 1988 DeVries was close to performing his fifth artificial-heart transplant when a human donor heart was found for the patient. In January 1990 the FDA withdrew its approval of the Jarvik-7, ending the innovative program.

Sources:
The Schroeder Family with Martha Barnette, *The Bill Schroeder Story* (New York: Morrow, 1987);

Jeff Wheelright, Donna E. Haupt, and William Strode, "Bill's Heart; the Troubling Story Behind a Historic Experiment," *Life* (May 1985): 33+.

ROBERT C. GALLO

1937-

AIDS RESEARCHER

The First Human Retrovirus. In May 1984 Dr. Robert C. Gallo's research team at the National Cancer Institute (NCI) claimed to have identified the Human T-cell Lymphotropic Virus (HTLV-III) as the cause of AIDS. Earlier, in the fall of 1981, Kaposi's sarcoma, the strange disease striking the homosexual community, began to interest the National Cancer Institute, part of the National Institutes of Health (NIH), located in Bethesda, Maryland. Gallo, a lively and imaginative young researcher at NCI, previously identified the first human retrovirus in 1978–1979. It was the first time a cancer-causing virus was found in humans. For his pioneering discovery of how these RNA tumor viruses cause cancer, Gallo was awarded the prestigious Albert Lasker Award, often called "America's Nobel Prize," in 1982. Retroviruses were important to the NCI because they can cause severe diseases such as cancer. The rare form of cancer striking the gay community was thought by many scientists possibly to have a viral cause. When Kaposi's sarcoma was identified as a symptom of Acquired Immunodeficiency Syndrome (AIDS), Robert Gallo and his colleagues thought the culprit was a retrovirus. By 1984 they had it identified.

A Family Tragedy Leads to a Medical Career. When Robert Gallo was a thirteen-year-old in Waterbury, Connecticut, his younger sister became ill with leukemia. Although the cancer treatment available to her in the 1950s brought about a temporary remission, she died of the disease. The pathologist who diagnosed his sister's fatal leukemia became Gallo's mentor, fascinating him with stories of the medical world. The experience led to his interest in medical research, rather than patient care. In 1963 he graduated from Jefferson Medical College in Philadelphia. As a medical student he performed experiments involving the growth of red blood cells. The publication of his research led to his career at the National Cancer Institute where he was soon drawn to the growth patterns of leukocytes, or white blood cells. Intrigued by the theory that certain human cancers were triggered by viruses, Gallo began his research on the retroviruses that ultimately led him to his discovery of the AIDS virus. The discovery was a challenging one. It took months to isolate HTLV-III because it disappeared once it killed a cell. But when Gallo's team found a way to mass-produce the virus, they cornered their suspect.

Scientific Rivalry and the Race for the Nobel Prize. Gallo's 1984 announcement came a year after scientists at the Pasteur Institute in Paris, led by Dr. Luc Montagnier, revealed they had identified a differently named virus (lymphadenopathy-associated virus, or LAV) as the cause of AIDS. Gallo's team and the French researchers became involved in one of the most bitter disputes in science over the priority of the discovery. Isolation of the causative agent of an infectious disease is important for many reasons. It helps lead to accurate diagnoses by blood tests, prevention by vaccination, and treatment by chemotherapy. And in the case of the AIDS epidemic, it could lead to a Nobel Prize or other recognition for the researchers and their institutes. The rivalry between the two research groups slowed a comparison of their results. Montagnier told Gallo about his team's discovery in 1983, and scientific materials and information were exchanged. Before he isolated his own HTLV-III, Gallo received samples of LAV from the French labs. At first, Gallo claimed his retrovirus differed from that of the French, but once serological tests, cloning, and gene sequencing were complete, there was no doubt — the viruses were the same. What, then, should be the name for the AIDS virus? LAV, since the French team had been the first to discover it, or HTLV-III? For a brief period, as recommended by the World Health Organization, the virus was known by the tongue-twisting double abbreviation, LAV/HTLV-III. In May 1986 an international commission on naming viruses put an end to the dispute and gave the virus another abbreviation: HIV, for human immunodeficiency virus. In order to compromise, the commission took away the French team's right to name their discovery, but also found fault with the American team, and refused to allow them to affiliate the name of their virus with the HTLV family. In 1986 the Albert and Mary Lasker Foundation gave both Gallo and Montagnier a shared award, noting that both teams had made "unique contributions to the understanding of AIDS."

An Important Test. Many observers felt that the vitriolic dispute was an unseemly distraction from the real task at hand — discovering a solution for AIDS. The isolation of the AIDS virus and the production of large amounts of it resulted in the development of a test to screen blood for antibodies to the virus. The test was important, both to identify individuals with the virus to treat them, but especially to protect the nation's donated blood supply. With an estimated 3 million Americans getting close to 23 million transfusions each year, contaminated blood was a major threat in the spread of the disease. Gallo and his colleagues continued to study the biochemistry of AIDS to find a way to cure its victims and to create a vaccine that could prevent its transmission. But by the decade's end the medical solution to the deadly, slow-acting, mutating virus still remained a scientific mystery.

Sources:

Monty Brower and Michael J. Weiss, "The Medical Sleuth Who Tracked the Cause of AIDS, Now Tries to Find the Cure," *People* (24 September 1984): 49+;

Mirko D. Grmek, *History of AIDS: Emergence and Origin of a Modern Pandemic* (Princeton: Princeton University Press, 1990).

CAROL GILLIGAN

1936-

DEVELOPMENTAL PSYCHOLOGIST

Are Women and Men Different? In 1982 Harvard University psychologist Carol Gilligan published her book In a *Different Voice* and startled a country trying to understand male and female differences. In the early 1980s the prevailing approach to sex differences was to ignore them. Differences implied inequality. But Gilligan's ten years of research convinced her that men and women really were different. They differed in the way they thought, in their sense of values and morality, and in the way they connected with other people. According to Carol Gilligan, "The spirit in which I wrote the book was to raise questions." Her research questioned traditional psychological concepts of human development that had always been drawn on a male model.

Putting Girls and Women on the Map. Carol Gilligan was an associate professor in the Graduate School of Education at Harvard University where she taught adolescent and moral development. Forty-five years old at the time of the publication of her research, she was the wife of a psychiatrist and the mother of three sons. She completed her Ph.D. at Harvard between the birth of her first and second sons, and spent years in what she called women's "kitchen world." As a graduate student in psychology, Gilligan noticed that most theories of human psychological development were based on studies of boys and men. She set out to develop a theory based on the experiences of girls and women. Gilligan "wanted to ask men to listen to women's voices — and to say to women that if men hadn't listened in the past, it wasn't simply a matter of being narrow-minded or biased. They simply didn't know what to do with these voices. They did not fit."

A Different Voice. In 1975 when she was listening to pregnant women considering abortion, Gilligan first heard "the different voice." After researching these "voices" of girls and women, she defined two orientations or systems of moral values. The highest moral value for women was not justice, as it was for men, but care. "Morality for a woman was being responsible to oneself and others; as opposed to doing one's duty, fulfilling one's obligations," she said. Men resolved questions of right or wrong by looking at a broad ruling. Women questioned what was the responsible thing to do, not what was the right thing to do. In the past, the responses of girls to stories of moral choice were often considered wrong. The connection between this past research and the self-effacement typical of girls from puberty on up also interested Gilligan. She concluded that something happened to girls when they were about twelve. The confident eleven-year-old who offered an opinion on a moral dilemma would hold out for her point of view, but the fifteen-year-old would yield. Gilligan suspected that the older girls began to realize that bringing in their own values would make trouble in a world where male values were considered the norm. So the girls started waiting and watching for other people to give them their cues as to what their values should be. For Gilligan, a crucial question for the future was: "How do we get females not to abandon what they know at eleven?"

Toward a New Understanding. Before Gilligan published her studies, researchers sometimes dropped women from their samples because the women's different responses complicated the research. The publication of her landmark work made it much harder for researchers to equate "human" with male or to see female experience as simply an aberration. Gilligan hoped she had pointed the way for other researchers to pick up her research where she had left off. She put women on the map of human development and hoped her ideas about the differences between the sexes would change the way men and women understood themselves. For Gilligan, to label the different voice a female voice was too limiting. "I want to call it a human voice," she said, " both to emphasize for women that they're in touch with the human condition — this is a real contribution to human thought — and to get rid of the phrase, 'as a woman and as a person.'"

Sources:

Carol Gilligan, *In a Different Voice: Psychological Theory and Women's Development* (Cambridge, Mass.: Harvard University Press, 1982);

"Carol Gilligan: When Girls Talk, She Listens," *NEA Today* (September 1990): 9;

Amy Gross, "Thinking Like a Woman," *Vogue* (May 1982): 268+;

Lindsy Van Gelder, "Carol Gilligan: Leader for a Different Kind of Future," *Ms.* (January 1984): 37+.

G. TIMOTHY JOHNSON

1936-

NETWORK DOCTOR

Medicine and the Media. By the 1980s Americans were much more aware of their role as medical consumers. The growing health-industry conglomerates and the uncertainties of medical practice during the 1970s led to the breakdown of traditional barriers between the paternalistic doctor and the passive, unquestioning patient. In the past the physician controlled information and gave it out to his patient as he thought appropriate. But in the 1980s Americans demanded more direct information about medicine. The media responded with such television entertainment offerings as *St. Elsewhere,* which provided viewers with portraits of physicians, diseases, and the "medical crisis of the week." Many networks, aware that health information was a high priority with their viewers, also looked for charismatic and articulate medical sources. One of these was the ABC's Dr. Tim Johnson.

Communicating Medical Information. Tim Johnson was born and grew up in Illinois where he was first attracted to the ministry and graduated with honors at Chicago's North Park Seminary. After a stint as a college admissions officer, Johnson applied to medical school, graduating summa cum laude from Albany Medical College in New York. He came to Massachusetts to practice medicine in the early 1970s, and as sometimes happens with unexpected twists of fate, was drawn into the world of television. Dr. John Knowles, then the head of the Massachusetts General Hospital, was also one of the founding stockholders of Boston Broadcasters, which took over the local ABC affiliate television station. Knowles asked Johnson to host a local half-hour morning television talk show that allowed viewers to call in with their questions. The show soon became so popular that it moved to prime time. In the mid 1970s Johnson became nationally known when *Good Morning America* asked him to join them. As he became a familiar figure on *Good Morning America, World News Tonight,* and *20/20,* Johnson found himself increasingly divided between the medical profession and broadcasting. In 1984 he stopped actively practicing medicine to devote himself full-time to communicating information to medical consumers over national television.

The Unexpected Challenges of Television Medicine. Making "house calls" via television presented Johnson with some unexpected challenges. Television looked to Johnson for "sound bites"; simple, direct, and conclusive statements; and an authoritative presence. But scientific medicine insists that there are no final truths, and simple answers are even rarer. Conflicts arose from the medical profession, which saw medicine differently than did the media. Johnson found himself caught in the middle. As the medical editor for a major network, he had to mediate the complexities of medical information and television's need to present programs that would attract viewers.

A Fateful Prediction. When Johnson first began broadcasting in the 1970s, he felt a need to learn more about public health. In 1976 he received his Master of Public Health degree from the Harvard School of Public Health. As one of the nation's most recognizable public-health doctors, he considered himself to be privileged to be able to communicate both medical news and medical and health information over a major television network. One of his more memorable experiences in reporting medical breakthroughs came in the early 1980s. To get information for his broadcasts, Johnson pored over such medical statistics as the Centers for Disease Control's weekly morbidity and mortality reports, where he noticed

a report of unusual cases of cancer occurring among gay men in California. That week Johnson appeared on *Good Morning America* and reported on a new and unusual form of disease that should be a worry for gay men. He suggested it looked "ominous" and might be a "cause for alarm." A Boston newspaper columnist heard his report and wrote a critical editorial suggesting Johnson had overreacted. When it became apparent that the cancer, Kaposi's sarcoma, was indeed a cause for alarm, representing as it did the first wave of the AIDS epidemic, the columnist publicly recanted and admitted he was wrong. For Johnson, the bottom line was keeping medical science and responsible reporting in perspective. His careful reporting and reassuring manner made him a major source of medical news for many Americans.

Sources:

G. Timothy Johnson, "Media," *Journal of the American Medical Association* (23 October 1987): 2303–2304;

Johnson, "Sounding Board. Restoring Trust Between Patient and Doctor," *New England Journal of Medicine* (18 January 1990): 195–197.

CHARLES EVERETT KOOP

1916-

SURGEON GENERAL

The Nation's Family Doctor. C. Everett Koop always knew he would grow up to be a surgeon. As a teenager in Brooklyn, he pretended to be a medical student so he could sneak into hospitals and watch operations. Koop was a renowned pediatric surgeon, known for his successes in separating Siamese twins and in surgical procedures for dealing with formerly fatal birth defects. He played a major role in stopping the 1950s practice of X-raying children's feet in shoe stores, which exposed children to harmful radiation. In the fall of 1981 he became President Reagan's surgeon general of the United States, the nation's leading spokesman on public-health issues. As a passionate evangelical Christian and foe of abortion, he became during his confirmation hearings the target of those who felt his conservative perspective made him the wrong man for the post. But by the time he resigned his post in July 1989, Dr. C. Everett Koop stood out as a model of integrity and courage in public office. He confounded everyone's expectations as he put aside his own personal beliefs and Reagan-administration policy on medicine and health and acted in the best medical interests of the American people.

The Confirmation Controversy. When Koop was first named in February 1981 as deputy assistant secretary for health in the Department of Health and Human Services, it was widely believed he and Reagan agreed on issues such as abortion. Koop's surgeon general nomination created tremendous controversy, not so much over

Koop himself as over the abortion issue. Even the American Public Health Association opposed him, as it had never done his predecessors, criticizing him for his lack of public-health experience. Massachusetts senator Edward M. Kennedy criticized Koop, charging that his concept of the role of women was based on "cruel, outdated, and patronizing stereotypes." When Koop was confirmed after an unprecedented nine-month battle, his new post was technically limited in scope, with no real authority, little staff, and almost no formal responsibilities. His chief duties included reporting on public-health issues and advising the White House on health policy. But Koop became one of the nation's most famous surgeon generals and a most influential and admired member of President Reagan's administration with his stance on many major public-health issues.

Smoking. Koop pledged that he would not use his position as "a pulpit for ideology," and pointed out that he did not always agree with the Reagan administration. He stirred up his first controversy in February 1982 with his strong stand against smoking, "the most important public-health issue of our time," linking it scientifically to some 30 percent of all cancer deaths. His "Smoke-Free Society" campaign during his tenure as surgeon general ruffled the Reagan administration and the strong tobacco lobby, but by the end of his term the percentage of U.S. smokers had dropped from one-third to one-quarter of the adult population, with much of that drop because of Koop's efforts.

AIDS. Although AIDS was a subject of national concern by the mid 1980s, the president remained silent on the subject. By 1986, as public pressure mounted, Reagan ordered his surgeon general to prepare a report. For the next two years Koop focused on the crisis: "I realized that if ever there was a disease made for a Surgeon General, it was AIDS." The country was panicked, and ill-founded rumors and incorrect information about the disease and its transmission were widespread. Once again, Koop stunned his president and his fellow citizens by his willingness to focus on the nation's health rather than the perspective of the administration. His report clarified the nature of the disease and told people how they could protect themselves. He spoke graphically and candidly about safe and unsafe sex practices. He used and publicized the taboo "C word" — condoms — and, disregarding Reagan-administration policy entirely, he argued for intensive sex education in the schools, beginning in the third grade. Over the strong objections of the White House, Congress approved a shortened version of Koop's report, which in May 1988 was sent to every American household.

Abortion. His public-awareness campaign was successful, but his stance was one of many that turned his conservative allies against him. Opposition mounted when Reagan asked him to write a report on the health effects of abortion on women. Koop was certain there would not be enough unbiased scientific evidence to support the White House's assumption that abortions damaged women's health. He delivered his opinion to newly elected George Bush in January 1989. Conservatives turned their backs on him, and Koop realized that the Bush White House wanted him gone. But after his July resignation, Koop found he had earned the liking and respect of the American people. He became a fixture on television, passing along important health information in news broadcasts and other media. The nation's family doctor had become the health conscience of America.

Sources:

Anne Bianchi, *C. Everett Koop: The Health of the Nation* (Brookfield, Conn.: Millbrook Press, 1992);

C. Everett Koop, *Koop: The Memoirs of America's Family Doctor* (New York: Random House, 1991).

SUSAN M. LOVE

1948-

SURGEON

A Major Killer. "More women have died of breast cancer than people died in the Vietnam war," according to Dr. Susan M. Love. "Every four minutes a woman is diagnosed with it, and every twelve minutes a woman dies of it." Trained in Boston to be a general surgeon, Love became one of the most visible experts in the nation on breast cancer, a disease that affected one in ten American women and claimed 42,000 lives in 1988. Television viewers saw her on the PBS science program *NOVA* and on an ABC *Nightline* program about breast cancer. Breast cancer was a disease greatly feared by American women, and with her down-to-earth and forthright manner, Love provided a reassuring voice. She became famous for educating American women about their choices for cancer treatment as well as for her skill in performing surgery. A controversial figure in her field, Love was also well known for her views that were contrary to what many doctors advocated for treating breast cancer.

A Fascination with Science and Religion. The oldest of five children, Susan Love grew up in Puerto Rico and Mexico and attended Catholic schools run by the Sisters of Notre Dame. One of her junior-high schoolteachers became her mentor in her biology class and began her involvement in science. During her high-school years in Mexico City, Love was involved in National Science Foundation summer programs in Connecticut and New York. After two years at a women's college, Notre Dame of Baltimore, Love was drawn to the religious life of her teachers. She entered the Order of Notre Dame, hoping to become a nun "to do good works," and enrolled at Fordham University as a premed student. "It was the '60s, and we were all being relevant in one way or another," she pointed out. But six months after she became a postulant, she left the order after a consultation with her mentor convinced her that it "was the right thing to do."

Medical School. In the late 1960s when she applied to medical school, Susan Love ran into discrimination and the quota system for women applicants. At that time, many medical schools only admitted enough women to make up 5 percent of their classes. After applying to several East Coast schools, she was accepted at SUNY Downstate Medical College in Brooklyn, one of the 10 percent of the college admissions allotted to women that year. Since "all the women did well because we had to be better than the men to get in in the first place," Love graduated among the top five — all women — in her class of 225. When she began her surgical practice after a grueling five years of surgical residency at Beth Israel Hospital in Boston, doctors began sending her breast-cancer patients since she was a woman surgeon. In 1981 she was appointed as surgical oncologist for the Dana Farber Cancer Institute Breast Evaluation Center. In 1988 the Faulkner Hospital offered her an appointment, and she set up a breast-cancer clinic run and staffed almost entirely by women.

A Feminist Physician. A good part of Love's fame lay in her criticism of the traditional treatment of breast cancer, which used major surgery, radiation, and chemotherapy. Love called this "slash, burn, and poison." In the 1980s controversies arose in the medical community over this treatment. In 1985 the *New England Journal of Medicine* published a study suggesting that simple removal of a woman's malignant breast lump and radiation treatment was as effective as the removal of her entire breast in treating early breast cancer. But many members of the medical community were slow to respond to this technique. Looking at the data from a feminist perspective, Love believed that lumpectomy along with other therapies was as effective as a total mastectomy. Her strongly worded criticisms of the medical establishment, whom she derided as "the boys," did not endear her to them, but her women patients found her comforting, safe, and reassuring. She placed a higher value on her role as a popular educator, rather than as an academic educator, since she felt that most women got their medical information from the media. Love believed her job was to be an educator, to teach her women cancer patients what they needed to make a choice about their cancer treatment. She authored a popular book, *Dr. Susan Love's Breast Book;* continued to educate the medical profession, collaborating with other surgeons on a breast-surgery textbook; and comforted her patients, telling them, "Surgery is a lot of ritual and a little science."

Sources:

Anita Diamant, "The Passion of Dr. Love," *Boston Magazine* (October 1988): 163+;

Elizabeth Gleick, "A Surgeon Crusades Against Breast Cancer," *People* (25 July 1994): 147+;

Susan M. Love with Karen Lindsey, *Dr. Susan Love's Breast Book* (Reading, Mass.: Addison-Wesley, 1990).

BERNARD LOWN

1921-

INTERNATIONAL PHYSICIANS FOR THE PREVENTION OF NUCLEAR WAR

Nobel Peace Prize Winners. The two cardiologists, Bernard Lown and Yevgeny Chazov, saw it as a straightforward procedure: clog the arteries of support for nuclear weaponry until the heart of the atomic arms race stopped beating. Although the operation was not yet fully completed, in 1985 the Nobel Peace Prize was awarded to International Physicians for the Prevention of Nuclear War (IPPNW), a worldwide federation of medical doctors and health professionals founded in 1980. Its founders and copresidents, Lown, a professor of cardiology at the Harvard School of Public Health in Massachusetts, and Chazov, director general of the Cardiology Research Center in Moscow, first bumped into each other in an elevator in New Delhi in 1960. Soon they began corresponding about medical matters and visited each other's medical facilities. In 1961 Lown became interested in the medical aspects of nuclear war and invited eight doctors to his home after he heard a speech about the nuclear arms race and the dangers of atomic conflict given by Nobel Peace Prize laureate Philip Noel-Baker. Shortly afterward, he cofounded Physicians for Social Responsibility and served as its first president. Physicians for Social Responsibility produced articles, talks, and forums on the medical effects of nuclear war. It later became one of the major affiliates of IPPNW.

An International Peace Movement. In 1979 Lown proposed to Chazov that they organize an international movement of physicians against the nuclear arms race as part of their professional duty to "address the greatest threat to human life." By 1985 the federation, sometimes popularly called Doctors Against Nuclear War, had more than 135,000 members in forty-one countries, with headquarters in Boston and London. The Norwegian Nobel Committee praised the group for performing "a considerable service to mankind by spreading authoritative information and by creating an awareness of the catastrophic consequences of atomic warfare." The prize was the first ever for an East-West citizens' group for the umbrella organization for the affiliated groups of doctors, nurses, and other health workers. Lown believed it was not an accident that the prize was announced just six weeks before the Reagan-Gorbachev summit in Geneva.

A Different Drummer. Lown, born in Utena, Lithuania, on 7 June 1921, had, in the words of one colleague, "always marched to a slightly different drummer." He fled Lithuania at fourteen when his father brought him to Lewiston, Maine. A Jew, he believed he was turned down by Harvard, Chicago, and other medical schools because "it was the '40s and they had their Jewish quota filled." He was accepted at Johns Hopkins University in Baltimore and got his medical degree in 1943. He briefly served in World War II as a first lieutenant, but was mustered out of the Korean War on an "undesirable" discharge — later changed to "honorable" — because he found himself caught up in the McCarthy era. A self-admitted "maverick," Lown refused to sign an organization-affiliation statement, fearing that earlier attendance at a Yale Marxist study group might be used against him. During his two-year blacklist from significant medical employment, he wrote a classic treatise on digitalis drugs in the treatment of heart disease. "I feel proud," he said, "that in many ways I didn't compromise my beliefs." Lown, Chazov, and other IPPNW members planned to use their $225,000 Nobel Prize money to continue worldwide lecture tours for its member physicians. "We take the position that we should not spread the arms race into space," said Lown.

Sources:

Ron Arias, "A Soviet Doctor and a Boston Cardiologist Celebrate Their Group's Nobel Peace Prize," *People* (28 October 1985): 59–60;

"Peace: Two from the Heart," *Science News* (19 October 1985): 246.

STEVEN A. ROSENBERG

1940-

CANCER RESEARCHER

A Headline-Making Discovery. Science has two principal stages of discovery. First is the dramatic, headline-making, often controversial revelation of an important new or preliminary discovery. In 1985 National Cancer Institute (NCI) surgeon Dr. Steven A. Rosenberg stirred national attention when he reported that eleven of twenty-five cancer patients improved dramatically after treatments involving interleukin-2 (IL-2), a genetically engineered hormone. This "adoptive immunotherapy" activated the body's natural immune system of white blood cells to fight cancerous tumors. The second stage of scientific discovery comes after more extensive clinical testing justifies the earlier excitement.

A Cancer Breakthrough? In 1985 cancer killed 462,000 Americans. The American public took its first notice of Rosenberg in July 1985 when the NCI specialist announced, "The President has cancer." As a member of the team that operated on President Reagan's cancerous colon, Rosenberg explained the procedure to the public and won high marks for his cool, careful explanations. In early December Rosenberg emerged with news of an exciting approach to cancer treatment, and the switchboards at the NCI nearly melted from phone calls as dying patients around the country deluged their physicians and the NCI with demands for the treatment. But some of Rosenberg's colleagues in the cancer war were

dubious about his first stage of discovery, and claimed that IL-2 didn't live up to its press notices. Rosenberg characterized his work as experimental therapy, but it received so much publicity as a medical "breakthrough" that a critical backlash followed. In an unusually harsh editorial in the *Journal of the American Medical Association*, a Mayo Clinic physician declared that Rosenberg had inappropriately described his IL-2 results as a "breakthrough" and charged that the treatment caused "devastating toxic reactions," including jaundice, low blood pressure, and anemia. Again IL-2 hit the news.

The Road to Immunotherapy. The media's medical superstar was born in the Bronx, the youngest child of Jewish immigrants from Poland who owned a luncheonette. Rosenberg couldn't "remember a day when I didn't want to be a doctor." His elder brother Jerry was his role model, and when Jerry was in medical school, Steve read his big brother's medical textbooks. Rosenberg went to the well-known "mother of scientists," the Bronx High School of Science, and earned his M.D. in a special program at Johns Hopkins University in Baltimore in 1963 after six years of study instead of the usual eight. He added a Ph.D. in biophysics from Harvard. When he was a young surgeon in training at Harvard, a sixty-three-year-old man checked in to the Veterans Administration hospital in Roxbury. Rosenberg was astonished when he read his patient's medical history. Twelve years earlier, the same man was found to have a stomach tumor the size of his fist, with extensive spread of the cancer to his lymph nodes and liver. The doctors cut the tumor out of his stomach, but they thought he was a hopeless case and sent him home to die. Yet there he was, twelve years later, alive and well except for his gallstones. Rosenberg was fascinated with his first case of a truly spontaneous remission of cancer. This marked the beginning of his career aimed at proving a long-held and intriguing theory — that the immune system could be enlisted to rid the body of cancer. Rosenberg joined the National Cancer Institute in Bethesda, Maryland, in 1970 as a clinical associate in immunology. Four years later he was named chief of surgery to oversee an eighty-member surgical department and an immunotherapy team.

The Second Stage of Research. Even after some researchers thought that the potential of IL-2 had been blown out of all proportion, Rosenberg continued to work with it, and the National Cancer Institute approved additional trials of IL-2. "Desperate diseases demand desperate responses," Rosenberg said. Entering the second stage of scientific research and discovery — more clinical testing and a refinement of IL-2 using TIL (tumor-infiltrating lymphocytes) to verify his earlier work — Rosenberg and his team reported some successes. Adding a third ingredient — the immunosuppressant cyclophosphamide — to TIL and IL-2 resulted in the long-term cure of all Rosenberg's cancerous laboratory mice. The mechanisms were only beginning to be understood, and there were still many questions about the toxicity of IL-2. But Rosenberg believed that the side effects could be medically managed. At the same time, his colleagues in oncology were cautious. When all the research was added up, it revealed a few amazing successes, a reasonable number of partial remissions, and many failures. More than 650 patients had been treated with one form of adoptive immunotherapy or another by 1989. Some 20 percent had responded. Rosenberg had the first real evidence that immunotherapy worked in humans. There was still a long way to go, but for Rosenberg it was one step more in a long journey.

Sources:

Jerry Adler, Mary Hager, and Diane Weathers, "The Rise of a Superstar," *Newsweek* (16 December 1985): 63;

"Cancer: Backlash Against a 'Breakthrough,'" *Newsweek* (22 December 1986): 57;

Barbara J. Culliton, "Fighting Cancer with Designer Cells," *Science* (23 June 1989): 1430–1433;

"Steven Rosenberg," *People* (23 December 1985): 46–47.

(KAROLA) RUTH WESTHEIMER

1928-

MEDIA THERAPIST

Success Story. Known to her public simply as "Dr. Ruth," the New York psychologist, broadcaster, and writer Dr. Ruth Westheimer became known for giving out sexual advice "like good hot chicken soup" to Americans in the 1980s. Orphaned by the Third Reich when her German-Jewish family perished after sending her to safety in Switzerland, she immigrated to Palestine where she became a fervent Zionist and member of the Haganah, the Jewish underground movement. The tiny woman, only four feet seven inches tall, briefly married a young Israeli soldier, and the couple moved to Paris where she earned a degree in psychology from the Sorbonne. In 1956 Dr. Ruth moved to New York with her second husband. After this marriage ended, she supported herself and her young daughter by working as a maid while she learned English and earned a master's degree at the New School for Social Research. After meeting her third husband on a ski trip to the Catskills, she earned her doctorate in education at Columbia University.

Media Celebrity. Dr. Ruth learned about sex early when she sneaked into her father's library to read his hidden marriage manual. At Columbia she studied family counseling and sex counseling, and her big break came in 1977 when she gave a lecture to a group of New York broadcasters about the need for more broadcast programs to promote "sexual literacy." Contacts at this lecture evolved into a phenomenally popular two-hour syndicated radio talk show called *Sexually Speaking*, a cable television show, *The Dr. Ruth Show*, several best-selling books, and celebrity status throughout the country.

"Grandma Freud." Dr. Ruth's accent, witty humor, eccentric style, and commonsense advice made her enormously popular with the American public. On a typical night four thousand callers jammed the radio station's switchboards, and her talk show became the top-rated radio show in the New York City area in 1983. She stirred controversy with both political and religious leaders because of her frank answers about homosexuality, sex education, and contraception. Her ability to say anything and get away with it gave her both detractors and admirers. Critics warned she verged on entertainment rather than psychology and accused her of being frivolous and irresponsible. Her admirers praised her conviction and "knack of translating new technological information about sex into sound practical advice." A firm believer in traditional marriage and family, her enthusiasm for her work also kept her in her active private practice as a psychologist and family counselor.

Spicy Advice and the Ratings. To her loyal followers who counted on her, no question was too outrageous and no problem was insoluble. When a caller asked what to do about his girlfriend who had given him an inflatable love doll and "wants to watch," Dr. Ruth fired back, "Give the doll a name and have a good time." Concern about instant advice to unseen callers prompted the American Psychiatric Association to caution the growing ranks of media therapists against providing actual therapy or trying to solve a problem conclusively over the air. But Dr. Ruth's spicy advice, conventional morality, and upbeat approach continued to help media ratings whether or not they actually helped the nation's sexual psyche.

Sources:

Patricia Bosworth, "Talking with Doctor Goodsex," *Ladies' Home Journal* (February 1986): 82+;

Georgia Dullea, "Therapist to Therapist: Analyzing Dr. Ruth," *New York Times*, 26 October 1987, p. 8B;

George Hackett, "Talking Sex with Dr. Ruth," *Newsweek* (3 May 1982): 78.

RYAN WHITE

1971-1990

AIDS VICTIM

A Terrible Diagnosis. For most sufferers, an AIDS diagnosis was a death sentence. Most AIDS patients died within two years of their diagnosis. Some patients who tested positive for HIV were able to live for years without symptoms of active AIDS, but they had to live with the likelihood of an early death as well as disabling medical symptoms. Some people had mild symptoms which physicians called ARC, or AIDS-related complex. People with many symptoms had "full-blown AIDS," which required a host of often painful treatments. Compounding the psychological and medical costs of the illness was social rejection and prejudice. Victims had to fear their neighbors, friends, and even their families because of the dread associated with the disease. The initial victims of the epidemic were homosexual men and intravenous drug users. In the beginning of the epidemic, scientists thought only gay men got AIDS, and many Americans came to think of it as "the gay disease." Victims of AIDS often suffered extreme prejudice from homophobes, and many in the public considered AIDS just punishment for what they considered to be deviant sexual behavior. In the background were other victims: the partners of AIDS victims in heterosexual relationships, infants who contracted the disease from their infected mothers, and hemophiliacs and other people who needed blood transfusions and injections of blood products and received HIV-contaminated blood. In the early 1980s popular knowledge of how the disease was transmitted combined scientific evidence, ignorance, mythology, and prejudice. Victims had to contend with discrimination and stigma as well as the ravages of their illness.

A Young AIDS Victim. In 1984 hemophiliac Ryan White was looking forward to turning into "a typical obnoxious teenager" in Kokomo, Indiana, when his physicians discovered that he had contracted AIDS. He got the disease through the tainted blood products he was given for his hemophilia. As the word of his illness began to spread around his church and neighborhood, Ryan soon knew that AIDS would be even harder to live with than hemophilia. When the family went to church, parishioners watched the family warily, and they were asked to sit either in the first or the last pew, so everyone would know where they were at all times. Homophobic jokes about Ryan made the rounds at his school, but the worst

came in late July 1985, when officials at the school denied him the right to return that fall. The school claimed it needed guidelines from the state Board of Health for handling children with AIDS, and there were none. Ryan White and his family went to court, where they had to fight not only the angry, fearful school district but the whole community. His legal battle made headlines all over the world; but although he won his battle to return to school, his problems were not over.

Making AIDS a Disease, Not a Dirty Word. After a bullet was fired into the Whites' home and they were shunned at their church, the family moved to Cicero, Indiana. Ryan began to speak out about the ignorance and misconceptions of the disease and spoke of the sufferings of its victims. In Cicero, Ryan's new school made an effort to step up its AIDS-education program, and the president of the student body at his high school came by to welcome him, telling him, "No one is planning on treating you badly. We just want to be normal." Throughout the decade Ryan White and his family kept up their campaign against ignorance and fear. He appeared at schools and fund-raisers across the country and testified before the President's Commission on AIDS. He appeared on national television programs, and celebrities such as Elizabeth Taylor, Elton John, and Michael Jackson became his friends. Ryan became a celebrity, too, to his chagrin, because "it's creepy to be famous because you're sick." A film of his life and struggle, *The Ryan White Story*, was made in 1988, and his life changed for the better. Before his death on 8 April 1990 at the age of eighteen, Ryan White knew he was good at something besides being sick. He had made a major contribution in his effort to "make AIDS a disease — not a dirty word."

Source:
Ryan White and Ann Marie Cunningham, *Ryan White: My Own Story* (New York: Dial, 1991).

PEOPLE IN THE NEWS

On 21 March 1981 **Drs. Benjamin Aaron** and **Joseph Giordano** of the George Washington University Hospital in Washington, D.C., performed two hours of surgery on President **Ronald Reagan** to remove a bullet from his left lung after he was shot in the chest in an assassination attempt.

On 20 September 1984 former heavyweight boxing champion **Muhammad Ali** was revealed to be suffering from Parkinson's syndrome, renewing the debate over the safety of boxing because doctors theorized that repeated blows to the head could damage brain cells, bringing on Parkinson's syndrome.

On 5 January 1986 **Donna Ashland,** a fourteen-year-old California girl who suffered from cardiomyopathy, a degeneration of the heart muscle, received a heart transplant from her fifteen-year-old boyfriend, **Felipe Garcia.** Garcia, who died after a blood vessel burst in his brain, had earlier told his mother of his premonition of his impending death and his wish for his girlfriend to receive his heart.

Education Secretary **William Bennett** released a handbook for teachers and parents on 6 October 1987, urging them to promote abstinence as the best way for young people to avoid AIDS.

The Supreme Court of Connecticut ruled on 3 June 1982 that **Dr. Anthony P. Borelli** must bear the child-rearing costs for the child of a woman on whom he had unsuccessfully performed a sterilizing operation.

On 23 March 1980 **Dr. Joseph Boutwell,** deputy director of the U.S. Centers for Disease Control, reported that as many as 14 percent of medical laboratory tests were inaccurate.

On 7 November 1985 **Dr. Otis R. Bowen** was nominated by President Reagan to succeed **Margaret M. Heckler** as health and human services secretary.

On 18 March 1987 the National Institute of Mental Health accused **Stephen E. Breuning,** a prominent researcher of mental retardation, of fabricating many of his results and of being "knowingly, willfully, and repeatedly, engaged in misleading and deceptive practices."

Joyce Brown, a forty-year-old former secretary who became a test case for a New York City policy of forcibly hospitalizing the mentally ill homeless, was released from Bellevue Hospital on 19 January 1988, after it was ruled that she could not be given antipsychotic medication against her will.

Dr. John F. Burke and researchers from the Massachusetts Institute of Technology developed an artificial skin to use in treating burn victims, announced on 24 April 1981.

On 2 January 1980 **President Jimmy Carter** vetoed a bill requiring the Department of Health, Education, and Welfare to conduct a study of the health effects of dioxins, the chemicals used in Agent Orange, a defoliant widely used during the Vietnam War and blamed by some vets for causing health problems. Carter supported investigative efforts but felt the bill contained an unconstitutional infringement by Congress on presidential power.

Lillian Carter, President Carter's eighty-two-year-old mother, underwent surgery for a hip fracture after slipping on a rug in her home on 2 October 1980.

On 9 February 1986 a Phoenix, Arizona, woman, **Bernadette Chayrez,** became the first person known to have received a second artificial heart, in surgery performed at the University of Arizona Medical Center in Tucson.

On 2 December 1982 **Barney B. Clark,** a sixty-one-year-old retired dentist, received the first permanent artificial heart, the Jarvik-7, in surgery in Salt Lake City, Utah. Clark died 112 days after surgery, on 23 March 1983.

On 24 July 1981 the FDA criticized **Dr. Denton Cooley**'s use of an artificial-heart device that had not been approved by the agency for human use.

Dr. James Curran, director of the AIDS program at the Centers for Disease Control, said on 12 June 1986: "We recognize now that the disease is transmitted through heterosexual contact as well as homosexual contact. This is a problem that all people have to be concerned about."

On 11 November 1982 **Nan Davis,** a twenty-two-year-old woman who had been paralyzed, managed to walk a few steps with the aid of a "computerized electrical stimulation and feedback system" using brief bursts of electricity to stimulate major muscle groups in her paralyzed legs.

Dr. Charles W. Denko reported on 4 June 1981 that his studies showed that arthritis sufferers produced lower than normal endorphins, a naturally occurring pain-killer, thus making the arthritic pain more intense for disease victims.

On 23 November 1981 **Robert P. Diaz,** a California male hospital nurse, was charged with murdering twelve elderly patients by administering lethal overdoses of a drug that caused fatal heart attacks.

On 29 August 1985 **Michael Drummond,** twenty-five, became the youngest recipient of a permanent artificial heart in a Tucson, Arizona, operation

San Francisco mayor **Dianne Feinstein** signed a landmark law regulating smoking in the workplace on 3 June 1983.

On 23 November 1988 **Dr. Shevert H. Frazier,** a prominent psychiatry professor at Harvard Medical School in Boston, resigned after admitting to plagiarism in papers he had written.

Drs. Nancy Gutensohn and Philip Cole reported on 15 January 1981 that their study linked Hodgkin's disease, an often fatal lymph cancer, to common viral infections.

On 22 May 1980 **Dr. Dale E. Hammerschmidt,** a University of Minnesota Medical School researcher, reported that a tree fungus common in Chinese cooking might curb heart disease.

On 22 July 1985 **Dr. Michael R. Harrison** headed a surgical team that partly removed a twenty-three-week-old fetus from its mother's womb, operated on it to correct a blocked urinary tract, and then returned it to the uterus; nine weeks later the baby boy was born in good condition.

Donald Harvey, a thirty-five-year-old Ohio resident, pleaded guilty on 18 August 1987 to killing twenty-one patients during the time he worked as an orderly in a Cincinnati hospital.

On 12 February 1986 **Dr. William A. Haseltine** reported that the AIDS virus reproduced itself by stepping up the production of protein by messenger RNA by as much as one thousand times.

On 17 February 1985 **Murray P. Haydon,** a fifty-eight-year-old retired auto worker, received a permanent artificial heart, the Jarvik-7, in the third operation of its kind.

On 12 January 1983 **Margaret M. Heckler** was named secretary of health and human services by President Reagan.

Margaret M. Heckler on 14 June 1983 quoted the Reagan administration's view that "for the over-whelming majority of Americans, there appears to be little or no risk of falling victim to [AIDS], in particular, through normal, daily social contacts," and said that concerns the disease was increasingly affecting the general population were not founded on facts.

On 16 October 1987 **Paul Holc** became the world's youngest heart transplant patient, undergoing surgery two and a half hours after his birth by caesarean section, in Loma Linda University Medical Center in California.

On 20 February 1987 **Dr. Peter H. St. George Hyslop** identified a small area of chromosome 21 that appeared to contain the gene causing familial Alzheimer's disease, the inherited form that accounted for at least 10 percent of all cases of the disease.

"Baby Jesse," a sixteen-day-old infant, received a new heart in a transplant operation on 10 June 1986, at Loma Linda University Medical Center in California; the hospital had caused a national stir by first turning down the child, reportedly because of the unstable home situation of the child's unmarried parents.

Kenneth K. Kidd, a Yale University geneticist, reported on 5 January 1980 that stuttering, a problem for 100,000 to 200,000 Americans, was linked to genetic factors, contradicting a long-held belief that it was caused by psychological or emotional factors.

On 11 February 1989 a comatose New York woman, **Nancy Klein,** thirty-two, underwent an abortion following a two-week court battle between her husband and antiabortion activists in an attempt to increase her chances of survival.

On 7 January 1988 New York City mayor **Edward I. Koch** signed a comprehensive antismoking law banning smoking in many retail stores and other public establishments.

C. Everett Koop released a report on 27 July 1988 calling on Americans to cut the amount of fat to 30 percent in their diets, saying dietary fat was a major health problem.

On 27 March 1984 **Gov. Richard D. Lamm** of Colorado drew sharp criticism after his statement that terminally ill people had a "duty to die and get out of the way."

On 13 March 1981 murder charges were dropped against **Dr. Raymond L. LaScola** because of the suspicion of perjured testimony by a witness after the physician was charged with the insulin-injection slaying of an eighty-nine-year-old woman who had legally adopted him and made him the sole heir to her estate.

Dr. Claude Lenfant, director of the National Heart, Lung, and Blood Institute, questioned the artificial-heart surgery program on 25 April 1985.

On 19 December 1985 **Mary Lund** became the first woman to receive a permanent artificial heart in Minneapolis.

Cindy Martin, twenty-six, became the world's first recipient of a transplanted heart, liver, and kidney, in surgery performed by **Dr. Thomas Starzl** and **Dr. John Armitage** in Pittsburgh on 3 December 1989.

On 7 March 1988 pioneer sex researchers and therapists **Dr. William H. Masters** and **Virginia E. Johnson** challenged the prevailing notion that the AIDS threat to heterosexuals was small.

On 4 January 1980 **Dr. Mary B. Meyer** of the Johns Hopkins School of Hygiene and Public Health and **Dr. Kenneth Jones** of the University Hospital of San Diego said heavy smoking and drinking during pregnancy caused spontaneous miscarriages, stillbirths, and as many as 35 percent of premature births in the United States.

Dr. Donald Miller, assistant director of the U.S. Centers for Disease Control, reported on 19 January 1980 that few changes were expected in the human life span in the next twenty years because the leading killers were no longer infectious diseases, but chronic illnesses, accidents, and violence. Any future gains in life expectancy would have to occur through changes in habits and lifestyles.

Consumer advocate **Ralph Nader** urged the Federal Trade Commission to require health warnings on packages of chewing tobacco and snuff on 14 February 1984.

On 9 May 1988 **Stella Nickell,** forty-four, was convicted of killing her husband and another person in the nation's first death-by-product-tampering trial; she laced Excedrin capsules with cyanide.

Drs. Roy Patterson and **Stephen Hendrix** of the Northwestern University Medical School reported on 23 March 1980 a major breakthrough in the treatment of hay fever sufferers that would immunize them in fifteen weeks instead of the current three to four years.

First Lady Nancy Reagan underwent surgery on 17 October 1987 to remove her left breast after a biopsy had revealed cancer.

On 23 June 1983 **President Reagan**'s weekly radio address asked for organ donations; more than five thousand people in forty-seven states responded.

On 13 July 1985 **President Reagan** had a cancerous growth removed from his large intestine.

On 30 July 1985, only two weeks after intestinal cancer surgery, **President Reagan** had a cancerous skin patch removed from his nose. **First Lady Nancy Reagan** at first denied reports of the nature of the lesion.

President Reagan announced on 12 February 1987 that he would propose legislation to help expand the Medicare system to help cover the costs of catastrophic illness.

On 31 May 1987 **President Reagan** called for "routine" AIDS testing of marriage-license applicants and of individuals seeking treatment for drug abuse or sexually transmitted diseases.

U.S. Surgeon General **Dr. Julius Richmond** said on 14 January 1980 that lung cancer among women was rapidly increasing and within three years could become the leading cancer killer of women.

Dr. Darrell Rigel of New York University reported on 7 March 1985 that severe sunburns in childhood appeared to increase the risk of adults developing malignant melanomas of the skin.

On 23 June 1982 Health and Human Services secretary **Richard S. Schweiker** proposed changes in the Food and Drug Administration's procedure for approving new drugs, including reduction of paperwork and time needed for approval.

Allyssa Smith, twenty-one months, became the first U.S. recipient of a liver transplant from a living donor when she received a section of her mother's liver in surgery in Chicago on 27 November 1989.

Dr. Thomas E. Starzl reported in the 30 July 1981 *New England Journal of Medicine* that a fungus-derived drug called cyclosporine-A was successfully used in liver-transplant patients to avoid rejection of the new organ.

On 21 September 1987 Illinois governor **James R. Thompson** signed into law a broad range of bills aimed at fighting AIDS, becoming the first U.S. governor to approve sweeping AIDS legislation.

On 4 September 1986 former Democratic senator from Massachusetts **Paul Tsongas** underwent a bone-marrow transplant; Tsongas had decided not to run for reelection in 1984 after learning he had a form of cancer known as non-Hodgkin's lymphoma.

On 26 August 1985 **Ryan White** of Kokomo, Indiana, began his school year with lessons over the telephone when local authorities barred the thirteen-year-old AIDS victim from classes.

On 21 September 1989 **Judge W. Dale Young** awarded custody of seven frozen embryos to a divorced woman, **Mary Sue Davis,** in a decision likely to impact the abortion debate because Young ruled life began at conception.

AWARDS

NOBEL PRIZE WINNERS IN MEDICINE OR PHYSIOLOGY

1980

Baruj Benacerraf (United States, born in Venezuela), **George Snell** (United States), and **Jean Dausset** (France) for their studies of antigens, the protein-carbohydrate complexes found on every cell membrane of the body, leading to the development of rules for the transplantability of human organs, explanations of the body's immunology system, and development of transplant immunology.

1981

David H. Hubel (Canadian-born American) and **Torsten Wiesel** (Sweden) for their discoveries concerning information processing in the visual system; and **Roger W. Sperry** (United States) for his discovery concerning the functional specialization of the cerebral hemispheres of the brain.

1982

Sune Bergström (Sweden), **Bengt Samuelsson** (Sweden), and **John R. Vane** (Great Britain) for their discoveries concerning prostaglandin and related biologically active substances.

1983

Barbara McClintock (United States) for her discovery of transposable genetic systems.

1984

Niels K. Jerne, (Britain and Denmark), **Georges Köhler,** (Germany), and **César Milstein** (Argentina) for their discovery and development of principles for production of monoclonal antibodies by the hybridoma technique.

1985

Michael S. Brown (United States) and **Joseph L. Goldstein** (United States) for their revolutionary discoveries about the regulation of cholesterol metabolism and treatment for disorders of blood cholesterol levels.

1986

Biochemist **Stanley Cohen** (United States) and developmental biologist **Rita Levi-Montalcini** (United States and Italy) for their discovery of cell growth factors.

1987

Susumu Tonegawa (Japan) of the Massachusetts Institute of Technology, a molecular biologist, for the elucidation of the unique capacity of the immune system to produce an enormous diversity of antibodies.

1988

Shared by American researchers **George H. Hitchings** and **Gertrude B. Elion,** and a Briton, **Sir James W. Black,** for work that led to the introduction of drugs widely used to treat heart disease, ulcers, and leukemia.

1989

American medical researchers **J. Michael Bishop** and **Harold E. Varmus** of the University of California, San Francisco, for their discovery of how normal cell growth can go awry and cause cancer.

ALBERT LASKER AWARDS

The Albert Lasker Awards are given in honor of medical research or public service of a pioneering nature. The awards are viewed by some as America's Nobel Prize.

Albert Lasker Basic Medical Research Awards

1980

Paul Berg, Stanley N. Cohen, A. Dale Kaiser, and **Herbert W. Boyer** for their work with recombinant DNA, the genetic material in cells of all living things that has helped inaugurate a new, promising age of biomedical achievements.

1981

Barbara McClintock for her achievement in first discovering that certain genetic elements are not static, but can move from one location to another on DNA.

1982

J. Michael Bishop, Raymond L. Erikson, and **Harold E. Varmus** for their studies of the nature of oncogenes and their roles in cell growth and regulation; and **Robert C. Gallo** and **Hidesaburo Hanafusa** for their pioneering studies of how RNA tumor viruses cause cancer.

1983

Eric R. Kandel for his application of cell-biology techniques to the study of behavior, revealing the mechanisms underlying learning and memory; and **Vernon B. Mountcastle** for his original discoveries that illuminate the brain's ability to perceive and organize information, and to translate sensory impulses into behavior.

1984

Georges J. F. Köhler for his achievement in fusing plasma and myeloma cells to form the first hybridoma; **César Milstein** for his creation of the first hybridomas; and **Michael Potter** for his fundamental research into the genetics of immunoglobulin molecules, paving the way for the development of hybridomas.

1985

Michael S. Brown and **Joseph L. Goldstein** for their discovery of the basic mechanisms controlling cholesterol metabolism, opening the way to a new pharmacologic approach to the treatment of cardiovascular disease.

1986

Rita Levi-Montalcini and **Stanley Cohen** for their discoveries of natural chemicals known to control cell growth.

1987

Molecular biologist **Susumu Tonegawa** for research that proved that the immense diversity of antibodies is achieved by a previously unknown shuffling of the genes that serve as blueprints for antibody production;

Philip Leder for his studies of the genetic basis of antibody diversity and role of genetic rearrangement in carcinogenesis; and **Leroy Hood** for studies that show how the body manipulates fundamental parts of antibody molecules to create the great diversity of antibodies.

1988

Molecular biologists **Thomas R. Cech** of the University of Colorado and **Phillip A. Sharp** from the Massachusetts Institute of Technology for their work on RNA.

1989

Edwin G. Krebs, Michael J. Berridge (Great Britain), **Alfred G. Gilman,** and **Yasutomi Nishizuka** (Japan) for the discovery and elucidation of signal transduction, the process that enables each cell to receive and respond to signals from extracellular messengers such as hormones, growth factors, and neurotransmitter molecules, allowing cells within an organism to communicate with each other.

Albert Lasker Clinical Medical Research Awards

1980

Vincent J. Freda, John Gorman, and **William Pollack;** and **Sir Cyril A. Clarke** and **Ronald Finn,** two groups of researchers who independently arrived at utilizing immunological principles to create a vaccine for preventing Rh disease in the newborn.

1981

Louis Sokoloff for developing a pioneering method of mapping and measuring brain function, both as a whole and in localized areas — a major breakthrough in the understanding and diagnosis of brain diseases.

1982

Roscoe O. Brady for his pioneering contribution to the understanding of hereditary diseases, the development of effective genetic counseling procedures, and initiation of possible treatment by replacement of missing enzymes; and **Elizabeth F. Newfeld** for clarifying the molecular basis and diagnosis of certain hereditary lysosomal storage disorders that may cause growth abnormalities, mental retardation, blindness, deafness, and death.

1983

F. Mason Sones Jr. for combining the techniques of cardiac catheterization and coronary artery cinematography, thus beginning the modern era of diagnosis and treatment of coronary artery disease.

1984

Paul C. Lauterbur for his theoretical and technical contributions that made possible a new form of medical imaging based on nuclear magnetic resonance.

1985

Bernard Fisher for his influence in shaping the character of modern breast cancer treatment, thus lengthening the lives of women suffering from the disease.

1986

Robert C. Gallo and Luc Montagnier for their discovery that a retrovirus is the cause of AIDS.

1987

Mogens Schou for long-term research that proved lithium was an effective drug for treating manic-depression and recurring episodes of severe depression.

1988

Vincent P. Dole for his discovery that methadone can treat heroin addiction.

1989

Etienne-Emile Baulieu (France) for discoveries of primary importance in endocrinology.

Albert Lasker Public Service Awards

1980

No award

1981

No award

1982

No award

1983

Maurice R. Hilleman and Saul Krugman for their discoveries of the causes of certain viral diseases and pioneering development of vaccines, especially against hepatitis B.

1984

Henry J. Heimlich for developing the Heimlich maneuver, a simple and practical technique for the prevention of death from choking.

1985

Lane W. Adams for his skills in expanding the American Cancer Society into the major volunteer force in the battle against cancer; and Ann Landers (Eppie Lederer) for her respected advice and practical translations of medical information and her tireless commitment to the health and well-being of the American people.

1986

Ma Haide and George Hatem for their legendary conquest of venereal disease and the eradication of leprosy in China.

1987

No award

1988

Sen. Lowell P. Weicker Jr. for his compassion and dedication in the fight to eradicate disease and disability through federal funding of medical research and public-health programs.

1989

Lewis Thomas, the author of *Lives of a Cell*, for opening the wonders of twentieth-century medical research and practice to the average person.

Albert Lasker Special Public Health Award

1980

Robert I. Levy and the Heart, Lung and Blood Institute (National Institutes of Health) for creation of a landmark hypertension detection and follow-up program derived from a monumental five-year study of 10,940 men and women with high blood pressure.

1981

No award

1982

No award

1983

No award

1984

Dorothy T. Krieger for her contributions to the field of neuroendocrine research.

1985

No award

1986

No award

1987

Centennial Salute to the **National Institutes of Health** for one hundred years of leadership in biomedical research establishing the preeminence of the United States in the fight against death, disease, and disability.

1988

No award

1989

No award

AMERICAN MEDICAL ASSOCIATION DISTINGUISHED SERVICE AWARD RECIPIENTS

The AMA Distinguished Service Award honors a member of the association for general meritorious service.

1980

Frank H. Mayfield, Cincinnati, Ohio

1981

John W. Kirklin, Birmingham, Alabama

1982

J. Englebert Dunphy, San Francisco, California

1983

Merrill O. Hines, New Orleans, Louisiana

1984

William D. Holden, Cleveland, Ohio

1985

George Valter Brindley Jr., Temple, Texas

1986

Kenneth M. Brinkhous, Chapel Hill, North Carolina

1987

Raymond T. Holden, Washington, D.C.

1988

M. T. Jenkins, Dallas, Texas

1989

Eben Alexander Jr., Winston-Salem, North Carolina

ALFRED P. SLOAN JR. MEDAL, GENERAL MOTORS CANCER RESEARCH FOUNDATION

This award, for recognition of outstanding recent basic scientific contribution to cancer research, was first presented in 1979.

1980

Isaac Berenblum

1981

César Milstein

Wallace P. Rowe

1982

Stanley Cohen

1983

Raymond L. Erikson

1984

J. Michael Bishop

Harold E. Varmus

1985

Robert T. Schimke

1986

Phillip Allen Sharp

1987

Robert A. Weinberg

1988

Yasutomi Nishizuka

1989

Donald Metcalf

Leo Sachs

BRISTOL-MEYERS AWARD

The Bristol-Meyers Award for Distinguished Achievement in Cancer Research is given annually to a scientist for an outstanding contribution to the progress of cancer research.

1980

Howard Earle Skipper, Southern Research Institute, Birmingham, Alabama, and Kettering-Meyer Laboratory.

1981

Van Rensselaer Potter, McArdle Laboratory for Cancer Research, University of Wisconsin, Madison.

1982

Denis P. Burkitt, St. Thomas' Hospital Medical School, London, England.

Michael Anthony Epstein, Nuffield College, Oxford University, England.

1983

Leo Sachs, Weizmann Institute of Science, Rehovot, Israel.

1984

Robert A. Weinberg, Whitehead Institute for Biomedical Research and the Massachusetts Institute of Technology.

1985

William S. Hayward, Memorial Sloan-Kettering Cancer Center.

Philip Leder, Harvard Medical School.

1986

Susumu Tonegawa, Massachusetts Institute of Technology.

1987

Donald Metcalf, Walter and Eliza Hall Institute of Medical Research, Melbourne, Australia.

1988

George W. Santos, Johns Hopkins University School of Medicine.

1989

Peter K. Vogt, University of Southern California.

PASSANO FOUNDATION AWARDS

Passano Foundation Awards honor distinguished work done in the United States in medical research. Originally one award was endowed. Beginning in 1974 there were two awards, a Senior Award and a Junior Award.

Passano Foundation Senior Awards

1980

Seymour Solomon Kety for his original and creative contribution to our knowledge of brain function and the biology of mental illness.

1981

Hugh O. McDevitt for his research on the relationships between the immune response, histocompatibility antigens, and human disease.

1982

Roscoe O. Brady for elucidating the molecular basis of a series of formerly incurable hereditary diseases of complex lipid metabolism.

Elizabeth F. Neufeld for her contributions to the understanding of the molecular basis of a group of hereditary diseases known as mucopolysaccharide storage diseases.

1983

J. Michael Bishop and **Harold E. Varmus** for their pioneering research on the molecular biology of tumor viruses, and in particular for their key discovery that the cancer-causing genes of a major class of tumor viruses are present as normal components of the chromosomes of all vertebrates, including humans.

1984

Peter C. Nowell for the discovery of the first characteristic and consistent chromosomal abnormality in cancer cells.

1985

Howard Green for his pioneering research in cell biology.

1986

Eugene Patrick Kennedy for his contributions to the understanding of the mechanism of synthesis of complex lipids and of the function and organization of cellular membranes.

Albert Lester Lehninger for his important contributions to bioenergetics and its relation to mitochondrial calcium metabolism and to proton transport.

1987

Irwin Fridovich for the discovery of the biological significance of oxygen radicals and the mechanisms employed by living organisms to defend themselves against their toxic effects.

1988

Edwin G. Krebs and Edmund H. Fischer for their pioneering studies on the role of protein phosphorylation/dephosphorylation cycles in cellular regulation.

1989

Victor A. McKusick for his important contributions to the field of medical genetics.

Passano Foundation Junior Awards

1980

No award

1981

William A. Catterall for his pioneering contributions to the understanding of the relationship of ion transport to electrical excitability.

Joel Moss for his contribution to an understanding of the action of bacterial toxins and his exemplary combination of clinical and scientific skills.

1982

Roger D. Kornberg for his contributions to the current understanding of the structure of chromatin.

1983

Gerald M. Rubin and Allan C. Spradling for their outstanding research in developmental genetics.

1984

Thomas R. Cech for his highly original discovery that ribonucleic acids (RNA) are capable of catalyzing their own splicing reactions in the absence of conventional enzymes.

1985

Mark M. Davis for his discovery of the genes that encode the antigen receptors of T lymphocytes.

1986

James Edward Rothman for his clarification of the functions of a specific and highly characteristic set of stacked intracellular membranes known as the Golgi apparatus.

1987

Jeremy Nathans for his contribution to the molecular biology of color vision.

1988

Peter Walter for his characterization of a signal recognition particle that identifies newly synthesized proteins and directs them to their membrane locations.

1989

Louis M. Kunkel for his discovery of the genetic defects responsible for Duchenne muscular dystrophy.

PSYCHIATRY AWARDS

AMERICAN PSYCHIATRIC ASSOCIATION DISTINGUISHED SERVICE AWARD

The American Psychiatric Association Distinguished Service Award honors individuals and/or institutions for exceptional meritorious service to American psychiatry.

1980

Daniel Blain

Seymour S. Kety

1981

Milton Greenblatt

Margaret S. Mahler

1982

Lester Shapiro

1983

Viola Bernard

Lawrence Kolb

1984

Hayden Donahue

Francis Gerty

1985

Charles Prudhomme

Fritz Redlich

1986
Melvin Sabshin

1987
Henry W. Brosin
Robert J. Campbell III

1988
Eward W. Busse
National Alliance for the Mentally Ill
Raymond W. Waggoner

1989
American Association of Chairmen of Departments of Psychiatry Robert Wood Johnson Foundation
Erik R. Kande
Solomon H. Snyder

WILLIAM R. McALPIN MENTAL HEALTH RESEARCH ACHIEVEMENT AWARD

The National Mental Health Association began giving the McAlpin Award in 1972 for outstanding research in the causes and prevention of mental illness.

1980
Floyd Elliott Bloom, Salk Institute Center for Behavioral Neurobiology.

1981
Jerome D. Frank, Johns Hopkins University.
Douglas W. Heinrich, Maryland Psychiatric Research Center.

1982
No award

1983
No award

1984
No award

1985
No award

1986
Richard J. Wyatt, St. Elizabeth's Hospital.

1987
Paul Greengard, Rockefeller University.

1988
Donald Klein, New York Psychiatric Institute.

1989
William T. Carpenter Jr., Maryland Psychiatric Research Center.

PUBLIC-HEALTH AWARDS

SEDGWICK MEMORIAL MEDAL, AMERICAN PUBLIC HEALTH ASSOCIATION

This American Public Health Association medal recognizes distinguished service in the advancement of public-health knowledge and practice.

1980
Lorin E. Kerr

1981
Dwight F. Metzler

1982
C. Rufus Rorem

1983
Milton I. Roemer

1984
Milton Terris

1985
Henrik L. Blum

1986
C. Arden Miller

1987
Larry J. Gordon

1988
Dorothy P. Rice

1989

Clarence L. Brumback

MARTHA MAY ELIOT AWARD, AMERICAN PUBLIC HEALTH ASSOCIATION

This American Public Health Association award honors unusual achievement in the field of maternal and child health.

1980

Pauline G. Stitt

1981

Eunice R. Ernst

1982

Edwin M. Gold

1983

Kathryn E. Barnard

1984

C. Arden Miller

1985

Marian Wright Edelman

1986

George A. Silver

1987

Vince H. Hutchins

1988

Mary C. Egan

1989

Frederick C. Green

NURSING AWARDS

AMERICAN NURSES' ASSOCIATION HONORARY RECOGNITION AWARD

The American Nurses' Association presents this award to recognize persons who have rendered distinguished service or valuable assistance to the nursing profession and whose contributions are of national and international significance to nursing.

1980

Marilyn Goldwater

1981

No award

1982

Sen. Daniel K. Inouye
Margaretta M. Styles

1983

No award

1984

Veronica Driscoll
Hildegard Peplau

1985

No award

1986

Faye G. Abdellah
Barbara Nichols

1987

No award

1988

Claire Fagin

1989

No award

MARY ADELAIDE NUTTING AWARD

The Mary Adelaide Nutting Award is given every two years by the National League for Nursing to honor outstanding leadership and achievement in nursing education or nursing service.

1981

Anne K. Kibrick

1983

Faye G. Abdellah

1985

Mary Dineen

1987

Faculty of the Department of Nursing Education, 1907–1986, Teachers' College, Columbia University

1989

Verle Waters

DEATHS

Dr. Howard B. Andervont, 83, virologist and cancer researcher who helped establish the National Cancer Institute in the 1930s, in Sarasota, Florida, 11 March 1981.

Dr. Gould Arthur Andrews, 62, pioneer in the use of nuclear medicine, who introduced the use of radioisotopes in cancer therapy, in Royal Oak, Michigan, 1 July 1980.

Dr. James Z. Appel, 74, surgeon and general practitioner who served as president of the American Medical Association from 1965 to 1966 and helped coordinate the structuring of Medicare, in Lancaster, Pennsylvania, 31 August 1981.

Dr. Silvano Arieti, 67, Italian-born psychoanalyst, author, and teacher who was a specialist in schizophrenia; winner of a National Book Award in 1975 for his book *Interpretation of Schizophrenia;* he was the editor in chief of the reference text *American Handbook of Psychiatry,* in New York City, 7 August 1981.

Dr. Franklin L. Ashley, 69, noted plastic surgeon who treated Hollywood celebrities and numerous deformed African and Vietnamese children, in Saint Petersburg, Florida, 14 February 1985.

Frederik Barry Bang, 64, Johns Hopkins University biologist and teacher known for his research on infectious and parasitic diseases, in New York City, 3 October 1981.

George Wells Beadle, 85, 1958 Nobel Prize–winning geneticist who demonstrated how genes control basic chemical processes in living cells, in Pomona, California, 9 June 1989.

Lauretta Bender, 88, child psychiatrist known for the 1923 development of the Bender Gestalt Visual Motor Test, a neurophysiological exam, in Annapolis, Maryland, 4 January 1987.

Dr. Harry Benjamin, 101, pioneering researcher into the phenomenon he called "transsexualism" who helped win acceptance of medical treatment for transsexuals, including sex-change surgery, in New York City, 24 August 1986.

Dr. Edgar Berman, 68, personal physician to former vice president Hubert Humphrey; he was prominent in Democratic Party politics until 1970 when he was forced to resign from the Democratic National Committee planning council after he angered women by saying they were physiologically unfit for leadership roles, in Baltimore, 25 November 1987.

Dr. George F. Bond, 67, navy doctor who was an authority on the medical effects of deep-sea diving and underwater pressure, and who pioneered the Sealab program of the 1960s, in which teams of "aquanauts" lived for days in a small capsule anchored to the seafloor, in Charlotte, North Carolina, 3 January 1983.

Dr. George F. Boyd, 79, researcher who in 1945 discovered lectins, natural chemicals that react to certain blood types — a discovery important in the development of modern immunology, in Falmouth, Massachusetts, 11 February 1983.

Bernard Beryl "Steve" Brodie, 81, medical scientist whose discovery that animals and humans had similar reactions to drugs laid the basis for chemical pharmacology, in Charlottesville, Virginia, 27 February 1989.

Dexter M. Bullard, 83, psychiatrist and pioneer in adopting psychoanalytic methods over simple confinement or drug therapy in the treatment of major psychiatric illnesses, in Rockville, Maryland, 5 October 1981.

Jack C. Burcham, 62, died ten days after receiving the fifth permanent artificial heart implant, in Louisville, Kentucky, 24 April 1985.

Barney B. Clark, the first recipient of a permanent artificial heart, died 112 days after its implantation; the heart worked until the end when it was turned off after Clark was "essentially dead," in Salt Lake City, Utah, 23 March 1983.

Dr. Irving S. Cooper, 63, leading brain surgeon who developed cryogenic surgery for treating Parkinson's disease, in Naples, Florida, 30 October 1985.

George Washington Corner, 91, embryologist whose research on hormones in the female menstrual cycle led to the discovery of the hormone progesterone, the key to the development of the birth control pill, in Huntsville, Alabama, 28 September 1981.

Dr. Andre Frederic Cournand, 92, French-born physician and physiologist; 1956 Nobel laureate for his work with the heart catheter, in Great Barrington, Massachusetts, 19 February 1988.

Dr. Burrill B. Crohn, 99, who in 1932 identified and defined the disease ileitis, an inflammation of the digestive tract, also known as Crohn's disease, in New Milford, Connecticut, 29 July 1983.

"David," 12, a Houston, Texas, child who had spent all but the last fifteen days of his life enclosed in a germ-free plastic bubble, from diseases related to his birth with severe combined immune deficiency syndrome, in Houston, 22 February 1984.

Dr. Loyal Davis, 86, distinguished neurosurgeon and stepfather of First Lady Nancy Reagan, in Scottsdale, Arizona, 19 August 1982.

Max Delbruck, 74, 1969 Nobel Prize winner in medicine or physiology for his work in modern molecular genetics; he proved that viruses were able to undergo spontaneous mutations and attack cells that were normally resistant to viral invasion, in Pasadena, California, 9 March 1981.

Dr. Derek Ernest Denny-Brown, 79, New Zealand–born physician and pioneering researcher on degenerative nervous disorders; he introduced the theory that an insufficient supply of blood to the brain could cause a stroke, in Cambridge, Massachusetts, 20 April 1981.

Edward Adelbert Doisy, 92, 1943 Nobel Prize–winning biochemist who isolated vitamin K and the female sex hormones estrone and estradiol, in Saint Louis, 23 October 1986.

Dr. Albert Dorfman, 66, discoverer of the cause of Hurler's syndrome, a genetic defect that leads to mental retardation, in Chicago, 27 July 1982.

John Franklin Enders, 88, Nobel Prize–winning virologist who codeveloped a method for culturing the poliovirus in large quantities, thus paving the way for the mass production of a safe polio vaccine, in Waterford, Connecticut, 9 September 1985.

Dr. Milton H. Erickson, 79, psychiatrist who was considered one of the world's leading authorities on the uses of hypnosis in therapy and medicine, in Phoenix, 25 March 1980.

Leslie H. Farber, 68, psychoanalyst and a leading theoretician of the existential movement in psychiatry; he stressed the link between culture and therapy, in New York City, 24 March 1981.

Dr. Benjamin Franklin Feingold, 81, pediatrician and allergist who in 1973 introduced the controversial theory that hyperactivity in childhood could be controlled by eliminating artificial food colorings and additives from the diet, in San Francisco, 23 March 1982.

Andrew W. Fleischer, 101, pharmacist and inventor who developed a device to measure blood pressure in 1911, and an improved stethoscope in 1913, in Ridgewood, New Jersey, 11 January 1983.

Charlotte Friend, 65, microbiologist who discovered a virus that causes leukemia in mice and emerged as a major tool for studying the links between cancer and viruses, in New York City, 13 January 1987.

Dr. William Horsley Gantt, 87, a behavioral psychiatrist whose work on behavior patterns and conditioned heart reflexes in animals led to greater understanding of the causes of high blood pressure, in Baltimore, 26 February 1980.

Muriel Gardiner, 83, psychoanalyst who specialized in the treatment of children; in Vienna in the 1930s she joined the antifascist underground and helped hundreds of Austrians escape from the Nazis, in Princeton, New Jersey, 6 February 1985.

Dr. Norman Geschwind, 58, whose pioneering work on the functional differences between the right and left sides of the brain led to a new understanding of learning disabilities and other behavioral and emotional patterns, in Boston, 4 November 1984.

Dr. Frank Gollan, 78, polio victim who isolated the poliovirus in 1948; and who invented the heart-lung machine for use in open-heart surgery, in Miami, 5 October 1988.

Dr. Andres Gruentzig, 46, German-born physician who developed the revolutionary balloon catheter technique for cleaning arteries of fatty deposits, in Forsyth, Georgia, 27 October 1985.

Dr. William Haddon Jr., 58, known for his work in the field of automobile safety; a pioneer researcher in the field of alcohol-related accidents, he pressed for tougher drunk-driving laws, in Washington, D.C., 4 March 1985.

E. Cuyler Hammond, 74, biologist and epidemiologist who published the first results of a 1952 landmark study linking cigarette smoking to lung cancer, in New York City, 3 November 1986.

Dr. H. Keffer Hartline, 79, 1967 cowinner of the Nobel Prize for medicine or physiology for his research on the electrical activities of the optic nerve, in Fallston, Maryland, 17 March 1983.

Dr. George (born Shafick) Hatem, American physician who devoted his career to public-health efforts in China; he was widely credited with eradicating syphilis and gonorrhea from China, in Beijing, 3 October 1988.

Dr. Starke Hathaway, 80, codeveloper of the Minnesota Multiphasic Personality Inventory test, the world's most widely used psychological test, in Minneapolis, 4 July 1984.

Gayelord Hauser, 89, an early advocate of health foods who helped shape the eating habits of many famous film stars from the 1920s to the 1950s, in North Hollywood, California, 26 December 1984.

Louis Hazam, 72, pioneering television documentary writer and producer who was the first to produce a live telecast of a medical operation, the birth of a baby, and television coverage of the inside of a mental hospital, in Silver Spring, Maryland, 6 September 1983.

Lt. Gen. Leonard Dudley Heaton, 80, army surgeon-general under Presidents Eisenhower, Kennedy, Johnson, and Nixon who received the Legion of Merit for his treatment of victims of the Japanese attack on Pearl Harbor in 1941, in Washington, D.C., 10 September 1983.

Dr. Charles Heidelberger, 62, cancer researcher who was best known for developing 5-fluorouracil, a powerful anticancer drug and for research into the chemical processes of cancer, in Pasadena, California, 11 January 1983.

Dr. Hudson Hoagland, 82, neuroendocrinologist who pioneered in the study of brain waves and the use of the electroencephalogram, and cofounded the Worcester, Massachusetts, Foundation for Experimental Biology, which developed the birth control pill, in Southborough, Massachusetts, 4 March 1982.

Rock Hudson (born Roy Scherer Jr.), 59, American actor whose good looks propelled him to superstardom, of AIDS; the public disclosure of his illness in July — the first known major celebrity case of AIDS — gained worldwide attention and focused public support on the disease, in Beverly Hills, California, 2 October 1985.

Dr. Charles Anthony Hufnagel, 72, cardiac surgeon who developed and implanted the first artificial human heart valve in 1952, in Washington, D.C., 31 May 1989.

Dr. Frances L. Ilg, 78, pediatrician and expert on child behavior who cofounded the Gesell Institute of Human Development in New Haven, Connecticut, in Manitowish Waters, Wisconsin, 26 July 1981.

Dr. Franz J. Ingelfinger, 69, editor of the *New England Journal of Medicine* and an international authority on diseases of the bowel, in Boston, 26 March 1980.

Dr. Leo Kanner, 86, Austrian-born child psychiatrist who first identified early infantile autism (also known as Kanner syndrome); he founded the Johns Hopkins Children's Psychiatric Clinic in 1930, in Sykesville, Maryland, 3 April, 1981.

Dr. Henry Kaplan, 65, radiologist whose pioneering work was responsible for making Hodgkin's disease one of the most curable forms of cancer, in Palo Alto, California, 4 February 1984.

Abraham Kardiner, 89, psychoanalyst who was one of the leading proponents of the environmental school of psychiatry that stressed the importance of social conditions to human behavior; a student-patient of Freud, he was a cofounder of the first psychoanalytical training school in the United States, the New York Psychiatric Institute, in 1930, in Easton, Connecticut, 20 July 1981.

Pearl L. Kendrick, 90, microbiologist who helped develop a whooping-cough vaccine that led to the near eradication of the childhood illness; she also developed the standard DPT shot against diphtheria, whooping cough, and tetanus, in Grand Rapids, Michigan, 8 October 1980.

Dr. Nathan S. Kline, 66, psychiatrist who pioneered in the use of tranquilizers and antidepressants in treating mental illness, in New York City, 11 February 1983.

Heinz Kohut, 68, Viennese-born psychoanalyst who introduced a controversial reinterpretation of Freudian theory called "self psychology," which stressed the importance of family and social relationships over sexual and aggressive drives in childhood in the development of mental illness, in Chicago, 8 October 1981.

Dr. Henry Kunkel, 67, who was recognized for major contributions to the study of immunologically linked diseases, in Rochester, Minnesota, 14 December 1983.

Walter Langer, 82, psychoanalyst commissioned by the Office of Strategic Services in 1943 to write a psychological profile of Adolf Hitler, and who correctly predicted Hitler's suicide, in Sarasota, Florida, 4 July 1981.

Dr. Richard Lawler, 86, who successfully performed the world's first kidney transplant in 1950; he never again performed the operation, saying he "just wanted to get it started," in Chicago, 24 July 1982.

Dr. Philip Levine, 87, medical researcher regarded as one of the founders of the field of immunohematology; he was codiscoverer of the Rh factor in human blood, in New York City, 18 October 1987.

Fritz A. Lipmann, 87, German-born American biochemist and 1953 Nobel Prize cowinner, whose work provided a basis for understanding how cells convert food into energy, 24 July 1986.

Dr. Margaret S. Mahler, 88, psychiatrist whose research into the psychological development of very young children led her to conclude that the foundation for the adult personality was laid in the first three years of life, in New York City, 2 October 1985.

Foster G. McGaw, 89, founder and longtime chairman of American Hospital Supply Corporation and a philanthropist who donated more than $100 million, in Chicago, 16 April 1986.

Dr. John P. Merrill, 67, Boston physician who led the medical team that performed the first successful human organ transplant of a kidney in 1954, in the Bahamas, 4 April 1984.

Dr. William Nolen, 58, small-town Minnesota physician whose book, *The Making of a Surgeon,* became a 1970 best-seller and led to his appearances on many television talk shows, in Minneapolis, 20 December 1986.

Dr. Marie Nyswander, 67, psychiatrist who became one of the first to advocate treating drug addiction as a medical problem; she and her research group were credited with the development of the methadone treatment of heroin addiction, in New York City, 20 April 1986.

Dr. Alton Ochsner, 85, internationally famous heart surgeon, teacher, and researcher who was the first, in 1936, to suggest a link between cigarette smoking and lung cancer, in New Orleans, 24 September 1981.

Dr. M. Murray Peshkin, 88, pediatric allergist who was a leader in the diagnosis and treatment of emotionally based allergies such as childhood and juvenile asthma, in New York City, 17 August 1980.

Rev. Michael R. Peterson, 44, Roman Catholic priest who died of AIDS two months after making his illness public; he was also known as a psychiatrist specializing in the treatment of alcohol and drug abuse among priests and nuns, in Washington, D.C., 9 April 1987.

Abe Plough, 92, founder of Plough Chemical Company, who started as a sixteen-year-old with a $125 investment and eventually parlayed it into a multimillion dollar medical business empire, in Memphis, Tennessee, 14 September 1984.

Dr. Seymour Pollack, controversial forensic psychiatrist who performed mental evaluations of famous criminals, among them Charles Manson family members, Sirhan Sirhan, and Patricia Hearst, in Culver City, California, 9 April 1982.

Hans Popper, 84, Viennese-born pathologist known as the founder of hepatology, the study of the liver and its diseases, in New York City, 6 May 1988.

Norman Pritikin, 69, controversial self-taught nutritionist who claimed his diet and exercise program could prevent and even reverse heart disease, in Albany, New York , 21 February 1985.

Karen Ann Quinlan, 31, the New Jersey woman whose adoptive parents won a landmark 1976 legal victory allowing them to disconnect her from the respirator to which she had been attached; she remained comatose from her drug and alcohol overdose, breathing on her own and fed through a nasogastric tube until her death from pneumonia, in Morris Plains, New Jersey, 11 June 1985.

Joseph Banks Rhine, 84, psychologist whose pioneering experiments led to his theory of extrasensory perception and made ESP a commonplace term; he helped open the new and controversial field of parapsychology research at Duke University, in Hillborough, North Carolina, 20 February 1980.

Dr. John Rock, 94, obstetrician-gynecologist who played a key role in developing the first oral contraceptive pill in the 1950s; he was also the first scientist to fertilize a human egg in a test tube (in 1944), in Peterborough, New Hampshire, 4 December 1984.

Rufus C. Rorem, 93, economist whose early advocacy of prepaid health care and group medical practice led to the founding of Blue Cross and Blue Shield, in Cherry Hill, New Jersey, 19 September 1988.

Dr. Samuel Rosen, 84, famous ear surgeon who developed the "Rosen stapes" operation, a revolutionary surgical technique for curing a common cause of deafness when the stapes, a tiny bone in the middle ear, was improperly positioned, in Beijing, China, 5 November 1981.

Wallace P. Rowe, 57, internationally known virologist and cancer researcher whose work provided insights into how retroviruses relate to the cells in which they grow and how they can produce cancer, in Washington, D.C., 4 July 1983.

Dr. Howard Archibald Rusk, 88, pioneer in rehabilitation science; during World War II he developed physical and psychological programs to rehabilitate soldiers, in New York City, 4 November 1989.

Dr. Arthur M. Sackler, 73, research psychiatrist who became known as one of the United States' leading art patrons, and endowed the Arthur M. Sackler Gallery at the Smithsonian Institution, in New York City, 26 May 1987.

Virginia M. Satir, 72, pioneer family therapist, in Menlo Park, California, 10 September 1988.

Dr. Louis W. Sauer, 94, pediatrician who developed a technique for manufacturing a whooping-cough vaccine and who helped develop and popularize vaccines against whooping cough, diphtheria, and tetanus, in Coral Gables, Florida, 10 February 1980.

Forrest Shaklee, 91, chiropractor who founded Shaklee Corporation, a San Francisco–based marketer of nutritional supplements and health-care products, in Castro Valley, California, 15 December 1985.

Dr. David Shakow, 80, psychiatrist who conduced pioneering research on schizophrenia; he was chief of the National Institute of Mental Health's clinical, developmental, and experimental psychology laboratory and received numerous awards for his professional accomplishments, in Washington, D.C., 26 February 1981.

Dr. Michael B(oris) Shimkin, 76, medical researcher who helped establish the link between smoking and lung cancer, in La Jolla, California, 6 January 1989.

William Bradford Shockley, 79, Nobel Prize winner in physics who later alienated his colleagues and the public with his statements that African Americans were genetically inferior to whites, 12 August 1987.

Louise Sloan, 83, vision expert who developed the lettering used on eye charts, in Baltimore, 1 March 1982.

Dennis Slone, 52, South African–born epidemiologist whose 1977 study, *Birth Defects and Drugs in Pregnancy,* was the definitive work linking drug-taking by pregnant women to fetal deformities, in Lexington, Massachusetts, 10 May 1982.

Reidar Sognnaes, 72, Norwegian-born pioneer of forensic dentistry who claimed to have confirmed the deaths of Adolf Hitler and Martin Bormann by comparing dental remains with X rays; he also discredited the story that George Washington had wooden false teeth, in Thousand Oaks, California, 21 September 1984.

Dr. Harry Solomon, 92, famous for his efforts to revolutionize mental-health care, replacing virtual imprisonment of patients with rehabilitative care, in Boston, 23 May 1982.

Dr. Sol Spiegelman, 68, microbiologist and Columbia University professor known for his pioneering research on genetics and on the molecular basis of cancer, in New York City, 14 January 1983.

Dr. Julian Caesar "Jules" Stein, 85, founder and president of the entertainment conglomerate Music Corporation of America and founder of the Jules Stein Eye Institute at UCLA, in Los Angeles, 29 April 1981.

Dr. William Howard Stein, 68, Rockefeller University biochemist who shared the 1972 Nobel Prize in chemistry for his studies on the chemical structure of a pancreatic enzyme, in New York City, 2 February 1980.

Curt Stern, 79, German-born geneticist who helped develop the modern science of genetics and who discovered many of the fundamental rules of heredity; during World War II he was a researcher with the Manhattan Project that developed the atomic bomb and pioneered the study of radiation effects on living organisms, in Sacramento, California, 24 October 1981.

Albert Szent-Györgyi, 93, Hungarian-born 1937 Nobel Prize–winning biochemist for his isolation of vitamin C; 1954 Albert Lasker award winner for his research on heart muscle contraction, in Woods Hole, Massachusetts, 22 October 1986.

Vic Tanny (born Victor Iannidinardo), 73, physical-fitness buff who pioneered the development of aesthetically appealing health clubs when dingy gyms were the norm, in Tampa, Florida, 11 June 1985.

Dr. Herman Tarnower, 69, a prominent physician and author of the best-selling *The Complete Scarsdale Medical Diet;* shot and killed by Jean S. Harris, a longtime friend, in Purchase, New York, 10 March 1980.

Dr. Helen Brooke Taussig, 87, recognized as the founder of pediatric cardiology; in the 1940s she and Dr. Alfred Blalock developed the first successful "blue baby" operation to save children born with a congenital heart defect; in the early 1960s she played a key role in preventing in the United States a repeat of the epidemic of birth defects in Europe among babies born to women who had taken the tranquilizer thalidomide, in West Chester, Pennsylvania, 20 May 1986.

Dr. Luther Leonidas Terry, 73, who as surgeon general of the United States from 1961 to 1965 was responsible for the historic government report linking cigarette smoking to lung cancer and other diseases; in 1965, at his urging, Congress introduced the requirement that cigarette packages carry a health warning, in Philadelphia, 29 March 1985.

Dr. Walter Robert Tkach, 72, M.D. who served as assistant White House physician for Presidents Eisenhower and Kennedy, and as senior physician to President Nixon, in Scripps Ranch, California, 1 November 1989.

Dr. Owen Wagensteen, 82, heart surgeon whose "Wagensteen suction approach," a now standard procedure used in preventing intestinal blockage after abdominal surgery, is credited with saving more than one hundred thousand lives, in Minneapolis, 13 January 1981.

Shields Warren, 82, Harvard University pathologist and pioneer specialist in the biological effects of radiation, in Mashpee, Massachusetts, 1 July 1980.

Dr. Jack Edward White Sr., 66, African American surgeon and medical researcher who was a role model for aspiring black physicians during his years on the faculty of Howard University, in Washington, D.C., 2 July 1988.

Roger J. Williams, 94, biochemist and nutrition researcher who discovered the growth-promoting vitamin pantothenic acid, in Austin, Texas, 20 February 1988.

Maxwell M. Wintrobe, 85, inventor of the hematocrit, a device to count the number and concentration of red blood cells; he was also the first to use chemotherapy to treat Hodgkin's disease, in Salt Lake City, Utah, 9 December 1986.

Dr. Norman E. Zinberg, 67, psychoanalyst whose research examined the effects of illegal drugs on individuals and society; his advice helped convince Congress to pass drug education and treatment measures, in Cambridge, Massachusetts, 2 April 1989.

PUBLICATIONS

Drew Altman, *AIDS in the Mind of America* (Garden City, N.Y.: Anchor, 1986);

Altman, Richard Greene, and Harvey M. Sapolsky, *Health Planning and Regulation: The Decision-Making Process* (Washington, D.C.: AUPHA, 1981);

L. B. Andrews, *New Conceptions: A Consumer's Guide to the Newest Infertility Treatments* (New York: St. Martin's Press, 1984);

L. Bachrach, ed., *New Directions for Mental Health Services: Deinstitutionalization* (San Francisco: Jossey-Bass, 1983);

Ross J. Baldessarin, *Chemotherapy in Psychiatry: Principles and Practice,* revised edition (Cambridge, Mass.: Harvard University Press, 1985);

David Baltimore and S. Wolf, eds., *Confronting AIDS: Directions for Public Health, Health Care and Research* (Washington, D.C.: National Academy Press, 1986);

Yvonne Baskin, *The Gene Doctors* (New York: Morrow, 1984);

William Bennett and Joel Gurin, *The Dieter's Dilemma* (New York: Basic Books, 1982);

Richard A. Berk, ed., *The Social Impact of AIDS in the USA* (Cambridge, Mass.: Abt, 1988);

Henry S. Berman and Louisa Rose, *Choosing the Right Health Plan* (Mount Vernon, N.Y.: Consumer Reports Books, 1990);

D. Black, *The Plague Years: A Chronicle of AIDS, the Epidemic of Our Times* (New York: Simon & Schuster, 1986);

D. Bolognesi, ed., *Human Retroviruses, Cancer and AIDS: Approaches to Prevention and Therapy* (New York: Liss, 1988);

Marlene Boskind-White and William White, *Bulimarexia: The Binge/Purge Cycle* (New York: Norton, 1987);

A. M. Brandt, *No Magic Bullet: A Social History of Venereal Disease in the United States since 1800. With a New Chapter on AIDS,* second edition (New York & Oxford: Oxford University Press, 1987);

Dennis L. Breo and Noel Keane, *The Surrogate Mother* (New York: Everest House, 1981);

Joan Jacobs Brumberg, *Fasting Girls: The Emergence of Anorexia Nervosa as a Modern Disease* (Cambridge, Mass.: Harvard University Press, 1988);

A. Cantwell Jr., *AIDS, the Mystery and Solution* (Los Angeles: Aries Rising Press, 1986);

Edward K. Chung, *One Heart, One Life* (Englewood Cliffs, N.J.: Prentice-Hall, 1982);

H. M. Cole and G. D. Lundberg, *AIDS: From the Beginning* (Chicago: American Medical Association, 1986);

S. Connor and S. Kingman, *The Search for the Virus: The Scientific Discovery of AIDS and the Quest for a Cure* (Harmondsworth, U.K.: Penguin, 1988);

Gene Corea, *The Mother Machine: Reproductive Technologies from Artificial Insemination to Artificial Wombs* (New York: Harper & Row, 1985);

P. G. Crosignani, *In Vitro Fertilization and Embryo Transfer* (London & New York: Academic Press, 1983);

H. L. Dalton and S. Burris, *AIDS and the Law* (New Haven: Yale University Press, 1987);

S. Davidson and R. Hudson, *Rock Hudson, His Story* (New York: Morrow, 1986);

R. G. Edwards and P. C. Steptoe, *A Matter of Life* (New York: Morrow, 1980);

John Elkington, *The Gene Factory: The Science and Business of Biotechnology* (New York: Carroll & Graf, 1987);

Alain C. Enthoven, *Health Plan: The Only Practical Solution to Soaring Health Costs* (Reading, Mass.: Addison-Wesley, 1980);

Rashi Fein, *Medical Care. Medical Costs. The Search for a Health Insurance Policy* (Cambridge, Mass.: Harvard University Press, 1986);

A. G. Fettner and W. A. Check, *The Truth about AIDS: Evolution of an Epidemic* (New York: Holt, Rinehart & Winston, 1984);

Seymour Fisher and Roger Greenberg, *The Scientific Credibility of Freud's Theories and Therapy* (New York: Basic Books, 1985);

A. F. Fleming, ed., *The Global Impact of AIDS* (New York: Liss, 1988);

Robert C. Gallo and F. Wong-Staal, eds., *Retrovirus Biology: An Emerging Role in Human Diseases* (New York: Dekker, 1988);

Lawrence Galton, *Med Tech: The Layperson's Guide to Today's Medical Miracles* (New York: Harper & Row, 1985);

Paul E. Garfield and David M. Garner, *Anorexia Nervosa: A Multidimensional Perspective* (New York: Brunner/Mazel, 1982);

Jeff Charles Goldsmith, *Can Hospitals Survive? The New Competitive Health Care Market* (Homewood, Ill.: Dow Jones–Irwin, 1981);

M. S. Gottlieb and others, eds., *Current Topics in AIDS* (New York: Wiley, 1987);

Ellen Greenfield, *House Dangerous: Indoor Pollution in Your Home and Office — and What You Can Do About It* (New York: Vintage, 1987);

Cynthia S. Gross, *The New Biotechnology: Putting Microbes to Work (Discovery series)* (New York: Lerner, 1987);

M. Haug and B. Lavin, *Consumerism in Medicine* (Beverly Hills, Cal.: Sage, 1983);

Health & Medical Horizons 1986 (New York: Macmillan, 1986);

Judi Hollis, *Fat Is a Family Affair* (Center City, Minn.: Hazelden Educational Materials, 1985);

H. B. Holmes, B. B. Hoskins, and M. Gross, eds., *The Custom-Made Child* (Clifton, N.J.: Humana Press, 1981);

A. F. Ide, *AIDS Hysteria* (Dallas: Monument Press, 1986);

Institute of Medicine, National Academy of Sciences, *Confronting AIDS: Directions for Public Health, Health Care, and Research* (Washington, D.C.: National Academy Press, 1986);

Elisabeth Kübler-Ross, *AIDS, the Ultimate Challenge* (New York: Macmillan, 1987);

Elaine Landau, *Surrogate Mothers* (New York: Franklin Watts, 1988);

Landau, *Why Are They Starving Themselves: Understanding Anorexia Nervosa and Bulimia* (New York: Messner, 1983);

Mark Lappe, *Broken Code: The Exploitation of DNA* (San Francisco: Sierra Book Clubs Press, 1984);

Judith Lasker and Susan Borg, *In Search of Parenthood: Coping with Infertility and High Tech Conception* (Boston: Beacon, 1988);

Gerald Leinwald, *Transplants* (New York: Franklin Watts, 1985);

Martin R. Lipp, *The Bitter Pill* (New York: Harper & Row, 1980);

Harold S. Luft, *Health Maintenance Organizations: Dimensions of Performance* (New York: Wiley, 1981);

John Francis Marion, *The Fine Old House: Smith Kline Corporation's First 150 Years* (Philadelphia: Smith Kline, 1980);

Jeffrey M. Masson, *The Assault on Truth: Freud's Suppression of the Seduction Theory* (New York: Farrar, Straus & Giroux, 1984);

W. A. Masters, E. Johnson, and R. C. Kolodny, *Crisis: Heterosexual Behavior in the Age of AIDS* (New York: Grove, 1988);

Aubrey Milunsky, ed., *Genetic Disorders and the Fetus* (New York: Plenum Press, 1986);

Ian I. Mitroff and Ralph H. Kilmann, *Corporate Tragedies: Product Tampering, Sabotage, and Other Catastrophes* (New York: Praeger, 1984);

National Research Council, National Academy of Sciences, *Indoor Pollutants* (Washington, D.C.: National Academy Press, 1981);

Ranganath Nayak and John M. Ketteringham, *Breakthroughs!* (New York: Rawson, 1986);

Dorothy Nelkin and Laurence Tancredi, *Dangerous Diagnostics: The Social Power of Biological Information* (New York: Basic Books, 1989);

Eve K. Nicholas, ed., *Human Gene Therapy* (Cambridge, Mass.: Harvard University Press, 1988);

E. K. Nichols, *Mobilizing against AIDS: The Unfinished Story of a Virus* (Cambridge, Mass.: Harvard University Press, 1986);

L. G. Nungasser, *Epidemic of Courage: Facing AIDS in America* (New York: St. Martin's Press, 1986);

S. Panem, *The AIDS Bureaucracy: U.S. Government Response to AIDS in the First Five Years* (Cambridge, Mass.: Harvard University Press, 1988);

John Parascandola, ed., *The History of Antibiotics: A Symposium* (Madison, Wis.: American Institute of the History of Pharmacy Press, 1980);

B. Peabody, *The Screaming Room: A Mother's Journal of Her Son's Struggle with AIDS* (San Diego, Cal.: Oak Tree, 1986);

Harrison G. Pope Jr. and James I. Hudson, *New Hope for Binge Eaters: Advances in the Understanding and Treatment of Bulimia* (New York: Harper & Row, 1984);

President's Commission for the Study of Ethical Problems in Biomedical Research, *Splicing Life: A Report on the Social and Ethical Issues of Genetic Engineering* (Washington, D.C.: U.S. Government Printing Office, 1982);

Tom Riley, *The Price of a Life: One Woman's Death From Toxic Shock* (Bethesda, Md.: Adler & Adler, 1986);

B. K. Rothman, *The Tentative Pregnancy: Prenatal Diagnosis the Future of Motherhood* (New York: Viking, 1986);

David Rousseau, David, W. J. Rea, Jean Enwright, *Your Home, Your Health, and Well-Being* (Berkeley, Cal.: Ten Speed Press, 1988);

Margery W. Shaw, ed., *After Barney Clark* (Austin: University of Texas Press, 1984);

Randy Shilts, *And the Band Played On: Politics, People, and the AIDS Epidemic* (New York: St Martin's Press, 1987);

Edward Shorter, *Bedside Manners: The Troubled History of Doctors and Patients* (New York: Simon & Schuster, 1985);

Shorter, *The Health Century* (New York: Doubleday, 1987);

Shorter, *History of Women's Bodies* (New York: Basic Books, 1982);

P. Singer and D. Wells, *Making Babies: The New Science and Ethics of Conception* (New York: Scribners, 1985);

Walter Sneader, *Drug Discovery: The Evolution of Modern Medicine* (New York: Wiley, 1985);

Patricia Spallone, *Beyond Conception: The New Politics of Reproduction* (Granby, Mass.: Bergin & Garvey Publishers, 1989);

David B. Starkweather, *Hospital Mergers in the Making* (Ann Arbor, Mich.: Health Administration Press, 1981);

Paul Starr, *The Social Transformation of American Medicine: The rise of a sovereign profession and the making of a vast industry* (New York: Basic Books, 1982);

DeWitt Steten Jr., *NIH: An Account of Research in Its Laboratories and Clinics* (Orlando: Academic Press, 1984);

Lewis Thomas, *The Lasker Awards: Four Decades of Scientific Medical Progress* (New York: Albert and Mary Lasker Foundation, 1985);

Isaac Turiel, *Indoor Air Quality and Human Health* (Stanford, Cal.: Stanford University Press, 1985);

Elliot Valenstein, *Great and Desperate Cures: The Rise and Decline of Psychosurgery and Other Radical Treatments for Mental Illness* (New York: Basic Books, 1986);

Ruth Westheimer, *All in a Lifetime* (New York: Warner, 1983);

Westheimer, *Dr. Ruth's Guide to Good Sex* (New York: Warner, 1983);

Westheimer, *First Love: A Young People's Guide to Sexual Information* (New York: Warner, 1983);

P. R. Wheale and Ruth McNulty, *Genetic Engineering: Catastrophe or Utopia?* (New York: St. Martin's Press, 1987);

Mary Beth Whitehead (with Loretta Schwartz-Nobel), *A Mother's Story: The Truth About the Baby M Case* (New York: St. Martin's Press, 1989);

C. Wood and A. Westmore, *Test-Tube Conception* (Englewood Cliffs, N.J.: Prentice-Hall, 1984);

G. P. Wormser, R. E. Stahl, and E. J. Bottone, eds., *AIDS: Acquired Immunodeficiency Syndrome and Other Manifestations of HIV Infection* (Park Ridge, N.J.: Noyes, 1987);

Burke K. Zimmerman, *Biofuture: Confronting the Genetic Era* (New York: Plenum Press, 1984);

Zimmerman and Raymond A. Zilinkas, eds., *Reflection on the Recombinant DNA Controversy* (New York: Macmillan, 1984).

CHAPTER ELEVEN
RELIGION

by MARC D. BAYARD

CONTENTS

Sidebars and tables are listed in italics.

1980

- Marilyn Ferguson's *The Aquarian Conspiracy,* expounding the philosophy and ideas of the New Age movement, is published.

18 Jan. A Gallup Youth Survey reports that one-fourth of teenagers in the United States have never read the Bible and that about one teenager in ten reads it daily.

24 Jan. Delegates from ten Protestant denominations seeking church unity approve a proposal for a common ministry for a projected united church. The new church would be known as the Church of Christ Uniting.

Apr. The Church of Jesus Christ of Latter-Day Saints (Mormons) celebrates 150 years of institutional existence.

29 Apr. More than two hundred thousand evangelical Christians gather in Washington, D.C., for a "Washington for Jesus" rally and march.

4 May Pope John Paul II issues a directive banning all Roman Catholic priests and nuns from serving in public office.

4 Aug. Roman Catholic nun and 1979 Nobel Prize winner Mother Teresa visits the United States on a four-day mission.

11 Oct. Rev. Jerry Falwell says that he believes that God hears the prayers of Jews, reversing his earlier position.

4 Nov. Ronald Reagan is elected president after being greatly supported by the New Christian Right.

1981

- Richard A. Viguerie's book *The New Right: We're Ready to Lead,* revised after the national elections, is published.

- The Dalai Lama conducts a six-week tour of the United States.

26 Mar. The Moral Majority launches an advertising campaign to counter criticism that it is anti-Semitic, opposed to women's rights, and that its concerns are really political and not moral.

17 Apr. The National Council of Churches and several major Protestant denomination leaders stage a Good Friday protest in Washington, D.C., against the United States giving military aid to El Salvador.

13 May Pope John Paul II is shot in the abdomen by a Turkish terrorist, Mehmet Ali Agca, while being driven into Saint Peter's Square in Vatican City.

28 July Antiwar activists Father Daniel Berrigan and his brother, former priest Philip Berrigan, are sentenced to three to ten years in prison for participating in an antinuclear protest and damaging warheads in Pennsylvania.

1982

4 Mar. The Coalition for Better Television calls for a nationwide boycott of the National Broadcasting Company (NBC) and its parent company, RCA Corporation, claiming too much violence, sex, and anti-Christian messages are on the airwaves.

23 Mar. President Ronald Reagan is given a humanitarian award by the National Conference of Christians and Jews.

6 May President Reagan endorses a constitutional amendment authorizing voluntary group prayer in public schools.

1983

7 May Baptist evangelist Rev. Billy Graham leads more than six hundred religious leaders in a weeklong antinuclear conference held in the Soviet Union.

3 June The Equal Rights Amendment (ERA), attacked by the New Right and the Catholic Church since its inception, is defeated after falling three states short of ratification.

16 July Rev. Sun Myung Moon, leader of the Unification Church (Moonies), is sentenced to eighteen months in prison and fined $25,000 for tax fraud and conspiracy to obstruct justice.

29 Aug. A Gallup poll shows American public opinion almost evenly divided between belief in biblical accounts of creation and belief in the theory of evolution.

3 Nov. A federal appeals court in Pawtucket, Rhode Island, rules that the city has violated the constitutional prohibition on the establishment of religion by displaying a Christian nativity scene.

22 Nov. A federal district judge rules unconstitutional a Louisiana law requiring the teaching of "scientific creationism" in the state's public schools.

- The White House declares 1983 as the Year of the Bible.

- Episcopal Church membership is at 2,794,690, according to the *Yearbook of American and Canadian Churches.*

23 Feb. The Synagogue Council of America issues a statement urging President Reagan and Soviet leader Yuri V. Andropov to seek "a total cessation of the production and deployment of nuclear weapons."

3 May The National Conference of Catholic Bishops publishes "The Challenge of Peace: God's Promise and Our Response."

The California State Board of Equalization strips away the tax-exempt status of Rev. Robert H. Schuller's $18 million Crystal Cathedral.

8 June A diverse group of U.S. religious leaders calls for Congress to limit genetic research and ban genetic engineering.

10 June The Presbyterian Church U.S.A. is formed by the merger of the Northern and Southern branches of the denomination.

14 Oct. The National Council of Churches publishes a nonsexist translation of the Bible that changes the practice of referring to God and humanity as solely male.

3 Nov. Rev. Jesse Jackson declares his candidacy for the 1984 Democratic presidential nomination.

8 Nov. The People's Temple is officially dissolved as a legal and corporate entity nearly five years after the tragic suicides of hundreds in Jonestown.

20 Nov. New Right organizations condemn the antinuclear television film *The Day After,* calling it leftist, prodisarmament propaganda.

1984

- *The Christian Science Monitor* observes its 75th anniversary.

- The Assemblies of God creates a satellite television network to broadcast across the nation.

- Membership in religious congregations in the United States rises almost 1 percent in 1984, according to the National Council of Churches.

10 Jan. The United States and the Vatican establish full diplomatic relations after a 116-year hiatus.

26 Feb. Rev. Jesse Jackson apologizes for referring to Jews as "Hymies" and New York City as "Hymietown."

5 Apr. The Reorganized Church of Jesus Christ of Latter-Day Saints votes to accept a revelatory document authorizing the ordination of women.

13 Apr. A two-year study reveals that 13.3 million Americans watch religious television programs regularly.

May The United Methodist Church celebrates the two hundredth anniversary of American Methodism.

24 June John Cardinal O'Connor of New York declares that no Catholic "in good conscience" can vote for a prochoice candidate for elected office.

28 June Rev. Jesse Jackson disavows minister Louis Farrakhan and his Nation of Islam for their anti-Semitic remarks.

11 Nov. The National Conference of Catholic Bishops releases the first draft of its pastoral letter on the state of the United States' economy.

1985

24 Jan. The heads of the three major Lutheran Churches protest the indictments of the Sanctuary movement supporters.

14 Feb. The U.S. Rabbinical Assembly of Conservative Judaism announces its acceptance of women rabbis.

24 Apr. The Procter & Gamble Company announces that it is phasing out its distinctive emblem carried on its products because of intense criticism from Christian groups who believe the emblem is a symbol for Satan.

5 May President Reagan infuriates American Jews with his visit to a West German cemetery at Bitburg.

19 Aug. Rev. Jerry Falwell, after visiting South Africa, declares his support for the Pretoria regime and vows to oppose U.S. economic sanctions on that nation.

2 Oct. Rabbi Meir Kahane is stripped of his U.S. citizenship after assuming a seat in the Israeli parliament in 1984.

28 Oct. U.S. authorities arrest Indian guru Bhagwan Shree Rajneesh in Oregon after he had made his rich followers give him money to buy a fleet of Rolls Royces.

1986

- *The Christian Science Monitor* expands its monthly television news broadcast to a weekly program.

- The American Baptist Churches in the U.S.A. announces a new $30 million national church-building campaign titled "Alive in Mission."

3 Jan. Rev. Jerry Falwell founds his Liberty Federation.

16 Jan. The British government announces that it has barred minister Louis Farrakhan from entering their country in the belief that his presence there "would not be conducive to the public good."

23 June The Unitarian-Universalist Church marks the twenty-fifth anniversary of the two churches' merger.

18 Aug. Father Charles E. Curran is barred by the Vatican from teaching theology because of his dissenting views on sexual matters.

1 Oct. The Christian Broadcasting Network (CBN) celebrates its twenty-fifth anniversary.

1987

- Robert Peel's *Spiritual Healing in a Scientific Age* is published and reaffirms the Christian Scientist belief in faith healing.

Mar. Evangelical preacher, Rev. Oral Roberts, begins his month-long campaign to raise $4.5 million or he claims "God could call Oral Roberts home."

19 Mar. Praise the Lord (PTL) founder Rev. Jim Bakker resigns after revelations that he committed adultery and stole funds from his ministry.

30 June The United Church of Christ adopts a declaration on Judaism acknowledging the continuing religious validity of the Jewish faith.

July The North American Congress on the Holy Spirit, in the largest Pentecostal gathering of the year, adopts the goal of converting half the world's population to Jesus Christ by the year 2000.

16 Aug. The Harmonic Convergence, a two-day gathering of New Agers, begins.

7 Sept. A *Time* magazine poll reveals that 53 percent of Catholics in the United States believe priests should be allowed to marry.

10 Sept. Pope John Paul II begins his ten-day tour of the United States titled "Unity in the Work of Service."

7 Dec. *Time* magazine devotes its cover story, "New Age Harmonies," to the growing New Age movement in the nation.

10 Dec. U.S. Catholic bishops release a position paper on AIDS, which allows for the teaching of condom usage.

1988

- The National Missionary Baptist Convention is founded.

1 Jan. The Evangelical Lutheran Church in America is formed.

6 Apr. Rev. Marion "Pat" Robertson declares that he will no longer campaign actively for the Republican presidential nomination.

8 Apr. Rev. Jimmy Swaggart is defrocked by the Assemblies of God for refusing to accept discipline by church leadership.

3 May The United Methodist Church revises its hymnal and book of worship to represent a less sexist tone.

15 May Rev. Pat Robertson files papers to create a new PAC, Americans for the Republic, that will train and fund conservative Christian political candidates.

12 Aug.	The film *The Last Temptation of Christ* opens to much criticism and protest by Christian and Jewish groups.

1989

22 Jan.	President George Bush signs a proclamation establishing a National Day of Prayer and Thanksgiving.
11 Feb.	Rev. Barbara Clementine Harris becomes the first woman consecrated as a bishop in the Episcopal Church.
	The Vatican officially condemns racism as sinful and identifies the United States and South Africa as nations with major racial problems.
21 Feb.	The Supreme Court upsets a Texas law exempting the Bible and other religious publications from sales tax.
25 Feb.	More than four thousand American Muslims pray and burn effigies of writer Salman Rushdie in front of the New York offices of Viking Penguin, the American publisher of *The Satanic Verses*.
2 June	The Episcopal Synod of America is formed after dissenting conservative Episcopalians splinter from the main branch because of their opposition to the ordination of female priests and bishops.
10 June	The Moral Majority is officially disbanded.
2 July	Father George A. Stallings Jr. establishes an African American Catholic congregation.
29 Aug.	The Evangelical Lutheran Church of America adopts a neutral stance on abortion.
24 Oct.	Former PTL leader Jim Bakker is sentenced to forty-five years in prison and fined $500,000 for fraud and conspiracy convictions.

OVERVIEW

The Great Divide. The decade of the 1980s was a great period of restructuring for the majority of religions in the United States. Coming off the turbulent eras of the 1960s and early 1970s many traditional religious groups in the United States attempted to refocus themselves and sharpen their definitions. In the course of their doing so, several distinct factions and conflicts emerged. Among the most prominent were the divisions between religious liberals and a newer, more boisterous religious conservative movement. While by the mid 1980s many surveys were acknowledging the decline in mainline Protestant sects, Gallup polls by 1986 were reporting that three in ten Americans (31 percent) felt comfortable referring to themselves as evangelicals or born-again Christians. The meteoric rise of religious conservatism into the mainstream had an impact on many of the religious and nonreligious events of the period as all of society was forced to reckon with this once-fringe segment of the population. The basis of the schism appeared to be the longstanding dispute of what role religion and faith should play in a person's life. Liberal churches stressed the message of the social gospel, while conservatives emphasized an obedience to a higher power and piety. Conferences and symposiums were held on the subject, but the rift continued to grow with no sign of closing the chasm. As Peggy L. Shriver, a mainline Protestant scholar and assistant general secretary at the National Council of Churches, declared in an article written for the *Christian Century* in 1984 after meeting with a fundamentalist, "I must admit that he and I surely do differ on many things that matter to both of us, but I grieve that our unity in Christ does not override those differences."

Protestant Membership. Protestantism in its many incarnations remained the dominant faith in the United States, attracting more than 55 percent of the population. Baptists were the largest Protestant body, with twenty-seven denominations making up 20 percent of the general population. Included in the overall Baptist numbers was the Southern Baptist Convention (SBC), who made up half the Baptist membership with 15 million believers and were the most conservative and active segment of the religion. Second to the Baptists in numbers were the Methodists. The United Methodist Church (UMC), the largest Methodist denomination, had 9.1 million members and more than thirty-seven thousand local churches and was, because of its consistently moderate to liberal positions on most social and political issues, generally considered the standard by which mainline Protestantism could be defined. Ecumenism was a trend adopted by mainline churches in the 1980s in an effort to consolidate limited resources. The Presbyterian Church U.S.A. was created in 1983 from the merger of the Northern and Southern Presbyterian branches that had split apart during the Civil War. The new church had a membership of 3.1 million and twenty-one thousand ministers nationwide. The Lutheran Church also merged on 1 January 1988, forming the Evangelical Lutheran Church in America (ELCA). The ELCA was created by the merger of the three leading Lutheran bodies — the Lutheran Church in America, the American Lutheran Church, and the Association of Evangelical Lutheran Churches. The ELCA included 5.3 million members, eleven thousand congregations, and sixteen thousand clergy. These events aside, the biggest change to affect Protestantism in membership and in theology was the phenomenal growth of conservative or evangelical sects. Evangelicals did not constitute a specific denomination, nor were they all Protestants; yet their conservative and fundamentalist views on the Bible and on questions of morality made them a cohesive body. With a steady to explosive growth from the 1950s forward, evangelicals numbered somewhere between 40 million and 60 million persons in this country. The most prominent evangelical church was the Assemblies of God. The Assemblies of God, a Pentecostal body, had more than 2.1 million members and some eleven thousand churches in the United States. Between 1973 and 1983 the Assemblies of God grew a phenomenal 71 percent because of the denomination's relentless evangelism and the use of the "electronic church." Other major evangelical churches were the 3.6-million-member Church of Jesus Christ of Latter-Day Saints (Mormons), and the 700,000-member Seventh-Day Adventists.

Catholics. With the installation of Pope John Paul II in 1978, a stronger conservative message began to be issued from the Vatican. Response to the stringent moral doctrines — no ordinations of female priests, no use of contraceptives or abortion, and no remarriage in the church after having been divorced — caused some stormy relations between American Catholics and their church. Nevertheless, Catholicism was the largest religious denomination in the United States with more than 54 million members — making it the fourth largest Catholic community in the world behind Brazil, Mexico, and Italy. The Catholic Church membership grew a solid 16 percent during the decade and maintained 7 active cardinals, 47 archbishops, 309 bishops, 53,000 priests, and 153 dioceses. Catholic laity in the 1980s were having smaller families, earning higher incomes, and becoming better educated than Protestants. With this improved socioeconomic status, Catholics began to question their church's doctrines and to seek greater flexibility from the church hierarchy. Of those surveyed in 1987, 31 percent of U.S. Catholics labeled Pope John Paul II's positions too conservative. A clash was brewing between American Catholics' individualism and the Vatican's needs for obedience and order. The greatest influx of new Catholics came from the Hispanic community, whose numbers, because of immigration and high birth rates, swelled on the West Coast and in urban areas.

Judaism. Jews constituted 2 percent of the population of the United States, as they had since the late 1960s. The biggest change in the Jewish community of 5.8 million was in demographics. Many Jews left the traditional confines of the Northeast to better experience other growing regions of the country, such as the Midwest and Southwest. Jews continued to be one of the most upscale American groups in terms of income and education. Jews also remained one of the least religiously attached groups in the nation. The four branches of American Judaism reported membership numbers as follows: Conservative Judaism, 1.5 million; Reform Judaism, 1.2 million; Orthodox Judaism, 1 million; and Reconstructionist Judaism, 60,000 members. Ideologically, Jews took various positions on the political spectrum and were heavily involved in Jewish national organizations. *The American Jewish Year Book* found that in more than 225 larger towns and cities Jews maintained at least one central local organization. It also found some two hundred periodicals and newspapers dealing with Jewish issues. Of primary concern to many Jews on the political front was the United States' position toward Israel.

An Increased Pluralism. Americans, even in this time of great modernity, still cherished a love of religion. Poll after poll showed that the majority of the populace had a strong belief in an all-powerful God and in an afterlife; yet, as American society became more pluralistic, it became increasingly difficult for many churchgoers to adhere to the rigid traditions of their churches. With advances in wealth, education, and science and technology, and with a overall new skepticism toward power structures, Americans tended to listen less to authorities and more to their own opinions and consciences. Religion, therefore, became more personalized in the 1980s, and that personalization took on many forms. The decade saw growth spurts in more popular television- and media-

hyped religions. The unstructured and mystical New Age Movement grew apace, as did its polar opposite, the populist born-again evangelical movement. Traditional churches faced dissent and decline and struggled to keep pace with society while maintaining their foundation. The decade was one of new ideas clashing with traditional values, one in which self-assertive people felt that they, not a hierarchy, could best decide the role of the churches, and one in which the boundaries of church-state relations would be tested on almost a daily basis. Several new leaders, movements, and sects developed in this period that rivaled the traditional churches for power, influence, and loyalty of membership. Extremism became the norm and a search for purity and simplicity the ultimate goal. The victors in these skirmishes were to decide which direction faith would take in the next century.

Politics from the Pulpit. The line between religion and politics continued to lose its definition as religious groups and organizations strived to use the pulpit to expound political ideologies. With the presidential elections of 1980 featuring three declared born-again Christian candidates — Jimmy Carter, Ronald Reagan, and John Anderson — religion and religious rhetoric was abundant. The births of several new fundamentalist Christian organizations, such as the Moral Majority, headed by the Reverend Jerry Falwell, and the Campus Crusade for Christ, run by political and religious conservative Bill Bright, fueled what became known as the New Christian Right. These groups believed that they had a mission to bring a strong, fundamentalist Christian morality into politics. Their ability to use the electronic and media resources of the time, mixed with a strong grassroots populist effort, enabled them to shift the focus of political debate from the liberal court, where it had been for the past two decades, to a more culturally conservative one. One of the highlights of this movement was when the conservative television commentator and fundamentalist preacher Marion "Pat" Robertson left his post as host of the powerful *700 Club* to seek the nation's highest political office in the 1988 election.

Liberal Religious Activism. Several mainline Protestant denominations and the Catholic Church raised the question of how a nation that considered itself moral could continue to manufacture and potentially use weapons of mass destruction — nuclear arms. Mainline churches also questioned the nation's involvement in what they considered unjust wars in Central America and elsewhere around the globe. Cultural issues, such as the equality of the sexes, also could no longer be ignored by churches who traditionally labeled themselves as liberal. Other social issues, such as the decline of the cities, homelessness, and poverty were raised by the Reverend Jesse Jackson, an African American Baptist minister and political activist who ran for the presidency in 1984 and 1988. His crusade for social justice encouraged church involvement in social causes and urged the disenfranchised to enter the political arena.

TOPICS IN THE NEWS

ACRIMONY WITHIN MAINLINE PROTESTANTISM

Declining Membership. The 1980s marked the third consecutive decade of declining membership for America's top mainline Protestant churches. The United Methodist Church, the Episcopal Church, the Evangelical Lutheran Church in America, the United Church of Christ, and the Presbyterian Church U.S.A. all experienced decreases in membership. For the Presbyterian Church U.S.A. and the Episcopal Church the decline was 25 and 28 percent, respectively, between 1965 and 1989, while the United Methodists, the nation's second largest Protestant body, reported losses of 18 percent during that same period. The loss of membership was accompanied by severe decreases in revenue for some denominations. The National Council of Churches (NCC), the umbrella organization for mainline Protestant denominations, suffered great financial hardship in 1989 and was forced to eliminate four hundred staff positions. Mainline churches also faced decreasing enrollments in their programs; Sunday school programs, once a staple of Protestantism, for example, had declined 55 percent during the previous two decades. Missionary work abroad had also declined: in 1965 mainline churches had more than four thousand missionary workers, but by 1989 the number was down to slightly more than twelve hundred. With these losses, mainline churches found it difficult to remain the shapers of American values. Faced with this reality, mainline churches sought recommendations on how to stem the tide of losses, and several conferences were held and works written on the subject. Analysis showed a relationship between demographic trends and church membership. Protestant birthrates continued to decline in the 1980s, becoming lower than they had been since the 1960s. The loss of young adults in the churches had also greatly disrupted growth. In 1983, 24 percent of all Americans were young adults between eighteen and twenty-nine. The percentage of Protestants in that age group was also 24 percent. By 1987, however, the percentage of young adults in the United States rose to 29 percent, while the percentage of young Protestants dropped to 23 percent. While there were more young church members, the rate of growth in church member-

ship lagged alarmingly behind the population growth. The mainline churches' inability to pass their traditions on to the next generation greatly reduced their chances for future growth. Other factors that contributed to the continuing decline of membership included the loss of the "baby boom" generation, increasing diversity of religions, and the churches' inability to tailor their spiritual messages to attract non-Protestants.

Inclusiveness. Mainline churches continued mission to promote social justice, create equality, and foster an atmosphere of inclusiveness. Trying to move the nation into a more progressive era, churches spoke out against perceived injustices in the United States and abroad. Internal reforms were also made as the churches tried to keep pace with the thinking of their memberships. Several mergers of churches occurred during the decade — the two biggest taking place in the Lutheran and Presbyterian denominations. Controversial issues such as racism, sexism, and homosexuality were confronted. Though they realized that some of their liberal positions were not fully supported by their congregations, the majority of mainline church officials felt it important not to bow down to the new conservative trends.

A Battle from Within. The long-standing conflicts between mainline churches and fundamentalist ones continued to take center stage. The two spheres had been at odds for almost a hundred years, and by the 1980s they were separated by more than their opposing views of Scripture. A host of economic, social, and educational factors had a great influence on whether potential members would affiliate themselves with the liberal Protestant mainline denominations or the more-conservative evangelical ones. The liberalism of mainline churches, such as the Unitarian-Universalists, Society of Friends (Quakers), United Methodists, and Episcopalians stemmed from a tradition of modernism, while more conservative sects, such as the Assemblies of God, Seventh-Day Adventists, and other evangelical churches, traced their roots to a fundamentalist background that stressed personal morals and adherence to the Bible over social activism. In poll after poll throughout the decade the most crucial factor that determined the side on which Americans fell on this issue was education. A survey in

1981, for example, showed that approximately half of college-educated Americans identified themselves as "religious liberals," while only one person in seven among those who had only a grade-school education identified himself or herself in that way. The same pattern appeared when more- and less-educated respondents were asked how they viewed the Bible. A Gallup poll in the mid 1980s showed that 45 percent of those with less than a high school degree and 34 percent of those who had graduated from high school but had not attended college believed in a literal interpretation of the Bible, while those with a college education were much less apt to believe that the Bible is literally true. The gap between the educated and the uneducated has fueled much of the controversy between religious liberals and conservatives, as it represents a difference not only in religious beliefs but also in cultural attitudes.

The Southern Baptist Convention. The Southern Baptist Convention (SBC) is the nation's largest Protestant denomination, with nearly 15 million members. With the election in 1981 of Baily Smith as president of the SBC, a new era of conservatism swept over the once-moderate sect. Smith, a strong conservative and fundamentalist, made belief in an "inerrant Bible" a litmus test for SBC members. He also stirred up controversy with several flagrant anti-Semitic remarks toward Jews and prayer. By 1983 Jimmy Draper, the new president of the SBC, attempted to move the denomination back toward the center by lowering the voices on the issue of biblical inerrancy and by reversing the support that the SBC had given President Ronald Reagan's policies in 1982. There was a massive conservative revolt in 1984, and Draper was ousted as president of SBC. Charles Stanley, a pastor and former director of the Moral Majority, became his replacement. Stanley wished to restructure the church and systematically weed out its liberal elements. One of Stanley's major policy changes was a resolution barring the further ordination of women. In 1986 another fundamentalist conservative, Adrian Rogers, was elected president of the SBC. His victory demonstrated that fundamentalism was now the dominant force in the SBC, as moderate to liberal members could do little to stop his election. By the end of the decade such members held little hope that the SBC would hold any place for them, and questions of a schism began to loom on the horizon.

Mormons in the Mainstream. The Mormon religion turned 150 years old in April 1980. This celebration was marked with much fanfare and some controversy. Becoming part of the mainstream had now exposed the Mormons to much outside criticism and ideas. By far the most prominent example of this was the excommunication of dissident feminist Sonia Johnson in 1979 for her views on the ERA. Her harsh treatment provoked strong responses within and without the Mormon community. On the theological front the church also faced great turbulence. In 1981 new historical documents were found that raised questions about the historical succession of Mormon authority. Mark W. Hofmann, a collector of rare Mormon documents, claimed to have discovered writings that showed that Joseph Smith III, son of Joseph Smith, the religion's founder, was to have been named the head of the Mormon Church in 1844 and not Brigham Young. The document caused some stir in the Mormon Church; yet it did not change any of the current power structure or heal the rift Utah Mormons had with the Reorganized Church of Jesus Christ of Latter-Day Saints based in Missouri. Worldwide Mormon membership passed the 5-million mark in 1982, and by 1984 the church attempted again to shed its image as a Christian cult by starting to associate more frequently with other Christian sects and by adding the subtitle "Another Testament of Jesus Christ" to the *Book of Mormon.* In 1985 the Mormons elected a new president, Ezra Taft Benson, a former cabinet official in the Eisenhower administration. Also that year the church was rocked in controversy as a letter was found indicating that the religion's first leader, Joseph Smith, had been part of a superstitious cult before founding the Mormons. By 1987 it was found that the letter concerning Smith and countless other Mormon documents were forged by Mark W. Hofmann, who later pled guilty to two counts of felony theft as well as to two counts of second-degree murder. By the end of the decade Mormon membership had surpassed the 7-million mark with the majority of membership residing in North America. The struggle to remain unique while gaining acceptance in the mainstream remained the denomination's greatest challenge.

Sources:

Wade Clark Roof and William McKinney, *American Mainline Religion: Its Changing Shape and Future* (New Brunswick: Rutgers University Press, 1987);

Robert Wuthnow, *The Restructuring of American Religion: Society and Faith Since World War II* (Princeton: Princeton University Press, 1988).

ACTIVISM AND THE MAINLINE CHURCH

Antinuclear Movement. Mainline churches were heavily involved in the growing antinuclear movement of the 1980s. The Religious Society of Friends (Quakers), the Unitarian-Universalists, and the United Church of Christ launched separate large-scale campaigns against the creation and use of nuclear weapons. The Quakers' "New Call to Peacemaking" campaign, which was first launched in 1979, stressed the role that churches had in the peace process and encouraged mainline churches to become more involved in this crucial issue. In 1982 the Reverend Billy Graham, the respected Baptist minister and friend to several U.S. presidents, became involved in the antinuclear movement despite being urged not to by the Reagan administration. Graham traveled to the Soviet Union to attend the World Conference on Religious Workers for Saving the Sacred Gift of Life from Nuclear Catastrophe, sponsored by the Russian Orthodox Church. This event brought together more than six hun-

Billy Graham, center, with President and Mrs. Ronald Reagan in 1981

dred religious leaders from around the world to denounce nuclear weapons as immoral. In 1983 the United Church of Christ (UCC), long a peacekeeping church, decided to endorse the pastoral peace letter adopted by the National Conference of Catholic Bishops. Many mainline Protestant laity participated in antinuclear demonstrations held throughout the early and mid 1980s. One of the firmest stances to be taken by a mainline church was in 1986 when the United Methodist Church approved a pastoral letter calling on all Methodists to say no to and rally against weapons of mass destruction.

Controversy. The United Methodist Church found itself embroiled in controversy in 1983 over its liberal political stances on issues and its use of membership funds. A neoconservative group called the Institute on Religion and Democracy (IRD) charged that the church had Marxist and Communist leanings and had diverted some NCC funds to those causes. The issue made national attention when the television news show *60 Minutes* and the magazine *Reader's Digest* ran stories on the allegations. The NCC president, United Methodist bishop James Armstrong, denied the charges that the group had funded Communist governments, but he did state that the UMC gave money to progressive social

groups working to better the living situation for people in Third World and in Communist nations. The NCC wrote off the attack as an attempt by conservative religious groups and the conservative press to discredit it.

Social Gospel. Direct social action was used at various times throughout the 1980s by liberal Protestant groups who felt that some U.S. laws were dramatically wrong and had to be corrected by acts of disobedience. In 1984 the Denominational Ministry Strategy, a Pennsylvania clergy group largely made up of radical Lutherans and Episcopalians, joined with some militant labor unions in an attempt to force U.S. Steel and the Mellon Bank to invest more money back into the local economy. Encouraged by Lutheran activist minister D. Douglas Roth, the groups went on a crusade to harass the executives of these corporations at their homes, offices, and places of worship. Roth was ordered by the regional bishop, Kenneth May, and the Lutheran Church in America to cease his involvement in this militant effort. He refused and was ousted from his post, but instead of vacating the church Roth barricaded himself inside until he was finally removed forcibly by the police. He was later sentenced to ninety days in jail and fined for contempt of court. Upon release from jail in 1985, Roth was immediately defrocked by the Lutheran Church in America, as they claimed that he had acted in "willful disregard and violation" of church law when he refused to vacate his pulpit.

Foreign and Domestic Causes. In terms of foreign policy, mainline churches vehemently decried the injustice in South Africa and called for an end to the system of apartheid and continued U.S. sanctions. Several churches held demonstrations, protested, and divested whatever interests they had in South Africa. The efforts of Nobel Prize winner and South African Anglican bishop Desmond Tutu were fully supported by the majority of his counterparts in the United States. More direct action was also deemed appropriate by some church members. The case of the Sanctuary Movement, a liberal religious group that smuggled Central American refugees into the United States, was resolved in 1986 by a U.S. District Court in Tucson, Arizona. Sanctuary saw six of its members sentenced by the federal government for conspiring to bring Salvadorans and Guatemalans across the border. Two more members were found guilty of harboring and transporting illegal aliens. Despite being sentenced, members of the group claimed that it was their moral obligation to help save lives and asserted that they would continue with their activities. More than three hundred churches and synagogues were involved in this movement. In another development, by the end of the decade more than 240 religious leaders declared their support in a written statement to the United Mine Workers, who were on strike in West Virginia against the Pittston Coal Group. The mission of a social gospel still remained at the core of many mainline churches.

The Role of Women. Women, both clergy and lay, took bold strides forward in mainline Protestant churches. Mainline denominations traditionally opposed the ordination of women, but between the years of 1956 and 1977 the five major denominations — Methodists, Baptists, Presbyterians, Episcopalians, and Lutherans — reversed their stance on the issue, which opened the gates for major changes in the 1980s. By the mid 1980s more than eighty Protestant denominations in America allowed for the ordination of women. The first woman bishop in the United Methodist Church (UMC), Majorie S. Matthews, was elected in 1980. By 1985 two more women were elected as bishops in the UMC. Bishop Leontine Kelly was appointed to San Francisco, becoming the UMC's first black woman bishop. Bishop Judith Craig was appointed to Detroit. If not for the growing influence of women in the UMC, events like this would not have been possible. The UMC had the largest number of women in pastorates and provided more opportunities for women than most other denominations. Both female and male mainline Protestants worked for the passage of the Equal Rights Amendment (ERA) in 1982, seeing it as an important step toward ending sexism and promoting equality and fairness in our culture. Other mainline churches also joined in the new trend to elevate the status of women in their denomination. Sandra An-

toinette Wilson became the first black female priest of the Episcopal diocese of New York in 1982, and Barbara Clementine Harris was elected to the title of bishop in the Episcopal Church on 11 February 1989. Harris became the first woman bishop in the worldwide Anglican Communion. Her elevation was heralded by most as a crowning achievement of equality; yet some in the church, including Robert Runcie, the archbishop of Canterbury and leader of the church of England, said he would not recognize women bishops in England.

Quest for Equality. The significance of women's influence in the church in the 1980s is still an issue of considerable debate. Though many women chose to pursue a career in religious service and entered programs in record numbers a "glass ceiling" still existed throughout the period. Surveys in the early 1980s revealed that on average one-third of seminarians in the UMC, Lutheran Church in America, or the United Presbyterians were women; yet the majority of women ordained remained in lower status positions, such as assistant pastor or educator as opposed to pastor or bishop. Overall this quest for equality has been met without any major repercussions.

Sources:

Roberta Hestens and others, "Women in Leadership: Finding Ways to Serve the Church," *Christianity Today*, 30 (3 October 1986): 4I–10I;

Richard N. Ostling, "Defrocking a Contentious Pastor," *Time*, 125 (25 March 1985): 64.

BORN AGAIN: THE EVANGELICAL MOVEMENT

Growth. The growth of evangelicalism and fundamentalism in the 1980s was a phenomenon that extended well beyond the religious sphere into the cultural and political. Known by many names (born-again Christians, evangelicals, Pentecostals, The New Religious Right) these Christians, mostly Protestants, grew in numbers like no single Protestant denomination. In the 1980s fundamentalists, or militant evangelicals, shared a disregard for modernity as sinful and insisted on the inerrancy of the Bible, the doctrine of dispensational premillennialism in regard to the Second Coming of Christ (the Rapture), and the separation of their churches from other Christian groups that did not believe as they did. They also actively pursued an entrance into the arena of conservative politics. The premier fundamentalist preachers of the era were the Reverend Jerry Falwell, Rev. Richard Zone, Rev. James Robison, and the Rev. Marion "Pat" Robertson. While Evangelicals, or Protestants actively involved in converting others to their beliefs about Jesus Christ, generally hold conservative beliefs toward religion and issues of morality, they may or may not interpret the Bible literally and are not opposed in principle to interacting with other Christian churches. A survey taken in 1986 showed that 31 percent of the American population identified themselves as evangelicals. The major evangelical churches of the decade were the Southern Baptist

Tammy and Jim Bakker, 1987

Convention, Church of Jesus Christ of Latter-Day Saints, Assemblies of God, Seventh-Day Adventists, and the Church of the Nazarene. Leading evangelical preachers of the era were the Reverend Jimmy Swaggart, Rev. Jim Bakker, Rev. Oral Roberts, and Rev. Robert Schuller. The two factions' explosion into the mainstream of American society came primarily from their diligent recruiting techniques, their use of modern media tools, the backlash against moderate and liberal religious groups, and strategic political involvement.

Entrance into Politics. The evangelical entrance into the politics first occurred in the mid 1970s with the election of Jimmy Carter as president. Americans watched to see what an evangelical really looked liked and how one would function as president of the United States in a changing pluralistic society. In 1979 a Lynchburg, Virginia, television preacher and fundamentalist, Rev. Jerry Falwell, founded the Moral Majority, a religious organization whose goal was to mobilize Christian believers for conservative political purposes. Falwell, who had long preached a firebrand conservative political message over the airwaves on his "Old Time Gospel Hour" syndicated program, felt that the time was ripe to launch

directly into the realm of politics. The Moral Majority formed chapters and local affiliates in all fifty states and sought to register conservative voters; influence local, state, and national elections; support conservative candidates; and combat liberal groups whom, it was argued, had come to dominate the nation. Estimates of Moral Majority membership varied, but it was conservatively held to be about four hundred thousand. Joining Falwell on his crusade to correct the morality of American politics was Richard Zone of the Christian Voice, a conservative political lobbying group formed in 1978. The Christian Voice stated plainly that it would help fund national campaigns for conservative, mainly Republican candidates that met their strict criteria. Another religious group that entered the political arena in the early 1980s was the Roundtable founded by Edward McAteer of Memphis, Tennessee. McAteer wanted his group to focus on "pro-God, pro-family, pro-American causes" and created an institute to train leaders to do just that. Conservative Bill Bright's Campus Crusade for Christ and Ronald Sider's Evangelicals for Social Action also intertwined the political realm with fundamentalist Christianity, and together these groups helped form what became known as the New Christian Right or simply the New Right.

Direct Action. The New Right wasted no time in taking their conservative Christian message to the high-

Moral Majority founder Jerry Falwell

est authorities — the White House, the U.S. Congress, and the Supreme Court. On 29 April 1980 more than two hundred thousand evangelical Christians gathered in Washington, D.C., for a mammoth "Washington for Jesus" rally. This event was put together as a coming-out party for a group of Christians that had traditionally steered clear of politics and to show government that they were a force to be reckoned with. The elections of 1980 were the first real challenge for the political evangelical machine, and they were well prepared. The presidential candidate of choice for the majority of evangelicals and fundamentalists was Ronald Reagan, who appealed to them with his antigovernment rhetoric and stances on critical moral issues. His 4 November 1980 landslide victory, as well as the victories of several conservative members of Congress, were claimed by the New Right as the result of their own efforts. Falwell boasted that the Moral Majority had registered millions of voters who had contributed heavily in time and money to campaigns. Instead of resting with these victories, the New Right sought in the early 1980s to assert their moral agenda onto the political landscape. Issues such as prayer in the public schools and opposition to the Equal Rights Amendment (ERA), homosexual rights, abortion, and pornography became top priorities for the New Right. Moral crusades were launched by preachers such as the Rev. Donald E. Wildmon and his Coalition for Better Television against stations and advertisers that they deemed offensive. Jerry Falwell fought hard in 1982 for President Reagan's proposed constitutional amendment legalizing prayer in the public schools. With the 1984 presidential elections evangelicals again gave their support in great numbers (81 percent) to Ronald Reagan. In reality the president had done little in terms of passing any legislation that benefited the New Christian Right directly; yet he was still seen as the best hope to carry out their mission. By 1986 the power and stability of the New Christian Right coalition began to wane. Jerry Falwell, leader of the Moral Majority, reduced his participation in the organization, while he formed a new organization called the Liberty Federation to focus on foreign policy and national defense instead of social issues. Other once-dominating New Right organizations also began to lose ground and change their scope. The Religious Round-table folded in the mid 1980s, while the Christian Voice lost strength and began to back away from the moral absolutism that it held as a litmus test for candidates. The

Robert Schuller's $18 million Crystal Cathedral in Garden Grove, California, designed by architect Philip Johnson

flame that had stirred these groups to form at the beginning of the decade appeared to have engulfed them by its end. The New Right's influence was still apparent at the close of the decade; it had simply taken a smaller role as it concentrated on community-level races rather than national campaigns.

The Run for the Presidency. The power of the New Christian Right was put to the test in the presidential race of 1988, after Marion "Pat" Robertson, televangelist and head of the Christian Broadcasting Network (CBN), announced his candidacy. Robertson, who had been pondering and praying over the idea for several months, decided to announce his intentions formally on 1 October 1987, after winning the Iowa Republican caucus. His campaign faced several major drawbacks from its inception because major fundamentalists, such as the Reverend Jerry Falwell and Gary Jarmin of the Christian Voice, had already pledged their support to other prominent Republican candidates. Robertson also faced the question of whether the American public was ready to

have a fundamentalist preacher and television host as their president. Robertson's base of support came from his popularity among conservative Christians. CBN and its flagship program *The 700 Club* had a reported weekly audience of 12 million viewers for the program and 29 million cumulative viewers during the course of an average month, according to the A. C. Nielsen Company. Robertson was labeled an extremist by his opponents for his fundamentalist views of the world and his religious solutions to the cultural problems facing the nation; yet, unlike many fundamentalists, Robertson was a well-educated man (with a law degree from Yale University) and a charismatic speaker who could articulate statements with a secular emphasis. Although Robertson did not win the Republican nomination for president in 1988, his entrance into the race did shift the focus of the political debate and strengthened the conservative forces in the Republican Party.

Battle with the Courts. Evangelical conservatives' greatest political setbacks may have come in their court-

Assembly of God televangelist Jimmy Swaggart

Pentecostal minister Oral Roberts, who thanked his followers for donating $8 million in 1987 to prevent God from "calling me home."

room battles. Infuriated by the *Roe* v. *Wade* abortion decision of 1973, fundamentalists have consistently denounced it as a moral outrage that legalized a form of murder. A strong antiabortion movement has been led by conservative Christians throughout the nation to revoke this decision. The 1989 *Webster* v. *Reproductive Health Services,* which limited women's rights to abortions, was viewed as a major victory for fundamentalists, who felt that with their grassroots campaigns they could muster greater influence in state courts rather than the Supreme Court. *Roe* v. *Wade,* however, remained the law of the land. In other battles the issue of "scientific creationism" was revived in 1982, when federal judges in both Arkansas and Louisiana struck down state laws passed in 1981 that allowed for the teaching of creationism in public schools. Both judges cited the importance of separation of church and state in making their decisions. A Supreme Court decision in 1985 ruled that public-school officials in New York City and Grand Rapids, Michigan, should not permit public-school teachers to lead special education classes in parochial schools. Other Supreme Court decisions invalidated a Connecticut law that allowed employees the right to observe the Sabbath and an Alabama law allowing for a moment of silent prayer in public schools. These opinions caused many conservative Christian leaders to claim that the courts had waged war on them. Several New Right groups, such as the American Coalition for Traditional Values (ACTV), declared that the courts were preaching secular humanism and that they would not allow it.

The Rise of Televangelism. The intermingling of religion and mass communication reached new heights in the 1980s with the explosive merger of evangelical preachers and cable television, allowing television preachers to reach a broader congregation than they had ever deemed possible. The premier players in this new

televangelism, as it was labeled by the media, were Jerry Falwell, Pat Robertson, Robert Schuller, Jim and Tammy Faye Bakker, Oral Roberts, and Jimmy Swaggart. Each of them represented different segments of the fundamentalist and evangelical movements; yet, they all profited from their ability to tailor their message to a television format, and they became superstars of the new religious circuit of the airwaves. The amount of money generated by televangelists through their radio and television ministries reportedly reached $2 billion a year. Televangelists reached millions of Americans daily as they tuned into such popular Christian programs as *The 700 Club,* the *PTL Club,* and the *The Hour of Power.* Combined, these new "electronic churches" drew weekly audiences of almost 20 million viewers. The astonishing growth of televangelists and their empires in such a short time caught much of the American public by surprise.

Downfall. As televangelism and the electronic church continued to grow year after year, the preachers and their finances began to inspire increasing public scrutiny. One of the first televangelists to receive major public criticism was the Reverend Robert Schuller. A self-described preacher and apostle of Norman Vincent Peale's ideas of positive thinking, Schuller had amassed a gigantic empire in Garden Grove, California, that included the $18 million Crystal Cathedral and a popular Sunday morning television service, *The Hour of Power,* that reached almost 3 million persons annually. Schuller's empire was first attacked by the California courts, who in 1983 took away the tax-exempt status of the Crystal Cathedral. The state claimed that the cathedral had been used for profit-making concerts and thus the church had forfeited its tax status. By the mid to late 1980s Schuller's church began to lose substantial amounts of money as contributions began to dwindle and church listeners began to be less responsive to his positive message.

Oral Roberts. Rev. Oral Roberts, a prominent Pentecostal preacher and healer for several decades based in Tulsa, Oklahoma, also saw his economic fortunes take a dramatic slide by the late 1980s. Roberts, whose syndicated half-hour program was carried by 210 television stations, reached some 1.1 million people a year, but viewership and contributions had been steadily decreasing since 1978. Realizing the magnitude of his financial situation, Roberts in 1987 faced the fact that he could lose his whole church empire, including his twenty-two-year-old medical school and Oral Roberts University. He made a desperate plea to his viewing audience to donate $8 million by the end of March or "God could call Oral Roberts home." Roberts's plea for money shocked both the televangelist community and the general public, as it amounted to a form of biblical blackmail. His credibility suffered greatly; yet, the funds were raised and his ministry saved. By 1989 Roberts's empire and power finally crumbled as he was forced to close his City of Faith Hospital and medical school and then sell his home in order to pay off the enormous debt that Oral Roberts University had accumulated.

PTL Ministries. The fall of the PTL (Praise the Lord or People that Love) empire in 1987 was a scandal that fully exposed the hidden side of a corrupt televangelist empire. Rev. Jim Bakker, the popular "president for life" of the PTL, based in Charlotte, North Carolina, which owned and operated Heritage USA, confessed on 19 March 1987 to having had an adulterous encounter in 1980 with a Long Island church secretary named Jessica Hahn and paying her $265,000 in church funds to keep quiet. He then resigned from his position as head of his $129 million empire, handing it over to fundamentalist Jerry Falwell. As the investigation into the Bakkers' affairs unfolded, it was learned that in the three and a half years before his resignation, Bakker and his wife, Tammy Faye, had taken salaries, bonuses, and retirement benefits of more than $4.76 million. The bulk of PTL revenue was generated from fund-raising schemes presented on the PTL Television Network, which featured programs hosted by the Bakkers. Their programs were among the most popular and entertaining of the televangelist world, reaching 140 television stations daily. An Assemblies of God minister, Bakker had sought to make Pentecostals more secular, and he was not afraid to be materialist in his approach to the world. His Heritage USA (often referred to as a "Biblical Disneyland"), located in Fort Mill, South Carolina, was America's largest gospel theme and amusement park and drew in yearly revenues of more than $6 million. Space in the Heritage Towers Hotel at Heritage Park was sold to 152,903 "Lifetime Partners," who sent $1,000 each between 1984 and early 1987 in return for a promise of four days and three nights accom-

Long Island church secretary Jessica Hahn, who had an adulterous affair with PTL minister Jim Bakker in 1980

modations per year for life at the as yet unbuilt hotel. By April 1987, $70 million had been raised for the hotel, yet only $12 million went toward construction. PTL was generating revenues of $4.2 million per month but was spending $3 million more than it raised. When Falwell took over, he announced that the ministry was $72 million in debt. In April 1987 the PTL scandal claimed another victim as Rev. Richard Dortch, second in command at PTL, was dismissed by Falwell for his involvement in the attempted cover-up of the scandal. Both Bakker and Dortch were then stripped of their credentials as ministers by the Assemblies of God, and by June

1987 the PTL corporation had declared bankruptcy. Jerry Falwell abandoned his commitment to help save PTL in October 1987, upon learning that he would not maintain full control of the reorganizing process since the courts had ruled that previous PTL creditors and supporters would have some say in the organization's structure. Bakker, for his part, was investigated by a federal grand jury on fraud charges and in 1989 was sentenced to forty-five years in prison and fined $500,000 for having defrauded his followers of more than $158 million.

Sources:

Nancy Tatom Ammerman, *Bible Believers: Fundamentalist in the Modern World* (New Brunswick: Rutgers University Press, 1987);

Jeffrey K. Hadden and Anson Shupe, *Televangelism: Power and Politics on God's Frontier* (New York: Holt, 1988);

Stewart M. Hoover, *Mass Media Religion: The Social Sources of the Electronic Church* (Newbury Park: Sage Publications, 1988);

Richard A. Viguerie, *The New Right: We're Ready to Lead* (Falls Church, Va.: Viguerie, 1981).

CATHOLIC CONTROVERSIES

Development. The diversity of Catholics in the United States reflected the diversity of the nation. Catholicism remained the largest single religious organization in the nation, representing 28 percent of the general population. The decade of the 1980s marked the bicentennial of the Catholic hierarchy in the independent United States and the church proved in this decade that it had become a formidable force in the United States, particularly in the areas of politics, policy, and morality. The Catholic Church continued its mission to reach out to immigrants. One in five Catholics belonged to a minority group. The two largest new Catholic populations were Hispanics, who made up 16 percent of Catholics, and African Americans who were about 3 percent of the population, or 2 million people. Struggling to meet the special needs of these new groups as well as tackle the growing dissent in its ranks was the contemporary challenge of the Catholic Church. John Paul II, the newly elected pope, faced a sometimes belligerent American public and clergy who felt that many of the old ideas of the Catholic Church were not fully applicable to the United States and needed to be updated to fit the times. The battle of tradition versus modernity was a conflict that was fought on all levels throughout the decade.

Transition. American Catholicism faced a difficult paradox in the fact that it was on the surface a strong, vibrant, growing religion; yet the infrastructure that supported the Catholic Church was continually weakening without any sign of relief. Structurally the Catholic Church had lost ground in the 1980s as the number of priests in the church was not growing to keep pace with membership, and the number of new seminarians entering the church fell by 16 percent during the past twenty-five years. The number of nuns serving the Catholic Church also decreased sharply, perhaps primarily because many women felt the church was too male dominated and

Children at a church-sponsored demonstration against nuclear weapons

hierarchical. In 1962 there were 173,351 nuns, but the number had decreased by 1988 to 106,912. Another seeming contradiction the church dealt with was the curious fact that membership had grown consistently every year, but attendance at services was down. Tied in directly with declining mass attendance was the decrease in church revenues despite the increasing prosperity of Catholics, who had the same average income as Protestants. In response to these problems the Catholic hierarchy made dramatic cutbacks. Cardinal Szoka of Detroit symbolized this best in 1988 when he eliminated 43 of Detroit's 112 parishes, citing lack of funds and declining membership in urban Catholic Churches. American Catholics, for their part, felt it much less important to adhere to strict Catholic teachings, prompting some theologians to refer to their mind-set as "cafeteria style," picking and choosing what they liked. The independence of the Catholic laity as they became more educated, wealthier, and worldly increased the opportunities for friction between them and the traditional hierarchy.

Politics. The Catholic Church had been no stranger to the political arena; yet in 1980 the Vatican decreed that no priest or nun could hold a public office in the government. This decree, which was specifically aimed at the rebellious, liberal priest and U.S. Congress member from Massachusetts, Father Robert Drinan, forced him to resign his seat in May 1980; but the larger implication of the decree resonated throughout the period. The Vatican was taking a hard-line stance against liberal to radical priests and nuns who veered away from traditional church teachings. Drinan, in his ten years in the House of Representatives, often voted for abortion rights — an act that infuriated the Vatican and conservative Catholics everywhere. The antipolitics decree served the Vatican greatly in disciplining several nuns who joined campaigns for women's rights and abortion rights. Sister Agnes Mary Mansour, acting director of the Michigan Department of Social Services and a nun in the Sisters of Mercy of the Union order for thirty years, was ordered by the Vatican in 1983 to step down from her position in social services or to resign as a nun. The controversy surrounding Mansour involved the issue of abortion as the social-services department she worked for administered funds for public abortions. Mansour, though personally opposed to abortion, felt that her position in government was helping many people and that the Catholic Church was doing a disservice to women. Therefore, she abandoned her position as a nun. Similarly Sisters Elizabeth Morancy and Arlene Violet were forced out of the Sisters of Mercy after they were elected to public office in Rhode Island. Several other clergy members and Catholic organizations, such as the National Coalition of American Nuns and Catholics for a Free Choice, clashed with the Vatican on this ban, seeing it as skewed toward only liberal groups, while conservative cardinals, priests, and bishops were given free rein to state publicly their staunch opposition to issues such as abortion and gay rights and the candidates that supported them.

Abortion. The issue of abortion was at the forefront of much of the heated debate that occurred between liberal Catholics and more traditional ones. American Catholics for the most part believed in theory that abortion was wrong, but few believed it a mortal sin, an act of murder. Catholics felt that issues of contraception, abortion, and sexuality were personal matters that could be handled without the church's interference. Many Catholics regarded the encyclical *Humanae Vitae* (1968), the Vatican's doctrine on sexuality and contraception, as too intrusive, and Pope John Paul II's desire to enforce it too draconian. Father Charles E. Curran, a Catholic theologian at Catholic University in Washington, D.C., had his license revoked in 1986 by Joseph Cardinal Ratzinger, head of the Vatican's Congregation for the Doctrine of the Faith, for preaching against the Vatican's official teachings on sexuality and abortion. Curran's dismissal served as a warning to church officials to abide by official teachings or be severely reprimanded. Abortion had been labeled an unspeakable crime by the Vatican, and therefore church leaders were urged to act against it. Newly

PAPAL VISIT TO THE UNITED STATES

Pope John Paul II was famous for his globe-trotting. Since assuming the papacy in 1978, John Paul II had traveled the world around, preaching a staunch conservative Catholicism. His September 1987 trip to the United States was his fourth overall visit to the nation and his second as the Pope. The official title of the ten-day trip was "Unity in the Work of Service"; it covered nine cities, including major Catholic strongholds such as Miami, San Antonio, and Los Angeles. The pontiff's journey was greatly anticipated, especially since American Catholics had often criticized several of the official church teachings on social issues. The Pope, born and raised in communist Poland, was unfamiliar with the concept of public dissent and came to America in some measure to put U.S. Catholics back in line. According to a *Time* magazine poll, 93 percent of American Catholics believed that one could still be a good Catholic and disagree with the Pope, and many felt that they, not the church, could best decide personal moral issues. Many Catholics in America believed that it was time for priests to have the opportunity to be married and raise families, that women should be allowed to be priests, and that birth control and abortion were not necessarily sins. The media, always interested in controversy, played up the differences between the Vatican and American Catholics for weeks before the Pope's arrival, adding to the tension between traditional and liberal Catholics. The trip, however, produced few fireworks as the Pope steered clear of opposition forces and reiterated traditional church teachings to friendly crowds of worshipers and clergy.

Sources: Pope John Paul II, *John Paul II in America* (Boston: St. Paul Books & Media, 1987);

George Weigel, *Catholicism and the Renewal of American Democracy* (New York: Paulist Press, 1989).

appointed cardinals, such as Bernard Law of Boston and John O'Connor of New York placed the issue on the forefront of the Catholic agenda in 1984. O'Connor, who labeled the issue his "No. 1 priority," compared abortion to the Holocaust and directly criticized Democratic vice presidential candidate Geraldine Ferraro, a Catholic, for her prochoice position. This direct reference to politics and a highly visible political figure caused Mario Cuomo, the governor of New York and also a prochoice Catholic, to enter the debate and defend a Catholic's right to choose without compromising her church membership. The church remained unyielding in its belief in a prolife stance, so much so that in 1985 the National Conference of Catholic Bishops updated the ten-year-old prolife document "Pastoral Plan for Pro-Life Activities: A Reaffirmation." The issue struck a chord with Catholic women and nuns, many of whom viewed the question of this debate as woman's right to decide the fate of her own body and not a decision that should be made by a male-dominated church. Activist nuns, such as Sister Traxler, a member of the School Sisters of Notre Dame for more than forty years, saw the issue of abortion as the most prominent example of the church's debasement of women. The National Coalition of American Nuns helped to sponsor a prochoice advertisement in 1984 to counterattack the harassment they felt that women were receiving from an overruling Vatican. The strong, rebellious stance of female clergy symbolized the rift that was developing in the church because of perceived sexism.

Women and the Church. Americans led in the battle for equality of the sexes in the Catholic Church. The Vatican, realizing the growing need to legitimize women's role in the church and in the modern era, attempted to walk a fine line balancing tradition with progress. The results of these efforts left both traditionalists and modernists unsatisfied. Against the backdrop of the women's movement and the great progress that had been made in mainline Protestant churches, progressive nuns and laity demanded a larger, more visible role for women in the Catholic Church. The demands by women to be become priests and have a greater say in church policy were seen as major goals in fostering equality. Nuns fighting the two-thousand-year-old, male-dominated church joined together to form groups to enhance their strength and shed their image as "docile." Organizations such as the National Assembly of Religious Women, The National Coalition of American Nuns, The Leadership Conference of Women Religious Speakers, and The Black Sisters Conference saw their membership increase, and all worked for feminist causes in and out of the church. Another sign of the rebellion of women in the church was the sheer drop in the number of women who chose to enter convents. Seeing no hope for equality and justice in Catholicism, many young Catholic women steered away from it as a vocation. The nuns who remained in the church were highly educated, with 65 percent having master's degrees and 25 percent possessing doctorates. Conservative Catholic women, such as Phyllis Schlafly, opposed all facets of women's equality in the church and were staunch opponents of the ERA. She and many conservative Catholics joined with fundamentalists to lobby against women's rights and abortion. Though well funded and strident, activists such as Schlafly grew dimmer and dimmer among Catholic women as the quest for equality entered the mainstream. In 1985 Gallup polls found that 47 percent of Catholics were in favor of women priests. In 1988 U.S. Catholic bishops, realizing the need for some new official statement on women's role in the church, published the "Partners in the Mystery of Redemption." The document dif-

fered from previous bishops' documents in that some nuns were allowed to participate in discussing and drafting it, but in the end the document broke very little new ground on the issues that interested female Catholics. The church condemned sexism as a sin; yet it still did not favor women priests, contraception, or abortion. In 1989 out of desperation at the realization of the shortage of priests, the bishops issued the "Order for Sunday Celebrations in the Absence of a Priest." This decree allowed a bishop to assign a deacon or nun to lead a prayer service based on the Scriptures. Some nuns felt that this act was a first step toward real changes in the Catholic Church.

Homosexuality. The Catholic Church's condemnation of homosexuality remained consistent in the 1980s, but with the emergence of AIDS the church found that criticism of its policies intensified. One of the church's most militant crusaders against homosexuality was New York's John Cardinal O'Connor. O'Connor, appointed in 1984, believed wholeheartedly in the strict Vatican teaching that homosexuality was a sin against God and nature. O'Connor vehemently refused an organization of gay Catholics called Dignity to hold masses in New York churches. He also attacked the New York City Council for sponsoring a gay-rights bill that would have made it illegal to discriminate against homosexuals. In October of 1986 Joseph Cardinal Ratzinger of the Vatican issued an order forbidding Father John J. McNeill, author of the book *The Church and the Homosexual,* from preaching to the gay community and from speaking publicly about his ideas and works. McNeill's silencing followed that of Father Curran the year before for his statements on sexuality, contraception, and homosexuality. The Vatican's crackdown continued on 30 October 1987 with what gay activists referred to as the "Halloween letter," a directive that ordered all Catholic bishops to withdraw support from any organization that opposed the official church teaching on homosexuality. Greatly impacted by this letter were the many Dignity groups located across the country that used church facilities to hold their masses. Homosexual Catholics vowed to continue their services with or without official approval, as they felt it possible to be gay and still be a good Catholic. Surveys showed that American Catholics for the most part did not view homosexuality in the abstract as a threatening concept. Church officials held their ground, viewing homosexual acts as immoral, and were unwilling to compromise with the current sentiment. Only the epidemic of AIDS, which had caused about eighteen thousand fatalities in the United States by 1988, prompted U.S. bishops to action. The Catholic Church, after substantial debate, allowed in 1987 for the educational discussion of the use of condoms to help control the AIDS virus. Condoms, considered a form of contraception, were previously forbidden to be discussed. Several conservative cardinals, among them Law of Boston, O'Connor of New York, and John Krol of Philadelphia, voted against the measure, believing that it condoned sex and homosexuality, but

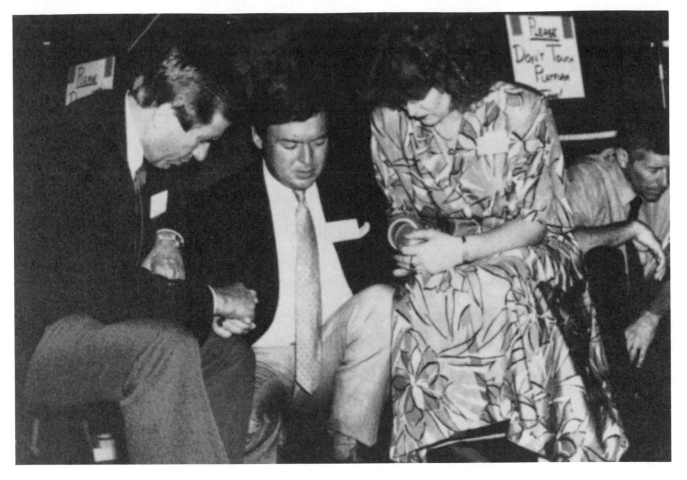

Prayer session at a Southern Baptist Convention annual meeting, 1986

more-liberal cardinals, such as Joseph Bernardin of Chicago, pushed the issue. The question of homosexuality was also an internal one for the Catholic Church in the 1980s. Several works were written by homosexual priests and nuns exposing to the world the church's internal dilemma. A book that caused the biggest stir in the church was the 1984 publication of the biography of the late Francis Cardinal Spellman of New York by John Cooney. The work entitled *The American Pope* exposed evidence of the cardinal's homosexuality. Another work *Lesbian Nuns: Breaking Silence* (1985) documented the stories of present and former nuns. The Catholic Church's official response to the majority of these accusations was denial.

Sources:

George Gallup Jr. and Jim Castelli, *The American Catholic People: Their Beliefs, Practices, and Values* (Garden City, N.Y.: Doubleday, 1987);

Andrew M. Greeley, *The Catholic Myth: The Behavior and Beliefs of American Catholics* (New York: Scribners, 1990);

Lawrence Lader, *Politics, Power and the Church: The Catholic Crisis and Its Challenge to American Pluralism* (New York: Macmillan, 1987).

CATHOLICS SPEAK OUT

Antinuclear Beliefs. In possibly its boldest maneuver of the decade the Catholic Church launched an official condemnation of nuclear warfare and the military buildup that was taking place in the United States. The official pastoral letter titled "The Challenge of Peace: God's Promise and Our Response" was a 155-page statement issued by the National Conference of Catholic Bishops on 3 May 1983. The document was two years in the making. During that difficult period bishops debated the merits of issuing such a statement, the political implications of their action, the theory of just war, and United States national security concerns. While the bishops were slow to act, several priests from around the nation took it upon themselves to respond to what they saw as the biggest moral crisis of recent decades. Archbishop Raymond Hunthausen of Seattle, Washington, became an ardent protester against nuclear weapons, so much so that in 1982 he publicly stated that he would withhold half of his federal taxes as a symbolic gesture. Hunthausen was later punished by the Vatican for his association with radical peace-activist groups. Prior to Hunthausen's reprimand Father Daniel Berrigan, a long-time activist, was arrested in 1980 for damaging warhead cones in a Pennsylvania factory.

Impact. The bishops' pastoral letter when it was issued had greater impact than all of these smaller protests combined because it was not a message from the fringe but a change in the hierarchy's approach to the notion of peace. The primary advocates for the pastoral letter were

Auxiliary Bishop Thomas Gumbleton of Detroit and Joseph Cardinal Bernardin of Chicago. Bernardin faced strong opposition from John Cardinal O'Connor, Terrence Cardinal Cooke, and others, who believed that it was not the Catholic Church's role to interfere in national security issues. The most highly contested point of the document was the question of the morality of nuclear war. In 1976 the U.S. Catholic hierarchy as a whole opposed the use of nuclear weapons and threats to fire those weapons at the Soviet Union, but in this debate the morality of even possessing such weapons was questioned. The bishops criticized the doctrine of nuclear deterrence, arguing that the balance-of-terror game both nations played was demoralizing and would never eliminate nuclear weapons. The bishops dramatically called for a halt in the spread of weapons that effectively endorsed a nuclear-freeze resolution. The pastoral letter was attacked by the Reagan administration, which feared that it could stir a nationwide peace movement. Catholics, for the most part, had traditionally supported the administration's policies and were an important constituency to the president. Conservative Catholics also attacked the letter, stating that the bishops had gone too far in an area outside their expertise. One of the major lay critics was Michael Novak, a conservative writer and scholar at the American Enterprise Institute who was in favor of the status quo. The bishops followed up the letter with several actions. In 1984 they opposed funding for the MX missile, claiming that the money could be better spent in America's cities and for the poor. The bishops' official change on military policy was approved by the Vatican and inspired many churches and denominations to issue their own condemnations of nuclear weapons. The letter was not deemed an absolute moral teaching, but it did signal the end of the Catholic Church's support of any policy that claimed to deter communism.

Economic Justice. With the decline of mainline churches came the decline of their influence in America. The Catholic Church, with its millions of members and prominent scholars, concluded by the 1980s that it had now come time to reach out past their traditional immigrant constituency and assume responsibility as the moral voice of the nation. Vatican II, the document of revolutionary change in Catholic teachings issued in 1963, had already made it possible for the church to broaden its mission in the modern era and now the changes in the 1980s made it possible for the United States Catholic hierarchy to act on their social beliefs as well as preach about them. The bishops' pastoral letter on nuclear arms was a gigantic first step in the Catholic Church becoming what religious scholar and historian Martin E. Marty labeled a "public church," and the church's follow-up letter on economic justice, which was first issued in 1984, solidified the church's new role in American policy decision making. The final draft of the National Conference of Catholic Bishops' pastoral letter on economics was titled "Economic Justice for All: Cath-

olic Social Teaching and the U.S. Economy" and was issued in 1986. The letter focused on the flaws of a capitalist system, problems in the United States economy, and the crime of massive inequality. The tone of the letter was drawn from Liberation Theology, which had become a powerful force in Central and Latin America because of its mix of the basic tenets of socialism with traditional Catholicism. The bishops, of course, realized all of these beliefs would not be accepted in the United States, but they also believed that the United States' economic system was hurting millions of people and felt it important to take a firm stance. Criticized by the Christian Right, officials in the Reagan administration, and conservative Catholics, the bishops, led by Archbishop Rembert G. Weakland of Milwaukee, held to their belief that if the nation did not make changes in its economic system, problems such as poverty would never be eliminated. The battle waged over the merits of the letter were fierce in Washington, D.C., and throughout the scholarly world, but the church expressed its new desire to set the moral tone in the nation and its willingness not to back down when faced with a challenge.

Sources:

Robert N. Bellah and others, *Habits of the Heart: Individualism and Commitment in American Life* (Berkeley: University of California Press, 1985);

Lawrence Lader, *Politics, Power and the Church: The Catholic Crisis and Its Challenge to American Pluralism* (New York: Macmillan, 1987);

George Weigel, *Catholicism and the Renewal of American Democracy* (New York: Paulist Press, 1989).

CULTURAL CHANGE AND JUDAISM

Identity. The quest to maintain individual identity in the ever-growing pluralist society was a struggle that constantly plagued Jewish culture and increased in the 1980s because of several cultural and demographic factors. The Jewish population had remained steady at less than 6 million since the early 1970s, but with increasingly low birth rates and growths in intermarriage the future of Judaism was in question in the 1980s. In November 1983 a conference on Jewish Population Growth was held in New York to look at these trends and consider ways to reverse them. Jewish intermarriage reached a rate of 30 percent and had tripled in the last three decades. Most traditional faiths frowned on intermarriage, but in Jewish culture this issue was a matter of premier importance. All four divisions of American Judaism viewed intermarriage as a crisis, and all found different ways to cope with this latest threat to the integrity of the culture. Conversion, the process by which a Gentile converts to Judaism, had increased dramatically, easing some tensions in the process of intermarriage, but it was accepted with reservations by some, particularly Orthodox Jews. A major issue to spin off from the intermarriage debate was the question of what religion to consider children born of that union. The Reformed Jewish Church, the second largest division of American Judaism, declared that a child born of a Jewish parent, mother or father, was Jewish. Prior to this historic ruling, only children born to Jewish mothers were considered Jewish. The three other remaining Jewish divisions — Conservative, Reconstructionist, and Orthodox — stood by the traditional definition of Jewish children.

Anti-Semitism. According to surveys taken in the mid 1980s many Jews believed that any outward support of the state of Israel, particularly in Arab-Israel relations, could provoke domestic anti-Semitism. Tensions over the rights of Palestinians split liberal and conservative Jews. The most controversial anti-Semitic statements came from blacks, Jews' once-strong allies in the civil rights era. In 1984 Rev. Jesse Jackson, Democratic presidential candidate and black Baptist minister, in an off-the-record conversation with a reporter referred to New York Jews as "Hymies" and New York City as "Hymietown." These remarks angered many Jews throughout the nation who were shocked that Jackson, preaching a message of unity, could utter such remarks, even in private conversation. Jackson quickly apologized for his remarks, yet substantial damage had been done. Adding to black-Jewish tensions, minister Louis Farrakhan, leader of the Nation of Islam, a strong supporter of Jackson, issued several controversial statements about Judaism, questioning the religion's merit, the integrity of its leaders, and the historical accuracy of the Holocaust. Tensions between blacks and Jews were mended toward the end of the decade as conferences and lectures were held to better inform both groups about each other's history and culture. President Ronald Reagan angered many Jews with his 1985 visit to a West German cemetery at Bitburg, the burial site of two thousand German soldiers, many of them part of Adolf Hitler's Nazi SS. Jews saw Reagan's appearance as a demonstration of his failure to understand the importance of symbolism and the depth of the scars that still remained from the Holocaust.

Changing Philosophy. Judaism saw changes in both its secular and theological beliefs. Jews, once overwhelmingly Democrats in their political identification, began to switch allegiances to the Republican Party; by 1986, 16 percent of Jews were Republicans. New Jewish organizations, such as the American Jewish Forum, were created in an attempt to integrate some traditional Jewish concepts with more conservative political beliefs. Some Jews began to veer away from their liberal civil rights positions of the 1960s and sought a more conservative approach to the social issues of the day. On the religious front Conservative Judaism broke a long-standing tradition in 1984 when the Jewish Theological Seminary of America allowed women to be ordained rabbis. Amy Eilberg in May 1985 became the first woman to be ordained in Conservative Judaism. Factional tension continued between the four divisions of American Judaism, as each vied for precious limited membership and definition as the true Judaism.

Israel. United States foreign policy focused heavily on Israel in the 1980s. As one of the few allies in the turbu-

lent Middle East, Israel was supported heartily by the Reagan administration, the New Right, and conservative Jews. Radical advocates for Israel's supremacy in the region, such as Meir Kahane, irritated many moderate to liberal Jews because of his harsh rhetoric. Orthodox and Conservative Jews supported Israel and all of its policies without reservation. Acts of terrorism on both sides of the Arab-Israeli conflict deepened divisions in the American Jewish population. The question of whether Israel should be seen as simply a nation-state or the biblical Jewish homeland raged on. Zionist advocates pushed for Jewish nationalism at any cost. Many American Jews preferred a compromise where they were allowed to support Israel without being fanatical Zionists.

Apathy. American Jews showed a distressing lack of interest in religious participation. Synagogue affiliation and attendance steadily declined in the 1980s. Orthodox Jews had the highest rate of synagogue affiliation. Religious observance of ritual and ritual events, such as Passover Seder and Yom Kippur fasting, were highest among Orthodox Jews, followed by Conservatives and members of the Reformed Church. Over the last generation more and more Jews were changing denominational identification and moved toward Reformed Judaism and Conservative Judaism, if they chose a denomination at all. Many Jews have chosen simply to remain secular in religious beliefs while maintaining cultural ties. According to a 1986 Gallup poll, 35 percent of American Jews said that religion was "not very important" in their lives.

Sources:

George Gallup Jr. and Jim Castelli, *The People's Religion: American Faith in the 90's* (New York: Macmillan, 1989);

Marshall Sklare, *Observing America's Jews* (Hanover, N.H. & London: University Press of New England, 1993);

Jack Wertheimer, *A People Divided: Judaism in Contemporary America* (New York: Basic Books, 1993).

EMPOWERMENT AND THE AFRICAN AMERICAN RELIGIOUS COMMUNITY

Black Church Growth. The connection between African Americans and their churches remained a tie that bound, as they consistently led poll after poll as the most religious people in the United States. *Ebony* magazine estimated in 1984 that there were between 18 million to 20 million nominal black Christians in the United States, of whom approximately one-fourth were regular churchgoers. The largest single African American religious organization throughout the 1980s was the National Baptist Convention, U.S.A., Inc., (NBCUSA), which boasted a membership of more than 7 million. The NBCUSA, long a conservative religious group in both its sermons and politics, entered the mainstream with the election of T. J. Jemison as its president in 1982. Jemison wanted to take this century-old organization into the mainstream to help combat some of the social ills that had inflicted the black community. NBCUSA actions, long overdue in the eyes of many African American

FATHER STALLINGS AND THE CATHOLIC CHURCH

Father George A. Stallings Jr., the black director of evangelization for the Roman Catholic Archdiocese of Washington, D.C., announced on 21 June 1989 that he planned to form an African American Catholic Church over the specific objections of his archbishop, James A. Cardinal Hickey, and the Catholic hierarchy. Stallings named his new congregation the Imani Temple African American Catholic Congregation. He chose the word *imani* because it means "faith" in Swahili. The decision to create a new Catholic Church specifically for African Americans stemmed from Stallings's beliefs that the Catholic Church was too hierarchical and at times racist and that some bishops were imperialistic in their views toward nonwhites. Stallings claimed he loved the Catholic church but had to create a new body in order to improve it. The Catholic Church's thirteen black bishops agreed with Stallings's concerns but not his tactics and urged him to come back to the fold. Stallings refused, and the Imani Temple was inaugurated on 2 July 1989. The following day he was suspended from the Catholic Church. Many African American Catholics in Washington, D.C., and around the nation supported Stallings's actions as they too believed that the Catholic Church had to do more to hold onto its 2 million black members. Stallings continued to preach despite the suspension, and membership in his congregation grew at a steady pace.

Source: Felician A. Foy, O.F.M., ed., *Catholic Almanac* (Huntington, Ind.: Our Sunday Visitor, 1990).

preachers, came at the perfect time for Democratic presidential candidate Rev. Jesse Jackson, who enlisted the support of the black churches for his political campaigns in 1984 and 1988. The influence of African American preachers on their constituencies remained high. With the growth in gang violence, drugs in the inner city, and teenage pregnancy, African American church leaders focused much of their time dealing with the targeted problems in order to heal their community. The National Baptist Convention of America, the second largest African American denomination with 4 million members, devoted the majority of its efforts to social issues and condemned its fellow Baptists in the New Right for their simplistic solutions to complex societal issues.

Jesse Jackson. The rise of Rev. Jesse Jackson on the national political scene did more to invigorate black churches than anything else since the civil rights movement. Jackson's two runs for the presidency of the United States in 1984 and 1988 relied heavily on the black

church for financial as well as spiritual support. A Baptist minister and civil rights advocate, Jackson had pushed since the 1960s for African American churches to get involved in the political arena, and with his campaign of empowerment and unity many felt it was now time to join. The NBCUSA estimated in 1984 that 90 to 95 percent of the denomination's ministers supported Jackson. Jackson's campaign strategy was wholly progressive and appealed beyond a religious base, attracting liberal whites, Hispanics, unions, the poor, and others that were energized by his populist message. His Rainbow Coalition, as he called this political amalgam, was not simply a scheme to boost Jackson to the presidency, it also focused on empowerment and voter registration. The idea of empowerment, particularly to the black churches, was a powerful force. Few church leaders expected Rev. Jackson to win the presidency, but they supported him because of the hope he brought to his community, especially young black males who searched for role models. Jackson's campaign in 1984 was plagued by several problems, such as his having never held an elected office, financial constraints, and his off-putting remarks about Jews — traditionally strong Democratic supporters. His 1988 race was better financed as he won ten states and finished second in total delegates in the Democratic primaries. Jackson's efforts were not enough for him to win the presidency in 1984 or 1988, but he did move African American churches and the Democratic Party more toward the Left with his progressive message of social change and community action. Along with Pat Robertson, he proved that a religious candidate could be seen as a legitimate contender for the presidency.

Black Catholics. The growth of African American membership in the Catholic Church has been rapid since the 1970s. With this growth in numbers has been a demand for more control and representation in the church's structure. African American Catholics numbered slightly more than 2 million members in the late 1980s, yet the church only had 350 black priests and some 700 nuns. Questions of equal treatment weighed heavily on black Catholics' minds, and in 1984 the U.S. black Roman Catholic bishops voiced their concerns on this issue in a pastoral letter. Pope John Paul II on hearing those concerns in 1989 stated that he favored doing whatever was necessary to better represent African American Catholics. One of the leading priests pushing the pope was Bishop Eugene A. Marino, a longtime activist in the cause of elevating the role of blacks in the church, who acknowledged that blacks had never felt completely welcomed by the Catholic Church in the United States. Historically Protestants had spent considerably more time and effort evangelizing blacks, while the Catholic Church focused its attention on immigrants and ethnic groups. Some African American priests, such as Father Robert A. Stallings felt that revolutionary change was needed. Despite tensions the Roman Catholic Church reaffirmed its commitment to increasing its diversity and promoting equality.

The Nation of Islam. Perhaps the most controversial of all African American religions is the Nation of Islam (or the Black Muslims, as they are often referred). Consisting of 100,000 to 750,000 members, the Nation of Islam made news in the 1980s with several angry and sometimes anti-Semitic statements by its leader, minister Louis Farrakhan, who decreed Judaism a "gutter religion" in 1984 and supported Jesse Jackson's reference to Jews as "Hymies" long after Jackson himself had apologized for his remarks. Later Farrakhan went on to belittle the Holocaust in a 1985 speech in New York's Madison Square Garden. Officially Islam and America's 2 million Muslims did not recognize the Nation of Islam as a true Islamic group. Warith Muhammad, son of the late Elijah Muhammad, the Nation's founder, also disassociated himself from the Nation of Islam as he headed the American Muslim Mission. Farrakhan's followers were mostly young black men ages seventeen to thirty-five who turned to Islam for a sense of self-worth and discipline. The Nation of Islam primarily worked in the nation's inner cities and in the prison system to help turn men away from drugs and gangs, fostering an alternative in Islam and Allah.

Sources:

George Gallup Jr. and Jim Castelli, *The People's Religion: American Faith in the 90's* (New York: Macmillan, 1989);

Jesse Jackson, *Keep Hope Alive* (Boston: South End Press, 1989);

Frank S. Mead and Samuel S. Hill, *The Handbook of Denominations in the United States* (Nashville: Abingdon Press, 1985).

THE NEW AGE MOVEMENT

Birth. The New Age movement was not a religion as much as it was an amalgamation of several Eastern philosophies blended with postmodernism. Initially somewhat of a fringe movement, New Age broke into the mainstream in the mid 1980s and soon found its way into contemporary society in several ways. New Age music, speakers, and books became readily available across the United States as stores selling New Age materials proliferated, unashamed to mix consumerism with religious tenets. *American Bookseller* in 1988 lists more than twenty-five hundred New Age bookstores, twenty-five thousand titles in print, and $1 billion in sales in 1987 alone. New Age became an immensely profitable endeavor, as well as a somewhat contradictory one. The contradictions arose because the movement's teachings of individuality, counterculture sensibility, oneness with nature, and simple lifestyles clashed with its commercial obsession and use of the media and celebrities — as one *Time* magazine reporter observed in 1987, its "slightly greedy tone." Curiously, the movement was easily accepted by Americans, many of whom were not particularly religious or already belonged to an established church.

THE HARMONIC CONVERGENCE

No one event typified the New Age movement of the 1980s more than the Harmonic Convergence. The Convergence, marked by a gathering of 144,000 persons at more than 350 sacred locations around the globe on 16 and 17 August 1987, was the brainchild of José Argulles, an art historian from Colorado. Its goal was to generate a universal energy that would help create world peace and harmony. The rituals of dance, prayer, and prophecy were expected to reach out to the stars and attract extraterrestrial powers that would help people on Earth achieve peace. Argulles claimed he came up with the idea for this event from studying ancient Mayan and Aztec calendars. He found patterns, or "great cycles," that occurred throughout the ages where the earth sent out a beacon to the stars and rejuvenated itself. He calculated that the time had come for another one of these "great cycles." The Convergence drew media attention as well as ridicule from people in and out of the movement. In the end no extraterrestrials were spotted at the Convergence, but adherents still believed the power that they had unleashed in the two-day event would benefit the world.

Source: Russell Chandler, *Understanding the New Age* (Dallas: Word Publishing, 1988).

Defined. The New Age movement avoided specific theology, but some of its basic tenets included a belief in reincarnation, spiritual healing, out-of-body experiences, meditation, yoga, astrology, and some belief in the supernatural or extraterrestrial. The movement was not truly new in many senses because it borrowed from several earlier mystical or occult teachings. Native American Shamanism, early Christianity, and the 1960s counterculture all played prominent roles in the movement, but its largest influence stemmed from Eastern religious traditions. Buddhism and its predecessor, Hinduism, provided much of the structure of the new movement. Early New Age pioneers, such as Marilyn Ferguson, presented these various ways of seeing the world in a simplified form to an American audience. Ferguson's 1980 book, *The Aquarian Conspiracy* touched a chord in the American public because it tapped into ideas and mystic concepts that people had believed in for centuries but gave them a modern interpretation. Surveys done in the late 1980s showed that about 30 million, or one in four, American adults believed in the idea of reincarnation. The movement exploded in 1987 when Shirley MacLaine, actress and celebrity, brought her own story of New Age reincarnation to television in a miniseries. Once this much attention was placed on the movement, it began to grow dramatically.

L. Ron Hubbard, founder of the Church of Scientology, testing tomatoes for an emotional response

founders, all equally important, were believed to have taught a universal message of oneness. New Age thinking was extended into political views that were primarily liberal to radical. A call to end nationalism, opposition to nuclear weapons, and expansion of environmental awareness formed the core politics of believers. The New Age movement was not a cult or an organized church because it possessed few temples, or official places of worship. Instead the movement was unified by an optimistic, simple message that appealed to millions of Americans in one version or another. One of the largest segments of the population to support New Age beliefs was the "baby boom" generation, many of whom had left the mainline churches. The appeal of nonthreatening rituals, such as meditation and yoga, as well as celebrity endorsements drew in hundreds of eager participants.

Conflict. The explosion of the New Age movement into the mainstream offended many Christians and Jews because of its apparent similarities to the occult and its denigration of biblical figures. Evangelical magazines, such as *Christianity Today*, cast a doubtful eye on the movement, believing it too commercial, unstructured, and potentially dangerous. Some fundamentalist preachers labeled the movement a cult and its teachings that Jesus Christ was only a prophet, blasphemous. To combat these allegations New Age leaders attempted to show how their movement incorporated the best of all religions and did not seek to downgrade any. Their "umbrella" approach also created much controversy as theologians and religious scholars labeled the movement shallow, unoriginal, and postmodern because of its need to borrow so heavily from other religions. Skeptics and the media often labeled the movement a fraud, an American fad that had no roots and would eventually disappear. Leaders of the movement, most of whom lacked academic or religious credentials, claimed the New Age was moving toward community and providing hope to many who had given up on conventional faith. Instead of shying away from publicity, New Age leaders relished the media and became celebrities in the process.

Teachings. Humanity acting as its own god was the core New Age belief. Man was felt to possess unknown and untapped resources that modern society had suppressed because of its rigorous structure. New Age gurus, such as MacLaine, J. Z. Knight, and Jack Pursel preached a message of self-love, which to some nonbelievers appeared to border on narcissism. Both the New Age and the self-help movements emphasized the power of human potential to reinvigorate itself. New Agers stressed that every man, woman, and child was a spiritual entity and was interconnected with one another, going so far as to claim that all people and nations — past and present — were interconnected in the cosmos. All is one, including God, was the pantheistic theme of New Age thinking. Ancient religious figures, such as Buddha, Jesus Christ, Lao-tse, Krishna, and other important religious

Sources:

Russell Chandler, *Understanding the New Age* (Dallas: Word Publishing, 1988);

Henry Gordon, *Channeling Into the New Age* (Buffalo: Prometheus Books, 1988).

HEADLINE MAKERS

JOSEPH CARDINAL BERNARDIN

1928-

ROMAN CATHOLIC CARDINAL

Symbol. Joseph Cardinal Bernardin became the symbol, even if unknowingly, of the U.S. Catholic Church's struggle with modernity. A quiet, devout man, he rose in the ranks of the church in the 1980s to lead American Catholicism into a more progressive era. He was an instrumental part of the creation of the National Conference of Catholic Bishops' pastoral letters on nuclear weapons, the economy, and AIDS. Bernardin's positions ranged between innovation and traditional Vatican teachings; yet, with his skills of negotiation he was almost always able to forge a compromise. It was his ability to listen clearly as well as speak strongly that separated his vision and actions from other officials in the Catholic Church hierarchy. Bernardin's modesty did not allow him to view himself as a pure instrument of change, but only as a symbol doing the work that was required of him. As he once said in an interview with *Time* magazine, "There is a real spiritual hunger on the part of the people. They are not reaching out to me. They are reaching out to the Lord. Perhaps there is a personal dimension, but I am just a symbol."

Background. Born on 2 April 1928 in Columbia, South Carolina, to a family of Italian immigrants, Bernardin was the only Catholic boy on his block. These early experiences helped him acquire a great understanding and tolerance for other religions and opposite points of view. Initially intent on choosing a career in medicine, he attended the University of South Carolina for a year. Later, after deciding to enter the priesthood, he graduated with a degree in philosophy from St. Mary's Seminary in Baltimore in 1948. He received a master's in education from Catholic University in Washington, D.C., and was ordained a priest in 1952. Once ordained, Bernardin's skills shined, as he soon climbed the hierarchical ladder, moving to Atlanta and becoming the youngest bishop in

the country by 1966. By 1968 Bernardin made Washington, D.C., his home as he became the general secretary of the National Conference of Catholic Bishops (NCCB) and its social action agency, the United States Catholic Conference. In 1972 he was named the archbishop of Cincinnati, Ohio, and was elected president of the NCCB in 1974, serving in that role until 1977. Bernardin brought to every position a strong confidence and a progressive agenda toward church policies. In 1982 Bernardin was named archbishop of Chicago, the largest archdiocese in the nation. This new foothold of power placed Bernardin in a prominent location to express his social activism.

Pastoral Letters. In February 1983 Bernardin was elevated to the Sacred College of Cardinals by Pope John Paul II. Bernardin succeeded the late John Cardinal Cody, who in his last days had been plagued by financial scandals and dissent by priests and followers who believed him to be uncaring and rigid. With Bernardin now in power, Chicago's more than 2.4 million Catholics felt they had a leader who would listen. Bernardin's outspoken position on social issues was evident in 1982 when the first draft of the NCCB's antinuclear weapons letter was issued — "The Challenge of Peace." The letter questioned the morality of possessing nuclear weapons, let alone the use of such destructive forces. After much debate, discussion, and modifications, the pastoral letter was issued 3 May 1983. Bernardin's determination did not stop there; he urged his fellow bishops, both liberal and conservative, to fight for reductions in the amounts of government money spent on the military in general, believing it wrong to waste resources on weapons while urban neighborhoods fell to ruin. In 1984 the NCCB examined the United States' economic structure. Once again Bernardin led the charge for the Catholic Church to take a moral stand, and the resulting pastoral letter, "Economic Justice for All," cited systematic flaws. Although seen as too much of an activist by some officials and church laity, Bernardin continued to work within the framework of the Catholic Church, always seeking biblical and Vatican confirmation for all maneuvers. In 1987 he witnessed the scourge of the AIDS virus sweeping the nation and felt it was time for the church to react officially. The issue of AIDS was complex for the Catholic Church, as it touched upon several issues — condoms, homosexuality, sexual activity — that the church preferred not to deal with publicly. Bernardin, acknowledging this, pushed for the Catholic Church to allow teaching the use of condoms as a prevention of future transmission of the disease. Opposition was severe as some bishops and cardinals felt any change in the official stance would appear as if the church were condoning sexual behavior outside of marriage. Bernardin saw silence and a lack of information as a sinful act on the church's part. In the end the document was adopted and discussion of the use of condoms was permitted on a limited basis.

Vision. Joseph Cardinal Bernardin was a visionary in the Catholic Church, always looking toward the future but never neglecting the Church's rich past. His strong relationships with the laity and to John Paul II in the early 1970s before his elevation to pope served Bernardin well during difficult periods in his career. His open style created a level of comfort not known to many elder Catholics, as he symbolized the pinnacle of post–Vatican II Catholicism. Unafraid to challenge the status quo, he became a star of the American Catholic Church. In 1995 Bernardin was diagnosed with pancreatic cancer, but he continues to lead his Chicago archdiocese and the Catholic Church toward change.

Sources:
D. J. R. Bruckner, "Chicago's Activist Cardinal," *New York Times Magazine*, 132 (1 May 1983): 42–45, 60, 63, 69, 82, 92;

Richard N. Ostling, "Bishops and the Bomb," *Time*, 120 (29 November 1982): 68–77.

JERRY FALWELL

1933-

FUNDAMENTALIST

Leader. The integration of fundamentalist religion with electoral politics in the 1980s was largely designed by the Reverend Jerry Falwell. Falwell was the spokesman for the conservative religious organization known as the Moral Majority, and he was also the premier symbol for the New Right movement. His realization of the impact that conservative religious leaders blended with impassioned followers and modern media could have on politics hoisted him to the forefront of a political movement.

Foundations. Jerry Falwell built his conservative base of operations in the small town where he was born in 1933, Lynchburg, Virginia. He began studying fundamentalism about the age of eighteen and attended Bible Baptist College in Springfield, Missouri. Falwell eventually became a popular fundamentalist preacher and host of his own syndicated television program, *The Old Time Gospel Hour.* His Thomas Road Baptist Church grew to

feature several social services as well as an academic Bible college. Financially, Falwell's empire generated more than $100 million a year in revenues and employed two thousand workers. By the end of the decade, his church grew to have more than twenty thousand members and his weekly television sermon was aired on more than 350 stations to 438,000 households.

The Moral Majority. The birth of the Moral Majority in 1979 heralded a new dimension in fundamentalist thinking. Before Falwell's leadership fundamentalists spent little time with things they perceived as secular or earthly. Falwell's skill was the ability to create an atmosphere in politics where the once apolitical could now have a strong voice. The Moral Majority utilized grassroots as well as the most sophisticated tactics of the times to get their message across. Chapters formed in all fifty states and pushed for a moral agenda in what they saw as an immoral society. Falwell stated in his 1987 autobiography, *Strength for the Journey,* that the Moral Majority had a simple fourfold platform: "We are pro-life, pro-traditional family, pro-moral, and pro-American," and that platform was the exact prescription that many had been looking for. Falwell's group was not alone in the new conservative revolution. Several other Christian conservative organizations had formed in a backlash response to the 1960s and 1970s liberalism, and with the rise of Ronald Reagan as president the movement grew even more powerful. Reagan's election was viewed as a moral victory, but there remained questions as to how much real impact the Moral Majority had in it. The New Right also found later victories few and far between as Americans, for the most part, were not ready to have their public policy formulated by religious zealots. The conservatism that motivated these groups also stifled them as they learned that the rigidity of their beliefs was not compatible with the pluralistic nature of issue politics. Realizing this, Falwell created a new organization in 1986 entitled the Liberty Federation that portrayed a broader message than the Moral Majority had done. The success of this new group was limited, and by 1989 Falwell retreated from the world of politics to spend more time at his church in Lynchburg, Virginia.

Methodology. Falwell's increasing rigidity cast him in a harsh light to the American public. His controversial dealings with the South African government, President Marcos of the Philippines, and Israel all appeared to be ill-timed and generated controversy. Often apparently acting impulsively, Falwell spent as much time defending his reputation as he did elevating it. A skilled statesman, his ability to build ecumenical coalitions with other fundamentalists and conservatives in the Catholic and Mormon churches served him well. He was a natural leader, but he appeared to abandon situations if they did not immediately go his way, as he did PTL reconstruction. After Jim Bakker's removal from the PTL corporation in April 1987, Falwell was named as new chairman of the board for the organization and chose his board members. Bakker anticipated a friendly successor, but Falwell disappointed him; for the next six months what was called a "Holy War" of separation raged between them. Falwell was unable to save PTL from bankruptcy and resigned from the group in 1987. Subsequently the influence of the New Right declined and Falwell's power diminished. The coalition Falwell helped to foster, however, continues to influence American politics. His contribution to the debate over issues of church and state is still being understood. The powerful merger of conservative politics with Christianity would probably have occurred without Falwell, yet he contributed significantly to the impact of the movement in the 1980s.

Sources:
Jerry Falwell, *Strength for the Journey* (New York: Simon & Schuster, 1987);

Charles H. Lippy, ed., *Twentieth-Century Shapers of American Popular Religion* (Westport, Conn.: Greenwood Press, 1989).

BARBARA CLEMENTINE HARRIS

1930-

EPISCOPAL BISHOP AND ACTIVIST

Voice of the Voiceless. Destined never to take the well-traveled or easy path to success, Barbara Clementine Harris made history in 1989 when she became the first woman bishop in the Worldwide Anglican Communion. Harris, an African American Episcopal pastor, had always chosen to be a leader and not a follower, both within and outside her church. Her elevation to bishop amazed many, as it provided a towering example of how far women had come in their struggle for equality in mainline Protestant churches. Harris's goal was to extend the boundaries of her church, continually pushing for a more progressive message from Episcopalians on issues of civil rights, sexism, and fairness. Harris's history as a social activist before joining the priesthood remained ingrained and served as a guide in all her religious actions.

Background. Harris was born on 12 June 1930 in Philadelphia, Pennsylvania. As a youth Harris attended Saint Barnabas Episcopal Church in Philadelphia and developed a strong relationship with her church and its vision. Harris completed high school and enrolled in college, but did not complete her course work. In 1958 a public relations firm, Joseph Baker Associates, hired Harris, believing that she had great potential to enter this field and succeed. Two years later, Harris married. The relationship was short-lived and she was divorced by 1963. Politically, Harris was greatly affected by her surroundings. As a young African American woman, she felt it her duty to be a part of the civil rights struggle. Her participation in freedom rides, voter registration, and

marches with Dr. Martin Luther King in Selma, Alabama, focused Harris's attention on the importance of fighting injustice and inequality. She went on to work as a chief public relations executive at the Sun Oil Company but always held her interests in the Episcopal Church, religion, and in the struggle for justice. Harris's voice increased in the church in 1974 when she lent her support to a group of Episcopal bishops who defied a ban on ordaining women as priests. Harris became so engulfed in the issue of women's rights in the church that she contemplated becoming a priest herself. By October 1980 her dream became a reality as she was ordained. Harris's early assignments varied from serving as chaplain in a Philadelphia County prison and working in small parishes to becoming executive director of the Episcopal Church Publishing Company. While at the Publishing Company Harris wrote for the liberal Episcopal magazine *Witness* and began to receive worldwide coverage in the Anglican community.

Election. Harris's ascension as bishop was a major event in the religious world. The Lambeth Conference, the once-a-decade meeting of the international Anglican hierarchy, decided in early August 1988 to allow for the ordination of women as bishops in the church, and this decision set the stage for Harris to be elected. Her election in September 1988 to be the Episcopal bishop for the state of Massachusetts occasioned great celebration as well as turmoil. She defeated many prominent candidates, including other female priests, in order to achieve her status. In response to her victory counterprotests were launched. Several conservative priests revolted, some breaking ties with the church completely, while top Anglican leaders, such as Robert Runcie, the archbishop of Canterbury, refused to acknowledge female bishops in England. Ecumenical ties between the Roman Catholic Church and the Anglican Church were also strained as the Catholic Church wholeheartedly opposed women entering the priesthood. Harris, for her part, took the controversy in stride and did not let the spotlight detract her from her mission. She had always been outspoken, and she was willing to battle potential challenges to her election as bishop, a stand that won her the admiration of many of her critics.

Aftermath. Once elected and consecrated bishop, Harris continued to advocate for continued diversity in the Episcopal Church and the entire Anglican community. Her command of a ninety-six-thousand member Boston-based diocese made her a powerful force to be reckoned with in deciding church policy and programs. Realizing that with great power came greater responsibility, Harris toned down her rhetoric but did not alter her message. She remains today what she always was, an activist critic of the status quo who constantly strives to break new ground.

Sources:
Larry G. Murphy, J. Gordon Melton, and Gary L. Ward, eds., *Encyclopedia of African American Religions* (New York: Garland, 1993);

Richard N. Ostling, "The Bishop is a Lady," *Time*, 132 (26 December 1988): 80.

MEIR KAHANE

1932-1990

RABBI, ZIONIST, AND FOUNDER OF JDL

Radical. Rabbi Meir Kahane was obsessed with what he believed to be rampant anti-Semitism in America and abroad. He chose to be always on the offensive, attacking his enemies, allies, or fellow Jews if they disagreed with his tactics. He founded the Jewish Defense League, or JDL, in the late 1960s for the specific purpose of defending American Jews from any form of persecution — real or perceived. He popularized the post-Holocaust slogan "Never Again," vowing that Jews would from this point forward always be prepared. Kahane's extremist views were well beyond the mainstream; he was seen as fanatic by most. In the 1970s after being in trouble with the law in the United States, he turned his attention toward Israel, where his ultra-Zionist views and actions brought him worldwide attention. His entrance into Israeli politics and his racist position toward Arabs added fire and tension to an already volatile situation in a sensitive part of the world.

Background. Kahane was born in Brooklyn, New York, on 1 August 1932, into a distinguished heritage of Jewish rabbis. His great-grandfather had been a rabbi in the Austro-Hungarian Empire and his grandfather and father were rabbis in Palestine. As a child Kahane was prone to getting into trouble in his Flatbush neighborhood, but he turned his zeal toward sports and excelled. Until the age of twenty-five Kahane used his birth name, Martin David, but in 1957, when he was ordained an Orthodox rabbi, he changed his name to Meir. Kahane also studied at Brooklyn College, earning a master's degree in international law and international relations. He later received an LL.B. degree from New York Law School but failed to pass the state bar examination. Serving as a rabbi in a small synagogue in Queens, Kahane was expelled from his post because of his Zionist rhetoric and controversial statements. He remained determined in his pursuits and began writing about them in such periodicals as the *Jewish Press*, where he later became an editor.

FBI. In the late 1950s to early 1960s Kahane led a life of secrecy. His strong anti-Communist views landed him a position as a consultant with the Federal Bureau of Investigation (FBI). His assignment was to infiltrate the right-wing John Birch Society and report his findings back to the FBI. For this position Kahane took on the false name Michael King and spent nearly two and a half years posing as a Christian, learning all he could about the John Birch Society. Once his assignment was completed, Kahane retained his double-life status as King, becoming increasingly involved with other government agencies, such as the CIA, Pentagon, and the Cointelpro project. Upon ending his contract with the federal government, Kahane went on to become the director of the Center for Political Studies, a private research organization, and then to writing a book with an associate titled *The Jewish Stake in Vietnam* (1967). When the work was completed, Kahane left Washington, D.C., and returned to New York.

Jewish Defense League. Created out of the tensions that arose because of the Six-Day War and inner-city urban fears, the Jewish Defense League was formed in July 1968. The organization's goals were, according to its charter, "to combat anti-Semitism in the public and private sectors of life in the United States of America; to support all agencies of government charged with the responsibility of maintaining law and order . . . and to safeguard and transmit to posterity the principles of justice, freedom and democracy." Officially Kahane headed the group and pushed the ideas of Jewish pride, self-defense, and political power. The organization's base was located primarily in Jewish neighborhoods of New York. Pride soon turned to violence as the JDL's urban street patrols acted as vigilantes in their quest to root out anti-Semitism. Many moderate Jews saw Kahane's tactics as bordering on terrorism and thuggery, but the JDL appealed to militant youths looking for direction and respect. In order to enlarge its base of support the JDL began to focus on the issue of Soviet Jews by 1970. Kahane and his followers protested vehemently and violently against the Soviet Union. Eventually Kahane and other JDL members were arrested on illegal weapons charges and bomb possession in 1971. Police also suspected Kahane's involvement in a series of previous bombings that had taken place at Soviet installations. Kahane denied all charges but was sentenced on 23 July 1971 to five years' imprisonment (suspended) and a $5,000 fine. These events and court trial did not mellow Kahane's rhetoric but did hasten his departure from the United States.

Israel. With the move to Israel Kahane found a new enemy to attack — Arabs. Initially welcomed in Israel, Kahane's inflammatory statements proved too militant for many Israelis. In 1973 he decided to run for political office in the Knessett, Israel's parliament, and formed the reactionary Kach Party. He lost this election and lost again in 1977 and 1981, but in 1984 Kahane won a seat in the Knessett. His triumph was deemed a sign of the growing tensions between Arabs and Jews. Terrorism and violence had become rampant in the West Bank; the PLO had grown substantially; and Jews began to wonder if Israel could continue to exist under a veil of uncertainty. Kahane fed off this anger and fear of conflict. His agenda was to rid Israel of its Arab influence, and with his newfound power he was in a position possibly to make his dreams a reality. His Kach Party was antidemocratic but pushed a populist, nationalist message of hatred and an "eye for an eye."

Racism. In assessing the life of Kahane words such as *racist* and *fascist* often come to mind. Many Israeli politicians condemned him outright for his ultraright-wing views toward Arabs. The Kach Party was eventually banned in 1988 for its "Nazi-like" stances. Kahane's support came primarily from the poor in Israel, the young, and the military. He decried the left and moderates for their weak positions toward Arabs. They were, in his opinion, Israel's biggest problem and had to be dealt with swiftly if the nation was to survive. Israel to him was God's gift, and he swore that he would protect it unto his death. Kahane was assassinated in New York on 5 November 1990, by an American of Egyptian descent. His legacy of hatred and defiance continued to shape Arab-Israeli relations well past his death.

Sources:

Yair Kotler, *Heil Kahane* (New York: Adama Books, 1986);

Raphael Mergui and Philippe Simonnot, *Israel's Ayatollahs: Meir Kahane and the Far Right in Israel* (London: Saqi Books, 1987).

JIMMY SWAGGART

1935-

TELEVANGELIST

Prophet or Charlatan? With as much fame and power as any other televangelist preacher in the 1980s, Jimmy Swaggart was on top of the conservative religious world. From his base in Baton Rouge, Louisiana, Swaggart created an empire based on fundamentalist interpretations of the Bible, charismatic performances, and on the condemnation of all groups and religions that did not bow down to his limited perspectives of faith. His devastating fall from grace in February 1988 shocked the nation and put into question the merit of the entire evangelical movement. Swaggart's adultery considerably dimmed the halo of the electronic church.

Rise to Fame. Swaggart was viewed as a controversial figure even as a youth because of his early relationship with his famous rock 'n' roll cousin, Jerry Lee Lewis. Swaggart was born in Ferriday, a small town in rural Louisiana on 15 March 1935. His impoverished family actively participated in the local Assemblies of God congregation. Swaggart was a rebellious youth and a high-school dropout. His discovery of religion was the catalyst to his personal turnaround. He met his wife in a Pentecostal church, and by the age of seventeen he was married and fathering children. Searching for viable employment to support his new family, Swaggart conducted informal church meetings in his neighborhood. He also

had the ability to sing and began recording gospel albums in 1959. His recordings increased his popularity immensely and created a strong congregational base for his sermons. Swaggart's album sales remained consistently high and profitable, earning him more than $200 million. Swaggart branched out into radio, and by 1977 his daily religious program was heard on more than six hundred stations. In the 1980s his new television ministries boomed. His weekly program soon became the number one syndicated religious program in the nation. Millions of dollars poured into his ministries, feeding his growing televangelist empire. At the height of his success, Swaggart's average yearly gross was about $150 million. The growth of his power was only stifled by his own harsh rhetoric, which repulsed many and offended others.

Philosophy. Fire and brimstone was the message of Jimmy Swaggart's ministries. Preaching extremist views on the Bible, faith, and sin, Swaggart made few friends outside his evangelical circles and several enemies. His attack on individuals and religious groups that did not view the world as he did caused many television stations to remove Swaggart from the airwaves despite the popularity of his program. Such setbacks did not soften Swaggart's tone but only inspired him to provoke more controversy. Unlike his premier Assemblies of God and televangelist rival Jim Bakker, Swaggart pushed a traditional Pentecostal message that worldly goods were sinful and that only a pious born-again life could protect one from the wrath of God. Swaggart had little tolerance for nonbelievers or those of other faiths, particularly Roman Catholics and Jews. In his sermons he lambasted these religions as false and their followers sinners, and he repeated the attacks in his monthly magazine, the *Evangelist*. Tension flared when in the early 1980s Swaggart claimed that Mother Teresa, Nobel Prize winner and Catholic nun, would burn in hell with the rest of the sinners unless she received the born-again experience and that Jews had suffered because they had turned their backs on Jesus Christ. Swaggart carefully avoided any direct entrance into the political arena. Believing little to be gained and much to be lost by attaching himself to any political figure or ideology, he focused his message on personal religious experience rather than New Right coalition building.

Destruction. Swaggart's downfall may have culminated with his adulterous relationship in 1988, but the seeds for his destruction were planted much earlier on. His denouncement of material possessions as sinful rang hollow as news leaked out about the millions of dollars his religious empire acquired and spent every year. Living a lavish lifestyle Swaggart built a $30 million world headquarters and a recording studio. His empire relied on the donations of his followers, which were often obtained under questionable circumstances. An example of his suspect fund-raising occurred in 1981 when a wealthy California widow, obsessed with achieving piety, willed her entire $10 million fortune to Swaggart. Controversy flared over Swaggart's acceptance of this money despite the widow's family's objections and a heated court battle. Events such as these caused many to question the morality of preachers who preyed on weak victims. Swaggart's sexual transgression was the final straw, as his immorality and hypocrisy exploded onto the airwaves and his tirades against sex, adultery, and pornography came back to haunt him. Once Swaggart had faltered in the public's eyes, he could not go back.

Fall from Grace. The religious empire that Swaggart had taken years to build crumbled as news of his disgrace spread around the country and the world. Followers ceased contributing the large sums they once did, and Swaggart's moral high ground eroded. Stripped of his credentials as an Assemblies of God minister, Swaggart continued to preach despite sharp drops in revenue and dwindling support. He did manage a recovery of sorts and retained enough support to continue his ministry.

Sources:

Marshall Fishwick and Ray B. Browne, eds., *The God Pumpers: Religion in the Electronic Age* (Bowling Green, Ohio: Bowling Green University Popular Press, 1987);

Joanne Kaufman, "The Fall of Jimmy Swaggart" *People Weekly*, 29 (7 March 1988): 35–39;

Charles H. Lippy, ed., *Twentieth-Century Shapers of American Popular Religion* (Westport, Conn.: Greenwood Press, 1989).

PEOPLE IN THE NEWS

On 11 November 1985 **Ezra Taft Benson,** a former agriculture secretary in President Dwight Eisenhower's cabinet, became president of the Church of Jesus Christ of Latter-Day Saints.

On 13 May 1980 a Chicago theologian, **Ralph Wendell Burhoe,** became the first American to receive the prestigious Templeton Prize for Progress in Religion.

Richard Dortch, PTL president, was dismissed by Jerry Falwell following revelations of his role in the PTL scandal on 28 April 1987.

Fundamentalist Moral Majority leader **Rev. Jerry Falwell** scolded the United States for "bellyaching" and urged that it give "unswerving support" to President Ferdinand Marcos of the Philippines on 11 November 1985.

Controversial Nation of Islam leader minister **Louis Farrakhan** announced on 1 May 1985 that he had accepted a $5 million interest-free loan from Libyan leader Col. Mu'ammar al-Gadhafi.

Rev. Billy Graham issued a bold, controversial speech to a convention of religious broadcasters in Washington, D.C., warning of the "dangers" of television evangelism on 28 January 1981.

In September 1982 **T. J. Jemison** became the president of the NBCUSA, succeeding Joseph H. Jackson, the president of the organization for twenty-nine years.

On 15 March 1988 **Bishop Eugene Antonio Marino** was named Roman Catholic archbishop of Atlanta, making him the first African American Catholic archbishop in the United States.

Rev. Patricia Ann McClurg, a Presbyterian minister, was installed on 5 November 1987 as the first female minister to head the National Council of Churches.

On 1 July 1982 former Episcopal priest, now Roman Catholic, **Father James Parker** became the first married priest to say mass in the Catholic Church.

Rev. Norman Vincent Peale received the Presidential Medal of Freedom on 26 March 1984.

Father Donald E. Pelotte on 6 May 1986 became the first Native American to be ordained a bishop in the Roman Catholic Church .

On 21 February 1988 televangelist **Rev. Jimmy Swaggart** was removed from his pulpit by the Assemblies of God after he confessed his sin of adultery.

James Watt, President Ronald Reagan's secretary of the interior, on 22 January 1981 became the first Pentecostal to hold a cabinet position.

DEATHS

Rev. Herbert W. Armstrong, 93, religious evangelist, broadcaster, and founder of the Worldwide Church of God, 16 January 1986.

Eugene Carlson Blake, 78, religious leader and a dominant figure in mainline Protestantism expounding the ideas of ecumenicalism, 31 July 1985.

John Patrick Cardinal Cody, 74, head of the Roman Catholic Church's largest U.S. archdiocese, Chicago, for more than fifteen years, 25 April 1982.

Terrence Cardinal Cooke, 62, Roman Catholic Church cardinal of New York City, 6 October 1983.

Dorothy Day, 83, activist, pacifist, and founder of the Catholic Worker movement, 29 November 1980.

John Francis Cardinal Dearden, 80, Roman Catholic cardinal of the archdiocese of Detroit and head of the National Conference of Catholic Bishops, 1 August 1988.

Father John J. Dougherty, 78, Catholic priest and host of *The Catholic Hour* on radio and television, 20 March 1986.

Rev. V. Carney Hargroves, 85, former president of the American Baptist Churches in the U.S.A. and the Baptist World Alliance, 25 June 1986.

L. Ron Hubbard, 74, founder of the controversial Church of Scientology, 24 January 1986.

Rabbi Mordecai Menahem Kaplan, 102, founder of the Jewish Reconstructionist movement and author of several prominent works on Jewish history, 8 November 1983.

Spencer W. Kimball, 90, leader of the Church of Jesus Christ of Latter-Day Saints, 5 March 1985.

Rev. Martin Luther King Sr., 84, pastor, civil rights leader, and father of the Reverend Martin Luther King Jr., 11 November 1984.

Humberto Cardinal Medeiros, 67, conservative Roman Catholic Church cardinal for the archdiocese of Boston, 17 September 1983.

C. Kilmer Myers, 65, politically active radical theologian and Episcopal bishop, 27 June 1981.

Patrick Aloysius Cardinal O'Boyle, 91, Roman Catholic cardinal of the archdiocese of Washington, D.C., and former director of Catholic Charities, 10 August 1987.

Hryhorij Osijchuk, 87, prelate of the Ukranian Church and founder of Saint Pokrova's Ukranian Cathedral in Chicago, 13 February 1985.

Rev. Jeanette Ridlon Piccard, 86, high-altitude balloonist, scientist, and Episcopal priest, 17 May 1981.

H. M. S. Richards, 90, founder of the international radio broadcast *The Voice of Prophecy*, 24 April 1985.

Rev. Ernest Edwin Ryden, 94, Lutheran minister, journalist, and hymnologist who wrote and translated more than forty hymns, 1 January 1981.

Rev. Francis August Schaeffer, 72, evangelical theologian and leading scholar of fundamentalist Protestantism, 15 May 1984.

Lawrence Joseph Cardinal Shehan, 86, liberal Roman Catholic Church cardinal and civil rights advocate, 26 August 1984.

Rev. Henry Knox Sherrill, 89, Episcopal bishop and the first president of the National Council of Churches, 11 May 1980.

Rabbi Seymour Siegel, 60, theologian and religious liberal Jew who helped shape contemporary Conservative Jewish theology, 24 February 1988.

PUBLICATIONS

Nancy Tatom Ammerman, *Bible Believers: Fundamentalism in the Modern World* (New Brunswick: Rutgers University Press, 1987);

Karen Armstrong, *The Gospel According to Women: Christianity's Creation of the Sex Wars in the West* (Garden City, N.Y.: Anchor/Doubleday, 1987);

William Sims Bainbridge, *The Future of Religion: Secularization, Revival and Cult Formation* (Berkeley: University of California Press, 1985);

Randall Balmer, *Mine Eyes Have Seen the Glory: A Journey into the Evangelical Subculture of America* (New York: Oxford University Press, 1989);

Robert N. Bellah and others, *Habits of the Heart: Individualism and Commitment in American Life* (Berkeley: University of California Press, 1985);

Richard C. Brown, *The Presbyterians: Two Hundred Years in Danville, 1784–1984* (Danville, Ky.: Presbyterian Church, 1983);

Kennon L. Callahan, *Twelve Keys to an Effective Church* (San Francisco: Harper & Row, 1983);

Joseph Castelli and Jim Gremillion, *The Emerging Parish: The Notre Dame Study of Catholic Life Since Vatican II* (San Francisco: Harper & Row, 1987);

Steven M. Cohen, *American Assimilation or Jewish Revival* (Bloomington: Indiana University Press, 1988);

John Cooney, *The American Pope* (New York: Times Books, 1984);

Harvey Cox, *Religion in the Secular City* (New York: Simon & Schuster, 1984);

Herbert M. Danzger, *Returning to Tradition: The Contemporary Revival of Orthodox Judaism* (New Haven: Yale University Press, 1989);

John Deedy, *American Catholicism: And Now Where?* (New York: Plenum Press, 1987);

James T. Draper and Forrest E. Watson, *If the Foundations Be Destroyed* (Nashville: Oliver Nelson, 1984);

Wilber Edel, *Defenders of the Faith: Religion and Politics from the Pilgrim Fathers to Ronald Reagan* (New York: Praeger, 1987);

Ronald Enroth, *Lure of the Cults and New Religions* (Downers Grove, Ill.: InterVarsity Press, 1987);

Jerry Falwell, *The Fundamentalist Phenomenon: The Resurgence of Conservative Christianity* (Garden City, N.Y.: Doubleday, 1981);

Marilyn Ferguson, *The Aquarian Conspiracy: Personal and Social Transformation in the 1980s* (Los Angeles: J. P. Tarcher, 1980);

Marshall Fishwick and Ray B. Browne, eds., *The God Pumpers: Religion in the Electronic Age* (Bowling Green, Ohio: Bowling Green University Popular Press, 1987);

William F. Fore, *Television and Religion: The Shaping of Faith, Values, and Culture* (Minneapolis: Augsburg Publishing House, 1987);

J. W. Fowler, *Stages of Faith* (New York: Harper & Row, 1981);

Andrew Greeley, *Religious Change in America* (Cambridge, Mass.: Harvard University Press, 1989);

Douglas R. Groothuis, *Unmasking the New Age* (Downers Grove, Ill.: InterVarsity Press, 1986);

Andres Gonzales Guerrero, *A Chicano Theology* (Maryknoll, N.Y.: Orbis Books, 1987);

Patricia Gundry, *Neither Slave nor Free: Helping Women Answer the Call to Church Leadership* (San Francisco: Harper & Row, 1987);

Jeffrey K. Hadden and Anson Shupe, *Televangelism: Power and Politics on God's Frontier* (New York: Holt, 1988);

James Hennesey, *American Catholics: A History of the Roman Catholic Community in the United States* (Oxford: Oxford University Press, 1981);

Peter G. Horsefield, *Religious Television: The American Experience* (New York: Longman, 1984);

James Davidson Hunter, *American Evangelicalism: Conservative Religion and the Quandary of Modernity* (New Brunswick: Rutgers University Press, 1983);

William R. Hutchenson, *Between the Times: The Travail of the Protestant Establishment in America, 1900–1960* (Cambridge: Cambridge University Press, 1989);

Erling Jorstad, *Being Religious in America* (Minneapolis: Augsburg Publishing House, 1986);

Robert B. Kaiser, *The Politics of Sex and Religion* (Kansas City: Leaven Press, 1985);

Lawrence Lader, *Politics, Power and the Church: The Catholic Crisis and Its Challenge to American Pluralism* (New York: Macmillan, 1987);

Charles H. Lippy, ed., *Twentieth-Century Shapers of American Popular Religion* (New York: Greenwood Press, 1989);

Robin W. Lovin, ed., *Religion and American Public Life* (New York: Paulist Press, 1986);

Isidro Lucas, *The Browning of America: The Hispanic Revolution in the American Church* (Chicago: Fides/Claretian, 1981);

Shirley MacLaine, *Dancing In the Light* (Toronto: Bantam Books, 1985);

Gregory Martire and Ruth Clark, *Anti-Semitism in the United States* (New York: Praeger, 1982);

Martin E. Marty, *Modern American Religion* (Chicago: University of Chicago Press, 1986);

Egon Mayer, *Love and Tradition: Marriage Between Jews and Christians* (New York: Schocken, 1985);

Michael A. Meyer, *Response to Modernity: A History of the Reform Movement in Judaism* (New York: Oxford University Press, 1988);

Ida Rousseau Mukenge, *The Black Church in Urban America* (Lanham, Md.: University Press of America, 1983);

Mark A. Noll and others, *The Search for Christian America* (Westchester: Crossway Books, 1983);

Richard Quebedeaux, *By What Authority: The Rise of Personality Cults in American Christianity* (San Francisco: Harper & Row, 1982);

James Randi, *The Faith-Healers* (Buffalo: Prometheus Books, 1987);

James A. Reich, *Religion in American Public Life* (Washington, D.C.: Brookings Institution, 1985);

Pat Robertson, *America's Dates with Destiny* (Nashville: Thomas Nelson, 1986);

Wade Clark Roof and William McKinney, *American Mainline Religion: Its Changing Shape and Future* (New Brunswick: Rutgers University Press, 1987);

Marshall Sklare, ed., *Understanding American Jewry* (New Brunswick: Transaction Books, 1982);

Timothy L. Smith, *Revivalism and Social Reform in the Mid-Nineteenth Century America* (Baltimore: Johns Hopkins University Press, 1980);

Richard A. Viguerie, *The New Right: We're Ready to Lead* (Falls Church, Va.: Viguerie, 1981);

Kenneth D. Wald, *Religion and Politics in the United States* (New York: St. Martin's Press, 1987);

George Weigel, *Catholicism and the Renewal of American Democracy* (New York: Paulist Press, 1989);

Sharon D. Welch, *Communities of Resistance and Solidarity: A Feminist Theology of Liberation* (Maryknoll, N.Y.: Orbis Books, 1985);

Bryan R. Wilson, ed., *The Social Impact of New Religious Movements* (New York: Rose of Sharon Press, 1981);

Jonathan Woocher, *Sacred Survival: The Civic Religion of American Jews* (Bloomington: Indiana University Press, 1986);

James E. Wood Jr., ed., *Religion and the State* (Waco: Baylor University Press, 1985);

Robert Wuthnow, *The Restructuring of American Religion: Society and Faith Since World War II* (Princeton: Princeton University Press, 1988);

American Jewish Year Book, periodical;

The Catholic Review, periodical;

Christian Century, periodical;

Christianity Today, periodical.

SCIENCE AND TECHNOLOGY

by JOHN LOUIS RECCHIUTI, MARC D. BAYARD, and GUILLAUME DE SYON

CONTENTS

Sidebars and tables are listed in italics.

1980

1 Jan. Physicist Luis Alvarez proposes that the extinction of the dinosaurs was because of the collision of an asteroid with the Earth.

16 Jan. The Boston office of Biogen, a Swiss bioengineering firm, announces it has produced a disease-fighting protein, interferon.

2 Feb. *Science News* reports that 170 Adirondack lakes have become fishless due to acid rain.

26 Feb. The nuclear containment building at Crystal River, Florida, suffers the spillage of thousands of gallons of radioactive water.

20 Mar. *New Scientist* publishes the discovery of a contact binary system — two stars that rotate around each other every six hours.

2 Apr. University of California scientists discover evidence that life on earth is 3.5 billion years old — 400 million years older than previous evidence had shown.

18 May In Washington State, Mount St. Helens erupts, spewing forth 51 million cubic yards of volcanic ash, dirt, and rocks, leveling nearby forests and killing sixty-one people.

16 June In *Diamond* v. *Chakrabarty* the Supreme Court rules that a biologically engineered organism may be patented.

12 Nov. The spacecraft *Voyager 1* reaches Saturn, making new discoveries about Saturn's moons and rings.

1981

- During the early summer, a live Mediterranean fruit fly is discovered in California, leading to fears of infestation and devastation of the state's agricultural crops. Widespread quarantines and pesticide spraying commence. When no further flies are found by fall, fears abate.

3 Mar. In *Diamond* v. *Diehr* the Supreme Court rules that a technological process that relies on a computer program can be patented.

12 Apr. NASA's reusable spacecraft, the space shuttle *Columbia*, is successfully launched from Cape Canaveral, Florida.

12 Aug. International Business Machines (IBM) introduces its first personal computer, with an operating system by Microsoft.

25 Aug. The spacecraft *Voyager 2* comes within sixty-three thousand miles of Saturn.

1982

- A Gallup poll reports the American public almost evenly divided between supporters of the theory of evolution and those who believe in the biblical account of creation.

- Boeing aircraft introduces the commercial airliner 767, which it claims is 35 percent more fuel efficient than older jets.

- In the Mojave Desert the largest solar energy generating plant ever built, capable of producing ten thousand kilowatts of electricity, is finished.

5 Jan. • A federal judge in Arkansas, citing the separation of church and state, strikes down a law mandating the teaching of creationism in the public schools.

1983

28 Jan.	The Federal aviation administration announces efforts to update the nation's twenty-year-old air traffic control system.
29 Jan.	The Nuclear Regulatory Commission (NRC) fines Boston Edison Company $500,000 for violations at its Pilgrim Station Unit 1 in Plymouth, Massachusetts.
1 Mar.	Two unmanned Soviet probes land on Venus, surviving long enough to transmit data on the soil and atmosphere.
30 Aug.	In Kenya anthropologists report the discovery of a "humanlike" jawbone reportedly 8 million years old.
10 Dec.	Two Soviet cosmonauts set a new world record for time in space, 211 days.
23 Dec.	The Centers for Disease Control (CDC) calls for the evacuation of Times Beach, Missouri, after soil samples reveal toxic levels of dioxin contamination.
30 Dec.	Harvard scientists receive federal permission to begin genetic engineering experiments with the dangerous diphtheria bacterium.

1984

26 Jan.	Scientists announce the apparent discovery of one of the four assumed basic forces in nature. The W, for weak force, assumed to be the force responsible for the radioactive splitting of atoms, joins gravity, electromagnetism, and the strong force (which holds atomic nuclei together) as the physical constants of nature.
8 Mar.	Apple Computer introduces a new machine, called Lisa, that features a hand-held electronic pointer, or "mouse."
30 Mar.	At the San Diego Zoo the first California condor born in captivity is hatched.
11 May	The newly discovered IRAS-Araki-Alcock comet comes within 2.9 million miles of Earth, the closest a comet has come since 1770.
9 Aug.	Scientists at the Jet Propulsion Laboratory announce the discovery of evidence that there are solar systems other than earth's. Satellites had detected solid objects orbiting the star Vega.
14 Sept.	IBM announces the development of a computer chip capable of storing 512,000 bits of information (512K).

13 Jan.	For the first time in history, the Nuclear Regulatory Commission refuses an operating license for a nearly completed nuclear plant.
24 Jan.	Apple Computer unveils its long-awaited personal computer, the Macintosh.
7 Feb.	Two shuttle astronauts, Bruce McCandless and Robert Stewart, become the first humans to fly freely in space. Rather than being tethered to their spacecraft, they sport jet backpacks to maneuver.
26 Mar.	In the first major eruption since 1950, Hawaii's Mauna Loa volcano erupts.
16 May	U.S. District Judge John J. Sirica orders a delay in outdoor experiments with genetically engineered organisms.

3 July Scientists announce they have found convincing evidence of the "top" quark — one of the basic building blocks of subatomic theory.

22 Aug. Anthropologists Richard Leakey and Alan Walker announce the discovery of 18-million-year-old bones of the common ancestor of man and apes.

24 Sept. The Carnegie Museum of Natural History in Pittsburgh announces a rich find of fossils in central Wyoming.

11 Dec. University of Arizona at Tucson astronomers announce they have discovered the first planet outside the solar system.

20 Dec. A one-megabite random access memory (RAM) chip, capable of storing four times as much information as any previous computer chip, is introduced by Bell Laboratories.

1985

- The scanning tunneling microscope is developed by IBM researchers, making it possible to obtain atomic-resolution pictures of surfaces.

- British scientists report the existence of a giant "hole" in the ozone layer over Antarctica.

4 Mar. The EPA bans virtually all leaded gasolines in the United States.

13 Mar. The United States government agrees to clean up Bikini atoll, a ring of tiny islands in the Pacific where nuclear tests were conducted after World War II.

12 Apr. In what becomes the most soaring example of congressional logrolling to date, Sen. Jake Garn of Utah becomes the first nonastronaut to fly aboard a space shuttle.

1 Sept. Explorer Robert D. Ballard, leading a joint French-U.S. team, discovers the wreck of the Titanic in the Atlantic Ocean five hundred miles south of Newfoundland.

24 Sept. According to the Congressional Office of Technology Assessment, the Reagan administration's Strategic Defense Initiative (SDI) does "not appear feasible."

11 Oct. University of Chicago scientists announce evidence that continent-sized wildfires raged across the globe 65 million years ago.

13 Oct. The Fermi National Accelerator Laboratory in Illinois activates a new cyclotron that is the world's most powerful atom smasher.

14 Nov. The EPA approves the release into the environment of the first genetically engineered microorganisms, bacteria designed to prevent frost damage in strawberries.

1986

- Swiss, German, and American physicists make news as they explore zero electrical resistance — "superconductivity" — in ceramic materials frozen at temperatures below -283°F.

24 Jan. The space probe *Voyager 2* passes within fifty-one thousand miles of Uranus.

28 Jan. The space shuttle *Challenger* explodes following liftoff in Cape Canaveral, Florida. All crew members are killed, including Christa McAuliffe, a New Hampshire schoolteacher who was intended to be the first "citizen-observer" in space.

6 Mar.   James C. Fletcher, NASA administrator from 1971 to 1977, is once again named head of the space program.

14 Mar.   The European Space Agency's *Giotto* spacecraft passes within 335 miles of the core of Halley's Comet.

26 Apr.   The perils of nuclear energy are frighteningly dramatized by an accident at the Chernobyl power plant near Kiev, Ukraine, which releases fallout across much of Europe and renders thousands of acres of land near the accident site uninhabitable and unarable for thousands of years.

3 June   President Reagan names William R. Graham his chief science adviser.

9 June   A presidential commission investigating the *Challenger* disaster releases its report, highly critical of NASA.

31 July   American and Japanese trade representatives sign a five-year accord resolving a dispute over computer chips.

23 Dec.   Pilots Richard Rutan and Jeana Yeager complete the first nonstop flight around the globe on a single load of fuel in the experimental airplane *Voyager*.

1987

•   The race to find materials capable of superconductivity at higher temperatures continues, with major breakthroughs announced on 16 February and 27 March.

15 Jan.   The British journal *Nature* publishes a study that concludes that scientific fraud is far more common than heretofore assumed.

30 Jan.   President Reagan approves the construction of a gigantic $6 billion atomic particle accelerator.

9 Mar.   Scientists testifying before Congress announce that the ozone layer has undergone a sharp depletion in the last ten years.

2 Apr.   IBM unveils the next generation of its personal computer.

3 Apr.   President Reagan approves a scaled-down version of the proposed space station.

16 Apr.   The federal government announces it will grant patents for genetically engineered animals, although it prohibits the manufacture of genetic characteristics in human beings.

19 Apr.   In an effort to prevent their extinction, the last California condor left in the wild is captured by biologists forty miles southwest of Bakersfield.

24 Apr.   The first release of a genetically engineered organism into the environment occurs. Frostban, a frost-retardant bacteria, is introduced into a strawberry patch in northern California. By summer, researchers at Advanced Genetic Sciences, Inc., a bioengineering firm, will announce that Frostban successfully protects against frost.

17 June   Canadian geologists announce the discovery of a vast meteor impact crater on the North Atlantic Ocean floor.

19 June   The Supreme Court invalidates the teaching of creationism in public schools when the intention is to promote religious belief.

26 July   Scientists announce the discovery of strong evidence suggesting black holes in nearby galaxies.

1988

16 Sept.	A world environmental summit in Montreal passes measures designed to reduce the presence of ozone-depleting chlorofluorocarbons.
4 Nov.	Genentech, Inc., a bioengineering firm, wins a broad patent covering basic techniques of bioengineering.

28 Jan.	The Public Service Corporation of New Hampshire, a power company responsible for building the controversial Seabrook, New Hampshire, nuclear plant, files for bankruptcy.
14 Mar.	The Senate ratifies an international agreement to phase out the use of ozone-depleting chlorofluorocarbons.
12 Apr.	Scientists at Harvard University patent a genetically engineered mouse, made to be susceptible to cancer and thus of use in medical experiments.
13 May	According to *Nature* magazine, scientists have succeeded in deciphering a second genetic code responsible for the synthesis of proteins inside cells, a problem geneticists had been working on for over twenty years.
29 Sept.	With the successful launch of the space shuttle *Discovery*, NASA resumes shuttle flights, suspended for thirty-two months following the destruction of the shuttle *Challenger* in 1986.

1989

23 Mar.	Stanley Pons of the University of Utah and Martin Fleischmann of the University of Southampton, England, announce they have achieved a controlled nuclear fusion at room temperature. So-called "cold fusion" would represent a revolution in power generation, but many in the scientific world are skeptical about the phenomenon.
24 Mar.	In the worst oil spill in American history, the oil tanker Exxon *Valdez* runs aground in Alaska, discharging 240,000 barrels of oil into Prince William Sound.
12 Apr.	President Bush chooses Rear Adm. Richard Truly to replace James C. Fletcher as head of NASA.
23 May	IBM, AT&T, and the Massachusetts Institute of Technology form the Consortium for Superconducting Electronics to advance the research into high-temperature superconductors.
21 June	Seven leading computer firms form U.S. Memories, Inc., a consortium to produce dynamic random access memory (DRAM) chips for computers.
24 Aug.	The *Voyager 2* spacecraft passes within three thousand miles of the planet Neptune.
27 Aug.	McDonnell-Douglas Space Systems Co. launches the first privately owned orbital rocket carrying a satellite in history.
17 Oct.	San Francisco experiences its worst earthquake since 1906, measuring 7.1 on the Richter scale, killing ninety people, and causing $6 billion in property damage.
19 Nov.	Scientists at the California Institute of Technology announce they have discovered the oldest and most distant object yet known, a quasar at the edge of the observable universe.

OVERVIEW

Anxiety. The general anxiety the American public felt toward science and technology in the 1970s deepened during the 1980s. In the 1970s many Americans began to doubt a long-standing faith that science and technology worked together to improve the human condition. Widespread environmental pollution, the discovery of toxic waste sites such as New York's Love Canal, and the nuclear accident at Three Mile Island suggested to many that the dangers of technology outweighed its merits. The continued threat of nuclear annihilation and the brutality of the war technologies employed in Vietnam strengthened the arguments of those who maintained that rather than advance progress, science and technology retarded human improvement. Such fears deepened during the 1980s. The dangers of environmental pollution became more acute and expensive as thousands of hazardous waste sites were identified and Congress moved to clean them up via Superfund appropriations. The discovery in 1985 of a hole in the Earth's protective ozone layer, a hole allegedly caused by chlorofluorocarbon refrigerants, fed concerns that technology was destroying the basic ecological foundation of human life. The 1986 nuclear disaster at Chernobyl in the Soviet Union spewed radioactive material into the atmosphere, depopulated entire areas of the Ukraine, and confirmed the worst fears of nuclear-power opponents. Massive increases in arms expenditures under the Reagan administration fueled another antinuclear movement, one dedicated to the abolition of nuclear weapons. It did little to dispel public fears that war technology was hurtling the world toward annihilation, especially as reflected in books such as Jonathan Schell's *The Fate of the Earth* or television programs such as *The Day After*. Thankfully, by the end of the decade the willingness of Mikhail Gorbachev's Soviet regime to disarm quelled many of these fears.

Big Science. In the 1970s many critics expressed concern over what they termed "big science": huge, expensive, government-sponsored projects that paid few immediate returns and diverted resources from social programs. Large-scale physics projects, such as particle accelerators and NASA space shots, were particularly criticized. The criticisms increased in the 1980s and had their impact. Congress scaled back the funding for a gigantic supercollider particle accelerator, and NASA's long-projected space station was continually down-graded and defunded throughout the decade. Public confidence in such expensive projects was deeply shaken by the explosion of the space shuttle *Challenger* shortly after its launch on 28 January 1986. For many critics it proved the program was not worth the cost: space shuttles were expensive and complex, and their failures, as in the case of *Challenger*, were far too costly. Many suggested that NASA could accomplish the same mission objectives using unmanned robot vehicles — a suggestion backed by the success of the *Voyager* deep-space probes. NASA hung tough, weathering congressional criticism and improving the safety defaults of the shuttles, and renewed flights within three years of the *Challenger* disaster. But the criticisms of big science continued. To many observers the explosion of the *Challenger* and the meltdown of the Chernobyl power plant symbolized the limits of science: both were expensive, complex endeavors that admitted no error. Despite the best efforts of scientists and engineers to operate these projects perfectly, they failed spectacularly. Their failures only increased public anxiety over other big science projects.

Biological Manipulation. In the 1980s, biological engineering became the focus of big science. Spurred by technical advances during the 1970s that made possible genetic recombination, universities and private corporations moved quickly into the research and production of new genetic codes and modified biological lifeforms. The potential benefit to humanity of genetic engineering was limitless. Genetic engineering could develop hardy, disease- and weather-resistant food sources, eradicate deadly diseases, and modify lifeforms to accomplish highly specialized tasks. In 1988 Harvard University was granted the first patent on a genetically engineered organism: in this case a mouse susceptible to cancer, that could facilitate medical research. Many among the public, however, were deeply troubled by genetic engineering. They feared, above all, errors of the type plaguing nuclear power or the space program. A genetically engineered virus, for example, might mutate into a toxic plague; modified plant life might destroy the world's food stocks. Of even more concern was the potential to modify the genetic structure of human beings, producing "superhumans," or the use of the technology to eradicate particular racial groups. Many scientists, such as Nobel Prize–winners Paul Berg and David Baltimore, recommended careful progress in the field, constantly guarding against the dangers of biological disasters. Despite these fears, in 1989 the government began funding the Human Genome Project, an effort to map the entire 3 billion nucleotides of human DNA, a project estimated to cost $3 billion. For the moment the potential returns on big biological science seemed to outweigh the potential risks of the technology.

SDI. Other big science projects fared less well. Among the most controversial was the Reagan administration's effort to build an impenetrable "space shield" to protect the United States from nuclear attack. Exactly how the space shield would work was unclear. The impetus for the program apparently came from Reagan himself, convinced that it would provide a platform for future peace. Scientists developed several proposals for implementing the program, from high-energy particle beams to exploding satellites, but the mathematical and physical barriers to intercepting thousands of ballistic missiles simultaneously were formidable. Many experts considered the program, named the Strategic Defense Initiative (SDI, commonly called "Star Wars" after the popular science-fiction movie), impossible. And the program also complicated disarmament talks with the Soviet Union. Most important, SDI was expensive, estimated to cost upward of $1 trillion. The technical difficulties, high cost, and complicated politics behind the program doomed it. In 1993 the administration of Democratic president Bill Clinton killed the SDI program — one of the few technical defense programs of the 1980s to be killed. Many others, extremely expensive — including the radar-evading "Stealth" aircraft, the cruise missile, the neutron bomb, and the multiple-warhead Trident submarine — were deployed before the decade was out.

Spurious Science. SDI was not the only big scientific program plagued by formidable technical barriers. Nuclear fusion, long holding the potential for vast power generation, continued to frustrate engineers seeking to harness its power. Over the decade the disappointing returns on fusion resulted in the loss of half the funding for fusion research, and fusion technology remained in the experimental stage. As the decade closed, hopes were raised by the announcement that two Utah chemists had achieved nuclear fusion in a test tube at room temperature — a miraculous feat with the potential to unleash a vast new energy source. It was too good to be true, and, in fact, close scrutiny by the scientific community revealed that the scientific basis for the discovery was badly flawed. Other areas of science were also plagued by poor or misleading methodology. In 1991 a young scientist alerted the academic community to a 1986 research paper by Nobel Prize–winner David Baltimore that was based on falsified research. A subsequent cover-up brought an investigation by Congress into the problem of scientific method and proper protocols and led to Baltimore's resignation from the presidency of Rockefeller University.

Success Stories. Failure and sloppy science were not the only stories in science during the 1980s. One new technology in particular delivered the type of progressive improvement Americans had formerly associated with science. Computers had a profound impact on the decade. Capable of replicating a host of intellectual functions, computers revolutionized basic science and increased the speed and accuracy of technical applications. Moreover, when International Business Machines (IBM) introduced its personal computer in 1981, it began a revolution in business practices, personal finance, and communications technology whose full impact cannot yet be assessed. Computers were an old-fashioned scientific success story, dramatically improving the quality of life and restoring the faith of many in the potential of technology. Superconductivity — the discovery in 1986 of ceramic materials capable of conducting electricity with little loss of energy — was another success story. Superconducting materials had the potential to dramatically increase the world's energy resources. Unlike computers, however, superconductive technology remained in the early stages as the decade closed, capable of much but as yet unproved.

Transforming the Natural. The success stories in science in the 1980s, especially genetic engineering and computers, had broad implications for the public's sense of the natural. Both technologies imitated and manipulated cognitive and natural functions. Science was, in other words, transforming the sense of the natural. Many controversies during the decade were centered around this transformation: environmental disputes were grounded in the desire of many to restore the natural wilderness to a pristine state; as scientists continued to manipulate the basic matter of life, antiabortionists insisted on the sanctity of even unborn life; and a fixed sense of the natural — regardless of the scientific evidence — was part of the disputes over gay rights, feminism, and race relations. In the 1980s conservatives and fundamentalists insisted on forms of the natural and normal even as scientists continued to prove that the natural and normal could be altered and manipulated. In a sense, conservatives and fundamentalists were expressing their anxieties over the pace of scientific change by rejecting modern science. But as the decade closed, even environmentalist and antiabortion groups were networking via computer. Science and technology would press forward. But the question implicit in the rejection and anxiety over science in the 1980s — was it pressing forward on a human scale? — remained unanswered.

TOPICS IN THE NEWS

AVIATION

Innovation and Consolidation. Aeronautics in the 1980s experienced many technological improvements built on achievements from the previous two decades. Such progress was hampered in some fields by economic realities and enhanced in others by political imperatives. Issues such as safety, pollution, the arms race, and government spending became fully intertwined with aerospace technology. As a result, aviation developed into a field with enormous socio-economic implications ranging from leisure travel to high-technology industrial development. Some observers nevertheless argue that the fluctuations the field underwent in the 1980s point to its having yet to reach maturity.

No-Frills Flying. The 1980s were a period of upheavals for the commercial aviation industry. Following the deregulation trend begun in the United States in 1978, economic control of the industry was lifted in favor of letting market forces act. The rationale that high levels of competition would winnow out inefficient airlines and lower the costs of flying led to the appearance of low-cost "no-frills" airlines, operating a limited number of routes and offering little or no on-board service. The practice had been initiated by Sir Freddie Laker, a British businessman, with his low cost "Skytrain," a DC-10 that flew daily between New York and London. In the case of U.S. no-frills airlines, such policies were quite successful in the short term, allowing many people who would have otherwise traveled on the ground or not at all to fly to their destination. One of the more notorious airlines was the now-defunct People Express, which bought used jets and flew them out of its Newark, New Jersey, base to cities throughout the United States. It competed directly with Eastern Airlines on the New York-to-Boston shuttle route (one of the busiest air links in the nation). In 1984, at the height of People Express's short success, a one-way ticket between the two cities cost as low as $29 for an off-peak flight, against $60 for an Eastern ticket and $35 for an Amtrak train ticket.

Market Problems. No-frills airlines found themselves fighting each other for the same market, with little overhead left to face losses. On the other hand, older, more stable airlines were established in a variety of markets that guaranteed income (businesspeople flying to a meeting, no matter what the cost), while the no-frills airlines, in an attempt to increase profits, started opening new routes at a pace too fast for their own good. People Express and others suffered fatal growing pains. When expected revenues failed to materialize, these airlines either went bankrupt or had to consolidate their operations. There were a few notable exceptions, such as Southwest Airlines, a short-haul operator that carefully expanded into other markets. As for big, established airlines, they also suffered from the competition prompted by deregulation. Big airlines were able to compete by matching the low fares of no-frills airlines. While they profited considerably from the low cost of fuel (in the mid to late 1980s it cost about the same as in 1979), they also faced a series of slumps when recessions hit the United states in the early and late 1980s. This forced several airlines into bankruptcy court, while others fared somewhat better, depending on their structure. Some never recovered, such as Pan Am and Eastern Airlines.

The Civil Aircraft War. New technologies developed in the 1970s allowed aircraft manufacturers to build safer, more efficient, and less polluting aircraft. This situation caused considerable competition for airline contracts: from the mid 1960s until the late 1970s, U.S. airlines usually bought American-built aircraft, citing quality of manufacture, better financing, and better servicing as reasons. The European Airbus Industry Consortium broke the U.S. consensus when it leased and sold its A-300 model to Eastern Airlines in 1978. Soon other Airbus models followed into the breach, as did those of other aircraft manufacturers. In 1982 the British Aerospace Corporation, for example, built a four-engine jet, the 146, designed for short-haul links between airports with limited space. The technical solutions devised to reduce noise pollution made the aircraft the only jet allowed to operate at such airfields as the Orange County, California, airport. Other foreign manufacturers offered new commuter aircraft (Brazilian Ambraer, Franco-Italian ATR, Dutch Fokker, German Dornier).

U.S. Manufacturers Respond. Calls for U.S. governmental protection of domestic aircraft builders against foreign aircraft caused confusion among business and po-

The B-2 Stealth bomber during its maiden flight over California in July 1989

litical leaders, as most foreign aircraft used parts and engines built by American firms, thereby nullifying the claim that the U.S. aerospace industry deserved governmental help. In fact, U.S. manufacturers did not remain idle. McDonnell-Douglas offered updated versions of its highly successful DC-9 model, while Boeing launched two new models. The 757, designed to replace the aging 727, offered a vastly improved wing design and a cockpit centered around digital displays rather than the traditional dials that had characterized commercial aircraft until then. The other model, the 767, a twin-engined wide-body aircraft designed to compete with the European Airbus 310 model, became the first twin-engine passenger aircraft used regularly on Transatlantic routes. Overall, many of the technical improvements made to civil and commercial aviation came in part from trickle-down effects of military innovations from the 1960s and 1970s.

Military Aviation. In the 1980s military aviation arguably got its greatest boost since the Vietnam War. Political events, framed within the implications of the Cold War, prompted a massive military buildup under the two Republican administrations that controlled the White House in the 1980s. The most notorious aspect of this buildup was a call for a six-hundred-ship navy, including a series of nuclear aircraft carriers. At the aviation level President Ronald Reagan ordered the reactivation of the B-1 supersonic nuclear bomber program (which had been canceled under President Carter), to be built by the Rockwell company. Other aircraft, in particular F-14, F-15, and F-16 jet fighters, were ordered in large quantities, and the new F-18 "Hornet" also entered service. This buildup became popular in the public mind in part through the release of such movies as *Top Gun* (1986) and *Iron Eagle* (1986). The rationale for such an increase in military spending pointed to the failure of negotiations with the Soviet Union concerning arms reductions and the discovery that new aircraft with vastly superior capabilities to previous Soviet and American models were under development in Russia.

New Missile Technology. New missile technology was also developed during the decade. Air-launched cruise missiles (ALCMs) were installed on aging B-52 bombers. These automatic machines, fitted with either nuclear or conventional explosives, could cruise hundreds of miles thanks to satellite navigation (a signal from a satel-

Halley's Comet on its closest approach to Earth in April 1986

lite in orbit gives the missile its exact position second by second) to reach their target without requiring human control and strike within yards of their intended goal. These ALCMs weren't used, however, until the Persian Gulf War in 1991. Missiles intended for air-to-air and air-to-sea or -ground combat were also perfected, in particular those nicknamed "fire and forget," which implied that, once aimed on target, the device keeps track of the target without assistance from the operator. Finally, at the tactical level, the U.S. Army completed development of the Pershing II missile, capable of carrying several warheads that would drop on different targets (the term assigned to these warheads is MIRV — Multiple Independently Targeted Reentry Vehicle). The development of the Pershing II was part of a NATO defense program known as "dual track," which involved negotiations for armament reduction with the Soviet Union while at the same time developing new weaponry for deployment in case negotiations failed. The Soviet Union, for a variety of reasons, refused to remove its new SS-20 missile from Eastern Europe, and in October 1983 the Pershing II was deployed in West Germany.

Invisible Planes. In an effort to put new research and development results to practical use, the Pentagon also pushed forward the "stealth" program. Stealth technology's goal is to render an object invisible to radar detection. Methods used since the 1940s ranged from building machines out of wood (early radar could detect metal only in large quantity) to covering aircraft with a wave-absorbing substance that would not reflect back to the radar dish. The Lockheed Aircraft Corporation, whose "Skunk Works" secret aircraft project unit had already developed such aircraft as the U-2 and the SR-71 "Blackbird" spy planes, set about in the 1970s to develop a stealth aircraft. The first prototype, named "Have Blue," has never been shown in public and remains classified, although some blurry pictures of it exist. Following the testing of the machine, probably in the late 1970s, a production model, the F-117, was built and first flew in 1983. It was first used in combat during the U.S. invasion of Panama in 1989.

The B-2. In parallel, the Northrop company was contracted to build a stealth bomber, the B-2, that would help perpetuate the nuclear deterrence aspect of American defense policy (a B-2 might have a better chance of breaking through the Soviet defense perimeter than an aging, very vulnerable B-52). While the end result (a massive, carefully engineered flying wing) makes the B-2 one of the great marvels of American aerospace technology, its cost (over $1 billion per plane) along with budgetary problems and the end of the Cold War have led critics to question its usefulness when military objectives seem to be shifting to other regions of the globe where other machines, such as helicopters, would be more useful. Other critics argue that spending the money on space flight would be preferable.

Commercial Satellites. In the 1980s, private companies were formed to launch commercial satellites into space. These satellites were to be used for weather, ground observation (geological studies), television relays, and long-distance phone service. The increase in demand for such services and the loss of availability of the space shuttle (only U.S.–sanctioned payloads are allowed) opened the market to other launchers. In the United States, Titan and Delta rockets were put to use, competing against the European Ariane space consortium. The increase in competition in this highly lucrative market has lowered launch costs and prompted further demand for such services, which companies from other nations are eager to offer.

New Promises and Concerns. The aerospace industry in the 1980s offered hope in solving long-distance transportation problems. More people could afford to fly, and, despite occasional recurrence of terrorism, flying remained the safest mode of transportation. Military aviation was used extensively in fulfilling U.S. foreign policy goals, whether to carry out political objectives or to provide relief missions. Finally, the conquest of space allowed new applications, in particular in the field of telecommunication. All these factors contributed to shrinking further the planet, yet also raised new concerns with regard to noise and air pollution. The depletion of the ozone layer remains a central issue to the development of new aircraft, in particular those intended to fly supersonically. Increases in air traffic are encountering the opposition of people residing near airports, and airlines operating at break-even levels worry about maintaining a steady passenger flow. Nevertheless, aviation has become central to many aspects of life in the United States in the 1980s and will likely increase in importance as the United States moves into the next millennium.

Sources:

Michael E. Brown, *Flying Blind: The Politics of the U.S. Strategic Bomber Program* (Ithaca, N.Y.: Cornell University Press, 1992);

Steven Morrison and Clifford Winston, *The Economic Effects of Airline Deregulation* (Washington, D.C.: Brookings Institute, 1986);

John Newhouse, *The Sporty Game* (New York: Knopf, 1982);

James Ott and Raymond E. Neidl, *Airline Odyssey* (New York: McGraw-Hill, 1995);

George C. Wilson, *Flying the Edge* (Annapolis, Md.: Naval Institute Press, 1982).

CLEANING UP TOXIC WASTE

A Problem of Plenty. During the 1980s the people of the United States lived a life of comfort unheralded in human history for so large and diverse a people. Astonishing advances in technology were largely responsible for the nation's material success. The country's comparative affluence had, however, a major side effect: pollution. From the earliest days of the Industrial Revolution the country's factories, chemical plants, and even (beginning with the use of manmade chemical fertilizers and insecticides) the nation's farms were culpable. While producing an expansive profusion of goods for market, the nation's economy had also been pouring vast quantities of pollutants into the soil, water, and air.

Superfund. In 1980 Congress established the Superfund to clean up toxic waste dumps across the country. The Superfund was only one part of the Comprehensive

Environmental Response, Compensation, and Liability Act (CERCLA), but CERCLA was judged an awkward acronym, and the law was commonly referred to as the Superfund Act of 1980. The Superfund provided three essential things in the fight against toxic waste sites: it put the federal government in charge of identifying public sites; it provided for fines to be levied on chemical manufacturers to assist in funding the cleanup; and it held companies that had contributed to a toxic site, however large or small their contribution to the total pollution present, liable. The new act initially provided more than $1 billion for a Hazardous Substance Response Trust Fund, but it was soon clear that even this amount might not be enough to clean up the tons of toxic chemicals buried and abandoned in sites scattered all across America. There were 1,224 sites on the Superfund inventory list of toxic dump sites in need of cleanup by mid 1989. Conversely, during the 1980s only twenty-seven sites had been cleaned so thoroughly that they were removed from the Superfund list of hazardous sites.

Superfund Expanded. A series of amendments to CERCLA in 1986 increased the public's legal right to information from corporations. The 1986 revisions gave the public access to industrial data on the use of chemicals in industry. The information corporations supply must, according to the law, describe the toxicity of the chemicals they use and the manner in which the companies are disposing of them. Large users of chemicals are required by the law to file annual Toxics Release Inventory (TRI) reports with the EPA. The 1986 amendments also increased funding of the Superfund. The new federal funding of $9.6 billion was a substantial increase from the 1980 provision of $1.6 billion, but many environmental organizations were estimating that the actual costs might run to over $100 billion. By 1987, however, a contingent of Environmental Protection Agency analysts were asserting that toxic dumps were overrated as a danger to the environment. In their view ozone depletion and naturally occurring radon were much greater risks to public health.

Corporate Responsibility. By 1989 the federal Superfund had $8.5 billion for cleanup of toxic sites. It was also increasingly wielding an important provision of the 1980 Superfund Act: the provision authorizing the government to bring suit against the corporations responsible for creating the toxic sites. Using this proviso, federal bureaucrats were able to alleviate some of the taxpayers' burden. Further, the very creation of the Superfund Act had inspired corporate action: striving to keep their companies off the Superfund list, many corporations initiated investigations and cleanup efforts on their own. Indeed, with public attention and concern focused on air, water, and land pollution, companies began to voluntarily reduce the amounts of pollutants they spewed into the environment. In 1987 the Monsanto Corporation vowed to reduce its air pollution emissions by 90 percent, and other companies such as Union Carbide and Du Pont also set out to reduce the pollutants they released into the

Prototype developed in 1989 by the U.S. Department of Energy for an underground nuclear waste dump. Radioactive uranium used for fuel would be stored in cylindrical casks.

environment. Lastly, though governmental fines associated with a Superfund site were modest, the repercussions of being declared a responsible party for polluting a site could, in civil court, be enormous. Private liability lawsuits often followed quickly on the heals of modest Environmental Protection Agency fines. For example, Xerox was fined $95,000 by the EPA for failing to report chemical pollutants at one site. The company, however, suffered $4.75 million in losses to two families who sued them as a result.

The Problem of Pollution. The Superfund was made necessary because chemicals had been disposed of inappropriately for decades. The symbol in the 1980s of the toxic waste site was Love Canal, a section of Niagara Falls, New York, used as a dump site by a chemical and plastics company in the 1940s and 1950s. The company had dumped nearly twenty thousand tons of toxic pollutants in improperly sealed metal drums into the empty canal and covered over the barrels with earth. Subsequently, the company donated the land to the city of Niagara Falls. Houses and an elementary school were built at the dump site. By the 1970s local children suffered from a variety of disorders, including malformed bones, retardation, cleft palates, and kidney disease. The

unusually high rate of birth defects, miscarriages, and cancers in the area were blamed on the discarded chemicals, which had leached into the soil from leaking barrels. Love Canal, however, was only the most publicly visible toxic site. Also infamous as the nation's worst polluted areas during the 1980s were "cancer alley" outside Baton Rouge, Louisiana, and two West Virginia valleys. By 1983 the fifty worst hazardous waste sites on the Superfund's National Priorities List included the municipalities of Jacksonville, Arkansas; New Castle County, Delaware; Swartz Creek, Michigan; Bridgeport, New Jersey; and Kent, Washington. One of the largest Superfund sites was twenty-seven square miles of Rocky Mountain Arsenal outside Denver, Colorado. Every region of the nation was affected.

The Fix. Agents of the Environmental Protection Agency declared "toxic-substance emergencies" at many of the more than twelve hundred identified toxic waste sites during the 1980s. The declaration of an emergency did not, however, mean that the government was swift to act. Often, little more was done than fencing off the sites and posting notices that they were hazardous. When the EPA actively pursued cleanup of a toxic waste site they often chose between a series of expensive options, including cap and contain, a process whereby packed clay is used to cap the polluted area; the incineration of contaminated soils; chemically "washing" soils to remove contaminants and then collecting the runoff; and removal of the soil to one of the few government-approved toxic waste storage sites. Another option was to improve the laws so that pollution is stopped before it starts, as in a 1984 law calling for a strict "land ban" on PCBs and dioxins. Such chemicals, Congress decreed, must be destroyed by incineration or chemical neutralization.

Source:
"Yesterday's Toxics: Superfund," *Newsweek,* 114 (24 July 1989): 36–38.

COMPUTER REVOLUTION

Personal Computers. The personal computer revolution was a phenomenon of immense importance in the 1980s. What the average American commonly refers to as a PC, or personal computer, did not even exist before the 1970s. Mainframe computers had been the norm, and they were primarily relegated to business and scientific use. With the dawn of the personal computer all Americans were allowed potential access to computers. As competition and modernization increased, issues of cost became less and less of an inhibitor, and it appeared that a new technological "populism" had developed. Companies such as Apple Computer became household names, and words such as *software* and *downloading* became commonplace. It was predicted that by 1990, 60 percent of all the jobs in the United States would require familiarity with computers. Already by 1985, some 2 million Americans were using personal computers to perform various tasks in the office. The impact of the personal computer to the average American has been enormous — in addition to its usefulness at the office, it has become a source of entertainment, culture, and education.

Apple. Founded in 1976 by Steven Jobs and Stephen Wozniak, Apple Computer was to be the spearhead of the personal computer revolution. Apple had achieved moderate success in the late 1970s, but in the 1980s the company developed its innovative vision of how computers could relate to the average person. By 1982 Apple became the first personal computer company to have an annual sales total of $1 billion. In 1983 Apple introduced the Lisa. Lisa was to be the successor of the Apple II and was the first computer to widely introduce the concept of windows, menus, icons, and a mouse to the mainstream. The Lisa computer was phased out by 1985 and surpassed by the Macintosh in 1984. Macintosh was faster, smaller, and less costly than the Lisa; it retailed for around $2,500 and was packaged as a user-friendly machine that was economical enough to be in every home. Although the machine possessed less processing capability than IBM PCs, one did not need any programming capability to run the machine effectively, and it became popular.

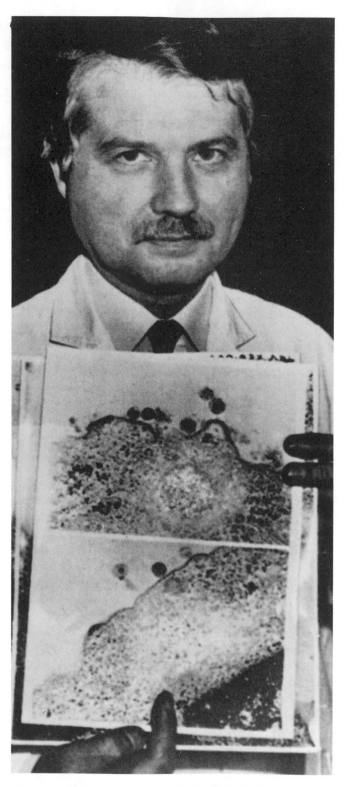

French microbiologist Dr. Luc Montagnier displaying slides of a virus he had discovered. He shared his research with Dr. Robert Gallo, who subsequently announced that he had found a strikingly similar virus, which, he said, caused AIDS.

Beyond Simplicity. Not satisfied to be simply "the easy PC," Apple in 1986 introduced the Mac Plus, PageMaker, and the Laserwriter. The infusion of these three, particularly PageMaker, an easy-to-use graphics

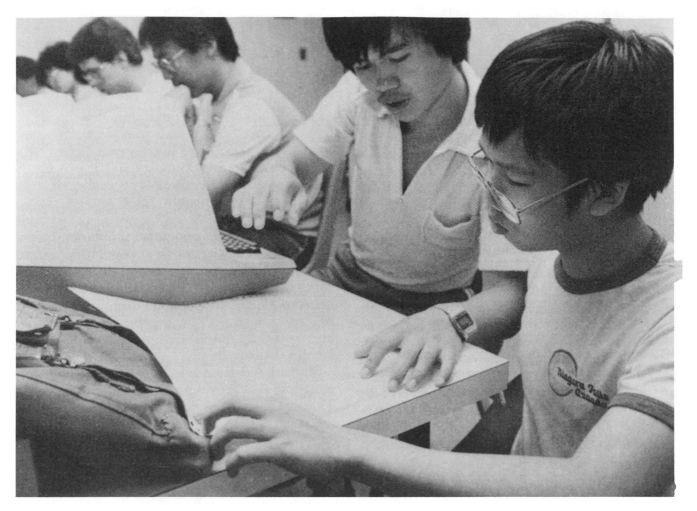

New York City high-school students studying computer programming during a summer-school session at New York University in 1982

page-layout program, helped give rise to a new medium known as desktop publishing. Creating this new niche made Macintosh the premier, efficient publishing computer. Apple expanded its hold on the graphics market in 1987 with the introduction of the Mac II computer. Its color graphic capability fostered the introduction of color printers capable of reproducing the color images on the computer screen. By 1988 Apple introduced Macs capable of reading DOS and OS/2 disks, thereby closing some of the separation between Macintosh and IBM PCs.

IBM. On 12 August 1981 International Business Machines (IBM) created its first personal computer. Simply called the IBM PC, it became the definition for the personal computer. IBM was the largest of the three giant computer firms in the world, and the other two, Hewlett-Packard (HP) and Xerox, had previously attempted to make efforts into the new PC market but failed. IBM initially was not convinced that the American public was interested in computers, particularly for their own home usage, but after viewing the early successes of Apple they were determined to enter the race.

In creating the software for the PC, IBM turned to a young company called Microsoft to formulate MS-DOS.

Market Success. IBM PCs were immensely powerful, fast machines, and their entrance into the market legitimized the personal computer and created a new cottage industry. In 1983 IBM introduced the PCjr, a less expensive version of the PC. Despite strong advertisement PCjr was not a success and cost IBM quite a bit in reputation and money. Undiscouraged by these results, IBM pressed onward. By the mid 1980s, IBM PCs had inspired many clones that emulated IBM's functions at a lower cost to consumers. Constantly setting the standard, IBM in 1987 introduced the PS/2 and the OS/2, the first IBM 386 models. IBM also established agreements with software companies such as Lotus to develop sophisticated programming for their company. Attempts were also made by the company to launch a line of portable computers over the decade. The success of these various portable models was somewhat limited, due to size and cost, as well as improper promotion. Even with several marketing setbacks throughout the decade, however, IBM remained the largest computer firm in the world. By

1989 IBM was producing personal computers that dwarfed earlier models in speed, capability, and technology.

Software. As the personal computer explosion continued to grow, it spawned more and more cottage industries. One of the largest new markets to develop was that of the software industry, and one of the largest companies in that industry was Microsoft, founded in 1975 by William Gates and Paul Allen in Redmond, Washington. In 1981 Microsoft created MS-DOS, short for Microsoft Disk Operating System. Although it was initially licensed only to the IBM Corporation, by the end of the decade it became the industry-standard operating software for all PCs. The ability to corner this lavish, fast-growing market solidified Microsoft's software leadership position in the 1980s. Microsoft also began work late in the decade on Windows and OS/2 software programs for PCs and introduced programs for Apple Computer. Another growing software company was Lotus Development Corporation, who created its innovative 1–2–3 spreadsheet programs. Desktop publishing software was advanced greatly thanks to the growth of Apple Computer's graphics capabilities. Countless other software programs, from playful (video games) to statistical (accounting programs), began to saturate the market, attempting to feed the growing desires of the American public.

Information Society. Computers have touched most aspects of how Americans function. Through their ability to link groups across great distances, they have made the world, at least theoretically, a smaller place. The computer was not the first technological advancement to impact the nation so greatly, but the speed in which it swept across the country and the pace in which change within the field continues to occur have been remarkable. As technology advanced, the cost of computers also significantly declined. Schools on all levels began to integrate computer literacy into their academic programs as it was seen that this knowledge would be as essential as reading in the next century. Sales for computer companies skyrocketed as they rushed to meet demand. Computer magazines, such as *Byte, PC World,* and *PC Magazine* were either born in the 1980s or grew substantially as interest around the issue grew. Backlash regarding the growth of computers and their infiltration into society also occurred. Fear of an unfeeling technical society where human contact has been replaced by machines has been voiced by some extreme critics. On the more moderate side are criticisms that computer technology will only improve the lives of those who could afford the high costs of a PC. Thus, the computer, instead of unifying, could potentially increase the gap between the rich and the poor.

Sources:
Paul Freiberger and Michael Swaine, *Fire in the Valley: The Making of the Personal Computer* (Berkeley, Cal.: Osborne/McGraw-Hill, 1984);

MACHINE OF THE YEAR

In 1983 *Time* magazine solidified the personal computer's arrival into mainstream society when it named the PC its 1982 Machine of the Year. *Time's* Man of the Year award was given to a prestigious man or woman that had made a significant mark on the world in the preceding year; by adapting the honor for a machine, *Time* acknowledged the immense contribution this technology had made upon society. Computers, once available only to trained programmers, now became increasingly commonplace in homes across the country. They changed the way the average American received and processed information at work and at home. Some critics scoffed at the fact that the magazine had bestowed a machine with such an important title, but *Time* defended the decision, stating, "There are some occasions, though, when the most significant force in a year's news is not a single individual but a process, and a widespread recognition by a whole society that this process is changing the course of all other processes. That is why, after weighting the ebb and flow of events around the world, *Time* has decided that 1982 is the year of the computer."

Source: Otto Friedrich, "The Computer Moves In," *Time,* 121 (3 January 1983): 14–24.

Gene Smarte and Andrew Reinhardt, "1975–1990: 15 Years of Bits, Bytes, and other Great Moments," *Byte,* 15 (September 1990): 369–400;

Tom Thompson, "The Macintosh at 10," *Byte,* 19 (February 1994): 47–54;

Edward Yourdon, *Nations at Risk: The Impact of the Computer Revolution* (New York: Yourdon, 1986).

FUSION

Disappointment. Fusion, once touted as the energy source of the future because of its cleanliness and low demand for raw materials, became immensely difficult to produce. To extract all this energy required the ability to fuse two atomic nuclei, an act that is extremely difficult to achieve since like charges repel one other. To overcome this basic problem, scientists spent millions of dollars on machines and research. Rarely were these machines able to replicate, even for a minute, what the sun accomplishes constantly — fusion reactions. With limited sustainable results and waning interest, the fusion program in the United States appeared destined for hard times. By 1989 funding for fusion research had been cut to slightly more than $500 million, about half of its peak in the 1970s. Decreased funding led to internal fighting within the field as each potential program promised more than it could ever possibly deliver in such a short period.

Magnetic Confinement. Magnetic confinement remained the most widely used approach in the attempt to harness fusion reactions. Two-thirds of U.S. efforts and a larger percentage worldwide pursued this method, which called for the heating up and the compressing of plasma confined in a magnetic field. The process was accomplished using a gigantic machine called a tokamak. Modern tokamaks, such as Princeton's Tokamak Fusion Test Reactor, have been able to heat plasma hotter than the interior temperature of the sun; yet their ability to capture the energy created by the plasma has been limited. The other major flaw of modern tokamaks is that they lack the ability to produce ignition: the point at which the fusion reaction produces enough heat to sustain itself without further heating by the machine. Without the ability to sustain themselves, fusion reactions would never be able to create the endless cost-efficient energy source that United States researchers demanded and would not be able to justify continued funding. In 1984 the pursuit of the magnetic-confinement fusion program cost U.S. taxpayers $350 million, and funding remained close to that level throughout the decade.

Reactions. Late in the decade scientists at Princeton University, one of the top research facilities in this field, looking to improve reaction time and duration, combined deuterium (*d*), a heavy form of hydrogen, with tritium (*t*), believing that a *dt* reaction would release two hundred times more energy per fusion than a *dd* reaction alone. Tritium was not an easy substance to obtain, however, and was also quite costly. Innovative research was further postponed near the end of the decade when the Bush administration, frustrated with a consistent lack of results in fusion research, reduced federal funding and caused severe cutbacks at Los Alamos, Oak Ridge National Laboratory, and Princeton.

Internal Confinement. Internal confinement, better know as laser fusion, became increasingly used in the 1980s as a potential means of harnessing fusion. It too brought with it many unforeseen and costly complications. Its basic premise involved blasting small amounts of deuterium and tritium from all sides with radiation to create a fuel so hot that it ignited. The Lawrence Livermore National Laboratory and the University of Rochester took the lead in this technology in the 1980s. In 1989 scientists at Lawrence Livermore were constructing a free-electron laser (FEL) coupled to a tokamak. They discovered that high-frequency FELs in visible and infrared wavelengths yielded greater plasma heat control. At Rochester scientists used a neodymium-glass laser split through a complex optic array to vaporize deuterium and tritium. Their experiments yielded the highest thermonuclear efficiency of any laser fusion facility up to that time. The full benefits of this technology have yet to be completely determined, but cost overruns have caused the federal government to assess whether it should continue to be funded at its present stage. Other problems faced the internal confinement program, primarily political

ones since the official goal of the U.S. program was not to produce new sources of energy but to help workers study weapons-related physics. This official position made much of the laser research top secret and prohibited any significant international cooperation.

Cold Fusion. On 23 March 1989 the scientific world stood in awe as two obscure chemists working in Utah announced that they had done the nearly impossible — they had created fusion in a test tube. B. Stanley Pons and Martin Fleischmann claimed that they had accomplished, simply and inexpensively, what scientists had attempted to accomplish for the preceding thirty years. Pons, a professor at the University of Utah, and Fleischmann, of Britain's University of Southampton, were neither elite physicists nor chemists, so their discovery was greeted with skepticism in the scientific community but hailed by the general public. Labeling the process "cold fusion" because the reaction had occurred at room temperature, Pons and Fleischmann claimed that the reaction was simple to produce. In sum, they had placed palladium encircled by platinum into heavy water — water enriched with deuterium. From that point electricity separated the oxygen from the deuterium, and the deuterium was left to fuse with the palladium. Once the fusion reaction had occurred, large amounts of energy were released.

Criticism. Instantly questions arose as to whether this discovery was valid and whether fusion could occur so easily. Scientists around the nation attempted to replicate these findings — the majority to no avail. Pons and Fleischmann defended their experiment, but with potential millions riding on their discoveries, they refused to reveal the specific details of their work. With no way to replicate their experiment and with later revelations that Pons and Fleischmann had not been particularly precise with their scientific methodology, their findings were eventually labeled invalid.

Cold Fusion Continues. In 1989 Steven Jones of Brigham Young University in Utah also claimed to have created cold fusion. Jones's fusion discovery produced a much smaller energy output than that of Pons and Fleischmann, but it did have a larger output than the initial input. His research was also received with some skepticism but appeared more plausible than his Utah colleagues. By the end of the decade, the bang of cold fusion was less than a fizzle as it was consistently debunked and refuted by the scientific community.

Sources:
Sharon Begley, Harry Hurt, and Andrew Murr "The Race for Fusion," *Newsweek,* 113 (8 May 1989): 49–54;

Frank Close, *Too Hot to Handle* (Princeton: Princeton University Press, 1991);

John Horgan, "Fusion's Future: Will Fusion-Energy Reactors be 'Too Complex and Costly'?," *Scientific American,* 260 (February 1989): 25–28.

The largest magnetic fusion-energy test reactor, assembled at Princeton University and tested successfully in December 1982

HUMAN GENOME PROJECT

Mapping the Human Genetic Blueprint. Humans are made up of billions of cells, each of which performs a specific function. The coding for these functions is located in the "blueprint" held in each cell's chromosomes, and the collection of genes on the twenty-three pairs of chromosomes constitutes the human genome. Mapping the precise sequence of the 3 billion nucleotides that make up the genetic sequence in the human genome became the focus of many geneticists' work during the 1980s. "The total human sequence," as Walter Gilbert noted, "is the grail of human genetics."

Big Science. Judged technically feasible at conferences of biologists in 1985 and 1986, the U.S. government committed itself to funding the effort to map the blueprint of human life in 1989. In January 1989, partly spurred on by an awareness that scientists in Japan and the European nations were beginning to catch up with America's lead in the field, the U.S. National Institutes of Health launched a multiyear project to map the human genome. Initial cost estimates were projected to be around $3 billion, putting the Human Genome Project, as it came to be called, into the category of "Big Science"

projects funded by U.S. taxpayers. By comparison the supercollider project of the mid 1980s was to have cost $3 billion; NASA's several projects, including a future space station, were estimated at around $8 billion.

New Era in Human Understanding. Knowledge of the exact nucleotide sequence of the human genome could be a tool for understanding every aspect of human function. Precisely what will be learned when the mapping is completed is uncertain, but in the 1980s there was reason to believe that the Human Genome Project would offer insights into the biological basis of such things as brain development, evolution, and human intelligence. Indeed, a complete genetic map could unlock the answers to the etiology of more than a thousand known genetic diseases, making possible the development of unheralded cures for such afflictions as cancer, heart disease, diabetes, sickle-cell anemia, Huntington's disease, cystic fibrosis, and Alzheimer's disease. Nevertheless, some people worried that a complete knowledge of human genetics, if it fell into the wrong hands, could be used to produce genetically engineered "superhumans," or, perhaps less invidiously, that parents would ask scientists to rearrange those elements of their unborn children's genetic structures to make their progeny highly intelligent, more resistant to disease, or more physically attractive.

Technical Difficulties. Mapping 3 billion microscopic nucleotides is no simple task. Researchers David Ward and Peter Lichter at Yale University used X rays and a complex system of chemical color coding to identify gene sequences in the 1980s, but further advances will be necessary. Automation will speed up the sequencing process. Furthermore, hundreds of millions of dollars will have to be spent on computer software and hardware merely to keep track of the results geneticists achieve in the lab. Storing and handling the data collected, and making it accessible to researchers, is essential. In 1989 James Watson — codiscoverer of the double-helix structure of DNA — was optimistic. As director for human genome research at the National Institutes of Health, Watson was confident that an initial "low resolution" map of the human genome could be completed within several years and that a "high resolution" map was in sight.

Sources:

"Genome Mapping Goal Now in Reach," *Science,* 244 (28 April 1989): 424–425;

"Genome Project Under Way, At Last," *Science,* 243 (13 January 1989): 167–168;

"Proposal to Sequence the Human Genome Stirs Debate," *Science,* 232 (27 June 1986): 1598–1600.

MOUNT ST. HELENS

Early Signs of Activity. Located seventy miles from Portland, Oregon, in a sparsely populated region of southwestern Washington State, Mount St. Helens erupted in 1980 in one of the largest volcanic explosions in North American history. The mountain's last eruption had been recorded by the American soldier, explorer, and political leader John C. Fremont in 1857. Signs of significant seismic and volcanic activity began as early as 27 March 1980, when the first venting of smoke and ash began. As many as 250,000 residents in nearby counties, including several hundred loggers, forest rangers, and residents in the immediate vicinity of Mount St. Helens, were either evacuated or warned.

The Volcano Erupts. At 8:32 A.M. on Sunday 18 May 1980 Mount St. Helens erupted. Millions of tons of earth were shot as high as 65,000 feet into the air. Heated rock and ash poured down the mountain's northern side. In a short time, what had been a 9,677-foot mountain measured only 8,364 feet. A crater two and one-half miles long and one mile wide had been created. One scientist compared the force of the explosion to five hundred Hiroshima-sized atomic bombs. Sixty-one people lost their lives as a result. Thousands of elk and coyotes; hundreds of deer, bobcats, and black bears; and an estimated fifteen mountain lions were also killed in the blast. Ash from the volcanic eruption fell on half of the state of Washington as the public witnessed the awesome event on television.

Subsequent Activity. A second eruption occurred a week after the initial blast, on 25 May. A dome of molten rock had formed by October 1980, and another, less spectacular, eruption took place on 11 April 1981. Five years later, in May and June 1985, a series of minor earthquakes accompanied by mild volcanic activity worried residents, but no major volcanic activity followed. Scientists predicted, however, that the volcano would erupt again early in the twenty-first century.

Sources:

D. E. Bilderback, ed., *Mount St. Helens, 1980: Botanical Consequences of the Explosive Eruption* (Berkeley: University of California Press, 1987);

"Eruption of Mount St. Helens," *Scientific American,* 244 (March 1981): 68–80;

"Mt. St. Helens is Calm," *Science News,* 127 (29 June 1985);

"Volcano, Dormant for 123 Years, Begins Erupting in Washington State," *New York Times,* 28 March 1980.

NUCLEAR POWER

A Deceiving Calm. During the 1980s proponents of nuclear power had much to celebrate. The technology worked, and it did so without burning up the earth's coal and oil reserves and without spewing noxious fossil-fuel pollutants from conventional power plants into the atmosphere. By 1989 there were 426 nuclear power plants worldwide, and the 110 plants located in the United States that year supplied nearly one-fifth of the nation's electricity. All, however, was not well in the nation's nuclear power industry.

A Torrent of Problems. The nuclear power industry in the United States was beset with problems. During the 1980s not one new order was placed for a nuclear power plant anywhere in the country. Cost overruns in construction and maintenance of reactors was much higher than had been anticipated. It was not uncommon for the final price tag of a nuclear plant to exceed tenfold the initial estimates. Safety, too, was a major concern. The events of 28 March 1979 at Three Mile Island, Pennsylvania — two hundred thousand citizens fled the region when severe core damage in one of the site's reactors was reported to be nearing a dreaded meltdown — had shaken public confidence in the industry. The issue of what to do with spent nuclear fuel rods — the used-up, highly radioactive isotopes at the heart of the reactors — also plagued the industry. These problems, coupled with an unanticipated reduction in the growth of demand for electricity nationwide (experts had predicted that demand for electricity would grow at the rate of about 7 percent annually, but in 1981 demand was up only 0.3 percent, and in 1982, amid a national campaign to conserve energy, demand actually fell by 2.3 percent), resulted in a major setback for those who had envisioned meeting half of the country's electrical demand with nuclear power by the end of the century.

Generating Electricity. A nuclear power plant is something like a giant tea kettle. The intense thermonuclear reaction at its heart is used to boil water. The controlled fission reaction at the reactor's core gives off extraordinary amounts of heat. Water passed nearby the core absorbs the heat and turns to steam, which is then used to generate electricity. By focusing high-pressure steam onto the blades of a turbine, they can spin the turbine's coils of wire through giant magnetic fields. The result is the electricity that illuminates otherwise darkened streets, powers air conditioners on sultry summer nights, energizes computers, and serves the nation in many other ways. The tricky part is boiling the water. In conventional power plants water is boiled by burning coal or oil. What attracts engineers to nuclear power is the fact that fission can provide a trillion times more energy than a windmill and a million times more energy than the combustion process at the center of conventional coal, gas, or oil power plants. The use of fission to boil water is, however, fraught with problems. Even a minuscule amount of highly radioactive uranium is deadly.

Nuclear Disaster at Chernobyl. Though thousands of miles away from America's shores, the events of 26 April 1986 near the town of Pripyat in the Soviet Union focused concern once again on the issue of safety in the nuclear power industry. One of four nuclear reactors at the Chernobyl Nuclear Power Station in the Ukraine exploded with such force that the roof of the building was completely blown off. Eight tons of radioactive material was scattered about the region immediately surrounding the plant. Airborne radioactivity from the blast rained down on northern Europe and Scandinavia — fallout was measured as far away as Scotland — contaminating farm produce. Engineers at Chernobyl had accidently initiated an uncontrolled chain reaction in the reactor's core during an unauthorized test in which they unlawfully incapacitated the reactor's emergency systems. In the immediate aftermath of the catastrophe, more than thirty people lost their lives, and one estimate placed the number who would eventually live shortened lives as a result of the effects of their exposure to radiation from the accident at twenty thousand.

Reaction. In the United States experts argued that the disaster at Chernobyl was not pertinent to the domestic nuclear industry. They noted that the technology employed at Chernobyl was not being used in the United States. The Soviets, they pointed out, were using a weapons-material production reactor to generate electricity for their domestic market — something not done in the United States. Furthermore, the Chernobyl reactor lacked a containment building — a required safety component mandated for all U.S. reactors. Nevertheless, many Americans drew uneasy parallels between Chernobyl and Three Mile Island: operator error and equipment failure were possible in the nuclear industry. The consequences of a single major mistake could be catastrophic.

Seabrook and Shoreham. Both proponents and opponents of nuclear power persistently articulated their views — sometimes in strident tones — during the 1980s. Proponents hailed the small number of nuclear power plant safety violations. Opponents pointed out that a single mistake could be extremely costly both in environmental and human terms. During the 1980s scores of "anti-nuke" organizations warned of the hazards of nuclear energy and protested plant construction and operation. In Seabrook, New Hampshire, protesters rallied around a citizens' action group — the Clamshell Alliance — to oppose the building of two nuclear reactors. By 1987, in part due to the increased vigilance of oversight safety committees insisted upon by the Clamshell Alliance, the utility that owned Seabrook was near bankruptcy. At Long Island's Shoreham nuclear facility the story was much the same. By 1988, besieged by civic-group opposition, the Shoreham "nuke," having far exceeded initial cost estimates of $241 million (its actual cost to the utility had surpassed $5 billion), was closed by the state government. The utility that owned Shoreham had failed to develop an adequate evacuation plan of that region of Long Island that would be affected in the event of a meltdown. Sold to the state government for one dollar, the completed plant was to be dismantled even before it opened.

Cost Overruns, Problematic Workmanship. Repeatedly the industry discovered that cost overruns and construction problems were an issue. Florida's St. Lucie 2 plant cost about four times its original estimate of $360 million, but this price, as it would turn out, was a relative bargain. By middecade Michigan's Midland nuclear

Eruption of Mount St. Helens in Washington State, 18 May 1980

power plant (initial cost estimate: $267 million) had cost the utility constructing it $4.4 billion, and it was nine years behind schedule. In the West, at the Diablo Canyon Plant, earthquake supports were installed backward. At the Shoreham reactor workers had to craft makeshift elbow joints when, during construction, they discovered that pipes failed to meet at the proper point. As one commentator noted, it was no wonder that problems cropped up, because constructing a nuclear plant was "like building a giant Swiss watch" using subcontractors.

The Problem of Disposal. Reactors in the 1980s were inefficient. Only about 1 percent of the uranium atoms in the rods fission; the remaining 99 percent of the uranium remains in the rods even after they are no longer useful for producing power. The pellets of uranium, which are packed into long rods and lowered into the core of a nuclear reactor, remain extremely radioactive even after they are "spent," and remain so for thousands of years. These irradiated fuel rods must be disposed of, but no one wants them in his backyard. During the 1980s utility companies stored these rods on site, at the power plants, in large vats resembling swimming pools, but this was considered a temporary solution. In 1982 Congress passed the Nuclear Waste Policy Act. The act called upon the Department of Energy (DOE) to find a suitable site to bury the radioactive waste. DOE, however, was unsuccessful in locating a site that included both the necessary stable rock formation (free of groundwater) and the requisite local public support. At decade's end, no solution to the problem of nuclear waste had been found.

Sources:
"Energy from Nuclear Power," *Scientific American,* 263 (September 1990): 136–142;

"The $5 Billion Nuclear Waste," *Time,* 131 (6 June 1988): 55;

"Memories of a Near Meltdown," *Time,* 123 (13 February 1984): 41;

"Pulling the Nuclear Plug," *Time,* 123 (13 February 1984): 34–38;

"We are in a Heap of Trouble," *Time,* 130 (26 October 1987): 114.

OZONE

Problems with Ozone. When three atoms of oxygen bond they form a molecule of ozone (O_3). Ozone is both much rarer and much more chemically active than O_2 molecules — the common form of oxygen found on earth. Nevertheless, ozone posed two significant health risks during the 1980s. The first problem was that there was too much of it in urban areas near the planet's surface. The second problem was that there was not enough of it at high altitudes. Both problems were "man-made."

Ozone as an Urban Problem. At low altitudes, in the earth's troposphere, automobiles and factories poured tons of organic gases into the atmosphere. When these chemicals mix with nitrogen oxides they form smog — one ingredient of which is the highly poisonous ozone. During the 1980s the government issued "ozone alerts" — cautioning citizens to stay indoors or curtail vigorous out-

---

CALIFORNIA CONDOR

The most visible aspect of the government's endangered species program in the 1980s was its $10 million effort to save the California condor from extinction. The largest vulture in North America, the California condor (*Gymnogyps californianus*) has a nine-foot wingspan and can achieve top flight speeds of 60 MPH. It is the only surviving large bird from the late Pleistocene era. California's expanding population, and the concomitant rise in hunters, poison bait intended to kill other predatory animals such as coyotes, and the introduction of pesticides for farming, all contributed to the diminution of the condors' numbers. In the 1940s the Audobon Society counted approximately sixty condors in California, but by the early 1960s only forty-two birds could be found. It was clear that many of environmental hazards were leading toward the condor's extinction. The government stepped in with a plan in the 1980s. It would capture the remaining condors, breed them, and then, having built up the species's numbers, repopulate the wilds with the majestic animals. The captured birds were kept at the San Diego Wild Animal Park and at the Los Angeles Zoo. The last of the wild condors was captured from the San Joaquin Valley by the California Fish and Game Commission on 19 April 1987. By 1989 the condor population had increased from twenty-four to thirty-five, and plans were being laid to release some birds back into the wild.

Sources: "Ancient Death and Modern Survival," *Science News,* 132 (29 August 1987): 136;

"Condor Recovery Effort," *Science,* 231 (17 January 1986): 213–214;

"Last Days of the Condor?," *Time,* 126 (30 December 1985): 68;

"The Last Days of the Wild Condor?," *Science,* 229 (30 August 1985): 844–845..

---

door activities that might cause them to inhale large quantities of ozone and thereby injure their lung tissue. In many urban areas, where automotive exhaust and industries are highly concentrated, the problem was often very serious. In 1987 Los Angeles's ozone levels exceeded federal health standards on 141 days. But California was not the only affected state. In 1987 ozone levels exceeded federal standards on 19 days in New York City, on 21 days in Houston, and on 23 days in Philadelphia.

Ozone Depletion. High above the Earth's surface during the 1980s there was another problem. In the earth's stratosphere — from around nine to thirty miles above sea level — ozone was being destroyed. The depletion of enormous quantities of stratospheric ozone led scientists to beseech governments to act. Stratospheric ozone, it turned out, was a major component in blocking the sun's dangerous ultraviolet rays from reaching the earth's surface.

Chlorine Destruction. In 1974 scientists Mario Molina and Sherwood Rowland wrote a groundbreaking paper describing the potential harm to the stratosphere caused by chlorine. What they found was that chlorofluorocarbons (CFCs), chlorinated hydrocarbons, methyl chloroform, and halons (used in extinguishing fires) were finding their way into the upper atmosphere and destroying the protective blanket of ozone. As it turned out, chlorine molecules break ozone molecules into ordinary oxygen. When even small quantities of chlorine interact with ozone it forms chlorine monoxide by stealing an oxygen atom from ozone. But the process does not stop there. The chlorine rapidly releases the oxygen atom it steals, and turns again to breaking apart other O_3 molecules. The resultant two-atom oxygen molecules are ineffective in absorbing the energy of ultraviolet light. As a result, increased ultraviolet radiation reaches the earth's surface — since it is no longer absorbed by the stratospheric ozone — and causes increases in skin cancer and cataracts among humans and other animals, as well as adversely affecting sea algae, soybean crops, and other plant life. Ozone depletion may also promote the growth of organisms that are better adapted to higher levels of ultraviolet light.

The Culprit. Chlorofluorocarbons were invented in 1928 for use as a refrigerant. CFCs are excellent for use in refrigerators and are also cheap and effective as cleaning agents, in plastic foams used in styrofoam (for disposable coffee cups and in packaging for fast-food chains), and as propellant in aerosol sprays. By 1978 CFCs were banned in aerosol sprays, but problems persisted. In 1985 scientists discovered the Antarctic ozone hole — the first irrefutable evidence of the destruction of upper-atmosphere ozone by CFCs. The cold above the poles (especially above the South Pole) creates ideal conditions in ice clouds to unleash ozone-destroying chlorine from CFCs. Two years later, in the Montreal Protocol of 1987, many countries agreed to cut their production of CFCs by the year 2000 to one-half and to hold production of halons to 1986 levels. Soon, however, many considered even this curtailment inadequate. In 1989 the European Economic Community (EEC) countries agreed to stop CFC production altogether by the year 2000, and later that year, in Helsinki, Finland, eighty-one countries, including the United States, agreed to stop the production of CFCs by 2000.

Alternative. In 1986 the Du Pont corporation developed an alternative to the ozone-depleting CFCs, which were commonly marketed under the name Freon. The company was hopeful that CFC-22 (which breaks down in the earth's troposphere but is much more expensive than Freon) might serve as a practical substitute for Freon. Nevertheless, chlorofluorocarbons already released into the atmosphere will continue to destroy the ozone layer for another century, and some researchers predict that as many as eight hundred thousand people may die from the ill effects caused by the additional ultraviolet radiation that will reach the earth's surface during those years.

Sources:

"Chemistry Ties CFCs Firmly to Ozone Hole," *Science News*, 134 (10 December 1988): 373;

"Decline of the CFC Empire," *Science News*, 133 (9 April 1988): 234–236;

"More Bad News for the Planet," *Newsweek*, 111 (28 March 1988): 63;

"Ozone Breakaway," *Newsweek*, 112 (29 August 1988): 48–49;

"Ozone Hits Bottom Again," *Science*, 246 (20 October 1989): 324;

"Ozone Hole Hikes Antarctic Ultraviolet," *Science News*, 135 (15 April 1989): 228;

"Ozone in the Danger Zone: Cities at Risk," *Newsweek*, 107 (5 May 1986): 66;

"Putting a Freeze on Freon," *U.S. News and World Report*, 101 (17 November 1986): 72.

PATENTING LIFE

Genetic Engineering. In 1980 a team of scientists at the University of California, headed by Professor Martin Cline, successfully transferred a gene from one mouse to another. Cline's team of researchers took genetic material from the bone marrow of a drug-resistant strain of mice and placed it into mice not possessing the gene. Such gene-replacement techniques, researchers hoped, might eventually lead to applications in healing sick people. They had potential use in increasing the drug tolerance of human cancer patients undergoing chemotherapy or in helping sickle-cell anemia patients overcome this malady.

Giant Mice. In yet another genetic experiment researchers at four U.S. laboratories collaborated during the early 1980s in engineering genetically altered mice. Their endeavors resulted in offspring twice the size of the parents. They achieved this outcome by placing a growth hormone from rats into the reproductive eggs of laboratory mice. The growth hormone became active in the livers of the genetically manipulated mice — causing them to grow into comparative giants. Following their successes with the rat growth hormone, researchers successfully repeated the experiment using human growth hormones — the first instance in history in which human genes had been transplanted into another living mammal — and found that a similar doubling in the size of the mice offspring occurred.

The Harvard Mouse. In April 1988 the first U.S. patent for an animal was granted to Harvard University for a genetically altered mouse. The research culminating in the patent had been conducted by researchers Philip Leder and Timothy Stewart in 1982 at Harvard. Seeking to better understand how genetic inheritance contributed to the development of human cancers, these researchers altered the molecular structure of a gene within the mice to make them more susceptible to carcinogens. Leder and Steward were not the first geneticists to be granted a patent on a living thing. The first organisms to be protected by a U.S. patent were oil-eating bacteria, and patents had been granted to geneticists in the United States for several plant varieties, including an insect-resistant tobacco plant, blight-resistant potatoes, and genetic alterations to a strain of cotton plants that made them sturdier. What made the "Harvard Mouse" patent unique was the fact that it was the first time in the United States that the power of the government had been invoked — via the U.S. Patent Office — to grant a patent on a genetically manipulated animal.

Should Life Be Patentable? A wide range of legal, moral, and political issues were opened when the U.S. Patent Office awarded the "Harvard Mouse" patent. In reaction some members of Congress called for a two-year moratorium on such genetic patents so that the question could be further studied. And the nation's farmers were concerned with the precedent. A spokesman for the National Farmers' Union asserted that animal patenting was "an economic issue." Patenting animal life would have important consequences on the nation's farms. Genetically altered livestock herds might yield greater quantities of milk or meat, but would farmers be required to pay royalties to scientists each time a genetically altered animal gave birth to a foal, lamb, or piglet? Would the offspring also be covered under the initial patent?

Mutant Dangers. There was also concern over the potential impact of genetically altered life on the biosphere. Unforeseen problems with potentially devastating consequences might result from having a genetically altered animal escape into the wilds. Moreover, if scientists created a cow that produced four times as much milk as a Jersey cow, the resultant animal, as the founder of the Cambridge Committee for Responsible Research noted, might well live in "continual agony." Still, a major counterpressure on the efforts to curtail U.S. patents was international competition. The Japanese and nine other countries allowed animal patents in the late 1980s. If the United States failed to do so it might slow research in the field while other countries bounded ahead. Additionally, geneticists argued that the laboratory results they achieved were only a more efficient version of animal husbandry, which had been practiced for hundreds of years by farmers and breeders. Amid the continuing debate, the transgenetic experiments continued.

Sources:
"The Gene Hunt," *Time*, 133 (20 March 1989): 62–67;

"A Mouse that Roared," *Time*, 131 (25 April 1988): 83;

"Patenting Life," *Scientific American*, 264 (March 1991): 40–46.

SPACE EXPLORATION

Triumph to Chaos. The National Aeronautics and Space Administration (NASA) witnessed both great triumph as well as immense downfall in the 1980s. With the formulation of the Space Transportation System (STS), more commonly referred to as the space shuttle, NASA fundamentally shifted its approach to space travel. The space shuttle was to supersede traditional expendable launch vehicles (ELVs), as it was to be the first in the line of reusable spaceships. Competition in the race for space had increased in recent years, as both Europe and the Soviet Union had found more-economical methods of exploration. With the shuttle in operation all appeared in order for NASA, an organization that had long been underfunded by the federal government and was searching for a new symbol to retain its prestige as the premier space exploration organization in the world. The 1986 space shuttle *Challenger* explosion derailed this progress, and the entire space program was placed in great jeopardy. The explosion and its subsequent scrutiny by the government, scientists, and the media left NASA reeling and searching for stability, respect, and direction. NASA was scolded for its emphasis on style and gimmickry over science and safety, and the organization was ill prepared to fend off such attacks. In 1988 NASA attempted to revive its tarnished image with a remodeled and internally redesigned *Discovery* shuttle. NASA also achieved a great level of success with its outer-space probes, such as *Voyager 2*, which had been launched in 1977 and surpassed all the expectations of its creators.

Space Shuttles. NASA launched the space shuttle *Columbia* on 12 April 1981. *Columbia* was to be the first in a long line of reusable, cost-efficient spacecraft. The shuttles were multifunctional vehicles designed to provide reliable and consistent travel into space. Their shape was similar to that of airplanes; yet shuttles could carry with them up to seven passengers, several satellites, and had a cargo bay fifteen feet wide and sixty feet long that could haul payloads up to sixty-five thousand pounds. They were launched with the aid of two solid booster rockets and an external tank, expendable pieces that separated from the shuttle once it had cleared the earth's atmosphere. NASA touted the craft as being able to perform dozens of missions a year with minimal repair. The shuttle was unable to perform under the vigorous standards that were set for it, however, and as a result NASA frequently cut corners and sacrificed safety to meet their goals.

Successes. Despite problems with the program, the shuttle accomplished a string of historic successes, one of which was the fifth shuttle flight on 11 November 1982, the first operational mission, which launched two communication satellites. Sally K. Ride made history on 18 June 1983, when she became the United States' first woman astronaut in space. Other memorable flights included those in which members of the United States Congress rode on board and flights in which commercial satellites were deployed, retrieved, and repaired in space. NASA intended to have a team of shuttles constantly deployed; yet its schedule was severely obstructed by technical, financial, and weather constraints. Other space

Challenger astronauts killed when the rocket exploded on liftoff, 28 January 1986: Ellison S. Onizuka, Michael J. Smith, Christa McAuliffe, Francis R. Scobee, Gregory B. Jarvis, Judith A. Resnik, and Ronald E. McNair

efforts, such as President Reagan's Strategic Defense Initiative (SDI) and several military and commercial satellites, were either tabled or delayed due to the inconsistency of shuttle launch flights and cost overruns.

Disaster. On 28 January 1986 the United States witnessed a terrible disaster as the space shuttle *Challenger* exploded seventy-four seconds after liftoff. The seven crew members on board were killed as the shuttle became engulfed in flames. The astronauts, five males and two females, were pilot Michael J. Smith, flight commander Francis R. Scobee, physicist Ronald E. McNair, electrical engineer Judith A. Resnik, aeronautical engineer Ellison S. Onizuka, electrical engineer Gregory B. Jarvis, and high-school social studies teacher Sharon Christa McAuliffe. After twenty-four successful missions NASA and the country had come to see space shuttle launches as routine, but this event changed those perceptions forever.

Inquiry. The causes of the *Challenger* explosion were studied by the Rogers Commission, which identified two primary reasons for the shuttle's destruction. The first lay in the faulty design of the craft's rubber O-rings, the seals used to join sections of the two solid-rocket boosters on either side of the shuttle. The rings' function was to keep certain gases from escaping by expanding to fill the gaps. They were sensitive to temperature shifts, and their designer, Morton Thiokol, and NASA were both familiar

with the fact that the rings had sometimes failed to expand properly, but they had underestimated the importance of the problem. The second major flaw the commission named was the fact that the *Challenger* was launched at a much colder temperature than any other previous launch. Other discoveries of the commission shed a harsh light on NASA, suggesting that it was an organization riddled with incompetence and a top-heavy bureaucracy. The House Science and Technology Committee concurred with the Rogers Commission's finding, which blamed NASA for creating unachievable aims in such short periods of time. On 15 August 1986 President Reagan commissioned NASA to begin construction of a new shuttle and to place safety issues as a primary concern.

Voyager 2. The success of the *Voyager* satellite program enabled the world to witness what could be accomplished when human ingenuity was put to the ultimate test. The *Voyager 2* satellite continued to make history as it zoomed across the solar system surveying the Earth's neighboring planets. Launched on 20 August 1977, *Voyager 2* was one of two probes created by NASA's Jet Propulsion Laboratory (JPL) to help give scientists and humanity a more accurate view of the solar system and what lay beyond it. *Voyager 2* examined the planet Saturn on 25 August 1981 and the planet Uranus on 24 January 1986, recording spectacular findings from both locations. The satellite's

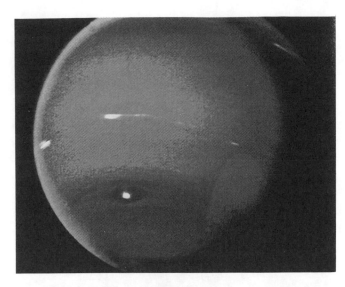

View of Neptune photographed by cameras aboard *Voyager 2* in August 1989

future upon clearing the solar system appeared unsure. By 1989 *Voyager 2* had outdone even the greatest of expectations as it reached the planet Neptune. The satellite's recording instruments captured data about this amazing cold planet and its many moons and broadcast them to scientists on Earth. Although its recording cameras were expected to break down subsequently, the satellite's other instruments, powered by radioactive plutonium thermal generators, were expected to function for quite some time to come. By the year 2025 all communications with *Voyager 2* were expected to cease because of increased distance and declining power levels. With the hope that the satellite might be retrieved by other intelligent life in the galaxy, a recording of greetings and sounds of the Earth was placed on a twelve-inch copper disc and installed inside *Voyager 2*.

Space Stations. Many scientists in NASA viewed man's ultimate goal as living in space, and talk of the creation of the world's most sophisticated space station grew more spirited in the 1980s. Inspired by the Soviet *Mir* space station and earlier United States efforts such as *Skylab*, NASA pushed for the creation of a large modern space station to be constructed 250 miles above the Earth. NASA envisioned experiments in chemistry, biology, and physics to be performed on this space station, and it was touted as the perfect point from which to launch spacecraft to Mars and other planets. Lastly, the space station was to ensure United States dominance in the race for space into the next century. The ultimate station design was called *Freedom* and was to begin construction in 1995. It would be five hundred feet long, contain four modules for living and working, and be powered by solar panels. NASA faced severe criticism to its "orbiting dream house," much of which came from members of Congress who questioned the need for such a large-scale space program and balked at the possible $16

billion price tag. Other criticism came when blueprint plans and timelines for construction were announced. By 1989 the station's future was questionable.

Sources:

Jerry Adler, "We Mourn Seven Heroes," *Newsweek,* 107 (10 February 1986): 26;

Stuart F. Brown, "20 Years After Apollo: Is the U.S. Lost in Space?," *Popular Science,* 235 (July 1989): 63–75;

Steve Budiansky and Robert Kaylor, "What's Wrong with America's Space Program," *U.S. News and World Report,* 103 (28 December 1987 – 4 January 1988): 32–34;

Leon Jaroff, "The Last Picture Show," *Time* (4 September 1989);

Jerry Kluger, "NASA's Orbiting Dream House," *Discover,* 10 (May 1989): 68–72;

Larry Martz, "America Grounded," *Newsweek,* 110 (17 August 1987): 34–42;

Frank Trippett, "Milk Run to the Heavens," *Time,* 117 (12 January 1981): 10–14.

STAR WARS

Growth of the Arms Race. Scientists in the United States created the world's first atomic bombs in 1945. In 1949 the Soviet Union built its own atomic bomb, and the arms race was on. In the 1950s and 1960s airplanes were the method of choice for delivering nuclear warheads to their destinations, and President Eisenhower developed an anti-aircraft defense system to guard against Soviet bombers. In the 1960s, with the introduction of the technology of rocketry, the preferred delivery system became the intercontinental ballistic missile (ICBM). The development of ICBMs led the United States, during President Nixon's administration, to develop and deploy antiballistic missiles (ABMs) that could shoot down incoming enemy missiles. The development of ABMs led both sides to search for further means of delivering their bombs to their targets, and multiple independently targetable reentry vehicles (MIRVs) were developed in the 1970s. MIRVs, consisting of one launch rocket with several nuclear bombs aboard, were able to overwhelm ABM defenses. During the 1970s increasing accuracy, speed, and miniaturization of nuclear warheads lent increased credibility to the notion that a first strike by the Soviet Union on the United States (or the reverse) was increasingly possible.

Star Wars. In March 1983 President Ronald Reagan called for a space-based military system to be used to defend against potential nuclear attack by the Soviet Union. As part of an expanded national defense system, Reagan's Strategic Defense Initiative (SDI) was to make use of the latest technology — and develop new technologies where necessary — in deploying a protective shield (based both in space and on earth) around the United States in the event of a Soviet nuclear missile attack. SDI had two essential components: first, surveillance of Soviet activities so that a launch could be detected at the earliest possible moment; and second, the necessary weaponry to incapacitate Soviet nuclear warheads before they reached the United States. SDI, its proponents asserted, would do

Target destroyed by a laser beam during testing of weapons in the "Star Wars" defense program

what ABMs could not, protect Americans in the event of a nuclear war. Initial estimates put the project's price at around $30 billion — but experts were soon pointing out that the cost might be as high as $1 trillion. (The 1987 budget for SDI was $6 billion.) Because President Reagan's proposed system was to employ nuclear X-ray lasers, subatomic particle beams, "bullets" launched from electromagnetic rail guns, and other "space age" technologies, it was dubbed "Star Wars" — after the popular 1977 science-fiction film. By the mid 1980s the goals of SDI were made more modest. Rather than assuring that no Soviet missiles would reach enemy U.S. targets, Reagan administration officials asserted that the project's goal would be downsized. The new aim was to insure that enough Soviet MIRVs would be stopped so that the United States could effectively retaliate.

Diplomacy and SDI. From the earliest days of the atomic age, the diplomatic theory of how a nuclear war would be avoided was grounded in a theory of "mutually assured destruction" (MAD), which reasoned that, since both the Soviet Union and the United States could completely destroy the other in the event of a nuclear war, neither could gain an advantage by initiating such a con-

flict. Critics argued that Reagan's Strategic Defense Initiative would end MAD and lead to undesirable instabilities in international affairs. On the other hand, proponents of SDI asserted that it was the next step in the deterrence of nuclear war, and that it would have the additionally desirable effect of "putting the squeeze" on the Soviet economy by forcing the Soviets to spend ever larger amounts of money to keep pace with the U.S. initiative. In any event, with the collapse of the Soviet Union in the early 1990s — some said a result achieved in part by the threat of SDI — the need for such an expensive defensive arsenal had diminished. By 1993 President Clinton's secretary of defense, Les Aspin, had announced that SDI was ended. It was to be replaced by a Ballistic Missile Defense Program with a substantially reduced budget.

Sources:

"In Defense of Star Wars," *Science,* 228 (3 May 1985): 563;

"New Doubts About Star Wars," *Science,* 229 (26 July 1985): 367–368;

"OTA Study Highlights Star Wars Difficulties," *Science,* 230 (4 October 1985): 50;

"Star War Games: The Stakes Go Up," *Time,* 128 (23 June 1986): 16–21.

HEADLINE MAKERS

LUIS W. ALVAREZ

1911-1988

PHYSICIST

Background. Luis Alvarez, winner of the 1968 Nobel Prize for physics, was born in San Francisco on 13 June 1911. A graduate of the University of Chicago, Alvarez's intellectual interests spanned a variety of scientific fields. During World War II Alvarez was a group leader among scientists who developed the atomic bomb, and he was one of a select few observers who flew in a companion aircraft with the Enola Gay to witness the detonation of the atomic bomb over Hiroshima on 6 August 1945. During the early years of the war Alvarez, then working at the Massachusetts Institute of Technology, developed a radar system that assisted aircraft in landing during heavy fog and other low-visibility circumstances. In 1946 Alvarez developed the proton linear accelerator known as LINEAC using tubular wave guides and other components. Using his invention, scientists were able to accelerate protons to a speed of 32 MeV. After World War II he returned to the University of California, Berkeley and began the work with cloud chambers that resulted in his Nobel Prize.

Bubble Chamber Experiments. In his work with, and development of, liquid hydrogen cloud chambers in the mid 1950s, Alvarez experimented with atomic and subatomic particles and mapped out many of their properties. He found that when atomic particles passed through a cloud chamber — a dish-sized container, its walls blackened, in which hydrogen liquid, kept near its boiling point, sat in a magnetic field — atomic particles that passed through the chamber would cause wisps of evaporating hydrogen to leave a trail of bubbles behind. From the patterns of these trails Alvarez was able to deduce many properties of the subatomic particles. Among his discoveries with the bubble chamber were tritium, as well as ephemeral meson and baryon particles.

Photographing a Pyramid. During the 1960s Alvarez applied his knowledge of high-energy physics to a question that had long haunted archaeologists. Most pyramids had been found to contain secret, treasure-laden chambers at their cores. In the Egyptian pyramid Chephren, however, archaeologists had been unable to discover such a chamber. Alvarez devised a system using sensitive detectors placed underneath the pyramid to "photograph" cosmic ray (radiation from the sun) absorption patterns in the pyramid's structure. If the original Egyptian architects had devised a hidden chamber it would show up in the detectors under the pyramid as a bright spot in the cosmic ray absorption patterns. The results of Alvarez's experiment, in which no such bright spots were detected, confirmed the suspicions of archaeologists that, in the Chephren pyramid at least, there was no hidden chamber.

Theory of the Dinosaurs' Extinction. In 1981 Alvarez and his son Walter proposed the view that dinosaurs had become extinct after a giant meteorite smashed into the earth 65 million years ago. Their theory had its genesis in geologic explorations done by Walter Alvarez in Italy during the 1970s. Walter had noted that an iridium-rich sediment little more than an inch thick was to be found in layers of earth situated between the Cretaceous and the Tertiary periods' geologic strata. Recognizing that meteorites generally contain high levels of iridium, the father-son team postulated that a gigantic meteorite — perhaps an asteroid or comet — smashed into the planet 65 million years ago. A cloud of dust was thrown into the upper atmosphere, causing temperatures on the planet's surface to plummet. The atmospheric changes associated with the impact choked off the sunlight needed by the cold-blooded dinosaurs to keep their body temperatures up and disturbed or destroyed food sources. After conducting a series of geochemical studies of rock strata which confirmed the view, the elder Alvarez chided a group of paleontologists who disagreed with his conclusions: "I don't like to say bad things about paleontologists, but they're not very good scientists. . . . They're more like stamp collectors."

Sources:
Luis R. Alvarez, *Alvarez: Adventures of a Physicist* (New York: Basic Books, 1987);

Discovering Alvarez: Selected Works of Luis W. Alvarez (Chicago: University of Chicago Press, 1987).

DAVID BALTIMORE

1938-

BIOCHEMIST

Education and Awards. David Baltimore was born in New York City, graduated from Swarthmore College with a B.S. in chemistry in 1960, and received a Ph.D. from Rockefeller University in 1964. In 1968 he became an associate professor of microbiology at the Massachusetts Institute of Technology, and in 1970 he won the Gustav Stern Award in Virology. Three years later he was awarded a prestigious American Cancer Society professorship. "My life," he told a *Time* correspondent in 1979, "is dedicated to increasing knowledge."

Nobel Laureate. In 1975 he shared the Nobel Prize for medicine or physiology (along with Renato Dulbecco and Howard Termin) for the discovery of reverse transcriptase, an enzyme that carries out one of the basic processes in a cell. He discovered that viral RNA (ribonucleic acid) can pass information to DNA (deoxyribonucleic acid) and replicate. This ground breaking discovery explained the perplexing problem of the replication of a group of retroviruses, whose genetic center consists of RNA rather than DNA. Scientists had been puzzled by the ability of some RNA viruses in tumors to transform healthy cells that they had infected. Since a better understanding of this cellular process potentially held answers to questions about the etiology of cancer, microbiologists toiled over the problem for years. In the 1960s and early 1970s Baltimore's colleague and cowinner of the Nobel Prize, Howard Temin, had promoted the view that genetic information might be passed from RNA to DNA. Temin's theory was ridiculed by many in the microbiological community, but it paid off.

Activist for Honest Science. Baltimore is well-known for his efforts to develop guidelines for genetic engineering research. Of the burgeoning field of genetic engineering, he said in an interview with *Time* magazine in 1974, "science fiction fantasies may come true very soon, we should be prepared." The following year he took a leading role in setting up a forum in which scientists discussed the need for self-policing their experiments in recombinant DNA. In 1976 he was appointed as a member of the government's Recombinant DNA Advisory Committee (RAC) to establish federal guidelines for funding genetic engineering research. In the mid 1980s he remained active in the debate about what genetic experiments should be attempted. In an interview in *Technology Review* in 1986 he noted that "We certainly need to examine every case on its merits to decide when concern is reasonable and when it's not. But generally I don't think such organisms will pose a problem for a number of reasons. First, the manipulations we're doing in the laboratory are minimal compared with what evolution has done. Evolution has made you and me out of bacterium, and we're not doing anything close to that."

Controversy. In 1974 he was elected to the American Academy of Arts and Sciences and to the National Academy of Sciences. In 1983 he was appointed director of the Whitehead Institute for Biomedical Research, a position he held for seven years. In 1990 Baltimore was named president of Rockefeller University. In 1991, after a research paper which he had co-authored in 1986 was found to be based on falsified data, he resigned the university's presidency under faculty pressure. The case represented something of a cause célèbre in the academy. Margaret O'Toole, a young scientist, discovered clear evidence that the 1986 article was fraudulent. When she confronted the authors with her findings she was demoted — and later claimed that her career had been ruined by her superiors. The United States House of Representatives held an inquiry into the matter, as did the Office of Scientific Integrity, and both found O'Toole's claims credible. Baltimore, however, was cleared of any wrongdoing. For, it appeared, his co-author, Imanishi-Kari, was responsible for those aspects of the paper called into question by O'Toole. Baltimore continued on as a professor at Rockefeller University following his resignation of the presidency.

Sources:

"David Baltimore: Setting the Record Straight on Biotechnology," *Technology Review* (October 1986): 38–46;

"The 1975 Nobel Prize for Physiology or Medicine," *Science,* 190 (1975): 650;

"A Troubled Homecoming," *Scientific American,* 226 (1992): 33–35.

PAUL BERG

1926-

BIOCHEMIST

Education and Early Career. Born on 30 June 1926, Paul Berg earned a B.S. in biochemistry at Pennsylvania State University in 1948. After serving three years in the Navy, Berg returned to school, earning a Ph.D. from Case Western Reserve University in Cleveland, Ohio, in 1952. He continued his postgraduate research in Denmark and subsequently in Saint Louis, Missouri, at Washington University. In 1956 he was appointed to an assistant professorship in microbiology at Washington University's School of Medicine and in 1959 accepted a professorship in biochemistry at Stanford University. It was at Stanford that Berg made the discoveries that won him the Nobel Prize in chemistry in 1980.

Recombining Bits of DNA. Berg has made a variety of important contributions to the study of biochemistry. He developed a technique for splicing deoxyribonucleic acid (DNA) from different organisms together. This splicing technique has proved to be of inestimable importance in studying viral chromosomes. It has also served as the cornerstone for much subsequent biochemical research into human genetic diseases and has allowed scientists to use rudimentary organisms as chemical mills, turning out useful medical drugs. The commercial production of many medicines has at its root the methodologies developed by Berg. The recombination of DNA fragments (recombinant DNA) made possible by Berg's work is the basis of the growing field of gene therapy. When the Royal Swedish Academy of Sciences announced Berg as winner of the 1968 Nobel Prize they specifically cited his "fundamental studies of the biochemistry of nucleic acids with particular regard to recombinant DNA." Techniques he developed and mastered in the field of recombinant DNA hold enormous promise for understanding, and perhaps curing, genetically based diseases in humans.

Continuing Contributions. Working in the complex world of cellular proteins, genes, and amino acids, Berg has repeatedly made important discoveries. In 1956 he demonstrated that a molecule specific to methionine played the role — suggested by some theoreticians at the time — of "joiner" in the intricate interactions between RNA and certain amino acids. In the 1960s he undertook the study of genes in the primate tumor virus known to biologists as SV40. By the 1970s he had charted the location of various viral genes on DNA and used his results to hypothesize that it is an interaction between genes and the biochemistry of cells that turn normal cells into cancerous ones.

Scientific Activist. Concerned with the destructive potential of some genetic engineering experiments, Berg headed a nationwide drive to insure proper laboratory practices by scientists working in the field. On 26 July 1974 he and a group of colleagues published their recommendations for future precautions in recombinant DNA research. Subsequently known as the "Berg letter," their missive to the scientific community cautioned that "There is serious concern that some of these artificial recombinant DNA molecules could prove biologically hazardous." The letter called for the prohibition of certain areas of experimentation (those creating harmful genetic mutants in the laboratory, which, if they escaped or were otherwise introduced into the environment, might cause increased cancer or other diseases among human or other animal populations). There were, Berg and his colleagues noted, inestimable goods that might redound to humankind from genetic research. It was necessary, however, to guard against potential disasters.

Sources:

Paul Berg and Maxine Singer, *Genes and Genomes: A Changing Perspective* (Mill Valley, Cal.: University Science Books, 1991);

Nick Wade, *The Ultimate Experiment* (New York: Walker, 1977).

GUION S. BLUFORD JR.

1942-

ASTRONAUT

Education. Guion Stewart Bluford Jr. was the first U.S. astronaut of African American descent. Born in Philadelphia, Pennsylvania, on 22 November 1942, Bluford earned his B.S. in aerospace engineering in 1964 from Penn State University and his Ph.D. from the Air Force Institute of Technology, in the same field, in 1978. While working toward his doctorate he engaged a broad spectrum of aerospace engineering problems and did research in laser physics. His dissertation was titled "A Numerical Solution of Supersonic and Hypersonic Viscous Flow Fields Around Thin Planar Delta Wings."

Air Force Pilot in Vietnam. Beginning in 1967 Bluford served as an Air Force pilot with the 557 Tactical Fighter Squadron in Vietnam. During his service in Vietnam he flew 144 combat missions and served with distinction. Bluford received the Vietnam Campaign Medal, the Vietnam Cross of Gallantry with Palm, the Vietnam Service Medal, ten Air Force Air Medals, and three Air Force outstanding unit awards.

Becoming an Astronaut. Chosen from a field of ten thousand candidates, Bluford became one of thirty-five astronauts chosen in 1978 to join the space program. Bluford's intellectual and military training served him well in the astronaut corps. Becoming an astronaut, as he noted in 1979, "gives me a chance to use all my skills and do something that is pretty exciting," and he relished the NASA training he received in oceanography, geology, celestial mechanics, and space navigation. "The job is so fantastic, you don't need a hobby. The hobby is going to work," he told an interviewer.

The First African American in Space. At 2:32 A.M. on 30 August 1983, in a spectacular nighttime launching, Bluford became the first American of African ancestry to travel in space. (He was not, however, the first person of African lineage to fly in space. Arnaldo Tamayo Mendez, a Cuban astronaut flying aboard the Soviets' *Soyuz 38* in 1980, holds that distinction.) One of two mission specialists aboard the *Challenger*, Bluford headed numerous scientific and technical experiments, including the deployment of a communications and weather satellite, tests on the shuttle's mechanical arm, and medical experiments on cell tissues which, it was hoped, would prove useful in fighting a variety of illnesses from diabetes to heart disease. Given his flight experience as a U.S. Air Force pilot, Bluford was also assigned the task of assisting the shuttle's commander during their nighttime landing in California's Mojave Desert on 5 September. In a 1983 interview Bluford noted the importance of his achievements: "From a black perspective, my flight on the shuttle was important because it represented another step forward." And, addressing a group of young African Americans, he said, "What I want to pass on to you is that it's very important to set high goals for yourself and realize that if you work hard you will get them."

Source:
"Astronaut Guion Bluford," *Jet,* 84 (5 July 1993): 32.

STEPHEN JAY GOULD

1941-

PALEONTOLOGIST AND AUTHOR

Background. Born in New York City on 10 September 1941, Gould was from an early age intrigued by dinosaurs and fossils. He received his B.A. from Antioch College in 1963 and earned a Ph.D. from Columbia University in 1967. That same year he began his illustrious career as a teacher at Harvard University.

Punctuated Equilibrium. In 1972 Gould and his colleague Niles Eldredge produced a paper, "Punctuated Equilibria: An Alternative to Phyletic Gradualism," in which they challenged the theory of phyletic gradualism, which contends that species evolve gradually over long periods of time. Gould and Eldredge argued that new species arise over a relatively short period of geologic time through rapid change in small groups of species. They promoted their view after noting the paucity of transitional varieties of animals found in the fossil record.

Creationism versus Evolution. In 1981 Gould was called as an expert witness in a trial in Arkansas. The state legislature had required the teaching of the biblical account of creation in school classrooms. By labeling the Judeo-Christian account of creation given in Genesis — which states that God created the world and all its creatures in six days, sometime around six thousand years ago — as "Creation science," Arkansas legislators had hoped to mandate its teaching in public schools. The constitutionality of the law was questioned, and in the subsequent trial Gould asserted that the views of "Creation science" belied all scientific evidence and cannot, therefore, properly be called scientific. Gould's testimony helped win the case, and the decision to keep the teaching of creationism out of public schools was upheld by appellate courts.

Celebrated Author and Teacher. Stephen Jay Gould teaches geology, paleontology, and the philosophy of science at Harvard University and is widely acclaimed for the eloquence of his exposition in his writings on a variety of scientific subjects, foremost among them evolution. Gould's writing made him a scientific celebrity in the 1980s. His column in the journal *Natural History,* "This View of Life," and his many books, including *The Panda's Thumb: More Reflections in Natural History* (1980), *Hen's Teeth and Horse's Toes: Further Reflections in Natural History* (1983), *The Flamingo's Smile* (1985), and *Bully for Brontosaurus* (1991), have attracted a wide audience and built the author's reputation. His *The Mismeasure of Man* (1981) won the National Book Critics Circle Award.

Sources:
"Good as Gould," *American Spectator* (August 1991): 9–11;

Stephen Jay Gould, "The Verdict on Creationism," *New York Times Magazine,* 19 July 1987, p. 32;

Gould, *Wonderful Life: The Burgess Shale and the Nature of History* (New York: Norton, 1989);

"Paean to a Leader in Evolutionary Theory," *Science News* (23 August 1986): 121.

BARBARA McCLINTOCK

1902-1992

GENETICIST

Background. Barbara McClintock was born in Hartford, Connecticut, and grew up in Flatbush, Brooklyn. McClintock later described herself in youth as someone who enjoyed social occasions well enough but who valued most of all the time she spent "thinking about things." Her mother initially opposed her daughter's pursuit of a college degree as "unfeminine" — and worried that she might become "a strange person, a person that didn't belong to society." As a result, after completing high school, the highly talented young scientist spent a year working for an employment agency. In 1919, however, she enrolled at Cornell University, where in 1923 she earned her B.S. in biology, and in 1927 she completed her Ph.D. in the same field.

Early Research. While in graduate school McClintock began her research on the chromosome structure of the maize plant. It was this research that eventually led to her Nobel Prize–winning discoveries. From 1929 to 1931 she published nine papers, and in the early 1930s she was awarded a National Research Council fellowship. In 1933 she traveled to Germany expecting to take up a position as a Guggenheim Fellow, but witnessing the horrors of Nazism upon her arrival, she quickly returned to the United States. Thereafter, she landed a position at the University of Missouri and taught there for four years. She found her abilities only haltingly acknowledged at Missouri and so sought employment elsewhere, ultimately finding work as a researcher at the Cold Spring Harbor Laboratory on Long Island, New York.

Amazing Discovery. In 1951, during her research into the chromosome structure of Indian corn (maize) at the Cold Spring Harbor facility, McClintock made one of the most fundamental discoveries in genetics in the twentieth century. By observing succeeding generations of maize she found that genetic material could shift unpredictably from one generation to the next. Through painstaking research over the course of six years, McClintock observed that these generational changes were attributable to the unexpected fact that some genetic elements on maize chromosomes were mobile — they "jumped" from one location to another. The view that genes were fixed in linear units on chromosomes, the prevailing view at the time, was, she announced, simply untenable.

Revolutionary Discovery Ignored. When researchers observe phenomena which challenge the accepted paradigm of "normal science" in their field, their claims customarily initiate a flurry of around-the-clock activity in scores of laboratories. Scientists rush to "see for themselves" whether the persons reporting the astonishing findings have, in fact, made a revolutionizing discovery, or if, as is often the case, the scientists making the novel claim have erred. Amazingly, however, none of this occurred with McClintock's research. Though she published her results in the appropriate scientific journals, there was no rush to substantiate her claims. Instead, her announcement was met by a resounding silence. "They called me crazy, absolutely mad," she reminisced years later. Indeed, her biographer, Evelyn Fox Keller, argues convincingly that McClintock's work was neglected, in large part, because the biological sciences were dominated by male researchers who were prejudiced against women. In short, sexism blinded the profession from acknowledging one of the greatest discoveries in twentieth-century genetics for more than a decade.

A Nobel Laureate at Last. Though her work in the 1920s and 1930s had been acknowledged as groundbreaking, though she had been elected President of the Genetics Society in 1944, and though she was only the third woman nominated to the American Academy of Science, McClintock's most important achievement had been ignored. By the late 1960s there was, however, no denying the brilliance of her achievements in understanding mobile genetic elements. In 1970 McClintock was awarded the National Medal of Science and in 1982 Columbia University's Horwitz Prize. Finally, and at the age of eighty-one, thirty-two years after her discovery, McClintock was given her profession's greatest recognition, the Nobel Prize in medicine or physiology (1983) — the first woman to be the sole recipient of a Nobel Prize in that field. James Watson, the codiscoverer of the double-helix structure of DNA, said of her discoveries, "No one thinks of genetics now without the implications of her work."

Source:
Evelyn Fox Keller, *A Feeling for the Organism: The Life and Work of Barbara McClintock* (San Francisco: W. H. Freeman, 1983).

SALLY KIRSTEN RIDE

1951-

ASTRONAUT

Education. Born on 26 May 1951 in the suburbs of Encino, California, Sally Kirsten Ride's intellect and athleticism — both necessities for an astronaut — earned her a place in history as America's first woman to fly in space. She earned both a B.A. in literature and a B.S. in physics in 1973 at Stanford University, and in 1977 she received her Ph.D. in physics from Stanford. Her research in graduate school focused on X-ray astronomy and lasers, and her dissertation research engaged the theory of the influence of magnetic fields on free electrons.

Answering an Ad. While in graduate school Ride happened, almost by accident, to read an advertisement in the campus newspaper soliciting résumés for work as "mission specialists" on future space flights. NASA had placed the ads hoping that young, talented scientists would identify themselves. They received more than tewn thousand responses. Sally Ride was one of the select few chosen. In her youth she had trained for, and for a time seriously considered, a career as a professional tennis player — physical training which was to stand her in good stead during the rigors of the flight training she had to endure alongside the twenty-nine men and five other women who entered the U.S. space program as astronauts-in-training with her in 1978. As an astronaut she learned to fly a jet and became experienced in performing complex tasks in a weightless environment. In 1981 and 1982 she worked in mission control as the chief communicator (Capcom) between ground engineers and the orbiting space shuttle.

First U.S. Woman in Space. Ride rocketed into space aboard the seventh space shuttle mission on 18 June 1983. For six days she and the other members of the space shuttle *Challenger* orbited the earth and carried out a series of scientific experiments. In space Ride deployed two communications satellites, monitored or executed about forty onboard scientific experiments, and tested the shuttle's fifty-foot-long mechanical arm. She conducted experiments in growing crystals, producing pharmaceuticals, and in manufacturing superfine alloys in zero gravity. As the first U.S. woman astronaut to travel into space, Ride's *Challenger* flight was viewed by many as a significant achievement in the movement then going on in U.S. society to remove barriers to women's equality of opportunity with men. (Ride was not the first woman in space, however. Valentina Tershkova had flown for the Soviet Union in 1963.)

Hero. On returning to earth, Ride was widely celebrated as a great American hero. Much of the United States was "smitten with 'Sallymania.'" Ride became a popular celebrity as T-shirts trumpeting her accomplishments, and newspaper and magazine articles about her life, appeared across the nation. Ride, while acknowledging the accolades, remained a dedicated scientist. "I didn't come into the space program to be the first woman in space, I came in to get a chance to fly as soon as I could," she said. And, after her first flight in space, she noted, "The thing that I'll remember most about the flight is that it was fun. In fact, I'm sure it was the most fun that I'll ever have in my life."

Second Flight and Subsequent Career. Ride flew on her second, and as it would turn out, her final, space flight on an eight-day mission in 1984. She was not aboard when the space shuttle *Challenger* blew up during takeoff on 28 January 1986, but she did serve as the only astronaut on the presidential investigating commission into the tragedy. In 1987 she became a leading force at NASA for the development of future lunar bases and for the exploration of Mars by astronauts. That same year she joined the faculty at Stanford at the Center for International Security and Arms Control. In 1989 she became a professor of physics at the University of California, San Diego, and was appointed director of the California Space Institute.

Sources:

"Hero for Our Time," *Vogue*, 174 (January 1984): 86;

"Sally Ride on the Future in Space," *Ms.*, 12 (January 1984): 86;

"Sally Ride to Leave NASA Orbit," *Physics Today*, 40 (July 1987): 45.

KENNETH G. WILSON

1936-

PHYSICIST

Background. Wilson was born on 8 June 1936 in Waltham, Massachusetts, the oldest of six children. His father, Edgar B. Wilson Jr., was a Harvard physicist. From an early age Kenneth Wilson displayed an interest in science. He earned his B.A. from Harvard and a Ph.D. in 1961 from the California Institute of Technology. At Cal Tech, Wilson worked on quantum theory under Murray Gell-Mann, whose own work had garnered him the Nobel Prize in physics for his theoretical work on quarks. From 1959 to 1962 Wilson was a junior fellow at Harvard University's Society of Fellows, and in 1962–1963 he worked at the European Organization of Nuclear Research (CERN) in Geneva. Wilson became a member of Cornell University's faculty in 1963. In 1975 he was elected to the National Academy of Sciences. Wilson won the Heinemann Prize in 1973, the Botzmann Medal in 1975, and the Wolf Prize in 1980. In 1981 he was awarded an honorary doctorate from Harvard University.

Nobel Laureate. Kenneth Wilson won the Nobel Prize in physics in 1982 for his brilliant theoretical insights into the problem of how to account for what physicists refer to as "critical phenomena" in matter. Under certain temperatures and pressures a variety of chemicals display curious qualities. Iron and nickel, for example, when heated to 1,044 K — the "Curie point" — lose their magnetic properties. Similarly, under certain temperatures and pressures water cannot properly be called either a liquid or gas. For decades physicists believed that there might well be some commonality among these physical phenomena. It was Kenneth Wilson who developed a theoretical explanation for these disparate "critical phenomena." Though intensive use of the renormalization group theory at times brought Wilson but few results, he pointed out that "It should be kept in mind that the problems to which the method is being applied are among the hardest problems known to the physical sciences. If they were not, they would have been solved by easier methods long ago."

Theoretical Work Continued. At Cornell, Wilson turned his theoretical acumen to the problem of critical phenomena. Using a theory developed by Murray Gell-Mann called the "renormalization group," Wilson was able to describe critical phenomena with unheralded accuracy. In 1971 he published two papers, now classics in the field, on his theoretical breakthrough. These papers, as P. W. Anderson noted in 1982, offer "what is now accepted as the full solution in principle of the behavior at critical points and other continuous phase transitions." The field of research in which Wilson focused his efforts during the 1970s and 1980s holds out the possibility of generating the elusive unified field theory. Wilson's research is viewed in the scientific community for its potential in contributing to the discovery of a theory in which Einstein's theory of relativity on the macroscopic level, and the laws governing quantum physics on the microscopic level, may be unified.

Source:

Kenneth Wilson, "Renormalization Group and Critical Phenomena," *Physical Review B* (1 November 1971): 3174–3205.

PEOPLE IN THE NEWS

With a tight budget on research dollars in the late 1980s, large and small science projects had to compete for government funds in a zero-sum game. "Science in the United States is dying of giantism" argued Noble Prize–winning physicist **Phillip Anderson** in 1988. "Big projects are the worst way to arrive at basic discoveries."

In December 1980, after a five-year study of the mathematical ability of some ten thousand students, psychologists **Camilla Persons Benbow** and **Julian C. Stanley** conclude that "Sex differences in achievement in and attitude toward mathematics result from superior male mathematical ability." Critics charge the finding is flawed since environmental factors were not properly screened.

In an experiment in deep-sea diving conducted by physiologist **Peter Bennett** at Duke University in April 1980, three volunteers, **Delmar Shelton**, **William Bell**, and **Stephen Porter**, worked under pressures equivalent to 2,132 feet underwater — more than 100 feet beyond the deepest simulated dive ever before made — with no symptoms of high-pressure nervous syndrome (HPNS).

In 1987 **Paul Chu** and colleagues published the recipe for an yttrium-based ceramic that can superconduct at temperatures as high as 92 K (-294°F). Previously even the best superconductors had to be cooled to nearly -400°F.

Martin J. Cline, head of a research team at UCLA, announced in April 1980 that in experiments with mice scientists had successfully transferred genes for the first time into living tissue.

In one of the most intensive investigations of science fraud ever conducted at Harvard, an ad hoc committee in February 1982 reported "serious questions of credibility" in the work of medical researcher **Dr. John Darsee.**

Fred Gillett of Arizona's Kitt Peak National Observatory and **H. H. Aumann** of the Jet Propulsion Laboratory announced in August 1983 the discovery of rocky material orbiting the star Vega, the first evidence of planet formation occurring beyond the solar system.

Carl Sagan calls the discovery "an epochal finding in the history of astronomy."

In 1980 **Robert K. Graham,** a seventy-three-year-old optometrist, said that five Nobel laureates in science, including 1956 cowinner **William Shockley,** were participating in his experiment to use artificial insemination to produce superior children. "My slogan is, the more intelligent you are, the more children you should have," said Graham.

On 20 January 1987 **Peter Hagelstein,** the scientist whose work on a nuclear-powered X-ray laser inspired President Ronald Reagan's concept of the Strategic Defense Initiative, returned to work at the Lawrence Livermore National Laboratory. He had quit the lab to protest weapons research and returned only as a consultant for nonmilitary research.

In October 1988, thirty-two months after the *Challenger* disaster, Commander **Fred Hauck** leads a crew of four as the *Discovery* revives the U.S. manned space program.

At the first American conference on animal cognition, held at Columbia University in June 1982, psychologists report the results of experiments showing that some animals actually form categories, construct intricate mental maps of the world, and follow a process of reasoning that cannot be explained by behavioral conditioning. The experiments of **Louis Herman** suggest that dolphins are able to understand syntax, not just the meaning of individual words.

In 1983 the International Society of Cryptozoology is formed, a group that is interested in unknown forms of snails as well as reports of the Sasquatch ("Bigfoot"). President **Bernard Heuvelmans** says the group "aspires to a true skepticism, that which opposes both a priori incredulity and a naive willingness to believe."

Paleontologists digging in Arizona's Painted Desert in summer 1981 found the jawbone of a shrew-size animal 180 million years old. The discovery suggested that in addition to the Morganucodontids, the ancestor of the platypus, and the Kuehneotheriids, which evolved into all other mammals, a third order of mammals existed during the late Triassic period. "This discovery shows us that mammals were more diverse than we thought," said expedition leader **Farish Jenkins Jr.** of Harvard University.

On a sunny day in July 1981 a solar-powered plane designed by American physicist **Paul MacCready** flew across the English Channel. "It's actually the most ridiculous use I can think of for solar cells," said MacCready of the plane piloted by **Stephen Ptacek.** "But we wanted to point out just how much solar power can do."

On 28 January 1986 the *Challenger* space shuttle exploded barely a minute into its tenth mission, killing six astronauts and teacher **Christa McAuliffe.**

At the annual meeting of the American Astronomical Society in 1987, astronomers led by **Patrick McCarthy** of the University of California, Berkeley, report observations of a massive galaxy, some 12 billion light-years distant, discovered in its formation stages.

On 26 July 1989 the Justice Department announced indictments for computer fraud and abuse against **Robert Tappan Morris,** a Cornell University graduate student believed to be responsible for the release of a computer virus that shut down a nationwide computer network in November 1988.

"Archeological chemistry has come into its own in the last ten years," asserted **George Rapp** of the University of Minnesota in 1983. For example, **Dr. Arthur Aufderheide** theorized that subjects too poor to afford pewter dishes and piped water in colonial America can be identified by analyzing the lead concentration of their skeletons.

On 15 April 1987 Nobel laureate **Burton Richter** and physicists at Stanford University unveiled the Stanford Linear Collider, a low-cost, high-energy particle accelerator.

In June 1980 **J. William Schopf** announced in Los Angeles that researchers had confirmed the age of the most ancient living things yet discovered, 3.5-billion-year-old biological cells that were found inside rocks in Western Australia.

Chosen by Western Electric's **Lawrence Stern,** forty-seven stunning photographs celebrating the color and geometric forms inherent in new microtechnologies were exhibited at Chicago's Museum of Science and Industry in October 1983.

In his study of the fossil record of Kenya's Lake Turkana Harvard paleontologist **Peter Williamson** found support for the new model of evolution called puctuated equilibrium, which holds that species remain the same for long periods until environmental changes spark evolutionary spurts. Williamson writes in November 1981 that his research on mollusk evolution over several millions of years is especially significant since "for the first time we see intermediate forms" between old and new species.

In April 1981 **John W. Young** and **Robert J. Crippen** piloted the space shuttle *Columbia* on its maiden voyage, the first American manned space mission since 1975.

AWARDS

NOBEL PRIZES

1980

James W. Cronin and **Val L. Fitch,** Physics; **Paul Berg, Walter Gilbert,** and **Frederick Sanger,** Chemistry.

1981

Nicolass Bloembergen and **Arthur Schaalow,** Physics; **Roald Hoffmann,** Chemistry.

1982

Kenneth G. Wilson, Physics.

1983

Subrahmanyan Chandrasekhar and **William A. Fowler,** Physics.

1984

Bruce Merrifield, Chemistry.

1985

Herbert A. Hauptman and **Jerome Karle,** Chemistry.

1986

Dudley Herschbach and **Yuan T. Lee,** Chemistry.

1987

Donald J. Cram and **Charles J. Pederson,** Chemistry.

1988

Leon M. Lederman, Melvin Schwartz, and **Jack Steinberger,** Physics.

1989

Norman F. Ramsey, Physics; **Thomas R. Cech** and **Sidney Altman,** Chemistry.

DEATHS

George Abell, 57, astronomer whose discovery, the Abell Galaxy, was for many years the largest known object in the universe, 7 October 1983.

Luis W. Alvarez, 77, Nobel Prize–winning physicist and proponent of the theory that the dinosaur extinctions were caused by a comet striking the earth, 1 September 1988.

Frederik Barry Bang, 64, biologist and expert on parasitic disease, 3 October 1981.

Gregory Bateson, 76, British-born anthropologist and former husband and collaborator of Margaret Mead, 4 July 1980.

William Behrens, 63, naval admiral and oceanographer, 21 January 1986.

George Packer Berry, 87, virologist and dean of the Harvard Medical School (1949–1966), 5 October 1986.

Junius Bouton Bird, 74, prominent archaeologist with the American Museum of Natural History in New York, 2 April 1982.

Walter Houser Brattain, 85, physicist and coinventor of the transistor, 13 October 1987.

Harrison Brown, 69, atomic scientist who played a key role in developing the atomic bomb, 8 December 1986.

Kurt Heinrich Debus, 74, electrical and rocket engineer, director of the Kennedy Space Center at the time of the first moon landing, 10 October 1983.

Paul Adrian Maurice Dirac, 82, physicist and cowinner of the 1983 Nobel Prize for physics, 20 October 1984.

Donald W. Douglas, 88, aircraft designer and businessman, 2 February 1981.

Richard G. Drew, 81, chemist who invented Scotch transparent tape, 7 December 1980.

René Jules Dubos, 81, French-born bacteriologist and crusader against pollution, 20 February 1982.

Richard F. Feynman, 69, Nobel Prize–winning physicist, 15 February 1988.

Paul John Flory, 75, Nobel Prize–winning chemist and human-rights activist, 9 September 1985.

Diane Fossey, 53, American naturalist famous for studying the mountain gorillas of Africa, 26 December 1985.

R. Buckminster Fuller, 87, futurist and inventor of the geodesic dome, 3 July 1983.

Paul Gross, 91, specialist in physical inorganic and fluorine chemistry, 4 May 1986.

Gaylord P. Harnwell, 78, atomic physicist and educator, 18 April 1982.

Banesh Hoffmann, 79, British-born mathematician and collaborator with Albert Einstein, 5 August 1986.

James R. Killian Jr., 83, first presidential assistant (to Dwight D. Eisenhower) for science and technology, and former president of MIT, 29 January 1988.

Choh Hao Li, 74, Chinese-born biochemist who synthesized human pituitary growth hormone in 1971, 28 November 1987.

George M. Low, 58, rocket scientist and driving force in the Apollo space program, 17 July 1984.

Henry William Menard, 65, marine geologist whose work contributed to plate tectonics theory, 9 February 1986.

John H. Northrop, 95, cowinner of the 1946 Nobel Prize for chemistry, 27 May 1987.

George Polya, 97, professor of mathematics and author of the best-selling *How to Solve It,* 7 September 1985.

Isidor Isaac Rabi, 89, Nobel Prize–winning atomic scientist, 11 January 1988.

James Rainwater, 68, atomic physicist, cowinner of 1975 Nobel Prize, 31 May 1986.

Joseph Rhine, 84, pioneering parapsychologist, 20 February 1980.

Charles F. Richter, 85, seismologist who developed the Richter scale of earthquake magnitude, 30 September 1985.

Hyman G. Rickover, 86, naval admiral who oversaw the development of the nuclear submarine fleet, 8 July 1986.

Julia Bowman Robinson, 65, first woman mathematician elected to the National Academy of Sciences, 30 July 1985.

Emilio Gino Segre, 84, Nobel Prize–winning nuclear physicist and discoverer of the antiproton, 22 April 1989.

William Bradford Shockley, 79, Nobel-Prize–winning physicist whose coinvention of the transistor was later overshadowed by his repeated assertions that blacks were genetically inferior to whites, 12 August 1989.

Stanislaw Marcin Ulam, 75, Polish-born mathematician who worked on the hydrogen bomb, 13 May 1984.

Harold Urey, 87, Nobel Prize–winning chemist who discovered deuterium, an element of the hydrogen bomb, 5 January 1981.

Cornelis Bernardus Van Niel, 87, Dutch-born microbiologist who first explained the chemical basis of photosynthesis, 10 March 1985.

Sewall Wright, 98, geneticist who developed a mathematical model for evolution, 3 March 1988.

Jerrold R. Zacharias, 81, science educator and designer of the first atomic clock, 16 July 1986.

PUBLICATIONS

Isaac Asimov, *Frontiers: New Discoveries about Man and His Planet, Outer Space, and the Universe* (New York: Dutton, 1989);

Asimov, *The Universe: From Flat Earth to Black Holes — And Beyond* (New York: Walker, 1980);

David Attenborough, *Life on Earth: A Natural History* (London: Reader's Digest, 1980);

Anthony Aveni, *Empires of Time: Calendars, Clocks, and Cultures* (New York: Basic, 1989);

John D. Barrow and Frank J. Tipler, *The Anthropic Cosmological Principle* (Oxford: Oxford University Press, 1988);

John Boslough, *Stephen Hawking's Universe* (New York: Morrow, 1985);

Richard A. Carrigan Jr. and W. Peter Trowers, eds., *Particle Physics in the Cosmos* (New York: Freeman, 1989);

Nathan Cohen, *Gravity's Lens* (New York: Wiley, 1988);

Paul Davies, *Superforce* (New York: Simon & Schuster, 1984);

Freeman Dyson, *Infinite in All Directions* (New York: Harper & Row, 1985);

Richard P. Feynman, *QED: The Strange Theory of Light and Matter* (Princeton: Princeton University Press, 1983);

Feynman, *Surely You're Joking, Mr. Feynman!* (New York: Norton, 1985);

Julius T. Fraser, *Time: The Familiar Stranger* (Boston: University of Massachusetts Press, 1987);

Stephen Jay Gould, *The Flamingo's Smile* (New York: Norton, 1985);

Stephen Hawking, *A Brief History of Time: From the Big Bang to Black Holes* (New York: Bantam, 1988);

Werner Heisenberg, *Encounters with Einstein* (Princeton: Princeton University Press, 1989);

Douglas R. Hofstadter, *Godel, Escher, Bach: An Eternal Golden Braid* (New York: Vantage, 1980);

David Macaulay and Neil Ardley, *The Way Things Work* (London: Kindersley, 1988);

Heinz Pagels, *The Cosmic Code* (New York: Simon & Schuster, 1982);

Carl Sagan, *Cosmos* (New York: Random House, 1980);

Gary Taubes, *Nobel Dreams* (New York: Random House, 1986);

Steven Weinberg, *The First Three Minutes* (New York: Bantam, 1984).

SPORTS

by DAN NATHAN

CONTENTS

Sidebars and tables are listed in italics.

1980

1 Jan.   Alabama defeats Arkansas 24–9 in the Sugar Bowl and is later voted the national champion of college football for 1979.

7 Jan.   The Philadelphia Flyers' National Hockey League (NHL) record-setting streak of 35 games without a loss comes to an end when they are beaten by the Minnesota North Stars 7–1.

20 Jan.   The Pittsburgh Steelers win their fourth Super Bowl in six years with a 31–19 victory over the Los Angeles Rams; also, the United States announces that it will not participate in the 1980 Summer Olympics in Moscow in protest of the Soviet Union's invasion of Afghanistan.

12 Feb.   The XXIII Winter Olympic Games open in Lake Placid, New York. Bobsledders Willie Davenport and Jeff Gadley become the first black athletes to represent the United States in the Winter Olympics.

22 Feb.   The United States Olympic ice hockey team upsets the Soviet Union 4–3. Two days later the U.S. team wins the gold medal by defeating Finland 4–2.

23 Feb.   American speed skater Eric Heiden wins the gold medal in the 10,000-meter event in a world-record-setting time of 14 minutes, 28.13 seconds. It is his fifth gold medal in five events.

24 Feb.   Closing ceremonies for the Winter Olympics are held.

14 Mar.   A Polish airliner crashes, killing eighty-seven people, including twenty-two boxers and officials of a U.S. amateur boxing team.

24 Mar.   Louisville defeats UCLA 59–54 to win their first men's NCAA basketball championship.

26 Mar.   Nancy Lieberman of Old Dominion University wins her second straight Margaret Wade Trophy as the player of the year in women's college basketball.

6 Apr.   Hockey legend Gordie Howe, fifty-two, plays the final regular season game of his thirty-two-year career.

12 Apr.   Milwaukee Brewers' Cecil Cooper and Don Money both hit grand slams in the second inning against the Boston Red Sox.

16 Apr.   Arthur Ashe, the first black man to win major professional tennis tournaments, announces his retirement.

21 Apr.   Rosie Ruiz apparently wins the eighty-fourth Boston Marathon, but is later disqualified when it is discovered that she cheated by cutting the course.

6 May   The National Broadcasting Company (NBC) announces that it will not televise the 1980 Summer Olympics in the United States, at a loss of approximately $22 million.

16 May   The Los Angeles Lakers win the National Basketball Association (NBA) championship by defeating the Philadelphia 76ers in six games.

19 May   Con Errico is found guilty of bribing jockeys to fix nine races at New York State race tracks in 1974 and 1975.

29 May   Larry Bird of the Boston Celtics wins the NBA's Rookie of the Year award; Kareem Abdul-Jabbar of the Los Angeles Lakers wins the league's Most Valuable Player award, the sixth of his career.

31 May   Johns Hopkins wins its third NCAA lacrosse title in a row by defeating Virginia in a second overtime period 9–8.

3 June   The New York Mets make Darryl Strawberry the first pick in the amateur draft.

6 June   Nineteen-year-old Wayne Gretzky of the Edmonton Oilers wins the Hart Memorial Trophy (the league's MVP award) and the Lady Byng Memorial Trophy, thus becoming the youngest player ever to win two major NHL awards in the same season.

7 June   Temperence Hill, a 53–1 longshot, wins the Belmont Stakes.

9 June   The Boston Celtics trade the first and thirteenth picks in the NBA draft to the Golden State Warriors for Robert Parish and the third pick in the draft, which the Celtics use to select Kevin McHale.

12 June   Jack Nicklaus sets a record for the lowest 72-hole score in any U.S. Open championship, with a total of 272. It is his fourth Open win since 1962.

20 June   Roberto Duran defeats Sugar Ray Leonard in fifteen rounds to win the World Boxing Council (WBC) welterweight championship.

5 July   Bjorn Borg defeats John McEnroe in the Wimbledon finals in five sets.

19 July   The XXII Summer Olympic games in Moscow begin, the first Olympics ever staged in a communist nation. The United States and sixty-four other countries boycott the games to protest the Soviet invasion of Afghanistan.

30 July   Houston Astros pitcher J. R. Richard suffers a stroke during practice.

3 Aug.   Closing ceremonies for the Summer Olympics are held; also, Al Kaline and Duke Snider are among those inducted into the Baseball Hall of Fame.

10 Aug.   Jack Nicklaus wins the nineteenth major tournament of his career by winning the Professional Golf Association (PGA) championship in Rochester, New York.

11 Aug.   Reggie Jackson of the New York Yankees hits his 400th home run.

19 Aug.   The *Los Angeles Times* reports that between 40 and 75 percent of the players in the NBA use cocaine.

7 Sept.   John McEnroe beats Bjorn Borg to win his second straight U.S. Open singles championship.

25 Sept.   The U.S. yacht *Freedom* completes the twenty-fourth consecutive defense of the America's Cup.

2 Oct.   WBC heavyweight champion Larry Holmes defeats Muhammad Ali in ten rounds in Ali's penultimate fight.

4 Oct.   Alabama football coach Paul "Bear" Bryant wins his 300th game.

5 Oct.   George Brett finishes the season with a .390 batting average, the highest major-league mark in thirty-nine years.

15 Oct.   Manny Mota of the Los Angeles Dodgers collects his major-league record 150th career pinch hit.

21 Oct.   The Philadelphia Phillies defeat the Kansas City Royals in six games to win the World Series.

3 Nov.   In Los Angeles, British and European bantamweight champion Johnny Owen dies as the result of injuries suffered in a 19 September title bout with WBC champion Lupe Pintor.

25 Nov.   Sugar Ray Leonard avenges his loss to Roberto Duran to regain the WBC welterweight championship when Duran turns his back on Leonard in the eighth round and says, "No más."

29 Nov.   The three-point field goal line is used in college basketball for the first time on an experimental basis by the Southern Conference.

15 Dec.   Outfielder Dave Winfield becomes the highest-paid player in the history of U.S. team sports when he signs a ten-year contract with the New York Yankees worth at least $22 million.

20 Dec.   As an experiment NBC broadcasts an NFL game between the Miami Dolphins and the New York Jets without a play-by-play announcer and color commentator.

1981

1 Jan.   Georgia defeats Notre Dame 17–10 in the Sugar Bowl and is later voted the college football national champion for 1980.

13 Jan.   The NCAA votes to sponsor Division I women's championships in twelve sports after the 1981–1982 season.

25 Jan.   The Oakland Raiders defeat the Philadelphia Eagles 27–10 in Super Bowl XV.

29 Mar.   Phil Mahre is the first American to win the men's overall World Cup skiing championship.

30 Mar.   Led by sophomore guard Isiah Thomas, Indiana beats North Carolina 63–50 to win the men's NCAA basketball championship.

5 Apr.   Edmonton Oiler Wayne Gretzky, twenty, becomes the youngest player to win an NHL points title, with 55 goals and 109 assists for a league-record 164 points.

9 Apr.   Frank Robinson of the San Francisco Giants becomes the first African American manager in the National League.

24 Apr.   Jockey Bill Shoemaker wins his 8,000th race.

29 Apr.   Steve Carlton of the Philadelphia Phillies becomes the first left-handed pitcher to strike out 3,000 batters.

1 May   Tennis star Billie Jean King reveals she had a lesbian affair with her former secretary. King is the most prominent sports figure ever to admit involvement in a homosexual relationship publicly.

14 May   The Boston Celtics defeat the Houston Rockets in six games to win their fourteenth NBA championship.

15 May   Len Barker of the Cleveland Indians pitches a perfect game.

27 May   Julius "Dr. J" Erving of the Philadelphia 76ers wins the NBA's Most Valuable Player (MVP) award, the first noncenter to do so in sixteen years.

23 June   The longest game in the history of organized baseball ends when the Triple-A Pawtucket Red Sox beat the Rochester Red Wings, 3–2, in 33 innings.

26 June   Magic Johnson of the Los Angeles Lakers signs the richest and longest contract in the history of professional sports: a $1-million-a-year, twenty-five-year agreement that begins in 1984.

3 July   Chris Evert Lloyd wins her third women's singles lawn tennis championship at Wimbledon by defeating Hana Mandlikova.

4 July   John McEnroe upsets Bjorn Borg to win his first men's singles tennis championship at Wimbledon.

31 July   A midseason strike by Major League Baseball players comes to an end. The forty-nine-day strike, which saw 713 games canceled, is the longest in the history of professional sports.

2 Aug.   The Baseball Hall of Fame inducts Bob Gibson, Johnny Mize, and Rube Foster.

10 Aug.   Pete Rose collects his 3,631st hit, breaking Stan Musial's all-time National League mark.

12 Sept.   Tracy Austin wins her second U.S. Open women's singles title by defeating Martina Navratilova.

13 Sept.   John McEnroe beats Bjorn Borg to win his third consecutive U.S. Open men's singles title.

16 Sept.   Sugar Ray Leonard defeats Thomas Hearns in the fourteenth round in their bout to unify the welterweight championship of the world in the single richest sports event in history, grossing approximately $35 million.

20 Sept.   Gary Gaetti, Kent Hrbek, and Tim Laudner of the Minnesota Twins all hit home runs in their first major-league game.

26 Sept.   Nolan Ryan of the Houston Astros pitches his major-league record fifth no-hitter; also, the Chicago Sting beat the New York Cosmos 1–0 in a shootout to win the Soccer Bowl, the championship of the North American Soccer League (NASL).

28 Sept.   South Africa's national rugby team, the Springboks, leaves the United States and returns home after three controversial matches.

25 Oct.   Alberto Salazar sets a record for the fastest time in the New York City Marathon: 2 hours, 8 minutes, 13 seconds; Allison Roe of New Zealand sets a record for the best women's time: 2 hours, 25 minutes, 28 seconds.

28 Oct.   The Los Angeles Dodgers defeat the New York Yankees to win the World Series in six games after trailing two games to none.

23 Nov.   A former Boston College basketball player and four others are convicted of conspiring to manipulate the scores of six games during the 1978–1979 season.

28 Nov.   Alabama coach Bear Bryant becomes the all-time winningest coach in major-college football with his 315th victory.

2 Dec.   Less than a month after winning the National League Cy Young award, Fernando Valenzuela of the Los Angeles Dodgers wins the National League Rookie of the Year award. Valenzuela is the first player to win both awards in the same season.

22 Dec.   John Henry, a six-year-old gelding, is named Horse of the Year at the annual Eclipse Awards.

1982

1 Jan.   Clemson beats Nebraska 22–15 in the Orange Bowl and is later voted the national champion of college football for 1981.

11 Jan. WBC heavyweight champion Larry Holmes knocks out Gerry Cooney in the thirteenth round of their title bout; each man earns $7 million for his efforts.

10 Jan. Joe Montana of the San Francisco 49ers completes a 6-yard touchdown pass to Dwight Clark with 51 seconds left to beat the Dallas Cowboys in the National Football Conference (NFC) championship game 28–27.

24 Jan. The San Francisco 49ers win Super Bowl XVI by beating the Cincinnati Bengals, 26–21.

27 Feb. Earl Anthony becomes the first bowler to win $1 million in his career.

13 Mar. Scott Hamilton and Elaine Zayak win gold medals at the world figure skating championships in Copenhagen, Denmark.

18 Mar. The first NCAA women's swimming and diving championship is held in Gainesville, Florida.

22 Mar. The NFL owners unanimously approve the richest television contract in the history of sports.

28 Mar. Louisiana Tech defeats Cheyney State of Pennsylvania 76–62 to win the first women's Division I NCAA basketball championship.

29 Mar. Freshman guard Michael Jordan hits a game-winning jump shot with 32 seconds left to lead North Carolina over Georgetown 63–62, winning the men's NCAA basketball championship.

4 Apr. Edmonton Oiler center Wayne Gretzky sets three NHL single-season records: in goals (92), assists (120), and total points (212).

18 Apr. George Gervin of the San Antonio Spurs wins his fourth NBA scoring title by averaging 32.3 points per game.

6 May Gaylord Perry of the Seattle Mariners wins his 300th career game.

7 May A federal district court decides in favor of the Oakland Raiders in that team's civil antitrust suit against the NFL, clearing the way for the team to move to Los Angeles.

12 May The twelve-team United States Football League (USFL) is founded.

16 May The New York Islanders sweep the Vancouver Canucks four games to none to become the first U.S.-based NHL team to win three consecutive Stanley Cups.

30 May Gordon Johncock wins the Indianapolis 500 by the narrowest margin in the race's history, .16 of a second ahead of Rick Mears; also, Cal Ripken Jr. of the Baltimore Orioles begins his record-setting consecutive-games-played streak.

8 June Wayne Gretzky of the Edmonton Oilers becomes the first player to win an NHL MVP award by a unanimous vote.

3 July Martina Navratilova wins her third women's singles championship at Wimbledon by defeating Chris Evert Lloyd. The following day Jimmy Connors wins his second men's Wimbledon singles title by defeating John McEnroe.

1 Aug. Hank Aaron and Frank Robinson are among those inducted into the Baseball Hall of Fame.

4 Aug. Joel Youngblood gets hits for two different teams in two different cities on same day when he is traded from the New York Mets to the Montreal Expos.

8 Aug.	Ray Floyd wins the sixty-fourth PGA championship at the Southern Hills Country Club in Tulsa, Oklahoma.
12 Sept.	Jimmy Connors wins his fourth U.S. Open men's singles championship. The previous day Chris Evert Lloyd won her sixth U.S. Open women's singles title.
19 Sept.	The New York Cosmos win their fourth NASL title in five years by edging the Seattle Sounders 1–0 to win the Soccer Bowl.
21 Sept.	NFL players strike for the first time in the league's sixty-three-year history.
25 Sept.	Eddie Robinson, head football coach at Grambling, wins his 300th game as Grambling beats Florida A & M 42–21.
20 Oct.	The St. Louis Cardinals win the World Series four games to three over the Milwaukee Brewers.
26 Oct.	Steve Carlton of the Philadelphia Phillies wins a record fourth Cy Young award.
13 Nov.	Duk Koo Kim suffers fatal brain damage in a fight with Ray "Boom Boom" Mancini for the World Boxing Association (WBA) lightweight championship.
17 Nov.	The NFL players' strike comes to an end after fifty-seven days. The strike led to the cancellation of 112 of 224 scheduled games and lost players, owners, television networks, cities, and businesses an estimated $450 million.
20 Nov.	On the last play of the game, trailing Stanford 20–19, the California football team receives a kickoff and, via five laterals, proceeds to score an improbable touchdown to win the game while the Stanford marching band is coming onto the field.
28 Nov.	The United States wins its twenty-eighth Davis Cup by beating France, 4–1.
24 Dec.	Chaminade defeats number-one-ranked Virginia 77–72 in one of the biggest upsets in men's college basketball history.

1983

1 Jan.	Penn State defeats Georgia 27–23 in the Sugar Bowl and is later awarded its first national championship in college football.
3 Jan.	Dallas Cowboy running back Tony Dorsett runs for a 99-yard touchdown against the Minnesota Vikings.
11 Jan.	At the annual NCAA convention Proposition 48 is passed by a 4–1 margin. Applying only to Division I schools, the proposal mandates minimum scores on entrance tests and graduation from high school with a 2.0 GPA in a core curriculum.
13 Jan.	The International Olympic Committee (IOC) presents Jim Thorpe's children with two Olympic gold medals, reversing the decision to strip Thorpe of his 1912 decathlon and pentathlon victories.
30 Jan.	The Washington Redskins defeat the Miami Dolphins 27–17 in Super Bowl XVII. The game draws a record 111.5 million national television viewers.
23 Feb.	Heisman Trophy running back Herschel Walker signs a contract with the New Jersey Generals of the USFL.
2 Apr.	Seven-foot four-inch Ralph Sampson of Virginia wins his third consecutive Adolph Rupp Trophy as the men's college basketball player of the year.

4 Apr.   North Carolina State upsets Houston 54–52 on a last-second shot to win the men's NCAA basketball championship. The game draws a record fifty million television viewers.

18 Apr.   Joan Benoit sets a world record for women in the Boston Marathon, winning the race in 2 hours, 22 minutes, 42 seconds.

26 Apr.   San Diego Chargers' quarterback Dan Fouts becomes the highest-paid player in the NFL, signing a $7.2-million contract for six years.

27 Apr.   Nolan Ryan of the Houston Astros breaks Walter Johnson's career strikeout record with strikeout number 3,508.

17 May   The New York Islanders defeat the Edmonton Oilers in four games to win their fourth Stanley Cup in a row, only the second NHL team to do so.

20 May   Quarterback Art Schlichter of the Baltimore Colts is suspended indefinitely from the NFL for betting on ten games during the 1982 season.

27 May   Tom Sneva wins the sixty-seventh Indianapolis 500. His average speed of 162.117 MPH is the second fastest in the race's history.

31 May   The Philadelphia 76ers win the NBA championship by sweeping the Los Angeles Lakers.

2 July   Martina Navratilova wins her fourth women's singles championship at Wimbledon. The following day John McEnroe wins his second men's Wimbledon singles title.

6 July   The American League breaks its eleven-game losing streak in the All-Star Game by beating the National League 13–3 at Comiskey Park.

17 July   Golfer Tom Watson wins his fifth British Open; also, the Michigan Panthers beat the Philadelphia Stars 24–22 to win the first USFL championship.

24 July   George Brett of the Kansas City Royals hits his famous "pine tar" home run against the New York Yankees to give the Royals a 5–4 lead in the 9th. The homer was disallowed at the time because the pine tar extended too far on the barrel of the bat, but the umpire's decision was reversed on appeal.

25 July   NFL commissioner Pete Rozelle suspends four players for their admitted involvement with cocaine.

29 July   Steve Garvey's National League–record 1,207 consecutive-games-played streak ends when he breaks his thumb.

31 July   Brooks Robinson, Juan Marichal, George Kell, and Walter Alston are inducted into the Baseball Hall of Fame.

19 Aug.   Billy Cannon, college football's Player of the Year in 1959, is sentenced to five years in prison and fined $10,000 for masterminding a multimillion-dollar counterfeiting scheme.

11 Sept.   Jimmy Connors wins his fifth U.S. Open men's singles championship. The previous day Martina Navratilova won her first U.S. Open women's singles title.

16 Sept.   Philadelphia Phillies pitcher Steve Carlton wins his 300th game.

26 Sept.   *Australia II* beats the U.S. yacht *Liberty* to win the America's Cup, the first American loss in the competition in the 132-year history of the event.

16 Oct. The Baltimore Orioles defeat the Philadelphia Phillies to win the World Series four games to one.

8 Nov. Dale Murphy of the Atlanta Braves wins his second consecutive National League MVP award.

10 Nov. Middleweight champion "Marvelous" Marvin Hagler scores a unanimous fifteen-round victory over Roberto Duran.

16 Nov. Cal Ripken Jr. becomes the first player in major-league history to win Rookie of the Year and Most Valuable Player awards in consecutive seasons.

21 Nov. Darryl Strawberry of the New York Mets is named National League Rookie of the Year.

3 Dec. Ray Meyer, men's basketball coach at DePaul for more than forty years, wins his 700th game.

1984

2 Jan. Miami defeats Nebraska 31–30 in the Orange Bowl and is later voted its first national championship in college football.

22 Jan. The Los Angeles Raiders win Super Bowl XVIII by beating the Washington Redskins 38–9.

27 Jan. Edmonton Oiler Wayne Gretzky's NHL record-setting fifty-one-game scoring streak comes to an end against the Los Angeles Kings.

8 Feb. The XIV Winter Olympic Games open in Sarajevo, Yugoslavia.

16 Feb. Bill Johnson becomes the first American to win a gold medal in the Olympic downhill skiing event.

19 Feb. The XIV Winter Olympic Games end. The Soviet Union wins the most medals, 25, while the United States finishes tied for fifth, with 8 medals.

29 Mar. The Baltimore Colts of the NFL leave Baltimore for Indianapolis. The team had been in Baltimore since 1953.

1 Apr. Southern California (USC) defeats Tennessee 72–61 to win its second consecutive women's Division I NCAA basketball championship.

2 Apr. Georgetown beats Houston 84–75 to win the men's college basketball championship. John Thompson becomes the first black coach to win an NCAA Division I basketball title.

5 Apr. Kareem Abdul-Jabbar of the Los Angeles Lakers becomes the NBA's all-time scorer by breaking Wilt Chamberlain's record of 31,419 points. Abdul-Jabbar finishes his career in 1989 with 38,387 points.

13 Apr. Twenty-one years to the day after his first major-league hit, Pete Rose of the Cincinnati Reds doubles against the Philadelphia Phillies to become the first National League player to accumulate 4,000 hits.

7 May The Soviet Union announces that it will not attend the 1984 Summer Olympic games in Los Angeles.

15 May	Magic Johnson of the Los Angeles Lakers sets an NBA playoff-game record by passing for 24 assists.
19 May	The Edmonton Oilers, led by Wayne Gretzky, win their first Stanley Cup with a 5–2 victory over the New York Islanders, taking the NHL championship series four games to one.
12 June	The Boston Celtics defeat the Los Angeles Lakers in seven games to win the NBA championship.
18 June	Fuzzy Zoeller wins the eighty-fourth U.S. Open in a 18-hole playoff against Greg Norman.
19 June	After the Houston Rockets select Akeem Olajuwan and the Portland Trail Blazers choose Sam Bowie, the Chicago Bulls take Michael Jordan with the third pick in the NBA college draft.
27 June	The Supreme Court rules 7–2 that the NCAA had violated federal antitrust law by preventing individual schools from negotiating the rights to football telecasts.
29 June	Pete Rose of the Cincinnati Reds sets a major-league record by playing in his 3,309th baseball game.
28 July	The XXIII Summer Olympics open in Los Angeles.
3 Aug.	Mary Lou Retton wins the Olympic gold medal in the all-around women's gymnastic competition by earning perfect scores in the floor exercise and the vault.
4 Aug.	Carl Lewis wins the gold medal in the 100-meter dash, his first of four in the Summer Olympics.
8 Aug.	Greg Louganis wins the springboard and platform Olympic diving competitions, setting world records in both events.
10 Aug.	Mary Decker and Zola Budd collide during the 3,000-meter run at the Olympics. Maricica Puica of Romania wins the race.
12 Aug.	Closing ceremonies held for the Summer Olympics.
20 Aug.	Nancy Lopez wins the richest prize on the Ladies' Professional Golf Association (LPGA) tour, $65,000, with a victory in the World Championship of Women's Golf.
23 Aug.	Controversial television sportscaster Howard Cosell quits ABC's *Monday Night Football* after fourteen years of telecasts.
17 Sept.	Reggie Jackson of the California Angels hits the 500th home run of his career.
30 Sept.	California Angel Mike Witt pitches a perfect game against the Texas Rangers; also, New York Yankee Don Mattingly goes 4 for 5 to finish the season with .343 batting average, and thus becomes only the seventh major-league player since 1900 to win a batting crown in his first full season.
1 Oct.	Peter Ueberroth succeeds Bowie Kuhn as baseball commissioner.
7 Oct.	Walter Payton of the Chicago Bears rushes for 154 yards against the New Orleans Saints to bring his career rushing total to 12,400 yards, breaking the previous mark of 12,312 held by Jim Brown. Payton finished his career in 1987 with 16,726 yards.
11 Oct.	Mario Lemieux makes his NHL debut with the Pittsburgh Penguins.

14 Oct.	The Detroit Tigers beat the San Diego Padres four games to one to win the World Series.
17 Oct.	The USFL files a $1.3 billion antitrust suit against the NFL.
27 Oct.	Running back Ruben Mays rushes for 357 yards for Washington State against Oregon, setting an NCAA record for most rushing yards in a game; also, Mississippi Valley State wide receiver Jerry Rice sets a Division I-AA record with five touchdown catches in one game.
6 Nov.	Relief pitcher Willie Hernandez of the Detroit Tigers wins the American League MVP award to go with his American League Cy Young award.
19 Nov.	Twenty-year-old New York Mets pitcher Dwight Gooden becomes the youngest player to win the National League Rookie of the Year award.
23 Nov.	With six seconds left in the game, Boston College quarterback Doug Flutie scrambles and then completes a 64-yard touchdown pass to lead BC over Miami 47–45. A week later Flutie wins the Heisman Trophy.
9 Dec.	Eric Dickerson of the Los Angeles Rams rushes for 215 yards against the Houston Oilers to break O. J. Simpson's single-season mark of 2,003 yards. Dickerson finishes the season with 2,105 yards.
16 Dec.	Washington Redskins wide receiver Art Monk catches eleven passes against the St. Louis Cardinals to set an NFL record for receptions in a season with 106.
17 Dec.	Dan Marino of the Miami Dolphins throws his 48th touchdown of the year, setting an NFL single-season record.
19 Dec.	It is announced that the Los Angeles Summer Olympics netted a surplus of $215 million.

1985

3 Jan.	Brigham Young University, the nation's only undefeated and untied football team, narrowly becomes the 1984 college football champion.
14 Jan.	Tennis great Martina Navratilova wins her 100th career singles title.
19 Jan.	Mary Decker sets a world indoor record in the 2,000 meters with a time of 5:34.52.
20 Jan.	The San Francisco 49ers win Super Bowl XIX by beating the Miami Dolphins 38–16. Las Vegas bookmakers report that a record $40 million is bet on the game.
22 Jan.	O. J. Simpson, Joe Namath, Roger Staubach, Pete Rozelle, and Frank Gatski are elected into the Pro Football Hall of Fame.
27 Jan.	Chris Evert Lloyd beats Martina Navratilova for the first time in more than two years.
6 Feb.	Diann Roffe becomes the first American woman to win a gold medal at the World Alpine Skiing Championships.
18 Feb.	Olympic diver Greg Louganis wins the 1984 Sullivan Award as the amateur athlete of the year.
3 Mar.	Bill Shoemaker becomes the first jockey to win $100 million in purses.

6 Mar.	Heavyweight Mike Tyson knocks out Hector Mercedes in the first round to win his first professional fight.
28 Mar.	The North American Soccer League announces that it will not operate an outdoor league in 1985.
1 Apr.	Villanova University upsets Georgetown 66–64 to win the NCAA men's basketball championship.
4 Apr.	A New Orleans grand jury indicts eight people, including three members of the Tulane men's basketball team, on charges connected to point shaving during the 1984–1985 season.
14 Apr.	Steve Garvey of the San Diego Padres plays in his 193rd straight game without committing an error, a major-league record for first basemen.
15 Apr.	Marvin Hagler knocks out Thomas Hearns in the third round of their fight for the undisputed middleweight world championship.
26 Apr.	Utaz Jazz center Mark Eaton blocks 10 shots versus the Houston Rockets to set an NBA playoff-game record.
16 May	Michael Jordan of the Chicago Bulls is named the NBA Rookie of the Year.
30 May	The Edmonton Oilers win their second consecutive Stanley Cup by beating the Philadelphia Flyers in five games.
9 June	The Los Angeles Lakers beat the Boston Celtics four games to two to win their third NBA championship of the decade.
11 June	Von Hayes of the Philadelphia Phillies leads off a game against the New York Mets with a home run. Later that same inning he hits a grand slam, becoming the first player ever to hit 2 home runs in the first inning.
11 July	Nolan Ryan, 38, of the Houston Astros strikes out his 4,000th batter.
14 July	The Baltimore Stars beat the Oakland Invaders 28–24 to win their second straight USFL championship. It is the USFL's final game.
4 Aug.	Tom Seaver of the Chicago White Sox wins his 300th game; also, Rod Carew of the California Angels raps his 3,000th hit.
7 Aug.	A major-league players' strike is settled after just one day when a new five-year basic agreement is reached.
23 Aug.	Martina Navratilova and Pam Shriver beat Vitas Gerulaitus and sixty-seven-year-old Bobby Riggs to win $300,000 in a battle-of-the-sexes doubles tennis exhibition.
25 Aug.	Twenty-year-old Dwight Gooden of the New York Mets becomes the youngest major-league pitcher to win 20 games in a season.
11 Sept.	Pete Rose, the forty-four-year-old player-manager of the Cincinnati Reds, cracks his 4,192nd career hit, breaking Ty Cobb's fifty-seven-year-old record for career hits. Rose retires as a player in 1986 with 4,256 hits.
20 Sept.	A Pittsburgh drug trial implicates eleven major-league players as having "in some fashion facilitated the distribution of drugs in baseball."
21 Sept.	Light-heavyweight champion Michael Spinks upsets previously undefeated heavyweight world champion Larry Holmes by winning a unanimous fifteen-round decision.

5 Oct.   Eddie Robinson of Grambling becomes the winningest coach in college football history with his 324th win.

6 Oct.   New York Yankees pitcher Phil Niekro, forty-six, wins the 300th game of his twenty-two-year career.

8 Oct.   Former college basketball all-American and 1984 Olympic team captain Lynette Woodard is the first woman to make the Harlem Globetrotters' roster.

13 Oct.   Dallas Cowboy Tony Dorsett becomes only the sixth player in NFL history to rush for more than 10,000 yards.

26 Oct.   Patrick Ewing of the New York Knicks makes his NBA debut.

27 Oct.   After being down three games to one, the Kansas City Royals beat the St. Louis Cardinals in seven games to win the World Series.

9 Nov.   Running back Joe Dudek of Plymouth State, a Division III college in New Hampshire, sets three NCAA records against Curry College: he rushes for his 76th touchdown, the 79th touchdown of his career, and scores the 474th point of his career.

13 Nov.   Dwight Gooden of the New York Mets becomes the youngest winner of the National League's Cy Young award after leading the league in wins (24), earned run average (1.53), and strikeouts (268).

27 Nov.   Lou Holtz is named football coach at Notre Dame.

7 Dec.   Auburn University running back Bo Jackson wins the Heisman Trophy.

22 Dec.   Roger Craig of the San Francisco 49ers becomes the first player in NFL history to gain 1,000 yards rushing and receiving in a season.

1986

1 Jan.   Oklahoma defeats Penn State 25–10 in the Orange Bowl and is named the national champion of college football for the 1985 season.

4 Jan.   Navy basketball center David Robinson sets an NCAA record with fourteen blocked shots in a game against North Carolina–Wilmington.

13 Jan.   NCAA adopts Proposition 48, which had been passed in early 1983.

25 Jan.   Mike Tyson knocks out his seventeenth straight opponent to break Rocky Marciano's heavyweight record.

26 Jan.   The Chicago Bears rout the New England Patriots 46–10 in Super Bowl XX.

28 Jan.   Denis Potvin of the New York Islanders scores his 271st goal to break Bobby Orr's goal-scoring record for defensemen.

8 Feb.   Five-foot seven-inch Spud Webb of the Atlanta Hawks wins the NBA's slam dunk competition.

24 Feb.   Marathoner Joan Benoit Samuelson wins the Sullivan Award as the nation's top amateur athlete.

25 Feb.   Alvin Robertson of the San Antonio Spurs achieves a "quadruple double" — 20 points, 11 rebounds, 10 assists, and 10 steals; also, Micheal Ray Richardson of the New Jersey Nets is banned from the NBA for cocaine use. It is his third such violation.

13 Mar. Susan Butcher wins the 1,158-mile Iditarod dogsled race.

15 Mar. The University of Iowa wins its ninth consecutive NCAA wrestling championship.

21 Mar. Debi Thomas becomes the first African American to win a women's world figure skating championship.

30 Mar. Texas thrashes USC 97–81 to win the NCAA women's basketball championship. Texas finishes the season 34–0.

31 Mar. Louisville beats Duke 72–69 to win the NCAA men's basketball championship.

2 Apr. The NCAA approves the use of the 19-foot 9-inch three-point field goal in college basketball for the 1986–1987 season.

8 Apr. With the first swing of his first major-league at-bat, Will Clark of the San Francisco Giants hits a home run off Houston Astro pitcher Nolan Ryan.

13 Apr. Jack Nicklaus becomes the oldest player to win the Masters, his record-setting sixth victory at Augusta.

20 Apr. Michael Jordan of the Chicago Bulls scores an NBA playoff-record 63 points in a losing cause against the Boston Celtics.

29 Apr. The Boston Red Sox's Roger Clemens strikes out twenty Seattle Mariners, including eight in a row.

3 May Riding Ferdinand, fifty-four-year-old Bill Shoemaker becomes the oldest jockey to ever win the Kentucky Derby.

15 May Patrick Ewing is honored as the NBA's Rookie of the Year.

28 May Larry Bird wins his third consecutive NBA MVP award.

31 May Bobby Rahal sets a record for the fastest Indianapolis 500, averaging almost 171 MPH.

1 June Pat Bradley wins the LPGA championship and becomes the first woman to win all four of the top women's tournaments: the du Maurier Classic, the U.S. Open, the Dinah Shore, and the LPGA.

8 June The Boston Celtics win their sixteenth NBA championship in six games over the Houston Rockets.

10 June Former college star Nancy Lieberman becomes the first woman to play in a men's professional basketball league, the U.S. Basketball League.

18 June Forty-one-year-old pitcher Don Sutton wins his 300th career game.

19 June Maryland basketball player Len Bias dies from a drug overdose. Two days before, Bias was selected in the NBA college draft by the Boston Celtics.

6 July The Atlanta Braves' Bob Horner hits 4 home runs in a game, which the Braves lose.

27 July Greg LeMond wins pro cycling's Tour de France, an American first.

29 July The USFL is awarded one dollar in their federal antitrust civil suit against the NFL.

26 Aug.	With less than two months to live, former Washington Redskins tight end Jerry Smith discloses that he is suffering from Acquired Immune Deficiency Syndrome (AIDS). Smith is the first prominent athlete known to have AIDS.
23 Sept.	Jim Deshaies of the Houston Astros sets a major-league record by striking out the first eight batters of a game.
25 Sept.	Mike Scott of the Houston Astros pitches a no-hitter to clinch the National League Western Division title.
12 Oct.	In game five of the American League Championship Series (ALCS) Donnie Moore of the California Angels gives up a two-out, two-run home run to Dave Henderson of the Boston Red Sox in the ninth inning, propelling the Red Sox to a 7–6 victory in 11 innings. Three years later the game is said to be a contributory cause in Moore's suicide.
25 Oct.	In game six of the World Series Bill Buckner's fielding error on a slow roller in the tenth inning enables the New York Mets to defeat the Boston Red Sox 6–5. Two nights later the Mets win game seven and the World Series.
18 Nov.	Roger Clemens of the Boston Red Sox wins the American League MVP; he already had won the American League Cy Young award after going 24–4 with a 2.24 earned-run average and 238 strikeouts.
22 Nov.	Mike Tyson knocks out WBC champion Trevor Berbick in the second round to become, at twenty, the youngest heavyweight champion in history.
13 Dec.	Augustana wins its fourth straight Amos Alonzo Stagg Bowl to claim the NCAA Division III national championship.
25 Dec.	Linebacker Brian Bosworth of Oklahoma is prohibited from playing in the upcoming Orange Bowl because he tests positive for steroids.
27 Dec.	Doug Jarvis of the Hartford Whalers plays in his record-breaking 915th consecutive NHL game.

1987

2 Jan.	Penn State defeats Miami 14–10 in the Fiesta Bowl and is later voted the 1986 national college football champion.
25 Jan.	The New York Giants beat the Denver Broncos 39–20 in Super Bowl XXI.
4 Feb.	*Stars & Stripes*, captained by Dennis Conner, wins the America's Cup trophy for yachting, avenging Conner's 1983 loss.
8 Feb.	With her 35th career victory Nancy Lopez qualifes for the LPGA Hall of Fame.
25 Feb.	The NCAA announces sanctions for the scandal-ridden Southern Methodist University (SMU) football program, including the cancellation of its 1987 season.
7 Mar.	Mike Tyson wins the WBA title by beating James "Bonecrusher" Smith in twelve rounds.
9 Mar.	George Foreman, former heavyweight world champion, wins his first fight after his ten-year retirement by knocking out Steve Zouski.

21 Mar. Iowa State snaps Iowa's NCAA wrestling championship streak at nine.

30 Mar. Bobby Knight wins his third NCAA men's national college basketball championship when Indiana beats Syracuse 74–73 on a shot by Keith Smart with five seconds left in the game.

6 Apr. Sugar Ray Leonard defeats Marvin Hagler on points to win the WBC middleweight championship. It is Leonard's first fight in three years; also, Los Angeles Dodgers' vice president Al Campanis reveals racist attitudes during an interview on *Nightline*.

9 Apr. Wayne Gretzky of the Edmonton Oilers breaks the all-time NHL playoff scoring mark of 176 points set by Jean Beliveau.

12 Apr. Golfer Larry Mize wins the Masters in a sudden death playoff when he holes an improbable pitch from 140 feet.

18 May Magic Johnson of the Los Angeles Lakers becomes the first guard in twenty-three years to win the NBA's MVP award.

24 May Al Unser Sr. wins his fourth Indy 500.

30 May All-Star guard Isiah Thomas of the Detroit Pistons says that if Larry Bird of the Boston Celtics were black instead of white he would be considered "just another good guy." Six days later Thomas maintains he was joking but asserts that he is disturbed by how the media portrays black athletes.

4 June Edwin Moses loses in the 400-meter hurdles. It is his first loss in almost ten years and ends his record-setting victory streak at 122.

14 June The Los Angeles Lakers win the NBA championship by beating the Boston Celtics in six games.

27 June The longest winning streak in baseball history comes to an end as the Salt Lake Trappers, a rookie-league team, loses for the first time in 30 games.

18 July New York Yankee first baseman Don Mattingly ties a major-league record by hitting a home run in eight straight games.

1 Aug. Mike Tyson defeats Tony Tucker in twelve rounds to become the undisputed world heavyweight champion by unifying the IBF, WBA, and WBC titles.

9 Aug. Golfer Larry Nelson wins the PGA Championship in sudden death.

26 Aug. Paul Molitor of the Milwaukee Brewers sees his 39-game hitting streak come to an end, the longest streak in the American League since Joe DiMaggio's 56-game streak in 1941.

19 Sept. Freshman running back Emmitt Smith in his first start rushes for a school-record 224 yards as Florida upsets Alabama, 23–14.

21 Sept. An arbiter rules that Major-League Baseball owners are guilty of collusion after they fail to sign free agents following the 1985 season.

29 Sept. Don Mattingly hits his sixth grand slam of the season to set a major-league record.

19 Oct. Billy Martin is hired by George Steinbrenner to manage the New York Yankees for the fifth time. He is fired 23 June 1988.

25 Oct. The Minnesota Twins beat the Saint Louis Cardinals four games to three to win the World Series.

1 Nov. Kansas City Royals outfielder Bo Jackson makes his NFL debut with the Los Angeles Raiders. Jackson says professional football will be a "hobby."

6 Nov. Jack Ramsay sets an NBA record for most games coached with 1,559.

4 Dec. Kareem Abdul-Jabbar of the Los Angeles Lakers is held to only 7 points by the Milwaukee Bucks, breaking his streak of 787 games in which he scored at least 10 points a game.

6 Dec. San Francisco 49er quarterback Joe Montana completes an NFL record 22 straight passes against the Green Bay Packers.

8 Dec. Philadelphia Flyer goaltender Ron Hextall is the first goalie in NHL history to shoot and score a goal.

1988

1 Jan. Unbeaten Miami defeats previously unbeaten Oklahoma 20–14 on their way to winning the 1987 college football national championship.

9 Jan. Brian Boitano wins his fourth straight U.S. men's figure-skating championship.

16 Jan. CBS broadcaster and oddsmaker Jimmy "The Greek" Snyder is fired for making racist remarks.

17 Jan. In the American Football Conference (AFC) championship game, Cleveland Browns running back Ernest Byner fumbles at the goal line as the Browns lose 38–33 to the Denver Broncos.

31 Jan. The Washington Redskins score 35 points in the second quarter on their way to winning Super Bowl XXII over the Denver Broncos 42–10.

13 Feb. The Calgary Winter Olympic Games open.

22 Feb. Bonnie Blair wins the 500-meter speed-skating gold medal at the Winter Games.

28 Feb. The Winter Olympic Games close with the Soviet team winning the most medals (29). The United States finishes a disappointing ninth with 6 medals.

15 Mar. The NFL approves the St. Louis Cardinals' proposed move to Arizona.

24 Mar. The NFL announces that referee John Grier will lead an umpiring crew in the upcoming season. He is the first African American official to head a crew.

4 Apr. George Bell of the Toronto Blue Jays becomes the first player to hit three home runs on opening day.

28 Apr. The Baltimore Orioles lose their record-setting 21st game in a row.

2 May National League president A. Bartlett Giamatti suspends Cincinnati Reds manager Pete Rose for thirty days and fines him $10,000—the toughest penalty ever imposed for an on-field infraction—for twice shoving umpire Dave Pallone during an argument.

17 May John Stockton of the Utah Jazz passes for 24 assists in a playoff game to tie Magic Johnson's NBA record.

26 May	The Edmonton Oilers win the Stanley Cup, their fourth in five years.
29 May	Rick Mears wins the Indy 500 for the third time.
30 May	More than twenty thousand people witness Syracuse defeat Cornell in the Carrier Dome to win the NCAA lacrosse championship.
21 June	By defeating the Detroit Pistons 108–105, the Los Angeles Lakers become the first team since 1969 to win back-to-back NBA championships.
27 June	Heavyweight champion Mike Tyson knocks out former champ Michael Spinks in the first round.
2 July	Steffi Graf defeats Martina Navratilova to win the women's singles championship at Wimbledon, ending Navratilova's record streak of 6 straight Wimbledon titles.
9 July	Baseball manager Sparky Anderson wins his 800th game with the Detroit Tigers to become the first manager to win 800 games in both the American League and the National League. He had won 863 with the Cincinnati Reds (1970–1978).
16 July	Florence Griffith Joyner sets a world record time of 10.49 in the 100-meter dash at the U.S. Olympic trials.
17 July	First baseman Willie Stargell of the Pittsburgh Pirates is inducted into the Baseball Hall of Fame.
8 Aug.	The first night game at Wrigley Field in Chicago is played.
9 Aug.	The Edmonton Oilers trade superstar Wayne Gretzky to the Los Angeles Kings in a multiplayer, multimillion-dollar deal.
16 Sept.	Cincinnati Reds' pitcher Tom Browning throws a perfect game.
17 Sept.	The Summer Olympic Games open in Seoul, South Korea.
18 Sept.	Arnold Palmer wins his first golf tournament in three years, the Crestar Classic for Seniors in Richmond, Virginia.
23 Sept.	José Canseco of the Oakland Athletics becomes the first major leaguer to steal forty bases and hit forty home runs in the same season.
24 Sept.	Canadian runner Ben Johnson wins the 100-meter dash at the Olympics and sets a world record with a time of 9.79. Two days later Johnson is stripped of his gold medal when he tests positive for steroids.
25 Sept.	Swimmer Matt Biondi wins his fifth gold medal (and seventh medal overall) at the Olympics by helping the U.S. team win the 400-meter medley relay.
27 Sept.	On his final dive Greg Louganis wins the 10-meter platform event, becoming the first man to win two diving gold medals in two Olympics in a row.
29 Sept.	Sisters-in-law Jackie Joyner-Kersee and Florence Griffith Joyner both win gold medals and set world records in their respective events: Joyner-Kersee in the heptathlon and Griffith Joyner in the 200-meter dash.
2 Oct.	The Summer Olympics close.
8 Oct.	The Columbia football team snaps its 44-game losing streak by beating Princeton 16–13.

9 Oct.   In Bayston, Texas, Eddie Hill sets a record for the fastest time in drag racing, completing the quarter-mile race in 4.936 seconds.

20 Oct.   The Los Angeles Dodgers win the World Series by upsetting the Oakland Athletics four games to one.

24 Oct.   Mike Bossy, whose 573 goals is sixth on the NHL all-time list, retires.

11 Nov.   Dallas beats John Brown 76–68 to snap college basketball's longest losing streak at 86 games.

20 Nov.   The North Carolina women's soccer team wins its seventh NCAA national championship in eight years.

3 Dec.   Oklahoma State running back Barry Sanders wins the Heisman Trophy.

14 Dec.   CBS wins the right to televise Major League Baseball for four years beginning in 1990 for $1.1 billion.

19 Dec.   Oklahoma's football program is penalized for "numerous and major" violations of NCAA rules.

1989

1 Jan.   Undefeated Notre Dame defeats West Virginia 34–21 in the Fiesta Bowl and is later voted the national champion for the 1988 college football season.

11 Jan.   The NCAA passes controversial Proposition 42, which disallows athletic scholarships to those students who fail to meet minimum academic standards set by Proposition 48.

14 Jan.   Georgetown basketball coach John Thompson walks off the court before a game against Boston College to protest the passage of Proposition 42.

20 Jan.   Mario Lemieux of the Pittsburgh Penguins becomes only the second player in NHL history (Wayne Gretzky is the other) to score 50 goals in less than 50 games. Lemieux scores goal number fifty in the forty-fourth game of the season.

22 Jan.   The San Francisco 49ers win Super Bowl XXIII by coming from behind to beat the Cincinnati Bengals 20–16.

25 Jan.   Chicago Bulls guard Michael Jordan scores his 10,000th NBA point in his 303rd game. Only Wilt Chamberlain scored as many points in fewer games.

31 Jan.   The Loyola Marymount and U.S. International men's basketball teams combine to score a record 310 points in a game, which Loyola Marymount wins 181–130.

3 Feb.   Former St. Louis Cardinal outfielder Bill White is named president of the National League. White is the first African American man to head a major U.S. professional sports league.

13 Feb.   Oklahoma quarterback Charles Thompson is arrested for selling cocaine.

25 Feb.   The Dallas Cowboys of the NFL are sold to Jerry Jones. Coach Tom Landry is replaced by former University of Miami coach Jimmy Johnson.

17 Mar.   Julie Croteau of St. Mary's becomes the first woman to play in a men's college baseball game.

22 Mar.   Pete Rozelle, commissioner of the NFL for twenty-nine years, announces his resignation.

3 Apr.   Rumeal Robinson sinks two free throws with three seconds left in overtime to help Michigan defeat Seton Hall 80–79 in the NCAA's men's basketball championship final.

7 Apr.   The International Basketball Federation (FIBA) votes to allow professional basketball players to participate in the Olympics beginning in 1992.

13 Apr.   Sports agents Norby Walters and Lloyd Bloom are found guilty of racketeering, mail fraud, and extortion in their dealings with college athletes.

23 Apr.   Kareem Abdul-Jabbar plays his final NBA regular season game; also, the NFL holds its annual college draft: the first five picks are quarterback Troy Aikman (Dallas), offensive lineman Tony Mandarich (Green Bay), running back Barry Sanders (Detroit), linebacker Derrick Thomas (Kansas City), and defensive back Deion Sanders (Atlanta).

28 Apr.   High-school pitcher Jon Peters wins his record 51st consecutive game. His streak is snapped at 53 a month later.

4 May   Soviet hockey player Alexander Mogilny defects to Sweden and thereafter immigrates to the United States to play for the Buffalo Sabres of the NHL.

21 May   Nancy Lopez wins the LPGA Championship.

26 May   Hobart College wins its 10th consecutive NCAA division III lacrosse championship.

12 June   Sugar Ray Leonard and Thomas Hearns fight to a draw in their twelve-round WBC super-middleweight title fight.

13 June   The Detroit Pistons complete a sweep of the Los Angeles Lakers in the NBA finals to win their first world championship.

18 June   Golfer Curtis Strange wins his second consecutive U.S. Open Championship.

19 June   Pitcher Dwight Gooden of the New York Mets, twenty-four, wins his 100th career game.

23 July   Greg LeMond wins cycling's Tour de France for the second time; also, the Baseball Hall of Fame inductees include Johnny Bench and Carl Yastrzemski.

22 Aug.   Nolan Ryan, forty-two, of the Texas Rangers collects the 5,000th strikeout of his career.

24 Aug.   Cincinnati Reds manager Pete Rose agrees to a lifetime suspension from baseball for gambling; also, Victoria Brucker becomes the first girl from the United States to play in the Little League World Series.

26 Aug.   A team from Trumbull, Connecticut, wins the Little League World Series.

1 Sept.   Baseball commissioner A. Bartlett Giamatti dies of a heart attack.

2 Sept.   SMU plays its first football game since the NCAA "death penalty" was imposed in 1987.

5 Sept.   Chris Evert Lloyd plays her last match at the U.S. Open, losing to Zina Garrison.

13 Sept.   Fay Vincent is named baseball commissioner.

16 Sept.   In college football action number one Notre Dame defeats number two Michigan 24–19. Raghib "Rocket" Ismail returns two kickoffs of 88 and 92 yards for touchdowns.

3 Oct.   Art Shell is hired as the Los Angeles Raiders coach, making him the first African American NFL coach since Fritz Pollard was a player-coach for the Hammond (Indiana) Pros (1923–1925).

15 Oct.   Wayne Gretzky of the Los Angeles Kings scores a goal against the Edmonton Oilers to become the NHL's all-time leading scorer with 1,850 points.

17 Oct.   An earthquake in the San Francisco Bay area prior to game three of the World Series forces a ten-day delay in the series, which the Oakland Athletics eventually win by sweeping the San Francisco Giants.

26 Oct.   Paul Tagliabue is named commissioner of the NFL.

9 Nov.   The Milwaukee Bucks defeat the Seattle SuperSonics 155–154 after five overtime periods. The game takes four hours and seventeen minutes to complete, the third-longest game in NBA history.

19 Nov.   The U.S. soccer team wins a berth in the final round of the World Cup.

7 Dec.   Sugar Ray Leonard wins a unanimous twelve-round decision against Roberto Duran to retain his WBC super-middleweight championship.

23 Dec.   Wide receiver Steve Largent of the Seattle Seahawks plays his final game. He retires as the NFL's all-time leader in touchdown receptions (100), total catches (819), and receiving yardage (13,089).

OVERVIEW

A Matter of Scale. For most of the twentieth century mass-entertainment spectator sports have been big business. American sporting contests have been commercialized to varying degrees since their inception, contrary to claims of some critics who yearn for a time when games were not sullied by money. Throughout the 1980s sports enjoyed unprecedented financial prosperity and mass popularity, even eclipsing the so-called Golden Age of Sport during the 1920s, when, in the words of Roderick Nash, "the nation went sports crazy." Without a doubt money dramatically changed the sporting world during the 1980s; those changes, however, were primarily a matter of scale, not kind. For instance, the amount of money generated from television contracts for the broadcast rights to professional leagues, big-time college athletics, and the Olympics increased tremendously. In 1982 television revenue provided $14 million a year per NFL team. By the 1990 season the per-team annual payout had risen to $26 million. As early as the 1980 season 30 percent of Major League Baseball's revenue was derived from television contracts, and in 1988 CBS agreed to pay $1.1 billion to televise four years worth of the national pastime. In 1989 NBC won the right to televise NBA basketball games for four years for $600 million. The NCAA signed a billion-dollar deal with CBS for the television rights to the men's college basketball tournament. Notre Dame forged its own multimillion dollar contract with NBC to televise Fighting Irish football games. Though the Olympics Games were long thought to be about amateurism and sport for its own sake, the Games became increasingly lucrative for the International Olympic Committee. For instance, ABC paid $25 million to televise the 1976 Summer Olympics from Montreal. Eight years later ABC paid $225 million for the rights to the 1984 Los Angeles Summer Olympics. Eight years later NBC paid $401 million to broadcast the 1992 Summer Olympics from Barcelona. Though a handful of small-market professional teams struggled financially, the financial value of professional teams reflected the prosperity of the industry. Perhaps one team best illustrates this development. Famous trial lawyer Edward Bennett Williams bought the Baltimore Orioles baseball club in 1979 for $12 million. In 1988 the executors of his estate sold the team for $70 million. Five years later the Orioles were sold again, this time for $173 million.

Earnings. To the annoyance of many sports fans, the salaries of both superstar and middling professional athletes skyrocketed. Outfielder Dave Winfield began the decade by signing a record-setting ten-year contract with the New York Yankees worth at least $22 million. Less than a year later, Earvin "Magic" Johnson of the Los Angeles Lakers signed what was then the richest and longest contract in the history of professional sports: a $1 million a year, twenty-five-year agreement. By the end of the decade both of these contracts had been surpassed many times over in terms of their annual salary. In 1989, for instance, eight major leaguers signed multiyear contracts for at least $3 million per season. In fact, professional sport was infused with so much money that even athletes of mediocre talent were able to command multimillion dollar contracts.

Serious Business. The sports industry grew in other ways, as well. The retailing of sports equipment and clothing, the construction and maintenance of sports stadiums, health and fitness clubs, racetracks, golf courses, tennis courts, bowling alleys, and skating rinks were multimillion-dollar ventures. Moreover, corporate sponsorship of sports was everywhere. Major companies sponsored youth leagues, events at various professional games, race car driving teams, college football bowl games, the Olympic Games, and thousands of athletes. Trading in baseball cards and other sports cards became big business. Sports agents, lawyers, and business managers for athletes became ever more wealthy and powerful. Product endorsements by athletes became more visible and lucrative than ever. Sports medicine and sports insurance were growth industries. Finally, it was not only competitive games that were big business. Hunting, fishing, and boating were also highly profitable enterprises in the 1980s especially for manufacturers. All told, by the close of the 1980s the sports industry was a $50 billion annual business. As these numbers suggest, sports were not simply escapist diversions but intensely serious endeavors. They were deeply rooted in American cultural values and traditions, such as individualism, teamwork, a belief in meritocracy, and laissez-faire capitalism.

Television. The influence of television in the decade on the commercialization of sport cannot be overestimated. Sport historian Benjamin Rader argues, "Nothing was more central to the history of organized sports during the second half of the twentieth century than television." Millions of Americans loved to watch televised athletics, and it often seemed as though the public's appetite for televised sports was insatiable. Ratings for most televised sports rose steadily. Moreover, some sports which had rarely been televised in the past, like ice figure skating and beach volleyball, were increasingly on the air. The growth of the Entertainment and Sports Programming Network (ESPN) and the cable television industry was a boon for sports fans. These developments, however, were not problem free. "Sport has been glorified by television. It is the best that television does," notes writer John Underwood. "But it is also the worst." According to Underwood television "bribes and bullies and makes whores of sport, and helps make money-grubbing freaks of its heroes. It even modifies and distorts the ways sports are played." Without a doubt, the power of television to create and sustain viewing markets has influenced the playing of the games. In some cases the rules were changed to accommodate programming. Changes such as the shot clock and the three-point field goal in basketball were not necessarily mandated by television, but they were adopted to speed up the game and to make it more appealing to viewers. In the case of professional golf, a different scoring system and the sudden-death playoff were added to stimulate interest in the game. The tiebreaker introduced to shorten televised tennis matches was adopted for regular tournament play. The number of timeouts allowed during games was increased to allow for more commercials. The two-minute warning near the end of each half in professional football was used for commercials. Television was also responsible for changes in the scheduling of games. "We think TV exposure is important to our program and so important to this university that we will schedule ourselves to fit the medium," said Alabama football coach Paul "Bear" Bryant. "I'll play at midnight, if that's what TV wants." Because of television marketing, Major League Baseball was primarily played at night. Most World Series games, except for those played on weekends, were broadcast at night. For better or worse, the relationship between television and sports in the 1980s was symbiotic, and produced in many the indiscriminate desire for even more televised athletic contests.

Athletes. Many Americans seemed almost schizophrenic in their view of athletes in the 1980s. On the one hand, sports figures were never more popular as celebrities and genuine folk heroes. They enjoyed tremendous wealth and social status, were praised lavishly by cultural critics and fans alike, and were often treated as secular deities. For many, athletic superstars became personifications of certain kinds of values which Americans wanted to believe they too possessed. On the other hand, for many of those same celebrants, professional athletes were most notable for their "obscene salaries, grandiose lifestyles, out-for-number-one philosophies, and lack of commitment to the teams that employed them or the cities in which they performed," wrote journalist Haynes Johnson. Despite their on-the-field heroics, many athletes were castigated for their arrogance and braggadocio. "What ever happened to humble heroes?" asked sportswriter Thomas Boswell. "If Lou Gehrig were alive, would he wear a Mohawk haircut? Or write a tell-all biography at age twenty-two about his former college team? Course not." Some sports fans, longing for the good old days when sports and athletes seemed more noble, were probably in the grip of nostalgia. Looking back on the 1980s and early 1990s, Robert Lipsyte wrote: "Sports no longer reflect the America of our dreams, and the stars of sport are no longer the idealized versions of ourselves." Perhaps. But American sports heroes—at least since the days of John. L. Sullivan and later Ty Cobb—have been dubious role models. Writer Gerald Early notes that "since the time of the Roman gladiators when the glory of Greek athleticism was made totally contemptible, the athlete has always been a suspect person in the Western mind—a hero to be sure, but a cheap and crude one." This was never more so the case than in the decade of the 1980s in America.

Scandals. Due in part to the possibility of the tremendous financial rewards to be won, in part to a more permissive ethical climate, sports scandals came in all varieties during the decade. Cheating of all sorts was preeminent, but the era also witnessed more than its fair share of gambling, drug, and sex-related scandals. The abuses that beset intercollegiate athletics alone during the 1980s were daunting. There were many cases of recruiting violations, athletes receiving improper benefits from coaching staffs and alumni, falsified transcripts and other forms of academic cheating, illegal steroid use, recreational drug abuse, and incidents of violence. Institutions of higher learning—such as the University of Maryland, Tulane, the University of Kentucky, Memphis State, the University of Oklahoma, the University of San Francisco, and Southern Methodist University, to name but a few—were severely punished by the NCAA for assorted rules violations. Though college athletics received the lion's share of the media's attention, no sport was immune from scandal. Baseball witnessed the Pittsburgh drug trial, owner collusion, and the Pete Rose betting controversy. Professional basketball suffered from persistent revelations of drug abuse. The specter of steroids and other performance-enhancing drugs haunted football, track and field, swimming, and weightlifting. Some sports scandals were probably the result of heightened ethical sensitivities and distaste for practices and behavior that were previously accepted or ignored. In any event, if sport was a primary expression of American society at the end of the twentieth century, then it revealed a deeply troubled nation.

Gender Equity. In 1984 Jane O'Reilly observed that the "dazzling accomplishments of U.S. women at this year's [Summer Olympic] Games were the direct result of changes in personal attitude and public policy brought about by two inseparable revolutions: the women's movement and the growth of women's sports." Thanks in large part to Title IX of the 1972 education amendments, women and girls made significant gains in the world of sports and beyond. In the early 1980s, for instance, almost two million girls participated in high-school varsity sports every year, a dramatic increase from the number who played in 1970s before Title IX. Said USC basketball great Cheryl Miller, "Without Title IX, I'd be nowhere." Still, sport historian Allen Guttmann points out that Title IX "has not wrought miracles." Women athletes did not compete on a level playing field. Men still controlled sport. Intercollegiate athletics played by men continued to receive significantly more funding than sports played by women. Men continued to earn more prize money than women on the professional golf and tennis tours. Men continued to have more opportunities than women to pursue professional athletic careers and sports-related jobs. Although superior athletes such as Miller, Martina Navratilova, Chris Evert, Joan Benoit, Florence Griffith Joyner, and Jackie Joyner-Kersee dispelled ancient myths about female athletic inferiority and provided young women with important role models, athletic gender equity in the 1980s remained an elusive goal. "In spite of enormous changes since the mid-1970s, the world of sport still promotes and preserves traditional gender differences, and patriarchal ideology is still firmly entrenched in American institutions and social practices," writes sport sociologist George Sage. "More females playing sports does not signify that a revolution has been won for women, not so long as the organization of sport promotes and sustains the dominance of men in social relations."

Race Relations. Race relations in the sports world were complicated. On the one hand, after decades of struggling for civil rights, racial minorities achieved a degree of equal opportunity. Overt racial segregation and explicit discrimination were largely relics. It was not uncommon for the rosters of professional basketball, football, and baseball teams to be composed of players from a variety of ethnic and racial backgrounds. African American athletes such as Michael Jordan, Magic Johnson, and Mike Tyson enjoyed tremendous popularity across the racial spectrum. "On the face of it, sports would seem to be a model for racial progress," notes Philip Hoose. "But, although appearances may have changed, four decades after Jackie Robinson's major league debut [in 1947], racial prejudice remains as deeply rooted in America's sports as it is in American society in general." Indeed, racial discrimination in sports continued, but in new, less visible forms. Racial minorities, for instance, tended to be relegated to certain positions and excluded from others, a phenomenon known as "stacking." In Major League Baseball, for example, African American ballplayers were most often played in the outfield or at first base. In 1989 only 5 percent of big-league pitchers were Americans of African descent and only 8 percent were Latinos or Hispanic Americans. In professional and college football stacking was even more conspicuous. Benjamin Rader writes, "Blacks were more likely to be found playing at a wide receiver or running back position than at quarterback or in the middle of the offensive line. On defense blacks usually constituted a majority of the cornerbacks and safeties, but few of them played linebacker positions." In addition to the prevalence of stacking, racial minorities generally had difficulty receiving equal financial rewards for equal performance. In spite of the astronomical salaries of African American superstars, data on salary equality and endorsement income suggests that racial minorities earned less than their white counterparts. Again, despite some notable exceptions—such as Maury Wills, Frank Robinson, Cito Gaston, Art Shell, Lenny Wilkins, Wes Unseld, Wayne Embry, Bernie Bickerstaff, and Bill White—racial minorities were rarely hired as Major League Baseball managers or coaches, professional football and basketball coaches, or upper-level front office executives. Mass-media representations of racial minorities were not much better. According to Hoose, "by the words and images they choose, broadcasters and writers continue to convey racial stereotypes—portraying blacks as undisciplined brutes, Latins as explosive little firecrackers, and whites as heady, gutty leaders who overcome their damned inferior equipment through Puritan effort. Blacks are described in terms of hang time, are encouraged to say 'hi, Mom' after touchdowns, are said to make mental mistakes and to have innate 'athletic ability.'" While a great deal of progress was made in terms of the athletic participation of racial minorities in professional sports, in other ways little of significance changed.

Another End of Innocence. Though sports enjoyed tremendous popularity and prosperity in the decade, for many Americans professional and big-time college athletics had gone too far in their desire for glory and profits. Indeed, the amateur ideal had become so debased over the course of the decade that it was difficult for some to discern the difference between the two enterprises. Simply put, argued Craig Neff, "Sports had grown out of all proportion to the rest of society." Others argued that the mindless pursuit of athletic victory and financial gain had despoiled and disillusioned generations of sports fans. Even in the midst of an era of plenty, some respected critics like Robert Lipsyte suggested that the sports world had sown the seeds of its own destruction, that games were no longer meaningful. "Sports are over because they no longer have any moral resonance," lamented Lipsyte looking back on the 1980s and early 1990s. "They are merely entertainment, the bread and circuses of a New Rome." If sports are a social mirror, continued Lipsyte, "truly reflecting who and what we are now, we are selfish, short-sighted, morally bankrupt, approaching impotence." It was an era in which sportsmanship and humility appeared to be in decline and the ethos expressed by Oakland Raiders managing partner Al Davis held sway: "Just win, baby." But if sports represented some of the worst America had to offer in the 1980s, they also probably offered some of the best. Many American athletes exhibited tremendous courage, quested for excellence, and tried to transcend their social and physical limitations. Rick Telander noted, "At their best, the competition lifted us all. The Lakers against the Celtics. Notre Dame against Miami. The 49ers against the whole NFL." The list could go on and on. Good and bad, American sport in the 1980s, rich in metaphoric possibilities, symbolized the culture.

TOPICS IN THE NEWS

BASEBALL

Survival. Perhaps the best thing that can be said about Major League Baseball in the 1980s is that it survived. Although the decade witnessed superb individual and team performances on the field, it was probably more notable for its labor disputes, strikes, threats of strikes, owner-collusion scandals, many substance abuse revelations, the Pete Rose betting affair, and, in general, the shortsightedness of those who ran the game. But despite these and other serious problems, baseball somehow remained vibrant and popular. In 1980, for instance, a record forty-three million people paid to see Major League Baseball games, income from baseball television contracts accounted for a record 30 percent of the game's $500 million revenue, and television ratings for the World Series had never been higher. Over the course of the decade all of these leading indicators would continue to improve, which suggests that baseball's place as the national pastime was not as diminished as some critics maintained. "In the coming decade, profits, salaries, attendance, and general excitement over things baseball would be greater than ever," observed historian Charles Alexander, "but it would be an unprecedentedly strife-filled period. If baseball's best of times, the 1980s, in some ways, would also be its worst."

Parity. Baseball dynasties were abundant in the 1970s: the Baltimore Orioles won three consecutive American League (AL) pennants (1969–1971); the Oakland Athletics took three World Series in a row (1972-1974); the Cincinnati Reds were victorious in two straight World Series (1975–1976); and the New York Yankees returned to championship form by winning the World Series in 1977 and 1978. The 1980s, however, were a time of surprising parity in both the AL and the National League (NL). Though several teams won more than one pennant in the 1980s—the St. Louis Cardinals won three, while the Kansas City Royals, Los Angeles Dodgers, Oakland Athletics, and Philadelphia Phillies won two apiece—no team was able to win the World Series back-to-back. Why this was the case is difficult to answer. Some observers suggested that the players' free-agent status contributed to the unprecedented parity. Others noted that the inception of the amateur draft in 1965, more liberal trading rules, the contraction of minor-league farm systems, and expansion of major league clubs helped even out competition. As Benjamin Rader put it, "Stockpiling players became more difficult than in the past." No matter what the reasons were, the decline of baseball dynasties clearly did not hinder the game. In fact, it probably contributed to baseball's popularity by giving fans genuine hope that next year would bring their team a championship.

Third Sacker Series. The 1980 season concluded with the Kansas City Royals meeting the Philadelphia Phillies in the World Series. A well-rounded club with a great deal of playoff experience from the late 1970s, the Royals were led by third baseman George Brett. During the regular season Brett flirted with the .400 mark and ended up hitting .390 with 24 home runs and 118 runs batted in (RBI) in 117 games to win the AL Most Valuable Player (MVP) award. The Royals won their first ever pennant by sweeping the AL East champion New York Yankees in the American League Championship Series (ALCS). The Phillies were also loaded with playoff veterans, such as Cy Young award–winning pitcher Steve Carlton and first baseman Pete Rose, and were also led by a slugging third baseman, Mike Schmidt. The NL MVP, Schmidt set career highs with 48 home runs and 121 RBI. The NL Championship Series (NLCS) between the Phillies and the NL West winner Houston Astros was particularly dramatic, with the final four games going into extra innings. The Phillies won the World Series in six games behind the pitching of Carlton and reliever Tug

It was often said in the 1980s that America was slipping as a superpower, that Americans had lost their competitive edge in the world marketplace. As proof of this phenomenon in sports, some pointed to the loss of the America's Cup in 1983. After the United States held the most prestigious trophy in yachting for 132 years, the longest winning streak in sports history was broken when *Australia II* beat *Liberty*, skippered by Dennis Conner. "Remember how it was when the U.S. hockey team beat the Russians at the 1980 Olympics and Americans who had never seen a hockey game and who had given up saluting the flag after fifth grade were swept up overnight on a tidal wave of patriotic fervor?" asked Sarah Pileggi of *Sports Illustrated*. "Multiply that ardor a hundredfold and you'll have some idea of what winning the America's Cup . . . meant to Australians." Not one to take losing lightly, Conner worked tirelessly over the next four years, working with designers to improve yachting technology and raising millions of dollars. "Competition is life's blood," said Conner, "and I'm a vampire." In February of 1987 Conner captained *Stars & Stripes* to a four-race sweep of the Australian yacht *Kookaburra III* to regain the America's Cup. In the process he transformed the twemty-six-inch silver cup from a trophy signifying yachting supremacy into an expansive national symbol. Thomas Boswell listed the meanings attached to the victory: "Let's see? America loses something on the world stage that it once held unquestionably. The United States wakes up, works hard and gets it back. Could we be talking about economic strength vis-à-vis the Japanese? Or military power compared with the Russians? Or the persuasive power of moral authority in the world community? Or maybe 'all of the above,' plus whatever else you want to throw in the pot?" For many the America's Cup, previously little known outside the sailing community, became a national treasure during a time of national insecurity.

Sources: Thomas Boswell, "The America's Cup: Reductio ad Absurdum" in *Game Day: Sports Writings 1970–1990* (New York: Doubleday, 1990);

Sarah Pileggi, "It Isn't America's Cup Any Longer," *Sports Illustrated* (3 October 1983): 82–85;

Roger Vaughan, "Obsessed," *Life* (September 1988): 82–85.

12 June to the end of July and led to the cancellation of 713 games, a third of the schedule. The strike resulted from a dispute over compensation for players who switched teams as free agents. Several public opinion polls suggested widespread hostility toward the players, whose average salaries had ballooned with the advent of free agency in the late 1970s; according to one report, in 1970 the average major leaguer's salary was $25,000; in 1976 it was $52,000; and by 1980 it had reached $185,000. The fifty-day strike cost the players approximately $30 million in lost salary and the owners about $166 million in lost revenue. After the strike was resolved noted baseball writer Roger Angell of *The New Yorker* argued: "If the strike proved anything, it was that the owners do not hold themselves accountable in any way to their customers. The crisis left a very sour feeling, not just because of the loss of the dailiness and flow of summer baseball, or because of the bitterness and hostility of the negotiations, but because no one on the owners' side could ever put forward a brief, reasonable explanation of the deadlock or prevent its prolongation until the last moment at which some vestige of the season could be retrieved. From first to last, the crisis was an invention of the owners—the inevitable result of their determination to radically alter or put an end to the basic structure of player free-agency, and thus to win back by force what they had lost in bargaining and in the courts and through mediation." As if to prove that neither management nor the players' union had learned much from their previous conflict, in 1985 another baseball strike was called. Thankfully, though, that midseason work stoppage lasted only two days. In an attempt to salvage the 1981 season, baseball commissioner Bowie Kuhn implemented a split-season format. According to Kuhn's plan the division leaders before the strike would be declared the first-half winners, and the teams that finished atop their division after the strike were declared the second-half winners. The first- and second-half winners in each division then played a best-of-five-game miniplayoff before the regular playoff between the division champions. The results were mixed. The plan produced more postseason revenue for the owners, but the two teams with the best records in the NL, the Cincinnati Reds and the St. Louis Cardinals, failed to make the playoffs. Still, the 1981 World Series was an exciting affair. The Los Angeles Dodgers, led by Steve Yeager, Ron Cey, Pedro Guerrero, and phenomenal rookie pitcher Fernando Valenzuela, beat the New York Yankees in six games after they had been down two games to none.

Iron Cal. From 30 May 1982 onward there was at least one constant in Major League Baseball: Cal Ripken Jr. Ripken played for the Baltimore Orioles, and for the rest of the decade—and well beyond it—Ripken did not miss a single game. "The Streak is baseball's most amazing feat and Ripken perhaps the game's most respected performer," noted one writer. "He commands adulation from his peers and fans alike." In many ways a throwback

McGraw, Schmidt's power hitting, and fine all-around defensive play. It was their first world championship.

Labor Woes. In 1981 the Major League Baseball season was marred by a bitter player strike that lasted from

to an earlier era when ballplayers seemed more dignified and humble, the 6-foot 4-inch, 220-pound Ripken established a new offensive standard by which shortstops would be measured. By the end of the decade Ripken had collected 204 home runs and averaged 93 RBIs a year, astonishing numbers for his position. At the same time Ripken was an excellent defensive player: what he lacked in speed and range he made up for with a strong throwing arm, intelligence, and experience. He led AL shortstops in assists five times in the 1980s and in 1984 set an AL single-season mark for assists with 583. Although he won the Rookie of the Year (1982) and Most Valuable Player (1983) awards in consecutive seasons, and he was on seven straight All-Star teams in the 1980s, Ripken was better known for his assault on Lou Gehrig's all-time record of 2,130 consecutive games played. For many the most incredible thing about Ripken's streak was that he played all but 27 of his games at shortstop. "In an age when the concept of a sports hero is justifiably under attack," wrote Mike Lupica, "Ripken has actually behaved like one. Baseball fans identify with Ripken more than with the loud chest-thumpers of sports because he is like them in this one crucial way: He goes to work every day." On 6 September 1995 Ripken played his 2,131st consecutive game.

The Year of the Tiger. The 1984 season marked the debut of New York Mets pitcher Dwight Gooden. A nineteen-year-old right-hander, Gooden won 17 games and struck out 276 batters (a major-league rookie record) in just 218 innings on his way to winning the NL Rookie of the Year award. Because of his youth and pitching skill, some observers called Gooden "the Mozart of baseball." Nevertheless, after having been acquired from the Cleveland Indians in June, veteran Rick Sutcliffe of the Chicago Cubs won the NL Cy Young award by going 16–1. Sutcliffe, along with NL MVP second baseman Ryne Sandberg and relief pitcher Lee Smith, led the Cubs to their first-ever NL East division title, but Chicago could not get past the San Diego Padres in the NLCS. The Padres met the Detroit Tigers in the World Series. The Tigers began the season with a 35-5 record, ended up 104–58 in the regular season, and swept the Kansas City Royals in the ALCS. In the World Series the Tigers roared to a five-game victory over the Padres behind Kirk Gibson's clutch power hitting. The Tigers got productive years from Darrell Evans, Alan Trammell, Jack Morris, and Willie Hernandez, who became only the second relief pitcher to win the league MVP and Cy Young award in the same season. Unfortunately, the Tigers' World Series victory precipitated riots in Detroit in which eighty-two people were injured and one man was killed.

Drug Scourge. "A cloud called drugs is permeating our game," said baseball commissioner Peter Ueberroth in the wake of the 1985 Pittsburgh drug trial, which saw seven alleged drug dealers, most of whom had dealings with major-league ballplayers, prosecuted for smuggling, distributing, and selling cocaine and other drugs. Despite the embarrassing revelations coming out of federal court in Pittsburgh, which suggested that approximately two dozen current and former ballplayers allegedly used cocaine and amphetamines, drug abuse was nothing new to the national pastime. The year before, for instance, pitcher Pasqual Perez was jailed in Santo Domingo for cocaine possession. Also in 1984 Willie Aikens, Jerry Martin, Willie Wilson, and Vida Blue of the Royals served three months apiece in federal prison for possessing or trying to buy cocaine. Lonnie Smith of the Cardinals entered a drug rehabilitation program the same year. Regrettably, these were not isolated incidents. Steve Howe first sought professional help for his cocaine addiction in 1982. That same year fellow Dodger Bob Welch wrote of his battle with alcoholism in *Five O'Clock Comes Early.* Future Hall of Fame pitcher Ferguson Jenkins was arrested by Canadian police in 1980 for possession of cocaine, marijuana, and hashish. Before the 1980 season All-Star catcher Darrell Porter became one of the first ballplayers to admit his drug problems publicly. Dock Ellis played most of his twelve-year career while on drugs and supposedly threw a no-hitter while under the influence of LSD. Moreover, when those ballplayers who battled the bottle are considered, the list becomes even more lengthy and luminous: it includes former stars such as Mickey Mantle, Jimmie Foxx, Hack Wilson, Grover Cleveland Alexander, and Babe Ruth, among many others. In any event Ueberroth responded to the 1985 public confessions by suspending Dave Parker, Keith Hernandez, Joaquín Andújar, Lonnie Smith, and seven others. Under the terms of Ueberroth's punishment, the offending players could have their suspensions lifted if they agreed to donate a percentage of their salaries to drug abuse programs, perform community service, and submit to random drug testing. Not surprisingly, all the implicated players accepted these conditions. Still the problem continued. Alan Wiggins, LaMarr Hoyt, Otis Nixon, and Leon Durham all abused illegal drugs after Ueberroth's symbolic housecleaning. Most famous, Dwight Gooden of the Mets entered the Smithers Alcoholism and Treatment Center in 1987 after testing positive for cocaine. Three years later, Gooden's former teammate Darryl Strawberry sought treatment at Smithers for alcohol abuse.

Baseball At Its Finest. The 1986 postseason was the most memorable of the decade. In the ALCS the Boston Red Sox met the California Angels to decide the pennant. With the Angels leading three games to one, Dave Henderson of the Red Sox smashed a two-out, two-run home run in the ninth inning to save the game. The Red Sox eventually won game five 7–6 in eleven innings and the series in seven games. The NLCS between the powerful New York Mets and the pitching-rich Houston Astros was just as dramatic. A tight series, in which four contests were decided by one run, the Mets were trailing for most of game six when they tied it in the ninth. The

Mets took a 7–4 lead into the sixteenth inning, but Houston scored twice before Mets reliever Jesse Orosco struck out Kevin Bass with two runners on base to end the game and the series. Following the game Mets manager Davey Johnson said, "This was major league baseball at its finest. If you didn't enjoy this, you don't enjoy anything." The final two games of the World Series were no less exciting. After five contests the Red Sox led the Mets three games to two. In game six the Red Sox were winning 5–3 going into the bottom of the tenth frame, poised to win their first world championship in sixty-eight years. But after two quick outs, the Mets staged a comeback. Three hits and a wild pitch later, the Mets had tied the score. With the winning run on third base in the person of Ray Knight, veteran first baseman Bill Buckner allowed Mookie Wilson's routine ground ball to go between his legs as Knight scored to win the game. Thomas Boswell of the *Washington Post* wrote that "the Red Sox defeat will live, vivid and symbolic, growing in the retelling for years." Game seven was almost as devastating for Red Sox fans. Their team took a 3–0 lead into the sixth inning but could not hold it and eventually lost 8–5. It was, wrote Boswell, "the most brutal team disappointment in baseball history." Of course, for the Mets and their fans it was a tremendously gratifying series.

Necessities. The 1987 season began with a jolt. Baseball commissioner Peter Ueberroth had previously announced that the season would be dedicated to the memory of Jackie Robinson, the legendary second baseman for the Brooklyn Dodgers who broke baseball's color line forty years earlier. To commemorate that anniversary, Ted Koppel invited Al Campanis, the Los Angeles Dodgers' vice president for player personnel and one of Robinson's former teammates, to be a guest on the 6 April episode of the television program *Nightline*. Early in the show Koppel asked Campanis why there were no black baseball managers, general managers, or owners: "Is there still that much prejudice in baseball today?" Campanis replied: "No, I don't believe it's prejudice. I truly believe they may not have some of the necessities to be, let's say, a field manager or perhaps a general manager." A stunned and incredulous Koppel allowed Campanis to continue. "I have never said that blacks are not intelligent. I think many of them are highly intelligent," said Campanis, "but they may not have the desire to be in the front office. . . . They're outstanding athletes, very God-gifted, and they're very wonderful people, and that's all I can tell you about them." Campanis was fired two days later for his racist remarks and for inadvertently revealing the fact that after forty years of integration many of those who ran the game still maintained troubling views with regard to race. "Name baseball's 100 most powerful people—owners, league executives and general managers—and 99 are white males," wrote Thomas Boswell a year later. "Many are conservative, a few reactionary. Al Campanis was typical." The Campanis debacle led some to point out that less than 2

Widely celebrated as he reached the 5,000-strike-out mark on 22 August 1989, Nolan Ryan finished his career in 1993 with the all-time record of 5,714.

percent of the top administrative positions in baseball were held by racial minorities and that African American players continued to be relegated primarily to certain positions, such as the outfield and first base. "Baseball had tried to portray itself for years as a beacon of racial enlightenment," noted writer Richard Scheinin. "But now the truth was out: the systemic racism of American society remained woven into the fabric of the game." Fortunately some in the baseball establishment seemed willing to try to rectify this deplorable situation. After the Campanis incident Ueberroth hired outspoken African American sociologist Harry Edwards as a consultant on minority affairs. One of Edwards's first acts was to hire Campanis to his staff. "We are going to have to deal with the Campanises in baseball," explained Edwards, "and it's good that I have a person in-house who knows how they think." In 1988 racial minorities comprised approximately 10 percent of baseball's front-office personnel, and Frank Robinson and Cito Gaston were hired as managers. A year later former ballplayer and broadcaster Bill White became president of the National League. These and other developments led Dan Gutman to write that "Campanis probably did more to advance the progress of blacks in sport than all the speeches, protests, and articles on the subject combined."

Dramatic Dodgers. Orel Hershiser and Kirk Gibson of the Los Angeles Dodgers had big years in 1988. Hershiser went 23–8 with a 2.26 earned-run average (ERA) and finished the season with a 59-inning scoreless streak to win the NL Cy Young award. In his first year in the National League Gibson hit .290 with 25 home runs and 76 RBI to win the NL MVP award. Many thought Darryl Strawberry of the New York Mets was a more worthy recipient considering his 39 home runs and 101 RBIs. Despite productive years from their star players, the Dodgers surprised many by beating the New York Mets in the playoffs to take the pennant. They won in large part because Gibson hit decisive home runs in games four and five and because Hershiser had a 1.09 ERA in 24 2/3 innings in the NLCS, shutting out the Mets in game seven. Waiting for the Dodgers in the World Series were the Oakland Athletics. Led by AL MVP Jose Canseco, Mark McGwire, Dave Stewart, and Dennis Eckersley, the powerful A's swept the Boston Red Sox in the ALCS to take the first of their three straight AL flags. The conclusion of the first game of the World Series provided Major League Baseball with its most dramatic moment of the decade. The Dodgers trailed 4–3, with one on and one out. Dodger manager Tommy Lasorda summoned the injured Gibson to pinch hit. Gibson, barely able to walk, made what would be his only appearance of the series. He worked the count to 3–2 against ace reliever Eckersley. After fouling off four pitches, Gibson delivered a two-run homer to lift the Dodgers to a 5–4 victory and the most spectacular comeback in World Series history. "Down to his last strike, Gibson hit a home run that, in some still photos, seemed to have been struck with one hand," wrote Boswell. "No player, not in the entire twentieth century, had hit a sudden-death homer to turn a World Series defeat into victory." Propelled by Gibson's heroics, superior pitching, and outfielder Mickey Hatcher's inspired play, the Dodgers beat the A's in five games. "The Dodgers' unexpected triumph in the century's eighty-fifth World Series capped a tremendously successful baseball season," noted Charles Alexander, "one that saw attendance and television ratings reach all-time highs."

The Saddest Year. According to political columnist George Will, the "1989 season was baseball's saddest season in seventy years." Negotiations continued between baseball owners and labor representatives to compensate those players who had been victims of owner-collusion scandals in the mid 1980s. Former Dodgers star Steve Garvey, who was said to be "so clean that he squeaked," had paternity suits filed against him by two women. Red Sox third baseman Wade Boggs was publicly humiliated when his four-year extramarital affair with Margo Adams was revealed. Donnie Moore, a former relief pitcher with the California Angels, reportedly never got over giving up an important home run in the 1986 ALCS against Boston: he shot his wife and then committed suicide. Dave Dravecky of the San Francisco Giants broke his arm pitching while making a comeback from cancer, and then broke it again in the on-field celebration after the Giants won the pennant. After a summer of intrigue, denial, and impassioned recriminations, Cincinnati Reds manager Pete Rose was banned from baseball for allegedly gambling on baseball games. Rose, baseball's all-time hit leader and a personification of the self-made man, denied the accusations. "I'd be willing to bet you, if I was a betting man," he said, "that I have not bet on baseball." Be that as it may, on the basis of a league-sponsored investigation, which writer Roger Kahn described as "an unconvincing mix of allegation and distortion," baseball commissioner A. Bartlett Giamatti was convinced that Rose had wagered on the game. In late August Giamatti announced that Rose had agreed to a lifetime suspension from baseball. "The matter of Mr. Rose is now closed," declared Giamatti. "It will be debated and discussed. Let no one think it did not hurt baseball. That hurt will pass, however, as the great glory of the game asserts itself and a resilient institution goes forward." According to many, the Rose controversy was the worst episode in baseball history since the Black Sox scandal of 1919. The fifty-one-year-old Giamatti died of a heart attack eight days after concluding the Rose case. The former president of Yale University, Giamatti was commissioner of baseball for five months. "He added a touch of class to the game, but was hopelessly out of touch with its soulless reality," lamented Richard Scheinin. Less than seven weeks after Giamatti's death, as the Oakland Athletics and the San Francisco Giants were preparing for game three of the World Series at Candlestick Park, a massive earthquake shook the Bay Area. The quake registered 7.1 on the Richter scale, killed more than sixty people, left thousands homeless and frightened, and caused billions of dollars in damage; needless to say, the World Series was postponed. Lastly, combative and self-destructive former New York Yankee player and manager Billy Martin was killed in December in a drunk-driving accident. Despite some impressive on-the-field achievements, such as Kevin Mitchell's 49-home-run, 125-RBI performance and the Baltimore Orioles' dramatic 32 1/2 game improvement over the previous year, the final baseball season of the 1980s was most memorable for its tragedies.

Breaking Records. For all its problems baseball provided fans with a great deal of pleasure in the 1980s, largely because many ballplayers performed brilliantly and established some remarkable single-game, regular-season, postseason, and career records and achievements. Len Barker, Tom Browning, and Mike Witt each pitched perfect games during the decade. In all, the period witnessed seventeen no-hitters, including Nolan

Ryan's record-setting fifth. In 1986 Roger Clemens set a major-league record by striking out twenty hitters in a single game. That same season Bob Horner tied a major-league record by slugging four home runs in a game and Mike Scott established a first by throwing a no-hitter to clinch a division title. Kirk Gibson hit one of the most dramatic home runs ever, a ninth-inning, pinch-hit, two-run shot to lift the Los Angeles Dodgers over the Oakland Athletics in the first game of the 1988 World Series. From a single-season perspective there were more than a few performances of historic caliber. George Brett hit a phenomenal .390 batting average in 1980, which remains the highest major-league batting average since Ted Williams hit .406 in 1941. In 1982 Rickey Henderson obliterated Lou Brock's single-season stolen base record by swiping 130 bases. Dwight Gooden's 1985 season must rank among the greatest of all time: he led the NL in wins (24), ERA (1.53), and strikeouts (268) and thus earned the "pitcher's triple crown." In 1987 Paul Molitor hit in 39 straight games, the fourth-longest streak in AL history. The following year Orel Hershiser set a major-league mark with 59 consecutive scoreless innings pitched, and Jose Canseco became the first player ever to steal 40 bases and hit 40 home runs in the same season.

Milestones. Over the course of the decade milestones were passed and dominant players emerged. The exclusive 300-win club admitted Steve Carlton (329 career wins), Don Sutton (324), Phil Niekro (318), Gaylord Perry (314), and Tom Seaver (311). Rollie Fingers set an all-time mark for saves with 341. Ferguson Jenkins earned his 100th AL win to become only the fourth pitcher to win 100 games in both leagues. Steve Carlton became the all-time left-handed strikeout leader. Carlton and Nolan Ryan dueled one another for the all-time strikeout mark: Carlton ended up with 4,136 while Ryan pitched until 1993 and collected 5,714. Mike Schmidt won three NL MVP awards, while Dale Murphy and Robin Yount won two league MVPs apiece. Wade Boggs won five AL batting crowns and had seven consecutive 200-hit seasons. Tony Gwynn won four NL batting titles. Rickey Henderson led the AL in stolen bases nine times, and Ozzie Smith won all ten NL Gold Glove awards at shortstop. Jack Morris was the decade's winningest pitcher with 162 victories. Dwight Gooden won his 100th game before he was twenty-five years old.

Grand Finales. The 1980s were also a time of transition. Willie Stargell retired in 1982 as the Pittsburgh Pirates' all-time home run leader with 475. After twenty-three years with the Boston Red Sox, Carl Yastrzemski retired in 1983, having played in more AL games than anyone else in history: he also collected 3,419 hits and 452 home runs. Johnny Bench, the preeminent catcher of his generation, hung up his mask for good at the conclusion of the 1983 season. Jim Palmer ended his career as one of the finest pitchers in AL history in 1984 with 268 wins. That same season Joe Morgan broke Rogers Hornsby's record for career home runs by a second base-

man and retired. A year later Rod Carew rapped his 3,000th hit and retired at the end of the season with a lifetime batting average of .312. On 11 September 1985 Pete Rose stroked hit number 4,192 to break Ty Cobb's fifty-seven-year-old record: Rose retired in 1986 with 4,256 hits, his legendary reputation for hard, intelligent

---

WINNING ATTITUDE

Jim Abbott's baseball career was one of the more compelling stories during the 1980s. Though his major-league win-loss record does not yet indicate it, there is little doubt that Abbott is special. "Abbott's goal is to blend in and be a great pitcher, but to millions of Americans he'll always be more," wrote Steve Marantz. Born without a right hand, Abbott inspired a generation of people (not all of whom were sports fans) to challenge convenient, simplified definitions and so-called physical limitations. "Any type of definition that puts me or anybody like me in the category of disabled is completely wrong," Abbott explained. "I feel blessed with what I've been given. My missing five fingers have been compensated [for in] so many other ways. I've been given a frame, a throwing arm, and so many other things. I'm not sure there's a lot of people within those parameters who wouldn't feel the same way." In high school he was a two-sport star: a magnificent pitcher and a talented quarterback. At the University of Michigan he won the Golden Spikes award as the best college player in the country. In 1986 he pitched for the U.S. team at the Pan American games and became the first American in twenty-five years to win a game in Cuba. The following year Abbott won the Sullivan Award, the annual honor given to the top amateur athlete in the nation. He played for the 1988 U.S. Olympic team and pitched the gold medal–winning game in Seoul. The number one pick of the California Angels in the 1988 amateur draft, he ended up being one of the few players never to play in the minors. As a major leaguer he quickly established himself as a fierce competitor and won twelve games as a rookie on a weak Angels team. At every level of competition Abbott transformed doubters into believers. Perhaps Abbott put it best when he said, "Just because other people think you are handicapped, that does not make it so." To prove his point yet again, Abbott pitched a no-hitter for the New York Yankees on 4 September 1993.

Sources: Norman Macht, *Jim Abbott: Major League Pitcher* (New York: Chelsea House, 1994);

Steve Marantz, " 'Courage is so much more than playing baseball with one hand,' " *Sporting News,* 216 (19 July 1993): 12–15.

---

play intact. Reggie Jackson called it quits in 1987 with 563 home runs, sixth on the all-time list. Four-time Cy Young award–winner Steve Carlton finished his career in 1988. Eight-time NL home run titlist Mike Schmidt retired in 1989 with 548 home runs to finish directly behind Jackson on the all-time homer register. With the notable exception of Rose, they were all elected to the Baseball Hall of Fame in their first year of eligibility.

State of the Game. For Most Major League Baseball players and owners the 1980s were tremendously prosperous. By the end of the decade over fifty million fans annually attended major-league games and baseball's gross revenues were more than $1 billion a year. Up-and-coming players like Roberto Alomar, José Canseco, Joe Carter, Dave Cone, Randy Johnson, Dave Justice, Barry Larkin, Mark McGwire, Greg Maddux, and perhaps most notably Ken Griffey Jr. emerged to take the place of fading stars. Of course, the 1980s were also a troubled time. Some small-market clubs faced fiscal limitations that hindered their competitiveness, and many players continued to experience drug problems. The most pressing concern, however, remained the power struggle between team owners and the Major League Baseball Players' Association. Despite being a lucrative industry, baseball suffered terribly from acrimonious labor conflicts, which more than anything else threatened the game's stronghold on the American imagination.

Sources:
Charles C. Alexander, *Our Game: An American Baseball History* (New York: Holt, 1991);

Roger Angell, *Late Innings: A Baseball Companion* (New York: Ballantine Books, 1982);

Thomas Boswell, *The Heart of the Order* (New York: Penguin, 1990);

Dan Gutman, *Baseball Babylon: From the Black Sox to Pete Rose, the Real Stories Behind the Scandals that Rocked the Game* (New York: Penguin, 1992);

Benjamin G. Rader, *Baseball: A History of America's Game* (Urbana & Chicago: University of Illinois Press, 1992);

Richard Scheinin, *Field of Screams: The Dark Underside of America's National Pastime* (New York: Norton , 1994);

George F. Will, *Men At Work: The Craft of Baseball* (New York: Harper & Row Perennial Library, 1990).

BASKETBALL: PROFESSIONAL

Rebirth. As the National Basketball Association (NBA) staggered toward the close of the 1970s, attendance was down in almost every market and television ratings were declining. The public was disenchanted with players' bouts with alcohol and drug abuse and uninspired by the parity which left the league without any dominant teams or captivating new superstars. Revenues fell and interest waned. In what many now regard as the low point in NBA history, game six of the 1980 league finals between the Los Angeles Lakers and the Philadelphia 76ers was televised late at night on taped delay. NBA commissioner David Stern would later call it "our biggest public relations disaster of the decade." At this moment, however, the league began its return to public popularity.

Game six showcased the talents of Earvin "Magic" Johnson, the Laker rookie who, along with the Boston Celtics' Larry Bird, had riveted public attention in the NCAA finals a year earlier. Johnson, filling in for the injured Kareem Abdul-Jabbar, put on a tremendous show. He collected 42 points, 15 rebounds, and 7 assists. It was a performance that foreshadowed the Lakers' nearly decade-long stranglehold on the championship. From 1980 to 1989 the Lakers played for the title eight times and won five of them. "Never fear," Johnson told his teammates as they boarded a flight for game six without their captain and star player, "E.J. is here." He might as well have been speaking to the entire league and most of its fans. In the years to come, clashes between Johnson's Lakers and Bird's Celtics would resuscitate fan interest and inspire fellow players toward remarkable individual and team accomplishments. As Golden State Warrior Chris Mullin later explained, "what they did, for the player and the spectator, was to give the lesson that you played hard on every play, every night, every season. You were unselfish and you were fundamentally sound. And if you did those things, you won." In addition to the Lakers' success with Johnson, Boston with Bird in the lineup returned to the finals in 1981 and each year from 1984 to 1987, winning three titles. The level at which Bird and Johnson played and the heights to which they took their respective teams enthralled the basketball-watching public and inspired a financial and popular resurgence that carried the league toward astronomical revenue totals, player contracts, and television ratings as well as to expansion in new markets by the decade's end.

The Trey. Looking to spice up their product, the league's board of governors voted to introduce a three-point shot into the professional game at the start of the 1980–1981 season. The shot had worked well in the old American Basketball Association (ABA), leading to higher scores and last-second drama. The NBA was in need of both elements and was willing to alter the shape of the game in order to get them. Not since the narrowing of the key (and the penalty for spending three seconds there) and the introduction of the 24-second clock had the game been so consciously and so profoundly altered. Inevitably, there was resistance to the change from those who thought that it suggested a kind of pandering to the public and represented a threat to the game. Among the dissenters was Golden State Warrior owner Franklin Miculi, who stormed out of the vote and declared that "changing the 2-point basket is immoral!" Such protests aside, NBA commissioner Lawrence O'Brien successfully guided the idea into the rule book. At the meeting's end O'Brien gushed, "I think that I shall never see a thing more lovely than a three." In what began as a one-year trial, the three-point line was established at 22 feet from the basket in the corners and 23 feet 9 inches at the top of the arc. Teams and players alike were slow to understand and exploit the significance of the new rule, thinking of it mainly as a desperation shot at the end of games. In its first year of existence teams collectively took just over 5,000 shots from three-point land, making 28 percent of them. The Boston Celtics, who would post the league's best record and win the championship over Houston, were quick to realize that this new shot had strategic benefits. It opened up the middle of the court for their dominant inside players and forced the opposition to play more honest man-to-man defense. They began shooting the shot in the course of their regular offense and had the league's most efficient shooter from "downtown" in Chris Ford. Fans were excited by the new rule and its potential to infuse games with drama at any moment. The rule also provided an opportunity for experienced ABA transplants to succeed in the NBA. The Celtics' successful approach to the shot was soon mimicked by other clubs, and the one-year trial became an established part of the NBA game. By the end of the 1980s teams collectively attempted more than 13,400 threes a season and hit nearly one-third of them. Efficient three-point marksmen like Dale Ellis and Danny Ainge managed to extend their careers well into the 1990s because of their ability to "knock down the trey" consistently.

All But Unstoppable. In stark contrast to the flash and hype surrounding Johnson and Bird stood the relentless rebounder and scorer Moses Malone. Malone dominated the backboards and thought of the lane as his territory. "I love to rebound," said Malone. "Scorers will have off nights. But the boards. They'll be there." One of the few players to make the jump from high school straight to the professional ranks, Malone felt he had something to prove and set about proving it every night. Without a college education he was often considered slow or unpolished by reporters who mistook his reticence for dimwittedness. But he understood the workings of the game as well as any other player of his time, and he understood the nature of the challenges he faced like no one else: "people thought we [those players who skipped college] had problems and that's why I didn't go to college. But they're the fools. We had to have strong minds to do what we did . . . All along, I thought that if I make mistakes, it's going to be *me* that makes 'em." Malone's determination propelled the underdog Houston Rockets to the NBA finals in 1981, where they were defeated in six games despite Malone's efforts. His teammates at the time recognized Malone's talents and were the first to speak of his place in history. "When my grandkids grow up, I'm going to tell them about this big fella," said guard Robert Reid. "By then he'll be known as the best of them all." Malone won the league's MVP award in 1980 and again in 1982, but he was unable to win a championship in Houston. In 1982 he became a free agent. Remarkably, there were no bids for Malone's services, and he did not find a new home until he was traded to Philadelphia before the start of the 1982–1983 season. Upon his arrival in Philadelphia Malone assured 76er fans and the media that they were in good hands. "I can do so many things," he said. Eager to fit in with an already impressive

Kareem Abdul-Jabbar shoots a "sky hook" against Patrick Ewing.

team, Malone explained that it was still Julius Erving's team and that he was just there to "work hard." The combination of Malone's inside strength and Erving's play in the open court made Philadelphia nearly unstoppable. They rolled through the regular season and marched toward the playoffs. Asked to predict their performance in the postseason, Malone responded, "Fo', fo' and fo'," to indicate that they were untouchable and would not lose a single game. He was not far off. With the exception of a second-round loss to Milwaukee, the Sixers played flawlessly in capturing their first championship since 1967. Malone would stay with Philadelphia through 1986 and then play four productive years with the Washington Bullets before slowing down in the early 1990s. By the time he retired Malone had established himself as one of the game's all-time greats. He played in eleven All-Star games and won three MVP awards and five rebounding titles.

Direction. NBA commissioner Lawrence O'Brien stepped down after the 1983 season and was replaced by his executive vice president, David Stern. If one half of the league's formula for renewal was found on the court in the figures of Larry Bird, Magic Johnson, and Michael Jordan, the other half lay in David Stern's vision and determination. At the time, the league's gross nonretail

On 23 March 1985 New York Knicks star forward Bernard King made such a powerful turn toward the basket that, in the words of sportswriter Bruce Newman, "he simply ran out of his knee the way someone else might twist out of his shoe." At the time of his injury King was leading the National Basketball Association (NBA) in scoring, and the diagnosis of a torn anterior cruciate ligament (ACL) left the Knicks' workhorse shattered. "I cried my eyes out," King admitted. "I never knew how far this thing would go, if I would have to retire because of it." His concern was warranted. The knee's flexibility is dependent on a series of ligaments connecting the femur and tibia; the ACL is one of two ligaments (the other is the posterior cruciate ligament) that cross between the thigh and shin, preventing the bones from slipping out of joint. While ACL injuries once portended the twilight of an athlete's career, especially in a sport such as basketball, which requires speed, explosiveness, and lateral quickness, the 1980s saw the refinement of sophisticated procedures aimed at reconstructing damaged knees. With the development of fiber optics in the mid 1970s, arthroscopic surgery — the insertion of a tubal telescopic lens through a small slit in the skin to survey joint damage before and during its eventual repair — became a less invasive procedure, and advances in physical therapy regimes lessened an athlete's rehabilitation time. The rise of sports medicine during the decade brought considerable acclaim to prominent surgeons such as Dr. Robert Jackson, a pioneer in arthroscopy, and Dr. Frank Jobe, a specialist on rotator cuff surgery who saved the careers of major-league pitchers Tommy John and Orel Hershiser. As Dr. Norman Scott observed, "I've put out six books and 80-some articles, and yet I'll go down as Bernard King's doctor. I just hope that in his lifetime, Bernard has someone who makes him as proud as he has made me." Scott repaired King's ACL by replacing the damaged tissue with a strip of the tough sheath that runs from the hip to the tibia along the outside of the thigh muscles. The advances in arthroscopic procedures have not, however, lightened the emotional and psychological burden of rehabilitation. Danny Manning, the first pick in the 1988 NBA draft who tore up his knee in 1989, reported his experience: "You wake up with two scars on your legs — you know you weren't born with them. Even if you're no different physically, you're different psychologically." King himself went into seclusion for almost two years ("I felt I had to protect myself emotionally from the game"), but when he returned to the NBA for the 1987 season he once again reigned as one of the game's most creative scorers. By doing so he became a symbol of promise to every athlete who experienced the fragility of the body.

Sources: Richard Demak, "One False Move," *Sports Illustrated,* 74 (29 April 1991): 52–58;

Richard Hoffer, "Dr. Robert Jackson," *Sports Illustrated,* 81 (18 September 1994): 139;

Bruce Newman, "A King Eyes a Court Comeback," *Sports Illustrated,* 66 (30 March 1987): 32–33.

revenue, including ticket sales and television fees, was $160 million. By the close of the 1980s that figure would reach $500 million and was augmented by a staggering $750 million in gross retail revenues. While the game was thriving on the court, Stern made sure the league was also financially and commercially successful. His leadership made him the undisputed champion of professional sports commissioners. Looking back on Stern's tenure, E. M. Swift suggested that the former lawyer "reshaped a floundering, financially strapped league into an entity that is the envy of professional sports—an innovative, multifaceted, billion-dollar global marketing and entertainment company whose future literally knows no bounds." He accomplished this by stressing innovation and improvement. After the 1980–1981 season sixteen of the NBA's twenty-three teams lost money, and teams played to an average of only 10,201 fans per game, only a little more than 50 percent of capacity. The commissioner's office had one person working in public relations, and advertisers wanted nothing to do with the league. From the beginning Stern brought a determinedly progressive perspective to bear upon the workings of the league. As Richard Bloch, part owner of the Phoenix Suns, suggested, "David changed the direction of the league." Stern charmed a fractured group of team owners and players into forming alliances and rethinking the way they conducted business. Creating a Team Services division to monitor the workings and public relations of individual franchises, Stern managed to package the league as a single product. Perhaps the most crucial element in this packaging was negotiated by Stern before assuming the commissioner's post. In search of a financial agreement between players and owners which would ensure the survival of all NBA teams, the league and the Players Association agreed to a salary cap under which players received 53 percent of gross revenues and the owners 47 percent. As Charles Grantham, onetime head of the NBA Players Association, indicated, the cap was agreed upon because "players and management were in the gutter together" and both sides had to work together if they hoped to survive. Stern then set about the task of revitalizing the league's relationship with its fans. He understood that the league was in the entertainment business and worked to woo a large and loyal audience. Borrowing ideas from the ABA and Major League Baseball, the NBA turned its All-Star game into a fan-friendly extravaganza, complete with slam-dunk and three-point-shooting contests and an old-timers' game. By the end of the 1980s it was clear that the changes had paid off. The league broke its attendance record seven straight years; player salaries rose 177 percent (from an average of $325,000 to $900,000 by decade's end), and television fees skyrocketed from $22 million per year to more than $150 million.

Draft Boon. The NBA unveiled some of its stars of the future at the 1984 college draft. The Houston Rockets, who had selected Ralph Sampson number one in the previous year's draft, again picked first. They took University of Houston standout Hakeem Olajuwon and began fantasizing about a vaunted "Twin Towers" offense. Next, the Portland Trail Blazers selected Kentucky center Sam Bowie, who would struggle with injuries, later suffering severe breaks to each of his legs. With the third pick the Chicago Bulls chose North Carolina junior Michael Jordan. For years fans and executives associated with the game would refer to Portland's blunder and Chicago's good fortune. Jordan's impact on the league was immediate and long lasting. He won the NBA Rookie of the Year award in 1985. In 1986 he averaged 37.1 points per game and became the first player since Wilt Chamberlain to score more than 3,000 points in a season. He signed unprecedented shoe contracts with Nike and established an amazing career in commercials within his first two years in the league. More important, he transcended the game and transformed the fortunes of his franchise. By the early 1990s he had the Bulls poised to win three consecutive NBA championships. The mark of the 1984 draft went still deeper. In the fourth position Philadelphia, looking to energize its aging frontcourt, selected Auburn forward Charles Barkley. Like Jordan, Barkley was not only a talent but a personality, one who would help shape the future of the league and sustain fan interest after Bird and Johnson retired. He toiled ferociously for the Sixers throughout the 1980s, running the floor like no man his size had ever done before. As if these players were not enough to distinguish this draft in terms of its depth and impact, buried near the end of the first round lay another jewel. Out of little-known Gonzaga University stepped point guard John Stockton. A steady playmaker and precision passer, Stockton did not play much for the Utah Jazz in 1985, but by the close of the decade he had amassed over 4,000 assists on his way to becoming the NBA's all-time assist leader. In response to Houston's consecutive first selections, the draft structure was changed the following year. A lottery process to determine which of the league's seven bottom teams got to draft first was instituted. As a result, the lottery became a popular television event whose first prize was Georgetown center Patrick Ewing, picked by the New York Knicks in 1985.

Policy. While the NBA was making financial gains by the mid 1980s it had not yet fully emerged from the shadow of drug abuse which had characterized it during much of the 1970s. More than a few players were unable to handle the pressures of daily life in the NBA and were incapable of managing their enormous salaries responsibly. Micheal Ray Richardson, the New Jersey Nets' point guard and one of the league's most promising young stars, spent much of the 1980s in and out of the league and drug rehabilitation centers. Upon his departure from training camp before the 1983–1984 season, Richardson said, "I don't want any more part of basketball." That same year John Drew of the Utah Jazz and John Lucas of the Houston Rockets were waived from the league because of drug abuse. Each would return and be suspended again before finally making it back to regular playing status. Such incidents prompted the league to establish what many still regard as the most progressive drug policy in sports: players were quietly granted rehabilitation opportunities in response to voluntary confessions of drug usage; the league claimed the right to test players randomly with reasonable cause; failure to pass a drug test meant a minimum two-year suspension. In 1988 the policy was expanded to include incoming rookies, a practice which was part of an extensive orientation program wherein young players would be counseled, often by former users such as Lucas, on how to deal with the lure of drugs, the scrutiny of the media, financial concerns, and the pressure of life in the NBA. Though the problem was not completely eradicated, it was largely contained, and the league's approach was widely praised and emulated in other professional sports.

Expansion. Eager to strengthen its image and revenue base, the NBA's board of governors voted to add four expansion teams at the close of the 1980s. The new teams—the Charlotte Hornets and Miami Heat in 1988, and the Minnesota Timberwolves and Orlando Magic in 1989—provided the league with new life and new sources of revenue. When these teams entered the league, the NBA was flourishing. Within three years all four expansion teams were worth double the $32.5 million they paid to enter the league. Under Stern's direction the NBA boldly spoke of "looking for new places to conquer." On the court, however, things moved much more slowly, for the new teams floundered. After drafting Rex Chapman number one, Charlotte finished the 1988–1989 season with 20 wins and 62 losses. Miami selected Rony Seikaly and Kevin Edwards in the first round, endured an unprecedented 0–17 stretch to open the season, and managed just fifteen wins all year. Neither Minnesota nor Orlando fared much better the next year, securing 22 and 18 wins respectively. However, attendance figures for all four franchises were consistently impressive. Charlotte led the league in attendance in 1988 and was second in 1989, while Minnesota set the standard in 1989. Orlando began the 1990–1991 season having amassed thirty-two straight sellouts; Charlotte collected seventy-one; and Miami garnered fifty-four. Patient fans in Charlotte, Miami, and Orlando were rewarded with playoff teams by the mid 1990s, at which point the league began making plans for Canadian franchises in Toronto and Vancouver. By the end of the 1980s, the expansion impulse and its attendant financial success moved overseas. The league's pledge to claim new territory pushed them into foreign markets such as Italy, Spain, and France. The opening of European markets in the mid 1980s to officially licensed NBA products meant even greater financial success for the league and its owners. "The key thing to remember is that we've barely scratched the surface internationally," Stern explained, apparently unconcerned with what Jack McCallum of *Sports Illustrated* termed "cries of Yankee colonialism."

Farewell. On 13 June 1989 the Detroit Pistons completed a sweep of the Los Angeles Lakers with a 105–97 victory to claim the NBA title. It was the end of an era dominated by Los Angeles and Boston. Detroit would repeat in 1990 before surrendering the top spot to the Chicago Bulls between 1991 and 1993. But the conclusion of the series also closed another chapter in the story of professional basketball: it was Kareem Abdul-Jabbar's final game. As the NBA's all-time leader in points, games and minutes played, field goals made and attempted, and blocked shots left the court, the crowd chanted, "Kareem, Kareem, Kareem." The only six-time winner of the NBA's MVP award, Abdul-Jabbar retired after twenty seasons of unsurpassed grace and skill. He was, from the very beginning, a unique combination of athlete and public figure. The man whose Muslim name means "generous and powerful servant of Allah" towered above the league for much of his career and outlasted several prominent players who began and ended their own basketball careers during the course of his tenure. In addition to his longevity, it was his integrity that characterized Abdul-Jabbar as a player and a man. More comfortable in a redwood forest than in a crowd of people, he confounded the media and the public by making political statements and gestures but usually refused to speak about himself. He went about his business in a quiet manner that some interpreted as aloof. Though he may have lacked the charisma of Michael Jordan, Magic Johnson, or Charles Barkley, his game was remarkable for its rare combination of talent and determination. Abdul-Jabbar "gave his position grace, agility, quickness and elegance never before possessed by one man," wrote Paul Attner. Abdul-Jabbar's full impact on the game was rarely recognized during his playing years. In fact a chorus of voices insisted that the forty-two-year-old center had hung on too long. His retirement was a time for Abdul-Jabbar to reflect on his accomplishments. "My legacy? That I played as well

as I have for as long as I have," he said. His numbers were astounding: 38,387 points, 787 straight games in double figures, six NBA championships, and a record nineteen All-Star appearances. He was arguably the best player in the history of the league. At the close of the 1985 playoffs, in which the thirty-eight-year-old Abdul-Jabbar managed 21.9 points along with 8.1 rebounds and nearly two blocks per game, Lakers coach Pat Riley put the big man's feats in perspective for historians and fans alike: "He defies logic. He's the most unique and durable athlete of our time, the best you'll ever see. You better enjoy him while he's here." With the conclusion of the 1989 season, that time had passed.

Sources:

Larry Bird with Bob Ryan, *Drive: The Story of My Life* (New York: Doubleday, 1989);

David Halberstam, *The Breaks of the Game* (New York: Ballantine, 1981);

Dave Heeren, *The Basketball Abstract* (New Jersey: Prentice-Hall, 1988);

Earvin Johnson Jr. and Roy S. Johnson, *Magic's Touch* (New York: Addison-Wesley, 1989);

Roland Lazenby, *The Lakers: A Basketball Journey* (New York: St. Martin's Press, 1993);

Terry Pluto, *Tall Tales* (New York: Simon & Schuster, 1992);

Bob Ryan and Terry Pluto, *Forty-Eight Minutes: A Night in the Life of the NBA* (New York: Macmillan, 1987);

Alex Sachare, ed., *The Official NBA Basketball Encyclopedia*, second edition (New York: Villard Books, 1994).

BASKETBALL: COLLEGE

"March Madness." College basketball became a national obsession in the 1980s. Once a regionalized pastime, the college game became virtually omnipresent due to expanding cable television networks (particularly ESPN) and the media's rigorous marketing of the National Collegiate Athletic Association (NCAA) championship tournament; even the phrase for the championship tournament, "March Madness," is a registered trademark. The major network covering the monthlong men's tournament, CBS, bid $16 million for exclusive rights to the Final Four in 1982, and then renegotiated its pact with the NCAA every few years until in November 1989, when it reached an agreement on a seven-year, $1 billion contract. Capitalizing on the phenomenal popularity of the Magic Johnson–Larry Bird matchup in the title game in 1979, network television poured money into the sport like never before and promoted the Final Four as a media spectacle to rival the Super Bowl. The NCAA responded by enlarging the tournament field from forty-eight to sixty-four teams (beginning with the 1985 tourney), establishing a 45-second shot clock to eliminate stalling (1986), and introducing a three-point shot at 19 feet 9 inches (1987), changes designed to increase scoring, competitiveness, and fan appeal. The title games were close throughout the decade, each contest seemingly undetermined until the final nerve-wracking moments.

Only then did a misthrown pass, an improbable shot, or a couple of clutch free throws decide the issue.

The Women's Game. The decade also saw a marked increase in the popularity of women's basketball, bolstered in part by the dazzling grace and physical prowess of players such as Kansas's Lynette Woodard, Southern California's Cheryl Miller, and Texas's Clarissa Davis. While the women's game cultivated a new, more athletic image, it lacked the media attention enjoyed by the men's game; in fact, negotiations over television rights proved divisive early in the decade. The Association of Intercollegiate Athletics for Women (AIAW), a student- and women-centered organization that put on the first national championship for women in 1972, collapsed under the NCAA's renewed interest in women's basketball, which was motivated in part by the mandates of Title IX. Because the NCAA could offer a women's tournament package that included promises for more television exposure and program expansion, many of the top women's teams shifted their allegiance from the AIAW to the NCAA. After some intense rhetoric and a series of lawsuits, the AIAW disbanded after eleven years of promoting women's athletics. By 1989 the women's tournament was popular enough to be included in CBS's billion-dollar television deal with the NCAA.

Parity. After more than a decade of college dominance, the presence of the UCLA Bruins in the 1980 NCAA championship game ironically represented not a return to dynastic rule, but the emergence of team parity. These were not the Bruins of Lew Alcindor and Bill Walton, but a scrappy group of youngsters unranked when the regular season ended and seeded eighth in the West Regional when the tournament began. Although the Bruins lost to the Louisville Cardinals and their all-American guard Darrell Griffith in the championship game 59–54, their 77–71 victory over number-one-ranked DePaul in the second round gave credence to an age-old dictum, "on any given night a lesser team can upset a great one." Indeed, the NCAA Tournament throughout the decade was characterized by unfulfilled expectations and underdog champions. In 1981 DePaul, ranked number one in the final regular season poll, as well as highly regarded Oregon State and Arizona State, all lost their opening game in the tournament, and Indiana, with nine losses on the season, won the title. North Carolina State, relying on coach Jim Valvano's shrewd and opportunistic game plan and the long-range bombing of guards Dereck Whittenburg and Sidney Lowe, made an improbable and dramatic run through the tournament field in 1983, beating a Houston team with future pro stars Clyde Drexler and Hakeem Olajuwon on a buzzer-beating dunk by sophomore Lorenzo Charles. Villanova stunned Big East rival Georgetown in the 1985 final, and Kansas upset conference foe Oklahoma in 1988: in both cases the eventual champions entered the tournament with ten or more losses, and both avenged two of those losses in the final. While there were cer-

Steve Alford, who led Bobby Knight's Indiana Hoosiers to the national championship in 1987, slips a pass by Chris Conway of Montana State.

tainly great teams and dominant players throughout the decade, the period from 1982 to 1991 saw ten different schools win titles, and only two teams (Louisville and Indiana) were able to win twice during the 1980s. Every year the early rounds of the NCAA tournament were marked by improbable upsets, and the new atmosphere of parity allowed underdogs such as Cleveland State, Arkansas–Little Rock, and Siena to enjoy an unexpected moment in the sun.

Sampson. If the Johnson-Bird duel in March 1979 heralded the return of majesty to college basketball, the heir to the decade's newly vacated throne was a sinewy 7-feet 4-inch, 207-pound freshman named Ralph Sampson. Virginia's head coach, Terry Holland, who won the recruiting sweepstakes when he signed Sampson, said of his new center, "He has a chance to be the best who ever played," and opposing coaches quickly compared the towering Sampson to a young Lew Alcindor (Kareem Abdul-Jabbar). Blessed with grace and agility that belied his seeming gawkiness, Sampson quickly displayed an array of offensive moves under the basket and showed a deft shooting touch when pushed away from it. At the defensive end of the court Sampson's eighty-eight-inch arm span seemed to swallow up anyone who dared to venture into the lane. As a freshman Sampson led the Cavaliers to the 1980 NIT championship and was named the tourney's MVP. Resisting pressures to turn professional after his initial college campaign (the Celtics' Red Auerbach was said to be enamored with Sampson's breathtaking potential), he appeared to come of age early in his sophomore season, pouring in 40 points against Ohio State before a national television audience. Over the next three seasons the Virginia center dominated the college game, winning the national Player of the Year award at the end of each season (1981–1983), thereby joining the select company of Oscar Robertson and Bill Walton as three-time honorees. In 1981 Virginia earned a trip to the Final Four, but Sampson struggled offensively throughout the tournament and the Cavaliers lost to North Carolina in the national semifinals. In both 1982 and 1983 Virginia entered the NCAA tournament as a top seed, only to lose to teams on a hot streak (Alabama–Birmingham and North Carolina State). While his critics pointed to Sampson's inability to lead his school to prominence consistently, pro scouts were won over by his size and offensive repertoire, and the Houston Rockets selected him as the first pick overall in the 1983 NBA draft.

Beast of the East. On 11 December 1982 Sampson's Virginia squad took on the Georgetown Hoyas, led by their intimidating sophomore center Patrick Ewing. The matchup in the middle was perhaps the most anticipated confrontation since UCLA's Alcindor and Houston's Elvin Hayes locked horns in the Astrodome in 1968. While Sampson outbattled his younger counterpart and Virginia won 68–63, the game reconfirmed the emergence of Georgetown as a basketball power. The Hoyas had narrowly missed capturing an NCAA title the previous spring when North Carolina's own brilliant freshman, a teenager named Michael Jordan, buried a sixteen-foot jump shot with sixteen seconds left to secure the Tar Heels' 63–62 win, Coach Dean Smith's first championship. Relying on Ewing's presence in the paint, Georgetown coach John Thompson fashioned the closest thing to a basketball dynasty in the 1980s, reaching three championship games in Ewing's four years. Thompson's teams induced a different version of March Madness, a condition known as "Hoya Paranoia," which was said to afflict opponents who wilted in the face of Georgetown's intense and menacing defense. In one of their more devastating displays of suffocating the opposition, Ewing and company erased a seven-point halftime deficit in the 1984 national semifinal by limiting a potent Kentucky team to 9 percent shooting in the second half (3 for 33). Buoyed by key substitute Michael Graham, a bald, rugged freshman forward, the Hoyas then defeated Hakeem Olajuwon and the Houston Cougars 84-75 in the championship game. Ewing was named the tournament's Most Outstanding Player despite scoring only eighteen points in the two Final Four games, a testament to his awesome defensive presence. The rise of Georgetown coincided with the emergence of the Big East Conference as a prominent basketball power, and forced a reconsideration of the "East is Least" tag that plagued East Coast basket-ball during the UCLA reign. This ascent culminated in the 1985 NCAA tournament in which three Big East members—Georgetown, St. John's, and Villanova—advanced to the Final Four.

'Nova. In the 1985 title game in Lexington, Kentucky, defending champion Georgetown, a team that drew comparisons with the great Indiana and UCLA teams of the 1970s, played their typically ferocious defense, forcing their opponent into seventeen turnovers, and shot an impressive 55 percent from the field. The trouble was that the Villanova Wildcats shot an incredible 79 percent and pulled the upset of the decade, 66-64. A eighth seed in their region when the tournament began, Rollie Massimino's squad responded to one formidable challenge after another, upending Michigan, Maryland, North Carolina, and Memphis State on their way to the finals. But Georgetown was, presumably, another matter altogether. Patrick Ewing was a senior, and the Hoyas, sporting a gaudy 35-2 record, seemed destined for history. In the semifinals the Hoyas routed conference rival St. John's, holding the Redmen's star forward Chris Mullin (the 1985 national Player of the Year) to a mere eight points; since they had beaten Villanova twice during their conference schedule, Georgetown was considered a heavy favorite to repeat as champions. But the senior-laden Wildcats displayed uncommon composure in the face of Georgetown's relentless pressure and coolly turned in what Paul Attner called "the greatest shooting exhibition in college history." They refused to unravel after three straight monstrous dunks by Ewing in the first half and led 29-28 at intermission. In the second half each offensive possession was an exercise in patience as Villanova controlled the pace of the game and calmly waited for high-percentage shots. The strategy worked: they only missed one shot in the entire second half and kept their lead by making their free throws once the Hoyas desperately turned to fouling in the game's final minutes. When it was over the Georgetown players stayed on the bench watching as Wildcat center Ed Pinckney pounded the floor in ecstasy and his teammates climbed up on the press tables to celebrate with fans. As the Villanova players walked to the podium to be honored, the Hoyas stood and applauded. The 1985 championship offered the best college basketball had to offer: an underdog who succeeded by virtue of savvy play and a disappointed champion willing to lose gracefully.

Propositions 48 and 42. On 14 January 1989, just as the Georgetown Hoyas and the Boston College Eagles were gathering to jump center, Georgetown coach John Thompson removed his signature white towel from his shoulder and draped it over the shoulder of assistant coach Mike Riley. Then he walked off the court in protest. At issue was Thompson's displeasure with the NCAA's new standards for academic eligibility, known as Propositions 48 and 42. Proposition 48 was passed at the NCAA's 1983 convention in San Diego: it stipulated that an incoming Division I freshman athlete had to attain a prescribed minimum score on one of the two national standardized tests, as well as graduate from high school with at least a C average, to be eligible to compete in his or her freshman year. Nonqualifiers would maintain their scholarships during that first year, and future athletic eligibility would then be conditioned upon satisfactory academic performance. The measures immediately inspired debate. Initially the strongest outcry against the proposition came from officials representing sixteen historically black colleges. They protested that black educators were not consulted during the drafting of the proposal and, had they been, they would have pointed out that a disproportionate number of black students perform poorly on standardized tests because the tests reflect cultural and racial biases. Penn State football coach Joe Paterno gave an impassioned speech in support of the proposal, arguing that big-time athletics had educationally "raped" athletes, and that those who opposed the mandate were underestimating the "pride and competitiveness" of black athletes. Despite the controversy, the NCAA membership began enforcing the provisions of Proposition 48 in 1986. Thompson's boycott was in response to Proposition 42, passed 11 January 1989 by the NCAA, a measure that eliminated the partial-qualifier loophole of Proposition 48. With the tougher rule, schools could tender athletic scholarships only to incoming freshmen who met all of Proposition 48's requirements. Nonqualifiers would either have to pay their own way or attend a junior college (where these academic requirements were not applicable). In the first few years under Proposition 48 roughly eighteen hundred football and basketball players lost a year of eligibility, 86 percent of whom were African American. Thompson and the Black Coaches Association insisted that Proposition 48's stipulations were not only susceptible to charges of racial bias but also put athletes from low-income backgrounds at a disadvantage.

Scandal. With money flooding the sport from large-scale television contracts (millions of which was funneled back into the athletic programs and conferences that performed well in the NCAA tournament) and academic restrictions limiting the pool of potential Division I athletes, the recruiting process took on added significance, and many schools were tempted into wooing the star athletes with something more than the promise of a college education. One might call the 1980s "the decade of probation," since many of college basketball's most tradition-rich programs violated NCAA rules and were penalized. Kentucky, Kansas, UCLA, Maryland, North Carolina State, Memphis State, Cincinnati, Minnesota, Auburn, Wichita State, Bradley, San Francisco, and New Mexico all served probationary terms for recruiting violations and academic improprieties, and the sanctions against these prominent basketball powers belied the long-held notion that some schools were "untouchables." Cars, cash, imaginary summer "jobs," and relaxed academic standards were most often the lures in what was

THE ODDS ON THE DREAM

Throughout the United States in the 1980s millions of young men and women dreamed of becoming professional athletes. Inevitably, however, only a comparative few would have their fantasies come true. According to the National Federation of State High School Associations (NFSHSA), the odds of a high-school athlete making it in professional football at the end of the 1980s were more than six thousand to one. Becoming a professional basketball player was even less likely, ten thousand to one. The NFSHSA went on to report that the odds against an African American high-school athlete becoming either a professional football or a basketball player exceeded five thousand to one. These and other statistics prompted sociologist Harry Edwards to note that young black men and women "have a better chance of getting hit by a meteorite in the next ten years than getting work as an athlete." Still, young and not-so-young people continue to dream of becoming star athletes if they work hard and receive a few breaks. "Because the few rags-to-riches athletes are made so visible, the social mobility theme is maintained," writes sociologist George Sage. "This reflects the opportunity structure of society in general — the success of a few reproduces the belief in social mobility among the many."

Sources: Richard Lapchick, *Five Minutes to Midnight: Race and Sport in the 1990s* (New York: Madison Books, 1991);

George Sage, *Power and Ideology in American Sport: A Critical Perspective* (Champaign, Ill.: Human Kinetics Books, 1990).

increasingly becoming a bidding war for basketball talent. The rise of college basketball as an enormous profit venture revealed its darker side in two prominent point-shaving scandals during the decade as well. On 16 February 1981 *Sports Illustrated* reported that a mobster named Henry Hill claimed he had fixed six Boston College basketball games during the 1978–1979 season, making an estimated $100,000 over an eleven-week period as a result of the arrangements. On 23 November 1981 Rich Kuhn, a former Boston College player who was said to have netted as much as $2,500 per game, and four others were convicted of conspiring to manipulate the scores of those games. Then, as the country prepared to enjoy the 1985 Final Four, a story broke concerning Tulane University and another point-shaving scheme. Four Tulane starters, including Metro Conference Player of the Year John "Hot Rod" Williams, and a key reserve were paid approximately $23,000 to ensure that Tulane not cover the point spread in a 2 February game against Southern Mississippi and not lose to Memphis State by more than the seven-point spread on 20 February. Continued investigations revealed that cocaine was often given to players as a goodwill gesture by the conspirators (former Tulane students) who masterminded the fix. Furthermore, it was discovered that Williams had been paid handsomely to attend Tulane after high school, that head coach Ned Fowler often gave him as much as $100 per week, and that academic improprieties had taken place to ensure the eligibility of players. Fowler's resignation, along with two assistant coaches, was followed by Tulane president Eamon Kelly's decision to disband the university's basketball program, an act Kelly characterized as "the only way I know to demonstrate unambiguously this academic community's intolerance of the violations and actions we have uncovered."

The Cruelest Thing. The University of Maryland was one of many prominent basketball programs put on probation by the NCAA's ruling body during the 1980s. The story of how they got there begins with a tragic episode. Len Bias, the Terrapins' 6-foot-8-inch senior forward, was drafted by the Boston Celtics on 17 June 1986, the second player selected in the NBA lottery. The Celtics' general manager, Red Auerbach, claimed that Bias "was as happy as any player I ever signed," and Larry Bird was said to be so excited about Bias's arrival that the veteran promised to show up at rookie camp in the fall. Forty hours after his moment of triumph, Bias was dead of cardiorespiratory arrest precipitated by an overdose of cocaine. Bias, who roamed the court with an almost regal bearing, had never missed a college game due to injury, and yet in the end he let his body down, and his heart gave out. On being told of the young star's death, Bird said, "It's the cruelest thing I've ever heard." The subsequent criminal and intercollegiate investigations uncovered widespread drug use among players, academic and financial improprieties, and a possible attempt to tamper with evidence. Both Maryland athletic director Dick Dull and head basketball coach Lefty Driesell resigned in October 1986. The situation at Maryland once again raised questions about the responsibilities that athletic departments owe to the athletes who generate substantial revenues for their universities as well as the difficulties faced by young men and women who are thrust into the limelight. Reflecting on the Bias story, sportswriter Thomas Boswell may have put it best, "Athletes not only have to cope with fame, wealth, and hero worship; they have to face the possibility that they are frauds. Our image-making apparatus seems to insist that scoring average and virtue be connected.... Those who exaggerate the importance and the virtue of athletes do them no favor."

Knight in Tarnished Armor. Only two men's college basketball coaches won more than one NCAA championship in the 1980s, and while Louisville's Denny Crum (who led his team to titles in 1980 and 1986) certainly established himself as one of the preeminent coaches in the game, it was Indiana's Bobby Knight who captured the country's imagination—and indignation. Knight seemed intent on matching his every success with some

outrageous act. Widely regarded as one of the acutest basketball minds in the coaching ranks, Knight preached aggressive man-to-man defense and an intricate and highly disciplined offensive scheme. His teams were most successful when directed by skillful guards such as Quinn Buckner, Isiah Thomas, and Steve Alford, who anchored his three NCAA titlists in 1976, 1981, and 1987 respectively. (Knight himself was a substitute guard at Ohio State on the great Jerry Lucas–John Havlicek teams of the 1950s.) Knight was respected as a coach who ran a clean program in a period of scandal, and his players almost always graduated. Despite these accomplishments Knight's erratic behavior, explosive temper, and lack of judgment often overshadowed his coaching prowess. In 1979 he assaulted a police officer at the U.S. Pan American Games in Puerto Rico, where a six-month sentence remains pending after Knight was convicted in absentia. In 1981 he shoved a Louisiana State fan into a trash can after a tournament game. Then there was the infamous "chair incident" on 23 February 1985, when Knight flung a chair out onto the court to protest a technical foul that was called against him: the chair narrowly missed the Purdue player stepping to the foul line to shoot the technical. On another occasion he pulled his team off the court during an exhibition game against the Soviet national team because he did not agree with the referee's calls. At once shrewd and rash, loyal and abusive, resistant to change and wildly unpredictable, Knight stands out as one of the most complicated figures in the college game. Even his former players struggle to define their relationship with their coach. As Isiah Thomas put it, "You know, there were times when, if I had had a gun, I think I would have shot him. And there were other times when I wanted to put my arms around him, hug him, and tell him that I loved him."

Sources:

John Feinstein, *A Season Inside: One Year in College Basketball* (New York: Villard Books, 1988);

Feinstein, *A Season on the Brink: A Year With Bob Knight and the Indiana Hoosiers* (New York: Macmillan, 1986);

Peter Golenbock, *Personal Fouls* (New York: Carroll & Graf, 1989);

Jim Savage, *The Encyclopedia of the NCAA Basketball Tournament* (New York: Dell, 1990);

C. Fraser Smith, *Lenny, Lefty, and the Chancellor: The Len Bias Tragedy and the Search for Reform in Big-time College Basketball* (Baltimore: Bancroft Press, 1992);

Alexander Wolff and Armen Keteyian, *Raw Recruits: The High Stakes Game Colleges Play to Get Their Basketball Stars—and What it Costs to Win* (New York: Pocket Books, 1990).

BOXING

Sugar Ray. Although no single boxing champion dominated the 1980s as Muhammad Ali did the 1970s, the era witnessed the emergence of several extraordinarily talented and charismatic fighters and many noteworthy bouts. In retrospect, professional boxing in the decade appears to have experienced one of its periodic heroic cycles. Larry Holmes, Roberto Duran, Thomas "Hit

Man" Hearns, Marvelous Marvin Hagler, and Mike Tyson provided fight fans with many inspired and courageous displays of boxing prowess. Yet in surveying the boxing world of the 1980s, one fighter stands apart for his skill, style, and longevity: Sugar Ray Leonard. Three years after winning a gold medal at the 1976 Olympics, the twenty-three-year-old Leonard relieved Wilfred Benitez of the World Boxing Council (WBC) welterweight title. On 20 June 1980, however, Leonard lost a fifteen-round decision and his title to the hard-hitting Duran in Montreal. It would be Leonard's only defeat in the decade. Five months later, on 25 November, Leonard avenged his loss to Duran with "flashing combinations, glorious boxing skills and audacious courage," in Thomas Boswell's words. With sixteen seconds left in the eighth round, Duran gave up his hard-won title when he turned his back on Leonard and said, "No más." In June of the following year Leonard temporarily moved up a weight class, and knocked out Ayub Kalule in the ninth round, thus earning the World Boxing Association (WBA) junior middleweight title. Three months later, on 16 September 1981, Leonard and Hearns fought for the undisputed welterweight crown since Leonard held the WBC title and Hearns the WBA version of the championship. After fourteen tough, mostly evenly fought rounds, Leonard was awarded a technical knockout over the previously undefeated Hearns, improving his record to 33–1. In recognition of his accomplishments, *Sports Illustrated* named Leonard its Sportsman of the Year for 1981, declaring that he "has gained a nearly unanimous affection that not even Ali could claim." Following one successful title defense in 1982, Leonard announced he was retiring from boxing because of a medically repaired detached retina. His retirement, however, was short-lived. In 1984 Leonard returned to the ring, beat Kevin Howard unconvincingly, and again retired. Three years later, though, Leonard signed on to fight WBC middleweight champion Hagler. On 6 April 1987, despite having fought only once in the previous five years, Leonard beat the rugged Hagler, winning a split decision in one of the richest bouts in boxing history: it reportedly grossed over $100 million. Nineteen months later, on 7 November 1988, Leonard beat Donny Lalonde in nine rounds to claim the WBC light-heavyweight and super-middleweight titles. Finally, in 1989 the thirty-three-year-old Leonard again took on Hearns and Duran: on 12 June he fought Hearns to a draw to retain the title, and on 7 December he outpointed Duran. Thus by the end of the 1980s, Leonard was 36–1–1, had held world championship titles at five different weights, and had earned in excess of $100 million from fight purses, television contracts, and endorsements. He had also won a great deal of praise as a boxer of rare artistry, grace, intelligence, and surprising toughness. According to Boswell and others, Leonard was simply "the greatest fighter of his generation."

Holmes. WBC heavyweight champion Larry Holmes essentially ended a boxing era on 2 October 1980 when

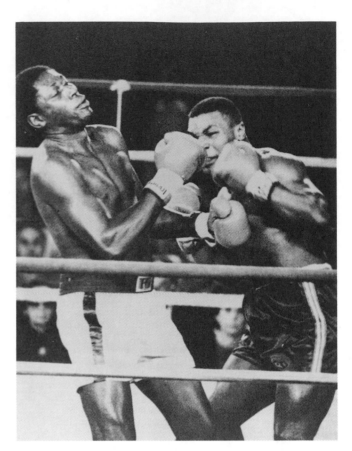

Mike Tyson (right) pummels Robert Colay in a bout that lasted just 37 seconds.

he thoroughly defeated former three-time champion Muhammad Ali in ten rounds. It was a bittersweet victory for Holmes, for Ali had been his boyhood hero. After the fight Holmes said, "I love that man and didn't want to see him getting hurt." Although he held the heavyweight crown from 1978 to 1985 and defended his title an impressive twenty times, Holmes was never a truly popular champion; for all his success he never captured the public's imagination the way Sugar Ray Leonard did, to say nothing of Ali. Often noted for his defensiveness and his belief that he was underappreciated, Holmes lashed out at the media after one title defense: "I'm sorry I'm not what all you guys want me to be. I'm not Muhammad Ali, I'm not Joe Louis, I'm not Leon Spinks. I can't continue to prove myself again and again." Nevertheless Holmes certainly proved himself in one of the decade's most publicized and richest fights. On 11 June 1982 the thirty-two-year-old Holmes met twenty-five-year-old challenger Gerry Cooney in Las Vegas before 32,500 fans. The fight garnered tremendous national publicity for a variety of reasons. "One is a boxer and one is a puncher, one a mover and the other a plodder," wrote William Nack in *Sports Illustrated* before the fight, "but that is only the beginning of the difference between them. Rarely in the history of heavyweight championship competition have two men who contrast more sharply—both in and out of the ring—been brought together." The fight's racial politics—Holmes was black, Cooney was white—also made the bout interesting for many people. At one point in the months leading up to the fight Holmes referred to Cooney as the "Great White Hoax" and suggested that the only reason the he had been given a title shot was because he was white in a weight division where the majority of the fighters were black. Holmes dominated the fight from the opening bell. He knocked Cooney down with an overhand right late in the second round and took charge in the middle rounds on the strength of his stinging left jab and swift combinations. The fight was stopped with less than twenty seconds left in the thirteenth round when Cooney's trainer jumped into the ring and signaled that Cooney had had enough, thus earning Holmes a TKO and improving his record to 40–0. Though Cooney proved to be a courageous challenger, the champion's performance lent credence to the claim that Holmes was the best heavyweight of his era. Late in his career Holmes offered the following self-appraisal: "As a boxer, you got to put me up there with all the top three . . . [Rocky] Marciano, [Joe] Louis, and Muhammad Ali. I just didn't have the charisma." After a lengthy feud with the WBC Holmes relinquished his title in 1983 and became the heavyweight champion of the newly formed International Boxing Federation (IBF). In his fourth defense of his new crown in September 1985, Holmes lost a unanimous decision to light-heavyweight champion Michael Spinks, the brother of former heavyweight champ Leon Spinks. Less than a year later Holmes again lost on points to Spinks. Finally, after a two-year layoff, Holmes was enticed to fight heavyweight titlist Mike Tyson for $2 million in 1988. Tyson dispatched the thirty-eight-year-old Holmes in the fourth round.

The Mouth That Roared. In early December 1982, six days after heavyweight champion Larry Holmes brutally punished the badly mismatched Randall "Tex" Cobb for fifteen rounds, controversial sportscaster Howard Cosell declared that he would no longer announce professional boxing matches for ABC television. "The Cobb fight did it for me," said Cosell. "I don't want to be a party to the sleaziness. I'm worn out by it all." Noted for his recognizable voice, presence, and intelligence—as well as for his arrogance and self-righteousness—Cosell was boxing's only nationally known television commentator; he had earned the respect of many by championing Muhammad Ali's cause during the heavyweight champ's three-year exile from boxing in the 1960s. Though Cosell significantly contributed to the popularity of the sport and was made famous in return, he nonetheless expressed the view that if professional boxing could not be cleaned up and regulated, then it should not be permitted to exist. Later Cosell would go even further in his denunciation of the sport, declaring that "professional boxing is no longer worthy of civilized society. It's run by self-serving crooks, who are called promoters. They are buttressed with the

look of nicety about them by the television networks, which are in fact corrupt and unprincipled in putting up the front money that continues boxing in its present form. Quite frankly, I now find the whole subject of professional boxing disgusting. Except for the fighters, you're talking about human scum, nothing more. Professional boxing is utterly immoral. It's not capable of reformation. I now favor the abolition of professional boxing. You'll never clean it up. Mud can never be clean."

The AMA on Boxing. While boxing and the medical profession had been at odds for years, the American Medical Association (AMA) in the early 1980s intensified calls for tighter medical supervision of the sport. Responding in part to the highly publicized death of South Korean fighter Duk Koo Kim, who suffered irreversible brain damage in a 1982 fight with Ray "Boom Boom" Mancini, and in part to new medical studies suggesting that 87 percent of boxers suffer some degree of brain damage in their lifetimes, the AMA's Council on Scientific Affairs commissioned a study on the death and injury rates in various high-risk sports. Surprisingly, boxing ranked relatively low, seventh overall, with a fatality rate per 1,000 participants of 0.13. According to the AMA study, college football (0.3), scuba diving (1.1), and skydiving (12.3), were more life-threatening activities than boxing. Still, in the January 1983 issue of the *Journal of the American Medical Association,* Dr. George Lundberg editorialized that prizefighters pay too heavy a price for occasional success and that boxing should be abolished since it is the only sport where the objective is to cause injury. Following Lundberg's lead, the AMA in 1984 passed a resolution calling for the abolition of amateur and professional boxing. Historian Jeffrey Sammons observed, "the AMA renewed its call for a ban on professional boxing amid evidence that serious eye injuries occurred far more frequently than boxers, officials, promoters, or even doctors admitted." The AMA's position probably contributed to the reduction of title fights from fifteen to twelve rounds and the imposition of a standing eight-count when a boxer appears defenseless. Despite these and other reforms, opinion in the medical community remained divided on the boxing issue, both on scientific and ethical grounds.

Hagler versus Hearns. Without a doubt, one of the most exciting fights of the decade, if not of all time, was between undisputed middleweight champion Marvelous Marvin Hagler and WBC junior-middleweight champion Thomas Hearns on 15 April 1985 in Las Vegas. The bout "lasted only a second longer than eight minutes," wrote Pat Putnam, "but for those who saw it, the memory of its nonstop savagery will remain forever." The powerful Hagler was the aggressor throughout the fight, but the tall and muscular Hearns gave nearly as good as he got in the ferocious first round, opening a cut above and below Hagler's right eye. The pace of the second round was nearly as frenzied with Hagler continuing to pressure Hearns. In the third Hagler unleashed a devastating combination and Hearns went down. Though Hearns managed to get to his feet by the count of nine, the referee wisely ended the contest. Novelist Joyce Carol Oates came away from the "fight with the vision of the dazed Hearns, on his feet but not fully conscious, saved by referee Richard Steele from what would have been serious injury, if not death—considering the extraordinary ferocity of Hagler's fighting that night, and the personal rage he seems to have brought to it." According to Phil Berger, "The hellbent way in which he [Hagler] demolished Hearns in three rounds instantly upgraded his standing among fight fans and among the advertising wizards who decide which athletes get the commercials." From the fight alone Hagler reportedly earned at least $7.5 million, while Hearns collected approximately $7 million.

The King. Perhaps more than any prizefighter, controversial promoter Don King dominated the boxing world in the 1980s. Yet even before the decade began, the colorful King had become one of the two most powerful promoters in boxing (Bob Arum was the other) and one of the most successful black businessmen in America, and he had done a tremendous amount to popularize the sport and to make his fighters wealthy. At the same time, King's business methods, connections, and personal style came under unrelenting criticism and led many to question whether King was good for the sport. "Don King is certainly not a saint," wrote Sammons. "Like all promoters his overriding aim has been to profit from boxing, and to that end he could employ charm, devious persuasion, and outright coercion." Or as Larry Holmes once put it, King "looks black, lives white, and thinks green." In his own defense King said, "People don't like me for the same reason they didn't like Muhammad Ali. We're the wrong kind of nigger. We're not quiet. We stand up to be counted. We're the best, and we're heard." Over the course of the decade King's stable included such fighters as Holmes, Greg Page, Tim Weatherspoon, James "Bonecrusher" Smith, Trevor Berbick, Julio Cesar Chavez, and Mike Tyson. Several of these men filed civil suits against King alleging that he exploited them in one way or another. "You can't believe anything anybody tells you in boxing," King reportedly said in response to those critical of him. "The business is predicated on lies. You are dealing with people who very rarely tell the truth."

Tyson. By winning a twelve-round unanimous decision against IBF heavyweight titlist Tony Tucker on 1 August 1987, WBC/WBA champ Mike Tyson became the first undisputed heavyweight world champion since Leon Spinks defeated Muhammad Ali in 1978. Although the twenty-one-year-old Tyson was heralded before beating Tucker, he could now legitimately claim to be boxing's most exciting, popular, and dominating performer. Beginning his career in 1980 under the tutelage of Cus D'Amato, who had trained and managed world champions Floyd Patterson and José Torres in the 1950s and 1960s and who ran an informal boxing camp in Catskill, New York, Tyson quickly became D'Amato's protégé. After a brief but highly successful amateur career, he turned professional in 1985. In his first two years as a pro Tyson won all of his twenty-eight fights; on 22 November 1986 he knocked out Trevor Berbick in the second round to win the WBC heavyweight crown, becoming the youngest heavyweight champion in history. A talented and ferocious boxer, Tyson took on mythic proportions as his opponents continued to fall; many believed that he could develop into the greatest heavyweight of all time. Unfortunately, Tyson's personal life was unstable due to the death of D'Amato in 1985 and trusted manager Jim Jacobs in 1988, and it further deteriorated after his disastrous marriage to actress Robin Givens and (according to some) his alliance with promoter Don King. At the end of the 1980s Tyson remained undefeated, running his record to 37-0, but his aura of invincibility was forever shattered by an ignominious loss to James "Buster" Douglas early in 1990. In July of that year, while attending the Miss Black America pageant in Indianapolis, Tyson allegedly raped a beauty contestant named Desiree Washington. The ensuing trial began in February 1991, lasted two weeks, and garnered tremendous national media attention. After his conviction Tyson began serving his six-year sentence at the Indiana Youth Center in Plainfield, Indiana. He was released on 25 March 1995.

Foreman's Return. On 9 March 1987 thirty-eight-year-old former heavyweight champion George Foreman began an improbable comeback by knocking out unheralded Steve Zouski. It was Foreman's first fight in over ten years. While the 6-foot 4-inch, approximately 250-pound Foreman was ponderously slow, he possessed powerful punching ability. As he continued his quest to regain the heavyweight crown, Foreman won eighteen of nineteen consecutive fights by knockout. Nevertheless, he was the subject of much derision, with critics pointing to his opponents' lack of experience and skill, Foreman's advanced age, and his apparent lack of conditioning. Foreman, a self-ordained evangelical preacher, combated such criticism with self-deprecating humor and knockouts. In 1990 he stopped Gerry Cooney in the second round to position himself for a title shot. Although he lost to then-champion Evander Holyfield in their 19 April 1991 title bout, Foreman's performance was impressive and he continued to fight. Remarkably, on 6 November 1994, twenty years after he lost the title to Muhammad Ali in Zaire, Foreman at the age of forty-five won the heavyweight championship of the world by knocking out Michael Moorer in the tenth round, thus becoming an inspiration for millions of aging baby boomers.

Sources:

Phil Berger, *Punch Lines: Berger on Boxing* (New York: Four Walls Eight Windows, 1993);

Nigel Collins, *Boxing Babylon: Behind the Shadowy World of the Prize Ring* (New York: Carol Publishing Group, 1990);

Thomas Hauser, *The Black Lights: Inside the World of Professional Boxing* (New York: Simon & Schuster, 1986);

Joyce Carol Oates, *On Boxing* (New York: Kensington, 1987);

Jeffery T. Sammons, *Beyond the Ring: The Role of Boxing in American Society* (Urbana & Chicago: University of Illinois Press, 1988).

FOOTBALL: PROFESSIONAL

Futility. Few would have thought that when the Los Angeles Raiders defeated the Washington Redskins 38–9 in Super Bowl XVIII on 22 January 1984 the game would signal the end of the era of American Football Conference (AFC) dominance. The mighty Pittsburgh Steeler dynasty last won the title in the 1980 Super Bowl and the nucleus of players that made up their championship teams had retired by 1984, but the future was apparently bright for the AFC. Marcus Allen, the Raiders' catalyst that January evening, had run wild, including a breath-taking change-of-direction touchdown gallop of 74 yards that seemed like a bit of playground mischief. Meanwhile, the pretenders to the Raiders' AFC crown had armed themselves with a cluster of strong-armed and strong-willed quarterbacks in the 1983 National Football League (NFL) draft. Yet the rest of the 1980s and half of the 1990s would pass without an AFC victory in the title game; moreover, the National Football Conference (NFC) representative typically won with remarkable ease (a 26-point average margin of victory from 1985 to 1990), thus turning every season's anticipated spectacle into a predictable, often unwatchable, affair. San Francisco, Washington, Chicago, and the New York Giants, each bolstered by an aggressive defense and methodical, ball-control offense, showcased their talents by crushing their AFC rivals before millions of television viewers. But perhaps it was the Denver Broncos who best epitomized AFC futility during the latter half of the decade. Led by their young and confident quarterback, John Elway, the Broncos won the AFC championship in 1987, 1988, and 1990, only to lose three Super Bowls by a combined score of 136–40. Having already stumbled in a title game in 1977, the hapless Broncos tied an NFL record for most losses in the Super Bowl (held by the NFC's Minnesota Vikings and later equaled by the AFC's Buffalo Bills in the 1990s).

Year of the Quarterback. On 26 April 1983 the AFC began building for the future. That year's senior class was considered one of the deepest talent pools in college football history, so when the NFL draft rolled around, many of the league's weaker teams sought an immediate change of fortune. Scouts were particularly intrigued by the wealth of fine quarterbacks available, and six signal-callers were selected in the first round, all of them by AFC squads. Beginning in 1985, four of those six—Stanford's John Elway, Miami's Jim Kelly, Illinois's Tony Eason, and Pittsburgh's Dan Marino—would go on to quarterback the AFC's Super Bowl representative in nine of the next ten title games. They would, however, lose every one of them. The number one pick of the draft was

Miami quarterback Dan Marino in the last minutes of the Dolphins' loss to the San Francisco 49ers in Super Bowl XIX

Elway, a big, strong-armed gunslinger who thrived in Stanford's pro-style offense. He refused to come to terms with the Baltimore Colts, who selected him with the first overall pick in the draft despite Elway's repeated warnings that he would play only for a West Coast franchise or a championship contender. The woeful Colts fit neither description. On 2 May the Denver Broncos acquired Elway in a trade with Baltimore, and he proceeded to lead the Broncos through the 1980s and beyond. But it was the last quarterback selected in the first round, Marino, who outshone them all. Chosen by the Miami Dolphins with the twenty-seventh pick, Marino exploded into the league, earning Rookie of the Year honors and a Pro Bowl invitation in his first season. Marino shattered long-standing league records in his sophomore campaign, passing for a phenomenal 5,084 yards and 48 touchdowns. Possessing a powerful arm, a lightning-quick release, and the ability to see opportunity amid defensive chaos, Marino soon established himself as one of the game's all-time greats. The careers of Elway, Marino, and Kelly—who took the Buffalo Bills to four straight Super Bowls in the 1990s after a three-year tenure in the ill-fated United States Football League (USFL)—symbolized the AFC's accomplishments and its disappointments.

The Hogs. The Washington Redskins, who were the last NFC team to lose a Super Bowl, were nonetheless one of the great teams of the decade. What set the Redskins apart from other successful franchises was the versatility displayed in their two championship seasons (1982–1983 and 1987–1988). Although both teams were coached by the dignified and cerebral Joe Gibbs, they attained their laurels with dissimilar quarterbacks — Joe Theismann and Doug Williams — and with contrasting offensive styles. The 1982–1983 team, in the words of Paul Zimmerman, "grabbed modern NFL football by the scruff of the neck and tossed it back a few decades into a simpler era — a big guy running behind bigger guys blocking." The "big guy running" was the incomparable John Riggins, a human sledgehammer with startling speed; the "bigger guys blocking" were known simply and fondly as the Hogs. The 27–17 victory over Miami in the title game was definitive Redskins football: Riggins shouldered the load, carrying 38 times for a then-record 166 yards, including a rumbling 43-yard touchdown run on fourth and one that put the Redskins on top for good. Gibbs occasionally threw in a bit of trickery to keep the Dolphins' defense from keying on his star, including an offensive set called the "Explode Package" in which all five eligible receivers scramble and shift places before the snap. The formation, used sparingly, resulted in two short touchdown passes from Theismann. Where the 1983 titlists ground out victories with brutal and methodical ease, the 1988 Super Bowl champions were an explosive bunch and saved their most electrifying moments for the championship game itself. Trailing the Denver Broncos 10-0 at the start of the second quarter, the Redskins scored 35 unanswered points before halftime. The quarter resulted in some astonishing statistics: five possessions resulting in five touchdowns and 356 yards of offense. Williams completed nine of eleven passes, including throws of 80, 27, 50, and 8 yards for touchdowns, all in one quarter. By the end of the 42–10 Redskin romp, rookie halfback Timmy Smith, who had totaled only 126 yards rushing during the entire season, had gained 204 yards on the ground.

Strikes. The NFL suffered through two significant labor disputes during the decade, both of which resulted in the suspension of play. In 1982 a fifty-seven-day strike resulted in the cancellation of seven weeks of play. The strike occurred after the league signed a five-year, $2.1 billion contract with the three major television networks; the NFL Players Association (NFLPA) responded by demanding a larger cut of the guarantees, 55 percent of the league's gross revenues. NFL team owners kept camps closed throughout the strike in the fear that a series of makeshift games conducted with replacement players might irredeemably tarnish the league's image. After weeks of unproductive bargaining sessions a mediator was finally brought in, and the NFLPA agreed to a contract in which the team owners guaranteed to spend $1.6 billion over four years on players' salaries, including $60 million in "money now" bonuses for ending the strike. The settlement was, many observed, a far cry from the union's initial demands. "The strike was a complete failure," one player representative noted afterward. "If we'd kept the old agreement, we would have been better off." Two games into the 1987–1988 season a second work stoppage of play occurred, but this time franchises reloaded their rosters with replacement players immediately, and the league determined that any games played during the strike would count in the final league standings. While free agency was not the principal motivating factor in the earlier strike, the NFLPA in 1987 initially demanded unlimited free agency; they later proposed freedom of movement after a four-year tenure in the league. Despite the fact that the average NFL career is less than the four-year minimum proposed, the owners rejected the condition outright. Failing to reach a new collective bargaining agreement, the players' union ended the strike after twenty-four days and three weeks of "replacement" games. The conflict was a study in obstinacy and futility. Law professor John Weistart found the owners' stubbornness to be particularly troubling when compared with comparable labor disputes in other sports: "Management was surprisingly intransigent in its position on free agency, more so than in past contract talks. Their position was harsh in light of the fact that the increase in free agency hasn't led to the demise of baseball and basketball. It was tough economic posturing, a flat refusal to bargain, which is the definition of bad-faith bargaining. There was no evidence of give-and-take." The owners did pay for their unyielding position, at least in the short term, by forsaking $104 million in potential revenue due to the suspension of play, but in the long run they maintained significant leverage in the constant battle over player autonomy.

Moving. The NFL was a bit unsettled in the 1980s, largely due to the efforts of the Oakland Raiders' managing general partner, Al Davis. A shrewd and somewhat eccentric figure within the league's corridors of power, Davis decided to move the Raiders from Oakland to Los Angeles for the start of the 1982 football season, despite twelve straight years of capacity crowds in the Bay Area, because Los Angeles offered a larger venue and the opportunity to operate in one of the country's media capitals. Davis's decision represented a conscious violation of the league constitution, which required the approval of three-quarters of the league's owners before a franchise could relocate. Davis, the Raiders, and the Los Angeles Coliseum Commission sued the NFL for $213 million on the grounds that the league was in violation of the Sherman Antitrust Act when they tried to block the Raiders' move. Following a five-week trial, a jury ruled in favor of the Raiders, a judgment which prompted commissioner Pete Rozelle to lament that the NFL's "basic structure and stability" was under attack. He warned that the ruling might result "in the relocation of clubs under auction-type conditions." Many speculated that Rozelle's anxiety was heightened because Davis was depriving the NFL of a chance to sell L.A.'s "territorial rights" to a new franchise for an extravagant expansion fee. Nevertheless, the

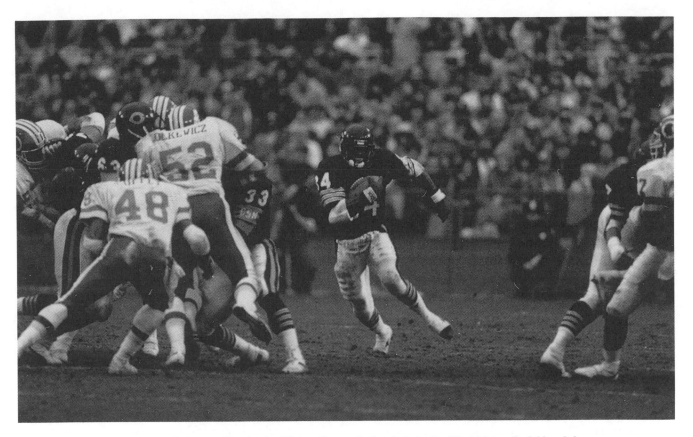

Chicago Bears' all-time rushing leader Walter Payton finds a hole in the Washington Redskins defense.

Oakland Raiders became the Los Angeles Raiders and went on to win the 1984 Super Bowl under their new name (they would, ironically, move back to Oakland during the summer of 1995). Davis's legal triumph opened the way for further movement. In the early morning of 29 March, Baltimore Colts owner Robert Irsay stealthily moved all of the Colts' possessions to Indiana with a fleet of moving vans, thus establishing the Indianapolis Colts in a sleek new domed stadium. Despite the strangeness of Irsay's machinations, the league, according to Pete Axthelm, "had no stomach for a fight with an owner who wanted to sneak out of town" after the Davis fiasco. The abandonment of Baltimore left a sour taste in the mouths of true Colts fans. Frank Deford wrote, "A man who could screw up professional football in Baltimore would foul the water at Lourdes or flatten the beer in Munich." Finally, in 1988 the St. Louis Cardinals moved to Phoenix, thanks to the efforts of team owner Bill Bidwill. St. Louis, long acknowledged as a "baseball town," consistently had trouble attracting a substantial football crowd. For star quarterback Neil Lomax, therefore, the move to Phoenix was convenient: "We won't have to apologize anymore because we don't play baseball." After the Davis challenge and the Irsay covert operation, some observers were relieved that at least the Cardinals' Bidwill went through the proper channels before abandoning St. Louis.

A Special Case. The desire to expand the professional game inspired in part the formation of the United States Football League (USFL). Initially the foundling league set out to avoid direct competition with the NFL by structuring their eighteen-game season for the spring and early summer months when the older league was dormant. The USFL gained considerable legitimacy by luring veterans such as Greg Landry, Stan White, and Raymond Chester, as well as college stars such as North Carolina's Kelvin Bryant and Michigan's Anthony Carter, away from the NFL. But the *coup de grace* was the New Jersey Generals' signing of running back Herschel Walker, a junior at Georgia and the 1980 Heisman Trophy winner. Even though both leagues possessed a mandate prohibiting the signing of undergraduates, USFL commissioner Chet Simmons, obviously eager to add a marketable name to the fold, conceded that he personally approved of the negotiations and argued that Walker was such an exceptional athlete that he represented a onetime "special case." The Generals sold seven thousand season tickets within hours of Walker's signing. On 6 March 1983 the league began play with twelve teams in three divisions. By summer it had crowned its first champion, the Michigan Panthers, who defeated the Philadelphia Stars 24–22 before 50,906 fans at Denver's Mile High Stadium. To its credit the league featured a host of experimental offensive schemes and saw many young players hone their considerable talents, but it was soon doomed by the team owners' collective frenzy to obtain the services of football's next generation of superstars. Steve Young, Mike Rozier, Marcus Dupree, Jim Kelly, Doug Flutie, and many others signed multimillion-dollar contracts, even while their franchises were struggling to stay afloat financially. Donald Trump, who purchased the New Jersey team after its disappointing inaugural year, still imagined the USFL eventually challenging the hegemony of the senior league: "Institutions are sometimes the most vulnerable elements of our society, and the NFL is very vulnerable." Despite Trump's confidence the league oversaw frequent franchise moves and mergers. When the USFL planned to compete head-on with the NFL in the fall of 1986, it could not negotiate a network television contract. After only three seasons of competition and nearing bankruptcy, the USFL filed a $1.69 billion antitrust suit against the NFL, charging that the senior league constituted a monopoly. In a curious decision a jury, after thirty-one hours of contentious deliberation, allowed the USFL's claim to stand, but awarded the league only one dollar in damages. Needing an estimated $300 million to proceed, the USFL suspended its upcoming fall schedule on 4 August 1986, never to resume play. Most of the league's stars went on to sign with NFL franchises.

Drugs. The USFL's attempt to maneuver into the NFL's competitive markets was hardly the only threat to football's collective peace. Tales of drug and anabolic steroid abuse by NFL players frequently surfaced during the decade, and on occasion the league took action against prominent players. In July 1983 commissioner Pete Rozelle suspended four players—Cincinnati's Ross Browner and Pete Johnson, St. Louis's E. J. Junior, and New Orleans's Greg Stemrick—for the first four games of the 1984 season after Junior and Stemrick were arrested for possession of cocaine and Browner and Johnson confessed to cocaine use during a trial of a suspected drug dealer. Don Reese, a former NFL player, related in a lengthy 1982 *Sports Illustrated* cover story the harrowing tale of his cocaine addiction. Said Reese, "cocaine is a .38 at the head of every player in the game" and "controls and corrupts the game, because so many players are on it." By the end of the decade the NFL had established large-scale drug-testing measures and had put into place prescribed penalties for each successive positive test result, including a thirty-day suspension for a second infraction and a ban from the league after a player's third violation. Some teams initiated their own drug counseling and rehabilitation programs modeled after the Cleveland Browns' system, "The Inner Circle." But despite disciplinary measures, rehab groups, and plaintive warnings like Reese's, the problem often led to tragedy before abuse was detected. Former defensive lineman Lyle Alzado felt that his twenty-year addiction to steroids and human growth hormone exacerbated the brain cancer that caused his eventual death. In June 1986 Cleveland Browns defensive back Don Rogers overdosed on cocaine

and died of heart failure. Rogers, the 1984 AFC Rookie of the Year, was to be married the next day. The tragedy, following closely on the heels of the cocaine-related death of college basketball star Len Bias, prompted Rick Reilly to pronounce, "The Big Lie is over. Sports can't bury its head in the sand anymore; there are too many bodies buried there. . . . This is not a party anymore. Somebody just called the paramedics."

Sweetness and Joy. In the midst of the various lawsuits, suspensions, tragedies, and covert transactions unfolding off the field, the NFL thrived by virtue of some marvelous performances on it. In particular Chicago's Walter Payton, known as "Sweetness," erased the bitterness of league turmoil with his unique blend of grace, agility, and power. Although a small running back, Payton seemed to enjoy contact. When Payton did not stutter-step a lineman off his feet or beat the linebacker to the corner, he simply flattened an unsuspecting cornerback with a stiff-arm or a lowered shoulder. In 1984 Payton broke Jim Brown's all-time rushing mark of 12,312 yards, and by the time he retired in 1987 he had tacked another 4,000 yards onto the standard. For much of his career Payton was the stellar member of mediocre Chicago teams, but in the mid 1980s head coach Mike Ditka and defensive coordinator Buddy Ryan assembled an extraordinary squad. With Payton and maverick quarterback Jim McMahon leading a ball-control offense, and Mike Singletary, Wilber Marshall, Richard Dent, and William "Refrigerator" Perry disrupting NFL offenses, the Bears ripped through the 1985 postseason with surprising ease. After shutting out both the New York Giants and the Los Angeles Rams, Chicago destroyed the New England Patriots in Super Bowl XX, 46–10. Ryan's innovative defensive schemes helped limit New England to minus-19 yards of total offense in the first quarter, and the run-oriented Patriots only generated seven yards rushing for the entire game. Perhaps the Bears' enthusiastic defensive play was best summed up by middle linebacker Singletary when he described a devastating hit on running back Eric Dickerson in the NFC championship game: "I don't feel pain from a hit like that. What I feel is joy. Joy for the tackle. Joy for myself. Joy for the other man. You understand me; I understand you. It's football, it's middle-linebacking. It's just . . . good for everyone."

L. T. While Chicago had the decade's most stubborn, unyielding defense, the New York Giants possessed the NFL's most ferocious marauder, linebacker Lawrence Taylor. When Taylor entered the league in 1981 as the second player chosen in the draft, Paul Zimmerman likened him to "an emissary from another planet." Indeed, "L. T." redefined the linebacker position. Strong enough to fill holes in the middle of the defense and agile enough to drop back into pass coverage (he once returned an interception 97 yards for a touchdown), Taylor also routinely ran down halfbacks with his breathtaking speed. But L. T. seemed to save his most spectacular brand of menacing for quarterbacks. Spinning around or simply leaping over offensive linemen, Taylor swooped in on unsuspecting quarterbacks before they could even find the laces on the ball, burying them in a one-man avalanche of Giant blue. His defensive coordinator, Bill Belichick, tried to pinpoint the source of Taylor's ferocity: "What makes L. T. so great, what makes him so aggressive, is his total disregard for his body." Stories abound of Taylor's capacity to "play through" his pain. In a 1988 game against New Orleans he tore a deltoid muscle severely and had to play in a shoulder harness but still managed to record ten tackles, two sacks, and two forced fumbles. Early in his career he suffered a concussion during a game against archrival Philadelphia, and the Giants' trainer had to hide Taylor's helmet to keep him from returning to the fray. Taylor had his best year in 1986, recording over twenty sacks during the season and becoming the first defensive player in history to be named consensus league MVP. Not coincidentally, the New York Giants dominated the NFC that season and won their first Super Bowl on 25 January 1987 against the Denver Broncos, 39–20. Mercilessly double- and triple-teamed throughout the game, L. T. was neutralized by the Broncos' offensive scheme—which allowed fellow linebacker Carl Banks to record ten unassisted tackles—but it was the Giants' offense that stole the show. Giant coach Bill Parcells kept the Denver defense off balance by unexpectedly passing on first down and mixing in trick plays (a fake punt, a flea-flicker), and quarterback Phil Simms ran the offense to near perfection, completing a remarkable 22 of 25 passes and earning Super Bowl MVP honors for his efforts. Taylor would get a second Super Bowl ring after the Giants' victory in Super Bowl XXV in 1991. Finally, worn down from a decade of double-teams and his continual struggles to curb his substance abuse, Taylor retired in 1994 as perhaps the most intimidating player of his generation.

Niners. Make no mistake, the dominant team of the 1980s was the San Francisco 49ers. Where the Bears and Giants dictated each game with their ferocious defenses, the Niners demoralized the opposition with a precise, nearly unstoppable offense. Designed by their innovative head coach, Bill Walsh, and mastered by quarterback Joe Montana, the San Francisco system depended on short passes, the "ready" of options by the quarterback and his receivers, and players who could run after they caught the ball. It did not hurt that Walsh coached two of the best players ever to play their positions, Montana and receiver Jerry Rice, but Montana was quick to give Walsh his due, saying "there's no coach I could have played for who would have been better for my career. Absolutely none." What made the Niners offense so potent was its flexibility: in their first Super Bowl in 1982, Walsh implemented an assortment of trick plays and new formations (some designed the day before the championship game) in order to confuse the Cincinnati Bengals early in the game. San Francisco led 20–0 at halftime and won

SWOOSH!

Although sports in the 1980s were, in Craig Neff's words, "awash in logos, brand names and marketing gimmicks," there is little doubt that Nike led the way. Named after the mythological winged goddess of victory, the Nike athletic footwear company was founded in 1972, but it was not until the 1980s that it became a force in the sports world. Led by founder and chairman Phil Knight, recognized as one of the most powerful men in sports, Nike made its mark through innovative product design and shrewd marketing, especially of superstars such as Michael Jordan and Bo Jackson. Recognizing that "nobody roots for a product," Knight sought to project images of heroism and glory onto gifted athletes. According to writer Donald Katz, "people would come to these heroes and listen to what they had to say, Knight believed, because superior athletic ability speaks to everyone's belief in some primordial capacity for a kind of true greatness that has been obscured over time by expediency and disappointment and the general clutter of contemporary life." Of course the corollary is that people would then want to buy Nike products. To enhance its image further Nike outfitted elite athletes in sportswear emblazoned with its swoosh icon, which was ubiquitous during the 1980s. Katz reports that by the early 1990s it was estimated that seven times as many athletes had "working agreements with Nike than with any other company. Over half of the NCAA championship basketball teams of the past ten years had worn Nikes, and more than sixty big-time colleges were 'Nike schools' — this, in most cases, because their coaches were Nike coaches. Well over 200 of the 324 NBA players wore Nike shoes, over 80 of them by contract. Two hundred seventy-five pro football players wore Nikes, as did 290 major-league baseball players." Collectively, these associations translated into a multi-billion dollar enterprise. By the end of the decade and beyond, argues Katz, Nike came "to signify status, glamour, competitive edge and the myriad intricacies of cool. Especially for the young, Nike shoes conjure up a yearning and fascination that for much of the century has been inspired by cars." At a time when sports were plagued by a variety of ills Nike promoted the nobility of competition and athletic excellence and in the process significantly shaped the way many Americans thought about sports.

Sources: Donald Katz, *Just Do It: The Nike Spirit in the Corporate World* (New York: Random House, 1994);

Craig Neff, "The Selling of Sport," in *The Best of Sports Illustrated* (New York: Oxmoor House, 1990);

J. B. Strasser and Laurie Becklund, *Swoosh: The Unauthorized Story of Nike and the Men Who Played There* (New York: Harcourt, Brace, Jovanovich, 1991).

26–21. In January 1985 Montana simply outgunned the Dolphins' Dan Marino in Super Bowl XIX, hitting on 24 of 35 passes for 331 yards and three touchdowns. Then, after four years of missing the Super Bowl, the 49ers returned in 1989 and 1990 to win the first back-to-back titles since the great Pittsburgh teams of the 1970s. For all of Montana's accomplishments, perhaps it was Rice who best embodied what might be deemed the 49er spirit. Widely regarded as the best receiver ever to snare a pass, Rice appeared to prepare for each game with a continual fear that he would be supplanted from his lofty perch. Dismissing those who said they would love to be in his shoes, Rice sighed, "They don't know what it's like. The pressure. Before games I can't sleep. Before Super Bowl XXIII I woke up at 4 a.m. and just paced. I can't relax. I should be able to enjoy it, but I can't. The table can turn." Perhaps it is such vigilance that makes champions.

A Chapter Closed. The once-proud Dallas Cowboys franchise in 1988 posted the NFL's worst record at an anemic 3–13. On 13 February 1989 Dallas head coach Tom Landry, sixty-four, declared proudly that he intended to guide the club for at least four more years, "because I just don't want to leave the Cowboys when they're down." Landry's loyalty to a sinking ship is understandable when one considers that he was the only head coach the franchise had ever had, and after twenty-nine years of dignified service he refused to reconcile himself to mediocrity, or worse. But less than two weeks later, Cowboy owner H. R. "Bum" Bright sold the team to Jerry Jones, an Arkansas millionaire who summarily fired the stone-faced Landry and replaced him with Jones's close friend, Jimmy Johnson, the coach of the University of Miami. The $140-million business deal and the sudden and seemingly unfeeling dismissal brought recriminations against Jones, but he maintained that the move was both painful and necessary. "This man is like Bear Bryant to me, like Vince Lombardi to me," said Jones. "If you love competitors, Tom Landry's an angel." Yet Jones noted, "I wouldn't have bought the Dallas Cowboys if Jimmy Johnson couldn't be my coach!" While NFL commissioner Pete Rozelle and many of Landry's former players treated the news as if it were an obituary, the old coach himself was more philosophical: "I was looking forward to this year. I thought it was going to be a tremendous challenge. But that's over with. It's a chapter closed. This is the worst scenario, I guess, but I'm not bitter." Dallas stumbled to a 1–15 record in Johnson's first year, but through a series of shrewd draft choices and trades the Cowboys rose to prominence again, winning consecutive Super Bowls in 1993 and 1994. The close bond between Jones and Johnson collapsed, however, and after the second championship Johnson was replaced by another of Jones's old friends, former University of Oklahoma coach Barry Switzer.

Sources:

Jim Byrne, *The $1 League: The Rise and Fall of the USFL* (New York: Prentice-Hall, 1986);

David Harris, *The League: The Rise and Decline of the NFL* (New York: Bantam, 1986);

Peter King, *Inside the Helmet: A Player's Eye View of the NFL* (New York: Simon & Schuster, 1993);

Michael LeBlanc, ed., *Professional Sports Team Histories: Football* (Detroit: Gale Research, 1994);

John Wiebusch and Brian Silverman, eds., *A Game of Passion: The NFL Literary Companion* (Atlanta: Turner Publishing, 1994);

Paul Zimmerman, *The New Thinking Man's Guide to Pro Football* (New York: Simon & Schuster, 1984).

FOOTBALL: COLLEGE

"Numerous and Major." "There is a firm feeling that we have turned the corner when it comes to major violations. We are getting on top of this integrity issue.... Ninety-nine percent of everything that is going on in intercollegiate athletics today is exceptionally positive." Such was the summation of NCAA executive director Dick Schultz at the 1988 national convention of the National Collegiate Athletic Association (NCAA). But given the sequence of events that unfolded in Norman, Oklahoma, in January 1989, it became difficult to credit Schultz's confident assertion. The University of Oklahoma finished atop the polls following the 1985 season, thus winning the mythical national championship, and narrowly missed winning another crown in 1987 when they lost the 1988 Orange Bowl to the University of Miami, 20–16 on New Year's Day. The winningest college football program in the 1950s and the 1970s, the Sooners of the 1980s were a brash, flamboyant, and talented lot, shaped in the image of their carefree and confident head coach, Barry Switzer. But Oklahoma was soon to become an unhappy example of the dangers of success. In December 1988 the football program was placed on three years probation by the NCAA Committee on Infractions for "numerous and major" recruiting violations. The NCAA declared that "for at least several years, the university has failed to exercise appropriate institutional control." Indeed, Switzer freely admitted, "We don't inhibit, muzzle, or restrict our players. You can't manage kids that way. *I* don't want to be managed that way." After the disciplinary measures were handed down, the Oklahoma program spun completely out of control. On 13 January 1989 redshirt freshman Jerry Parks shot sophomore offensive lineman Zarak Peters in the chest after a late-night argument. Eight days later three more Oklahoma players were under arrest, this time for allegedly raping a woman in the athletic dorm. Then, just five days later, the FBI brought star quarterback Charles Thompson into custody, charging him with selling $1,400 worth of cocaine to an undercover agent. As the athletic department desperately tried to condemn the crimes as a series of "isolated incidents," the public perception flourished that Oklahoma was a lawless program where the players ran the show. Ironically, had any of the criminal charges constituted an NCAA rules infraction, Switzer's team could conceivably have received the "death penalty," and the football program would have been shut down entirely. These criminal activities, however, fell outside of NCAA jurisdiction. Driven by the grandiose expectations of alumni, boosters, and fans, Switzer, who resigned in 1989, was fond of saying that "Bud Wilkinson [OU coach from 1947 to 1963] created this monster. I just have to keep feeding it. I like feeding it. It is exciting." He apparently never foresaw how monstrous it would all become.

Death Penalty. On 25 February 1987 the NCAA did hand down its first "death penalty," which was meted out to the Southern Methodist University (SMU) Mustangs. Forced to suspend football operations for the entire 1987 season and allowed only seven games (all on the road) for the 1988 campaign, the university voluntarily canceled that season as well. The sanctions also included limitations on off-campus recruiting and scholarships through the 1989 football season. The NCAA's Committee on Infractions designed the penalties "to compensate for the great competitive advantage that Southern Methodist has gained through long-term abuses and a pattern of purposeful violation of NCAA regulations." Never before had the NCAA suspended a football program, but rarely had college athletics seen a program so determined to circumvent the rules. The Mustangs had been caught cheating for a record seventh time; worse yet, the revelation that an unnamed booster had paid thirteen SMU players $61,000 from a slush fund—with the approval of prominent members of the athletic department—came while SMU was already on probation for infractions cited in 1985. According to a 1985 NCAA mandate any school found guilty of rules violations twice in the same sport within a five-year period could receive a one- or two-year "death penalty" sentence. Watching as SMU's first-string players rushed to sign with other prominent universities, Mustang supporters quickly recognized the long-term effects of the ban. One prominent booster asked ruefully, "My Lord, they killed the program. Why do they pick on one small school all the time?" When SMU football did return in 1989, the team was manned by a collection of freshmen, walk-ons, and a few remaining veterans, and they suffered a series of humiliating defeats while trying to compete in the tough Southwest Conference. Whereas the University of Oklahoma had seemingly handed control over to a collection of renegade players, SMU was perceived to be in the grip of affluent alumni. One backup quarterback put it most simply, "They were trying to buy us a better program and they bought us no program."

Rushing. In an era of increasingly sophisticated offensive schemes and pro-style passing attacks, many college football coaches still relied on the game's most elemental play, the handoff, and the 1980s saw a procession of phenomenal running backs. In 1980 the University of Georgia earned the mythical national championship behind the powerful running of a teenager named Herschel Walker. Built like a prototypical fullback, Walker possessed the acceleration of a world-class sprinter. In three

University of Miami quarterback and Heisman Trophy winner Vinny Testaverde in action against Florida State

seasons he gained 5,259 yards, won the 1982 Heisman Trophy, and seemed destined to break Tony Dorsett's record of 6,083 career yards, but he left school before his senior season to sign a multimillion-dollar contract with the newly emergent United States Football League. Despite his accomplishments Walker was upstaged during his sophomore year by the exploits of Marcus Allen, another in the long line of explosive backs at the University of Southern California (USC). Allen's sleek, graceful running style and slashing moves reminded many of O. J. Simpson, and he put up statistics that surpassed the former USC great, becoming the first back to gain over 2,000 yards rushing in a season (2,342 in 1981). The middle of the decade saw the arrival of another Walker-like talent in Auburn's Bo Jackson, who won the 1985 Heisman despite missing two games due to injury. An extraordinary athlete who would go on to star in both the National Football League (NFL) and Major League Baseball, Jackson parlayed his various talents and charismatic personality into a national media phenomenon with his "Bo knows" commercials for Nike shoes. Finally, there was Oklahoma State's Barry Sanders, who never seemed to get hit cleanly, except when he lowered his shoulder and surprised defensive backs who got in his way. Small and muscular, Sanders spun, stutter-stepped, and danced his way to an astonishing 2,628 yards rushing in 1988 (including four games with more than 300 yards) and a record 39 touchdowns. While all of these great backs received Heisman Trophies (Sanders and Walker in their junior years), only Walker was able to lay claim to a national championship ring.

Juggernauts. Perhaps the richness of college football in the 1980s was best expressed in the distinctive styles of its two best teams, the Penn State Nittany Lions and the Miami Hurricanes, who together won five national championships during the decade. Penn State's longtime coach, Joe Paterno, ran a clean and disciplined program; his teams, especially his championship squads in 1982 and 1986, relied on a strong, sound defense and a rugged, error-free offense that methodically conquered its opponents. While Paterno could be curmudgeonly at times, his teams earned the respect and admiration of the media and fans alike. On the other hand the Hurricanes, champions in 1983, 1987, and 1989, were perhaps the brashest, most flamboyant team in the history of the college game. Before the 1987 Fiesta Bowl against Penn State, a dozen Miami players showed up in Arizona sporting combat fatigues, and the entire team walked out of a pregame steak fry with the Nittany Lions. On the field the Hurricanes utilized their frightening team speed and sophisticated passing scheme (led by future pro quarterbacks Jim Kelly, Bernie Kosar, Vinnie Testaverde, and Steve Walsh) to demoralize opponents, often rubbing salt in the wounds with trash talk and unsportsmanlike behavior. Nevertheless, they were the closest thing to a football dynasty in the 1980s, compiling the second highest winning percentage during the decade with an 87–19 record (behind only Nebraska's 93–17 record). Miami seemingly contended for every title after the 1983 season, when they upset the highly favored Nebraska Cornhuskers in the season-ending Orange Bowl to capture their first NCAA crown. However, the unsavory (and occasionally criminal) exploits of the Miami team over the years provoked a continual barrage of stern condemnation, including a 1995 cover story in *Sports Illustrated* that called for the dismantling of the football program. In a long open letter addressed to University of Miami president Tad Foote II, Alexander Wolff wrote, "Your football team is malignant, recidivist, and scarcely integrated into your campus. Your city has the Dolphins and hardly needs a jayvee pro team."

The Pass. Miami was beatable, however. Just ask Doug Flutie. Standing 5-feet 9-inches in a game routinely dominated by massive, muscled bodies, he hardly seemed the stuff of legend, and yet when Flutie began flinging the ball to his sure-handed receiving corps, he made up for his supposed lack of stature. One of the most prolific quarterbacks in history, Flutie won the 1984 Heisman Trophy while leading Boston College back to national prominence. When the Eagles met defending national champion Miami on 23 November 1984, the diminutive Flutie was already the favorite to win college football's most prestigious award. His performance that afternoon insured that Flutie would be remembered for more than simply his statistics and accolades. The Hurricanes were coming off one of the most devastating single-game collapses in college football history when they blew a 31–0 halftime lead over Maryland and lost 42–40. Flutie and Miami sophomore phenom Bernie Kosar ignited an offensive explosion, combining to throw for 919 yards in a game in which the two teams produced 92 points. In the game's final minutes Kosar led the Hurricanes on a gutsy 79-yard drive to score the go-ahead touchdown with twenty-eight seconds left. But then Flutie and his receiver/roommate Gerard Phelan pulled off the decade's most improbable bit of magic. On the game's last play Flutie scrambled right with Miami's Jerome Brown in pursuit. After sidestepping the lunging defensive lineman, Flutie launched a pass that traveled 64 yards in the air and was caught by Phelan, who had somehow slipped behind the Hurricanes' last line of defense. Phelan afterward speculated that Miami freshman defensive back Darrell Fullington had misplayed the ball: "He must have thought Doug couldn't throw it that far." Fullington was guilty of a common sin, selling Flutie short. Flutie set the record straight, "I can throw 75 yards if I have to. Actually, I had to take a little off it to keep it in the end zone."

Futility. Not once between 12 November 1983 and 1 October 1988 did the Columbia University Lions pull out a victory in dramatic, Flutiesque fashion. In fact, the Lions did not celebrate a victory of any fashion during that five-year span, thus setting the all-time Division I record for futility: 44 consecutive losses. Sadly, an entire class of Columbia football players passed their college careers without experiencing the sweet taste of a win or even a tie. The Columbia streak of ignominy eclipsed the decade's other prominent losing streak, Northwestern's 34 consecutive defeats from 1979 to 1982. Northwestern's streak was understandable, for it was a small private school with demanding academic standards trying to survive in the cutthroat Big Ten Conference. Columbia competed on a more level playing field in the Ivy League, where athletic scholarships are not available and freshman are not allowed to play, but it had to struggle to entice quality Division I athletes to attend America's most urban campus, in the heart of New York City. To hear one rabid Lions fan tell it, they suffered the larger philosophic quandaries of their liberal, well-heeled, college community: "To liberals, to beat somebody on the field is to be morally aggressive. The entire liberal philosophy is based on passivity. You're better if you're a victim. If we ever won the Ivy League title, the administration would have us investigated by the ACLU!" Despite these complications Columbia finally won a game on 8 October 1988, defeating Princeton 16–13. After the gun sounded a weary band of Lions finally added their roar to the din of America's loudest city.

The CFA. Few people had heard of the College Football Association (CFA) before 1981. But when the organization that represented 61 major football powers approved its own $180-million television contract with the National Broadcasting Company (NBC) that summer, the CFA challenged the NCAA's stranglehold on network television rights. Formed in 1977 as a lobbying body within the NCAA, the CFA allowed member schools the opportunity to pitch their "product" directly to the networks, eliminating the NCAA's "middleman" role. Previously the NCAA negotiated all television sports packages involving the 139 Division I-A schools, but would not guarantee which of the member schools would appear on television. Given that the CFA included squads from every major conference except the Big Ten and Pacific Ten as well as independent powers such as Notre Dame and Penn State, the NBC deal left the NCAA with few viable options for attracting a national audience. To make matters worse for the NCAA, on 27 June 1984 the Supreme Court ruled 7–2 that college sports' governing body had violated federal antitrust law by preventing individual schools from negotiating their own contracts. The majority opinion, written by Justice John Paul Stevens, held that the NCAA acted as a cartel because college football constituted a "separate market for which there is no reasonable substitute," and was thus liable for restraint of trade under antitrust acts. Stevens wrote that under the NCAA's existing television contract "individual competitors lose their freedom to compete. Price is higher and output lower than they should otherwise be, and both are unresponsive to consumer preference. This latter point is perhaps the most significant, since Congress designed the Sherman (Anti-Trust) Act as a consumer welfare prescription." As a consequence of this decision Notre Dame, a powerful football program with a national fan base, was able to sign its own five-year television deal with NBC in 1990, thus separating itself from even the CFA's deal.

Good Things in Small Packages. Some exceptional football players competing for Division I-AA and II teams fell outside the often complicated purview of the CFA and NCAA television contracts. While Herschel, Marcus, and Bo eventually entered America's consciousness on a celebrated first-name-only basis, thousands of fans at smaller colleges eagerly followed the exploits of their own stars. Typically these players grabbed the mainstream media's attention with statistical feats such as Neil Lomax's seven touchdown passes in a single quarter in 1980, or Willie Totten's 56 touchdown passes in the 1984 season, or Johnny Bailey's 6,320 career yards rushing from 1986 to 1989. While critics quickly noted that Division I-AA and II football lacked the overall talent of its more prominent cousin, many coaches at small schools saw their players as works-in-progress. As one coach put it, "The big schools may get the blue-chippers, but we *make* the blue-chippers." Furthermore, a surprising number of stars on the professional level toiled in the intimate confines of smaller-college stadiums. The league that nurtured Jerry Rice—the Southwestern Athletic Conference (SWAC)—also produced pro football receiving greats Otis Taylor, Charlie Joiner, Harold Jackson, Harold Carmichael, and Trumaine Johnson. Rice held almost every receiving record on the NCAA books by the end of the 1980s, including most catches in a game (24 versus Southern University in 1983), most career yards receiving (4,693), and most career touchdown catches (50). Blessed with big, powerful hands strengthened from working with his father, a brick mason, Rice could "catch a BB in the dark" according to his Mississippi Valley State coach, Archie Cooley. Operating in the "Satellite Express" offense designed by Cooley and run by Totten, Rice thrived in a wide-open attack that was at once a prodigious offensive force, an entertaining spectacle, and a savvy recruiting tool. Later in the decade another small-school athlete captured the media's attention and even garnered some of the year-end Heisman Trophy hype. Holy Cross's Gordie Lockbaum became the first Division I player to play both offense and defense since Leroy Keyes in 1968. The Crusaders' starting halfback and cornerback, Lockbaum also spent time each game at flanker and as a kick returner and generally served as a special-teams demon, breaking wedges and blocking punts. Lockbaum's versatility even made the team's quarterback noticeably paranoid. "Every once in a while I check the sideline to see if Gordo's warming up his arm," said Jeff Wiley. Lockbaum was no slouch at any of his positions, averaging nearly six yards per carry, seventeen yards per reception, and once recording 22 tackles in a game against Army. Being on the field for 80 to 85 percent of a game's plays suited the modest Lockbaum. "I love it. Anybody would love it," said Lockbaum. "Not only do you get to handle the ball, but you get to intercept passes, hit guys, blitz. It's great." In an age of specialization, Lockbaum proved to be a throwback, and his career suggested that football on the small-college level was indeed a breed apart.

Sources:

Willie Morris, *The Courting of Marcus Dupree* (New York: Doubleday, 1983);

Robert M. Ours, *College Football Encyclopedia: The Authoritative Guide to 124 Years of College Football* (Rocklin, Cal.: Prima, 1994);

Tom Perrin, *Football: A College History* (Jefferson, NC: McFarland, 1987);

Murray Sperber, *College Sports Inc.: The Athletic Department vs. The University* (New York: Holt, 1990);

Rick Telander, *The Hundred Yard Lie: The Corruption of College Football and What We Can Do to Stop It* (New York: Simon & Schuster, 1989).

GOLF

Jack is Back. "These are interesting times," Jack Nicklaus mused. In the 1980s the Golden Bear was, by many accounts, growing old and losing his competitive edge. At forty his drives were not as prodigious as they once were, his legendary concentration often seemed to wane at critical junctures, and even his fans feared that their hero invested too much of his time and passion into the business and architectural ventures that cluttered his schedule. Furthermore, critics of the game described a professional tour overrun by country-club clones with mechanical swings and little imagination. Even golf's veterans shook their heads: "Pro golf is dull," grumbled Tommy Bolt, "It's a chorus line of blond towheads you can't even tell apart." Ironically, the blond Nicklaus himself had once been condemned as a talented player with few charms, especially when he dared to challenge golf's reigning demigod, Arnold Palmer, in the early 1960s. Now, the tour looked to Nicklaus for an infusion of character, and during the summer of 1980 he gave the game what it yearned for. After a two-year winless streak and endless tinkering with his swing mechanics and short game, Nicklaus unexpectedly seized control of the U.S. Open at Baltusrol Country Club with an Open-record 63 in the first round. He went on to lead the tournament from start to finish, wrapping up his fourth Open championship with birdies on the seventy-first and seventy-second holes to maintain his two-shot lead over Japan's Isao Aoki. In the process Nicklaus won over fans and competitors alike: cries of "Jack is back!" filled the gallery between shots, and in the locker room old rival Lee Trevino shouted at the television screen as he watched Nicklaus stalk up the eighteenth fairway, "Get away and let the big dog eat!" The title was Nicklaus's eighteenth major championship, five more than anyone else in history. But he was not through. In August the rejuvenated Nicklaus routed the field in the Professional Golfers' Association (PGA) Championship, winning by seven shots on the treacherous Oak Hill course in Rochester, New York. By claiming two major titles in 1980, Nicklaus accomplished an incredible feat. He had won majors in four different decades dating back to his 1959 U.S. Amateur Championship, solidifying through longevity what he had already confirmed in countless moments of competitive excellence: that he was the greatest golfer the game had ever known. And he still was not finished.

Watson. Despite Nicklaus's stunning reemergence, the early years of the decade belonged to Tom Watson. In the mid 1970s Watson endured a reputation as a choker after letting two U.S. Open titles slip from his grasp, but in 1977 he bested Nicklaus in two thrilling matches at the Masters and the British Open and thus gave notice of his ascendancy. By the 1980s it was apparent that Watson's occasional failures were largely a product of being in contention nearly every week. Each year he seemed to set a new season-earnings record, gathering

PGA Player of the Year honors in 1977 through 1980, 1982, and 1984 (more than any other golfer in history), and winning a total of eight major championships between 1975 and 1983. But in many ways Watson's legacy is indelibly linked to a single shot played at the 1982 U.S. Open at Pebble Beach. Capturing the Open title had become Watson's obsession ("Just winning money is not enough. . . . I must win the U.S. Open to be considered one of the great players"), and so when he came to the second-to-last hole tied once again with Nicklaus, Watson resisted the conservative approach into the center of the green and instead fired a two-iron toward the seventeenth's perilous pin placement. The gamble failed, and his ball settled in the deep Open rough between the green and the rocky shores of the Pacific Ocean. Watson faced a shot that demanded the nerves of a surgeon: a delicate wedge shot out of the viney grass to a slick green sloping away from him. When Watson's caddie whispered nervously, "Get it close," Watson responded confidently: "I'm not trying to get it close. I'm gonna make it." And he did, sending him into an ecstatic victory dance around the green's perimeter, at the conclusion of which he swung and pointed at his caddie and exclaimed, "Told ya!" Making a birdie when a bogey seemed inevitable, Watson had the Grail in his clutches, and when he birdied the final hole for good measure, he had staggered the Golden Bear once again. Watson's playing partner that day, Bill Rogers, rated the shot afterward, "He couldn't have hit a better shot if he'd dropped down a hundred balls." To which Nicklaus chimed in, "Try about a thousand." For many Watson had stared down the ghosts of blown opportunities past, or, as Thomas Boswell wrote afterward: "Golf allows its champions to develop genuine dignity. They play completely alone, more free of owners, managers and teammates than even professional boxers. . . . Because of their solitude—each reaches moments like Watson's at the seventeenth when he is framed by nothing but sky and history—great golfers seldom find it possible to hide their bedrock character, even if they would prefer it."

Senior Tour. Nicklaus's "comeback" at the age of forty would prove to be a portent of things to come. One might argue that the 1980s represented golf's "gray years," a period during which established figures such as Raymond Floyd, Lee Trevino, and Hale Irwin, all in their forties, wrested one last major championship from the young and hungry. Even the venerable Arnold Palmer, fifty-three, opened the 1983 Masters with a bit of magic, a four-under-par 68, and briefly tantalized those members of "Arnie's Army" longing for one last charge from their hero. Significantly, the decade gave the game's legendary names new life in the form of a tour of their own. The PGA Senior Tour grew out of the popular success of the "Legends of Golf" tournament, a team event begun in 1978 that not only brought the likes of Sam Snead and Billy Casper out of retirement, but showed that they could still play scintillating golf. In 1980 the United

States Golf Association established the U.S. Senior Open for players fifty-five years of age and older (the minimum age was dropped to fifty in 1981 to coincide with PGA Seniors Tour entry age), and the inaugural event was won by Roberto de Vicenzo at Winged Foot in Mamaroneck, New York. By 1987 the PGA had scheduled a circuit of thirty-seven Senior tournaments. Two years later there was a "Senior Slam" in place, consisting of the U.S. Senior Open, the Senior Players Championship, The Tradition, and the PGA Seniors' Championship. Financially, the Senior Tour was a colossal success. Capitalizing on the popularity of their members, including by 1990 such players as Trevino, Nicklaus, Palmer, Gary Player, and Chi Chi Rodriguez, the tour was driven financially by large-scale corporate sponsorship and by the revenues generated from two-day Pro-Ams before each tournament, in which amateur golfers paid thousands to play and socialize with their idols. As a result many of the Senior Tour's stars, such as Bob Charles and Jim Dent, earned nearly as much in one year on the fifty-and-older circuit as they had during their entire PGA careers. Still able to break par but unwilling to undergo the rigors of the regular tour, older golfers reveled in the opportunity to reclaim their competitive fire. The once gruff Billy Casper showed up for each round in brightly colored knickers and argyle plus fours, while the rejuvenated Trevino gushed, "This is the most fun I've had with my clothes on." Even Nicklaus, who initially dismissed the tour by asserting that "the problem for me is that the guys who are competing are the same guys I have beaten for thirty years," warmed to the challenges offered and in 1991 won three quarters of the Senior Slam.

European Invasion. During the decade golf increasingly distinguished itself as an "international" game. While there had long been a coterie of skilled foreign-born golfers laboring on the PGA and Ladies PGA (LPGA) tours, the 1980s saw a notable shift away from the customary dominance of American players. On the women's circuit Britain's Laura Davies and Sweden's Liselotte Neumann won U.S. Opens in 1987 and 1988, and Ayako Okamoto of Japan was selected as the 1987 LPGA Player of the Year after leading all female golfers in earnings. South Africa's Sally Little continued to win frequently on the women's circuit and captured three different major championships during the decade. On the men's tour the presence of international players was even more pronounced. European players won nearly half of the Masters and British Opens contested during the 1980s, and Australians David Graham and Greg Norman each captured one major during that span. It was perhaps Seve Ballesteros from Spain who best exemplified the challenge to the supremacy of U.S. players on the American tour. Ballesteros was a handsome and compelling figure, attacking each course with youthful exuberance, daring, and an endless arsenal of imaginative shots. At times it seemed like Ballesteros won every tournament with a cunning shot from a strand of trees, the wrong

Jack Nicklaus stroking a putt in his record sixth win at the Masters

fairway, or an out-of-the-way parking lot. By the age of twenty-one he had used his precocious talents to capture victories on four different continents (including the 1979 British Open), and a year later he became the youngest champion ever at the Masters. By contrast, Nick Faldo of Great Britain was a model of consistency, negotiating a golf course with almost geometric precision. Fittingly, Faldo won the 1987 British Open by parring every hole in the final round, while his competitors struggled in the gorse and brambles that penalize the wayward. Perhaps the most telling sign of the European preeminence came in the Ryder Cup series, a biannual team competition pitting an American squad against a contingent of golfers from Europe. When the Europeans captured the cup in 1985, it was their first victory since 1957. They proved the feat was no fluke by winning again in 1987, and, after a tie in 1989, retained the cup into the 1990s.

For Old Time's Sake. If Nicklaus's victories in 1980 surprised those who thought his best golf was behind him, then his winning the Masters at the age of forty-six must have seemed unthinkable. When the tournament

The appeal for most occasional bowlers (and the thorn in most professional bowlers' sides) is that bowling is a sport anyone can play well. Bowling began the 1980s as one the most popular participant sports in the country. Three out of every eight Americans were sanctioned league bowlers in 1980. Its popularity flagged over the next ten years, however, due in part to the fact that the public increasingly perceived it as a recreational rather than an athletic practice. Many believed that lanes were so oiled and grooved that any hack off the street could stroll into an alley, drink a few beers, chew the fat, and still post a high score. The gap between "Joe Bowler" and bowling legend Earl Anthony was perceived as decreasing, and the American Bowling Congress (ABC) grew anxious about the standards within which bowling scores were considered legitimate. The effort to maintain the integrity and stature of bowling as a sport was perhaps never more clear than in the curious case of Glenn Allison. Allison stood with one foot in each bowling world. He was a retired professional bowler — winner of four ABC championships and five Professional Bowlers Association (PBA) titles — who, as a liquor store manager and league member, rolled three consecutive 300 games on his girlfriend Jessie's birthday. The 900 series on 1 July 1982 was the highest score in bowling history, surpassing the 886 total Allie Brandt bowled in 1939. Allison's "gift" (he had told Jessie he would bowl a 300 game for her moments before his first strike sent the pins crashing) was witnessed by an awestruck alley full of spectators, bowlers, employees, and family members who celebrated the accomplishment with enthusiastic abandon. The general manager at La Habra 300 Bowl later mounted Allison's portrait over Lanes 13 and 14 and put his name on the pinsweeps which guard the now-hallowed ground. The ABC was not nearly as enthusiastic. After inspecting the lanes the organization's representative refused to sanction the 900 series, citing lane-dressing conditions that were not "in compliance with Article 7, Section 3" of the bowlers rule book. Despite assurances from local inspectors, appeals from Allison, and complaints from critics of the ABC (including many members of the professional tour) who had long contended that lane-dressing standards were vague and arbitrarily policed, the Congress did not waiver. Although never officially recognized, Glenn Allison's feat remains for many a significant achievement. "I think it's a remarkable feat," said Earl Anthony. "It's like a golfer hitting three or four straight holes in one." For his part Allison felt that he needed the sanction in order to secure a spot at the top of the bowling world. "The 900 series, if it were sanctioned, that's something that could never be broken," said Allison. "I would always be at the top of the record books, and as far as I'm concerned that would make me immortal." The claim to immortality was later made by Thomas Jordan who rolled an ABC-recognized 899 (and a four-game total of 1,198) in New Jersey in 1989. But for many bowling fans, Jordan's near-perfect score is only a reminder that perfection's name is Glenn Allison.

Sources: Frank Deford, "Frank Deford Goes Bowling," *Sports Illustrated*, 68 (25 January 1988): 50–59;

John Garrity, "Thrice Perfect, Once Scorned," *Sports Illustrated*, 57 (15 November 1982): 76–90.

began he was 160th on the money list, had missed three of seven cuts (and withdrawn from a fourth), and was once again said to be anxious about his business interests. He began the final round five shots behind the leader, Greg Norman, and had eight players ahead of him on the leader board. Nevertheless, on 13 April 1986 the Golden Bear roared again. Having missed a series of makable putts on the front nine, Nicklaus suddenly caught fire, shooting a phenomenal 30 on the back nine for a round of 65 to win his sixth green jacket. With the crowd exploding with each stroke and their shouts resounding through the azaleas, the rest of the field came unglued. The title was safe only after Ballesteros hooked his iron shot into Rae's Creek on the fifteenth and Greg Norman pushed his approach shot into the bleachers on the eighteenth. The unfolding scenario reconfirmed the power of Nicklaus's sheer presence during a stretch run at Augusta.

But for the Golden Bear himself his extraordinary play and the gallery's adoration led to an unexpected consequence: he began to struggle with powerful emotions during his round. Four or five times he fought back tears and had to lecture himself, "We have to play golf. This isn't over. . . . What I really don't understand is how I could keep making putts in the state I was in." Moreover, he admitted that he often failed to see the·ball land because of his weakening eyesight. "I'm missing the pleasure of seeing my ball finish," he said. The golfing world, on the other hand, celebrated the flight of each drive and the curl of each putt. As Rick Reilly wrote afterward, "It is a trick no other golf god has pulled, not Palmer or Hogan or Snead or Sarazen. Nicklaus had beaten young men at a young man's game on young men's greens and beaten them when they were at their youthful best."

Saturday Slam. One of the men caught in the wake of Nicklaus's Augusta run was Greg Norman, who was only just beginning a summer of amazing golf and astounding misfortune. By the mid 1980s Norman was being touted as another in the long line of "Bear-apparents." In the 1984 U.S. Open he nearly broke through with a major win, losing an 18-hole playoff to Fuzzy Zoeller after the two had tied after 72 holes. But in 1986 it appeared that Norman, called the Great White Shark for his blond locks and his tales of deep-sea fishing off the Australian coasts, had positioned himself for greatness. Norman led each of the four major tournaments going into the final rounds, but could secure only one victory. The press dubbed the impressive feat the "Saturday Slam," but for Norman it amounted to a trail of disappointment. He seemed to lose each tournament in some new, excruciating manner. Nicklaus's tremendous back nine momentarily stunned the normally resolute Norman, and after he double-bogeyed the par-four tenth hole, it seemed as if his chances were slipping away. "When we got to the fourteenth hole, there were only about fifty people left in our gallery," said Norman afterward. "They were all up with Nicklaus. . . . I told Nick [Price, Norman's playing partner], 'Let's wake these people up and show them we're still here.' " And he did, reeling off four straight birdies to tie Nicklaus, who had finished his round. On the last hole, needing only a par to force a playoff, Norman's four-iron approach shot careened into the bleachers to the right of the green, and he had to settle for a bogey and second place. In the final round of the 1986 U.S. Open at Shinnecock, Norman's putting stroke abandoned him and he shot a 75, as Raymond Floyd emerged from the pack to win. To his credit Norman dominated the field at the British Open that summer and earned his first major title. The jinx seemed to be over. But in August Norman saw the PGA Championship ripped from his grasp when Bob Tway holed a shot from a bunker beside the eighteenth green to beat the Shark by a stroke. As if 1986 were not torturous enough, golf's furies victimized Norman once again at the 1987 Masters, where Larry Mize sank an improbable 140-foot pitch on the second hole of sudden death to take victory from Norman. In the history of the game, no golfer had ever made a shot from off the final green to win a major title.

Pat Bradley. While Norman saw his chance at the Grand Slam crumble, Pat Bradley nearly accomplished the rare feat on the ladies' tour that same summer. By the mid 1980s the LPGA tour was flourishing, bolstered by the charismatic rise of Nancy Lopez and Jan Stephenson in the late 1970s, and the continued fine play of JoAnne Carner, the tour's reigning matriarch. In a period of seeming parity Bradley won three legs of the women's slam in 1986 — the LPGA Championship, the Nabisco Dinah Shore Tournament, and the du Maurier Classic — and finished an impressive fifth in the U.S. Women's Open. Excluding Bobby Jones, who inspired the notion of golf's Grand Slam when he won the U.S. Open, U.S. Amateur, British Open, and British Amateur in 1930, only three other professional golfers had captured three-quarters of the prize: Ben Hogan (1953) on the PGA Tour, and Babe Zaharias (1950) and Mickey Wright (1961) on the LPGA. Having already triumphed in the U.S. Open in 1981, Bradley also became the first woman to win all four majors in her career. Before the summer of 1986 Bradley's reputation bore a certain similarity to Norman's, for though she possessed remarkable concentration — her peers referred frequently to "the Stare" to describe her otherworldly intensity during competition — she had garnered notoriety as a frequent bridesmaid. Critics pointed to her remarkable record of 21 wins and 42 second-place finishes to attest to both her preeminence on the tour and her purported lack of a "killer instinct." But that summer Bradley won tournaments as dramatically as Norman lost them. At the LPGA Championship, for instance, Bradley birdied the last hole with a twelve-foot putt that left runner-up Patty Sheehan pounding her fists on the ground in frustration. At the du Maurier, Bradley found herself nine shots back after thirty-six holes, only to shoot a 67 followed by a 67 to gain a sudden-death playoff with Ayako Okamoto, whom she ousted with yet another birdie on the first playoff hole. In the only major that eluded her, Bradley struggled to a 76 in the first round, only to play herself back into contention with rounds of 71, 74, and 69. By the end of the year Bradley had put together one of the greatest seasons any golfer had ever known: five victories (three of them majors) and six second-place finishes. She was the LPGA's leading money winner, its Player of the Year, and the recipient of the Vare Trophy for low stroke average.

Repeat. No one had won the U.S. Open in consecutive years since Ben Hogan returned from a near-fatal car accident to grab the crown in 1950 and 1951. Tom Watson nearly accomplished the repeat in 1983, finishing second to Larry Nelson, but for many a defending champion the rigors of the Open (slick greens, narrow fairways, unyielding rough, intense pressure) seemed to dissolve quickly any visions of grandeur repeated. Few would have pegged Curtis Strange as the man to accomplish such a feat before the 1988 Open. The tour's leading money winner in 1985, 1987, and 1988, Strange was widely regarded as one of the best golfers in the world, but he won mostly in the small tourneys. Many fans cringed at the memory of Strange's collapse at the 1985 Masters, when he lost a commanding lead in the final round, twice hitting approach shots into the water on the back nine. But in 1988 Strange played himself into contention in the second and third rounds of the Open, and despite losing two shots to par on the final day, gained an eighteen-hole playoff with Nick Faldo when he artfully escaped a greenside bunker on the final hole. In the Monday playoff Strange putted extraordinarily well and defeated the usually steady Faldo. Having finally "broken through," Strange was considered one of the favorites entering the 1989 Open at Oak Hill Country Club, and he did not disappoint. However, even after a spectacular 64 on Friday, Strange and the rest of the field found themselves on Sunday chasing Tom Kite, who had broken par in each of the first three rounds. Kite, heir to the "best golfer to never win a major" tag previously attributed to Strange, struggled mightily during his final round, never quite recovering from a triple-bogey on the fifth hole. Meanwhile, Strange performed with Hogan-esque calm and precision. Beginning his round with fifteen straight pars, Strange watched the rest of the field wilt in the heat of competition. When he birdied the sixteenth with a fifteen-foot putt, Strange pushed his lead to two shots and coasted to his second consecutive Open victory. Entering the press tent after his victory, Strange broke the stoic demeanor that had carried him through the day's travails and shouted, "Move over, Ben." Curtis Strange had earned the right to share the pedestal with the great Hogan.

Sources:

Thomas Boswell, *Strokes of Genius* (New York: Doubleday, 1987);

Rhonda Glenn, *The Illustrated History of Women's Golf* (Dallas: Taylor Publishing, 1991);

Steven Goodwin, *The Greatest Masters: The 1986 Masters and Golf's Elite* (New York: Harper & Row, 1988);

Dan Jenkins, *Fairways and Greens: The Best Golf Writings of Dan Jenkins* (New York: Doubleday, 1994);

George Peper, *Grand Slam Golf* (New York: Abrams, 1991).

HOCKEY

1980 Olympic Attention. The new heights of popularity achieved by the National Hockey League (NHL) in the 1980s stems in part from the interest in the sport generated when the United States hockey team shocked the world by upsetting the mighty Soviets and later winning the gold medal at the 1980 Winter Olympics. The "Miracle on Ice" at Lake Placid "wound up being, quite literally, an icebreaker in terms of the sport's visibility at home and the new stature American hockey attained with the National Hockey League," wrote Robin Finn of *The New York Times* on the tenth anniversary of the event. "Suddenly hockey gained viability as a career for aspiring athletes who might otherwise have looked to other sports as their launching pads." Moreover, the U.S. hockey team's victory brought the sport to millions of viewers who were caught up in the excitement of the unfolding national drama but who had no previous knowledge of or interest in the game. "Winning the gold medal gave our hockey program some visibility and some credibility," said Herb Brooks, coach of the U.S. team in 1980, "and it brought the thing into a certain degree of focus, opening doors that had only been partly opened before. It was a catalyst and a springboard." Or as hockey superstar Wayne Gretzky succinctly put it, the 1980 Olympics were "the greatest thing to happen to hockey in twenty years."

Realignment. After a period of great expansion in the 1970s, the NHL opened the 1979–1980 season with a record twenty-one teams, including four from the defunct World Hockey Association (WHA). Late in 1980 in an attempt to lend some geographical logic (in terms of regional rivalries, traveling expenses, and television scheduling) to the organization of divisions, the league's board of governors unanimously approved a realignment plan for the 1981–1982 season. "This is a major step — our business has changed," said league president John Ziegler. During the season each team would continue to play eighty games, but with the realignment teams would play each of the opponents in its division four times. Preliminary playoffs between the top four teams in each of the four divisions would now determine the semifinalists in the conference championships.

New York Islanders. The 1979–1980 season witnessed the beginning of the New York Islanders' dynasty. During the first half of the decade the Islanders' combination of offensive firepower and defensive ruggedness proved to be insurmountable for their opponents. With perennial all-stars such as high-scoring forward Mike Bossy, nifty-passing center Bryan Trottier, hard-hitting defenseman Denis Potvin, and intimidating goalie Billy Smith at his disposal, coach Al Arbour led the Isles to four consecutive Stanley Cups from 1979–1980 to 1982–1983. As one of the Islanders' opponents put it, they were "an almost perfect team." Much like the Montreal Canadiens of the late 1970s, the Islanders of the early 1980s thoroughly dominated the league. Unlike the Canadiens, however, the Islanders were a team without a glorious past. Having entered the NHL in 1972, the Islanders' accomplishments made them the winningest team in professional sports for its age and led some to ponder where they ranked in terms of other hockey dynasties. "As far as I'm concerned," said Potvin in the immediate afterglow of the Isles' fourth championship, "we're the best hockey team ever to lace on skates." Noted for their fierce competitiveness and poise, the aging and injured Islanders reached the Stanley Cup finals yet again in 1984 but were overwhelmed four games to one by the fleet, Gretzky-led Edmonton Oilers, whom the Isles had swept in the finals the year before. The Oilers' victory inspired journalist Jack Falla to quip, "the sleek may yet inherit the ice." The Islanders' dynasty had come to its inevitable end. "I don't feel badly about turning the Cup over to them," Potvin acknowledged. "They're truly a worthy champion. This is one great, great team passing the Cup along to a team that is great."

Edmonton Oilers. Well before the 1983–1984 season Wayne Gretzky of the Edmonton Oilers was hailed by many as the best hockey player in the world, if not of all time. By his fifth NHL season Gretzky had won virtually every award a professional hockey player could win, and he had set a myriad of NHL scoring records. Gretzky put up numbers that few people could have imagined a decade before. In 1981–1982, his third year in the league,

The jubilant New York Islanders after winning the Stanley Cup in 1980

he led the NHL in goals (92), assists (120), and total points (212), all of which were single-season records. But, as was frequently noted, he had not won a Stanley Cup. Critics suggested that the Oilers' brand of wide-open, high-scoring hockey won games but did not win championships. By the 1981–1982 season, finally surrounded by talented players such as forwards Mark Messier, Jari Kurri, and Glenn Anderson, defenseman Paul Coffey, and goaltenders Grant Fuhr and Andy Moog, Gretzky captained the Oilers through a period of tremendous success. The Oilers' first league championship in 1984 signified a changing of the guard in more than one way. Gretzky proclaimed, "We proved that an offensive team can win the Cup. That can't do anything but help hockey. We showed you can win by skating and by being physical without having to fight all the time." Powered by a combination of explosive scoring and surprisingly tough defensive mettle, the Oilers emerged as the best team in hockey for the rest of the decade. "They've got the mix of the Canadiens of the late 1970s and the Islanders of the 1980s," commented Philadelphia Flyer Ed Hospodar. "They can beat you by skating or playing tough, anyway they want." With Gretzky leading the way and playing superlative, unselfish, finesse hockey, the Oilers won four Stanley Cups over a five-season stretch and established themselves as one of the greatest hockey teams in history.

The Great One. When Wayne Gretzky joined the Edmonton Oilers of the World Hockey Association (WHA) in 1978, he was seventeen years old, the youngest player ever in professional hockey. At the end of the season he was named WHA Rookie of the Year. After skating on the same line with Gretzky at the WHA All-Star Game, the legendary Gordie Howe said, "It scares me how good he could become." The next season the Oilers merged into the NHL and Gretzky became the youngest player to ever win the Hart Trophy, the league's MVP award. During his nine years in Edmonton, Gretzky won the Hart Trophy eight times. He also set the NHL's single-season scoring mark and established more than fifty other regular-season and career scoring records. In playoff action he became the all-time points leader. In two of the four years in which he led the Oilers to Stanley Cup titles, Gretzky was voted MVP of the playoffs. Recognizing Gretzky's brilliance and importance, Hall of Famer Bobby Orr in 1982 noted: "Hockey would have survived the last three years without him: hockey will always *survive*. But if Wayne is influencing the hundreds of thousands, the millions of kids that I think he is — well, put it this way: Thank God he's around." As Gretzky continued to rewrite the record book and win championships, his popularity and legend grew. And it became clear that his famous sobriquet "The

Wayne Gretsky of the Edmonton Oilers scoring his record-breaking seventy-seventh goal, 24 February 1982

Great One" was not hyperbolic nor merely slick marketing. It therefore came as a tremendous surprise to the sporting world when Gretzky was traded to the Los Angeles Kings in a multiplayer, multimillion-dollar deal the summer after he led the Oilers to their fourth Stanley Cup. Though the trade serves as a useful line of demarcation for his career, Gretzky continued his unparalleled success with the Kings. In his first season in Los Angeles Gretzky scored 168 points and earned his ninth Hart Trophy. Early the next season he broke Howe's all-time scoring record of 1,850 points. Howe set the record over the course of twenty-six seasons; Gretzky broke it in less than ten. In the end Mark Stevenson was correct: Gretzky's "only standard of comparison is himself."

Violence. Although professional hockey has long been noted for its rugged, physical play, game-related violence in the 1980s escalated. The 1980–1981 season, for example, witnessed a rash of brawls, including the most fight-filled game in NHL history. On 26 February 1981 the Boston Bruins and the Minnesota North Stars started fighting seven seconds into the game and continued throughout the contest. At the end of the first period some of the North Stars exchanged blows with Bruins fans. All told, seven North Stars and five Bruins were ejected from the game, and a record 84 penalties and 406 penalty minutes were assessed. After reviewing the debacle the league suspended three North Stars for their ac-

tions, and over $15,000 in fines were imposed. Unfortunately, this was not an isolated incident. A week earlier seven New York Rangers had charged into the stands of Detroit's Joe Louis Arena and fought with Red Wings fans who had been taunting them and pelting them with debris. Two days before the infamous game in Boston, the Philadelphia Flyers and the Vancouver Canucks engaged in a vicious, bench-clearing melee. The behavior of some management was not much better. Earlier in the year Boston general manager Harry Sinden was fined for pursuing a referee onto the ice during a game. With the ascendance of the Edmonton Oilers, whose style of hockey was not predicated on ferocious checking or fighting, many hoped that the sport would become less violent. It did not. In 1986, for instance, there was a substantial increase in penalties and penalty minutes for fighting. "Intimidation is still a big factor in hockey," said Calgary Flames general manager Cliff Fletcher. "In fact it's probably the major factor. Every team likes to have one or two enforcers or designated hit men so that the rest of the team feels comfortable." This explains why a small number of players, such as Dave "Tiger" Williams and Chris Nilan, had a disproportionate share of major fighting penalties. Over the course of the decade NHL officials combated the outbursts of violence with increasingly stiff fines and suspensions, and some stars like Gretzky spoke out against fighting, but in general the league chose to accept what it described as "spontaneous combat which comes with the frustrations of the game."

Lemieux. After being drafted number one overall in 1984, Montrealer Mario Lemieux of the Pittsburgh Penguins won the NHL's Calder Trophy as the league's Rookie of the Year for the 1984–1985 season. By scoring 100 points, the third-highest total ever for a rookie, Lemieux almost immediately established himself as the second-best player in professional hockey. As *Sports Illustrated* later observed, "Where Wayne Gretzky once stood alone, Mario Lemieux presumes to tread." As both a goal scorer and passer, Lemieux was a dominating offensive force. Bigger and stronger than Gretzky, Lemieux was no less gifted and graceful than the Great One. "His imagination and creativity are endless," said coach Mike Keenan. "His reach is great, his talent is excessive." Following two superlative seasons, Lemieux blossomed into a full-fledged superstar in 1987. Playing with Gretzky in the Canada Cup tournament, Lemieux emerged as the Canadian team's star. Parlaying his success into added confidence, Lemieux broke Gretzky's streak of seven consecutive league scoring titles, with 168 points during the 1987–1988 season. The next season Lemieux again won the league scoring crown by amassing 199 points, setting an NHL regular-season record with 13 short-handed goals. He also became the Penguins' all-time leader in assists and the first player other than Gretzky to score 50 goals in fewer than the first 50 games of the season. Rewarded for his achievements in 1989, Lemieux signed a five-year, $12 million contract with the Penguins, joining Gretzky as the only other NHL player to make more than $2 million a year. "Had he arrived in the NHL in an era other than Gretzky's," wrote Austin Murphy, "he would have had the whole pantheon to himself." Following another great season in 1989–1990, Lemieux fell victim to a spate of serious injuries, most notably to his back, which forced him to miss more than half of the 1990–1991 season. Still, he came back to lead the Penguins to their first-ever Stanley Cup and won the Conn Smythe Trophy as the MVP of the playoffs. On 13 January 1993 it was announced that Lemieux was diagnosed with Hodgkin's disease, a form of cancer. Following a month of radiation treatment, he returned to the ice in time to lead the league in scoring with 160 points.

Soviet Invasion. Even before the fall of the Berlin Wall in November 1989, there were signs that the Cold War in hockey was nearly over. Nine former Soviet players were already signed to play in the upcoming 1989–1990 NHL season. The Soviet players — with the exception of Alexander Mogilny of the Buffalo Sabres, who defected in May — were allowed to join the NHL with the stipulation that a portion of their salaries was to be paid to the Soviet Ice Hockey Federation. Unlike the proliferation of Europeans in the league (mostly Swedes, Finns, Czechs, and Slovaks), the "arrival of the powerful Soviet contingent in the NHL came about as a result of the policies of *perestroika* (restructuring) introduced by

Soviet leader Mikhail Gorbachev," noted John Howse. The entry of Soviets into the league generated a great deal of fanfare and diplomatic goodwill, and many fans expected significant contributions from players such as Vladimir Krutov and Igor Larionov, members of the Soviet National Team's famed "KLM" line. Not everyone, however, was pleased by the arrival of the Soviets. "There is an undercurrent of resentment by [some] North American players," observed Jay Greenberg, "both because of jobs lost to the Soviet athletes and a lingering cold war antipathy." By the end of the season many were disappointed by the performance of the Soviet veterans. Aside from Sergei Makarov of the Calgary Flames, who won the Calder Trophy as the league's Rookie of the Year, Jim Matheson of *The Sporting News* concluded that the "Soviet invasion was a washout."

Sources:

Jay Greenberg, *NHL: The World of Professional Hockey* (New York: Rutledge Press, 1981);

Wayne Gretzky, *Gretzky: An Autobiography* (New York: HarperCollins, 1990);

Michael LeBlanc, ed., *Professional Sports Team Histories: Hockey* (Detroit: Gale Research, 1994);

Tim Wendel, *Going For The Gold* (Westport, Conn.: Lawrence Hill, 1980).

THE OLYMPICS: 1980

The Winter Games. The XIII Winter Olympics were held in Lake Placid, New York, from 12 to 24 February and included athletes from thirty-seven nations. It was the second time the Winter Games were held in the tiny upstate New York town, the first time being in 1932. Despite horrendous transportation problems the 1980 Winter Games were, as described by one observer, "a glistening festival in which superb athletes performed their feats in superb surroundings." Fortunately, the United States–led movement to boycott the 1980 Summer Games in Moscow because of the Soviet Union's invasion of Afghanistan had virtually no effect on the competition. Instead, the most noteworthy political controversy of the games was the absence of the Taiwanese team, who petitioned the International Olympic Committee (IOC) to be excused from the games due to the presence of a team from the People's Republic of China. Politics aside, the 150-member U.S. team enjoyed the advantage of hosting the games and did well, finishing third in the final medal standings, behind East Germany (23 total medals) and the Soviet Union (22), with a total of 12 medals (6 gold, 4 silver, 2 bronze). Moreover, American athletes provided the Winter Games with two of its most extraordinary, memorable, and historic performances.

America's Golden Boy. Over the course of eight days American speed skater Eric Heiden turned in an epic performance. The twenty-one-year-old Heiden won gold medals and set Olympic records in all five of the events in which he participated: the 500-, 1,000-, 1,500-, 5,000-,

The United States Hockey team provided the surprise of the 1980 Winter Olympics in winning the gold medal

Miracle on Ice. The U.S. hockey team's improbable 4–3 victory over the Soviets on 22 February ranks as one of the greatest upsets in the history of American sport and the Olympic Games. "For millions of people, their single, lasting image of the Lake Placid Games will be the infectious joy displayed by the U.S. hockey team following its 4–3 win over the Soviet Union," wrote E. M. Swift. The surprising victory led to euphoric, patriotic celebrations all over the country. Two days later, the inspired American team beat Finland 4–2 to win the Olympic gold medal, again prompting a national outpouring of pride and joy. Going into the Games the U.S. club was ranked seventh among the twelve teams competing in the Olympics. Coached by Herb Brooks, the U.S. team was composed of overachieving, "fuzzy-cheeked" collegians who were given little chance of competing with the powerful Soviets, the reigning Olympic and world champions. The unheralded U.S. team, led by goaltender Jim Craig, captain Mike Eruzione, and center Mark Johnson, played aggressive, fearless hockey throughout the seven-game tournament. Though the game with the Soviets meant little to the players politically, many others saw the victory in geopolitical terms. "At a time when international tension and domestic frustration had dampened traditional American optimism," wrote *Sports Illustrated,* "the underdog U.S. Olympic hockey team gave the entire nation a lift by defeating the world's top team, the Soviets, and ultimately winning the gold medal. Those youngsters did so by means of the old-fashioned American work ethic, which some people feared was disappearing from the land." For their performance the U.S. hockey team was named Sportsmen of the Year for 1980 by *Sports Illustrated.*

The Games Went On. The XXII Summer Olympics began 19 July 1980 in Moscow and were the first Games ever held in a communist nation. While eighty-one countries participated the United States, led by embattled President Jimmy Carter, and sixty-four other countries boycotted the competition to protest the Soviet invasion of Afghanistan. Secretary of State Cyrus Vance had articulated the Carter administration's position before the IOC in February: "We will oppose the participation of an American team in any Olympic Games in the capital of an invading nation. This position is firm. It reflects the deep convictions of the United States Congress and the American people." Though many Olympic purists argued that the Olympics should be divorced from politics, others pointed out that politics had always been present in the Games. Conservative political columnist Lance Morrow noted that the Olympics were "an immense and garish parade of nationalism." Although President Carter's decision understandably embittered many American athletes, he steadfastly defended the Olympic boycott and asserted that it was "the only correct course for our country." The competition, opened by Soviet president Leonid Brezhnev, did not encounter any serious disruptions. There were, however, a few minor protests

and 10,000-meter races. In so doing he became the first athlete ever to win five gold medals in individual events in one Olympics. He alone won more gold medals than any American team had in the Winter Games since 1932. By the end of the Winter Games he had become a speed-skating immortal. It should not lessen his accomplishments to note that Heiden's victories were expected. Before the competition began, Heiden was already considered the best speed skater in history. One commentator argued that "Heiden outstrips human comparison: he is [like] Secretariat, stronger, faster, possessed of a greater racing heart than has ever been known." A near-perfect combination of speed, power, stamina, technique, discipline, and competitive desire, Heiden was described by Thomas Boswell as a "young man whose name will go down with the greats of Olympic history." In recognition of his tremendous Olympic performance, Heiden was awarded the 1980 Sullivan Award as the nation's outstanding amateur athlete.

Mary Lou Retton during exercise on the balance beam in the 1984 Summer Olympics

throughout the Games, such as when New Zealand athletes carried a black flag with the Olympic symbol of five interlocking rings and an olive branch of peace during the opening ceremonies. The Soviet team won 197 medals (80 gold, 70 silver, and 47 bronze), far outdistancing its nearest rival. East Germany ended up with 126 total medals, followed by Bulgaria (40), Hungary (32), and Poland (31). "No Games, of course, could be representative of world sport without the Americans," wrote one observer. "The 1980 Olympics were always going to be a makeshift affair from the time the American government decided on a boycott. To the Olympic medal winners, though, a medal is a medal, whoever happened to be or not to be competing. The Games is already history, and the boycott will be a progressively smaller detail of that history as time passes." Unfortunately, the 1980 boycott would have a tremendous impact on the 1984 Summer Olympiad in Los Angeles.

Sources:

Peter Arnold, *The Olympic Games: Athens 1896 to Los Angeles 1984* (London: Optimum, 1983);

Allen Guttmann, *The Olympics: A History of the Modern Games* (Urbana & Chicago: University of Illinois Press, 1992);

John Hoberman, *The Olympic Crisis: Sport, Politics and the Moral Order* (New York: Caratzas, 1986);

Ben Olan, ed., *The Olympic Story 1980: Pursuit of Excellence* (Danbury, Conn.: Grolier Enterprises, 1980);

Martin Vinokur, *More Than A Game: Sports and Politics* (New York: Greenwood Press, 1988);

Tim Wendel, *Going For The Gold* (Westport, Conn.: Lawrence Hill, 1980).

THE OLYMPICS: 1984

Sarajevo. The XIV Winter Games, held in Sarajevo, Yugoslavia, from 6 to 19 February, included 1,437 athletes from forty-nine nations. Though initially hampered by a four-day blizzard with intermittent 80-MPH winds, the Games were a success. As one observer put it, despite the weather "everyone's mood was upbeat." Before the Games began, many thought that the United States was represented by its strongest Winter Olympic team ever. If strength translates into medals, this was not the case. Still, the American team did well, particularly in the alpine events. Bill Johnson became the first American to win a gold medal in the Olympic downhill skiing event. Debbie Armstrong and Christin Cooper finished first and second in the women's giant slalom. Twins Phil and Steve Mahre finished first and second in the men's slalom. The rest of the U.S. medals came in figure skating. Three-time world champion Scott Hamilton won the men's competition and set a new Olympic record in the process. Rosalynn Sumners finished second behind East Germany's Katarina Witt in the women's competition, and Kitty and Peter Carruthers won the silver in the pairs. The Soviet Union won the most medals with 25 (6 gold, 10 silver, and 9 bronze), followed by East Germany

Mary Decker falls after colliding with Zola Budd in the 3,000-meter race in the 1984 Summer Olympics.

publicized Ban the Soviet Coalition." Two months before the opening of the XXIII Summer Games the Soviets announced that they would not attend the competition. Historian Allen Guttmann contends that there is "little doubt that the Soviet decison was motivated mainly by the desire to retaliate for the damage done in 1980." A few days later East Germany, Czechoslovakia, Poland, and a host of other Warsaw Pact and communist nations announced that they too would not participate. Despite the notably weakened level of competition, 7,458 athletes from 139 countries did compete at the Los Angeles Olympiad. During the opening ceremonies Juan Antonio Samaranch, president of the IOC, noted that "our thoughts also go to those athletes who have not been able to join us." Politics aside, for writer Harvey Frommer the Los Angeles Games "were hype and hoopla, ceremony and celebration, anticipation and achievement. For those who were there as participants and witnesses, the feeling and the images of that Summer's fortnight will forever tarry in memory." The 1984 Summer Games were notable for other reasons as well. "The L.A. Olympics were a watershed," wrote Craig Neff of *Sports Illustrated*. "They reversed the course of the Olympic movement and demonstrated how sports could tap into the economic boom of the '80s." A huge popular and financial success — the LAOOC netted a surplus of over $200 million, only the second time since 1932 that the Games had not run a deficit — the 1984 Summer Games forever dispelled the notion that the Olympics were primarily about amateurism rather than commercialism and nationalism.

Carl Lewis Soars. "No chronicle of the Games of the XXIII Olympiad would be complete without giving full credit to the phenomenal performance of Carl Lewis," writer Mark Levine noted. The twenty-three-year-old sprinter and long jumper was the brightest of the many American stars at the Games. He won three individual gold medals — in the 100 meters, the 200 meters, and the long jump — and he anchored the gold medal–winning 4 x 100-meter relay team. In so doing Lewis matched the legendary 1936 Olympic performance of the late Jesse Owens. In the face of incredible media attention, Lewis demonstrated his remarkable athletic prowess before ninety thousand spectators at the Los Angeles Coliseum. "Success never seemed so smooth," wrote *Sports Illustrated*. When asked whether he competed for financial gain or to become a hero, Lewis responded: "My objective is to be the role model, not the rich man." Yet for all his accomplishments at the Games, Lewis was criticized by some for being aloof, self-important, and difficult. Sportswriter Pete Axthelm wrote that "with his sometimes whining attitude, Lewis threatened to turn victory into antiheroism. In sports history, he may relate to Owens much as Roger Maris relates to Babe Ruth, and may prove that mere records do not make legends."

America's Darling. Though Carl Lewis captured more gold medals at the 1984 Games, gymnast Mary Lou Retton probably captured more hearts. Described by one

(24), Finland (13), and Norway (9), while the United States tied with Sweden for fifth with eight medals (4 gold and 4 silver). Just eight years later, Sarajevo would be devastated by mortar and sniper fire as warring factions battled for control of the city.

Reciprocity. "Somehow Americans and the IOC assumed that the Soviet Union would attend the 1984 Los Angeles Games," wrote historians Randy Roberts and James Olson. Perhaps this was the case because they believed the Soviet Olympic committee chairman when he noted in 1983 that he did "not see any reasons" why the Soviet team would not participate in the upcoming Summer Games. Or because early the following February a Soviet IOC official commended Peter Ueberroth, president of the Los Angeles Olympic Organizing Committee (LAOOC), for the "excellent job" he and the committee had done. In the next few months, however, the Soviet position on the 1984 Summer Games was reversed, in large part due to the death of Soviet leader Yuri Adropov, who was replaced by Konstantin Chernenko. With the change in leadership came a change in attitude toward Soviet Olympic participation in the Los Angeles Games. According to Roberts and Olson: "Old slights were once again remembered. Suddenly Soviet sports officials had reservations about the job Ueberroth was doing. Publicly they fretted over security and the over-

observer as a "chunky, tiny dynamo," the four-foot nine-inch sixteen-year-old won national adulation for her historic individual all-around performance — the gymnastic equivalent of the decathlon — and endearing charm. Retton's primary rival in the all-around competition was Ecaterina Szabo of Romania. Trailing Szabo by the slimmest of margins going into the final event, the vault, Retton needed a perfect score to win. So she did it. Twice. Her performance won her the enthusiastic approval of over nine thousand spectators and a place in Olympic history. "The resulting 10 gave her not only the gold, but the first individual gymnastics medal ever won by an American," wrote Murray Olderman. It was, in fact, the first all-around gymnastics victory for an American in any international competition. "It was just like I dreamt it, the excitement, the tension, the crowd," said the ebullient Retton. In addition to her gold medal Retton also won a silver in the vault competition and two bronze medals for the uneven bars and floor exercises. In the opinion of her coach, Romanian-born Bela Karolyi, who previously trained the great Nadia Comaneci and Szabo before defecting to the United States in 1982, Retton represented a "new kind of gymnast." Said Karolyi: "She's strong and powerful and athletic; not a little flower, a little flyer."

Decker, Budd Collide. Perhaps the most controversial moment during the 1984 Summer Games was the collision between favored U.S. runner Mary Decker and the barefoot South African runner Zola Budd, who was granted British citizenship in order to compete in the Games since apartheid South Africa was barred from the competition. Decker and Budd collided after completing the fourth lap of the 3,000-meter race. The accident put Decker out of the competition and allowed Maricica Puica of Romania to win the gold. An unnerved Budd finished a disappointing seventh. Did Decker fall or was she tripped? Replays were inconclusive but suggested that both women were partially responsible for the mishap. "The incident was a tragedy for both women and for the Games, which was robbed of what would have been a classic finale to the race," wrote Cliff Temple. "The regrettable outburst by Decker afterwards, holding Budd responsible, made the incident even less palatable as was Decker's refusal to shake hands with the young runner who had always idolized her." For many the sight of the injured, wailing Mary Decker crumpled in a heap at the side of the track was one of the Games' most enduring images. "For every flying Carl Lewis there is a fallen Mary Decker," wrote *Time* magazine, "and the fullest appreciation of sport requires both."

The Best of the Rest. There were, also, many notable performances by American athletes other than Carl Lewis and Mary Lou Retton. The star-studded U.S. men's and women's basketball teams swept their opponents on the way to gold medals. Greg Louganis won the gold medal and set a world record in the 10-meter platform diving competition and also won the springboard event. Swimmers Carrie Steinseiffer and Nancy Hogshead tied for first in the 100-meter freestyle race to become the first athletes to win dual gold medals in one event. All told, Hogshead won four medals (three gold and one silver), while fellow American swimmer Tracy Caulkins won three golds. The water polo team took the silver. The men's volleyball team beat Brazil in straight sets to win the gold medal, while the women's contingent finished second to the Chinese team. The men's gymnastic team won seven medals, including the team championship, and the women's gymnastic team won the silver in the team competition, behind the Romanians. The U.S. boxing team won a record nine gold medals, and the wrestling team won thirteen medals, including nine gold, and provided perhaps the most inspirational performance of the games: Greco-Roman wrestler Jeff Blatnick, diagnosed with cancer two years earlier, won the gold medal in the super heavyweight division and wept for joy after his victory. The Los Angeles Coliseum was the site of some of the U.S. team's most stunning performances. Evelyn Ashford won the 100-meter dash and anchored the 4 x 100-meter relay victory. Valerie Brisco-Hooks set Olympic marks in the women's 400 meters and 200 meters and thus became the first sprinter to win both events in the same Games. Brisco-Hooks was also a member of the 4 x 400-meter gold-medal relay team. Sisters-in-law Florence Griffith Joyner and Jackie Joyner were both medalists: Griffith Joyner won a silver medal in the 200-meter race and Joyner took the silver in the heptathlon. Al Joyner, Florence's husband and Jackie's brother, won the triple jump competition. Edwin Moses won his 105th consecutive race and a gold medal in the 400-meter hurdles, and Roger Kingdom won the 110-meter hurdles. In both races Americans also finished second. Finally, Joan Benoit won the first women's Olympic marathon.

TV Coverage Criticized. The American Broadcasting Company (ABC) bought the television rights to the 1984 Summer Games for $225 million. After the Games ABC reported that over 180 million Americans watched at least some of its coverage. Many Americans were interested in the unfolding narratives the Games dramatized, while others reveled in the ubiquitous chants of "U.S.A! U.S.A!" every time an American athlete won an event or a medal. From the very beginning, though, non-American reporters, team officials, and some American commentators were critical of ABC's coverage of the Games, which they found too chauvinistic. Before the end of the first week of the Games IOC president Samaranch, and Ueberroth expressed concern over ABC's approach. Samaranch noted that the Olympic Charter mandated "unbiased" media coverage of the Games, and Ueberroth claimed he was troubled that ABC's broadcast was diluting the "international flavor" of the event. Later, others were more explicit. "What ABC sold was not so much athletic competition as American nationalism," argued historians Randy Roberts and James Olson. "No previous Olympics — including the 1936 Berlin Games and the

1980 Moscow Olympics — had seen such nationalistic displays." In its own defense a spokesperson for ABC explained that the network's U.S. coverage was not broadcast worldwide and that other nations could edit and provide commentary on the visual transmissions any way they pleased. "When it was all said and done, it wasn't ABC's opening-week jingoism that most indelibly marked the coverage of these Olympics after all," said William Taaffe of *Sports Illustrated*. Rather, he argued, it was that "ABC consistently captured emotions live on camera as sports television has never caught them before."

Medal Count. In large part due to the absence of the Soviets and the East Germans, the United States dominated the Summer Games by capturing 174 medals, including a record 83 gold. West Germany (59 total medals), Romania (53), and Canada (44) were the next highest medal-winning nations. Though most American sports fans were joyous at the end of the Games, the medal dominance of the home team was, in historian Allen Guttmann's words, "an embarrassment for anyone who recalled Pierre de Courbertin's dream of international harmony and good will." In the end, the XXIII Olympiad in Los Angeles will be remembered as an American spectacle, for better or worse.

Sources:

Mary T. Gaddie, ed., *Games of the XXIIIrd Olympiad Los Angeles 1984 Commemorative Book* (Salt Lake City: International Sport Publications, 1984);

Allen Guttmann, *The Olympics: A History of the Modern Games* (Urbana & Chicago: University of Illinois Press, 1992);

John Hoberman, *The Olympic Crisis: Sport, Politics and the Moral Order* (New York: Caratzas, 1986);

Randy Roberts and James Olson, *Winning Is the Only Thing: Sports in America since 1945* (Baltimore: Johns Hopkins University Press, 1989);

Martin Vinokur, *More Than A Game: Sports and Politics* (New York: Greenwood Press, 1988).

THE OLYMPICS: 1988

Calgary Winter Games. The XV Winter Olympics were held in Calgary, Alberta, from 13 to 28 February. They included 1,793 athletes from a record fifty-seven nations and marked the fourth time in twelve years that the Games were held at a North American venue. Free of political controversy, the Games suffered from high winds and unseasonably warm weather. Nonetheless, IOC president Juan Antonio Samaranch called the Calgary Games "the best ever." Many of the 180,000 visitors to Calgary no doubt agreed. The American team, however, did not fare well. The U.S. hockey team finished seventh and failed to make it to the medal round. Debi Thomas came up short in her attempt to supplant Katarina Witt of East Germany as the Olympic figure skating champion. After missing a series of jumps and slipping several times during her long program, Thomas ended up taking the bronze, behind Witt and silver medalist Elizabeth Manley of Canada. More disappointing,

speed skater Dan Jansen fell in both the 500-meter and 1,000-meter sprints. Jansen, who was world champion in the 500 meters, learned just prior to the first race that his sister had died of leukemia. Following Jansen's first fall, Thomas Boswell wrote that "millions of people all over America, perhaps hundreds of millions around the world, felt a pain of unaccountable sharpness." Although the U.S. team suffered its worst disappointments on the ice, they also won two gold medals on the surface. In the men's figure skating competition Brian Boitano of the United States outdueled Canadian Brian Orser for the Olympic championship. Said Boitano afterward, "I've never been so proud to be an American." Speed skater Bonnie Blair won the gold medal in the 500-meter race, setting new Olympic and world records. "The moment I crossed the finish line was the happiest of my life," said Blair. "And hearing the national anthem played when I got my medal was probably the second happiest." Blair later won a bronze in the 1,000 meters to become the only double medalist on the U.S. team. As was the case at the 1984 Winter Olympiad, the Soviet team won the most medals with 29 (11 gold, 9 silver, and 9 bronze), and East Germany finished second with 25 medals (9 gold, 10 silver, and 6 bronze). The United States finished a distant and disappointing ninth with 6 medals (2 gold, 1 silver, and 3 bronze).

A New Era. With the opening of the XXIV Summer Olympics in Seoul, South Korea, the era of the political boycott came to an end. The Seoul Summer Games drew entries from a record 160 countries, and 9,417 athletes participated in the competition. Only seven IOC-member nations failed to send teams, most notably North Korea and Cuba. The 1988 Summer Games were the first since 1964 in which no major political issues were disruptive. Still, there were political concerns. "The tension in South Korea was fierce," wrote William Johnson. "Student riots had engulfed sections of the city in the weeks leading up to the Olympics, and South Korea's hated Communist brothers to the north were suspected of preparing all sorts of bloody terrorist acts to disrupt the Games." Despite such concerns the games suffered no political disruptions. Adding to the success and high level of the competition was the fact that many of the issues regarding amateurism had finally been resolved. According to Randy Roberts and James Olson, "Amateurism had ceased to be a problem. IOC officials allowed 'professionals' to compete in some sports and 'amateurs' to become millionaires through endorsements and other payments." At the 1988 Summer Games virtually everyone was eligible. "Olympic athletes were free, at last, of the hypocritical need to pretend that they were really just ordinary blokes who trained a bit after work," wrote Allen Guttmann. Veteran sportswriter Frank Deford expressed the view of many respected Olympic observers: "The Games in Seoul showed that the Olympics have moved into a new era a few years before they move into their second century. For most of the Games' first 92 years the issues that commanded attention off the field were politics, money and amateurism (which is, of course, politics and money). The Seoul Games indicated that in large part these issues have been resolved, or perhaps simply dissolved, by compromise and evolution. In their stead is another major issue that will engage the Games at Barcelona in 1992 and beyond — drugs."

Drugs. Scandal shook the 1988 Summer Games during their first week. On 24 September Canadian sprinter Ben Johnson won the eagerly anticipated 100-meter dash and set a world record with a time of 9.79 seconds. Carl Lewis, the 1984 Olympic champion and Johnson's primary rival, finished second. Three days later, Johnson was stripped of his gold medal when it was discovered that he had tested positive for anabolic steroids. Johnson was not alone. Over the course of the 1988 Games nine other athletes, mostly weightlifters, were disqualified after tests revealed illegal drug use: four of them were deprived of their Olympic medals. At the previous quadrennial in Los Angeles, eleven athletes, two of whom who were medalists, were also disqualified for using performance-enhancing substances. Still, for many, Johnson tainted the 1988 Games. Although some South Korean Olympic officials resented the controversy, many Canadians were devastated by the news. According to William Johnson, "Some Canadians treated Johnson's bust as high treason, some as raw tragedy." One Toronto newspaper editorialized: "National celebration has become national wake. Parents struggle to answer questions from their teary-eyed children, even as our athletes in Seoul cover their uniforms in shame and sports fans contemplate the dreadful possibility that they may never see the fastest man in the history of the world run again, ever." Due to the revelations, second-place finisher Carl Lewis was awarded the gold medal in the 100 meters and became the first sprinter to defend his title. "I feel sad for Ben and for the Canadian public," said Lewis. "Ben is a great athlete, and my hope is that in the next two years [the length of his suspension] he can get himself together and return to our sport." Unlike most observers, former runner Mary Decker Slaney managed to put a positive spin on the misfortune: "I think it's wonderful. Not because of Ben, but because I want a clean sport. The fact that a thing this big can't be swept under the rug is a sign of hope."

A Family Affair. The most successful and flamboyant female athlete of the Olympics was Florence Griffith Joyner. Dubbed "Flo-Jo," Griffith Joyner won the gold medal in the 100 meters in 10.54 seconds. "Only a man could run faster than she can," said former gold medalist sprinter Evelyn Ashford. Griffith Joyner then won the 200 meters, setting a world record in the process. Next, Griffith Joyner ran the third leg of the gold medal–winning 4 x 100-meter relay team. Finally, she anchored silver medal–winning 4 x 400-meter relay squad. At the close of the competition Griffith Joyner said, "These days have been a dream come true." Though less flashy than

Carl Lewis (left) finishes second to Canada's Ben Johnson in the 100-meter dash in the 1988 Summer Olympics. Lewis was later awarded the gold medal when Johnson was disqualified following drug testing.

her sister-in-law, Jackie Joyner-Kersee performed no less spectacularly. She bested her own world record in the heptathlon and later won her second gold medal in the long jump competition. All told, Griffith Joyner and Joyner-Kersee accounted for five of the six gold medals won by the United States in the women's track-and-field competition. "By all odds Flo-Jo and her sister-in-law, Jackie Joyner-Kersee, should have come away from Seoul as prom queens to the world, like Mary Lou [Retton] and Olga [Korbut] before them," noted Frank Deford. "Instead, because of the ugly shadow of drugs, their achievements were held up to suspicion, and our affections wavered." Though speaking in her own defense, Joyner-Kersee could also have been referring to her sister-in-law when she said, "I worked hard to get here. I haven't used drugs. It's time and patience and work. So it's just not fair to point fingers, to blame us all."

Swimming and Diving. Although the U.S. swim team won only eight gold medals and eighteen medals overall, its poorest showing since the 1960 Games in Rome, there were several notable individual achievements at the Games. Preeminent among them was the remarkable performance turned in by Matt Biondi, who won five gold medals, one silver, and a bronze. Biondi's seven medals matched the number Mark Spitz amassed at the 1972 Games. But as his defenders were quick to note, Spitz won seven gold medals and set seven world records in Munich. "The Mark Spitz days are over," said Biondi during the competition. Nonetheless, Biondi set an individual world record (in the 50-meter freestyle), an Olympic record (100-meter freestyle), and was a member of three world-record-setting relay teams. Besides Biondi, Janet Evans was the only other American swimmer to win individual gold medals. The seventeen-year-old Evans won the 400-meter individual medley, the 800-meter freestyle, and the 400-meter freestyle; the latter two performances earned her Olympic and world records, respectively. Diver Greg Louganis provided compelling drama. A gold medalist in the springboard and platform competitions in 1984, Louganis was leading the springboard competition when he hit his head on the board during a dive and crashed into the water. Although he required four stitches, Louganis said, "I think my pride was hurt more than anything else." An hour later he recorded the highest score of the day. The next day he won the gold. In the platform competition Louganis proved to be just as resilient. On his final dive Louganis executed an extraordinarily difficult dive and edged out Xiong Ni of China 638.61–637.47. Louganis became the first man to win two diving gold medals in two Olympics in a row and solidified his claim to being the greatest diver in history.

Upsets. On 28 September the U.S. men's basketball team was upset by the Soviets, 82–76, in the semifinals of the medal round. It was just the second basketball game the U.S. had ever lost in the Olympics, the other being the controversial 1972 final against the Soviets. This time, however, after playing a nearly perfect game, the experienced Soviet team legitimately beat the American squad, which was coached by John Thompson of Georgetown University and composed of future NBA players such as David Robinson, Danny Manning, and Mitch Richmond. The Soviets went on to take the gold medal by beating Yugoslavia, while the Americans settled for the bronze after thrashing the Australian team. The disappointing third-place finish led many to second-guess Thompson's strategy, which emphasized defense, and the selection of his players. "If somebody's going to criticize us for striving for excellence and not being able to achieve it," said Thompson, "let it be." An upset of an entirely different sort occurred on 2 October. In the boxing finals of the light-middleweight division, Roy Jones of the United States was paired with Park Si-Hun of South Korea. After the three-round bout it was unanimously agreed upon by observers that Jones had dominated Park. Jones landed more punches and tagged his opponent with

---

FOREVER YOUNG

"If wrinkles must be written upon our brows, let them not be written upon the heart," implored President James A. Garfield, the twentieth president of the United States. "The spirit should never grow old." Over the course of the 1980s, hundreds of thousands of athletically inclined senior Americans took Garfield's exhortation seriously and participated in a variety of sports considerably more strenuous than shuffleboard. Many seniors played at levels which would have taxed people half or, in some cases, even a quarter their age. Inspiring examples of serious senior athletic accomplishment were legion. Seniors could be found on golf courses and tennis courts but also at organized senior Olympic-style competitions nationwide. By the end of the decade over one hundred thousand athletes from all over America competed in over fifty preliminary competitions in order to qualify for the second biennial U.S. National Senior Olympics in St. Louis. Though one octogenarian athlete explained that he was there to "kick some butt," ninety-one-year-old sprinter Guy Sibley probably more accurately reflected the ethos of the games: "Most people my age just retire and set, but that gets old. I like to keep going." The institutional origins of the Senior Olympics — later renamed the U.S. National Senior Sports Classic at the behest of the U.S. Olympic Committee — can be traced to the late 1960s when grass-roots organizations began sponsoring senior games. But the spiritual source of the games is ancient. One competitor, no doubt speaking for many, explained: "Senior athletics is one of the few areas where you look forward to your birthdays. Thus we remain forever young."

Sources: Leslie Lindeman, "Beating Time," *Modern Maturity* (June/July 1991): 26–35;

Demmie Stathoplos, "Silver Threads Among The Gold (Medals)," *Sports Illustrated* (3 July 1989): 38–40.

---

a standing eight-count. Inexplicably, the judges voted 3–2 for Park. The decision was a travesty. Jones was devastated and said he was considering quitting the sport. Before the medal ceremony Park said to Jones through an interpreter: "I am sorry. I lost the fight. I feel very bad." Recognizing the injustice of the decision, the International Amateur Boxing Federation (AIBA) awarded Jones the Val Baker Cup, which is bestowed upon the tournament's outstanding boxer. In addition to the Jones incident, the boxing tournament suffered other controversies, the most serious of which occurred when several South Korean boxing officials charged the ring and assaulted a referee after one of their fighters lost a decision.

Charges of bias and incompetence in the officiating at the boxing events resulted in two-year suspensions for several Korean officials, judges, and referees. The competition was so rife with controversy that at the conclusion of the Games IOC president Samaranch mused that boxing might be discontinued as an Olympic sport.

Other Stars. Carl Lewis did not match his 1984 performance in Seoul, but he came close. In addition to his successful defense of his Olympic championship in the 100-meter dash, he also defended his long jump title. Both of these accomplishments were unprecedented. In the 200 meters Lewis finished second to his training partner Joe DeLoach, who set a Olympic record by winning the race in 19.75 seconds. At the conclusion of the Seoul Games Kenny Moore wrote: "It's time to reexamine our perceptions of Lewis. When these bewildering Olympics recede enough to allow us a sense of proportion, we may not remember Johnson being found out as much as Lewis being revealed as the gentleman he has always been." As usual, Americans excelled in the track-and-field competitions. Steven Lewis, Butch Reynolds, and Danny Everett finished one, two, and three, respectively, in the 400 meters, and Lewis, Mike Powell, and Larry Myricks swept the long jump competition. The U.S. men's relay team set a world record in the 4 x 400 meters. The remarkable Edwin Moses competed in his third and final Olympics and took the bronze in the 400-meter hurdles. In other action Phoebe Mills was the only U.S. gymnast to win a medal, a bronze in the balance beam. The U.S. women's basketball team, led by Teresa Edwards and Katrina McClain, defeated Yugoslavia to win the gold. The U.S. men's volleyball team repeated as Olympic champions with a win over the Soviets in the finals, while the U.S. water polo team finished second to the Yugoslavs. The U.S. boxing team won eight medals, including three gold. Free-style wrestlers John Smith (137 pounds) and Kenneth Monday (163 pounds) won gold medals. The U.S. baseball team won the demonstration gold medal with a 5–3 victory over Japan in the finals. The winning pitcher was the one-handed Jim Abbott, who had won the 1987 Sullivan Award as the nation's best athlete.

Medal Count. The United States won 94 medals, including 36 gold, at the Summer Games to finish third in the final medal count behind the Soviet Union (55 gold and 132 overall) and East Germany (37 gold and 102 total). Though the U.S. team's performance was not as spectacular as it was in 1984, there was cause for enthusiasm. "Despite gloom-and-doom predictions and a stumbling start out of the blocks, the 1988 U.S. Olympic team came out of Seoul with pretty good results," affirmed E. M. Swift. "It was a team whose lack of depth was balanced out by the quality and maturity of its best athletes, and one that generally kept victory in perspective and showed grace in defeat. These last two qualities were reason enough to declare these Games a success for the Americans who participated."

Sources:

Lisa H. Albertson, ed., *Seoul Calgary 1988: The Official Publication of the U.S. Olympic Committee* (Sandy, Utah: Commemorative Publications, 1988);

Allen Guttmann, *The Olympics: A History of the Modern Games* (Urbana & Chicago: University of Illinois Press, 1992);

William Oscar Johnson, *The Olympics: A History of the Games* (Birmingham, Ala.: Oxmoor House, 1992);

David Wallechinsky, *The Complete Book of the Olympics* (Boston: Little, Brown, 1991).

PROFESSIONAL TENNIS

Epic. In the summer of 1980 a single afternoon marked the beginning of a break between one tennis era and another. At the Wimbledon men's singles finals on 5 July, Bjorn Borg of Sweden defeated American John McEnroe. However, Borg's amazing effort during the five-set battle was a closing argument. He played for only two more Grand Slam titles, retired from the tour in 1982, and never again beat McEnroe. McEnroe, on the other hand, had made an opening statement. The Swedish baseliner took the court ranked number one in the world, having won nine Grand Slam titles and four consecutive Wimbledon singles titles. McEnroe brought his crafty left-handed game, well suited to the quick grass-court surface, and a fiery, aggressive disposition. To the British and American media Borg was cool and collected, the possessor of a refined, graceful game, while McEnroe was brash, creative, and unpredictable. Three hours and fifty-three minutes, five sets and fifty-five games later, it was clear that each was perfect for the occasion. The match's momentum shifted repeatedly. McEnroe took the first set 6–1, then Borg managed two straight sets at 7–5 and 6–3. McEnroe won a remarkable fourth-set tiebreaker, 18–16. Finally, Borg won the fifth set, 8–6. It was the greatest Grand Slam match of the 1980s and one of the greatest matches of all time. "It will be almost impossible to deny Borg-McEnroe a place at or near the top of any championship match ever played," wrote journalist Neil Amdur. "The tiebreaker was the most exciting 22-minute patch of scintillating shotmaking that the sport will ever witness." Though several players, including McEnroe, Martina Navratilova, Stefan Edberg, and Steffi Graf, would reach greater heights in terms of individual excellence, this match's drama would never be approximated in the next ten years. After dropping the fourth set and struggling to begin the fifth, Borg ignored his doubts and delivered on an astonishing 25 of 31 first serves. "You have to forget and go forward," he said. McEnroe played valiantly, but he was in awe of the Swede's precision. Said McEnroe, "what he does out there, the way he plays, the way he thinks . . . I know I couldn't do it." As McEnroe walked off the court to the cheers of the British crowd, his task was only slightly different from Borg's: he would remember and move forward.

Genius. He was not much to look at. John McEnroe dominated tennis during the first half of the decade with a scrawny body and a predilection toward "bagging it" during practice. "I prefer the Häagen-Dazs diet," he explained to those who wondered aloud about his training methods. After dropping the 1980 Wimbledon title to Bjorn Borg, McEnroe bounced back with the second of three consecutive U.S. Open titles. Between 1980 and 1984 he won seven Grand Slam singles titles (including three at Wimbledon), nine doubles championships with Peter Fleming, and was ranked as the world's number one player at year's end four times. By the end of his career in the early 1990s, McEnroe had won seventy-seven tournament titles to finish third on the all-time list. As is often the case, however, numbers tell only part of the story. In a world of hard hitters, McEnroe played finesse tennis, reminiscent of Ken Rosewall's game and the graceful precision of Rod Laver. His command of the men's tour inspired critics and colleagues. Frank Deford argued that McEnroe was a magician. "McEnroe's 6–1, 6–1, 6–2 rout [in the 1984 Wimbledon finals] of Jimmy Connors was simply bedazzling, cadenza upon cadenza," he wrote. "No one who had the honor of watching McEnroe play tennis on Sunday could imagine anyone else ever having displayed so many gifts." McEnroe's game was instinctive, inventive, occasionally overpowering, but always and in all ways captivating for fans and frustrating for opponents.

Conduct. For all his brilliance John McEnroe also represented what many considered to be the worst of tennis in the 1980s. A trend toward crude and bombastic behavior, initiated by Ilie Nastase and Jimmy Connors in the 1970s, was continued by McEnroe and others in the 1980s. Sometimes unable to control himself during key matches, McEnroe berated officials for what he deemed to be missed calls. He loudly complained about fan noise and movement during matches. Such behavior was widely viewed as a blight upon the game and disenchanted some fans. In an era when the public was quick to criticize athletes, the men's tennis tour provided critics with a great deal of fodder. "You get into those obscenities," former tennis great Laver suggested, "you downgrade yourself, the game, the public, the way you're going to be remembered." The perception at the time was that professional tennis was played by "surly millionaires" and risked losing its audience. While there were those who insisted that McEnroesque outbursts were a necessary trade-off for the desired level of intensity and brilliance, the United States Tennis Association (USTA) was not convinced. In 1983 the USTA began leveling fines and enforcing policies of conduct on a more regular basis in hopes of recapturing the American tennis fan's imagination, attention, and respect.

Too Much Too Soon. In the wake of stories about injuries and burnout surrounding some of America's youngest and most promising players, the Women's International Professional Tennis Council established guidelines governing the participation of young players on the women's tour. The new rules enacted in Septem-

Bjorn Borg after defeating John McEnroe to win his fifth consecutive Wimbledon singles title

ber 1985 prohibited girls under the age of fourteen from playing in professional tournaments. The council's hope was to discourage the trend toward increased parental pressure and the stress of competition that had come to characterize youth tennis in the United States during the early 1980s. Hoping to produce the next great champion, parents had begun putting their children through intensive training sessions, enrolled them in tennis camps, and entered them in tournaments when they were seven and eight years old. "They [the parents] are out of control," said Florida tennis camp founder Nick Bollettieri, who was seen by some as emblematic of the teen tennis problem and by others as its solution. For years the junior circuit had been a pressure cooker. "I've never felt the pressure, not at Wimbledon, not at the U.S. Open, nowhere, that I went through in junior tennis," said Chris Evert. "Every match was life or death." In the mid 1980s this pressure, exacerbated by the desire to win increasingly large endorsement contracts and tournament purses, began to produce profoundly unhappy and ineffective young athletes, particularly on the women's tour. For some the council's recommendations were too late and too conservative. In 1984 and 1985 the tennis world watched two of its brightest lights flicker and fade under the weight of expectations and cutthroat competition.

Both Tracy Austin and Andrea Jaeger ascended to the top of the women's tour in the late 1970s and early 1980s, winning tournaments in their teens and playing for Grand Slam titles before they could vote. Austin was the world's number one women's player for a brief period in 1980, and Jaeger climbed to the number three spot, but they were unable to maintain such lofty heights. Many blamed their problems on the nature of the tour. Said Austin, later reflecting upon her struggle to overcome injury and adversity in the early part of the decade, "I had so much success at a young age, my life was almost perfect. I never faced adversity until I was 20. Then I didn't understand what was happening." For Jaeger the game was no longer fun, and she soon began playing with a lack of enthusiasm and commitment. "Four years after turning pro, she no longer seems to care whether she wins or loses," wrote Barry McDermott. After witnessing Austin's and Jeager's declines and then departures from the game, many on the tour reconsidered the emphasis on winning early.

Cash. The departure of several young players notwithstanding, tennis in the 1980s became increasingly "green." Little more than two decades into the open era, tournament prize money reached nearly unimaginable heights. By 1990 the men's tour held twenty tournaments with $1 million in prize money, and another fifty-plus tournaments averaged $500,000. The women's tour, while it enjoyed purses much larger than it had in the 1970s, did not fully participate in this boom. The women's tour had only one tournament with $1 million in prize money, and the ratio of purse totals between the Association of Tennis Professionals (men) and Virginia Slims Circuit (women) had increased from three to one in 1973 to ten to one at the close of the 1980s. The discrepancy meant that the women's tour, which had been roundly criticized for its seemingly incongruous relationship with Virginia Slims, was forced to extend its relationship with the cigarette manufacturer into the 1990s. As tournament sponsorship grew, individual players also profited. Thanks to advertising exposure and corporate links with television, tennis in the 1980s increasingly became a game of identifiable stars and heroes whose presence often ensured the financial success of an ATP tournament. As a result players began negotiating for appearance fees, even though such honoraria were not allowed. In the early part of the decade the Men's International Professional Tennis Council, eager to uphold the integrity of individual matches and tournaments, brought the hammer down. It fell hardest on Guillermo Vilas in 1983. Found guilty of accepting a payment of between $40,000 and $60,000, Vilas was fined $20,000 by the council and suspended from the tour for one year. His career was effectively over. While the measure served as a wake-up call for those eager to engage in illicit financial negotiations, it did little to assuage the concerns of players who wanted a piece of the tour's burgeoning pie. In an effort to appease the tour's elite players — at the expense of its lesser-known, unseeded participants — the council reversed its earlier position regarding incentives by announcing that beginning in 1990 contracts would be signed with players participating in Grand Prix tournaments based on their point standings and ATP computer rankings. The gap between tennis haves and have-nots grew wider.

Visibility. Having retired from playing early in the decade, Arthur Ashe spent much of the 1980s coaching the U.S. Davis Cup team. Off the court he became perhaps the game's most eloquent and powerful ambassador by the time of his death in 1993. In the latter part of the decade, as fans watched one impressive young foreign player after another make their way toward Grand Slam championships, American tennis officials worried about where they would find the next great American champion. Although he was not caught up in this nationalistic impulse, Ashe was concerned with "making tennis a more visible part of America's sports culture" because he believed it was a marvelous game that deserved more attention. More important, Ashe thought that people from every sector of society deserved the right to pursue the game, both recreationally and competitively. He believed that professionals had been coming from too narrow a sector of society. "They're from upper-middle-class homes," Ashe explained. "They belong to private clubs. They're overwhelmingly white and play most of their serious tennis outside the public school system." In an attempt to "democratize" the game Ashe turned to the private sector to secure funds for more college tennis scholarships, which he hoped would attract minority athletes to the sport. In addition to his efforts to increase opportunities for students, Ashe reached out to inner-city youth. In 1988 he and Nick Bollettieri established the Ashe-Bollettieri Cities program, which was designed to use tennis as "a way to gain and hold the attention of young people in the inner cities and poor environments." Ashe hoped to use the sport to teach children "about matters more important than tennis." He later changed the name of the organization to Safe Passage but continued his efforts to "help poor young people," receiving the support of several players from the pro tour who participated in fund-raising exhibitions.

Power. The way tennis was played on the professional level changed in the 1980s. Thanks to the development and introduction of stronger composite and graphite rackets, tennis became a power game. In the latter half of the decade several players had fashioned their games to fit the new technology and were claiming titles and high rankings. Ivan Lendl's cannon serve and devastating forehand, Pat Cash's ace-and-volley runs at Wimbledon, and Kevin Curran's and Boris Becker's tremendous power made for short points and quick matches. Many were impressed by the new punch the game offered and were interested in what it meant for the balance of power on the tour. "They're trying to copy Boris and me, and they have no choice," Lendl said. "If they don't they're going to go down the drain. Even though McEnroe has so much touch and talent, guys are overpowering him now." Meanwhile, others were concerned by the uniformity they saw in tennis. While Lendl, the world's number one ranked male player from 1985 to 1987, and Becker, the men's Wimbledon champion in 1985, 1986, and 1989, played tennis at a high level and were excellent shot makers, others were winning without as much skill. Their strategy was to pound their opponents into the court. "There's no doubt that today's players play differently," said Owen Davidson, a former Australian Davis Cup team member. "The ones that hit hard and do it well, do it unbelievably well . . . but if you get down slightly below Lendl's level, there are a lot of no-brainers out there." By the close of the 1980s tennis afficionados began calling for change. Commentator Bud Collins, a fan of McEnroe's clever style and of stalwarts like Chris Evert and Jimmy Connors, called for the return of wood rackets, particularly on the men's tour. His reasoning was simple: tennis had become boring and was hurting at the turnstiles and on television. According to Collins, "games would look better to the paying customer and televiewer if tempered with timber." His calls were largely ignored, however, and the boom-or-bust game continued to thrive well into the 1990s.

Sources:

Arthur Ashe and Arnold Rampersad, *Days of Grace* (New York: Knopf, 1993);

Bud Collins, *My Life With the Pros* (New York: Dutton, 1989);

John Feinstein, *Hard Court: Real Life on the Professional Tennis Tours* (New York: Villard Books, 1991);

Michael Mewshaw, *Ladies of the Court* (New York: Crown, 1993);

Martina Navratilova with George Vecsey, *Martina* (New York: Knopf, 1985).

RACING

Revving Up. Auto racing of nearly every kind — Indy, stock car, drag, formula one, and more — enjoyed increased popularity as the 1980s sped to a close. The sport's steadily rising popularity could be indexed by the increase in the number of spectators attending races. Though the Indianapolis 500 routinely drew at least 300,000 fans over the course of the decade, attendance at other Indy car races rose from 654,000 in 1979 to almost 2.5 million in 1988. As for the National Association for Stock Car Auto Racing (NASCAR), prior to the 1980s it was seen primarily as a southern sport. By the end of the decade, however, the sport's venues extended as far north as New York, Connecticut, New Hampshire, and Michigan, and over 3 million people annually attended NASCAR Winston Cup races. In fact, a survey conducted by Goodyear in 1990 indicated that over 25 percent of Americans considered themselves auto racing fans, including 14 million women. All of which led one racing expert to quip that "NASCAR probably is Dixie's rebuttal to the Civil War." Moreover, the sport's increased popularity could also be measured by the increase

Al Unser Sr. after his record-tying fourth victory in the Indianapolis 500, in May 1987

in the number of people watching races on network and cable television, the fact that more and more races were held, and the myriad of corporate sponsors pumping money into the sport. Although many profited from the sport's ascendance, drivers and their crews were the most obvious beneficiaries. Over the course of the 1980s the aggregate winners' purse on the NASCAR circuit grew from $6 million to $21 million. One way of accounting for the sport's increased popular and commercial success is that more people began to recognize that, as writer Peter Golenbock put it, every "race brings excitement, drama, danger, and heartbreak, as well as an exhilaration that goes with watching sleek, colorful cars rocket at top speeds for hundreds of miles, sometimes only inches apart." Also, as author J. M. Fenster explained, auto racing "differs from other American sports in that practically every spectator partakes in its form every day. Driving a passenger car is monumentally different from racing a competition car, obviously — but not obviously to the imagination. Racing in this country has existed not to make heroes out of drivers but to make self-imagined heroes out of every fan." Even so, race car drivers have always attracted devoted fans and have been the sport's primary attraction. As Dick Berggren of *Stock Car Racing Magazine* put it, "Drivers do amazing things with their cars. There's also tremendous competition between old veterans and young guns, and there are heroes and villains at every race."

Long Live the King. According to writer Louis Franck, the reigning princes of auto racing in the 1980s were Indy drivers Danny Sullivan and Rick Mears and NASCAR drivers Dale Earnhardt, Bill Elliott, Darrell Waltrip, and Rusty Wallace. But Richard Petty remained the king of the road, at least in terms of popularity and historical significance. A living legend, Petty has been described as "the Babe Ruth of stock car racing," in part because he was the sport's most dominant performer and in part because he paved the way for stock car racing's later popular and financial success. Universally acknowledged as NASCAR's first and biggest megastar, Petty was probably at the zenith of his career as the 1980s began. He had won seven NASCAR national championships and six Daytona 500s. Petty, however, was not content to rest on his laurels. In 1981, at the age of forty-four, he won his seventh and final Daytona 500. Three years later on the Fourth of July, Petty won his two hundredth race, the Firecracker 500. Though he failed to take another checkered flag, he continued to race until his retirement in 1992 and drew a huge following of fans wherever he raced. Petty's two hundred NASCAR victories were nearly twice as many as his closest competitor. He also held a host of other records, including most starts, most victories in a single season, and most consecutive victories. By any standard Petty's was a bountiful reign, for over the course of his thirty-five-year career he earned almost $7,500,000 in winnings. "The best race drivers have a way of transforming their cars into extensions of themselves, fusing man and machine into a single organism, pistons and heart beating as one at 15,000 revolutions per minute," wrote Bruce Newman of *Sports Illustrated,* reflecting on Petty's amazing career. "No driver ever got under the sheet-metal skin of a stock car better than Richard Petty, who revolutionized his sport, simonized his opposition and was canonized in his native South."

.16 of a Second. From start to finish the 1982 Indy 500 proved to be one of auto racing's most dramatic contests. Before the race officially began, as the field came out of the fourth turn toward the green flag for the start, an unfortunate series of events led to an accident that disabled four cars, one of which was driven by former Indy winner Mario Andretti. The race's conclusion, however, more than made up for the day's inauspicious start. With thirteen laps remaining, hard-luck underdog Gordon Johncock held a 12-second lead over the heavily favored former Indy winner Rick Mears, whose 207-MPH qualifying speed in the time trials set an Indy record. Steadily gaining on Johncock, Mears closed the lead to 3 seconds with four laps remaining. With two laps to go Johncock led Mears by a little less than a second. "Coming off the final turn, Mears chased Johncock down the straight toward the checkered flag," wrote Sam Moses of *Sports Illustrated.* "Mears swung out in a final, desperate attempt to slingshot past, but Johncock crossed the finish line slightly more than a car length ahead. As measured by the clock his margin was .16 of a second. It was the closest finish, and perhaps the most exciting, in the 66-year history of the 500." After the race the forty-five-year-old Johncock said, "There will never be another thrill like this." Soon thereafter Johncock had to speed home to see his ailing mother, who died hours later, never having learned of her son's victory. As for the second-place finisher, after losing by the narrowest margin in the race's history, Mears went on to win at the Brickyard (so-called because 3.2 million ten-pound bricks were used to pave the speedway) in 1984, 1988, and 1991 to join A. J. Foyt and Al Unser Sr. as the race's only four-time winners.

Spin and Win. Three years after Johncock's heroics Danny Sullivan and Mario Andretti raced wheel-to-wheel in another memorable duel at the 500 in Indianapolis. In the first turn of the 120th lap Sullivan attempted to pass the favored Andretti as the two were traveling approximately 200 MPH. Suddenly, Sullivan's car spun out of control to the right, narrowly missing Andretti, who skillfully drove to the left. Incredibly, after a 360-degree pirouette, Sullivan managed to control his car and continued to chase Andretti. "I thought that was all she wrote," said Sullivan. "But when the smoke cleared, I was headed in the right direction. I stuck it down in gear and took off." Twenty laps later, with sixty to go, Sullivan finally passed Andretti for good. At the finish line it was Sullivan by a mere 2.47 seconds. "When you start getting conservative, that's when you start getting into trouble," explained Sullivan after his first Indy 500 victory. Andretti finished second. "Second means nothing, especially here," said a disappointed Andretti. "When you get to a certain stage in your career, winning seems to be the only thing."

NASCAR. Indy drivers are often considered the original blue bloods of American auto racing, but during the 1980s stock car racers steadily gained on their Indy counterparts in popularity, purse winnings, and media exposure. There is little doubt that NASCAR was largely responsible for making auto racing one of the top spectator and fastest-growing sports in America during the decade. "Although there is not much that is actually 'stock' in a modern stock car," wrote J. M. Fenster, "all the entries are nominally based upon GM, Chrysler, or Ford cars." This points to a significant part of the sport's appeal: many fans seem to be able to identify with the cars. "I don't come to see any bang-up crashes," said one stock car racing enthusiast. "I like the close racing and the battle of those guys trying to get around each other at 180 mph. In baseball and football it's two teams against each other, but out here it's one driver against 40 others. And the cars look just like the ones people come to the track in." Another factor which contributed to NASCAR's popularity was that fans had some access to their racing heroes. "Going to a race is like going to a carnival," said one fan. "You can get passes to pit row before the start and meet the drivers and the crews. Try getting them to let you into the locker room at a football game." For NASCAR drivers and fans alike, the twisting two-and-a-half-mile high-banked course at the Daytona International Speedway is the zenith of stock car racing. "Daytona is stop number one on the NASCAR tour, the World Series and Super Bowl of stock car racing on opening day," wrote Peter Golenbock in *American Zoom*. "For race fans, it is Christmas and New Year's Day in February." The first Daytona 500 of the 1980s began auspiciously enough; Buddy Baker ran the fastest race ever: 177.6 MPH. Two-thirds of the decade's remaining races, however, would be won by either Bobby Allison, Bill Elliott, or Cale Yarborough — each a two-time winner. Yarborough, the first driver ever to qualify for the 500 at 200 MPH, is the man who best described the dangerous nature of his profession. "Driving a race car," he quipped, "is like dancing with a chain saw." At Daytona and all over the country it was an immensely popular dance.

Dragsters. Though less frequently covered by the media than Indy and stock car racing, drag racing and other forms of hot rodding became increasingly popular, annually drawing millions of people to thousands of races and auto shows. For the greater part of the decade the National Hot Rod Association (NHRA) circuit was dominated by dragsters such as Don "Big Daddy" Garlits, Shirley Muldowney, Darrell Gwynn, Joe Amato, and Gene Snow. Garlits, who in 1975 became the first driver to clock 250 MPH in an NHRA contest, won fifteen major races in the 1980s, and Muldowney, Gwynn, Amato, and Snow all earned membership in the exclusive "4-Second Club" — that is, they had completed a quarter-mile race in under five seconds. The single most notable achievement in the sport occurred in Bayston,

Texas, on 9 October 1988, when Eddie Hill set a world record by completing a quarter-mile race in a remarkable 4.936 seconds. Hill's accomplishment failed to garner significant media attention, because drag racing "is not an enthusiasm everybody can appreciate, and in the grand scheme of things it would not make much difference if nobody had ever dreamed the dreams of hot rodders," argued racing historian Robert Post. "But we need to remember that their dreams are, after all, not much different from the dreams of enthusiasts for superconducting supercolliders and manned space stations." For Post and many others there is something akin to virtue in the never-ending quest for death-defying speed for its own sake.

Death and Danger, Speed, and Safety. Motor racing of all sorts has endured a long tradition of criticism. In the early days of auto racing, notes Fenster, "outside observers grew outraged at the death and violence common to the sport. It was called commercial murder, spectacle on a par with Roman gladiator fighting and feeding of Christians to hungry lions." At different times in the 1980s — usually immediately after a racing-related fatality — the chorus of critics who assailed the sport was equally vociferous. In the spring of 1982, for instance, after Indy drivers Gordon Smiley and Gilles Villeneuve were killed within a week of each other, the sport experienced an avalanche of attacks. "Who has died is always news," wrote Tom Callahan in *Time* magazine, "but death in auto racing never is: it is an expected part of the game." Veteran sportswriter Frank Deford added that "there are some psycho-social critics who say that people come to Indy just to see drivers get killed." There is little question that auto racing is — and always will be — extraordinarily dangerous; that is, no doubt, a large part of its appeal as a spectator sport. "Not even an observer feels entirely safe at the Speedway," wrote cultural critic Paul Fussell, "and indeed the spectators are in literal danger all the time — from hurtling machines, tires, and fragments, and from the deadly methanol fuel, which burns with a scarcely visible flame, consuming ears and fingers before on-lookers are even aware that the victim's on fire." Partially in response to these and other like-minded observations, racing administrators worked hard on ways to improve the sport's safety record, as well as its image. Despite advances in technology (such as lighter, stronger materials and state-of-the-art aerodynamic engineering) that led to faster cars, their efforts were successful; even as speeds increased, fatalities decreased. This was accomplished in various ways: significantly improved racetrack design, protective equipment (such as better helmets and fire-retardant suits), and various mechanical and fuel-consumption restrictions. Reflecting on the state of racing at the end of the 1980s, Louis Franck observed that "of all the trends observed in the last ten years, perhaps the most gratifying is the most contradictory, at least on the surface — faster racing and more safety." It was a trend that would continue into the 1990s.

Sources:

J. M. Fenster, "Indy," *American Heritage* (May–June 1992): 66–81;

Peter Golenbock, *American Zoom: Stock Car Racing — From the Dirt Tracks to Daytona* (New York: Macmillan, 1993);

Robert Post, *High Performance: The Culture and Technology of Drag Racing, 1950–1990* (Baltimore: Johns Hopkins University Press, 1994);

Michael Silver, "A Day at the Races," *Sports Illustrated* (24 July 1995): 18–24;

Rich Taylor, *Indy: Seventy-Five Years of Racing's Greatest Spectacle* (New York: St. Martin's Press, 1991).

HEADLINE MAKERS

LARRY BIRD

1957-

EARVIN "MAGIC" JOHNSON

1958-

HEART AND SOUL OF THE NBA

The Two. On 26 March 1979 Earvin "Magic" Johnson, a brash and brilliant sophomore from Michigan State, and Larry Bird, the sharpshooting senior leader of Indiana State, held the first of many summit meetings. On that night Johnson's Spartans defeated Bird's Sycamores in front of the largest television audience ever to watch an NCAA title game. It was the beginning of a relationship between the two players which was fiercely competitive, consistently respectful, and always breathtakingly intense. The dramatic encounters between Bird and Johnson would characterize professional basketball at its best for much of the next decade and would permanently link the two in the annals of the game. As the scene changed from college to the professional stage — Johnson performed before the footlights in Los Angeles while Bird roamed the parquet floor of Boston — the association which began at the close of the 1970s was underscored and expanded by a series of memorable mid

and postseason head-to-head contests in the 1980s. Their place in history was ensured by a string of individual awards and organizational victories for both players: each was a three-time MVP and led his team to at least three world titles in the 1980s (Johnson's Lakers won five). Their position at the head of the NBA's class was accomplished by way of competition and respect. "Larry and I always had each other," Johnson once explained. "Athletes live to get so up that they can't sleep for two or three days before competition. Nobody did that to me except Larry Bird." Each man directed the return of his respective franchise to a position among the league's elite. The strength of the partnership lay in the watchful eye each player kept on the other. For Bird each morning of an NBA season began by looking "at the box scores to see what Magic did." Likewise, Johnson would "check out Larry's line first thing." Each was so intent upon tracking and surpassing the feats of the other and so dogged in his pursuit of a championship that the league and its fans were inevitably drawn to watch and admire them at every opportunity. A Bird versus Magic game became an event, a happening. Jack McCallum suggested that "you were either a Magic guy or a Larry guy." In the public imagination, not to mention the world of television programming and advertising revenue, they became bigger than the game itself. Johnson explained, "when the new schedule came out each year I'd grab it and circle the Boston games. To me it was The Two and the other 80." In addition to their two regular-season meetings each year, they would meet in the league finals three times in the middle of the decade and play opposite each other in a total of thirty-seven games. Johnson's Lakers won twenty-two; Bird's Celtics won fifteen. The NBA won them all. For most observers of the game the 1980s became the hundred or so men who played professional basketball and "The Two" who played it better than anyone else. They became the standard for each other and for those who would follow in their footsteps.

Savior. In the midst of drawn-out contract negotiations between the Celtics and Larry Bird during the summer of 1979, club president Red Auerbach suggested to local reporters that "Larry Bird can help, but he's not a franchise player." As he prepared for his rookie season and dealt with a glaring media spotlight and the mounting expectations of frustrated Boston fans, Bird issued a similar warning: "very few people can turn a team around by themselves, and I'm not one of them." While one man was interested in lowering the cost of a highly touted rookie and the other was hoping to ease the pressure which affected his every move, both men were conservative in their estimation of Bird's impact upon the Celtic organization. The Celtics of 1978–1979 managed only 29 wins during the regular season, their worst record since 1950 and a far cry from the consistent dominance of the teams which had won twelve titles between 1957 and 1974. The team won the league title in 1976 but had fallen off dramatically by the time of Bird's arrival. Despite Auerbach's contract-time assertions to the contrary, the six-foot nine-inch forward from French Lick, Indiana, was expected to have a major impact on the team's fortunes. Bird quickly recognized the significance of being a Celtic: "when I got there and saw all those championship banners . . . then [I realized] that the Boston Celtics is the greatest franchise that has ever been put together." At that point he took it upon himself to uphold their great tradition. On his way to Rookie of the Year honors, Bird combined with veterans Cedric Maxwell and Nate "Tiny" Archibald to lead the team to a 61–21 record in 1980. The 32-game swing is still the greatest single-season improvement in league history. Bird managed to restore Celtic pride and earn the support of Boston's loyal fans by way of his hard work, precision passing, unselfish play, and clutch shooting. Though a quiet, relatively unsophisticated figure, Bird was appealing because of his style and dedication. Jack McCallum suggested that he was a crowd favorite "mostly because of the effort he expended," effort that was essential to the Celtics' return to the championship series.

Charisma. Just as Larry Bird's game was characterized by his tireless dedication, Earvin Johnson's was marked by his equally relentless passion for the game. The standard interpretation was that the two men were opposites: one white and the other black, one from a small school and the other from a collegiate powerhouse, one on the East Coast and the other on the West, one a forward and the other a guard, one steadily intelligent and the other breathtakingly flashy. These apparent differences dissolve in the light of the single factor that united them: each man won NBA championships consistently. While Bird directed the resurgence of the Celtics, Johnson set about the work of invigorating a veteran Los Angeles Lakers team for a run at the 1980 title. As a rookie Johnson came to an experienced team fashioned around center Kareem Abdul-Jabbar, but they were struggling to put together a

championship season. The victim of injury and contract disputes as well as a largely apathetic public, the Lakers were in need of a boost. Enter Earvin "Magic" Johnson. Laker forward Jamaal Wilkes explained Johnson's impact in terms of his boundless energy and love for the game: "his enthusiasm was something out of this world, something I had never seen prior to him and . . . haven't seen since. It just kind of gave everyone a shot in the arm." The charismatic Johnson brought an unprecedented range of skills to the game, playing the point position at six feet nine inches and making seemingly impossible passes appear mundane. Along with Norm Nixon, he provided the Lakers with the best backcourt in the league and opened up the middle for a rejuvenated Abdul-Jabbar. Benefiting from this new chemistry, Los Angeles finished the regular season with a 60–22 record. If the beginning of Bird's NBA reign was revealed in the Celtics' remarkable turnaround in the standings, Johnson's long-range impact was foreshadowed in a single game. Throughout the playoffs he put up impressive individual numbers while facilitating Jabbar's resurgent game as the Lakers marched to a 3–2 lead over the Philadelphia 76ers in the finals. Abdul-Jabbar was injured in game five and was forced to watch game six from his home in Los Angeles. What he saw was Johnson's coming-out party. Playing all five positions at one time or another, the Laker rookie dazzled the crowd and confounded the Sixers with a transcendent performance. After the Lakers' victory Johnson said, "once we got the ball, we were gone. We beat Philadelphia in the transition game because they couldn't keep up." He finished with 42 points, 15 rebounds, 7 assists, 3 steals, and a block and left players everywhere wondering if they could keep up.

About Winning. Although Larry Bird's Celtics would win the NBA title in 1981 and Magic Johnson's Lakers in 1982, due to injuries and the ascendance of 76ers, led by Moses Malone and Julius Erving, the two did not meet in the finals until 1984. Roland Lazenby characterized that first series as the collision of forces of pride and ego between the two established superstars and suggested that the seven-game final was "the juice that grew the NBA." The Celtics claimed the title with a 111–102 victory in the seventh game. The series was marked by several dramatic turns; it is largely remembered as a series that the Lakers lost as much as one which the Celtics won. Bird's Celtics were not thought to be as talented as Johnson's Lakers, but they were tougher and more confident. Lazenby noted, "the Celtics had challenged them with psychological warfare and won." A new, more resilient brand of Laker basketball emerged in the next year's finals. This time Magic and Kareem were able to solve the Celtic puzzle and capture the championship on Boston's parquet floor. Johnson's "triple double" of 14 points, 10 rebounds, and 14 assists ended a long drought for the Lakers in head-to-head competition with the Celtics. The Celtics and Bird returned to reclaim the

NBA championship trophy with a six-game victory over the Houston Rockets in 1986, a series which saw Bird team up with former UCLA star Bill Walton. In 1987 both Bird and Johnson reestablished their grip upon the basketball world by staging one last championship battle, won by the Lakers in six games. Johnson's "junior sky hook" over Kevin McHale and Robert Parrish in the final seconds of game four prompted Bird to exude, "Magic plays basketball the way you *should* play the game." Though they would never meet in the finals again, Johnson and Bird left an indelible mark upon the game, providing the league and its fans with a dramatic centerpiece for the decade. They established themselves as the heart and soul of the league by never losing sight of its ultimate prize. As Johnson explained, "we weren't about stats, we were about winning."

Sources:

Larry Bird with Bob Ryan, *Drive: The Story of My Life* (New York: Doubleday, 1989);

Earvin Johnson Jr. and Roy S. Johnson, *Magic's Touch* (New York: Addison-Wesley, 1989);

Roland Lazenby, *The Lakers: A Basketball Journey* (New York: St. Martin's Press, 1993);

Jack McCallum, "Leaving a Huge Void," *Sports Illustrated,* 76 (23 March 1992): 20–25;

Bob Ryan, "The Two and Only," *Sports Illustrated,* 77 (14 December 1992): 44–55.

WAYNE GRETZKY

1961-

HOCKEY SUPERSTAR

The Great One. No individual dominated his or her sport in the 1980s the way Wayne Gretzky dominated professional hockey. Regardless of how greatness is measured, whether in terms of individual accomplishments such as statistics and awards, team championships, or peer respect, Gretzky distanced himself from virtually everyone over the course of the decade. According to Gretzky, "the best players in hockey are the ones who make their teammates look good, the ones who make their teams win." By that standard, too, Gretzky was in extraordinarily select company, including such players as Phil Esposito, Bobby Hull, Bobby Orr, and Gordie Howe. Even such players as these are unstinting in their praise of the "Great One." "No one I have ever seen has been able to think like Wayne Gretzky can on ice. You can hone that talent by studying the game, but believe me, it comes from God," testified Esposito. "No one can do the things he does out there — the back passes, toying with people with the puck right in front of them, and they can't get it from him. It's miraculous," marveled Hull. "There are great players, but no one can ever compare" to Gretzky, asserted Orr. "If you want to tell me he's the greatest player of all time, I have no argument at all," conceded Howe.

Accomplishments. Of course, numbers also tell a good deal of the Gretzky story. "I have to admit," said Gretzky, "my childhood was a little different from most. I could skate at two. I was nationally known at six. I was signing autographs at ten. I had a magazine article written about me at eleven and a thirty-minute national television show done on me at fifteen." He turned professional at seventeen. In his nine seasons with the Edmonton Oilers, from 1980 to 1988, Gretzky scored 583 goals and handed out 1,086 assists. For six of those years he *averaged* 73 goals and 130 assists a season, a remarkable achievement considering that no one else in the history of the NHL had managed to score 200 points in a season. He won eight MVP awards and led the Oilers to four Stanley Cup championships. Traded to the Los Angeles Kings before the 1988–1989 season, Gretzky continued his excellence. In his first year with the Kings he scored 54 goals, passed for 114 assists, and won the league's MVP award. The next season, on 15 October 1989, he broke Howe's all-time scoring record of 1,850 points. All this before the age of thirty. Perhaps just as important, wrote E. M. Swift, "Gretzky's style of play was changing hockey's image as a goon sport as night after night he put on a show of offensive creativity worthy of the highlight tapes."

Legend. A man of seemingly ordinary physical gifts, of average size and never the fastest or strongest player on his NHL teams, Gretzky was a hockey legend nonetheless. Noted for his modesty and teamwork, his consistency and endurance, his leadership and sportsmanship, Gretzky has been called by many the greatest athlete of the twentieth century. Such a claim is far from hyperbolic. One national newspaper poll rated him the fourth greatest athlete of this century, behind only Muhammad Ali, Babe Ruth, and Jim Thorpe. In 1985, years after his greatness had bloomed but years before it would begin to fade, Tom Callahan wrote that as "long as men beat sticks against the ice, not to mention each other, Gretzky will be remembered." He will be remembered for his statistical achievements and the way his name reappears time and time again in the hockey record book and on NHL trophies; for his ability to make clever passes and shots appear commonplace by their sheer frequency; for his ability to dominate the flow and pace of a game without monopolizing the puck; his grace, quiet determination, and competitive drive. But to truly understand why he was the best hockey player ever it has been suggested that one will have had to see him play.

Sources:

Tom Callahan, "Masters of Their Own Game," *Time,* 125 (18 March 1985): 52–60;

Wayne Gretzky, *Gretzky: An Autobiography* (New York: HarperCollins, 1990);

Allan Safarik & Dolores Reimer, *Quotations On The Great One: The Little Book of Wayne Gretzky* (Vancouver: Arsenal Pulp Press, 1992);

E. M. Swift, "Wayne Gretzky," *Sports Illustrated*, 81 (19 September 1994): 76–77.

MICHAEL JORDAN

1963-

BASKETBALL LEGEND

Air Jordan. Michael Jordan's spectacular style of play set the standard for athletic creativity and earned him a special place in basketball history. Jordan had the ability to make the apparently impossible routine and to remain airborne as long as necessary to score a graceful or explosive basket. Even as a rookie with the Chicago Bulls in 1984, Jordan was compared to such celebrated and legendary basketball acrobats as Elgin Baylor, Connie Hawkins, David Thompson, and Julius Erving. The comparisons proved prophetic, for Jordan dominated professional basketball — offensively, defensively, and aesthetically — during the latter part of the 1980s and into the 1990s. With the guidance of agent David Falk of ProServe, the affable Jordan also made his mark in the advertising world. He served as a spokesperson for Coca-Cola, McDonald's, Wheaties, and Gatorade. Because Jordan was so enthusiastically embraced as an athlete-endorser, Steve Wulf quipped, "Sometimes with Jordan, you don't know where the reality ends and the commercial begins." Nowhere was this blurring more evident than in Jordan's association with the Nike athletic shoe company. By selling Jordan's spectacular athleticism and approachable personality, Nike successfully marketed both an air-sole sneaker and the Air Jordan persona, creating an American icon. For many he was viewed as someone who "transcended race." According to Jack McCallum, Jordan "crossed all lines — gender, race, age — as smoothly as he crossed over his dribble. He had no hidden agenda, no dark side, and so his appeal was uncomplicated and thoroughly wonderful." In the process of arguing that Jordan had become "our new DiMaggio," novelist John Edgar Wideman wrote, "Perhaps MJ is proof there are no rules about race, no limits to what a black man can accomplish in our society." Sociologist John Hoberman saw this phenomenon more critically and suggested that Jordan's "cross-over" appeal represented "virtual" integration. While race relations during the 1980s proved to be volatile, Jordan was among only a handful of African American men and women wholeheartedly embraced by white America.

Cut from the Team. The genesis of Michael Jordan's carefully crafted, highly marketable image begins with an often-told tale. As a sophomore Jordan was cut from his high-school varsity basketball team. But by honing his skills all summer Jordan turned that setback to his advantage and emerged as a great player the following season.

Said Jordan, "When a lot of people figured I couldn't do something, that gave me the challenge to do it." Jordan's commitment to hard work and his competitive desire attracted the attention of University of North Carolina basketball coach Dean Smith. Though Jordan was not initially heavily recruited, Smith offered him a basketball scholarship. Smith's faith would be rewarded a year later when Jordan made the winning jump shot during the final seconds of the 1982 NCAA national championship game. As a collegian Jordan was a two-time all-American and was twice named *The Sporting News* National Player of the Year, before forsaking his final year of eligibility to play professionally. The summer before his rookie season Jordan was the leading scorer on the 1984 Olympic gold medal–winning U.S. basketball team. Jordan's professional accomplishments were even more impressive. Selected number three in the NBA college draft behind Hakeem Olajuwon (Houston) and Sam Bowie (Portland), Jordan finished his first season by being named the NBA's Rookie of the Year. Jordan won the NBA's regular season MVP award three times, was on the All-Star team nine times, won seven consecutive scoring titles, and was named Defensive Player of the Year in 1988. Prior to the 1986–1987 season, when Jordan scored 3,041 points, Wilt Chamberlain was the only other player in NBA history to score 3,000 points in a season. Jordan scored his 10,000th career point in his 303rd game, reaching that mark faster than any other player except Chamberlain. Jordan averaged 32.3 points per game during the first nine years of his career. After Jordan scored an NBA playoff-record 63 points in a losing cause against the Boston Celtics in 1986, fellow superstar Larry Bird remarked that "he's God disguised as Michael Jordan."

Triumph and Tragedy. Despite his achievements and appeal, Jordan received his share of criticism as well, including charges of individual basketball selfishness. According to some basketball afficionados, the measure of greatness in sport is winning; but for all of Jordan's skills he had trouble leading his team to an NBA championship. Jordan silenced his critics in 1991, leading the once-hapless Chicago Bulls to the NBA title. After this triumph the world gained a glimpse of his humanity: in the locker room after the game Jordan clutched the championship trophy and cried unashamedly and uncontrollably. Despite his squeaky-clean image Jordan could not escape controversy and came under media fire for his expensive gambling habit. Said Jordan, "I guess people just got tired of seeing me succeed." Tragedy also struck on 3 August 1993, when the body of Jordan's father, James, was pulled from a South Carolina creek. Reportedly despondent over his father's murder and media allegations that his own high-stakes gambling activities might have had something to do with the tragedy, Jordan stunned the athletic world on 6 October 1993 by announcing his retirement from professional basketball. Having led the Chicago Bulls to three consecutive NBA championships, Jordan was then at the peak of his athletic career. He also left the game an extraordinarily wealthy man. Even with his retirement from basketball, it was estimated that Jordan's 1993 "Madison Avenue" income topped all other athletes at $32 million. Insiders insisted that his father's murder and the pressures of living up to the phenomenal standards he had established for himself both figured into his retirement decision. His agent, David Falk, and NBA commissioner David Stern both dismissed suggestions that Jordan's retirement was linked to the continued investigation into his gambling activities. The day after he retired from basketball, a press release issued from the commissioner's office exonerated Jordan of any wrongdoing in connection to gambling and professional basketball. Jordan preferred to place a more philosophical and triumphant spin on his retirement: "I just feel that I don't have anything else to prove." He left at the top his profession, on his own terms. After Jordan's retirement Jack McCallum wrote, "no one in history has played the game of basketball as spectacularly well as Michael Jordan. Game after game, year after year, the man was *better* than his hype. And that is his most enduring accomplishment." Six months later Jordan was pursuing a baseball career. As an outfielder with the minor-league Birmingham Barons he was a .200 hitter. He returned to play for the Chicago Bulls in the latter part of the 1994–1995 season.

Sources:

Jack McCallum, "Michael Jordan," *Sports Illustrated*, 81 (19 September 1994): 52–53;

John Edgar Wideman, "Michael Jordan Leaps the Great Divide," *Esquire*, 114 (November 1990): 138–145, 210–216;

Steve Wulf, "Two champs are back," *Time*, 145 (3 April 1995): 56–57.

JACKIE JOYNER-KERSEE

1962-

WORLD'S GREATEST FEMALE ATHLETE

Beginnings. On the day she was born in early March 1962, Jacqueline Joyner was tabbed for greatness by a grandmother who had named her after President Kennedy's wife. "Someday the girl will be the First Lady of something!" That she might one day become part of American "royalty" seemed rather unlikely at the time, however. Jackie and her brother Al were born into the harsh, desolate, sometimes violent world of East St. Louis, Illinois, a far cry from the comparatively prosperous streets of neighboring St. Louis, Missouri, and a seemingly insurmountable distance from the Olympic Stadium in Seoul, South Korea, where she would eventually change the standard of women's track-and-field excellence. That she did reach such heights was due in no small part to the determination and will to survive instilled in both her and her brother by their mother, Mary, who worked tirelessly and transferred her own aspirations and desires into her chil-

dren. She simply would not allow them to submit to the pressure and limitations of their material surroundings and insisted that they be "roses that have grown through the cracks in the sidewalk." Both Jackie and Al managed to grow through athletic competition. They ran, jumped, shot baskets, and threw with and against each other. And from the beginning Jackie outperformed her older brother.

College Star. Having thrown herself into sport and school, Joyner landed a scholarship to attend the University of California–Los Angeles (UCLA) in 1980. She was an amazingly versatile and dedicated student-athlete, excelling in volleyball and basketball while maintaining a grade-point average in the top 10 percent of her class. She was a four-year starting forward for the UCLA basketball team and led the squad to a 20–10 record her senior season, averaging 12.7 points and 9.3 rebounds per game. It was at UCLA that Jackie caught the attention of assistant track coach Bob Kersee, who threatened to leave the university unless he was allowed to work with Joyner on a one-to-one basis. Kersee insisted that she dedicate herself to track and field and begin a rigorous training program for the heptathlon.

The Start of Something. If the 1984 Summer Olympics in Los Angeles were characterized by Carl Lewis's brash charm and blinding speed, they were no less indelibly marked by the loyalty and promise in two remarkable performances by the Joyner siblings. Jackie entered the heptathlon as a contender for the gold medal while Al was considered a longshot in the triple jump competition. On the evening of 4 August each would become part of the American imagination. Jackie led after the first day of the heptathlon and was locked in a close battle with rival Glynis Nunn of Australia. Unfortunately, Joyner did not feel well, and her slim lead was lost in the 800-meter race to Nunn, who won the gold with a total of 6,390 points to Joyner's 6,385. Beyond the remarkably narrow margin of victory, the world would remember the display of a brother's love. As she labored to complete the 800, Jackie was cheered on by Al, who shouted encouragement and bounded around the infield with his sister, stride-for-stride. Later that same evening Al would manage an surprising upset victory in the triple jump. Afterward Jackie would not comment upon her own disappointment, choosing instead to focus on the accomplishments of her brother. The night of competition and dedication was emblematic of Jackie's career, marking the beginning of her relentless run on the record book.

Unstoppable. Between the fall of 1984 and the summer of 1988, Joyner-Kersee (she had by then married her coach, Bob Kersee) won each of the nine heptathlons she entered and made the world record in that event her personal domain. However, her run on the record book actually began with an American best in the women's long jump in 1985, when she sailed 23 feet 9 inches. In 1986 she became the first woman to break the 7,000-point barrier with a total of 7,148. That same year she received the Sullivan Award as the outstanding amateur athlete in the nation, an honor she deserved after having again bested her own mark only twenty-six days after her first world record in the heptathlon. In the summer of 1988 she pushed the point total ever higher and managed a 7,215 score at the Olympic trials in Indianapolis. She would dominate the heptathlon and long jump that summer in Seoul with an Olympic best 24 feet 3 1/4 inches in the long jump and still another world record in the heptathlon (7,291 points).

Drive. Joyner-Kersee's march on the record book, which spanned the last half of the 1980s and continued well into the 1990s, was possible because of a unique combination of talent and will. Fellow heptathlete Jane Frederick suggested that Joyner-Kersee's talent is *"real . . . not forced."* While undoubtedly a singularly talented athlete, her developing talent was always only half of the equation of her performances between 1984 and 1990. She practiced and competed at a relentless pace, working to honor her mother and family and to maintain a genuine relationship with her countless supporters. Bob Kersee explained that "it's like she has a promise with the fans to give her very best" every time out. She fulfilled this promise by way of a relationship with her husband which was equal parts personal and professional. The coach in him would accept nothing less than the absolute best from the athlete in her. Their relationship was driven by a combined will to win and improve. For Bob Kersee, Jackie's performance was always about milestones and records. "I'm expecting two golds and two world records," he predicted before the 1988 Olympics. In fact, he would not let her take his name until she held the world record in the heptathlon: she did not become Jackie Joyner-Kersee until her 7,000-plus victory in Moscow on 7 July 1986, six months after their marriage. For Jackie Joyner-Kersee, meanwhile, performance was about improvement for its own sake. She ran and jumped for the joy of it, so that she might run and jump again, always faster and farther. After setting the Olympic long jump record in 1988, she exuded, "I couldn't be content but, boy was I happy!"

Sources:

Neil Cohen, *Jackie Joyner-Kersee* (Boston: Little, Brown, 1992);

Kenny Moore, "Ties That Bind," *Sports Illustrated*, 66 (27 April 1987): 76–86.

CHERYL MILLER

1964-

SUPERSTAR OF WOMEN'S BASKETBALL

High-School Legend. Before she played a minute of college basketball Cheryl Miller was the focus of a *Sports Illustrated* feature titled "She May Well Be the Best Ever." Such an audacious claim befit the six-foot three-inch Miller, who in four years at River-side Poly High School had already been compared to the finest female players in the history of the game. As Roger Jackson of *Sports Illustrated* asserted, "she already possesses the deftness and charisma of a Nancy Lieberman, the virtuosity of an Ann Meyers, and the speed and athleticism of a Lynette Woodard." Not only had Miller been the first woman to dunk a basketball during a regulation game — the same game in which she scored a national high-school record of 105 points — but she also led her team to a 132–4 record from 1979 to 1982, averaging 32.8 points per game throughout her high-school career. An accomplished scorer and rebounder, Miller was equally admired for her tenacious defense and charismatic presence on the court. The prize in a feverish recruiting battle, Miller chose to attend the University of Southern California, a decision that immediately cast USC as the preseason favorite to win the NCAA crown.

USC and the Olympics. Miller admirably lived up to the expectations generated by her entry into the college game. In her freshman year she led USC in scoring, blocks, and steals, and poured in 27 points in a 69–67 win over Louisiana Tech in the NCAA championship. In her sophomore year the Lady Trojans won a second consecutive NCAA title, beating Tennessee 72–61. After a less successful campaign in 1984–1985, in which Miller still averaged nearly 27 points and 16 rebounds per game, USC returned to the championship game in her senior year, only to lose to the Texas. To honor their four-time all-American and three-time recipient of the Naismith Award for college player of the year, USC retired Miller's number 31 jersey at the end of her senior year (the only number retired in the history of USC sports). In the summer of 1984 Miller played for the U.S. women's team in the Los Angeles Olympics. Playing beside many of the women with whom she had been compared during her precocious high-school career, Miller led the team in scoring, rebounding, assists, and steals. The U.S. women's team coasted to the gold medal, winning their games by an average margin of 32 points.

The Phenomenon. Miller's impact on the women's game transcended the various awards and accolades, however. Thriving in the media market of Los Angeles, Miller's arrival on the national scene coincided with the positive consequences of Title IX and the gains of the feminist movement. Miller played basketball with the speed, agility, and flamboyance often associated with the men's game, and even inspired rumors that she would try out for the NBA. Claiming that Miller "revolutionized the game," Nancy Lieberman compared the USC star to Larry Bird; sportswriter Curry Kirkpatrick wrote, "With apologies to Wayne Gretzky, back on the hardwood Miller probably is the most dominating individual in a team sport of this era." Miller's combination of stylish physical grace and intense, often brash, on-court demeanor gave women's basketball a captivating personality and contributed to the game's increasing visibility and drawing power during the 1980s. Showing her competitive spirit, Miller remarked, "Just because we're women doesn't mean we don't work or struggle or compete or want to win any less than men. I always feel like a gunfighter and everyone is after me. We can be friends later. On the court . . . I'll be in your mug all night and if you can be intimidated, I'll take advantage of that too."

Coaching. Miller won gold medals at the Goodwill Games and the World Basketball Championships in 1986, but missed the 1988 Olympics because of a knee injury. After working as a sports reporter for ABC in the late 1980s, she became the head women's basketball coach at USC in September 1993 amid considerable controversy because she replaced a popular predecessor.

Sources:
Roger Jackson, "She May Well Be the Best Ever," *Sports Illustrated*, 57 (29 November 1982) 90–91;

Curry Kirkpatrick, "Lights! Camera! Cheryl!" *Sports Illustrated*, 63 (20 November 1985): 124–130;

John McCormick, "A Heroine Who Plays Ball Like a Man," *Newsweek* (13 August 1984): 27.

JOE MONTANA

1956-

SUPER BOWL QUARTERBACK

Seventh String. Perhaps it was his only moment of indecision in a career devoted to imposing his will on circumstance. As a high-school senior in Monongahela, Pennsylvania, Joe Montana nearly accepted a basketball scholarship at North Carolina State University. But western Pennsylvania is blue-collar football country, the birthplace of legendary quarterbacks Johnny Lujack, George Blanda, John Unitas, and Joe Namath, and such a tradition ultimately swayed Ringgold High's star quarterback to attend Notre Dame on a football scholarship. However, as a homesick freshman Montana may have had lingering doubts about his decision-making skills when he calculated that he was the Fighting Irish's seventh-string quarterback — barely. Early in his college career Montana made the most of his infrequent appearances: as a sophomore he twice led Notre Dame back from fourth-quarter deficits for improbable wins, including a game against Air Force in which he came off the bench with just twelve minutes remaining to erase the Falcons' twenty-point lead. He inspired two more miraculous rallies as a junior and still two more as a senior. These exploits — what Rick Reilly called the "impossible, get-serious, did-you-hear-what-happened-after-we-left comeback" — quickly became Montana's signature. Still, Montana did not become Notre Dame's first-string quarterback until his senior year; in his very last game, the 1979 Cotton Bowl against Houston, he engineered a rescue of operatic proportions. With his team down 34–12 with only 7:37 left on the clock and suffering from hypothermia so disabling that the trainer spent halftime pumping him full of bouillon to raise his body temperature, Montana completed seven of his last eight passes to win the game 35–34. The game's final points came on a touchdown pass on fourth down with two seconds left — in an ice storm. Yet despite his almost supernatural football instincts and his documented savvy under pressure, Montana was not a highly touted prospect when he entered the 1979 NFL draft.

God or Something. Eighty-one players were selected before the San Francisco 49ers drafted Montana late in the third round. New 49ers coach Bill Walsh ignored the negative scouting reports on his rookie signal caller ("average" arm strength, no touch), and envisioned Montana as the orchestrator of his complex ball-control passing attack: "Joe's . . . an excellent spontaneous thinker, a keen-witted athlete with a unique field of vision. And he will not choke. Or rather, if he ever does, you'll know that everyone else has come apart first." Walsh's "system" depended on a nimble quarterback with an accurate arm who could adjust quickly to each defensive sequence as it unfolded. By the 1981 season Montana and the 49ers had become a sophisticated and virtually unstoppable offensive machine, but they met an old nemesis in the National Football Conference championship game, the Dallas Cowboys. The Cowboys had eliminated the 49ers from their last three playoff appearances, and after six San Francisco turnovers had led to a 6-point Dallas lead, it looked as if history would repeat itself. But Montana drove the 49ers 89 yards in the game's final minutes, and with 51 seconds left connected with flanker Dwight Clark for the winning touchdown on what was one of the most heralded plays of the decade. Known simply as "The Catch," the play began with Montana scrambling desperately to his right with three Cowboys in pursuit. Just before he was about to be thrown for a loss, Montana, throwing off his back foot, lofted a pass that appeared to be uncatchable. He later said he never saw Clark get open but knew his receiver would be sprinting across the back of the endzone as a safety valve on the play. Clark went high to catch the pass, landing just inside the boundary: afterward he marveled at the feat, "It was over my head. I thought, 'Oh, oh, I can't go that high.' Something got me up there. It must have been God or something."

Super Bowl Hero. San Francisco went on to win Super Bowl XVI over the Cincinnati Bengals 26–21, and Montana was named the game's Most Valuable Player (MVP). It was to become a familiar scenario during the decade. The 49ers would win four titles by 1990, including consecutive Super Bowls in 1989 and 1990, and Montana was awarded the MVP trophy on three occasions (his favorite receiver, Jerry Rice, won the award in 1989). Not only did Montana complete almost 70 percent of his passes in those four Super Bowl victories — outdueling the likes of Dan Marino, John Elway, and Boomer Esiason in the those title games — but he never threw an interception in 122 attempts. He drove the

49ers 92 yards in the waning moments of Super Bowl XXIII to beat Cincinnati again, 20–16, finishing the Bengals off with a 10-yard touchdown pass to receiver John Taylor with 34 seconds left. After the game Montana described the final drive and hinted that his mythic composure was susceptible to all-too-human frailties: "It's a blur. I hyperventilated to the point of almost blacking out . . . I was yelling so loudly in the huddle that I couldn't breathe. Things got blurrier and blurrier." Montana's performance in the clutch nevertheless left teammates grasping for comparisons; "He's like Lazarus," claimed 49er cornerback Tim McKyer. "You roll back the stone, Joe limps out — and throws for 300 yards." In Super Bowl XXIV Montana came back with an even more impressive performance, shredding the Denver Broncos' defense with five touchdown passes in a 55–10 rout. When he retired in 1995 Montana held NFL playoff records for completions, yards, and touchdowns, as well as single-season (1989) and career records for passing efficiency.

Intangibles. But statistics do not adequately measure Joe Montana's worth as a quarterback. Watching a young Montana practice in the early 1980s, coach Bill Walsh commented, "there was something hypnotic about him. That look when he was dropping back; he was poetic in his movements, almost sensuous, everything so fluid, so much under control." At six feet two inches and rather fragile, Montana was never physically imposing, and his career was twice suspended by major surgery (a back operation in 1986 to widen his spinal canal and elbow surgery that forced him to miss all of the 1992 season). He never appeared to be a brash and demonstrative leader, and by his own account he struggled to articulate how he seemed to perform miracles so effortlessly. Joe Montana simply had the ability to impose a quiet order on a raw and disorderly game. With his leadership there was always time enough.

Sources:

Rick Telander, "Joe Montana," *Sports Illustrated*, 81 (19 September 1994): 106–107;

Paul Zimmerman, "Born to Be a Quarterback (Part I of II)," *Sports Illustrated*, 73 (6 August 1990): 62–76;

Zimmerman, "The Ultimate Winner (Part II of II)," *Sports Illustrated*, 73 (13 August 1990): 72–88.

MARTINA NAVRATILOVA

1956-

PROFESSIONAL TENNIS PLAYER

Innovator. If Billie Jean King transformed the business of women's tennis off the court in the 1970s, Martina Navratilova redefined the game on the court the following decade. Noted for her remarkable speed, strength, and power (her left-handed first serve was timed at 93 MPH), Navratilova brought an attack mentality to a sport which had previously been dominated by the precision and patience of Chris Evert's baseline game. For Navratilova tennis was not a game of waiting out your opponent so much as it was a matter of taking what was yours. Her coach, Mike Estep, encouraged her to capitalize upon deep approach shots and rush the net behind them. "Go North!" he shouted during practice sessions and matches, and Navratilova heeded his advice, mounting a relentless assault upon the net and upon the nerves of her more hesitant foes. Her success as a "serve and volley" style player changed the face of the women's game. Having participated in an unprecedented strength and conditioning program, Navratilova was able to generate more pace with greater accuracy than any woman before her. Other players on the tour were unable to keep up with her throughout much of the 1980s as they struggled to rethink and redefine their own approaches to the game.

Belonging. Navratilova's success was due in large part to a newfound comfort in her private life. Having defected from Czechoslovakia in 1975, the young star had engaged in a tumultuous life of consumer excess and personal wandering in an effort to overturn the conventions and restrictions which characterized her early life. "I'm gonna buy one of everything," she said at the time. In one remarkable week in 1981, however, two experiences would mark the beginning of a sense of place and purpose for Navratilova which enabled her decade-long dominance of women's tennis. On 21 July she became a United States citizen. After six years of living without a country, Navratilova had found a home. The significance of this moment was dramatized later that same summer when she cried after losing in the U.S. Open — a tournament she described as "the embodiment of my adopted country" — to Tracy Austin. The New York crowd's ovation that afternoon felt like a welcoming. "I knew they were cheering me as Martina, but they were also cheering me as an American," she would explain later in her autobiography. Only nine days after gaining U.S. citizenship, Navratilova granted an interview to the *New York Daily News* in which she shared information about her personal life. During the course of that interview she discussed her long-standing relationship with lesbian author Rita Mae Brown. Immediately after the information went to press, she was nervous about what it might mean for her image (some sponsors did back away from the star because of her sexual orientation). However, the conversation also meant she had nothing more to hide. As Alexander Wolff of *Sports Illustrated* wrote, "as she dealt publicly with her private life, she was learning to grapple with some of the private issues that affected the public Martina, the woman who played tennis for a living." Becoming increasingly comfortable with herself and her public role, she developed a new attitude toward the critical moments of match play, resolving to "to hit out more when the pressure is on." The summer of 1981 was a renaissance of sorts for Navratilova. At twenty-five she had won only three Grand Slam titles, but she felt renewed and confident as she thought about her immediate tennis future: "I know there's still a place for me in the history of tennis. It's not too late."

Pinned to the Mat. Two years later Navratilova had succeeded in making history. In 1982 and 1983 she won 176 of 180 matches. She was, as Barry McDermott wrote, "simply too good" in every element of the game. After once being dismantled by her friend and rival 6–2, 6–0, Chris Evert spoke for the entire women's tour when she stated, "that was one of her better matches ... I hope." Indeed, the women's game seemed to wilt in the face of Navratilova's dominance in the early 1980s. Critics spoke of the threat her skills posed to fan interest, since the outcome of nearly every major tournament seemed preordained. "She has the women's game pinned to the mat," McDermott explained. In 1983 Navratilova captured her first U.S. Open title. She would win again in 1984 and twice more before the close of the decade. "She savaged the Open," wrote Frank Deford, after watching her drop but 19 games over two weeks. With her victory in the 1984 French Open she became only the third woman to win tennis's grand slam; at one point in the middle of the decade she would win six consecutive Grand Slam singles titles. From 1982 to 1986 her cumulative numbers were astounding: 12 Grand Slam titles (6 singles and 6 doubles) and an overall record of 427–114. By the early 1990s she had amassed an all-time record 166 tournament titles and 55 Grand Slam titles (second only to Margaret Court Smith's 66), 18 of them in singles competition and 37 in doubles. She was ranked number one in the world from 1978 to 1979 and from 1982 to 1986 and remained in the world's top five for an unprecedented eighteen years. Her place in history assured, Navratilova was named Female Athlete of the Decade by the *National Sports Review*, the Associated Press, and United Press International in 1990.

Team Navratilova. The story of Navratilova's rise to the top of women's tennis would be incomplete without a consideration of her methods. After struggling to harness her talent through much of the late 1970s, she began working with former player Renee Richards on the technical aspects of her game. While Richards worked out the kinks in Navratilova's backhand, former basketball standout Nancy Lieberman went to work on Martina's mental approach to the game. As part of a disciplined approach to the game, Lieberman forced her friend and charge to focus upon playing strategic, merciless tennis that would leave her opponents nowhere to hide. "It's just not good enough to play a good match against her anymore," Evert explained. In addition to Richards and Lieberman, Navratilova traveled with a nutritionist, a strength and conditioning coach, and a reflex trainer. The troupe was affectionately (sometimes mockingly) known as "Team Navratilova" and its star member as "Smartina." Navratilova lost weight, gained muscle, increased her

stamina, and established a new standard for fitness in women's tennis. By the mid 1990s top players on both the men's and women's tours had instituted similarly rigorous training regimens.

Partners. One of those who began to realize the importance of increased strength and conditioning was Chris Evert. In her attempt to keep pace with Navratilova, Evert trimmed down and got stronger to add pace to her ground strokes. Evert, who occupied tennis's top spot for much of the 1970s, maintained a fierce rivalry with Navratilova throughout the 1980s. The two would play 80 matches in the course of their careers. When all was said and done Navratilova held the edge at 43–37. Each woman's name and position in the sport is intimately tied to the other in both friendship and competition. "We're opponents on the court, but in the locker room ... we're part of something. Martina and I are linked, whether we like it or not," Evert said in 1986. When Navratilova won her first Wimbledon and U.S. Open titles, they were over Evert. When she established the record for match victories and tournament titles, it was Evert's totals of 1,308 and 157 which she surpassed. The media understood them as stark opposites: Evert's cool, methodical demeanor and conventional game versus Navratilova's fiery disposition and groundbreaking style. They thought of each other as friends who often consoled one another after emotional, face-to-face defeats. Finally, what bound them was a love of winning and an unflinching belief in their capacity to perform. As Navratilova's longtime doubles partner Pam Shriver once indicated, "there's an arrogance you must have" to be the very best, "and only two of them have it."

Sources:

Frank Deford, "A Pair Beyond Compare," *Sports Illustrated*, 64 (26 May 1986): 70–84;

Martina Navratilova with George Vecsey, *Martina* (New York: Knopf, 1985).

PETE ROSE

1942-

FALLEN BASEBALL SUPERSTAR

"Charlie Hustle." Pete Rose was named Player of the Decade for his exceptional and inspiring play in the 1970s, when he collected more hits (2,045) and scored more runs (1,068) than anyone else in the major leagues. As an integral cog in the famous Cincinnati Big Red Machine, Rose played baseball with unbridled passion and intensity. He ran to first base on walks and slid into bases headfirst. He stretched singles into doubles and challenged his teammates to do likewise. Though the name "Charlie Hustle" was intended to be derisive, Rose embraced it. According to Ron Fimrite of *Sports Illustrated*,

"He seemed to have come from an earlier time when professionals always played hard, and out of joy, not greed." Appearances, however, can be deceptive. Columnist George Will described Rose as "a man utterly defined by his vocation — perhaps too much so. The melancholy example of Rose shows that people with particularly narrow tunnel vision have no peripheral vision for adult responsibilities." By the beginning of the 1980s, advancing age had not significantly diminished Rose's skills, and he continued to play aggressive, intelligent baseball. In 1980, his second season with the Philadelphia Phillies after sixteen with the Reds, the thirty-nine-year-old Rose paced the National League (NL) in doubles (42) and helped the Phillies win their first World Series. The following strike-shortened year Rose rapped his 3,631st hit to pass Stan Musial as the NL's all-time hit leader, led the NL in hits (140) — the oldest player ever to do so — and batted .325. Two years later Rose again helped the Phillies reach the World Series. The oldest starting player in Series history, Rose hit .313 in the fall classic. In 1984, playing for the Montreal Expos, Rose tallied hit number 4,000 and collected 100 hits for the twenty-second straight year, a major league record. Before the end of the 1984 season Rose would find himself back in Cincinnati, his hometown, as the Reds' player-manager. The next year he would finally chase down an improbable dream.

4,192. The 1985 season was Rose's twenty-third year in the majors. Despite his many records, the single most impressive accomplishment still lay in front of him. After a five-month nationwide hit watch, on 11 September, before a hometown crowd at Riverfront Stadium, Rose stroked a first-inning single to left center. His 4,192nd major-league career hit, it broke Ty Cobb's career record of 4,191, which had stood since 1928. It was a monumental feat, a testament to consistency, endurance, and desire. Reds fans cheered him for seven minutes. Rose cried on first base. After the game Rose said, "I'm not smart enough to really have the words to describe my feelings." When he finished his career the next year, he had collected more hits (4,256), played in more games (3,562), been to bat more times (14,053), amassed more singles (3,215), and had more 200-hit seasons (10) than anyone else in major-league history. He set thirty-four major-league and NL records. "But it wasn't so much the record-busting that made Rose such an appealing national icon," wrote Fimrite, "it was the sheer gusto with which he played the game, the belly-sliding, glove-banging intensity he brought to the ballpark every day."

Disgrace. After retiring as a player Rose continued to manage the Reds. Early in 1988 in a game against the New York Mets Rose twice shoved umpire Dave Pallone during an argument over a close play at home plate. Pallone tossed Rose from the game, and Reds fans bombarded the field with debris for fifteen minutes. For his own safety Pallone was forced to leave the game. The next day NL president A. Bartlett Giamatti suspended Rose for thirty days and fined him $10,000. It was the most severe penalty for an on-field transgression in baseball

history, and it foreshadowed things to come. When gambling allegations hounded Rose in the spring of 1989, he quickly became an object of national ridicule. For many the name Charlie Hustle took on new meaning. After a lengthy — and some said inconclusive — investigation, first-year baseball commissioner Giamatti was convinced that Rose had bet on baseball and thus had damaged the integrity of the game. "Certainly Rose may have bet on baseball. His lawyers are slick and his denial skill is most ornate," wrote writer Roger Kahn. "It is impossible, of course, to prove the negative, that Rose did not bet [on] baseball, but it seems important here for both sides to go beyond assurances and pleas of 'trust me.'" Late in the season the issue came to a head. Rose accepted Giamatti's lifetime suspension from baseball with the right to apply for reinstatement in a year. Said Giamatti: "The banishment for life of Pete Rose from baseball is the sad end of a sorry episode. One of the game's greatest players has engaged in a variety of acts which have stained the game and he must now live with the consequences of those acts. It will come as no surprise that like any institution composed of human beings, this institution will not always fulfill its highest aspirations. I know of no earthly institution that does. But this one, because it is so much a part of our history as a people, and because it has such a purchase on our national soul, has an obligation to the people for whom it's played." Eight days later the fifty-one-year-old Giamatti died of a heart attack, which many argued was at least partially the result of the strain from the Rose controversy. "Pete Rose hardly seemed the stuff of Aristotelian poetics," Fimrite noted. "Ordinary in appearance and demeanor, sometimes crude, occasionally even vulgar, he certainly didn't reflect the Greek ideal of the Great Man. But through a combination of unabashed enthusiasm, sly intelligence and unshakable self-confidence, he did, in fact, achieve a form of greatness. And he had within him the Aristotelian 'fatal flaw' that led inevitably to his tragic fall."

Sources:

Ron Fimrite, "Pete Rose," *Sports Illustrated,* 81 (19 September 1994): 62–63;

Roger Kahn, *Games We Used to Play: A Lover's Quarrel With the World of Sport* (New York: Ticknor & Fields, 1992);

James Reston Jr., *Collision at Home Plate: The Lives of Pete Rose and Bart Giamatti* (New York: HarperCollins, 1991).

MIKE TYSON

1966-

HEAVYWEIGHT CHAMPION BOXER

Iron Mike. In 1986 twenty-year-old Mike Tyson became the youngest heavyweight world champion in history. In doing so he fulfilled the prophecy of legendary boxing trainer Cus D'Amato and captivated the public imagination in a way no prizefighter had since Muhammad Ali in the 1960s and 1970s. Although a skilled defensive boxer, Tyson was primarily known for his powerful punching ability, his gladiatorlike demeanor, and his well-deserved aura of invincibility. Unbeaten as a professional in the 1980s, Tyson completely dominated his weight division: all but four of his thirty-six fights ended in knockouts. "For many," wrote novelist Joyce Carol Oates in the mid 1980s, "Mike Tyson has become the latest in a lineage of athletic heroes — a bearer of inchoate, indescribable, emotion — a savior, of sorts, covered in sweat and ready for war." In the beginning of the 1990s, however, Tyson's heroic status was irreparably damaged, done in by the loss of his championship title and a conviction for rape.

Troubled Youth. Like virtually all prizefighters, Tyson was born into an impoverished family and community. As a child on the streets of Brooklyn he engaged in petty and serious criminal activities. By the age of eleven he was in and out of juvenile detention centers. A few years later Tyson was sentenced to the Tryon School for Boys in upstate New York. While at Tryon he came in contact with a counselor and former boxer named Bobby Stewart, who trained with Tyson and recognized his ability and potential. In March 1980 Stewart introduced Tyson to Cus D'Amato, a semiretired seventy-two-year-old fight trainer and manager who helped Floyd Patterson and José Torres to world championships in the 1950s and 1960s. After witnessing the thirteen-year-old Tyson participate in a brief sparring session, D'Amato reportedly said: "That's the heavyweight champion of the world."

Ascension. Transferred from Tryon to D'Amato's legal guardianship, Tyson lived and trained in Catskill, New York. He flourished under D'Amato's tutelage; it is, however, debatable whether his behavior improved outside the ring. After a brief amateur career — in which he won the 1981 and 1982 Junior Olympic heavyweight titles, the 1983 U.S. National Championships, and the 1984 National Golden Gloves Tournament, but lost to Henry Tillman at the 1984 Olympic trials — Tyson turned professional in 1985 with the financial backing of managers Jim Jacobs and Bill Cayton. D'Amato, however, would not see his protégé accomplish his prediction, dying of pneumonia on 4 November 1985. Still, Tyson improved as a fighter as Jacobs and Cayton orchestrated his career. They arranged for Tyson to fight as often as twice a month and carefully selected his opponents to maximize his success. In January 1986 *Sports Illustrated* wrote that Tyson "is the most electrifying young heavyweight prospect in years." Soon thereafter Jacobs and Cayton reached an agreement with the cable television network Home Box Office (HBO) on a $1.35 million three-fight deal.

Success. Less than two years after turning professional, Tyson won the heavyweight championship of the world on 22 November 1986 by knocking out Trevor Berbick for the World Boxing Council (WBC) version of

the title. According to Montieth Illingworth, "No other heavyweight ever captured the title in so short a span of time. No other heavyweight ever achieved as high a percentage of first-round knockouts as Tyson — 40.5 percent, or fifteen in twenty-seven fights — in his career leading up to the crown." On 7 March 1987 Tyson beat James "Bonecrusher" Smith in 12 rounds to win the World Boxing Association (WBA) heavyweight title, and on 1 August he outpointed Tony Tucker to win the International Boxing Federation (IBF) crown, thus becoming the undisputed world heavyweight champion at the age of twenty-one. In addition to respect and admiration, Tyson earned millions of dollars from fight purses and television contracts: in 1987 he signed a $26.5 million, seven-fight deal with HBO. "Like Joe Louis, Sugar Ray Robinson, Larry Holmes, et al.," wrote Oates, "Mike Tyson has become a model of success for 'ghetto youth,' though his personal code of conduct, his remarkably assured sense of himself, owes nothing at all to the ghetto. He is trained, managed, and surrounded, to an unusual degree, by white men, and though he cannot be said to be a white man's black man he is surely not a black man's black man in the style of, for instance, Muhammad Ali." Be that as it may, by the end of 1987 there was virtually unanimous agreement that Tyson was the sport's most exciting performer and arguably one of the greatest of all time.

Decline. In 1988 Tyson's life seemed to spin out of control: his ill-fated marriage to actress Robin Givens in February disintegrated after only eight months; manager Jim Jacobs died of leukemia in March; he secretly signed a deal with avaricious promoter Don King in May; he got into a street fight with Mitch "Blood" Green outside a Harlem clothing store at 4:30 A.M. in August; he wrecked his car in September; and he fired trainer Kevin Rooney in December. Nevertheless, Tyson defended his titles three times during the course of the year, the most impressive of which was a first-round knockout of former champion Michael Spinks. After the fight Tyson declared, "There is no fighter like me. I can beat any man in the world." Although he seemed unbeatable Tyson had only fought six times in the two years since he unified the heavyweight championship. In 1989 he fought twice, for a total of six rounds.

Fall. By the time he fought 42–1 underdog James "Buster" Douglas on 11 February 1990 in Tokyo, Tyson was relatively out of shape and psychologically unprepared: Douglas dominated the fight and knocked him out in the tenth round. At the time, the jolt of that upset shook the sporting world. Tyson began his quest to regain the heavyweight championship by knocking out Henry Tillman in the first round of their 16 June 1990 fight. Tyson subsequently won three other fights on his comeback trail and was scheduled to meet Evander Holyfield for the title in November 1991. But while attending the Miss Black America pageant in Indianapolis in July, Tyson allegedly raped a beauty contestant named

Desiree Washington. Indictments were handed down by an Indianapolis grand jury on 9 September. The ensuing trial began in February, lasted two weeks, and garnered tremendous national media attention. After Tyson's conviction sportswriter Richard Hoffer wrote, "a six-year career that will forever leave its mark on boxing is done. It happened so fast. Nine cars in a driveway, $60 million in earnings, the promise of countless millions more. All those men littered on the canvas. The sullen glare of a man pacing a ring, waiting to take a torn towel from over his head. All gone." On 26 March 1992 Tyson began serving his six-year sentence at the Indiana Youth Center in Plainfield, Indiana. He was released three years later on 25 March 1995.

Sources:

Richard Hoffer, "Destined to Fall," *Sports Illustrated*, 76 (17 February 1992): 24–31;

Montieth Illingworth, *Mike Tyson: Money, Myth, and Betrayal* (New York: Carol, 1991);

William Nack, "Ready to Soar to the Very Top," *Sports Illustrated*, 64 (6 January 1986): 22–27;

Joyce Carol Oates, *On Boxing* (New York: Ecco Press, 1995).

PEOPLE IN THE NEWS

Lev Alburt was the U.S. chess champion during 1984–1985.

Bobby Allison, Bill Elliott, and **Cale Yarborough** each won the Daytona 500 twice in the 1980s.

In 1985 **Les Anderson** caught a world-record (97 pounds, 4 ounces) chinook salmon in the Kenai River in Alaska.

Willie "Flipper" Anderson of the Los Angeles Rams gained 336 yards receiving against the New Orleans Saints in 1989 to set an NFL single-game record.

Racquetball player **Cindy Baxter** won a record four women's open titles in the 1980s.

Mookie Blaylock of the University of Oklahoma set an NCAA record for steals in a basketball season with 150 in 1988.

The 5-foot 3-inch **Tyrone "Muggsy" Bogues,** picked by the Washington Bullets in 1987, became the shortest player in NBA history.

The 7-foot 6-inch **Manute Bol,** picked by the Washington Bullets in 1985, became the tallest player in NBA history.

Dogsled racer **Susan Butcher** won the Iditarod in 1986, 1987, and 1988.

JoAnne Carner won the LPGA's Vare Trophy for the best annual scoring average three years in a row, beginning in 1981.

In 1982 **Tracy Caulkins** became the winningest swimmer in U.S. history when she broke Johnny Weissmuller's record of 36 national titles.

Julius "Dr. J" Erving concluded his basketball career in 1987 having scored 11,662 points in the American Basketball Association (1971–1976) and 18,364 points in the National Basketball Association (1976–1987).

Chris Evert retired from tennis in 1989, having won twenty-one Grand Slam titles.

Lewis Feild was the All-Around Cowboy champion from 1985 through 1987.

Carlton Fisk played in more games (1,063 compared to 945) and hit more home runs (174 compared to 144) for the Chicago White Sox in the 1980s than he did for the Boston Red Sox in the 1970s.

Dan Fouts ended his NFL career with the San Diego Chargers in 1987, having passed for 43,040 yards (second all-time) and 254 touchdowns (fourth all-time).

Defensive lineman **Mark Gastineau** of the New York Jets set an NFL record with 22 sacks in 1984.

Wayne Gretzky passed for seven assists in a hockey game three times in the 1980s.

In 1986 **Harriet Hamilton** was named the athletic director of Fisk University, the first African American woman to hold the post in the Southern Intercollegiate Athletic Conference.

In 1988 **Orel Hershiser** of the Los Angeles Dodgers won the National League Championship Series MVP, the World Series MVP, and the National League Cy Young award.

Whitey Herzog managed the St. Louis Cardinals to three National League pennants in 1982, 1985, and 1987.

In the 1980s Bo Jackson hit 81 home runs for the Kansas City Royals and rushed for 2,084 yards and scored 13 touchdowns for the Los Angeles Raiders.

In 1981 Sharon Richardson Jones was named director of outreach activities for the Oakland Athletics, thus becoming the first African American woman in the front office of a Major League Baseball team.

Bowler Thomas Jordan set a world record for the highest individual score, 899, for three games in 1989.

Instructor Jan Kemp successfully sued the University of Georgia for firing her because she had protested against giving academic favoritism to student-athletes.

LeChandra LeDay of the Grambling State University women's basketball team averaged 30.4 points a game in 1988, an NCAA women's single-season record.

Greg LeMond won the Tour de France bicycle race in 1986, 1989, and 1990. His margin of victory in 1989 was eight seconds, the closest Tour de France in history.

Ivan Lendl and John McEnroe were each rated number one by the ATP at the end of the year four times in the 1980s.

Basketball player Lisa Leslie won the 1989 Dial Award, which is presented annually to the national high-school athlete-scholar of the year.

Carl Lewis won seven Olympic track-and-field medals in the 1980s, six of them gold.

Nancy Lopez won five consecutive golf tournaments she entered in 1987.

Boston Celtics forward Kevin McHale won the NBA's sixth man award twice, in 1984 and 1985.

Dan Marino of the Miami Dolphins passed for 5,084 yards and 48 touchdowns in 1984, NFL single-season records.

Rick Mears won the Indianapolis 500 in 1984 and 1988.

Art Monk of the Washington Redskins caught an NFL record 106 receptions in 1984.

Swimmer Pablo Morales set U.S. national records in the 100-meter and 200-meter butterfly.

First baseman Eddie Murray led the major leagues in runs batted in during the 1980s, with 996.

Paula Newby-Fraser won the women's Triathlon championships in 1986, 1988, and 1989.

Chicago Bears running back Walter Payton finished his career in 1987 with 16,726 yards rushing, an NFL all-time record.

Gaylord Perry was ejected for the only time in his career for throwing a spitball in 1982, the same season he won his 300th career game.

In 1988 Pam Postema, a minor-league umpire, was almost chosen to become the first female Major League Baseball umpire.

Jerry Rice of the San Francisco 49ers caught 22 touchdown passes in 1987.

Nolan Ryan struck out 2,167 batters over the course of the 1980s. In 1989, when he was forty-two, Ryan averaged 11.3 strikeouts per nine innings.

Barry Sanders of Oklahoma State University set NCAA single-season records for touchdowns (39) and rushing yards (2,628) in 1988.

Dave Scott won six Ironman Triathlon championships in the 1980s.

Hockey players Peter and Anton Stastny of the Quebec Nordiques each scored eight points in a 1981 game against the Washington Capitals.

Bill Walsh coached the San Francisco 49ers to three Super Bowl wins in the 1980s.

Tom Watson was the PGA's Player of the Year three times in the 1980s.

Using a sabre, fencer Peter Westbrook won nine U.S. national championships in the 1980s.

Robin Yount of the Milwaukee Brewers led the major leagues in base hits during the 1980s with 1,731.

AWARDS

1980

Major League Baseball World Series — Philadelphia Phillies (National League), 4 vs. Kansas City Royals (American League), 2

Super Bowl XIV — Pittsburgh Steelers, 31 vs. Los Angeles Rams, 19

National Collegiate Athletic Association Football Champion — Georgia

Heisman Trophy, Collegiate Football — George Rogers (South Carolina)

Indianapolis 500, Automobile Racing — Johnny Rutherford

Daytona 500, Automobile Racing — Buddy Baker

National Basketball Association Championship — Los Angeles Lakers, 4 vs. Philadelphia 76ers, 2

National Collegiate Athletic Association Men's Basketball — Louisville, 59 vs. UCLA, 54

Association of Intercollegiate Athletics for Women Basketball — Old Dominion, 68 vs. Tennessee, 53

National Hockey League Stanley Cup — New York Islanders, 4 vs. Philadelphia Flyers, 2

Kentucky Derby, Horse Racing — Genuine Risk (Jacinto Vasquez, jockey)

Ladies' Professional Golf Association Championship — Sally Little

U.S. Open Golf Championship — Jack Nicklaus

Masters Golf Tournament — Seve Ballesteros

U.S. Open Tennis Tournament — Chris Evert Lloyd; John McEnroe

Athletes of the Year — U.S. Olympic Hockey Team and Chris Evert Lloyd (Tennis)

1981

Major League Baseball World Series — Los Angeles Dodgers (National League), 4 vs. New York Yankees (American League), 2

Super Bowl XV — Oakland Raiders, 27 vs. Philadelphia Eagles, 10

National Collegiate Athletic Association Football Champion — Clemson

Heisman Trophy, Collegiate Football — Marcus Allen (Southern California)

Indianapolis 500, Automobile Racing — Bobby Unser

Daytona 500, Automobile Racing — Richard Petty

National Basketball Association Championship — Boston Celtics, 4 vs. Houston Rockets, 2

National Collegiate Athletic Association Men's Basketball — Indiana, 63 vs. North Carolina, 50

Association of Intercollegiate Athletics for Women Basketball — Louisiana Tech, 79 vs. Tennessee, 59

National Hockey League Stanley Cup — New York Islanders, 4 vs. Minnesota North Stars, 1

Kentucky Derby, Horse Racing — Pleasant Colony (Jorge Velasquez, jockey)

Ladies' Professional Golf Association Championship — Donna Caponi

U.S. Open Golf Championship — David Graham

Masters Golf Tournament — Tom Watson

U.S. Open Tennis Tournament — Tracy Austin; John McEnroe

Athletes of the Year — John McEnroe (Tennis) and Tracy Austin (Tennis)

1982

Major League Baseball World Series — St. Louis Cardinals (National League), 4 vs. Milwaukee Brewers (American League), 3

Super Bowl XVI — San Francisco 49ers, 26 vs. Cincinnati Bengals, 21

National Collegiate Athletic Association Football Champion — Penn State

Heisman Trophy, Collegiate Football — Herschel Walker (Georgia)

Indianapolis 500, Automobile Racing — Gordon Johncock

Daytona 500, Automobile Racing — Bobby Allison

National Basketball Association Championship — Los Angeles Lakers, 4 vs. Philadelphia 76ers, 2

National Collegiate Athletic Association Men's Basketball — North Carolina, 63 vs. Georgetown, 62

National Collegiate Athletic Association Women's Basketball — Louisiana Tech, 76 vs. Cheyney State, 62

National Hockey League Stanley Cup — New York Islanders, 4 vs. Vancouver Canucks, 0

Kentucky Derby, Horse Racing — Gato Del Sol (E. Delahoussaye, jockey)

Ladies' Professional Golf Association Championship — Jan Stephenson

U.S. Open Golf Championship — Tom Watson

Masters Golf Tournament — Craig Stadler

U.S. Open Tennis Tournament — Chris Evert Lloyd; Jimmy Connors

Athletes of the Year — Wayne Gretzky (Hockey) and Mary Decker (Track)

1983

Major League Baseball World Series — Baltimore Orioles (American League), 4 vs. Philadelphia Phillies (National League), 1

Super Bowl XVII — Washington Redskins, 27 vs. Miami Dolphins, 17

National Collegiate Athletic Association Football Champion — Miami (Fla.)

Heisman Trophy, Collegiate Football — Mike Rozier (Nebraska)

Indianapolis 500, Automobile Racing — Tom Sneva

Daytona 500, Automobile Racing — Cale Yarborough

National Basketball Association Championship — Philadelphia 76ers, 4 vs. Los Angeles Lakers, 0

National Collegiate Athletic Association Men's Basketball — North Carolina State, 54 vs. Houston, 52

National Collegiate Athletic Association Women's Basketball — Southern California, 69 vs. Louisiana Tech, 67

National Hockey League Stanley Cup — New York Islanders, 4 vs. Edmonton Oilers, 0

Kentucky Derby, Horse Racing — Sunny's Halo (E. Delahoussaye, jockey)

Ladies' Professional Golf Association Championship — Patty Sheehan

U.S. Open Golf Championship — Larry Nelson

Masters Golf Tournament — Seve Ballesteros

U.S. Open Tennis Tournament — Martina Navratilova; Jimmy Connors

Athletes of the Year — Carl Lewis (Track) and Martina Navratilova (Tennis)

1984

Major League Baseball World Series — Detroit Tigers (American League), 4 vs. San Diego Padres (National League), 1

Super Bowl XVIII — Los Angeles Raiders, 38 vs. Washington Redskins, 9

National Collegiate Athletic Association Football Champion — Brigham Young

Heisman Trophy, Collegiate Football — Doug Flutie (Boston College)

Indianapolis 500, Automobile Racing — Rick Mears

Daytona 500, Automobile Racing — Cale Yarborough

National Basketball Association Championship — Boston Celtics, 4 vs. Los Angeles Lakers, 3

National Collegiate Athletic Association Men's Basketball — Georgetown, 84 vs. Houston, 75

National Collegiate Athletic Association Women's Basketball — Southern California, 72 vs. Tennessee, 61

National Hockey League Stanley Cup — Edmonton Oilers, 4, vs. New York Islanders, 1

Kentucky Derby, Horse Racing — Swale (Laffit Pincay, jockey)

Ladies' Professional Golf Association Championship — Patty Sheehan

U.S. Open Golf Championship — Fuzzy Zoeller

Masters Golf Tournament — Ben Crenshaw

U.S. Open Tennis Tournament — Martina Navratilova; John McEnroe

Athletes of the Year — Carl Lewis (Track) and Mary Lou Retton (Gymnastics)

1985

Major League Baseball World Series — Kansas City Royals (American League), 4 vs. St. Louis Cardinals (National League), 3

Super Bowl XIX — San Francisco 49ers, 38 vs. Miami Dolphins, 16

National Collegiate Athletic Association Football Champion — Oklahoma

Heisman Trophy, Collegiate Football — Bo Jackson (Auburn)

Indianapolis 500, Automobile Racing — Danny Sullivan

Daytona 500, Automobile Racing — Bill Elliott

National Basketball Association Championship — Los Angeles Lakers, 4 vs. Boston Celtics, 2

National Collegiate Athletic Association Men's Basketball — Villanova, 66 vs. Georgetown, 64

National Collegiate Athletic Association Women's Basketball — Old Dominion, 70 vs. Georgia, 65

National Hockey League Stanley Cup — Edmonton Oilers, 4, vs. Philadelphia Flyers, 1

Kentucky Derby, Horse Racing — Spend a Buck (Angel Cordero, jockey)

Ladies' Professional Golf Association Championship — Nancy Lopez

U.S. Open Golf Championship — Andy North

Masters Golf Tournament — Bernhard Langer

U.S. Open Tennis Tournament — Hana Mandlikova; Ivan Lendl

Athletes of the Year — Dwight Gooden (Baseball) and Nancy Lopez (Golf)

1986

Major League Baseball World Series — New York Mets (National League), 4 vs. Boston Red Sox (American League), 3

Super Bowl XX — Chicago Bears, 46 vs. New England Patriots, 10

National Collegiate Athletic Association Football Champion — Penn State

Heisman Trophy, Collegiate Football — Vinny Testaverde (Miami, Fla.)

Indianapolis 500, Automobile Racing — Bobby Rahal

Daytona 500, Automobile Racing — Geoff Bodine

National Basketball Association Championship — Boston Celtics, 4 vs. Houston Rockets, 2

National Collegiate Athletic Association Men's Basketball — Louisville, 72 vs. Duke, 69

National Collegiate Athletic Association Women's Basketball — Texas, 97 vs. Southern California, 81

National Hockey League Stanley Cup — Montreal Canadiens, 4, vs. Calgary Flames, 1

Kentucky Derby, Horse Racing — Ferdinand (Bill Shoemaker, jockey)

Ladies' Professional Golf Association Championship — Pat Bradley

U.S. Open Golf Championship — Ray Floyd

Masters Golf Tournament — Jack Nicklaus

U.S. Open Tennis Tournament — Martina Navratilova; Ivan Lendl

Athletes of the Year — Larry Bird (Basketball) and Martina Navratilova (Tennis)

1987

Major League Baseball World Series — Minnesota Twins (American League), 4 vs. St. Louis Cardinals (National League), 3

Super Bowl XXI — New York Giants, 39 vs. Denver Broncos, 20

National Collegiate Athletic Association Football Champion — Miami (Fla.)

Heisman Trophy, Collegiate Football — Tim Brown (Notre Dame)

Indianapolis 500, Automobile Racing — Al Unser

Daytona 500, Automobile Racing — Bill Elliott

National Basketball Association Championship — Los Angeles Lakers, 4 vs. Boston Celtics, 2

National Collegiate Athletic Association Men's Basketball — Indiana, 74 vs. Syracuse, 73

National Collegiate Athletic Association Women's Basketball — Tennessee, 67 vs. Louisiana Tech, 44

National Hockey League Stanley Cup — Edmonton Oilers, 4, vs. Philadelphia Flyers, 3

Kentucky Derby, Horse Racing — Alysheba (Chris McCarron, jockey)

Ladies' Professional Golf Association Championship — Jane Geddes

U.S. Open Golf Championship — Scott Simpson

Masters Golf Tournament — Larry Mize

U.S. Open Tennis Tournament — Martina Navratilova; Ivan Lendl

Athletes of the Year — Ben Johnson (Track) and Jackie Joyner-Kersee (Track)

1988

Major League Baseball World Series — Los Angeles Dodgers (National League), 4 vs. Oakland Athletics (American League), 1

Super Bowl XXII — Washington Redskins, 42 vs. Denver Broncos, 10

National Collegiate Athletic Association Football Champion — Notre Dame

Heisman Trophy, Collegiate Football — Barry Sanders (Oklahoma State)

Indianapolis 500, Automobile Racing — Rick Mears

Daytona 500, Automobile Racing — Bobby Allison

National Basketball Association Championship — Los Angeles Lakers, 4 vs. Detroit Pistons, 3

National Collegiate Athletic Association Men's Basketball — Kansas, 83 vs. Oklahoma, 79

National Collegiate Athletic Association Women's Basketball — Louisiana Tech, 56 vs. Auburn, 54

National Hockey League Stanley Cup — Edmonton Oilers, 4, vs. Boston Bruins, 0

Kentucky Derby, Horse Racing — Winning Colors (Gary Stevens, jockey)

Ladies' Professional Golf Association Championship — Sherri Turner

U.S. Open Golf Championship — Curtis Strange

Masters Golf Tournament — Sandy Lyle

U.S. Open Tennis Tournament — Steffi Graf; Mats Wilander

Athletes of the Year — Orel Hershiser (Baseball) and Florence Griffith Joyner (Track)

1989

Major League Baseball World Series — Oakland Athletics (American League), 4 vs. San Francisco Giants (National League), 0

Super Bowl XXIII — San Francisco 49ers, 20 vs. Cincinnati Bengals, 16

National Collegiate Athletic Association Football Champion — Miami (Fla.)

Heisman Trophy, Collegiate Football — Andre Ware (Houston)

Indianapolis 500, Automobile Racing — Emerson Fittipaldi

Daytona 500, Automobile Racing — Darrell Waltrip

National Basketball Association Championship — Detroit Pistons, 4 vs. Los Angeles, 0

National Collegiate Athletic Association Men's Basketball — Michigan, 80 vs. Seton Hall, 79

National Collegiate Athletic Association Women's Basketball — Tennessee, 76 vs. Auburn, 60

National Hockey League Stanley Cup — Calgary Flames, 4 vs. Montreal Canadiens, 2

Kentucky Derby, Horse Racing — Sunday Silence (Pat Valenzuela, jockey)

Ladies' Professional Golf Association Championship — Nancy Lopez

U.S. Open Golf Championship — Curtis Strange

Masters Golf Tournament — Nick Faldo

U.S. Open Tennis Tournament — Steffi Graf; Boris Becker

Athletes of the Year — Joe Montana (Football) and Steffi Graf (Tennis)

DEATHS

Walter Alston, 72, Hall of Fame manager of the Brooklyn and Los Angeles Dodgers, 1 October 1984.

Alan Ameche, 55, 1954 Heisman Trophy–winning running back at the University of Wisconsin who as a professional player with the Baltimore Colts scored the winning touchdown in the 1958 NFL championship game against the New York Giants, 8 August 1988.

Henry Armstrong, 75, legendary professional boxer who simultaneously held titles to three different weight divisions, 22 October 1988.

Emett Ashford, 66, first African American major-league umpire, 1 March 1980.

Earl Averill, 81, Hall of Fame outfielder and the first player to hit a home run in his first major-league at-bat, 16 August 1983.

Ricky Barry, 24, professional basketball player with the Sacramento Kings, 14 August 1989.

Cliff Battles, 70, Hall of Fame halfback with the Washington Redskins (1932–1938), 28 April 1981.

Clair Bee, 87, the second-winningest college basketball coach in history, he pioneered the 3-second rule in college basketball and the 24-second shot clock in the NBA, 20 May 1983.

Ricky Bell, 29, University of Southern California running back in the 1970s, played six years in the NFL, 28 November 1984.

Larry Bethea, 30, former Dallas Cowboys defensive lineman, 23 April 1987.

Len Bias, 22, University of Maryland all-American basketball player, 19 June 1986.

Tom Blackaller, 49, noted yachtsman who successfully defended the America's Cup, 7 September 1989.

Earl "Red" Blaik, 92, Army football coach who won national championships in 1944 and 1945 and weathered academic cheating scandals in the 1950s, 6 May 1989.

Ken Boyer, 51, noted third baseman for the St. Louis Cardinals (1955–1969), 7 September 1982.

Norm "The Dutchman" Van Brocklin, 57, professional football Hall of Fame quarterback and coach, 2 May 1983.

Paul "Bear" Bryant, 69, University of Alabama football coach (1958–1982), 26 January 1983.

Augie Busch Jr., 90, owner of the St. Louis Cardinals baseball team, 29 September 1989.

Clarence Campbell, 78, president of the NHL (1946–1977), he was the longest-serving head of any professional sport, 24 June 1984.

John Carmichael, 83, Baseball Hall of Fame sportswriter, 6 June 1986.

Norm Cash, 51, first baseman for the Detroit Tigers and 1961 American League batting champion, 12 October 1986.

Jocko Conlan, 89, Baseball Hall of Fame umpire, 16 April 1989.

Chuck Cooper, 57, the first African American basketball player drafted by an NBA team, 5 February 1984.

Stanley Coveleski, 94, Hall of Fame pitcher won three games in the 1920 World Series for the Cleveland Indians, 20 March 1984.

Herbert "Fritz" Crisler, 83, football coach at the University of Michigan (1938–1947), developed the two-platoon system of using one team for offense and one team for defense, 19 August 1982.

Joe Cronin, 77, Hall of Fame second baseman, 1930 American League MVP, and American League president (1959–1973), 7 September 1984.

Constantine "Cus" D'Amato, 77, legendary boxing trainer and manager of world champions Floyd Patterson, José Torres, and Mike Tyson, 4 November 1985.

Dan Daniel, 91, Baseball Hall of Fame sportswriter, 2 July 1981.

Duffy Daugherty, 72, Michigan State University football coach (1954–1972), 25 September 1987.

Paul "Daffy" Dean, 67, pitcher for the St. Louis Cardinals in the 1930s and brother of pitcher Dizzy Dean, 17 March 1981.

Esteban DeJesus, 37, WBC lightweight boxing champion (1976–1978), 12 May 1989.

Joe Delaney, 24, football player for the Kansas City Chiefs who died attempting to rescue drowning children, 29 June 1983.

Jack Dempsey, 87, popular world heavyweight champion (1919–1926), 31 May 1983.

William O. DeWitt Sr., 79, baseball executive and owner associated with nine pennant-winning teams, 3 March 1982.

Vince DiMaggio, 74, the eldest of three baseball-playing brothers, 3 October 1986.

Jack Drees, 71, noted radio and television sportscaster for nearly fifty years, 27 July 1988.

Ray Eliot, 74, football coach at the University of Illinois (1942–1960), 24 February 1980.

James "Jumbo" Elliot, 66, longtime track coach at Villanova University, 22 March 1981.

Charles "Rip" Engle, 76, Penn State University football coach (1950–1965), 7 March 1983.

John Facenda, 72, broadcaster who narrated NFL highlight films, 25 September 1984.

George Fazio, 75, professional golfer and later golf course designer, 6 June 1986.

Jim Fixx, 52, fitness enthusiast, lecturer, author of books on jogging, 20 July 1984.

Larry Fleisher, 58, organizer and former head of the NBA Players Association, 4 May 1989.

Carl Furillo, 66, strong-armed outfielder for the Brooklyn Dodgers in the 1940s and 1950s, 21 January 1989.

Terry Furlow, 25, professional basketball player with a variety of teams, 23 May 1980.

Mike Garcia, 62, fourteen-year veteran pitcher with the Cleveland Indians, 13 January 1986.

Bill George, 51, Hall of Fame linebacker with the Chicago Bears (1952–1965), 30 September 1982.

A. Bartlett Giamatti, 51, president of Yale University and commissioner of Major League Baseball, 1 September 1989.

Robert "Ruby" Goldstein, 76, former professional boxer who went on to officiate 39 championship fights in his twenty-one-year career, 22 April 1984.

Vernon "Lefty" Gomez, 80, Hall of Fame pitcher for the New York Yankees in the 1930s and 1940s, 17 February 1989.

Bryan "Bitsy" Grant, 75, popular amateur tennis champion who won more than fifty national championships, 4 June 1986.

Hank Greenberg, 75, Hall of Fame first baseman for the Detroit Tigers (1930–1946), 4 September 1986.

Burleigh Grimes, 92, Hall of Fame pitcher with 270 career wins, 6 December 1985.

Ralph Guldahl, 75, professional golfer who won the Masters in 1939 and the U.S. Open in 1936 and 1937, 11 June 1987.

George "Papa Bear" Halas, 88, one of the founders of the NFL, owner of the Chicago Bears, and for a time the winningest coach in NFL history, 31 October 1983.

Doug Harvey, 65, Hall of Fame defenseman with the Montreal Canadiens of the 1950s, 26 December 1989.

Billy Haughton, 62, Hall of Fame harness racing trainer and driver, 15 July 1986.

Woody Hayes, 74, legendary football coach who twice led Ohio State to national championships, 12 March 1987.

Floyd "Babe" Herman, 84, star player for Brooklyn Dodgers, who had a .324 batting average over his thirteen-year career, 27 November 1987.

Clarke Hinkle, 79, Professional Football Hall of Famer who starred for the Green Bay Packers, 9 November 1988.

Elston Howard, 51, star catcher of the New York Yankees and first African American player with the team, 14 December 1980.

Dick Howser, 51, manager of the New York Yankees and Kansas City Royals, led the Royals to their only World Championship in 1985, 17 June 1987.

Waite Hoyt, 84, Hall of Fame pitcher and member of the 1927 Yankees, 25 August 1984.

Carl Hubbell, 85, Hall of Fame pitcher for the New York Giants (1928–1943), 21 November 1988.

Flo Hyman, 31, "the best American woman volleyball player ever," 24 January 1986.

Ned Irish, 76, sportswriter and public relations agent who became a force behind the growth of the New York Knicks, 21 January 1982.

Tommy "Hurricane" Jackson, 50, popular heavyweight boxer, 14 February 1982.

Travis Jackson, 83, Hall of Fame shortstop for the New York Giants (1922–1936), 27 July 1987.

Irving Jaffee, 74, gold medal–winning Olympic speed skater, 20 March 1981.

Jackie Jensen, 55, Boston Red Sox outfielder (1954–1961) and American League MVP in 1958, 14 July 1982.

Gus Johnson, 48, nine-year veteran of the Baltimore Bullets who played in five NBA All-Star games, 28 April 1987.

William "Judy" Johnson, 89, Hall of Fame Negro League baseball player who played in the 1920s and 1930s, 14 June 1989.

George "Highpockets" Kelly, 89, Hall of Fame second baseman with the New York Giants, 13 October 1984.

John Kieran, 89, sportswriter and first by-lined columnist with *The New York Times*, 10 December 1981.

Duk Koo Kim, 23, South Korean boxer who suffered fatal brain damage in a bout with Ray Mancini, 17 November 1982.

Ted Kluszewski, 63, National League home-run champion with the Cincinnati Reds, 29 march 1988.

Harvey Kuenn, 57, 1959 American League batting champion who later led the Milwaukee Brewers to what was then their only World Series appearance, 28 February 1988.

Edward Lasker, 95, five-time winner of U.S. chess championship, 23 March 1981.

Bobby Layne, 59, quarterback who led the Detroit Lions to NFL championships in the 1950s, 1 December 1986.

Emil "Dutch" Leonard, 74, pitcher in the major leagues for twenty-one years, 17 April 1983.

Fred Lieb, 92, sportswriter and baseball historian for nearly seventy years, 3 June 1980.

Freddie Lindstrom, 75, Hall of Fame third baseman for the New York Giants (1924–1932), 4 October 1981.

Joe Don Looney, 45, eccentric former college and professional football player, 24 September 1988.

Tommy Loughran, 79, world lightweight champion (1927–1929), 7 July 1982.

Joe Louis, 67, legendary world heavyweight champion (1937–1949), 12 April 1981.

Ted Lyons, 85, Hall of Fame pitcher with the Chicago White Sox (1923–1946), 25 July 1986.

Pete Maravich, 40, greatest scorer in college basketball history and ten-year NBA veteran, 5 January 1988.

Roger Maris, 51, major leaguer who broke Babe Ruth's single-season home-run record by hitting 61 homers in 1961, 14 December 1985.

Richard "Rube" Marquard, 90, Hall of Fame pitcher with 201 career wins, 1 June 1980.

Billy Martin, 61, combative New York Yankee player and former manager, 25 December 1989.

John Matuszak, 38, former defensive lineman with the Oakland Raiders, 17 June 1989.

Frank McCormick, 70, professional baseball player, coach, scout, and broadcaster, 21 November 1982.

Chuck McKinley, 45, 1963 Wimbledon singles champion, 11 August 1986.

Davey Moore, 28, former WBA junior-middleweight champion, 3 June 1988.

Donnie Moore, 35, thirteen-year veteran major-league pitcher, 18 July 1989.

Van Lingle Mungo, 73, fourteen-year major-league pitcher, 12 February 1985.

David Overstreet, 25, professional football running back, 24 June 1984.

Jesse Owens, 66, legendary gold medal–winning Olympic track star, 31 March 1980.

Joe Page, 62, ace relief pitcher for the New York Yankees in the 1940s, 21 April 1980.

Leroy "Satchel" Paige, 75, Hall of Fame pitcher and superstar in the Negro leagues, joined the Cleveland Indians in 1948 at the age of forty-two, 8 June 1982.

Raymond "Buddy" Parker, 68, coach of the Detroit Lions (1950–1957) who led them to consecutive NFL titles in 1952 and 1953, 22 March 1982.

Maurice Podoloff, 95, first president of the NBA, 24 November 1985.

Fritz Pollard, 91, legendary African American football player and coach, 11 May 1986.

Vic Raschi, 69, New York Yankess pitcher during the 1940s and 1950s, 14 October 1988.

Katherine Rawls, 64, swimmer and diver who won 33 national swimming and diving titles, 8 April 1982.

Pete Reiser, 62, Brooklyn Dodgers outfielder (1940–1948) who led the National League in hitting in 1941, 25 October 1981.

Paul Richards, 77, former professional baseball player and manager, 4 May 1986.

Milton Richman, 64, noted sports columnist and editor for UPI, 9 June 1986.

Tim Richmond, 34, leading stock car racer, 13 August 1989.

Sugar Ray Robinson, 67, world welterweight (1946–1951) and middleweight champion (1951–1952, 1957–1960), 12 April 1989.

Don Rogers, 23, defensive back with the Cleveland Browns, 27 June 1986.

Art Rooney Sr., 87, founder and owner of the Pittsburgh Steelers, 25 August 1988.

Julian Roosevelt, 64, leading U.S. amateur sportsman, 20 March 1986.

Edd Roush, 94, Hall of Fame outfielder for the Cincinnati Reds (1916–1926) and the last surviving participant of the 1919 World Series, 21 March 1988.

Red Ruffing, 83, Hall of Fame pitcher considered the best hitting pitcher of his generation, 17 February 1986.

Al Schacht, 91, former Major League Baseball player who became known as the Clown Prince of Baseball, 14 July 1984.

Jackson Scholz, 89, gold medal–winning sprinter whose 1924 Olympic experiences were dramatized in the film *Chariots of Fire,* 26 October 1986.

Bob Shawkey, 90, pitcher for the New York Yankees and later team manager, 31 December 1980.

Eddie Shore, 82, the only defenseman to win the NHL's MVP award four times, 16 March 1985.

Robert Short, 65, owner who bought the Minneapolis Lakers and moved them to Los Angeles in 1957 and bought and moved the Washington Senators to Texas in 1961, 20 November 1982.

James Shuler, 26, former middleweight boxing champion, 21 March 1986.

Jerry Smith, 43, professional football player with the Washington Redskins, the first prominent athlete known to have AIDS, 15 October 1986.

Walter "Red" Smith, 76, nationally admired and syndicated sportswriter, 15 January 1982.

Conn Smythe, 85, founder of the Toronto Maple Leafs, 18 November 1980.

Monty Stratton, 70, Chicago White Sox pitcher in the 1930s who lost his leg in 1938 and subsequently had his story told in *The Stratton Story* (1949), 29 September 1982.

Lee Taylor, 42, leading powerboat racer, 13 November 1980.

Bill Terry, 90, Hall of Fame first baseman and manager of the New York Giants and the last National Leaguer to hit .400, 9 January 1989.

Joe Thomas, 61, football talent specialist with the Minnesota Vikings, Miami Dolphins, and San Francisco 49ers, 11 February 1983.

Stacey Toran, 27, defensive back with the Los Angeles Raiders, 5 August 1989.

James Tyrer, 41, professional football player and nine-time all-star, 15 September 1980.

Alec Ulman, 82, sports car racing pioneer, 23 April 1986.

Glenna Vare, 85, pioneer of women's golf and a charter member of the Women's Golf Hall of Fame, 3 February 1989.

Andy Varipapa, 93, member of the bowling Hall of Fame and considered by many to be the greatest bowler of all time, 25 August 1984.

Bill Veeck, 71, innovative and eccentric baseball team owner, 2 January 1986.

Fred "Dixie" Walker, 71, outfielder with the Brooklyn Dodgers (1940–1947), who was traded at his own request when Jackie Robinson joined the Dodgers, 17 May 1982.

Mickey Walker, 79, world welterweight (1922–1926) and middleweight champion (1927–1931), 28 April 1981.

Stella Walsh (Stanisława Walasiewicz), 69, Polish-born Olympic track star who became a U.S. citizen in 1947, 4 December 1980.

Bill Wambsganss, 91, professional baseball player who completed an unassisted triple play in the 1920 World Series, 8 December 1985.

Lloyd "Little Poison" Waner, 76, Hall of Fame outfielder with the Pittsburgh Pirates (1927–1940), 22 July 1982.

Bob Waterfield, 62, NFL Rookie of the Year in 1945, all-pro quarterback, professional football Hall of Famer, 25 March 1983.

Johnny Weissmuller, 79, gold medal–winning Olympic swimmer who later played Tarzan in the movies, 20 January 1984.

Vic Wertz, 58, American League first baseman for seventeen years, 7 July 1983.

Edward Bennett Williams, 68, famous trial lawyer and owner of the Baltimore Orioles, 13 August 1988.

Arthur Wirtz, 82, owner of the Chicago Black Hawks, the Chicago Bulls, and Chicago Stadium, 21 July 1983.

"Smoky" Joe Wood, 95, major-league pitcher who went 34–5 for the Boston Red Sox in 1912, 27 July 1985.

Claude "Buddy" Young, 57, pro football Hall of Fame running back, 4 September 1983.

Dick Young, 69, nationally syndicated, Baseball Hall of Fame sportswriter, 31 August 1987.

Fred Zollner, 81, founder and owner of the Fort Wayne Zollner Pistons who moved the team to Detroit in 1957 and sold it in 1974, 21 June 1982.

PUBLICATIONS

Ira Berkow, *Pitchers Do Get Lonely and Other Sports Stories* (New York: Penguin Books, 1988);

Thomas Boswell, *Game Day: Sports Writings 1970–1990* (New York: Doubleday, 1990);

John Feinstein, *A Season on the Brink: A Year With Bob Knight and the Indiana Hoosiers* (New York: Macmillan, 1986);

Peter Golenbock, *Personal Fouls* (New York: Carroll & Graf, 1989);

Jay Greenberg, *NHL: The World of Professional Hockey* (New York: Rutledge Press, 1981);

Allen Guttmann, *The Olympics: A History of the Modern Games* (Urbana & Chicago: University of Illinois Press, 1992);

Guttmann, *A Whole New Ball Game: An Interpretation of American Sports* (Chapel Hill: University of North Carolina Press, 1988);

David Halberstam, *The Breaks of the Game* (New York: Ballantine, 1981);

Thomas Hauser, *The Black Lights: Inside the World of Professional Boxing* (New York: Simon & Schuster, 1986);

John Hoberman, *The Olympic Crisis: Sport, Politics and the Moral Order* (New York: Caratzas, 1986);

Philip M. Hoose, *Necessities: Racial Barriers in American Sports* (New York: Random House, 1989);

Dan Jenkins, *"You Call It Sports, But I Say It's A Jungle Out There"* (New York: Simon & Schuster, 1989);

Leonard Koppett, *Sports Illusion, Sports Reality: A Reporter's View of Sports, Journalism, and Society* (New York: Houghton Mifflin, 1981);

Richard Lapchick, *Broken Promises: Racism in American Sports* (New York: St. Martin's Press, 1984);

Lapchick, *Fractured Focus: Sport as a Reflection of Society* (Lexington, Mass.: Lexington Books, 1986);

Helen Lenskyj, *Out of Bounds: Women, Sport, and Sexuality* (Toronto: Women's Press, 1986);

Richard D. Mandell, *Sport, A Cultural History* (New York: Columbia University Press, 1984);

Michael A. Messner, *Power at Play: Sports and the Problem of Masculinity* (Boston: Beacon, 1992);

Douglas A. Noverr and Lawrence E. Ziewacz, *The Games They Played: Sports in American History, 1865–1980* (Chicago: Nelson-Hall, 1983);

Joyce Carol Oates, *On Boxing* (New York: Kensington, 1987);

Benjamin G. Rader, *In Its Own Image: How Television Has Transformed Sports* (New York: Free Press, 1984);

Randy Roberts and James Olson, *Winning Is the Only Thing: Sports in America since 1945* (Baltimore: Johns Hopkins University Press, 1989);

Bob Ryan and Terry Pluto, *Forty-Eight Minutes: A Night in the Life of the NBA* (New York: Macmillan, 1987);

Mark Sabljak and Martin H. Greenberg, *Sports Babylon: Sex, Drugs, and Other Dirty Dealings In the World of Sports* (New York: Bell, 1988);

George Sage, *Power and Ideology in American Sport: A Critical Perspective* (Champaign, Ill.: Human Kinetics Books, 1990);

Jeffery T. Sammons, *Beyond the Ring: The Role of Boxing in American Society* (Urbana & Chicago: University of Illinois Press, 1988);

Rick Telander, *The Hundred Yard Lie: The Corruption of College Football and What We Can Do to Stop It* (New York: Simon & Schuster, 1989);

José Torres, *Fire & Fear: The Inside Story of Mike Tyson* (New York: Warner, 1989);

Oliver Trager, *Sports in America: Paradise Lost?* (New York: Facts On File, 1990);

Wiley Lee Umphlett, ed., *American Sport Culture: The Humanistic Dimensions* (Lewisburg, Penn.: Bucknell University Press, 1985);

John Underwood, *Spoiled Sport: A Fan's Notes On The Troubles Of Spectator Sports* (Boston: Little, Brown, 1984);

Ralph Wiley, *Serenity: A Boxing Memoir* (New York: Holt, 1989);

William Zinsser, *Spring Training* (New York: Prentice-Hall, 1989);

Facts On File, periodical;

The Sporting News, periodical;

Sports Illustrated, periodical.

GENERAL REFERENCES

GENERAL

James McGrgeor Burns, *Crosswinds of Freedom* (New York: Knopf, 1991);

William H. Chafe, *The Unfinished Journey: America Since World War II* (New York: Oxford University Press, 1986);

Chafe and Howard Sitkoff, eds., *A History of Our Times: Readings on Postwar America*, third edition (New York: Oxford University Press, 1991);

Chronicle of the 20th Century (Mount Kisco, N.Y.: Chronicle Publications, 1987);

Current Biography Yearbook (New York: Wilson, various years);

Day by Day: The Eighties, 2 volumes (New York: Facts On File, 1995);

Jane Duden and Gail B. Stewart, *1980s* (New York: Crestwood Press, 1991);

Encyclopaedia Britannica Book of the Year (Chicago: Encyclopaedia Britannica, 1981–1990);

Paul Johnson, *Modern Times: From the Twenties to the Nineties*, revised edition (New York: HarperCollins, 1991);

Walter LeFeber, *The American Century: A History of the United States Since 1941*, fourth edition (New York: McGraw-Hill, 1992);

Richard B. McKenzie, *What Went Right in the 1980s* (San Francisco: Pacific Research Institute for Public Policy, 1994);

Oxford Analytica, *America in Perspective: Major Trends in the United States through the 1990s* (Boston: Houghton Mifflin, 1986);

Norman L. Rosenberg, *In Our Times: America Since World War II* (Englewood Cliffs, N.J.: Prentice Hall, 1990);

Statistical Abstract of the United States (Washington, D.C.: U.S. Department of Commerce, various years);

Time Lines on File (New York: Facts On File, 1988);

James Trager, *The People's Chronology*, revised (New York: Holt, 1992).

ARTS

Christopher Andersen, *Madonna: Unauthorized* (New York: Simon & Schuster, 1991);

John Beardsley and Jane Livingston, *Hispanic Art in the United States* (New York: Abbeville Press, 1987);

Donald Boyle, *Blacks in American Films and Television: An Encyclopedia* (New York: Garland, 1988);

Douglas Brode, *The Films of Robert De Niro* (Secaucus, N.J.: Carol Publishing Group, 1993);

Brode, *The Films of the Eighties* (New York: Citadel Press, 1990);

Fred Bronson, *The Billboard Book of Number One Hits* (New York: Billboard Publications, 1992);

Edward D. C. Campbell, *The Celluloid South: Hollywood and the Southern Myth* (Knoxville: University of Tennessee Press, 1981);

Dennis Carroll, *David Mamet* (New York: St. Martin's Press, 1987);

Germano Celant, ed., *Keith Haring* (Munich: Prestel, 1992);

Charles R. Cross and the editors of *Backstreets Magazine*, *Backstreets: Springsteen, The Man and His Music* (New York: Harmony Books, 1989);

Francis Davis, *In the Moment: Jazz in the 1980s* (New York: Oxford University Press, 1986);

Anne Dean, *David Mamet: Language as Dramatic Act* (Rutherford, N.J.: Fairleigh Dickinson University Press, 1990);

Mark Eliot, with Mike Appel, *Down Thunder Road: The Making of Bruce Springsteen* (New York: Simon & Schuster, 1992);

Jonathan Fineburg, *Art Since 1940: Strategies of Being* (New York: Abrams, 1995);

Peter Frank and Michael McKenzie, *New, Used & Improved: Art for the '80s* (New York: Abbeville Press, 1987);

Benjamin Friedman, *Day Of Reckoning: The Consequences of American Economic Policy Under Reagan and After* (New York: Random House, 1988);

Gary Giddins, *Rhythm-a-ning: Jazz Tradition and Innovation in the '80s* (New York: Oxford University Press, 1986);

Giddins, *Riding on a Blue Note: Jazz and American Pop* (New York: Oxford University Press, 1981);

Tony Godfrey, *The New Image: Painting in the 1980s* (Oxford: Phaidon, 1986);

Donald J. Greiner, *Women Without Men: Female Bonding and the American Novel of the 1980s* (Columbia: University of South Carolina Press, 1993);

Richard Grenier, *Capturing the Culture: Film, Art, and Politics* (Washington, D.C.: Ethics & Public Policy Center, 1991);

Lawrence Grossberg, *We Gotta Get Out of This Place: Popular Conservatism and Postmodern Culture* (New York: Routledge, 1992);

Molly Haskell, *From Reverence to Rape: The Treatment of Women in the Movies* (Chicago: University of Chicago Press, 1987);

Paul Honeyford, *The Thrill of Michael Jackson* (New York: Quill, 1984);

Michael Jackson, *Moonwalk* (New York: Doubleday, 1988);

Leslie Kane, *David Mamet: A Casebook* (New York & London: Garland, 1992);

Paul Kingsbury and Alan Axelrod, eds., *Country: The Music and the Musicians* (New York: Abbeville Press, 1988);

Barbara Kruger, *Love for Sale*, with text by Kate Linker (New York: Abrams, 1990);

Kruger, *Remote Control: Power, Culture, and the World of Appearance* (Cambridge, Mass.: MIT Press, 1993);

Annette Kuhn, *Women's Pictures: Feminism and Cinema* (London & Boston: Routledge & Kegan Paul, 1982);

Bruce K. Kurtz, ed., *Keith Haring, Andy Warhol, and Walt Disney* (Munich: Prestel / Phoenix: Phoenix Art Museum, 1992);

Marco Livingstone, *Pop Art: A Continuing History* (New York: Abrams, 1990);

Lee Lourdeaux, *Italian and Irish Filmmakers in America* (Philadelphia: Temple University Press, 1990);

Edward Lucie-Smith, *Race, Sex, and Gender in Contemporary Art* (New York: Abrams, 1989);

Dave Marsh, *Glory Days: Bruce Springsteen in the 1980s* (New York: Pantheon, 1987);

Diana Maychick, *Meryl Streep: The Reluctant Superstar* (New York: St. Martin's Press, 1984);

Michael Medved, *Hollywood vs. America: Popular Culture and the War on Traditional Values* (New York: HarperCollins, 1992);

Mark Crispin Miller, ed., *Seeing Through Movies* (New York: Pantheon, 1990);

Donald R. Mott and Cheryl McAllster Saunders, *Steven Spielberg* (Boston: Twayne, 1986);

George Nelson, *Buppies, B-boys, Baps & Bohos: Notes on Post-Soul Black Culture* (New York: HarperCollins, 1992);

Norm N. Nite, *Rock On Almanac: The First Four Decades of Rock 'n' Roll* (New York: Harper & Row, 1989);

Tom O'Brien, *The Screening of America: Movies and Values from Rocky to Rain Man* (New York: Continuum, 1990);

Andreas Papadakis, Clare Farrow, and Nicola Hodges, eds., *New Art: An International Survey* (New York: Rizzoli, 1991);

Arlene Raven, *Crossing Over: Feminism and Art of Social Concern* (Ann Arbor, Mich.: UMI Research Press, 1988);

Robert V. Rozelle, Alvia Wardlaw, and Maureen A. McKenna, eds., *Black Art: The African Impulse in African-American Art* (New York: Abrams, 1989);

Martin Scorsese, *Scorsese on Scorsese* (London & Boston: Faber & Faber, 1990);

Adam Sexton, *Desperately Seeking Madonna: In Search of the Meaning of the World's Most Famous Woman* (New York: Delta, 1993);

David P. Szatmary, *Rockin' in Time: A Social History of Rock and Roll* (Englewood Cliffs, N.J.: Prentice-Hall, 1987);

David Thomson, *A Biographical Dictionary of Film*, third edition, revised (New York: Knopf, 1994);

Kirk Varnedoe and Adam Gopnik, *High and Low: Modern Art and Popular Culture* (New York: Abrams, 1990);

Steve Vineberg, *No Surprises, Please: Movies in the Reagan Decade* (New York: Schirmer, 1993);

John Walker, ed., *Halliwell's Film Guide*, tenth edition, revised and updated (New York: HarperCollins, 1994);

Walker, ed., *Halliwell's Filmgoer's and Video Viewer's Companion*, eleventh edition, revised and updated (New York: HarperCollins, 1995);

Joel Whitburn, *The Billboard Book of Top 40 Hits* (New York: Billboard Publications, 1991);

Whitburn, *Billboard Hot 100 Charts: The Eighties* (Menomonee Falls, Wis.: Record Research, 1991);

Mason Wiley and Damien Bona, *Inside Oscar: The Unofficial History of the Academy Awards* (New York: Ballantine, 1992).

BUSINESS

Alberto Alesina and Geoffrey Carliner, eds., *Politics and Economics in the Eighties* (Chicago: University of Chicago Press, 1991);

Barry Bluestone and Bennett Harrison, *The Deindustrialization of America: Plant Closings, Community Abandonment, and the Dismantling of Basic Industry* (New York: Basic Books, 1982);

Connie Bruck, *The Predators Ball: The Junk Bond Raiders and the Man Who Staked Them* (New York: American Lawyer/Simon & Schuster, 1988);

Paul Carroll, *Big Blues: The Unmaking of IBM* (New York: Crown, 1993);

Michael L. Dertouzos, Richard K. Lester, and Robert M. Solow, *Made in America: Regaining the Productive Edge* (New York: Harper & Row Perennial Library, 1989);

James M. Dobson, *A History of American Enterprise* (Englewood Cliffs, N.J.: Prentice Hall, 1988);

Irvin Farman, *Tandy's Money Machine: How Charles Tandy Built Radio Shack Into the World's Largest Electronics Chain* (Chicago: Mobium Press, 1992);

Martin Feldstein, ed., *American Economic Policy in the 1980s* (Chicago: University of Chicago Press, 1994);

Benjamin M. Friedman, *Day of Reckoning: The Consequences of American Economic Policy Under Reagan and After* (New York: Random House, 1988);

Alfonso Gambardella, *Science and Innovation: The U.S. Pharmaceutical Indusrty in the 1980s* (Cambridge: Cambridge University Press, 1995);

Neil E. Harl, *The Farm Debt Crisis of the 1980s* (Ames: Iowa State University Press, 1990);

Linda M. Hooks, *Bank Failures and Deregulation in the 1980s* (New York: Garland, 1994);

Paul M. Kennedy, *The Rise and Fall of the Great Powers: Economic Change and Military Conflict from 1500 to 2000* (New York: Random House, 1987);

Robert Emmit Long, ed., *The Farm Crisis* (New York: Wilson, 1987);

Martin Lowy, *High Rollers: Inside the Savings and Loan Debacle* (New York: Praeger, 1991);

Paul Zane Pilzer and Robert Deitz, *Other People's Money: How Bad Luck, Worse Judgment, and Flagrant Corruption Made a Shambles of a $900 Billion Industry* (New York: Simon & Schuster, 1989);

Clyde V. Prestowitz, *Trading Places: How We Allowed Japan to Take the Lead* (New York: Basic Books, 1988);

Robert Reich, *The Work of Nations: Preparing Ourselves for 21st Century Capitalism* (New York: Knopf, 1991);

Michael A. Robinson, *Overdrawn: The Bailout of American Savings: The Inside Story of the $2 Billion S & L Debacle* (New York: Dutton/Penguin, 1990);

Steven Schlosstein, *The End of the American Century* (New York: Congdon & Weed, 1989);

Robert Slater, *Portraits in Silicon* (Cambridge, Mass.: MIT Press, 1987).

Paul A. Tiffany, *The Decline of American Steel: How Management, Labor, and Government Went Wrong* (New York: Oxford University Press, 1988);

Kevin Phillips, *The Politics of Rich and Poor: Wealth and the American Electorate in the Reagan Aftermath* (New York: Random House, 1990);

Sandra Stringer Vance and Roy V. Scott, *Wal-Mart: A History of Sam Walton's Retail Phenomena* (New York: Twayne, 1994);

Daniel Yergin, *The Prize: The Epic Quest for Oil, Money, and Power* (New York: Simon & Schuster, 1991).

EDUCATION

Mortimer Adler, *The Paideia Proposal: An Educational Manifesto* (New York: Macmillan, 1982);

Bruno Bettelheim and Karen Zelan, *On Learning to Read: The Child's Fascination With Meaning* (New York: Knopf, 1982);

Ruth Bleier, *Science and Gender* (London & New York: Pergamon Press, 1984);

Allan Bloom, *The Closing of the American Mind: How Higher Education Has Failed Democracy and Impoverished the Souls of Today's Students*, foreword by Saul Bellow (New York: Simon & Schuster, 1987);

John Brademas, *The Politics of Education: Conflict and Consensus on Capitol Hill* (Norman: University of Oklahoma Press, 1987);

Godfrey Brandt, *The Realization of Anti-Racist Teaching* (Philadelphia: Falmer Press, 1986);

John Clements, *Changed Lives: The Effects of the Perry Preschool Project on Youths Through Age Nineteen* (Ypsilanti, Mich.: High Scope Press, 1984);

A Common Destiny: Blacks and American Society (Washington, D.C.: National Research Council, 1989);

Philip Cusick, *The Egalitarian Ideal and the American High School* (New York: Longman, 1983);

Joan Delfattore, *What Johnny Shouldn't Read: Censorship In America* (New Haven: Yale University Press, 1992);

Judith S. Eaton, *The Unfinished Agenda: Higher Education and the 1980s* (New York: Macmillan, 1991);

Thersa Escobedo, ed., *Early Childhood Bilingual Education: A Hispanic Perspective* (New York: Teachers College Press, 1982);

Rudolf Flesch, *Why Johnny Still Can't Read* (New York: Harper & Row, 1981);

Douglas Franzosa and Karen Mazza, comp., *Integrating Women's Studies into the Curriculum: An Annotated Bibliography* (Westport, Conn.: Greenwood Press, 1984);

Howard Gardner, *Frames of Mind: The Theory of Multiple Intelligences* (New York: Basic Books, 1983);

Carol Gilligan, *In a Different Voice: Psychological Theory and Women's Development* (Cambridge, Mass.: Harvard University Press, 1982);

Kenneth Goodman, *Language and Literacy* (Boston: Routlege & Kegan Paul, 1982);

Hugh Davis Graham, *The Uncertain Triumph: Federal Education Policy in the Kennedy and Johnson Years* (Chapel Hill: University of North Carolina Press, 1984);

Shirley Brice Heath, *Ways With Words* (Cambridge: Cambridge University Press, 1983);

Karen Klein and Deborah Strother, eds., *Planning for Microcomputers in the Curriculum* (Bloomington, Ind.: Phi Delta Kappa, 1984);

Herbert Kohl, *Basic Skills: A Plan for Your Child, A Program for All Children* (Boston: Little, Brown, 1982);

Jonathan Kozol, *Savage Inequalities: Children in America's Schools* (New York: Crown, 1991);

Arthur Levine, ed., *Higher Learning in America 1980–2000* (Baltimore: Johns Hopkins University Press, 1993);

Ken Macrorie, *Twenty Teachers* (New York: Oxford University Press, 1984);

Joseph Murphy, ed., *The Educational Reform Movement of the 1980s: Perspectives and Cases* (Berkeley, Cal.: McCutcheon, 1990);

Jeannie Oakes, *Keeping Track: How Schools Structure Inequality* (New Haven: Yale University Press, 1985);

David Owen, *None of the Above: Behind the Myth of Scholastic Aptitude* (Boston: Houghton Mifflin, 1985);

Arthur G. Powell, Eleanor Farrar, and David Cohen, *The Shopping Mall High School: Winners and Losers in the Educational Marketplace* (Boston: Houghton Mifflin, 1985);

Dianne Ravitch, *The Schools We Deserve: Reflections on the Educational Crises of Our Time* (New York: Basic Books, 1985);

Stanley Sharp, *The REAL Reason Johnny Still Can't Read* (Smithtown, N.Y.: Exposition Press, 1983);

Ira Shor, *Culture Wars: School and Society in the Conservative Restoration* (Boston: Routledge & Kegan Paul, 1986);

Larry Silver, *The Misunderstood Child: A Guide for Parents of Learning Disabled Children* (New York: McGraw-Hill, 1984);

Michael Timpane and Laurie Millar McNeill, *Business Impact on Education and Child Development Reform* (New York: Committee for Economic Development, 1991);

Sherry Turkle, *The Second Self: Computers and the Human Spirit* (New York: Simon & Schuster, 1984).

FASHION

Joel Warren Barna, *The See-Through Years: Creation and Destruction in Texas Architecture and Real Estate 1981–1991* (Houston: Rice University Press, 1992);

Juli Capella and Quim Larrea, *Designed by Architects in the 1980s* (New York: Rizzoli, 1988);

Vicky Carnegy, *Fashions of a Decade: The 1980s* (New York: Facts On File, 1990);

Farid Chenoune, *A History of Men's Fashion* (Paris: Flammarion, 1993);

Thomas Cowan, *Living Details: More than 500 Ways to Make a House a Home* (New York: Whitney Library of Design, 1986);

The Encyclopedia of Fashion (New York: Abrams, 1986);

Joel Garreau, *Edge City* (New York: Doubleday, 1991);

Annalee Gold, *90 Years of Fashion* (New York: Fairchild Fashion Group, 1991);

Paul Goldberg, *On the Rise: Architecture and Design in a Postmodern Age* (New York: Penguin, 1983);

William Dudley Hunt Jr., *Encyclopedia of American Architecture* (New York: McGraw-Hill, 1990);

Jim Kemp, *American Vernacular: Regional Influences in Architecture and Interior Design* (New York: Viking, 1987);

Spiro Kostof, *History of Architecture: Settings and Rituals* (Oxford: Oxford University Press, 1995);

Udo Kultermann, *Architecture in the 20th Century* (New York: Reinhold, 1993);

Sydney LeBlanc, *20th Century American Architecture* (New York: Watson-Guptill, 1993);

Diane Maddex, ed., *Master Builders: A Guide to Famous American Architects* (Washington, D.C.: Preservation Press, 1985);

Richard Martin and Harold Koda, *Jocks and Nerds: Men's Style in the Twentieth Century* (New York: Rizzoli, 1989);

Caroline Rennolds Milbank, *Couture: The Great Designers* (New York: Stewart, Tabori & Chang, 1985);

Milbank, *New York Fashion: The Evolution of American Fashion* (New York: Abrams, 1989);

Jonathan Moor, *Perry Ellis: A Biography* (New York: St. Martin's Press, 1988);

Ann Lee Morgan and Colin Naylor, eds., *Contemporary Architecture* (Chicago: St. James Press, 1987);

Jane Mulvagh, *"Vogue" History of 20th Century Fashion* (New York: Viking, 1988);

Blanche Payne, *The History of Costume* (New York: HarperCollins, 1992);

John Peacock, *20th Century Fashion: The Complete Sourcebook* (New York: Thames & Hudson, 1993);

Beverly Russell, *Architecture and Design 1970–1990: New Ideas in America* (New York: Abrams, 1989);

Lynn Schurnberger, *Let There Be Clothes* (New York: Workman, 1991);

Ray Smith, *Interior Design in 20th Century America: A History* (New York: Harper & Row, 1987);

Anne Stegemeyer, *Who's Who in Fashion* (New York: Fairchild, 1988);

Elizabeth Wilson, *Adorned in Dreams: Fashion and Modernity* (Berkeley: University of California Press, 1987);

Tom Wolfe, *From Bauhaus to Our House* (New York: Farrar, Straus & Giroux, 1981);

Doreen Yarwood, *Fashion in the Western World: 1500–1990* (New York: Drama Book Publishers, 1992).

GOVERNMENT AND POLITICS

Ken Auletta, *The Underclass* (New York: Random House, 1982);

Lucius J. Barker and Ronald W. Walters, eds., *Jesse Jackson's 1984 Presidential Campaign: Challenge and Change in American Politics* (Urbana & Chicago: University of Illinois Press, 1989);

Michael Barone, *Our Country: The Shaping of America from Roosevelt to Reagan* (New York: Free Press, 1990);

Terrel Bell, *The Thirteenth Man: A Reagan Cabinet Memoir* (New York: Free Press, 1988);

David H. Bennett, *The Party of Fear: From Nativist Movements to the New Right in American History* (Chapel Hill: University of North Carolina Press, 1988);

Michael R. Beschloss and Strobe Talbott, *At the Highest Levels: The Inside Story of the End of the Cold War* (Boston: Little, Brown, 1993);

Sidney Blumenthal, *Our Long National Daydream: A Political Pageant of the Reagan Era* (New York: Harper & Row, 1988);

Blumenthal, *Pledging Allegiance: The Last Campaign of the Cold War* (New York: HarperCollins, 1990);

Walter Dean Burnham, *The Current Crisis in American Politics* (New York: Oxford University Press, 1982);

Lou Cannon, *Reagan* (New York: Putnam, 1982);

William H. Chafe, *The Unfinished Journey: America Since World War II*, second edition (New York: Oxford University Press, 1991);

Leslie Cockburn, *Out of Control: The Story of the Reagan Administration's Secret War in Nicaragua, the Illegal Arms Pipeline, and the Contra Drug Connection* (New York: Atlantic Monthly Press, 1987);

Elizabeth O. Colton, *The Jackson Phenomenon: The Man, the Power, the Message* (Doubleday, 1989);

Robert Dallek, *Ronald Reagan: The Politics of Symbolism* (Cambridge, Mass.: Harvard University Press, 1984);

Michael Deaver, with Mickey Hershkovits, *Behind the Scenes* (New York: Morrow, 1987);

Theodore Draper, *A Very Thin Line: The Iran Contra Affair* (New York: Hill & Wang, 1991);

Wilbur Edel, *The Reagan Presidency: An Actor's Finest Performance* (New York: Hippocrene Books, 1992);

Bob Faw, *Thunder in America: The Improbable Presidential Campaign of Jesse Jackson* (Austin: Texas Monthly Press, 1986);

Ernest B. Furgurson, *Hard Right: The Rise of Jesse Helms* (New York: Norton, 1986);

John Kenneth Galbraith, *A Journey Through Economic Time: A Firsthand View* (Boston: Houghton Mifflin, 1994);

Galbraith, *Reaganonomics: Meaning, Means, and Ends* (New York: Free Press, 1983);

Jack W. Germond and Jules Witcover, *Wake Us When It's Over: Presidential Politics of 1984* (New York: Macmillan, 1985);

Larry Gerston, Cynthia Fraleigh, and Robert Schwab, *The Deregulated Society* (Pacific Grove, Cal.: Brooks/Cole, 1988);

Roy Gutman, *Banana Diplomacy: The Making of American Policy in Nicaragua, 1981–1987* (New York: Simon & Schuster, 1988);

Alexander M. Haig, *Caveat: Reaganism, Realism, and Foreign Policy* (New York: Macmillan, 1984);

Jerome L. Himmelstein, *To the Right: The Transformation of American Conservatism* (Berkeley: University of California Press, 1990);

J. David Hoeveler Jr., *Watch on the Right: Conservative Intellectuals in the Reagan Administration* (Madison: University of Wisconsin Press, 1990);

Ernest R. House, *Jesse Jackson & the Politics of Charisma: The Rise and Fall of the Push/Excel Program* (Boulder, Colo.: Westview Press, 1988);

Jesse Jackson, *Straight From the Heart* (Philadelphia: Fortress Press, 1987);

Haynes Johnson, *Sleepwalking Through History: America in the Reagan Years* (New York: Norton, 1991);

Hamilton Jordan, *Crisis: The Last Year of the Carter Presidency* (New York: Putnam, 1982);

Michael B. Katz, *The Undeserving Poor: From the War on Poverty to the War on Welfare* (New York: Pantheon, 1982);

Paul Kennedy, *The Rise and Fall of the Great Powers: Economic Change and Military Conflict from 1500 to 2000* (New York: Random House, 1987);

Penn Kimball, *Keep Hope Alive!: Super Tuesday and Jesse Jackson's 1988 Campaign for the Presidency* (Washington, D.C.: Joint Center for Political and Economic Studies Press, 1992);

Jeane J. Kirkpatrick, *The Reagan Phenomenon, and Other Speeches on Foreign Policy* (Washington, D.C.: American Enterprise Institute, 1983);

Jane Mayer and Doyle McManus, *Landslide: The Unmaking of the President, 1984–1988* (Boston: Houghton Mifflin, 1988);

Mark A. Noll, *Religion and American Politics: From the Colonial Period to the 1980s* (New York: Oxford University Press, 1990);

Thomas P. O'Neill, *All Politics Is Local, and Other Rules of the Game* (New York: Times Books, 1994);

O'Neill, *Man of the House: The Life and Memoirs of Speaker Tip O'Neill* (New York: Random House, 1987);

Kevin P. Phillips, *The Politics of Rich and Poor: Wealth and the American Electorate in the Reagan Aftermath* (New York: Random House, 1990);

Phillips, *Post-Conservative America: People, Politics and Ideology in a Time of Crisis* (New York: Random House, 1982);

Gerald M. Pomper, Ross K. Baker, Walter Dean Burnham, Barbara G. Farah, Marjorie Randon Hershey, Ethel Klein, and Wilson Carey McWilliams, *The Election of 1988: Reports and Interpretations* (Chatham, N.J.: Chatham House, 1989);

Pomper, Baker, Kathleen A. Frankovic, Charles E. Jacob, McWilliams, and Henry A. Plotkin, *The Election of 1980: Reports and Interpretations* (Chatham, N.J.: Chatham House, 1981);

Pomper, Baker, Jacob, Scott Keeter, and McWilliams, *The Election of 1984: Reports and Interpretations* (Chatham, N.J.: Chatham House, 1985);

Austin Ranney, ed., *The American Elections of 1984* (Durham, N.C.: Duke University Press, 1985);

Nancy Reagan, with William Novak, *My Turn: The Memoirs of Nancy Reagan* (New York: Random House, 1989);

Ronald Reagan, *An American Life: The Autobiography* (New York: Simon & Schuster, 1990);

Donald T. Regan, *For the Record: From Wall Street to Washington* (San Diego, New York & London: Harcourt Brace Jovanovich, 1988);

Robert Reich, *The Next American Frontier* (New York: Times Books, 1983);

Hobart Rowen, *Self-Inflicted Wounds: From LBJ's Guns and Butter to Reagan's Voodoo Economics* (New York: Times Books, 1994);

David R. Runkel, *Campaigning for President: The Managers Look at '88* (Dover, Mass.: Auburn House, 1989);

Michael Schaller, *Reckoning with Reagan: America and Its President in the 1980s* (New York: Oxford University Press, 1992);

George P. Shultz, *Turmoil and Triumph: My Years as Secretary of State* (New York: Scribners, 1993);

Gary Sick, *All Fall Down: America's Tragic Encounter With Iran* (New York: Random House, 1985);

Sick, *October Surprise: America's Hostages in Iran and the Election of Ronald Reagan* (New York: Times Books/Random House, 1991);

Paul Slansky, *The Clothes Have No Emperor: A Chronicle of the American '80s* (New York: Simon & Schuster, 1989);

Geoffrey Smith, *Reagan and Thatcher* (New York: Norton, 1991);

Larry Speakes, with Robert Pack, *Speaking Out: The Reagan Presidency from Inside the White House* (New York: Scribners, 1988);

David A. Stockman, *The Triumph of Politics: Why the Reagan Revolution Failed* (New York: Harper & Row, 1986);

Strobe Talbott, *Deadly Gambits: The Reagan Administration and the Stalemate in Nuclear Arms Control* (New York: Knopf, 1988);

Talbott, *The Master of the Game: Paul Nitze and the Nuclear Peace* (New York: Knopf, 1988)

Lester Thurow, *The Zero-Sum Solution: Building a World-Class American Economy* (New York: Simon & Schuster, 1985);

John Tower, Edmund Muskie, and Brent Scowcroft, *The Tower Commission Report: The Full Text of the President's Special Review Board* (New York: Bantam, 1987);

Caspar W. Weinberger, *Fighting For Peace: Seven Critical Years in the Pentagon* (New York: Warner, 1990);

Theodore H. White, *America in Search of Itself: The Making of the President, 1956–1980* (New York: Harper & Row, 1982);

Garry Wills, *Reagan's America: Innocents at Home* (Garden City, N.Y.: Doubleday, 1987);

Bob Woodward, *Veil: The Secret Wars of the CIA, 1981–1987* (New York: Simon & Schuster, 1987).

LAW AND JUSTICE

David Abramsen, *Confessions of Son of Sam* (New York: Columbia University Press, 1985);

Shana Alexander, *Very Much A Lady* (Boston: Little, Brown, 1983);

Nan Aron, *Liberty and Justice For All: Public Interest Law in the 1980s* (Boulder, Colo.: Westview Press, 1989);

Tim Cahill, *Buried Dreams: Inside the Mind of a Serial Killer* (New York: Bantam, 1989);

Deborah Cameron and Elizabeth Frazer, *The Lust To Kill* (New York: New York University Press, 1987);

Alan Dershowitz, *Reversal of Fortune: Inside the von Bulow Case* (New York: Random House, 1986);

Dominick J. Di Maio and Vincent J. Di Maio, *Forensic Pathology* (New York: Elsevier/Nelson, 1989);

J. H. H. Gaute and Robin Odell, *The New Murderers' Who's Who* (New York: International Polygonics, 1989);

Robert W. Greene, *The Sting Man: Inside ABSCAM* (New York: Dutton, 1981);

Jean Harris, *Stranger In Two Worlds* (New York: Zebra Books, 1986);

Ronald Holmes and James De Burger, *Serial Murder* (Newbury Park, Cal.: Sage, 1988);

Elizabeth Kendall, *The Phantom Prince: My Life with Ted Bundy* (Seattle, Wash.: Madrona, 1981);

Jack Levin and James Alan Fox, *Mass Murder: America's Growing Menace* (New York: Plenum, 1988);

Elliott Leyton, *Hunting Humans: Inside the Minds of Mass Murderers* (New York: Pocket Books, 1986);

Lillian B. Rubin, *Quiet Rage: Bernie Goetz in a Time of Madness* (New York: Farrar, Straus & Giroux, 1986);

Ted Schwarz, *The Hillside Strangler: A Murderer's Mind* (Garden City, N.Y.: Doubleday, 1981);

Carl Sifakis, *The Encyclopedia of American Crime* (New York: Facts On File, 1982);

Terry Sullivan and Peter Maiken, *Killer Clown* (New York: Grosset & Dunlap, 1983);

Mike Taibbi and Anna Sims-Phillips, *Unholy Alliances: Working the Tawana Brawley Story* (New York: Harcourt Brace Jovanovich, 1989);

Maury Terry, *The Ultimate Evil: An Investigation into a Dangerous Satanic Cult* (New York: Bantam, 1989);

Ronald Tobias, *They Shoot To Kill* (Boulder, Colo.: Paladin Press, 1981);

Colin Wilson and Donald Seaman, *Encyclopedia of Modern Murder* (New York: Arlington House, 1983, 1988).

LIFESTYLES AND SOCIAL TRENDS

David F. Allen and James F. Jekel, *Crack: The Broken Promise* (New York: St. Martin's Press, 1991);

Margaret K. Ambry, *Consumer Power: How Americans Spend Their Money* (Ithaca, N.Y.: New Strategists Publications, 1991);

Beth L. Bailey, *From Front Porch to Back Seat: Courtship in Twentieth-Century America* (Baltimore: Johns Hopkins University Press, 1988);

David Bender and Bruno Leone, eds., *Child Abuse: Opposing Viewpoints* (San Diego: Greenhaven Press, 1994);

Merton C. Bernstein and Joan Brodshaug Bernstein, *Social Security: The System That Works* (New York: Basic Books, 1988);

George Beschner and Alfred S. Friedman, *Teen Drug Use* (Lexington, Mass.: Lexington Books, 1986);

Allan Bloom, *The Closing of the American Mind: How Higher Education Has Failed Democracy and Impoverished the Souls of Today's Students*, foreword by Saul Bellow (New York: Simon & Schuster, 1987);

Toni Carabillo, Judith Meuli, and June Bundy Csida, *Feminist Chronicles: 1953–1993* (Los Angeles: Women's Graphics, 1993);

F. M. Christensen, *Pornography: The Other Side* (New York, Westport, Conn. & London: Praeger, 1990);

Robine E. Clark and Judith Freeman Clark, *The Encyclopedia of Child Abuse* (New York: Facts On File, 1989);

Stephanie Coontz, *The Way We Never Were: American Families and the Nostalgia Trap* (New York: Basic Books, 1992);

John D'Emilio and Estelle B. Freedman, *Intimate Matters: A History of Sexuality in America* (New York: Harper & Row, 1988);

Barbara Ehrenreich, *The Worst Years Of Our Lives: Irreverent Notes From A Decade of Greed* (New York: Pantheon, 1990);

Susan Faludi, *Backlash: The Undeclared War against American Women* (New York: Crown, 1991);

Rick Fantasia and Maurice Isserman, *Homelessness: A Sourcebook* (New York: Facts On File, 1994);

David Finkelhor, Linda Meyer Williams, and Nanci Burns, *Nursery Crimes: Sexual Abuse in Day Care* (Newbury Park, Cal.: Sage, 1988);

Peter Francese and Rebecca Piirto, *Capturing Customers: How To Target The Hottest Markets of the '90s* (Ithaca, N.Y.: American Demographics Press, 1990);

Richard A. Gardner, *Sex Abuse Hysteria: Salem Witch Trials Revisited* (Cresskill, N.J.: Creative Therapeutics, 1991);

A. Bartlett Giamatti, *Take Time for Paradise: Americans and Their Games* (New York: Summit Books, 1989);

Patrick Glynn, *Closing Pandora's Box: Arms Races, Arms Control, and the History of the Cold War* (New York: Basic Books, 1992);

Judith Graham, ed., *Current Biography Yearbook: 1992* (New York: Wilson, 1992);

Susan Gubar and Joan Hoff, eds., *For Adult Users Only: The Dilemma of Violent Pornography* (Bloomington & Indianapolis: Indiana University Press, 1989);

Jonathan Harris, *Drugged America* (New York: Four Winds Press, 1991);

David Hey, *The Oxford Guide to Family History* (New York: Oxford University Press, 1986);

Joan Hoff-Wilson, *Rights of Passage: The Past and Future of the ERA* (Bloomington: Indiana University Press, 1986);

Mary Ellen Hombs, *American Homelessness: A Reference Handbook* (Santa Barbara, Cal.: ABC-CLIO, 1990);

Jerome H. Jaffe, ed., *Encyclopedia of Drugs and Alcohol* (New York: Simon & Schuster Macmillan, 1995);

Morris Janowitz, *The Reconstruction of Patriotism: Education for Civic Consciousness* (Chicago: University of Chicago Press, 1983);

Milton S. Katz, *Ban the Bomb: A History of SANE, the Committee for a Sane Nuclear Policy, 1957–1985* (New York: Greenwood Press, 1986);

James Kinsella, *Covering the Plague: AIDS and the American Media* (New Brunswick, N.J.: Rutgers University Press, 1989);

Albert D. Klassen, Colin J. Williams, and others, *Sex and Morality in the U.S.* (Middletown, Conn.: Wesleyan University Press, 1989);

William Severini Kowinski, *The Malling of America: An Inside Look at the Great Consumer Paradise* (New York: Morrow, 1985);

Bart Landry, *The New Black Middle Class* (Berkeley: University of California Press, 1987);

Paul Rogat Loeb, *Hope in Hard Times: America's Peace Movement and the Reagan Era* (Lexington, Mass.: Lexington Books, 1987);

Richard Maltby, *Passing Parade: A History of Popular Culture in the Twentieth Century* (New York: Oxford University Press, 1989);

Jane J. Mansbridge, *Why We Lost the ERA* (Chicago: University of Chicago Press, 1986);

Nancy F. McKenzie, ed., *The AIDS Reader: Social, Political, and Ethical Issues* (New York: Meridian, 1991);

Richard A. Melanson, *Reconstructing Consensus: American Foreign Policy Since the Vietnam War* (New York: St. Martin's Press, 1991);

Joan Moore and Harry Pachon, *Hispanics in the United States* (Englewood Cliffs, N.J.: Prentice-Hall, 1985);

Dorothy Nelkin, David P. Willis, and Scott V. Parris, eds., *A Disease of Society: Cultural and Institutional Responses to AIDS* (Cambridge, New York, Port Ches-

ter, Melbourne & Sydney: Cambridge University Press, 1991);

Charles Panati, *Panati's Parade of Fads, Follies, and Manias: The Origins of Our Most Cherished Obsessions* (New York: HarperPerennial, 1991);

Erdman B. Patmore, *Handbook on the Aged in the United States* (Westport, Conn.: Greenwood Press, 1994);

Kevin Phillips, *The Politics Of Rich and Poor: Wealth and the American Electorate in the Reagan Aftermath* (New York: Random House, 1990);

Harry A. Ploski and James Williams, eds., *The Negro Almanac: A Reference Work on the African American*, fifth edition (Detroit: Gale Research, 1989);

Rosalind Rosenberg, *Divided Lives: American Women in the Twentieth Century* (New York: Hill & Wang, 1992);

Kirkpatrick Sale, *The Green Revolution: The American Environmental Movement, 1962–1992* (New York: Hill & Wang, 1993);

Robert B. Settle and Pamela L. Alreck, *Why They Buy: American Consumers Inside and Out* (New York: Wiley, 1986);

Shelby Steele, *The Content of Our Character: A New Vision of Race in America* (New York: St. Martin's Press, 1990);

D. T. Suzuki, *An Introduction to Zen Buddhism* (New York: Grove, 1991);

Cynthia Taeuber, ed., *Statistical Handbook on Women in America* (Phoenix: Oryx Press, 1991);

U.S. Advisory Board on Child Abuse and Neglect, *Child Abuse and Neglect: Critical First Steps in Response to a National Emergency* (Washington, D.C.: Department of Health and Human Services, Office of Human Development Series, 1990);

Paul L. Wachtel, *The Poverty Of Affluence: A Psychological Portrait of the American Way of Life* (New York: Free Press, 1988);

Jill Waterman, Robert J. Kelly, Mary Kay Oliveri, and Jane McCord, *Behind the Playground Walls: Sexual Abuse in Preschools* (New York: Guilford Press, 1993);

Lenore J. Weitzman, *The Divorce Revolution* (New York: Free Press, 1985);

Geraldine Woods, *Drug Abuse In Society: A Reference Handbook*, Contemporary World Issues Series (Santa Barbara, Cal.: ABC-CLIO, 1993).

MEDIA

David Armstrong, *A Trumpet to Arms: Alternative Media in America* (Los Angeles: J. P. Tarcher, 1981);

Ken Auletta, *Three Blind Mice: How the TV Networks Lost Their Way* (New York: Random House, 1991);

Thomas G. Aylesworth, *Great Moments of Television* (New York: Exeter Books, 1987);

Ben H. Bagdikian, *Media Monopoly* (Boston: Beacon, 1990);

Eric Barnouw, *Tube of Plenty: The Evolution of American Television,* second edition (New York: Oxford University Press, 1990);

Gwenda Blair, *Almost Golden: Jessica Savitch and the Selling of the American News* (New York: Simon & Schuster, 1988);

Alex Ben Block, *Outfoxed: Marvin Davis, Barry Diller, Rupert Murdoch, Joan Rivers, and the Inside Story of America's Fourth Television Network* (New York: St. Martin's Press, 1990);

The Bowker Annual of Library & Book Trade Information (New York & London: R. R. Bowker, 1981–1990);

David S. Broder, *Behind the Front Page* (New York: Simon & Schuster, 1987);

Les Brown, *Les Brown's Encyclopedia of Television* (New York: New York Zoetrope, 1982);

Jack Casserly, *Scripps: The Divided Dynasty* (New York: Donald I. Fine, 1993);

Jannette L. Dates and William Barlow, eds., *Split Image: African Americans in the Mass Media* (Washington, D.C.: Howard University Press, 1990);

R. Serge Denisoff, *Inside MTV* (New Brunswick, N.J.: Transaction Books, 1988);

Edwin Diamond and Stephen Bates, *The Spot: The Rise of Political Advertising on Television* (Cambridge, Mass.: MIT Press, 1988);

Michael Emery and Edwin Emery, *The Press and America: An Interpretive History of the Mass Media,* seventh edition (Englewood Cliffs, N.J.: Prentice Hall, 1992);

Martin Esslin, *The Age of Television* (San Francisco: Freeman, 1982);

Todd Gitlin, *Inside Prime Time* (New York: Pantheon, 1983);

Robert Goldberg and Gerald Jay Goldberg, *Citizen Turner* (New York & San Diego: Harcourt Brace, 1995);

Andrew Goodwin, *Dancing in the Distraction Factory: Music Television and Popular Culture* (Minneapolis: University of Minnesota Press, 1992);

Mark Hertsgaard, *On Bended Knee: The Press and the Reagan Presidency* (New York: Farrar, Straus & Giroux, 1989);

David H. Hosley and Gayle K. Yamada, *Hard News: Women In Broadcast Journalism* (Westport, Conn.: Greenwood Press, 1987);

Douglas Kellner, *Media Culture: Cultural studies, identity and politics between the modern and the postmodern* (London & New York: Routledge, 1995);

Thomas Kiernan, *Citizen Murdoch* (New York: Dodd, Mead, 1986);

Richard Kluger, *The Paper: The Life and Death of the New York Herald Tribune* (New York: Knopf, 1986);

J. Fred MacDonald, *Black and White TV: Afro-Americans in Television Since 1948* (Chicago: Nelson-Hall, 1983);

Thomas Maier, *Newhouse: All the Glitter, Power, and Glory of America's Richest Media Empire and the Secretive Man Behind It* (New York: St. Martin's Press, 1994);

George Mair, *Oprah Winfrey: The Real Story* (New York: Birch Lane Press, 1994);

David Marc and Robert J. Thompson, *Prime Time, Prime Movers* (Boston: Little, Brown, 1992);

Alvin H. Marrill, *Movies Made For Television: The Telefeature and the Miniseries, 1964–1986* (New York: New York Zoetrope, 1987);

Barbara Matusow, *The Evening Stars* (Boston: Houghton Mifflin, 1983);

Richard H. Meeker, *Newspaperman: S. I. Newhouse and the Business of News* (New Haven & New York: Ticknor & Fields, 1983);

Kathryn C. Montgomery, *Target Prime Time: Advocacy Groups and the Struggle Over Entertainment Television* (New York: Oxford University Press, 1989);

Ron Powers, *The Beast, the Eunuch, and the Glass-eyed Child: Television In the '80s* (San Diego: Harcourt Brace Jovanovich, 1990);

Carl Rowan, *Breaking Barriers: A Memoir* (Boston: Little, Brown, 1991);

Jessica Savitch, *Anchorwoman* (New York: Putnam, 1982);

Madelon Golden Schlipp and Sharon M. Murphy, *Great Women of the Press* (Carbondale: Southern Illinois University Press, 1983);

Michael Schudson, *The Power of News* (Cambridge, Mass.: Harvard University Press, 1995);

William Shawcross, *Murdoch* (New York: Simon & Schuster, 1992);

Anthony Smith, *Goodbye Gutenberg: The Newspaper Revolution of the 1980s* (New York: Oxford University Press, 1980);

Ronald L. Smith, *Cosby* (New York: St. Martin's Press, 1986);

James D. Squires, *Read All About It: The Corporate Takeover of America's Newspapers* (New York: Times Books, 1993);

Christopher H. Sterling, ed., *Electronic Media: A Guide to Trends in Broadcasting and Newer Technologies, 1920–1983* (New York: Praeger, 1983);

Gerald Stone, *Examining Newspapers: What Research Reveals About America's Newspapers*, Vol. 20, Sage CommText Series (Newbury Park, Cal.: Sage, 1987);

Doug Underwood, *When MBAs Rule the Newsroom: How the Marketers and Managers Are Reshaping Today's Media* (New York: Columbia University Press, 1993);

Ana Veciana-Suarez, *Hispanic Media, USA* (Washington, D.C.: Media Institute, 1987);

Hank Whittemore, *CNN: The Inside Story* (Boston: Little, Brown, 1990);

Michael Winship, *Television* (New York: Random House, 1988).

MEDICINE

Drew Altman, *AIDS in the Mind of America* (Garden City, N.Y.: Anchor, 1986);

Altman, Richard Greene, and Harvey M. Sapolsky, *Health Planning and Regulation: The Decision-Making Process* (Washington, D.C.: AUPHA, 1981);

L. B. Andrews, *New Conceptions: A Consumer's Guide to the Newest Infertility Treatments* (New York: St. Martin's Press, 1984);

L. Bachrach, ed., *New Directions for Mental Health Services: Deinstitutionalization* (San Francisco: Jossey-Bass, 1983);

Ross J. Baldessarini, *Chemotherapy in Psychiatry: Principles and Practice,* revised edition (Cambridge, Mass.: Harvard University Press, 1985);

David Baltimore and S. Wolf, eds., *Confronting AIDS: Directions for Public Health, Health Care and Research* (Washington, D.C., National Academy Press, 1986);

Yvonne Baskin, *The Gene Doctors* (New York: Morrow, 1984);

William Bennett and Joel Gurin, *The Dieter's Dilemma* (New York: Basic Books, 1982);

R. A. Berk, ed., *The Social Impact of AIDS in the USA* (Cambridge, Mass.: Abt, 1988);

Henry Berman and Louisa Rose, *Choosing the Right Health Plan* (Mount Vernon, N.Y.: Consumer Reports Books, 1990);

D. Black, *The Plague Years: A Chronicle of AIDS, the Epidemic of Our Times* (New York: Simon & Schuster, 1986);

D. Bolognesi, ed., *Human Retroviruses, Cancer and AIDS: Approaches to Prevention and Therapy* (New York: Liss, 1988);

Marlene Boskind-White and William White, *Bulimarexia: The Binge/Purge Cycle* (New York: Norton, 1987);

A. M. Brandt, *No Magic Bullet: A Social History of Venereal Disease in the United States since 1800. With a New Chapter on AIDS,* second edition (New York & Oxford: Oxford University Press, 1987);

Dennis L. Breo and Noel Keane, *The Surrogate Mother* (New York: Everest House, 1981);

Joan Jacobs Brumberg, *Fasting Girls: The Emergence of Anorexia Nervosa as a Modern Disease* (Cambridge, Mass.: Harvard University Press, 1988);

A. Cantwell Jr., *AIDS, the Mystery and Solution* (Los Angeles: Aries Rising Press, 1986);

Edward K. Chung, *One Heart, One Life* (Englewood Cliffs, N.J.: Prentice-Hall, 1982);

H. M. Cole and G. D. Lundberg, *AIDS: From the Beginning* (Chicago: American Medical Association, 1986);

S. Connor and S. Kingman, *The Search for the Virus: The Scientific Discovery of AIDS and the Quest for a Cure* (Harmondsworth, U.K.: Penguin, 1988);

Gene Corea, *The Mother Machine: Reproductive Technologies from Artificial Insemination to Artificial Wombs* (New York: Harper & Row, 1985);

P. G. Crosignani, *In Vitro Fertilization and Embryo Transfer* (London & New York: Academic Press, 1983);

H. L. Dalton and S. Burris, *AIDS and the Law* (New Haven: Yale University Press, 1987);

S. Davidson and R. Hudson, *Rock Hudson, His Story* (New York: Morrow, 1986);

R. G. Edwards and P. C. Steptoe, *A Matter of Life* (New York: Morrow, 1980);

John Elkington, *The Gene Factory: The Science and Business of Biotechnology* (New York: Carroll & Graf, 1987);

Alain C. Enthoven, *Health Plan: The Only Practical Solution to Soaring Health Costs* (Reading, Mass.: Addison-Wesley, 1980);

C. F. Farthing and others, *A Colour Atlas of AIDS* (Chicago: Yearbook Medical Publications, 1986);

Rashi Fein, *Medical Care, Medical Costs: The Search for a Health Insurance Policy* (Cambridge, Mass.: Harvard University Press, 1986);

A. G. Fettner and W. A. Check, *The Truth about AIDS: Evolution of an Epidemic* (New York: Holt, Rinehart & Winston, 1984);

Seymour Fisher and Roger Greenberg, *The Scientific Credibility of Freud's Theories and Therapy* (New York: Basic Books, 1985);

A. F. Fleming, ed., *The Global Impact of AIDS* (New York: Liss, 1988);

Robert C. Gallo and F. Wong-Staal, eds., *Retrovirus Biology: An Emerging Role in Human Diseases* (New York: Dekker, 1988);

Lawrence Galton, *Med Tech: The Layperson's Guide to Today's Medical Miracles* (New York: Harper & Row, 1985);

Paul E. Garfield and David M. Garner, *Anorexia Nervosa: A Multidimensional Perspective* (New York: Brunner/Mazel, 1982);

Jeff Charles Goldsmith, *Can Hospitals Survive? The New Competitive Health Care Market* (Homewood, Ill.: Dow Joines-Irwin, 1981);

M. S. Gottlieb and others, eds., *Current Topics in AIDS* (New York: Wiley, 1987);

Ellen Greenfield, *House Dangerous: Indoor Pollution in Your Home and Office — and What You Can Do About It* (New York: Vintage, 1987);

Cynthia S. Gross, *The New Biotechnology: Putting Microbes to Work* (New York: Lerner, 1987);

M. Haug and B. Lavin, *Consumerism in Medicine* (Beverly Hills, Cal.: Sage, 1983);

Health & Medical Horizons 1986 (New York: Macmillan Educational Co., 1986);

Judi Hollis, *Fat Is a Family Affair* (Center City, Minn.: Hazelden Educational Materials, 1985);

H. B. Holmes, B. B. Hoskins, and M. Gross, eds., *The Custom-Made Child* (Clifton, N.J.: Humana Press, 1981);

A. F. Ide, *AIDS Hysteria* (Dallas: Monument Press, 1986);

Institute of Medicine, National Academy of Sciences, *Confronting AIDS: Directions for Public Health, Health Care, and Research* (Washington, D.C.: National Academy Press, 1986);

Elisabeth Kübler-Ross, *AIDS, the Ultimate Challenge* (New York: Macmillan, 1987);

Elaine Landau, *Surrogate Mothers* (New York: Franklin Watts, 1988);

Landau, *Why Are They Starving Themselves: Understanding Anorexia Nervosa and Bulimia* (New York: Julian Messner, 1983);

Mark Lappe, *Broken Code: The Exploitation of DNA* (San Francisco: Sierra Book Clubs, 1984);

Judith Lasker and Susan Borg, *In Search of Parenthood: Coping with Infertility and High Tech Conception* (Boston: Beacon, 1988);

Gerald Leinwald, *Transplants* (New York: Franklin Watts, 1985);

Martin R. Lipp, *The Bitter Pill* (New York: Harper & Row, 1980);

John Francis Marion, *The Fine Old House: Smith Kline Corporation's First 150 Years* (Philadelphia: Smith Kline, 1980);

Jeffrey M. Masson, *The Assault on Truth: Freud's Suppression of the Seduction Theory* (New York: Farrar, Straus & Giroux, 1984);

W. A. Masters, E. Johnson, and R. C. Kolodny, *Crisis: Heterosexual Behavior in the Age of AIDS* (New York: Grove Press, 1988);

Aubrey Milunsky, ed., *Genetic Disorders and the Fetus* (New York: Plenum Press, 1986);

Ian I. Mitroff and Ralph H. Kilmann, *Corporate Tragedies: Product Tampering, Sabotage, and Other Catastrophes* (New York: Praeger, 1984);

National Research Council, National Academy of Sciences, *Indoor Pollutants* (Washington, D.C.: National Academy Press, 1981);

Ranganath Nayak and John M. Ketteringham, *Breakthroughs!* (New York: Rawson, 1986);

Dorothy Nelkin and Laurence Tancredi, *Dangerous Diagnostics: The Social Power of Biological Information* (New York: Basic Books, 1989);

Eve K. Nicholas, ed., *Human Gene Therapy* (Cambridge, Mass.: Harvard University Press, 1988);

E. K. Nichols, *Mobilizing against AIDS: The Unfinished Story of a Virus* (Cambridge, Mass.: Harvard University Press, 1986);

L. G. Nungasser, *Epidemic of Courage: Facing AIDS in America* (New York: St. Martin's Press, 1986);

S. Panem, *The AIDS Bureaucracy: U.S. Government Response to AIDS in the First Five Years* (Cambridge, Mass.: Harvard University Press, 1988);

John Parascandola, ed., *The History of Antibiotics: A Symposium* (Madison, Wis.: American Institute of the History of Pharmacy, 1980);

B. Peabody, *The Screaming Room: A Mother's Journal of Her Son's Struggle with AIDS* (San Diego: Oak Tree, 1986);

Harrison G. Pope Jr. and James I. Hudson, *New Hope for Binge Eaters: Advances in the Understanding and Treatment of Bulimia* (New York: Harper & Row, 1984);

President's Commission for the Study of Ethical Problems in Biomedical Research, *Splicing Life: A Report on the Social and Ethical Issues of Genetic Engineering* (Washington, D.C.: U.S. Government Printing Office, 1982);

Tom Riley, *The Price of a Life: One Woman's Death From Toxic Shock* (Bethesda, Md.: Adler & Adler, 1986);

B. K. Rothman, *The Tentative Pregnancy: Prenatal Diagnosis the the Future of Motherhood* (New York: Viking, 1986);

David Rousseau, W. J. Rea, Jean Enwright, *Your Home, Your Health, and Well-Being* (Berkeley, Cal.: Ten Speed Press, 1988);

Margery W. Shaw, ed., *After Barney Clark* (Austin: University of Texas Press, 1984);

Randy Shilts, *And the Band Played On: Politics, People, and the AIDS Epidemic* (New York: St Martin's Press, 1987);

Edward Shorter, *Bedside Manners: The Troubled History of Doctors and Patients* (New York: Simon & Schuster, 1985);

Shorter, *The Health Century* (New York: Doubleday, 1987);

Shorter, *History of Women's Bodies* (New York: Basic Books, 1982);

P. Singer and D. Wells, *Making Babies: The New Science and Ethics of Conception* (New York: Scribner, 1985);

Walter Sneader, *Drug Discovery: The Evolution of Modern Medicine* (New York: Wiley, 1985);

Patricia Spallone, *Beyond Conception: The New Politics of Reproduction* (Granby, Mass.: Bergin & Garvey Publishers, 1989);

David B. Starkweather, *Hospital Mergers in the Making* (Ann Arbor, Mich.: Health Administration Press, 1981);

Paul Starr, *The Social Transformation of American Medicine: The rise of a sovereign profession and the making of a vast industry* (New York: Basic Books, 1982);

DeWitt Steten Jr., *NIH: An Account of Research in Its Laboratories and Clinics* (Orlando: Academic Press, 1984);

Lewis Thomas, *The Lasker Awards: Four Decades of Scientific Medical Progress* (New York: Albert & Mary Lasker Foundation, 1985);

Isaac Turiel, *Indoor Air Quality and Human Health* (Stanford, Cal.: Stanford University Press, 1985);

Elliot Valenstein, *Great and Desperate Cures: The Rise and Decline of Psychosurgery and Other Radical Treatments for Mental Illness* (New York: Basic Books, 1986);

Ruth Westheimer, *All in a Lifetime* (New York: Warner Books, 1983);

Westheimer, *Dr. Ruth's Guide to Good Sex* (New York: Warner, 1983);

Westheimer, *First Love: A Young People's Guide to Sexual Information* (New York: Warner, 1983);

P. R. Wheale and Ruth McNulty, *Genetic Engineering: Catastrophe or Utopia?* (New York: St. Martin's Press, 1987);

Mary Beth Whitehead, with Loretta Schwartz-Nobel, *A Mother's Story: The Truth About the Baby M Case* (New York: St. Martin's Press, 1989);

C. Wood and A. Westmore, *Test-Tube Conception* (Englewood Cliffs, N.J.: Prentice-Hall, 1984);

G. P. Wormser, R. E. Stahl, and E. J. Bottone, eds., *AIDS: Acquired Immunodeficiency Syndrome and Other Manifestations of HIV Infection* (Park Ridge, N.J.: Noyes, 1987);

Burke K. Zimmerman, *Biofuture: Confronting the Genetic Era* (New York: Plenum Press, 1984);

Zimmerman and Raymond A. Zilinkas, eds., *Reflection on the Recombinant DNA Controversy* (New York: Macmillan, 1984).

RELIGION

Nancy Tatom Ammerman, *Bible Believers: Fundamentalism in the Modern World* (New Brunswick, N.J.: Rutgers University Press, 1987);

Karen Armstrong, *The Gospel According to Women: Christianity's Creation of the Sex Wars in the West* (Garden City, N.Y.: Anchor/Doubleday, 1987);

William Sims Bainbridge, *The Future of Religion: Secularization, Revival and Cult Formation* (Berkeley: University of California Press, 1985);

Randall Balmer, *Mine Eyes Have Seen the Glory: A Journey into the Evangelical Subculture of America* (New York: Oxford University Press, 1989);

Robert N. Bellah and others, *Habits of the Heart: Individualism and Commitment in American Life* (Berkeley: University of California Press, 1985);

Richard C. Brown, *The Presbyterians: Two Hundred Years in Danville, 1784–1984* (Danville, Ky.: Presbyterian Church, 1983);

Kennon L. Callahan, *Twelve Keys to an Effective Church* (San Francisco: Harper & Row, 1983);

Joseph Castelli and Jim Gremillion, *The Emerging Parish: The Notre Dame Study of Catholic Life Since Vatican II* (San Francisco: Harper & Row, 1987);

Steven M. Cohen, *American Assimilation or Jewish Revival* (Bloomington: Indiana University Press, 1988);

John Cooney, *The American Pope* (New York: Times Books, 1984);

Harvey Cox, *Religion in the Secular City* (New York: Simon & Schuster, 1984);

Herbert M. Danzger, *Returning to Tradition: The Contemporary Revival of Orthodox Judaism* (New Haven: Yale University Press, 1989);

John Deedy, *American Catholicism: And Now Where?* (New York: Plenum Press, 1987);

James T. Draper and Forrest E. Watson, *If the Foundations Be Destroyed* (Nashville: Oliver Nelson, 1984);

Wilber Edel, *Defenders of the Faith: Religion and Politics from the Pilgrim Fathers to Ronald Reagan* (New York: Praeger, 1987);

Ronald Enroth, *Lure of the Cults and New Religions* (Downers Grove, Ill.: InterVarsity Press, 1987);

Jerry Falwell, *The Fundamentalist Phenomenon: The Resurgence of Conservative Christianity* (Garden City, N.Y.: Doubleday, 1981);

Marilyn Ferguson, *The Aquarian Conspiracy: Personal and Social Transformation in the 1980s* (Los Angeles: J. P. Tarcher, 1980);

Marshall Fishwick and Ray B. Browne, eds., *The God Pumpers: Religion in the Electronic Age* (Bowling Green, Ohio: Bowling Green University Popular Press, 1987);

William F. Fore, *Television and Religion: The Shaping of Faith, Values, and Culture* (Minneapolis: Augsburg Publishing House, 1987);

J. W. Fowler, *Stages of Faith* (New York: Harper & Row, 1981);

Andrew Greeley, *Religious Change in America* (Cambridge, Mass.: Harvard University Press, 1989);

Douglas R. Groothuis, *Unmasking the New Age* (Downers Grove, Ill.: InterVarsity Press, 1986);

Andres Gonzales Guerrero, *A Chicano Theology* (Maryknoll, N.Y.: Orbis Books, 1987);

Patricia Gundry, *Neither Slave nor Free: Helping Women Answer the Call to Church Leadership* (San Francisco: Harper & Row, 1987);

Jeffrey K. Hadden and Anson Shupe, *Televangelism: Power and Politics on God's Frontier* (New York: Holt, 1988);

James Hennesey, *American Catholics: A History of the Roman Catholic Community in the United States* (Oxford: Oxford University Press, 1981);

Peter G. Horsefield, *Religious Television: The American Experience* (New York: Longman, 1984);

James Davidson Hunter, *American Evangelicalism: Conservative Religion and the Quandary of Modernity* (New Brunswick, N.J.: Rutgers University Press, 1983);

William R. Hutchenson, *Between the Times: The Travail of the Protestant Establishment in America, 1900–1960* (Cambridge: Cambridge University Press, 1989);

Erling Jorstad, *Being Religious in America* (Minneapolis: Augsburg Publishing House, 1986);

Robert B. Kaiser, *The Politics of Sex and Religion* (Kansas City: Leaven Press, 1985);

Lawrence Lader, *Politics, Power and the Church: The Catholic Crisis and Its Challenge to American Pluralism* (New York: Macmillan, 1987);

Charles H. Lippy, ed., *Twentieth-Century Shapers of American Popular Religion* (New York: Greenwood Press, 1989);

Robin W. Lovin, ed., *Religion and American Public Life* (New York: Paulist Press, 1986);

Isidro Lucas, *The Browning of America: The Hispanic Revolution in the American Church* (Chicago: Fides/Claretian, 1981);

Shirley MacLaine, *Dancing In the Light* (Toronto: Bantam, 1985);

Gregory Martire and Ruth Clark, *Anti-Semitism in the United States* (New York: Praeger, 1982);

Martin E. Marty, *Modern American Religion* (Chicago: University of Chicago Press, 1986);

Egon Mayer, *Love and Tradition: Marriage Between Jews and Christians* (New York: Schocken, 1985);

Michael A. Meyer, *Response to Modernity: A History of the Reform Movement in Judaism* (New York: Oxford University Press, 1988);

Ida Rousseau Mukenge, *The Black Church in Urban America* (Lanham, Md.: University Press of America, 1983);

Mark A. Noll and others, *The Search for Christian America* (Westchester, Ill.: Crossway Books, 1983);

Richard Quebedeaux, *By What Authority: The Rise of Personality Cults in American Christianity* (San Francisco: Harper & Row, 1982);

James Randi, *The Faith-Healers* (Buffalo: Prometheus Books, 1987);

James A. Reich, *Religion in American Public Life* (Washington, D.C.: Brookings Institution, 1985);

Pat Robertson, *America's Dates with Destiny* (Nashville: Thomas Nelson, 1986);

Wade Clark Roof and William McKinney, *American Mainline Religion: Its Changing Shape and Future* (New Brunswick, N.J.: Rutgers University Press, 1987);

Marshall Sklare, ed., *Understanding American Jewry* (New Brunswick, N.J.: Transaction Books, 1982);

Timothy L. Smith, *Revivalism and Social Reform in the Mid-Nineteenth Century America* (Baltimore: Johns Hopkins University Press, 1980);

Richard A. Viguerie, *The New Right: We're Ready to Lead* (Falls Church, Va.: Viguerie, 1981);

Kenneth D. Wald, *Religion and Politics in the United States* (New York: St. Martin's Press, 1987);

George Weigel, *Catholicism and the Renewal of American Democracy* (New York: Paulist Press, 1989);

Sharon D. Welch, *Communities of Resistance and Solidarity: A Feminist Theology of Liberation* (Maryknoll, N.Y.: Orbis Books, 1985);

Bryan R. Wilson, ed., *The Social Impact of New Religious Movements* (New York: Rose of Sharon Press, 1981);

Jonathan Woocher, *Sacred Survival: The Civic Religion of American Jews* (Bloomington: Indiana University Press, 1986);

James E. Wood Jr., ed., *Religion and the State* (Waco: Baylor University Press, 1985);

Robert Wuthnow, *The Restructuring of American Religion: Society and Faith Since World War II* (Princeton: Princeton University Press, 1988).

SCIENCE AND TECHNOLOGY

Isaac Asimov, *Frontiers: New Discoveries about Man and His Planet, Outer Space, and the Universe* (New York: Dutton, 1989);

Asimov, *The Universe: From Flat Earth to Black Holes — And Beyond* (New York: Walker, 1980);

David Attenborough, *Life on Earth: A Natural History* (London: Reader's Digest, 1980);

Anthony Aveni, *Empires of Time: Calendars, Clocks, and Cultures* (New York: Basic Books, 1989);

John D. Barrow and Frank J. Tipler, *The Anthropic Cosmological Principle* (Oxford: Oxford University Press, 1988);

John Boslough, *Stephen Hawking's Universe* (New York: Morrow, 1985);

Richard A. Carrigan Jr. and W. Peter Trowers, eds., *Particle Physics in the Cosmos* (New York: Freeman, 1989);

Nathan Cohen, *Gravity's Lens* (New York: Wiley, 1988);

Paul Davies, *Superforce* (New York: Simon & Schuster, 1984);

Freeman Dyson, *Infinite in All Directions* (New York: Harper & Row, 1985);

Richard P. Feynman, *QED: The Strange Theory of Light and Matter* (Princeton: Princeton University Press, 1983);

Feynman, *Surely You're Joking Mr. Feynman!* (New York: Norton, 1985);

Julius T. Fraser, *Time: The Familiar Stranger* (Boston: University of Massachusetts Press, 1987);

Stephen Jay Gould, *The Flamingo's Smile* (New York: Norton, 1985);

Stephen Hawking, *A Brief History of Time: From the Big Bang to Blackholes* (New York: Bantam, 1988);

Werner Heisenberg, *Encounters with Einstein* (Princeton: Princeton University Press, 1989);

Douglas R. Hofstadter, *Godel, Escher, Bach: An Eternal Golden Braid* (New York: Vantage, 1980);

David Macaulay and Neil Ardley, *The Way Things Work* (London: Kindersley, 1988);

Heinz Pagels, *The Cosmic Code* (New York: Simon & Schuster, 1982);

Carl Sagan, *Cosmos* (New York: Random House, 1980);

Gary Taubes, *Nobel Dreams* (New York: Random House, 1986);

Steven Weinberg, *The First Three Minutes* (New York: Bantam, 1984).

SPORTS

Charles C. Alexander, *Our Game: An American Baseball History* (New York: Holt, 1991);

Peter Arnold, *The Olympic Games: Athens 1896 to Los Angeles 1984* (London: Optimum, 1983);

Arthur Ashe and Arnold Rampersad, *Days of Grace* (New York: Knopf, 1993);

Arthur R. Ashe Jr., *A Hard Road to Glory: A History of the African-American Athlete Since 1946* (New York: Warner, 1988);

Larry Bird, with Bob Ryan, *Drive: The Story of My Life* (New York: Doubleday, 1989);

Thomas Boswell, *Strokes of Genius* (New York: Doubleday, 1987);

Neil Cohen, *Jackie Joyner-Kersee* (Boston: Little, Brown, 1992);

Bud Collins, *My Life With the Pros* (New York: Dutton, 1989);

John Feinstein, *Hard Court: Real Life on the Professional Tennis Tours* (New York: Villard, 1991);

Rhonda Glenn, *The Illustrated History of Women's Golf* (Dallas: Taylor, 1991);

Peter Golenbock, *American Zoom: Stock Car Racing — From the Dirt Tracks to Daytona* (New York: Macmillan, 1993);

Steven Goodwin, *The Greatest Masters: The 1986 Masters and Golf's Elite* (New York: Harper & Row, 1988);

Wayne Gretzky, *Gretzky: An Autobiography* (New York: HarperCollins, 1990);

Allen Guttmann, *The Olympics: A History of the Modern Games* (Urbana & Chicago: University of Illinois Press, 1992);

Guttman, *A Whole New Ball Game: An Interpretation of American Sports* (Chapel Hill: University of North Carolina Press, 1988);

John Hoberman, *The Olympic Crisis: Sport, Politics and the Moral Order* (New York: Caratzas, 1986);

Montieth Illingworth, *Mike Tyson: Money, Myth, and Betrayal* (New York: Carol Publishing Group, 1991);

Dan Jenkins, *Fairways and Greens: The Best Golf Writings of Dan Jenkins* (New York: Doubleday, 1994);

Earvin Johnson Jr. and Roy S. Johnson, *Magic's Touch* (Reading, Mass.: Addison-Wesley, 1989);

William Oscar Johnson, *The Olympics: A History of the Games* (Birmingham, Ala.: Oxmoor House, 1992);

Roger Kahn, *Games We Used to Play: A Lover's Quarrel With the World of Sport* (New York: Ticknor & Fields, 1992);

Donald Katz, *Just Do It: The Nike Spirit in the Corporate World* (New York: Random House, 1994);

Richard Lapchick, *Five Minutes to Midnight: Race and Sport in the 1990s* (New York: Madison Books, 1991);

Roland Lazenby, *The Lakers: A Basketball Journey* (New York: St. Martin's Press, 1993);

Michael LeBlanc, ed., *Professional Sports Team Histories: Hockey* (Detroit, Mich.: Gale Research, 1994);

Lee Lowenfish, *The Imperfect Diamond: A History of Baseball's Labor Wars* (New York: Da Capo, 1991);

Norman Macht, *Jim Abbott: Major League Pitcher* (New York: Chelsea House, 1994);

Robert Mechicoff and Steven Estes, *A History and Philosophy of Sport and Physical Education* (Dubuque, Iowa: William C. Brown, 1993);

Michael Mewshaw, *Ladies of the Court* (New York: Crown, 1993);

Martina Navratilova, with George Vecsey, *Martina* (New York: Knopf, 1985);

Joyce Carol Oates, *On Boxing* (New York: Ecco Press, 1995);

George Peper, *Grand Slam Golf* (New York: Abrams, 1991);

Robert Post, *High Performance: The Culture and Technology of Drag Racing, 1950–1990* (Baltimore: Johns Hopkins University Press, 1994);

James Reston Jr., *Collision at Home Plate: The Lives of Pete Rose and Bart Giamatti* (New York: HarperCollins, 1991);

Randy Roberts and James Olson, *Winning Is the Only Thing: Sports in America since 1945* (Baltimore: Johns Hopkins University Press, 1989);

Allan Safarik and Dolores Reimer, *Quotations On The Great One: The Little Book of Wayne Gretzky* (Vancouver: Arsenal Pulp Press, 1992);

George Sage, *Power and Ideology in American Sport: A Critical Perspective* (Champaign, Ill.: Human Kinetics Books, 1990);

J. B. Strasser and Laurie Becklund, *Swoosh: The Unauthorized Story of Nike and the Men Who Played There* (New York: Harcourt Brace Jovanovich, 1991);

Rich Taylor, *Indy: Seventy-Five Years of Racing's Greatest Spectacle* (New York: St. Martin's Press, 1991);

Martin Vinokur, *More Than A Game: Sports and Politics* (New York: Greenwood Press, 1988);

David Wallechinsky, *The Complete Book of the Olympics* (Boston: Little, Brown, 1991).

CONTRIBUTORS

ARTS	JAMES ZRIMSEK *Chicago, Illinois*
BUSINESS AND THE ECONOMY	PHILLIP D. PAYNE *Institute of Industrial Technology* PENNY MESSINGER *Ohio State University*
EDUCATION	HARRIETT WILLIAMS *University of South Carolina*
FASHION	JULIA TAYLOR *Somerville, Massachusetts*
GOVERNMENT AND POLITICS	ROBERT M. ROOD *University of South Carolina* KAREN L. ROOD *Bruccoli Clark Layman Inc.*
LAW AND JUSTICE	PAUL L. ATWOOD *University of Massachusetts — Boston* MICHAEL PIERCE *Wakefield, Massachusetts*
LIFESTYLES AND SOCIAL TRENDS	KENNETH GRAHAM *Bruccoli Clark Layman Inc.* DARREN HARRIS-FAIN *Shawnee State University*
MEDIA	JAMES W. HIPP *Bruccoli Clark Layman Inc.* KAREN L. ROOD *Bruccoli Clark Layman Inc.* CHARLES D. BROWER *Columbia, South Carolina*
MEDICINE AND HEALTH	JOAN LAXSON *Boston, Massachusetts*
RELIGION	MARC D. BAYARD *Cambridge, Massachusetts*
SCIENCE AND TECHNOLOGY	JOHN LOUIS RECCHIUTI *Lawrence Technological University* MARC D. BAYARD *Cambridge, Massachusetts* GUILLAUME DE SYON *Albright College, Pennsylvania*
SPORTS	DANIEL A. NATHAN *University of Iowa*

INDEX OF PHOTOGRAPHS

GENERAL INDEX

A

A. C. Nielsen Company 86, 424, 547

A. H. Robbins Company 471

A. M. Chicago 454

Aaron, Benjamin 513

Abbott, Jim 634

ABC. *See* American Broadcasting Company

ABC (band) 29, 32, 84

ABC World News Tonight 442

Abdnor, James 284

Abdul, Paula 40, 88, 91

Abdul-Jabbar, Kareem 606, 639–640, 678

Abel, I. W. 168

Abell, George 603

Abell Galaxy 603

ABM Treaty 264

Abortion 258, 278–279, 281–282, 287, 289, 295–296, 301, 311–312, 315, 334–335, 348, 350, 370, 372–373, 376–378, 398–399, 462, 474–475, 479, 506–508, 514–515, 536, 538–539, 546, 548, 551–552, 576

About Last Night . . . 80

Above the Law 75

"Abracadabra" 27

Abraham, F. Murray 30, 82

Abrams, Elliot 342

Abrams, Robert 353

Abscam 248, 257, 284, 324, 328, 332–333

Abstract Expressionism 50, 132

"Academic Preparation for College" (College Board) 196

Academy Awards (Oscars) 45–46, 67–69, 75, 77–78, 87–88, 128, 245, 382, 388, 454

The Accidental Tourist (Tyler) 32, 82

The Accidental Tourist (movie) 38, 73

The Accused 38

The Acquitaine Progression (Ludlum) 30

Acrobat and Young Harlequin (Picasso) 39

ACT (American College Test) 186

Act of Will (Bradford) 34

Action for Children's Television 198

Action for Excellence (Hunt Report; Education Commission of the States) 196

Acupuncture 481

Ad Age 384

Adair, Edwin R. 319

Adam and the Ants 84

Adams, Ansel 129

Adams, Bryan 29, 32, 45, 89

Adams, Lane W. 518

Adams, Margo 633

Adams, Sherman 319

Adam's Daughter (Samuels) 61

Adamson, George 418

Adamson, Joy 418

Addabbo, Joseph P. 319

"Addicted to Love" 35

Addonizio, Hugh J. 319

Adelman, Clifford 184

Adidas 66, 225

Adler, Kurt 129

Adler, Mortimer 201, 212

Adoration of the Magi (Mantegna) 33

Adorno, Henry 344

Advance Publications 448, 451–452

Advanced Genetic Sciences Inc. 573

Aerosmith 38, 40, 45, 65

Affirmative action 190, 289–290, 300, 310, 330, 332, 348, 350, 406, 414

Afghanistan Invasion 259

AFI Communications Group 439

AFL-CIO 141, 168, 260, 288

AFL-CIO Committee on Political Education 311

"Africa" 29

Africa, Birdie 345

Africa, Conrad 345

Africa, Ramona 345

African Americans 29, 44, 46–47, 58, 60, 63–66, 69, 81, 88, 123, 163, 169, 172, 174, 178, 180, 182, 186–187, 189–192, 200, 206, 214–215, 267, 274, 279, 283–285, 289, 291, 293–295, 312–314, 318, 321–324, 360, 368, 372, 407, 414, 436, 449–450, 455–456, 538, 544, 550, 555–557, 561, 565, 597, 642, 680, 688

Afrika Bambaataa 27, 63, 65

"After All" 40

After Hours 32, 77

After the Fire 29

"Against All Odds" 30

Agca, Mehmet Ali 534

The Age of Innocence 112

"Agenda for Progress" (Heritage Foundation) 173

Agent Orange 469, 513

Agnes of God 99

Agnew, Spiro 360

Ahearn, Charlie 27, 64

Aichi Corporation 49

Aid to Families With Dependent Children (AFDC) 401

AIDS 34, 37, 46–47, 55–57, 97, 178–179, 181, 187, 368, 371–383, 397, 412, 418, 463–464, 466–479, 480, 482–485, 505,

507–508, 511–515, 518, 537, 552, 559

AIDS and the Education of Our Children 187

AIDS quilt 383, 475

Aiello, Danny 36, 39

Aiken, George D. 319

Aikens, Willie 631

Ailey, Alvin 58, 129

"Ain't Nothin' Goin' On But the Rent" 35

Air Jordan sneakers 66

Air Supply 24, 26, 29

Air Transportation Act of 1978 306

Airplane! 24, 76

Airplane II: The Sequel 76

Akutsu, Tetsuzu 487

Al Shiraa 275

Alabama (band) 27, 103

Alan Guttmacher Institute 471

The Alan Parsons Project 27, 31

Alaska (Michener) 38

Albany Medical College, New York 507

Albert and Mary Lasker Foundation 505

Albert Einstein Peace Prize 389

Albert Lasker Awards 505, 516–518

Albertson, Jack 129

Albright, Ivan 129

Alburt, Lev 688

Alcindor, Lew 640

Alcohol abuse 43, 62, 173, 181, 194, 200, 407, 462, 465, 479, 485, 631, 635

Aldrich, Robert 129

Alexander, Eben Jr. 519

Alexander, Grover Cleveland 631

Alexander, Lamar 184, 202, 212

Alexander Dawson School 213

Alford, Steve 643

Alfred A. Knopf (publishing house) 169, 442, 451

Alfred P. Sloan Jr. Medal 519

Algren, Nelson 129

Ali, Muhammad 513, 607, 643–645, 687

Alice Tully Hall, New York City 34

"Alice Walker and the Temple of Doom" (Kehr) 69

Alien 72

Aliens 34, 67

"All Night Long" 31, 87

All of Me 30, 75

"All That Money Wants" 39

All Things Considered 426, 444

"All Those Years Ago" 26, 45

Allen, Barry 354

Allen, Nancy 24–25, 36

Allen, Paul 161, 584

Allen, Woody 28, 30, 32, 34, 36, 39, 77–78, 124

"Allentown" 29, 86

Alley, Kirstie 40

Allied Bank Tower, Dallas 223

Allott, Gordon L. 319

Almond, J. Lindsay Jr. 319

Alomar, Roberto 635

"Alone" 36

Alpert, Herb 36

"Alphabet St." 39

Alreck, Pamela L. 386

Alsop, Joseph 319

Altered States 24

Altman, Robert 28, 67

Alvarez, Luis 570, 595, 603

Alvarez, Walter 595

Alvin Ailey Dance Theater, New York City 116

Alvor Agreements of 1988 268

"Always On My Mind" 27

Alzheimer, Alois 486

Alzheimer's Disease 274, 413, 485–487, 514, 586

Amadeus 30

The Amal 269

"Amanda" 35

Amazing Stories 69, 119

Amblin Entertainment 69

Ameche, Don 32, 45, 65, 78

"America" 26

American Academy of Arts and Sciences 596

American Academy of Pediatrics 478

American Academy of Science 599

American Association of Retired Persons (AARP) 413

American Association of School Administrators 174, 177, 180

American Association of University Women 212

American Astronomical Society 602

American Ballet Theater 25

American Baptist Churches in the U.S.A. 536, 566

American Basketball Association (ABA) 635, 637–638, 688

American Bookseller 557

American Bowling Congress (ABC) 658

American Broadcasting Company (ABC) 145, 152, 389, 422–424, 426–427, 431, 434, 441–442, 445–446, 448, 453–454, 456–457, 507–508, 626, 667

American Cancer Society 468–470, 518, 596

American Civil Liberties Union (ACLU) 62, 199, 418

American Civil War 399, 539, 674

American Coalition for Traditional Values (ACTV) 548

American College Health Association 478

American College of Obstetricians and Gynecologists 465

American College Test. *See* ACT

American Council of Teachers 176

American Council on Higher Education 189

American Dance Theater 58

American Enterprise Institute 302, 554

American Express 84, 391

American Federation of Labor. *See* AFL-CIO

American Federation of Labor and Congress of Industrial Organizations. *See* AFL-CIO

American Federation of Teachers (AFT) 195, 211, 213

American Federation of Television and Radio Artists 140

American Film Academy 416

American Football Conference (AFC) 647, 650

American Gigolo 24, 68, 75

"American Girl" 90

American Health 438

American Health Foundation 462

American Heart Association 469, 471

The American Heritage Dictionary 61

American Hiking Society 416

American Humane Association (AHA) 393

American Institute for Research 181

American Institute of Architects (AIA) 245

American Jewish Forum 555

The American Jewish Year Book 540

American League (baseball) 629, 631, 634

American League Championship Series 629

American Library Association 60
American Lung Association 469
American Lutheran Church 539
American Medical Association (AMA) 463–464, 468–470, 472–473, 475, 645
American Medical Association Distinguished Service Award 519
The American Mercury 459
American Messenger Company 168
American Motors 142
American Museum of Natural History 603
American Music Awards 31, 87
American Muslim Mission 557
American National Theater, Washington, D.C. 125
The American Pope (Cooney) 553
American Psychiatric Association (APA) 469, 511
American Public Health Association 508
American Red Cross 381, 402, 471
The American Scholar 414
American Sign Language 213
American Society of Interior Designers (ASID) 245
American Telephone & Telegraph (AT&T) 140, 142, 150, 153, 155, 169, 185, 357, 422, 574
American University 184
American Zoom (Golenbock) 676
The Americanization of Emily (Huie) 459
Americans for Democratic Action 311
Americans for the Republic 537
America's Cup (yachting) 445, 630, 694
America's Most Wanted 332, 435
Amnesty International 39, 376
The Anatomy Lesson (Roth) 29
Anchorwoman (Savitch) 453
Ancient Evenings (Mailer) 29
Ancier, Garth 434
"... And Ladies of the Club" (Santmyer) 30
"And the Beat Goes On" 24
"And We Danced" 33
Anderson, Carl 35
Anderson, J. Reid 159
Anderson, John 29
Anderson, John B. 165, 248, 277–278, 282–284, 430, 540
Anderson, John R. 455
Anderson, John Z. "Jack" 319

Anderson, Kris 416
Anderson, Laurie 45–46, 53, 56–57
Anderson, Les 688
Anderson, Maxie 416
Anderson, P. W. 600
Anderson, Phillip 601
Anderson, Poul 38
Anderson, Robert B. 319
Anderson, W. French 494
Anderson, Willie "Flipper" 688
Andre, Maurice 106
Andretti, Mario 675
Andrews, Cecil 456
Andrews, Julie 25, 27
Andropov, Yuri V. 262, 419, 535
"Angel" 33, 38
Angel of Light (Oates) 25
"Angel of the Morning" 26
Anglican Church 544, 561
Anglican Communion 544
Angolan Civil War 252, 267–268, 316
Anheuser-Busch Company 168
Animal House 72
Animotion 32
The Annals of the Heechee (Pohl) 36
Anne Klein and Company 219, 232, 243
Annenberg, Walter 424, 451
Anorexia nervosa 471, 491–493
"Another Brick in the Wall" 24
"Another Day in Paradise" 40
"Another One Bites the Dust" 26
Answered Prayers (Capote) 36
Ant, Adam 29
Anthony, Earl 658
Anthrax 111
Anti-Semitism 61, 289, 294, 313–314, 339, 374, 407, 510, 534, 536, 542, 555, 557, 562
Antiballistic Missile (ABM) Treaty of 1972 260
Antibiotics 464, 469
Antioch College 598
"Any Day Now" 27
Anything for Billy (McMurtry) 38
"Anything for You" 38
Apartheid 46, 97, 188, 190, 253, 268, 295, 312, 544, 667
Apollo space program 603
Apollo Theater, New York City 114
Aponte, Angelo 49
Aponte, Hector Escudero 363
Appelonia 88
Apple Computers 155, 158, 161, 384, 432–433, 571, 582, 584

The Aquarian Conspiracy (Ferguson) 534, 557
Aquino, Benigno Jr. 268–269
Aquino, Corazon 252, 269
Arafat, Yassir 255, 270, 314
Arbuckle, Ernest 214
Area (club), New York City 44, 54
Arends, Leslie C. 319
Argulles, Jose 557
Arias, Joey 57
Arkansas Gazette 439
Arledge, Roone 442
Arlen, Harold 129
Armani designs 50
Armco Steel 148
Armitage, John 515
Arms Export Control Export Act 342, 356
Armstrong, Gillian 77
Armstrong, Rev. Herbert W. 566
Armstrong, Bishop James 543
Armstrong, Orland Kay 319
Arnaz, Desi 458
Arnold, Roseanne 448
Arnold, Tom 448
Arquette, Rosanna 32
Arquitectonica 233, 238
Art (exhibition) 54
Art Dealers Association of America 48
Art Deco 234
Art of Noise 30, 35, 40
Artforum 116
Arthur 25, 75, 80
Arthur M. Sackler Gallery of Asian and Near Eastern Art 37
"Arthur's Theme" 26
Artificial hearts 468, 470–472, 476, 481, 487–488, 504, 513–515
Artists United Against Apartheid 32, 66
ARTnews 33
Aryan Nations World Congress 374
ASCAP 87
Ashbrook, John M. 319
Ashby, Hal 129
Ashe, Arthur 606, 673
"Ashes to Ashes" 24, 83
Ashland, Donna 513
Ashley, Elizabeth 383
Ashley, Laura 245
Ashmore, Robert T. 319
Asian Americans 314, 407
Asimov, Isaac 27, 29, 34, 36
Askew, Reuben 289
Aspartame 464, 467

Bass, Kevin 632
Bass, Sid 70
Bassett High, La Puente, Cal. 195
Bassi, Lauri 167
"Batdance" 41
Bateson, Gregory 603
Bathurst, David 49
Batman 39, 43–44, 66–67, 73, 75, 88
Batts, Sharon 416
Bauer Group 439
Bauhaus 107
Baulieu, Etienne-Emile 518
Bavarian Motor Works (BMW) 386
Baxter, Anne 129
Baxter, Cindy 688
Bay City Blues 447
Bayh, Birch 284
Bayh, Evan 300
Baylor College of Medicine 462
"Be Near Me" 32
Beach Boys 38, 45
Beals, Jennifer 28, 86
The Beans of Egypt, Maine (Chute) 32
Beard, James 418
Beastie Boys 36, 65
"Beat Box" 30
"Beat It" 29, 86–87
Beat Street 30, 64–65
Beatles 87, 364
Beaton, Cecil 245
Beatrice International Foods 145, 163
Beattie, Ann 24, 27, 32
Beatty, Warren 25, 36, 78
Beck, Michael 24
"Beds Are Burning" 39
Bee Gees 40, 45
The Beet Queen (Erdrich) 34
Beethoven, Ludwig von 37
Beetlejuice 38, 73
Behrens, William 603
Belafonte, Harry 65
Belcher, Page 319
Bell, Terrel H. 176, 193, 204, 212, 274
Bell, William 601
Bell Laboratories 572
Bellefleur (Oates) 24
Bellevue Hospital 513
Bellow, Saul 27, 36, 81, 202, 411
Beloved (Morrison) 36, 82
Belushi, James 34
Belushi, John 24, 45, 75, 129
Benacerraf, Baruj 516

Benatar, Pat 24, 26, 30, 32, 46, 85–86
Benbow, Camilla Persons 212, 601
Benitez, John "Jellybean" 32, 64
Benitez, Wilfred 644
Benjamin, Adam Jr. 319
Bennett, Michael 46
Bennett, Peter 601
Bennett, Robert Russell 130
Bennett, Tony 45
Bennett, William J. 176, 178–179, 187–189, 194, 204–207, 211. 397. 513
Benoit, Joan 628, 667
Benson, Ezra Taft 542, 565
Benton, Thomas Hart 31
Bentsen, Lloyd 295, 309, 314
Berenblum, Isaac 519
Berendzen, Richard 184
Berenger, Tom 28, 34
Berg, Paul 494, 516, 576, 596–597
Bergen, Edgar 274
Berger, Thomas 24–25
Bergland, David 317
Bergman, Ingrid 130
Bergström, Sune 516
Berkeley Barb 455
Berle, Milton 423
Berlin (band) 30, 35
Berlin Wall 56, 113, 204, 258, 265
Berman, Emile Z. 365
Bernardin, Cardinal Joseph 553–554, 559–560
Bernbach, William 458
Bernhard, Sandra 28, 91
Bernstein, Leonard 124
Bernstein, Robert 452
Berridge, Michael J. 517
Berrigan, Daniel 534, 553
Berrigan, Philip 534
Berry, Chuck 124
Berry, George Packer 603
Bertelsmann AG (publishing house) 442
Bessie Award (dance) 58
"The Best of Times" 26
Beth Israel Hospital, Boston 509
Bethpage Park Authority, New York 322
"Bette Davis Eyes" 26
"Better Be Good to Me" 33
"Better Man" 40
Beverly Hills Cop 30, 44, 68, 72, 76, 86
Beverly Hills Cop II 35, 76, 89
Beverly Hills 90210 435

Bi-Lingual Education Act of 1967 188–189
Biafra, Jello 47, 62–63
Biaggi, Mario 363
Bianchi, Kenneth 346
Bias, Len 363, 397, 643, 650
Bible, Alan H. 319
Bible 61, 178, 198–199, 207, 312, 381, 534–535, 538–539, 541–542, 544, 549, 555, 558–560, 563, 570
Bible Baptist College 560
Bickerstaff, Bernie 628
Bickerton, Ashley 52
Bickle, Travis 112
Biden, Joseph R. Jr. 293
Bidwill, Bill 649
Big 38, 75, 77
Big Business 38, 75, 80
The Big Chill 28, 43–44, 72–73, 78–79, 393
Big Country 27
The Big Easy 35, 78
Big Science (Anderson) 57
"Big Time" 36
Bigelow, Kathryn 77
Bill & Ted's Excellent Adventure 39, 76
The Bill Cosby Show 449
Bill T. Jones/Arnie Zane Dance Company 58
Billboard 39, 65, 85, 436
"Billie Jean" 29, 86–87
Billionaire Boys Club 376
Billy Bathgate (Doctorow) 40
Billy Phelan's Greatest Game (Kennedy) 81
Billy Vera and the Beaters 37
Billygate 281, 320
Bingham, Barry Sr. 458
Bingham, Jonathan B. 319
Binoche, Juliette 38
Biofeedback 481
Biogen 570
Biomedicine and Behavioral Research 464
Biondi, Matt 670
Bird, Junius Bouton 603
Bird, Larry 606, 635–636, 638–640, 643, 677–680, 682
Birmingham Barons 681
Birnbach, Lisa 455
Birth control 301, 374, 376, 419, 463–464, 467, 471, 474, 476, 478–480, 511, 537, 539, 551–552, 560
Bishop, J. Michael 516–517, 519

"Brilliant Disguise" 37, 89
Brimley, Wilford 32, 78
Brindley, George Valter Jr. 519
Brinkhous, Kenneth M. 519
Brinkley, Christie 90, 232, 239
Bristol-Meyers Award 520
British Aerospace Corporation 577
British Open Golf Tournament 656–657
Broadcast News 35, 78
Broadcasting 441
Broadway, New York City 24–26, 28–29, 42–44, 46, 97
Broadway Danny Rose 30, 77
Brock, Lou 634
Brock, William 184, 212
Broderick, Matthew 28, 40
Brodie, Fawn McKay 214
Brokaw, Tom 441–442, 453, 455
"Broken Hearted Me" 24
"Broken Wings" 35
Brolin, Josh 32
Bronski Beat 32, 46, 85
Bronx High School of Science 510
Brooklyn College 562
Brooklyn Dodgers 632
Brooklyn Museum 48
Brooklyn Philharmonica 105
Brooks, Albert 32, 35
Brooks, Garth 104
Brooks, Herb 660
Brooks, Louise 130
Brooks Brothers 392
The Brother from Another Planet 77
Brothers and Keepers (Wideman) 30
Broughton High School 177
Brown, Blair 24
Brown, Bobby 36, 38, 40, 88
Brown, Daniel 62
Brown, Edmund G. "Jerry" Jr. 279–280
Brown, Harrison 603
Brown, James 35, 38, 88
Brown, Joyce 513
Brown, Louise 490
Brown, Michael S. 516–517
Brown, Rita Mae 684
Brown, Rosellen 30
Brown, Shirley 130
Brown, Sterling Allen 214
Brown, Tina 439, 448, 451
Brown Brothers 309
Brown University 188, 193, 371
Brown v. *Board of Education* 191
Browning, Tom 633
Brownson, Charles B. 319
Broyhill, James T. 292

Bruce Hornsby and the Range 36
Bruckheimer, Jerry 68, 72
Bryant, Paul "Bear" 627
Brzezinski, Zbigniew 339
Buchanan, Patrick 300, 359, 484
Buchwald, Art 124
Buckley, William 317
Buckner, Bill 632
Buckner and Garcia 27
Budd, Zola 667
Buddhism 557–558
Budweiser 84
Buffalo Bills 647
Buffalo Courier-Express 439
Buffalo Sabres 663
"Buffalo Stance" 40
Buffett, Jimmy 40
The Buggles 26, 436
Buick 237
Bujold, Genevieve 30
Bulimia 471, 491–493
Bull Durham 38, 75
The Bulletin Of Atomic Scientists 389
Bundy, Ted 345–346
Bunker, Ellsworth 319
Buono, Angelo 346
Burford, Anne Gorsuch 250, 306
Burger, Warren 212, 330, 332, 348, 363
Burgess, Anthony 61
Burhoe, Ralph Wendell 565
Burke, Dr. John F. 513
Burnham, James 458
The Burning House (Beattie) 27
"Burning Up" 90
Burns, Arthur F. 319
Burton, Dan 312
Burton, Phillip 319
Burton, Sala 319
Burton, Scott 54
Burton, Tim 32, 38–39, 73
Busch, August Anheuser Jr. 168
Busch Publishing 438
Bush, Barbara 220, 243, 286, 309
Bush, Dorothy Walker 309
Bush, George 59–60, 140, 145, 147, 156, 167, 189, 193–194, 202, 208, 220, 255–258, 260, 265–266, 268, 277–279, 282, 286–287, 291, 295–300, 303, 306–310, 318, 328, 332, 341–343, 351–352, 368, 376–378, 381, 389, 399, 408, 414, 441, 475, 508, 538, 574, 585
Bush, Prescott Sheldon 309
Bushinsky, Ned 430

Business Impact on Education and Child Development Reform (Timpane) 184
Business Roundtable 301–302
Business Week 384, 392
Business-Higher Education Forum 197
"Bust a Move" 41
Butcher, Susan 688
The Butthole Surfers 63, 110
Butz, Earl 153, 363
Byrd, Harry F. Jr. 284
Byrd, Robert 317
Byrne, Jane 280
Byrnes, John W. 320
Byte 584

C

Caan, James 36
Cabey, Darrell 354
Cable Music Channel (CMC) 446
Cable News Network (CNN) 86, 140, 152, 422, 426–431, 440–441, 445–446
Cable Satellite Public Affairs Network (C-SPAN) 441
Caddyshack 24, 76
Cadillac 237
Caesarean sections 416, 474
Cage, John 34
Cage, Nicolas 28, 34, 36
Cagney, James 25, 130, 359
Cagney and Lacey 422, 457
Caine, Michael 24, 27, 34
Calder Trophy (hockey) 662
Caldwell, Millard F. 320
Caldwell, Philip 140
Cali drug cartel 351–352
California Angels 631, 633
California Board of Education 179, 205
"California Girls" 33
California Gold (Jakes) 40
California Institute of Technology 574. 600
California Space Institute 600
California State Board of Equalization 535
"Call Me" 24, 85
Callahan, Tom 676, 679
Calvin Klein designs 228
Cambridge Committee for Responsible Research 591
Cambridge University 240, 361
Camden High School 191
Cameo 30, 35

Control 36, 88
Control Data Corporation 433
"Controversy" 28
Cook, Carrie 393
Cook, Robin 32, 36
Cooke, Cardinal Terrence 554, 566
Cooking Light 438
"Cool It Now" 33
Cooley, Dr. Denton A. 487, 513
Coolidge, Calvin 257
Coolidge, Martha 77
Cooney, Gerry 644–646
Cooney, John 553
Coonts, Stephen 34, 38, 40
Cooper, Alice 40
Cooper, Gary 75
Cooper Union School 240
Coors, Joseph 302
Cop Rock 448
Copiague Drive-In, Long Island, N.Y. 455
Copland, Aaron 34, 124
Coppola, Francis Ford 36, 67, 81, 112, 124
COPS 332
Corcoran Gallery of Art, Washington, D.C. 59, 377
Cornell University 188, 240, 360, 411, 598, 600, 602
— Law School 360
Corporation for Public Broadcasting 444
Corrections Corporation of America 337
Corrosion of Conformity (COC) 110
Cosby, Bill 423, 449
Cosby, Camille 449
The Cosby Show 423, 449, 457
Cosell, Howard 645
Costello, Elvis 40
Costner, Kevin 36, 38, 40, 75
Cotter, William R. 320
Cotton, Norris 320
The Cotton Club 81
Coty American Fashion Critics' Award (Winnie) 240, 243–244
"Could've Been" 39
Coulson, Dr. Williams 199
Council for Basic Education 177
Council of Fashion Designers of America 241, 243–244
Council of Fashion of America 243
The Counterlife (Roth) 36
Country 30, 46
"A Country Boy Can Survive" 28
Courageous 445

The Covenant (Michener) 24
"Cover Me" 31
"Coward of the County" 24
Cowboy Junkies 40
Cowles, Gardner Jr. 458
Cox, Alex 30, 34, 77
Cox, Archibald 334, 349
Cox, Courteney 43, 89
Coyle, Joseph William 363
Crabbe, Buster 131
Crack cocaine 66, 194, 352, 370, 380, 394, 397
Craft, Christine 370, 416
Craig, Jim 664
Craig, Bishop Judith 544
Crane, Phillip 301
Cranston, Alan 289
Crawford, Broderick 458
Crawford, Cindy 239, 243
"Crazy for You" 33, 72, 91
"Crazy Little Thing Called Love" 24
Creationism 173, 176, 178, 200, 570–571, 573, 598
Creationist-Science Research Center 200
Creepshow (King) 82
Crescent City (Plain) 30
Criden, Howard 333
Crimes & Misdemeanors 39, 77
Crimes of the Heart 34
Crippen, Robert J. 60
Crocker, Chester A. 265, 268, 312
Crocodile Dundee 75
Cronenberg, David 76–77
Cronkite, Walter 422, 441, 455
Cronyn, Hume 32, 78
Crosby, Mary 455
Crosby, Stills, & Nash 27
Cross, Christopher 24, 26
"Crossfire" 41
Crossings (Steele) 27
Crouch, Stanley 414
Crouse, Lindsay 36, 118
Crowded House 36
Crown Publishing Group 452
The Crucifucks 63
Crude Oil Windfall Profits Tax Act of 1980 248
"Cruel Summer" 30
Cruise, Tom 28, 34, 38–39, 43, 45, 71, 74–75, 80, 218
"Cruisin'" 24
Crumpacker, Shephard J. Jr. 320
"Crush On You" 35
Cry Freedom 35, 46
A Cry in the Dark 38

"Cry Myself to Sleep" 36
"Crying My Heart Out Over You" 28
Crystal, Billy 40
Crystal Cathedral, Garden Grove, Cal. 535, 548
Cuban Missile Crisis of 1962 389
Cuellar, Javiar Perez de 277
Cujo (King) 25, 82
Cukor, George 131
Culp, Robert 449
The Cult 40
"Cult of Personality" 40
Culture Club 29–30, 35, 46, 85
The Culture of Narcissism (Lasch) 183
The Culture Wars (Shor) 183
"Cum On Feel the Noize" 31
Cunningham, Merce 58
Cuomo, Mario 285, 290, 293, 295, 353, 355, 551
"Cupid/I've Loved You for a Long Time" 24
The Cure 40
Curran, Fr. Charles E. 537, 551–552
Curran, James 483, 513
A Current Affair 427
Curtis, Jamie Lee 38
Curtis, Laurence 320
Cusack, John 32, 40
Cutrone, Ronnie 45, 54
Cutting Crew 36, 84
Cyborg 75
Cyclosporin A 515
Cyclosporine 467, 489
Cystic fibrosis 479

D

D. J. Jazzy Jeff and the Fresh Prince 38, 43
"Da'Butt" 38
Dade County School District, Fla. 172
Dafoe, Willem 34, 38
Dailey, Janet 36
Daily Express 450
Daily Racing Form 424
Dalai Lama 534
Daley, Richard J. 317
Daley, Richard M. 317
The Daley Planet 422
Dalkon Shield 468, 471, 481, 480
Dallas 218–219, 368, 422, 455
Dallas Cowboys 652, 683
Daly, Timothy 27

DeVito, Danny 34, 36, 38, 75
Devo 26, 84
DeVries, Dr. William Castle 488, 504
Dexter, Pete 38
Dexy's Midnight Runners 29
Diabetes 469, 493–494, 586
The Dial 439
Diamandis Communications, Inc. 424
Diamond, Neil 26
Diamond v. Chakrabarty 570
Diamond v. Diehr 570
"Diamonds" 36
"Diamonds Are a Girl's Best Friend" 90
Princess Diana 448
The Diary of Anne Frank (Frank) 61
Diaz, Robert P. 514
Dick Tracy (Gould) 458
Dickerson, Earl B. 365
Dickey, James 125
Dickey, Lucinda 30
Dickinson, Angie 24
Dickinson, Emily 178
The Dicks 63
"Didn't We Almost Have It All" 36, 87
Die Hard 38, 44, 75
A Different Kind of Christmas (Haley) 38
Different Seasons (King) 27
Diggs, Ira 344
Digital Equipment 155, 159
Diller, Barry 43, 68, 434
Dillon, Matt 28, 40
Diner 27, 78
Dinnan, James 212
Dinner at the Homesick Restaurant (Tyler) 27, 82
Dirac, Paul Adrian Maurice 603
Dire Straits 32
Director's Guild 69
Dirty Dancing 35, 43, 72, 78
"Dirty Diana" 39, 87
"Dirty Laundry" 29
Dirty Mind (Prince) 88
DiSalle, Michael V. 320
"Disappointed" 41
Discover 438
Discovery 574, 591, 601
Disney, Roy 69
Disney, Walt 69, 142, 452
Disney World 71, 87, 115, 142
Disneyland, Cal. 71, 423
Disneyland, Tokyo 71
Distinguished Flying Cross 309

Ditka, Mike 650
"Dixie Road" 33
"DJ" 83
"Do That to Me One More Time" 24
Do the Right Thing 39, 47, 66, 77
"Do You Really Want to Hurt Me" 29, 85
The Dr. Ruth Show 511
Dr. Ruth's Guide To Good Sex (West-heimer) 456
Dr. Strangelove 74
Doctorow, E. L. 24, 30, 32, 40
Doctors (Segal) 38
Doctors Against Nuclear War 509
Dodd, Mead (publishing house) 61
Dodson, Gary 363
Dogmatic Wisdom (Jacoby) 184
Dohrn, Bernadette 364
Dolan, John Terry 300
Dolby, Thomas 29, 84
Dole, Elizabeth 143, 317
Dole, Robert J. 60, 269, 277–278, 296–297, 305, 317, 410
Dole, Vincent P. 518
Dollywood, Pigeon Forge, Tenn. 35
Domenici, Pete 297
Domingo, Placido 25
Dominick, Peter H. 320
Donahue 454
Donahue, Phil 453–455
Donaldson, Stephen R. 27, 29, 34
Donna Karan New York (DKNY) 232, 243
Donnelly, Patrice 27
Donner party 204
Donovan, Raymond J. 251
"Don't Answer Me" 31
"Don't Be Cruel" 38
"Don't Close Your Eyes" 39
"Don't Come Around Here No More" 89
"Don't Do Me Like That" 24
"Don't Dream It's Over" 36
"Don't Know Much" 41
"Don't Rush Me" 40
"Don't Stand So Close to Me" 26
"Don't Stop Til You Get Enough" 24, 86
"Don't Talk to Strangers" 28
"Don't Worry, Be Happy" 39
"Don't You (Forget About Me)" 33, 72
"Don't You Want Me" 27
Doogie Howser, M.D. 448
Doonesbury 393, 456

"Dope Smokin Moron" 110
Doris Day: Her Own Story (Burgess) 61
Dorn, Francis E. 320
Dornan, Robert 312
Dorsett, Tony 653
Dortch, Rev. Richard 549, 565
Dosti, Arben 376
"Double Dutch Bus" (Smith) 26
Double Trouble 41
Doubleday, Frank 26
Dougherty, Fr. John J. 566
Douglas, Donald W. 603
Douglas, Helen Gahagan 320
Douglas, James "Buster" 646
Douglas, Melvyn 131
Douglas, Michael 30, 35–36, 40, 79–80
Douglas, William O. 335, 365
Down and Out in Beverly Hills 34, 70, 75
Down by Law 77
"Down Under" 29
Downey, Robert Jr. 80
Down's Syndrome 177, 479, 494, 500
Doyle, Frank 185
Doyle Dane Bernbach 458
Dozier, Terry 212
Dragonsdawn (McAffrey) 38
Draper, Jimmy 542
Dravecky, Dave 633
The Dream Academy 35
Dreiser, Theodore 26
Dress for Success (Molloy) 227
"Dress You Up" 33, 91
Dressed to Kill 24, 77
Drew, John 638
Drew, Richard G. 603
Drexel, Burnham, and Lambert 143, 163
Drexler, Clyde 640
Dreyfuss, Richard 34, 36, 45
Driesell, Lefty 643
Drinan, Fr. Robert 551
"Drive" 30, 85
Driving Miss Daisy 40, 78, 100
Drug abuse 43, 45, 62, 65–66, 172–173, 176–177, 180–181, 183, 193–195, 199–200, 205, 214, 257, 286, 295, 299–300, 317, 332, 352, 363, 368, 370, 380–381, 394, 396–397, 417, 453, 462, 464, 466–467, 473, 476–478, 480, 482, 484–485, 512, 515, 556–557, 627, 631, 635, 643
Drug testing 253

Gephardt, Richard 293–294, 305
Gere, Richard 24, 27–28, 74–75
Gernreich, Rudi 245
Gershwin, Ira 131
Gertz, Jamie 80
"Get Outta My Dreams, Get Into My Car" 39
Getman, Debra 343
Getty, J. Paul 28
Getty Museum, Malibu, Cal. 28, 31, 33
Ghostbusters 30–31, 67, 72, 75–76, 86
Ghostbusters II 40, 76
Giamatti, A. Bartlett 212, 214, 364, 633, 686
Giants and Dwarfs (Bloom) 412
Gibb, Barry 26
Gibbons, Edward F. 168
Gibbons, Fred 159
Gibbs, Joe 648
Gibson, Debbie 36, 38, 40, 43
Gibson, Mel 27–28, 30, 32, 36, 75, 82
Gideonse, Hendrick 202
Gielgud, John 25, 78
Giger, H. R. 62
Gilbert, Walter 586
Gilchrist, Ellen 30
Gildea, James H. 321
Gilder, George 380, 383
Gillett, Fred 601
Gilliam, Dubois 361
Gilliam, Terry 32, 77
Gilligan, Carol 203, 506
Gilman, Alfred G. 517
Ginsburg, Douglas H. 330, 349, 375
Giordano, Joseph 513
Giorgio Armani designs 219
Gipp, George 73
Giraldi, Bob 86
"Girl I'm Gonna Miss You" 40
"The Girl Is Mine" 29
"Girl You Know It's True" 40
"Girlfriend" 36, 39
"Girls Just Want to Have Fun" 31
"Girls on Film" 26
Gish, Lillian 416
"Give It to Me Baby" 26
"Give Me Wings" 36
"Giving You the Best That I Got" 38
Gladys Knight and the Pips 39
"The Glamorous Life" 30
Glamour 239, 492
Glass, David Dayne 167

Glasser, Ronald 61
Glassey, Donald 345
Gleason, Jackie 458
Glen and Company 443
Glengarry Glen Ross (Mamet) 42
Glenn, John 74, 289
Glenn, Scott 28
The Glitter Dome (Wambaugh) 25
Glitz (Leonard) 32
"Gloria" 27
Glory 40
"Glory Days" 33, 45, 86, 89
Glover, Danny 32, 36
"God Bless America" 47
"God Bless the U.S.A." 47, 387
God Emperor of Dune (Herbert) 25
God Knows (Heller) 30
The Godfather, Part II 112
Godfrey, Arthur 458
Goetz, Bernhard 354
Gogh, Vincent van 37, 49, 375, 384
The Go-Go's 27, 30, 85
Goldberg, Whoopi 32
Goldberger, Paul 233
Goldblum, Jeff 28, 34
The Golden Child 76
The Golden Cup (Plain) 34
Golden Earring 29
The Golden Girls 457
The Golden Palominos 50
Golden State Warriors 635
Goldman, Sylvan N. 418
Goldsmith, Sir James 155
Goldstein, Joseph L. 516–517
Goldwater, Barry 287, 291, 300–301, 315, 322, 334
Golenbock, Peter 675–676
Gone With the Wind 446
Gonorrhea 465
Gonzaga University 638
Good Morning America 441, 507
Good Morning, Vietnam 36, 70, 75
The Good Mother 34, 38, 47, 78
"Good Thing" 40
Goodbye, Janet (Robbins) 25
Goode, Wilson 345
Goodell, Charles E. 321
Gooden, Dwight 618, 631, 634
Goodlad, John I. 208–209
Goodman, Robert 313
Goodrich, Frances 131
Goodwill Games 683
"Goody Two Shoes" 29
Goodyear Tire and Rubber Company 674
The Goonies 32, 67

Gorbachev, Mikhail S. 252–256, 258, 262–265, 268, 270, 315, 318, 339, 375, 391, 448, 509, 575
Gorbachev, Raisa 263
Gordon, Dexter 34
Gordon, Lawrence 71
Gordon, Mary 32
Gordon, Ruth 132
Gordon, Slade 284
Gore, Albert A. Jr. 61, 292–294
Gore, Tipper 47, 61–62, 66, 88
Gorky Park (Smith) 25
Gorman, John 517
"Got My Mind Set on You" 39
Gottlieb, Robert 451
Gould, Chester 458
Gould, Glen 132
Gould, Stephen 598
Graceland (Simon) 46
Graceland, Memphis, Tenn. 28
Grady, John 212
Grady, William 353
Graf, Steffi 671
Graffiti 42, 44, 51–52, 54–55, 63–64, 81
Graham, Rev. Billy 535, 542, 565
Graham, Martha 35, 58, 116
Graham, Michael 641
Graham, Dr. Robert 175
Graham, Robert K. 601
Graham, William R. 573
Grambling State University 689
Gramm, Lou 36
Gramm, Phil 292, 305
Gramm-Rudman-Hollings Act of 1985 143, 252–253, 305, 307
Grammy Awards 31, 44, 85–87, 415
Grand Hyatt Hotel, New York City 368
Grandmaster Flash 65
Grandmaster Flash and the Furious Five 24
Grandmaster Melle Mel 65
Grant, Amy 36
Grant, Cary 132, 228
Grant, Eddy 29
The Grapes of Wrath (Steinbeck) 61
Grasso, Ella T. 321
"Grate American Sleep-Out" 374
Grateful Dead 36, 45, 92, 97
Graves, Michael 54, 222, 233, 237, 243
Gray, Ed 157
Gray, William 214
Gray Panthers 412–413
Grazer, Brian 68

Grease 25
Great Depression 146–147, 156–157, 165–166, 307
The Great Gatsby (Fitzgerald) 61
Great Peace March for Global Nuclear Disarmament 391
The Great Santini 24
Great Society programs 185, 300, 303, 379–380, 400
Great White 40
"Greatest Love of All" 35, 87
Greeley, Andrew M. 25, 32, 82
Green, Edith S. 321
Green, Mitch "Blood" 687
Green, Richard 214
Green-Brown, Ruthie 191
Greenberg, Robert 371
Greenblat, Rodney Alan 52, 54
Greenspan, Alan 145, 167
Greenwood, Lee 33, 47, 387
The Greg Kihn Band 29
Gregg, Judd 300
Gregory, Andre 25
Gregory's Girl 77
Greider, William 185
Greist, Kim 32
Gremlins 30, 67, 69
Grenada Invasion 250, 258, 269, 313, 315
Gretzky, Wayne 607, 660–663, 679, 688
Grey, Jennifer 35
Griffey, Ken Jr. 635
Griffin, John Howard 418
Griffith, D. W. 416
Griffith, Darrell 640
Griffith, Melanie 30, 34, 38
Grisham, John 40
Gromyko, Andrei A. 251, 263
"Groovy Kind of Love" 38
Gross, Harold Royce 321
Gross, Harvey 207
Gross, Paul 603
Gross national product (GNP) 303–306
Grossman, Larry 441
Grotberg, John E. 321
Group W 441
Grove, Andrew 159
Grove, Barry 213
Grove Press 423
Growing Without Schooling 214
Guarino, Michael 62
Guccione, Bob Jr. 412, 415
Guccione, Bob Sr. 412
Guernica (Picasso) 51
Guerrilla Girls 58

Guest, Christopher 30
Guibourge, Philippe 246
"Guilty" 26
"Guitars, Cadillacs" 35
Gulf 442
Gulf and Western 442
Gulf of Sidra 249, 253, 271
Gulf War 579
Gull, Sir William 491–492
Gumbel, Bryant 455
Gumbleton, Auxiliary Bishop Thomas 554
Gund, Graham 234
Guns N' Roses 39–40
Gurganus, Allan 40
Gustav Stern Award 596
Guston, Philip 132
Gutensohn, Dr. Nancy 514
Guthrie, Gwen 35
Guttenberg, Steven 27, 30, 32, 36, 76
Guttmann, Allen 668
Guyer, Tennyson 321
"Gypsy" 27

H

Haagen-Dazs 386
Hack, Shelley 36
Hackman, Gene 25, 38
Hagelstein, Peter 601
Hagerty, James C. 321
Hagerty, Julie 24, 32
Haggard, Merle 104
Hagler, Marvin 645
Haglund, Carolla 210
Hagman, Larry 455
Hagnes, Helen 125
Hahn, Jessica 375, 549
Haide, Ma 518
Haig, Alexander M. Jr. 249, 260, 274, 296
Haim, Corey 36
Haines, Randa 77
Haircut 100 84
The Haj (Uris) 30
Haley, Alex 38
Haley, James A. 321
Hall, Anthony Michael 30, 32, 80
Hall, Arsenio 435
Hall, Daryl 26–27, 29–30
Hall, Joyce Clyde 168
Halleck, Charles A. 321
Halley, Peter 52
Halley's Comet 573
Hallmark Company 168
Hallmark Hall of Fame 207

Halloween 76
"Halloween Letter" 552
Halston designs 232, 243
Hamburger Hill 36, 74
Hamill, Mark 24, 28
Hamilton, Alexander 451
Hamilton, Harriet 688
Hamilton, Margaret 132
Hamlin, Harry 27
Hammer, Armand 125, 376
Hammer, Jan 33
Hammerschmidt, Dale E. 514
Hammill, Pete 440
Hammond, Tommy 62
Hanafusa, Hidesaburo 517
Hancock, Herbie 29
Hands Across America 374
"Hands to Heaven" 38
"Hangin' Tough" 40
Hanks, Tom 30, 38, 75–76, 382
Hannah, Daryl 30, 36
Hannah and Her Sisters 34, 77
Hansen, George 317
Hanson, Howard 132
Harcourt Brace Jovanovich 423, 442
"Hard Habit to Break" 30
Hard to Kill 75
"Hard to Say I'm Sorry" 27
Harden, Cecil Murray 321
"Harden My Heart" 28
Hare, David 100
Hargroves, Rev. V. Carney 566
Haring, Keith 43–46, 50–51, 53–58, 64, 113, 383
Harkin, Tom 292
Harlow, Bryce N. 321
Harmonic Convergence 537, 557
Harnwell, Gaylord P. 603
Harper and Row 423, 425, 442, 451, 458
HarperCollins 424, 442, 451
Harper's 81, 414
Harper's Bazaar 239, 404
Harriman, W. Averell 321
Harriman and Company 309
Harrington, Michael 168, 401
Harris, Bishop Barbara Clementine 538, 544, 561
Harris, Ed 28, 32, 74
Harris, Emmylou 46, 103
Harris, Gary 456
Harris, James 354
Harris, Jean 354–355, 416
Harris, LaDonna 317
Harris, Patricia R. 321
Harris polls 188, 191, 286, 394

Harrison, George 26, 39, 45, 125
Harrison, Michael R. 514
Harry, Debbie 85
Hart Trophy (hockey) 662
Hart, Corey 30
Hart, Gary 213, 289–290, 293, 391
Hart, Lois 429
Hartley, Marilee 393
Hartman, Dan 31
Hartz Mountain Products Corporation 169
Harvard Business Review 377
Harvard University 161, 188, 191, 203, 212, 362, 450, 464, 472, 506, 510, 571, 574, 590–591, 598, 600, 602
— Business School 392
— Law School 330
— Medical School 213, 472, 477, 510, 514, 603
— School of Education 506
— School of Public Health 477, 479, 507, 509
— Society of Fellows 600
Harvey, Donald 364, 514
Haseltine, William A. 514
Hasenfus, Eugene 341
Hatch, Orrin 176, 185, 348
Hatcher, Mickey 633
Hatem, George 518
Hauck, Fred 601
Hauer, Rutger 34, 76
The Haunted Mesa (L'Amour) 36
Hauser, Gayelord 418
"Have Mercy" 35
Hawk missiles 252
Hawn, Goldie 24, 75, 77
Hayden, Carl 318
Hayden, N. S. 455
Haydon, Murray P. 488, 504, 514
Hayes, Elvin 641
Haynsworth, Clement F. Jr. 321, 365
Hays, Brooks 321
Hays, Robert 24
Hays, Wayne L. 321
Hayworth, Rita 486
Hazardous Substance Response Trust Fund 580
Hazelwood v. *Kuhlmeier* 179
Hazzard, Shirley 24
"Head Over Heels" 30, 33
Head, Murray 33
Head Start 191–192
"Head to Toe" 37
Health and Racquet Club 404
Healy, Rev. Timothy 213

Hearing Education and Awareness for Rockers (HEAR) 97
Hearns, Thomas 645
Hearst Corporation 440, 451
Heart 35–36, 45
"Heart and Soul" 29
Heart disease 462, 464–465, 468, 472, 474, 476–479, 487, 492, 494, 504, 510, 513–514, 516, 586
"Heart Mender" 24
"The Heart of Rock'n'Roll" 31
Heart, Lung and Blood Institute 518
"Heartbeat" 31
"Heartbreaker" 24, 85
"The Heat Is On" 33
Heathers 40
"Heaven" 32, 41, 89
Heaven and Hell (Jakes) 36
"Heaven Is a Place on Earth" 38
Heaven's Gate 25
Heavy D 66
Heavy D & The Boyz 40
Heckerling, Amy 77
Heckler, Margaret M. 317, 513–514
Heiden, Eric 606
The Heidi Chronicles (Wasserstein) 46
Heifetz, Jascha 132
Heimlich, Henry J. 518
Heimlich Maneuver 471, 518
Heinemann, Larry 34
Heinemann Prize 600
Heinlein, Robert A. 30, 32, 413, 458
Heinz, John 213
Heiress (Dailey) 36
Heisman Trophy 655, 690
Heller, Joseph 30
Heller, Walter W. 321
"Hello" 31, 86–87
"Hello Again" 26
Helmich, Joseph George 364
Helms, Jesse 47, 59, 173, 292, 305, 311–312, 377
Helmsley, Harry 167
Helmsley, Leona 167, 377
Helmsley Hotels chain 167
Helprin, Mark 29
Hemingway, Ernest 34, 458
Hemingway, Mariel 27
Hemingway, Mary Welsh 458
Hemophilia 375, 382, 467–468, 475, 480, 484, 512
Henderson, Ken 445
Hendrix, Dr. Stephen 515

Henley, Beth 44, 46
Henley, Don 29, 33, 92
Hennard, George 347
Hennings, Sally 214
Henry Hudson Parkway Authority, New York 322
Hepatitis 177, 465, 473, 518
Hepburn, Katharine 25, 45, 78
Herald American 451
Herbert, Frank 25, 30, 32, 458
"Here Comes the Rain Again" 30, 85
"Here Comes Your Man" 41
"Here I Go Again" 37
Heretics of Dune (Herbert) 30
Heritage Foundation 173, 302
Heritage USA, Fort Mill, S.C. 549
Herman, Louis 601
Herman, Pee-Wee 32
Hermitage Museum, Leningrad 25
Hernandez, Keith 631
Heroin 52, 351–352, 462
Herpes 464–465, 470, 473, 479
Herrara, Carolyn 243
Hershiser, Orel 633, 637, 688
Hertz car-rental agency 418
Herzog, Whitey 688
Heterograft 470
Heuvelmans, Bernard 601
Hewlett, Sylvia Ann 400
Hewlett-Packard 143, 159, 583
Hickey, Cardinal James A. 556
Hicks, James L. 458
High Museum of Art, Atlanta 219
High Tide 77
Higher Education Act 185, 192
"Higher Love" 35
Highway 101 40
Highway of Eternity (Simak) 34
"Highwayman" 33
Hill, Eddie 676
Hill, Lister 321
Hill Street Blues 392, 422, 447–448, 456
Hilleman, Maurice R. 518
Hiller, Wendy 27
Hillery, Judith 353
Hilton Hotel, Washington, D.C. 248, 260
Hinckley, John W. Jr. 248, 260, 270
Hinduism 557
Hines, Earl 132
Hines, Gregory 32
Hines, Merrill O. 519
Hinojosa-Smith, Rolando 32
"Hip to Be Square" 37

Huston, John 32
Hutchinson, Edward 321
Hutton, Lauren 24, 239
Hutton, Timothy 24
Hyatt Regency Hotel, Kansas City, Mo. 369
Hyde, Henry 359
Hyde Amendment 399, 462–463
Hyslop, Dr. Peter H. St. George 514

I

"I Beg Your Pardon" 40
"I Can Dream About You" 31
"I Can't Go for That (No Can Do)" 27
"I Can't Stand It" 26
"I Can't Wait" 35
"I Could Never Take the Place of Your Man" 39, 88
"I Don't Know a Thing About Love" 31
"I Don't Need You" 26
"I Don't Want to Go On with You Like That" 39
"I Feel for You" 31
"I Found Someone" 38
"I Get Weak" 38
"I Guess That's Why They Call It the Blues" 31
"I Just Called to Say I Love You" 31, 87
"I Just Can't Stop Loving You" 36
"(I Just) Died in Your Arms" 36
"I Knew You Were Waiting for Me" 36
"I Love a Rainy Night" 26
"I Love Rock'n'Roll" 27, 85
I. M. Pei and Associates 243
"I Need Love" 36
"I Ran" 27
I Spy 449
"I Still Haven't Found What I'm Looking For" 37
"I Think We're Alone Now" 37
"I Wanna Be Your Lover" 24, 88
"I Wanna Dance with Somebody (Who Loves Me)" 36, 87
"I Want a New Drug" 31
"I Want Her" 39
"I Want to Know What Love Is" 33
"I Want Your Sex" 37
"I Wonder If I Take You Home" 33
"I Won't Back Down" 41
"I Would Die 4 U" 88
Iacocca, Lee 146, 167

IBM 48, 142, 155, 157–159, 161, 385, 432, 442, 570–574, 576, 582–584
Ibuprofen 469
The Icarus Agenda (Ludlum) 38
Ice-T 39, 65–66
Iditarod Trail Sled Dog Race 417
Idol, Billy 27, 36, 107
"If I Could Turn Back Time" 40
"If It Isn't Love" 39
"If She Knew What She Wants" 35
"If This Is It" 31, 89
If Tomorrow Comes (Sheldon) 32, 82
"If You Could Change Your Mind" 38
"If You Leave" 35
"If You Love Somebody Set Them Free" 33
Iglesias, Julio 31
"I'll Always Love You" 38
"I'll Be Loving You (Forever)" 40
"I'll Be There For You" 40
"I'll Be You" 41
I'll Take Manhattan (Krantz) 42
"I'll Tumble 4 Ya" 29
"I'll Wait" 31
Illusions of Love (Freeman) 32
"I'm Goin Back to Cali" 39, 65
"I'm on Fire" 33, 86, 89
"I'm Real" 38
"I'm So Excited" 31, 88
"I'm That Type of Guy" 40
Imani Temple African American Catholic Church 556
Immediate Family 78
Immigration Control and Reform Act 373, 376
"An Imperiled Generation" 191
"In a Big Country" 27
In Another Country (Kenney) 30
In Country 32, 40, 44, 74
"In No Time at All" 24
In View 438
In vitro fertilization 462, 479, 490
Independent Television News Association 429
Indiana Jones movies 67, 69, 75
Indiana Jones and the Last Crusade 40, 67, 69
Indiana Jones and the Temple of Doom 30, 67, 69, 119
Indiana National Guard 297
Indiana University 186
Indiana Youth Center, Plainfield, Ind. 646
Indianapolis 500 675, 690

Individual Education Plans 213
Industrial Light and Magic 69
INF (Intermediate Nuclear Forces) Treaty 254–255, 265, 391
"Inflammatory Essays" (Holzer) 42, 56
Inflation 140–144, 151, 167, 180, 205, 257, 278–279, 281–282, 303–305, 307, 383, 442–443, 467–468, 495
Influenza 462, 464
Ingram, James 29, 37
Ingrassia, Angelo 353
The Ink Truck (Kennedy) 81
Inland Steel 148
Innerspace 69
Inouye, Daniel 358
Inside Edition 427
Inside, Outside (Wouk) 32
Institute for Contemporary Art 59
Institute on Religion and Democracy (IRD) 543
Instructional-theory-into-practice (ITIP) model 209
Insulin 362, 465, 480, 493–494, 514
Intel 155, 159
Interagency Council on the Homeless 402
Interchange (de Kooning) 41
Intercontinental Ballistic Missiles (ICBMs) 259, 339
Interferon 468, 472–473, 477, 493, 570
Intermediate Nuclear Forces Treaty. See INF Treaty
Internal Revenue Service (IRS) 351, 433, 443
International Amateur Boxing Federation (IABA) 670
International Boxing Federation (IBF) 645, 687
International Brotherhood of Teamsters 169
International Court of Justice 251, 253, 275
International Freedom Foundation 312
International Ladies Garment Workers Union (ILGW) 168
International Olympic Committee 626, 663–664
International Physicians for the Prevention of Nuclear War (IPPNW) 509–510
International Society of Cryptozoology 601

Lance, Bert 364
"Land of Confusion" 36
Landau, Jon 120
Landers, Ann 518
Landgrebe, Earl F. 322
Landis, John 72, 86, 125, 364
Landon, Alfred M. 322
Landry, Greg 649
Landscape #20 (Giger) 62
Lane, Diane 30
Lane, Kenneth Jay 243
Lane Bryant, Inc. 439
Lang, K. D. 40, 47
Lange, Jessica 27, 30, 32, 34, 46, 78
Langella, Frank 82
Langer, Susanne K. 418
Lansing, Sherry 43, 68–69, 77, 125
Lao-tse 558
Laosa, Luis 213
LaRouche, Lyndon 364
Larson, Kay 52
Lasch, Christopher 183
LaScola, Dr. Raymond L. 514
Laser therapy 480, 497–498
Lasorda, Tommy 633
The Last Temptation of Christ 38–39, 60, 77, 376
The Late Show Starring Joan Rivers 434–435
Lau v. *Nichols* 188
Lauper, Cyndi 31, 35–36, 45–46, 65, 92
Laura Ashley designs 236, 392
Lauren, Ralph 218, 240, 243
Lauterbur, Paul C. 518
Lavelle, Rita 364
Laver, Rod 672
Law, Cardinal Bernard 551–552
Lawford, Peter 133
Lawrence Livermore National Laboratory 585, 601
Lay, Herman W. 169
Leach, Jim 287
Leadership Conference of Women Religious Speakers 552
Leakey, Richard 572
"Lean on Me" 36
Leaphart, Vincent 345
Lear, Norman 423
Lear Publishing 436
"Learning to Fly" 37
Lear's 439
"Leave a Light On" 40
Leaving Home (Keillor) 36, 82
Leavitt, David 30, 34, 46, 82
Lebanese Civil War 269
LeBon, Simon 84, 94

LeBrock, Kelly 30
Le Carre, John 82
Leder, Philip 517, 590
Lederer, Raymond 248
Lee, Spike 34, 39–40 47, 66, 77–78
The Legacy (Fast) 25, 36
Legal Eagles 78
Legs (Kennedy) 31, 81
Lehigh University 180
Lehmann-Haupt, Christopher 202
Leigh, Jennifer Jason 27, 34, 80
Leland, George Thomas "Mickey" 322
LeMat, Paul 24
Lemieux, Annie 59
Lemieux, Mario 662–663
Lemmon, Jack 27
LeMond, Greg 689
Lend Me a Tenor 101
Lendl, Ivan 689
Lenfant, Dr. Claude 514
Lennon, Alton 312
Lennon, John 26, 31, 33, 45, 364
Lennon, Julian 33
Lennox, Annie 45, 85
Leonard, Elmore 32
Leonard, Sugar Ray 607, 644
Leonardo da Vinci 49
Leowy, Raymond Fernand 246
Leprosy 518
Lesbian Nuns: Breaking Silence 553
Leser, Tina 246
Leslie, Lisa 689
Less Than Zero 32, 42, 46, 80–81
A Lesser Life (Hewlett) 400
"Let It Whip" 27
"Let the Music Play" 31
Lethal Weapon 36, 44, 75
"Let's Dance" 29, 86
"Let's Fall to Pieces Together" 31
"Let's Get Serious" 24
"Let's Go Crazy" 31, 88
"Let's Groove" 27
"Let's Hear It for the Boy" 31
"Let's Wait Awhile" 36
Letterman, David 117
Level 42 35
LeVert 36
Levi Strauss 240
Levi-Montalcini, Rita 516–517
Levin, Jennifer 363
Levine, Alan 61
Levine, James 125
Levinson, Barry 78
Levitation, Five Fictions (Ozick) 27
Levy, Robert I. 518
Lewis, Carl 666, 669, 671, 689

Lewis, Drew 151, 304
Lewis, Emmanuel 87
Lewis, Huey 29, 31, 33, 35, 37, 72, 89
Lewis, Jerry 28
Lewis, Jerry Lee 563
Lewis, Michael 417
Lewis, Reginald F. 163
Lewis, Rob 393
Li, Choh Hao 603
Lianna 28, 46
Liberace 46, 49, 133
Liberation Theology 554
Libertarian Party 317
Liberty 630
Liberty Federation 536, 546, 560
Libra (DeLillo) 38
Library of America 28
Lichtenstein, Roy 34, 50, 53
Lichter, Peter 587
Lie Down With Lions 34
Lieberman, Myron 176
Lieberman, Nancy 606, 682, 685
"Lies" 29
Life 78, 504
The Life and Adventures of Nicholas Nickleby 26, 97–98
"Life in a Northern Town" 35
Lifestyles of the Rich and Famous 42, 384
Lightning (Koontz) 38
Like a Prayer 40, 91
"Like a Virgin" 33, 90
Limbaugh, Rush 426
Limbo Lounge, New York City 54
The Limelight, New York City 54
Limited Nuclear Test Ban Treaty of 1963 321
Lincoln (Vidal) 30
Lincoln Center for the Performing Arts 323
Lindbergh Middle School 194–195
Lindquist, Mark 81
Ling, Rev. Jeff 62
Liposuction 467
Lipps Inc. 24, 84
Lisa Lisa and Cult Jam 33, 37
Listen Like Thieves (INXS) 92
Lithgow, John 27–28
Little, Sally 657
"Little Red Corvette" 29, 88
Litton Publishing Group 438
Live Aid 33, 45, 66, 95, 372
"Live to Tell" 35, 91
Lives of a Cell (Thomas) 518
Lives of the Poets (Doctorow) 30
"Livin' on a Prayer" 36

Madonna 31–37, 40, 42–44, 46, 53, 60, 72, 86, 88, 90–91, 98, 113, 116, 218, 230, 232, 383, 437

Mafia 311, 352, 365

Magdalene, Mary 60

"Magic" 24

The Magician (Stein) 61

Magna Carta 371

Magnetic Resonance Imaging (MRI) 433

Magnuson, Ann 57

Magnuson, Warren G. 284, 322

Mailer, Norman 29–30, 125

Major League Baseball Players Association 635

"Major Tom (Coming Home)" 31

"Make It Real" 39

Making Love 27, 46

"Making Love Out of Nothing at All" 29

The Making of Michael Jackson's Thriller 44

Malamud, Bernard 29, 61, 133

Malkovich, John 35, 38

The Malling of America (Kowinski) 385

Malone, Moses 636, 678

Mama Day (Naylor) 38

"Mama He's Crazy" 31

Mamet, David 36, 42, 44–46, 91, 100, 117

The Mammoth Hunters (Auel) 32, 82

The Man from St. Petersburg (Follet) 27

"Man in the Mirror" 39, 87

Manchester Guardian Weekly 289

Mancini, Ray "Boom Boom" 645

"Mandolin Rain" 36

Mandrell, Barbara 31, 103, 125

"Maneater" 29

Mangione, Chuck 105

Manhattan Transfer 26

"Maniac" 29

"Manic Monday" 35, 88

Mankiewicz, Frank 444

Mankiller, Wilma 373

Manon Lescaut 25

Mansion, Gracie 51

Mansour, Sister Agnes Mary 551

Mantegna, Andrea 33

Mantegna, Joe 36

Mantle, Mickey 631

Mapplethorpe, Robert 44–47, 58–59, 133, 377, 383

Marantz, Steve 634

Marathon Oil 141

March of Dimes 465

Marchetti, Victor 352

Marciano, Rocky 645

Marcos, Ferdinand 252, 268–269, 560, 565

Marcus, Greil 63

Margaret Wade Trophy (basketball) 606

Marijuana 173, 194, 310, 330, 347, 369, 462

Marine Parkway Authority, New York 322

Marino, Bishop Eugene Antonio 556, 565

Marino, Dan 689

Marley, Ziggy 40

Maronite Christian Community 269

Marrero, Alex 344

Married to the Mob 38, 77

Married . . . With Children 435

Marriott, J. Willard 169

Marriott Corporation 169

M/A/R/R/S 39

Marsalis, Branford 106

Marsalis, Wynton 43, 46, 105–106

Marshall, Fred 322

Marshall, Penny 77

Marshall, Prentice 328

Marshall, Thurgood 407

Marshall Plan 321

Marshner, Connaught 417

Martha Stewart Living 415

Martha Stewart Weddings (Stewart) 414

Martha Stewart, Inc. 414

Martha Stewart's Christmas (Stewart) 414

Martha Stewart's Quick Cook Menus (Stewart) 414

Martin, Billy 633

Martin, Cindy 515

Martin, Dean 45

Martin, Jerry 631

Martin, Judith 417

Martin, Steve 30, 36, 40, 75

Martinez v. *School Board of Hillsborough County* 187

Marty, Martin E. 554

Marx, Richard 39

Marxism 248, 258, 267, 269, 273, 275, 315, 352, 358, 510, 543

Mary Boone Gallery 56

The Mary Tyler Moore Show 447, 459

Marymount College 310

M*A*S*H 422

Mask 32, 78, 89

Mason, Bobbie Ann 27, 32

Mason, C. Vernon 353

Massachusetts General Hospital 473, 507

Massachusetts Institute of Technology (MIT) 472, 513, 516–517, 574, 595–596

Massimino, Rollie 641

"Master Blaster" 26

Master of the Game (Sheldon) 27, 42

Master Teachers 202, 209

Mastercard 385

Masters, Dr. William H. 515

Masters Golf Tournament 656–657, 659, 690–691

"Material Girl" 33, 42, 90

Matewan 36, 77

Matlin, Marlee 34

Mattea, Kathy 104

Mattel toy company 416

Matthews, Bishop Marjorie S. 544

Mattingly, Mack 293

Maurice 40, 46

Maximum Overdrive 82

Maxwell, Cedric 678

Maxwell, Robert 423, 442

May, Elaine 77

May, Bishop Kenneth 543

Mayans 557

Mayer, Louis B. 67

Mayfield, Frank H. 519

Maynard, Robert 450

Mayo Clinic 470, 510

"The Mayor of Simpleton" 41

Mays, Benjamin 418

Mays, Kimberly Michelle 378

Mazda 142

MC Lyte 65–66

MCA 39

McAteer, Edward 545

McAuliffe, Caroline 210

McAuliffe, Christa 210, 572, 592, 602

McAuliffe, Scott 210

McAuliffe, Steven 210

McBride, Lloyd 169

McCaffrey, Anne 29, 38

McCall Pattern Company 163

McCall's 169, 309

McCallum, Jack 678

McCandless, Bruce 571

McCarthy, Andrew 32, 80

McCarthy, John 405

McCarthy, Joseph R. 320, 323, 365

McCarthy, Mary 133

McCarthy, Patrick 602

Miller, William M. "Fishbait" 322
Milli Vanilli 40, 44, 88
Millie (dog) 318
Milliken 149
Millionaire 438
Mills, Juliet 82
Milsap, Ronnie 24, 26–27, 33
Milstein, César 516–517, 519
Milwaukee Brewers 606, 689
Mindbend (Cook) 32
Minimalism 48, 52
Minnelli, Liza 25, 112
Minnelli, Vincente 134
Minnesota Multiphasic Personality Inventory 479
Minnesota North Stars 606, 662
Minnesota Timberwolves 638
Minor Threat 46
Minotaur (Coonts) 40
The Minutemen 110
Miporn 328
Mir 593
Mirabella, Grace 231, 439, 452
Mirabella 439
"Mirror in the Bathroom" 26
Mirth and Girth (Nelson) 60
MIRVs 259
Les Miserables 44, 98
Misery (King) 36
"Misled" 33
Miss America pageant 43, 368, 415–417
"Miss Me Blind" 30
Miss Saigon 44, 99
Miss USA pageant 375
"Miss You Much" 40, 88
Missing 27
Missing in Action 30, 47, 74
"Missing You" 31
The Mission 34
Mississippi Burning 38
Mississippi University for Women 213, 465
Mrs. Soffel 30, 77
Mr. Mister 35
Mr. Mom 28, 78
"Mr. Roboto" 29
Mistral's Daughter (Krantz) 27
Mitchell, Clarence 365
Mitchell, John N. 322, 365
Mitchell, Michael 95
Mitla Pass (Uris) 38
Mitsubishi 142
Mize, Larry 659
Modern Classicism (Stern and Gastil) 220
"Modern Love" 29

Modernism (architecture) 218, 233
Modernism (religion) 541, 552
Modine, Matthew 28, 35
Molina, Mario 590
Molloy, John T. 227
Mommie Dearest 25
Mona Lisa 34
Mondale, Walter "Fritz" 74, 143, 213, 251, 281, 288–291, 293, 310–311, 328
Mondavi, Robert 417
MONEY 383
"Money for Nothing" 32
"Money's Too Tight to Mention" 33
Monk, Art 689
Monk, Thelonious 134
The Monkees 436
"Monkey" 39
Monroe, Marilyn 90
Monroe, Marion 214
Monroney, A. S. "Mike" 322
Monsanto Corporation 581
Montagnier, Dr. Luc 505, 518
Montalban, Ricardo 27
Montana, Joe 683–684
Montgomery, Robert 134
Montgomery Ward 385
Montreal Expos 686
"Mony Mony" 36
Moon, Rev. Sun Myung 535
Moonstruck 36, 45, 79
Moore, Arch A. Jr. 300
Moore, Demi 32, 43, 80, 448
Moore, Don W. 459
Moore, Dudley 25, 75
Moore, Gordon 159
Moore, Mary Tyler 24, 110
Moore, Roger 82
Moore, Samuel 61
Moore, Stanley 213
Moorhead, William S. 322
Moral Majority 212–213, 301, 312, 381, 399, 534, 538, 540, 542, 545–546, 560, 565
Morales, Pablo 689
Morancy, Sister Elizabeth 551
Moranis, Rick 30, 40, 75
Morano, Albert P. 322
Morantz, Paul 416
Mordant's Need (Donaldson) 34
More Die of Heartbreak (Bellow) 36
Moreta (McCaffrey) 29
Morgan's Passing (Tyler) 24, 82
Morial, Ernest N. 322
Morita, Pat 30

Mormons. *See* Church of Jesus Christ of Latter-Day Saints 542
Morning Edition 444
"Morning Train" 26
Morris, Jack 634
Morris, Mark 46, 58
Morris, Robert Tappan 602
Morris, Wright 24
Morrison, Toni 25, 36, 46, 82, 214
Morrow, Vic 28, 364
Morton, Rogers 308
Morton, Thurston B. 322
Moses, Edwin 667
Moses, Robert 322, 418
Moses, Sam 675
The Mosquito Coast (Theroux) 27
Mossad 338
The Motels 27
Motion Picture Association of America 31
Motor Carrier Act 140
Motorola 188
Motown Records 39
Mould, Bob 40, 110
Mount St. Helens Curriculum Materials Project 172
"Mountain Music" 27
Mountain States Legal Defense Foundation 151
"Mountains" 35, 88
Mountcastle, Vernon B. 517
MOVE 345, 372
"Move Away" 35
"Move Somethin'" 62, 66
The Movie Channel (TMC) 427, 436
Moyers, Bill 455
Moynihan, Daniel Patrick 410
Mozert, Bob 198–199
Mozert v. *Board of Education* 198–199
MPLA (Popular Movement for the Liberation of Angola) 267–268
Ms. 418
MTM Enterprises 447–448
Mtume 29
MTV (Music Television) 26, 42, 44, 60, 65, 72, 74, 80–82, 84–87, 92–95, 230, 422, 427, 435–437, 446, 448
Mudd Club, New York City 54, 64, 113
Muhammad, Elijah 557
Muhammad, Warith 557
Muhlenberg, Frederick A. 323
Mujahideen guerrillas 267
Mullin, Chris 635

Multer, Abraham J. 323
Multimedia Audiences 444
Multiple sclerosis 479
Murdoch, Sir Keith 450
Murdoch, Rupert 143, 152, 423–424, 434, 439, 442, 450–451
Murdoch Magazines 439
Murmur 110
Murphy, Austin 663
Murphy, Dale 634
Murphy, Eddie 27–28, 30, 35, 38, 43, 45–46, 75–76, 88
Murphy, John M. 248
Murray, Anne 24
Murray, Bill 24–25, 30, 40, 45, 75–76
Murray, Charles 313
Murray, Eddie 689
Murrow, Edward R. 441
Museum of African Art, Washington, D.C 37
Museum of Modern Art, New York City 25, 31, 48, 51, 58
Museum of Science and Industry, Chicago 602
Musial, Stan 686
Music for Life 37
Musical Youth 29
Muskie, Edmund 253, 276
Muskovites 263
Mutual Assured Destruction (MAD) 261
MX missiles 259, 261
"My Adidas" 65
My Beautiful Laundrette 46
My Dinner with Andre 25
My Favorite Year 27
"My Heart Can't Tell You No" 41
"My Hometown" 33, 45, 89
"My Love" 29
"My Prerogative" 38, 88
My Turn (Reagan) 413
Myers, C. Kilmer 566
Myers, Michael 248
Mystery Train 77
Mythologies (Morris) 58

N

N.W.A. 66
Nabisco Dinah Shore Tournament 659
Nack, William 644
Nader, Ralph 515
Naked Gun 38, 76
Naked Raygun 109–110
Namath, Joe 683

The Name of the Rose (Eco) 82
Names Project 383
Napier, Frank 206
Nash, Roderick 626
Nashua Telegraph 277
Nashville Network 85
Nassau Country Club, N.Y. 360
"Nasty" 35, 88
The Nation 459
A Nation at Risk 180, 183, 185
Nation of Islam 289, 314, 407, 536, 555, 557, 565
National Academy of Design for Interior Design 245
National Academy of Sciences 474, 476, 478, 596, 600, 604
National Advisory and Coordinating Council on Bi-Lingual Education 189
National Aeronautics and Space Administration (NASA) 210, 570, 572–575, 586, 591–593, 597, 599–600
National Airport, Washington, D.C. 369
"National Anthem" 66
National Antiapartheid Protest Day 188
National Archives, Washington, D.C. 371
National Assembly of Religious Women 552
National Assessment of Educational Progress 173, 178, 182
National Association for Stock Car Auto Racing (NASCAR) 674–676
National Association for the Advancement of Colored People (NAACP) 180, 191, 324, 365, 407, 419
National Association of Broadcasters 455
National Baptist Convention of America 556
National Baptist Convention, U.S.A., Inc. 555–556, 565
National Basketball Association (NBA) 446, 606, 626, 635–639, 641, 643, 678, 680–682, 688, 690
National Book Critics Circle Awards 81–82, 598
National Broadcasting Company (NBC) 145, 152, 422–423, 426–427, 431, 434, 436–437, 441, 445, 447, 449, 453, 455–458, 534, 606, 626 655

National Cancer Institute (NCI) 462, 464, 476, 494, 505, 510
National Center for Educational Information 179, 201
National Center for Educational Statistics 177, 182
National Center for Health Statistics 463, 470, 485
National Coalition of American Nuns 551–552
National Coffee Association 464
National Collegiate Athletic Association (NCAA) 186–187, 626–627, 635, 639–643, 651–655, 677, 680, 682, 688–690
National Commission on Excellence in Education (NCEE) 183, 192, 195–196
National Commission on Graduate Education 197
National Commission on Social Security Reform 410
National Conference of Catholic Bishops (NCCB) 535–536. 543, 552–554, 559, 566
National Conference of Christians and Jews 534
National Council for Better Education 175
National Council of Churches (NCC) 417, 534–536, 539, 541, 543, 565–566
National Council of State Legislatures 180
National Council on Year-Round Education 178
National Day of Prayer and Thanksgiving 538
National Drug Control Strategy 194
National Education Association (NEA) 172, 175, 178, 191, 201, 211, 214
National Endowment for the Arts (NEA) 57–60, 179, 377–378
National Endowment for the Humanities 204
National Enquirer 49
National Farmers' Union 591
National Federation for Decency 60, 406
National Federation of State High School Associations (NFSHSA) 642
National Football Conference (NFC) 647, 650–651, 683

National Football League (NFL)
427, 439, 446, 626, 629, 647–
650, 652, 688–689

National Football League Players
Association (NFLPA) 648

National Gallery of Art, Washington, D.C. 126

National Geographic Traveler 438

National Golden Gloves Tournament 687

National Heart, Lung, and Blood Institute 465, 468, 494, 514

National Hockey League (NHL) 606, 660–663, 679, 694, 696

National Humanities Center 204

National Institute Against Prejudice and Violence 407

National Institute of Allergy and Infectious Diseases 479

National Institute of Dental Research 477

National Institute of Mental Health 513

National Institute on Aging 485

National Institute on Drug Abuse 374, 396, 473

National Institutes of Health (NIH) 373, 468–469, 471, 473, 475–476, 478, 494, 505, 518–519, 586–587

National Lampoon's Christmas Vacation 40

National Lampoon's European Vacation 32, 77

National Lampoon's Vacation movies 72, 75

National League (NL) 629, 631, 633–634, 686, 688

National League Championship Series 629

National Legal Foundation 199

National Low-Income Housing Coalition 401

National Medal of Science 599

National Missionary Baptist Convention 537

National Organization for Women (NOW) 291, 373, 399

National Playwrights Conference 123

National Press Club 261

National PTA 212

National Public Radio (NPR) 426, 444, 455

National Research Council (NRC) 180, 189, 598

National Review 411, 458

National School Boards Association 213

National Science Board 196

National Science Board — Commission on Precollege Education in Math, Science and Technology 182

National Science Foundation 182, 494, 508

National Security Act 342

National Security Administration 338

National Security Council (NSC) 272, 275–276, 309, 342, 352, 357–359

National Socialist Party of America 260

National Sports Review 685

National Survey on Drug Abuse 396

National Teacher of the Year Award 183, 212

National Trails System 416

National Urban League 66, 364, 368, 372–373, 407

Nation's Business (Brock) 184, 212

Native Americans 234, 313–314, 347, 371, 407, 557, 565

NATO 249, 262, 264–265, 296, 309, 579

The Natural 30, 78

Natural History 598

Nature 573–574

"Naughty Girls (Need Love Too)" 38

Navajo tribe 373

Navratilova, Martina 610, 671, 684–685

Naylor, Gloria 38

Nazism 33, 58, 108, 122, 318, 330, 364, 373, 407, 511, 555

NBC. *See* National Broadcasting Corporation

NBC News 441, 453

NBC News at Sunrise 441

NBC Nightly News 441, 452–453, 455

Near Dark 36, 77

Nebraska (Springsteen) 88

Nebraska Cornhuskers 654

NEC 155

"The Necessary Revolution in Teacher Education" (Gideonse) 202

"Need You Tonight" 39

Needham, John 418

Neel, Alice 134

Neeson, Liam 38

Negri, Pola 134

Neighbors (Berger) 24

Neill, Sam 38

Nelson, David 60

Nelson, Gaylord 284

Nelson, Judd 32, 80

Nelson, Rick 134

Nelson, Willie 24, 27, 31, 33–34

Nelson Fine Arts Center 234

Nena 31

Neo, Chicago 84

Neo-Expressionism 42, 44, 46, 50, 52

Neo-Geo 52

Neo-minimalism 52

Nesbitt, Lowell 59

Nesmith, Michael 436

Neumann, Liselotte 657

Nevelson, Louise 134

"Never" 35

"Never Be You" 35

"Never Gonna Give You Up" 38

"Never Tear Us Apart" 39

"Never You Done That" 33

Neverland 87

Nevil, Robbie 37

Neville, Aaron 41

"New Age Harmonies" 537

New Age movement 534, 537, 540, 557–558

The New American Poverty (Harrington) 401

"New Attitude" 33

The New Bill Cosby Show 449

New Bohemians 38

"New Call to Peacemaking" 542

New Christian Right. *See* Religious Right

New Deal 151, 157, 258, 350, 360, 400

New Deal Coalition 284, 289, 291, 299

New Edition 33, 39, 88

New England Journal of Medicine 463–469, 471–474, 476, 478–479, 509, 515

New England Monthly 438

New England Monthly, Inc. 438

New Federalism 185, 249

New Jersey Nets 638

New Jersey Superior Court 491

New Jersey Supreme Court 179, 201, 491

New Jewel political movement 269

New Journalism 81

New Kids on the Block 39–40, 43

North American Congress on the Holy Spirit 537

North American Soccer League (NASL) 610

North and South (Jakes) 27

North Carolina Agricultural and Technical University 313

North Carolina Mutual Insurance Company 169

North Carolina State University 640, 683

North Park Seminary 507

Northrop, John Knudsen 169

Northrop Corporation 169, 579

Northrup, John H. 603

Northwestern University 654
— Medical School 515

Norton, Andre 34

"Nothing's Gonna Stop Us Now" 37

"Notorious" 36

Notre Dame College 508

NOVA 508

Novak, Michael 554

Novak, Robert 59

Noyce, Robert 159

Nu Shooz 35

Nuclear Magnetic Resonance (NMR) 433

Nuclear Propulsion 323

Nuclear Regulatory Commission (NRC) 571

Nuclear Waste Policy Act of 1982 589

Nuclear weapons 56, 74, 188, 213, 249, 254, 258, 260–261, 264–265, 281, 283, 286, 289–290, 295, 318, 323, 370, 389, 391, 417, 422, 509, 534–535, 540, 542–543, 553–554, 558–559, 570, 575

Nueharth, Allan H. 439

Numan, Gary 24, 84

Nunn, Sam 269

Nunn, Trevor 43

NutraSweet 476

O

"O Superman" 57

Oak Hill Country Club 659

Oak Ridge Boys 26, 103

Oak Ridge National Laboratory 585

Oakland Athletics 629, 633–634

Oakland Raiders 629, 648

Oakland Tribune 450

Oates, John 26–27, 29–30

Oates, Joyce Carol 24–25, 27

O'Boyle, Cardinal Patrick Aloysius 566

O'Brien, George M. 323

O'Brien, Lawrence 635

O'Brien, Leo 323

O'Brien, Pat 134

"Obsession" 32

Ocasek, Ric 85

Occidental Petroleum Corporation 376

Occupational Safety and Health Administration 150, 494

Ocean, Billy 31, 39

O'Connor, John III 359, 536, 551–552, 554

O'Connor, Archbishop John J. 311

O'Connor, Sandra Day 57, 249, 332, 335, 348, 350, 359–360, 369

Off the Wall 24, 86, 114

An Officer and a Gentleman 27, 74–75

The Official Preppy Handbook 218, 455

Offit, Avodah K. 417

"Oh Father" 40

"Oh L'Amour" 35

"Oh Sheila" 33

O'Hara, James G. 323

O'Hara, Mary 134

Ohio State University 239

Ohio University 176

Oingo Boingo 84–85

O'Keeffe, Georgia 134

Oklahoma State University 689

O'Konski, Alvin E. 323

Olajuwon, Hakeem 638, 640, 680

The Old Forest and Other Stories (Taylor) 32

Old Time Gospel Hour 301, 545, 560

"Old Time Rock and Roll" 89–90

The Oldest Living Confederate Widow Tells All (Gurganus) 40

Oldman, Gary 34, 36

Oldsmobile 237

Olin, Lena 38, 40

Oliveri, Alfred 64

Ollie and Jerry 31

Olmos, Edward James 208

Olson, James 25

Olson, James Elias 169

Olympic Games, 1936 667

Olympic Games, 1960 669

Olympic Games, 1976 626

Olympic Games, 1980 248, 259, 279–280, 606, 660, 663

Olympic Games, 1984 64, 626, 628, 665, 668, 681

Olympic Games, 1988 88, 446, 668, 671, 682

Olympic Games, 1992 626, 669

Omni 412

Omnibus Education Bill 193

On Golden Pond 25, 78

"On My Own" 35

"On Our Own" 40

On the Beach 74

"On the Other Hand" 35

"On the Road Again" 24

On Wings of Eagles 164

"Once Bitten, Twice Shy" 40

Once Is Not Enough (Susann) 82

Once Upon a Time in America 30

One (Bach) 38, 40

"The One I Love" 37

"One Moment in Time" 39, 88

"One More Night" 32

"One More Try" 39

"One Night in Bankok" 33

"The One That You Love" 26

The One Tree (Donaldson) 27

"1-2-3" 38

O'Neill, Cherry Boone 493

O'Neill, Thomas P. "Tip" 286, 311

"Only a Lonely Heart Knows" 31

"Only a Memory" 39

"Only in My Dreams" 36

"Only the Lonely" 27

Ontkean, Michael 27

OPEC (Organization of Petroleum Exporting Countries) 141, 282, 303

"Open Arms" 27

"Open Your Heart" 37, 91

Operation Breadbasket 313

Operation Rescue 273

Oppenheimer and Company 438

Oprah Winfrey Show 453–454

O'Quinn, Terry 36

Oral History (Smith) 29

Oral Roberts University 549

Orange Bowl 652, 654

"Orange Crush" 41

Orbison, Roy 40, 134

Orchestral Manoeuvres in the Dark 35, 84–85

Order 373

"Order for Sunday Celebrations in the Absence of a Priest" 552

Order of Notre Dame 508

Ordinary People 24, 78

O'Reilly, Jane 628

Organized crime 169, 329–330, 351–352, 363
Orlando Magic 638
Orosco, Jesse 632
Orr, Bobby 679
Orr-Cahall, Christina 59
Orser, Brian 668
Ortega, Daniel 273
Orthodox Judaism 540, 555, 562
Osbourne, Ozzy 40
Osijchuk, Hryhorij 566
Oslin, K. T. 37
Osmond, Donny 41, 92
The Other America (Harrington) 168
O'Toole, Margaret 596
O'Toole, Peter 24, 27
"Our Lips Are Sealed" 27, 85
Out of Africa 32, 78, 219
"Out of the Blue" 38
"Out of Touch" 30
Out the Window (Johns) 37
Outbreak (Cook) 36
Outrageous Fortune 70, 75
Outside Providence (Farrelly) 81
The Outsiders 28
Overnight 441
Owens, Buck 39, 104
"Owner of a Lonely Heart" 31
Oxford University 448
— Worcester College 450
Ozick, Cynthia 27, 36

P

P.S. 1 52, 56, 64
Pace Gallery, Manhattan 51
Pacino, Al 28, 118
Paco's Story (Heinmann) 34
Pac-Man 432
"Pac-Man Fever" 27
Page, Geraldine 32, 78, 134
Pagones, Stephen 354
Pahlavi, Shah Mohammed Reza 266–267
The Paideia Proposal 201
Paisley Park Records 88
Pale Kings and Prices (Parker) 36
Palestine Liberation Organization (PLO) 255, 269–270, 289, 313–314, 338, 562
Paley, William S. 423, 459
Palin, Michael 38
The Palladium, New York City 44, 54, 57
Pallone, Dave 686
Palmer, Arnold 656

Palmer, Robert 35, 39, 92
Pan Am Airlines 577
Pan American Games 643
"Panama" 31
Panama Canal Treaty 282
Panama Invasion 277
Pantheon (publishing house) 442, 452
Pap smear 462, 475
"Papa Don't Preach" 35, 91
"Paper in Fire" 37
Papp, Joseph 122
"Paradise City" 40
Paramount Communications 443
Paramount Pictures 68, 70, 442
Paré, Michael 30
Parenthood 40, 78
Parenting 438
"Parents Just Don't Understand" 38
Parents' Music Resource Center (PMRC) 47, 61–63, 66, 437
Paris, Texas 30, 77
Paris peace talks (1969) 321–322
Paris Trout (Dexter) 38
Parker, Charlie 52, 105
Parker, Father James 565
Parker, Ray Jr. 31
Parker, Robert B. 36
Parkinson's disease 478–479, 513
Parks, Bert 368, 417
Parks, Rosa 417
Parr, John 33
Parrish, Robert 679
The Parsifal Mosaic (Ludlum) 27
Parsons School of Design 115
Partners in Crime (Hinojosa-Smith) 32
"Partners in the Mystery of Redemption" (U.S. Catholic bishops) 552
Parton, Dolly 24, 26, 31, 35, 103–104
"Part-time Lover" 33
"Party All the Time" 35, 88
Pasdar, Adrian 36
"Pass the Dutchie" 29
"Passion" 26
Passman, Otto E. 323
Pasteur Institute 505
"Pastoral Plan for Pro-Life Activities" (National Conference of Catholic Bishops) 552
PATCO (Professional Air Traffic Controller's Organization) 141, 151, 304
Paterno, Joe 642, 654

Paterson Education Association 206
"Patience" 40
Patinkin, Mandy 28
Patric, Jason 36
Patriot Games (Clancy) 36, 82
Patterson, Alicia 440
Patterson, Floyd 646, 687
Patterson, Frederick Douglass 215
Patterson, James T. 323
Patterson, Dr. Roy 515
Patterson v. *McLean Credit* 350
Paul, Ron 318
Pauling, Linus 390
Pavarotti, Luciano 37, 102
Payne, Donald 453
Payton, Wayton 689
PBS. *See* Public Broadcasting System
PC Magazine 584
PC World 584
Peabody, Mary Parkman 419
Peale, Rev. Norman Vincent 548, 565
Peale, Rembrandt 37
Pebbles 39
Peck, Gregory 75
"Peek-A-Boo" 39
Peel, Robert 537
Pee-Wee's Big Adventure 32, 73
Peggy Sue Got Married 34, 78
Pei, I. M. 41, 223
Pell, Claiborne 185
Peller, Clara 417
Pelli, Cesar 220
Pelotte, Fr. Donald E. 565
Pelton, Ronald William 338
Pendleton, Clarence M. Jr. 323
Penicillin 465
Penn Central Railroad 166
Penn, Sean 27, 34, 38–39, 43, 76, 80, 90, 117
Penney, John Cash 166
Pennsylvania State University 214, 596–597
The Pentagon 387, 562, 579
Penthouse 43, 61–62, 90, 117, 371, 406, 412, 415
People 42, 54, 407, 449
People Are Talking 453
People Express Airline 140, 577
People for the American Way 198–199
People Like Us (Dunne) 38
People United to Save Humanity. *See* PUSH
People's Temple 535

Presbyterian Church U.S.A. 372, 535, 539, 541

President's Commission for the Study of Ethical Problems in Medicine 464

President's Commission on AIDS 512

President's Commission on Obscenity and Pornography 406

President's Commission on Organized Crime 330

President's Task Force on Food Assistance 175

Presidential Medal of Freedom 565

Presley, Elvis 28, 37, 85, 114, 417

Presley, Lisa Marie 115

Presley, Priscilla 38

Presser, Jackie 169, 365

Preston, Peter 289

Preston, Robert 27

Presumed Innocent (Turow) 36, 82

The Pretenders 24, 29, 84

Pretty in Pink 80

Prevention 438

Price, Charles Melvin 323

Price, Leontyne 37, 125

Price, Reynolds 34, 82

Prick Up Your Ears 36, 46

Pride, Charley 29

Prime Time (Collins) 38

Prime Time Sunday 453

Prince 24, 27, 29–31, 34, 36–37, 39, 41, 45–46, 61, 88, 230

Prince & The Revolution 31, 33, 35, 88

The Prince of Tides (Conroy) 34

Princess Daisy (Krantz) 24, 443

Princeton University 308, 418, 585, 654

Pritzker, Abram Nicholas 169

Private Benjamin 24, 75

Private Dancer (Turner) 33, 88

"Private Eyes" 27

Prizzi's Honor (Condon) 27, 32

Pro 439

Pro-Family Coalition 417

Procter & Gamble 465, 503, 536

Prodigy 385

Professional Air Traffic Controllers Organization (PATCO) 141

Professional Golfers' Association (PGA) 656–657, 659, 689

Progressive Architecture 220

Progressive Party 323

Proposition 48 (NCAA) 186–187

ProServe 680

Protestantism 292, 296, 399, 414, 534, 539–544, 550, 552, 556, 561, 566

"Prove Your Love" 38

Provenzano, Anthony 365

Providence-St. Mel High School 207

Prudden, Bonnie 177

Pryce, Jonathan 32

Pryor, Richard 28

Psychedelic Furs 31, 39

Psycho 76

Psychology 174, 209, 212–213, 479, 486, 492, 506, 511

Ptacek, Stephen 602

PTL (Praise the Lord) Ministries 375, 377, 537–538, 549–550, 560–561, 565

PTL Club 548

PTL Television Network 549

Public Broadcasting System (PBS) 244, 296, 439, 449, 453, 508

Public Enemy 41, 47, 66

Public Image Ltd. 41, 107

Public Service Corporation 574

Publishers Weekly 443

Pueblo Indians 234

Puica, Maricica 667

Pulitzer Prize for Drama 46, 99, 126

Pulitzer Prize for Fiction 46, 81–82, 126

Pulitzer Prize for Music 126

Pulitzer Prize for Poetry 126

Pulitzer Prizes for Journalism 456–457

"Pulling Back the Reins" 40

"Pump Up the Jam" 41

"Pump Up the Volume" 39

The Punisher 75

Purdy, Claude 123

Purdy, Patrick Edward 364

Pure Food and Drug Act of 1906 351

Puritanism 257

Puritans 285

Purple Rain 30–31, 86, 88

The Purple Rose of Cairo 32, 77

Pursel, Jack 558

PUSH (People United to Save Humanity) 313

"Push It" 39

PUSH/Excel 313

Putnam, Emily Jane 212

Puttnam, David 68, 71

Puzo, Mario 30

Pyramid Club, New York City 54

Pythagoras 207

Q

Quaid, Dennis 28, 35

Quakers. *See* Society of Friends

Quarterflash 28

Quayle, J. Danforth 185, 284, 297, 300

Que Pasa 438

Quebec Nordiques 689

Queen 24, 26, 31, 45

Queen Latifah 37, 65–66

"Queen of Hearts" 26

The Queen of the Damned (Rice) 38, 82

The Queen's Gambit (Tevis) 29

Quiet Riot 31

Quigley, Joan 270, 413

Quinlan, Karen Ann 419

Quinn, Aidan 30, 32

Quinn, Sally 34

Quinn's Book (Kennedy) 81

Quinones, Adolfo (Shabba-Doo) 30

Quinones, Lee 27, 64

QVC Network 385

R

R.E.M. 37, 41, 45

Ra'anan, Uri 338

Rabbit Is Rich (Updike) 25, 42, 82

Rabbitt, Eddie 26, 29

Rabi, Isidor Isaac 604

Rabins, Peter 486

Race discrimination 46–47, 57–60, 65–66, 174, 178, 186, 188, 190–191, 200, 207, 215, 298, 306, 311, 313, 328, 334–335, 353–354, 360, 370, 408, 414, 436, 454, 538, 541–542, 556, 563, 604

Race relations 46–47, 63, 65, 81, 190–191, 214, 343, 368, 376–377, 406–408, 449, 628

Rachel and Her Children (Kozol) 401

RAD (Rockers Against Drugs) 437

Radiant Child (Haring) 113

Radio Corporation of America (RCA) 157, 423, 442, 445, 534

Radio Days 36, 78

"Radio Ga-Ga" 31

Radio Shack 161, 432

Radner, Gilda 30

Radon 180, 502

Rafelson, Bob 86

Rhythm Nation 1814 88
"Rhythm of the Night" 32
Rice, Anne 32, 38, 46, 82
Rice, Donna 293
Rice, Jerry 689
Richard J. Daley College 422
Richards, Ann 295
Richards, H. M. S. 566
Richards, Renee 685
Richardson, Elliot 334
Richardson, Michael Ray 638
Richardson, Miranda 35
Richie, Lionel 26, 29, 31, 35, 46, 86–87, 91
Richmond, Julius 481, 515
Richmond Board of Education, Va. 172
Richmond Newspapers v. *Virginia* 422
Richmond v. *Croson* 350
Richter, Burton 602
Richter, Charles F. 604
Richter Scale 174, 378, 574, 604, 633
Rickover, Adm. Hyman George 318, 323, 604
Riddles, Libby 417
"Ride Like the Wind" 24
Ride, Sally K. 210, 591, 599–600
Riekehof, Lottie 213
Rigel, Dr. Darrell 515
Riggins, John 648
The Right Stuff 28, 39, 74, 78, 289
Riker's Island Prison, New York City 66
Riley, Rev. Miles O'Brien 417
Riley, Richard 285
Ringling Bros. & Barnum and Bailey Circu 419
Ringwald, Molly 30, 32, 43, 80
Rio 29, 84
Ripken, Cal Jr. 630
Risky Business 28, 42, 75, 80, 89, 218
The River 30, 46, 88
Rivers, Joan 434–435
The River's Edge 36, 45, 77
Rizzo, Frank 345
The Road Warrior 27
Robards, Jason 24, 82
Robb, Charles S. 293, 300
Robbins, Harold 25, 27
Robbins, Jerome 125
Robbins, Tim 38
Robbins, Tom 24, 30
Robert, Ed 161
The Robert Cray Band 36

Robert Wood Johnson Foundation 402, 468
Roberts, Kenneth A. 323
Roberts, Rev. Oral 537, 545, 548–549
Roberts, Randy 666
Robertson, Rev. Marion "Pat" 62, 199, 296–297, 301, 303, 312, 537, 540, 544, 547–548, 556
Robinson, Aubrey 339
Robinson, Frank 628
Robinson, Julia Bowman 604
Robinson, Max 442
Robinson, Smokey 24, 37
Robinson, Sugar Ray 687
Robison, Rev. James 301, 544
Robocop 36, 67
The Robots of Dawn (Asimov) 29
Rock, John 419
Rock and Roll Hall of Fame, Cleveland 35
"R.O.C.K. in the U.S.A" 35, 45
"Rock Me Amadeus" 35
Rock Star (Collins) 38
Rock Steady Crew 64
"Rock the Casbah" 29
Rock the Vote 437
"Rock with You" 24, 86
"Rock You Like a Hurricane" 31
Rockefeller Plaza West, New York City 220
Rockefeller University 576, 596
Rockefeller, John D. I 147
Rockefeller, John D. "Jay" IV 284, 292
Rockefeller, Nelson 312
"Rocket 2 U" 39
"Rockit" 29
Rockwell, Norman 89
Rockwell Company 31, 87, 578
Rocky IV 32, 47, 74–75
Rocky Mountain News 455
Rocky movies 72, 74
Rodale Press 438
Rodriguez, Chi Chi 657
Roe v. *Wade* 335, 348–350, 398–399, 548
Rogaine 474, 477
Rogers, Adrian 542
Rogers, Bill 656
Rogers, Carl R. 419
Rogers, Don 650
Rogers, Kenny 24, 26, 29, 31, 87, 103
Roger's Version (Updike) 34
Rolex 102
"Roll With It" 39

Rolling Stone 120, 405, 412, 436, 439
Rolling Stones 24, 26
Rollins, Howard E. Jr. 25
Rolls Royce 373, 386, 536
Roman Catholic Church 210, 311, 534, 556, 561, 563, 565–566
— College of Cardinals 559
Romancing the Stone 30, 73, 75
The Romantics 31, 84
Romeo Void 84
Romney, Hervin 238
"Roni" 40, 88
Ronstadt, Linda 37, 41, 104
Rooney, Andy 441
Roosevelt, Franklin D. 168, 214, 280, 299, 323, 347, 365
Roosevelt, Franklin D. Jr. 323
Roosevelt, John A. 169
Roosevelt, Theodore 322
"Rosanna" 28
Rosato, Frank 404
Rose, Pete 364, 627, 629, 633–634, 685–686
"The Rose" 24
Rosenberg, Edgar 435
Rosenberg, Jerry 510
Rosenberg, Dr. Steven A. 494, 510–511
Rosenthal, Benjamin S. 323
Ross, Diana 24, 26, 87, 114
Rossellini, Isabella 32, 34
Rossner, Judith 29
Rotary clubs 375
Roth, D. Douglas 543
Roth, David Lee 33
Roth, Philip 25, 29, 32, 36, 81
Rothschild, Baron Phillipe de 417
Rotten, Johnny 107
"Round and Round" 31
Round Midnight 34
Rourke, Mickey 27–28
Rousseau, Jean-Jacques 411
"Route 66" 38
Rowe, James H. 365
Rowe, Nicholas 32
Rowe, Wallace P. 519
Rowland, Sherwood 590
Roxanne 36, 75
Roxette 41
Rozelle, Pete 648
Rozier, Mike 649
Rubens Peale with a Geranium (Peale) 37
Rubik's Cube 369
Rubin, Jerry 391, 417
Rubinstein, Artur 134

Ruckelshaus, William D. 250, 334
Rudman, Warren 284, 305
Rudolph, Alan 30, 77
Ruiz, Rosie 606
Rukeyser, William 198
Rumble Fish 28
Rumsfeld, Donald 312
Run, Shelley, Run (Samuels) 61
"Run to You" 32, 89
Run-D.M.C. 29, 31, 33, 35, 45–46, 62, 65–66, 229
The Runaways 85
Runcie, Robert, Archbishop of Canterbury 544, 561
Runnels, Harold 323
Runner's World 455
"Runnin' Down a Dream" 41, 89
The Running Man 75
Running on Empty 38, 45
"Running with the Night" 31, 86
Rushdie, Salman 42, 538
Russell, Brenda 39
Russell, Charles H. 323
Russell, Kurt 25, 28
Russian Orthodox Church 542
Russo, Aaron 68
Rustin, Bayard 323
Rutan, Richard 573
Rutgers University 188, 387
— Medical School 462
Ruth, Babe 631
Ruthless People 34, 70, 75
Ryan, Meg 40
Ryan, Nolan 633
Ryan, Sheelah 418
Ryan Foundation 418
The Ryan White Story 512
Ryden, Rev. Ernest Edwin 566
Ryder, Winona 38, 40
Ryder Cup (golf) 657
Rykiel, Sonia 232

S

Saatchi, Charles 49
Saccharin 462, 472
Sachs, Leo 519
Sad Movies (Lindquist) 81
"Sad Songs (Say So Much)" 31
Saddler, Joseph 65
Sade 33
Safe City, U.S.A. 394
"The Safety Dance" 29
Safire, William 339
Sagan, Carl 32, 443, 601
"Sailing" 24

St. Barnabas Episcopal Church, Philadelphia 561
St. Elizabeths Hospital for the Criminally Insane, Washington, D.C. 260
St. Elmo's Fire 32–33, 43, 80, 396
St. Elsewhere 507
Saint George's University School of Medicine 269
St. John, Adela Rogers 459
St. Louis Cardinals 629, 631, 649
St. Louis Globe-Democrat 439
St. Mary's Seminary, Baltimore 559
St. Nicholas Players 118
St. Peter's Square, Vatican City 534
St. Pokrova's Ukranian Cathedral, Chicago 566
Salinger, J. D. 47, 61
Salk, Lee 394
Salle, David 50–51, 53, 115
SALT II Treaty 248, 259, 279–280
Salt-N-Pepa 39, 65
Salvador 34, 46
Salvador Dali Museum, Saint Petersburg, Fla. 28
Salvation Army 402, 418
Samaranch, Juan Antonio 668
Samaritan 402
Sammons, Jeffrey 646
SAMO 51, 64
Sampson, Ralph 640
Sam's Wholesale Club 167
Samuels, Gertrude 61
Samuelsson, Bengt 516
San Antonio Express 451
San Antonio Museum 26
San Diego Padres 631
San Francisco Ballet 64
San Francisco 49ers 629, 651, 683
San Francisco Giants 633
San Jose State University 414
San Jose Unified School District 197
San Quentin Prison 365
Sanctuary movement 536
Sanctuary Movement Case 544
Sanders, Barry 653, 689
Sanders, Col. Harland 169, 419
Sanders, Lawrence 25, 32, 34, 36, 38, 40
Sandinistas (Nicaragua) 248, 250, 273–275, 277, 289, 313, 352, 358
Sandman, Charles W. Jr. 323
The Sands of Time (Sheldon) 38
SANE (Committee for a Sane Nuclear Policy) 389
Sanford, Terry 292

Santa Fe Southern Pacific 143
Santmyer, Helen Hooven 30
"Sara" 35
Sarandon, Susan 25, 36, 38, 78
Sarnoff, David 423
Sassy 425, 439
SAT (Scholastic Aptitude Test) 173, 176, 178–179, 182, 186, 190, 201, 206, 213
The Satanic Verses (Rushdie) 538
Satellite News Channel (SNC) 426, 431, 441, 445
Satterfield, David E. III 323
Saturday Evening Post 359
Saturday Night Live 43, 45, 75–76, 110
Saturday Review 422
Savage Beliefs 109–110
"Saving All My Love for You" 33, 87
Savitch, Jessica 452–453
Sawyer, Diane 442
Say Anything 40
"Say It Isn't So" 30
"Say Say Say" 31, 86–87
"Say You, Say Me" 35, 87
Sayles, John 28, 36, 77, 86
Scaife Foundation 302
Scalia, Antonin 330, 335, 348–350
Scandal 31, 40
Scanners 77
Scarbury, Joey 26
Scarecrow (Mellencamp) 46
Scarface 28, 77
Scarsdale Medical Center 355
Schaeffer, Rev. Francis August 566
Schaller, Michael 185
Scharf, Kenny 44–46, 50–51, 53–54, 57, 113
Scheinin, Richard 632–633
Schell, Jonathan 390, 575
Scherer, Gordon H. 323
Schilling, Peter 31
Schimke, Robert T. 519
Schindler, Oskar 120
Schindler's List 120
Schlafly, Phyllis 301, 399–400, 552
Schlumberger, Jean 246
Schmidt, George 207
Schmidt, Mike 629
Schnabel, Julian 43–44, 50–51, 125
Schnayerson, Philip 62
Schneider, Alan 135
Scholastic Aptitude Test. *See* SAT
Scholastic, Inc. 438
Schonfeld, Reese 429

The Sonny and Cher Comedy Hour 24

Sony Corporation 26, 28, 41, 71

Soon to Be a Major Motion Picture (Hoffman) 317

Sophie's Choice 27

Sorbel, Carol 62

Sorbonne, Paris 511

S.O.S. Band 24

Sotheby's auction house, New York City 26, 37, 48–49, 375

Soul Asylum 110

Soul on Ice (Cleaver) 61

Soul II Soul 41

The Source 432

South African Defense Fund 312

South Florida Task Force 310

Southeastern Center for Contemporary Art 59

Southern Baptist Convention 539, 542, 545

Southern Christian Leadership Conference (SCLC) 407

"Southern Cross" 27

Southern Intercollegiate Athletic Conference 688

Southern Living 438

Southern Living Classics 438

Southern Methodist University 627, 653

Southern Poverty Law Center 408

Southern Regional Education Board 176

Southern Travel 438

Southland Corporation 61

Soviet Border Law 261

Soviet grain embargo 249

Soviet Ice Hockey Federation 663

Sowell, Thomas 414

"Sowing the Seeds of Love" 41

Space (Michener) 27, 82

Space Transportation System (STS) 591

Spacek, Sissy 24, 27, 30, 34, 46, 78

Spader, James 40

Spanish-American War 268

Sparkman, John J. 323

Spartina (Casey) 38

Speakes, Larry 260, 318

"Speaking in Tongues" 29

Speaking Out (Speakes) 318

Special Weapons and Tactics (SWAT) team 345

Spectacolor board, Times Square 56

Specter, Arlen 284, 335

Spectrum Gallery, New York City 114

Speed-the-Plow (Mamet) 42, 91, 100

Spellbinder (Robbins) 27

Spellman, Cardinal Francis 553

Spencer Davis Group 93

Sperry, Roger W. 516

Spheeris, Penelope 77

Spielberg, Steven 25, 27–28, 32, 35, 43, 66–67, 69, 72–73, 87–88, 114, 118, 454

Spin 412, 425

Spinks, Leon 644, 646

Spinks, Michael 645

Spinners 24

Spiritual Healing in a Scientific Age (Peel) 537

Splash 30, 68, 70, 78

Spock, Benjamin 390

Sports Club, Los Angeles 404

Sports Illustrated 239, 445, 630, 639, 642, 644, 663–664, 682, 684, 686

The Sportswriter (Ford) 34, 82

Spring 438

Spring Break 76

Spring Training 439

Springfield, Dusty 39

Springfield, Rick 26, 28

Springsteen, Bruce 26, 31, 33, 37, 39, 43, 45–47, 65, 86, 88–89, 120, 437

Sprint 153

Sprouse, Stephen 53, 81

Spy 412

Spy Line (Deighton) 40

Squeeze 107

Squier, Billy 26

Stacey Q 35

Stakeout 70

Stalin, Joseph 262

Staller, Ilona 53

Stallings, Fr. George A. Jr. 538, 556

Stallings, Fr. Robert A. 556

Stallone, Sylvester 27, 32, 43, 46, 74, 388

Stamats Communication 438

"Stand" 41

Stand and Deliver 208

Stand by Me 34, 78, 82

Chief Standing Bear 318

Stanford Law Review 359

Stanford University 188, 191, 214, 338, 359, 596, 599–600, 602

— Hoover Institute 302

— Law School 359

Stanley, Charles 542

Stanley, Julian C. 601

Stanley Cup (hockey) 660–663, 679, 690–691

Stanton, Harry Dean 30, 77

Stapleton, Maureen 25, 78

Star (newspaper) 451

Star (Steel) 40

"The Star-Spangled Banner" 387

Star Trek 67, 72

Star Trek II: The Wrath of Khan 27, 69

Star Trek III: The Search for Spock 30

Star Trek IV: The Voyage Home 34

Star Trek V: The Final Frontier 40

Star Wars 66–67, 69, 250, 252, 260–261, 264, 296, 305, 307, 311, 315–316

Star Wars. *See* Strategic Defense Initiative

USS *Stark* 254, 277

Stars & Stripes 630

Starship 33, 35, 37, 45

START (Strategic Arms Reduction Talks) 249, 261, 265, 300

"Start Me Up" 26

"Starting Over" 26

Starzl, Dr. Thomas E. 515

Stastny, Anton 689

Stastny, Peter 689

"State of Shock" 31

State University of New York 205

— Downstate Medical College 509

The Statler Brothers 35

Statue of Liberty 330, 374, 388

Stealth aircraft 248, 256

Steed, Thomas J. 323

Steel, Danielle 27, 29–30, 32, 34, 36, 38, 40, 82

Steel, Dawn 68–69, 77

Steel Magnolias 100

Steele, Shelby 414

Steenburgen, Mary 24–25

Steichen, Edward 49

Stein, Sol 61

Steinbeck, John 47, 61

Steinberg, Joel B. 365, 377, 394

Steinberg, Lisa 394

Steinberg, Saul 69

Steinem, Gloria 200, 399, 418

Stelling, Bill 51, 64

Stemrick, Greg 650

Stennis, John C. 299, 318

The Stepfather 36, 76

Stephens, Stan 300

The Untouchables 36, 77, 100, 112
"Up Where We Belong" 27
Updike, John 25, 30, 34, 42, 82
UPI Television News 429
Upland College 205
"Upside Down" 24
"Uptown" 88
"Uptown Girl" 31, 90
Urban Cowboy 24
Urban, Matt 318
Urey, Harold 604
Uris, Leon 30, 38
US 42
U.S. News and World Report 339
USA for Africa 33, 46, 87, 94, 115, 371, 374
USA Network 85–86
USA Today 142, 422, 425, 439–440
Ustinov, Peter 82
Utah Jazz 638
Utah State Prison 346
U2 37, 39

V

"Vacation" 27, 85
Valium 463
Vallee, Rudy 135
Valley Girl 28, 45, 77, 80
Valley of the Dolls 82
The Valley of the Horses (Auel) 27, 82
"Valotte" 33
Valvano, Jim 640
The Vampire Lestat (Rice) 32, 82
Van Damme, Jean Claude 75
Van Halen 31, 39
Van Metre, Peter 346
Van Niel, Cornelis Bernardus 604
Van Sant, Gus 40, 47
Van Sauter, Gordon 441
Van Zandt, James E. 324
Van Zandt, Steve 62, 120
Vance, Cyrus 664
Vance, Robert 331
Vancouver Canucks 662
Vandross, Luther 37
Vane, John R. 516
Vangelis 28
The Vanishing Family 454
Vanity 88
Vanity Fair 47, 425, 439, 448, 451
Vare Trophy (golf) 659
Varmus, Harold E. 516–517, 519
Vassar College 122, 214, 413
Vatican 174, 277, 374, 494, 536–538, 539–540, 550–554, 559

Vatican II 554, 560
Vatican Congregation for the Doctrine of the Faith 551
Vaughan, Stevie Ray 41
Vega, Suzanne 37
Veil: The Secret Wars of the CIA (Woodward) 342
Venereal disease 518
Venturi 233
"Venus" 35
Vera, Billy 37
Vera Companies 240
Veranda 425, 438
Verbatim Corporation 159
The Verdict 27
"Veronica" 40
VH1 (Video Hits 1) 427
Viacom 86, 443
Vice President's Task Force on Combating Terrorism 310
Vicious, Sid 107
Victor/Victoria 27, 46, 85
Victory Over Japan (Gilchrist) 30
Vidal, Gore 30, 82
Video Digest 439
"Video Killed the Radio Star" 26, 436
Video Music Conference 436
Vienna Philharmonic 37
Vietnam Campaign Medal 597
Vietnam Cross of Gallantry with Palm 597
Vietnam Service Medal 597
Vietnam Veterans Memorial, Washington, D.C. 218, 369, 388
Vietnam War 44, 61, 74, 89, 165, 185, 284, 297, 303, 318–319, 322, 351, 357–359, 387–388, 412, 456, 469, 508, 513, 575, 578
"A View to a Kill" 32
Viguerie, Richard A. 300–302, 534, 545
Viking Press 81
Viking Penguin 538
Vilas, Guillermo 673
The Village Voice 80, 451
USS *Vincennes* 255, 277
Vinson, Carl 324
Violet, Sister Arlene 551
Virgin and Martyr (Greeley) 32, 82
Virginia State Board of Education 181
Visa 385
VisiCalc 432
Vision Quest 72
Vitale, Alberto 456

Vogue 219, 231, 244, 404, 439
The Voice of Prophecy 566
"Voices Carry" 33
Volcker, Paul 145, 151, 162, 167, 303, 307
von Bulow, Claus 361, 448
von Bulow, Cosima 362
von Bulow, Sunny 362
Vonnegut, Kurt 32, 36, 61
Voorhis, Jerry 324
Voyager 573, 575, 592
Voyager I 570
Voyager 2 570, 572, 574, 591–593
Vreeland, Diana 244, 452

W

W 439
Wachtel, Paul L. 386
Waite, John 31
"Waiting For a Girl Like You" 27
"Waiting for a Star to Fall" 40
Wake Forest University 311
"Wake Me Up Before You Go-Go" 31
Waldheim, Kurt 330
"Walk Like an Egyptian" 36
"Walk This Way" 35, 65
Walken, Christopher 25
Walker, Alan 572
Walker, Alice 27, 40, 46–47, 69, 81, 454
Walker, Arthur J. 339
Walker, Dave 429
Walker, Herschel 653
Walker, John Anthony 338–339
Walker, Michael L. 339
"Walking on Sunshine" 33
Walkman (Sony) 26, 42, 236
Wall Street, New York City 48, 81, 142, 147, 159–160, 309, 384, 414
Wall Street 36, 42, 80, 383, 393
Wall Street Journal 291, 359, 393, 466, 472, 475
Wallace, George C. 285, 318
Wallace, John H. 200
Wallace, Rusty 675
Wallach, E. Robert 357
Wallenberg, Raoul 318
Wallenstein, Alfred 135
Wal-Mart 61, 166–167, 418
Walsh, Bill 651, 683, 689
Walsh, Lawrence E. 276–277, 343, 356, 358
Walt Disney Concert Hall, Los Angeles 220
Walt Disney Studios 45, 69–71, 75